Sea

obruk

Alexandria
Cairo ✪
Suez
Canal

EGYPT

Al Jawf

*Lake
Nasser*
Aswān

Red Sea

Port Sudan

20°

Khartoum ✪

SUDAN

Asmara
ERITREA

Nyala

White Nile
Blue Nile

DJIBOUTI ✪ Djibouti

Gulf of Aden

Erigavo

RICAN
PUBLIC

Juba

Addis Ababa ✪

ETHIOPIA

10°

*Lake
Albert* **UGANDA**
Kisangani

SOMALIA

INDIAN

Kampala ✪

Mogadishu ✪

OCEAN

LAIRE
RWANDA
Kigali ✪
KENYA

Nairobi ✪

*Lake
Turkana*

Bujumbura ✪

Equator
0°

BURUNDI

*Lake
Victoria*

Victoria ✪

Kananga

*Lake
Tanganyika*

Pemba I.

TANZANIA

Zanzibar I.

SEYCHELLES

pa

Dar es Salaam ✪

Mafia I.

Mbala

*Îles Glorieuses
(FRANCE)*

Lubumbashi

MALAWI

COMOROS

Kitwe
Lilongwe ✪

*Lake
Malawi*

Moroni ✪

Dzaoudzi
Antsiranana

ZAMBIA

Nampula

*Mayotte
(FRANCE)*

*Cargados Carajos
Shoals (MAURITIUS)*

Lusaka

*Juan de Nova
(FRANCE)*

Mahajanga

*Tromelin
(FRANCE)*

ga

Harare ✪

MOZAMBIQUE

Antananarivo ✪

*Rodrigues I.
(MAURITIUS)*

uhembo

ZIMBABWE

Mozambique

Port
Louis

Bulawayo

*Bassas da India
(FRANCE)*

MADAGASCAR

St.-Denis

MAURITIUS

OTSWANA

Inhambane

*Îles Europa
(FRANCE)*

Toliara

*Réunion
(FRENCH AFRICAN
DEPENDENCY)*

20°

Tropic of Capricorn

Gaborone ✪

Pretoria ✪

Channel

Johannesburg
Mbabane ✪ **Maputo**

SWAZILAND

Maseru ✪
LESOTHO

UTH
RICA

Port
Elizabeth

30°

30° 40° 50° 60° 70°

WORLDMARK ENCYCLOPEDIA OF THE NATIONS

Volume 2

WORLDMARK
ENCYCLOPEDIA OF THE NATIONS

AFRICA

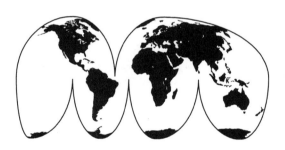

Formerly published by Worldmark Press, Ltd.

 **Gale Research Inc.**

An International Thomson Publishing Company

I(T)P

NEW YORK • LONDON • BONN • BOSTON • DETROIT • MADRID
MELBOURNE • MEXICO CITY • PARIS • SINGAPORE • TOKYO
TORONTO • WASHINGTON • ALBANY NY • BELMONT CA • CINCINNATI OH

Gale Research Inc. Staff

Jane Hoehner, *Developmental Editor*
Allison McNeill, Rebecca Nelson, and Kelle S. Sisung, *Contributing Developmental Editors*
Marie Ellavich, Jolen Gedridge, and Camille Killens, *Associate Developmental Editors*
Lawrence W. Baker, *Senior Developmental Editor*

Mary Beth Trimper, *Production Director*
Evi Seoud, *Assistant Production Manager*
Mary Kelley, *Production Associate*

Cynthia Baldwin, *Product Design Manager*
Barbara J. Yarrow, *Graphic Services Supervisor*
Todd Nessell, *Macintosh Artist*

Library of Congress Cataloging-in-Publication Data

Worldmark encyclopedia of the nations. — 8th ed.
   5 v.
   Includes bibliographical references and index.
   Contents: v. 1. United Nations — v. 2. Africa — v. 3. Americas —
v. 4. Asia & Oceania — v. 5. Europe.
   ISBN 0-8103-9878-8 (set). — ISBN 0-8103-9893-1 (v. 1). — ISBN
0-8103-9880-x (v. 2)
   1. Geography—Encyclopedias. 2. History—Encyclopedias.
3. Economics—Encyclopedias. 4. Political science—Encyclopedias.
5. United Nations—Encyclopedias.
G63.W67 1995
903—dc20   94–38556
                                       CIP

Printed in the United States of America by Gale Research Inc.
Published simultaneously in the United Kingdom
by Gale Research International Limited
(An affiliated company of Gale Research Inc.)

10 9 8 7 6 5 4 3 2 1

The trademark **ITP** is used under license.

CONTENTS

For Conversion Tables, Abbreviations and Acronyms, Glossaries, World Tables, Notes to the Eighth Edition, and other supplementary materials, see Volume 1.

GUIDE TO COUNTRY ARTICLES

All information contained within a country article is uniformly keyed by means of small superior numerals to the left of the subject headings. A heading such as "Population," for example, carries the same key numeral (6) in every article. Thus, to find information about the population of Albania, consult the table of contents for the page number where the Albania article begins and look for section 6 thereunder. Introductory matter for each nation includes coat of arms, capital, flag (descriptions given from hoist to fly or from top to bottom), anthem, monetary unit, weights and measures, holidays, and time zone.

FLAG COLOR SYMBOLS

Yellow   Red   Green   Blue   Orange   Brown   White   Black

SECTION HEADINGS IN NUMERICAL ORDER

1 Location, size, and extent
2 Topography
3 Climate
4 Flora and fauna
5 Environment
6 Population
7 Migration
8 Ethnic groups
9 Languages
10 Religions
11 Transportation
12 History
13 Government
14 Political parties
15 Local government
16 Judicial system
17 Armed forces
18 International cooperation
19 Economy
20 Income
21 Labor
22 Agriculture
23 Animal husbandry
24 Fishing
25 Forestry
26 Mining
27 Energy and power
28 Industry
29 Science and technology
30 Domestic trade
31 Foreign trade
32 Balance of payments
33 Banking and securities
34 Insurance
35 Public finance
36 Taxation
37 Customs and duties
38 Foreign investment
39 Economic development
40 Social development
41 Health
42 Housing
43 Education
44 Libraries and museums
45 Media
46 Organizations
47 Tourism, travel, and recreation
48 Famous persons
49 Dependencies
50 Bibliography

SECTION HEADINGS IN ALPHABETICAL ORDER

Agriculture 22
Animal husbandry 23
Armed forces 17
Balance of payments 32
Banking and securities 33
Bibliography 50
Climate 3
Customs and duties 37
Dependencies 49
Domestic trade 30
Economic development 39
Economy 19
Education 43
Energy and power 27
Environment 5
Ethnic groups 8
Famous persons 48
Fishing 24
Flora and fauna 4
Foreign investment 38
Foreign trade 31
Forestry 25
Government 13
Health 41
History 12
Housing 42

Income 20
Industry 28
Insurance 34
International cooperation 18
Judical system 16
Labor 21
Languages 9
Libraries and museums 44
Local government 15
Location, size, and extent 1
Media 45
Migration 7
Mining 26
Organizations 46
Political parties 14
Population 6
Public finance 35
Religions 10
Science and technology 29
Social development 40
Taxation 36
Topography 2
Tourism, travel, and recreation 47
Transportation 11

FREQUENTLY USED ABBREVIATIONS AND ACRONYMS

ad—Anno Domini
am—before noon
b.—born
bc—Before Christ
c—Celsius
c.—circa (about)
cm—centimeter(s)
Co.—company
Corp.—corporation
cu ft—cubic foot, feet
cu m—cubic meter(s)
d.—died
e—east
e—evening
e.g.—exempli gratia (for example)
ed.—edition, editor
est.—estimated
et al.—et alii (and others)

etc.—et cetera (and so on)
f—Fahrenheit
fl.—flourished
FRG—Federal Republic of Germany
ft—foot, feet
ft³—cubic foot, feet
GATT—General Agreement on Tariffs and Trade
GDP—gross domestic products
gm—gram
GMT—Greenwich Mean Time
GNP—gross national product
GRT—gross registered tons
ha—hectares
i.e.—id est (that is)
in—inch(es)
kg—kilogram(s)
km—kilometer(s)

kw—kilowatt(s)
kwh—kilowatt-hour(s)
lb—pound(s)
m—meter(s); morning
m³—cubic meter(s)
mi—mile(s)
Mt.—mount
Mw—megawatt(s)
n—north
n.d.—no date
NA—not available
oz—ounce(s)

pm—after noon
r.—reigned
rev. ed.—revised edition
s—south
sq—square
St.—saint
UK—United Kingdom
UN—United Nations
US—United States
USSR—Union of Soviet Socialist Republics
w—west

A fiscal split year is indicated by a stroke (e.g. 1987/88).
For acronyms of UN agencies and ther intergovernmental organizations, as well as other abbreviations used in text, see the United Nations volume.
A dollar sign ($) stands for us$ unless otherwise indicated.
Note that 1 billion = 1,000 million = 10^9.

ALGERIA

Democratic and Popular Republic of Algeria
Al-Jumhuriyah al-Jaza'iriyah ad-Dimuqratiyah ash-Sha'biyah

CAPITAL: Algiers (Alger).

FLAG: The national flag consists of two equal vertical stripes, one green and one white, with a red crescent enclosing a five-pointed red star in the center.

ANTHEM: *Kassaman (We Pledge).*

MONETARY UNIT: The Algerian dinar (DA) is a paper currency of 100 centimes. There are coins of 1, 2, 5, 10, and 50 centimes and 1, 5 and 10 dinars, and notes of 10, 20, 50, 100, and 200 dinars. DA1 = $0.0385 (or $1 = DA25.945).

WEIGHTS AND MEASURES: The metric system is the legal standard.

HOLIDAYS: New Year's Day, 1 January; Labor Day, 1 May; Overthrow of Ben Bella, 19 June; Independence Day, 5 July; Revolution Day, 1 November. Muslim religious holidays include 'Id al-Fitr, 'Id al-'Adha', 1st of Muharram (Muslim New Year), and Milad an-Nabi. Christians observe their own religious holidays.

TIME: GMT.

¹LOCATION, SIZE, AND EXTENT

Situated in northwestern Africa along the Mediterranean Sea, Algeria is the second-largest country on the continent. Comparatively, it is slightly less than 3.5 times the size of Texas, with a total area of 2,381,740 sq km (919,595 sq mi). Extending about 2,400 km (1,500 mi) E–W and 2,100 km (1,300 mi) N–S, Algeria is bounded on the N by the Mediterranean Sea, on the E by Tunisia and Libya, on the SE by Niger, on the SW by Mali, on the W by Mauritania, and on the W and NW by the Western Sahara and Morocco; the total boundary length is 7,341 km (4,561 mi). Land boundary and claims disputes and claims with Libya and Tunisia were unresolved as of late 1994.

Algeria's capital city, Algiers, is located on the northern boundary of the country on the Mediterranean Sea.

²TOPOGRAPHY

The parallel mountain ranges of the Tell or Maritime Atlas, comprising coastal massifs and northern inland ranges, and the Saharan Atlas divide Algeria into three basic longitudinal zones running generally east–west: the Mediterranean zone or Tell; the High Plateaus, including the regions of Great and Small Kabilia; and the Sahara Desert, accounting for at least 80% of Algeria's total land area. About half of Algeria is 900 m (3,000 ft) or more above sea level, and about 70% of the area is from 760 to 1,680 m (2,500 to 5,500 ft) in elevation. The highest point is Mount Tahat (2,918 m/9,573 ft), in the Ahaggar Range of the Sahara.

Only the main rivers of the Tell have water all year round, and even then the summer flow is small. None of the rivers are navigable. The mountainous areas of the High Plateaus are poorly watered; most of the rivers and streams (oueds) flow irregularly, since they depend for water upon an erratic rainfall. In the High Plateaus are many salt marshes and dry or shallow salt lakes (sebkhas or shotts). Farther south, the land becomes increasingly arid, merging into the completely dry desert.

Northwestern Algeria is a seismologically active area. Earthquakes on 10 October 1980 in a rural area southwest of Algiers left over 2,500 persons dead and almost 100,000 homeless.

³CLIMATE

Northern Algeria lies within the temperate zone, and its climate is similar to that of other Mediterranean countries, although the diversity of the relief provides sharp contrasts in temperature. The coastal region has a pleasant climate, with winter temperatures averaging from 10° to 12°C (50° to 54°F) and average summer temperatures ranging from 24° to 26°C (75° to 79°F). Rainfall in this region is abundant—38 to 69 cm (15 to 27 in) per year, and up to 100 cm (40 in) in the eastern part—except in the area around Oran (Ouahran), where mountains form a barrier against rain-carrying winds. When heavy rains fall (often more than 3.8 cm/1.5 in within 24 hours), they flood large areas and then evaporate so quickly that they are of little help in cultivation.

Farther inland, the climate changes; winters average 4° to 6°C (39° to 43°F), with considerable frost and occasional snow on the massifs; summers average 26° to 28°C (79° to 82°F). In this region, prevailing winds are westerly and northerly in winter and easterly and northeasterly in summer, resulting in a general increase in precipitation from September to December and a decrease from January to August; there is little or no rainfall in the summer months.

In the Sahara Desert, temperatures range from –10° to 34°C (14° to 93°F), with extreme highs of 49°C (120°F). There are daily variations of more than 44 degrees Celsius (80 degrees Fahrenheit). Winds are frequent and violent. Rainfall is irregular and unevenly distributed.

⁴FLORA AND FAUNA

Characteristic trees of northern Algeria are the olive and the cork oak. The mountain regions contain large forests of evergreens (Aleppo pine, juniper, and evergreen oak) and some deciduous trees; the forests are inhabited by boars and jackals, about all that remain of the many wild animals once common. Fig, eucalyptus, agave, and various palm trees grow in the warmer areas. Esparto grass, alfa, and drinn are common in the semiarid regions. On the coastal plain, the grape vine is indigenous.

Vegetation in the Sahara is sparse and widely scattered. Animal life is varied but scarce. Camels are used extensively. Other mammals are jackals, jerboas, and rabbits. The desert also abounds with poisonous and nonpoisonous snakes, scorpions, and numerous insects.

5ENVIRONMENT

Algeria's principal environmental problem is encroachment of the desert on the fertile northern section of the country. To impede desertification, the government in 1975 began to erect a "green wall" of trees and vegetation, 1,500 km (930 mi) long and 20 km (12 mi) wide, along the northern fringes of the Sahara. This afforestation project costs about $100 million annually and was expected to take 20 years to complete.

Other significant environmental problems include water shortages and pollution. Algeria has 4.5 cubic miles of water reserves. The small amount of water available in Algeria is threatened by regular droughts. The problem is further complicated by lack of sewage control and pollutants from the oil industry. Algeria contributes 0.2% of the total gas emissions in the world.

Endangered species in 1987 included the Barbary hyena, Barbary leopard, Barbary macaque, and Mediterranean monk seal. The African elephant is extinct in North Africa. Of the 97 species of mammals, 12 are endangered. Fifteen species of birds are also threatened. One hundred and forty-five of the 3,139 plant species in Africa are endangered as of 1994.

6POPULATION

The 1987 census listed the population of Algeria at 23,038,942, while the estimated population in 1994 was 27,989,792. The projected population for the year 2000 was 32,693,000, assuming a crude birthrate of 32.8 per 1,000 population, a crude death rate of 6.0, and a net natural increase of 26.8 during 1995–2000. Average population density in 1987 was estimated at 11.8 per sq km (30 per sq mi). The population is concentrated in the cultivated areas of the north (over 90% in the northern eighth of the country) and sparsely distributed in the plateau and desert regions.

Algeria was an estimated 56% urban in 1992, when greater Algiers had about 3,033,000 people. Other large cities and their estimated 1987 populations were Oran, 590,000; Constantine (Qacentina), 438,000; Annaba (Bône), 310,000; Batra, 182,000; Sétif, 168,000; and Blida, 165,000.

7MIGRATION

In 1962, some 180,000 Algerian refugees were repatriated from Tunisia and Morocco; after independence was declared that July, about 650,000 French Algerians and more than 200,000 harkis (Algerian Muslims who fought on the French side during the war of independence and chose to retain French citizenship) emigrated to France. The exodus reduced the French population from about 10% of the total in 1961 to less than 1% in 1981. As a result of the war between the Polisario guerrillas and Morocco over the Western Sahara, about 150,000 Sahrawi refugees fled to Algeria. There were 165,000 at the end of 1992, when Algeria was also harboring 50,000 people from Mali and Niger who had sought refuge in southern Algeria. About 620,000 Algerians were living in France in 1990.

8ETHNIC GROUPS

Apart from about 1 million Europeans, who had immigrated or were descended from immigrants who had come since 1830, and about 140,000 Jews, the population before independence consisted almost entirely of Muslims. Muslims in Algeria are chiefly of Berber derivation, particularly in the Kabilia and Aurès areas and in the Sahara oases, or admixtures of Berbers with Arabs and other invaders from earlier periods. The Berbers, who resemble the Mediterranean subrace of Southern Europe, are descendants of the original inhabitants of Algeria and are divided into many subgroups. They account for about one-fifth of the population. The Kabyles (Kaba'il), mostly farmers, live in the compact mountainous section in the northern part of the country between Algiers and Constantine. The Chaouia (Shawiyyah) live in the Aurès Mountains of the northeast. The Mzab, or Mozabites, include sedentary date growers in the Ued Mzab oases. Desert groups include the Tuareg, Tuat, and Wargla (Ouargla).

Europeans are of French, Corsican, Spanish, Italian, and Maltese ancestry. Algeria's European population was estimated at 75,000 in the early 1980s. About half the Jews in Algeria were descended from converted Berbers, and the remainder were mainly descendants of Spanish Jews. Within a month after Algeria became independent, about 70,000 emigrated to France and 10,000 to Israel. Almost all the rest left Algeria during the next seven years; fewer than 200 Jews remained as of 1985, and virtually all synagogues had been converted to mosques.

9LANGUAGES

The sole official and majority language is Arabic, with many variations and dialects, but many Algerians also speak French; "Arabization" has been encouraged by the government. About one-fifth of the population speaks a wide variety of Berber dialects, particularly in Kabilia, in the Aurès, and in smaller, relatively protected areas in the mountains and the Sahara. Berber is a distinct branch of the Hamitic language group; dialects vary from district to district. In antiquity, the Numidians wrote Berber in script form.

10RELIGIONS

About 99% of the population adheres to Islam. Except for a small minority of Kharijites (Ibadhis) in the Mzab region, most Muslims are adherents of the Maliki rite of the Sunni sect, with a few Hanafi adherents. In 1993 there were 27,000 Roman Catholics and small Protestant and Jewish communities.

11TRANSPORTATION

In 1991, Algeria's nationally owned railroad had about 4,146 km (2,576 mi) of track. The system consists principally of a main east–west line linked with the railways of Tunisia and Morocco and of lines serving the mining regions of Béchar (formerly Colomb Béchar); the esparto grass country on the High Plateaus; the date-producing areas of Biskra, Touggourt, and Tebessa; and the main port cities.

Roads are most adequate in the Tell zone; in the mountainous and rural areas, they are relatively poor. In 1991 there were 80,000 km (49,712 mi) of roads, of which about 75% were paved, used by 760,000 passenger cars and 510,000 commercial vehicles. The French colonial administration built a good road system, partly for military purposes, which after independence was allowed to deteriorate to some extent; however, new roads have been built linking the Sahara oil fields with the coast. Algeria's portion of the trans-Saharan highway, formally known as the Road of African Unity, stretching about 420 km (260 mi) from Hassi Marroket to the Niger border south of Tamanrasset, was completed in 1985.

Algiers is the principal seaport. Other important ports are Arzew, Bejaïa (Bougie), Skikda (a large gas-exporting center also known as Philippeville), Oran, Annaba, Ghazaouet, and Mostaganem. Algeria's merchant fleet numbered 67 ships totaling 858,000 GRT as of 1 January 1992.

An extensive air service uses 124 airports and airstrips; the main international airport is about 20 km (12 mi) from Algiers. Constantine, Annaba, Tilimsen (Tlemcen), and Oran have smaller modern airports that can accommodate jet aircraft. Air Algérie, the national airline, provides international service, and carried 3,551,100 people in 1992.

ALGERIA

| 0 | 100 | 200 | 300 Miles |
| 0 | 100 | 200 | 300 Kilometers |

MEDITERRANEAN SEA

Alboran Sea

Golfe de Bejaïa

Algiers ✪
Blida
Bejaïa
Skikda
Annaba

Oran
Mostaganem
Setif
Constantine

Sidi Bel Abbès
Batna

Tlemcen
Djelfa
Biskra

Oujda
Laghouat
Touggourt
Redeyef

Taza
Ghardaïa
Golfe de Gabès

M O R O C C O

A T L A S   M O U N T A I N S

A T L A S   S A H A R I E N

T U N I S I A

Béchar
Ouargla

Zagora

Oued Draa

Oued Saoura

Grand Erg Occidental

El Golea

Grand Erg Oriental

Dirg

Akka

Tabelbala

Plateau du Tademaït

I-n-Amenas

Adrar

El Mansour
Titaf
I-n-Belbel

L I B Y A

Tindouf

WESTERN SAHARA

Tarat

Chenachane

Erg Chech

MAURITANIA

Ghat

I-n-Amguel

A H A G G A R   M T S.

Djanet

Silet

Mt. Tahat 9,573 ft. 2918 m.

Tamanrasset

S A H A R A   D E S E R T

N
W   E
S

M A L I

Ti-n-Zaouâtene

N I G E R

Algeria

LOCATION: 18°57′ to 37°5′N; 8°44′W to 12°E. **BOUNDARY LENGTHS:** Mediterranean coastline, 1,104 km (686 mi); Tunisia, 958 km (595 mi); Libya, 982 km (610 mi); Niger, 956 km (594 mi); Mali, 1,376 km (855 mi); Mauritania, 463 km (288 mi); Morocco, 1,637 km (1,017 mi). **TERRITORIAL SEA LIMIT:** 12 mi.

¹²HISTORY

Before the period of recorded history, the North African coastal area now known as Algeria was inhabited by Berber tribal groups, from whom many present-day Algerians are descended. Phoenician sailors established coastal settlements, and after the 8th century BC, the territory was controlled by Carthage. Roman dominance dates from the fall of Carthage in 146 BC. Completely annexed in AD 40, the region, known as Numidia, became a center of Roman culture. Christianity flourished, as did agriculture and commerce; Numidian wheat and olives were shipped to

Rome. By the mid-3d century there were some 20 Numidian bishops. Despite the prosperity of the Roman cities and the cereal-growing countryside, there were frequent Berber revolts. The Roman influence gradually declined, especially after the Vandal invasion of 430–31. The Byzantine conquered eastern Numidia in the 6th century.

After the Arab conquest began in 637, the area was known as Al-Maghrib al-Awsat, or the Middle West and continued for a century. The Berbers accepted Islam but preserved their own traditional political and social institutions, in effect absorbing the invaders. Arabs from the east attacked in the 11th century. These newcomers, unlike their predecessors, were nomadic herders rather than farmers; they destroyed many of the towns and farms and reinforced a more pastoral type of economy. Almoravids from Morocco also took possession of part of the region in the 11th century, and they were succeeded by Almohads a century later. Although these and other dynasties and individuals united the territory and consolidated it with Morocco and Spain, local rulers retained considerable autonomy. Meanwhile, seafaring and piracy became important.

Spain conquered part of the coast in the early 16th century, and Algerians asked the aid of 'Aruj, known as Barbarossa, a Turkish pirate. He expelled the Spaniards from some of their coastal footholds, made himself sultan, and conquered additional territory. The area of Barbarossa's control was extended by his brother, Khayr ad-Din, also called Barbarossa, who placed his territory under the suzerainty of the Ottoman sultan in Constantinople. Until 1587, Algiers was governed by beylerbeys; from 1587 to 1659, by pashas, who were appointed for three-year terms; and after 1659, by aghas and finally by deys (28 deys in all, 14 of whom were assassinated). Other parts of what is now called Algeria were ruled either by Turkish officials or by local chieftains. Spain held a small area around Oran until 1708 and controlled it again from 1732 to 1791.

Algiers became increasingly independent of Constantinople and, joining with other states of the Barbary Coast, thrived on piracy. At this time, it had diplomatic and trade relations with many European countries, including France. But with the defeat (though not suppression) of the Barbary pirates by US and European fleets during 1815–16, and with the growing European interest in acquiring overseas colonies, Algiers was seen as a possible addition to either the British or the French empire. In 1830, the French took over the principal ports; they gradually subjugated the Berbers, annexed the northern regions, and set up a system of fortified posts. Thereafter, sporadic revolts broke out, notably the guerrilla war from 1830 to 1847, led by the legendary hero, Abd al-Qadir, and the Kabyle rebellion in 1871. Other sections, however, remained independent of France until the first decade of the 20th century.

Al-Jazair, as it was called in Arabic, became, in French, Algérie, a name that France applied to the territory for the first time in 1839. In 1848, northern Algeria was proclaimed an integral part of France and was organized into three provinces. Following the Franco-Prussian War of 1870–71, large numbers of Alsatians and other French colonizers settled the most fertile confiscated lands, as did other Europeans at the invitation of France. Muslims had no political rights except for limited participation in local financial delegations.

Following World War I, France took the first steps toward making all Algeria an integral part of France. In 1919, voting rights were given to a few Muslims, based on education and military service qualifications. (French citizenship had previously been open to Muslims who renounced their Koranic status.)

During World War II, in exchange for loyalty to France, many Muslims hoped for political concessions, and moderates believed that France might be persuaded to grant Algeria a separate status while retaining close diplomatic, economic, and defense ties. In 1957, all Muslims became French subjects, but about 9 million Muslims and 500,000 Europeans voted on separate electoral rolls for a joint assembly. Unsuccessful in obtaining further reforms and faring poorly in several apparently rigged elections, the moderate Muslim nationalist group led by Ferhat Abbas was greatly weakened.

Meanwhile, younger nationalists had formed what would become known as the National Liberation Front (Front de Libération Nationale—FLN), and a guerrilla war was launched on 1 November 1954. The FLN's National Liberation Army

(Armée de Libération Nationale—ALN) perpetrated acts of terrorism and sabotage throughout Algeria and gained increasing mass support. Eventually, France was forced to maintain at least 450,000 troops in Algeria. During the hostilities, the French army completely cleared many rural areas of their civilian populations and evacuated some 2 million Muslims to army-controlled regroupment centers or new large villages. Although the army gradually eliminated the power of the ALN to carry out large-scale attacks, the latter continued its terrorist acts against the French army, French settlers, and pro-French Muslims. Terrorist activities, mainly as a result of factional disputes, also were carried on by Algerian Muslims in France. During more than seven years of civil war, well over 100,000 Muslim guerrillas and civilians and 10,000 French soldiers lost their lives.

The war in Algeria toppled several French governments before causing the demise of the Fourth Republic in May 1958. Gen. Charles de Gaulle was then brought to power by French rightists and military groups in Algeria. To their surprise, however, he pursued a policy of preparing for Algerian independence. He offered self-determination to Algeria in September 1958. Referendums in France and Algeria on 8 April and 1 July 1962 approved a settlement, and independence was formally proclaimed on 3 July, despite a program of counterterrorism by the French Secret Army Organization in Algeria.

With independence achieved, a seven-man Political Bureau, set up as the policymaking body of the FLN, took over effective control of the country on 5 August 1962. Ahmed Ben Bella became the first premier, and Ferhat Abbas was chosen speaker of the Assembly. The Assembly adopted a constitution, which was endorsed by referendum in September 1963.

Elected president in October, Ben Bella began to nationalize foreign-owned land and industry. Opposition to his authoritarian regime led to an outbreak of armed revolts in the Kabilia and Biskra areas in July 1964 and to open attacks on the regime by leading political figures. On 19 June 1965, the Ben Bella government was overthrown in a bloodless coup directed by Col. Houari Boumedienne, first deputy premier and defense minister. The 1963 constitution was suspended, and a revolutionary council headed by Boumedienne took power. The new government shifted to a gradualist approach to national development, with deliberate economic planning and an emphasis on financial stability. During the 1970s, the council nationalized the oil industry and initiated agrarian reforms. Boumedienne ruled by decree until June 1976, when a national referendum approved a Socialist constitution providing for a one-party state with a strong presidential system and an elected National Assembly. Boumedienne was elected president in December 1976 but died two years later.

The FLN Central Committee, with strong army backing, chose Col. Chadli Bendjedid as the party's leader, and his presidential candidacy was ratified by the electorate on 7 February 1979. He was reelected without opposition in January 1984 for a second, five-year term. After a period of maintaining continuity with the previous regime, the Bendjedid government moved toward more moderate policies, expanding powers for the provinces and state enterprises and attempting to revitalize the FLN and government agencies. In foreign affairs, Algeria reduced its earlier support for liberation groups around the globe and for hard-line non-aligned positions. It patched up its dispute with Morocco over the Western Sahara and sharply reduced its aid to the Polisario. Algeria played a key role in helping the US resolve the hostage crisis in 1981 and worked hard for the Arab Maghreb Union, a planned EC for North Africa. Serious internal trouble developed in 1988 when young Algerians rioted over high prices, unemployment, and the dictatorship of an aging, inept, and corrupt revolutionary regime. Shocked by the 500 deaths in the streets, Bendjedid moved to liberalize his government. Political parties were allowed to form outside the FLN and the prime minister and cabinet were made responsible to the National Assembly. He won a third term in 1989, supported by 81% of the electorate.

Burdened by heavy debts and low oil prices, Bendjedid was obliged to pursue austere economic policies and to abandon socialism for the free market—actions which further inflamed his opposition, now led by the Islamic Salvation Front (FIS). In 1989, the party won 55% of urban election seats while the FLN maintained power in the countryside. Elections to the National Assembly, postponed six months, were held in December 1991 under relatively free conditions. FIS candidates won 188 out of 231 contested seats, needing only 28 more places in a second vote to control the 430-member Assembly. The FLN won only 16 seats.

The army intervened, arresting FIS leaders and postponing indefinitely the second stage vote. Bendjedid resigned under pressure from the army and Mohammed Boudiaf, a hero of the revolution, returned from exile to lead the High State Council which the army established. A harsh crackdown on Islamists began; the FIS was banned and its local councils were closed. As acts of terrorism continued by both sides in 1992 and 1993, the regime declared a state of emergency, set up special security courts and arrested more than 5,000 persons. Boudiaf was assassinated in June 1992 to be replaced by Ali Kafi with Redha Malek as Prime Minister in August 1993. In January 1994, Defense Minister Liamine Zeroual was named President and the five-man presidential council was abolished. During this period, Islamic militants carried out threats against secular intellectuals and foreigners (30 killed by April 1994); security forces have responded with overwhelming force and harsh treatment and reportedly employed death squads against Muslim militants. An average of 11 persons a day were being killed in early 1994. Despite the stated Zeroual government's interests in talks with Islamists, many observers feared a prolonged, Lebanon-like civil war in Algeria.

13GOVERNMENT

The constitution of 1976, as subsequently amended, provides for a strong executive headed by a president who is nominated as the sole candidate by the FLN congress and elected by universal adult suffrage for a five-year term. The president appoints the prime minister and cabinet ministers. Until 1992, the highly centralized government was guided in policy matters by the Political Bureau of the FLN's Central Committee. Since 1992, the army has exercised real power behind the appointed High State Council and, in 1994, the president.

The legislative body is the National Assembly, whose 430 deputies are elected to five-year terms. In the single-party balloting of 26 February 1987, 885 candidates contested the 295 seats; all had been nominated by FLN local cells. In the 27 December 1991 elections, Algeria's first free and multi-party vote, 30 parties participated. The FIS took 188 of 430 seats with 44% of the vote; the FLN won 16 seats and the Front for Socialist Forces had 20 places. Runoff elections, scheduled for January 15, were canceled when the army assumed control of the government.

14POLITICAL PARTIES

One of the earliest active figures in the struggle for Algerian self-determination was Messali Hadj, who in 1925 formed the Star of North Africa (Étoile Nord Africaine) movement among Algerian workers and intellectuals in Paris and in 1937 founded the Algerian People's Party (Parti Populaire Algérien—PPA). Banned in 1939, the PPA operated illegally and militantly under the Vichy regime, with strong support from students and workers.

In 1944, Ferhat Abbas formed the Friends of the Manifesto and of Liberty (Amis du Manifeste et de la Liberté—AML), a moderate reform group that was later transformed into the Democratic Union of the Algerian Manifesto (Union Démocratique du Manifeste Algérien—UDMA). In 1946, some AML members joined the PPA and, under Messali Hadj's leadership, formed a

legal front organization, the Movement for the Triumph of Democratic Liberties (Mouvement pour le Triomphe des Libertés Démocratiques—MTLD). On a program favoring "the return of the Algerian people to national sovereignty," the MTLD won 5 of the 15 elected seats in the National Assembly elections of 1 November 1946; in 1948, however, the MTLD lost all its seats and was reduced to semi-illegality. Two years later, it was suppressed by the police.

In 1947, a small group of MTLD members led by Ahmed Ben Bella formed the Secret Organization (Organisation Secrète—OS) to prepare for an armed rebellion. French authorities discovered and suppressed the OS in 1950, and most of its leaders fled to Cairo.

In 1951, an Algerian Front was formed by the MTLD, the UDMA, the Algerian Communist Party, and the Society of 'Ulema, a political-cultural organization. Policy differences in the following years resulted in the creation of three groups: supporters of Messali Hadj; centrists, who hoped to obtain constitutional advances by cooperating with the French administration; and a militant group who proposed violent action. By 1954 there was an open split. The centrist majority repudiated Messali Hadj's leadership. An activist group of nine former OS members then established the Revolutionary Committee for Unity and Action (Comité Révolutionnaire d'Unité et d'Action—CRUA) with headquarters in Cairo, divided Algeria into six military zones and appointed commanders for each, and launched a war with France on 1 November 1954.

Shortly thereafter, the CRUA changed its name to the National Liberation Front (Front de Libération Nationale—FLN), and its forces became known as the National Liberation Army. The FLN was an amalgamation of various nationalist tendencies in Algeria. Its membership gradually incorporated most members of the former MTLD, most members of the UDMA, and members of the Society of 'Ulema, as well as former independents and young people with no previous political allegiance. Its goal was the complete independence of Algeria, and it appeared to have the support of the great majority of Muslims. After Messali Hadj broke with the FLN, he formed the National Algerian Movement (Mouvement National Algérien—MNA), supported mainly by Algerians in France. The MNA attacked both the FLN and the war through acts of terrorism in France, but became almost completely without influence following Messali's imprisonment.

In August 1956, an FLN congress established an embryo parliament, the 34-member National Committee of the Algerian Revolution, enlarged in 1957 by 20 more members to a total of about 50, and a 5-member executive body, the Executive and Coordinating Committee, enlarged in Cairo in 1957 by additional members. In September 1958, a provisional government was established with Ferhat Abbas as president and with headquarters in Cairo and Tunis. (Benyoussef Ben Khedda succeeded Abbas as premier in August 1961.) President de Gaulle in effect recognized the FLN as the only political organization that had the authority to speak for the Muslims during peace negotiations with the French government. During this period, French expatriates in Algeria organized the Secret Army Organization, which violently opposed Algerian independence.

After independence, differences of opinion arose among the members of the Political Bureau, the FLN's policy-making body, regarding the organization of the FLN. While Ben Bella envisaged the creation of an elite party, Mohammed Khider (assassinated in Spain in January 1967) sought to create a broader mass party. The FLN mobilized popular political participation by forming mass organizations for peasants, youth, guerrilla veterans, and women. It organized itself into departmental federations, sections, and cells, staffed largely by former guerrillas (mujahidin). In April 1964, the first congress of the FLN adopted the Charter of Algiers, a guideline for government policy that provided for a wide range of agricultural, industrial, and social reforms. The FLN's National Charter of April 1976 outlined a plan for creating a Socialist system commensurate with Islamic principles. A new National Charter adopted in January 1986 deemphasized Socialism and placed greater stress on Islam. The chief organs of the FLN are the Central Committee, the highest policy-making body of both the FLN and the nation, the Political Bureau and the Secretariat. The Islamic Salvation Front is an umbrella organization of groups which support a government guided by Islamic law. In September 1989 the government approved a multiparty system, and as of 31 December 1990, over 30 legal political parties existed, including Islamic Salvation Front (FIS), National Liberation Front (FLN), and Socialist Forces Front (FFS).

15LOCAL GOVERNMENT

In 1969, a governorate of 48 provinces (wilayats) system replaced the departments which had been established by the French. Each wilaya has its own elected people's assembly, executive council, and appointed governor (wali), who is responsible to the Ministry of the Interior. The 48 wilayats have 160 subdivisions called da'iraats (districts) and 691 communes. The commune is the basic collective unit, governed by an assembly elected for four years.

16JUDICIAL SYSTEM

After independence, Algeria's judicial system was reorganized. The former French magistrats were replaced by Algerians and the judiciary was extended into regions of the country previously ignored.

The judicial system now includes civil, military and antiterrorist courts. Within each wilayat is a court of first instance for civil and some criminal cases. At the head of the system is the Supreme Court. Special courts for eliminating economic fraud are presided over by members of the FLN. A special Court of State Security tries all cases involving political offenses.

The constitution guarantees independence of the judiciary. Judges are appointed by the executive branch without legislative approval.

Algeria's present legal codes, adopted in 1963, are based on the laws of Islam and of other Northern African and Socialist states, as well as on French laws. Efforts were made to harmonize the laws and legal procedures with those of the Maghreb nations. A first plan for judicial reorganization was approved in 1965; this was followed in 1966 with the beginning of large-scale structural reforms. A new civil code was promulgated in 1975 and a new penal code in 1982.

In civilian courts, Shari'a (Islamic law) is applied in resolving social issues. Defendants in civilian courts are afforded a wide range of procedural protections including a public trial, right to counsel, right to confront witnesses and right of appeal.

Military courts have jurisdiction in cases involving military personnel and recently have heard some cases in which civilians are charged with security-related offenses. Special antiterrorist courts were set up in 1992. These courts afford few procedural projections and produce a high rate of convictions including over 300 death sentences in 1993.

17ARMED FORCES

Six months' military service is compulsory for males. Algeria's armed forces in 1993 totaled 139,000 personnel. The army had 120,000 officers and men, plus reserves of up to 150,000; weaponry included 960 main battle tanks. The navy had 7,000 men; vessels included 2 submarines, 3 frigates, 3 corvettes, and 11 OSA missile patrol craft. The air force had 12,000 men, about 242 combat aircraft, and 58 combat helicopters. The gendarmerie totaled 35,000, and the Ministry of Interior guards 16,000. Algeria's defense budget is the equivalent of about $1 billion (1991) or around 1.5% of GDP. It imports $100 million in arms.

18INTERNATIONAL COOPERATION

Algeria was admitted to the UN on 8 October 1962 and is a member of ECA and all the nonregional specialized agencies except the IFC. Algeria also participates in the African Development Bank, G-77, League of Arab States, OAU, and OPEC. The nation is a signatory of the Law of the Sea and a de facto adherent of GATT.

19ECONOMY

Although almost 25% of Algerians make their living directly from the soil, agriculture produced only 9.6% of Algeria's GDP in 1990. Saharan oil and natural gas have been important export items since 1959, and they now dominate Algeria's economy, accounting for over 95% of total export value and 26% of GDP. During the late 1970s, as oil prices rose, real economic growth topped 20% annually, with the manufacturing sector averaging about 15%; during 1980–81, however, the rate dropped to 7–8% because of the weakening oil market, and a decline of 5% was registered in 1982, followed by an average annual growth rate of 4.5% during 1983–86. Because of the weak oil market, growth fell to 3.4% in 1989, 1.1% in 1990, and less than 2% in 1993.

Before independence, the Algerian economy was almost completely dependent on the Europeans, who employed more than 90% of those working in industry and commerce, accounted for about 90% of gross business earnings, and provided some 90% of the country's private investment. The exodus of most Europeans in 1962 temporarily disrupted Algeria's economic life. The FLN governments have established a Socialist economy by nationalizing the mining industry and creating state farms and state-owned industries on abandoned farms and on expropriated French landholdings. The nationalization with compensation of all foreign-owned companies was completed in 1974, although certain companies operating in partnership with Algerian state enterprises were allowed to continue. In the 1980s, decentralization was emphasized, with over 90 state corporations split into 300 specialized units. It was announced in 1987 that these enterprises would adopt their own annual plans, decide on the prices of their products, and invest their profits freely.

The dramatic decline in oil prices in 1985/86 affected Algeria at a time when it also faced a heavy foreign debt burden. The Algerian government thus attempted to diversify the economy. In 1990 the money and credit law opened the way for substantial international participation in Algeria's economy.

20INCOME

In 1992 Algeria's GNP was $48,326 million at current prices, or $1,830 per capita. For the period 1985–92 the average inflation rate was 18.4%, resulting in a real growth rate in per capita GNP of –2.0%. In 1992 the GDP was $45,196 million in current US dollars.

21LABOR

Of a labor force estimated at 6.2 million in 1992, 25% were in agricultural sectors. Over 40% of the population is under the age of 15. The informal sector provides work for an estimated 270,000 Algerians. The private sector employs 47% of the labor force, even though it only controls 5–10% of the industrial base. At least 21.1% of the work force was unemployed in 1991. From 1985 to 1991, the labor force size increased by about 3.7% per year. About 27% of the labor force has been organized, but strikes are illegal in the public sector.

Before 1956, many European and Muslim workers belonged to the General Labor Federation. This organization was Communist controlled after 1947 and organized in Algeria as the General Union of Algerian Syndicates. Realizing the importance of trade union activity in organizing and strengthening a nationalist movement, the two Algerian nationalist groups formed trade unions in

1956: the Trade Union of Algerian Workers, which found its greatest strength among Algerian laborers in France, and the General Union of Algerian Workers (Union Générale des Travailleurs Algériens—UGTA), founded by the FLN.

In July 1956, because of its obvious strength among the Muslims and because of the support it had received from the General Union of Tunisian Workers, UGTA was admitted to the ICFTU. Working closely with the FLN leadership, UGTA was more of a political weapon in the struggle for independence than a means for improving the economic lot of the worker. Since independence, it has combined its political and economic roles. The largest group within UGTA represents the workers on self-management farms, organized in the Federation of Land Laborers. In 1962, the UGTA formed the first two women's organizations: the Committee of the Union of Algerian Women and the Movement of the Young Women of Algiers. After its disaffiliation with the ICFTU in 1963, UGTA played a significant role in the revival of the All-African Trade Union Federation.

The 1990 Law of Work Relations permits strikes after 14 days of conciliation, mediation, or arbitration efforts; the law also permits collective bargaining for all unions. Minimum wages are set by the government with the advice of the UGTA. Algerian workers are eligible for workers' compensation and disability, maternity, and death benefits, as well as family allowances. Workers and employers contribute to a social security program. A growing xenophobic sentiment in Algeria has recently resulted in increased harassment and threats toward non-Arab contract workers.

[22]AGRICULTURE

Although almost 25% of the population is engaged in agriculture (including subsistence farming), only 3% of Algeria's land is cultivated. The soil is poor and subject to erosion, and the water supply is generally irregular and insufficient; about one-quarter of northern Algeria is completely unproductive. Agriculture contributed 15.1% to GDP in 1992, up from 10.7% in 1985.

Before independence, European-owned agriculture accounted for about two-thirds of vegetable production and employed about 800,000 farm laborers, 700,000 of them Muslims. Most Muslim-owned farms were small—10 hectares (25 acres) or less—and were located mainly in marginal areas on the interior plains and on mountain slopes. The Muslim sector, comprising the bulk of the agricultural population, accounted for only one-third of vegetable production but nearly all the livestock raising.

Within six months after independence was declared, at least half the European-owned land had been vacated. Algerian peasants soon began to work on these abandoned farms under a self-management system. During the 1960s, the government established more than 2,300 state farms on expropriated French landholdings; by the end of the decade, these farms accounted for two-thirds of total agricultural production and employed about 500,000 workers. In July 1971, President Boumedienne announced an agrarian program providing for the breakup of large Algerian-owned farms and their reorganization into cooperatives. The first stage of the plan, the registration of land ownership, began in March 1972. In the second stage, many absentee landlords were forced to hand over part of their land to the state. By July 1973, of a total of 5 million hectares (12.4 million acres) of public land, 1 million hectares (2.5 million acres) of cultivable land had been redistributed to 54,000 families of landless peasants (fellahin), and 1,348 cooperatives had been created. By 1980, the number of cooperatives had increased to about 6,000; in the early 1980s, however, the government split large cooperatives into smaller units to improve efficiency. In 1982–83, about 450,000 hectares (1.1 million acres) of land previously nationalized were returned to private ownership, mostly in plots of 10 hectares (25 acres) or less. In 1987, a further breakup of large state-owned farms into private cooperatives was implemented.

Long-term leases of land to cooperatives were begun. Farmers were given autonomy in production and investment decisions, including the right to keep profits. The National Union of Algerian Peasants, established in March 1973, played a leading role in the land reform program and has about 1,200,000 members.

Government policy aims at increased use of fertilizers and improved seeds, conversion of vineyards to the production of cereals and other staple foods, and achievement of self-sufficiency in food production. Estimated agricultural output in 1992 included 1,750,000 tons of wheat, 1,370,000 tons of barley, 900,000 tons of potatoes, 500,000 tons of tomatoes, 300,000 tons of citrus fruits, 260,000 tons of grapes, and 210,000 tons of wine. In 1992, for every $1 of agricultural products exported, over $43 of agricultural products were imported. That same year, 4.6 million tons of cereals were imported, including 3.6 million tons of wheat and 900,000 tons of corn. The total cost for imported cereals was $697.4 million.

[23]ANIMAL HUSBANDRY

About half of the livestock is owned by only 5% of the herdsmen. In 1992 there were an estimated 18,600,000 sheep, 2,500,000 goats, 1,420,000 head of cattle, 340,000 donkeys, 130,000 camels, 107,000 mules, and 84,000 horses. There were also 76 million chickens. Algeria has a severe shortage of milk, meat, and cheese and must therefore rely on imports.

[24]FISHING

Fishing is fairly extensive along the coast, but the industry is relatively undeveloped. Sardines, bogue, mackerel, anchovies, and shellfish are caught. The 1991 catch was estimated at 80,115 tons.

[25]FORESTRY

Less than 2% of the land is forested. The mountain ranges contain dense forests of evergreens (evergreen oak, Aleppo pine, and cedar) and deciduous trees, whereas the warmer regions contain large numbers of fruit and palm trees. Algeria is an important producer of cork; other forestry products are firewood, charcoal, and wood for industrial use. Roundwood production was estimated at 2,221,000 cu m in 1991.

Two-thirds of the French-planted forests in eastern Algeria were burned by French forces during the 1954–62 war. Reafforestation was begun on 12,100 hectares (30,000 acres) of unused land in the semiarid region in 1960. By 1964, 25 million trees had been planted: eucalyptus in clay soils, Aleppo pine in calcareous regions, and olive trees. Current reafforestation projects include the planting of a "green wall" across Algeria from the Moroccan to the Tunisian frontier to halt the encroachment of the Sahara. During the first half of the 1980s, reafforestation proceeded at a rate of 52,000 hectares (128,000 acres) per year, but from 1987 to 1991, deforestation averaged about 40,400 hectares (99,800 acres) per year, so that Algeria now has 1.7% less forested land than in 1976.

[26]MINING

Algeria's phosphate deposits at Djebel Onk, in the northeast, are among the largest in the world, covering about 800 sq mi (2,100 sq km) with an output of 1,090,000 tons in 1991. There are deposits of high-grade iron ore at Ouenza, near the Tunisian border; production totaled 2,344,000 tons in 1991, of which half was exported. Other mineral production in 1991 included zinc ore, 2,610 tons; bentonite, 25,803 tons; and lead concentrates, 900 tons. Silver, mercury, kaolin, barites, sulfur, fuller's earth, and salt are also mined.

[27]ENERGY AND POWER

Natural gas and petroleum dominate the economy; in 1992, hydrocarbon exports were valued at $8.2 billion, or 97% of total exports. In the 1950s, natural gas was found in the east, near the Libyan border, and at Hassi R'Mel in the Sahara. Algeria's natural gas deposits are the world's sixth largest, totaling an estimated 3.6 trillion cu m in 1992, or 2.6% of the world's proven reserves. Production of natural gas that year totaled 52.1 billion cu m. A 500-km (310-mi) main pipeline connecting Hassi R'Mel to Arzew (between Oran and Mostaganem) was opened in 1961, and branch lines to Oran and Algiers were completed four years later. The Hassi R'Mel field accounts for about 67% of proven reserves and 25% of annual natural gas output. Since then, six other pipelines have been constructed, including the first trans-Mediterranean gas pipeline to Europe via Sicily, built at a cost of $3 billion. In December 1990, Italy and Algeria agreed to expand the capacity of the pipeline by 26%. A $2.5-billion pipeline to Spain and Portugal via Morocco was scheduled to be completed in 1996. There were four gas liquefaction plants in 1991, three at Arzew and one at Skikda, all operating well below capacity because of disrepair and lack of funds for spare parts.

Oil was discovered at Edjeleh and Hassi Messaoud in 1956 and at Al-Gassi in 1959; by 1969, the Franco-Algeria Cooperative Association (ASCOOP), a petroleum development company, had discovered eight major fields. Proved reserves of crude oil amounted to 9.2 billion barrels in 1993; production averaged 1,325,000 barrels per day in 1992, up 18% from 1986. There are four main pipelines linking the wellheads in the eastern Sahara with Algerian ports and a fifth with the Tunisian port of Sekhira; there are also several branch pipelines.

The Société Nationale pour la Recherche, la Production, le Transport, la Transformation et la Commercialisation des Hydrocarbons (SONATRACH), founded in 1964 as the state-owned petroleum company, handles the distribution and transport of oil. On 24 February 1971, President Boumedienne announced the Algerian takeover of controlling interest in all French oil company subsidiaries and the nationalization of all pipelines and natural gas deposits. Holdings of all other foreign petroleum interests in Algeria were nationalized by the end of 1971. Subsequent agreements have generally treated foreign companies as minority partners in Algerian state enterprises. Contracts for sales of natural gas to Western Europe and the US increased spectacularly in the 1970s but decreased in the 1980s as world energy prices fell, pushing Algeria into severe debt. By 1991, SONATRACH was reversing its monopolistic policy, and is now forming joint ventures for new exploration contracts. SONATRACH has recently joined forces with a Canadian and an Australian company for an exploratory project which began in 1993. SONATRACH will keep 51% of the production from any discovery at the site, which is due west of the Hassi R'Mel field. Another contract with a German consortium involves the sinking of three exploratory oil wells at Hassi Massaoud.

Installed electrical generating capacity in 1991 totaled 5,369,000 kw; power production was 17,345 million kwh, of which only 1.7% was hydroelectric. Under the 1985–89 plan, Algeria planned to achieve a national electrification rate of 96%.

28INDUSTRY

Industries, which are concentrated around Algiers and Oran, include carpet mills, cement factories, chemical plants, automobile assembly plants, food-processing installations, oil refineries, soap factories, and textile plants. Other major industries produce bricks and tiles, rolled steel, farm machinery, electrical supplies, machine tools, phosphates, sulfuric acid, paper and cartons, matches, and tobacco products.

Before independence, industry made significant gains. New enterprises were developed in food processing and packaging, textiles, leather, chemicals, metalworking, building materials, and farm machinery. A new large steel plant was built at Annaba, a petroleum refinery at Algiers, a petrochemical complex at Arzew,

and a phosphate production center at Djebel Onk, near the Tunisian border. Other industries were set up to produce automobiles, tractors, cement, rubber tires, and ammonia. The natural gas produced at Hassi R'Mel provides the basis for heavy industry in the Arzew-Mostaganem region.

Since independence, the industrial sector has been widely nationalized; the last European-owned enterprises—in the steel, chemicals, textiles, engineering goods, and mineral water industries—were taken over in December 1974. About 100 French firms were nationalized between 1962 and 1974.

In 1989, industrial production (in tons) included cement, 6,519,000; pig iron, 1,478,000; crude steel, 1,041,000; and phosphate fertilizers, 193,000. Liquid petroleum gas (LPG) production totaled 4.4 million tons in 1992.

The government has put great emphasis on the development of the hydrocarbons sector, including the building of refineries and natural gas liquefaction plants. Algeria had five oil refineries with a capacity of 470,000 barrels per day in 1989. A refinery built at Arzew with Japanese technical cooperation began operating in 1973, and a vast petrochemical complex built at Skikda by Italian and Japanese firms produces polyethylene, polyvinyl chloride, caustic soda, and chlorine. Three other petrochemical centers, including fertilizer factories, were built in the 1980s.

Algeria assembles small numbers of trucks and buses (6,671 and 730, respectively, in 1986). In 1987, a contract with Fiat of Italy provided for the nation's first auto production plant, a joint venture sited at Ain-Bouchekif, about 150 miles southwest of Algiers, with production to begin in the mid–1990s of 30,000 units a year. A second plant is planned with Peugeot. Metalsider, the first Algerian private steelmaker, started operations in 1992.

In recent years the industrial sector, which accounted for 10% of GDP in 1991, has been adversely affected by lack of supplies and spare parts because of import controls. Thus most companies are operating only at about 50% of production capacity. Since 1986 industrial production has declined at an annual rate of 2.5%.

29SCIENCE AND TECHNOLOGY

Since independence, Algeria has made major technological advances, especially in the steel and petrochemical industries. However, Algeria still has a severe shortage of skilled workers and is heavily dependent on foreign technologies. Scientific training is conducted at the Boumedienne University of Science and Technology, founded at Algiers in 1974, and in several other universities and colleges nationwide. The government's National Scientific Research Organization operates 18 research centers in various technologies, nuclear science, renewable energy sources, and other fields. Several research institutes conduct research in renewable sources of energy, hygiene, and microbiology.

30DOMESTIC TRADE

European trading firms formerly played a major role in the economy; however, many Europeans, fearful of eventual Muslim control, sold their holdings or gave them up in 1961–62. After independence, about one-half of the country's shops closed down, and in 1963 the Ben Bella government empowered local authorities to take over small businesses and hotels. Boumedienne returned them to their owners in 1965, but state agencies have taken over nearly all wholesaling and marketing.

The principal cities of the north are the largest trade centers. While most trade is done on a cash or credit basis, some bartering still goes on among the rural dwellers and in the Muslim quarters of cities. In the mountain regions there are local market days or special local fairs for the exchange of products during different seasons.

Normal business hours in winter are 8 AM to noon and 2:30 to 6 PM, Sunday–Wednesday, and 8 AM to noon on Thursday; afternoon hours in summer are 3 to 6:30. Banks are generally open in the winter months from 8:45 AM to 12 noon and 2:15 to 5 PM, Saturday–Wednesday; in summer, 8:15 AM to 12 noon and 3 to 5:30 PM.

31 FOREIGN TRADE

Crude oil and natural gas account for nearly all of Algeria's export value; industrial equipment and semifinished goods and foodstuffs dominate the country's imports. Trade deficits were recorded throughout the colonial period, but with the departure of the Europeans the trade balance steadily improved. However, as the pace of development quickened, imports began to increase, and deficits were recorded during the early 1970s. Surpluses accrued with the oil and gas price increases beginning in the mid-1970s and continuing through 1985, with the exception of 1978. In 1986, however, because of a severe drop in oil prices, exports came to only DA37,034 million as compared to imports of DA47,872 million—the first trade deficit since 1978 and the largest ever. With continued government control over the level of imports, Algeria was able to register trade surpluses in the following years.

The trend of Algeria's foreign trade is as follows (billions of US dollars):

	1990	1991	1992
Exports (fob)	12.93	12.33	12.22
Imports (cif)	–9.79	–6.85	–6.75
Balance	3.14	5.48	5.47

The main items of trade from 1988 to 1990 were (millions of DA):

	1988	1989	1990
EXPORTS			
Energy & lubricants	45,598	65,237	93,362
Semi-finished products	1,059	—	—
Food	178	—	—
IMPORTS			
Industrial equipment	11,838	17,777	33,324
Semi-finished products	11,489	15,213	15,884
Food	10,605	22,257	19,206
Consumer goods	5,171	7,390	10,068

In recent years, a leading purchaser of Algeria's oil has been the US. Roughly two-thirds of Algeria's trade is with EEC countries.

Algeria's main trading partners were as follows (% of total):

	1989	1980	1991
EXPORTS TO:			
Italy	21.0	19.2	21.7
USA	19.5	21.0	16.8
France	14.0	13.8	15.1
Germany	7.7	7.4	8.3
Spain	5.8	5.3	7.6
Netherlands	6.7	7.4	5.8
IMPORTS FROM:			
France	24.9	28.5	26.3
Italy	14.6	12.3	13.4
Germany (includes East Germany)	9.6	9.8	8.9
USA	9.4	10.0	8.8
Spain	4.6	6.1	7.8
Japan	3.3	3.5	4.4

32 BALANCE OF PAYMENTS

Algeria long had a current-accounts deficit, which before independence was covered by French army expenditures, private capital investment, and direct French aid. While the departure of Europeans after independence contributed to an improved balance of trade (Europeans were the chief consumers of foreign goods), it also caused a heavy withdrawal of capital and a decrease in French aid, resulting in a continued deterioration of Algeria's payments position. However, with the continued growth of the petroleum sector, Algeria recorded substantial payments surpluses during the 1970s. In 1991, many import restrictions were abolished, although foreign exchange and external credit access were still restricted.

In 1991 merchandise exports totaled $12,330 million and imports $6,852 million. The merchandise trade balance was $5,478 million. The following table summarizes Algeria's balance of payments for 1990 and 1991 (in millions of US dollars):

	1990	1991
CURRENT ACCOUNT		
Goods, services, and income	1,087	2,151
Unrequited transfers	333	216
TOTALS	1,420	2,367
CAPITAL ACCOUNT		
Direct investment	–4	–39
Other long-term capital	–921	–961
Other short-term capital	–74	–21
Other liabilities	54	—
Reserves	–138	–1,047
TOTALS	–1,083	–2,068
Errors and omissions	–336	–299
Total change in reserves	142	–436

33 BANKING AND SECURITIES

The Central Bank of Algeria, created in December 1962, is the sole bank of issue. The Algerian Development Fund was established in 1963 to provide financial assistance for economic development. Following the separation of the French and Algerian treasuries in late 1962, the Directorate of Treasury and Credit was established as the government's fiscal agent. The state has also established cooperative banks. The money supply as measured by M2, totaled DA523.2 billion at the end of 1992.

Foreign banks ceased operations after the nationalization of banks in 1963 and were absorbed by three government-owned banks including the Foreign Bank of Algeria, the National Bank of Algeria, and the People's Credit of Algeria. There are also four government banks for financing economic development and a savings institution that offers housing loans. Foreign banks in Algeria include The Banque Nationale de Paris, Beogrosssska Banka, Credit Lyonnais and Societe Generale.

There are no securities exchanges in Algeria.

34 INSURANCE

In May 1966, a state monopoly began to replace existing foreign insurance companies, which were permitted to wind up their operations but not to issue new policies. Four Algerian insurance companies were operating in 1985. In 1990, Algerians spent US$18.5 per capita on insurance premiums, or 1.4% of the country's GDP.

35 PUBLIC FINANCE

Algeria's fiscal year coincides with the calendar year. Because of the rise in petroleum revenues, government expenditures have increased rapidly since 1973. In 1992 revenues were US$14.4 billion and expenditures were US$14.6 billion of which US$3.5 billion were for capital expenditures.

36 TAXATION

The most important sources of government revenue are oil and gas royalties. Algeria's tax system has been streamlined through the replacement of a number of different taxes by a value-added tax, a personal income tax, and a corporate profits tax. Corporation tax is 50% on distributed profits and 20% on reinvested earnings. Many fiscal advantages are granted to developing and expanding industries. There is a tax on production (a single tax that is passed on to the consumer) and a tax on industrial and commercial activities.

37 CUSTOMS AND DUTIES

A customs union between Algeria and France allows regulations applicable in the metropole to apply also in Algeria, making Algeria a de facto adherent of GATT. By a special agreement with the EC, Algerian industrial products are granted duty-free entry into the EC market, and its agricultural products get seasonal tariff reductions, while Algeria gives reciprocal treatment to EC imports. Algeria has also concluded preferential customs agreements with Tunisia and Morocco.

Goods from France are admitted at a preferential rate; next come goods from other Common Market countries and finally come goods from countries that grant Algeria most-favored-nation treatment which are subject to a basic standard taridd. As of 1993, the government was revising the tariff schedule to reduce the number of tariff levels to eight and lower the maximum tariff rate from 120% to 42%.

38 FOREIGN INVESTMENT

According to the 1962 cease-fire agreement, French companies in Algeria were to be free to continue their normal activities without discrimination; all oil and other mining rights previously granted by France were confirmed; and for a six-year period, French companies were to receive preference in the granting of oil exploitation rights. As a result of the government's nationalization policy, however, almost all the private foreign investment in Algeria has been liquidated since independence. The takeover of all foreign companies except those in joint-partnership agreements with Algerian state enterprises was completed in 1974.

The investment code of 1966 was designed to attract foreign and domestic capital and to define the role of private capital in Algeria's economic development. Under the new code, approved projects were eligible for exemption from the real estate tax, from production tax on the purchase of domestically manufactured equipment, and from profits taxes; in addition, delays were granted on the payment of customs duties and production taxes for the purchase of imported equipment. In allowing these concessions, consideration was to be given to the additional employment created by prospective enterprises, the possibility of improving skills of workers, and geographical location. Annual repatriation of profits was authorized for up to 15% of a company's capital investment. Assurances were also given that industry would be nationalized only in case of overriding national need and that compensation would be paid in full and the proceeds transferable abroad within nine months. Compensation was paid for enterprises nationalized through 1974.

In August 1983, a new foreign investment code was approved, and still another one was issued in 1986. The government's aim was to encourage the inflow of foreign capital, private as well as public. Foreign investment would be permitted only in joint ventures with state-owned companies, but repatriation of profits is guaranteed.

The money and credit law of March 1990 allows majority foreign-owned joint ventures in almost all sectors. The law provides for the safe transfer of capital and terms for international arbitration. The hydrocarbon law of November 1991 allows foreign firms to exploit, in partnership with the state oil firm, existing oil fields. The Investment Code of October 1993 does not distinguish between investments made by foreigners and Algerians and grants new investors limited tax exemptions and reductions in duty on imported goods.

39 ECONOMIC DEVELOPMENT

Following independence, Algeria adopted an economic policy favoring a Socialist organization of society. The new developmental guidelines were contained in the Charter of Algiers, issued by an FLN congress in April 1964. The basis of Algerian policy was self-management of farms, industry, and commercial enterprises. Under this system, the workers themselves were responsible for management, while ownership of the property was maintained by the state. Two-thirds of the profits were to be divided among the workers and the government, with one-third earmarked for reinvestment. All new major industries were to be state owned.

The agrarian reform of 1963 provided for the creation of self-managed state farms and producers' cooperatives, the latter serving as a transitional stage. In May 1963, it was agreed that one-third of France's financial aid to Algeria would be used to compensate French landowners whose holdings had been expropriated. A program for the nationalization of large estates owned by Algerians was announced in 1967. The nationalized land was conveyed to the National Agrarian Reform Fund and then redistributed, wherever possible, on a collective basis for exploitation under the self-management system. A further agrarian reform in 1971 involved redistribution of public and private landholdings, resettlement of the rural population in model villages, and various water and soil conservation measures.

The Boumedienne regime, while reaffirming Algeria's commitment to socialism, followed a gradual national development policy with deliberate economic planning and an emphasis on financial stability. The government's desire to create an atmosphere of confidence in Algeria's economy was reflected in the cautious pace of agrarian reform and the introduction of a new investment code in September 1966.

The first stage of development, covering 1967–69, set up a basis for expansion of industry, improvement of agriculture, and training of personnel. Expenditures totaled DA5,400 million, 75% of which was spent on heavy industry. The development plan for 1970–73 involved a total planned expenditure of DA27.7 billion. Overall growth of the economy was projected at 9%; in fact, during the 1970–73 plan period, the GDP in current prices grew by 11.2% annually, and real annual growth was about 7%. The 1973 GDP of DA31,420 million exceeded expectations by 40%, partly because of inflation but largely because of growth in the petroleum sector.

The second four-year plan (1974–77) projected an annual economic growth rate of 10%. The plan established a heavy industrial base for the economy and largely completed agricultural reforms. The period 1978–79 was used to consolidate economic gains. In 1979, the government decided to limit oil and gas exports and to decentralize industry away from Algiers in order to build up the country's less developed regions. The new five-year plan for 1980–84 switched the emphasis from heavy to light industry and to neglected social areas, especially housing. Of the plan's total investment of DA400 billion, nearly half was to be used to complete projects held over from the first two plans. The second five-year plan (1985–89) emphasized agriculture and water supply in order to reduce the chronic food deficit, but industry (32%) and social infrastructure (27%) were allotted the largest shares of the proposed total investment of DA550 billion. The third five-year plan (1990–94) defined broader national policy objectives. Under the aegis of former Prime Minister Belaid Abdesselam, the government set forth three principal goals for its economic program: increasing domestic production, opening and diversifying the economy, and fulfilling external commitments.

By OPEC standards, Algeria has a relatively high population and low per capita income; hence, it has concentrated on its own development requirements rather than on aid to other countries. Net disbursements of official development assistance by Algeria from 1976 through 1981 amounted to $536.8 million, of which

$270.2 million went in 1979 in the form of a grant to Arab nations classified as "confrontation states" because of their hostile relations with Israel. In the early 1980s, Algeria said it would allocate 1% of its GDP to aiding third world countries, with about 80% going to other African countries. Algeria was chiefly a recipient of aid, however. In 1984, it received $701 million from Arab sources, and in 1984–85, it received two IBRD loans worth $552 million for water and sewage projects. Austria and France were the chief bilateral donors during 1982–85.

Algeria's debt burden has increased since the mid-1980s due to lower oil prices and dollar weakness. At the end of 1991, the external debt totaled $27 billion. The 1991 debt service was about 77% of export earnings. A 10-month IMF standby program was implemented in June 1991. Since 1992 Algeria has received a $7.2-billion Italian bilateral multi-year credit package, $400-million EEC balance of payments support for 1993, and various other bilateral aid packages mainly from France, Japan, and Spain. World Bank lending to Algeria is forecast to reach up to $3 billion in 1990–95, compared with $1.4 billion in 1985–89.

40SOCIAL DEVELOPMENT

Since the early 1960s, the government has repeatedly sought to implement a proposed family code, based on Islamic principles, that would, in effect, treat any woman as a legal minor for life, under the authority of her father, husband, or other male head of the family; permit polygamy; recognize as a legal divorce a man's repudiation of a wife (although not a wife's repudiation of a husband); proscribe marriage between a Muslim woman and a non-Muslim man (while allowing a Muslim man to marry outside the faith); and permit a woman to work at a profession only with the approval of her husband. In part because of concerted opposition by the National Union of Algerian Women, the proposed code was withdrawn by the Council of Ministers after it had been submitted to the National Assembly in early 1982. A compromise code was passed in 1984 that did not fully meet the objections of women's groups.

It was estimated in 1987 that the average Algerian family lived with about five children in a dwelling of three rooms or less. Because of the high fertility rate and the high population growth rate (about 3.1% annually in the late 1980s), the government supports the goal of family planning; funding, however, is modest, and only the most highly educated Algerians practice birth control to any significant extent. The lives of most Algerians are burdened by unemployment, high prices, a severe housing shortage, government corruption, harsh repression, and inadequate social services.

41HEALTH

The Ministry of Health has overall responsibility for the health sector, although the Ministry of Defense runs some military hospitals. In 1990, Algeria had 284 hospitals with 60,124 beds (2.4 per 1,000 people); 1,309 health centers; 510 polyclinics; and 475 maternity hospitals (64 privately owned). Medical personnel in 1990 included 23,550 doctors, 2,134 pharmacists, and 7,199 dentists.

Free medical care was introduced in 1974 under a Social Security system, which reimburses 80% of private consultations and prescription drugs.

The principal health problems have been tuberculosis, malaria, trachoma, and malnutrition. By 1990, the incidence of tuberculosis was 53 in 100,000. In 1992, the average life expectancy was 66 years, with a death rate of 7 per 1,000 people. Infant mortality in 1992 was 60 per 1,000 live births, with 901,000 births that same year. The government is interested in creating public awareness of birth control.

From 1988 to 1991, 88% of the population had access to health services. Algeria's immunization rates between 1990 and 1992 for one-year-old children were: tuberculosis (87%); diphtheria, pertussis, and tetanus (89%); polio (89%); and measles (82%).

Algeria's government has been developing plans to boost domestic production of pharmaceuticals (which currently covers only 13% of requirements), as well as to remedy a serious shortage of dentists and pharmacists.

42HOUSING

The need for adequate housing is a pressing problem for Algeria. The average number of persons per dwelling was 6.9 in 1987, compared to 5.9 in 1966.

In 1964, the Ministry for Housing and Construction was created; its first task was the reconstruction and upgrading of damaged and substandard dwellings. The government's 1965 financial reform provided for regularization of ownership and collection of rents from some 500,000 nationalized or sequestered apartments and houses in the major cities.

Migration to the coastal cities during the 1960s and 1970s aggravated the housing problem, and in the 1974–77 development plan the government took steps to curb the flow. The 1980–84 plan called for the construction of 450,000 new housing units; the building effort failed to meet the target because of shortages of construction materials. In 1982, the government committed more than $1.5 billion to prefabricated housing, some of it as part of a program to build "model villages" for workers on state farms or in state-owned enterprises. Private housing construction is also permitted and is subsidized at the local level; more than 100,000 building permits were issued during 1981–82. In 1985, 44.5% of all housing units were individual houses, 19.9% were traditional houses called "haouches," and 14.7% were flats, while 20.9% were shacks and other marginal arrangements. In the same year, 63% of all housing units were owner occupied, 24.6% were rented, and 12.4% were occupied free of charge. Roughly three-fourths of housing units had electricity and half were connected to common sewage systems. The 1985–89 development plan called for construction of 250,000 new units per year; 115,000 were built in 1986. Almost 100% of the urban population and 80% of the rural population had access to safe water in the mid-1980s.

43EDUCATION

Education in Algeria largely continues to follow the pattern laid down during the French administration, but its scope has been greatly extended. Public primary and secondary schools were unified in 1976 and private schools were abolished. Expenditure on education has steadily increased since independence. The government has given priority to teacher training, technical and scientific programs, as well as adult literary classes.

Education is officially compulsory for children between the ages of 6 and 15. Arabic is the official language although French and Berber are also in wide usage. Adult literacy stood at 57.8% in 1990 (males, 69.8% and females, 45.5%). In 1991–1992 there were a total of 48,953 teachers and 831,798 students in schools. In 1991 there were 10 universities along with 5 centers, 7 colleges, and 5 institutes for higher learning. The University of Algiers (founded in 1909), its affiliated institutes, and other regional universities enrolled about 300,000 students in 1988. The universities provide a varied program of instruction that stresses development-related subjects. Many technical colleges also are in operation.

44LIBRARIES AND MUSEUMS

The largest libraries in Algeria are those of the University of Algiers (800,000 volumes) and the National Library (over 1,020,000 volumes). Other collections of size are the Municipal Library in Constantine and the Aubert Library in Oran. The Pasteur Institute in Algiers has a special library of over 47,000 volumes.

Museums of importance in Algiers include the Bardo National Museum of Prehistory and Ethnography, the National Museum of Fine Arts of Algiers, the National Museum of Antiquities and Islamic Art, and the Museum of the Revolution. Various regional museums are located at Constantine, El Biar (west of Algiers), Oran, Sétif, and Skikda.

45MEDIA

On 30 September 1964, the Algerian Press Service (established in 1961) was given a monopoly over the distribution of news items within Algeria. Until then, foreign press agencies were permitted to distribute information directly to their Algerian clients. The following daily newspapers (all with FLN orientation) were in circulation in 1991:

	LANGUAGES	CIRCULATION
Al-Mujahid (Algiers)	French and Arabic	280,000
Horizons 2000 (Algiers	French and Arabic	220,000
Al-Chaab (Algiers)	Arabic	150,000
El-Masaa (Algiers)	Arabic	90,000
Al-Jumhuriyah (Oran)	Arabic	90,000
An-Nasr (Constantine)	Arabic	70,000

In 1990 there were 48 periodicals with a total circulation of 803,000.

In 1991, Algeria had Arabic and French radio networks with a total of 26 AM stations and a total of 18 television stations operated by the national television network. There were some 6 million radios and 1.9 million television sets in use and telephones numbered 1,050,951. Satellite, cable, and radiotelephone services link Algeria with most other parts of the world.

46ORGANIZATIONS

There are foreign and domestic chambers of commerce, industry, and agriculture in the major cities. Red Cross and Red Crescent societies are active. The leading trade union, UGTA, sponsors many organizations in Algeria. The "professional trade sectors" affiliated with the UGTA include food, agriculture, construction, teachers, energy, finance, information sciences, light and heavy industry, health social security, and telecommunications. There is also a national peasant and laborers union, a youth movement, and a war veterans organization. Learned societies are active in such fields as anthropology, archaeology, geography, history, and various branches of medicine. Muslim brotherhoods once played a considerable part in political affairs, but their influence has greatly diminished recently.

47TOURISM, TRAVEL, AND RECREATION

Visitors need a valid passport and a visa. Smallpox vaccinations are required. Vaccination against yellow fever is required of those coming from an infected area; inoculations against typhoid, tetanus, and cholera are recommended.

Among popular tourist attractions are the Casbah and Court of the Great Mosque in Algiers, as well as the excellent Mediterranean beaches, Atlas Mountains resorts, and tours of the Sahara Desert. The government has encouraged tourism as an increasingly important source of foreign exchange. In 1991, there were 1,193,210 visitor arrivals, 43% from Africa and 13% from Europe. Hotel rooms numbered 27,493 with 54,986 beds. Receipts from tourism came to US$64 million in 1990.

The most popular Algerian sport is soccer, which is played throughout the country by professionals and amateurs alike. Tennis is widely played as well.

48FAMOUS ALGERIANS

The most famous Algerian of antiquity was St. Augustine (Aurelius Augustinus, 354–430), a Church father and theologian who was born in eastern Numidia. An important 19th-century figure

was Abd-el-Kader ('Abd al-Kadir bin-Muhyi ad-Din al-Hasani, 1808–73), emir of Mascara, who led the resistance against the French invaders from 1830 to 1847. Two early figures in the drive for Algerian independence were Messali Hadj (1898?–1974), who organized several political movements, and Ferhat Abbas (1900–86), who led the first provisional government and was elected first speaker of the National Assembly in 1962. Other important nationalist leaders include Ahmed Ben Bella (b. 1916), a founder of the FLN and the first premier of independent Algeria, who, after becoming president in 1963, was overthrown and imprisoned for 15 years (until 1980); Belkacem Krim (1922–70), political leader in Kabilia; Benyoussef Ben Khedda (1922–67), head of the provisional government in 1961–62; and Houari Boumedienne (Muhammad Boukharrouba, 1927–78), who overthrew Ben Bella in 1965 and became president in 1976. Boumedienne's successor as president and FLN leader was Col. Chadli Bendjedid (b. 1929).

Two renowned French Algerian writers are playwright Jules Roy (b. 1907) and novelist, playwright, and essayist Albert Camus (1913–60), winner of the Nobel Prize for literature in 1957. Frantz Fanon (b. Martinique, 1925–61), a psychiatrist, writer, and revolutionary, was a leading analyst of colonialism.

49DEPENDENCIES

Algeria has no territories or colonies.

50BIBLIOGRAPHY

American University. *Algeria: A Country Study.* Washington, D.C.: Government Printing Office, 4th ed., 1985.

Bennoune, Mahfoud. *The Making of Contemporary Algeria, 1830–1987: Colonial Upheavals and Post-independence Development.* New York: Cambridge University Press, 1988.

Christelow, Allan. *Muslim Law Courts and the French Colonial State in Algeria.* Princeton, N.J.: Princeton University Press, 1985.

Confer, Vincent. *France and Algeria: The Problems of Civil and Political Reform, 1879–1920.* Syracuse, N.Y.: Syracuse University Press, 1966.

Entelis, John P. *Algeria.* Boulder, Colo.: Westview, 1985.

Fanon, Frantz. *The Wretched of the Earth.* New York: Grove Press, 1966 (orig. 1961).

Heggoy, Alf A., and Robert R. Crout. *Historical Dictionary of Algeria.* Metuchen, N.J.: Scarecrow, 1981.

Hutchinson, Martha C. *Revolutionary Terrorism: The FLN in Algeria.* Stanford, Calif.: Hoover Institution Press, 1978.

Joly, Daniele. *The French Communist Party and the Algerian War.* Houndmills, England: Macmillan, 1991.

Kaye, Jacqueline. *The Ambiguous Compromise: Language, Literature, and National Identity in Algeria and Morocco.* London and New York: Routledge, 1990.

Kettle, Michael. *De Gaulle and Algeria, 1940–1960: from Mers el-Kebir to the Algiers Barracades [sic.].* London: Quartet Books, 1993.

Knauss, Peter R. *The Persistence of Patriarchy: Class, Gender, and Ideology in Twentieth Century Algeria.* New York: Praeger, 1987.

Ottaway, David, and Marina Ottaway. *Algeria.* Berkeley: University of California Press, 1970.

Ruedy, John (John Douglas). *Modern Algeria: the Origins and Development of a Nation.* Bloomington: Indiana University Press, 1992.

Smith, Tony. *The French Stake in Algeria, 1945–1962.* Ithaca, N.Y.: Cornell University Press, 1978.

Spencer, William. *Algiers in the Age of the Corsairs.* Norman: University of Oklahoma Press, 1976.

State and Society in Algeria. Boulder, Colo.: Westview Press, 1992.

ANGOLA

Republic of Angola
República de Angola

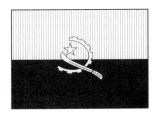

CAPITAL: Luanda.

FLAG: The upper half is red, the lower half black; in the center, a five-pointed yellow star and half a yellow cogwheel are crossed by a yellow machete.

ANTHEM: *Angola Avanti.*

MONETARY UNIT: The Angolan escudo (AE) was the national currency until 1977, when the kwanza (Kw) of 100 lwei replaced it. There are coins of 50 lwei and 1, 2, 5, 10, and 20 kwanza, and notes of 20, 50, 100, 500, and 1,000 kwanza. Kw1 = $0.0334 (or $1 = Kw29.918).

WEIGHTS AND MEASURES: The metric system is used.

HOLIDAYS: New Year's Day, 1 January; Anniversary of Outbreak of Anti-Portuguese Struggle, 4 February; Victory Day, 27 March; Youth Day, 14 April; Workers' Day, 1 May; Armed Forces Day, 1 August; National Heroes' Day, 17 September; Independence Day, 11 November; Pioneers' Day, 1 December; Anniversary of the Foundation of the MPLA, 10 December; Family Day, 25 December.

TIME: 1 PM = noon GMT.

¹LOCATION, SIZE, AND EXTENT

Angola is located on the west coast of Africa, south of the equator. Angola is slightly less than twice the size of Texas, with a total area of 1,246,700 sq km (481,353 sq mi), including the exclave of Cabinda (7,270 sq km/2,810 sq mi), which is surrounded by Zaire and the Congo. Angola proper extends 1,758 km (1,092 mi) SE-NW and 1,491 km (926 mi) NE-SW; Cabinda extends 166 km (103 mi) NNE-SSW and 62 km (39 mi) ESE-WNW. Angola proper is bounded on the N and NE by Zaire, on the SE by Zambia, on the S by Namibia (South West Africa), and on the W by the Atlantic Ocean. Its total boundary length, including Cabinda's, is 6,798 km (4,224 mi).

²TOPOGRAPHY

Topographically, Angola consists mainly of broad tablelands above 1,000 m (3,300 ft) in altitude; a high plateau (planalto) in the center and south ranges up to 2,400 m (7,900 ft). The highest point in Angola is Mt. Moco, at 2,620 m (8,596 ft), in the Huambo region; other major peaks are Mt. Mejo (2,583 m/8,474 ft), in the Benguela region, and Mt. Vavéle (2,479 m/8,133 ft), in Kuanza Sul.

Rivers are numerous, but few are navigable. There are three types of rivers in Angola: constantly fed rivers (such as the Zaire River), seasonally fed rivers, and temporary rivers and streams. Only the Kuanza, in central Angola, and the Zaire, in the north, are navigable by boats of significant size.

³CLIMATE

Angola's climate varies considerably from the coast to the central plateau and even between the north coast and the south coast. The north, from Cabinda to Ambriz, has a damp tropical climate. The zone that begins a little to the north of Luanda and extends to Namibe, the Malanje region, and the eastern strip has a moderate tropical climate. Damp conditions prevail south of Namibe, dry conditions in the central plateau zone, and a desert climate in the southern strip between the plateau and the frontier with Namibia. There are two seasons: a dry, cool season from June to late September, and a rainy, hot season from October to April or May. The average temperature is 20°C (68°F); temperatures are warmer along the coast and cooler on the central plateau. The Benguela Current makes the coastal regions arid or semiarid. The annual rainfall is only 5 cm (2 in) at Namibe, 34 cm (13 in) at Luanda, and as high as 150 cm (59 in) in the northeast.

⁴FLORA AND FAUNA

Thick forests (especially in Cabinda and in the Uíge area in the north) cover the wet regions, and in the drier areas there is a thinner savanna vegetation. Fauna includes the lion, impala, hyena, hippopotamus, rhinoceros, and elephant. There are thousands of types of birds and a wide variety of insects.

⁵ENVIRONMENT

The existing environmental problems in Angola have been aggravated by a 30-year war. The main problems are land abuse, loss of forests and impure water. The productivity of the land is continually threatened by erosion and drought. The cutting of tropical rain forests for the commercial value of the wood contributes to the destruction of the land.

Endangered species in Angola included the black-faced impala, three species of turtle (green, olive ridley, and leatherback), the giant sable antelope, the African slender-snouted (or long-snouted) crocodile, the African elephant and the black rhinoceros. Of the 275 species of mammals in Angola, 14 are endangered. Twelve of the 872 species of birds are threatened. Nineteen of the 5,000 species of plants in Angola are also endangered as of 1994.

⁶POPULATION

Angola's population was estimated at 9,390,720 in 1994 by the US Census Bureau but 11,072,000 by the UN for 1995. The government's own estimate was 10,900,000 for mid-1993. This may include refugees abroad. A total of 13,074,000 was projected by the UN for the year 2000, assuming a crude birthrate of 48.4 per 1,000 population, a crude death rate of 16.9, and a net natural increase of 31.5 during 1995–2000. The average density in 1994 was 7.5 per sq km (19.5 per sq mi). About 32% of the population was urban in 1995.

Luanda, the capital, had 1,642,000 people in 1990. Other principal cities are Huambo (about 400,000), Benguela, Lobito, Cabinda, Malanje, and Lubango.

7MIGRATION

According to the UN High Commissioner for Refugees, at the end of 1992 there were 10,800 Zairian and 200 South African refugees in Angola. About 198,000 Angolan refugees were residing in Zaire, and 101,800 in Zambia. An estimated 400,000 whites and mestiços left Angola between May and December 1975; many of them fled to Portugal. There has also been internal migration from rural areas to urban; by 1992 at least 700,000 Angolans had been displaced and as many as 3.5 million peasants were estimated to have migrated to the cities.

8ETHNIC GROUPS

The overwhelming majority (more than 95%) of the population is Bantu, divided into a number of ethnolinguistic groupings. The main ones are, roughly from north to south, the Kongo, Mbundu, Lunda, Chokwe, Ovimbundu, Nganguela, Nyaneka-Humbe, Ovambo, Xindonga, and Herero. A few thousand people in southern and eastern Angola belong to the Khoisan group (Bushmen). The most numerous are the Ovimbundu of west-central Angola (about 37% of the population). Next come the Mbundu of northwest Angola, including the Luanda (about 25%) and the Kongo (some 15%).

The mestiço population is about 200,000. Since the mestiços are generally better educated than the black population, they exercise influence in government disproportionate to their numbers. About 10,000 whites, mostly of Portuguese extraction, remain in Angola from a peak of 335,000.

9LANGUAGES

Portuguese remains the official language, although African languages (and their dialects) are used at the local level.

10RELIGIONS

In 1994, Roman Catholics were believed to be as much as 55% of the population, and Protestants anywhere from 15% to 20%. Perhaps half the population follows African traditional beliefs as well, with some 9.5% doing so exclusively. During the colonial period, Roman Catholicism was the official religion; this ended after independence was declared in 1975.

11TRANSPORTATION

According to Portuguese estimates, there were 72,323 km (44,939 mi) of roads at the time of independence, of which only 8,371 km (5,201 mi) were paved, all-weather highways. In the mid-1980s, these figures had increased to perhaps 80,000 km (50,000 mi), but by 1991 had fallen back to 73,828 km (45,877 mi), of which 8,577 km (5,330 mi) were paved. The government estimated that the renovation of the road system would take 30 years to finish. In 1991 there were 120,000 passenger cars and about 40,000 commercial vehicles.

The rail network had a total extension in 1991 of about 2,879 km (1,789 mi) of 1.067-m-gauge and 310 km (193 mi) of 0.600-m-gauge track. There were three main railway lines, of which only the Luanda railway, which connects the national capital with the provincial capital of Malanje in the north, was functioning normally in 1991. The Namibe railway, which theoretically runs from Angola's port of Namibe to the provincial capital of Menongue in the south (but was running only as far as Matala in 1987), formerly hauled an average of 6 million tons of iron ore a year from the Kassinga mines. The Benguela railway was for-

merly the main exit route for Zairian and Zambian copper, extending through the country from the port of Benguela to the border with Zaire. The Benguela line was shut down by the 1975–76 civil war and, although formally reopened in 1978, ran only sporadically during the next decade, being subject to attacks by insurgents. In 1987, the insurgents offered to cease their attacks so long as the line did not carry military equipment or troops. As of 1991, service had resumed between Lobito and Huambo. By mid-1992, normal passenger traffic resumed from Lobito to Ganda. East of Ganda, however, the route was still severely damaged, with at least 75 bridges in serious disrepair. The Southern African Development Coordination Conference could not obtain the estimated $600 million in funds needed to repair the entire line, so a modest partial repair of the section from Lobito to Kuito was approved, for an estimated cost of $17 million. A national maritime company, Angonave, had eleven ships in 1991, totaling 65,000 GRT.

There is an international airport at Luanda. International and domestic services are maintained by Transportes Aéreos de Angola (TAAG), which performed 1,301 million passenger-kilometers (807,820 passenger-miles) and 43 million freight ton-kilometers (26.7 million freight ton-miles) of service in 1992. There are airstrips for domestic transport at Benguela, Cabinda, Huambo, Namibe, and Catumbela (near Lobito).

12HISTORY

Originally inhabited by people of the Khoisan group (Bushmen), Angola was occupied by various Bantu peoples from farther north and east between 1300 and 1600. By the 15th century, several African kingdoms had developed; the most notable were the kingdoms of the Kongo and Mbundu peoples. The Portuguese arrived on the coast in the late 15th century, and Luanda was founded as a trading settlement in 1575. The Portuguese developed trade with African nations, particularly with the Mbundu, whose ruler was called the ngola (from which the name of Angola comes). The slave trade assumed paramount importance during the 17th century, when slaves were carried to Portuguese plantations in Brazil. From the late 16th through the mid-19th century, Angola may have provided the New World with as many as 2 million slaves.

Slavery was formally abolished (with a 20-year grace period) in 1836, although under Portuguese rule forced labor was common until the early 1950s. Trade in other commodities was needed to replace the slave trade, and between 1870 and 1903 the Portuguese claimed control over more and more of the interior of the country. To spread their control into the interior, the Portuguese began building the Benguela railway in 1902. European domination spread until, in 1951, Angola was made an overseas province of Portugal. Increasing numbers of Portuguese settlers came to Angola, and by 1960 there were about 160,000 Europeans in the country.

Organized armed resistance to Portuguese rule began on 4 February 1961, when urban partisans of the Popular Movement for the Liberation of Angola (MPLA) attacked the São Paulo fortress and police headquarters in Luanda. Within six weeks, the war had been spread throughout the north by the rural guerrillas of another organization, the Union of Angolan Peoples, which later became the National Front for the Liberation of Angola (FNLA). The FNLA, headed by Holden Roberto, set up a revolutionary government-in-exile in Zaire on 3 April 1962. A third movement, the National Union for the Total Independence of Angola (UNITA), headed by Jonas Savimbi, came into being as the consequence of a split in the government-in-exile, of which Savimbi had been foreign minister. The three movements, which were divided by ideology, ethnic considerations, and personal rivalries, were all active militarily when the Portuguese decided to end their African empire after the coup in Portugal on 25 April

LOCATION: Angola proper: 5°49′ to 18°3′s; 11°40′ to 24°5′E. Cabinda: 4°21′ to 5°46′s; 12°2′ to 13°5′E. **BOUNDARY LENGTHS:** Zaire, 2,285 km (1,420 mi); Zambia, 1,086 km (675 mi); Namibia (South West Africa), 1,376 km (855 mi); Atlantic coastline, 1,434 km (891 mi). Cabinda: Zaire, 225 km (140 mi); Congo, 201 km (125 mi). **TERRITORIAL SEA LIMIT:** 20 mi.

1974. After negotiations with FNLA, MPLA, and UNITA leaders, the Portuguese agreed on 15 January 1975 to grant complete independence to Angola on 11 November 1975. The agreement also established a coalition government headed by a three-man presidential council including MPLA leader António Agostinho Neto, Roberto, and Savimbi. As independence day approached,

however, the coalition government fell apart; mediation attempts by other African countries failed.

Thus, when Angola became independent, each of three rival organizations had its own army and sphere of influence. Based in Zaire, the FNLA, which primarily represented the Kongo people, received financial support mainly from China and the US. UNITA and the FNLA together established the Popular Democratic Republic of Angola (with its capital at Huambo), supported by US funds, South African troops, and some white mercenaries (mostly former commandos in the Portuguese armed forces). UNITA had the support of the Ovimbundu, the largest ethnic group in Angola. The MPLA, a Marxist-oriented party, drew its supporters from mestiços in Luanda and other urban areas and from the Mbundu people. It received military as well as financial assistance from the USSR and from some 15,000 Cuban soldiers. The MPLA and Cuban forces soon seized the initiative, and by mid-February 1976 the FNLA and UNITA strongholds had fallen. On 11 February, the OAU formally recognized the MPLA government in Luanda as the legitimate government of Angola. South African troops subsequently withdrew, but the Cuban forces remained to consolidate the MPLA's control over the country and provide technical assistance. By 1982 there were 18,000 Cuban troops in Angola, with the number reportedly rising to 25,000 during the first half of 1983 and to 30,000 in late 1986.

A coup attempt on 27 May 1977 by an MPLA faction opposed to the Cuban involvement was suppressed and followed by a massive purge of the party. Activist groups were reined in, and the organization became more centralized. Meanwhile, UNITA, which had never been rooted out of southern Angola, began to regroup. Despite the Cuban troops and Soviet-bloc military assistance, the MPLA government remained vulnerable to the UNITA insurgency, operating from the southern Angolan countryside and from Namibia. Implicated in this conflict was the government of South Africa, whose continual incursions into southern Angola in the late 1970s and early 1980s were aimed chiefly at the forces of the South West Africa People's Organization (SWAPO), who were using Angola as a base in their bid to force South Africa to give up Namibia. By 1983, 500–1,500 South African soldiers were said to be permanently stationed in southern Angola; in December, South Africa launched a major offensive in the region. In addition to harassing SWAPO, South Africa was continuing to provide supplies to UNITA. The Angolan government resisted efforts by the US to secure the withdrawal of Cuban troops in return for Namibian independence and a South African pullback.

Under an agreement brokered by the US, South African troops withdrew from southern Angola in 1985 but continued to raid SWAPO bases there and to supply military aid to UNITA, including air support. In 1986, the US sent about $15 million in military aid to UNITA, reportedly through Zaire.

Fighting escalated in 1987 and 1988 even as negotiations for a settlement progressed. An Angolan settlement became entangled with the resolution of civil war in and the independence of Namibia. A controversial battle at Cuito Cuanavale in 1988, at which South African and Angolan/Cuban forces were stalemated, led to a South African willingness to agree to end its involvement in Angola and eventually to withdraw from Namibia. Included in the settlement was the Cuban commitment to a phased withdrawal of its military forces from Angola by mid-1991.

Those two agreements, signed on 22 December 1988, in New York by Angola, South Africa, and Cuba, also included a pledge that the signatories would not permit their territories to be used "by any state, organization, or person in connection with any acts of war, aggression, or violence against the territorial integrity...of any state of southwestern Africa." This meant that South Africa would be prohibited from aiding UNITA and Angola would remove the ANC's training bases.

All the major parties had been brought to the conclusion that a settlement was better than a prolongation of the fighting. The Soviet Union wanted to disentangle itself from Angola. The Reagan administration wanted to take the lead in a successful resolution, and its Assistant Secretary of State for African Affairs, Chester A. Crocker, took the lead in the negotiations.

But as settlement in Namibia was moving forward, it proved much harder to bring the Angolan government and UNITA to terms. At a summit at Gbadolite involving 19 African leaders, dos Santos and Savimbi shook hands publicly and endorsed the "Gbadolite Declaration" (cease-fire and reconciliation plan) on 22 June 1989. But from the start, the terms were disputed and swiftly unraveled. The parties returned to the battlefield.

Yet, the powers began to scale back their support. The relaxation of cold war tensions provided the basis for contacts between the warring parties. Progress moved in fits and starts and in April 1991, Savimbi and dos Santos initialed an agreement which led to the establishment of a UN-supervised cease-fire and a process of national reconciliation.

The culmination of that process was to have been national elections, held on 29 and 30 September 1992. The run-up to the election went smoothly. Representatives of 18 parties participated in a non-partisan National Electoral Commission. All 18 parties ran candidates in the legislative election. There were 11 presidential candidates.

Dos Santos won 49.6% of the presidential vote and Savimbi got 40.1%. Thus, a run-off was required. The MPLA took 53.7% to UNITA's 34.1% of the legislative vote, giving the ruling party a 129 to 70 margin in the 220-seat legislature. Holden Roberto's FNLA got 2.1% of the vote.

Savimbi, upset by his unexpected defeat, charged fraud and threatened to take up arms again. Yet, the UN and other international observers certified the absence of systematic fraud and urged Savimbi to accept the results.

Tension increased when UNITA took de facto control of several provinces, and its generals were withdrawn from the officially "merged" national army. Fighting broke out in Luanda in October and more than 1,000 were killed in a week. UNITA gained control of around 75% of Angola. Its refusal to accept UN-brokered cease-fire terms agreed to by the government in May led to a Security Council resolution on 1 June 1993, condemning unanimously UNITA for endangering the peace process and to US recognition of the Angolan government on 19 May. In 1994, it was estimated that 1,000 were dying every day in the fighting. In September 1993, the Security Council placed a mandatory oil and arms embargo on UNITA.

A stable cease-fire proves elusive. By mid-year 1994, UNITA threatened several major cities. Yet, UNITA lost its sources of South African support after an ANC-coalition government was installed there in April. US pressure led to a resumption of talks in Lusaka, Zambia, in October 1993, but they dragged on for months.

[13]GOVERNMENT

The constitution of 1975, amended in 1976 and 1980, was promulgated and revised by the MPLA. The Council of Ministers, chaired by the president of Angola, formed the executive. In 1980, a 223-member National People's Assembly, indirectly elected, replaced the Council of the Revolution as the supreme organ of the State; in January 1987, the Assembly was enlarged to 289 members. The president of the republic is the president of the MPLA–Workers' Party. The president may rule by decree, exercising legislative functions delegated to him by the People's Assembly.

This was changed by the 1988 accords and the agreements between government and UNITA leading up to the September 1992 legislative and presidential elections. In those elections, 220 seats were contested. MPLA won 129 and UNITA took 70. A run-off was called for in the presidential election, since dos Santos got just 49.6% to Savimbi's 40.7%, but Savimbi, charging fraud, plunged Angola into major war. UNITA now controls three-quarters of the territory and a good many of the cities. No date has been set for the run-off.

A transitional government was set up in December 1992. It is dominated by the MPLA. UNITA has six cabinet posts. Four other parties are represented, but the central government cannot administer what it cannot control.

14POLITICAL PARTIES

Until 1974, Portuguese policy did not recognize the legitimacy of any nationalist movements for self-determination and independence, and political parties advocating territorial independence were suppressed. The three leading political organizations at the time of independence were the Popular Movement for the Liberation of Angola (Movimento Popular de Libertação de Angola—MPLA), founded in 1956; the National Front for the Liberation of Angola (Frente Nacional de Libertação de Angola—FNLA), founded in 1962; and the National Union for the Total Independence of Angola (União Nacional para a Indepêndencia Total de Angola—UNITA), founded in 1966. After the victory of the MPLA and Cuban forces and the recognition of the MPLA government by the OAU and by most non-African countries, the MPLA-Workers' Party (MPLA–Partido de Trabalho, or MPLA–PT), a Marxist-Leninist vanguard party, was created in December 1977. UNITA remained in de facto control of part of the country, while the remnants of the FNLA continued low-level guerrilla activity in the northwest, as did the Front for the Liberation of the Cabinda Enclave.

Some 18 parties contested the 1992 legislative elections. MPLA took 53.7% of the vote to UNITA's 34.1% and the FNLA's 2.1%. Also represented are the Angolan Democratic Forum (FDA), the Democratic Renewal Party (PRD), and the Angola Youth Worker, Peasant Alliance Party (PAJOCA). Separatist groups in Cabinda, such as the Frente Nacional de Libertação do Enclave de Cabinda (FLEC) and the National Union for the Liberation of Cabinda (UNLC) demand independence. They did not take part in the national elections.

15LOCAL GOVERNMENT

Angola consists of 18 provinces, one of which, Cabinda, is physically separated from the others by the Zaire River. The provinces are divided into districts and communes. Commissioners, directly responsible to the prime minister but appointed by the president on the recommendation of the MPLA–PT, direct these units. Provincial legislatures, each of 55–85 members, were created in 1980; in 1986, these legislatures were enlarged and had up to 100 members each. In the 1992 elections, MPLA carried 14 of the provinces and UNITA carried four. That order collapsed in the fighting since late 1992.

16JUDICIAL SYSTEM

Before independence, Portuguese civil and military law was applied by municipal courts, labor courts, ordinary courts, and administrative tribunals; final appeal was to the Metropolitan High Court in Lisbon. A 1978 law declared that people's courts with working class representatives would be courts of first instance. Criminal, police, and labor courts would have lay judges whose voices would be equal to those of professional judges. Higher courts were to be located in Luanda and each provincial capital, and there were to be a court of appeals and a Supreme Court in Luanda. As of 1986, regional military councils had jurisdiction over state security cases, including those involving economic crimes.

The judicial system currently consists of municipal and provincial courts at the trial level and a Supreme Court at the appellate level. Municipal court judges are usually laymen. Provincial courts located in each of the 18 provincial capitals are administered by the Ministry of Justice. Provincial court judges are nominated by the Supreme Court. The judge of the provincial court, along with two laymen, acts as a jury.

In 1991, the Constitution was amended to guarantee an independent judiciary. In practice, however, the President appoints the 16 judges of the Supreme Court for life terms upon recommendation of an association of magistrates but without confirmation by the General Assembly.

A 1992 law called for a constitutional court, but as of early 1994, this court had not yet been established.

In 1993, the National Union for the Total Independence of Angola (UNITA) controlled most of national territory. There is now little in the way of an organized judicial system in the areas under UNITA control.

17ARMED FORCES

Defense responsibilities are vested in the Armed Popular Forces for the Liberation of Angola (Forças Amadas Populares de Libertação de Angola—FAPLA), now divided into an army, navy, air and air defense force, people's defense organization and territorial troops (a militia), and frontier guard. Conscription was imposed in 1978. In 1993, the army had 73 brigades of about 1,000 men each and a total force of 120,000, armed with perhaps 500 Soviet-made tanks and other combat vehicles; the navy had 1,500 personnel and 17 vessels; and the air force had 6,000 personnel and 150 combat aircraft and 40 armed helicopters. Cuban forces and European advisors have left the country, but reorganization and reduction of the government and rebel forces is moving slowly. Defense expenditures are impossible to estimate with confidence, but may reach $500 million. UNITA and other opposition forces probably number no more than 28,000 soldiers.

18INTERNATIONAL COOPERATION

Angola, a UN member since 1 December 1976, participates in ECA and all the nonregional specialized agencies except IAEA, IBRD, IDA, IFAD, IFC, IMF, and WIPO; the nation is a de facto adherent of GATT and a signatory to the Law of the Sea. Angola also participates in the African Development Bank, G-77, and OAU.

During the struggle against Portuguese rule, economic and political support was provided to the revolutionary groups by the OAU and its member states, organizations such as the World Council of Churches, and some Western nations, including Sweden. The MPLA had strong ties with the former USSR and Cuba, from which it received financial and military aid.

19ECONOMY

Angola is a potentially rich country of abundant natural resources, a surplus-producing agricultural sector and a sizable manufacturing potential. This promise has remained unfulfilled due to the effects of a 20-year-long civil war.

Having both temperate and tropical zones, Angola has the potential for producing a wide variety of agricultural products. Prior to the outbreak of hostilities, Angola produced major surpluses of coffee, sisal, cotton, and maize. Cassava is the staple food crop and the leader, though consumed almost entirely domestically, in terms of volume of agricultural output.

Petroleum production and diamond mining lead Angola's minerals sector. Angola also has significant deposits in high-grade iron ore, copper, manganese, phosphates, and uranium.

The petroleum sector has benefited from major investments, totaling over $2 billion since 1987, and from a relative immunity from the civil war. Angola is not a member of OPEC.

20INCOME

In 1992 Angola's GDP was $760 million in current US dollars. It is estimated agriculture contributed 10.3%, while mining produced 5.7%. Petroleum refining and other manufacturing combined added 3.2% and trade accounted for 4.4%.

[21] LABOR

Until 1975, the great bulk of the Angolan African population consisted of traditional subsistence farmers or wage workers on expatriates' plantations. With the boom the country experienced during the 1960s and early 1970s, especially in mineral-related industries, a number of Africans were training in mining and in road, railway, and housing construction.

Nationwide employment figures are not available. The labor force was estimated at 4.1 million in 1990. Wage policy was made the prerogative of the state in 1976, when penalties of two to eight years were established for unauthorized strikes and slowdowns. The official national labor federation, the União Nacional de Trabalhadores Angolanos (which is controlled by the MPLA), is still the primary workers' organization in the country. There are two other groups, the National Confederation of Free Trade Unions of Angola and the Democratic Confederation of Angolan Workers. Reversing earlier policy, the 1991 Constitution recognizes the right for Angolans to form unions, bargain collectively, and to strike. In 1992 there were numerous strikes, including those by the Ministry of Finance workers, hospital personnel, and teachers at Luanda.

[22] AGRICULTURE

Agriculture has long been the backbone of the Angolan economy. In 1991, even though an abundance of arable land was available, less than 3% was cultivated. Diverse climatic conditions favor a wide variety of crops, and there is also considerable irrigation potential. Coffee, primarily of the robust variety, at one time made Angola the world's fourth-largest producer, but during the civil war almost all the main plantations were abandoned, and crop disease set in.

Marketed cash crops in 1992 included 5,000 tons of coffee (down from 225,000 tons in 1972), 11,000 tons of cotton (48,000 in 1972), and 1,000 tons of sisal. The principal food crops are cassava, with an estimated 1,885,000 tons in 1992, corn, 369,000 tons, and sweet potatoes, 170,000 tons. Other 1992 estimated yields included bananas, 280,000 tons; citrus fruits, 80,000 tons; millet, 75,000 tons; dry beans, 36,000 tons; palm oil, 40,000 tons; potatoes, 40,000 tons; raw sugar, 33,000 tons; rice, 18,000 tons; and peanuts (in shell), 18,000 tons.

[23] ANIMAL HUSBANDRY

Lack of a pastoral tradition among northern Angolans, abundance of the tsetse fly in many regions, and the poor quality of natural pastures are some of the factors most frequently cited to explain the lag in animal husbandry in Portuguese Angola. What little there was of the livestock industry was virtually destroyed in the 1975–76 civil war.

Estimated livestock in 1992 included cattle, 3,200,000 head; goats, 1,550,000; hogs, 810,000; and sheep, 250,000. There were 6 million chickens. Livestock products included an estimated 57,000 tons of beef and veal and 148,000 tons of milk in 1992.

[24] FISHING

Fresh fish, fish meal, dried fish, and fish oil are produced for the domestic market and for export. During 1975–76, some of the processing plants were destroyed, and most of the modern fishing boats departed with refugees. In 1991, the Angolan catch was only 75,062 tons (down from 106,941 tons in 1990). Some of the Spanish, Japanese, and Italian vessels fishing under license also pay in kind. The majority of the catch consists of cunene horse mackerel.

[25] FORESTRY

In 1991, about 42% of the country was covered by forests and woodland. Angola's large timber resources include the great Maiombe tropical rain forest in Cabinda. In addition, eucalyptus, pine, and cypress plantations cover 140,000 hectares (346,000 acres). In 1991, roundwood production was estimated at 6,593,000 cu m. Timber exports were banned after independence.

[26] MINING

Angola is very rich in mineral resources, especially crude oil, diamonds, iron ore, magnetite, copper, phosphates, gypsum, uranium, gold, asphalt, and feldspar. Diamond production, consisting mainly of gem stones, totaled 960,558 carats in 1991. The mines, mainly in Lunda Norte Province, have been government controlled, but in 1986 the government began a policy of awarding production-sharing concessions to foreign companies. In the early 1980s, about 30% of the diamond output was being smuggled out of the country, primarily to Portugal. In 1990, an estimated 500,000 carats may have been smuggled across the border to Zaire. Large iron ore deposits have been discovered in many areas; the deposits at Kassinga, in southern Angola, with an estimated reserve of 1 billion tons of high-grade hematite iron ore, annually yielded millions of tons of ore exports before the civil war halted mining in 1975. Ferrangol, the state iron ore mining company, produced a slight quantity of ore in 1988, but has shown no output since. Clay, granite, marble, and crushed stone were also reportedly mined throughout the country. As of 1991, the state was considering a joint-venture contract with a South African–British group to mine high quality quartz from the Conda–Pocarica mine near Sumbe.

[27] ENERGY AND POWER

Angola has extensive hydroelectric power resources that far exceed its present needs. The Cambembe Dam, on the Kuanza River, provides Luanda's industries with cheap power. Two dams on the Catumbela River produce power for the Lobito and Benguela areas. Matala Dam in southern Cunene provides power to Lubango and Namibe. The Ruacaná Falls Dam, near the Namibian border, was completed in the late 1970s, but the power station is in Namibia. A 520-million-kwh hydroelectric station on the Kuanza River at Kapanda, the first turbine of which was to have come on stream in December 1992, is still not completed. Installed capacity rose from 429,000 kw (67% hydroelectric) in 1985 to 617,000 kw (about 67% hydro) in 1991. Total production in 1991 was 1,840 million kwh, of which 74% was hydroelectric. Angola's hydroelectric power distribution has come under rebel attack; from 1984 to 1990, rebels destroyed 217 pylons to the powerlines that supply Luanda.

Crude oil, in the production of which Angola ranks fifth in Africa, has been Angola's chief export since 1973; it is also the leading source of government revenue. All production is along the Atlantic coast, mostly off Cabinda. In 1992, several oil companies were engaged in production, of which the largest was a subsidiary of Chevron. This firm has a 49/51% participation agreement with Sonangol, the state oil company. Other firms included Fina Petróleos de Angola (a Belgian subsidiary), Elf Aquitaine, and Texaco. In 1992, 27 million tons were produced; output increased by 5.5% from 1991. At the beginning of 1993, proven oil reserves totaled 200 million tons. About 560 million cu m of natural gas was produced in 1992. Total natural gas reserves were estimated at 50 billion cu m. On 12 January 1993, UNITA forces destroyed five oil wells in the northwestern province of Zaire. Although oil experts have been relatively unaffected, continued fighting could seriously disrupt service.

[28] INDUSTRY

In its pre-1975 prime, the Angolan industrial sector centered on petroleum refining and machinery, construction inputs, food processing, electrical products, chemicals, steel, and vehicle assembly. As a consequence of the civil war, Angola's industrial sector is operating at a fraction of pre-war levels. Prospects for a peaceful resolution of the conflict and a retreat from Marxist-Leninist principles have encouraged investors in certain industries. The 1988 foreign investment code, while liberalizing foreign rights over profits and property, still prevents foreign investment in the telecommunications and media, transport, defense, and banking industries. Angola's hydroelectric power potential is considerable and is a key to Angola's industrial future. A $1,230 million World Bank project is planned to double Angola's post-war hydroelectric capacity, which stood at 1.8 billion kwh in 1990.

29SCIENCE AND TECHNOLOGY

Angola has the Cotton Scientific Research Center in Catete, the Agricultural Research Institute and the Institute for Veterinary Research in Huambo, and the Medical Research Institute and the Hydrological and Geophysics Institute in Luanda. The University Agostinho Neto, founded in 1963, has faculties of sciences, agriculture, medicine, and engineering, and the National Scientific Research Center. The National Museum of Natural History has zoology exhibits.

30DOMESTIC TRADE

Practically all domestic trade was in Portuguese hands before independence, when state people's stores and consumer cooperatives were established in the cities. Today, the Angolan domestic economy is in shambles. The rural population has been displaced by the civil war and is unable to fully engage in agricultural production. It is projected that less than 40% of cereal needs will be met in 1994. Food assistance requirements for over 2 million people are met through food aid and emergency assistance programs. According to the Angolan industrial association, 60% of all workers were unemployed by mid-1991. Meanwhile inflation is soaring; it stood at 1,680% for the year ending September 1993. Imports are strictly controlled due to a lack of foreign exchange. Barter is common.

31FOREIGN TRADE

Angola is a major exporter of crude oil and diamonds, which have been the backbone of its enviable trade surplus record since the late 1970s.

Imports in 1989 totaled Kw34,362 million. The principal items imported in 1985 were food and food products, civil engineering equipment, motor vehicles and parts, metal products, and medicines and pharmaceuticals.

In 1985, Angola's principal trading partners were the US (43.4%), Spain (11.8%), the United Kingdom (10.4%), and Brazil (6.3%). Imports came primarily from Portugal (13.2%), France (11.2%), and Brazil (10.7%).

32BALANCE OF PAYMENTS

Oil exports produced substantial trade surpluses during the late 1970s and early 1980s. Despite this positive cash flow, Angola in 1979 began to request lines of credit in order to finance its reconstruction projects. By 1991 the government's economic policies encouraged neither private investment nor non-oil exports. Furthermore, poor monetary policy created price distortions which have exacerbated a trade deficit and rapidly diminished agricultural exports. Import restrictions were reintroduced after the 1986 oil price slump.

In 1992 merchandise exports totaled $3,259 million and imports $2,977 million. The merchandise trade balance was $1,860 million. The oil sector accounted for $2,977 million in exports.

33BANKING AND SECURITIES

In 1976, the government nationalized the two major banks, the Bank of Angola and the Commercial Bank of Angola. The former became the central bank, renamed the National Bank of Angola; the latter was renamed the People's Bank of Angola. The Bank of Commercial and Industrial Commerce also operates, and in 1985 the Banque Paribas opened an office. There are no securities exchanges.

34INSURANCE

The conflicts of the mid-1970s greatly shook the insurance industry, which was nationalized in 1978. At that time, the National Insurance and Reinsurance Co. of Angola was created. All private company policies were declared null and void except for life insurance.

35PUBLIC FINANCE

Liberal monetary policies have financed large public sector deficits, which has led to high inflation and price distortions. In 1991, the budget deficit amounted to 23% of GDP. Angola's external debt in 1992 amounted to an estimated $8.1 billion; more than half was owed to the former Soviet Union, and the majority of the debt was incurred from the war.

Government finances are precarious. Military expenditures continue to consume an enormous portion of the national budget. Since the 1970s, Angola has relied heavily on oil exports for revenue. However, revenues from oil sales are down as the result of a fall in the international price of oil. Revenues from diamond sales have likewise declined due to the capture of some of the producing fields by the anti-government forces. As a result, the current-account deficit for 1992 was $511 million and is thought to have widened in 1993. In the absence of a debt-structuring agreement with international creditors, debt-service arrears had expanded to over $4 billion by the end of 1992. With the civil war unresolved, the Angolan government does not feel prepared to enter into a structural adjustment agreement with the IMF.

36TAXATION

Corporation tax is 35% of net profits, with a surtax ranging from 2% to 28%. Income tax for individuals ranges from 1–40% for employees and 3–60% for self-employed professionals. Also levied are inheritance and gift taxes, a payroll tax for social security, and a value-added tax ranging from 5%–80% on 100 listed products.

37CUSTOMS AND DUTIES

Both specific and ad valorem duties are levied. Specific duties are assessed by weight. Additional taxes are levied on luxury items, and preferential treatment is accorded to goods from Portugal, Mozambique, Guinea-Bissau, Cape Verde, and Sao Tome and Principe. All imports require a license and are handled by one of several state companies. Most exports are similarly handled by state agencies.

38FOREIGN INVESTMENT

In spite of the civil war and the socialist legacy, investors retain their interest in Angola. In an action pivotal to future foreign investment, Angola initiated a financial restructuring program in 1988 and became a member of the IMF in September 1989. In October 1990, the government brought about a return to a market economy, and in April 1991, 100 previously nationalized companies were returned to their original owners.

The sizable investments in the petroleum sector continue. Elf oil and Chevron both have major new investments underway, with Chevron talking of a $2.5 billion program over the next five years. De Beers, in a 1991 agreement with the government diamond company, is investing in new diamond exploration. The African Development Bank is preparing a loan in support of the phosphate industry.

The fishing industry is reviving. A joint Angolan-Spanish company has begun exporting lobsters. The French government is financing the redevelopment of the Boavista fishing port and a $10 million Italian investment in artisanal fishing has been made.

39 ECONOMIC DEVELOPMENT

With the exception of the petroleum industry and possibly the fishing industry, economic development in Angola depends upon a political settlement of the civil war. There are signs that an agreement is now possible between the government and UNITA, but negotiations continue over an increased role for UN peace-keeping forces, the terms of the amnesty for UNITA forces, and the package of national reconciliation measures to be adopted.

40 SOCIAL DEVELOPMENT

Until recently, social services for Africans were almost entirely the responsibility of the various tribal groups. The Roman Catholic Church also played an integral part in the administration of welfare, health, and educational programs. The MPLA has established a number of self-help organizations. A number of international nongovernmental organizations have also gotten involved, particularly in the provision of health care.

Human rights organizations such as Amnesty International have complained to the Angolan government concerning arbitrary arrest and detention of persons suspected of political crimes and physical intimidation of prisoners by prison guards. Military forces, the Ministry of State Security, and the police reportedly have independent powers of arrest, and prisoners may be held without trial. UNITA is even more responsible for coercion and the violent denial of human and civil rights. Hundreds of thousands of deaths and far more brutal injuries, particularly from hidden land mines, have grown out of the post-1992 renewal of the civil war.

41 HEALTH

Only a small fraction of the population receives even rudimentary medical attention (an estimated 30% in 1992). In 1990, there were 389 doctors and, in 1989, there were 8 pharmacists and 6 dentists. In 1992, average life expectancy was estimated at only 46 years, and infant mortality was estimated at 170 per 1,000 live births. The incidence of tuberculosis in 1990 was 225 per 100,000 people. Immunization rates for one-year-old children in 1992 were: tuberculosis, 27%; diphtheria, pertussis, and tetanus 12%; polio, 13%; and measles, 26%. In 1992, 50% of deaths were attributed to malaria, malnutrition, measles, and diarrheal diseases, and from 1975 to 1992, there were 300,000 civil war-related deaths. The overall death rate was 19.2 per 1,000 in 1993.

42 HOUSING

The rapid growth of Angola's industrial centers has meant the rapid growth of urban slums. Demolition of shantytowns around Luanda is a principal aim of the government. According to the latest available figures for 1980–88, the total housing stock numbered 1,750,000 with 5.1 people per dwelling.

43 EDUCATION

In 1990 the adult literacy rate was estimated as 58.3% (males: 44.4% and females: 71.5%). Education for children between the ages of seven and 15 years is compulsory and free. Primary education is for four years and secondary for seven years. While Portuguese was the language of instruction in earlier times, the vernacular is more commonly used now. Angolan primary schools had 990,155 pupils and 31,062 teachers in 1990. The secondary schools had 186,499 pupils the same year.

The University Agostinho Neto in Luanda was established in 1963 and has a faculty for science, engineering, law, medicine, economics, and agriculture. In 1990 all higher level institutions had 6,534 students and 439 teaching staff.

44 LIBRARIES AND MUSEUMS

The National Library of Angola, founded in Luanda in 1969, had 30,000 volumes in 1986. The Municipal Library in Luanda has more than 14,000 volumes.

The Angola Museum, which contains Angola's historical archives, and the Coffee Museum, Museum of Geology, Museum of Natural History, National Museum of Archaeology, Central Museum of the Armed Forces, and National Museum of Anthropology are all located in Luanda. There are regional museums in Dondo, Namibe, Huambo, Lobito, Lubango, and Uíge.

45 MEDIA

All media were nationalized in 1992. Daily newspapers in 1986 were *Jornal de Angola*, with a circulation of 41,000; *Provincia de Angola*, 35,000; and *ABC Diario de Angola*, 8,500. All were published in Portuguese in Luanda. The official government organ is the *Diario da Republica*.

There were 77,000 telephones in 1991. Rádio Nacional de Angola broadcasts in Portuguese, English, French, Spanish, and major local languages. There were about 270,000 radio sets in 1991. Televisão Popular de Angola was received by about 21,000 television sets during the same year.

46 ORGANIZATIONS

Organizations established by the MPLA include the Organization of Angolan Women, the Medical Assistance Service, and the Centers for Revolutionary Instruction.

47 TOURISM, TRAVEL, AND RECREATION

Tourism was an important activity until 1972, when the guerrilla war and the subsequent civil war led to a precipitous drop in the number of tourists and hence of tourist revenues. Since the mid-1980s the government has severely restricted the number of foreigners allowed into the country, and all visitors require visas.

48 FAMOUS ANGOLANS

António Agostinho Neto (1922–79), a poet and physician who served as the president of MPLA (1962–79) and president of Angola (1975–79), was Angola's dominant political figure. José Eduardo dos Santos (b.1942) succeeded Neto in both these posts. Jonas Malheiro Savimbi (b.1934), the son of a pastor, founded UNITA in 1966.

49 DEPENDENCIES

Angola has no territories or colonies.

50 BIBLIOGRAPHY

Angola, Mozambique, and the West. New York: Praeger, 1987.

Bender, Gerald J. *Angola Under the Portuguese: The Myth and the Reality.* Berkeley: University of California Press, 1978.

Black, Richard. *Angola.* Santa Barbara, Calif.: Clio Press, 1992.

Broadhead, Susan H. (Susan Herlin). *Historical Dictionary of Angola.* 2nd ed. Metuchen, N.J.: Scarecrow Press, 1992.

Changing the History of Africa: Angola and Namibia. Melbourne, Australia: Ocean Press, 1989.

Ebinger, Charles K. *Foreign Intervention in Civil War: The Politics and Diplomacy of the Angolan Conflict.* Boulder, Colo.: Westview, 1986.

Henderson, Lawrence W. *Angola: Five Centuries of Conflict.* Ithaca, N.Y.: Cornell University Press, 1979.

James, W. Martin. *A Political History of the Civil War in Angola, 1974–1990.* New Brunswick, N.J.: Transaction Publishers, 1992.

Jaster, Robert S. *The 1988 Peace Accords and the Future of South-western Africa.* London: Brassey's for the International Institute for Strategic Studies, 1990.

Marcum, John. *The Angolan Revolution.* 2 vols. Cambridge, Mass.: MIT Press, 1969–78.

Spikes, Daniel. *Angola and the Politics of Intervention: From Local Bush War to Chronic Crisis in Southern Africa.* Jefferson, NC: McFarland & Company, 1993.

BENIN

Republic of Benin
République du Bénin

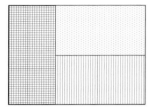

CAPITAL: Porto-Novo.

FLAG: Two equal horizontal bands of yellow (top) and red with a vertical green band on the hoist side.

ANTHEM: *L'Aube Nouvelle (The New Dawn).*

MONETARY UNIT: The Communauté Financière Africaine franc (CFA Fr) is a paper currency. There are coins of 1, 2, 5, 10, 25, 50, 100, and 500 CFA francs, and notes of 50, 100, 500, 1,000, 5,000, and 10,000 CFA francs. CFA Fr1 = $0.0017 (or $1 = CFA Fr586.20).

WEIGHTS AND MEASURES: The metric system is the legal standard.

HOLIDAYS: New Year's Day, 1 January; Anniversary of Mercenary Attack on Cotonou, 16 January; Labor Day, 1 May; Independence Day, 1 August; Armed Forces Day, 26 October; National Day, 30 November; Harvest Day, 31 December. Most religious holidays have been abolished, but Good Friday, Easter Monday, Christmas, 'Id al-Fitr, and Id al-'Adha' remain public holidays.

TIME: 1 PM = noon GMT.

¹LOCATION, SIZE, AND EXTENT

The People's Republic of Benin (formerly Dahomey) is situated in West Africa on the northern coast of the Gulf of Guinea, and has an area of 112,620 sq km (43,483 sq mi), extending 665 km (413 mi) N–S and 333 km (207 mi) E–W. Comparatively, the area occupied by Benin is slightly smaller than the state of Pennsylvania. Roughly wedge-shaped, Benin is bounded on the N by Niger, on the E by Nigeria, on the S by the Gulf of Guinea (Atlantic Ocean), on the W by Togo, and on the NW by Burkina Faso, with a total boundary length of 2,110 km (1,311 mi). The capital city of Benin, Porto-Novo, is located in the southeastern corner of the country.

²TOPOGRAPHY

Difficult of access because of sandbanks, the coast has no natural harbors, river mouths, or islands. Behind the coastline is a network of lagoons, from that of Grand Popo on the Togo border (navigable at all seasons) and joined to Lake Ahémé, to that of Porto-Novo on the east, into which flows Benin's longest river, the Ouémé, navigable for some 200 km (125 mi) of its total of 459 km (285 mi). Besides the Ouémé, the only other major river in the south is the Couffo, which flows into Lake Ahémé. The Mono, serving from Parahoué to Grand Popo as the boundary with Togo, is navigable for 80 km (50 mi) but subject to torrential floods in the rainy season. Benin's northern rivers, the Mékrou, Alibory, and Sota, which are tributaries of the Niger, and the Pandjari, a tributary of the Volta, are torrential and broken by rocks.

North of the narrow belt of coastal sand is a region of lateritic clay, the main oil palm area, intersected by a marshy depression between Allada and Abomey that stretches east to the Nigerian frontier. North of the hills of Dassa, the height ranges from 60 to 150 m (200–500 ft), broken only by the Atakora Mountains, stretching in a southwesterly direction into Togo; their high point is 641 m (2,103 ft).

³CLIMATE

South of Savalou, especially in the west, the climate is typically equatorial—hot and humid, with a long dry season from December to March, in which the dry harmattan blows in a northeasterly to southwesterly direction. Temperatures range between 22°C (72°F) and 35°C (95°F), with the average 27°C (81°F). The great rains fall from March to July; there is a short dry season from July to September and a short wet season from mid-September to mid-November. In the southwest, average rainfall is considerably lower and the dry season longer: at Grand Popo, for example, average rainfall is about 82 cm (32 in) as compared with about 127 cm (50 in) in Porto-Novo and Cotonou. Northern Benin has only one wet season (May to September, with most rain in August) and a hot dry season in which the harmattan blows for three or four months. Temperatures range from a maximum of 40°C (104°F) in January to a minimum of 13°C (56°F) in January. Although rainfall, which is highest in central Benin (135 cm/53 in), decreases as one moves northward, it remains high (97 cm/38 in), in most of northern Benin.

⁴FLORA AND FAUNA

Apart from small isolated patches, little true forest remains. The coconut plantations of the coastal strip give way to oil palms and ronier palms growing as far north as Abomey; these are in turn succeeded by savanna woodland, in which the vegetation of the Guinea forest and the vegetation of the southern Sudan are intermingled, and then by characteristic Sudanic savanna. Trees include coconut, oil palm, ronier palm, ebony, shea nut, kapok, fromager, and Senegal mahogany. Among the mammals in Benin are the elephant, lion, panther, monkey, and wild pig, as well as many kinds of antelope. Crocodiles and many species of snakes (including python, puff adder, and mamba) are widely distributed. Partridge, guinea fowl, and wild duck, as well as many kinds of tropical birds, are common. Insects include varieties of tsetse fly and other vectors of epidemic disease.

⁵ENVIRONMENT

Benin has two national parks and several game reserves. In addition, the government has set aside 5,900 hectares (14,580 acres) for nurseries to foster reforestation. In 1986, 297,800 trees were planted. Among the government organizations with responsibility for the environment are the National Commission for Combating Pollution and for the Protection and Improvement of the Environment, which is under the Ministry of Public Health, and the Ministry of Rural Development and Cooperative Action. In 1994, the main environmental issues facing the people of Benin are desertification, deforestation, wildlife endangerment and water pollution. The spread of the desert into agricultural lands in the north is accelerated by regular droughts. Benin has also lost 59% of its forests from uncontrolled agricultural practices and fires. Benin has 6.2 cubic miles of water supply. Twenty-seven percent of the city dwellers and 57% of the people in rural areas do not have water. Factors which contribute to the endangerment of the wildlife in Benin are the same as those which threaten the forests. By 1994, of the 187 species of mammals, 11 were threatened with extinction. Of 630 bird species, one was endangered. Three plant species out of a total of 2,000 were also threatened. As of 1994, the chimpanzee was extinct.

⁶POPULATION

Total population mid-1994 was estimated at 5,338,095, as compared with a 1992 census population of 4,855,349. A population of 6,269,000 is projected for the year 2000, assuming a crude birthrate of 45.8 per 1,000 population, a crude death rate of 16, and a net natural increase of 29.8 during 1995–2000. The average annual growth rate is about 3.1%. The average population density in 1992 was 43 per sq km (112 per sq mi). Almost three-fourths of the population are clustered in the southern half of the country, where the density reaches more than 120 per sq km (290 per sq mi). An estimated 42% of the population was urban in 1995. Porto-Novo, the nominal capital, had a population of about 213,000 in 1990. In the early 1990s, Cotonou, the administrative and economic center and port, had a population of about 400,000. Other important towns are Abomey, Ouidah, and Parakou.

⁷MIGRATION

Seasonal labor migration, to both Nigeria and Ghana, is considerable and of long duration, but estimates of its extent are not available. Thousands of Beninese were expelled from Nigeria in early 1983, and thousands were expelled from Gabon in 1977–78. It was estimated in 1984 that over 100,000 people living abroad could be regarded as political refugees. There were some 200 Chadian refugees in Benin at the end of 1992.

⁸ETHNIC GROUPS

Although several of the larger groups in southern Benin are culturally and socially closely related, Benin is not ethnically or linguistically homogeneous, and there is a particularly marked division between the peoples of the south and those of the north. The largest ethnic group is that of the Fon or Dahomeyans (about 25%), the closely related Adja (about 6%), and the Aizo (about 5%), who live in the south of the country and are predominantly farmers. The Goun (about 11%), who are related to the Adja, are concentrated around Porto-Novo. The Bariba (about 12%) are the dominant people in northern Benin. The Yoruba (more than 12%), who came from Nigeria and are settled along the eastern boundary of the country, are essentially a farming people. In the northeast, the Somba (more than 4%) subdivide into a number of distinct groups. The Fulani (about 6%), traditionally nomadic herders, gradually are becoming sedentary. Other groups include the Holli, the Dendi, and the Pilapila (or Yowa).

⁹LANGUAGES

The official language is French. Many African languages are spoken. Fon and Yoruba are the most important in southern Benin, Bariba (a subgroup of the Voltaic group in which the Mossi language is most important) and Fulani in the north.

¹⁰RELIGIONS

In 1992, it was estimated that 70% of the people of Benin follow traditional African religions, particularly those involving fetishism. Fetishes may take the form of images, trees, or animals (the python is considered sacred in southern Benin). There are convents where novices undergo periods of training before returning to the outside world. Christian missions were established in the middle of the 19th century (Wesleyan Methodist, 1852; Roman Catholic, 1863), and missionary effort was more concentrated in Benin than in the rest of French West Africa, especially in educational work. In 1982, Pope John Paul II visited Benin during his tour of Africa. Some independent African Christian churches, eschewing European influence or control, have also been established. In 1992, about 20% of the population was Roman Catholic; some 13% of the people, mainly those in the north, profess Islam.

¹¹TRANSPORTATION

In 1991, Benin had 578 km (359 mi) of meter-gauge railroad. The Benin-Niger Joint Railway and Transport Organization, a public corporation, operates the passenger and freight railroad, with Benin owning 63% of the corporation and Niger 37%. The main line runs north from Cotonou to Parakou, with a branch to Segboroué in the west. The eastern line runs from Cotonou to Porto-Novo and Pobé.

Of Benin's 5,050 km (3,138 mi) of roads (excluding tracks), only about 920 km (572 mi) are tarred. The major roads are the coastal highway linking Benin with Lagos in Nigeria and Lomé in Togo; the road from Cotonou to Parakou (terminus of the railroad) and its extension via Kandi to Malanville on the Niger River; and the road north from Tchaourou that links Benin with Burkina Faso. In 1992, Benin had about 25,000 passenger cars and 13,000 commercial vehicles.

Regular transportation services from Parakou to Malanville and thence to Niamey (in Niger), either by road or, in the season when the Niger River is navigable, by river steamer, are important for the movement of produce to and from Niger via Cotonou, Benin's one port. Until 1965, the port was serviced by a wharf built in 1891. In 1965, a new deepwater port, constructed with French and European Development Fund assistance and capable of handling 1 million tons annually, was opened. In the mid-1980s, the port was expanded to handle 3 million tons a year. Landlocked Niger has a free zone in the port area of Cotonou. Because of overcrowded conditions at the port of Lagos, Cotonou has served as a relief channel for goods destined for Nigeria. It also serves as the chief port for Niger. There is boat traffic on the lagoons between Porto-Novo and Lagos, Nigeria, as well as on the rivers. An oceanic shipping line, which is 51% Beninese-owned and 49% Algerian-owned, received its first vessel in 1978; in 1985, it had only one small freighter and functioned mainly as an agent.

There is an international airport at Cotonou and direct international jet service to Accra, Niamey, Monrovia, Lagos, Ouagadougou, Lomé, and Douala, and connections to other West African cities. Direct services also link Cotonou to Paris. International airlines include UTA and Air Afrique. There is a major airport at Parakou, and airfields of lesser importance at Natitingou, Kandi, and Abomey. Transports Aériens du Bénin (TAB), offering services to Parakou, Natitingou, Djougou, Savé, and Kandi, and abroad to Lagos, Lomé, Ouagadougou, and Niamey, was founded in 1978. Benin also has a 7% share in Air Afrique.

¹²HISTORY

Benin (formerly Dahomey) has no geographical or historical unity and owes its frontiers to Anglo-French rivalry in the late-19th-century partition of Africa. This is especially marked in northern Benin, whose affinities are rather with the neighboring countries of West Africa than with the peoples of the south. Southern Benin has some historical unity, owing to the existence there of several kingdoms, all traditionally related and peopled by Fon and Adja (related to the Ewe of southern Togo and southeastern Ghana). Traditionally, the kingdoms of Allada, Abomey (or Dahomey), and Adjatché (later Porto-Novo) were founded when two brothers of the king of Allada created new states, respectively, north and southeast of Allada. Abomey conquered Allada in 1724, seized the port of Ouidah in 1727, and became a famous slave-trading kingdom. At this time, women soldiers ("Amazons") were recruited by Abomey for regular service.

The Portuguese—the first Europeans to establish trading posts on the West African coast—founded the trading post of Porto-Novo on what is now the Benin coast. They were followed by English, Dutch, Spanish, and French traders as the slave trade developed. The French established posts at Ouidah and Savé in the middle of the 17th century, and the English and Portuguese also built forts nearby in the early 18th century. The Portuguese fort at Ouidah, which remained Portuguese territory until 1961, was built in 1727. French, English, and Portuguese coastal trade continued, and as Yoruba power weakened, Abomey continually raided the Yoruba and westward toward the Ashanti. Prisoners seized in these campaigns were sacrificed or exported as slaves until the latter half of the 19th century. European traders were closely controlled by the yevogan of Ouidah, the Abomey functionary stationed there, and subjected to substantial levies. It was not until the mid-19th century, with the gradual replacement of the slave trade by trade in palm oil, that European activity brought forth new developments. In 1857, the French established themselves in Grand Popo. In 1868, the French made a treaty with the king of Abomey by which they were permitted to establish a trading post at Cotonou. The British meanwhile established themselves in Lagos, which they annexed in 1861 in order to eliminate the slave trade. Anglo-French rivalry in Porto-Novo, in which successive local kings took different sides, eventually ended with a French protectorate there (1882) and British posts at various points farther west, which were abandoned by the Anglo-French agreements of 1888–89. But Abomey remained outside French control, and its levies on European trade became increasingly irksome. War between Abomey and Porto-Novo broke out in 1889 over France's rights of sovereignty to Cotonou, and Béhanzin, who succeeded to the throne of Abomey in that year, attacked the French posts there. His forces included some 2,000 Amazons. Béhanzin next attacked Porto-Novo and Grand Popo in 1891. In 1893, a French expeditionary force commanded by Dodds took Abomey, and a French protectorate was declared. Renewed hostilities were followed by Béhanzin's surrender to the French in 1894. (He died in exile in Martinique in 1906.) His successor, his brother Agoli Agbo, was exiled in 1899 for maladministration, and the kingdom of Abomey finally came to an end.

From 1892 to 1898, the territory took its modern shape with the exploration and extension of French control in the north. The construction of the railroad to the north was begun in 1900. Dahomey became a component colony of the federation of French West Africa in 1904. In 1946, under the new French constitution, it was given a deputy and two senators in the French parliament, and an elected Territorial Assembly with substantial control of the budget. Under the reforms of 1956–57, the powers of the Territorial Assembly were extended, and a Council of Government elected by the Assembly was given executive control of most territorial matters. Universal adult suffrage and a single electorate were established at the same time. In September 1958, the territory accepted the French constitution proposed by Gen. de Gaulle's government and opted for the status of an autonomous republic within the French Community, as provided by the new constitution.

On 4 December 1958, the Territorial Assembly became a national constituent assembly and the Republic of Dahomey was proclaimed a member of the French Community. On 14 February 1959, a constitution was adopted; the first Legislative Assembly was elected on 3 April. Hubert Maga, chairman of the Dahomeyan Democratic Rally, was named prime minister on 18 May 1959. On 1 August 1960, Dahomey proclaimed its complete independence, and on 25 November a new constitution, calling

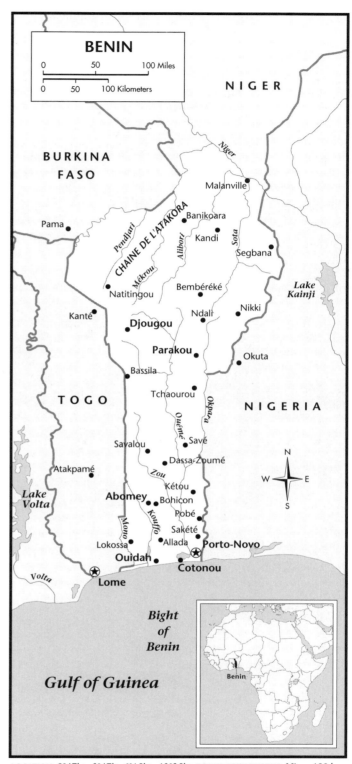

LOCATION: 0°47′ to 3°47′E; 6°15′ to 12°25′N. **BOUNDARY LENGTHS:** Niger, 190 km (118 mi); Nigeria, 750 km (466 mi); Atlantic coastline, 125 km (78 mi); Togo, 620 km (385 mi); Burkina Faso, 270 km (168 mi). **TERRITORIAL SEA LIMIT:** 200 mi.

for a strong unitary state, was adopted. Other constitutions were adopted in 1963, 1965, and 1968.

After independence, the country suffered from extreme political instability, with military coups in 1963, 1965 (twice), 1967, 1969, and 1972. The numerous and often ingenious efforts at constitutional government (including, from 1970–72, a three-man presidential council with a rotating chairman) failed for a number of reasons. The major ones were regionalism (especially the north–south differences) and the country's poor economic situation; unemployment has been high for the relatively large number of educated Beninese, and economic growth has been minimal.

The coup on 26 October 1972 established Maj. Mathieu Kérékou as the leader of a military regime. It represented a clear break with all earlier Dahomeyan administrations, introducing revolutionary changes in the political and economic life of the country. In late 1974, President Kérékou said that the national revolution would follow a Marxist-Leninist course, and the state sector was rapidly expanded by nationalization. As of 1 December 1975, the country's name was changed to the People's Republic of Benin by presidential proclamation.

On 16 January 1977, about 100 persons, including 27 Africans and 62 European mercenaries, made a poorly organized assault on Cotonou. After directing small-arms fire on the presidential palace, they departed three hours later on the DC-8 jet on which they had arrived. The government blamed "international imperialism" in general and France, Morocco, and Gabon in particular.

In 1979, a National Revolutionary Assembly was elected from the single list of candidates offered by the Party of the People's Revolution of Benin, the only legal political organization. This body elected Kérékou to a new term as president in 1980. In that year, in the course of an official visit to Libya, he converted to the Islamic faith in the presence of the Libyan leader, Col. Mu'ammar al-Qadhafi, and accordingly took the first name Ahmed. During the visit the two countries signed a major bilateral cooperation agreement.

Through the years, hundreds of government opponents have been incarcerated, often without trial. Opposition centered in the banned Communist Party (Parti Communiste du Dahomey—PCT) and among student protesters. Since 1990, however, arbitrary arrest and detention are no longer routinely practiced by government.

In February 1990, after weeks of unrest and economic disorder, Kérékou convened a National Conference of Active Forces of the Nation to discuss Benin's future. It became a public critique of Kérékou's 17 years of rule. On 2 December 1990, a new constitution was adopted by popular referendum. The National Conference forced Kérékou to turn over effective power to a transitional government which held presidential and parliamentary elections on 10 March 1991, and run-offs on 24 March. It has been called a "civilian coup."

Prime Minister Nicephore Soglo won 68% of the votes versus Kérékou's 32%. In the elections to the 64-seat National Assembly, no party or coalition of parties gained more than 12 seats and 11 parties or coalitions of parties are represented. The new government took office on 4 April 1991.

In late 1993, the working coalition of approximately 34 parties referred to as the Presidential majority dissolved. Since then, there have been tensions between the executive and legislature. In January 1994, a National Convention of Forces of Change met and adopted a report on the organization of the next elections. It urged the creation of a national electoral commission.

13GOVERNMENT

Maj. Mathieu Kérékou assumed the presidency after the military coup of October 1972 and ruled essentially by decree. In 1973, the National Council of the Revolution, headed by President Kérékou, became the ruling authority. This body disbanded itself in 1979 in accordance with a fundamental law it issued in 1977. The supreme authority of the state became the 336-member National Revolutionary Assembly (NRA), elected from a single list in November 1979 and June 1984. In 1984, this body was reduced to 196 members. The NRA elected the incumbent president, Mathieu Kérékou, as president on 5 February 1980 and reelected him on 31 July 1984.

On 29 July 1988, the Cabinet was restructured. Cabinet Ministers, as well as six "prefets" (provincial governors) made up the National Executive Council.

The 1990 Constitution led to multiparty elections. The president is elected by popular vote for a five-year term. A directly elected National Assembly has a maximum life of four years. The country's name was changed from the People's Republic to the Republic of Benin. The coalition government was dissolved in late 1993.

14POLITICAL PARTIES

The political evolution of Benin since the end of World War II has been largely outside the main currents of French West African politics and determined mainly by local factors. The leading political figures in the 1950s and 1960s were Sourou Apithy and Justin Ahomadegbé in the south and Hubert Maga in the north.

As a result of the first Legislative Assembly elections in April 1959, Apithy's Dahomeyan Republican Party (Parti Républicain du Dahomey—PRD) obtained 28 seats; Maga's Dahomeyan Democratic Rally (Rassemblement Démocratique Dahoméen—RDD), 22; and Ahomadegbé's Dahomey Democratic Union (Union Démocratique Dahoméenne—UDD), 20. A coalition of the three parties took office, with Maga as prime minister. In November 1960, after losing a vote of confidence, the UDD ministers resigned, and the PRD and RDD united first in the Dahomeyan Nationalist Party (Parti des Nationalistes de Dahomey) and then in the Dahomeyan Unity Party (Parti Dahoméen de l'Unité—PDU), again under Maga as prime minister. At the end of 1960, the PDU's single list of candidates won overwhelmingly over the UDD and thereby gained complete control of the executive and the legislature. In 1961, the UDD was banned, and Dahomey became a one-party state.

After the fall of the Maga government in October 1963, the PDU was disbanded and replaced by the Dahomeyan Democratic Party (Parti Démocratique Dahoméen), which was in turn dissolved following the 1965 military coup. The Union for Dahomeyan Renewal (Union pour le Renouveau du Dahomey) was later formed, but it was dissolved after the military coup of December 1969.

The Kérékou regime, which took power in 1972, appeared at first to be unwilling to return to party government, but following the adoption of a Marxist-Leninist policy in 1974, the government formed a political organization as the basis of a one-party state. This organization, which became known as the Party of the People's Revolution of Benin (Parti de la Révolution Populaire du Benin—PRPB), was the sole legal party until 1990. An illegal opposition group, the Front for the Liberation and Rehabilitation of Dahomey, was reportedly responsible for the 1977 coup attempt. The three major political and regional leaders—Maga, Apithy, and Ahomadegbé—remained under house arrest in Benin until 1981, when they were allowed to leave the country.

In 1986, President Kérékou began to modify his Marxism-Leninism and, by December 1989, the ideology was officially abandoned.

Partisan politics are characterized by frequent splits and mergers. Party allegiances in the National Assembly are fluid. The 1990 multiparty general elections produced a National Assembly in which the largest bloc of votes (12 of 64) are held by a Coalition of Democratic Forces (RFD), made up of The Forces of

Progress (UDFP), the Movement for Democracy and Social Progress (MDPS), and the Union for Liberty and Development (ULD). This group was renamed the Union Pour le Triomphe du Renouveau Democratique (UTRD-Union for the Triumph of Democratic Renewal) in March 1992. At its peak, it could count on 34 deputy votes. It was replaced on 30 October 1993 by the African Assembly for Progress (RAP) and is composed of 11 parties and associations. The second largest bloc, with nine seats, is the Alliance of the National Party for Democracy and Development (PNDD) and the Démocratic Renewal Party (PRD). Kérékou's PRPB had been reduced to one of a number of opposition groups, although it was popular in the armed forces.

The National Convention for the Forces of Change, formed in February 1993, is an alliance of opposition groups. The Communist Party of Benin was registered in October 1993.

15LOCAL GOVERNMENT
The country is divided into six provinces for administrative purposes, and these in turn are divided into 84 districts. There are elected provincial, district, town, and village councils.

16JUDICIAL SYSTEM
The legal system in Benin was formerly based on French and customary law. However, on 4 September 1981, Kérékou announced the creation of people's courts presided over by a Central People's Court which would control all judicial activities under the supervision of the executive and legislature. Each district has a court with the power to try cases, and each province has a court that acts as an appeals and assizes court. At the lowest level, each commune, village, and city ward has its own court.

The 1990 Constitution provided for establishment of a new Constitutional Court responsible for judicial review of the constitutionality of legislation. This court began functioning in 1993. The new Constitution also establishes a High Court of Justice to be responsible for hearing charges of crimes against the nation committed by the President or other government officials. The highest court for nonconstitutional judicial review under the new Constitution is the Supreme Court. Under the new constitution, detainees must be brought before a magistrate within 48 hours of arrest.

17ARMED FORCES
In 1993, the armed forces had some 4,350 personnel. The army of 3,800 included 3 infantry battalions, a parachute/commando battalion, a service battalion, an engineering battalion, an artillery battery, and an armored squadron. There were 350 personnel in the air force, which had one attack helicopter and 14 support helos and aircraft. There was a navy of 150 personnel and 1 patrol boat. A paramilitary gendarmerie totaled 2,000. All forces are run by the army headquarters.

18INTERNATIONAL COOPERATION
Benin was admitted to UN membership on 20 September 1960, and is a member of ECA and all the nonregional specialized agencies except IAEA and IFC. It is a signatory of GATT and the Law of the Sea, and a member of the African Development Bank, ECOWAS, G-77, the OAU, and OCAM. Relations with France, strained following the January 1977 attempted coup, improved markedly after 1981.

Benin has joined with Côte d'Ivoire, Niger, Burkina Faso, and Togo in the Conseil d'Entente, a loose grouping of likeminded states with a common loan guarantee fund. Benin, as a member of the Niger Basin Authority, cooperates with other riparian states of the Niger River in planning the further use and development of the river for fishing, transportation, flood control, and hydroelectricity. The Organisation Commune Bénin-Niger regulates common problems of transportation and communications. Benin

became a member of the Association of African Petroleum Producers in 1987. Benin is a signatory to the Lomé Convention.

19ECONOMY
Benin's economy is recovering from the economic problems which led to the collapse of the socialist government in power between 1974 and 1989. Privatization of previously nationalized companies is current policy. However, recovery efforts are complicated by the fact that Benin's economy is strongly influenced by economic trends in Nigeria. Over the past decade, this effect has caused Benin's GDP to fluctuate considerably between recovery and decline.

Agriculture is the most important sector in the Benin economy, accounting for some 35.4% of GDP (1990). About 90% of this output is produced on family farms using low-technology inputs and focusing primarily on domestically consumed crops, such as maize, sorghum, millet, paddy rice, cassava, yams, and beans. Typically, Benin is self-sufficient in food. Cotton, palm oil, and groundnuts are grown and exchanged for cash.

Livestock, forestry, and fishing make up another 10% of GDP. Benin's livestock population has increased an estimated 40% over the past 10 years, though it still does not satisfy local demand. Wood production for local fuel consumption also falls behind national demand. The fishing sector, made up of artisanal fishers, has overfished the stock and is in decline.

Benin's mineral resources are limited. Limestone, marble, and petroleum reserves are exploited commercially. Gold is produced at the artisanal level. Phosphates, chromium, rutile, and iron ore have been located in the north but remain undeveloped resources. Given the current petroleum price levels on the international market, it is estimated that Benin will exhaust its oil reserves by the end of 1993.

In January 1994 France suddenly devalued the CFA franc, causing its value to drop in half overnight. Immediately, prices for almost all imported goods soared, including prices for food and essential drugs, like those to combat malaria. Since 1948 France had guaranteed a fixed parity of one French franc to 50 African francs. The resulting stability in the currency had generally kept inflation low and helped to maintain a steady rate of growth. However, in the 1980s, the economies of the CFA countries began to stagnate in relation to other African nations, and France came under increased pressure from the World Bank, the IMF, and western countries to stop subsidizing the CFA franc. The devaluation, long expected in the investment community, is designed to enourage new investment, particularly in the export sectors of the economy, and discourage the use of hard currency reserves to buy products that could be grow domestically.

In the short term, however, the move has left the economy reeling and provoked anger and confusion among the population. Price-gouging by local merchants and a sharp rise in inflation led the government to impose temporary price controls on existing stocks of imports. Long-term prospects are uncertain.

20INCOME
In 1992 Benin's GNP was $2,058 million at current prices, or $410 per capita. For the period 1985–92 the average inflation rate was 1.2%, resulting in a real growth rate in per capita GNP of −1.5%.

In 1992 the GDP was $2,181 million in current US dollars. It is estimated that agriculture, hunting, forestry, and fishing contributed 36% to GDP; mining and quarrying, 1%; manufacturing, 9%; electricity, gas, and water, 1%; construction, 3%; wholesale and retail trade, 17%; transport, storage, and communication, 7%; finance, insurance, real estate, and business services, 11%; and other sources, 14%. A very active informal sector, cross-border trade, represents economic activity typically not included in official statistics.

[21] LABOR

The total labor force was about 2 million in 1992, of which 80% were primarily engaged in agriculture. There is a great disparity between the income of the wage earner and that of the uneducated traditional laborer, whose yearly income is less than the average monthly income of the salaried worker.

The fundamental labor legislation provides for collective agreements between employers and workers, for the fixing of minimum wages by the government on the advice of advisory committees, and for a 40-hour basic workweek (except for agricultural workers, for whom longer working hours are permitted), subject to an annual maximum of 2,400 hours. The legislation also provides for paid annual leave and for family allowances for children. These arrangements affect only the small proportion of the total labor force that is in wage-paid employment. The minimum industrial wage (CFA Fr81.21 per hour in 1983), was still in effect in 1992 but was only enough to provide rudimentary food and shelter for a family.

Trade union activity is concentrated in urban areas and particularly in the south, where most wage and salaried workers are employed. The Kérékou regime consolidated all previous trade union organizations into the National Union of Syndicates and Workers of Benin in 1973. The National Workers' Union of Benin (UNSTB) declared its independence from the former ruling party in 1990 and now claims 26 affiliated unions in Benin. The Confederation of Autonomous Unions, a separate and larger federation formed in 1991, represents 23 more unions, mostly in the public sector. The December 1990 Constitution gives workers the right to organize, join unions, meet, and strike. About 75% of wage earners are unionized.

[22] AGRICULTURE

Benin is predominantly an agricultural country. About 75% of the population is engaged in the agricultural sector, which accounted for 37% of GDP in 1992 and about one-third of foreign exchange earnings. Small, independent farmers produce 90% of agricultural output, but only about 17% of the total area is cultivated, much of it in the form of collective farms since 1975. The agricultural sector is plagued by a lack of infrastructure, poor utilization of rural credit, and inefficient and insufficient use of fertilizer, insecticides, and seeds. Smuggling of crops for export or the domestic black market results in understating of crop figures. An estimated 20% of output is informally traded with Nigeria. The main food crops are manioc, yams, corn, sorghum, beans, rice, sweet potatoes, pawpaws, guavas, bananas, and coconuts. Production estimates for the main food crops for 1992 were yams, 1,177,000 tons; manioc, 932,000 tons; corn, 399,000 tons; millet and sorghum, 129,000 tons; beans, 50,000 tons; sweet potatoes, 28,000 tons; and rice, 9,000 tons. Benin is self-sufficient in food crops, given favorable weather conditions.

Palm products were long Benin's principal export crop, but in recent years cotton has increased in importance, with production increasing tenfold since 1981. Despite improved production, however, cotton storage and ginning capacity are still insufficient. Production of most cash crops fell between 1976 and 1986 because of drought and state mismanagement. In 1992 cotton was grown on some 68,000 hectares (168,000 acres), and the crop was managed by the National Agricultural Society for Cotton. Cotton production was 65,000 tons in 1992, down from 76,000 tons in 1991. Peanut production has also recently become important; in 1992, 70,000 tons of shelled groundnuts were produced. These statistics are distorted by the smuggling of cash crops to and from Nigeria, depending on which country's prices are more attractive. Some 400,000 hectares (990,000 acres) of natural palms are exploited, and there are 30,000 hectares (74,000 acres) of palm plantations, the largest of which is managed by SOBEPALH, a government enterprise producing palm oil

and cottonseed oil. Palm oil production was 40,000 tons in 1992 and palm kernel output was 9,000 tons. Other crops with their 1992 production figures were cashews, 1,200 tons, bananas, 13,000 tons, mangoes, 12,000 tons, and coconuts, 20,000 tons.

[23] ANIMAL HUSBANDRY

In 1992 there were an estimated 1 million head of cattle, 920,000 sheep, 1,120,000 goats, 750,000 hogs, and 25 million chickens. Most of Benin's cattle are in the north beyond the main trypanosomiasis (sleeping sickness) zone inhabited by the tsetse fly, but there is also a small hardy type in the lagoon area. Horses are rare owing to the ravages of trypanosomiasis. Poultry are mainly confined to the south of the country.

Estimated output of livestock products in 1992 included 14,000 tons of beef, and veal, 6,000 tons of sheep and goat meat, and 8,000 tons of pork. Although the livestock population has increased by 40% over the last decade, Benin still imports substantial amounts of meat and poultry to meet local demand.

[24] FISHING

Ocean fishing, which had been carried on largely by Ghanaian fishermen, is gaining importance at Cotonou (where a fishing port was opened in 1971) and other coastal centers. Under an agreement with the Senegal government, Senegalese fishermen introduced deep-sea-fishing methods to the Beninese, and a national fishing company was established as a joint venture with Libya. Production increases, however, have not kept pace with the demand of a growing population; in 1991, 7.6 tons of fresh, chilled, or frozen fish had to be imported. Lagoon and river fishing remain of primary importance; of an estimated catch of 41,000 tons in 1991, 32,000 tons were from inland waters. The production of fish has steadily declined since the 1980s due to overfishing and ecological degradation. A survey of the ecological changes and fish stocks is underway.

[25] FORESTRY

There are about 3.4 million hectares (nearly 8.4 million acres) classified as forest and woodland, about 31% of the total land area. Most forests are in northern Benin, and exploitation is subject to public control. Timber production is small. Firewood, charcoal, and building wood for local use are the most important forest products. In 1991, an estimated 5,203,000 million cu m of roundwood were produced. A project to increase wood production and processing is underway with substantial assistance from Germany. American Peace Corps volunteers are also assisting with the development of the forestry sector, with special attention on the dilemma between ecological balance and fuelwood production.

[26] MINING

With the exception of oil, Benin is relatively poor in mineral resources. Exports of mineral commodities accounted for 9.5% of total estimated 1991 exports of $291.4 million. There is iron ore in the north, but of low-grade quality; limestone is quarried for use in cement plants. The potential for small-scale gold mining exists in the northwest.

[27] ENERGY AND POWER

Production from the Sémé offshore oil field began in October 1982 by Saga Petroleum, a Norwegian firm working under a service contract. The field yielded 1,353,000 barrels of oil in 1991. In 1990, Benin exported an estimated 1.27 million barrels of crude oil. In 1986, the contract was transferred to Pan Ocean Oil (Panoco), a Swiss-based US firm, but loans to Benin from international development agencies were frozen because the company could not furnish satisfactory financial and capability statements; it withdrew, forcing Benin to take over oil production. Reserves, which were estimated at 44 million barrels, were considered sufficient to meet domestic needs, but there is currently no refinery in Benin; consequently, refined petroleum products have to be reimported. In 1991, imports of refined petroleum products amounted to $55 million, or 11% of total imports.

Electrical power generated in Benin is entirely thermal. Installed capacity in 1991 was an estimated 15,000 kw; total domestic power output in 1991 was 5 million kwh. An agreement was signed with Togo and Ghana in 1967 under which Benin receives low-cost electric power from the Akosombo Dam on the Volta River in Ghana; in 1991 this came to about 98% of national consumption. Electricity imports in 1991 were estimated at $10 million. Togo and Benin are constructing a dam on the Mono River, along the Togo border, that will feed a 62-Mw power station to supply the southern regions of both countries.

28INDUSTRY

Benin's industrial sector accounts for 9% of GDP (1990) and centers primarily on construction materials and the processing of agricultural products. Excess capacity at enterprises such as the Onigbolo cement factory and the Savé sugar refinery have characterized Benin's industrial sector. The nation's palm oil production capacity of 215,000 metric tons is underutilized. In 1986, for example, Benin produced 12,096 tons of oil, 704 tons of palm-kernel oil, and 896 tons of palm cake. Likewise, Benin's cotton ginning capacity of 120,000 tons far exceeds current use levels. An exception to this trend is the textile factory at Parakou. This plant is being revitalized, thanks to financing from the West African Development Bank, with capacity scheduled to reach 3.5 million meters of fabric and 1,254 tons of garments.

Benin's electricity needs are met by hydroelectric power from Akosombo dam in Ghana and the Nangbeto dam on the Mono River. A second Mono River dam is currently under construction at Adjarala. The two Mono River dams should produce enough power to provide for Benin's needs into the foreseeable future.

29SCIENCE AND TECHNOLOGY

Much of the scientific and technical research conducted in Benin is directed toward agriculture and is supported by France. The Directory of Mines, Geology, and Hydrocarbons, which is attached to the Ministry of Industry, Trade, and Tourism, is located at Cotonou; the Institute of Applied Research is at Porto-Novo. The National University in Cotonou has faculties of scientific and technical studies, health sciences, and agriculture. In 1989, expenditures for research and experimental development totaled CFA fr 3.3 billion; 242 technicians and 794 scientists and engineers were engaged in research and development.

30DOMESTIC TRADE

Benin is an important West African trading center. Except in Cotonou and Porto-Novo, retailers deal in a wide variety of goods rather than specializing in a few products. In the two larger towns, some shops specialize in such lines as dry goods, foodstuffs, and hardware. In the smaller towns, bazaars and individual merchants and peddlers deal in locally grown products and a few imported items. Domestic trade is generally on a cash basis, but in the countryside barter is common.

Advertising is not widely used. Business hours are from 9:30 AM to 1 PM and from 4 to 7 PM Monday through Friday, from 3 to 7 PM on Saturday, and from 9 to 11 AM on Sunday. Banks are open on weekdays from 7 to 11 AM and on Saturdays from 7 to 9 AM.

31FOREIGN TRADE

Benin consistently runs a trade deficit; this pattern continued in 1991 when the deficit reached $191.1 million on $291.4 million worth of exports. Exports declined by 50% in the 1985 to 1987 period and declined another 28% between 1987 and 1990.

In 1987 the leading exports (in millions of CFA francs) were as follows:

Ginned cotton	17,903
Palm products	1,421
Cacao beans	314
Cottonseed	1,164
Fuels	9,429
Other exports	4,035
TOTAL	34,266

The leading imports in 1987 (in millions of CFA francs) were as follows:

Manufactured articles:	40,375
Cotton products	10,973
Food products	20,514
Electrical and mechanical machinery	8,909
Tobacco and beverages	7,971
Chemicals	5,925
Road transport equipment	5,202
Refined petroleum products	4,299
Other imports	11,785
TOTAL	104,980

In 1987, Benin exported to Portugal 21.0%; the US, 16.8%; Italy, 13.8%; and Nigeria, 7.3%. Benin's imports came primarily from France, 17.6%; Thailand, 14.1%; and the Netherlands, 7.1%.

32BALANCE OF PAYMENTS

Large annual transfers from the French government and other sources are necessary for Benin to offset its chronic trade deficit. Substantial long-term capital investments during the late 1960s and 1970s also helped Benin finance the deficit. Benin's current account has deteriorated sharply from the years of high prices for crude oil exports. A growing dependence on imports has also increased the deficit, but official statistics do not include substntial amounts of informal trade flows to neighboring countries.

In 1992 merchandise exports totaled $369.1 million and imports $551.6 million. The merchandise trade balance was $-182.5 million. The following table summarizes Benin's balance of payments for 1991 and 1992 (in millions of US dollars):

	1991	1992
CURRENT ACCOUNT		
Goods, services, and income	-200.2	-261.1
Unrequited transfers	189.6	232.0
TOTALS	-10.6	-29.1
CAPITAL ACCOUNT		
Other long-term capital	81.2	-18.9
Other short-term capital	-28.4	-26.3
Exceptional financing	42.2	141.3
Reserves	-104.0	-67.5
TOTALS	-9.0	28.6
Errors and omissions	19.7	0.5
Total change in reserves	-113.3	-54.5

Benin has historically maintained a sizeable trade deficit. As producer prices declined in the late 1980s, Benin's export revenues fell sharply. By 1989 and 1990, foreign aid matched export earnings. Arrears on debt payments accumulated until by the end of 1988, Benin had a projected debt-service ratio in excess of 30%.

Benin accepted an IMF structural adjustment program in 1989, which was followed by a phase-two program in 1991. The IMF formula called for modest real GDP growth, reducing public sector employment, improving tax collection and privatizing of public-sector enterprises. In addition, Benin's government has initiated tariff reforms and lifted price controls. While debt cancellations by the US and France helped bring the debt-service ratio down to 7.0%, Benin still has a serious debt problem which has only partially been resolved.

33BANKING AND SECURITIES
In 1959, the Central Bank of the West African States (Banque Centrale des États de l'Afrique de l'Ouest—BCEAO) succeeded the Currency Board of French West Africa and Togo as the bank of issue for the former French West African territories. In 1962, it was reorganized as the joint note-issue bank, and in 1983 included Benin, Côte d'Ivoire, Niger, Senegal, Togo, and Burkina Faso. BCEAO notes, known as CFA francs, are unreservedly guaranteed by France. Foreign exchange receipts of the member states go into the franc area's exchange pool, which in turn covers their foreign exchange requirements.

In December 1974, the government nationalized the banking sector, amalgamating the three main commercial banks into the Commercial Bank of Benin. There is also the Benin Development Bank. Other commercial banks include the Bank of Africa (1990), Banque Internationale du Benin (1984), Ecobank-Benin (1989), and the Financial Bank (1988).

As of 1993, deposit money banks held CFA Fr84.6 billion in demand deposits and CFA Fr59.3 billion in time and savings deposits. The money supply, as measured by M2, totaled CFA Fr171.0 billion. There is no securities market in Benin.

34INSURANCE
Insurance companies were nationalized in 1974, and the National Society of Insurance and Reinsurance is the state agency.

35PUBLIC FINANCE
Benin has both an ordinary and a development budget. High personnel costs have been a continuing problem in Benin, which has a surfeit of civil servants. Many government-backed enterprises are near bankruptcy and some are barely functioning. The fiscal year follows the calendar year.

Most investment expenditure is financed by foreign loans and grants. From 1985 to 1988, current government expenditures increased from 13% to 15% of GDP, and the budget deficit averaged 11% of GDP. During the 1980s, the external debt nearly tripled, and stood at $909 millions of US dollars by 1988. In 1989, the government rescheduled its arrears through the Paris Club, and has been reducing the public sector's role in the economy ever since. As a result, public finances have improved, with the overall deficit declining from 10.6% of GDP in 1989 to 7.2% in 1991.

36TAXATION
In 1987, direct taxes were expected to provide 27% of government revenues, and indirect taxes, 58.6%.

37CUSTOMS AND DUTIES
In general, two main taxes make up the tariff system. A fiscal import duty is applied ad valorem to all incoming goods regardless of origin and serves as a source of revenue. A customs duty is levied on goods coming from places other than franc-zone countries and serves to protect goods of franc-zone origin. Goods imported from countries that have trade agreements with Benin pay a minimum customs duty, while those from other countries are subject to a substantially higher tariff.

Benin has bilateral customs agreements with Côte d'Ivoire, Niger, Nigeria, and Togo. Goods from EC countries other than France are dutiable at below the standard minimum rate. Some goods are admitted duty-free if they are considered essential to Benin's economic development. The country has practically no specific import duties other than those assessed on tobacco and cigarettes, alcohol and alcoholic beverages, and petroleum products. As part of an ongoing trade reform, most quantitative import restrictions have been removed, and all remaining import licensing ended in March 1993. Additional measures planned include tariff simplifications and reduction of duty exemptions.

38FOREIGN INVESTMENT
With government privatization of the nationalized industrial sector well under way, it is a period of considerable investment activity in Benin. In the financial sector, Rasmal Finance, a Swiss banking interest backed by American Express and Citicorp; Ecobank, based in Togo and correspondent for the Midland Bank; the Bank of Africa, a Malian financial interest; and the Banque Internationale de Bénin, a Nigerian consortium, have started commercial operations in Benin since 1989.

Rothmans-UK has invested in the formerly state-run cigarette factory. An American private investor has entered the steel industry, manufacturing reinforcing bars and roofing materials. While current oil reserves are negligible, investments in further exploration possibilities have been considerable. Formerly state-owned cement, auto parts, and stationery supply operations have also been privatized, and the privatization of the brewery and cashew nut factory are planned. In terms of legislation, Benin has adopted a new investment code in the hope of attracting additional private-sector investment. For example, though both Sheraton and the French PLM chains have hotels in Benin, the tourist industry is considered underdeveloped.

39ECONOMIC DEVELOPMENT
Benin's economic development program is conducted within the context of an IMF structural adjustment program. The recent devaluation of the CFA franc, the local currency, has made imports more expensive and brought the CFA closer in value to the Nigerian currency. This should inhibit imports while stimulating local production and raw material exports.

40SOCIAL DEVELOPMENT
All public employees receive family allowances for up to six children. There is also a system of old-age benefits, and medical care is free.

The Kérékou government subjected many of its citizens to arbitrary arrest and imprisonment, chiefly in times of political tension. These detainees were usually held for indefinite periods.

41HEALTH
Most serious epidemic diseases have been brought under control by mobile health units and other facilities. Yaws has been almost totally eradicated in the northern part of the country. Sleeping sickness (trypanosomiasis) has also been greatly reduced in the north, and yellow fever has all but disappeared. Meningitis, once endemic in the north, now appears only sporadically, and measures against tuberculosis have been intensified. In 1990, there were 135 cases of tuberculosis per 100,000 people. However, in 1990, malnutrition was prevalent in 35% of children under 5 years old, and by 1991, still only 51% of the population had access to safe water. Estimated average life expectancy in 1992 was only 46 years, with a death rate of 17.8 per 1,000 people in 1993.

From 1988 to 1992, there were 7 doctors per 100,000 people, and only 18% of the population (5.1 million in 1993) had access to health services. Total health care expenditures for Benin were $79 million in 1990.

There were 243,000 births in 1992, with 9% of married women (age 15 to 49) using contraception from 1980 to 1993. The infant mortality rate in 1992 was 88 per 1,000 live births.

As of 1993, the government of Benin planned to expand its health care system, upgrade the quality of first referral care, promote private sector care, and improve public sector care.

[42]HOUSING

Improvement in overall appearance and in sanitation facilities in towns and villages has been fostered by the government. Low-cost housing has been provided by a public corporation backed by French development funds.

In the rural areas, the typical dwelling of northern Benin is a round hut of beaten mud with a conical roof of thatch. In southern Benin, rectangular huts with sloping roofs of palm or straw thatch are more usual. Along the coastal lagoons, houses are often built on stilts.

As of 1979, 24% of housing units were modern houses, 74% were traditional dwellings, and less than 1% were categorized as flats or villas. Owners occupied 76% of housing units, 10% were rented, and 11.5% were occupied rent free, with the remaining percentage unaccounted for.

[43]EDUCATION

During the French colonial period, Benin produced the educational elite of French West Africa. The percentage of primary-school attendance was higher than in any other French West African territory, largely because of intense missionary activity. The educational system is patterned on that of France, but changes have been introduced to modify the elitist system and to adapt the curriculum to local needs and traditions. The most significant change has been the takeover of mission schools following legislation in 1975, by which the state made all education free, public, secular, and compulsory from ages 6 to 12. In 1988–89, enrollment of children at the primary level was 52% and the comparable ratio for the secondary level was 13%.

The adult illiteracy rate was 76.6% (68.3% for males and 84.4% for females) in 1990. In 1991 there were 2,952 primary schools with 505,970 pupils enrolled. In the general secondary schools, there were 76,672 pupils and 2,178 teachers.

The National University of Benin at Cotonou, founded in 1970, offers courses in agriculture, medicine, liberal arts, science, law, economics, and politics. According to consolidated estimates, 12.8% of the total government expenditure is devoted to education.

[44]LIBRARIES AND MUSEUMS

The National Archives and National Library, which has around 35,000 volumes, are in Porto-Novo. The Institute of Applied Research, also in Porto-Novo, maintains a research collection of 8,000 volumes. There are historical museums in Abomey and Ouidah, an ethnography museums in Porto-Novo, and a museum of natural history and ethnography in Parakou.

[45]MEDIA

Virtually all media in Benin are controlled by the government. The state provides telegraph and telephone service, and a government-owned radio and television service broadcasts in French, English, and 18 indigenous languages. In 1991 there were about 428,000 radios and 24,000 television sets in use and 16,918 telephones.

In 1991, the only daily newspaper was *La Nation* (formerly *Ehuzu*), the government organ, with a daily circulation of about 12,000.

[46]ORGANIZATIONS

The Chamber of Commerce, Agriculture, and Industry of Benin is in Cotonou. There are numerous youth and student groups in Benin.

[47]TOURISM, TRAVEL, AND RECREATION

Benin has great potential for tourism, and the government is striving to develop this sector of the economy. The country has a rich cultural heritage, varied scenery, and impressive national parks. However, except for hotels managed by the Sheraton and French PLM chains, the tourist industry remains underdeveloped. Cotonou has an international class hotel, the Benin Sheraton, opened in 1982. The Hotel Aledjo, run by the French-PLM chain, also is first class. Less expensive is the Hotel de la Plage. In the north, the PLM runs an excellent hotel in Natitingou—the Tata-Somba. There is a good hotel in Parakou (Les Routiers); For trips to the Pendjari game park, there is a small (21-room) hotel in Porga. Abomey also has an adequate hotel. In 1991, there were 1,500 hotel rooms, with 3,200 beds and a 58% occupancy rate. In that year there were an estimated 401,000 visitor arrivals, 72% from Africa and 20% from Europe, and tourism payments totaled US$29 million.

Tourist attractions include the lake village of Ganvie, two game parks in the north, the ancient royal city of Alromey, several museums, and beaches. Hunting lodges have been built to foster safaris in the two national parks, where strenuous efforts have also been made to preserve wild game. In the south are picturesque villages built on stilts over the waters of the coastal lagoons. Visitors must have a passport, a visa (except for citizens of France, Denmark, Germany, and African countries), and proof of vaccination against yellow fever.

[48]FAMOUS BENINESE

Perhaps the most famous historical ruler in the area now known as Benin was Béhanzin (d.1906), who was king of Abomey from 1889 until he was defeated by the French in 1894. The best-known modern Beninese are the political leaders Hubert Maga (b.1916); Sourou-Migan Apithy (b.1913); Justin T. Ahomadegbé (b.1917); and Brig. Gen. Ahmed Mathieu Kérékou (b.1933).

[49]DEPENDENCIES

Benin has no territories or colonies.

[50]BIBLIOGRAPHY

Argyle, William J. *The Fon of Dahomey.* London: Oxford University Press, 1966.

Burton, Richard F. *Wanderings in West Africa from Liverpool to Fernando Po.* New York: Johnson Reprints, 1971.

Chatwin, Bruce. *The Viceroy of Ouidah.* New York: Summit Books, 1980.

Cornevin, Robert. *Histoire du Dahomey.* Paris: Berger-Levrault, 1962.

Decalo, Samuel. *Historical Dictionary of Benin,* 2nd ed. Metuchen, N.J.: Scarecrow Press, 1987.

Diamond, Stanley. *Dahomey: Transition and Conflict in State Formation.* South Hadley, Mass.: J.F. Bergin, 1983.

Herskovits, Melville Jean. *Dahomey: An Ancient West African Kingdom.* Evanston, Ill.: Northwestern University Press, 1967.

Law, Robin. *The Slave Coast of West Africa, 1550–1750: the Impact of the Atlantic Slave Trade on an African Society.* New York: Oxford University Press, 1991.

Manning, Patrick. *Slavery, Colonialism, and Economic Growth in Dahomey, 1640–1960.* New York: Cambridge University Press, 1982.

Obichere, Boniface I. *West African States and European Expansion: The Dahomey-Niger Hinterland, 1885–1898.* New Haven, Conn.: Yale University Press, 1971.

Ronen, Dov. *Dahomey: Between Tradition and Modernity.* Ithaca, N.Y.: Cornell University Press, 1975.

Tevoedjré, Albert. *Pan Africanism in Action: An Account of the* *UAM.* Cambridge, Mass.: Harvard University Press, 1965.

Thompson, Virginia, and Richard Adloff. *French West Africa.* Stanford: Stanford University Press, 1958.

BOTSWANA

Republic of Botswana

CAPITAL: Gaborone.

FLAG: The flag of Botswana consists of five horizontal stripes. The top and bottom stripes are light blue and wider than the middle stripe, which is black. The blue stripes are separated from the black by thin white stripes.

ANTHEM: *Fatshe La Rona (Blessed Country).*

MONETARY UNIT: On 23 August 1976, the pula (P) of 100 thebe replaced the South African rand (R) as Botswana's legal currency. There are coins of 1, 2, 5, 10, 25, 50 thebe and 1 pula, and notes of 2, 5, 10, 20, 50 and 100 pula. P1 = $0.3899 (or $1 = P1.5878).

WEIGHTS AND MEASURES: The metric system is the legal standard.

HOLIDAYS: New Year's Day, 1 January; Good Friday; Easter Monday; Ascension; President's Day, 15 July; Botswana Days, 30 September–1 October; Christmas, 25 December; Boxing Day, 26 December.

TIME: 2 PM = noon GMT.

¹LOCATION, SIZE, AND EXTENT

A landlocked country in southern Africa, Botswana has a total area of 600,370 sq km (231,804 sq mi), extending 1,110 km (690 mi) NNE–SSW and 960 km (597 mi) EWE–WNW. Comparatively, the area occupied by Botswana is slightly smaller than the state of Texas. It meets Zambia at a point in the N and is bordered on the NE by Zimbabwe, on the SE and S by South Africa, and on the W and N by Namibia (South West Africa), with a total boundary length of 4,013 km (2,494 mi).

²TOPOGRAPHY

The country is a broad tableland with a mean altitude of 1,000 m (3,300 ft). A vast plateau about 1,200 m (4,000 ft) in height, extending from near Kanye north to the Zimbabwean border, divides the country into two distinct topographical regions. The eastern region is hilly bush country and grassland (veld). To the west lie the Okavango Swamps and the Kalahari Desert. The only sources of year-round surface water are the Chobe River in the north, the Limpopo in the east, and the Okavango in the northwest. In seasons of heavy rainfall, floodwaters flow into the Makgadikgadi Salt Pans, Lake Ngami, and Lake Xau.

³CLIMATE

Most of the country has a subtropical climate, with cooler temperatures prevailing in the higher altitudes. Winter days are warm and nights are cool, with heavy frost common in the desert. Temperatures range from average maximums of 33°C (91°F) in January and 22°C (72°F) in July to average minimums of 18°C (64°F) in January and 5°C (41°F) in July. In August begin the seasonal winds that blow from the west and carry sand and dust across the country. Rainfall normally averages 45 cm (18 in) but ranges from 69 cm (27 in) in the north to less than 25 cm (10 in) in the Kalahari; drought conditions prevailed in the early and mid-1980s.

⁴FLORA AND FAUNA

Although about 90% of Botswana is covered by some kind of savanna, even the Kalahari Desert contains adequate vegetation to support tens of thousands of wild animals. Common trees are the mopane, camel-thorn, motopi (shepherd's tree), and baobab. Botswana is a natural game reserve for most animals found in southern Africa, including lions, leopards, cheetahs, elephants, giraffes, zebras, hippopotamuses, rhinoceroses, African buffalo, hyenas, and 22 species of antelope. The duiker (a small, horned antelope), wildebeest (gnu), and springbok (gazelle) are familiar. Also indigenous to Botswana are an estimated 549 bird species.

⁵ENVIRONMENT

Overgrazing, due to the rapid expansion of the cattle population, is a continuing threat to the vegetation and wildlife of Botswana. There are five game reserves, three game sanctuaries, and 40 controlled hunting areas. Almost 20% of the land has been set aside as national parks and game reserves. Other environmental problems include the preservation of wildlife and water shortages. The expansion of grazing areas for cattle has reduced the amount of land available to other forms of wildlife and threatened their survival.

Botswana has a very limited water supply that is inadequate for its increasing population. One major factor in Botswana's water supply problem is that 66% of the country is part of the Kalahari desert. It has 0.2 cubic miles of water, 85% of which is used for farming. As of 1994, 100% of Botswana's urban dwellers and 88% of its rural people have pure water.

In a total of 154 species of mammals, nine are endangered. Six bird species of 549 are also endangered. One reptile in a total of 158 and four plant species in a total of 2,800 are threatened with extinction as of 1994. The African elephant and the black rhinoceros are examples of endangered mammals.

⁶POPULATION

The 1991 census population was 1,326,796, and the 1994 population was estimated at 1,359,413; a total of 1,650,000 was projected for the year 2000, assuming a crude birthrate of 36.1 per 1,000 population, a crude death rate of 7.9, and a net natural increase of 28.2 for the period of 1995–2000. The population increased by 2.4% annually between 1990 and 1995. The average population density in 1991 was 2.3 per sq km (6 per sq mi), but nearly 80% of the population lives on the better soils of the eastern strip of the country. About 31% of the population was urban in 1995. Gaborone, the capital, had an estimated population of 138,471 in 1991. Other cities and their 1991 populations are Mahalapye, 104,450; Serowe, 95,041; Tutume, 86,405; Bobonong, 55,060; Francistown, 52,725; Selebi-Phikwe, 49,542; Boteti, 32,711; and Lobatse, 26,841.

[7]MIGRATION

At least 50,000 Botswanans are working in South Africa at any particular time. In 1991 21,468 South African residents were listed as born in Botswana. Botswana had some 500 refugees at the end of 1992, about 40% from South Africa.

[8]ETHNIC GROUPS

The population, predominantly of Tswana stock (70%), is distributed among eight tribes: the Bamangwato, Batswana, Bakwena, Bangwaketsi, Bakgatla, Barolong, Bamalete, and Batlokwa. Each tribe has its own territory, and tribal land comprises about 71% of the country. Other indigenous peoples include the Kalanga, Yei, Mbukushu, Subiya, Herero, Kgalagadi, Basarwa (Bushmen), and Hottentots. In the mid-1980s, the non-African population included small numbers of Asians (about 15,000), Europeans, and people of mixed race.

[9]LANGUAGES

English is the official language. Setswana, however, is spoken by most Botswanans.

[10]RELIGIONS

It is presently estimated that about one-half the population followed traditional African religions, almost all the rest being nominally Christian. Nearly 12% of the Christians belong to African independent churches, and 3.6% are Roman Catholics. The largest of the affiliated churches was the United Congregational Church of Southern Africa. Freedom of religion is constitutionally guaranteed.

[11]TRANSPORTATION

In 1991, Botswana had 11,514 km (7,154 mi) of roads: 1,700 km (1.056 mi) were gravel, 1,600 km (994 mi) bitumen, and 8,214 km (5,104 mi) earth or sand. Bituminized roads have been extended to the Zambian and Zimbabwean borders, thereby reducing Botswana's economic dependence on South Africa. There were some 60,000 registered road motor vehicles in 1991, of which 42% were passenger cars and the rest commercial vehicles.

The main railroad from Cape Town in South Africa to Bulawayo in Zimbabwe runs through Botswana for a distance of 641 km (398 mi), connecting Lobatse, Gaborone, and Francistown. Two branch lines totaling 71 km (44 mi) connected the coal field of Morupule and the copper-nickel complex at Selebi-Phikwe with the main line; these lines were owned by Botswana but operated by National Railways of Zimbabwe. In 1991, a new 165 km (103 mi) spur connecting Sua Pan to Francistown was completed, at a cost of $45 million.

The government-owned Air Botswana operates scheduled flights to Francistown, Gaborone, Maun, and Selebi-Phikwe. There is international service to Johannesburg, South Africa; Mbabane, Swaziland; and Harare, Zimbabwe. A new international airport near Gaborone was opened in 1984. Air passengers arriving and departing via Air Botswana during 1992 totaled 111,200.

[12]HISTORY

According to tradition, the founder of the Batswana tribe was a 14th-century chief named Mogale. His great-great-grandson Malope had three sons, Kwena, Ngwaketse, and Ngwato, who became the chiefs of the major tribes that now inhabit Botswana.

The foundations of the modern state lie in the 1820–70 period, when the Batswana suffered many tribulations at the hands of the Matabele. In 1872, Khama III became chief of the Bamangwato. He was the son of Chief Sekgoma, the only Batswana chief who had succeeded in turning back the Matabele. Up to that time, the Batswana had had no permanent contact with Europeans, except for the missionaries Robert and Mary Moffat and David Livingstone, who had established missions in the first half of the 19th century. But with increased exploration and the partition of southern Africa among the European powers, hostility developed between the Batswana and the Boer trekkers from the Transvaal. Khama III appealed to the UK for assistance, and in 1885 the whole of what was then known as Bechuanaland was proclaimed to be under the protection of Queen Victoria. The territory south of the Molopo River was constituted a crown colony called British Bechuanaland, and in 1895 it was incorporated into South Africa. The northern part of the territory, the Bechuanaland Protectorate, remained under the protection of the British crown, the powers of which, beginning in 1891, were exercised by the high commissioner in South Africa. The South African Act of Union of 1909, which created the Union (now Republic) of South Africa, provided for the eventual transfer to South Africa of Bechuanaland and the two other High Commission Territories, Basutoland and Swaziland, despite their requests to the contrary. The provision was dropped in 1961, after the withdrawal of South Africa from the Commonwealth.

The first significant political progress was made in 1921–22 with the creation of European and African advisory councils, added to which was a joint advisory council. In 1961, executive and legislative councils were created. A major step on the road to independence was taken in 1965 with the implementation of Bechuanaland's self-government constitution under Seretse Khama, the former chief-designate of the Bamangwato, who had become prime minister after Bechuanaland's first general elections. Final constitutional talks were held in London in February 1966, and on 30 September 1966, under the leadership of President Khama, the newly named Republic of Botswana came into being.

On 18 October 1969, the Botswana Democratic Party (BDP), under the leadership of Sir Seretse Khama, was returned to power in the general elections, and he was sworn in for a second term as president on 22 October. Khama was reelected president after the BDP won 27 out of 32 regular elective seats in the National Assembly in national elections held on 26 October 1974. During this first decade of independence, Botswana refused to support UN sanctions against South Africa because, although officially opposed to apartheid, Botswana recognized its own economic dependence on South Africa. Following the 1969 elections, President Khama banned the import of goods from the white minority regime in Rhodesia (now Zimbabwe). Tensions were high in the 1970s as Botswana harbored 20,000 refugees from Rhodesia, and Rhodesian forces several times crossed into Botswana on "hot pursuit" raids against guerrillas.

In elections held in October 1979, the BDP won 29 of the 32 elective seats, and Khama was elected to a fourth presidential term. He died in 1980 and was succeeded by Vice-President Quett Ketumile Joni Masire, who was elected to a full five-year term on 10 September 1984. South Africa repeatedly, but fruitlessly, pressed Botswana to sign a mutual-security agreement, and it accused Botswana of harboring insurgents opposed to the Pretoria regime and allowing them to mount acts of terrorism and sabotage against South Africa, a charge Botswana denied. An attack by South African commandos on 14 June 1985, aimed at South African refugees, killed at least 15 people in Gaborone. Further South African border violations and attacks on targets in

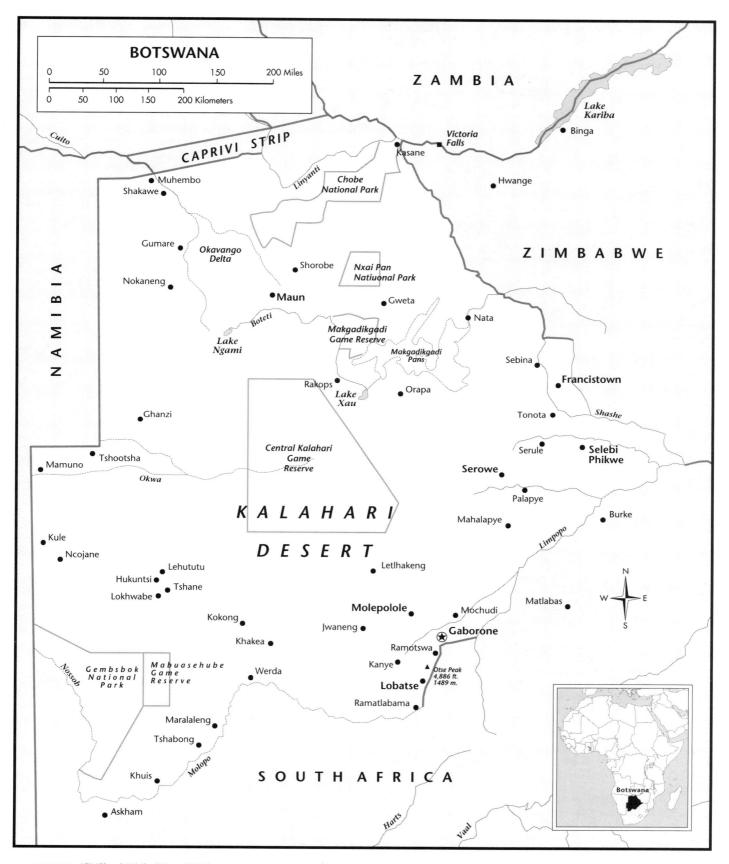

BOTSWANA

| 0 | 50 | 100 | 150 | 200 Miles |
| 0 | 50 | 100 | 150 | 200 Kilometers |

ZAMBIA

Lake Kariba

CAPRIVI STRIP

Victoria Falls

Kasane

Binga

Muhembo

Shakawe

Hwange

Linyanti

Chobe National Park

ZIMBABWE

Gumare

Okavango Delta

Shorobe

Nxai Pan Natiuonal Park

NAMIBIA

Nokaneng

Maun

Boteti

Gweta

Nata

Lake Ngami

Makgadikgadi Game Reserve

Makgadikgadi Pans

Sebina

Ghanzi

Rakops

Lake Xau

Orapa

Francistown

Tonota

Shashe

Mamuno

Tshootsha

Central Kalahari Game Reserve

Okwa

Serule

Selebi Phikwe

Serowe

K A L A H A R I

Palapye

Kule

D E S E R T

Mahalapye

Burke

Limpopo

Ncojane

Lehututu

Letlhakeng

Matlabas

Hukuntsi

Tshane

N

Lokhwabe

Kokong

Molepolole

Mochudi

W

E

Jwaneng

Gaborone

S

Khakea

Ramotswa

Nossob

Gembsbok National Park

Mabuasehube Game Reserve

Werda

Kanye

▲ Otse Peak 4,886 ft. 1489 m.

Lobatse

Maralaleng

Ramatlabama

Tshabong

S O U T H   A F R I C A

Khuis

Molopo

Askham

Harts

Vaal

Botswana

LOCATION: 17°47′ to 26°54′s; 20° to 29°21′ε. **BOUNDARY LENGTHS:** Zimbabwe, 813 km (505 mi); South Africa (including Bophuthatswana), 1,778 km (1,105 mi); Namibia (South West Africa), 1,461 km (908 mi).

Botswana took place during 1986, but such incursions had ended by 1988 and in 1992 the two countries established formal diplomatic relations.

Masire was reelected on 7 October 1989 and the BDP won 31 and the BNF 3 of the elected assembly seats. Allegations of corruption in 1994 may lead to a reduced BDP majority in the October, 1994 elections. Botswana is an active member of the Southern Africa Development Community (SADC) and Gaberone serves as headquarters to the secretariat of the ten-state organization.

13GOVERNMENT

Under the 1965 constitution, as subsequently modified, Botswana is a republic. The president is the chief of state, chief executive, and commander-in-chief of the armed forces. He is elected by a simple majority of the National Assembly. The president appoints a cabinet from among the National Assembly members, including the vice-president, who also serves as a cabinet minister. The president also has the power to declare war, and he can summon or dissolve the National Assembly at any time. He can veto any bill, but if it is passed again within six months, he must either sign it or dissolve the Assembly.

The National Assembly consists of 34 directly elected members and four appointed members. In 1993, in preparation for the 1994 elections, that number was increased to 40 elected seats. All citizens of Botswana aged 21 and over are eligible to vote. Both the President and the Assembly are elected for five-year terms. After a no-confidence vote, the Assembly must be dissolved, or the president must resign. The House of Chiefs consists of the chiefs of the eight principal tribes, and four chiefs elected from minority districts. This group serves as an advisory body to government. Any proposed bill relating to matters of tribal concern must be referred to the House of Chiefs before the Assembly can pass it.

Botswana has both a High Court and traditional village councils, called "kgotla", which serve as public forums at which villagers can express opinions.

As one of Africa's few stable multiparty democracies with an open political system and a commendable human rights record, Botswana is a model of participatory democracy.

14POLITICAL PARTIES

Botswana's leading party, the Botswana Democratic Party (BDP), was founded in late 1961 as the Bechuanaland Democratic Party by Seretse Khama. The BDP advocated a gradual approach to independence and pledged itself to democracy, nonracialism, and a multiparty state. In foreign affairs, while maintaining opposition to the policy of apartheid, the BDP acknowledged Botswana's economic dependence on South Africa and the need to maintain friendly relations. Other parties include the Botswana People's Party (BPP), founded in 1960; the Botswana Independence Party (BIP), founded in 1964 under the leadership of Motsamai Mpho; and the Botswana National Front (BNF), which put up its first candidates in 1969.

In the March 1965 elections, the BDP won 28 of the 31 contested seats, and the BPP took the other 3. Seretse Khama became prime minister and appointed Quett Masire as deputy prime minister. Under the transitional constitutional provisions for the immediate postindependence period, they automatically acceded to the offices of president and vice-president, respectively. The members elected to the Legislative Assembly in 1965 continued to hold office in the new National Assembly. The first postindependence elections were held on 18 October 1969; the BDP won 24 seats, the BPP 3 seats, the BNF 3 seats, and the BIP 1 seat (only 31 seats were contested).

In the elections of 26 October 1974, the ruling BDP raised its total of elective seats to 27, while the BNF won 2 seats, the BPP 2,

and the BIP 1. In the elections of October 1979, the BDP won 29 seats, the BNF 2, and the BIP 1. In elections held in September 1984, the BDP won 29 seats, the BNF 4, and the BPP 1. The division in the October, 1989 elections was BDP 31 and BNF 3. Since then, the opposition parties, largely concentrated in urban areas, have moved toward a common front. The next scheduled elections will be October, 1994. There are emerging splits in both the BDP and the BNF. The BNF leader has threatened to boycott the 1994 elections unless electoral reform is enacted.

15LOCAL GOVERNMENT

Local government is carried out by 10 district councils and five town councils. Executive authority in each district is vested in the district commissioner, who is appointed by the central government. The commissioner is assisted by the district council and the district development committee, which are partly appointed and partly elected.

16JUDICIAL SYSTEM

The 1965 constitution provides for a high court, a court of appeal, and subordinate first-, second-, and third-class courts. The chief justice, appointed by the president, is chairman of the Judicial Services Commission, which advises the president on the appointment of other judges and magistrates. The African Courts Proclamation of 1961 provides for courts with competence in matters of tribal law and custom, presided over by chiefs and headmen. A court of appeals for such cases was created in 1986. The customary courts handle marital and property disputes as well as minor offenses. The judiciary is independent of the executive and the legislative branches.

17ARMED FORCES

The Botswana Defense Force was established in 1977 in response to Rhodesian incursions. The total strength of the armed forces of ground and air units was estimated at 6,000 or more, armed with NATO weapons in 1993. There were also about 1,000 paramilitary police. The defense budget (1992) was $136.4 million or 4.4 percent of gross domestic product.

18INTERNATIONAL COOPERATION

Botswana became a member of the UN on 17 October 1966 and is a member of ECA and all the nonregional specialized agencies except IAEA, IMO, and WIPO. It is a member of the OAU, adheres to GATT, and is a signatory of the Law of the Sea. It belongs to a customs union including South Africa, Lesotho, and Swaziland. Botswana also participates in the African Development Bank, the Commonwealth, G-77, and the Southern African Development Coordination Conference, which maintains a secretariat at Gaborone.

19ECONOMY

Botswana is regarded by some as one of Africa's success stories. Botswana's economy was dependent almost entirely on livestock production until the 1970s, when the country became an important exporter of diamonds and other minerals.   Then, the Botswana Development Corp., adopting a conservative investment policy, actively sought foreign capital for investments in crop agriculture, tourism, and secondary industries.   The rapid growth in diamond production helped Botswana achieve average annual economic growth of 8.4% from independence through 1984.   Real growth of 10% was recorded between 1985 and 1987, slowing to 8.7% in the following two years (1987–89).

Diamond mining in Botswana began in 1971. Developed in cooperation with De Beers Consolidated Mines, diamond production peaked at 17.3 million carats (70% gem quality) before dropping back to 15.9 million carats in 1992. Botswana also produces copper-nickel matte production, which peaked at

50,000 tons in 1988 before declining in the face of lowering world prices. A second copper-nickel mine began production in 1988, and a third is expected to begin production in the mid-1990s. Botswana has significant coal deposits which, in the face of low world coal prices, have been used only to meet local energy needs. A new soda ash and salt production center began production in 1991, but continuing technical difficulties have kept output well below capacity. Botswana has exploitable deposits in platinum, gold, and silver as well. Exploration for petroleum and natural gas deposits is underway in western Botswana.

In spite of the gains recorded by the mining sector, agriculture employs an estimated 62.1% of the labor force (1991). Commercial farms play a critical role in agricultural and livestock production. Of Botswana's total output of sorghum, maize, millet, beans and pulses, 37% was produced by 100 of the 360 commercial farms. Ownership of the national herd is highly concentrated: 5% of households own over 50%.

Botswana is drought-prone and has suffered severe drought nine of the last 11 seasons. As a consequence, the government has abandoned its earlier food self-sufficiency policy. Water for cattle is a major concern: one-third of national demand goes to livestock. Intense competition for water resources has affected industrial development plans.

Tourism is an important part of the economy, with an estimated 899,000 tourists in 1991. This was an improvement over the preceding year.

20 INCOME
In 1992 Botswana's GNP was $3,797 million at current prices, or $2,790 per capita. For the period 1985–92 the average inflation rate was 12.9%, resulting in a real growth rate in per capita GNP of 8.1%. The government has responded to high inflation rates with periodic devaluations. Nonetheless, wages have been kept low so as not to stimulate inflation or to encourage greater migration to Botswana.

In 1992 the GDP was $3,700 million in current US dollars. It is estimated that agriculture, hunting, forestry, and fishing contributed 6% to GDP; mining and quarrying, 46%; manufacturing, 4%; electricity, gas, and water, 2%; construction, 6%; wholesale and retail trade, 13%; transport, storage, and communication, 2%; finance, insurance, real estate, and business services, 5%; community, social, and personal services, 2%; and other sources 15%.

21 LABOR
The vast majority of the estimated labor force of 443,455 in 1991 was engaged in stock raising and subsistence agriculture. In 1992 there were 227,500 people in wage employment. In addition, about 16,000 citizens of Botswana were working in South African mines. The public sector accounts for 31% of formal employment. The other principal sectors of formal employment are commerce, 18%; construction, 15%; manufacturing, 12%; services, 10%; and mining, 4%.

There are well-developed unions in mining, railways, banking, and among blue-collar government workers, all members of the Botswana Federation of Trade Unions. An employment act controls employment contracts, work by women and children, wage guarantees, conditions of work, and paid holidays. Formerly, public sector salary levels were set by the government to serve as a benchmark for private sector wages, but that practice was ended by Parliament in 1990. Unemployment exceeded 25% in 1992.

22 AGRICULTURE
About 2.4% of total land area is engaged actively in crop production. Crop production is hampered by traditional farming methods, recurrent drought, erosion, and disease. Most of the land under cultivation is in the eastern region. The principal crops for domestic use are sorghum, corn, and millet. In 1992, the sorghum and corn harvests only comprised 10% of the annual requirement of 250,000 tons. Grain is usually imported from Zimbabwe and South Africa. Smaller quantities of cowpeas, beans, and other pulses are also grown. The 1985/86 output of all these crops was about 25,000 tons; Botswana imported 70% more (by value) than it exported in agricultural products during 1992.

Agricultural research has been devoted to soil conservation, grazing experiments, and developing and distributing improved strains of grain. The construction of dams and the drilling of boreholes to tap underground water are continuing government programs. In early 1990, the government changed its official agricultural policy to emphasize the production only of those foodstuffs which can be raised economically. The Arable Lands Development Program and the Tribal Grazing Land Policy are government programs designed to help farmers in communal areas.

23 ANIMAL HUSBANDRY
In 1991, the cattle population was about 2,500,000. Other livestock included 2,090,000 goats, 325,000 sheep, 34,000 horses, 153,000 donkeys, and 2,000,000 poultry. Cattle are valued for wealth and prestige and are used in the payment of bride price, but there is little of the cultural prohibition against selling cattle found in some other parts of Africa. Herds are grazed in the open veld where water and grass are available; the borehole-drilling program is extending the available grazing land. A gradual upgrading of stock quality has been achieved through selective breeding, culling, and controlled grazing. A system of disease-control fences has been installed. A vaccine institute was opened in 1981 to deal with the threat of foot-and-mouth disease. In the mid-1980s, the Botswana Meat Commission's plant at Lobatse was the largest export abattoir in Africa. In 1992, 55% of Botswana's annual beef production was exported, mostly to South Africa or Western Europe. About 170,000 cattle were slaughtered that year. Beef and beef products are Botswana's second largest export earner (after minerals). In 1991, beef exports earned $72 million, or 4% of total exports.

24 FISHING
Botswana is landlocked, but some fishing for local consumption is carried out by the inhabitants of the Limpopo River Valley and the Okavango region. Landings were estimated at 1,900 tons in 1991.

25 FORESTRY
The indigenous forests of northeast Ngamiland include the valuable mukwa, mukusi, and mopane woods. Some small-scale exploitation has taken place. Roundwood production was an estimated 1,440,000 cu m in 1991.

26 MINING
Mining and mineral commodoties account for more than 50% of a GDP estimated at more than $3 billion, and almost 90% of about $2 billion in exports; yet mining employed only 3% of the economically active population in 1991. Botswana's mineral resources are still largely unexplored. The northeast contains copper, nickel, and precious metals; the nothwest has coper and silver; and the south holds base and precious metals. De Beers Botswana Mining (Debswana) and Botswana Concessions, Ltd. (BCL), both partly owned by the government, developed major mineral fields in the eastern and central regions during the 1970s. The Debswana diamond mine at Orapa produced about 6.1 million carats of diamonds in 1991, half of

gem quality; starting in 1981, Debswana had to stockpile diamonds to brake the decline in world prices. The world's largest gem diamond mine was opened at Jwaneng in 1982, with production of 9.4 million carats in 1991, making Botswana the world's third-ranking diamond producer. Total production was 16.5 million carats in 1991. After diamonds, the next most valuable mineral commodity is smelted nickel-copper-cobalt matte. Diamond reserves were reported to be 300 million carats, or 20 years at current production. Nickel-copper ore reserves were reported by BCL as 95 million tons at 0.68% nickel and 0.71% copper at the end of 1991. BCL developed a nickel-copper complex at Selebi-Phikwe during the 1970s. Output totaled 48,319 tons of nickel-copper-cobalt matte in 1991. A soda ash plant was expected to open at Makgadikgadi in 1988—production commenced in June 1991 and amounted to 62,000 tons for the year.

27ENERGY AND POWER

Most electric power is generated thermally in installations run by the Botswana Power Corp., a public enterprise established in 1970. Total production of electricity in 1991 was 630 million kwh, nearly 20 times the 1972 output. Coal production was 783,873 tons in 1991, mined solely at Morupule by Anglo American, mostly for the generation of electricity. The government is considering constructing a 2,400 Mw coal-fired power plant at the same coal field, which would be designed to export power to South Africa beginning next century.

Several companies are prospecting for oil, but none had been discovered as of 1993. Petrocanada has an exploratory well in the western Kalahari. In 1992, Amoco was studying the possibility of extracting methane from coal beds.

28INDUSTRY

Botswana has a small, but dynamic, manufacturing sector, which contributed 4% of GDP in 1991. Average growth in this sector during the 1980s was 7.5%, with formal employment reaching 26,000 in 1991. The sector has diversified into textiles, beverages, chemicals, metals, plastics, and electrical products. The government parastatal, the Botswana Development Corp., has declined in significance relative to private initiatives, but still is a major promoter of industrial development with interests in brewing, sugar, furniture, clothing, tourism, milling, and concrete. Though promising, industrial development is limited by a small domestic market, weak infrastructure, import dependence, and small skilled labor force.

Local coal supplies the fuel required for Botswana's energy sector. Peak requirements are generally supplied by the South African grid. In 1991, Botswana also linked to the Zambian and Zimbabwean grids.

29SCIENCE AND TECHNOLOGY

Botswana has three universities and colleges offering training in science, agriculture, and engineering. The Geological Survey of Botswana, founded in 1948, conducts research in regional and economic geology, hydrogeology, and geophysics.

30DOMESTIC TRADE

Small general stores usually carry a variety of items, but food, fuel, and clothing staples make up most of their stock. There are also a few wholesalers, and some traders act as local agents for larger firms. To augment their incomes, other traders operate postal or transport services, restaurants, butcheries, and bakeries. The traders play an important role as middlemen between the local livestock and crop producers and the slaughterhouses, factories, and exporters. Business hours are 8 AM to 1 PM and 2:15 to 5:30 PM, Monday through Friday, and 8 AM to 10:45 AM on Saturday.

31FOREIGN TRADE

In the mid-1970s diamonds replaced beef as Botswana's principal export. Beef now accounts for about 4% of exports (1991), trailing copper-nickel matte's 6.8%.

Principal exports (in millions of pula) where estimated in 1990 at:

Diamonds	2,664.9
Meat and byproducts	130.9
Copper-nickel matte	287.6
Textiles	75.0
Other items (including reexports)	163.8
TOTAL	3,322.2

Imports in 1990 were estimated at 3,527.2 million pulas. Machinery and electrical goods made up 24.7% of imports, followed by vehicles and transport equipment at 15%. Food, beverage, and tobacco products accounted for 10.4%. With recurrent drought and only 5% arable land, Botswana imports much of its food and other basic needs, primarily through South Africa. In the drought year of 1991/92, an estimated 90% of Botswana's food was imported.

The bulk of Botswana's exports went to Europe (85.9%) in 1988, while 13.5% went to African countries. Of imports, 77.1% came from the countries of the Southern African Customs Union, primarily South Africa. The United Kingdom furnished another 6.1% of imports.

32BALANCE OF PAYMENTS

In 1991 Botswana registered a trade surplus of $363 million, up about one-third over 1990, but down from other previous years. The strong export performance can be largely attributed to favorable conditions in the world market for diamonds (the main export) as well as to increased diamond production. The total value of 1991 exports was $1.67 billion, with a balance on the current account of $37.7 million and a balance on the capital account of $225 million. Botswana has maintained a positive balance of payments position every year from 1978 to 1991, except in 1981. Reserves in mid-1992 came to $4.1 billion, or about 24 months of import cover, although they are expected to fall if diamond revenues plateau or decline in coming years.

33BANKING AND SECURITIES

Prior to 1976, Botswana belonged to the South African Monetary Area. Its currency, like those of Lesotho and Swaziland, was issued by the South African Reserve Bank. On 23 August 1976, however, the Bank of Botswana was established, and Botswana began issuing its own currency. In 1992, the bank had international reserves of P767.2 million. The Standard Bank and Barclays Bank had numerous branches in Botswana at the end of 1986. The National Development Bank was established in 1964 to promote economic development.

34INSURANCE

In 1987, five insurance companies had offices in Gaborone. The government took over third-party vehicle insurance in 1987.

35PUBLIC FINANCE

Mineral revenues, which accounted for 45% of treasury receipts in 1992/93, and a tight fiscal policy have allowed Botswana to accumulate surpluses since 1983. The 1992/93 budget surplus was estimated at $51 million. Customs and excise receipts account for an additional 25% of revenues; earnings on reserve holdings, 15%.

The following table shows actual revenues and expenditures for 1990 and 1991 (in millions of pula).

	1990	1991
REVENUE AND GRANTS		
Tax revenue	1,939.5	2,037.1
Non-tax revenue	1,642.3	1,920.4
Capital revenue	14.7	11.5
Grants	117.8	70.0
TOTAL	3,714.3	4,039.0
EXPENDITURES & LENDING MINUS REPAYMENTS		
General public services	323.8	429.4
Defense	315.7	359.1
Public order and safety	85.6	98.1
Education	485.9	565.1
Health	119.7	127.3
Social security and welfare	15.6	17.2
Housing and community amenities	367.8	859.9
Recreation, cultural, and religious affairs	32.2	43.4
Economic affairs and services	396.8	464.0
Other expenditures	225.1	227.8
Adjustments	6.5	−50.0
Lending minus repayments	552.6	587.2
TOTAL	2,920.9	3,278.5
Deficit /Surplus	793.4	760.5

In 1991 Botswana's total public debt stood at P965.8 million, of which P965.8 million was financed abroad.

36TAXATION
The income tax law establishes for individual incomes progressive rates ranging up to 50%. There is a basic corporate tax of 40%, as well as taxes on interest, on dividends, and payments for professional services. Special tax advantages have been granted by treaty to South African, Swedish, and UK firms. A local government tax is paid to the district or town council to finance social and sanitary services.

37CUSTOMS AND DUTIES
Botswana belongs to a customs union with South Africa, Lesotho, Swaziland, and Namibia. South Africa levies and collects most of the customs, sales, and excise duties for the five member states, paying a share of the revenues to the other four. In addition, all customs duties are eliminated among the five countries.

38FOREIGN INVESTMENT
Botswana began actively encouraging foreign investment in the mid-1980s. Government policies offered attractive tax rates, including a five-year tax holiday, capital grants on new projects, and duty-free access to the large South African market. Botswana also enjoys duty-free access to the European Economic Community for most of its products. Its liberal policies allow unrestricted repatriation of earnings and capital. Furthermore, it has a substantial financial assistance policy for foreign investors and has established an export processing zone in Selebi-Pikwa. Investment law is scrupulously observed by the Bostwanan bureaucracy and courts. Investment incentives, including cash grants, have been offered to smalland medium-scale investors for labor-intensive schemes, particularly outside urban areas.

Foreign investment is chiefly in the mining sector, with the Anglo-American Corp., AMAX, and De Beers leading the way. The British Commonwealth Development Corp. invested £714,000 in the Lobatse slaughterhouse and in three large cattle ranches, two in the northern part of the country and one on the Molopo River in the Kalahari. Colgate-Palmolive and H. J. Heinz have investments in Botswana, as does a Houston-based brick manufacturer, Interkiln Corp. Other areas of investment include specialty agricultural production, construction, and manufacturing of textile, health and beauty, and agricultural and construction equipment products. Investments in infrastructure, telecommunications, tourism, and housing development are sought by the government.

39ECONOMIC DEVELOPMENT
As in the 1986–91 development plan, which called for spending of P1.2 billion, Botswana has made job creation a top priority of government planning in the past few years. Though formal sector employment has been expanding at a 10% annual rate over much of the last decade, unemployment in mid-1993 was estimated at 30–35%.

The government has a long-standing policy of promoting human capital development and health care. All education through the university level is free (1992). Great importance is placed on the development of rural areas so as to reduce rural-urban migration.

In light of the limited resources, Botswana's government now follows "food security" agricultural policy of promoting only those foodstuffs which can be grown economically.

40SOCIAL DEVELOPMENT
Many social welfare needs are met through the provisions of tribal custom, and social security on a national scale has not yet been introduced. The infant mortality rate in the early 1990s was 43 per 1,000 live births, and the fertility rate was 6.9 children per woman during the childbearing years. Women made up about 28% of the wage labor force in 1983. Potable water supplies, public schools and health clinics have been established in almost every village.

41HEALTH
In 1992, comprehensive health services were available to approximately 90% of the population, from 15 general hospitals. The government stresses primary health care with emphasis on disease prevention and healthy living. In 1990, there was one doctor for every 5,150 people.

The major health problems are malnutrition and tuberculosis. In 1990, 15% of children under 5 years of age were considered malnourished. Public health teams conduct tuberculosis and malaria control campaigns. From 1985 to 1992, 89% of the population had access to health services.

There were 51,000 births in 1992 with 33% of married women (ages 15 to 49) using contraception from 1980 to 1993. From 1990 to 1992, immunized children one year of age were as follows: tuberculosis (71%); diphtheria, pertussis, and tetanus (82%); polio (82%); and measles (65%).

The average life expectancy in in 1992 was 61 years, with a death rate of 9.3 per 1,000 people in 1993. The infant mortality rate in 1992 was 45 per 1,000 live births.

42HOUSING
There is no overcrowding in tribal villages, but slums have developed in the larger towns. The Botswana Housing Corp., a public enterprise, concentrates its efforts on the main urban centers, where growth, and therefore demand, is greatest. Projects owned, managed, and maintained in 1985 totaled 7,215.

As of 1981, 96% of all housing units were categorized as "conventional," which included flats, bungalows, huts, and all other structures intended for human use. Squatter-occupied "improvised" units accounted for 2.3%, with the remainder categorized ads "unconventional" or "movable." Of all housing units, 29.4% were acquired through tribal authorities and 18.6% by land hoards. Rentals accounted for 17.1%, "self allocation" for 15.2%, and inheritance for 9.9%. Sanitation facilities included pit latrines (16.8%), and flush toilets (8.6%); however,

64% of housing units had no facilities. The water supply was piped (56.1%), or drawn from wells (21.2%), river beds (8.5%), rivers (5%), or other sources.

43 EDUCATION

In 1990, the literacy rate was 73.6% (males, 83.7%; and females, 66.1%). In 1992, 22% of government expenditure was on education. The ultimate aim is universal education. Education at the primary level lasts for seven years, though it is not compulsory. Subsequent to that is five years of secondary education (two years followed by three years). In 1992 Botswana had 654 primary schools, with 308,840 students and 9,708 teachers. Secondary schools had 78,804 students and 4,437 teachers in 1991. Until 1961, primary schooling was completely financed by tribal treasuries, with some tribes spending up to 70% of their budgets on education.

The University of Botswana, founded in 1976, has a faculty of social sciences, education, sciences, agriculture, and humanities. Universities and equivalent institutions in 1991 had 3,567 pupils with 376 teaching staff.

44 LIBRARIES AND MUSEUMS

The Botswana National Library Service was founded in 1967 to provide nationwide public library service and act as the national library. The main library is located in Gaborone, with 21 branches located throughout the country. Mobile library service is also provided. The library service has 378,000 volumes, and the University of Botswana has over 60,000. The National Archives, with 13,000 items, are in Gaborone.

The recently renovated National Museum and Art Gallery, in Gaborone, houses a collection of the ethnography and natural history of Botswana and of sub-Saharan African art. There are also ethnographic museums in Kanye and Mochudi and a postal museum in Lobatse.

45 MEDIA

The government publishes the *Daily News* (circulation 32,000 in 1991) in both English and Setswana. It also publishes, in a bilingual edition, the monthly magazine *Kutlwaro* (circulation 24,000). In 1991, five independent newspapers were publishing on a weekly or semiweekly basis. The major political parties publish monthly journals.

Radio Botswana broadcasts, in English and Setswana, a variety of news, educational, cultural, and entertainment programs. An earth satellite station was erected in 1980. Botswana had 15 radio transmitters and 155,000 radio receivers in 1991. There was no television service, but the 21,000 owners of television sets could receive South African programming. The number of telephones was 34,318 in 1991.

46 ORGANIZATIONS

Most towns have women's clubs, and there is a chamber of commerce in Gaborone. The Boy Scout movement is popular. The government has sponsored the formation of cooperatives.

47 TOURISM, TRAVEL, AND RECREATION

Botswana's beautiful and well-stocked game reserves are its principal tourist attraction, with both hunting and photographic safaris available. Popular with tourists is the Okavango Delta region, which during the rainy season is a maze of waterways, islands, and lakes; it includes the Moremi Wildlife Refuge.

Nearby is Chobe National Park. In all, eight national parks and game reserves cover almost 20% of the land area. The Kalahari Desert is another attraction, as are the country's tapestry weavers, potters, and rugmakers. The Tsodilo Hills have cave paintings by the ancestors of the Basarwa (Bushmen), the earliest known inhabitants of Botswana. The governments "National Conservation Strategy and Tourism Policy" is intended to promote tourism while protecting wildlife areas. Citizens of the US, South Africa, Commonwealth countries, and most Western European countries do not need visas. Proof of yellow fever and cholera vaccination is required of travelers from an infected area. Antimalarial precautions are advisable. As of 1990, there were 1,143 hotel rooms with 2,134 beds and a 58% occupancy rate, and tourism receipts totaled $65 million. In 1991, 899,000 visitors arrived in Botswana, 46% from South Africa and 37% from Zimbabwe.

48 FAMOUS BOTSWANANS

Khama III (1837–1923), chief of the Bamangwato and a Christian convert, reigned for 48 years. His grandson, Sir Seretse Khama (1921–80), was Botswana's first president. Quett Ketumile Joni Masire (b.1925) succeeded him in 1980.

49 DEPENDENCIES

Botswana has no territories or colonies.

50 BIBLIOGRAPHY

Alverson, Hoyt. *Mind in the Heart of Darkness: Value and Self-Identity Among the Tswana of Southern Africa.* New Haven, Conn.: Yale University Press, 1978.

Black, David R. *Foreign Policy in Small States: Botswana, Lesotho, Swaziland and Southern Africa.* Halifax, N.S.: Centre for Foreign Policy Studies, Dalhousie University, 1988.

Chirenje, J. Mutero. *A History of Northern Botswana, 1850–1910.* Rutherford, N.J.: Fairleigh Dickinson University Press, 1976.

Colclough, Christopher, and Stephen McCarthy. *The Political Economy of Botswana.* London: Oxford University Press, 1980.

Hartland-Thunberg, Penelope. *Botswana: An African Growth Economy.* Boulder, Colo.: Westview, 1978.

Harvey, Charles (ed.). *Papers on the Economy of Botswana.* London: Heinemann, 1981.

Hitchcock, R. Renee, and Mary R. Smith. *Settlement in Botswana.* London: Heinemann, 1982.

Holm, John and Patrick Molutsi (eds.). *Democracy in Botswana.* Athens: Ohio University Press, 1989.

Morton, Fred. *Historical Dictionary of Botswana.* Metuchen, N.J.: Scarecrow Press, 1989.

Schapera, Isaac. *The Tswana.* London: International African Institute, 1962.

Sillery, Anthony. *Botswana: A Short Political History.* London: Methuen, 1974.

Stedman, Stephen John (ed). *Botswana: the Political Economy of Democratic Development.* Boulder, Colo.: L. Rienner Publishers, 1993.

Vengroff, Richard. *Botswana: Rural Development in the Shadow of Apartheid.* Rutherford, N.J.: Fairleigh Dickinson University Press, 1976.

Wiseman, John A. *Botswana.* Oxford, Eng.; Santa Barbara, Calif.: Clio Press, 1992.

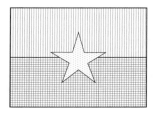

BURKINA FASO

Republic of Burkina Faso
Burkina Faso Jamahiriya

CAPITAL: Ouagadougou.

FLAG: The flag consists of two equal horizontal stripes of red and green divided by a narrow gold band. A five-point gold star is at the center.

ANTHEM: The national anthem begins "Contre le férule humiliante il y a déjà mille ans" ("Against the humiliating bondage of a thousand years").

MONETARY UNIT: The Communauté Financière Africaine franc (CFA Fr) is a paper currency with one basic official rate based on the French franc (100 CFA Fr = Fr1). There are coins of 1, 2, 5, 10, 25, 50, 100, and 500 CFA francs, and notes of 50, 100, 500, 1,000, 5,000, and 10,000 CFA francs. CFA Fr1 = $0.0018 (or $1 = CFA Fr571).

WEIGHTS AND MEASURES: The metric system is the legal standard.

HOLIDAYS: New Year's Day, 1 January; Anniversary of the 1966 Revolution, 3 January; Labor Day, 1 May; Independence Day, 5 August; Assumption, 15 August; All Saints' Day, 1 November; Christmas, 25 December. Movable religious holidays include Id al-Fitr, 'Id al-'adha', Milad an-Nabi, Easter Monday, Ascension, and Pentecost Monday.

TIME: GMT.

¹LOCATION, SIZE, AND EXTENT

Burkina Faso (formerly Upper Volta), a landlocked country in West Africa, has an area of 274,200 sq km (105,869 sq mi), with a length of 873 km (542 mi) ENE–WSW and a width of 474 km (295 mi) SSE–NNW. Comparatively, the area occupied by Burkina Faso is slightly larger than the state of Colorado. Bounded on the E by Niger, on the SE by Benin (formerly Dahomey), on the S by Togo, Ghana, and Côte d'Ivoire, and on the W and N by Mali, Burkina Faso has a total boundary length of 3,192 km (1,983 mi).

The capital city of Burkina Faso, Ouagadougou, is located in the center of the country.

²TOPOGRAPHY

Burkina Faso consists for the most part of a vast lateritic plateau in the West African savanna, approximately 180–300 m (600–1,000 ft) above sea level. The highest point (749 m/2,457 ft) is near the Mali border, northwest of Orodara. The land is slightly inclined toward the south and notched by valleys formed by the three principal rivers, the Black, White, and Red Voltas, and their main tributary, the Sourou. They are alternately dry or in flood and all are unnavigable. In general, the land is dry and poor.

³CLIMATE

The climate is characterized by high temperatures, especially at the end of the dry season. The humidity, which increases as one moves south, ranges from a winter low of 12% to 45% to a rainy season high of 68% to 96%. The harmattan, a dry east wind, brings with it spells of considerable heat from March to May, when maximum temperatures range from 40°C to 48°C (104° to 119°F); from May to October, the climate is hot and wet, and from November to March, comfortable and dry. January temperatures range from 7°C to 13°C (44° to 55°F). Average annual rainfall varies from 115 cm (45 in) in the southwest to less than 25 cm (10 in) in the extreme north and northeast. The rainy

season lasts from four months in the northeast to six months in the southwest, from May through October. From 1969 to 1974, Burkina Faso suffered from drought, especially in the north, which is in the semiarid Sahel zone.

⁴FLORA AND FAUNA

The area is largely wild bush country with a mixture of grass and small trees in varying proportions. The savanna region is mainly grassland in the rainy season and semidesert during the harmattan period. Fauna, possibly the widest variety in West Africa, includes the elephant, hippopotamus, buffalo, monkey, crocodile, giraffe, various types of antelope, and a vast variety of bird and insect life.

⁵ENVIRONMENT

The major environmental problems facing Burkina Faso are recurrent drought and the advance of the northern desert into the savanna. This trend toward desertification has been increased by overgrazing of pastureland, slash-and-burn agriculture, and overcutting of wood for fuel. Almost all the trees within 40 km (25 mi) of the capital have been felled. The frequency of droughts in Burkina Faso and its location in the Sahara desert contribute to the nation's water supply problems. The country has 6.7 cubic miles of water but 56% percent of the city dwellers and 30% of the rural people do not have safe water. According to the World Health Organization, 80% of all disease in Burkina Faso is caused by unsafe water. Pollution problems result from uncontrolled disposal of sewage and industrial wastes. Burkina Faso contributes 0.1% of the world's total gas emissions. The Ministry of Environment and Tourism is the principal government agency concerned with the environment. In 1985, Burkina Faso had 11 national parks and wildlife reserves totaling 1,140,700 hectares (2,817,000 acres). Of 147 species of mammals, 10 are considered endangered. One bird species in a total of 497 and two reptiles are also threatened. As of 1994, no plant species are in danger of extinction.

6POPULATION

The 1994 population was estimated at 10,278,771, with an average annual growth rate of about 2.8%. The projected population for 2000 is 11,833,000, assuming a crude birthrate of 44.1 per 1,000 population, a crude death rate of 164, and a net natural increase of 27.7 for 1995–2000.

Average density in 1994 was 37 per sq km (97 per sq mi). Most people live in the south and center of the country, and over 80% of the population is rural. Ouagadougou, the capital, had a population of about 689,000 in 1990. The only other big city is Bobo-Dioulasso.

7MIGRATION

Seasonal labor migration in Burkina Faso began in the colonial period as a means of obtaining money for taxes and continues today as a remedy for economic deficiencies. In 1985, 372,907 persons were listed as absent residents, 748,380 as émigrés, and 143,359 as visitors. According to some estimates, as many as 2 million Burkinabe live abroad at any one time, about half in Côte d'Ivoire and the rest throughout West Africa, where many are employed on coffee and cocoa plantations.

8ETHNIC GROUPS

The principal ethnic group in Burkina Faso is the Mossi, who make up about 55% of the total population. They are mainly farmers and live in the central portions of the country.

The Bobo, the second-largest ethnic group (about 1 million), are mostly farmers, artisans, and metalworkers living in the southwest around Bobo-Dioulasso. Other groups include the Senufo in the southwest, the Gourmantché in the east, and the nomadic Fulani, or Peul, who inhabit the areas near the country's northern borders. The number of nomads in the north has diminished since the Sahelian drought of the 1970s.

9LANGUAGES

French is the official language of Burkina Faso, and Moré, spoken by 55% of the population, is the most important indigenous language. The various ethnic groups speak their own languages.

10RELIGIONS

An estimated 65% of the population presently follows traditional animist religions. Of the remainder, 25% are Muslim, and 10% are Christian, primarily Roman Catholic, who comprise 9.2% of the entire population.

11TRANSPORTATION

In 1991, Burkina Faso had 16,500 km (10,253 mi) of roads and tracks, of which 1,300 km (808 mi) were paved. Many of the secondary roads are not open all year. Vehicles in 1991 included about 12,500 passenger cars, and 13,500 commercial vehicles.

The 510-km (317-mi) Mossi Railroad in Burkina Faso is part of the line that begins at Abidjan, Côte d'Ivoire, and ends in Niger, some 1,145 km (710 mi) away. The line serves the towns of Banfora, Bobo-Dioulasso, Koudougou, and Ouagadougou; 25–40% of the railway traffic passes through Burkina Faso. Planning for the construction of a railroad from Ouagadougou to Tambao (353 km/219 mi) to exploit the mineral deposits in the area was begun in October 1981. Constructed by volunteers, the line reached Donsin, 33 km (21 mi) from Ouagadougou, in 1987, and the second stage to Kaya (77 km/48 mi) was completed by 1991.

There are international airports at Ouagadougou and Bobo-Dioulasso and numerous smaller airfields. Burkina Faso owns 7% of Air Afrique, which provides the country with international service. Air Burkina, which began in 1967, is government-run and has a monopoly on domestic service. It also flies to neighboring countries.

12HISTORY

Until the end of the 19th century, the history of Burkina Faso is the history of the empire-building Mossi. According to legend and tradition, supported by some ethnographic evidence, the Mossi entered the region from the 11th to the 13th century as a warrior group from Central or East Africa and subjugated the weaker aboriginal Ninigi tribes. They called their land Mogho ("country of the Mossi") and established five independent kingdoms—Tenkodogo, Yatenga, Gourma, Zandoma, and Ouagadougou—each ruled by a king, the mogho or moro naba ("ruler of the Mossi"). Ouagadougou was the most powerful of the kingdoms.

Through the centuries, the Mossi population was augmented by groups of immigrants, such as the Hausa and the Fulani, who settled in Mossi territory but retained their ethnic identity. Contact and conflict with Islam came early. The Mossi were engaged, beginning in the 14th century, in recurrent wars with the neighboring empires of Mali and Songhai, and they occupied Timbuktu (now in Mali) at various times. They were decisively defeated by Askia Daoud of Songhai in the 16th century and thereafter ceased fighting their powerful neighbors. Their warrior tradition and their internal unity continued, however.

By the 19th century, Mossi power seems to have declined, and when the first known European incursions occurred, late in the 19th century, internal dissensions made the Mossi prey to the invaders. A French lieutenant, Voulet, was sent with an infantry column to subjugate the territory in 1896. Ouagadougou fell to Voulet in September of that year. The Mossi accepted French domination as a form of protection from their hostile neighbors.

In 1919, the French created a separate colony called Upper Volta (now Burkina Faso), but in 1932, Upper Volta's territory was divided among Niger, French Sudan (now Mali), and Côte d'Ivoire. Throughout the colonial period, the traditional political structure of the Mossi was retained, and the moro naba of Ouagadougou was regarded by the French as the emperor of the Mossi. When World War II broke out, the moro naba sent his two eldest sons to fight for France, and more than 10,000 youths in the territory followed suit. The restoration of Upper Volta as a territorial unit, long the aim of the traditional chiefs, was made a reality in 1947. In 1958, voters in Upper Volta overwhelmingly approved the new constitution of the Fifth French Republic, and Upper Volta's territorial assembly voted to make the country an autonomous state within the French Community. By this time, the traditional chiefs had lost most of their influence, and political power was in the hands of the young, European-educated elite.

The republic achieved independent status on 5 August 1960. Maurice Yaméogo, leader of the Volta Democratic Union, became president. His government quickly took on an authoritarian cast and banned all opposition parties. In 1965, a single election list was offered to the people, and the opposition—joined by civil servants, trade unionists, and students—fomented riots. Yaméogo was replaced in January 1966 by Lt. Col. (later Gen.) Sangoulé Lamizana, a former army chief of staff, who suspended the 1960 constitution, dissolved the National Assembly, and formed a military-civilian cabinet.

During the 1970s and early 1980s, Upper Volta suffered from severe political instability. A constitution that provided for an elected assembly was adopted in 1970, but factional struggle broke out and became so disruptive that in February 1974, President Lamizana announced that the military had again taken over the government. A new constitution was approved in 1977; under this constitution, Lamizana won election to the presidency in 1978. On 25 November 1980, however, Lamizana was deposed in a bloodless coup led by Col. Sayé Zerbo, who became president. Zerbo's government was overthrown on 7 November 1982 by yet another army coup, and Maj. Jean-Baptiste Ouédraogo was named president.

BURKINA FASO

| 0 | 50 | 100 | 150 Miles |
| 0 | 50 | 100 | 150 Kilometers |

Burkina Faso

MALI

Yatakala

Gorom Gorom

Kiri

Djibo   Aribinda   Dori   NIGER

Ouahigouya

Niamey

Tikaré   Kongoussi

Tougan   White   Volta   Kaya   Bogandé

Yako   Boulsa   Sirba

Nouna   Ziniaré

Dédougou   Réo   Ouagadougou   Kantchari

Koudougou   Kombissiri   Zorgo   Koupéla   Diapaga

Boromo   Red Volta   Fada N'Gourma

Mossi   Manga   Tenkodogo

Sikasso   Bobo   Highlands   Pama

Dioulasso   Black Volta   Pendjari

Orodara   Diébougou   Léo   Pô   Porga

Téna Kourou   Bawku

2,450 ft.   Dapong   BENIN

747 m.   Bougouriba

Banfora   Black

Léraba   Gaoua   Volta   GHANA   TOGO

Komoé   Wa

Léraba

CÔTE D´IVOIRE

LOCATION: 9°30′ to 15°N; 2° to 5°W. **BOUNDARY LENGTHS:** Niger, 628 km (390 mi); Benin, 270 km (168 mi); Togo, 126 km (78 mi); Ghana, 544 km, (338 mi); Côte d'Ivoire, 531 km (330 mi); Mali, 1,202 km (747 mi).

Under the moderate Ouédraogo regime, a military faction emerged that was suspected of having close ties to Libya. Prominent in this group was Capt. Thomas Sankara, who served as prime minister from January until May 1983, when he was purged by Ouédraogo. On 4 August 1983, in what was Upper Volta's third coup in three years, Sankara seized power. As many as 20 persons may have died in the disturbances. After the coup, Sankara, who emerged at the head of the ruling National Revolutionary Council, sought to retain Upper Volta's traditional foreign aid ties with the West while establishing warm relations with such nations as Ghana, Libya, the USSR, and Cuba.

Sankara sought to instill his nation with a spirit of revolutionary fervor. In August 1984, on the first anniversary of his rule, he renamed the nation Burkina Faso, meaning roughly "Land of Upright Men." He led a campaign against corruption and tax evasion, and he trimmed government spending by cutting the salaries of civil servants, an action that earned him the enmity of the nation's small but influential labor unions. A substantial number of politicians, soldiers, government officials, and labor leaders were jailed, and seven men were executed in 1984 for allegedly plotting to overthrow the government.

During December 1985, Burkina Faso fought Mali over possession of a 20- by 160-km (12- by 100-mi) disputed border strip (there had previously been clashes in 1974 and 1975). On 22 December 1986, the International Court of Justice ruled in favor of dividing the territory into roughly equal parts, a decision both nations accepted.

On 15 October 1987, faced by opposition among the trade unions and civil servants, the government was overthrown by an army unit led by Capt. Blaise Compaoré, the president's chief adviser, said also to have been his inseparable companion. Sankara and 12 aides (including two of the coup plotters) were immediately shot, and Compaoré assumed the presidency. Executions of highly placed military men followed a coup attempt on 18 September 1989.

At the start of the 1990s, the authorities sought to legitimize their position at the ballot box. Controversial presidential (December 1991) and parliamentary elections (24 May 1992) led to no governmental change. Compaoré ran unopposed for president and his party, the Popular Democratic Organization—Worker's Movement (ODP-MT), carried the legislative elections. Only three opposition parties contested seats nationwide; 35 parties boycotted the poll.

Since Compaoré took over, Burkina Faso has conducted an active foreign policy in West Africa. It sent troops to Liberia and harbors dissidents from Gambia. This has alienated Compaoré from his fellow West African leaders and from western governments. Human rights violations are commonplace and government seeks to suppress a vocal independent press. The security forces regularly use excessive force against demonstrations and government critics.

[13] GOVERNMENT

Under the constitution of 27 November 1960, the nation was governed by a president, a council of ministers, and a National Assembly of 50 members. On 5 January 1966, President Lamizana suspended the constitution and dissolved the National Assembly, announcing that he would exercise legislative and executive power by ordinance and decree. A constitution approved in 1970 provided for eventual restitution of democratic institutions, although with a formal role in the government for the military. The 1970 constitution was suspended in February 1974, when the army again assumed full power.

A democratic constitution, adopted in 1977, provided for a president and a 57-member National Assembly. This document was abolished after the coup of 25 November 1980, and the Military Committee for Reform and National Progress (Comité Militaire de Redressement pour le Progrès National—CMRPN), led by Col. Sayé Zerbo, assumed power. The military coup of 7 November 1982 led to the abolition of the CMRPN and the formation of the People's Salvation Council (Conseil du Salut du Peuple—CSP) under Maj. Jean-Baptiste Ouédraogo. The CSP was itself dissolved by the military coup of 4 August 1983, which established the National Revolutionary Council (Conseil National de la Révolution—CNR), a body that included radical former CSP members. Under Capt. Thomas Sankara, its chairman and the head of state, the CNR was the supreme governmental authority and was assisted by a Council of Ministers. Following the October 1987 coup, this body was renamed the Popular Front, with Capt. Blaise Compaoré as its chief.

A new constitution, establishing the Fourth Republic, was for an Assembly adopted on 2 June 1991 and called for an Assembly of People's Deputies with 107 seats. Capt. Compaoré is Chief of State and Head of Government and he chairs a Council of Ministers. Current law calls for a second, purely consultative chamber, and proposals to formally constitute it have been set in motion by the Assembly.

[14] POLITICAL PARTIES

After the 1978 competitive presidential and legislative elections, the government recognized only the three largest parties in the National Assembly: the Voltaic Democratic Union–African Democratic Rally, the National Union for Democracy, and the Voltaic Progressive Union. The last subsequently merged with smaller groups to form the Voltaic Progressive Front.

Following the coup of 25 November 1980, all political parties were banned. To disseminate government views on a grass-roots level, the CNR, which took power in 1983, sponsored the formation of Committees for the Defense of the Revolution.

The Compaoré government legalized parties prior to holding elections on 24 May 1992. Compaoré's Popular Democratic Organization—Worker's Movement (ODP-MT) gained 78 seats. The National Convention of Progressive Patriots—Social Democratic Party (CNPP-PSD) won 12 seats and the African Democratic Assembly (ADA) won 6. Eight other parties are represented in the Assembly of People's Deputies. Despite the introduction of multiparty elections, however, critics call the reforms "shamocracy."

[15] LOCAL GOVERNMENT

As of 1986, Burkina Faso was divided into 30 provinces. The provinces were subdivided into 300 departments and 7,285

villages. By the end of 1995, a decentralization program is supposed to be in place which will involve the election of local governing councils.

[16] JUDICIAL SYSTEM

At the apex of the judicial system are the courts of appeal at Ouagadougou and Bobo-Dioulasso. Courts of the first instance in Ouagadougou, Bobo-Dioulasso, Ouahigouya, and Fada N'Gourma deal with cases involving civil, criminal, and commercial law, and a court at Ouagadougou specializes in common law. The courts of appeal are in the capital. Following the 1983 coup, the CNR created tribunals to try former government officials for corruption and mismanagement. These "people's tribunals" infringed to some degree on the functions of courts of the first instance. In 1993, the "people's tribunals" were abolished.

In addition to the courts described above, traditional courts at the village level apply customary law in cases involving divorce and inheritance.

In June 1991, a new Constitution was adopted which provides a number of safeguards including a right to public trial, right to access to counsel and a right to appeal.

Although the judiciary in operation is independent of the executive, the President has considerable power over appointment of judges.

[17] ARMED FORCES

In 1993, Burkina Faso had an army of 7,000 personnel. The army consisted of 5 small infantry regiments, 1 airborne regiment, 1 artillery battalion, 1 tank battalion, and 1 engineering battalion. The 200-member air force had 18 combat aircraft. Paramilitary forces totaled 1,750, and 45,000 men and women serve in a "people's militia." The country spent $108 million or about 4% of gross domestic product in 1991.

[18] INTERNATIONAL COOPERATION

As Upper Volta, Burkina Faso was admitted to UN membership on 20 September 1960 and is a member of ECA and all the nonregional specialized agencies except IAEA and IMO. It is a signatory to GATT and the Law of the Sea and is a member of the African Development Bank, ECOWAS, G-77, and OAU. Together with other countries of former French West Africa, it participates in the Council of the Entente. The headquarters of the Communauté Economique de l'Afrique de l'Ouest are in Ouagadougou. Burkina Faso also belongs to the Niger Basin Authority.

[19] ECONOMY

Burkina Faso is an agricultural country where about 85% of the labor force produces food, primarily for domestic consumption. Food staples—millet and sorghum, maize and rice—are the principal crops. In addition, Burkina is a surplus producer of shea nuts, sesame, groundnuts, sugar, cashews, and garden vegetables. Cotton is the principal export crop; its cultivation, however, is notably price sensitive. Cotton output in 1992 was on the order of 170,000 metric tons. The livestock sector is also quite substantial, accounting for fully 15% of export earnings. Burkina livestock sales increased dramatically after the devaluation of the CFA in 1994.

The environmental conditions for agriculture are often precarious. Northern Burkina is at the edge of the Sahara Desert and, over the past 20 years, has been subject to severe drought. Furthermore, Burkina soils are generally poor and lateritic. However, expansion of agriculture to more fertile fields in river valleys is now possible thanks to a regional, multimillion-dollar UN project to eradicate "river blindness" (onchocerciasis) which had previously rendered these locations uninhabitable.

Burkina's mineral sector is largely undeveloped. Long underestimated, the Poura gold reserves have proven to be capable of generating export earnings in excess of us$30 million annually. Zinc and silver deposits at Perkoa have been judged commercially viable, with production expected to begin in 1994.

Mineral deposits in the north of the country are hostage to the extension of the Abidjan-to-Ouagadougou rail line to Dori. This off-again on-again project has been extended only as far as Kaya, 100 km north of Ouagadougou. Significant limestone deposits basic to cement manufacturing are located near Tambao at Tin Hrassan. Other mineral resources are manganese, vanadium-bearing magnetite, bauxite, lead, nickel, and phosphates. The start of manganese production at Tambao was reported to be near under a plan where trucks would transport the deposits to the Kaya rail head.

In January 1994 France suddenly devalued the CFA franc, causing its value to drop in half overnight. Immediately, prices for almost all imported goods soared, including prices for food and essential drugs, like those to combat malaria. Since 1948 France had guaranteed a fixed parity of one French franc to 50 African francs. The resulting stability in the currency had generally kept inflation low and helped to maintain a steady rate of growth. However, in the 1980s, the economies of the CFA countries began to stagnate in relation to other African nations, and France came under increased pressure from the World Bank, the IMF, and western countries to stop subsidizing the CFA franc. The devaluation, long expected in the investment community, is designed to enourage new investment, particularly in the export sectors of the economy, and discourage the use of hard currency reserves to buy products that could be grow domestically.

Unlike exporting countries, however, Burkina Faso imports most of its food and has little to export and therefore may benefit little from the devaluation. In the meantime, price-gouging by local merchats and a sharp rise in infaltion has caused the government to impose temporary price controls on existing stocks of imports.

20INCOME

In 1992 Burkina Faso's GNP was $2,908 million at current prices, or $290 per capita. For the period 1985–92 the average inflation rate was 1.8%, resulting in a real growth rate in per capita GNP of 0.9%.

In 1992 the GDP was $2,918 million in current US dollars. It is estimated that in 1985 agriculture, hunting, forestry, and fishing contributed 47% to GDP; manufacturing, 11%; electricity, gas, and water, 1%; construction, 1%; wholesale and retail trade, 10%; transport, storage, and communication, 7%; finance, insurance, real estate, and business services, 3%; and other sources, 19%.

21LABOR

Over 85% of the population was engaged in agriculture and animal husbandry in 1992, mostly at a subsistence level. Four employment offices in the country reported 29,784 unemployed workers in 1992.

In 1992 there were five labor federations who participated in the drafting of the 1991 Constitution. Although small, the unions claim a membership of 60% of government employees and 40% of private-sector salaried employees. The unions were active in the political turmoil of the 1980s and often took an adversary role toward the government. However, organized labor (about 60,000 non-agricultural workers in 1992) lost much of its influence under the Sankara and Compaoré military regimes.

22AGRICULTURE

Agriculture employs the vast majority of the work force and accounts for an estimated 30% of GDP. In 1991, however, only an estimated 13% of the total land area was under annual or perennial crops. Government attempts to modernize the agricultural sector have met with some success, especially with cotton, whose export accounted for 35% of total exports in 1992. The resistance to improvement has been due mostly to the insufficient water supply and poor soil. Burkina Faso is not self-sufficient in food, and in 1992, a deficit of 145,300 tons of cereals was registered.

In the early 1980s, local laborers constructed a 1,144-km (711-mi) canal to bring water for irrigation from the Black Volta to the newly constructed Sourou Dam. This work was part of a plan to establish 40,000 hectares (100,000 acres) of irrigated land for smallholders and state projects. Production figures for principal subsistence crops in 1992 were sorghum and millet, 1,964,000 tons; corn, 310,000 tons; and rice, 49,000 tons. Commercial crops (with 1992 production figures) included cottonseed (100,000 tons), karité (78,036 tons), cotton fiber (71,000 tons), groundnuts (110,000 tons), and sesame (8,000 tons). Other important crops are cassava, cowpeas, sweet potatoes, and tobacco. Sugarcane has been introduced on a large scale and is becoming an important cash crop; 340,000 tons were produced in 1992.

23ANIMAL HUSBANDRY

In 1992 there were an estimated 6,860,000 goats, 5,350,000 sheep, 427,000 asses, 530,000 pigs, and 22,000 horses. About 120,000 head of cattle were exported in 1992, many to Côte d'Ivoire. In 1992, 5,580 tons of cattle hides, 5,040 tons of goatskins, and 2,860 tons of sheepskins were produced. In recent years, livestock production has leveled off; since 1985 it has remained below 15% of GDP. Further development depends on the availability of pasturage and water, as well as the import policies and tax levels of neighboring countries.

24FISHING

The country has no access to the sea, and freshwater areas are limited. Fish still are caught by traditional methods, and production amounted to 7,012 tons in 1991.

25FORESTRY

Almost all vestiges of Burkina Faso's primitive forest have been cut down for fuel or to make way for farmland, and reforestation did not begin until 1973. In 1991, 24% of the total land was considered forest or woodland. Tree planting was stepped up to 8,400 hectares (21,000 acres) a year, but deforestation proceeded at the rate of some 5,000 hectares (12,000 acres) per year during 1981–85. Roundwood removals were estimated at 8,995,000 cu m in 1991, 95% of them for fuel.

26MINING

Burkina Faso has a potential for mineral development. As of 1991, however, there was virtually no commercial production except for 3,000 tons of phosphate rock. Exploitation of an estimated 15 million tons of high-grade manganese ore at Tambao awaits better commercial prospects and completion of a railway extension from Ouagadougou to Tambao. In 1981, work was begun to reopen the gold mine at Poura, 180 km (112 mi) southwest of Ouagadougou; it is estimated to contain 1.4 million tons of ore, grading 7.6 g of gold per ton. Production, which ceased in 1966, increased after extensive repairs in 1989; mine output amounted to 1,067 kg in 1991. Total gold production by formal operations and artisanal miners in 1991 was estimated at 5,300 kg; an estimated 50%–60% of artisanal gold production is smuggled out of the country.

Bauxite deposits have been located in the regions of Kaya and Bobo-Dioulasso. Four main deposits of limestone have also been discovered. Other deposits include cassiterite, copper, graphite, nickel, cobalt, diamonds, uranium, vanadium, and possibly zinc and lead. For many years, iron has been worked at Ouahigouya and near Banfora to make farm and home implements.

27ENERGY AND POWER

The burning of wood accounts for about 92% of energy requirements, and all petroleum products are imported. Total installed electrical capacity in 1991 was 59,000 kw, all of it thermal. Production rose from 42 million kwh in 1973 to 157 million kwh in 1991. Construction of a 15,000 kw hydroelectric facility at Kompienga was finished in 1989. Power stations are planned to be built along the White and Black Volta rivers. Production and distribution of electricity and water are controlled by the state-owned Société Nationale d'Électricité du Burkina (SONABEL), established in Ouagadougou in 1968. In 1992, fuel and energy accounted for 8.7% of total imports.

28INDUSTRY

Manufacturing accounts for 15% of Burkina's GDP (1991). The principal centers for economic activity are Bobo-Dioulasso, Ouagadougou, Banfora, and Koudougou, cities on the rail line to Abidjan, Côte d'Ivoire. Burkina's industries reflect an interesting diversity. There is a brick-and-ceramics factory, a plastics factory, a tire factory, two plants producing beer and soft drinks, a cigarette factory, five cotton-ginning plants, rice and flour mills, a shoe factory, a sugar mill at Banfora that refines local sugar, and a bicycle assembly plant, in addition to soap and cottonseed oil plants. A textile complex at Koudougou, the largest industrial enterprise in Burkina Faso, began production in 1970 and was enlarged in 1989. A second sugar mill is under construction at Sourou. Industrial production figures for 1990 included 822 million packs of cigarettes, 24,000 metric tons of sugar, and 63,000 assembled bicycles, motorcycles, and scooters. In 1990, 108,000 hectoliters of soft drinks and 350,000 hectoliters of beer were produced.

Burkina Faso has made a major effort to improve its hydroelectric resources. A 15 MW hydroelectric station has been built on the Kompienga River, and a 7.5 MW station has been erected on the Nankabe River, with a 60 MW plant planned for Noumbiel on the Mouhoun River. In addition, Côte d'Ivoire and Burkina have agreed to an extension of the Côte d'Ivoire grid to Banfora and Bobo-Dioulasso. Studies are underway for a possible extension of the Ghanaian grid to Ouagadougou.

29SCIENCE AND TECHNOLOGY

Burkina Faso has a shortage of skilled scientists and technicians. Scientific and technical aid comes chiefly from France (70 technicians in 1987). Burkina Faso has seven institutes conducting research in agriculture and geology and two French institutes conducting research in medicine, hydrology, and geology. The University of Ouagadougou has institutes of mathematics and physics, chemistry, natural science, technology, and health sciences. A 13-nation school of engineering and rural equipment is in Ouagadougou.

30DOMESTIC TRADE

Because of the demand for a wide variety of products and the comparatively small number of persons engaged in commerce, importers and exporters specialize little. Importers generally are their own wholesalers and often their own retailers, dealing in everything from matches to farm equipment. A state-owned marketing organization had 30 retail outlets in 1986. In Ouagadougou and Bobo-Dioulasso, French commercial practices prevail.

31FOREIGN TRADE

The principal imports in 1989 (in millions of CFA francs) were miscellaneous manufactured articles (24.8%), cereals (12.3%), chemicals (12.2%), and non-electrical machinery (10.8%).

France is Burkina Faso's most important single trading partner, with 29.2% of Burkina's exports going to France and 28.8% of

imports coming from France in 1989. After France, Burkina's exports went to Taiwan (16.9%), Côte d'Ivoire (12.5%), Togo (6.1%) and Belgium/Luxembourg (5.1%). After France, imports came from Côte d'Ivoire (14.5%) and Thailand (9.2%).

Burkina's trade balance is improved with the addition of some CFA Fr 106.4 billion in private remittances from emigrants working outside the country, principally in the Côte d'Ivoire. The size of the Burkina population in Côte d'Ivoire is put at anywhere from 1 to 2 million people. Higher cotton prices and increased gold production brought the trade deficit down to the CFA Fr 90 billion level in 1990.

32BALANCE OF PAYMENTS

Burkina Faso's balance of payments is chronically negative, as receipts from exports of goods and services typically only cover 30–40% of imports. It has had to rely heavily on remittances from Burkinabe working abroad and on international credits and other forms of borrowing to help offset widening trade imbalances. These factors, together with net capital inflows, generated a slight surplus from 1986 to 1988. Declining gold exports and falling cotton prices in 1989, coupled with increased imports and declining remittances from abroad, seriously deteriorated Burkina Faso's trade balance. By 1990, however, recovery in the gold and cotton sectors reduced the current account deficit to about 14% of GDP (from over 17% in 1989).

Burkina Faso and the IMF agreed upon a structural adjustment program in 1990 in which rigorous financial control was made a priority. Tax collections were improved and salaries stabilized to the point that budget surpluses were attained in 1989 and 1991. A value-added tax took effect in 1993. An enhanced structural adjustment program negotiated in 1993 sought growth of 3–11% annually while curbing ongoing financial imbalances.

In 1992 merchandise exports totaled $280.3 million and imports $642.3 million. The merchandise trade balance was $−361.9 million. The following table summarizes Burkina Faso's balance of payments for 1991 and 1992 (in millions of US dollars):

	1991	1992
CURRENT ACCOUNT		
Goods, services, and income	−532.4	−587.9
Unrequited transfers	442.0	496.4
TOTALS	−90.4	−91.4
CAPITAL ACCOUNT		
Other long-term capital	−35.8	105.8
Other short-term capital	6.2	−26.0
Exceptional financing	−12.4	4.2
Reserves	−35.7	−16.0
TOTALS	−91.5	63.8
Errors and omissions	181.9	27.6
Total change in reserves	−36.6	4.4

33BANKING AND SECURITIES

In 1959, the Central Bank of West African States (Banque Centrale des États de l'Afrique de l'Ouest—BCEAO) succeeded the Currency Board of French West Africa and Togo as the bank of issue for the former French West African territories. In 1962, it was reorganized as the joint note-issue bank of Benin (then Dahomey), Côte d'Ivoire, Mauritania (which withdrew in 1973), Niger, Senegal, Togo, and Burkina Faso (then Upper Volta). BCEAO notes, known as CFA francs, are guaranteed by France without limitation. Foreign exchange receipts of Burkina Faso go into the BCEAO's exchange pool, which in turn covers its foreign exchange requirements. As of 31 March 1987, Burkina Faso's foreign assets in the central bank totaled CFA Fr113.0 billion.

Other banks are the International Bank for Commerce, Industry, and Agriculture of Burkina Faso, the National Development Bank (80% government-owned), the National Fund of Agricultural Credit of Burkina Faso (54% state-owned), the state-owned National Fund of Deposits and Investment, and the International Bank of Burkina.

34INSURANCE

Insurance companies must have government approval and are subject to government supervision. Automobile third-party liability insurance is compulsory. Two French companies provide most types of insurance, as does the National Society for Insurance and Reinsurance (51% state-owned). In 1986, non-life insurance accounted for 95.7% of all premiums.

35PUBLIC FINANCE

Burkina Faso's revenue sources are limited, and the country depends heavily on subsidies from France. Over 40% of government income is derived from customs duties. Personnel expenses account for over 40% of outlays. Budget deficits averaging 13% of GDP during 1986–90 added significantly to the debt service burden. By 1990, the external principal and interest and domestic interest arrears were equivalent to one fiscal year of revenue. An extensive fiscal adjustment program was begun in 1991 with the help of the IMF, which helped lower the fiscal deficit to 7.2% of GDP that year.

36TAXATION

The contribution of direct taxation of all kinds to the governmental revenue is relatively low. Individuals pay a single income tax, varying from 2–30% on salaries, tips, and other remuneration, and 10–45% on business income. Companies pay a tax on profits, a forfeit tax, and taxes on income from debt and investments. There are also a number of real estate taxes. Sales and transaction taxes are shared by most of the population. Indirect taxes include customs duties and license fees.

There are consumption taxes on specified items, such as petroleum products and tobacco, and local taxes on motor vehicles.

37CUSTOMS AND DUTIES

As of 1992, a number of duties and taxes were imposed on most incoming goods and served as an important source of revenue. Rates were highest on goods coming from places other than franc-zone countries that did not have trade agreements with Burkina Faso. The fiscal duty on imports was the chief revenue raiser, but there were also a 5% customs duty, a turnover tax, and levies to support various government agencies. A new, streamlined system was scheduled to take effect in 1993, including a special tariff to protect domestically produced finished products. This tariff was slated for gradual elimination by 1996.

38FOREIGN INVESTMENT

Most foreign investments in Burkina Faso come from private French sources; however, investment capital from other EEC members has increased in recent years. Investment has been sought for hotels, textile factories, agroindustrial projects, communications, minerals, and other fields. Foreign firms must reserve at least 35% of capital for Burkinabe participation and 50% for priority-sector investments.

39ECONOMIC DEVELOPMENT

Development of the agricultural sector and of infrastructure have been the priorities established by Burkina's recent development plans. The 1991–95 plan estimates that almost 75% of the CFA fr 508 billion investment total would go to agriculture.

The country regularly receives bilateral and multilateral aid, primarily in technical assistance. France, which pledged Fr377 million for 1987, and the US are the leading bilateral aid donors. Total outstanding debt stood at $956 million, with a debt-servicing ratio of 10% in 1991.

40SOCIAL DEVELOPMENT

Social welfare services in the larger towns serve basically as extensions of medical aid. Classes are offered in prenatal care and in the care and feeding of infants. The very nature of tribal organization carries with it a type of social welfare, in that basic needs of the individual are cared for by the group. However, there is a veterans' pension system, and there are old-age and workers' insurance schemes for the small-wage sector.

The average woman gives birth to 6.5 children during her childbearing years. Abortion is legal only to save the woman's life. Polygamy was outlawed in 1964. Women played a prominent role during the Sankara regime, holding several government ministries.

41HEALTH

In 1993, the government of Burkina Faso took on the project of improving the quality of health services by upgrading facilities and skills, achieving control of endemic parasitic diseases, and strengthening sector institutions. The country's population in 1993 was 9.8 million, and total health care expenditures for 1990 were $219 million.

In 1989, there were 252 doctors, 101 pharmacists, 19 dentists, 909 nurses, and 297 midwives. Between 1988 and 1992, there were 3 doctors per 100,000 people. There was 1 nursing person for every 1,680 people in 1990.

From 1985 to 1990, there were 3 hospital beds per 10,000 inhabitants. The hospital at Ouagadougou is one of the most modern in Africa. Medical centers at Bobo-Dioulasso carry on research on insect-borne diseases. Mobile medical units attempt to control leprosy, sleeping sickness, yellow fever, and other contagious diseases.

One of Burkina Faso's most serious health problems is onchocerciasis (river blindness), which touches 84% of the total land area and causes many thousands of people to desert settlements infected by the fly vector. A control program has had some success.

The infant mortality rate in 1992 was 101 per 1,000 live births, with 449,000 births that same year. The birth rate in 1993 was 46.7 per 1,000 people. From 1980 to 1993, only 8% of married women (ages 15 to 49) used contraception. From 1990 to 1992, Burkina Faso immunized children up to one year old as follows: tuberculosis (66%); diphtheria, pertussis, and tetanus (39%); polio (39%); and measles (41%). However, in 1990, 46% of the country's children under 5 years of age were considered malnourished.

In 1990, there were 289 cases of tuberculosis per 100,000 people. Average life expectancy in 1992 was estimated at 48 years, and the death rate was 17.6 per 1,000 in 1993. In the same year, 70% of the population had access to health care.

42HOUSING

Architecture in the metropolitan centers is essentially French. Many African people, especially the Mossi, live in round huts with conical straw roofs or in rectangular huts with flat roofs. There is a housing shortage in the urban centers. According to the latest available figures for 1980–88, the housing stock totaled 1,267,000 with 6.3 people per dwelling.

43EDUCATION

Though education is listed as compulsory for all children aged 6 to 15, attendance is not enforced. All public education is free. The language of instruction is French. Primary education lasts for six years and secondary for seven years. In 1993 adult literacy was estimated at only 18.2% (males, 27.9%; and females, 8.9%).

In 1991 there were 2,590 primary schools with 530,013 pupils and 9,165 teachers. At the secondary level, students numbered 105,542. Of these, 8,022 were in vocational training and 350 in teachers' training.

The Center for Higher Education was established in 1969, and in 1974 it became the University of Ouagadougou. In 1990 there were 5,422 students in all higher level institutions.

44LIBRARIES AND MUSEUMS

The largest library, now part of the University of Ouagadougou, was founded in 1969 and has 55,000 volumes. Other libraries are attached to institutes such as the Center for Economic and Social Studies of West Africa. The National Museum in Ouagadougou has a collection of the ethnography, costumes, and domestic artifacts of Burkina Faso.

45MEDIA

Radio, telephone and telegraph service is available to Paris and to the neighboring countries. In 1991 there were about 16,769 telephones in use, most of them in Ouagadougou and Bobo-Dioulasso.

Two radio stations, one in Ouagadougou and one in Bobo-Dioulasso, are run by Radiodiffusion Nationale, the government radio corporation. Broadcasts are in French and 13 indigenous languages. In 1991 there were 150,000 licensed radios and 49,000 television sets. Télévision Nationale du Burkina, the government-owned television transmitting station, was established in 1963. Transmissions are made six days a week and are received only in Ouagadougou and Bobo-Dioulasso. The government has been establishing public viewing centers.

Burkina Faso had four daily newspapers in 1991, all published in Ouagadougou, with a total circulation of 19,500. L'Observateur Paalya had the highest circulation (8,000). Periodicals, all issued in Ouagadougou, include the Bulletin Economique et Social, published by the Chamber of Commerce six times a year, and Carrefour Africain, published monthly with government sponsorship.

The press agency Agence d'Information du Burkina is based in Ougadougou.

46ORGANIZATIONS

The Chamber of Commerce, Industry, and Handicrafts of Burkina Faso has its headquarters in Ouagadougou. There is also an Office for the Promotion of Burkinabe Enterprises. The National Farmers Union was created in 1987. Cooperative groups and unions are active, as are employers' and professional groups.

47TOURISM, TRAVEL, AND RECREATION

All visitors must have a passport and a certificate of yellow fever vaccination. A visa is required of all tourists except nationals of former French Africa and certain European countries. Tourist attractions include the Nazinga, Arly, and "W" park game preserves, the National Museum and artesian centers in Ouagadaugow and market towns such as Gorom-Gorom. The Division of Tourism and Hotels has its headquarters in Ouagadougou. In 1991 there were 80,100 tourist arrivals at hotels, and tourists spent $8 million.

48FAMOUS BURKINABE

The best-known persons are Maurice Yaméogo (b.1921), a former president of Upper Volta during 1960–66, who has been living in Côte d'Ivoire since 1970; Moro Naba Kougri (1930–82), the traditional sovereign of the Mossi; and Sangoulé Lamizana (b.1916), a former army chief of staff, who was president of Upper Volta from 1966 to 1980. Capt. Thomas Sankara (1949?–87), who gained a following in the 1974 clashes with Mali, seized power in a 1983 coup; he was overthrown and executed in 1987. Capt. Blaise Compaoré (b.1951?) assumed the presidency after Sankara's execution.

49DEPENDENCIES

Burkina Faso has no territories or colonies.

50BIBLIOGRAPHY

African Bibliographic Center. French-speaking West Africa: Upper Volta Today, 1960–1967; a Selected and Introductory Bibliographical Guide. New York: Negro Universities Press, 1969.

Institut National de la Statistique et de la Demographie. Annuaire Statistique du Burkina Faso. Ouagadougou, 1986.

McFarland, Daniel Miles. Historical Dictionary of Upper Volta. Metuchen, N.J.: Scarecrow Press, 1978.

Skinner, Elliott P. African Urban Life: The Transformation of Ouagadougou. Princeton, N.J.: Princeton University Press, 1974.

———. The Mossi of Burkina Faso: Chiefs, Politicians and Soldiers. Prospect Heights, Ill.: Waveland Press, 1989.

BURUNDI

Republic of Burundi
République du Burundi
Republika yu Burundi

CAPITAL: Bujumbura.

FLAG: The national flag consists of a white saltire with arms extending from a circle in the center. The circle contains three red stars with green borders. Upper and lower fields formed by the saltire are red; the fields at the hoist and the fly are green.

ANTHEM: *Burundi Bwacu (Our Burundi),* beginning "Burundi bwacu, Burundi buhire" ("Our Burundi, O blessed land").

MONETARY UNIT: The Burundi franc (BFr) is a paper currency. There are coins of 1, 5, and 10 francs, and notes of 10, 20, 50, 100, 500, 1,000, and 5,000 francs. BFr1 = $0.0039 (or $1 = BFr257.26).

WEIGHTS AND MEASURES: The metric system is the legal standard.

HOLIDAYS: New Year's Day, 1 January; Labor Day, 1 May; Independence Day, 1 July; Assumption, 15 August; Victory of UPRONA, 18 September; 13 October; All Saints' Day, 1 November; Christmas, 25 December. Movable religious holidays include Easter Monday, Ascension, and Pentecost Monday.

TIME: 2 PM = noon GMT.

¹LOCATION, SIZE, AND EXTENT

Burundi is a landlocked country in east-central Africa with an area of 27,830 sq km (10,745 sq mi), of which about 7% consists of lakes. Comparatively, the area occupied by Burundi is slightly larger than the state of Maryland. It extends 263 km (163 mi) NNE–SSW and 194 km (121 mi) ESE–WNW. Burundi is bounded on the N by Rwanda, on the E and S by Tanzania, and on the W by Zaire, with a total boundary length of 974 km (605 mi).
Burundi's capital city, Bujumbura is located in the western part of the country.

²TOPOGRAPHY

Burundi is a country mainly of mountains and plateaus, with a western range of mountains running north–south and continuing into Rwanda. The highest point is 2,760 m (9,055 ft). The only land below 914 m (3,000 ft) is a narrow strip of plain along the Ruzizi River (about 800 m/2,600 ft), which forms the western border north of Lake Tanganyika. From the mountains eastward, the land declines gradually, dropping to about 1,400 m (4,600 ft) toward the southeastern and southern border. The average elevation of the central plateau is about 1,700 m (5,600 ft). The major rivers form natural boundaries for most of the country. The Akanyaru and the Kagera separate Burundi from Rwanda along many sections of the common border. The Kagera and the Ruvuvu are important as the southernmost sources of the Nile. Most of Burundi's southern border is formed by the Malagarazi River. The principal lakes are Tanganyika, Cohoha, and Rweru.

³CLIMATE

Burundi in general has a tropical highland climate, with a considerable daily temperature range in many areas. Temperature also varies considerably from one region to another, chiefly as a result of differences in altitude. The central plateau enjoys pleasantly cool weather, with an average temperature of 20°C (68°F). The area around Lake Tanganyika is warmer, averaging 23°C (73°F); the highest mountain areas are cooler, averaging 14°C (57°F). Bujumbura's average annual temperature is 25°C (77°F). Rain is

irregular, falling most heavily in the northwest. Dry seasons vary in length, and there are sometimes long periods of drought. However, four seasons can be distinguished: the long dry season (June–August), the short wet season (September–November), the short dry season (December–January), and the long wet season (February–May). Most of Burundi receives between 130 and 160 cm (51–63 in) of rainfall a year. The Ruzizi Plain and the northeast receive between 75 and 100 cm (30–40 in).

⁴FLORA AND FAUNA

Most of the country is savanna grassland. There is little forest left; Burundi is one of the most eroded and deforested countries in all of tropical Africa. Of the remaining trees, the most common are eucalyptus, acacia, fig, and oil palms along the lake shores.

Wildlife was abundant before the region became agricultural. Still found are the elephant, hippopotamus, crocodile, wild boar, lion, antelope, and flying lemur, as well as such game birds as guinea fowl, partridge, duck, geese, quail, and snipe. Some 633 bird species have been reported, and several—the redheaded passat, the petilla, and some varieties of weather birds—can be found only in Burundi. The crowned crane is also prevalent. As the region becomes more densely populated, some species are dwindling or disappearing.

In Lake Tanganyika there is a great variety of fish, including the Nile perch, freshwater sardines, and rare tropical specimens. Most of the 133 fish species in Lake Tanganyika are found nowhere else in the world.

⁵ENVIRONMENT

There are no national parks, and laws against hunting and poaching are not enforced. Wildlife survives only in those areas of the country not heavily cultivated, and rapid population growth is reducing the amount of uncultivated land. The cutting of forests for fuel is uncontrolled despite legislation requiring permits. Soil erosion due to deforestation and improper terracing is also a serious problem. Burundi also has a problem with maintaining the purity of its water supply. It has only 0.9 cubic miles of water of which 64% is used for agricultural purposes. Ninety-two percent of the nation's urban population has access to pure water while 57% of the rural population does not.

In 1994, three species of mammals in a total of 103 were considered threatened. An example is the mountain gorilla whose existence is endangered due to poaching and damage to its living environment from deforestation. Five species of birds in a total of 633 were similarly threatened. One type of reptile was also endangered. Of 2,500 plant species in Burundi, none are currently threatened.

6POPULATION

One of the most densely populated countries in Africa, Burundi in mid-1994 had an estimated total of 6,417,932 inhabitants, for an average of 231 persons per sq km (597 per sq mi). The density is greatest in north-central Burundi. A population of 7,237,000 is projected for the year 2000, assuming a crude birthrate of 42.5 per 1,000 population, a crude death rate of 6, and a net natural increase of 26.5 during 1995–2000. The present rate of increase is nearly 3% annually. Apart from Bujumbura, the capital, which had a population of about 240,000 in 1990, urban areas are small and serve mainly as commercial and administrative centers. Only 6% of the population is urban.

7MIGRATION

At the end of 1992 there were about 271,700 refugees in Burundi. Some 25,800 were from Zaire and 245,600 from Rwanda; most of the latter were Tutsi from Hutu-ruled Rwanda. When ethnic massacres broke out anew in Rwanda in 1994, more refugees streamed across the border into Burundi. At the end of 1992 Tanzania was harboring 149,500 refugees from Burundi, Rwanda had 25,200 and Zaire 9,500. Hundreds of thousands of Hutu from Burundi crossed into Rwanda in late 1993 to escape massacre at the hands of the Tutsi-dominated army.

8ETHNIC GROUPS

The population is made up mainly of Hutu (also known as Bahutu), a Bantu people, traditionally farmers, who constitute about 85% of the inhabitants. A tall warrior people, the Tutsi (Watutsi, Watusi, Batutsi) constitute less than 15% of the population but dominate the government and military. The earliest known inhabitants of the region were the Twa (Batwa), a Pygmy tribe of hunters, related to the Pygmies of Zaire. They now make up less than 1% of the population. There are about 82,000 immigrant Africans. Europeans, Arabs, and Asians number about 6,000.

9LANGUAGES

The main language is Kirundi, a Bantu language. Kirundi and French are the official languages. In all the larger centers, Swahili is used as a lingua franca.

10RELIGIONS

Roman Catholic and Protestant missions have had much influence. In 1992, it was estimated that over 85% of the population was Christian, of which in 1993 59.9% were Roman Catholic. Many inhabitants follow African traditional practices, centered around belief in spirits. The Bagaza government regarded the Catholic Church as pro-Hutu and restricted Masses, prohibited religious gatherings without prior approval, nationalized Catholic schools, banned the Catholic youth movement, and shut down the Catholic radio station and newspaper. The Jehovah's Witnesses and Seventh Day Adventists were banned in 1986. Following Bagaza's ouster in September 1987, Maj. Pierre Buyoyo, the new president (a Catholic), stated that he would end all restrictions on the Catholic Church.

Only about 1% of the people are Muslims, but a $20-million Libyan-financed mosque and Islamic center was opened in Bujumbura in 1985.

11TRANSPORTATION

A great hindrance to Burundi's economic development is lack of adequate transportation. The country is landlocked, and there are no railroads. Roads total 5,900 km (3,666 mi), and only about 7% of them remain open in all weather; the rest are classed as local roads or tracks. In 1991 there were 8,500 passenger cars and 11,000 commercial vehicles.

Burundi is dependent on Tanzania, Uganda, Zambia, and Zaire for its imports. Through Bujumbura, Lake Tanganyika serves as a link with Kigoma in Tanzania for rail shipment to Dar es Salaam. In 1987, the African Development Bank awarded a 50-year loan of CFA Fr218 billion to finance the construction of a shipyard in Bujumbura.

Air service is maintained by Air Burundi, which operates domestic service and flies to Rwanda, Tanzania, and Zaire. International service is also provided by Air Zaïre, Sabena, and other airlines. Bujumbura has an international airport, and there are five smaller airports as well as a number of helicopter landing strips. Bujumbura airport handled 70,000 passengers by means of 2,700 commercial air transport movements in 1991.

12HISTORY

The first known inhabitants of what is now Burundi were the Twa, a Pygmy tribe of hunters. Between the 7th and 10th centuries AD, the Hutu, a Bantu agricultural people, occupied the region, probably coming from the Congo Basin. In the 15th and 16th centuries, tall warriors, the Tutsi, believed to have come originally from Ethiopia, entered the area.

The Tutsi, a nomadic pastoral people, gradually subjugated the Hutu and other inhabitants of the region. A feudal social system based on caste—the conquering Tutsi and the subject Hutu—became the dominant feature of social relations, and especially of economic and political relations. The Hutu did the farming and grew the food in return for cattle, but generally had no part in government. The Tutsi were the ruling caste and did no manual labor. To a certain extent, however, the castes were open to each other. Custom allowed a particularly worthy Twa or Hutu to rise to the rank of a Tutsi; conversely, an impoverished Tutsi who had fallen from his former estate could be assimilated into the Hutu.

The Tutsi conquest initiated a process of political integration. The ownership of land was gradually transferred from the Hutu tribes to the mwami, the king of the Tutsi. The first mwami, Ntare I Rushatsi, is thought to have come to power in the 16th century. While the ruling mwami was in theory an absolute king, he was often regarded as *primus inter pares* among the Ganwa, aristocrats of royal lineage. But he had his court and his army and could not easily be removed from office.

The first European known to have reached the territory was John Hanning Speke, who traveled with Richard Burton to Lake Tanganyika in 1858. They paddled to the north end of the lake in their search for the headwaters of the Nile. In 1871, Stanley and Livingstone landed at Bujumbura and explored the Ruzizi River region. Subsequently, other explorers, principally German, visited Burundi. After the Berlin Conference of 1884–85, the German zone of influence in East Africa was extended to include Rwanda and Burundi. A German, Count von Götzen, discovered Lake Kivu in 1894. The first Roman Catholic missionaries came in 1898.

The German authorities made no changes in the indigenous organization. They administered the territory through the traditional authorities in accordance with the laws and customs of the region. However, the history of Burundi under the German administration was marked by constant factional struggles and rivalry, in contrast to the peaceful state of affairs in Rwanda.

When Belgian troops occupied the country in 1916, they found it in dissension and the three-year-old mwami, Mwambutsa IV, the center of court intrigue. In 1923, the League of Nations awarded Belgium a mandate in the region, which was known as Ruanda-Urundi (present-day Rwanda and Burundi). The Belgians adopted the same policy of indirect administration employed by the Germans, retaining the entire established structure. In 1946, Ruanda-Urundi became a UN trust territory under Belgian administration.

On 18 September 1961, elections for the National Assembly were held in Urundi under the auspices of the UN. The result was a sweeping victory for UPRONA, the party headed by Prince Louis Rwagasore, eldest son of the mwami. On 13 October 1961, shortly after Prince Rwagasore had become premier, he was assassinated. Two leaders of the Christian Democratic Party were charged, convicted of responsibility for the murder, and executed.

The UN had strongly urged that Urundi and Ruanda come to independence united, since their relationship had long been close, their economies were integrated, and their people were ethnically one. However, the UN reluctantly decided that there was insufficient support for the union in both regions, and on 27 June 1962, the UN General Assembly passed a resolution that called for the creation of two independent nations, Burundi and Rwanda.

On 1 July 1962, Burundi became an independent kingdom headed by Mwami (King) Mwambutsa IV. He was deposed in July 1966 and was succeeded in September by his heir, Mwami Ntare V. On 29 November 1966, Mwami Ntare V in turn was overthrown by a military coup headed by Premier Michel Micombero, and Burundi was declared a republic with Micombero as president.

In 1969, an alleged Hutu coup attempt ended in the arrest of 30 prominent businessmen and officials. Another Hutu-led coup attempt in April 1972 led to widespread civil war, in which mass killings of Hutu by Tutsi and of Tutsi by Hutu were reported. On 21 July 1973, the UN High Commissioner for Refugees reported that there were at least 85,000 Hutu refugees from Burundi, of whom an estimated 40,000 were in Tanzania, 35,000 in Zaire, and 10,000 in Rwanda. President Micombero later conceded that more than 100,000 persons had been killed in the course of the 1972 insurgency. Most of the deaths were among the Hutu, and educated Hutu were systematically massacred. During 1973, rebel bands conducted raids into Burundi from across the Rwandan and Tanzanian borders, and Burundi's relations with those two neighbors deteriorated. By the end of 1973, however, the government was fully in control.

On 1 November 1976, President Micombero was stripped of all powers by a military coup led by Lt. Col. Jean-Baptiste Bagaza, and the Supreme Revolutionary Committee (SRC) that subsequently took power named Bagaza president. The new regime, like the old one, was dominated by Tutsi. At a party congress of UPRONA in 1979, a party central committee, headed by President Bagaza, was selected to replace the SRC, and civilian rule was formally restored. In reality, however, the military remained active in both the party and in the government. A new constitution was adopted in a national referendum in 1981, and a National Assembly was elected in 1982. Bagaza was reelected unopposed to a new five-year term in 1984, but in September 1987, he was overthrown by the military while he was attending a conference in Canada. Maj. Pierre Buyoyo became president.

Ethnic violence erupted again in 1988. In response to rumors of the murder of Tutsis in the north, the army massacred between 5,000 and 25,000 Hutu. Over 100,000 were left homeless and 60,000 took refuge in Rwanda.

Maj. Buyoyo agreed to the restoration of multiparty politics in 1991 and a new constitution was approved in March 1992. Competition between approved, ethnically balanced parties in the June, 1993 election brought to office Burundi's first elected presi-

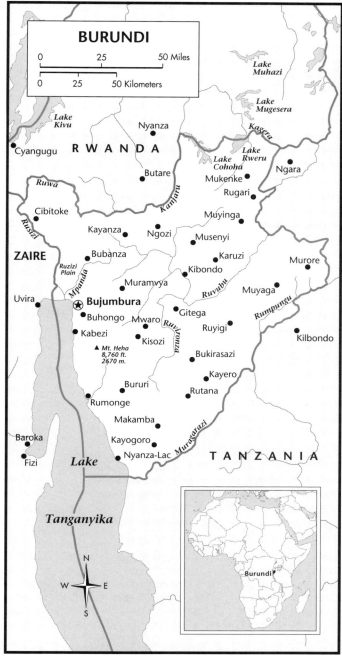

LOCATION: 2°20′ to 4°28′s; 29° to 30°50′E. **BOUNDARY LENGTHS:** Rwanda, 290 km (180 mi); Tanzania, 451 km (280 mi); Zaire, 233 km (145 mi).

dent and its first Hutu president, Melchior Ndadaye. Ndadaye got 66% of the vote, Buyoyo received just 33%. Ndadaye began to talk of reform of the Tutsi-dominated armed forces. But, on 21 October 1993, Ndadaye and several cabinet members were assassinated by Tutsi soldiers. Other cabinet officers, including Prime Minister Sylvie Kinigi, a Tutsi, took refuge in the French embassy. Ethnic violence continued, with some 10,000 murdered and 800,000 fleeing the country. Reliable figures are hard to get. Some estimate that as many as 100,000 may have been killed in this round of violence. The military coup attempt, however, failed.

In February, Ndadaye's successor, Cyprien Ntaryamira, was inaugurated. But his coalition, crossethnic government was unable to restore order. In an effort to negotiate peace, he went to Tanzania for consultations. On his flight home, the plane in which he was returning, along with Rwanda's President Habyarimana, was shot down near Kigali, Rwanda's airport, on April 6, 1994. Two other members of his cabinet also died in the attack. Yet, the levels of post-crash violence are considerably below that occurring in Rwanda or that after Ndadaye's assassination.

13 GOVERNMENT

Under the 1981 constitution, the president of the republic was elected by universal adult suffrage. The sole candidate was the president of UPRONA, the only legal political party. The president, who was head of state, was assisted by a council of ministers. Legislative power was vested in the 65-member National Assembly, of which 52 were elected and 13 appointed by the president. The president and legislators served five-year terms. Following the September 1987 coup, President Pierre Buyoyo dismissed all members of the government and ruled as head of the newly established Military Committee of National Redemption, until it was disbanded in December, 1990. A new constitution which recognized "democracy, human rights and development" was adopted on 13 March 1992, after a popular referendum. It provides for a directly elected president, a prime minister, and an 81-seat National Assembly.

In the elections of June, 1993, Buyoyo was defeated by Melchior Ndadaye. Ndadaye's government was broad based, with nine Tutsis (including the prime minister) among the 23 ministers. He was murdered in a failed coup attempt in October, 1993. His replacement, Cyprien Ntaryamira, was elected in January, 1994, and died in a plane crash in March, 1994.

14 POLITICAL PARTIES

Before independence, no fewer than 23 political parties were officially registered. Of these, only two retained political significance in the years following independence: the National Progress and Unity Party (Parti de l'Unité et du Progrès National—UPRONA), founded by Prince Louis Rwagasore, and the People's Party (Parti du Peuple—PP), an all-Hutu party. UPRONA, which initially controlled 58 seats in the National Assembly out of a total of 64, was soon torn by internecine leadership rivalries. In time, these rivalries took on the qualities of a racial feud between Tutsi and Hutu. In the National Assembly, the PP merged with the Hutu wing of UPRONA to form the so-called Monrovia Group, while the Tutsi wing of UPRONA referred to itself as the Casablanca Group.

In June 1965, legislative elections were held for the first time since independence. UPRONA won 21 seats, the PP 10, and independents 2. President Micombero, a Tutsi, proclaimed UPRONA to be the sole legal political party by a decree promulgated on 23 November 1966. On 1 November 1976, leaders of the coup that deposed Micombero announced that UPRONA had been dissolved, but in 1979, the party was incorporated into the government structure. According to the 1981 constitution, it was the only legal political organization. The president of UPRONA was president of the republic and also head of the party's 70-member Central Committee and 8-member Politburo.

Fifty-two members of the National Assembly were elected under the auspices of UPRONA in October 1982 from 104 candidates, about 75% of them Tutsi, chosen by local UPRONA committees. Several cabinet members and high party officials were defeated. In September 1987, following the coup that ousted President Bagaza, all members of UPRONA were dismissed.

The June 1, 1993 presidential election and the June 29 parliamentary election that year led to the defeat of UPRONA. President Ndadaye's party, the Burundi Democratic Front (FRODEBU) received 72% of the vote and 65 of parliament's 81 seats. UPRONA won the remaining seats with 21% of the ballots cast. Other parties include the Burundi People's Party (RPB), the Party for the Reconciliation of the People (PRP), and the People's Party (PP).

15 LOCAL GOVERNMENT

Burundi was formerly divided into 8 provinces, but a redistricting plan in 1982 increased the number to 15, each under a military governor. Each province is subdivided into arrondissements and communes; the latter total 114.

16 JUDICIAL SYSTEM

The legal system of Burundi is based on German and French civil codes and customary law. In 1987 there were 64 tribunals of first instance. The Court of Appeal and the Supreme Court are located in Bujumbura. The constitution provides for a state security court.

The 1992 constitution establishes a number of new courts including a constitutional court to review all new laws for conformity to the constitution. There will also be a High Court responsible for resolving charges of high level crimes by high level government officials. A military court will have jurisdiction over crimes by members of the military.

Under the new constitution, the judiciary is declared independent; in practice, however, the President appoints the judges and the system remains dominated by the Tutsi ethnic group. The coup attempt in 1993 severely disrupted the normal functioning of the legal system.

17 ARMED FORCES

In 1993, Burundi had an army with about 5,500 personnel. The troops include two infantry battalions, a battalion of commandos, and a battalion of paratroopers. The naval force had 50 personnel and 3 patrol boats; the air force, 150 with 3 counterinsurgency aircraft and 14 support air craft and helicopters. Paramilitary gendarmerie numbered 1,500. The defense budget (1989) was $28 million or 3.7% of gross domestic product.

18 INTERNATIONAL COOPERATION

Burundi was admitted to UN membership on 18 September 1962 and is a member of ECA and all the nonregional specialized agencies except IAEA and IMO. It also belongs to the African Development Bank, G-77, and OAU and is a signatory to GATT and the Law of the Sea. Burundi, Rwanda, and Zaire form the Economic Community of the Great Lakes Countries, which fosters development in the region of lakes Kivu and Tanganyika. Burundi also cooperates with Rwanda and Tanzania in the development of the Kagera River Basin. In addition, Burundi is a member of the 15-nation Preferential Trade Area of Eastern and Southern Africa, and the organization's Trade Development Bank is in Bujumbura.

19 ECONOMY

Burundi's is an agricultural and livestock economy. Bananas, plantains, sweet potatoes, and manioc are Burundi's staple crops, followed by beans, taro, and maize. Coffee and tea are the main export crops. Coffee provides roughly 80% of export earnings. Tea is Burundi's second leading export crop at 9.1% of total export earnings. Cotton is emerging as an important export (5.7% of export earnings in 1987), but recent production has been plagued by excessive rain. Livestock sales are discouraged by a tradition which encourages the maintenance of large herds. Sales of hides and skins amounted to 2.6% of exports.

Burundi's mineral sector is currently small, with a potential that remains undetermined. Gold, tungsten, columbo-tantalite, bastnaesite, and cassiterite are each mined in small quantities. Explorations have revealed petroleum under Lake Tanganyika and in the Ruzizi Valley, as well as large nickel deposits at

Musongati. Copper, cobalt, and platinum are expected to be found in association with the nickel. Phosphate rock deposits have also been located.

[20]INCOME

In 1992 Burundi's GNP was $1,193 million at current prices, or $210 per capita. For the period 1985–92 the average inflation rate was 4.3%, resulting in a real growth rate in per capita GNP of 1.0%.

In 1992 the GDP was $1,097 million in current US dollars. It is estimated that agriculture, hunting, forestry, and fishing contributed 48% to GDP; mining and quarrying, 1%; manufacturing, 18%; construction, 3%; wholesale and retail trade, 10%; transport, storage, and communication, 3%; community, social, and personal services, 2%; and other sources 15%.

[21]LABOR

The total labor force in 1990 was 2,779,777, mostly in small subsistence farming. Of the total labor force, over 90% was engaged in agriculture in 1992.

A labor organization, the Organization of Free Unions of Burundi (formerly the Burundi Workers Union), was formed in 1967, and was formerly with UPRONA. In 1981, a presidential decree made strikes by government officials illegal. As of 1992, the new Constitution and draft labor code protected the rights of Burundi workers to form unions, but did not protect collective bargaining rights, or fundamentally alter workers' right to strike, which requires 15 days' notice.

The government is seeking to boost training and employment opportunities in carpentry, masonry, furniture making, vehicle repair, and other crafts.

[22]AGRICULTURE

About 90% of the population depends on agriculture for a living. Most agriculture consists of subsistence farming, with only about 15% of the total production marketed. An estimated 1,350,000 hectares (3,336,000 acres), or about 52.6% of the total area, was arable or under permanent crops in 1991; 74,000 hectares (182,800 acres) were irrigated. The average farm family plot is 0.8 hectares (2 acres). Agriculture accounts for half the GDP. Coffee and tea exports comprise the majority of foreign earnings; coffee along accounted for 74% of exports of goods between 1989 and 1992. Principal crops for local consumption are manioc, beans, bananas, sweet potatoes, corn, and sorghum. Production in 1992 included bananas, 1,645,000 tons, mostly for wine; manioc, 597,000 tons; sweet potatoes, 710,000 tons; beans, 346,000 tons; sorghum, 67,000 tons; corn, 178,000 tons; peanuts, 99,000 tons; and potatoes, 46,000 tons.

The primary export crop is coffee, chiefly of the arabica variety. The government regulates the grading, pricing, and marketing of the coffee crop, and all coffee export contracts require approval. In 1992, coffee production was 34,000 tons. Other export crops are cotton and tea. Seed cotton production was 8,000 tons, and cotton fiber production (after ginning) was about 3,000 tons in 1992. That year, tea production was 6,000 tons. Tea exports in 1991 of 5,143 tons represented 9.2% of total exports (up from only 4% during the 1980s); the government has been encouraging cotton and tea production in order to diversify exports. The export of cotton, however, has been less successful. Whereas in 1990, cotton export earnings totaled $182,500, by 1992, exports had fallen to nearly zero. Palm oil is obtained from trees in plantations along the shore of Lake Tanganyika. Tobacco and wheat cultivated in the highland areas also yield some cash income.

Much of the land has suffered a loss of fertility because of soil erosion from poor agricultural practices, irregularity of rainfall, lack of fertilizer, and shortened fallow periods.

[23]ANIMAL HUSBANDRY

Livestock in 1992 included some 440,000 head of cattle, 932,000 goats, 370,000 sheep, and 105,000 pigs. There are also large numbers of beehives; honey production was estimated at 1,010 tons in 1992. Social prestige has traditionally been derived from ownership of cattle. This, together with improved sanitary conditions, has resulted in the accumulation of large herds of poor-quality stock; for example, the average milk yield per cow is only 350 kg a year (17% of world average). Meat consumption is estimated at only 48 calories per person per day, only one-tenth of the world's average. The herds retard economic development by cutting down the amount of land available for food growing, and they destroy pastureland by overgrazing. Through various technical assistance programs, the government is seeking to eliminate excess cattle, improve the remaining livestock, and introduce modern stock-raising methods.

[24]FISHING

There are three main methods of fishing in Lake Tanganyika: industrial, native, and traditional. Industrial fishing, which developed after 1946, is carried on by small trawlers accompanied by several rowboats. Native fishing is in catamarans equipped with lights, nets, and engines. Traditional fishing is in pirogues equipped with lights and landing nets. The total for native and traditional fishing was 23,094 tons in 1991.

[25]FORESTRY

Erosion and cutting, chiefly for fuel, have almost entirely eliminated Burundi's forests. The harvesting of wood has increased only slightly since the late 1970s, and the emphasis has now shifted to reforestation. Natural forest covered 67,000 hectares (165,600 acres) of 1991, up 8% from 1981 as a result of reforestation efforts. Forestry output should continue to grow as the result of a World Bank-sponsored tree-planting program. Of an estimated 4,343,000 cu m in roundwood production in 1991, 99% was for fuel.

[26]MINING

Tin production has significantly increased in recent years; from 5 tons in 1987 to 124 tons in 1991. Peat offers an alternative to increasingly scarce firewood and charcoal as a domestic energy source. The most significant mineral deposits in Burundi include gold, kaolin (china clay), limestone for cement, nickel, phosphate, platinum-group metals, rare-earth metals, and vanadium. Gold production was 25 kg in 1991. Nickel reserves, found in 1974, are estimated at 370 million tons (3–5% of world reserves), but high transportation costs and low world market prices have delayed their exploitation. Tin production has significantly increased in recent years; from 5 tons in 1987 to 124 tons in 1991.

[27]ENERGY AND POWER

Bujumbura and Gitega are the only two cities in Burundi that have municipal electricity service. Burundi's total installed capacity was 43,000 kw in 1991. Two dams completed since 1984 have increased the amount of power production from hydroelectric installations. In 1991, recorded production was about 136 million kwh, 99% of which was hydroelectric. Burundi imports all of its petroleum products from Kenya and Tanzania. A subsidiary of Amoco has an oil exploratory concession in and around Lake Tanganyika. Wood and peat account for 94% of energy consumption in Burundi. The government is promoting peat production and is fostering the development of renewable energy resources, such as solar electricity and biogas.

[28]INDUSTRY

Industrial activities are almost exclusively concentrated in Bujumbura and accounted for 10.5% of the GDP (1990). The industrial sector transforms to varying degrees agricultural and forestry products: cotton, coffee, tea, vegetable oil, and woods. There are also several small plants for soft drinks, blankets, footwear, soap, insecticides, building materials, furniture, and metal goods. In 1991, production included 1,084,000 hectoliters of beer, 296,840 pairs of shoes, 450 million cigarettes, and 276,000 blankets. The future of industrial development is largely linked to the development of electric power and transportation, as well as improved commercial relations with neighboring countries.

29SCIENCE AND TECHNOLOGY

Technical aid is supplied by many donors, including the EEC, IBRD, Belgium, France, the Federal Republic of Germany (FRG), the US, Switzerland, and China. The National Center of Hydrometeorology, the Ministry of Geology and Mines of Burundi, the Institute of Agronomical Sciences of Burundi, and a medical laboratory devoted to nutritional studies are located in Bujumbura. The University of Burundi, in Bujumbura, has faculties of sciences, medicine, agriculture, and applied sciences. The capital also has a technical school. The Higher Institute of Agriculture is in Gitega. In 1989, expenditures for research and development totaled 536 million francs; 168 technicians and 170 scientists and engineers were engaged in research and development.

30DOMESTIC TRADE

Burundi's economy is characterized by subsistence agriculture; commercialization and nationwide distribution of daily necessities and foodstuffs are practically nonexistent. Rural markets are the principal distribution centers. The National Office of Commerce is a state trading concern. Smaller trading operations are often in the hands of Greeks, Indians, and Arabs. All domestic trade is influenced by the coffee harvest, which during the harvest season (June–September) provides increased income and stimulates trading, with a somewhat inflationary effect.

Business hours are usually 8 AM to noon and 2 to 5 PM on weekdays and 8 AM to noon on Saturday. Banks are open 8 to 11:30 AM Monday–Friday.

31FOREIGN TRADE

Burundi's export income is highly volatile and, since 1987, has fluctuated sharply with shifts in world coffee prices. Revenue from coffee exports were relatively strong in 1991 at 13,482 million Burundi francs. Principal exports in 1991 (in millions of Burundi francs) were as follows:

Coffee	13,481.6
Tea	1,514.2
Hides and skins	433.5
Minerals	34.7
Other exports	1,180.9
TOTAL	16,644.9

Imports consist mainly of processed foods, textiles, foodstuffs, vehicles, and fuel. Import costs have risen steadily, and following a trade surplus in 1977, deficits were recorded in every year through 1991. Imports in 1985 (in millions of Burundi francs) were as follows:

Intermediate goods	17,607.4
Capital goods	16,479.0
Consumption goods	12,067.8
TOTAL	46,154.2

In 1991, the United States bought 38.5% of Burundi's exports while Germany bought 34.8%, almost all in coffee. Belgium accounted for 14.1% of imports, followed by France and Germany (9.8% and 8.8% respectively).

32BALANCE OF PAYMENTS

In 1991, Burundi's balance of payments improved significantly, mainly because of larger aid inflows, and the effects of a structural adjustment program implemented with the World Bank and IMF. The Burundi Franc was devalued by 15.5% in 1989 and by another 17.5% in 1991, making Burundi's exports more competitive.

In 1992 merchandise exports totaled $80.2 million and imports $181.8 million. The following table summarizes Burundi's balance of payments for 1991 and 1992 (in millions of US dollars):

	1991	1992
CURRENT ACCOUNT		
Goods, services, and income	−227.0	−231.0
Unrequited transfers	195.7	177.8
TOTALS	−31.3	−53.8
CAPITAL ACCOUNT		
Direct investment	0.8	0.6
Other long-term capital	56.0	90.0
Other short-term capital	13.7	8.2
Reserves	62.6	−25.5
TOTALS	133.1	73.4
Errors and omissions	−101.7	−19.6
Total change in reserves	−22.4	−16.5

33BANKING AND SECURITIES

Until the Congo (Zaire) became independent in 1960, the monetary and banking systems of Ruanda-Urundi were integrated with those of the Congo. Thereafter, Ruanda-Urundi had its own monetary structure and central bank. Shortly after the UN-sponsored Addis Ababa conference of July 1962, Rwanda and Burundi entered into an economic agreement providing for a continuation of the monetary union. After the breakup of the economic union in December 1963, Burundi's banking operations were transacted through the Bank of the Kingdom of Burundi, which in 1967 became the Bank of the Republic of Burundi, the central bank and bank of issue. Burundi has four commercial banks, which handle a substantial portion of short-term credit (vital for the coffee season) that include: the Commercial Bank of Burundi, the Credit Bank of Bujumbura, and the Belgian-African Bank of Burundi. Commercial bank reserves totaled BFr1,761 million at the end of 1993. There are also a savings bank, a postal savings bank, and a joint Libyan-Burundian financial institution. Other financial institutions are the National Economic Development Bank and the Central Fund for Mobilization and Finance.

As of 30 December 1990, the money supply, as measured by M2, was BFr35,381 million. At that time, demand deposits in the commercial banks totaled BFr14,721 million; savings deposits came to BFr10.085 million. There is no stock exchange in Burundi.

34INSURANCE

As of 1986, there were two insurance companies in Burundi, the partly state-owned Insurance Co. of Burundi (Société d'Assurances du Burundi—SOCABU) and branch of General Insurance of France. Motor vehicle insurance is the only compulsory coverage.

35PUBLIC FINANCE

Government expenditures have generally exceeded reserves. The fiscal deficit (excluding grants) during 1986–92 averaged 12.3%

of GDP, down from an average of 12.3% during 1980–85. In 1992, the fiscal deficit amounted to 14.1% of GDP before grants. By the end of 1992, Burundi's outstanding foreign debt amounted to over $1.2 billion, or 110% of GDP.

36 TAXATION

There are income taxes on businesses and individuals, and a tax on transactions. Other direct taxes are on vehicles and real estate. About twice as much money is collected from indirect taxes, of which the most important are import and export duties and a tax on beer. Taxes accounted for 95% of government revenues in 1984.

37 CUSTOMS AND DUTIES

Import duties, which are levied mainly ad valorem, include a revenue duty averaging 15–35% and an import duty averaging 2-5%. The government also levies a 4% statistical tax on all imports. As a party to the Lome Convention, Burundi receives preferential treatment by the EC.

38 FOREIGN INVESTMENT

Because of its limited domestic market and lack of infrastructure, Burundi has attracted few private foreign investors. Current foreign investment is generally limited to participation in semi-public corporations, though in 1986 a flower-growing and exporting company, financed by US interests, began operations. The 1979 investment code provides basic guarantees to foreign investors, but repatriation of profits is subject to delays. The corporation tax may be waived for five years.

39 ECONOMIC DEVELOPMENT

Burundi began a complete review of economic and financial policy with the help of the UN in 1986, when a reform of the currency and the first of a series of devaluations occurred. The first five year plan was designed to improve economic growth, reduce inflation, and diversify export production. Few of these objectives were met and the program was continued in 1991. A second reform of the currency and further devaluation took place in 1992. Growth of 5.0% in GDP and 8.8% inflation on 1991 indicated the program was beginning to take effect. An external debt of $961 million and a debt-servicing ratio of 31.6% are still causes of concern.

Burundi is dependent on foreign assistance for both development programs and current operations. Diversification of its export base and financial stability are key goals.

Belgium, France, Japan and Germany are Burundi's principal providers of development financial and technical support. Substantial support has been forthcoming to expand Burundi's coffee sector. Development of the hydroelectric resources of the Kagera River continue, under restrictions imposed by the decline in export earnings. The United Nations Development Programme and FAO are promoting integrated development plans focusing on cotton and rice production. Sugar production is supported by the African Development Bank, the Arab Bank for Economic Development, and the OPEC Fund.

40 SOCIAL DEVELOPMENT

Under the tribal system, the individual's basic welfare needs have traditionally been the responsibility of the group. Even now, the family remains the most important social welfare institution. There are social centers for women and youth. Missions help to look after orphans and the aged. For the small percentage of wage earners, there is a government social security system that insures against accidents and occupational diseases and provides pensions.

The women's affiliate of UPRONA is engaged in several social programs. The fertility rate in the early 1980s was estimated to be

6.4. Abortion is legal on broad health grounds.

41 HEALTH

Following independence, WHO assisted in the organization of public health services and the training of sanitarians and public health nurses for Burundi. Students from Burundi received medical training at universities in France and in Zaire. WHO coordinated all public health programs and helped in campaigns against smallpox, tuberculosis, and malaria. WHO, FAO, and UNICEF also provided aid for nutrition and maternal and child health programs.

Trypanosomiasis (sleeping sickness), borne by the tsetse fly, is a problem in the Ruvuvu River Valley. Malaria and schistosomiasis (bilharziasis) are common along the Ruzizi River. Intake of animal protein and fat is inadequate, and almost all diseases associated with malnutrition are found in Burundi. There was a cholera epidemic in 1978, due to insufficient sewage facilities. A four-year program covering 30–40% of the country, begun in 1986, was intended to rehabilitate and expand rural water supplies.

In 1990, there were 317 doctors, 55 pharmacists, and 9 dentists. From 1988 to 1992, there were 6 doctors per 100,000 people, and from 1985 to 1990, there were 1.3 hospital beds per 1,000 people. Total health care expenditures for 1990 were $36 million. In 1991, 80% of the population had access to health care.

In 1992, the infant mortality rate was 108 per 1,000 live births, with 271,000 births that year (46 per 1,000 birth rate). From 1980 to 1993, only 9% of married women (ages 15 to 49) practiced contraception. Between 1990 and 1992, Burundi immunized children up to one year of age as follows: tuberculosis (91%); diphtheria, pertussis, and tetanus (80%); polio (80%); and measles (70%). In 1990, 38% of children under 5 years were considered to be malnourished.

Average life expectancy in 1992 was estimated at 48 years. In 1990, there were 367 cases of tuberculosis per 100,000 people. The death rate in 1993 was 17 per 1,000, and due to the war between the Tutsis and Hutus from 1988 to 1992 in Burundi, there were approximately 8,000 war-related deaths.

42 HOUSING

The basic type of housing in the rural areas is the hut, most commonly beehive shaped, made of strips of wood woven around poles, and now covered with tin (thatch has become scarce). The huts are generally not grouped into villages but are organized in groups on a family basis. According to the latest available figures for 1980–88, the total housing stock stood at 900,000 with 5.4 people per dwelling.

43 EDUCATION

Until 1954, all education was provided by religious missions; it was almost entirely limited to the primary grades. Fewer than half of the children of school age attended classes. Education is now compulsory for children between the ages of 7 and 13. Primary education lasts for six years. The languages of instruction in schools are Kisundi and French. Secondary education lasts for seven years. In fact, the percentage of eligible children attending school decreased from 28% in 1967 to 18% in 1975 before rising to 39% in 1984. Only about 4% of the eligible young people attend secondary or technical schools. The shortage of trained teachers and administrators is acute. The rate of literacy has, however, risen from 34% in 1985 to 50% in 1990 (males: 60% and females: 39.8%). In 1991 Burundi had 1,373 schools at the primary level with 9,582 teachers and 631,039 students. At the secondary level, there were 2,211 teachers and 48,398 students. A total of 1,890 were attending teacher training schools and 6,174 were in vocational schools in 1991.

The University of Burundi, in Bujumbura (founded in 1960), is the country's only institution of higher learning. At all higher level institutions, a total of 3,830 students were enrolled with 492 teaching staff.

44LIBRARIES AND MUSEUMS

Libraries in Bujumbura include the Public Library, which has 26,000 volumes; the library of the University of Burundi, with 192,000 volumes; and a specialized collection at the Department of Geology and Mines. The National Museum in Gitega houses a collection of musical instruments, weapons, and witchcraft implements. The Musee Vivant, established in 1977 in Bujumbura, contains exhibits reflecting all aspects of life in the country. It also includes a reptile house, aquarium, aviary, open air theater, and botanical gardens.

45MEDIA

Burundi has a radio broadcasting station, the government-run Voice of the Revolution. It transmits FM broadcasts in Kirundi, Swahili, English, and French. A television service, Télévision Nationale du Burundi, was established in 1984. It began color transmissions in 1985. In 1991 Burundi had 340,000 radios and 5,000 television sets, and there were 9,600 telephones. The government issues a French-language daily, *Le Renouveau de Burundi,* with a circulation of 20,000 in 1991, and a weekly newspaper, *Ubumwe,* published in Kirundi, with a 1991 circulation of 2,000.

46ORGANIZATIONS

Various commercial, agricultural, cultural, social, and welfare organizations exist in Burundi. Most are located in Bujumbura. UPRONA has affiliate labor, youth, and women's organizations.

47TOURISM, TRAVEL, AND RECREATION

The tourist industry is still in its infancy, but there is ample opportunity for development. Lake Tanganyika is internationally famous for its scenic beauty. Points of interest include Bujumbura, the capital, on Lake Tanganyika; Gitega, the former capital, with its museum and traditional handicraft center; and the Mosso area in the southeast, with its fairly abundant wildlife. The northeast has a great variety of tropical birds. Burundi is rich in folk art; the dances and drummers of the Tutsi are particularly well known. In 1991, 125,000 tourists visited Burundi, 47% from Africa and 37% from Europe, and tourist receipts came to US$4 million. That year there were 719 hotel rooms and 1,364 beds with a 49% occupancy rate.

All visitors require a valid passport and visa. A certificate of vaccination against yellow fever is required of persons arriving from an infected area.

48FAMOUS BURUNDIANS

Mwami Ntare I Rushatsi (c.1500), a warrior and astute administrator, succeeded in unifying the country under Tutsi rule. Mwambutsa IV (1913–78), the last mwami under the Belgian administration, was deposed in July 1966. Prince Louis Rwagasore (1930–61), the son of Mwambutsa, was the founder of UPRONA. Michel Micombero (1940–83) was president from 1966 until 1976, when he was replaced by Jean-Baptiste Bagaza (b.1946).

49DEPENDENCIES

Burundi has no territories or colonies.

50BIBLIOGRAPHY

Daniels, Morn. *Burundi.* Oxford, England; Santa Barbara, Calif.: Clio Press, 1992.

Foster, F. Blanche. *East Central Africa: Kenya, Uganda, Tanzania, Rwanda, and Burundi.* New York: Watts [1981], 1980.

Gahama, Joseph. *Le Burundi sous Administration Belge.* Paris: Editions Karthala, 1983.

Lemarchand, René. *Rwanda and Burundi.* New York: Praeger, 1970.

McDonald, Gordon C, et al. *Area Handbook for Burundi.* Washington; Government Printing Office, 1969.

Weinstein, Warren, and Robert Schrire. *Political Conflict and Ethnic Strategies: A Case Study of Burundi.* Syracuse, N.Y.: Syracuse University Foreign and Comparative Studies Program, 1976.

———. *Historical Dictionary of Burundi.* Metuchen, N.J.: Scarecrow, 1976.

CAMEROON

Republic of Cameroon
République du Cameroun

CAPITAL: Yaoundé.

FLAG: The flag is a tricolor of green, red, and yellow vertical stripes with one gold star imprinted in the center of the red stripe.

ANTHEM: The national anthem begins "O Cameroun, berceau de nos ancêtres" ("O Cameroon, cradle of our ancestors").

MONETARY UNIT: The Communauté Financière Africaine franc (CFA Fr) is a paper currency. There are coins of 1, 2, 5, 10, 25, 50, 100, and 500 CFA francs, and notes of 50, 100, 500, 1,000, 5,000, and 10,000 CFA francs. CFA Fr1 = $0.0018 (or $1 = CFA Fr571).

WEIGHTS AND MEASURES: The metric system is the legal standard.

HOLIDAYS: New Year's Day, 1 January; Youth Day, 11 February; Labor Day, 1 May; National Day, 20 May; Christmas, 25 December. Movable religious holidays include Ascension, Good Friday, Easter Monday, End of Ramadan (Djoulde Soumae), and Festival of the Lamb ('Id al-Kabir or Djoulde Laihadji).

TIME: 1 PM = noon GMT.

[1]LOCATION, SIZE, AND EXTENT

Situated in West Africa, Cameroon, shaped like an elongated triangle, contains an area of 475,440 sq km (183,568 sq mi), extending 1,206 km (749 mi) N–S and 717 km (446 mi) E–W. Comparatively, the area occupied by Cameroon is slightly larger than the state of California. It is bordered on the N and NE by Chad, on the E by the Central African Republic, on the E and S by the Congo, Gabon, and Equatorial Guinea, on the SW by the Gulf of Guinea (Atlantic Ocean), and on the W and NW by Nigeria, with a total boundary length of 4,993 km (3,103 mi).

Cameroon's capital city, Yaoundé, is located in the southern part of the country.

[2]TOPOGRAPHY

There are four geographical regions. The western lowlands (rising from sea level to 600 m/2,000 ft) extend along the Gulf of Guinea coast and average about 100 km (60 mi) in width. The northwestern highlands consist of forested volcanic mountains reaching over 2,440 m (8,000 ft) in height. Mt. Cameroon (4,095 m/13,435 ft), which stands isolated on the coast to the south, is the nation's only active volcano and the highest peak in West Africa. The central region extends eastward from the western lowlands and northwest highlands to the border with the Central African Republic and northward to the Bénoué (Benue) River. It includes the Adamoua Plateau, at elevations of 900 to 1,500 m (2,950 to 4,920 ft). This is a transitional area where forest gives way to savanna. The northern region is essentially a vast savanna plain that slopes down to the Chad Basin. Of the two main rivers, the Bénoué is navigable several months during the year, and the Sanaga is not navigable. Part of Lake Chad is in Cameroonian territory.

[3]CLIMATE

The southern and northern regions of the country are two distinct climatic areas. On the coast, the average annual rainfall ranges between 250 and 400 cm (100 and 160 in); in the inland south, between 150 and 250 cm (60 and 100 in). The western slopes of Mt. Cameroon receive 600 to 900 cm (240 to 350 in) a year. The mean temperature ranges from 22° to 29°C (72° to 84°F) along the coast. In the south there are two dry seasons, December to February and July to September. The northern part of the country has a more comfortable climate. Total rainfall drops from 150 cm (60 in) a year in the central plateau to 60 cm (24 in) northward near Lake Chad, and the mean temperature ranges from 23° to 26°C (73° to 79°F), although it can reach 50°C (122°F) in the far north. The dry season in the north is from October to April.

[4]FLORA AND FAUNA

Cameroon possesses practically every variety of flora and fauna found in tropical Africa. Dense rain forest grows along the coast and in the south. This gives way northward and eastward to open woodland and savanna. Wooded steppe is found in the northern panhandle. Major game animals include buffalo, elephant, hippopotamus, antelope, Derby eland, and kudu. Twenty-two primate species are known in the coastal forests along the Gabon border.

[5]ENVIRONMENT

Cameroon has 14 national parks and equivalent reserves covering about 2.5 million hectares (6.2 million acres), more than 5% of the country. Nevertheless, poaching is a major problem because of insufficient guards. Destruction of the remaining forests is heavy, even within reserved lands. Fires and commercial exploitation of the forests result in the elimination of 200,000 hectares per year. Overgrazing is degrading the semiarid northern range lands. Air pollution is a significant environmental problem in Cameroon. In 1994, the nation contributed 0.3% of the world's total gas emissions. The main sources of pollution are industrial chemicals and vehicle contaminants. The same pollutants that affect the air also affect the water. Cameroon has 49.9 cubic miles of water, but 58% of the urban areas and 55% of the rural areas do not have pure water. As of 1994, the drill and Preuss's red colobus were endangered species. In a total of 257 mammal species, 27 are threatened with extinction. Of 848 bird species, 17 are endangered. Two reptiles, one amphibian, and 11 species of fresh-water fish are also threatened. Seventy-four plant species of 8,000 are endangered as of 1994.

The country also has a problem with volcanic activity, flooding, and insect infestation. In August 1986, poisonous gases emanating from Lake Nyos in northwestern Cameroon killed 1,746 villagers, by official count. The lake lies within the crater of a dormant volcano, and scientists speculated that the toxic gases were released by molten rock that had seeped into the lake.

6POPULATION

The 1994 population was estimated at 12,333,904, as compared with a 1987 census report of 10,483,655. However the UN estimated a population of 13,275,000 for 1995. A population of 15,293,000 was projected by the UN for the year 2000, assuming a crude birthrate of 39.4 per 1,000 population, a crude death rate of 10.7, and a net natural increase of 28.7 during 1985–2000. The average population density in 1994 was 26 per sq km (67 per sq mi). In 1990, the capital, Yaoundé, had about 823,000 inhabitants. Douala had about 810,000 in 1991, Garoua 142,000, Maroua 123,000, and Bafoussam 113,000. The urban population was about 38% in 1991.

7MIGRATION

There is some migration to and from Nigeria and other neighboring states, but there are no statistics on the volume. In 1981, nearly 10,000 Cameroonians living in Gabon were repatriated following anti-Cameroonian demonstrations there, and an estimated 120,000 Cameroonians were involved in the expulsion of foreigners from Nigeria in 1983. At the end of 1980 there were 110,000 refugees from Chad at a camp in Kousséri, but by the end of 1981, all but 25,000 had returned to Chad. The camp was closed in March 1982, with the remaining refugees transferred to the Poli region. At the end of 1992 there were an estimated 41,700 Chadian refugees in Cameroon.

8ETHNIC GROUPS

Cameroon has an extremely heterogeneous population, consisting of approximately 200 ethnic groups. The principal groups are Bantus (including Duala, Bassa, Fang, Bulu, and Eton), Semi-Bantus (Bamiléké, Tikar, Widekum, and Bamoun), Adamawa and Chadic peoples (Matakam, Masa, Tupuri, Mofu, Musgu, Mundan, Kapsiki), and the Fulani peoples. The Bantu peoples generally are in the south, and the Fulani in the north. The Bamiléké are by far the largest group (about 15% of the total). There were about 18,000 French in the mid-1980s.

9LANGUAGES

French and English are the official languages. Many African languages and dialects are spoken; most belong to the Bantu and Semi-Bantu (or Sudanic) language groups.

10RELIGIONS

Freedom of conscience and freedom of religion are guaranteed by the constitution. The Fulani people in the north are mainly Muslim, but Christian missionaries (Protestants since 1845 and Roman Catholics since 1890) have been particularly active in other areas. The Protestant missionaries are united in the Federation of the Protestant Churches and Missions in Cameroon. Some 53% of the population identifies itself as Christian, of whom 28.1% are Roman Catholics. As many as 22% are Muslims, 18.8% tribal religionists, and 18% Protestants.

11TRANSPORTATION:

In 1991, Cameroon had 65,000 km (40,400 mi) of roads, of which 50% were unpaved. These unpaved roads are not usable in all seasons. The government recently has been rerouting and paving heavily used roads in order to provide all-weather links between agricultural areas and commercial shipping centers. A major highway between Yaoundé and Douala was opened in 1985. In 1991 there were 94,000 automobiles and 82,000 other vehicles in use.

There are 1,003 km (623 mi) of railways, of which 85% is meter-gauge track, and the remainder 0.6 meter gauge track. The oldest, constructed before 1927 and rebuilt in the mid-1980s, links Douala to Yaoundé (307 km/191 mi) and Douala to Nkongsamba (172 km/107 mi). On the Douala-Yaoundé line there is a spur from Ngoume to Mbalmayo (30 km/19 mi). Kumba is linked to the Douala-Nkongsamba line by another spur. The Trans-Cameroon Railway, Cameroon's most recently constructed line, extends the Douala-Yaoundé line northward 622 km (386 mi) to Ngaoundéré, a cattle-marketing city on the Adamoua Plateau.

Of the operating maritime ports in Cameroon, Douala is the busiest and most important. Lesser ports include Kribi, used chiefly for the export of wood, and Limbé, used only for palm-oil exports. Garoua, on the Benoué River, is the main river port, but it is active only from July to September. Cameroon Shipping Lines, S.A., 67% government owned, had a fleet of two freighters, totaling 24 GRT as of January 1992.

The main international airport is at Douala. Secondary international airports are at Yaoundé and Garoua. In total, there are 9 other airports, 31 private airfields, and 21 rough landing strips. Cameroon Airlines, which went into operation 1 November 1971, flies to Paris, London, Frankfurt, Brussels, and many African cities; it also operates all scheduled domestic flights. In 1991, it carried 260,700 passengers. Cameroon Airlines is 75% owned by the government and 25% by Air France. Among the other airlines serving Cameroon are Pan Am, Air Afrique, Alitalia, Swissair, Iberia, Air Zaire, Air Mali, and Nigeria Airways.

12HISTORY

Linguistic evidence indicates that the area now known as Cameroon and eastern Nigeria was the place of origin of the Bantu peoples. After the 12th century AD, the organized Islamic states of the Sudanic belt, especially those of the Kanem and Fulani peoples, at times ruled the grasslands of northern Cameroon. Small chiefdoms dominated the western highlands and coastal area. Portuguese travelers established contact with the area in the 15th century, but no permanent settlements were maintained. Slaves, however, were purchased from the local peoples.

The modern history of Cameroon began in 1884, when the territory came under German rule after the explorer Gustav Nachtigal negotiated protectorate treaties with the local chiefs. Although British missionaries had been active in the area since 1845, the UK recognized the German protectorate, called Kamerun, which included areas that were later to become British Cameroons and French Cameroun. During their occupation from 1884 to 1914, the Germans advanced into the interior, cultivated large plantations, laid roads, and began constructing a railroad and the port of Douala. When World War I broke out, the territory was invaded by French and British forces. After the war, one-fifth of the former German Kamerun, which was contiguous with eastern Nigeria, was assigned to the UK, and the remaining four-fifths was assigned to France under League of Nations mandates.

During the period 1919–39, France made notable contributions to the development of the territory. Agriculture was expanded, industries were introduced, roads were built, medical services were broadened, and more schools were established. Political liberty was restricted, however, and the system of compulsory labor introduced by the Germans continued. In August 1940, Col. Philippe Leclerc, an envoy of Gen. Charles de Gaulle, landed at Douala and seized the territory for the Free French. The

CAMEROON

0   100   200 Miles
0   100   200 Kilomteres

NIGER

Lake Chad

N'Djamena

CHAD

Kousséri

Chari

Mokolo

Maroua

Mubi

MANDARA MTS.

Kaélé

Yagoua

NIGERIA

Garoua

Pala

Lagdo Reservoir

Bénoué

MBANG MTS.

Niger

Bénoué

Makurdi

Ngaoundéré

Enugu

Wum

Tibati

Adamawa Plateau

Cross

Bamenda

Mbam

Djérem

CENTRAL

Foumban

Lom

AFRICAN

Dschang

Bafoussam

REPUBLIC

Bafang

Kadéi

Port
Harcourt

Calabar

Nkongsamba

Kumba

Bafia

Sanaga

Bélabo

Bertoua

Batouri

Cameroon Mt.
13,435 ft.
4095 m.

Buea

Douala

Nanga-
Eboko

Limbe

Edéa

Yaoundé

Isla de
Bioko

Nyong

Mbalmayo

Kribi

Ebolowa

Dja

Gulf of Guinea

Sangmélima

Ntem

Moloundou

PRÍNCIPE

EQUATORIAL
GUINEA

Rio
Muni

GABON

CONGO

LOCATION: 1°40′ to 13°5′N; 8°30′ to 16°11′E. **BOUNDARY LENGTHS:** Chad, 1,047 km (651 mi); Central African Republic, 822 km (511 mi); Congo, 520 km (323 mi); Gabon, 302 km (188 mi); Equatorial Guinea, 183 km (114 mi); Gulf of Guinea coastline, 364 km (226 mi); Nigeria, 1,921 km (1,194 mi). **TERRITORIAL SEA LIMIT:** 50 mi.

birth of the Fourth French Republic and the UN trusteeship in 1946 signified a new era for the territory. French Cameroun was granted representation in the French National Assembly and the Council of the Republic. An elected territorial assembly was instituted and political parties were recognized, thus establishing a basis for Cameroonian nationalism.

Immediately after the setting up of the trusteeship in 1946, many parties began to emerge, but only one had effective organization and strength, the Union of Cameroon Peoples (Union des Populations du Cameroun—UPC). The party demanded immediate reunification of the British Cameroons and French Cameroun and eventual independence. In 1955, the UPC, accused of being under extreme left-wing influence, launched a campaign of sabotage, violence, and terror that continued sporadically until 1971, 11 years after independence. The death toll from this struggle has been estimated at between 10,000 and 80,000.

A new stage in self-government was reached in 1957, when the French government created the autonomous state of Cameroun, and Cameroonian institutions were created along the lines of French parliamentary democracy. In 1958, the Legislative Assembly of Cameroun voted for independence by 1960, and France and the UN General Assembly assented. In 1959, the last step in the evolution of political institutions prior to independence took place when a government of Cameroun was formed and given full internal autonomy. Ahmadou Ahidjo became prime minister. Earlier in the year, on 1 January 1959, the Kamerun National Democratic Party had won the general elections in Southern British Cameroons, and John Foncha had become prime minister. Soon Foncha and Ahidjo were discussing the possibilities of unification upon the achievement of independence.

On 1 January 1960, Cameroun became an independent republic. Fierce UPC-led riots in the Dschang and Nkongsamba areas caused Ahidjo to summon French reinforcements to suppress the rebellion, but intermittent rioting continued. A draft constitution was approved in a referendum of 21 February, and on 10 April a new National Assembly was elected. Ahidjo's Cameroun Union Party won a majority, and Ahidjo, who ran unopposed, was elected president in April 1960.

During 1960, consultations between Foncha and Ahidjo continued, and a proposed federation was tentatively outlined. On 11 February 1961, separate plebiscites were held in the Southern and Northern British Cameroons under the auspices of the UN. The voters in Southern Cameroons chose union with the Cameroun Republic, while those in Northern Cameroons opted for union with Nigeria, which was accomplished on 1 June 1961. During the months that followed, terrorist activity was renewed and the Cameroun Republic had to devote one-third of its national budget to the maintenance of public order.

A draft constitution for the federation was approved by the Cameroun National Assembly on 7 September 1961, and the new federation became a reality on 1 October. The Cameroun Republic became the state of East Cameroon and Southern British Cameroons became the state of West Cameroon in the new Federal Republic of Cameroon, with Ahmadou Ahidjo as president and John Foncha as vice-president. Both were reelected in 1965, but Foncha was later replaced as vice-president, and the office was abolished in 1972.

A proposal to replace the federation with a unified state was ratified by popular referendum on 20 May 1972; the vote was reportedly 99.97% in favor of unification. A new constitution went into effect on 2 June, under which the country was renamed the United Republic of Cameroon. Ahmadou Ahidjo remained president of the republic; running unopposed, he was reelected for a fourth five-year term on 5 April 1975. In June, by constitutional amendment, the office of prime minister was created, and Paul Biya was appointed to the post. Ahidjo, reelected unopposed, began his fifth five-year term as president in May 1980. In November 1982 he resigned and was succeeded by Biya; Ahidjo remained head of the ruling party.

Biya proved more independent than Ahidjo had anticipated. Following allegations of a military coup plot allegedly masterminded by Ahidjo, the former president retired to France in August 1983, and Biya became party chairman. Ahidjo was sentenced to death (later commuted to life imprisonment) in absentia in February 1984. Biya's own presidential guard attempted to overthrow the government in April; the rebellion was stamped out by the army. Purges followed, and 46 of the plotters were executed. A state of emergency was declared, which was still in effect at the end of 1987. Late in 1984, the position of prime minister was abolished, and the name of the country was changed to the Republic of Cameroon.

Despite democratic reform begun in 1990, political power remains firmly in the hands of President Biya and a small circle of RDPC members from his own ethnic group. Biya was reelected on 11 October 1992 amid accusations of voting irregularities. Biya reportedly got 39% of the vote to 35% for John Fru Ndi. In contrast, the 1 March 1992 legislative election was considered free and fair by international observers, although many parties boycotted the elections and the RDPC won several constituencies by default. But even though opposition parties are well-represented in the legislature (92 of 180 seats), there are, according to the 1992 constitution, few legislative or judicial checks on the president. As a result, the Biya government is widely unpopular and instability and fractious politics prevail. Government is weak and the opposition is divided.

13GOVERNMENT

Under the 1972 constitution, as amended in 1984, Cameroon is a republic headed by a president who is elected by universal suffrage to successive five-year terms. The president appoints the ministers and vice-ministers and can dismiss them, is the head of the armed forces, and promulgates the laws. The president can decree a state of national emergency and can be invested with special powers.

The legislative branch is composed of a National Assembly of 180 members. The Assembly is directly elected to a five-year term by universal suffrage. It meets twice a year, the duration of each session being limited to 30 days. There is also a Social and Economic Council that advises the government.

President Biya agreed in May 1993 to hold a so-called Great National Constitutional Debate and in June he began preparing a draft of a new constitution, to be adopted either by referendum or by the National Assembly. The opposition refused to participate and no debate took place.

14POLITICAL PARTIES

The Cameroon National Union (Union Nationale Camerounaise—UNC) was Cameroon's sole legal political party until 1990. It was formed in 1966 through a merger of the Cameroon Union (Union Camerounaise) and the Kamerun National Democratic Party, the major political organizations, respectively, of the eastern and western regions, and four smaller parties. The UNC sponsors labor, youth, and women's organizations and provided the only list of candidates for the 1973, 1978, and 1983 legislative elections.

Ahmadou Ahidjo became the first head of the UNC in 1966 and continued in that capacity after his resignation as the nation's president in 1982. Following President Biya's assumption of emergency powers in August 1983, Ahidjo, then in France, resigned as party leader. Biya was subsequently elected party chief at a special party congress in September. In 1985, the UNC was renamed the Cameroon People's Democratic Movement (CPDM or Rassemblement Démocratique du Peuple Camerounaise—RDPC).

Opposition parties were legalized in 1990. In the elections to the National Assembly on 1 March 1992, the RDPC won 88 of the 180 seats; the National Union for Democracy and Progress (UNDP), 68 seats; the Union of Cameroonian Populations (UPC), 18 seats; and the Movement for the Defense of the Republic (MDR), 6 seats. The RDPC and the MDR have formed a coalition.

In the presidential election of 11 October 1992, an election with widespread irregularities alleged, the votes were split—CPDM 40%; Social Democratic Front (SDF), 36%; and UNDP 18%.

The SDF and its allies in the Union for Change still dispute the results of the presidential election and call for new elections. They are also critical of France, which they call an "accomplice of those in power." Dissident movements in the northwest and southwest seek independence for the English-speaking regions or a return to a federal state, which had been terminated in 1984.

15LOCAL GOVERNMENT

The Republic of Cameroon is divided into 10 administrative provinces, each placed under the jurisdiction of a governor appointed by the head of state. Each province is subdivided into departments, totaling 58 in 1993, which are under the administrative control of divisional officers (préfets). In turn, departments are composed of subdivisions (arrondissements), totaling 269 in 1993, headed by assistant divisional officers (sous-préfets). Municipal officials are elected for five-year terms. Traditional institutions such as chiefdoms were in noticeable decline during the 1970s and 1980s, although traditional rulers are treated as administrative adjuncts and receive a governmental salary.

16JUDICIAL SYSTEM

Cameroonian law has three main sources: local customary law, the French civil code, and British law, although drafting of a unified code was reported under way in the 1980s. The Supreme Court, in addition to its other powers and duties granted by the constitution, gives final judgment on such appeals as may be granted by the law from the judgments of the provincial courts of appeal. The system also includes magistrate's courts in the provinces and a 15-member High Court of Justice, appointed by the National Assembly. Proposals for appointments and sanctions against magistrates throughout the republic are started by the Higher Judicial Council, of which the head of state is president. A Court of Impeachment has the right to try the president for high treason and cabinet ministers for conspiracy against the security of the state.

A State Security Court established in 1990 hears cases involving internal or external state security. Traditional courts that resolve domestic, probate, and minor property disputes remain an important element in the judicial system. These courts vary considerably according to region and ethnic group. Appeal is possible in most cases to traditional authorities of a higher rank.

The judiciary is supervised by the Ministry of Justice, a part of the executive, and does not function as an independent branch of government. The 1972 constitution contains few provisions guaranteeing an independent judiciary.

17ARMED FORCES

Cameroon's armed forces totaled 7,700 in 1993. The army had 6,600 personnel organized in 5 infantry battalions, 1 paratroop commando battalion, 1 artillery battalion, 1 engineering battalion, a presidential guard of infantry and armored car battalions, and various support units. The navy had 800 personnel, 2 small ships, and 34 patrol boats. The air force had 300 personnel and 16 combat aircraft. Paramilitary gendarmerie totaled 4,000. In 1990 Cameroon spent $219 million on defense, or 1.7% of gross domestic product.

18INTERNATIONAL COOPERATION

Cameroon was admitted to UN membership on 20 September 1960 and is a member of ECA and all the nonregional specialized agencies. Cameroon is also a member of the African Development Bank, G-77, OAU, and UDEAC and is a signatory to GATT and the Law of the Sea. The country is an associate member of the EEC under the Lomé conventions. It withdrew from OCAM in July 1973.

In August 1986, diplomatic relations with Israel were renewed after a 13-year gap, and the visit to Cameroon by Israeli Prime Minister Shimon Peres was the first by an Israeli leader to a black African nation in 20 years.

19ECONOMY

A rising economic star among African nations, Cameroon has nonetheless seen its economy suffer since the mid-1980s. The external debt to GDP ratio has skyrocketed to 77% (1993 est.); GDP has declined by 12.6%. Foreign project assistance fell from us$570 million in 1990 to us$180 million in 1993, a decline of 68.4%; net foreign financing completely collapsed, going from us$1,230 million to zero in the year ending 1993. The causes of this about-face were the simultaneous sharp declines in petroleum, coffee, and cacao prices and the appreciation of the currency of account—the US$—relative to the French franc.

However, Cameroon's economy retains a number of fundamental strong points. It is based on a diversified and self-sufficient agriculture supplemented by substantial petroleum production and a sizable manufacturing sector. Coffee and cocoa are Cameroon's principal agricultural exports, accounting for 32.1% of export earnings (1989). Cork, wood, and cotton account for an additional 16.4%. Petroleum provided 18.0% of exports in 1989, while basic manufactures (19.0%) and machinery and transport equipment (5.2%) provided additional export revenues.

Coffee production declined from 126,000 metric tons level in 1988–89 to 86,500 tons by 1990–91 as a result of less favorable climatic conditions and weak product prices. The robusta-to-arabica ratio is 80–20. Cocoa production of 140,300 tons was recorded in 1990–91. Cotton production fell by 65.4% from the 1988–89 season to the 1990–91 season, due primarily to unsatisfactory prices paid to producers. Palm oil production has shown signs of strength, but the product is not marketed internationally. Cameroon bananas are sold internationally, and the sector was reorganized and privatized in 1987. Similarly, rubber output has grown in spite of Asian competition. Cameroon is rich in forests, but sector development is hampered by transport limitations. However, output has regained the level attained in the early 1980s.

Cameroon is self-sufficient in its food staples: millet, sorghum, and maize. Rice is grown by both traditional and modern farm operations and has benefited from government interest. Sugar production reached 70,000 tons in 1991–92. Livestock and fishing subsectors are both significant contributors to the domestic economy.

Mineral production is mixed. Cameroonian petroleum production peaked in 1985 at 916 million tons before declining to 7.6 million tons in 1991. Reserves are limited, and without further discoveries, are expected to be exhausted in the 1990s. Natural gas reserves are limited. Cameroon's bauxite reserves are undeveloped, as are the identified iron ore and uranium deposits. Limestone is produced and processed into cement at Garoua.

In January 1994 France suddenly devalued the CFA franc, causing its value to drop in half overnight. Immediately, prices for almost all imported goods soared, including prices for food and essential drugs, like those to combat malaria. Since 1948 France had guaranteed a fixed parity of one French franc to 50 African francs. The resulting stability in the currency had generally kept inflation low and helped to maintain a steady rate of growth. However, in the 1980s, the economies of the CFA countries began to stagnate in relation to other African nations, and France came under increased pressure from the World Bank, the IMF, and western countries to stop subsidizing the CFA franc. The devaluation, long expected in the investment community, is designed to enourage new investment, particularly in oil, and discourage the use of hard currency reserves to buy products that could be grown domestically. As an interim measure, France has said that it will nearly halve Cameroon's debt, a move that has encouraged the international financial community.

20INCOME

In 1992 Cameroon's GNP was $10,003 million at current prices, or $820 per capita. For the period 1985–92 the average inflation rate was –0.6%, resulting in a real growth rate in per capita GNP of –6.7%.

In 1992 the GDP was $10,397 million in current US dollars. It is estimated that agriculture, hunting, forestry, and fishing contributed 22% to GDP; mining and quarrying, 12%; manufacturing, 12%; electricity, gas, and water, 1%; construction, 7%; wholesale and retail trade, 16%; transport, storage, and communication, 6%; finance, insurance, real estate, and business services, 11%; community, social, and personal services, 1%; and other sources 11%.

21LABOR

There were 4,200,000 people in the labor force in 1992, most of whom were in agriculture. In 1992, the estimated national unemployment rate was 15–20%. The parapublic sector's employment has been cut from 75,000 to 60,000 since 1988.

The nation's three major trade union confederations dissolved themselves in 1971, when the National Union of Cameroon Workers (Union Nationale des Travailleurs du Cameroun—UNTC) was formed. Renamed the Organization of Cameroon Workers' Associations (Organisation des Sociétés de Travailleurs Camerounais—OSTC) in 1985, it was affiliated with the Cameroon People's Democratic Movement prior to 1992. In August 1992, the National Assembly passed a new labor code, permitting workers to form and join unions of their choosing. Under the new rules, groups of at least 20 workers may organize a union provided they register with the Ministry of Labor.

22AGRICULTURE

Agriculture was the main source of growth and foreign exchange until 1978 when oil production replaced it as the cornerstone of growth for the formal economy. In 1992, agriculture contributed 22% to GDP. Agricultural development and productivity declined from neglect during the oil boom years of the early 1980s. Agriculture remains the principal occupation of the vast majority of the population, although only about 15% of the land is arable. The most important cash crops are cocoa, coffee, cotton, bananas, rubber, palm oil and kernels, and peanuts. The main food crops are plantains, cassava, corn, millet, and sugarcane.

Cameroon is among the world's largest cocoa producers; 94,000 tons of cocoa were produced in 1992. Two types of coffee, robusta and arabica, are grown; production was 85,000 tons in 1992. About 85,000 hectares (210,000 acres) are allocated to cotton plantations. Some cotton is exported, while the remainder is processed by local textile plants. A total of 108,000 tons of seed cotton were produced in 1992; ginned cotton output was 48,000 tons. Bananas are grown mainly in the southwest; 1992 estimated production was 520,000 tons. The output of rubber, also grown in the southwest, was 42,000 tons in 1992. Estimated production in 1992 of palm kernels and oil was 53,000 and 107,000 tons, respectively. For peanuts (in the shell) the figure

was 100,000 tons. Small amounts of tobacco, tea, and pineapples are also grown.

Estimated 1992 production of food crops was as follows: sugarcane, 1,400,000 tons; plantains, 860,000 tons; cassava, 1,230,000 tons; corn, 380,000 tons; millet, 55,000 tons; yams, 80,000 tons; sweet potatoes, 160,000 tons; potatoes, 32,000 tons; dry beans, 70,000 tons; and rice, 90,000 tons.

23ANIMAL HUSBANDRY

In 1992 there were 4,730,000 head of cattle, 3,560,000 each of goats and sheep, and 1,380,000 hogs. Most stock breeding is carried out in the north. Ngaoundéré has one of the largest and best-equipped slaughterhouses in Africa. Livestock products in 1992 included 73,000 tons of beef and about 12,400 tons of eggs. Meat products are exported to UDEAC countries. Attempts to improve livestock and hides and skins have been hindered by the social system, in which livestock constitutes a source of prestige, security, and wealth; by slowness in developing an effective transportation system; and by difficulty in controlling the tsetse fly.

24FISHING

The fishing industry is not highly developed. Most fish are caught by artisan fishermen in rudimentary motorized pirogues. The total catch was an estimated 78,000 tons in 1991.

25FORESTRY

In 1991, the forest area of 24.4 million hectares (60.2 million acres) included about 52% of the land area. The principal types of trees felled are assié, azobe, dussil, eloorba, mahogany, sapele, sipo, illomba, ayus, iroko, dibetu, and silk cotton. Timber exports in 1991 were about 728,000 cu m of logs and 253,000 cu m of sawn timber. In 1991, roundwood production was estimated at 14,637,000 cu m. Wood sales make up the fourth largest source of foreign revenue, but infrastructural problems and weak demand for lower-quality wood limits the development of the forestry sector.

26MINING

While Cameroon has steadily increased its oil production, the discovery and exploitation of other mineral resources have been slow. Bauxite deposits, in the Minam and Martap region, are estimated at 1 billion tons. Iron deposits containing an estimated 200 million tons have been discovered south of Kribi.

There is a large variety of other mineral deposits, including diamonds, tin, gold, mica, columbo-tantalite, cassiterite, lignite, and rutile, but only gold is commercially exploited. Limestone production was 57,000 tons in 1991, and pozzolana production (a rock used in cement) was 130,000 tons.

27ENERGY AND POWER

Cameroon began offshore oil production in 1977, and output amounted to 7 million tons in 1992 (about 140,000 barrels per day), down 7.1% from 1991. In 1991–92, oil accounted for 40% of total exports and 7% of GDP. As of 1993, oil exploration had resumed. If new discoveries are not found soon, Cameroon may cease being a net petroleum exporter by 2000, and production would, essentially, stop by 2005. A 1978 law provided a 60% share in all producing fields and a 50% share in all exploration areas for the newly created government oil company, National Association of Hydrocarbons (Société Nationale des Hydrocarbures—SNH). Cameroon reportedly has large reserves of liquid petroleum gas which are largely untapped.

Hydroelectric resources remain the most readily exploitable form of energy in Cameroon. Electrical energy is produced primarily by two hydroelectric stations on the Sanaga River. Nearly 60% of the power from these stations goes to the aluminum smelter at Edéa. Cameroon's installed capacity was 627,000 kw in 1991; total production of electricity was 2,712 million kwh (97% hydroelectric) during the same year.

In the 1980s, hydroelectric capacity was expanded by an additional complex on the Sanaga River (Songo-Loulou) and a 72-Mw generator (built with Chinese aid) on the Bénoué; the latter, at Lagdo, began production in 1983. However, despite Cameroon's impressive waterpower resources, the national electricity grid runs principally from Douala to Yaoundé and from Douala to Bafoussam. Most other areas are served by diesel-generated electricity or have no electricity at all. Cameroon's National Energy Plan attempts to prepare for a diminishing petroleum output. Hydro-Quebec of Canada is conducting a feasibility study of the Nachtigal Power Station, which could provide 280 Mw of hydroelectric power on the Sanaga River north of Yaounde.

28 INDUSTRY

Manufacturing accounted for 13.1% of GDP in 1990. Considerable advances in industrial development have been made in recent years, mostly in the south. The government, once a large shareholder in many industries, including aluminum, wood pulp, and oil refining, now advocates increased privatization.

Before the establishment of the Cameroonian Aluminum Refining Co. in 1957, all important enterprises were connected with processing agricultural and forestry products. The most significant of these early enterprises were the peanut and palm oil mills at Edéa, Douala, Bertoua, and Pitoa; soap factories at Douala and Pitoa; tobacco factories at Yaoundé; a rubber factory in the Dizangué region; and numerous lumber mills. Other concerns include a factory at Kaélé that produces cotton fiber and a cotton oil plant there that produces oil for export. There is a textile-weaving factory in Douala and a bleaching, dyeing, and printing factory in Garoua. Cement plants are at Figuil and near Douala, and several breweries supply both internal demand and surplus for export.

Cameroon's first oil refinery opened at Limbé in May 1981. It has a capacity of about 50,000 barrels a day and produced about 3,241,000 metric tons of motor and heating fuels in 1984. Another major industrial enterprise is the aluminum plant at Edéa, which began operations in 1957 with ore imported from Guinea. Output was 87,500 metric tons in 1990. There are also about 20 large sawmills and 5 plywood factories. In 1988, cement production was 586,000 tons; beer and soft drinks, 6,277,000 hectoliters; soap, 23,400 tons; and footwear, 1,733,000 pairs. In 1990, raw sugar production was at 81,000 tons and cigarettes, 4,300 million units.

A disastrous 65% government-owned pulp factory, which opened at Edéa in 1981, is the largest industrial plant in Central Africa. The capacity was 122,000 tons of bleached sulfate pulp a year, but after the first year (production was only 13,000 tons) the mill closed, its costs being far higher than possible sales. This investment may have cost the state as much as CFA Fr260 billion.

Since independence, Cameroon has had a favorable attitude toward industry. State involvement was in the form of shares held by the SNI (Société Nationale d'Investissement du Cameroun). In 1986, Cameroon announced its intention to divest its shares in 62 companies. By 1990, 15 had been privatized and the remaining parastatals were subject to performance-based contracts.

Electric power reached 2,702 kwh in 1990, nearly 50% of which went to process aluminum. Hydropower supplies 85% of the total, with the key plants located at Edéa (263 Mw) and Song-Loulou (384 Mw). A 200 Mw facility is projected for Nachtigal Falls on the Sanaga River.

29 SCIENCE AND TECHNOLOGY

The Ministry of Higher Education and Scientific Research is charged with formulating research policy and programs in Cameroon. It is divided into institutes and research centers dealing with specific disciplines and coordinates research throughout the country in agronomy, animal husbandry, fishing, forestry, hydraulic and geological surveys, statistical studies, economics, social sciences, and public health. In 1985–86 there were 362 researchers working for five government research institutes. Foreign institutes include a French overseas scientific and technical research mission in Yaoundé. The University of Yaounde, founded in 1962, has a faculty of science. The University Center of Dschang, founded in 1977, offers training in agricultural sciences.

Cameroon has ten institutes conducting research in forestry, meteorology, agriculture, geology, medicine, veterinary science, and botany. The French Institute of Scientific Research for Development and Cooperation is located in Yaoundé.

30 DOMESTIC TRADE

Most imported consumer goods are distributed among the European population and the salaried and urban African workers. The internal markets are run by African entrepreneurs, while important import-export houses are controlled by Europeans, usually French. The main firms are found in Douala and Yaounde. The internal markets deal mainly with cattle, locally produced foodstuffs, and textiles, sewing machines, and radios. Trade in capital equipment and construction materials is practically restricted to the local industrialists and government contractors. Some commodities are price-controlled, but there is a thriving black market in goods smuggled from Nigeria. Agricultural extension, modernization programs, cooperatives, and provident societies have all assisted in expanding markets. Credit, marketing of produce, transport of produce, and storage fall within their jurisdiction.

Usual business hours are from 8 AM to noon and from 2:30 to 5:30 PM, Monday through Friday, and 8 AM to noon Saturday. Banks are open 8 to 11:30 AM and 2:30 to 3:30 PM.

31 FOREIGN TRADE

Cameroon's leading exports are crude oil and petroleum products, coffee and cocoa, cork and wood, and aluminum. The principal exports in 1989 (in millions of US dollars) were as follows:

Petroleum	230.9
Coffee and coffee products	214.7
Cocoa and cocoa products	196.2
Wood and wood manufactures	141.3
Aluminum and aluminum manufactures	144.6
Cotton and cotton products	68.7
Other exports	285.2
TOTAL	1,281.6

The leading imports are machinery and transportation equipment, basic manufactures (textiles and paper), chemicals (medicines and insecticides), and food. The principal imports in 1984/85 (in millions of US dollars) were as follows:

Machinery and transport equipment	391.9
Basic manufactures	292.8
Chemicals and related products	193.9
Food and live animals	179.6
Beverages and tobacco	21.0
Crude materials (not fuels)	47.9
Misc. manufactured articles	109.0
Other imports	37.2
TOTAL	1,273.3

France is by far Cameroon's leading trade partner. It received 23.5% of Cameroon's exports and shipped 36.5% of Cameroon's imports in 1989. Cameroon sent 19.3% of its exports to Belgium, 10% to the US, and 8.8% to Germany. After France, the Netherlands was Cameroon's next leading supplier of imports (9.1%).

32BALANCE OF PAYMENTS

In the late 1970s, increased oil production compensated for the low world market prices of Cameroon's agricultural exports and helped the country achieve a favorable balance of payments. Cameroon last enjoyed a balance of payments surplus in 1985. As of 1991–92, the deficit was about $950 million, or 9.2% of GDP.

In 1991 merchandise exports totaled $1,317.8 million and imports $936.9 million. The merchandise trade balance was $380.9 million. The following table summarizes Cameroon's balance of payments for 1990 and 1991 (in millions of US dollars):

	1990	1991
CURRENT ACCOUNT	—	—
Goods, services, and income	–312.1	–344.9
Unrequited transfers	–22.7	21.8
TOTALS	–334.8	–323.1
CAPITAL ACCOUNT		
Direct investment	–77.4	–22.0
Portfolio investment		
Other long-term capital	6.2	–116.0
Other short-term capital	–155.8	–26.8
Exceptional financing	729.8	160.9
Other liabilities	69.5	–26.6
Reserves	63.6	30.0
TOTALS	635.9	–0.5
Errors and omissions	–301.1	323.6
Total change in reserves	64.0	–17.2

33BANKING AND SECURITIES

The bank of issue is the Bank of the Central African States (Banque des États de l'Afrique Central—BEAC), which replaced the Central Bank of the State of Equatorial Africa and Cameroon in November 1972. Its headquarters are in Yaoundé. Cameroon's central bank assets as of 31 December 1986 included CFA Fr4.18 billion in foreign assets. The government's Exchange Control Office controls all financial transactions effected between Cameroon and foreign territories. The Cameroonian Development Bank, an 82% government-owned institution established in 1961, provides financial and technical assistance to development projects. The National Fund for Rural Development grants loans to farmers and artisans. Other Cameroonian financial institutions include the Mortgage-Loan Society of Cameroon, the Cameroon Bank Ltd., and SNI, which was established in 1964 to evaluate all investment proposals.

The major commercial banks, all with important French participation, are the International Bank of Commerce and Industry of Cameroon, Banque Meridian BIAO Cameroun SA, and the Societe Commerciale de Banque Credit Lyonnais-Cameroun. There were also a savings bank and a postal bank. Reserves of the commercial and development banks were CFA Fr12.39 billion in claims on the economy as of 1993. Demand deposits totaled CFA Fr150.0 billion, and time and savings deposits were CFA Fr278.67 billion. Informal savings and loan systems known as tontines take the place of banks for many tribal members, with repayment enforced by social pressure.

There is no securities exchange in Cameroon.

34INSURANCE

Insurance activities are regulated by the Ministry of Finance. In 1986 there were eight foreign insurance companies (predominantly French) and five domestic companies. The National Reinsurance Fund is the only professional reinsurer. In 1984, life insurance premiums came to CFA Fr2,461 million.

35PUBLIC FINANCE

Cameroon relies heavily on customs duties and direct taxes as sources of government revenue. Most of Cameroon's oil revenues do not appear in the national budget and are maintained in secret accounts abroad.

Cameroon's external debt rose sharply (25%) in 1986 and reached $6,278 million in 1991. International debt refinancing programs reduced the debt-service ratio from 31% in 1988 to 17.1% in 1990. The structural adjustment program and an IMF stand-by credit program agreed to in 1989 were suspended in 1990 due to noncompliance with negotiated performance requirements. The adjustment program was continued in 1991 and a new standby agreement reached with the IMF. Further rescheduling relief was agreed to by the "Paris Club" and by France in 1992. In 1992, the external debt exceeded 60% of GDP.

36TAXATION

The tax on individual income ranged from 10–60% in 1993. Also levied were housing fund and employment taxes, a tax to finance Cameroon television, and social security taxes. The corporate tax rate was 38.5%. Indirect taxes included an internal turnover tax, and taxes on business licenses and stock dividend distributions.

37CUSTOMS AND DUTIES

In accordance with the trusteeship agreement between France and the UN, all nations had equal tariff treatment in Cameroon when it was a trust territory. Many types of goods essential for economic, social, and educational development were exempt from duty. Export duties were moderate. Despite this situation, the direction of Cameroon's trade was to the franc-currency zone, and importers were required to secure import licenses for non-franc-zone products.

Following independence, the import licensing system was continued but does not apply to UDEAC countries. The 1984 investment code, designed largely to attract foreign capital, provided exemptions from import and export duties on necessary equipment and raw materials, as well as other liberal concessions and benefits for new enterprises in a broad range of categories. Legislation to establish free trade zones was enacted in 1990.

38FOREIGN INVESTMENT

The investment environment in the Cameroon has declined over the course of the eight-year-long contraction in the economy. The country has adjusted slowly to a 50% decline in its terms of trade since 1984–85. It has been hindered by a product mix that, until the recent devaluation of the CFA franc, was overvalued and uncompetitive in the international market. Furthermore, companies doing business in Cameroon have faced substantial security, credit convertibility, judicial, and political risks. As Cameroon overcomes these drawbacks to investment, the country's potential is considerable.

Under the terms of a structural adjustment program, Cameroon has liberalized its investment code, eliminated most price controls, reduced import and export duties, and sought to privatize its parastatals.

39ECONOMIC DEVELOPMENT

The context of the debate over economic development has shifted from sector analysis to structural adjustment. The decline in petroleum revenues has precipitated a period of financial insecurity which led Cameroon ultimately, in 1988, to subscribe to an IMF structural adjustment program. France is the major aid donor. Other important bilateral donors are Germany, the US, the UK, Italy, and Canada. Multilateral aid from the United Nations family of organizations and the EEC totaled $1,525.2 million between 1946 and 1986.

40SOCIAL DEVELOPMENT

Social services were introduced by the French in 1950. Social centers concern themselves with child care, hygiene, and juvenile delinquency and maintain kindergartens, orphanages, and classes in domestic sciences. There are no welfare services covering the whole population. However, a 1969 law established an employees' old age, invalid, and survivors' pension plan, financed by employee and employer contributions and administered by the National Social Insurance Fund. Benefits are also paid for occupational diseases and accidents. The Public Health Service ostensibly provides (or, is supposed to provide) the free medical, surgical, and pharmaceutical services to those unable to pay. But in 1993, government cut doctors' and teachers' salaries by more than half. Since 1 July 1956, various schemes of family allowances and prenatal and maternity allowances were instituted for wage earners. Assistance to one's kin is a part of the traditional social system.

The women's wing of UNC has created social and economic programs, and women are represented in high government positions. Abortion is legal on broad health grounds. In the mid-1980s, women surviving their childbearing years had borne an average of 5.8 children.

There have been serious human rights abuses, including political and extrajudicial murders. In March 1993, security forces fired on peaceful opposition demonstrators (killing two and wounding 20). Arbitrary detention and physical abuse of detainees is common. Although the press is independent and criticizes the government, the authorities seek to intimidate journalists. Yet in 1993, a military tribunal tried and convicted one officer and five soldiers for the summary execution in 1992 of Chra Arabs. It was the first case in which members of the security forces were publicly tried for human rights offenses. Usually security force personnel commit human rights abuses with no fear of punishment.

41HEALTH

The Ministry of Public Health is responsible for the maintenance of all public health services. Many missionaries maintain health and leprosy centers. The government is pursuing a vigorous policy of public health improvement, with considerable success in reducing sleeping sickness, leprosy, and other endemic diseases. The demand for all types of health services and equipment is high and constant. The need for modern equipment is especially urgent, with many clinics using outdated equipment, some of which is imported illegally from Nigeria.

Malaria is prevalent in the Bénoué River Valley, the basin of Lake Chad, the coastal region, and the forests of southern Cameroon. A large percentage of the adult population is affected. Other serious water-borne diseases are schistosomiasis and sleeping sickness, which is spread by the tsetse fly. In 1990, the annual incidence of tuberculosis was 194 cases per 100,000 people.

In 1990, there was only 1 physician per 12,190 people, and 1 nursing professional per 1,690 people. From 1985 to 1990, there were 2.7 hospital beds per 1,000 people. Total health care expenditures in 1990 were $286 million.

In 1992, the average life expectancy was 56 years, with a death rate of 12 per 1,000 people in 1993. In 1992, only 41% had access to health care services.

In 1993, the birth rate was 40.7 per 1,000 people. In a study made between 1980 and 1993, only 13% of the country's married women (ages 15 to 49) used any type of contraception. The infant mortality rate in 1992 was 74 per 1000 live births.

Between 1990 and 1992 Cameroon immunized children up to one year old for: tuberculosis (52%); diphtheria, pertussis, and tetanus (37%); polio (37%); and measles (37%).

42HOUSING

Differences in climate, building materials, and patterns of living have resulted in a variety of traditional structures in rural areas. After 1946, the French government took measures to cope with growing urbanization, particularly in Douala and Yaoundé. However, there is still a housing shortage, and many people live in thatched hovels of mud and wood, with no running water or modern facilities. The Cameroonian government has engaged in housing improvement and construction programs in urban and rural areas. As of 1976, 38.2% of all housing units were detached dwellings.

43EDUCATION

Education is free in state schools and compulsory between ages 6 and 13. Government funds are available to mission and private schools. Most secondary schools have been made bilingual, with instruction in both French and English. Working alongside the public schools are the missionary schools, which have been extremely important in the history of Cameroonian education. In 1990 a total of 1,964,146 pupils were attending 6,709 primary schools, with 38,430 teachers. Secondary schools had 500,272 students. Children go through six years of primary schooling followed by three years of secondary at the first stage and two years at the second. In 1990 the adult literacy rate was estimated at 54.1% (males: 66.1% and females: 42.6%).

At Yaoundé University (founded in 1962) and other equivalent institutions, there were 31,360 students and 761 instructors in 1990. There are faculties of science, law and economics, and arts at Yaoundé, which maintains four regional campuses. Higher institutions attached to the university include the University Health Sciences Center, the Higher School of Sciences and Techniques of Information, the Institute of International Relations, the Advanced Teachers Training College, and the Polytechnic School. There is also a national school of public administration and an institute of business administration.

44LIBRARIES AND MUSEUMS

The National Archives is in Yaoundé and has an annex in Buea, where documents on colonial conditions and administration are stored. The National Archives also serves as the National Library of Cameroon and has a library of 64,000 volumes in Yaoundé. The University of Yaoundé has 90,000 volumes.

The Museum of Douala has prehistoric and natural history galleries devoted primarily to the main Cameroonian ethnic groups. The Museum of Bamounian Arts and Traditions at Foumban maintains objects of ancient art and a small library. The museums of Diamaré and Maroua at Maroua have ethnographic materials. Dschang has an ethnographic museum devoted to the Bamiléké and a fine-arts museum. Yaoundé has a museum of art and archaeology and a museum of Cameroonian art. There are also museums in Bamenda, Kousséri, and Mokolo.

45MEDIA

The telecommunications network has been improving over the years. An automatic telephone exchange system links all important cities and towns. Cable, telegram, and telex services connect Cameroon to the outside world. In January 1974, a satellite telecommunications earth station was inaugurated, greatly improving the quality of Cameroon's international telephone service. As of 1991, some 61,567 telephones were in use.

In 1987 Cameroon's radio and television networks were merged to form the Office de Radiodiffusion–Télévision Camerounaise (CRTV), which operates under the authority of the Ministry of Information and Culture. There are broadcasting stations at Yaoundé, Douala, Garoua, Buea, Bertoua, Bamenda, and Bafoussam, offering programs in French, English, and many African languages. About 1,725,000 radios and 279,000 television sets were in use in 1991.

Most Cameroonian publications are issued irregularly and have small circulations. The majority are published in French, but some appear in Bulu, Duala, and other native languages of Cameroon.

The constitution guarantees freedom of the press, but in practice the threat of government censorship generally prevents opposition viewpoints from appearing in print, especially in the government-controlled press. The major daily is the *Cameroon Tribune,* published in French in Yaoundé, with a weekly English-language edition; circulation was 70,000 in French and 25,000 in English during 1991. The *Cameroon Outlook* and *Cameroon Times* are published in Limbé three times a week (circulation 5,000 each in 1991).

[46]ORGANIZATIONS

The various economic interests of the country are represented in the Chamber of Commerce, Industry, and Mines in Douala and the Chamber of Agriculture, Pasturage, and Forests in Yaoundé. The Cameroonian Union of Professional Syndicates acts as a coordinating agency of the 20-odd syndicates of merchants and producers. There are also the Professional Banking Association and the Confederation of Small- and Medium-Sized Enterprises. There is a Lion's Club at Yaoundé.

The government has encouraged the formation of cooperatives. The National Produce Marketing Office, created in 1978, has a monopoly on marketing cocoa, cotton, coffee, peanuts, and palm kernels. It is responsible for the prices paid the producers, the quality of produce, and the development of production.

There are many women's associations, cultural organizations, youth movements, and sporting associations.

[47]TOURISM, TRAVEL, AND RECREATION

All visitors to Cameroon must have valid passports, visas (available to tourists on arrival), onward tickets, and international health certificates showing yellow fever and cholera immunization.

Cameroon's chief tourist attractions are its forests, savanna, jungle, and wild game. The 16 national parks and game reserves are equipped with camps for tourists. The diverse ethnic groups and their cultures and Cameroonian art have also proved of interest to visitors. There are several good hotels in the major cities. In 1991, there were 7,397 hotel rooms with 10,639 beds. There were 70,672 foreign tourist arrivals, 57% from Europe and 30% from Africa. Tourist payments totaled US$15 million.

[48]FAMOUS CAMEROONIANS

Ahmadou Ahidjo (b.1924) was president of Cameroon from 1960 until 1982. Paul Biya (b.1933) became president in 1982 after having served as prime minister since 1975. William-Aurélien Eteki Mboumoua (b.1933) was OAU secretary-general during 1974–78 and foreign minister of Cameroon during 1984–87. The best-known literary figures are the novelists Ferdinand Oyono (b.1928) and Mongo Beti (b.1932).

[49]DEPENDENCIES

Cameroon has no territories or colonies.

[50]BIBLIOGRAPHY

Bjornson, Richard. *The African Quest for Freedom and Identity: Cameroonian Writing and the National Experience.* Bloomington: Indiana University Press, 1991.

Burnham, Philip. *Opportunity and Constraint in a Savanna Society: The Gbaya of Meganga Cameroon.* New York: Academic Press, 1981.

Clignet, Remi. *The Africanization of the Labor Market: Educational and Occupational Segmentations in the Cameroons.* Berkeley: University of California Press, 1976.

DeLancey, Mark. *Cameroon.* Oxford: Clio, 1986.

———. *Cameroon: Dependence and Independence.* Boulder, Colo.: Westview Press; London: Dartmouth, 1989.

———. *Historical Dictionary of the Republic of Cameroon,* 2nd ed. Metuchen, N.J.: Scarecrow Press, 1990.

Eyongetah Mbuagbaw, Tambi. *A History of the Cameroon Brain, Robin Palmer,* 2nd ed. Burnt Mill, Harlow, Essex, England: Longman, 1987.

Introduction to the History of Cameroon: Nineteenth and Twentieth Centuries. New York: St. Martin's Press, 1989.

Johnson, Willard R. *The Cameroon Federation.* Princeton, N.J.: Princeton University Press, 1970.

Joseph, Richard A. *Radical Nationalism in Cameroun: Social Origins of the UPC Rebellion.* New York: Oxford University Press, 1977.

Le Vine, Victor T. *The Cameroon Federal Republic.* 2d ed. Ithaca, N.Y.: Cornell University Press, 1971.

———. *The Cameroons: From Mandate to Independence.* Westport, Conn.: Greenwood, 1977.

Rudin, Harry Rudolph. *Germans in the Camerouns, 1884–1914: A Case Study in Modern Imperialism.* Westport, Conn.: Greenwood, 1969.

Schatzberg, Michael G., and William I. Zartman (eds.). *The Political Economy of Cameroon.* New York: Praeger, 1985.

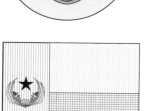

CAPE VERDE

Republic of Cape Verde
República de Cabo Verde

CAPITAL: Praia.

FLAG: The flag consists of two equal horizontal stripes, yellow over green, with a red vertical stripe at the hoist; on the red stripe is an emblem consisting of a black star above a yellow clam shell framed by two ears of corn, each having brown and light green husks and green leaves outlined in yellow.

ANTHEM: *É Patria Amada (This Is Our Beloved Country).*

MONETARY UNIT: The Cape Verde escudo (CVE) is a paper currency of 100 centavos. There are coins of 20 and 50 centavos and 1, 2 ½, 10, 20, and 50 Cape Verde escudos, and notes of 100, 500, and 1,000 Cape Verde escudos. CVE 1 = $0.0118 (or $1 = CVE 84.415).

WEIGHTS AND MEASURES: The metric system is used.

HOLIDAYS: New Year's Day, 1 January; National Heroes' Day, 20 January; Women's Day, 8 March; Labor Day, 1 May; Children's Day, 1 June; Independence Day, 5 July; Assumption, 15 August; Day of the Nation, 12 September; All Saints' Day, 1 November; Immaculate Conception, 8 December; Christmas Day, 25 December.

TIME: 10 AM = noon GMT.

¹LOCATION, SIZE, AND EXTENT

Cape Verde, containing an area of 4,030 sq km (1,555 sq mi), is situated in the Atlantic Ocean about 595 km (370 mi) west of Dakar, Senegal. Comparatively, the area occupied by Cape Verde is slightly larger than the state of Rhode Island. Extending 332 km (206 mi) SE–NW and 299 km (186 mi) NE–SW, it consists of 10 islands and 5 islets, divided into a northern windward group (Barlavento)—Santo Antão, São Vicente, Santa Luzia (uninhabited), São Nicolau, Sal, Boa Vista, and two islets—and a southern leeward group (Sotavento)—Brava, Fogo, São Tiago, Maio, and three islets. The total coastline is 965 km (600 mi).

Cape Verde's capital city, Praia, is located on the southeastern coast of São Tiago Island.

²TOPOGRAPHY

The island chain is of volcanic orgin. Fogo has the only active volcano, Pico do Cano, which reaches 2,829 m (9,281 ft) above sea level. Peaks on Santo Antão and São Tiago reach 1,979 m (6,493 ft) and 1,392 m (4,567 ft), respectively. All but three of the islands are quite mountainous, with prominent cliffs and deep ravines. High ground and southwestern slopes support lush vegetation because of moisture condensation. Only four islands have year-round running streams. Mindelo on São Vicente is the principal port, but there are several other fine harbors.

³CLIMATE

A cold Atlantic current produces an arid atmosphere around the archipelago. There are two seasons: December–June is cool and dry, with temperatures at sea level averaging 21°C (70°F); July–November is warmer, with temperatures averaging 27°C (81°F). Although some rain comes during the latter season, rainfall is sparse overall. Accumulations are generally around 13 cm (5 in) annually in the northern islands and 30 cm (12 in) in the south. The archipelago is subject to cyclical droughts; a devastating drought began in 1968 and was broken only briefly in 1975, 1978, 1984, and 1986.

⁴FLORA AND FAUNA

There are trees typical of both temperate and tropical climates, depending on elevation. The only native mammal is the long-eared bat.

⁵ENVIRONMENT

Much of the land used for raising crops or livestock is too arid or steep for these purposes, resulting in soil erosion. Drought contributes to Cape Verde's land problems along with cyclones, volcanic activity, and insect infestation. The intense demand for wood as fuel has led to the virtual elimination of native vegetation. By 1978, nearly all indigenous plants in farmed areas and within a half-day's walk of small villages had been removed. The land and water supply is adversely affected by insecticides, pesticides, and fertilization. In 1994, 13% of Cape Verde's urban dwellers and 35% of its rural areas do not have safe water. A resource still almost untapped is an estimated 80–90 million cu m of underground water, but the investment required to exploit it would be very large in relation to Cape Verde's resources.

As of 1994, endangered species in Cape Verde included the Mediterranean monk seal, the northern bald ibis, the green sea turtle, and the hawksbill turtle. In a total of 103 bird species, three are endangered. One type of reptile and 14 plant species of 659 total species are currently considered threatened.

⁶POPULATION

The population of Cape Verde was 341,491 in 1990, as compared with a 1980 census population of 296,063. It was estimated at 423,372 in 1994. A total of 479,000 was projected for the year 2000, based on a crude birthrate of 32.4 per 1,000 population, a crude death rate of 5.6, and a net natural increase of 26.8 during 1995–2000. The annual population growth rate for 1990–95 was 2.9%. The average population density was 85 per sq km (219 per sq mi) in 1990. More than half of the population lives on the island of São Tiago. (In 1990, Praia, the capital city, on São Tiago, was the largest town, with a population of about

62,000. Mindelo, on São Vicente, was second in population.) Some 68% of the population lived in rural areas in 1994.

[7]MIGRATION

Economic development has not kept pace with rapid population growth. This factor, in combination with the prolonged drought, has produced a sizable outflow of emigrants. By the early 1990s there were some 600,000 Cape Verdean emigrants in the US, Europe, Latin America, and other African countries. Some 325,000 were in the US alone—mostly in New England. Remittances to Cape Verde from emigrants enabled many of those who remained in the islands to survive the drought.

[8]ETHNIC GROUPS

About 70% of the inhabitants of Cape Verde are descendants of Portuguese colonists and their African slaves, who came, most often, from what is today Guinea-Bissau. Another 28% of the inhabitants are entirely African. There is a small minority (1–2%) of Europeans on the islands.

[9]LANGUAGES

Portuguese is the official language, but Crioulo, an archaic Portuguese dialect with a pronunciation that reveals African influences, is the spoken language of Cape Verde.

[10]RELIGIONS

Up to 97% of the population of Cape Verde is at least nominally Roman Catholic. Protestant churches, particularly the Church of the Nazarene, account for another 3%. Several African traditional religions are practiced, especially on São Tiago.

[11]TRANSPORTATION:

There are about 2,250 km (1,400 mi) of all types of roadway on the islands, of which some 600 km (370 mi) are paved. About 15,000 motor vehicles were in use in 1991. Commercial transportation is largely by coastal craft and domestic airlines. The ports of Mindelo on São Vicente and Porto Novo on Santo Antão are important as international fueling stops. In 1986 (the latest year available), the ports handled 394,000 tons of freight. The state-owned Companhia Nacional de Navigacão runs an interisland ferry service. As of the beginning of 1992, the merchant fleet of Cape Verde consisted of 7 ships with a capacity of 12,000 GRT. In November 1990, the IBRD announced the complete rehabilitation of two deepwater berths at Praia Port, which can now provide modern cargo handling techniques.

In 1975, the international airport on Sal was renamed the Amilcar Cabral International Airport, in honor of the former nationalist leader of the African Party for the Independence of Guinea-Bissau and Cape Verde. It is an important refueling point on many African flights; in 1991, there were some 7,600 aircraft take-offs and landings at that airport. There are smaller airports on seven islands. The national airline is Air Transport of Cape Verde, which began service to Lisbon in 1985 and Boston in 1987. In 1991, it carried about 96,000 passengers.

[12]HISTORY

Cape Verde was probably discovered in 1456 by Luigi da Cadamosto, who at that time was in service to Prince Henry the Navigator of Portugal (Henrique o Navegador); the islands showed no signs of any previous human settlement. São Tiago was the first island to receive settlers, in 1462. Plantation agriculture was established by the Portuguese community and worked by African slaves, who were brought in from the adjacent Guinea coast. There was a population of free Africans on the island of São Tiago from an early period, and that island retains the strongest cultural ties with the African mainland.

The islands produced trade goods; especially important were cattle, cotton cloths (pagnes) made by slave women, and alcoholic beverages. These goods were used to purchase slaves and consumer items from slavers seeking trade goods marketable in the African interior. The economy of the islands suffered from colonial restrictions on the production of potentially competitive export commodities, as well as from cyclical drought. Between 1747 and 1960, an estimated 250,000 Cape Verdeans died of famine.

The phaseout of the Atlantic slave trade and the abolition of slavery in the Portuguese Empire, coupled with an 1886 law providing for the settlement of former Cape Verde slaves on open lands, brought the end of Cape Verde's importance as a slave-trading center. The islands' historical role as a port of call became important again in the mid-twentieth century, when they were used by Portuguese troops as a staging area for their African campaigns. Portuguese control of the islands was strong enough to keep the African Party for the Independence of Guinea-Bissau and Cape Verde (Partido Africano da Independência da Guiné e Cabo Verde—PAIGC) in exile until 1974.

The military coup in Portugal in April 1974 brought a change in Portugal's African policy, however, and an independence agreement was signed between Portuguese and PAIGC representatives on 30 December 1974, leading to the establishment of the independent Republic of Cape Verde on 5 July 1975.

Cape Verde and Guinea-Bissau—where Luis de Almeida Cabral, a Cape Verdean, was president—were supposed to work toward unification, but a military coup in Guinea-Bissau toppled Cabral in November 1980. The Cape Verde wing of PAIGC subsequently broke its links with the mainland and temporarily abandoned the goal of unification. Diplomatic relations with Guinea-Bissau, severed at the time of the coup, were resumed in June 1982.

After 15 years of single-party rule by the African Party for the Independence of Cape Verde (PAICV), in 1990 people agitated to legalize opposition groups. A hastily assembled antigovernment coalition, the Movement for Democracy (MPD), won the 13 January 1991 parliamentary elections with 68% of the votes and 56 out of 79 seats in the National Assembly. In February, an independent candidate, Antonio Mascarenhas Monteaio, defeated Aristides Pereira, the incumbent, for the presidency with 72.6% of the vote. The governmental transition went smoothly and without violence. President Mascarenhas cooperates with the prime minister, Dr. Carlos Wahnon de Carvalho Veiga, and the MPD.

[13]GOVERNMENT

According to the 1980 constitution, the nation's first, the Republic of Cape Verde was a one-party state, under the guidance of the PAIGC; this party was replaced by the African Party for the Independence of Cape Verde (Partido Africano da Independencia do Cabo Verde—PAICV) in January 1981, after the coup in Guinea-Bissau. The president of the republic, Aristides Maria Pereira, secretary-general of the PAICV, was elected to his national office by the People's Assembly, the national legislative body. He was elected to a second five-year term in January 1986. He was replaced in a popular election on 17 February 1991, by President Mascarenhas. The prime minister, who heads the executive branch, was also elected by the Assembly, after being nominated by the president. The 83-member People's Assembly, which included the president and prime minister, was elected by direct universal suffrage for a five-year term. It seldom met and appeared to have little effective power.

The constitution, however, was amended on 28 September 1990 to legalize opposition parties and revised again in 1992. The People's Assembly now has 79 members and the president is elected directly by popular vote. It guarantees human rights and includes the principle of the separation of powers, a market-based economy, and individual rights and liberties.

14POLITICAL PARTIES

The African Party for the Independence of Cape Verde (Partido Africano da Independência do Cabo Verde—PAICV) was the sole legal political party from 1975 until 1990. On 28 September 1990, the constitution was amended to legalize opposition parties. In the 13 January 1991 parliamentary elections, the PAICV was defeated by the Movement for Democracy (MPD), which garnered 68% of the vote. PAICV is now the opposition in the National Assembly with 23 of the 79 seats.

In 1993 and 1994, divisions within the MPD led to the resignation of key members and the emergence of a new party.

15LOCAL GOVERNMENT

The islands are divided into 14 districts (conçelhos) and 31 freguesias, which are subdivisions of conçelhos. The islands of São Nicolau, Sal, Boa Vista, Maio, Brava, São Vicente, and Fogo each constitute a single conçelho. São Tiago is divided into 4 conçelhos: Praia, Tarrafal, Santa Cruz, and Santa Catarina. Santo Antão is divided into 3 conçelhos: Ribeira Grande, Porto Novo, and Paúl.

16JUDICIAL SYSTEM

In the preindependence period, Cape Verde was subject to the Portuguese civil and criminal codes. Most provisions of these codes remain in effect. A Supreme Tribunal of Justice hears appeals. from subregional and regional tribunals. Informal "popular tribunals" serve as courts of the first instance for minor disputes.

17ARMED FORCES

The Popular Revolutionary Armed Forces numbered 1,300 in 1993. Of these, 1,000 were in a two-battalion people's militia with Russian arms. The navy, which numbered 200, had five Russian patrol boats. The air force, which numbered perhaps 100, had two Russian-built transports. The budget is estimated at $71 million (1991).

18INTERNATIONAL COOPERATION

On 16 September 1975, the Republic of Cape Verde was admitted to the UN. It belongs to the ECA and all the nonregional specialized agencies except IAEA, IFC, and WIPO. It is also a member of the African Development Bank, ECOWAS, G-77, and the OAU. Cape Verde is a de facto adherent to GATT and a signatory to the Law of the Sea.

19ECONOMY

Agriculture, forestry, and fishing are the leading economic activities of the people of Cape Verde. Maize, beans, cassava, and sweet potatoes are the staple crops, produced on small, low-technology farms for domestic consumption. Some secondary crops, such as vegetables, sugarcane, and fruit are also produced; bananas are exported. Cape Verde is drought-prone, and less than 10% of food requirements are met by local producers. Cape Verdean fishing has potential and provided 53.8% of export earnings in 1992.

Mining is insignificant, with deposits of pozzolana, used in cement manufacturing, and salt constituting the principal resources. Remittances from Cape Verdeans living abroad accounted for 11% of GDP in 1988.

Perhaps Cape Verde's most important asset is its strategic economic location. It is an important refueling location for international air (Amilcar Cabral International Airport) and ocean traffic (at the port of Porto Grande, at Mindelo on São Vicente island). A 1993 World Bank-sponsored project was designed to upgrade the port facilities at Porto Grande.

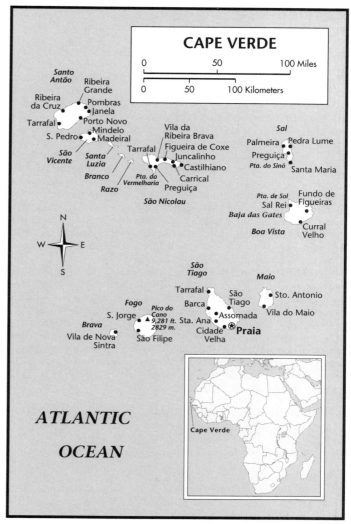

LOCATION: 14°48′ to 17°12′N; 22°40′ to 25°22′W.
TERRITORIAL SEA LIMIT: 12 mi.

20INCOME

In 1992 Cape Verde's GNP was $330 million at current prices, or $850 per capita. For the period 1985–92 the average inflation rate was 8.6%, resulting in a real growth rate in per capita GNP of 1.8%.

In 1992 the GDP was $351 million in current US dollars. It is estimated that hunting, forestry, and fishing contributed 20% to GDP; mining and quarrying, 1%; manufacturing, 5%; electricity, gas, and water, 1%; construction, 11%; wholesale and retail trade, 25%; transport, storage, and communication, 13%; finance, insurance, real estate, and business services, 9%; community, social, and personal services, 1%; and other sources 14%.

21LABOR

In 1990, the economically active population numbered 120,565, of whom 25% were engaged in services and agriculture; under drought conditions, however, a large proportion of the agricultural labor force is unemployed. All workers are free to form and join unions of their choosing; in 1992 seven new trade unions were organized, including unions for professors, fishermen, and public administrators. One labor union, the National Union of Cape Verdean Workers, once functioned under the direction of the PAICV, but has continued as an independent movement.

22AGRICULTURE

The most widespread agricultural activity of the islands is gardening for domestic consumption. Garden crops include corn, cassava, sweet potatoes, and bananas. Only about 9.6% of the land area is suitable for crop production. Frequent droughts often exacerbate an ongoing water shortage. Agriculture employs about one-quarter of the active population and contributes 13% to GDP. Estimated 1992 production figures were coconuts, 10,000 tons; sugarcane, 18,000 tons; potatoes, 3,000 tons; bananas, 6,000 tons; dates, 2,000 tons; cassava, 2,000 tons; sweet potatoes, 3,000 tons; and corn, 6,000 tons. Only the islands of São Tiago, São Vicente, São Nicolau, and Santo Antão have conditions suitable for raising cash crops. Bananas, the only agricultural export, are grown on irrigated land. Sugarcane, another cash crop, is used on the islands to produce rum.

Agriculture has been the focus of development aid programs since the 1960s, but progress has been frustrated by drought, locusts, overgrazing, and archaic cultivation methods. From 85–90% of food needs are met by imports; agricultural imports had a value of $53.9 million in 1992.

The PAIGC nationalized a few large-scale irrigated agricultural operations and began a program of land reform and cooperative agriculture; sharecropping was abolished. During 1976–80, 7,200 rainwater dikes were built. Torrential rains in 1984 destroyed much of this work, but in 1986, 17,000 dikes and 25,000 stone retaining walls had been completed. There has been little land redistribution, despite a 1982 law distributing farms over 5 hectares (12.5 acres)—1 hectare (2.5 acres) if irrigated—among the tenants if the land is not directly farmed by the owners.

23ANIMAL HUSBANDRY

Periodic droughts have significantly lowered the capacity of the islands to pasture livestock. In 1992 there were an estimated 110,000 goats, 19,000 head of cattle, 6,000 sheep, 11,000 asses, 2,000 mules, 1,000 horses, and 86,000 pigs.

24FISHING

The cold Canary Current, running adjacent to the islands, is an ideal environment for many kinds of marketable fish, and the fishing and fish-processing industries in the islands offer the best potential for expansion. São Vicente and Brava each have processing plants, and a fish-freezing plant was opened at Mindelo in 1991. Maritime resources are underexploited; of the estimated 50,000 tons of fish, lobster, and other marine products available for harvest, only some 1,500 tons of marine products reach the market annually, either for domestic consumption or export.

25FORESTRY

Forests on the island have been cut down for fuel, and the drought damaged many wooded areas. Large-scale reforestation is under way as part of a program of water-resource development. In 1991 there were about 1,000 hectares (2,470 acres) of forest plantations. A total of 4.3 million trees were planted during 1978–83.

26MINING

To date, the geological potential of the islands remains largely unexplored. Pozzolana (a volcanic rock used in pulverized form in the manufacture of hydraulic cement) and salt are the only minerals exploited commercially. In 1991, about 4,000 tons of salt and 53,000 tons of pozzolana were quarried. Sal and Boa Vista have sea-salt refineries, but production has decreased since 1985. Important new limestone deposits were found in 1982.

27ENERGY AND POWER

In 1991, the islands produced about 7 million kwh of electricity, entirely from thermal sources. Installed capacity totaled about 36,000 kw during the same year. Electra, the public electricity utility, maintains thermal power plants on Praia, Mindelo, and Sal; local councils operate 12 rural power plants. Ten wind generators of 30 kw each were in operation on Mindelo in 1991. Petroleum products were imported.

28INDUSTRY

The manufacturing sector contributes about 5% of GDP and employs about 1,700 Cape Verdeans. Besides the salt refining, Cape Verdean manufactures include frozen and canned fish, tobacco, bread and biscuits, soft drinks, and clothing. Rum is produced from locally grown sugarcane. Germany has sponsored the expansion of a butane gas factory.

29SCIENCE AND TECHNOLOGY

No information is available.

30DOMESTIC TRADE

Government policy is to base domestic trade on cooperative marketing of produce and foodstuffs. Most consumer goods are imported and sold or distributed in the major centers of Praia and Mindelo by EMPA, a state wholesale-retail company that controls the prices of many basic consumer goods. Business hours are 8 AM–12 noon and 2–6 PM, Monday through Friday, and 8 AM–12 noon on Saturday.

31FOREIGN TRADE

Cape Verde has been increasingly dependent upon imports, especially foodstuffs and manufactured goods, a situation which has led to a severe trade imbalance. Chronic drought has exacerbated the problem.

Exports in 1989 totaled $28,107,000. The principal exports were fish ($5,995,000), bananas ($1,726,000), petroleum and petroleum products ($16,822,000), basic manufactures ($632,000), and machinery and transport equipment ($2,427,000). Imports in 1989 totaled $111,937,000, of which food and live animals accounted for 25.2%. Of Cape Verde's imports, 30.7% came from Portugal, while Cape Verde's exports went primarily to Algeria (12.8%) and to Portugal (6.3%).

32BALANCE OF PAYMENTS

Cape Verde's massive annual trade deficit is only partially offset by remittances from Cape Verdeans employed abroad. In 1991, total remittances from abroad were approximately $57.4 million. Thus, annual payment deficits are substantial and can be met only through foreign assistance.

In 1992 merchandise exports totaled $4.43 million and imports $173.29 million. The merchandise trade balance was $–168.86 million. The following table summarizes Cape Verde's balance of payments for 1991 and 1992 (in millions of US dollars):

	1991	1992
CURRENT ACCOUNT		
Goods, services, and income	–96.97	–140.82
Unrequited transfers	89.04	137.27
TOTALS	–7.93	–3.55
CAPITAL ACCOUNT		
Direct investment	1.20	–0.75
Other Long-term capital	0.20	6.14
Other short-term capital	1.27	0.68
Exceptional financing	0.68	5.29
Reserves	11.87	–13.30
TOTALS	15.21	–1.94
Errors and omissions	–7.28	5.49
Total change in reserves	11.87	–10.66

33 BANKING AND SECURITIES

The Bank of Cape Verde is the central bank and also acts as a commercial bank. The main savings institution is the National Solidarity Fund. Other official banking institutions are the National Development Fund and the Cape Verde Institute, which handles foreign aid. There are no securities exchanges.

34 INSURANCE

In 1986, there was one insurance company in Cape Verde, and all insurance in force was non-life.

35 PUBLIC FINANCE

Before 1988, prudent management of public finances decreased the reliance on monetary borrowing or creation. The social sectors accounted for about 30% of the government's budgeted expenditures in 1992.

36 TAXATION

Recent information is unavailable.

37 CUSTOMS AND DUTIES

Cape Verde is a de facto adherent to GATT. Import licenses are required for goods above the value of CVE 100,000, and imports of nonessential goods are restricted. At the end of 1992, the value of imports entering Cape Verde was 24 times the value of goods exported. Sweden and Portugal were the major suppliers of non-food imports. A government decree has mandated establishment of a free trade zone, in which raw, semi-finished, and finished materials will be able to be imported without payment of customs duties.

38 FOREIGN INVESTMENT

Prior to 5 July 1975, Portuguese corporations were the principal investors in the islands. On that date, foreign corporate landholdings were nationalized by the government. In the mid-1980s there was no specific foreign investment code, but government policy was to encourage some Cape Verdean participation in foreign-owned enterprises. The shipbuilding and repair yard at Mindelo was jointly owned by the government and Portuguese investors, the fish-freezing plant there was jointly owned by the government and Dutch investors, and the clothing factory there was jointly owned by the government and 107 Cape Verdean nationals living abroad. Brazil signed an agreement in 1986 which would link Brazil more directly to West African and European markets.

Partial privatization of the parastatal sector is now government policy. In 1994, foreign banks were allowed to open branches in Cape Verde.

39 ECONOMIC DEVELOPMENT

The development plan adopted in 1992 seeks to transform Cape Verde into an open-market style economy. The development priorities include the promotion of the service-sector industries such as tourism, fishing, maritime services, and transhipping. A free-trade port is projected, and legislation permitting, the development of offshore banking is planned.

40 SOCIAL DEVELOPMENT

Social welfare services are being expanded by the government with UN assistance. The constitution bans sex discrimination, although social discrimination and violence against women have been reported. The Organization of Cape Verdean Women was founded in 1980 with party encouragement.

41 HEALTH

Malnutrition (exacerbated by the prolonged drought), influenza, and malaria are the major health problems in Cape Verde. The Portuguese government carried out a program of smallpox, yellow fever, and tuberculosis prevention throughout the 1960s. In 1986, there were 2 hospitals and 60 dispensaries, and from 1985 to 1990 there were 1.4 hospital beds per 1,000 people. In 1988, there were 112 doctors, 9 pharmacists, and 205 nurses. From 1988 to 1992 there were .12 doctors per 1,000 inhabitants, with a nurse-to-doctor ratio of 5.1.

There were 13,800 births in 1992, and a birth rate of 35.5 per 1,000 people in 1993. Average life expectancy in 1992 was 68 years. The overall death rate in 1993 was 6.8 per 1,000, and the maternal mortality rate in 1988 was 686 per 100,000 live births. Infant mortality in 1992 was 44 per 1,000 live births. In 1990, there were 220 cases of tuberculosis per 100,000 inhabitants, and from 1991 to 1992, 82% of children had been vaccinated against measles.

42 HOUSING

Housing on the islands varies greatly, from the elegant, Mediterranean-style homes of Europeans and middle-class Cape Verdeans to the simple timber and mud-block houses of peasants. As of 1980, 95% of all housing units were one-floor dwellings. External walls were mostly of stone and clay (39.3%), stone and cement (31%), or all stone (18.4%). Water supply was delivered by pipes (7%), wells (9.9%), tanks and cisterns (7.1%), and other sources (75.9%). A bath or shower was found in 85% of all housing units, and 88.7% of dwellings used neither public nor private sewage systems.

43 EDUCATION

In the preindependence period, education in the country followed the Portuguese system. Education under the independent government has been patterned after the program of popular education carried out in the liberated areas of Guinea-Bissau. The program stresses universal literacy and primary skills, with advanced education geared toward agricultural and technical skills for production. In 1983, primary and intermediate schools had 55,751 students, and secondary and technical schools had 4,596 students. Primary education is compulsory and lasts for six years. This is followed by three years of general secondary education. In 1989 there were an estimated 367 primary schools with 2,028 teachers and 67,761 students. At the secondary level, there were 7,866 students. The literacy rate was estimated at 66.5% in 1990.

44 LIBRARIES AND MUSEUMS

Reliable information is unavailable.

45 MEDIA

The government-run newspaper, *Vozde Povo* (1991 circulation 5,000) is published weekly. A cultural quarterly, *Pretextos*, was published monthly as of 1991. There are two government radio stations broadcasting to an estimated 61,000 receivers in Portuguese and Crioulo and one television channel. In 1991, Cape Verde had 2,384 telephones.

46 ORGANIZATIONS

Cooperative organizations in agriculture, marketing, and labor have been formed. Mass organizations for youth and women are tightly controlled by the government.

47 TOURISM, TRAVEL, AND RECREATION

Tourism is a potentially important source of revenue for the picturesque islands and has increased steadily since the mid-1980s. The number of hotels and other accommodations has grown from 24 in 1985 to 40 in the early 1990s. Between 1986 and 1990, the annual number of tourist arrivals nearly doubled from 13,626 to 22,470. The ruins at Cidade Velha on São Tiago and the beaches at Baia das Gates on Boa Vista hold considerable tourist interest.

48FAMOUS CAPE VERDEANS

Aristides Maria Pereira (b.1923) was the cofounder, with Amilcar Cabral (1921–73), of the PAIGC. He became PAIGC secretary-general after Cabral's assassination. Pereira was the first president of the independent Republic of Cape Verde. Luis de Almeida Cabral (b.1931), a brother of Amilcar, became the first president of Guinea-Bissau; after being ousted, he went into exile in Cuba.

49DEPENDENCIES

The Republic of Cape Verde has no territories or colonies.

50BIBLIOGRAPHY

Carreira, António. *The People of the Cape Verde Islands: Exploitation and Emigration*. Hamden, Conn.: Shoe String, 1982.

Duncan, T. Bentley. *Atlantic Islands, Madeira, the Azores and Cape Verde in the 17th Century: Commerce and Navigation*. Chicago: University of Chicago Press, 1972.

Foy, Colm. *Cape Verde: Politics, Economics, and Society*. London; New York: Pinter Publishers, 1988.

Henderson, Faye. *Cape Verde, a Country Profile*. Washington, D.C.: Government Printing Office, 1979.

Lobban, Richard and Marilyn Halter. *Historical Dictionary of the Republic of Cape Verde*. 2nd ed. Metuchen, N.J.: Scarecrow Press, 1988.

Meintet, Deirdre. *Race, Culture, and Portuguese Colonialism in Cabo Verde*. Syracuse, N.Y.: Syracuse University Foreign and Comparative Studies Program, 1984.

Shaw, Caroline S. *Cape Verde*. Oxford, England; Santa Barbara, Calif.: Clio Press, 1991.

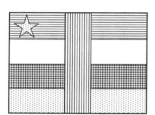

CENTRAL AFRICAN REPUBLIC

République Centrafricaine

CAPITAL: Bangui.

FLAG: The national flag consists of four horizontal stripes (blue, white, green, and yellow) divided at the center by a vertical red stripe. In the upper left corner is a yellow five-pointed star.

ANTHEM: *La Renaissance (Rebirth).*

MONETARY UNIT: The Communauté Financière Africaine franc (CFA Fr) is a paper currency. There are coins of 1, 2, 5, 10, 25, 50, 100, and 500 CFA francs, and notes of 50, 100, 500, 1,000, 5,000, and 10,000 CFA francs. CFA Fr1 = $0.0018 (or $1 = CFA Fr571).

WEIGHTS AND MEASURES: The metric system is the legal standard.

HOLIDAYS: New Year's Day, 1 January; Anniversary of President Boganda's Death, 29 March; Labor Day, 1 May; National Day of Prayer, 30 June; Independence Day, 13 August; Assumption, 15 August; All Saints' Day, 1 November; Proclamation of the Republic, 28 November; National Day, 1 December; and Christmas, 25 December. Movable religious holidays include Easter Monday, Ascension, Pentecost Monday.

TIME: 1 PM = noon GMT.

1 LOCATION, SIZE, AND EXTENT
Located in Central Africa, entirely within the tropical zone, the Central African Republic has an area of 622,980 sq km (240,535 sq mi), extending 1,437 km (893 mi) E–W and 772 km (480 mi) N–S. Comparatively, the area occupied by Central African Republic is slightly smaller than the state of Texas. Entirely landlocked, it is bordered on the N by Chad, on the E by Sudan, on the S by Zaire and the Congo, and on the W by Cameroon, with a total boundary length of 5,203 km (3,233 mi). The Oubangui and Mbomou rivers form much of the southern border; the eastern border coincides with the divide between the watersheds of the Nile and the Zaire rivers. The Central Afrian Republic capital city, Bangui, is located in the southwestern part of the country.

2 TOPOGRAPHY
The land consists of an undulating plateau varying in altitude from 610 to 760 m (2,000–2,500 ft). Two important escarpments are evident: in the northwest is a high granite plateau (rising to 1,420 m/4,659 ft), which is related to the Adamoua Plateau of Cameroon; in the northeast the Bongos Range rises to 1,368 m (4,488 ft) and extends into Sudan.

Soils are complex: sands and clays predominate, sometimes covered with a lateritic layer, over granite and quartz rocks. The land is well drained by two river systems: the Ubangi and its tributaries in the south, and the tributaries of the Chari and Logone rivers in the north.

3 CLIMATE
The climate is tropical, with abundant rainfall of about 180 cm (70 in) annually in the south, decreasing to about 80 cm (31.5 in) in the extreme northeast. There is one rainy season (April–November) and one long, hot, dry season. Floods are common. Temperatures at Bangui have an average daily minimum and maximum range from 21°C (70°F) to 32°F (90°F).

4 FLORA AND FAUNA
The tropical rain forest in the southwest contains luxuriant plant growth, with some trees reaching a height of 46 m (150 ft). Toward the north, the forest gradually becomes less dense, with wider patches of grassland, and eventually gives way to the rolling hills of the savanna, interrupted by taller growths along riverbeds. Almost every animal of the tropics is found, including the elephant; its ivory was once a major source of wealth but has declined in economic importance. The southwest has a colorful variety of butterflies.

5 ENVIRONMENT
The most significant environmental problems in the Central African Republic are desertification, water pollution, and the destruction of the nation's wildlife. The encroachment of the desert on the country's agricultural and forest lands is due to deforestation and soil erosion. The nation has 33.8 cubic miles of water, but 81% of all city dwellers do not have pure water. Only 26% of the rural population has pure water.

Due to mismanagement of the nation's wildlife, the Central African Republic reports major losses in its elephant population. In 1979, it was disclosed that three-quarters of what had been the nation's elephant population at independence (40,000–80,000) had been killed so that the tusks could be sold for ivory. As of 1994, it is estimated that 90% of the nation's elephant population has been eliminated over the last 30 years and 85% since 1982. Elephant hunting is now banned. Endangered species in the Central African Republic included the black rhinoceros and northern square-lipped rhinoceros. There are 12 national parks and wildlife reserves. As of 1994, in addition to the loss of the elephant population, 12 other species of mammals in a total of 208 were also threatened. Two types of birds in 668 total species were endangered along with two species of reptiles. Of the nation's 3,600 plant species, four were threatened with extinction.

6POPULATION

A census in 1988 reported the population as 2,539,051, and in 1994, the population was estimated at 3,187,466. A population of 3,862,000 was projected for the year 2000, assuming a crude birthrate of 42.1 per 1,000 population, a crude death rate of 18.4, and a net natural increase of 23.7 during 1995–2000. The average annual growth rate is about 2.6%. The estimated average density in 1994 was 5.1 persons per sq km (13.3 per sq mi), but large areas in the east are almost uninhabited. About half of the population is urban. Bangui, the capital and principal city, had an estimated population of 706,000 in 1990. Berbérati, had an estimated 82,492 people in 1988. Other cities, with 1988 population estimates, were Bouar (95,193) and Bambari (87,464). About 45% of the population is under 15 years of age.

7MIGRATION

Both internal and external migration is mainly seasonal. About 17,700 Sudanese and 1,200 Chadian war refugees were in the country at the end of 1992.

8ETHNIC GROUPS

The people belong to more than 80 ethnic groups, which are classified according to geographic location. The Banda (34%) in the east central region and the Baya (27%) to the west are estimated to be the most numerous groups. In the forest region are the Pygmies (Binga) and some Bantu groups (Mbaka, Lissongo, Mbinu). Along the rivers are the Sango, Yakoma, Banziri, and Buraka. In the savanna live the Mandjia, Mboum, Zande, Sara, Ndele, and Bizao, each of which has several subgroups. There were about 3,000 French civilians in 1993.

9LANGUAGES

Many languages and dialects are spoken, but Sango, the language of a group living on the Ubangi River, is spoken by a majority and is the national language. French is the official language of government and is taught in the schools.

10RELIGIONS

Much of the African population holds traditional religious beliefs. Christianity has spread slowly, and many Christian practices retain traditional overtones. Catholic and Protestant missions are scattered throughout the territory. Islam is followed primarily in the north. About 35% of the population is Protestant; 17.8% is Roman Catholic; 5% is Muslim; and 60% are nonexclusive adherents to traditional African beliefs.

11TRANSPORTATION

Transportation is limited to river, road, and air, with river transportation the most important for movement of freight. Some 1,200 km (750 mi) of the 7,080 km (4,400 mi) of inland waterways are navigable year-round, including the Ubangi River up to Bangui, and the Sangha to Nola, 100 km (62 mi) north of the Congo border. The important Ubangi River route leads to the Zaire River port of Brazzaville, Congo, where a rail line travels to the Atlantic port of Pointe-Noire. The Lobaye and several tributaries of the Chari and Logone rivers are partly navigable, but service is irregular during the dry season. Much river transport is in the hands of a company owned 51% by the state and 49% by foreign firms. The port of Kilongo (at Bangui) is the largest in the country. Both Kilongo and the port of Nola are being enlarged to accommodate steadily increasing maritime traffic.

In 1991, the country had 22,000 km (13,700 mi) of roads, of which only 2% were paved. A rehabilitation project, begun in 1974 and completed in 1984, centered on three highways running north, west, and south from Nola. Some 8,221 passenger cars and 8,541 commercial vehicles were in use in 1992. There are no railroads.

There is an international airport at Bangui-Mpoko and 22 secondary airfields and airstrips. Five airlines provide international transport. The Republic is a partner in Air Afrique, which carried some 66,300 passengers throughout Yaoundé Treaty countries in 1992. Inter-RCA, founded in 1980 and 52% state owned, provides domestic service.

12HISTORY

Before its colonial history, the area now known as the Central African Republic was settled by successive waves of peoples, mostly Bantu. Both European and Arab slave traders exploited the area in the 17th, 18th, and 19th centuries, and slave raids and intertribal wars were frequent until the French conquest. In the 19th century, the main population groups, the Baya and the Banda, arrived from the north and east, respectively, to flee the slave trade.

The French explored and conquered the country, chiefly from 1889, when an outpost was established at Bangui, to 1900, as part of a plan to link French colonies from the Atlantic to the Nile. The strongest and most sustained opposition to the French came from Sultan Senoussi, who was finally defeated in 1912. Isolated local revolts continued well into the 20th century, however. The strongest and bloodiest of these, known as the War of Kongo-Wara, lasted from 1928 to 1931.

The territory of Ubangi-Shari was formally established in 1894, and its borders fixed by treaties between the European colonial powers. The western border with the German Cameroons was fixed by a convention with Germany in 1884; a convention of 1887 with Belgium's King Leopold II delineated the southern border with the Independent State of the Congo; the eastern border with the Sudan was fixed by an 1899 convention. These boundaries were drawn with little knowledge of the human geography of the area, so that ethnic groups were sometimes separated into different territories. From 1906 to 1916, Ubangi-Shari and Chad were merged as a single territory. In 1910, Gabon, Middle Congo, and Ubangi-Shari (including Chad) were constituted administratively as separate colonies forming parts of a larger French Equatorial Africa. Ubangi-Shari's resources were exploited by French companies, and abuses of the forced labor system were common.

In 1940, the colony quickly rallied to the Free French standard raised at Brazzaville, Congo. After World War II, the territory elected Barthélémy Boganda as its first representative to the French Parliament in Paris. In a referendum on 28 September 1958, Ubangi-Shari voted to become an autonomous republic within the French community. The Central African Republic was proclaimed on 1 December 1958, with Boganda as president. On 30 April 1959, Minister of the Interior David Dacko was elected to succeed Boganda, who had died in a plane crash on 29 March. The country declared itself an independent republic on 13 August 1960, with Dacko as president. In 1961, the constitution was amended to establish a presidential government with a single-party system.

On 1 January 1966, a military coup d'etat led by Col. (later Field Marshal) Jean-Bédel Bokassa overthrew Dacko (who is Bokassa's cousin), abolished the constitution, and dissolved the National Assembly. Bokassa, who became president in 1968 and president for life in 1972, proclaimed himself emperor of the newly formed Central African Empire on 4 December 1976. A year later, on that date, he crowned himself emperor in a lavish ceremony at an estimated cost of $25 million—a quarter of the nation's annual export earnings.

On 20 September 1979, Dacko, with French support, led a bloodless coup that overthrew Bokassa while he was out of the country. The republic was restored, and Bokassa, who took refuge in Côte d'Ivoire and France, was sentenced to death in absentia for various crimes, including cannibalism. Moreover, an

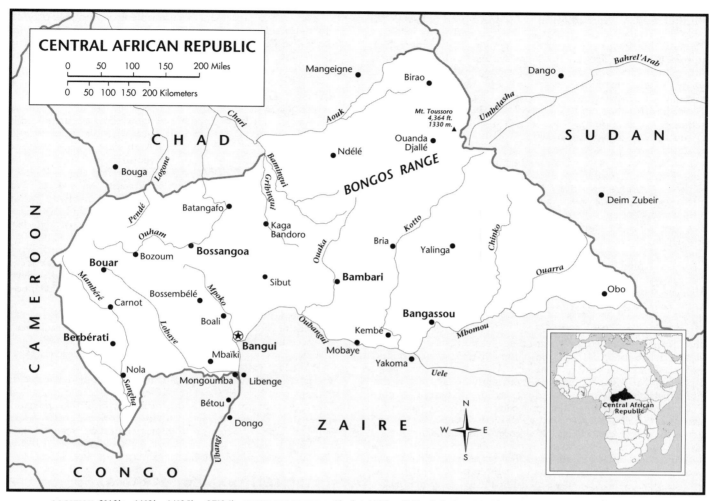

CENTRAL AFRICAN REPUBLIC

LOCATION: 2°13′ to 11°2′N; 14°25′ to 27°26′E. **BOUNDARY LENGTHS:** Chad, 1,199 km (745 mi); Sudan, 1,167 km (725 mi); Zaire, 1,577 km (980 mi); Congo, 467 km (290 mi); Cameroon, 822 km (511 mi).

African judicial commission reported that he had "almost certainly" taken part in the massacre of some 100 children for refusing to wear the compulsory school uniforms. In January 1981, six of his supporters, including two sons-in-law, were executed.

A new constitution allowing free political activity was approved by referendum in February 1981. A month later, Dacko was elected, polling a bare majority against four rivals. Violence followed the election, which the losers charged was fraudulent. Economic conditions failed to improve, and Dacko was overthrown on 1 September 1981 by a military coup led by army chief of staff Gen. André Kolingba. Kolingba became chairman of the ruling Military Committee for National Recovery, and the constitution and all political activities were suspended. The Kolingba regime survived an attempted coup in 1982 and an aborted return by Bokassa in 1983. On 21 November 1986, Kolingba was elected unopposed to a six-year term as president, and a new constitution was adopted establishing a one-party state. The new ruling party, the Central African Democratic Party (Rassemblement Démocratique Centrafricaine—RDC), nominated a list of 142 of its members, from which voters elected 52 to the new National Assembly on 31 July 1987.

Bokassa made an unexpected return in October 1986 and was retried. On 12 June 1987, he was convicted of having ordered the murders of at least 20 prisoners and the arrest of the schoolchildren who were murdered. He was sentenced to death, but this was commuted to a life term in February 1988. He was released

from prison on 1 September 1993, as a result of an amnesty.

In April 1991, under pressure from France, the IMF, and local critics, Kolingba agreed to legalize opposition parties, many of which had already formed a united front to press for further reforms. Elections were held on 25 October 1992, but widespread irregularities led to the Supreme Court dismissing the results for both the National Assembly and the presidency. Elections were rescheduled and on 19 September 1993, citizens elected Ange-Felix Patasse, head of the Movement for the Liberation of the Central African People (MLPC), president. A new National Assembly of 85 members was elected. Patasse's party won only 33 seats and Kolingba's RDC won 14 seats. Despite Kolingba's last-minute efforts to subvert the process and several incidents that marred the vote, an international observer delegation certified the validity of the outcome. The National Assembly convened on 8 November 1993 and elected Hugues Dodozendi of the MLPC as president of its Executive Bureau. The MLPC has six of the 11 seats in that Bureau.

The transition from military to elected government has gone smoothly, although the economy falters. The human rights picture has improved, yet the security forces still exercise arbitrary power and, in 1993, the military engaged in two brief mutinies.

13GOVERNMENT

The 1959 constitution was suspended after the January 1966 coup, and the National Assembly was dissolved. An imperial constitution issued in December 1976 lapsed with Bokassa's fall in 1979. A new constitution was promulgated on 6 February 1981 after 97.4% of the voters had approved it in a referendum. It provided for the election of a president and National Assembly by universal adult suffrage, and it allowed multiple parties. It was suspended after the military coup of 1 September 1981. All executive and legislative power was assumed by the ruling Military Committee for National Recovery (Comité Militaire pour le Redressement National), headed by Gen. André Kolingba. This committee was disbanded in 1985. A new constitution adopted by plebiscite on 21 November 1986 established a one-party state and a 52-member National Assembly; simultaneously, Kolingba was elected unopposed to a six-year term as president. The National Assembly provided a forum for debate, but it had little substantive impact on government policy.

In 1991, Kolingba was forced to legalize opposition parties and, after a 1992 election was invalidated by the Supreme Court, new elections were conducted successfully in September 1993. For the 1993 elections, the National Assembly was enlarged to 85 members. Kolingba was defeated. A new president, Ange-Felix Patasse, was installed and a graceful transition to multiparty democracy took place. The new coalition government is headed by the MLPC and includes members of three other parties.

14POLITICAL PARTIES

The Movement for Social Evolution of Black Africa (Mouvement d'Évolution Sociale de l'Afrique Noire—MESAN) was founded by Barthélémy Boganda in September 1949. Boganda, himself a deputy in Paris for some years, constantly fought for greater internal autonomy and an end to French administration.

Internal antagonism to Boganda came particularly from those who resented his electoral laws, which made it difficult to contest any seats with MESAN. In the election of 25 September 1960, MESAN received 80% of the votes, while the newly founded Movement for the Democratic Evolution of Central Africa (Mouvement d'Évolution Démocratique de l'Afrique Centrale—MEDAC) received 20%. MEDAC was dissolved by the government in February 1961. In December 1962, a constitutional amendment recognized MESAN as the sole party in the republic, but with the military coup d'état in January 1966 all political activity was banned. MESAN was revived in 1972 by Jean-Bédel Bokassa.

After Bokassa's fall, the single-party system was maintained, but the name of the party was changed to the Central African Democratic Union (Union Démocratique Centrafricaine—UDC) in 1980. The February 1981 constitution allowed other parties, and five competed in the presidential election of 15 March 1981. President David Dacko, the UDC candidate, received 50.2% of the vote. His chief opponent was Ange Patasse of the Movement for the Liberation of the Central African Republic (Mouvement pour la Libération du Peuple Centrafricain—MLPC), who received 38.1%. Following the military coup of 1 September 1981, all political activity was suspended. The MLPC was formally banned on 6 March 1982, after an unsuccessful coup that the government blamed on Patasse. Patasse subsequently fled to Togo.

The sole legal political party adopted by the Kolingba regime, the Central African Democratic Party (Rassemblement Démocratique Centrafricaine—RDC), held its founding assembly in February 1987. In 1987, three opposition parties in exile in Paris, including the MLPC, established a coalition called the United Front. In 1991, opposition parties were legalized and in October 1992, multiparty elections were held. The Supreme Court invalidated the results and on 19 September 1993, new elections led to Kolingba's defeat. His old nemesis, Patasse, became president and the MLPC gained 33 of the 85 seats in the National Assembly. The RDC won 14 seats.

Other parties in the government coalition include the Liberal Democratic Party, the Alliance for Democracy and Progress, and the David Dacko Movement (an informal grouping of supporters of the ex-president). In opposition, along with the RDC, are the Consultative Group of Democratic Forces (CFD), an alliance of 14 opposition groups; the Social Democratic Party; and the National Convention.

15LOCAL GOVERNMENT

The republic is divided into 16 prefectures, 47 subprefectures, and the autonomous commune of Bangui. Local elections held in mid-1988 created 176 municipal councils, each headed by a mayor.

16JUDICIAL SYSTEM

Justices of the peace in each prefecture hear cases in the first instance. There are several intermediate level civil courts including a criminal court and a court of appeal situated in Bangui. At the apex is a Supreme Court, also located in Bangui, the members of which are appointed by the President.

There are also provisions for a High Court of Justice, a body of nine judges created to try political cases against the President, members of Congress and government ministers, which has never convened. Administrative tribunals, several labor tribunals, and a military court also exist.

Detainees in nonpolitical cases must be brought before a magistrate within 96 hours of arrest. Because of inefficiency in judicial procedures, this deadline is not always respected.

17ARMED FORCES

The army, numbering about 3,500 in 1993, consisted of seven battalions and helicopters. The 300-man air force had 21 noncombatant aircraft and helicopters. Paramilitary gendarmerie numbered 2,700. France has a military base at Bouar, where about 1,200 men of a reinforced infantry battalion were stationed in 1993. The nation spent $19 million on defense in 1990 or 1.7% of gross domestic product.

18INTERNATIONAL COOPERATION

The Central African Republic was admitted to UN membership on 26 September 1960 and is a member of ECA and all the nonregional specialized agencies except IAEA, IFC, and IMO. In 1959, together with Chad, the Congo, and Gabon, it formed the Equatorial Customs Union (Union Douanière Equatoriale—UDE), a customs union in which merchandise, property, and capital circulated freely. The UDEAC, a subregional common market including the UDE nations and Cameroon, became operative in January 1966, superseding UDE. The country is also a member of the African Development Bank, G-77, OAU, and OCAM and is a signatory to GATT, the Lomé Convention, and the Law of the Sea treaty. OCAM headquarters are in Bangui.

19ECONOMY

The Central African Republic (CAR) has a basically agricultural economy supplemented by the export of diamonds. Coffee, cotton, and timber lead the list of agricultural exports. Economic growth, troubled before, stagnated between 1989 and 1991, severely affected by declining world prices for its exports. The country has also suffered as a result of its isolation from its major markets, deteriorating transportation infrastructure, and mismanagement of state funds and enterprises. To the extent that the devaluation of the CFA franc stimulates agriculture, the CAR should benefit.

In 1991, 41% of GDP came from the 70% of the population working in agriculture. Food crops—cassava, maize, millet, sorghum, groundnuts, and rice—are grown on low-technology farms for domestic consumption. Food production is believed to be only 80% of total consumption. Coffee is the CAR's principal export crop. As prices paid to producers were cut back in response to a fall in world prices, coffee production declined from a high of 20,200 tons in 1989 to 7,000 tons in 1992. Strong producer prices in the cotton sector led to an 82.3% jump in production between 1988 and 1991. Output declined 2.5% to 25,000 tons in 1992, however. Tobacco also contributes a small but consistent output to GDP.

Livestock production has grown in recent years as the northern limit of the tsetse fly zone retreats south and civil unrest continues in neighboring Chad and Sudan. The timber sector is a developing part of the CAR economy, though demand was discouraged by the high value of the CFA franc on international markets. Diamond output leads the mining sector.

20 INCOME

In 1992 Central African Republic's GNP was $1,307 million at current prices, or $410 per capita. For the period 1985–92 the average inflation rate was 1.3%, resulting in a real growth rate in per capita GNP of –2.4%.

In 1992 the GDP was $1,339 million in current US dollars. Agriculture, hunting, forestry, and fishing comprise 39.8% of the GDP, with the trade and transport sectors adding 23.7%. Mining's contribution to GDP is 3.5%, and manufacturing's is 9.5%.

In January 1994 France suddenly devalued the CFA franc, causing its value to drop in half overnight. Immediately, prices for almost all imported goods soared, including prices for food and essential drugs, like those to combat malaria. Since 1948 France had guaranteed a fixed parity of one French franc to 50 African francs. The resulting stability in the currency had generally kept inflation low and helped to maintain a steady rate of growth. However, in the 1980s, the economies of the CFA countries began to stagnate in relation to other African nations, and France came under increased pressure from the World Bank, the IMF, and western countries to stop subsidizing the CFA franc. The devaluation, long expected in the investment community, is designed to enourage new investment, particularly in the export sectors of the economy, and discourage the use of hard currency reserves to buy products that could be grow domestically.

21 LABOR

As of the 1988 census, the labor force was 1,186,972. About 70% were employed in agriculture. About 13,029 were private sector wage and salary workers in 1990.

The General Union of Central African Workers, the only central union since 1964, was dissolved in May 1981 by the Dacko regime, which formed the government-backed Confederation of Central African Workers. This body exists chiefly on paper, however, and has no collective-bargaining authority. In 1992, the government continued to inhibit labor activity by suspending four public service unions for four months. The government also briefly prevented the Labor Union of Central African Workers (USTC) from functioning in August 1992.

The 40-hour week has been established for nonagricultural workers, and the 42-hour week for agricultural and related workers. Labor tribunals with equal representation for workers and employers settle individual disputes, and advisory labor commissions intervene in the settlement of collective disputes. Labor offices provide free employment services.

22 AGRICULTURE

Agricultural output is dominated by subsistence crops. Agriculture (including forestry and fisheries) accounted for about 40% of GDP in 1992, and it employs about 70% of the labor force. In 1991, it was estimated that about 2,006,000 hectares (4,957,000 acres, or 3.2% of the total land area) were arable or under permanent crops, and 3,000,000 hectares (7,400,000 acres, or 4.8% of total land area) were in permanent pasture. The CAR is nearly self-sufficient in food production and has potential as an exporter.

Manioc, the basic food crop, is raised on about 200,000 hectares (494,200 acres); output was about 606,000 tons in 1992. Bananas are the second major food crop. Production was 94,000 tons in 1992, while plantain production was 68,000 tons. Other food crops in 1992 included 50,000 tons of corn, 6,000 tons of millet, and 10,000 tons of sorghum. Some tropical fruits are produced in small quantities, including 16,000 tons of oranges in 1992. An oil-palm plantation covering 2,500 hectares (6,200 acres) opened in 1986 at Bossongo, 35 km (22 mi) sw of Bangui. In 1992, production of palm oil totaled 2,000 tons.

The first commercial cotton production in French Equatorial Africa began in Ubangi-Shari in 1924. Cotton is grown in the Bamingui and Gribingui river valleys. In 1969–70, 58,000 tons of seed cotton were produced, a national high, but production quickly slumped: In 1992, it totaled 30,000 tons.

Another important cash crop is high-quality coffee, which is cultivated on the plateaus along with sisal and tobacco; coffee production was 14,000 tons in 1992; coffee exports were valued at $5 million that year, or 4.4% of total exports.

Production of peanuts, which are cultivated in conjunction with cotton, was an estimated 43,000 tons in 1992.

23 ANIMAL HUSBANDRY

Although most of the Republic is in the tsetse fly belt, some animal husbandry is carried on. In 1992 there were an estimated 2,700,000 head of cattle, 1,300,000 goats, 460,000 pigs, and 137,000 sheep. About 48,000 tons of beef were produced in 1992. Cow's milk production was around 48,000 tons the same year. There were an estimated 3,000,000 chickens in 1992, when some 1,341 tons of eggs were produced.

24 FISHING

Fishing is carried on extensively along the rivers, but most of the catch is sold or bartered on the Zaire side of the Ubangi. In 1950, the government began a fish-farming program, and by the end of 1968 there were almost 12,000 ponds. The 1991 fish catch was about 13,500 tons.

25 FORESTRY

There are 35.7 million hectares (88.2 million acres) of forest and savanna woodland (57.3% of the total land area), but only 3.4 million hectares (8.4 million acres) of dense forest, all in the south in the regions bordering Zaire. The CAR's exploitable forests cover 27 million hectares (68 million acres), or 43% of the total land area. Transportation bottlenecks on rivers and lack of rail connections are serious hindrances to commercial exploitation. Most timber is shipped down the Ubangi and Zaire rivers and then on the Congo railway to the Atlantic. More than a dozen types of trees are felled, but 95% of the total is composed of obeche, sapele, ebony, and sipo.

A dozen sawmills produced 2,290,000 m³ of sawn logs and veneer logs in 1991. The government is encouraging production of plywood and veneer. Roundwood removals were estimated at 3,444,000 m³ in 1991. Competition from lower-cost Asian and Latin American loggers has hurt the local industry, which is encumbered with high transportation and labor costs. In 1992, the country exported $15,104,000 of forest products, which accounted for 11.6% of total exports.

26 MINING

Small amounts of gold are produced, and uranium deposits have been located. Diamonds were discovered in alluvial deposits in various parts of the country in 1935 and in 1947. Production reached 609,360 carats in 1968. In 1991, controlled production was only 378,643 carats (78% of gem quality), but diamonds still accounted for 46% of exports. Sizable quantities are smuggled out of the country. About 60% of the nation's diamonds come from the upper Sangha region. Gold production, which began in 1930 and peaked at 521 kg in 1980, fell to only 26 kg in 1982 but rebounded to 176 kg in 1991. Diamonds and gold are still mined in alluvial deposits by individual prospectors.

Uranium was discovered in 1966 in the Bakouma region in the eastern part of the country, and there was further prospecting in the Berbérati and Bangassou areas. Exploitation, however, has not occurred, due to high start-up costs and poor transportation. Reserves are estimated at some 18,000 tons. Iron deposits estimated at 3,500,000 tons have been exploited, but production has ceased. The country also has deposits of nickel, manganese, cobalt, tin, copper, china clay, and limestone.

27ENERGY AND POWER

Wood supplies 80% of the country's energy needs. Electric power production was 96 million kwh in 1991. Bangui is supplied by two hydroelectric generators and one thermal plant. A new dam on the Mbali (a joint project with Zaire), which permits year-round hydroelectric generation, opened in late 1991. Installed capacity was 43,000 kw (51% hydroelectric) in 1991.

Exxon drilled an exploratory oil well in 1985, but futther work was deemed economically infeasible. Any oil production would depend on the connection of a pipeline from Chad to Douala, Cameroon. In 1989, the Central African Republic imported 80,620 barrels of distillate fuel oil, 64,767 barrels of kerosene and jet fuel, and 46,903 barrels of gasoline.

28INDUSTRY

Industry contributed 16% of GDP in 1990. Textile and leather manufacturing are the leading industries. The largest single factory is a joint-venture textile complex (51% French owned) in Bangui, which handles spinning, weaving, dyeing, and the manufacture of blankets. All cotton produced in the country is ginned locally, with cotton-ginning plants scattered throughout the cotton-producing regions Refined sugar and palm oil also are produced, as are soap and cigarettes. Beer production was 299,000 hectoliters in 1987, and bottled-water and soft-drink production was 68,000 hectoliters. Vehicle assembly operations were suspended in 1986.

Electricity production depends heavily on imported petroleum. Power from the Boali and M'Bali hydroelectric stations is to be supplemented by the Kembe station. Output in 1990 was 95 million kwh.

29SCIENCE AND TECHNOLOGY

Among the research institutes in the Central African Republic are a study center on animal sleeping sickness in Bouar, and an agricultural institute in Mbaïki. The National Institute of Textile Research and Food Crops is in Bambari. The Pasteur Institute in Bangui conducts research on diseases. French institutes include the Institute of Scientific Research for Development and Cooperation, at Bangui, and the experimental station of Maboké, in Mbaïki, under the direction of the National Museum of Natural History in Paris. The University of Bangui has faculties of science and technology, health science, a polytechnic institute, and a research institute for mathematics teaching. The Central School of Agriculture is located in Boukoko, and the Territorial School of Agriculture is in Grimari. Research and development expenditures in 1984 totaled 681 million CFA francs; in that year, 383 technicians and 196 scientists and engineers were engaged in research and development.

30DOMESTIC TRADE

Most local produce and imports are sold at markets in towns and villages. Company agents and independent middlemen buy export crops at local markets or directly from the producers for sale to large companies. Many trading businesses are French owned or operated. The government fosters the distribution of agricultural products through a monopolistic state trading company. Oil distribution is also a monopoly, owned by the government (60%) and foreign interests (40%).

A chamber of commerce at Bangui promotes trade and provides information to business firms. Advertising is found in local newspapers, company publications, and handbills and on billboards and radio. Normal business hours are from 7 AM to noon and 2:30 to 6:30 PM, Monday through Friday. Saturday hours are from 7 AM to noon.

31FOREIGN TRADE

Coffee, diamonds, timber, and cotton products represent almost all of the Republic's total exports, and machinery and transport equipment are the leading imports. Imports in 1991 were valued at US$4,853,000. Since 1981, imports have exceeded exports. The following table shows the estimated value of country's major exports for 1990 (millions of CFA francs):

Coffee	2,7304
Diamonds	15,970
Timber	3,348
Cotton	3,837
TOTAL	50,459

32BALANCE OF PAYMENTS

The Central African Republic's frequent deficits in trade and services are financed mainly through international aid. In the early 1980s, the Republic faced a severe balance-of-payments problem caused by low world prices for its exports and high fuel import costs. A structural adjustment program was begun in 1986 (and further developed in 1988 and 1990) to curb the public sector and to promote private-sector investment in an effort to decrease the reliance on infusions of foreign aid.

In 1992 merchandise exports totaled $123.5 million and imports $165.1 million. The merchandise trade balance was $−41.6 million. The following table summarizes the Central African Republic's balance of payments for 1991 and 1992 (in millions of US dollars):

	1991	1992
CURRENT ACCOUNT		
Goods, services, and income	−152.7	−150.7
Unrequited transfers	90.9	93.3
TOTALS	−61.8	−57.4
CAPITAL ACCOUNT		
Direct investment	−8.4	−8.7
Other long-term capital	52.1	61.6
Other short-term capital	−19.2	−20.0
Exceptional financing	29.2	
Other liabilities	−0.5	
Reserves	10.4	−0.3
TOTALS	63.6	32.6
Errors and omissions	−1.8	24.8
Total change in reserves	12.6	−0.1

33BANKING AND SECURITIES

In November 1972, a new central bank, the Bank of the Central African States (Banque des États de l'Afrique Central—BEAC), replaced the existing Central Bank of the States of Equatorial Africa and Cameroon, which had been controlled by French interests. This move was designed to strengthen the monetary solidarity and sovereignty of the Central African Republic and other member African nations, which would now control part of their foreign exchange and monetary policies. France continues to guarantee the convertibility of the CFA franc. As of the end of 1993, foreign assets of the BEAC for the Central African Republic were CFA Fr34,290 million. The money supply, as measured by M2, totaled CFA Fr14,430 million.

Other banks are the International Bank for Occidental Africa (20% state owned) and the Union Bank of Central Africa (60% state owned). The state has a one-third share in the Bank of Agricultural Credit and Development, established in 1984. As of 31 March 1987, commercial and development banks held CFA Fr17,368 million in demand, time, and savings deposits. There is no securities market.

[34] INSURANCE

In 1986, one state enterprise (SIRIRI) and eight foreign companies were represented in the Central African Republic. In the same year, over 99% of all premiums paid were for non-life insurance. Motor insurance is compulsory.

[35] PUBLIC FINANCE

A rapidly expanding civil service, nationalization of enterprises, and expensive short-term borrowing in the 1970s led to large budget deficits, which were made even worse in the early 1980s by falling commodity prices.

The Central African Republic and the IMF have worked together since 1980 to attempt to better manage the economy. The 1980 austerity plan focused on stabilizing budget and foreign deficits by concentrating on agricultural production. The 1982 Recovery Plan, also conducted within IMF frameworks, led to a formal structural adjustment plan in 1987. A second structural adjustment plan was agreed to in 1990, at a time when political instability began to affect the government's ability to reach its targets. Goals of the IMF-sponsored program were a reduction of the number of government employees and their salaries, price-policy reforms, and privatization of the parastatal sector.

[36] TAXATION

Current information is unavailable.

[37] CUSTOMS AND DUTIES

In 1959, the four territories of French Equatorial Africa joined the Equatorial Customs Union (Union Douanière Equatoriale—UDE), within which goods and capital flowed without obstruction. The UDE was expanded in December 1964 to include Cameroon, and together they formed the Central African Customs and Economic Union (Union Douanière et Economique de l'Afrique Centrale—UDEAC). The Republic therefore had no customs system of its own. In early 1968, the Central African Republic left the UDEAC to join an economic union with Zaire and Chad, but in December 1968 it returned to the UDEAC. As of 1993, the Central African Republic was a member of both UDEAC and CEEAC.

The UDEAC covers the entire range of commodity trade and bans all import and export taxes between member states. Goods and merchandise originating in member states are exempt from various taxes except in special circumstances. The gains derived from import duties in member states go into the state budgets, but to offset the advantages, especially to coastal countries, gained by transit trade, a share of import duties is deposited in a common fund. There is a uniform customs tariff levied against all third parties, but since the UDEAC countries are associated with the Common Market, imports from EC countries receive a reduction in customs duties. Imports from outside the franc zone require a license. Customs evasion through smuggling of goods across the Zaire and Cameroon borders is a serious problem.

Such goods are sold at 10–40% off the price of legitimate items, depriving the government of significant revenue.

[38] FOREIGN INVESTMENT

Until recently, almost all foreign investment in the Central African Republic was by the French government and private French firms. For many years, the territory had been worked by French concessionaires who obtained privileges in the area by decree, but with the decline of concessions, interest in private investment diminished. Foreign investment was further discouraged by the nationalization without compensation of private textile, oil-distribution, and river-transport interests in 1974.

In the early and mid-1980s, in an attempt to revitalize the nation's sagging economy, the Kolingba government reaffirmed its interest in foreign investment, stressing joint partnerships between private business and government. A 1982 investment code provided liberal incentives, including priority in the allocation of foreign exchange for the import of equipment and raw materials.

[39] ECONOMIC DEVELOPMENT

The 1981–85 five-year plan called for CFA Fr233,117 million in expenditures, including CFA Fr83,363 million for rural transport and CFA Fr54,935 million for agriculture and livestock raising. The 1986–90 plan called for CFA Fr261.4 billion in spending (86% from foreign sources), with 53% for infrastructure and 35% for rural and regional development. Development expenditures are financed almost exclusively by foreign donors. In 1985, international bilateral aid to the Central African Republic was $109 million; France, the largest donor, contributed $51 million. The World Bank extended a $30-million loan in 1986.

The 1994 devaluation of the CFA franc should serve to make products such as agricultural and forestry raw materials and diamonds more attractive on the world market. Transport costs to the coast are high, however, acting to restrain progress in this area.

[40] SOCIAL DEVELOPMENT

Social services based on the French model have been introduced slowly. Since 1 July 1956, family allowances have been paid to all salaried workers. Contributions are made by employers at a fixed percentage of the employee's wage. The funds are administered jointly by a council of employers, employees, and the government. Other payments include prenatal allowances, a lump sum payable at the birth of each of the first three children, and if the mother is employed, a recuperation allowance for 14 weeks. But government's commitment to social welfare and health were neglected in the 1990s because of a lack of funds.

Women completing their childbearing years in 1993 had borne an average of 5.47 children. Polygamy is widespread. Abortion is allowed only to save the mother's life.

[41] HEALTH

Mobile crews treat local epidemic diseases, conduct vaccination and inoculation campaigns, and enforce local health regulations. They conduct research on sleeping sickness, malaria, and other tropical diseases and devise prophylactic methods best suited to the rural population. The most common diseases are bilharziasis, leprosy, malaria, tuberculosis, and yaws. The Pasteur Institute at Bangui cooperates actively with vaccination campaigns. All medicine, antibiotics, and vaccine imports must be authorized by the Ministry of Health.

In 1990, there were 113 doctors (1 for every 25,930 people), 22 pharmacists, 6 dentists, 259 nurses, and 166 midwives.

In 1993, average life expectancy was 47 years, and the death rate was 18 per 1,000 people. In 1992, only 24% of the population had access to safe water, and only 45% had access to health care services. In 1990, there were 139 reported cases of tuberculosis per 100,000 people.

The country had 142,000 births in 1992 (45 per 1,000), with a birth rate of 44.5 per 1,000 people. In 1990, 42% of the population was under 15 years of age, with only 5% over 60 years. The infant mortality rate in 1992 was 105 per 1,000 live births. In 1992, the country immunized children up to one year old as follows: tuberculosis (94%); diphtheria, pertussis, and tetanus (77%); polio (77%); and measles (62%).

42HOUSING

The Central African Real Estate Investments Society makes small loans for the repair of existing houses and larger loans (amounting to almost the total cost of the houses) for new construction. Interest rates are low, and repayment extends over a long period. Because of their higher credit ratings, salaried civil servants and employees of large trading companies receive most of the loans.

Loans are made to mutual self-help groups and others for the construction of waterworks or electrical distribution systems and to individuals for the purchase of refrigerators, furniture, and other household equipment.

Between 1988 and 1990, 14% of the urban population and 11% of the rural population had access to a water supply; 36% of urban dwellers and 9% of rural dwellers had sanitation services.

43EDUCATION

The educational system is patterned on that of France, but changes designed by the government are being introduced gradually to adapt the curriculum to local needs. Education is provided free in government-financed schools. There are a few mission schools operated by religious groups; they receive little government aid but must comply with government guidelines. Education is compulsory between ages 6 and 14. Primary education lasts for six years; secondary lasts for seven years (four plus three). Adult illiteracy was about 62.3% in 1990 (males: 48.2% and females: 75.1%).

In 1989 there were 323,661 primary-school pupils and 49,147 secondary-school pupils. There were over 200 French teachers in the Central African Republic in the mid-1980s.

Specialized institutions include two agricultural colleges, a national college of the performing and plastic arts, and the University of Bangui, founded in 1969. In 1991, the university and equivalent institutions had 3,783 students with a teaching staff of 139.

44LIBRARIES AND MUSEUMS

The French Institute of Scientific Research for Development and Cooperation maintains a research collection of 1,730 volumes in Bangui. The Agricultural Research Center in Mbaïki has a library of 2,740 volumes. There is a municipal library in Bangui as well as a Roman Catholic mission library. The University of Bangui library has 28,000 volumes.

The Barthélémy Boganda Museum in Bangui (founded in 1966) includes collections on the ethnography, archaeology, and natural history of the country. There are regional natural history and anthropology museums in Bangassou, Bouar, and Mbaïki.

45MEDIA

Bangui is linked by satellite for telephone communication with France, the UK, the US, and Greece. The Republic has radiotele-

phone, telegraphic, and telex links with Paris. In 1991 there were 6,952 telephones.

Broadcasting services are government owned and operated by Radio–Télévision Centafrique. Television transmissions are available only in Bangui. There were 210,000 radios in 1991 and 14,000 television sets. Broadcasting is in Sango and French. The nation's first daily newspaper, the government controlled *E Le Songo,* began publication in 1986. Its circulation in 1991 was 1,000. *Rensorveau Centrafricaine* and *Terre Africaine* are weeklies, and the *Journal Officiel* is published every two weeks.

46ORGANIZATIONS

The Chamber of Agriculture, Livestock Raising, Water, Forests, Hunting, and Tourism and the Chamber of Commerce, Industry, Mines, and Handicrafts have their headquarters at Bangui. There are several youth centers. In rural areas, cooperatives promote the production and marketing of agricultural products.

47TOURISM, TRAVEL, AND RECREATION

The main tourist attractions are hunting, fishing, the waterfalls, and the many varieties of wild animals. Of special interest are the falls at Boali and Kembé, the megaliths of Bouar, and the Pygmies at Mongoumba. Hotels and guest bungalows are insufficient, although South African loans have financed a 278-room hotel and casino. In 1986, about 4,000 tourists visited the country. Except for those from France, French-speaking Africa, and a few other countries, visitors must have a visa and a certificate indicating that they have been inoculated against yellow fever.

48FAMOUS CENTRAL AFRICANS

Barthélémy Boganda (1910–59), a dynamic leader of Central African nationalism, worked toward independence and attained virtually complete political power. The first president of the independent Central African Republic was David Dacko (b.1930), who served from 1960 to 1966 and again from 1979 to 1981. Jean-Bédel Bokassa (b.1921) overthrew Dacko in 1966, proclaimed himself emperor in 1976, and was himself ousted by Dacko in 1979. Gen. André Kolingba (b.1936) seized power in 1981.

49DEPENDENCIES

The Central African Republic has no territories or colonies.

50BIBLIOGRAPHY

Brunschwig, Henri. *French Colonialism, 1871–1914: Myths and Realities.* New York: Praeger, 1966.

Decalo, Samuel. *Psychoses of Power: African Personal Dictatorships.* Boulder, Colo.: Westview Press, 1989.

Gide, André Paul Guillaume. *Travels in the Congo.* New York: Knopf, 1929.

Kalck, Pierre. *Central African Republic.* Santa Barbara, Calif.: Clio Press, 1993.

Kalck, Pierre. *Historical Dictionary of the Central African Republic.* Metuchen, N.J.: Scarecrow Press, 1980.

Le Vine, Victor T. *Political Leadership in Africa; Post-independence Generational Conflict in Upper Volta, Senegal, Niger, Dahomey, and the Central African Republic.* Stanford, Calif.: Hoover Institution on War, Revolution and Peace, 1967.

O'Toole, Thomas. *The Central African Republic: the Continent's Hidden Heart.* Boulder, Colo.: Westview Press, 1986.

CHAD

Republic of Chad
République du Tchad

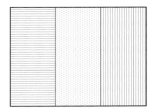

CAPITAL: N'Djamena (formerly Fort-Lamy).

FLAG: The flag is a tricolor of blue, yellow, and red vertical stripes.

ANTHEM: *La Tchadienne* begins "Peuple Tchadien, debout et à l'ouvrage!" ("People of Chad, stand up and set to work!").

MONETARY UNIT: The Communauté Financière Africaine franc (CFA Fr) is a paper currency. There are coins of 1, 2, 5, 10, 25, 50, 100, and 500 CFA francs and notes of 50, 100, 500, 1,000, 5,000, and 10,000 CFA francs. CFA Fr1 = $0.0018 (or $1 = CFA Fr398).

WEIGHTS AND MEASURES: The metric system is the legal standard.

HOLIDAYS: New Year's Day, 1 January; National Holiday, 11 January; Labor Day, 1 May; African Independence Day, 25 May; Independence Day, 11 August; Assumption, 15 August; All Saints' Day, 1 November; Proclamation of the Republic, 28 November; Christmas, 25 December. Movable religious holidays include 'Id al-Fitr, 'Id al-'Adha', Milad an-Nabi, Easter Monday, Ascension, and Pentecost Monday.

TIME: 1 PM = noon GMT.

¹LOCATION, SIZE, AND EXTENT

A landlocked country situated in northern Central Africa, the Republic of Chad has an area of 1,284,000 sq km (495,755 sq mi), extending 1,765 km (1,097 mi) N–S and 1,030 km (640 mi) E–W. Comparatively, the area occupied by Chad is slightly more than three times the size of the state of California. It is bounded on the N by Libya, on the E by the Sudan, on the s by the Central African Republic, on the sw by Cameroon, and on the w by Nigeria and Niger, with a total boundary length of 5,968 km (3,708 mi). The Aozou Strip of Chad, an area along the northern border of about 114,000 sq km (about 44,000 sq mi), was occupied and annexed by Libya in 1973. Armed clashes broke out in 1983 with Nigeria over several islands in Lake Chad that had emerged as the water level fell.

Chad's capital city, N'Djamena, is located in the southwestern part of the country.

²TOPOGRAPHY

The country's most marked feature is Lake Chad, which is situated at the foot of a gently sloping plain and is surrounded by vast marshes. Fed chiefly by the Chari and Logone rivers, it has an average depth of 0.9 to 1.2 m (3–4 ft). From this low point of 230 m (750 ft) above sea level, the land rises to a maximum of 3,415 m (11,204 ft) at Emi Koussi, an extinct volcanic peak in the Tibesti Mountains of northern Chad.

³CLIMATE

The three chief climatic zones are the Saharan, with a wide range of temperatures between day and night; the Sahelian, a semi-desert; and the Sudanic, with relatively moderate temperatures. Extreme temperatures range from –12° to 50°C (10°–22°F); at N'Djamena the average daily maximums and minimums are 42°C (108°F) and 28°C (73°F) in April and 33°C (91°F) and 14°C (57°F) in December. The rains last from April (in the south) or July (farther north) through October. At the capital, N'Djamena, average annual rainfall is about 76 cm (30 in). In the far south, it is as

much as 122 cm (48 in), but at Faya-Largeau in the north, it averages only 2.5 cm (1 in). A severe drought affected two-thirds of the country from 1967 through 1973 and again in the early 1980s, especially 1984.

⁴FLORA AND FAUNA

Animal and plant life correspond to the three climatic zones. In the Saharan region, the only flora is the date-palm groves of the oases. Palms and acacia trees grow in the Sahelian region. The southern, or Sudanic, zone consists of broad grasslands or prairies suitable for grazing. Elephants, lions, buffalo, hippopotamuses, rhinoceroses, giraffes, antelopes, leopards, cheetahs, hyenas, snakes, and a variety of birds are found in the savanna country.

⁵ENVIRONMENT

There are two national parks and five game reserves. The chief environmental problem is increasing desertification after a decade marked by below-normal rainfall. Other contributing factors to Chad's problems are drought and civil war. Drought eliminates vegetation, which causes the soil to erode. Warring factions in Chad have damaged the environment and hampered the efforts of the government to address environmental problems for 25 years. Locust swarms caused crop damage in 1978 and 1980. Elephant herds were reported greatly decimated in the 1970s. The availability of fresh water is also a major problem. Eighty-two percent of the water is used for farming activity.

As of 1994, endangered species in Chad included the black rhinoceros, scimitar-horned oryx, and African wild ass. Of 131 species of mammals in Chad, 18 are threatened with extinction. Four bird species out of 496 are also threatened. Two reptiles and 14 plant species out of 1,000 are in danger of extinction as of 1994.

⁶POPULATION

According to a 1993 census, the population was 6,288,261. The average annual growth rate was estimated in the mid-1990s at about 2.7%. A population of 7,307,000 was projected for the year 2000, assuming a crude birthrate of 41.8 per 1,000 population, a crude death rate of 16.8, and a net natural increase of 25 for 1995–2000. Overall density in 1993 was 4.9 per sq km (12.7 per sq mi), but almost half of the area is desert (where only about 110,000 people lived in 1986), and almost half the population lives in the southwestern 10% of Chad. In 1990, the largest communities were N'Djamena (formerly Fort-Lamy), capital and principal city, about 728,000; Sahr (formerly Fort-Archambault), 129,600; Moundou, 117,500; and Abéché, 95,800. The population was about 37% urban in 1994.

7MIGRATION

At least 200,000 Chadians fled the country during the civil war in 1979–81, mostly to Cameroon and Nigeria. About 150,000 returned in 1982. In 1983, up to 200,000 of the estimated 700,000 Chadians in Nigeria were expelled as part of a general expulsion of foreigners. Beginning in 1983, tens of thousands of Chadians fled from Libyan-controlled northern Chad and other areas of the country. The government of Chad reported that more than 152,000 Chadians returned home between November 1985, when a general amnesty was proclaimed, and the end of June 1987. At the end of 1992 there were about 16,000 Chadian refugees in Sudan, 1,200 in the Central African Republic, 41,700 in Cameroon, 3,400 in Niger, 2,200 in the Congo, 1,400 in Nigeria, and 200 in Benin. About 150,000 Chadians migrated from rural areas to towns in the early 1990s.

8ETHNIC GROUPS

The basic population of Chad derives from indigenous African groups, whose composition has been altered over the course of years through successive invasions from the Arabic north. The present population is a mixture of at least 192 ethnic groups.

The population can be broadly divided between those who follow the Islamic faith and the peoples of the south, by which is meant the five southernmost prefectures. The Arab invaders brought Islam, perhaps as early as the 8th century, and today their descendants form a relatively homogeneous group, localized in the regions of Chari Baguirmi and Ouaddai, but mostly semi-nomadic. Some indigenous groups, such as the Salamat and the Taundjor, were largely Arabized by intermarriage over the years. Other Muslim peoples include the Fulani, the great sheep and goatherders of Chad, and the Tubu (divided into Teda and Daza), living in the Tibesti region, who are thought to have originated in the valley of the Upper Nile.

Among the southern peoples, the most important (and the largest single group in Chad) are the Sara, about 30% of the population. They live in the valleys of the Chari and Logone rivers and are farmers of considerable skill.

9LANGUAGES

More than 100 languages are spoken by the different ethnic groups, but Arabic is commonly spoken in the north and Sara languages in the south. French and Arabic are the official languages.

10RELIGIONS

In 1985, an estimated 44% of the people were Muslims, 33% were Christians, and 23% were followers of African traditional religions. Most of the people of northern Chad are Muslims. Islam, brought both from Sudan and from northern Nigeria, spread through the area around Lake Chad long before the coming of Europeans. The people of the south, particularly those living in the valleys of the Shari and Logone rivers, follow African traditional religions. Protestant and Catholic missionaries have been in the territory only in this century.

11TRANSPORTATION

Chad suffers from poor transportation both within the country and to outside markets; its economic development depends on the expansion of transport facilities. During the rainy season, the roads become impassable and the economy slows down almost to a standstill. There are no railways.

In 1991 there were an estimated 31,322 km (19,463 mi) of roads, of which only 32 km (20 mi) were tarred. In 1992 there were about 9,000 passenger cars and 7,000 commercial vehicles in use, including trucks, buses, and tractors. The main export routes are to the Nigerian railhead of Maiduguri and the Cameroonian railhead of Ngaoundéré. A bridge across the Chari, linking N'Djamena to Kousséri, Cameroon, was completed in 1985. In the same year, a US$19.2 million loan for road rehabilitation was provided by the IDA.

Most rivers flow but intermittently. On the Chari, between N'Djamena and Lake Chad, transportation is possible all year round. In September and October, the Logone is navigable between N'Djamena and Moundou, and the Shari between N'Djamena and Sarh. Total waterways cover 4,800 km (3,000 mi), of which 2,000 km (1,250 mi) are navigable all year.

Chad has more than 55 airports and landing strips. Air Tchad (60% state owned) provides internal service to 12 locations but suffers from lack of fuel and equipment. The international airport at N'Djamena was damaged in fighting in 1981, but is now served by several international carriers including Air Afrique, which is 7% owned by Chad. Another major airport, developed as a military staging area, is located at Sarh.

12HISTORY

Fine prehistoric rock engravings and paintings can be found in northern Chad, dating between 5000–2000 BC. As early as the 8th century AD, Arabs entered from the north and their records tell of the existence of great African empires—Kanem, Bornu, Baguirmi, and Ouaddai—between the 9th and 16th centuries. By the end of the 19th century, many small states south of Lake Chad became vassals of the northern sultanates, which conducted a flourishing slave trade.

Chad was explored in part in 1822 by Dixon Denham and Hugh Clapperton, two British travelers. More detailed explorations were carried out by Heinrich Barth (1853) and Gustav Nachtigal (1870–71). In the decade after 1890, French expeditions gradually expanded French control of the lands to the south and east of Lake Chad. Full pacification of the territory was achieved by 1913. The borders of Chad as they presently stand were secured by conventions between France and Germany (1894) and France and the UK (1898). In 1910, Gabon, Middle Congo, and Ubangi-Shari (which included Chad) were constituted administratively as colonies; together they formed French Equatorial Africa. Chad was separated in 1916 and became a colony in 1920.

On 26 August 1940, during World War II, French officials in Chad rallied to the Free French standard, making Chad the first colony to do so. N'Djamena, formerly Fort-Lamy, was an important Allied air base on the route to the Middle East, and from there Col. Philippe Leclerc's troops departed to fight in the North African campaign. After 1945, Chad became one of the territories of French Equatorial Africa in the French Union, and in the referendum of 28 September 1958 the territory of Chad voted to become an autonomous republic within the French Community. On 26 November 1958, the territorial assembly became a constituent assembly and proclaimed the autonomous Republic of Chad. On 11 August 1960, Chad achieved full independence, with François (later Ngarta) Tombalbaye as head of state and prime minister. On 4 April 1962, a new constitution was proclaimed and a new government formed, with Tombalbaye as president.

ALGERIA

LIBYA

CHAD

| 0 | 150 | 300 Miles |
| 0 | 150 | 300 Kilometers |

Aouzou
Bardaï
Aozou Strip

TIBESTI

Zouar
DESERT

SAHARA

▲ Emi Koussi
11,204 ft.
3415 m.

Aozou Strip
The World Court, in
February of 1994, granted
administration of
the Aozou Strip to Chad.

Grand Erg de Bilma

NIGER

BORKOU
Faya-Largeau

Fada

Bodélé
Depression

ENNEDI

Ghazal

Howar

MASSIF DU
KERKOUR NOURENE

Berdoba

Miski

Mao

Biltine

SUDAN

Bol

Abéché

Lake
Chad

Ati

Batha

Farcha
N'Djamena

Mongo

NIGERIA

Massenya

Abou Deïa

Azoum

Chari

Melfi

Am Timan

Bousso

Bongor

Logone

Salamat

Aouk

N
W E
S

Léré

Chad

Pala

Laï

Sarh

Ouham

Doba

Moundou

CAMEROON

CENTRAL AFRICAN REPUBLIC

LOCATION: 7°26′ to 23°N; 13°28′ to 2°E. **BOUNDARY LENGTHS:** Libya, 1,054 km (655 mi); Sudan, 1,360 km (845 mi): Central African Republic, 1,199 km (745 mi); Cameroon, 1,047 km (651 mi); Nigeria, 88 km (55 mi); Niger, 1,175 km (730 mi).

After 1965 there was full-scale rebellion in the Muslim north country, largely the result of Muslim resentment toward the Christian- and animist-oriented government in N'Djamena. Prominent in the rebellion was the National Liberation Front (Front de Libération Nationale—FROLINAT). In late 1968, President Tombalbaye requested and received the aid of French troops in combating the rebels. French troops were officially withdrawn from Chad in 1972, although technical advisers remained. In 1973, Libya, a major source of covert aid for the rebels, occupied

and annexed the Aozou Strip in northern Chad.

On 13 April 1975, Tombalbaye's 15-year rule was ended with his assassination in an army coup. Gen. Félix Malloum became the new president. Like his predecessor, Malloum was a southerner whose rule was opposed by the Muslim north. In 1976, however, a faction led by Hissène Habré split with FROLINAT and eventually formed the Armed Forces of the North (Forces Armées du Nord—FAN). Goukouni Oueddei, with Libyan support, emerged as head of FROLINAT, but a FROLINAT advance south was stopped by additional French troops in 1978. In a government shuffle, Malloum named Habré prime minister in 1978, but the two broke in early 1979 as antagonism between Muslims and southerners intensified. After Habré's FAN seized control of the capital, Malloum resigned as president on 23 March 1979 and fled the country. In April Habré became defense minister and Oueddei interior minister in a coalition government, which in August was reconstituted with Oueddei as president. In November it became the interim Government of National Unity, representing 11 armed factions, with Oueddei remaining as president and Habré as minister of defense.

Fighting between FAN and government forces broke out in March 1980, and Habré was dismissed from the cabinet in April. France withdrew its forces from Chad in May, and the FAN occupied Faya-Largeau in June, as well as holding part of N'Djamena. By October, Libya had intervened on Oueddei's behalf, and, in December, an estimated 7,000 to 10,000 Libyan troops completed the conquest of Chad by occupying N'Djamena. Habré's forces fled to eastern Chad and the Sudan.

Libya's action and talk of a union with Chad angered other African leaders and France, and Oueddei himself may have become alarmed at the growth of Libyan influence. At Oueddei's request, Libyan troops withdrew in November 1981 and were replaced by a 3,600-man OAU peacekeeping force. These troops did nothing, however, to halt the FAN's subsequent advance from the east. On 7 June 1982, Habré's forces occupied the capital, and Oueddei fled to Algeria. Habré declared himself president of Chad on 19 October 1982.

By early 1983, the Habré regime had extended its control to southern Chad, but was meeting increasing difficulties in the north. Ousted president Oueddei formed a rival government and, with a rebel army of about 3,000, captured the northern town of Faya-Largeau on 10 August 1983, with the support of Libyan aircraft and artillery. France and the US rushed supplies to Habré, and France sent 2,000 to 2,500 troops. Zaire sent in another 2,700. As of early 1984, Chad was effectively partitioned, with a chain of French military posts stretching across the center of the country. To the south, the Habré regime was consolidating its position. France subsequently moved its defensive line 100 km (60 mi) to the north. Northern Chad, however, remained under the control of Libya and Oueddei's rebel forces, and there were growing fears that Libya was moving to annex the area.

A November 1984 agreement between France and Libya called for both countries to withdraw their forces from Chad, but although France complied, Libya reneged. French troops returned in 1985 to help repulse an enemy offensive. On 8 August, Aozou, and with it the entire disputed strip, fell to Chad, but a Libyan counteroffensive recaptured the settlement on 28 August. However, after a damaging Chadian raid on an air base within Libyan territory on 5 September, Libya agreed to a cease-fire, effective 11 September. During 1987 fighting, Chad captured $500 million to $1 billion worth of Libyan military equipment, most of it intact. US-supplied Stinger missiles allowed Habré's forces to neutralize Libya's air force.

The struggle for Chad took another twist in November 1990. After a three-week campaign by guerrillas loyal to an ex-army commander, Indriss Déby, the Habré regime fell. Déby was supported by Libya and Sudan, but he also was backed by the US, France, and Nigeria. A French force of 1,200 assisted Déby against pro-Habré rebels, who were eventually put down in 1993.

In May 1992, Déby appointed a new prime minister, Joseph Yodoyman, who formed a new cabinet that included several opposition figures. Parties were legalized and, by the end of 1992, 28 parties had registered. In April 1992, Yodoyman stepped down. He died in November.

A Sovereign National Conference that lasted from January to April 1993 brought together a diverse group of government,

economic, military, and special interest representatives. It confirmed Déby as Chief of State, established a new transitional government, elected 57 counselors to a Higher Transitional Council (a quasi-legislative body), and adopted the Transitional Charter, an interim constitution. This government was given a one-year mandate. Late in 1993, a technical commission of jurists was constituted, which began work on a new constitution, an electoral code, and a charter for political parties. In April 1994 Déby's mandate was extended by 12 months and the work of the jurists was continued. A presidential election is scheduled for March 1995.

In May 1993, the Transitional Council disbanded the Center for Research and Intelligence Coordination, a security organization. Nonetheless, serious human rights abuses and corruption continue under Déby. Also, Chad's long-standing territorial dispute with Libya over the Aozou Strip was taken up by the International Court of Justice in June 1993. On 3 February 1994, the Court rejected Libya's claim to Chadian territory. Libya has asked the OAU to supervise its withdrawal.

13GOVERNMENT

According to the constitution of 1962, Chad was an indivisible, secular, democratic, and social republic with a president and National Assembly. One-party rule was established and presidential elections were held on 15 June 1969, the first by universal suffrage. An official announcement on 16 June stated that President Tombalbaye, being the only candidate, had been reelected for a further seven years by 93% of the voters.

The National Assembly was dissolved after the coup of 13 April 1975 that ousted Tombalbaye. A provisional constitution which came into force 16 August 1975 was abolished on 23 March 1979, when President Malloum fled. The president heads a council of ministers with executive and legislative authority. In October 1982, a National Consultative Council was formed, with two representatives from each prefecture and two from N'Djamena. This body was to draft a new constitution by 1990, but it was replaced in the Déby coup on December 1, 1990.

The three-month-long National Conference in early 1993 established a new transitional government with a 57-member Higher Transitional Council (elected by the 254 Conference delegates) and a Transitional Charter.

Work on a new draft constitution began near the end of 1993 and presidential elections are scheduled for March 1995. The mandate of the transitional government was extended until April 1995.

14POLITICAL PARTIES

Prior to independence, Chad was split politically. The northerners, predominantly Muslim, were supporters of the Party of African Reunion (Parti de Regroupement Africain). The non-Muslim southern farmers were supporters of the Chad Progressive Party (Parti Progressiste Tchadien—PPT). In 1958, the Legislative Assembly of Chad was controlled by PPT members, who had a majority of 42 of the 65 seats. In the election of 31 May 1959, the PPT obtained 57 seats in the new Assembly, and François (later Ngarta) Tombalbaye of the PPT became prime minister. In February 1960, four smaller parties joined forces to form the opposition African National Party (Parti National Africain—PNA). In 1962, the PNA was dissolved, and Chad became a one-party state. In 1973, the name of the PPT was changed to the National Movement for Cultural and Social Revolution (Mouvement Nationale pour la Révolution Culturelle et Sociale—MNRCS). Following the 1975 coup, the MNRCS was banned and the National Assembly was dissolved. As a consequence, all formal political activity ceased.

In 1984, Habré established the National Union for Independence and Revolution (Union Nationale pour l'Indépendence et la

Révolution—UNIR), with a 14-member Executive Bureau headed by himself and an 80-member Central Committee. After the Déby coup, his Patriotic Salvation Movement (MPS) took over. Parties were legalized in 1992, and eventually 28 registered with the authorities.

A coalition of some 10 opposition parties and 15 associations, known as Alternative 94, requested and gained an extension period in preparation for elections in early 1995. But Déby still seems to dictate the pace of change.

[15]LOCAL GOVERNMENT

Chad is divided into 14 prefectures and 54 subprefectures. There are also 9 municipalities and 27 administrative posts. In many areas, the traditional chief still retains power as the head of his people.

[16]JUDICIAL SYSTEM

Since the 1990 coup, the structure and functioning of the judicial system has been seriously disrupted. Because of the breakdown of law and order, the judiciary has been unable to handle criminal cases. Interference by the government and by the military has contributed to the breakdown. Many magistrates went out on strike in 1993 to protest difficult working conditions and non-payment of salaries.

Traditionally, the legal system was based on French civil law and Chadian customary law. The judicial system consisted of four criminal courts, four magistrates' courts, four labor tribunals, 14 district courts (in major cities), 36 justices of the peace (in larger townships), and a court of appeal (the Appellate Court of N'Djamena). A Supreme Court was inaugurated in 1963 and abolished in 1975. A Court of State Security was established in 1976. In most rural areas where there in no access to these formal judicial institutions, sultans and chiefs preside over customary courts. Their decisions may be appealed to ordinary courts.

Under the Transitional Charter the Appellate Court of N'Djamena is charged with responsibility for constitutional review as well as review of decisions of lower courts and criminal convictions involving potential sentences of over 20 years.

[17]ARMED FORCES

In 1993, Chad's armed forces totaled about 25,200 men, all but 200 (air force) in the army, which is armed with French armored vehicles and weapons. The gendarmerie and other paramilitary forces totaled about 4,500. About 750 French troops were based in Chad. Insurgent strength is unknown. Chad spent $56 million for defense in 1990, or 5.4 percent of gross domestic product.

[18]INTERNATIONAL COOPERATION

Chad was admitted to UN membership on 20 September 1960 and is a member of ECA and all the nonregional specialized agencies except IAEA, IFC, IMO, and UNIDO. It is also a member of the African Development Bank, G-77, and OAU and an associate member of EEC. It is a signatory to the Law of the Sea and to GATT. Chad, Cameroon, Niger, and Nigeria are members of the Lake Chad Basin Commission, formed in 1964.

[19]ECONOMY

Water-resource limitations are the critical factor influencing the Chadian economy. Much of the country is desert suitable only for very limited agriculture and livestock production, while the remainder is threatened by periodic drought. Petroleum and natron are the principal mineral resources. Key industry is centered on cotton processing. Periodic civil war has compounded Chad's chronic negative trade imbalance. In spite of its problems, the World Bank estimates that the Chadian economy grew by an average of 5.5% in the decade ending in 1991.

Agriculture is Chad's primary sector, with 74% of the population accounting for 43% of the GDP (1991). Sorghum, millet, and groundnuts are the principal food crops, while cassava, rice, dates, maize, and wheat augment domestic consumption. While most groundnut production is consumed locally or turned into oil, Chadian groundnuts also make their way to Central African markets. Chad also has a successful sugar production agroindustry. Cotton is a principal export commodity, but the sector has suffered considerably from a variety of ills. The 75% state-owned cotton company was reorganized in 1986 and, after several promising years, the 1992 decline in cotton prices resulted in substantial losses.

Livestock production accounts for 13% of GDP and engages 40% of the labor force. Much of the industry is conducted following seasonal rain patterns and, as a result of the extended drought, is increasingly centered in the south.

In January 1994 France suddenly devalued the CFA franc, causing its value to drop in half overnight. Immediately, prices for almost all imported goods soared, including prices for food and essential drugs, like those to combat malaria. Since 1948 France had guaranteed a fixed parity of one French franc to 50 African francs. The resulting stability in the currency had generally kept inflation low and helped to maintain a steady rate of growth. However, in the 1980s, the economies of the CFA countries began to stagnate in relation to other African nations, and France came under increased pressure from the World Bank, the IMF, and western countries to stop subsidizing the CFA franc. The devaluation, long expected in the investment community, is designed to enourage new investment, particularly in the oil sector, and discourage the use of hard currency reserves to buy products that could be grow domestically.

[20]INCOME

In 1992 Chad's GNP was $1,261 million at current prices, or $220 per capita. For the period 1985–92 the average inflation rate was −0.2%, resulting in a real growth rate in per capita GNP of 1.3%. In the period 1988 to 1990, the cost of living declined by 4.3%.

In 1992 the GDP was $1,310 million in current US dollars. Agriculture, hunting, forestry, and fishing make up 48.6% of GDP; the trade, transport, and finance categories add an additional 28.9%. Manufacturing contributes 14.8% to GDP.

[21]LABOR

Over 80% of all Chadian workers are involved in subsistence agriculture, animal husbandry, or fishing. There were some 12,530 wage earners in 1991, with approximately 42% engaged in manufacturing. The National Charter of 1991 specifically addressed the right of labor to organize, and workers are free to form and join unions of their choosing; Chadian law, however, does not specifically protect collective bargaining.

[22]AGRICULTURE

Only 2.5% of Chad's land is cultivated. Prolonged periodic droughts and civil war and political instability have cut agricultural production and necessitated food relief. Because of drought, Chad's cereal production in 1990/91 totaled 604,700 tons, requiring 40,000 tons of food aid in the form of grains and flour to be imported that year.

Since the 1960s, cotton crops have accounted for a high percentage of Chad's export earnings. Cotton growing began about 1929 and spread gradually throughout southern Chad. Production was 60,000 tons in 1990 and 70,000 tons in 1992, still far below the high of 174,062 tons in 1975–76. Production is dominated by the parastatal Cotontchad, which regulates output, operates the ginneries and cottonseed-oil works, and markets and exports both cotton and cottonseed. Chad's medium staple cotton is sold to 20 different countries; Germany, Portugal, and Japan are the principal customers. Although most cotton is exported, factories in Chad produce cottonseed oil for domestic consumption.

Production of peanuts reached a peak of 150,000 tons in 1965; it was about 147,000 tons were produced in 1992. Millet is the basic foodstuff (except in the Lake Chad area, where corn is the main cereal). Production of millet and sorghum, another basic food crop, totaled 693,000 tons in 1967 and an estimated 674,000 tons in 1992. Rice production was about 52,000 tons in 1992; corn production amounted to 91,000 tons that year. Other products, with 1992 production figures, include cassava, 330,000 tons; yams, 240,000 tons; and sweet potatoes, 46,000 tons. Sugarcane production on a French-managed irrigated estate of 4,000 hectares (9,900 acres) on the Shari River yielded 37,000 tons of raw sugar in 1992.

23 ANIMAL HUSBANDRY

As of 1991, 35% of the total area of Chad was given over to pastureland. In 1992 there were about 5 million sheep and goats and 4.5 million head of cattle; more than 1.5 million cattle died during the 1984–85 drought. Despite the 1990 drought, Chad's livestock herd has increased. In 1992 there were about 570,000 camels and 4 million chickens. Actual totals may have been considerably higher because herders are reluctant to declare the extent of their herds and flocks, because all full-grown animals are subject to taxation.

Live cattle, sheep, and goats are exported, with considerable smuggling, to Nigeria. Also important are exports of meat, hides, and skins. In 1992, about 94,000 tons of meat were produced. Livestock is Chad's second most important export, after cotton.

24 FISHING

Fish, either fresh or dried, forms an important element in the diet of the people living in the major valleys. The catch from the Chari and Logone rivers and the Chad Basin was approximately 60,000 tons in 1991. Production is far below potential.

25 FORESTRY

Chad has wooded areas covering more than 10% of its land area but no real forests. The only exportable forest product is gum arabic, the yield of which has averaged 300 to 400 tons a year. Roundwood removals were estimated at 14,637,000 m^3 in 1991, 79% for fuel. Acacia trees were extensively planted in 1978.

26 MINING

Only natron, the natural form of sodium carbonate, is mined. It is used as salt for animal and human consumption, in the preservation of meat and hides, and in soap production. Annual production is a few thousand tons, but no production has been reported since 1982. There are important quartz deposits in the Ouaddai area. Minor gold deposits in the same region may someday be exploited in conjunction with surrounding alluvial gravels. Deposits of uranium and thorium have been discovered in Ennedi. The Aozou area is thought to contain uranium. In 1991, mining and quarrying employed 247 persons.

27 ENERGY AND POWER

Chad lacks both coal and sources of hydroelectricity. Continental Oil Co., in association with Shell Oil, struck oil in the Kanem area, north of Lake Chad, in 1978, and wells briefly produced 1,500 barrels a day (about 80% of national consumption) before fighting disrupted the operation in 1980. An Exxon-led consortium drilled eight wells in the south during 1985–86 but concluded that low oil prices made further development impracticable. Reserves were estimated at 10.5 million barrels. As of 1992, Chad imported 100% of its petroleum requirement from Cameroon and Nigeria. The World Bank has agreed to partially fund a pipeline, small refinery, and power plant that would bring crude oil found north of Lake Chad to N'Djamena.

All power plants are thermal. The two at N'Djamena provide most of the national output. Production of electricity rose from about 31 million kwh in 1968 to 85 million kwh in 1991. Installed capacity the same year was 31,000 kw.

28 INDUSTRY

Because it lacks power and adequate transportation, Chad is industrially one of the least developed countries in Africa. Cotton processing is the largest activity, though reduced in scope by the reorganization of the cotton sector in 1986 and competition from Nigeria. Cottonseed oil is processed at Sarh and Moundou.

Other enterprises include several modern slaughterhouses, a flour mill complex with a processing capacity of 6,000 tons of wheat a year, a sugar refinery, and a textile plant. There are also rice and peanut oil mills, a brewery, a soft-drink plant, a soap factory, and a cigarette factory. Factories at N'Djamena also produce bicycles and mopeds, radios, and perfume.

29 SCIENCE AND TECHNOLOGY

N'Djamena has an institute for cotton research. A French institute of livestock raising and veterinary medicine in tropical countries is at Farcha. The University of Chad has a faculty of sciences, and there is a national telecommunications school in Sarh. Most research in Chad is dependent on foreign scientists and technicians; however, many of these foreign personnel were evacuated during the fighting of the early 1980s.

30 DOMESTIC TRADE

Most local produce is sold directly to consumers or to intermediaries. Company agents and intermediaries buy export crops at local markets or directly from the producers for sale to large companies. The national marketing, distribution, and import-export company is SONACOT, 76% state-owned. Most other importing firms are branches of French companies.

There is some advertising in the local newspapers and through company publications, handbills, and billboards. Business hours are 8 AM to noon, Monday through Saturday, and 3–6 PM, Monday through Friday. Banks are open from 7 to 11:30 AM, Monday–Saturday.

31 FOREIGN TRADE

Chad's primary export—at 91.1% of the total—is cotton, making the economy's trade balance vulnerable to fluctuations in world cotton prices and the rising competition of synthetic materials. Live cattle, meat, and hides represent 2.2% of exports (1983).

According to data compiled from the trade figures of other nations, Chad's exports came to $120.05 million in 1986 and its imports to $203.48 million. Of exports, cotton accounted for $42.5 million and livestock for $34.7 million. The Federal Republic of Germany (FRG) was the leading buyer of Chad's exports in 1986, taking 8% of the total value. France was the leading source of imports, providing 22% of total value. Other important trade partners were Portugal, France, and Spain for Chad's exports, Italy for imports, and Cameroon for both imports and exports. Figures for Nigeria were not available.

32 BALANCE OF PAYMENTS

Normally Chad has a deficit in trade and services that is offset, or nearly offset, by foreign assistance, largely from France. Merchandise exports (mainly cotton and livestock) only amounted to about 65% of imports (mostly fuel and consumer goods) in 1990.

In 1991 merchandise exports totaled $193.9 million and imports $294.1 million. The merchandise trade balance was $−100.2 million. The following table summarizes the balance of payments for 1990 and 1991 (in millions of US dollars):

	1990	1991
CURRENT ACCOUNT		
Goods, services, and income	−237.2	−331.1
Unrequited transfers	191.6	258.4
TOTALS	−45.6	−74.7
CAPITAL ACCOUNT		
Other long-term capital	128.4	115.7
Other short-term capital	−72.3	0.8
Exceptional financing	14.7	8.5
Reserves	8.2	8.2
TOTALS	79.0	127.6
Errors and omissions	−33.3	−52.9
Total change in reserves	−9.1	8.2

33BANKING AND SECURITIES

In November 1972, a new central bank, the Bank of the Central African States (Banque des États de l'Afrique Centrale—BEAC), was established, replacing the Central Bank of the States of Equatorial Africa and Cameroon as the bank of issue. Banks other than the central bank were closed in 1979 because of the civil war. These included branches of two major foreign banks, the International Bank for Commerce and Industry of Chad (40% state owned) and the International Bank for West Africa (35% state owned); the latter later reopened. Other leading credit institutions are the Development Bank of Chad (58.4% state owned) and the Chad Credit and Deposit Bank (40% state owned). Money supply, as measured by M2, was CFA Fr47,470 million in 1993. There are no securities exchanges in Chad.

34INSURANCE

In 1986 there were three domestic and about a dozen French companies providing insurance in Chad.

35PUBLIC FINANCE

The military accounts for about 35% of expenditures, and more than half the sum is outside the budget, raised by "voluntary" contributions. Customs duties are the principal revenue source. Increased military and civil servant outlays caused the current fiscal deficit to increase from 2.2% of GDP in 1988 to 5% of GDP in 1990, but it fell to 4.7% in 1992.

Chad began working with the IMF in the preparation of the 1986 budget, which sought to limit the deficit. In return for help in covering the shortfall, Chad agreed to raise taxes and to lower spending on subsidies and the civil service. Consequently, a structural adjustment program covering 1987 to 1990 was funded by the IMF. However, the 1992 austerity budget precipitated civil disorder. In 1991 Chad's total public debt stood at CFA Fr176,918 million, of which CFA Fr150,597 million was financed abroad.

36TAXATION

A graduated income tax is imposed on civil servants and others who are paid fixed salaries or who have sufficient income. A head tax is imposed on all other persons, the amount varying according to regional levels of prosperity. There is also a domestic turnover tax, a corporate profits tax, and a corporate minimum tax. Further revenue is derived from business and professional licensing, from taxes on business transactions, real property, and profits, and from mining royalties.

37CUSTOMS AND DUTIES

In 1968, Chad left the Central African Customs and Economic Union (Union Douanière et Economique de l'Afrique Centrale—UDEAC) to join the Central African Economic Union (Union des États de l'Afrique Centrale—UEAC) with Zaire and the Central African Republic. The withdrawal of the Central African Republic later that year effectively ended the UEAC, and Chad's reentry into the UDEAC was delayed by its domestic turmoil until 1984.

Customs duties, which are ad valorem, range from 5% on essential items to about 20%. Between 1987 and 1990, 80% of all tariffs were reduced, and 20% were increased.

38FOREIGN INVESTMENT

The government has encouraged foreign private investment on two conditions: that the enterprise benefit the local population, and that local materials be processed as far as possible. The investment code, issued in 1960, offers benefits in any area except the commercial sector. These include preferential export duties and taxes, restrictions on the import of similar competitive products, preference in financial assistance from the Development Bank of Chad, and possible exemption from the sales tax and other fees and taxes for 15 years. Chad's environmental difficulties, compounded by years of civil war, have delayed significant foreign investments.

39ECONOMIC DEVELOPMENT

Foremost among governmental objectives are the expansion and improvement of the transportation network, the expansion and diversification of agriculture, and the attainment of food self-sufficiency. External aid was US$242 million in 1989. France supported Chad's 1990–1991 budget deficits with the equivalent of US$47.5 million.

40SOCIAL DEVELOPMENT

Social services were introduced in Chad very slowly and have been largely disrupted by warfare. Legislation calls for family allowances to be paid to all salaried workers. Contributions are to be made by employers at a fixed percentage (6%) of the employee's wage. Other mandated payments include prenatal allowances, a lump sum payable at the birth of each of the first three children to assist in purchasing clothing and, if the mother is employed, a recuperation allowance for 14 weeks.

The position of women in Chad is a subordinate one. The average woman completing her childbearing years in 1993 had borne an average of 5.3 children. Abortion is legal only to save the mother's life.

There was little regard for human rights during the civil war of the 1980s. It has been estimated that 10% of the total population had been killed in the fighting. In 1983, Amnesty International accused the Habré government of killing civilians suspected of disloyalty in southern Chad and its 1986 report noted the "disappearance" of hundreds of persons reportedly detained; many were believed to have been killed. A pattern of arbitrary regime violence continues, although less overtly, under Déby.

41HEALTH

In 1987 Chad had 4 hospitals, 44 smaller health centers, 1 UNICEF clinic, and 239 other clinics—half under religious auspices. Many regional hospitals were damaged or destroyed in fighting, and health services barely existed in 1987. Total health care expenditures were $76 million in 1990. In 1992, there was 1 physician per 30,030 people.

All medicine, antibiotic, and vaccine imports must be authorized by the Ministry of Health. The most common diseases are schistosomiasis, leprosy, malaria, spinal meningitis, tuberculosis, and yaws, as well as malnutrition. In 1990, there were 167 reported cases of tuberculosis per 100,000 people. Immunization rates in 1992 were very low for children up to one year of age: tuberculosis (43%); diphtheria, pertussis, and tetanus (17%); polio (17%); and measles (41%). In 1991, only 57% of the inhabitants had access to safe water.

Chad had 258,000 births in 1992 and a birth rate of 43.8 per 1,000 people. The infant mortality rate was 123 per 1,000 live births. Maternal mortality in 1991 was 960 per 100,000 live births. In 1993, only 1% of married women (ages 15 to 49) used any form of contraception

The average life expectancy in 1993 was estimated at 47 years, and the overall death rate was 18 per 1,000.

42HOUSING
Forty thousand buildings and homes were destroyed during the civil war. According to the latest available figures for 1980–88, the total housing stock numbered 700,000, with 7.2 people per dwelling.

43EDUCATION
The educational system is patterned on that of France, and the language of instruction is French. Private schools of an exclusively religious character (such as the catechism classes of Christian missions and the Muslim schools) receive no assistance from public funds, but the schools that conform to the officially prescribed educational programs are aided by government grants. Education is theoretically compulsory between ages 6 and 14. Primary education lasts for six years followed by secondary education which lasts for another seven years.

In 1991, there were 2,544 primary schools in Chad with 9,238 teachers and 591,417 pupils. In the general secondary schools, there were 2,062 teachers and 72,641 pupils. In 1990, UNESCO estimated that 57.8% of adult males and 82.1% of adult females were illiterate.

In 1971, the University of Chad was officially opened in N'Djamena. The university had three faculties—sciences; law and economics; and letters and human sciences. There is a zoological and veterinary institute at Farcha, a national communications college in Sarh, and a national college of administration in N'Djamena. In 1988, all higher level institutions had 329 teaching staff and 2,983 pupils.

44LIBRARIES AND MUSEUMS
Many of the libraries in Chad are small private collections of research institutes in N'Djamena. Among the largest are the Chadian National Institute for the Humane Sciences, with 3,196 volumes, and the Educational Documentation Center, with 2,500 volumes. The library of the University of Chad had about 12,000 volumes.

The National Museum in N'Djamena was founded in 1962 and has an excellent collection on the natural history, archaeology, and ethnography of Chad. The Museum of Abeche which was founded in 1962 and formally opened in 1984, features an ethnographical collection.

45MEDIA
Postal and telephone service are under the direction of the Minister of Posts and Telecommunications. There are direct telephone connections between N'Djamena and Paris and several African capitals. About 9,856 telephones were in service in N'Djamena in 1991. Radiodiffusion Nationale Tchadienne and Tele–Tchad have broadcasting stations in N'Djamena which broadcast in French, Arabic, and seven African languages. In 1991 there were 1,385,000 radios and 7,000 television sets.

The government press agency publishes the daily news bulletin *Info-Tchad* (circulation about 800 in 1991). Other publications include the weekly *N'Djamena Hebdo* (1991 circulation 12,000) and the monthly *La Democrate* (4,000).

46ORGANIZATIONS
The Chamber of Commerce, Agriculture, and Industry at N'Djamena has branches at Sarh, Moundou, Bol, and Abéché. In rural areas, cooperatives promote the production and marketing of agricultural products. Fishermen and artisans also maintain cooperatives. Self-help tribal societies have grown rapidly, particularly in the larger towns, where members of ethnic groups act together to assist newcomers and to maintain links with those remaining in traditional areas.

47TOURISM, TRAVEL, AND RECREATION
Visitors must have valid passports and visas (except visitors from France, Germany, Nigeria, and most French-speaking African countries). Evidence of a yellow fever vaccination is also required. There were 20,501 foreign visitors in 1991, 52% from Africa and 40% from Europe. The country had 275 hotel rooms with 550 beds and an 8% occupancy rate, and tourist receipts totaled us$10 million. Most tourists are attracted by hunting and the Zakouma National Park.

48FAMOUS CHADIANS
Ngarta Tombalbaye (1918–75) was the first president of the independent Republic of Chad. Gen. Félix Malloum (b.1932) became chief of state after the 1975 coup, but was ousted in 1979. Goukouni Oueddei (b.1944) served (1979–82) as president and subsequently led a Libyan-backed rival government in northern Chad. Hissène Habré (b.1942), a Muslim military leader, seized the capital in 1982 and became president.

49DEPENDENCIES
Chad has no territories or colonies.

50BIBLIOGRAPHY
Bouquet, Christian. *Tchad: Genese d'un Conflict.* Paris: L'Harmattan, 1982.

Collelo, Thomas, (ed.). *Chad: A Country Study,* 2nd ed. Washington, D.C.: Government Printing Office, 1990.

Chapelle, Jean. *Le Peuple Tchadien.* Paris: L'Harmattan, 1980.

Decalo, Samuel. *Historical Dictionary of Chad,* 2nd ed. Metuchen, N.J.: Scarecrow Press, 1987.

Kelley, Michael P. *A State in Disarray: Conditions of Chad's Survival.* Boulder, Colo.: Westview Press, 1986.

Lemarchand, Rene. *Chad: Background to Conflict.* Gainesville, Fla.: University of Florida Press, 1979.

Thompson, Virginia McLean. *Conflict in Chad.* Berkeley: Institute of International Studies, University of California, 1981.

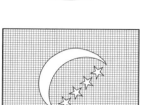

COMOROS

Federal Islamic Republic of the Comoros
République Fédérale Islamique des Comores
Jumhuriyat al-Qumur al-Ittihadiyah al-Islamiyah

CAPITAL: Moroni.

FLAG: On a green background appears a white crescent set at an angle and encompassing four white stars.

ANTHEM: No information available.

MONETARY UNIT: The Comorian franc (Co Fr) is the equivalent of the Communauté Financière Africaine franc (CFA Fr), which is linked with the French franc at a ratio of 75:1. There are notes of 500, 1,000, and 5,000 Co Fr. Co Fr1 = $0.0023 (or $1 = Co Fr428.25).

WEIGHTS AND MEASURES: The metric system is used.

HOLIDAYS: New Year's Day, 1 January; Second Coup d'État, 13 May; Independence Day, 6 July; Admission to UN, 12 November; Christmas Day, 25 December. The principal Muslim holidays are observed.

TIME: 3 PM = noon GMT.

¹LOCATION, SIZE, AND EXTENT

The Comoros are located at the northern entrance of the Mozambique Channel, between the eastern shore of the African continent and the island of Madagascar, which lies about 480 km (300 mi) to the SE. Comparatively, the area occupied by the Comoros Islands is slightly more than 12 times the size of Washington, D.C. The islands have a combined area of 2,170 sq km (838 sq mi), of which Grande Comore (Njazídja), the largest and northernmost island, comprises 1,148 sq km (443 sq mi); Mohéli (Mwali), lying to the s of Grande Comore, 290 sq km (112 sq mi); and Anjouan (Nzwani) to the E of Mohéli, 424 sq km (164 sq mi). There are also several small islands. The Comoros extend about 180 km (110 mi) ESE–WNW and 100 km (60 mi) NNE–SSW, with a total coastline of 340 km (211 mi). Mayotte, the fourth major island in the Comoros Archipelago, covering an area of 374 sq km (144 sq mi), is claimed by the Comoros but remains under French territorial administration. The capital city Moroni, is located at the western edge of the island of Grande Comore.

²TOPOGRAPHY

The islands are volcanic in origin, and their highest peak, Mt. Kartala (2,361 m/7,746 ft), located near the southern tip of the island of Grande Comore, is an active volcano. In the center of Grande Comore lies a desert lava field; to the north, a number of volcanic peaks rise from a plateau nearly 600 m (2,000 ft) in altitude. The island of Anjouan, to the southeast, has steep hills reaching heights of nearly 1,500 m (5,000 ft) in a central volcanic massif. Mohéli, to the west of Anjouan, has wide and fertile valleys, with a ridge in the center that reaches about 580 m (1,900 ft) above sea level, and a thick forest cover.

³CLIMATE

The climate in the Comoros is humid and tropical, with coastal temperatures averaging about 28°C (82°F) in March and 23°C (73°F) in August. The monsoon season lasts from November to April. Rainfall in January averages 42 cm (16.5 in), and in October, the driest month, 8.5 cm (3.3 in). Cyclones and tidal waves are frequent in the summer.

⁴FLORA AND FAUNA

The rich volcanic soils on the islands foster the growth of a profuse vegetation. Beyond the coastal zones, where mangroves predominate, there are coconut palms, mangoes, and bananas, and above them is a forest zone, with many varieties of tropical hardwoods. Broom, lichens, and heather grow on the highest peaks. The animal life is similar to that found on Madagascar. Comorian waters harbor the coelacanth, a rare primitive fish. Fossil remains of the coelecanth dating back 400 million years, have been found.

⁵ENVIRONMENT

Although Mohéli has large tracts of fertile land not yet cultivated, parts of Anjouan are so densely populated that farmers have been forced to extend cultivation to the higher slopes, leading to deforestation and soil erosion. Population growth has also increased the demand for firewood, threatening the remaining forest areas. Soil erosion is aggravated by lack of terracing. Comoras has .2 cubic miles of water. Forty-seven percent is used for agricultural purposes and 48% is used in urban centers and for domestic purposes. Five percent of the water supply is used in industry.

As of 1994, endangered species in the Comoros included the Anjouan sparrow hawk and Anjouan scops owl. Six of the 17 species of mammals in Comoros were endangered. Three types of birds in a total of 99 species and three plant species in a total of 416 are also endangered.

⁶POPULATION

The population of the islands in 1994 was estimated at 530,105, excluding Mayotte, which had a population of 94,410 in 1991. Grande Comore, the largest island, had an estimated population in 1991 of 255,800; Anjouan, 197,900; and Mohéli 25,200. The population density in 1994 was 285 persons per sq km (or 737 per sq mi); a population of 778,000 was projected for the year 2000, assuming a crude birthrate of 45.2 per 1,000 population and a crude death rate of 10.2, for a net natural increase of 35 during 1995–2000. Moroni, the capital, had an estimated population of 24,000 in 1990. Nearly half the population is under 15 years of age.

[7]MIGRATION

About 40,000 Comorians live in France and 25,000 in Madagascar. About 16,000 were expelled from Madagascar in 1977–78, following a massacre there of Comorians in December 1976.

[8]ETHNIC GROUPS

The islands' indigenous population consists almost entirely of persons of mixed African, Malagasy, Malay, and Arab descent. Small numbers of Indians, Malagasy, and Europeans play an important part in the economy.

[9]LANGUAGES

French and Arabic are the official languages. The main spoken language, Shaafi Islam (Comorian), is akin to Swahili but has elements borrowed from Arabic. Other languages spoken include French, Malagasy, Swahili, Arabic, and Makua (an African language).

[10]RELIGIONS

Islam, the state religion, is followed by more than 99% of Comorians. Almost all Comorians are Sunni Muslims. There are small numbers of Christians, mostly French of Malagasy descent, and of Baha'is.

[11]TRANSPORTATION

Each island has a ringed road, and there were some 750 km (466 mi) of roads in 1991, with 210 km (130 mi) paved. There is an international airport at Hahaia, on Grande Comore; other islands have smaller airfields. Air Comores (51% owned by Air France) provides regular inter-island flights. Air France and Air Madagascar provide service to Madagascar; Air Mauritius provides service to Mauritius; South African Airways makes a weekly stop; and there is also regular ship service between the Comoros and Madagascar. There is a year-round port at Dzaoudzi, off the island of Mayotte. Until recently, the other ports, at Moroni and Mutsamudu, could accommodate only small ships; larger vessels had to anchor offshore and be loaded and unloaded by dhows. Expansion of the port of Mutsamudu to allow direct access to Anjouan was completed in 1985.

[12]HISTORY

The Comoros were in all likelihood visited in antiquity by Phoenician sailors. The first settlers were probably Melanesian and Polynesian peoples, who came to the Comoros by the 6th century AD; later immigrants arrived from East Africa, Arab lands, Indonesia, Persia, and Madagascar. The Portuguese discovered the islands about 1503, and Frenchmen first landed in 1517. The Englishman James Lancaster visited the islands toward the end of the 16th century; at that time, and for many years afterward, Arab influence predominated over that of Europeans. Malagasy invasions also took place in the 16th century. In 1843, a Malagasy who ruled over Mayotte ceded the island to France, and in 1865, a Malagasy ruler of Mohéli signed a friendship treaty with France. A French protectorate was placed over Anjouan, Grande Comore, and Mohéli in 1886, and in 1908 the islands were joined administratively with French-ruled Madagascar. In World War II, the islands were occupied by a British force and turned over to the Free French. The Comoros were granted administrative autonomy within the Republic of France on 9 May 1946, acquiring overseas territorial status, and on 22 December 1961 achieved internal autonomy under special statute. This status was amended on 3 January 1968 to give the territory greater internal autonomy.

On 11 December 1958, the Territorial Assembly voted to remain in the Republic, but the cause of independence, championed by the Comoro National Liberation Movement, based in Tanzania, was eventually embraced by the ruling coalition on the islands. An agreement for independence within five years was signed in Paris on 15 June 1973, and in a referendum held on 22 December 1974, a large majority on all islands except Mayotte voted in favor of independence. The vote was ratified by the French parliament, which decided that each island should vote separately on a new constitution. On 6 July 1975, nevertheless, the Comoros legislature unilaterally declared independence for all the islands, including Mayotte. The French government, rejecting the Comorian claim to Mayotte, ordered a separate referendum for the island, which on 7 February 1976 voted to remain part of France. The UN General Assembly backed the Comorian claim to Mayotte in 1976 and 1979 resolutions.

Considerable domestic turmoil accompanied the birth of the new nation. The first Comorian government held power only a month before it was overthrown on 3 August 1975 with the aid of foreign white mercenaries. On 13 May 1978, 'Ali Soilih, who had led the 1975 military coup and had become head of state in January 1976, was overthrown by mercenaries, led by Bob Denard, whose previous exploits in Zaire and elsewhere made him infamous through Africa. They reinstalled the nation's first president, Ahmad 'Abdallah, who had been living in exile in Paris. Denard remained the true power behind Abdallah. Their government was close to right-wing elements in France and to South Africa, where the Comoros serve as a conduit for supplies to the Renamo rebels in Mozambique.

A new constitution was approved on 1 October 1978 by 99.31% of the voters, and on 22 October, 'Abdallah, the only candidate, was elected president with a reported 99.94% of the valid votes. Soon after, France agreed to restore economic and military aid, which had been suspended during the Soilih regime.

Chronic economic problems were worsened in January 1983 by tropical cyclone Elena, the worst in 30 years. The damage was estimated at Co Fr200 million; up to 80% of the crop was damaged.

'Abdallah was reelected unopposed in September 1984. There were coup attempts in 1985 and 1987. Elections to the Federal Assembly were held in March 1987. By 1989, however, resentment for the overbearing influence of Denard and his men grew. Even 'Abdullah grew disenchanted and, with the backing of France and South Africa, he moved to displace Denard's mercenaries. Before this could be implemented, however, on 26 November 1989, disgruntled mercenaries attacked the presidential palace and murdered 'Abdallah.

Said Mohamed Djohar, head of the Supreme Court, was appointed interim president. With the help of Paris and Pretoria, he forced Denard to relinquish power in exchange for safe passage to South Africa on 15 December 1989.

A French peacekeeping force enabled the government to lift political restrictions and conduct a presidential election. On 11 March 1990, Djohar won a runoff with 55% of the vote. His coalition government survived three coup attempts.

Legislative elections were held in November and December 1992. The Federal Assembly was badly divided (the largest party had 7 of the 42 seats) and could reach no consensus with the president on his choice of ministers. Governments fell frequently. On 18 June 1992, Djohar dissolved the National Assembly. In the long-delayed and controversial 12 and 20 December 1993 legislative elections, supporters of Djohar won 24 of the 42 seats in the Assembly. Members of the opposition parties rejected Djohar's appointment of Abdou Madi as prime minister as they contested the validity of both the election results and the choice of Djohar's son-in-law as president of the Assembly on 7 January. They accused the RDR (Djohar's new party) of being "usurpers". On 17 January, the main opposition parties agreed to coordinate their actions in a Forum for National Recovery (FRN).

[13]GOVERNMENT

Immediately prior to independence, the Comoros had partial autonomy and were governed by a 31-member Council of Ministers responsible to a Chamber of Deputies. The territory was represented in the French parliament by one senator and by two delegates to the National Assembly. A high commissioner represented the French president. After independence was declared, the Chamber of Deputies was reconstituted as a National Assembly. After the August 1975 coup, the National Assembly was abolished; supreme power was subsequently vested in the National Council of the Institutions, headed by President 'Ali Soilih.

The constitution of 1978, the first constitution of the Comoros, established a Federal Islamic republic. Under this document, as amended in 1982, the president was elected to a six-year term, and there was an elected Federal Assembly of 42 members. A new constitution was adopted in June 1992. The President and 42-member Federal Assembly are elected by universal suffrage for four- and five-year terms respectively. It also provides for a 15-member Senate to be chosen by an electoral college for a term of six years. The post of prime minister is held by a member of the majority party in the Assembly.

[14]POLITICAL PARTIES

In February 1982, the Comorian Union for Progress (Union Comorienne pour le Progrés—UCP) was established as the only legal party; in March, UCP members won 37 of 38 seats in the National Assembly in contested elections that also involved independents. In March 1987, UCP candidates won all 42 seats; despite earlier assurances of a free ballot, few opposition candidates were allowed to run, and dissidents were subject to intimidation and imprisonment.

The UCP (known as Udzima) had been President Djohar's party until November 1991. But it had no seats in the Assembly. On 10 September 1993, it merged with the Union for Democracy and Decentralization (UNDC), the largest party in the Assembly with just seven seats. Before the dissolution of the Assembly in June 1993, the Islands' Fraternity and Unity Party (CHUMA) had three seats and the MDP/NGDC had five seats. No other party had more than two seats. Djohar hastily created his own party, the RDR, to contest the December 1993 elections. After 1993, the party distribution in the Assembly was RDR, 24 seats, and the UNDC and its allies, 18 seats.

[15]LOCAL GOVERNMENT

Under the federal system, each island has its own elected legislature. The governors, formerly elected, were appointed by the president after the constitution was amended in 1982.

[16]JUDICIAL SYSTEM

The Supreme Court resolves constitutional questions, supervises presidential elections, and arbitrates any case in which the government is accused of malpractice. The Supreme Court also reviews decisions of the lower courts, including the superior court of appeals at Moroni Lower courts of the first instance are located in major towns. Religious courts on the islands apply Muslim law in matters relating to social and personal relationships.

The judiciary is largely independent of the executive and legislative branches. The 1992 Constitution provides a number of safeguards including equality of all citizens before the law and the right of the accused to access to defense counsel.

[17]ARMED FORCES

There is a small French-trained army of almost 1,000 men. A 300-man presidential guard is run by 30 French and Belgian mercenaries reportedly paid by South Africa, with additional contributions from France and Kuwait.

[18]INTERNATIONAL COOPERATION

On 12 November 1975, the Comoros became a UN member. The nation participates in the ECA, FAO, IBRD, IDA, IFAD, ILO, IMF, ITU, UNESCO, UNIDO, UPU, WHO, and WMO, as well

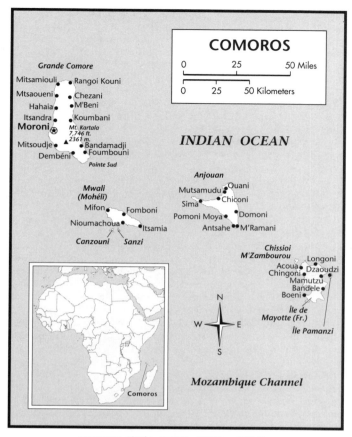

LOCATION: 43°1' to 44°32'E; 11°21' to 12°25'S.
TERRITORIAL SEA LIMIT: 12 mi.

as in the African Development Bank, G-77, and OAU. It is also a member of two new groups formed in the 1980s, the Indian Ocean Commission and the Preferential Trade Area for East and Southern Africa, and is a signatory of the Law of the Sea.

[19]ECONOMY

The economy of the Comoros is agriculture based, dependent on trade and foreign assistance. Foreign aid accounts for about half of GDP. Mineral resources are few; there is little industry. Tourism, however, increased considerably in 1991. After a period of low growth in the late 1980s, GDP returned in 1991 to its earlier growth rate of about 4%.

Agriculture accounts for 98% of export earnings (1988) and employs 78.6% of the population (1991). Cassava, sweet potatoes, rice, and bananas are the staple crops along with yams, coconuts, and maize. Meat, rice, and vegetables are leading imports. Comoros is the world's second largest producer of vanilla, with one-third of exports going to France, and the world's leading producer of ylang-ylang, a perfume oil. Cloves and copra are also exported. Land access is a problem, as is overpopulation. The fishing industry has potential but is still largely undeveloped.

In January 1994 France suddenly devalued the CFA franc, causing its value to drop in half overnight. Immediately, prices for almost all imported goods soared, including prices for food and essential drugs, like those to combat malaria. Since 1948 France had guaranteed a fixed parity of one French franc to 50 African francs. The resulting stability in the currency had generally kept inflation low and helped to maintain a steady rate of growth. However, in the 1980s, the economies of the CFA countries began to stagnate in relation to other African nations, and France came under increased pressure from the World Bank, the IMF, and western countries to stop subsidizing the CFA franc. The devaluation, long expected in the investment community, is designed to enourage new investment, particularly in the export sectors of the economy, and discourage the use of hard currency reserves to buy products that could be grown domestically.

20INCOME

In 1992 Comoros's GNP was $262 million at current prices, or $510 per capita. For the period 1985–92 the average inflation rate was 3.0%, resulting in a real growth rate in per capita GNP of –2.3%. In 1992 the GDP was $261 million in current US dollars. Agriculture contributes 38.8% to GDP, the category comprising trade, restaurants, and hotels contributes 15.1%, and construction and manufacturing 6.9% and 3.5% respectively.

21LABOR

The majority of the economically active population is engaged in subsistence agriculture, fishing, or petty commerce. The wage-earning labor force is small, consisting of fewer than 2,000 employees (or 9,500 employees including the public sector). Since 1990, teachers, civil servants, and dock workers have created unions for purposes of collective action. The minimum age for employment is 15 years, but children generally work with their families in the large subsistence farming and fishing sectors. The unemployment rate unofficially exceeded 70% in 1992.

22AGRICULTURE

The economy of the Comoros is primarily agricultural, with arable land comprising 44.8% of the total land area as of 1991. Among the chief crops in 1992, in tons, were manioc, 49,000; coconuts, 50,000; bananas, 53,000; sweet potatoes, 10,000; rice, 10,000; corn, 4,000; and copra, 5,000. Other crops include sugarcane, sisal, peppers, spices, coffee, and various perfume plants such as ylang-ylang, abelmosk, lemon grass, jasmine, and citronella. The chief export crops are vanilla, cloves, ylang-ylang, and copra. The Comoros, including Mayotte, account for about 80% of world production of ylang-ylang essence. Marketed exports in 1992 included copra, 200 tons, and dried vanilla, 236 tons.

Food demand is not met by domestic production, and so Comoros is highly dependent on imported foods, especially rice. Over half of all foodstuffs are imported, including 13,337 tons of rice in 1985. Agricultural productivity is extremely low, and cultivation methods are rudimentary. Fertilizer is seldom used by smallholders. About 20% of the cultivated land belongs to company estates; 20% to indigenous landowners who live in towns and pay laborers to cultivate their holdings; and 60% to village reserves allotted according to customary law. Agriculture contributes about 40% to GDP.

23ANIMAL HUSBANDRY

Small amounts of livestock are raised. In 1992 there were an estimated 126,000 goats, 47,000 head of cattle, 14,000 sheep, and 5,000 asses. An estimated 1,000 tons of beef and 1,000 tons of other meat were produced in 1992, along with 4,000 tons of milk and 640 tons of eggs.

24FISHING

The fish catch in the Comoros amounted to about 6,455 tons in 1991, half of which was tuna. A Japanese-funded fisheries training center was opened on Anjouan in 1985.

25FORESTRY

Forest and woodland areas declined from 44,000 hectares (109,000 acres) in 1968 to about 35,000 hectares (86,000 acres) in 1991 (including Mayotte). Numerous fruit trees and tropical hardwoods are found. Some timber is produced, notably on the island of Grande Comore, which has about half the remaining forest.

26MINING

There are no commercially exploitable mineral resources. Some sand, gravel, and crushed stone were produced for the domestic construction industry. Promotion of a new construction technique using lava and volcanic ash was expected to reduce cement imports and coral mining.

27ENERGY AND POWER

In 1991, 16 million kwh were generated. Installed capacity was about 5,000 kw, 80% of it thermal. Work began in 1985 on a 4,500-kw hydroelectric dam on Anjouan. All petroleum products are imported.

28INDUSTRY

There are various small-scale industries, mostly for processing the islands' agricultural products. Besides a few perfume distilleries, the Comoros had, in the mid-1980s, about 20 sawmills, a soap factory, a printing plant, a small plastics factory, a soft-drink plant, and metalworking shops.

29SCIENCE AND TECHNOLOGY

There are no research institutes or institutions of higher learning in the Comoros.

30DOMESTIC TRADE

Official policy in the mid-1980s was to control the prices of all products, with the government setting profit margins at the wholesale and retail levels. Business hours are 7:30 AM–noon and 3–5:30 PM Monday–Thursday, 7:30–11 AM Friday, and 7:30–noon Saturday. Banking hours are 7 AM–noon Monday–Thursday and 7–11:30 AM Friday.

31FOREIGN TRADE

Ylang-ylang essence, vanilla, cloves, copra, and other agricultural commodities make up the bulk of Comorian exports; of these, vanilla is by far the most important export earner. Imports include rice and other foodstuffs, petroleum products, and motor vehicles.

Exports in 1989 (in millions of French francs) were as follows:

Vanilla	72.5
Cloves	12.6
Ylang-ylang essence	25.5
Other exports	4.6
TOTAL	115.2

Principal imports in 1989 (estimated, in millions of French francs) were as follows:

Rice	55.2
Fuels	15.6
Transport equipment	15.2
Iron and steel	6.8
Cement	6.2
Other imports	172.51
TOTAL	271.51

France is the leading trade partner, accounting for 44.5% of exports and 58% of imports in 1989. Other leading trading partners that year were the United States, Botswana, Bahrain, Kenya, Brazil, and South Africa.

32BALANCE OF PAYMENTS

In general, the chronic deficit on current accounts is counterbalanced by foreign aid, especially from France. Domestic consumption has grown from 101% of GDP in 1986 to 104% in 1991.

In 1991 merchandise exports totaled $24.36 million and imports $53.60 million. The merchandise trade balance was $-29.24 million. The following table summarizes Comoros' balance of payments for 1990 and 1991 (in millions of US dollars):

	1990	1991
CURRENT ACCOUNT		
Goods, services, and income	-54.02	-49.85
Unrequited transfers	44.74	40.94
TOTALS	-9.29	-8.91
CAPITAL ACCOUNT		
Direct investment	-0.71	2.51
Other long-term capital	0.90	11.28
Other short-term capital	13.48	-9.63
Reserves	4.85	3.06
TOTALS	18.52	7.22
Errors and omissions	-9.23	1.70
Total change in reserves	3.77	-1.24

33BANKING AND SECURITIES

The Central Bank of the Comoros was established in 1981. The Banque Pour I' Industrie et de Commerce de Comores, is the main commercial bank; the French Commercial Bank is also represented. The Banque de Development de Comores is half state owned. There are no securities exchanges.

34INSURANCE

Société Comorienne d'Assurances is based in Moroni. The Paris-based Préservatrice Foncière d'Assurances has an agent in Moroni.

35PUBLIC FINANCE

From 1986 to 1989, the budget deficit (excluding grants) averaged 26% of GDP. The deficit was subsidized by foreign grants and loans, chiefly from France. In 1990 the deficit decreased to 17% of GDP, due to improved tax collection methods and a reduction of expenditures. The fiscal deficit was expected to fall from 19.6% of GDP in 1993 to 14% by 1995. From 1980 to 1992, the external medium- and long-term debt rose from $43 million to $165 million, due to massive public investment projects in the early 1980s.

The Comoros government and the IMF agreed in 1990 to a structural adjustment program covering 1991 to 1993. The program provides $135 million and proposes a plan whereby the government diversifies its exports, reduces public expenditures, and privatizes its parastatal sector. Furthermore, the plan called for the abolishment of levies on export crops, privatization of the state-owned hotels, liquidation of the state-owned meat marketing company, initiation of a number of environmental projects, and the reduction of the number of civil servants. This last measure prompted civil disorder and economic disruptions. Concerned over the progress of reforms in 1993, the IMF and the government reassessed the program. Measures were adopted which persuaded the IMF to continue its support of the program.

36TAXATION

Tax collection, formerly the role of the island governors, became a federal responsibility under the 1982 constitutional revision. Wage and salary earners were taxed in 1987 at a maximum rate of 15%.

37CUSTOMS AND DUTIES

Import and export licenses are required but often limited to a few firms. Since 1992, the government has reorganized the customs office, computerized customs, and introduced taxes on petroleum products and rice.

38FOREIGN INVESTMENT

Private foreign investment in the Comoros has been minimal since independence. The Comoros economy is supported by foreign aid and assistance, primarily from France but to a lesser extent from Japan, Saudi Arabia, Kuwait, and the United Arab Emirates. Recently, investment interest in the fishing industry and in hotel development has surfaced.

In the late 1980s France was subsidizing the Comoros budget with 30 million French francs annually. In 1990, France cancelled a Comoros debt of 229 million French francs and waived payment on a further 9-million-franc obligation. In 1992, France made pledges of some 80 million French francs to the Comoros government.

39ECONOMIC DEVELOPMENT

Development projects in the late 1980s and early 1990s focused on the agricultural sector, hydroelectric development, fishing, and start-up investment funds for small and intermediate enterprises. In addition, the European Development Funds provided resources for the redevelopment of the port at Moroni.

40SOCIAL DEVELOPMENT

Women occupy a subservient position in this extremely traditional society but retain some strength from the matrilineal social structure. In 1993, the fertility rate was estimated at 6.8, and the infant mortality rate was 82 per 1,000 live births. Although the government regards the fertility rate as too high, no major population control programs have been launched.

41HEALTH

In 1987 there were 6 main hospitals, 10 secondary hospitals and medical centers, and 4 maternity clinics. In 1990, there were 57 doctors (1 physician per 23,540 people), 6 pharmacists, 6 dentists, 155 nurses, and 86 midwives. In 1990 there were 1.4 hospital beds per 1,000 people.

In 1992, there were 28,700 births, which represents a birth rate of 48.5 births per 1,000 people. Average life expectancy in 1992 was 56 years. About 28% of all children were estimated to die before age 5. The overall death rate in 1993 was 11.7 per 1,000 people.

Lack of animal protein is a serious problem. In addition, a large percentage of the adult population suffers from malaria, and there is a high incidence of turberculosis and leprosy. In 1992, approximately 30% of children were immunized for measles.

42HOUSING

As of 1980, 65.4% of all housing units were straw huts with roofs of cocoa leaves, and 25.1% were made of durable materials including stone, brick, or concrete. Of all housing units, 87.5% were owned, 3.1% were rented, and 2.6% were occupied rent free. Traditional (non-flush) toilets were found in 92.3% of all housing units, gas lighting in 91.4%, and electric lighting in 5.7%.

43EDUCATION

Education is compulsory for children between the ages of 7 to 16 years. Primary education lasts for six years followed by seven years of secondary education, four years in the first stage followed by three years in the second stage. In 1987, the Comoros had 257 primary schools, with a total of 64,737 pupils and 1,777 teachers. Schools at the general secondary level had 14,472 pupils and 557 teachers in 1989. There is a teacher training college near

Moroni, and two technical schools. The higher-level institutions had 32 teaching staff and 248 students in 1989. About 52% of the population aged 15 or over was illiterate in the mid-1980s.

44 LIBRARIES AND MUSEUMS
At the time of independence there were two public libraries and three school libraries, with a total of 13,400 volumes.

45 MEDIA
The weekly newspaper *Al Watwany* (1991 circulation 1,200) is published by the government; *L'Archipel* is published independently. In 1991 there were 4,016 telephones and an estimated 72,000 radios. Radio-Comoros, a government agency, provides services on shortwave and FM in Comorian, French, English, Arabic, Malagasy, and Swahili. A television service was begun in 1986.

46 ORGANIZATIONS
There is a Chamber of Commerce, Industry, and Agriculture at Moroni.

47 TOURISM, TRAVEL, AND RECREATION
The tourist industry was undeveloped at independence and has stagnated since 1983. In 1991, there were 378 hotel rooms with a total of 750 beds. There were 16,942 tourists in 1991, 57% from Europe and 39% from Africa, and tourist receipts totaled about US$9 million. No vaccinations are required, but antimalarial precautions are advisable.

48 FAMOUS COMORIANS
Heads of state since independence include 'Ali Soilih (1937–78), who came to power as a result of the 1975 coup and who died after the 1978 takeover; and Ahmad 'Abdallah (b.1919), president briefly in 1975 and restored to power in 1978.

49 DEPENDENCIES
The Comoros have no territories or dependencies.

50 BIBLIOGRAPHY
American University. *Area Handbook for the Indian Ocean Territories*. 2nd ed. Washington, D.C.: Government Printing Office, 1982.

Chagnoux, H., and Ali Haribou. *Les Comores*. Paris: Presses Universitaires de France, 1980.

The Comoros: Current Economic Situation and Prospects. Washington, D.C.: World Bank, 1983.

Kerr, Alex (ed.). *Resources and Development in the Indian Ocean Region*. Boulder, Colo.: Westview, 1981.

Newitt, Malyn. *The Comoro Islands: Struggle Against Dependency in the Indian Ocean*. Boulder, Colo.: Westview, 1984.

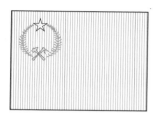

CONGO

People's Republic of the Congo
République Populaire du Congo

CAPITAL: Brazzaville.

FLAG: The flag consists of a red field with a gold crossed hammer and hoe, topped by a gold star and flanked by two green palm leaves, at the upper left quadrant.

ANTHEM: *The Congolaise.*

MONETARY UNIT: The Communauté Financière Africaine franc (CFA Fr) is a paper currency, tied to the French franc at the rate of CFA Fr50 = Fr1. There are coins of 1, 2, 5, 10, 25, 50, 100, and 500 CFA francs and notes of 50, 100, 500, 1,000, 5,000, and 10,000 CFA francs. CFA Fr1 = $0.0018 (or $1 = CFA Fr571).

WEIGHTS AND MEASURES: The metric system is the legal standard.

HOLIDAYS: New Year's Day, 1 January; Labor Day, 1 May; Three Glorious Days, 13–15 August (including Independence Day, 15 August); Christmas Day, 25 December. Movable religious holidays include Good Friday and Easter Monday.

TIME: 1 PM = noon GMT.

¹LOCATION, SIZE, AND EXTENT

Lying astride the Equator, the People's Republic of the Congo contains an area of about 342,000 sq km (132,000 sq mi), extending approximately 1,000 km (620 mi) NNE–SSW and 400 km (250 mi) ESE–WNW. Comparatively, the area occupied by the Congo is slightly smaller than the state of Montana. It is bounded on the N by Cameroon and the Central African Republic, on the E and S by Zaire, on the SW by Cabinda (an enclave of Angola) and the Atlantic Ocean, and on the W by Gabon, with a total boundary length of 5,625 km (2,874 mi).

The Congo's capital city, Brazzaville, is located in the southeastern part of the country.

²TOPOGRAPHY

The Congo is roughly divided into four topographical regions. The coastal region consists of a low, relatively treeless plain, with occasional high spurs jutting down from the Mayombé Escarpment. The escarpment region is made up of a series of parallel folds of moderate height (600–900 m/2,000–3,000 ft) that are almost completely forested. To the east and north of the escarpment, and forming the watershed between the Niari and Ogooué river systems, lies the plateau region, with savanna covering more than 129,000 sq km (50,000 sq mi) and separating the Zaire and Ogooué basins. The northeastern region of the country is a swampy lowland covering some 155,000 sq km (60,000 sq mi); flooding is seasonal, with different tributaries of the Congo/Zaire overflowing into one another. The country has two river systems: that of the coastal rivers, which flow into the Kouilou River, and that of the Zaire River and its tributaries.

³CLIMATE

The Congo has a tropical climate characterized by high humidity and heat. There are two wet and two dry seasons. At Brazzaville, in the south, the average daily maximum temperature is 30°C (86°F) and the average minimum temperature 20°C (68°F). At Souanké, in the far north, the extremes are 29°C (84°F) and 18°C (64°F). Annual rainfall varies from 105 cm (41 in) at Pointe-Noire, in the southwest, to 185 cm (73 in) at Impfondo, in the northeast.

⁴FLORA AND FAUNA

About half the land area is covered by okoumé, limba, and other trees of the heavy rainforest. On the plateaus, the forest gives way to savanna broken by patches of bushy undergrowth. The savanna supports jackals, hyenas, cheetahs, and several varieties of antelope; elephants, wild boar, giraffes, and monkeys dwell in the forest.

⁵ENVIRONMENT

The most significant environmental problems in the Congo are deforestation, increases in urban population, and the protection of its wildlife. The Congo's forests, which cover 50% of the nation's land area, are endangered by fires set to clean the land for agricultural purposes. The forests are also used as a source of fuel. The most accessible forest, that of the Kouilou-Mayombé Mountains, has been overexploited. During 1981–85, deforestation in the Congo proceeded at a rate of 22,000 hectares (54,400 acres) a year. In 1986, the Congo had 10 protected areas, covering some 13,500 sq km (5,200 sq mi). The two largest, the 7,800-sq-km (3,000-sq-mi) Léfini Reserve and the 2,600-sq-km (1,000-sq-mi) Odzala National Park, were established during the French colonial era.

The Congo's urban centers are hampered by air pollution from vehicles and water pollution from sewage. Its water purity problem is most apparent in rural areas where, as of 1994, 98% of the people do not have safe water.

By 1994, 12 of 198 species of mammals were endangered and 3 of 500 species of birds. In addition, 2 reptile species and 4 plant types were threatened with extinction.

⁶POPULATION

In 1984, the population was 1,912,429, and in 1994 it was estimated at 2,521,923; the projection for the year 2000 was 2,976,000, assuming a crude birthrate of 42.4 per 1,000 population, a crude death rate of 14.6, and a net increase of 27.8 during 1995–2000. The average density in 1994 was 7.4 persons per sq km (19.1 per sq mi). At least four-fifths of the people live in the southern third of the country; the greatest concentration is in the Brazzaville area, while the northernmost region is sparsely populated. In 1995, about 43% of the population lived in urban communities. Large cities in 1991 included Brazzaville, the capital, with 760,300 inhabitants; Pointe-Noire, 387,774; Loubomo (formerly Dolisie), 62,073; and Nkayi, 40,019.

7 MIGRATION

There is continuous migration to urban centers, but immigration from other African countries is negligible. Some French, Greek, and Lebanese immigrants have settled in the Congo. At the end of 1992, the Congo was harboring 9,500 African refugees. About 10,000 Zairians have been forcibly deported in recent years as economic migrants rather than political refugees.

8 ETHNIC GROUPS

The population belongs to four major ethnic groups—the Kongo, Bateke, Mboshi, and Sanga—which comprise more than 40 tribes. In addition, there are small groups of Pygmies, possibly Congo's original inhabitants, in the high forest region.

The major ethnic group, the Kongo, occupies the entire area southwest of Brazzaville and accounts for nearly half the nation's population. The Téké, who live north of Brazzaville, are chiefly hunters and fishermen. The Mboshi (or Boulangi) live where the savanna and the forest meet in the northwest; this group has furnished many immigrants to the urban centers, including the majority of Brazzaville's skilled workers and civil servants. The Gabonese inhabit the inundated forest zone of the northeast. There are about 12,000 Pygmies. The non-African community numbers at least 9,000.

9 LANGUAGES

French is the official language. Several related African languages and dialects of the Bantu family are spoken. Monokutuba (Kikongo) and Lingala are the most common.

10 RELIGIONS

Almost half of the population was Christian in the early 1990s, but much of it was considered only nominally so; 39.3% of the Christian population was Roman Catholic. Of the Protestants, about one-third belonged to the autonomous Evangelical Church of the Congo. Church activities have been limited by the state, which took over missionary schools in 1965. In 1978 the government limited the number of religions recognized by the state. Less than 2% of the population is Muslim, mainly in urban centers. About 5% of the people observe African traditional religions exclusively, but traditional beliefs and practices continue to be widespread and coexisting with Christianity.

11 TRANSPORTATION

The most important transportation system is the Congo-Ocean Railroad. Completed in 1934, the 510-km (317-mi) line runs between Brazzaville on Pool Malebo and the ocean port of Pointe-Noire. In the course of descending the Mayombé Escarpment, it crosses 172 bridges and goes through 12 tunnels. To relieve congestion on this stretch, a 91-km (57-mi) line was completed between Bilinga and Loubomo in 1985. The 285-km (177-mi) Comilog rail line was completed in 1962 to transport manganese ore extracted at Moanda, Gabon, from M'Binda on the Gabonese border to the Congo-Ocean line at Mont-Bélo. This traffic was expected to end in the late 1980s with the completion of a railway in Gabon that will transport the ore to the port of Libreville.

Dense tropical forests, rugged terrain, and swamps, together with a hot, humid climate and heavy rainfall, make construction and maintenance of roads extremely costly. In 1991 there were about 12,000 km (7,460 mi) of highways, but only about 560 km (348 mi) were asphalted, and it was considered extremely risky to venture more than 150–200 km (90–125 mi) from Brazzaville because of the poor road conditions. A Brazzaville-to-Duesso road was completed as far as Owando in the mid-1980s. In 1992, about 28,000 passenger cars and 17,418 commercial vehicles were in use.

River transportation is managed by the state-owned Trans-Congo Communications Agency. There are up to 5,000 km (3,100 mi) of navigable rivers: 1,200 km (750 mi) from Brazzaville to Bangui, Central African Republic, by way of the Zaire and Oubangui rivers; 1,300 km (800 mi) from Brazzaville to Nola, Central African Republic, on the Sangha; and the remainder on other internal rivers, especially in the north. The river port of Brazzaville, which is the junction point of the Congo-Ocean Railroad and the Zaire-Oubangui river system, is an important center for trade with the Central African Republic, Chad, and Zaire. A ferry connects Brazzaville with Kinshasa, Zaire. Pointe-Noire is the Congo's only seaport and the terminus of the Congo-Ocean Railroad.

Because of the great distances and the inadequacy of land transportation, air travel and air freight services are rapidly expanding. Brazzaville and Pointe-Noire airports are the hubs of a network of air routes that connect the four equatorial republics with several European cities. Of the other airfields, only Loubomo has a tarred runway. The state-owned Lina-Congo holds a monopoly on domestic routes; it also flew to Gabon and the Central African Republic as of 1987. The Congo is a member of Air Afrique, of which it owns a 7% share. Air Afrique and Union des Transportes Aériens (UTA) are the chief international carriers.

12 HISTORY

Although little is known of the early history of the Congo, it has been established that there was a Congo Empire that extended into present-day Angola and reached its height in the 16th century. The kingdom of Loango, which broke away from the Congo Empire, also prospered for a time. Another African state mentioned in the accounts of the first European explorers was the Anzico kingdom of the Teke. By the end of the 17th century, however, all these kingdoms had grown weak.

The coastal regions of the area were known to Portuguese sailors as early as the 15th century. The mouth of the Zaire River was discovered by Diogo Cão in 1484. French trading companies, interested in slaves and ivory, appeared on the scene during the 17th century; by 1785, more than 100 French ships annually sailed up the coast. After the French Revolution, however, French interest in the area waned.

With the abolition of the slave trade, merchants began to seek new sources of commerce. The first forays into the interior began at this time, but extensive exploration came only toward the end of the 19th century, with Pierre Savorgnan de Bràzza and Henry Morton Stanley. In 1880, Bràzza signed a treaty with the powerful Teke tribal ruler Makoko, bringing the right bank of the Zaire River under French control. The Congress of Berlin (1885) gave formal recognition to French claims to the region. The period after 1900 was marked by a slow but steady establishment of French administrative machinery. By 1910, Gabon, Middle Congo, and Ubangi-Shari (including Chad) were constituted administratively as colonies; together they constituted French Equatorial Africa, all under a governor general at Brazzaville. In 1940, French Equatorial Africa joined the Free French movement and the Allied war effort against the Axis powers. The first territorial assembly was elected in 1947. In a referendum held on 28 September 1958, the territory of Middle Congo voted to become an autonomous republic within the French Community.

CONGO

| 0 | 50 | 100 | 150 Miles |
| 0 | 50 | 100 | 150 Kilometers |

CENTRAL AFRICAN REPUBLIC

CAMEROON

EQUATORIAL GUINEA

GABON

ZAIRE

ATLANTIC OCEAN

Lopi

Bétou

Bangui

Motaba

Lokomo

Bomassa

Souanké

Sembé

Ouesso

Impfondo

Angouma

Zalangoye

Djoua

Lengoué

Sangha

Likouala aux Herbes

Oubangui

Giri

Zaire (Congo)

Belinga

Kemboma

Liouesso

Congo

Basin

Likouala

Etoumbi

Makoua

Owando

Likouala

Obili

Ewo

Alima

Lac Tumba

Mossaka

Congo

N W E S

Moanda

Franceville

Mbigou

M'Binda

Mayoko

▲ Lékéti Mts. 3,412 ft. 1040 m.

Djambala

N'Gao

Lac Mai-Ndombe

Moabi

Zanaga

Léfini

Mossendjo

Bouali

Makabana

Sibiti

Ngabé

Batéké Plateau

Djoué

Congo

Pool Malebo

Kayes

Loubomo

Nkayi

Madingou

Mindouli

Mafauati

Kinkala

Brazzaville

Kinshasa

Binza

Boko

Point-Noire

CABINDA (ANGOLA)

Ngounié

Ogooué

MAYOMBE MTS.

Kouilou

Niari

LOCATION: 3°42′N to 5°1′s; 11°7′ to 18°39′E. **BOUNDARY LENGTHS:** Cameroon, 520 km (323 mi); Central African Republic, 467 km (290 mi); Zaire, 1,625 km (1,010 mi); Angola, 201 km (125 mi); Atlantic coastline, 156 km (97 mi); Gabon, 1,656 km (1,020 mi). **TERRITORIAL SEA LIMIT:** 200 mi.

Two months later, on 28 November 1958, the Territorial Assembly of the Middle Congo proclaimed the Republic of the Congo. On 8 December, Fulbert Youlou, mayor of Brazzaville and leader of the Democratic Union for the Defense of African Interests (UDDIA), was elected to head the provisional government. The adoption of a constitution on 20 February 1959 transformed the provisional government into the first official government of the republic. Legislative elections were held that June. The new National Assembly elected Fulbert Youlou prime minister on 27 June and president on 21 November.

The constitutional law of 4 June 1960, adopted by the French

Parliament and by the Senate of the French Community, made it possible for a member state to become independent without thereby leaving the community. The Republic of the Congo thus proclaimed its independence on 15 August 1960. President Youlou resigned exactly three years later, on 15 August 1963, in the wake of antigovernment rioting that threatened to turn into civil war. Alphonse Massamba-Debat became provisional president and was formally elected to the presidency on 19 December 1963; a new constitution was approved by national referendum that same month. In 1964, relations were established with the USSR and China, and Massamba-Debat then announced the establishment of a "scientific Socialist state" with one-party control.

On 4 September 1968, Massamba-Debat resigned following a military coup that deprived him of most of his presidential powers. Capt. Marien Ngouabi then established a new revolutionary regime. Ngouabi was named president on 1 January 1969, and he proclaimed the People's Republic of the Congo the following December. Political stability proved difficult to achieve, however, and there were seven coup attempts during his seven years in office, which ended with his assassination on 18 March 1977. He was succeeded by Col. Joachim Yhombi-Opango, who abrogated the latest constitution, that of 24 June 1973. Yhombi-Opango resigned on 5 February 1979 (he was subsequently placed under house arrest and charged with treason) and was succeeded in March by Col. Denis Sassou-Nguesso. A 20-year treaty of friendship and cooperation with the USSR was signed in 1981. Sassou-Nguesso was reelected president in July 1984 and was chairman of the OAU during 1986–87.

In 1990, a conference of the ruling party agreed to abandon its Marxist ideology and its monopoly of power. A four-month-long National Conference in 1991 led to a new constitutional order. An interim government was appointed, pending elections, and Sassou-Nguesso was stripped of his powers, except for ceremonial tasks. André Milongo headed the interim government, which conducted free elections in 1992. A multiparty government with Pascal Lissouba as president was elected. His coalition, known as the Presidential Tendency, experienced much turbulence in 1993. A changing coalition of opposition parties, strikes, and violent civil unrest threatened the regime. First-round legislative elections on 2 May 1993, gave way to armed conflict in June and July. Also, the Supreme Court ruled that the second-round elections were flawed. The Organization of African Unity and the President of Gabon stepped in, seeking to mediate and to avoid a civil war. They reached an accord that accepted first-round results and called for second-round elections on 6 October. The opposition alliance, the Union for Democratic Renewal-Congolese Workers' Party (URD-PCT), won seven of the 11 seats contested at that time. Still, Lissouba's Pan-African Union for Social Democracy won 69 of the 125 seats and Lissouba's shaky presidency continued. Short-term success collapsed, however, as fighting again broke out in the capital in November 1993. Fighting continued into 1994 as armed forces loyal to Lissouba battled independent partisan militias.

On the one side is the northern Mbochi ethnic group, which had been aligned with the military government of Sassou-Nguesso. On the other sides are two main southern groups, the Pool Lari and the coastal Vili. Transitional prime minister Milongo surrounded himself with Lari and Bacongo. Lissouba replaced them with his own people, the Nibolek, and "cleansed" the presidential guard.

Although a mediation force was set up after a 30 January 1994 ceasefire, it has been difficult to disarm the tribally based factions.

13GOVERNMENT

The Congo was governed under a constitution, approved by referendum on 8 July 1979 and amended in July 1984. The chairman of the 75-member Central Committee of the Congolese Labor Party (PCT) was the president of the republic and head of state. He was elected for an unspecified term as chairman (and therefore as president) by the party congress. Executive powers resided with the Council of Ministers, appointed by the prime minister and chaired by the president. The 153-member National Assembly, the sole legislative body, was elected by universal suffrage at age 18 from candidates named by the PCT.

On 15 March 1992, voters approved a new constitution which provided for a mixed presidential-parliamentary form of government after the French model. Executive authority is vested in a directly elected president, who appoints the prime minister and cabinet. A National Assembly of 125 members was elected in two-round elections in June and July 1992. There is also a 60-member Senate. Pascal Lissouba was chosen president (61%) and his Pan-African Union for Social Democracy (UPADS) gained 39 seats. That legislature was dissolved in October and new legislative elections in May 1993 led to partisan fighting. A mediated settlement then confirmed a UPADS majority, yet fighting continued into 1994. In the view of many, the "democratic election" unleashed a pandora's box of tribal hatreds.

14POLITICAL PARTIES

Three political parties were active in the Middle Congo before the territory achieved its independence. Of these, the most important proved to be the Democratic Union for the Defense of African Interests (Union Démocratique de Défense des Intérêts Africain—UDDIA), founded by Abbé Fulbert Youlou. The UDDIA received 64% of the popular vote and won 51 of the 61 seats in the National Assembly elected in June 1959. Following the resignation of President Youlou and the dissolution of the Assembly in 1963, all political parties were banned. On 2 July 1964, the National Movement of the Revolution (Mouvement National de la Révolution—MNR), led by President Massamba-Debat, was officially established as the country's sole political party. A power struggle between the People's Militia and the army, tribal rivalries, and other conflicts led to Massamba-Debat's resignation in September 1968. The army commander in chief, Marien Ngouabi, then became head of state.

The Congolese Labor Party (Parti Congolais du Travail—PCT), created in December 1969 to succeed the MNR, had been based on the principles of Marxism-Leninism and democratic centralism. But at its 1990 conference, the PCT abandoned this ideology. The 1979 constitution recognized the PCT as the sole party: all other political parties and any political activity outside the PCT were illegal. In the National Assembly elections of 8 July 1979, all candidates were PCT members.

After his assassination on 18 March 1977, Ngouabi was succeeded by Col. Joachim Yhombi-Opango, and in March 1979 by Col. Denis Sassou-Nguesso, who was reelected in July 1984.

The 1991 National Conference led to an interim government and multiparty elections in 1992. Continual shifts in parties and in coalitions of parties have taken place since. The Pan-African Union for Social Development (UPADS) is currently the largest in the National Assembly and is the party of President Lissouba. His coalition is called the Presidential Tendency, and it also includes the Rally for Democracy and Development (RDD). The PCT is its principal opposition and the PCT has been joined by the Union for Democratic Renewal (URD).

15LOCAL GOVERNMENT

In 1994 there were nine administrative regions and one federal district, each under the authority of a government commissioner; these were subdivided into 46 districts.

16JUDICIAL SYSTEM

The Revolutionary Court of Justice, created in 1969, consists of nine judges who deal with cases involving state security. Judicial bodies include a Supreme Court (appointed by the president), a court of appeals, a criminal court, regional and magistrate's courts, labor courts, and courts of common law, where local chiefs apply traditional laws and customs. These courts are based on the French model. Traditional courts in rural areas handle local property, domestic, and probate disputes by applying local customary law. All special courts and secret trials were abolished in 1991. The 1992 constitution calls for a special court, not yet established, which will protect freedom of speech and press.

The 1992 constitution also affords a number of fundamental rights and freedoms including prohibition of arbitrary arrest and detention. In practice, judicial inefficiency often results in denial of bail and long pretrial detention.

¹⁷ARMED FORCES

In 1993, the Congo had an army of 10,000 men, a navy of 350, and an air force of 500. Its army included 2 armored battalions, 3 infantry battalion groups, 1 parachute commando battalion, 1 engineer battalion, and 1 artillery group, equipped with 83 BTR armored personnel carriers and 53 tanks. The navy had 6 patrol craft and the air force had 57 aircraft, including 22 MiG-17 and MiG-21 fighters. There was a paramilitary force of 6,100. The military budget in 1991 was $77 million or 3.7 percent of gross domestic product. The former USSR was the Congo's major supplier of arms, supplying $300 million in arms imports during 1983–88, but stopped shipments in 1989. The Congo still employs 20 Russian military advisors.

¹⁸INTERNATIONAL COOPERATION

The Congo was admitted to UN membership on 20 September 1960 and is a member of all of the specialized agencies except IAEA. It is also a member of the African Development Bank, the French Community, G-77, and the OAU. The country belongs, with the Central African Republic, Gabon, and Cameroon, to the UDEAC, in which merchandise and capital circulate freely, and it is a signatory to GATT, the Law of the Sea, and the Lomé Convention. In addition to close ties with France and other Western European nations, the Congo has established friendly relations with China. Brazzaville is the African headquarters of WHO.

¹⁹ECONOMY

The Congo's economy is built on its petroleum resources, transport services, and agriculture. After several prosperous years in the early 1980s, the price of oil declined and cast the Congolese economy into the financial turmoil which it has yet to stabilize. The country long flirted with state socialist approaches to its economy before embarking on market-style reforms in 1989.

In spite of its importance to the economy, the agricultural sector is in disarray. Over the last decade, per-capita food production has declined by some 8%. Some 27% of the population are not able to reliably meet their food needs. Early efforts at state-farm production of staple foods failed. Congo's staple food crops are cassava, maize, plantains, yams, and sweet potatoes. The livestock industry is small and subject to health limitations imposed by the prevalence of the tsetse fly. The fishing industry is small and undeveloped.

Petroleum is Congo's most significant resource, reaching a peak contribution of 90% of GDP in 1984. Production continues to increase as new fields are developed and in 1992 stood at 8.2 million tons. The oil refinery at Pointe-Noire continues to operate at less than capacity, however. Natural gas reserves are sufficient to foster interest in the construction of a gas condensation and ammonia plant.

In January 1994 France suddenly devalued the CFA franc, causing its value to drop in half overnight. Immediately, prices for almost all imported goods soared, including prices for food and essential drugs, like those to combat malaria. Since 1948 France had guaranteed a fixed parity of one French franc to 50 African francs. The resulting stability in the currency had generally kept inflation low and helped to maintain a steady rate of growth. However, in the 1980s, the economies of the CFA countries began to stagnate in relation to other African nations, and France came under increased pressure from the World Bank, the IMF, and western countries to stop subsidizing the CFA franc. The devaluation, long expected in the investment community, is designed to enourage new investment, particularly in oil, and discourage the use of hard currency reserves to buy products that could be grown domestically. As an interim measure, France has said that it will nearly halve Congo's debt, a move that has encouraged the international financial community.

²⁰INCOME

In 1992 the Congo's GNP was $2,502 million at current prices, or $1,030 per capita. For the period 1985–92 the average inflation rate was –0.3%, resulting in a real growth rate in per capita GNP of –3.0%.

In 1992 the GDP was $2,817 million in current US dollars. It is estimated that agriculture, hunting, forestry, and fishing contributed 13% to GDP; mining and quarrying, 28%; manufacturing, 7%; electricity, gas, and water, 2%; construction, 2%; wholesale and retail trade, 14%; transport, storage, and communication, 9%; finance, insurance, real estate, and business services, 9%; and other sources, 16%.

²¹LABOR

There were about 750,000 economically active people in 1985, the most recent year reported. Almost half of all salaried employees work for the government. On 21 December 1964, the National Assembly dissolved all existing trade unions and approved the formation of a single trade union movement, the Confederation of Congolese Syndicates, which in 1992 was still a powerful force and the only umbrella trade union organization. As of 1992, both the new constitution and the Congolese Labor Code affirm the right of workers to freely associate and form trade unions.

The 40-hour workweek has been established for wage employment. Labor tribunals with equal representation for workers and employers settle individual labor disputes, and advisory labor commissions intervene in the settlement of collective disputes.

²²AGRICULTURE

In 1991, total arable land was only 169,000 hectares (417,600 acres), or only 0.4% of the total land area. Agricultural activity is concentrated in the south, especially in the Niari Valley. Main crops for local consumption are manioc (790,000 tons in 1992), plantains (85,000 tons), yams, (13,000 tons), rice (1,000 tons), bananas (42,000 tons), sugarcane (450,000 tons), tobacco, peanuts, and corn. In 1992, 70% of food requirements were imported. Landholdings are small, averaging less than 1.4 hectares (3.5 acres) per plot.

Export crops are coffee, cocoa, and palm oil; in 1992, 1,000 tons of coffee and 2,000 tons of cocoa were produced. Palm trees are under the management of a state-owned company. Commercial production of oil from palm kernels, mainly from palm trees indigenous to the Niari Valley, the Pool Malebo, and the Bateke Plateau regions, fell from 4,935 tons in 1961 to 510 tons in 1992. The rural population has fallen from 80% in 1960 to less than 30% today. Since 1987, the government has encouraged agricultural development by abolishing state marketing boards and retail monopolies, freeing prices, removing tariffs on essential inputs, launching new agricultural credit institutions, and selling or closing most state farms. Sugar output rebounded after a 1989 restructuring of the sugar industry, which has since been privatized. By 2000, the Congo had hoped to be agriculturally self-sufficient, but that goal is not likely to be achieved by then, since per capita production has recently fallen.

²³ANIMAL HUSBANDRY

Animal husbandry has high government priority, and production is steadily increasing. In 1992 there were an estimated 385,000 sheep and goats, 55,000 hogs, 69,000 head of cattle, and 2 million chickens.

24FISHING

Most fishing is carried on along the coast for local consumption. The catch rose from 14,939 tons in 1970 to 45,577 tons in 1991, more than 40% of it from saltwater fishing.

25FORESTRY

Congolese forests cover some 21.1 million hectares (52.1 million acres), or over three-fifths of the total area of the country. There are three main zones. Mayombé forest, covering about 1 million hectares (2.5 million acres), is the oldest forest under commercial exploitation and is almost exhausted. The Niari forest, covering 3 million hectares (7.4 million acres), along the Chaillu River, was reopened for exploitation after completion of the Comilog railroad. The third zone, situated in the north, is the largest, with 15.5 million hectares (38.3 million acres); because of constant flooding, however, it is the least exploited. Total production of roundwood was estimated at about 3,760,000 m^3 in 1991. Okoumé, sapele, sipo, tiama, moaki, limba, and nioré were the main species cut. Eucalyptus and pine are raised commercially in southern and coastal Congo. Foreign private companies dominate commercial production. In 1992, exports of forestry products totaled $128,514,000, or 14% of total exports. The Congolese Forestry Office was set up in 1974 to implement an ambitious reforestation program. Forestry contributes only 3% to GDP, and development was neglected during the oil boom years. Isolated harvestable tracts, difficult weather conditions, and limited rail transport capacity inhibit the expansion of the forestry sector.

26MINING

Mining, begun in the Congo in 1905, is presently the most important sector of the economy. A Bureau of Mines was created in 1961 to intensify research and exploitation of mineral deposits, which, in addition to petroleum and natural gas, include bauxite, potassium, phosphate, gold, limestone, lead, zinc, copper, and iron.

Potash was the main mining product before the rapid growth of oil. Deposits are in the Kouilou Region and the Niari Valley. Production rose from 66,000 tons in 1969 to 475,000 tons in 1974, but even this total was not enough to make operations profitable; production dropped to 115,000 tons in 1977 before ceasing entirely. Gold, mined in the Mayombé area, reached 158 kg in 1967 but fell to 12 kg in 1991. Copper production at Mindouli ceased in 1978. Zinc and lead were extracted and processed at Mfouati; production, which began in 1938, reached 3,153 tons in 1972; the production of copper, lead, and zinc was suspended in 1984. Iron deposits estimated at 400 million tons have also been found; other mineral resource potential includes potash and phosphate in the southeast, and bentonite, granite, gypsum, kaolin, marble, and talc elsewhere.

27ENERGY AND POWER

Production of electricity rose from 29 million kwh in 1960 to 482 million kwh in 1991, over 98% hydroelectric. Another 65 million kwh were imported from Zaire. A new Chinese-built, 74-Mw hydroelectric project at Moukoukoulou Falls, on a tributary of the Niari River, came into operation in 1978. Another Chinese-aided hydroelectric project, the 100-Mw Imboulou Dam on the Léfini River, 225 km (140 mi) north of Brazzaville, was scheduled for completion in 1989.

Petroleum extraction began in 1960, with 31,847 tons, and did not increase substantially until 1972, when 336,000 tons were produced. The 1992 output was 180,000 barrels per day (about 8.8 million tons in total), up 17.9% from 1991. The cargo subsidiaries of the French ELF-Aquitaine and Italian AGIP companies produced 80% and 20%, respectively, of Congo's oil in 1991. Much of it, however, was considered unrecoverable by conventional methods, and since 1983 the Yanga/Sendji Field has

produced the most oil. A subsidiary of Amoco began offshore production in 1991, with the capacity of producing 35–40,000 barrels per day. Natural gas production was 368 million m^3 in 1991.

28INDUSTRY

Industry is concentrated in the southern part of the country around Brazzaville and Pointe-Noire. Many industries, until recently, were partially or completely nationalized.

In 1985, the largest industries were food processing, including beverages and tobacco, followed by chemicals and petroleum products, woodworking, metalworking and electrical industries, nonmetallic mineral products, paper and cardboard, and textiles. An oil refinery at Pointe-Noire, with capacity of 1.1 million tons, opened in 1982 as a joint government (60%) and ELF (40%) venture. In 1985, however, it turned out only 49,000 tons of petroleum products. Timber-related industries included about 20 sawmills, producing 43,641 m^3 of sawn timber in 1985. Breweries in 1985 produced 881,667 hectoliters of beer. Sugar production in 1985 was 51,010 tons, and cement production was 50,985 tons. Artisans create distinctive jewelry, ceramics, and ebony and ivory sculptures.

29SCIENCE AND TECHNOLOGY

Science-related institutions include an Agricultural Development Bureau and a National Council of Scientific and Technical Research in Brazzaville, a Technical Center of Tropical Forestry in Pointe-Noire, and a Research Institute for Oils in Sibiti. Marien Ngoubai University in Brazzaville has a faculty of sciences and attached institutes of sanitation and rural development. Sibiti has an agricultural college, and Brazzaville contains a technical, commercial, and industrial college and a school of railway engineering.

30DOMESTIC TRADE

Most local produce is sold directly to consumers or middlemen at local markets in towns and villages, where imported goods are also sold. Company agents and independent middlemen buy export crops at local markets or directly from the producers for sale to large companies. State companies have a monopoly on the distribution of certain products, including such staples as rice and flour.

There is some advertising in the local newspapers and through company publications, handbills, and billboards, but radio stations do not carry advertising. Normal banking hours are 6:30 to 11:30 AM, Monday through Saturday. Shops open by 8 AM, usually close for a midday break, and then stay open to at least 5:30 PM Tuesday through Friday, and are open Saturday morning. They may also be open Saturday afternoon, Sunday morning, and Monday morning.

31FOREIGN TRADE

Congo's foreign trade is led by its exports of petroleum products. Exports (in millions of CFA francs) for 1988 were:

	1988
EXPORTS	
Petroleum and petroleum products	178,289
Wood	34,935
Diamonds	4,768
Coffee	202
Iron and steel	251
Other exports	5,299
TOTALS	223,744

Imports totaled 161,958 million CFA in 1988, with machinery and the category of food, beverages, and tobacco leading all others at 22.4% and 21.3% respectively. Imports of chemicals amounted to 12.5% of all imports.

The US took almost 46% of exports in 1986, followed by France, Spain, Italy, Belgium, Germany, and Portugal. France accounted for 55% of Congo's imports.

[32]BALANCE OF PAYMENTS

Until the 1970s, the Congo's chronic trade deficit led to an annual payments deficit. With the growth of oil revenues, the balance of payments became positive; this trend did not last long, however, since the deficit in services grew even faster than the trade surplus during the early 1980s. In recent years, imports have represented over 70% of private consumption.

In 1992 merchandise exports totaled $1,190.4 million and imports $540.6 million. The merchandise trade balance was $649.8 million. The following table summarizes Congo's balance of payments for 1991 and 1992 (in millions of US dollars):

	1991	1992
CURRENT ACCOUNT		
Goods, services, and income	−506.5	−330.6
Unrequited transfers	79.4	22.7
TOTALS	−427.1	−307.9
CAPITAL ACCOUNT	—	—
Direct investment	—	—
Portfolio investment	—	—
Other long-term capital	−233.6	−241.1
Other short-term capital	74.4	18.1
Exceptional financing	500.2	451.1
Reserves	30.7	79.7
TOTALS	371.7	307.9
Errors and omissions	55.4	—
Total change in reserves	−4.0	—

[33]BANKING AND SECURITIES

The bank of issue is the Bank of the Central African States (BEAC), which serves all the members of the UDEAC. The Congo's central bank reserves as of June 1990 totaled CFA Fr192,566 million. The two commercial banks are the Congolese Union of Banks, and the International Bank of Congo. The state is the major shareholder in the two commercial banks. The National Development Bank of the Congo extends loans for economic development. The Congo has a 13% share in UDEAC's development bank, headquartered in Brazzaville.

There is no securities market in the Congo.

[34]INSURANCE

In March 1974, all private insurance companies were nationalized and put under the Congo Insurance and Reinsurance Co., which is 50% government owned.

[35]PUBLIC FINANCE

Oil revenues in the 1970s helped expand public sector employment. The collapse in oil prices in the mid-1980s dramatically decreased government revenues, which led to a surge in international borrowing. In 1985, Congo entered negotiation with the IMF for standby credits to satisfy domestic and foreign creditors. In 1986, Congo reluctantly joined with the IMF in a structural adjustment program for which Congo received US$40 million in funds and was able to reschedule its international payments. By 1988, the Congo's external debt had risen to an unsustainable $4.1 billion. In 1989, a second structural adjustment program was agreed to. By this time, the debt-service ratio stood at 29%, still high but at its lowest level since 1984. Critical to the success of the program was the reduction of the fiscal

and trade deficits and the privatization of the parastatal sector. Political unrest in late 1990 postponed quick enactment of the austerity measures, although the Congo has proceeded in liquidating its holdings in the economy's productive sectors. As of 1992, the external debt stood at 175% of GDP, one of the highest ratios in the world. An enormous civil service consumes 80% of government revenues.

[36]TAXATION

A graduated income tax at rates of 1–50% is levied, varying with an individual's marital status and number of dependents. Employees also pay social security taxes and regional income taxes. The corporate tax rate is 40%, with reduction for small businesses, joint ventures, and those engaging in certain activities. Also levied are a turnover tax, excise duties, and property taxes.

[37]CUSTOMS AND DUTIES

The Congo, Gabon, Central African Republic, and Cameroon are joined in a customs union, the UDEAC. The Congo is a part of the franc zone within which goods and capital flow freely. The country has no customs system of its own. Imports from outside the UDEAC require a license.

[38]FOREIGN INVESTMENT

Foreign investments, both private and in the form of joint ventures with the state, were growing in the early 1980s. The last nationalizations were in 1974. By 1979, petroleum companies were entering joint ventures with the Congolese government to develop the oil reserves. The 1982–86 development plan explicitly called for foreign private investment. A 1973 investment code guarantees the free transfer of capital, normally earned profits, and funds resulting from sales of foreign companies. According to legislation adopted in 1982, reduced import duties and taxes are offered on production equipment, and profits on manufacturing and trading are tax-exempt for the first five years. However, since the economy is very fragile overall, banks require a public guarantee before investing their funds.

[39]ECONOMIC DEVELOPMENT

The 1982–86 development plan called for expenditures of over $2.5 billion for the improvement of infrastructure (roads, electricity, water) and for the development of production in agriculture, forestry, and light industry; however, economic difficulties caused the plan to be cut back sharply. The 1987–91 development plan promoted agricultural self-sufficiency and rural development through the planned creation of 160 village centers and a mandatory national service program for youths. Reduction of the country's dependency on petroleum and the reform of the parastatal sector were set as priorities. The devaluation of the CFA franc in 1994 should boost those economic activities which do not rely on imports.

France is the leading foreign donor country (about $400 million between 1960 and 1985). France for a time reduced its participation (1985–89), but raised it to record levels in 1990 ($230 million). China and the former Soviet Union also provided substantial aid in the past. Between 1946 and 1986, Congo also received $107.7 million from the European Economic Community, $111.7 million from the World Bank, $74 million from International Development Agency, and $93.7 million from the African Development Bank.

[40]SOCIAL DEVELOPMENT

Social services based on the French model are being introduced slowly. Since 1 July 1956, family allowances have been paid to all salaried workers. Contributions are made by employers at a fixed percentage of the employee's wage. Other payments include a pension scheme, prenatal allowances, a lump sum payable at the birth of each of the first three children, and, if the mother is employed, a recuperation allowance for 14 weeks.

The population growth rate in the mid-1980s was considered satisfactory by the Congolese government, which regarded reductions in infant and maternal mortality as primary health goals. The fertility rate in 1993 was an average of about 5.4 children for every woman of childbearing years. Abortion was allowed on broad health grounds. Women are not prominent on the highest levels of political life. However, the Union of Congolese Women promotes the advancement of women and has launched large literacy and female education campaigns. Its activity in farming makes it a powerful economic force.

[41] HEALTH

In 1990, there were 613 doctors, 175 pharmacists, 35 dentists, 1,624 nurses, and 498 midwives. There were 12 doctors per 100,000 people, and a nurse-to-doctor ratio of 5.1. There were 1.4 hospital beds per 1,000 people. In 1992, 83% of the population had access to health care services.

In 1993, there were approximately 107,000 births (a rate of 45 per 1,000 people). The overall death rate was 14.8 per 1,000 people, while infant mortality was estimated at 112.7 deaths per 1,000 live births. In 1992, the average life expectancy was estimated at 52 years, with women living on average 2 years longer than men.

An endemic disease control service conducts vaccination and inoculation campaigns. All medicine, antibiotic, and vaccine imports must be authorized by the Ministry of Health. In 1990 there were 220 reported cases of tuberculosis per 100,000 people. However, immunization rates for children up to one year old were high between 1990 and 1992: tuberculosis (88%); diphtheria, polio, and tetanus (74%); polio (74%); and measles (64%). In 1990 24% of children under 5 years old were considered malnourished. From 1988 to 1991, only 38% of inhabitants had access to safe water.

[42] HOUSING

As of 1984, 88.3% of all housing units were private houses. Owners occupied 61.4% of dwellings, tenants 24.1%, and 9.4% were occupied rent free. Close to one-third of all units had brick external walls, 25.7% had stone walls, 15.9% had planks, and 10.5% cob.

[43] EDUCATION

The educational system is patterned on that of France, but changes are being introduced gradually to adapt the curriculum to local needs and traditions. The language of instruction is French. All private schools were taken over by the government in 1965. Education is compulsory between the ages of 6 and 16. Primary lasts for six years and secondary for seven years. Among adults, illiteracy was estimated in 1990 at 43.4%; 30.0% for men and 56.1% for women.

In 1990 there were 502,918 primary school pupils in 1,655 schools and 7,626 teachers; there were 183,023 secondary school students, 12,278 vocational school trainees, and 280 students in teachers' training schools. The National University, which opened in Brazzaville in 1971, was later renamed Marien Ngouabi University. Higher level institutions had 1,159 teachers and 12,045 students in 1991.

[44] LIBRARIES AND MUSEUMS

Brazzaville has Marien Ngouabi University Library, with 78,000 volumes in 1989, and the National Popular Library with 15,000 volumes. The National Museum of the Congo, also in Brazzaville, contains ethnography displays and historical displays. There is a regional museums in Pointe-Noire.

[45] MEDIA

In 1991 there were two daily newspapers: *Journal officiel de la République du Congo* and *Mweti*, both published in Brazzaville.

National and international communications are state-owned and -operated. Radio Brazzaville broadcasts in French and local languages. In 1991 there were 260,000 radios. The national television network began operations in 1963; a satellite communications station was inaugurated at Brazzaville in 1978. In 1991 there were 14,000 receiving sets, with telecasts in French, Kikongo, and Lingala. The Congo had 25,799 telephones in service in 1991.

[46] ORGANIZATIONS

There are Chambers of Commerce, Agriculture, and Industry in Brazzaville, Loubomo, Pointe-Noire, and Ouesso. Larger towns have youth centers; the national youth movement, Jeunesse, is very active. In rural areas, cooperatives promote the production and marketing of agricultural products. Among the tribes, self-help societies have grown rapidly, particularly in the larger towns.

[47] TOURISM, TRAVEL, AND RECREATION

Reforms and restructuring have enhanced the Congo's potential for tourism (especially ecotourism) contingent on attraction of investment capital. In 1990 there were 3,451 rooms in hotels with a 32% occupancy rate. About 30,786 tourists stayed at hotels and inns, 55% from Europe and 35% from Africa. International tourist receipts were about US$7 million. All visitors except nationals of France and most French-speaking African countries need passports and visas secured in advance. A vaccination certificate for yellow fever is also required, except from those arriving from noninfected areas and staying less than two weeks; antimalarial precautions are advisable.

[48] FAMOUS CONGOLESE

The best-known figures are Abbé Fulbert Youlou (1917–72), a former Roman Catholic priest who served as president from 1960 to 1963, as well as mayor of Brazzaville; Alphonse Massamba-Debat (1921–77), president from 1963 to 1968; and Marien Ngouabi (1938–77), who came to power in a 1968 coup and was president from 1968 to 1977. Denis Sassou-Nguesso (b.1941) became president in 1979.

[49] DEPENDENCIES

The Congo has no territories or colonies.

[50] BIBLIOGRAPHY

Allen, Chris, and Michael Raduin. *Benin and the Congo: Politics, Economics and Society*. New York: Lynne Rienner, 1987.

Allen, Chris, Michael S. Radu and Keith Somerville. *Benin, The Congo, and Burkina Faso*. New York: Pinter, 1989.

Fegley, Randall. *The Congo*. Santa Barbara, Calif.: Clio, 1993.

Gauze, Rene. *The Politics of Congo-Brazzaville*. Stanford, Calif.: Hoover Institution Press, 1973.

McDonald, Gordon C., et al. *Area Handbook for People's Republic of the Congo (Congo-Brazzaville)*. Washington, D.C.: Government Printing Office, 1971.

Millaure, Jean-Claude. *Patrinomialism and Changes in the Congo*. Stanford, Calif.: Stanford University Press, 1972.

Thompson, Virginia, and Richard Adloff. *The Emerging States of French Equatorial Africa*. Stanford, Calif.: Stanford University Press, 1960.

———. *Historical Dictionary of the People's Republic of the Congo*. Metuchen, N.J.: Scarecrow, 1974.

CÔTE D'IVOIRE

Republic of Côte d'Ivoire
République de Côte d'Ivoire

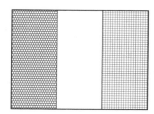

CAPITAL: Yamoussoukro.

FLAG: The flag is a tricolor of orange, white, and green vertical stripes.

ANTHEM: *L'Abidjanaise,* beginning: "Greetings, O land of hope."

MONETARY UNIT: The Communauté Financière Africaine franc (CFA Fr) is the national currency. There are coins of 1, 2, 5, 10, 25, 50, 100, and 500 CFA francs, and notes of 50, 100, 500, 1,000, 5,000, and 10,000 CFA francs. CFA Fr1 = $0.0018 (or $1 = CFA Fr571).

WEIGHTS AND MEASURES: The metric system is the legal standard.

HOLIDAYS: New Year's Day, 1 January; Labor Day, 1 May; Assumption, 15 August; All Saints' Day, 1 November; Independence Day, 7 December; Christmas, 25 December. Movable religious holidays include Good Friday, Easter Monday, Ascension, Pentecost Monday, 'Id al-Fitr, and 'Id al-'Adha'.

TIME: GMT.

¹LOCATION, SIZE, AND EXTENT

The Republic of Côte d'Ivoire, on the south coast of the western bulge of Africa, has an area of 322,460 sq km (124,502 sq mi). Comparatively, the area occupied by Côte d'Ivoire is slightly larger than the state of New Mexico. Roughly rectangular in shape, it extends 808 km (502 mi) SE–NW and 780 km (485 mi) NE–SW. It is bordered on the N by Mali and Burkina Faso, on the E by Ghana, on the S by the Gulf of Guinea and the Atlantic Ocean, and on the W by Liberia and Guinea, with a total boundary length of 3,625 km (2,252 mi).

In 1983, Côte d'Ivoire's capital was moved to Yamoussoukro, about 225 km (140 mi) northwest of the former capital, Abidjan, in the southcentral part of the country. However, the move is not complete, and Abidjan remains the nation's administrative center; foreign governments, including the US, maintain a presence there.

²TOPOGRAPHY

Except for the prolongation of the Guinea Highlands (in the northwest, from Man to Odienné), which has peaks of over 1,000 m (3,280 ft), reaching a high point of 1,302 m (4,272 ft), the greater part of Côte d'Ivoire is a vast plateau, tilted gently toward the Atlantic. It is drained by four major rivers running roughly parallel from north to south—the Cavally (on the Liberian frontier), Sassandra, Bandama, and Komoé. They are not of much value for transportation, since they are sluggish in the dry season, broken by numerous falls and rapids, and subject to torrential flooding in the rainy season. Lake Kossou, in the center of the country, has been formed by the impoundment of the Bandama. From Ghana to Fresco, the coast is almost a straight line, flat and sandy, with a series of deep lagoons behind it; from Fresco to the Liberian frontier, it is more broken, with small cliffs and rocky outcrops.

³CLIMATE

The greatest annual rainfall, 198 cm (78 in), is along the coast and in the southwest. The coastal region has a long dry season from December to mid-May, followed by heavy rains from mid-May to mid-July, a short dry season from mid-July to October, and lighter rains in October and November. Farther north, there is only one wet and one dry season, with rainfall heaviest in summer, culminating in September, and lightest in January. The country's lightest rainfall is in the northeast, averaging 109 cm (43 in) annually. Average temperatures at Abidjan range from 24° to 32°C (75° to 90°F) in January and from 22° to 28°C (72° to 82°F) in July. At Bouaké, in the center of the country, minimum and maximum temperatures in November, the hottest month, average 21° and 35°C (70° and 95°F); the range is from 20° to 29°C (68° to 84°F) in July, the coolest month. At Ferkéssédougou, in the far north, temperatures range from 21° to 36°C (70° to 97°F) in March and from 17° to 30°C (63° to 86°F) in November.

⁴FLORA AND FAUNA

The southern Côte d'Ivoire forest is a typical rain forest; it has a canopy at around 21–24 m (70–80 ft), with isolated trees pushing up above 37 m (120 ft). Farther north, the rain forest gives way to scattered stands of deciduous trees, and mahogany is widespread. Still farther north, oil palm, acacia, breadfruit, and baobab characterize the transition to true savanna, where shea nut and traveler's palm are common.

The jackal, hyena, panther, elephant, hippopotamus, numerous monkeys, and many other mammals are widely distributed. Crocodiles and chameleons, as well as venomous serpents (horned vipers, mambas, and many others) and pythons, are numerous. Among indigenous birds are vultures, cranes, pigeons, turtle doves, parrots, and herons. Venomous spiders and scorpions abound.

⁵ENVIRONMENT

Most of Côte d'Ivoire's forests, once the largest in West Africa, have been cut down by the timber industry, with only cursory attempts at reforestation. During the first half of the 1980s, deforestation averaged 290,000 ha (717,000 acres) per year, while reforestation was only 6,000 ha (15,000 acres) per year. The land is also affected by savanization and climate changes, including decreased rainfall. In 1994, Côte d'Ivoire had 17.8 cubic miles of water, of which 67% was used for farming and 22% for urban and domestic use. Water pollution is a significant environmental problem in Côte d'Ivoire due to chemical waste from agricultural, industrial, and mining sources: 43% of the country's city dwellers and 20% of the rural population do not have safe water. Reports indicate that as of 1992, the nation used 6,000 tons of pesticides and 78,000 tons of fertilizers per year. The country's lack of sanitation facilities also contributes to the pollution problem. Of the country's 11 million people, 6 million do not have access to a sewage system.

As of 1994, 18 of the nation's 226 mammal species and 9 of its 683 bird species were endangered, as well as one reptile and one type of amphibian. In addition, 70 of the country's 3,660 plant species were threatened with extinction.

6POPULATION

The 1988 census counted a population of 10,815,694; an estimate for mid-1994 was 14,566,749. A total of 17,065,000 was forecast for 2000, assuming a crude birthrate of 47.6 per 1,000 population, a crude death rate of 14.5, and a net natural increase of 33.1 during 1985–2000. Côte d'Ivoire's estimated population density in 1987 was 45.2 per sq km (117 per sq mi). About 49% of all Ivoirians are 14 years of age or younger.

Movement to the cities has been a problem in recent decades, the proportion of urban dwellers having increased from 13.2% in 1950 to an estimated 44% in 1995. The population of Abidjan, the former capital, was estimated at 2,751,000 for 1995. The other major urban areas are Bouaké (estimated at more than 390,000), the capital city of Yamoussoukro (120,000), and Daloa (102,000); other towns with populations of more than 20,000 include Gagnoa, Korhogo, Agboville, Abengourou, Dimbokro, Man, and Grand Bassam.

7MIGRATION

Flourishing economic activity in Côte d'Ivoire has attracted large numbers of workers from neighboring countries. In 1988 they constituted 28% of the national total. Migratory laborers from Burkina Faso, estimated at more than 1 million, work chiefly on the cocoa and coffee plantations. In addition, several hundred thousand Ghanaians, Guineans, Malians, Senegalese, and Mauritanians live in Côte d'Ivoire. The civil war in Liberia created a refugee population in Côte d'Ivoire that numbered 173,700 at the end of 1992. Most of the non-African population consists of French and other Europeans (at least 60,000) and Lebanese and Syrians (60,000–120,000). Foreigners can buy land and vote in Côte d'Ivoire; some cabinet ministers are foreign-born.

8ETHNIC GROUPS

The ethnic composition of Côte d'Ivoire is complex, and accurate statistics are not available. The Baulé, concentrated in the central and southeastern regions, account for about 15% of the population. Next come the Mandingo, or Malinké, in the northwest. Other large groups include the Agni, related to the Baulé, in the southeast; the Bété, a Kru people, in the southwest; the Sénoufo in the north; and the Dan, a Mandé people, in the west.

9LANGUAGES

The official language is French. Of the more than 60 African languages spoken by different ethnic groups, the most important are Agni and Baulé, spoken by the Akan group; the Kru languages; the Sénoufo languages; and the Mandé languages (especially Malinké-Bambura-Dioula).

10RELIGIONS

The state is secular, and the constitution provides for religious freedom. As of 1993, an estimated 60% of the inhabitants followed traditional animist religions. Muslims accounted for about 20% of the population, and the remaining 20% were Christians, with 1,585,000 belonging to the Roman Catholic Church. Roman Catholic missions were established toward the end of the 19th century, and Protestant missions, mainly British and American, also have done extensive work.

11TRANSPORTATION

Côte d'Ivoire has one of the best-developed and best-maintained transportation systems in Africa. The state controls a 660-km (410-mi) section of a 1,146-km (712-mi) railroad that runs north from Abidjan through Bouaké and Ferkéssédougou to Ouagadougou, Burkina Faso. In 1991, Côte d'Ivoire had 46,600 km of roads, of which 8% were paved. In the same year, there were 170,000 registered passenger automobiles and 92,000 registered commercial automobiles, trucks, and buses.

Harbor activity is concentrated at Abidjan (West Africa's largest container port), which has facilities that include a fishing port and equipment for handling containers, and San Pedro, a deepwater port that began operations in 1971. There are also small ports at Sassandra and Tabou. Two nationalized shipping lines serve West Africa and Europe. At the end of 1991, the merchant fleet consisted of 6 vessels, with a gross weight of 125,000 tons.

In 1991 Abidjan's international airport handled 13,700 commercial planes, but only 21% of all commercial traffic was domestic. Air Ivoire, government-owned since 1976, operates domestic services and also flies to Ouagadougou, Burkina Faso, and Bamako, Mali. In 1992, the airline carried 128,800 passengers. International flights to Paris, Dakar, and other African and European capitals are handled by Air Afrique, a joint venture owned by Côte d'Ivoire and other participating Yaoundé Treaty countries (72%) and by Air France and Union des Transports Aériens (28%). Secondary airports are located at Bérébi, Bouaké, Daloa, Man, Sassandra, Korhogo, Tabou, San Pedro, Guiglo, Bondoukou, Yamoussoukro, and Odienné.

12HISTORY

Little is known of the early history of the area now called Côte d'Ivoire. Most of its peoples entered the country in comparatively recent times, mostly from the northwest and the east, although the Kru-speaking peoples came from west of the Cavally River (modern Liberia). European travelers described flourishing and well-organized states in the north and east, with strongly hierarchical social organization and elaborate gold weights and ornaments. These states, such as the Agni kingdom of Indénié and the Abron kingdom of Bondoukou, were closely related linguistically and socially to the neighboring Ashanti of modern Ghana and formed with them, and with the Fon of Dahomey (now Benin) and the Yoruba and Bini kingdoms in Nigeria, an almost continuous string of relatively rich and developed states of the Guinea forest zone. Nearer the coast, the scale of social organization was much smaller, and innumerable small units recognized no political superior.

Modern European acquaintance with the west coast of Africa began with the Portuguese discoveries of the 15th century, culminating in the discovery of the route to India around the Cape of Good Hope in 1488 and the establishment of trading posts along the Senegal coast and the Gulf of Guinea. The Portuguese and Spanish were soon followed by the Dutch and English. Gold, ivory, ostrich feathers, gum arabic, and pepper were succeeded by slaves as the major trading commodities. French activity in what is now Côte d'Ivoire began in 1687, when missionaries landed at Assinié. In 1843, Adm. Louis-Édouard Bouet-Willaumez established French posts at Assinié and Grand Bassam, where treaties with the local chiefs provided for the cession of land for forts in exchange for tribute to the chiefs ("coutumes") at fixed rates and regular intervals.

After the Franco-Prussian War of 1870, the small garrisons of Assinié, Grand Bassam, and Dabou were withdrawn. French interests were confided to a resident trader named Verdier. He and a young assistant, Treich-Laplène, consolidated the French

CÔTE D'IVOIRE

0 50 100 Miles

0 50 100 Kilometers

LOCATION: 2°30' to 7°30'w; 4°20' to 10°50'N. **BOUNDARY LENGTHS:** Mali, 515 km (320 mi); Upper Volta, 531 km (330 mi); Ghana, 668 km (415 mi); Gulf of Guinea coastline, 507 km (315 mi); Liberia, 716 km (445 mi); Guinea, 605 km (376 mi). **TERRITORIAL SEA LIMIT:** 12 mi.

position along the coast. In 1887, Treich-Laplène signed treaties with Indénié, Bettié, Alangoa, and other chiefdoms of the interior, thus preventing British advances into eastern Côte d'Ivoire from Ashanti. Continuing northward to Kong, he joined forces with Col. Louis Binger, who had made his way from Bamako in French Sudan (Soudan Française, now Mali) to Kong and from there northeast to Ouagadougou in Upper Volta (now Burkina Faso) and back to Kong through Bondoukou. French claims to Upper Volta and northern Côte d'Ivoire, joining French Sudan and Niger in a continuous territory, were thus established. In 1893, the territory was renamed Côte d'Ivoire, and Col. Binger was appointed the first French governor. The new colony's frontier with Liberia was settled by a convention in 1892, and that with the Gold Coast (modern Ghana) by the Anglo-French agreement of 1893. The northern border was not defined until 1947.

French control of Côte d'Ivoire was, however, far from secured. Much of the region remained unexplored, and administrative control had still to be effectively organized in those areas whose chiefs had concluded treaties with the French. More serious still, Samory Touré, a Malinké from Guinea who periodically fought the French, had moved southeast after the French capture of Sankoro in 1892 and was continuing his struggle against the invaders in the region of Kong. Not until 1898, after prolonged fighting, was he finally captured near Man. Systematic military operations in the densely forested area between the upper Cavally and the upper Sassandra were carried out from 1908 onward before French rule was finally established in Côte d'Ivoire on the eve of World War I. In other parts of the colony, too, intermittent revolts continued throughout this period, stimulated by the imposition of a poll tax and opposition of many of the chiefs to the substitution of a tax rebate for the coutumes promised in the treaties. Nevertheless, some 20,000 Ivoirian troops were raised in the colony during World War I, when the greater part of the French forces was withdrawn.

In the interwar years, Côte d'Ivoire became a considerable producer of cocoa, coffee, mahogany, and other tropical products. Although European planters produced about one-third of the cocoa and coffee and most of the bananas, the share of African planters rapidly increased throughout this period. The railroad, begun in 1904, did not reach the northern part of the colony until 1925. The wharf at Grand Bassam (opened 1901) and that at Port Bouet (opened 1932) remained the principal ports until the cutting of the Ébrié Lagoon in 1950 and the opening of the deepwater port of Abidjan in 1954.

During World War II, Côte d'Ivoire, like the rest of French West Africa, remained under control of the Vichy government between 1940 and 1943. In 1941, the king of Bondoukou and thousands of his people made their way into the Gold Coast to join Gen. Charles de Gaulle's resistance forces. At the end of the war, Côte d'Ivoire was established as an overseas territory under the 1946 French constitution and given three deputies and three senators in the French parliament and an elected territorial assembly. By 1956, it produced 45% of all French West African exports, took in 30% of the imports, and seemed assured of continued economic advance.

Independence

In 1958, Côte d'Ivoire accepted the new French constitution in a referendum on 28 September and opted for the status of an autonomous state within the new French Community. On 4 December 1958, the Territorial Assembly, which had been elected by universal suffrage on 31 March 1957, formed itself into the Constituent Assembly and proclaimed the Republic of Côte d'Ivoire as a member state of the French Community. On 26 March 1959, the assembly adopted the first constitution of the new country. The legislature provided for in this constitution was chosen by a national election held on 17 April, and Félix Houphouët-Boigny was unanimously selected by the Assembly as prime minister on 27 April.

On 7 August 1960, the Republic of Côte d'Ivoire proclaimed its complete independence. On 31 October, a new constitution providing for a presidential system was adopted. In elections held on 27 November, Houphouët-Boigny was unanimously elected the country's first president. Although two plots to overthrow him, organized by government and party officials, were discovered in 1963, both failed, and in that year Houphouët-Boigny took over most key ministerial portfolios and consolidated his control over the Democratic Party of Côte d'Ivoire (PDCI).

Outbreaks of unrest plagued the Houphouët-Boigny government during the late 1960s and early 1970s. In 1969, some 1,500 unemployed youths were arrested in the course of widespread rioting. In 1970, disturbances broke out in Gagnoa, Bouaké, and Daloa. These incidents were followed in 1973 by an alleged conspiracy to overthrow the government. Following a brief trial, two army captains and five lieutenants were sentenced to death, while others were given jail sentences ranging from 15 to 20 years' hard labor. Before the sixth PDCI congress, in 1975, President Houphouët-Boigny pardoned some 5,000 persons, among whom were 145 political prisoners, some associated with the Gagnoa disturbances. All death

sentences were also commuted to 20 years' hard labor. Throughout this period, the government used a series of mass meetings called "dialogues" to win over new adherents. These public discussions were usually led by prominent members of the administration, and President Houphouët-Boigny often presided over them personally. During the second half of the 1970s, Houphouët-Boigny and the PDCI remained firmly in control, and Côte d'Ivoire became one of black Africa's most prosperous nations.

Houphouët-Boigny was reelected unopposed to his fifth five-year term as president in October 1980. The nation's first competitive National Assembly elections were held in the following month, as the ruling PDCI allowed 649 candidates to compete for the 147 seats, with a runoff between the two best-placed candidates in each constituency where there was no majority choice. A total of 121 new members were elected, while 54 of the 80 deputies who ran for reelection were defeated. Relations with neighboring countries have generally been favorable; in 1981, however, the death by suffocation of 46 Ghanaians who had been jailed near Abidjan on suspicion of drug smuggling led to friction with Ghana, which was resolved through Togolese mediation. Declining economic prospects in the early 1980s led to a series of strikes among professional workers, which Houphouët-Boigny accused a foreign power (presumed to be Libya) of fomenting.

Houphouët-Boigny won an unopposed sixth term as president in October 1985, reportedly receiving 100% of the vote in a turnout of over 99% of the eligible voters. In the following month, fewer than 30% turned out for the National Assembly elections, in which 546 candidates—all members of the PDCI but not screened—competed for 175 seats. Only 64 deputies were returned to office. Côte d'Ivoire celebrated the 25th anniversary of its independence on 7 December 1985 by releasing 9,500 convicted criminals from prisoners.

In 1990, Côte d'Ivoire entered a new political era as months of prodemocracy demonstrations and labor unrest led to the legalization of opposition parties, previously banned. Even within the PDCI, a progressive wing called for further liberalization. The first multiparty presidential and legislative elections were held on 28 October 1990 and 25 November 1990, respectively. Houphouët-Boigny was reelected as president with 81% of the vote. The PDCI carried 161 of the 175 seats and the Ivoirian Popular Front (FPI), 9 seats. Yet, outside observers saw the elections as less than free and fair. That November, the National Assembly passed a constitutional amendment to allow the Speaker to take over the presidency in the event of a vacancy (a provision eventually invoked on Houphouët-Boigny's death on 7 December 1993).

Meanwhile, popular disillusionment grew. Early in 1992, the president rejected the findings of his own investigative commission, which had found army chief of staff General Robert Guei responsible for the shootings at Yopougon University in May 1991. Then Houphouët-Boigny left for a four-month "private visit" to France. Rioting followed a mass demonstration in February 1992, and the government used this as a pretext to jail opposition leaders. In protest, the FPI withdrew from the National Assembly, leaving it a PDCI exclusive preserve. Houphouët-Boigny continued to manage affairs from Paris. He returned in June to release the opposition leaders as part of an amnesty that also shielded the soldiers.

After Houphouët-Boigny's death power was transferred smoothly to Henri Konan Bédíe, who became president until the 1995 elections.

13 GOVERNMENT

Under the constitution of 31 October 1960, as subsequently amended, executive power is exercised by a president, elected for a five-year term by direct universal suffrage (from age 21). The president, who appoints the Council of Ministers (cabinet), may initiate and veto legislation; the veto may be overruled by a two-thirds vote of the legislature. A 1980 constitutional amendment created the new post of vice-president, to be elected with the president and to become head of state automatically in the case of vacancy by death, resignation, or "absolute hindrance"; the post was left vacant, however, and a 1985 constitutional amendment eliminated it, making the president of the National Assembly the interim successor in the event of a vacancy. A 1990 amendment empowered its speaker to succeed the president. The unicameral National Assembly consists of 175 members, elected by direct universal suffrage for a five-year term in the same year as the president. The country had a de facto one-party system until May 1990, when opposition parties were allowed. The post of prime minister was created after the November 1990 elections.

¹⁴POLITICAL PARTIES

From 1959 to 1990, the only political party in Côte d'Ivoire was the Democratic Party of Côte d'Ivoire (Parti Démocratique de la Côte d'Ivoire—PDCI), headed by President Félix Houphouët-Boigny. The PDCI developed from the Côte d'Ivoire section of the African Democratic Rally (Rassemblement Démocratique Africain), formed in 1946. In the 1959 elections, Houphouët-Boigny made it clear that no party that did not fully accept Côte d'Ivoire membership in the French Community would be tolerated. After the elections, the number of constituencies was reduced to four for the whole country, and later a single nationwide constituency was established, with a single list of candidates for the National Assembly. In 1980, members of the National Assembly were chosen in 147 separate districts; in 1985, they were chosen from 175 districts.

In May 1990, opposition parties were legalized and contested the 1990 elections. Among the two dozen parties registered are the Ivoirian Popular Front (FPI), the Ivoirian Workers' Party (PIT), the Ivoirian Socialist Party (PSI), and the Ivoirian Human Rights League. In April 1994, some 19 parties formed a center-left opposition alliance, the Groupement pour la Solidarité (GPS).

¹⁵LOCAL GOVERNMENT

Côte d'Ivoire is divided into 7 regions and 49 prefectures, or departments. A prefect is delegated by the central government to represent the national interest. There are 163 subprefectures and 135 communes.

¹⁶JUDICIAL SYSTEM

The Supreme Court has four chambers—constitutional, judicial, administrative, and financial. Appeals courts sit at Abidjan and Bouaké. There are 28 courts of first instance (magistrates' courts). The High Court of Justice, composed of members elected from and by the National Assembly, has the power to impeach any government official, including the president. In January 1963, a special State Security Court was established. In rural areas, domestic and other local disputes are often handled though traditional village institutions.

The judiciary is independent of the legislative and executive branches in ordinary criminal cases. Under the Constitution and in practice, however, the judiciary accedes to the executive on political and national security issues.

¹⁷ARMED FORCES

Côte d'Ivoire's armed forces numbered 7,100 in 1993: 5,500 in the army, including three infantry battalions and one mechanized battalion; 700 in the navy; and 900 in the air force. There is also a paramilitary force of about 7,800. In 1993 the air force had 28 (6 combat) aircraft and helicopters. Côte d'Ivoire signed a defense agreement with France in 1961; as of 1993, a French marine infantry battalion of about 500 was stationed near Abidjan.

¹⁸INTERNATIONAL COOPERATION

Côte d'Ivoire was admitted to UN membership on 20 September 1960 and is a member of ECA and all the nonregional specialized agencies. It belongs to the OAU and various other intergovernmental organizations, including the African Development Bank and G-77. Together with other countries of former French West Africa, it participates in the West African Customs Union, and it was the organizer of the Conseil d'Entente, which unites Benin, Niger, Togo, and Burkina Faso in a customs union. It is an associate member of the EC and is a member of OCAM and CEAO. In May 1975, Côte d'Ivoire was one of the signatories to a treaty that created ECOWAS, an economic organization that includes both French- and English-speaking West African countries. Abidjan is the headquarters for the African Development Bank, the secretariat of the Conseil d'Entente, and the West African office of the World Bank and Air Afrique.

Strongly anti-Communist, Côte d'Ivoire broke diplomatic relations with the former USSR in 1969 but restored them in 1986.

¹⁹ECONOMY

Côte d'Ivoire's wealth rests essentially on the production for export of coffee, cocoa, cotton, and tropical woods. The nation is the world's sixth-largest producer of coffee and the world's largest producer of cocoa; bananas, palm oil, and pineapples are other products of importance. Industrial activity, consisting chiefly of processing industries, is well developed. Mining remains of limited significance, with diamonds and offshore oil the only important minerals produced.

For the first 15 years after independence, Côte d'Ivoire's economy expanded at a remarkable rate, owing both to increased prices for the country's agricultural exports and to maximal use of land and labor resources by the government's economic planners. During 1960-1970, the average annual GDP growth rate exceeded 11% and from 1970-80, 7%. During the 1980s, however, Côte d'Ivoire began experiencing an economic slowdown because of falling export prices, rising import prices, and heavy debt-service costs as a result of borrowing during the boom years. Between 1987 and 1991, the economy lost one-seventh of its GDP value and, with the help of the IMF, initiated a fiscal austerity plan of structural adjustment.

Côte d'Ivoire has diversified its agricultural base, although coffee is a main source of income for about half of all Ivoirians. Production of palm oil and palm products is now commercialized. It has become the largest cotton producer south of the Sahara and is also investing in rubber production, with the goal of joining Liberia as one of Africa's leading rubber producers. Sugar production has been rationalized following the rapid expansion of the early 1980s. Côte d'Ivoire is also a significant producer of pineapples; in 1991 exports had largely recovered from the drought-caused declines of 1982-84. The country is self-sufficient in maize, cassavas, plantains, and yams.

In January 1994 France suddenly devalued the CFA franc, cutting its value in half overnight. Immediately, prices soared for almost all imported goods, including food and essential drugs, like those to combat malaria. Since 1948 France had guaranteed a fixed parity of 1 French franc to 50 African francs. The resulting stability in the currency had generally kept inflation low and helped to maintain a steady rate of growth. However, in the 1980s, the economies of the CFA countries began to stagnate in relation to other African nations, and France came under increased pressure from the World Bank, the IMF, and Western countries to stop subsidizing the CFA franc. The devaluation, long expected in the investment community, is designed to encourage new investment, particularly in the export sectors of the economy, and discourage the use of hard currency reserves to buy products that could be grown domestically.

Marketplace fights have become commonplace as shoppers react to merchants' attempts to cut their losses by marking up the prices of existing stocks. To halt price-gouging and the sharp rise in inflation, the government imposed temporary price controls on existing stocks of imports.

Many analysts believe that France waited until the death of Côte d'Ivoire's president Felix Houphouët-Boigny in December 1993 to devalue the franc. Houphouët-Boigny, an opponent of devaluation, was a strong supporter of France.

[20]INCOME

In 1992 Côte d'Ivoire's GNP was $8,655 million at current prices, or $670 per capita. For the period 1985–92 the average inflation rate was –2.1%, resulting in a real growth rate in per capita GNP of –5.7%.

In 1992 the GDP was $10,158 million in current US dollars. It was dominated by the agricultural sector, which produced 38.3% of its value. The categories trade, transport, and finance together added another 18.7%, while manufacturing contributed 8.4%.

[21]LABOR

Over 80% of the labor force of about 4.2 million is engaged in agriculture, livestock raising, forestry, or fishing, while industry employs only about 8%.

A labor inspection service supervises conditions under which foreign workers—very numerous in Côte d'Ivoire—are employed. The National Union of Côte d'Ivoire was formed in 1959; it was dissolved and replaced in 1962 by the General Union of Côte d'Ivoire Workers (Union Générale des Travailleurs de Côte d'Ivoire), controlled by the PDCI. In 1991, several UGTCI-affiliated unions, including those representing transport, media, customs, and bank workers broke away and became independent. In 1992, 11 formerly independent unions joined together to form the Federation of Autonomous Trade Unions of Côte d'Ivoire(FESACI).

Labor legislation is still based on the French overseas labor code of 1952, which provides for collective agreements between employees and trade unions, the fixing of basic minimum wages by the government, and a 40-hour workweek for all except agricultural workers, for whom longer working hours are permitted. The minimum hourly industrial wage was last adjusted in January 1986. Legislation also provides wage earners with paid annual leave and children's allowances.

[22]AGRICULTURE

Agriculture provides a living for about 75% of Ivoirians and accounts for about one-half of the country's sizable export earnings. Only 11.6% of the land is cultivated, but farming is intensive and efficiently organized. Most production is in the hands of smallholders, but there are numerous European-owned plantations, far more than in neighboring West African countries.

The main food crops (with their production in tons) are yams, 2,450,000; manioc, 1,350,000; plantains, 1,170,000; rice, 700,000; and corn, 425,000. Sweet potatoes, peanuts, and in the northern districts, millet, sorghum, and hungry rice (fonio) are also grown. The government sought during the 1970s to reduce or eliminate rice imports, but in 1992, about 380,000 tons were imported. The economic decline during the 1980s coupled with high population growth has necessitated the modernization of agricultural production, with less dependence on coffee and cocoa.

However, they remain the principal cash crops and together provide about 45% of the country's export earnings. Côte d'Ivoire is Africa's leading producer of coffee, which is grown in the southern and central parts of the country, almost entirely on smallholdings. Coffee production reached a peak of 367,000 tons in 1981 and then declined because of drought and bush fires; in 1992 the total was 240,000 tons. Cocoa production has increased markedly since the early 1970s; it is now the nation's leading cash crop, and Côte d'Ivoire is the world's leading producer, accounting for 30% of world production in 1992. Output rose from 379,000 tons in 1980 to 417,000 tons in 1981 and to a record 804,000 tons in 1991, in part because of the use of high-yield plants and improvement in planting methods and upkeep.

Banana production (185,000 tons in 1992) fluctuates from year to year because of climatic conditions; exports in 1992 were 152,570 tons. Production of pineapples in that year was 240,000 tons; palm oil, 260,833 tons; and palm kernels, 41,113 tons. Rubber plantations yielded 76,000 tons, and cotton production reached 242,000 tons of seed cotton, and 87,000 tons of cotton fiber. Coconut production was 270,000 tons; copra production, 42,000 tons.

Six sugar complexes were established in the 1970s and early 1980s. These met domestic demand and provided an export surplus of over 60,000 tons of raw sugar in 1982, but the cost of production far exceeded the world market price, and two complexes were converted to rice plantations. Production of sugarcane was about 1.6 million tons in 1992.

[23]ANIMAL HUSBANDRY

Much of the country lies within tsetse-infested areas, and cattle are therefore concentrated in the more northerly districts. In 1992 there were an estimated 1,183,000 head of cattle (compared with 383,000 in 1968), 919,000 goats, 1,200,000 sheep, and 382,000 hogs. There are 26 million chickens; about 15,800 tons of eggs were produced in 1992.

[24]FISHING

In 1964 a modern fishing wharf was opened at Abidjan, which is Africa's largest tuna fishing port, handling about 100,000 tons of tuna each year. There are fish hatcheries in Bouaké, Bamoro, and Korhogo. Commercial fishing for tuna is carried on in the Gulf of Guinea; sardines are also caught in quantity. The total catch was 85,182 tons in 1991, almost 75% in Atlantic waters.

[25]FORESTRY

There are three types of forest in Côte d'Ivoire: rain forest, deciduous forest, and the secondary forest of the savanna region. At one time, mahogany was the only wood exploited, but now more than 25 different types of wood are utilized commercially. In 1983, the government acknowledged that the nation's forest area, which totaled approximately 16 million ha (40 million acres) at independence in 1960, had dwindled to about 4 million ha (10 million acres).

In 1991, timber and timber products accounted for $279 million in export value, providing the third most important source of foreign revenue (after coffee and cocoa). Total 1991 timber production was 13,061,000 cu m. In 1991, tropical hardwood production and exports (in parentheses) for logs totaled 2,122,000 cu m (367,000 cu m); for lumber, 608,000 cu m (470,000 cu m); for plywood, 37,000 cu m(14,000 cu m); and for veneer, 185,000 cu m(84,00 cu m). The increasing scarcity of forest resources is adversely impacting value-added industries, leaving lumber and veneer production in a steady state of decline.

[26]MINING

Both prospecting and mining are subject to government control under the Société pour le Développement Minier de la Côte d'Ivoire (SODEMI). Mineral commodities are estimated to account for 10% of the country's exports, excluding the value of smuggled gold and diamonds. Diamond output rose from 8,000 carats in 1948 to 549,000 carats in 1961 but declined to only 15,000 carats in 1991. Production from the manganese reserves at Grand Lahou rose to 127,000 tons in 1969, but quality and sale prices were low, and the mine was closed in 1970. In 1991, a French consortium began to exploit a mine estimated to contain some 500,000 tons of gold ore with a content of 7 grams of gold per ton. Gold production went from 20 kg in 1990 to 1,100 kg in 1991 with the opening of the new mine. Large nickel and cobalt resources, discovered in the early 1970s by SODEMI near Sipilou, were estimated to contain minable reserves of 77 million tons of ore. Copper, titanium, chromite, bauxite, and asphalt are among other known minerals not yet exploited commercially. Ilmenite fields containing an estimated 500,000 tons of the rare metal have been discovered near Grand Lahou, but these also await exploitation.

27ENERGY AND POWER

Until 1959, electric power generation was entirely thermal, using imported oil. Since then, however, substantial efforts have been undertaken to develop Côte d'Ivoire's hydroelectric potential, and by 1991, hydroelectricity supplied about 40% of electrical demand. The country's first hydroelectric plant opened in 1959 at Ayamé, on the Bia River, with a capacity of 19,200 kw; a second dam on the Bia was completed in 1964. The Kossou hydroelectric plant, on the Bandama River, began operations in the early 1970s. Subsequently, the government completed hydroelectric projects at Taabo, on the Bandama, and Buyo, on the Sassandra. The largest development project in the nation's history, a hydroelectric dam at Soubré, on the Sassandra, would nearly double the national power output on reaching full capacity. Bids for participation in the project, expected to cost at least CFA Fr650 billion, were being tendered in 1983, but drought and financial difficulties doomed the enterprise. In 1991, total installed capacity was 1,173,000 kw (52,000 kw in 1963); electric power production reached 2,376 million kwh in 1991 (18.3 million kwh in 1964).

Offshore oil was discovered in 1977. Production began three years later; in 1983, Côte d'Ivoire approached self-sufficiency, with an output of over 1,000,000 tons, but production was only 99,000 tons in 1991, as deposits proved smaller, more scattered, and in deeper water than expected. A 15% share in the first field to be developed, Bélier, about 25 km (16 mi) from Abidjan, was held by the Société Nationale d'Opérations Pétrolières de la Côte d'Ivoire (PETROCI), the state oil corporation. PETROCI holds a 10% stake in the larger Espoir field off Jacqueville, about 50 km (31 mi) east of Abidjan.

28INDUSTRY

Côte d'Ivoire's industrial activity is substantial by African standards. It accounts for 17% of GDP and was the sector which led the early expansion of the Ivoirian economy. The development of processing industries, especially in the Abidjan region, has been significant. Bouaké, situated in the cotton-, tobacco-, and sisal-growing region, has become a large industrial center, and numerous thriving industries have been built up in the forest zone of the southern coastal region. These include palm oil mills, soap factories, a flour mill, fruit canning factories, a tuna canning factory, breweries, beer and soft drink plants, rubber processing plants, sugar mills, cotton ginning plants, and coffee- and cocoa-bean processing plants. Local demand growth continues to drive this industrial sector.

The lumber industry, producing largely for export, includes plywood factories and numerous sawmills. The construction materials industry comprises brick works, quarries, and cement plants that produced 500,000 tons of cement in 1990.

29SCIENCE AND TECHNOLOGY

Scientific institutes in Côte d'Ivoire conduct research in such fields as tropical forestry, livestock and veterinary medicine, cotton and tropical textiles, coffee, cocoa, rubber, savanna food crops, and citrus fruits. The French Institute of Scientific Research for Development and Cooperation has centers in Abidjan and extensions in Bouaké and Man. The National University of Côte d'Ivoire (Abidjan) includes faculties of sciences, medicine, and pharmacy; institutes of tropical ecology, mathematical research, and renewable energy. A technical school in Bingerville offers training in electrical engineering, and a teachers' training college at Yamoussoukro includes schools of industrial technology and engineering.

30DOMESTIC TRADE

European firms play an important part in the economy, and the French and Lebanese dominate commerce. They buy and export lumber, coffee, cocoa, and palm oil products and import capital and consumer goods. Most European firms have their headquarters in Abidjan; many are also represented in Bouaké. In Abidjan and Bouaké there are specialty shops in such lines as dry goods, foodstuffs, hardware, electrical appliances, and consumer electronics. In the smaller towns of the interior, bazaars and individual merchants and peddlers deal in locally grown products and a few imported items.

Domestic trade is generally on a cash basis, but in the countryside, bartering is common. Many shopkeepers extend credit to farmers until the end of the harvest season. Installment purchase has been introduced for automobiles and major appliances. Prices and profit margins are regulated by the government for basic food products, many imported goods, and certain services.

Business hours are generally from 8 AM to noon and from 2:30 to 5:30 PM, Monday through Friday, and from 8 AM to noon on Saturday. Banks are normally open on weekdays from 8 to 11:30 AM and 2:30 to 4:30 PM.

31FOREIGN TRADE

Côte d'Ivoire has generally enjoyed a positive trade balance since independence. The major exports are cocoa beans and products, coffee, and fuels; the leading imports are miscellaneous manufactured articles, machinery and transportation equipment, and crude oil and petroleum products.

The principal exports in 1989 (in millions of CFA francs) were as follows

Cocoa and products	366,817
Coffee and products	95,849
Fuels	86,176
Timber and products	58,948
Cotton and cotton textiles	35,676
Fats and oils	17,811
Chemical products	30,589
Pineapples	12,019
Canned fish	24,760
Latex	18,461
Other exports	148,465
TOTAL	895,571

The principal imports in 1989 (in millions of CFA francs) were as follows:

Manufactured articles	153,327
Crude oil and petroleum products	143,121
Food, beverages, and tobacco	81,744
Chemical products	99,862
Machinery and transportation equipment	110,600
Other imports	84,793
TOTAL	673,447

Côte d'Ivoire exports primarily to the Netherlands (22.5%) and to France (13.6%), followed by Germany, the United States, and Ghana. The two principal sources of Côte d'Ivoire's imports are France (28.7%) and Nigeria (16.0%).

32BALANCE OF PAYMENTS

A formerly consistent trade surplus has been counterbalanced by repatriation of earnings by foreign enterprises, remittances by the large foreign population, and interest payments on the substantial foreign debt. Largely reflecting trends in the trade account, the current account plummeted from a surplus of $64 million in 1985 to a deficit of well over $1 billion in 1992. The current account deficit has continued to grow, however, to over 15% of GDP for both 1991 and 1992. Though the trade surplus strengthened somewhat in 1990, it deteriorated again in 1991 and 1992.

In 1992 merchandise exports totaled $2,880 million and imports $1,833.7 million. The merchandise trade balance was $996.3 million. The following table summarizes Côte d'Ivoire's balance of payments for 1991 and 1992 (in millions of US dollars):

	1991	1992
CURRENT ACCOUNT		
Goods, services, and income	−1,134.0	−1,044.2
Unrequited transfers	−262.7	−262.9
TOTALS	−1,396.6	−1,307.2
CAPITAL ACCOUNT		
Direct investment	46.1	49.1
Other long-term capital	90.8	184.8
Other short-term capital	−44.7	−365.7
Exceptional financing	1,324.3	1,272.8
Reserves	−59.1	−86.0
TOTALS	1,357.4	1,055.0
Errors and omissions	39.2	252.2
Total change in reserves	−60.5	−97.7

33BANKING AND SECURITIES

In 1959, the Central Bank of the West African States (Banque Centrale des États de l'Afrique de l'Ouest—BCEAO) succeeded the Currency Board (Institut d'Émission) of French West Africa and Togo as the bank of issue for the former French West African territories. In 1962, it was reorganized as the joint note-issue bank of Dahomey (now Benin), Côte d'Ivoire, Mauritania (which withdrew in 1973), Niger, Senegal, Togo, and Upper Volta (now Burkina Faso). BCEAO notes, known as CFA francs, are guaranteed by France without limitation. The board of directors of the BCEAO consists of representatives of each participating African country, as well as of France. Côte d'Ivoire has a monetary committee that reports to the BCEAO; the committee works under the general rules of the Central Bank but possesses autonomy in internal credit matters. As of December 1992, currency in circulation in Côte d'Ivoire totaled CFA Fr826.0 billion.

The 10 commercial banks in 1993 included subsidiaries of French banks. In 1992, the commercial banking sector had CFA Fr59.5 billion in foreign assets and held CFA Fr252.2 billion in demand deposits and CFA Fr326.6 billion in time and savings deposits.

Public credit institutions provide credit to farmers and agricultural cooperatives, mortgages and personal loans, real estate financing, and loans to small industries. The Ivoirian Industrial Development Bank was inaugurated in 1965 to provide medium- and long-term credit for industrial projects. The National Agricultural Development Bank, created in 1968, extends loans to the agricultural community. The National Bank for Savings and Credit is the state savings institution.

The Abidjan stock exchange is the local securities market.

34INSURANCE

Insurance companies are subject to government supervision. In 1981, 10 domestic insurance firms and 26 agencies of French, UK, Swiss, and other freign companies provided most types of insurance; domestic companies account for almost 80% of the business. Third-party motor liability insurance is compulsory.

35PUBLIC FINANCE

Côte d'Ivoire's central government budget is nominally balanced. Due to declining commodity prices, however, the fiscal deficit reached an unsustainable 15% of GDP in 1989, which caused the government to begin an adjustment program aimed at fiscal deficit reduction. By the early 1990s, the government was progressing in reducing the deficit. In 1991, the Ouattara Plan of fiscal austerity and market liberalization measures was inaugurated. By this plan the economy will grow by 3.2% annually between 1992 and 1995, the rate of investment growth will double, and the current-account deficit will be halved. Results have so far been disappointing. These fell short of IMF targets and, under pressure, Côte d'Ivoire reduced public sector employment by 25% in 1993.

36TAXATION

Most domestic state revenues come from indirect taxes on imports and exports, consumer products, and business. Direct taxes include a graduated income tax. There is also a tax on salaries of 1.2%, and a "contribution nationale" of 1%. The employer pays a 9–16% payroll tax and a small percentage of taxable salary for family benefits and workers' compensation. For old age and retirement insurance, 1.8% of the taxable salary is paid by the employer and 1.2% by the employee. As of 1993, the tax on industrial and commercial profits was 40%. Also levied are a value-added (sales) tax of 11-35%, a service tax of 25%, a business franchise tax, a real estate tax, a petroleum products tax, a tax on automobiles, withholding taxes on dividends and directors' fees, and taxes on bank deposit interest, interest from certificates of deposit, royalties, license fees, and management and service fees paid by Côte d'Ivoire companies to foreign companies. A national investment fund was established in 1964; resources for the fund come from compulsory loans to the government of percentages of the profits of corporate and unincorporated businesses and of all rental incomes.

37CUSTOMS AND DUTIES

A fiscal import duty, applied to all incoming goods regardless of origin, serves primarily as a source of revenue. A customs duty is levied on all goods coming from places other than franc-zone countries. Products from EC countries receive preferential customs treatment. An excise tax is levied on alcoholic beverages and tobacco; export duties and taxes are imposed on specified commodities. All imports valued at more than CFA Fr100,000 f.o.b. need licenses, which are issued on a quota basis. Bilateral customs agreements have been concluded with Burkina Faso, Niger, Benin, and some other countries.

38FOREIGN INVESTMENT

Foreign (that is, non-French) investment was negligible until the issuance of the 1959 investment code, which eliminated all special privileges for French companies. A new investment code was adopted in 1984. To finance national investment, all businesses must lend 10% of their profits to the government, but this loan is rebated if they reinvest twice that sum in government-approved industries. Investment incentives include tax holidays, export bonuses, duty-free imports of equipment and machinery, free repatriation of capital and profits, and tax stabilization clauses. The new code is particularly intended to help small- and medium-sized enterprises, with greater incentives for firms locating outside the Abidjan area. Foreign direct investment in Côte d'Ivoire totaled $20.8 million in 1985.

39ECONOMIC DEVELOPMENT

Since independence, Côte d'Ivoire has engaged in an economic program aimed at ending its reliance on outside assistance and at achieving self-sustained growth. Under current conditions, however, the Côte d'Ivoire economy will remain highly vulnerable to commodity price variations and dependent upon outside assistance into the foreseeable future, a future mortgaged by its earlier levels of borrowing. The recent devaluation of the CFA franc should provide a new framework for improving sales of Côte d'Ivoire's products.

40SOCIAL DEVELOPMENT

A social welfare service was established in 1950 to coordinate public and private social assistance activities; it occupies itself mainly with casework in the large towns. A system of family allowances for wage earners was instituted in 1956, and workers' compensation has also been introduced.

In 1964, the National Assembly abolished polygamy and set the legal marriage age at 18 for boys and 16 for girls. Family planning and sex education programs fall within the jurisdiction of the education and female promotion ministries. The fertility rate in 1993 was 6.7. In 1992 only 3% of married women (ages 15 to 49) used any type of contraception. Abortion is permitted in order to save the woman's life. There is a cabinet-level Ministry of Women's Affairs.

41HEALTH

The public medical services are more important than the small number of private physicians and clinics. In 1990, the country had 1,020 doctors, 135 pharmacists, 219 dentists, 3,691 nurses, and 1,533 midwives. From 1985 to 1990, there were 0.8 hospital beds per 1,000 population. Studies show that from 1985 to 1992, only 30% of the population had access to health care services. Total health care expenditures in 1990 were $332 million.

Malaria, yellow fever, sleeping sickness, yaws, leprosy, trachoma, and meningitis are endemic. A broad program was set up in 1961 to control these and other diseases: compulsory vaccination against smallpox and yellow fever was instituted, efforts by mobile health units to track down cases and provide treatment were intensified, and general health measures were tightened both within the country and at the borders. From 1990 to 1992, the country immunized children up to one year old as follows: tuberculosis (47%); diphtheria, pertussis, and tetanus (47%); polio (47%); and measles (51%). In 1990 there were 196 reported cases of tuberculosis per 100,000 people. Malnutrition affected 12% of children under 5 years old.

There were 650,000 births in 1992 (a rate of 50 per 1,000). The infant mortality rate in 1993 was 91 per 1,000 live births, and the overall death rate was 14.7 per 1,000. In 1992, average life expectancy in Côte d'Ivoire was estimated at 52 years for both men and women.

42HOUSING

Housing remains an issue of major concern in Côte d'Ivoire, particularly in Abidjan, which has been the focus of continued migration from rural areas. Extensive slum clearance has been carried out in the former capital, but shantytowns still persist on the outskirts. Police officers, soldiers, customs officials, top-level bureaucrats, and foreign salaried government employees receive free housing. In rural areas, some villages have been entirely rebuilt or replanned. According to the latest available figures for 1980–88, the housing stock totaled 1,800,000 units, with 5.5 people per dwelling.

43EDUCATION

Education is free at all levels. Primary education lasts for six years and secondary for seven years (four years followed by three years). Adult literacy rates in 1990 were estimated at 66.9% for men and 40.2% for women. In 1991, there were 6,844 schools with 39,057 teachers and 1,447,785 students. In the general secondary schools, there were 396,606 students. The National University of Côte d'Ivoire, located in Abidjan and established as a university in 1964, has six faculties.

44LIBRARIES AND MUSEUMS

The National Library, in Abidjan, was created in 1968 from the former library of the French Institute of Black Africa and has a primarily scientific collection; in 1986, it contained over 75,000 volumes. The Central Library in Abidjan-Treichville was founded in 1963 with the help of UNESCO; it is administered by the Ministry of National Education and has 14,000 volumes. Abidjan also has a municipal library with 50,000 volumes, the National University library with 80,000 volumes, and several small research libraries. The Museum of Côte d'Ivoire in Abidjan features ethnological, sociological, artistic, and scientific exhibits. The Native Museum of Costume was founded in 1981 in Grand Bassam. Regional museums are located in Bondoukou, Bingerville, and Abengourou.

45MEDIA

All news media are owned or controlled by the government or the ruling PDCI. The French-language daily *Fraternité Matin* had a circulation of 80,000 in 1991; its Sunday edition, *Ivoire Dimanche,* had a circulation of 60,000. Telephone and telegraph services are government owned; there were 87,700 telephones in use in 1991. The government also controls radio and television broadcasting. Radio broadcasts are in French, English, and indigenous languages; television is in French only. In 1991 there were an estimated 1,765,000 radios and 730,000 television sets in use.

46ORGANIZATIONS

Chambers of commerce, industry, and agriculture have their headquarters in Abidjan and elsewhere. The Red Cross Society is active. There are a number of employers' associations and agricultural producers' cooperatives; a consumer cooperative also functions. Côte d'Ivoire has many clubs devoted to various sports.

47TOURISM, TRAVEL, AND RECREATION

Tourism has developed significantly since the early 1970s. The country has excellent hotels and other tourist facilities, with approximately 12,000 beds in 6,000 hotel rooms and a 39% occupancy rate in 1991. There were about 200,000 tourist arrivals in that year, 115,000 from Africa, 69,000 from Europe, and 10,000 from the Americas. Receipts from tourism amounted to US$46 million during the same year. Fine beaches, specially built tourist villages, and photo safaris through the wildlife preserves are the principal attractions.

Nationals of many European and African countries and the US need no visas for stays of up to 90 days, but a vaccination certificate for yellow fever is required of all foreign visitors.

48FAMOUS IVOIRIANS

Queen Abia Pokou (b.1720), the legendary heroine of the Baule people, led them to Côte d'Ivoire from the territory that is now Ghana. Félix Houphouët-Boigny (1905–1993) was the first African to be a French Cabinet minister (1956–69); he was elected as Côte d'Ivoire's first president in 1960 and was continually reelected until his death. The nation's outstanding literary figure, Bernard Binlin Dadié (b.1916), is known abroad for several volumes of poetry and a novel; he has held many government posts, becoming minister of cultural affairs in 1977.

49DEPENDENCIES

Côte d'Ivoire has no territories or colonies.

50 BIBLIOGRAPHY

American University. *Area Handbook for the Ivory Coast*. Washington, D.C.: Government Printing Office, 1973.

Cote d'Ivoire (Ivory Coast) in Pictures. Minneapolis: Lerner, 1988.

Harshe, Rajan. *Pervasive Entente: France and the Ivory Coast*. Atlantic Highlands, N.J.: Humanities Press, 1984.

Kakwani, Nanak. *Poverty and Economic Growth*. Washington, D.C.: World Bank, 1990.

Masini, Jean, et al. *Multinationals and Development in Black Africa: A Case Study of the Ivory Coast*. New York: Praeger, 1980.

Mundt, Robert J. *Historical Dictionary of the Ivory Coast (Côte d'Ivoire)*. Metuchen, N.J.: Scarecrow, 1987.

Priovolos, Theophilos. *Coffee and the Ivory Coast: An Econometric Study*. Lexington, Mass.: Lexington Books, 1981.

Schneider, Hartmut. *Adjustment and Equity in Côte d'Ivoire*. Paris: Development Centre of the Organisation for Economic Cooperation and Development, 1992.

Weiskel, Timothy. *French Colonial Rule and the Baule Peoples: Resistance and Collaboration, 1889–1911*. New York: Oxford University Press, 1981.

Zartman, William, and Christopher L. Delgado (eds.). *The Political Economy of the Ivory Coast*. New York: Praeger, 1984.

Zolberg, Aristide R. *One-Party Government in the Ivory Coast*. Rev. ed. Princeton, N.J.: Princeton University Press, 1974.

DJIBOUTI

Republic of Djibouti
République de Djibouti

CAPITAL: Djibouti.

FLAG: A white triangle, with a five-pointed red star within, extends from the hoist; the remaining area has a broad light blue band over a broad light green band.

ANTHEM: No information available.

MONETARY UNIT: The Djibouti franc (DFr) of 100 centimes is the national currency. There are coins of 1, 2, 5, 10, 20, 50, 100, and 500 Djibouti francs, and notes of 500, 1000, 5000, and 10,000 Djibouti francs. DFr1 = $0.0056 (or $1 = DFr177.72).

WEIGHTS AND MEASURES: The metric system is in use.

HOLIDAYS: New Year's Day, 1 January; Labor Day, 1 May; Independence Day, 27 June; Christmas Day, 25 December. Movable religious holidays are Milad an-Nabi, Laylat al-Miraj, 'Id al-Fitr, 'Id al-'Adha', and Muslim New Year (1st of Muharram).

TIME: 3 PM = noon GMT.

¹LOCATION, SIZE, AND EXTENT

Djibouti (formerly known as French Somaliland and then as the Territory of the Afars and the Issas) is situated on the east coast of Africa along the Bab al-Mandab, the strait that links the Red Sea with the Gulf of Aden. It is bordered by Ethiopia N, S, and W, by Somalia on the SE, and by the Bab al-Mandab, Gulf of Tadjoura, and Gulf of Aden on the E. Djibouti encompasses approximately 22,000 sq km (8,494 sq mi) and has a total boundary length of 822 km (511 mi). Comparatively, the area occupied by Djibouti is slightly larger than the state of Massachusetts.

Djibouti's capital city, Djibouti, is located in the eastern part of the country.

²TOPOGRAPHY

Originally formed by volcanic action that accompanied the uplifting and faulting of the East African shield and the Rift Valley system, Djibouti consists of a series of high, arid tablelands surrounding faults, within which are low plains. Many areas exhibit thick layers of lava flow. There are three principal regions: the coastal plain, less than 200 m (660 ft) above sea level; the mountains, averaging about 1,000 m (3,300 ft) above sea level; and the plateau behind the mountains, rising from 300 to 1,500 m (1,000–4,900 ft). The highest point, Mt. Moussa Ali, rises to 2,010 m (6,594 ft) on the northern frontier. The saline Lake Assal, at 170 m (558 ft) below sea level, is the lowest point in Africa and the second lowest in the world. In general, the terrain is bare, dry, desolate, and marked by sharp cliffs, deep ravines, burning sands, and thorny shrubs. There is very little groundwater except in an area along the southern border with Somalia, and Djibouti is dependent on saline subterranean aquifers. Earthquakes are common.

³CLIMATE

The climate is torrid, and rainfall is sparse and erratic. During the hot season, from May to October, daytime temperatures average 35°C (95°F) and the northeastern monsoon blows. During the warm season, from October to May, average daytime temperatures moderate to 25°C (77°F). Humidity is high all year, but annual rainfall averages less than 13 cm (5 in).

⁴FLORA AND FAUNA

Djibouti is about 89% desert, 10% pasture, and 1% forest. On Mt. Goda, near Tadjoura, there are rare giant juniper trees, acacias, and wild olive trees. However, most of the vegetation is typical of the desert and semidesert, consisting of thorn scrubs and palm trees.

In its animal reserves, Djibouti has antelopes, gazelles, hyenas, and jackals.

⁵ENVIRONMENT

Djibouti's most significant environmental problems are deforestation, water pollution, and the protection of its wildlife. Djibouti's forests are threatened by agriculture and the use of wood for fuel. The rare trees on Mt. Goda are protected within a national park. The nation has 0.1 cubic miles of water. Fifty-one percent is used for farming, but the water supply is threatened by increasing salinity. Fifty percent of the country's urban dwellers and 79% of all rural people do not have safe water. Underwater reserves have been established in the Gulf of Tadjoura to prevent overfishing of tuna, barracuda, grouper, and other species. As of 1994, six of 22 mammal species and 3 of 311 bird species are endangered. Three of the nations 534 plant species are currently threatened with extinction. The Djibouti francolin was endangered in 1987. No hunting of wild animals is permitted, but abuses continue.

⁶POPULATION

In 1991, the population was estimated by the government at 542,000, of whom perhaps 317,000 lived in the city of Djibouti, the national capital. This includes the refugee population. Other estimates are lower: the US Census Bureau estimated the 1994 population at 374,733, and the UN the 1995 population at 511,000. The population density, according to the government figures, was about 23 per sq km (60.5 per sq mi). The annual population growth was estimated by the UN at 3%.

7MIGRATION

The peoples of Djibouti, Somalia, and Eritrea are historically nomadic, migrating with flocks of camels and goats across borders that now separate nations. Somalis from Djibouti have also historically sought work across the Gulf of Aden in Yemen and the Persian Gulf sheikdoms. The dominant migration in recent years has been from the rural areas of the republic to the capital. At the end of 1992, about 20,000 Somali refugees from Ethiopia's Ogaden region were living in Djibouti camps, and another 75,000 or so Somali nationals were also in the country. There were also 8,000 Ethiopian refugees in Djibouti.

8ETHNIC GROUPS

The Issa branch of the Somali people and related clans constitutes 40–65% of all Djibouti's inhabitants; most live in southern Djibouti or in the capital. The Afars, a related people of north and west Djibouti, who also live in the Danakil depression of neighboring Ethiopia, number about 25–35%. The remainder consists of Arabs of Yemeni background, French (about 3%), Ethiopians, Somali immigrants, and Italians.

9LANGUAGES

Although French and Arabic are the official languages, the home languages of the vast majority of Djiboutians are Somali and Afar, both of Cushitic origin.

10RELIGIONS

At least 94% of all indigenous Djiboutians are Muslims. Tadjoura is famous for its seven mosques. About 6% of all Djiboutians are Christian.

11TRANSPORTATION

About 97 km (60 mi) of the single-track, meter-gauge railway linking the capital with Addis Ababa traverses the Republic of Djibouti. It was closed during the Somali-Ethiopian War of 1977–78; by the time it reopened, the Ethiopians had developed their port of Assab (now part of Eritrea), so traffic did not return to its former level.

Djibouti had 2,900 km (1,800 mi) of road in 1991, over 280 km (174 mi) of which was paved. A tarred road runs most of the distance from Djibouti city to Dikhil, Yoboki, and Galafi, on the Ethiopian border, where it connects with the main Assab–Addis Ababa highway. Except for the 40-km (25-mi) road from Djibouti city to Arta, all other roads are rough. A secondary road connects Obock and Tadjoura, on the northern side of the Gulf of Tadjoura, with Randa and Dorra in the northern interior. A highway between Djibouti city and Tadjoura was completed by 1991. In 1991 there were an estimated 13,000 passenger cars and 2,500 commercial trucks, taxis, and buses in Djibouti.

Djibouti's improved natural harbor consists of a roadstead, outer harbor, and inner harbor. The roadstead is well protected by reefs and the configuration of the land. The inner harbor has five outer and six inner berths for large vessels. A quarter of Ethiopia's imports and half of its exports move through the port. Car ferries ply the Gulf of Tadjoura from Djibouti city to Tadjoura and Obock, which are ports of minor commercial importance.

Ambouli Airport, about 6 km (4 mi) from the city of Djibouti, is the country's international air terminal. There are local airports at Tadjoura and Obock. Air Djibouti, 62% government owned and 32.3% owned by Air France, provides domestic service to six centers and flies to a number of overseas destinations. It carried 50,325 passengers in 1986. Nine other airlines served Djibouti in 1986.

12HISTORY

Somali and Afar herders lived in and around Djibouti for hundreds of years before European explorers in the 19th century brought the region to the attention of the modern West. Obock and, later, Djibouti city were recognized as ports of great usefulness on the sea routes to India, Mauritius, and Madagascar. Inasmuch as the Italians and British were active colonizers farther south along the Somali coast, and Britain was gaining control in what are now Yemen, the Sudan, and Egypt. France decided to establish its colonial foothold in 1862 along what is now the northeastern coast of Djibouti. This tentative venture became in 1884–85 the protectorates of Obock and Tadjoura, which were merged to form French Somaliland.

The administrative capital of French Somaliland was moved from Obock to Djibouti in 1896, a year before the boundaries of the colony were officially demarcated between France and Ethiopia. In 1898, a French consortium began building the narrow-gauge railway that finally reached Addis Ababa in 1917. During the Italian invasion and occupation of Ethiopia in the 1930s and during the early part of World War II, there were constant border skirmishes between French and Italian forces. In December 1942, French Somaliland forces joined the Free French under Gen. Charles de Gaulle.

After World War II, French Somaliland gradually gained a measure of local autonomy. In 1957, it obtained a territorial assembly and a local executive council to advise the French-appointed governor-general. The following year, the voters of French Somaliland opted to join the French Community as an overseas territory, electing one deputy and one senator to the French National Assembly. In late 1958, the first elections to the local assembly were held under a system of proportional representation. In the second elections, held in 1963, plurality voting based on party lists in seven districts replaced proportional voting. The result was the election of an Afar leader as head of the executive council; the more numerous Issas felt they had been prevented by the new electoral procedures from gaining control of the council. In 1967, 60% of the voters in a special referendum opted to retain the colony's association with France, but the Issas again complained that the franchise lists had been unfairly restricted in a way that favored the Afars. After the referendum, French Somaliland became known as the Territory of the Afars and the Issas.

The country's independence movement had been led throughout the postwar period by the Issas, but their movement had been opposed by Ethiopia (which wanted French control to continue) and by the Afars, who feared Issa domination. Finally, in 1975, the French began to accommodate increasingly strident demands for independence. The territory's citizenship law, which had favored the Afar minority, was revised to admit more Issas. In a referendum in May 1977, the now-enlarged Issa majority voted decisively for independence, which was officially established on 27 June 1977. Hassan Gouled Aptidon, the territory's premier, had been elected the nation's first president by the territorial Chamber of Deputies three days earlier. Although Gouled, an Issa, appointed Afar premiers and the cabinet was roughly balanced, the dominance of the Issas in administration led to political conflict, including cabinet crises. Gouled was reelected without opposition by universal suffrage in June 1981 and April 1987. A one-party Chamber of Deputies list, elected without opposition in May 1982, consisted of 26 Issas, 23 Afars, and 16 Arabs. Only 12 seats were won by newcomers in the April 1987 election of a one-party list.

Dissatisfaction with Gouled grew in the late 1980s and contributed to an uprising by Afar guerrillas of the Front for the Restoration of Unity and Democracy (FRUD) in late 1991. FRUD gained control of some areas of the north and west. In February 1992, France deployed forces in Djibouti and the Afars declared unilaterally a cease-fire. Yet fighting continued and a government counter-offensive checked the FRUD by July. Rebel bases in the north were occupied, and many opposition leaders were imprisoned, including Ali Aref Bourhan, for an alleged coup attempt. He was released in December 1993. By the end of 1993, about 35% of the central government's budgetary expenditures went toward maintaining "security"; that is, the military occupation of the north by troops of Somali origin. The economy suffered markedly as the insurgency dragged on.

13 GOVERNMENT

Under the 1981 and 1992 constitutions, Djibouti is a parliamentary republic. The president, who according to the constitution must be an Issa, is elected by universal adult suffrage; the prime minister, who heads the cabinet, must be an Afar. The legislature consists of the unicameral Chamber of Deputies, whose 65 members are elected for five-year terms. Before 1992, candidates came from a single list submitted by the ruling party, the Popular Rally for Progress (RPP).

In January 1992, the Gouled government named a committee to draft a new constitution that would permit multiparty democracy, limit presidential powers, and establish an independent judiciary. On 4 September 1992, 75% of the voters approved the new constitution in a referendum. And on 18 December 1992, legislative elections were held, with the RPP gaining 74.6% of the vote and the Democratic Renewal Party (PRD) 25.4%. Other parties boycotted the elections on the grounds that Gouled did not consult the opposition in the "democratization" process. Most Afars did not vote. The RPP, therefore, won all 65 seats. Gouled was reelected, although not convincingly, on 7 May 1993. The four losing parties and FRUD accused the government of election fraud, a charge supported by international observers. Only 50% of the eligible voters were reported to have turned out.

14 POLITICAL PARTIES

A law passed in October 1981 restricted political activity to the ruling People's Rally for Progress (Rassemblement Populaire pour le Progrès—RPP). That year, the government temporarily detained the leaders of and banned the Djiboutian People's Party (Parti Populaire Djiboutien). There are also illegal Issa and Afar parties, including an Ethiopian-backed Afar party-in-exile and a Somali-backed Issa party-in-exile. For the 1987 elections to the Chamber of Deputies, a single list of candidates was drawn up by the RPP, headed by President Gouled; about 90% of the nation's 100,985 voters cast ballots.

Despite the 1992 constitutional changes that legalized opposition party political activity, Djibouti is a de facto one-party system. The RPP holds all seats in the legislature and the presidency. Two groups, the Democratic Renewal Party (PRD) and the Democratic National Party (PND) function openly. They contested the 1992 and 1993 elections. The Front for the Restoration of Unity and Democracy (FRUD), formed in August 1991, is in open armed rebellion, and the Movement for Unity and Democracy (MUD) allegedly is associated with the Somali National Movement operating out of northern Somalia. It is a coalition of Afar-oriented and Issa-oriented dissidents.

15 LOCAL GOVERNMENT

There are five *cercles,* or districts, with councils and appointed administrators: Ali Sabieh, Obock, Dikhil, Tadjoura, and Djibouti.

16 JUDICIAL SYSTEM

The judicial system consists of courts of first instance, a High Court of Appeal, and a Supreme Court. Each of the five administrative districts also has a customary court. The legal system is a blend of French codified law, Shari'a (Islamic law) and customary law of the native nomadic peoples.

The Constitution is modeled on the 1958 French Constitution. The judiciary is not completely independent of the executive branch. A state security court handles political trials and cases

LOCATION: 10°54′ to 12°43′N; 41°45′ and 43°27′E. **BOUNDARY LENGTHS:** total coastline, 370 km (230 mi); Somalia, 58 km (36 mi); Ethiopia, 459 km (285 mi). **TERRITORIAL SEA LIMIT:** 12 mi.

involving purported threats to national security. Political trials may be applied to the Supreme Court.

17 ARMED FORCES

About 4,000 French troops are based near the city of Djibouti to deal with threats to French interests in the region. The French forces are equipped with tanks, howitzers, antiaircraft guns, helicopters, and 10 Mirage-3 interceptors; a naval flotilla is based near the capital. Djibouti's own armed force of 3,800 members is divided into a 3,000-man army (three battalions), a 100-man navy with 9 patrol craft, and a 100-man air force with fifteen non-combatant planes and helicopters, excluding 18 MiGs and Mi helicopters from Ethiopia. A force of 4,500 insurgents opposes the government.

18 INTERNATIONAL COOPERATION

Admitted to UN membership on 20 September 1977, Djibouti belongs to ECA and all the nonregional specialized agencies except IAEA, UNESCO, UNIDO, and WIPO. It is also a member of the African Development Bank, G-77, League of Arab States, and OAU, as well as a signatory of the Law of the Sea. In 1981, treaties of friendship and cooperation were signed with Ethiopia, Somalia, Kenya, and the Sudan.

19ECONOMY

Djibouti has a market-based, free-enterprise economy. Its economy is dependent upon its strategic position at the narrow straits at the southern entrance to the Red Sea. The French military base in Djibouti is the country's largest single source of economic and commercial activity. The remainder of the money economy is service oriented and centered upon the free port of Djibouti, the railway terminus there, the airport, and government administration. There is also an active construction industry.

There is little arable farm land in Djibouti, and the country is subject to periods of severe drought. As a consequence, Djibouti produces only 3% of its food needs. Over half the population derives its income from livestock: goats, sheep, and camels. A fishing industry has emerged, and the Islamic Development Bank has helped finance a canning factory.

Construction of an oil refinery began in 1990 to process Saudi crude. Inauguration of production has been delayed due to factional conflict. Djibouti has a small tourist industry. The free port features a deep-water container terminal; France has committed $8 million to its continuing modernization.

20INCOME

In 1992 Djibouti's GNP was $1,030 per capita. In 1992 the GDP was $358 million in current US dollars. It is estimated that agriculture, hunting, forestry, and fishing contributed 4% to GDP; manufacturing, 8%; electricity, gas, and water, 3%; construction, 8%; wholesale and retail trade, 16%; transport, storage, and communication, 10%; finance, insurance, real estate, and business services, 11%; community, social, and personal services, 2%; and other sources, 39%.

21LABOR

Labor in the cash economy is concentrated in the city of Djibouti, particularly on the docks and in shipbuilding and building construction. The railway is a significant employer, as is the national government. Unemployment and underemployment are widespread. In 1992, the monthly minimum wage was DFr15,850—unchanged since 1980. By law, the standard workweek is 40 hours, often spread over 6 days. Unemployment may be as high as 70%.

Under the Constitution, workers are free to join unions and strike provided they legally comply with prescribed requirements. In 1992, less than 20% of persons in the age economy belonged to unions. The government-controlled General Union of Djiboutian Workers (UGTD) was opposed in 1992 by a new independent union confederation, the Democratic Labor Union (UDT), concerning the imposition of a 10% tax on all workers.

22AGRICULTURE

Agriculture in Djibouti is very limited, due to acute water shortages in rural areas. In 1990, agriculture contributes only 2.8% to GDP. In 1992, some 22,000 tons of vegetables were produced. Tomatoes are grown for domestic consumption. Date palms are cultivated along the coastal fringe. Famine and malnutrition in Djibouti have created a reliance on the distribution of food aid for millions of its people.

23ANIMAL HUSBANDRY

Cattle, fat-tailed sheep, goats, and camels are grazed in the interior; hides and skins are exported. In 1992, Djibouti had an estimated 506,000 goats and 450,000 sheep.

24FISHING

There is no local tradition of commercial fishing or seafaring, although the Gulf of Tadjoura, the Gulf of Aden, and the Red Sea are potentially rich sources of commercial and game fish. The catch was 380 tons in 1991.

25FORESTRY

There are protected forests on the slopes of the mountains north of the Gulf of Tadjoura. Less than 1% of the country's total land area is forested.

26MINING

Salt is extracted from evaporated pans in the marshes of Tadjoura, and lime is produced just west of Djibouti city from an old limestone quarry. Brick and tile clays, sand and gravel, and crushed and dimension stone also have been produced for domestic construction projects.

27ENERGY AND POWER

All of Djibouti's electricity is generated from an oil-fired generating station in the capital. Installed capacity was 38,000 kw in 1991, and production totaled 178 million kwh. One geothermal power station was in operation as of 1991. All petroleum products are imported. Fuel and energy generally account for one-quarter of total imports.

28INDUSTRY

Shipbuilding and urban construction are the only major industrial undertakings. Local manufacturing is limited to a mineral-water bottling facility and small plants that produce food, dairy products, beverages, furniture, building materials, and bottled gas.

With the help of France, Italy, the World Bank, OPEC, and the United Nations Development Programme, Djibouti is promoting a project to develop geothermal energy resources. Interest is focused on the Goubet-Lac Assal region and, through this project, Djibouti hopes to become self-sufficient in energy.

29SCIENCE AND TECHNOLOGY

Since Djibouti is an active volcanic zone, its two principal research organizations—the Higher Institute for Scientific and Technical Research and the Bureau of Geological and Mineral Research—concentrate on the earth sciences.

30DOMESTIC TRADE

Domestic trade is dominated by traffic in live sheep and camels, dates, and melons. The government maintains price controls on a number of essential commodities, including wheat flour, bread, sugar, and petroleum products. French citizens dominate the commerce of the city of Djibouti. Business hours normally are 7:30 AM to noon and 3:30 to 6 PM, Sunday through Thursday, and 7:30 AM to noon on Saturday. Banks are open Sunday–Thursday from 7:15 to 11:45 AM.

31FOREIGN TRADE

Imports exceeded exports by a large margin; in 1991, imports came to DFr38,103 million, and exports to only DFr3,080 million. Small amounts of hides and skins and live camels are exported; the reexport trade is of much greater significance. Exports in 1991 (millions of Djibouti francs) were:

Live animals	477
Food	395
Others	2,208
TOTAL	3,080

About 75% of imports are consumed or used in Djibouti, while the remainder is forwarded to Ethiopia or northern

Somalia. In 1991, 57% of exports went to France while 16% went to the Yemen; 26.1% of Djibouti's imports came from France while 8.3% came from Ethiopia, 7.2% came from Japan, and 6.5% came from Italy.

32BALANCE OF PAYMENTS

Since independence, Djibouti has run large trade deficits, which have been offset by surpluses on services and by transfers attributable to the French base, port receipts, the national airline, the national airport, and grants from donors. In 1991, increased services earnings and official transfers boosted foreign exchange reserves to five months of import cover. In 1992, however, the external account deficit (excluding transfers) increased to 26% of GDP due to a decline in exports.

33BANKING AND SECURITIES

The Djibouti franc was created in 1949 by the government of France. The Djibouti Treasury was replaced in 1983 as the bank of issue and central bank by the new National Bank of Djibouti. There were five commercial banks in 1993 and a National Development Bank, 51% government owned. The money supply came to Dfr58,498 million at the end of 1993. Demand deposits amounted to Dfr22,209 million. There is no securities exchange.

34INSURANCE

About 10 European insurance companies provide most of the insurance coverage.

35PUBLIC FINANCE

The budget deficit grew from 9% of GDP in 1989 to 18% by 1991, and exceeded 20% of GDP in 1992 because of increased military expenditures. Declining tax receipts and political unrest in bordering countries have exacerbated the deterioration of public finance in recent years.

36TAXATION

The individual income tax, payable by the employer, is collected by withholding from wages and salaries. In addition, the employee and the employer contribute to a medical and pension fund. There is a separate system for civil servants and soldiers. Private corporations and personal companies, as well as public companies and limited companies, pay a flat tax. Other taxes include property, stamp, and registration taxes. There is also an ad valorem consumption tax with a surtax on luxury items.

37CUSTOMS AND DUTIES

There are no customs duties on imports, but fiscal duties are levied by means of a general consumption tax of 30% on luxury items and 20% on all other goods. Although Djibouti was established as a "Free Zone," only its port is actually a free trade zone, not the entire territory.

38FOREIGN INVESTMENT

Foreign investment is predominantly French, largely in connection with the military base and the port. Saudi Arabia, Pakistan, China, Korea, and Uganda have cooperation agreements. The US contributes $3 million annually through its Economic Support Fund Djibouti (ESFD). There are no exchange controls, and investors are allowed to transfer their profits freely without tax. Tax relief is offered to some investors.

39ECONOMIC DEVELOPMENT

In 1990, the Djibouti government significantly expanded its public investment program. Projects in communications, agriculture, and fisheries, as well as in social and environmental areas, were planned. Execution of these plans was put on hold as a result of subsequent domestic disturbances. The Persian Gulf War also disrupted investment programs sponsored by Iraq, Kuwait, and Saudi Arabia.

French budgetary support of the Djibouti economy is crucial to its stability, providing some 45% of foreign aid. The long-standing French financial commitment has weakened since 1989, and the IMF in 1992 expressed serious concern over key budget and trade deficits.

40SOCIAL DEVELOPMENT

A social service fund covers medical and pension benefits. Although women have the franchise, they do not play a leadership role, and as of 1987 there were no women in the cabinet or legislature. Large numbers of refugees from the fighting in Somalia and Ethiopia have swelled Djibouti's population by about one-third which has increased demands on government services at the same time when government has diverted revenues to pursue anti-insurgency activities in the north and west. The latter itself has forced around 15,000 Djibouti nationals to take refuge in Ethiopia.

41HEALTH

Malnutrition is severe, and the incidence of tuberculosis high; malaria is endemic. There were 220 reported cases of tuberculosis in 1990. The city of Djibouti's publicly supplied water is suspect because the system is in disrepair.

In 1986 there were 18 hospitals, medical centers, and dispensaries, with a total of 1,283 beds; medical personnel included 89 physicians, 14 dentists, 20 pharmacists, and 1,314 paramedical personnel. In 1993, Djibouti's government was developing plans to improve public health and the management of hospitals. It also wanted to train more staff and rehabilitate existing facilities.

There were 21,900 births in 1992 with a birth rate of 47 per 1,000 people. Life expectancy in 1992 was 49 years, and the infant mortality rate was 113 per 1,000 live births. From 1991 to 1992, 83% of the country's children were vaccinated against measles. In 1993, there were 16.5 deaths per 1,000 inhabitants.

42HOUSING

Djiboutian nomads generally live in branch-framed, transportable huts (toukouls), which are covered with woven mats or boiled bark pulled into fine strands and plaited; they are carried from place to place on camels. Good-quality urban housing is in short supply. Construction of 5,000 low-cost dwellings was planned for the 1981–86 period, but only 729 were built. Between 1988 and 1990, 50% of the urban and 21% of the rural population had access to a water supply, while 94% of urban and 20% of rural dwellers had sanitation facilities.

43EDUCATION

In 1992 there were 68 primary schools, with 30,589 students. Secondary schools had a total of 9,740 students; of these 8,083 were in general education, 112 were in teachers' training, and 1,545 were in vocational training schools. Education is compulsory for six years at the primary level followed by seven years of secondary education. Adult literacy in 1985 was about 20%.

44LIBRARIES AND MUSEUMS

No information is available.

45MEDIA

All media are government controlled. In 1983, Djibouti inaugurated a powerful state-owned AM radio transmitting station, built with French and FRG funds. A television service was introduced in 1967. Both are state run and broadcast in French, Afar, Somali, and Arabic. In 1991 there were 1,385,000 radios and 24,000 television sets. From the city of Djibouti, telephone connections are available by satellite to Europe and the West and by land line to the main cities and towns of the interior; there were

7,500 telephones in 1991. Djibouti has one daily newspaper, *La Nation de Djebouti,* which had a circulation of 4,000 in 1991.

46 ORGANIZATIONS

A chamber of commerce and industry, founded in 1912, has its headquarters in the capital.

47 TOURISM, TRAVEL, AND RECREATION

In addition to several little-visited sandy beaches along the Gulf of Tadjoura, tourist attractions include islands in the Gulf of Tadjoura and the Bab al-Mandab. At Goubbet al-Kharab, at the western end of the Gulf of Tadjoura, there are steep cliffs and a bay turned dark green by black lava. Inland from this point is Lake Assal with a number of active volcanoes nearby. The Forest of the Day is a national park for rare trees on Mt. Goda. In the south, the alkaline Lake Abbé is visited by flocks of flamingos, ibis, and pelicans. Near Ali Sabieh are the famous red mountains and a national park full of various gazelles. All foreign nationals except French need a passport and visa secured in advance; antimalarial precautions are advisable.

48 FAMOUS DJIBOUTIANS

Hassan Gouled Aptidon (b.1916) has been president since independence.

49 DEPENDENCIES

Djibouti has no territories or colonies.

50 BIBLIOGRAPHY

Darch, Colin. *A Soviet View of Africa: an Annotated Bibliography on Ethiopia, Somalia, and Djibouti.* Boston, Mass.: G. K. Hall, 1980.

Schraeder, Peter J. *Djibouti.* Santa Barbara, Calif.: Clio Press, 1991.

Tholomier, Robert. *Djibouti: Pawn of the Horn of Africa.* Metuchen, N.J.: Scarecrow, 1981.

Thompson, Virginia, and Richard Adloff. *Djibouti and the Horn of Africa.* Stanford, Calif.: Stanford University Press, 1968.

Touval, Saadia. *Somali Nationalism: International Politics and the Drive for Unity in the Horn of Africa.* Cambridge, Mass.: Harvard University Press, 1963.

EGYPT

Arab Republic of Egypt
Jumhuriat Misr al-'Arabiyah

NAME: Egypt (Misr) is the name by which this ancient country has been known for more than 6,000 years. In 1958, the nation established by the merger of Egypt and Syria adopted the name United Arab Republic. Egypt retained this name (despite the breakaway of Syria in 1961) until 1971, when under a new constitution it became the Arab Republic of Egypt.

CAPITAL: Cairo (Al-Qahira).

FLAG: The flag is a tricolor of three horizontal stripes—red, white, and black—with the national emblem in the center white stripe.

ANTHEM: *The Arab Republic of Egypt Hymn*

MONETARY UNIT: The Egyptian pound (E£) is a paper currency of 100 piasters or 1,000 milliemes. There are coins of 1, 5, 10, and 20 piasters and notes of 25 and 50 piasters and 1, 5, 10, 20, 50, and 1000 pounds. Under a triple-tier exchange rate system, the official rate applies to petroleum and Suez Canal earnings; an "official incentive" rate governs most other official transactions; and the "own exchange" system employs a free-market rate. E£1 = US$3.38 (or US$1 = E£0.2959).

WEIGHTS AND MEASURES: The metric system is the official standard, but various local units also are used: 1 feddan, consisting of 333.3 kassabah, equals 0.42 hectare (1.038 acres).

HOLIDAYS: New Year's Day, 1 January; Evacuation Day, 18 June; Revolution Day, 23 July; Armed Forces Day, 6 October; Popular Resistance Day, 24 October; Victory Day, 23 December. Movable holidays include Sham an-Nassim (Breath of Spring), of ancient origin, as well as such Muslim religious holidays as 'Id al-Fitr, 'Id al-'Adha', and the 1st of Muharram (Muslim New Year).

TIME: 2 PM = noon GMT.

¹LOCATION, SIZE, AND EXTENT

Situated at the northeastern corner of Africa, the Arab Republic of Egypt has an area of 1,001,450 sq km (386,662 sq mi), extending 1,572 km (997 mi) SE–NW and 1,196 km (743 mi) NE–SW. However, the cultivated and settled area (Nile Valley, Delta, and oases) constitutes only about 3.5% of Egypt's land area; the Libyan and Western deserts occupy about 75% of the total. Comparatively, the area occupied by Egypt is slightly more than three times the size of the state of New Mexico. Beyond the Suez Canal in the east, the Sinai Peninsula overlaps into Asia; the Sinai was occupied by Israeli forces from 1967 to 1982.

Egypt is bounded on the N by the Mediterranean Sea, on the E by Israel and the Red Sea, on the S by the Sudan, and on the W by Libya. The total boundary length was 5,139 km (3,193 mi) following the 1982 withdrawal by Israel. Egypt's capital city, Cairo, is located in the northeastern part of the country.

²TOPOGRAPHY

The altitude of Egypt ranges from 133 m (436 ft) below sea level in the Libyan Desert to 2,640 m (8,660 ft) above in the Sinai Peninsula. The Nile Delta is a broad, alluvial land, sloping to the sea for some 160 km (100 mi), with a 250-km (155-mi) maritime front between Alexandria (Al-Iskandariyah) and Port Sa'id. South of Cairo, most of the country (known as Upper Egypt) is a tableland rising to some 460 m (1,500 ft). The narrow valley of the Nile is enclosed by cliffs as high as 550 m (1,800 ft) as the river flows about 900 km (560 mi) from Aswan to Cairo. A series of cascades and rapids at Aswan, known as the First Cataract (the other cataracts are in the Sudan), forms a barrier to movement upstream.

The bulk of the country is covered by the Sahara, which north of Aswan is usually called the Libyan Desert. East of the Nile, the Arabian Desert extends to the Red Sea. The Western Desert consists of low-lying sand dunes and many depressions. Kharijah, Siwah, Farafirah, Bahariyah, and other large oases dot the landscape; another lowland, the Qattarah Depression, is an inhospitable region of highly saline lakes and soils covering about 23,000 sq km (8,900 sq mi). The outstanding topographic feature is the Nile River, on which human existence depends, for its annual floods provide the water necessary for agriculture. Before the completion of the Aswan High Dam in 1970, the floods, lasting generally from August to December, caused the river level to rise about 5 m (16 ft). Now, however, floodwaters can be stored, making it possible to provide year-round irrigation and to reclaim about 1 million feddans (about 1.04 million acres) of land. Damming the Nile resulted in the creation of Lake Nasser, a reservoir 292 km (181 mi) long and 9–18 km (6–11 mi) wide.

³CLIMATE

Most of Egypt is a dry subtropical area, but the southern part of Upper Egypt is tropical. Northern winds temper the climate along the Mediterranean, but the interior areas are very hot. The temperature sinks quickly after sunset because of the high radiation rate under cloudless skies. Annual rainfall averages 2.5 cm (1 in) south of Cairo and 20 cm (8 in) on the Mediterranean coast, but sudden storms sometimes cause devastating flash floods. Hot, dry sandstorms, known as khamsins, come off the Western Desert in the spring. In Cairo, average temperatures range from 7° to 29°C (45° to 84°F) in January, while July averages range from 22° to

36°C (72° to 97°F). Relative humidity varies from 68% in February to over 70% in August and 77% in December.

4FLORA AND FAUNA

Plants are those common in dry subtropical and tropical lands, such as papyrus. Egypt has no forests but does have date palm and citrus groves; eucalyptus and cypress have been introduced. Sheep, goats, and donkeys are found throughout the country, and camels are found in all the deserts. Egypt has some 300 types of birds. Wild animals are few, except for the hyena, jackal, lynx, mongoose, and wild boar, the last-named inhabiting the Nile Delta. The ibex may be found in the Sinai, and gazelles in the deserts. The Nile is adequately stocked with fish, but crocodiles have been reduced to a few along the shores of Lake Nasser. Reptiles include the horned viper and the hooded snake.

5ENVIRONMENT

Egypt's environmental problems stem from its aridity, extremely uneven population distribution, shortage of arable land, and pollution. Soil fertility has declined because of overcultivation. The expansion of Egypt's cities eliminates land normally used for agriculture. Heavy use of pesticides, inadequate sewage disposal, and uncontrolled industrial effluents have created a major water pollution problem. The expanded irrigation of desert areas after completion of the Aswan High Dam in 1970 has increased soil salinity and aided the spread of waterborne diseases. As of 1994, 28% of Egypt's soils have been damaged by increased salinity. Egypt's cities produce 3.0 million tons of solid waste per year. Eighty-percent of the population living in the cities has adequate sanitation facilities. Half of Cairo's raw sewage is carried to the sea in open sewers, and some 100 of 120 towns do not have sewer systems at all. Even the existing sewers are decrepit; in December 1982, the bursting of a sewer main flooded a large area of Cairo with untreated waste and temporarily curtailed tap water for about two million people. To improve sewage disposal, the government earmarked E£2.9 billion under the 1983–87 five-year plan for sewage projects, allocating E£2 billion to Cairo alone. The nation has 0.4 cubic miles of water with 88% used for farming purposes. Ninety-five percent of all city dwellers have pure water. Fourteen percent of the rural population does not. The National Committee for Environment, within the Office of the Prime Minister, is the principal agency with environmental responsibilities.

The tremendous encroachment of human population in the Nile Valley over the centuries has decimated Egypt's wildlife in that region. The hunting of any bird has been prohibited by law. In 1994, 9 of Egypt's 105 mammal species are endangered. Sixteen birds, 2 types of reptiles and 1 type of fresh-water fish are also endangered. Ninety-three of the nation's 2,085 plant species are threatened with extinction. Endangered species include the Sinai leopard, northern bald ibis, and green sea turtle. The cheetah, Mediterranean monk seal, African ass, African wild ass, and Tora hartebeest are extinct.

6POPULATION

The population of Egypt was estimated at 58,274,848 in 1994, an increase of 20.8% over the 1986 census figure of 48,259,238. A population of 64,810,000 was projected for the year 2000, assuming a crude birthrate of 28.4 per 1,000 population, a crude death rate of 8, and a net natural increase of 20.4 for the period 1995–2000. The average population density in 1994 was estimated at 58.2 per sq km (150.7 per sq mi), but in the cultivated areas (only 35,000 square kilometers) it was closer to 1,650 per sq km (4,270 per sq mi), one of the highest densities in the world. Some 99% of all Egyptians live in the Nile Valley; in 1995, an estimated 44.8% of the population was urban, and 55.2% was rural. In 1990, Cairo, the capital, had a population of 6,542,000 (its metropolitan population was estimated at 9.6 million in 1995); Alexandria had 3,170,000; Giza (Al-Jizah), 2,156,000; Shubra Al Khayma, 811,000; Port Said, 461,000; and Suez, 392,000.

7MIGRATION

In the early 1960s, most of the Greek population emigrated as the result of the government's nationalization measures; nearly all Jews, who formed less than 0.3% of the population in 1966, left the country after the 1967 war with Israel. With the completion of the Aswan High Dam in 1970, up to 100,000 Nubian tribesmen were moved from flooded parts of the upper Nile and resettled in the plain downstream. During the 1970s there was significant internal migration from rural to urban areas. During the 1970s and first half of the 1980s, more than 3 million workers took jobs in other countries. In 1992 some 2,850,000 Egyptians were living abroad, including about 1 million in Libya and 850,000 in Saudi Arabia.

8ETHNIC GROUPS

Egyptians, who make up about 97% of the population of Egypt, are a product of the intermixture of ancient Egyptians with the invaders of many millennia from various parts of Asia and Africa. Minorities are mainly other Arabs, Berbers, Nubians, Armenians, Greeks, Maltese, and Indians, with a few remaining British and French residents. About 350,000 Greeks and 160,000 Nubians were living in Egypt in 1990. Several tribes of Bedouins live in the deserts and the Sinai Peninsula. Their numbers were estimated at 500,000 to 1,000,000 in 1990.

9LANGUAGES

The language of most of the population is Arabic, a Semitic tongue; the 1971 constitution declares Arabic to be Egypt's official language. Dialects vary from region to region and even from town to town. English and French are spoken by most educated Egyptians and by shopkeepers and others. The ancient language of Pharaonic Egypt, a Hamitic tongue, survives vestigially in the liturgy of the Copts, a sizable Christian sect dating back to the 5th century AD. The Nubians of Upper Egypt speak at least seven dialects of their own unwritten language. There are a small number of Berber-speaking villagers in the western oases.

10RELIGIONS

The majority religion is Islam, of which the Sunnis are the largest sect. The 1971 constitution declares Islam to be the state religion. According to the 1986 census, 90% of the population was Muslim and 5.9% was Christian. The latter figure includes Coptic Christians, Roman Catholics, and Orthodox, and is disputed by the religious authorities of those groups as too small. The small Jewish minority has virtually disappeared.

Religious tensions in Cairo, Alexandria, and other cities led President Anwar al-Sadat (as-Sadat) to order the arrest in September 1981 of militant Muslims and Copts. Sadat also stripped the Coptic Pope Shenuda III of his temporal powers, replacing him with a committee of five bishops; in 1985, however, Shenuda was allowed to resume his duties. Sadat had also authorized direct state supervision of the nation's mosques, estimated at 40,000, and required Muslim preachers to register with government authorities. During 1986 and 1987 there were numerous violent incidents involving Islamic fundamentalists and Copts, including bombings, riots, and burning of Coptic churches.

In February 1993, American workers were arrested on suspicion of attempted Christian proselytizing, an activity forbidden under Egyptian law. They were later released.

11TRANSPORTATION

Egypt's transportation system is well developed, with 51,925 km (32,266 mi) of roads in 1991, of which 34% were paved. In

LOCATION: 21°35′ to 31°35′N; 25° to 36°E. **BOUNDARY LENGTHS:** Mediterranean coastline, 957 km (595 mi). Israel, 266 km (165 mi). Gulf of Aqaba and Red Sea coastlines, 1,368 km (850 mi). Sudan: official, 1,275 km (792 mi); administrative, 357 km (222 mi). Libya, 1,115 km (693 mi). **TERRITORIAL SEA LIMIT:** 12 mi.

1992, 1,119,727 passenger cars and 466,650 commercial vehicles were registered. In 1982, in an attempt to alleviate Cairo's notorious traffic congestion, work began on a city subway system. The first phase, 5 km (3 mi) long, was completed in 1987 at a cost of some $370 million; Cairo Metro, modeled after the Paris Metro, is the first subway to be built in Africa. Railroads are managed by the state-owned Egyptian Railways, founded in 1852. Track totaling some 5,110 km (3,175 mi) links all parts of the country. Steamer service on the Nile is an important means of domestic transport, as are 3,100 km (1,926 mi) of navigable canals. Alexandria, Port Sa'id, and Suez are the principal ports. Egypt's

oceangoing merchant fleet of 134 ships totaled 986,000 GRT in 1991.

Attempts to link the Mediterranean Sea with the Gulf of Suez and the Red Sea date back at least 4,000 years. The modern Suez Canal, about 160 km (100 mi) long, was constructed between 1859 and 1869 under the supervision of the French engineer Ferdinand de Lesseps. Great Britain became the canal's leading shareholder in 1875. Under the Constantinople Convention (1888), Britain became the guarantor of the canal's neutrality; management of the canal was entrusted to the privately owned Suez Canal Co. British rights over the canal were reaffirmed in the Anglo-Egyptian Treaty of 1936, then repudiated by Egypt in 1951. In 1956, at Egypt's insistence, the British withdrew from the area, and Egypt nationalized the canal and placed it under the management of the Suez Canal Authority, which had paid former stockholders $64 million by 1963. The canal was closed during the 1967 war with Israel and remained closed until 5 June 1975, when it resumed operations after having been cleared of mines and debris by teams of US, UK, and Egyptian engineers. During its first six months after resuming operations, the canal provided passage for a substantial number of dry-cargo ships but was used by only a comparatively small number of oil tankers, since the newer supertankers could not navigate the canal's 38-ft depth. The first phase of a project to widen and deepen the canal was completed in 1980, permitting ships of 53-ft draft (up to 150,000 tons) to pass through. The second phase includes increasing the navigable depth to 67 ft (up to 270,000 tons). Egypt also announced plans to build five tunnels under the canal and dig a second channel to permit the two-way passage of convoys; the first tunnel at the southern end of the canal was opened to traffic in 1980. In 1990/91, the Suez Canal Authority earned about $1.8 billion in revenue, more than in any other year.

Cairo International Airport is used by numerous international airlines, including Egypt's own Egyptian; in 1991 it serviced 5.6 million passengers. Local flights are available to outlying airports.

12HISTORY

Egypt has the oldest recorded history in Western civilization, dating back 5,000 years. In early times, the desert provided protection against marauders, while the Nile River provided bread. Therefore, by 3400 BC the civilization of Egypt was well developed. The country was united about 3100 BC by Menes (or Narmer), king of Upper Egypt, who conquered Lower Egypt and established the first of some 30 dynasties, ruled over by a divine king, or pharaoh. Menes created a centralized state; under his dynastic successors, trade flourished, and the hieroglyphic form of writing was perfected. During the so-called Old Kingdom, the pharaohs of the fourth dynasty (c.2613–2494 BC), of whom Cheops (Khufu) was the most notable, began to build the great pyramids as royal tombs. The twelfth dynasty of the Middle Kingdom (c.1991–1786 BC) built vast irrigation schemes and developed a thriving civilization at Thebes; under their rule, a system of cursive writing was developed. After a century of domination by Semitic peoples known as the Hyksos, who introduced the horse-drawn chariot, ancient Egypt attained its apex during the eighteenth dynasty (c.1570–1320 BC) of the New Kingdom, under pharaohs Thutmose III, who extended the empire into Asia as far as the Euphrates; Amenhotep III and his son, Amenhotep IV (Akhenaten, or Ikhnaton), who, with his queen, Nefertiti, attempted forcibly to replace Egyptian polytheism with monotheistic worship of the sun god Aten, or Aton; and the boy-king Tutankhamen.

In subsequent centuries, political instability weakened the kingdom, and Egypt was invaded by Assyria (673–663 BC), annexed by Persia (525 BC), and conquered by Alexander the Great (332 BC). Alexander established the Macedonian dynasty of the Ptolemies, which ruled Egypt from 323 to 30 BC. During this period, the city of Alexandria flourished as the intellectual center of the Hellenistic world. The best-known ruler of this dynasty was Queen Cleopatra VII (sometimes designated as VI), who was defeated, together with her lover Mark Antony, at the Battle of Actium in 31 BC by Caius Octavius, later the Roman emperor Augustus. After the official division of the Roman Empire following the death of Theodosius in AD 395, Egypt became part of the Eastern Roman (Byzantine) Empire.

Egypt played an integral role in the Muslim world after the Arab conquest by 'Amr ibn-al-'As in 639–42. Egypt's conquerors brought in settlers from Arabia and established firm control under the Abbasid caliphate (established in 749) and the Fatimids (909–1171), who founded Cairo as their capital in 969. The Fatimids were overthrown by Saladin (Salah ad-Din), founder of the Ayyubid dynasty, which gave way about 1250 to a local military caste, the Mamluks. The Mamluks continued to control the provinces after the conquest of Egypt by the Ottoman Turks in 1517.

Egypt remained a Turkish satrapy for four centuries. In 1805, an energetic Albanian soldier, Muhammad 'Ali, was appointed ruler (wali) of Egypt. He succeeded in establishing his own dynasty, which ruled the country, first under nominal Ottoman control and later as a British protectorate. Muhammad 'Ali destroyed Mamluk feudalism (already weakened by Napoleon's Egyptian campaign in 1798), stabilized the country, encouraged the planting of cotton, and opened the land to European penetration and development.

After the completion of numerous ambitious projects, including the Suez Canal (1869), Egypt became a world transportation hub and heavily burdened by debt. Ostensibly to protect its investments, England seized control of Egypt's government in 1882 and, at the time of the outbreak of World War I, made Egypt a protectorate. After the war, in 1922, the UK took account of the gathering momentum of Egyptian nationalism and recognized Egypt as a nominally sovereign country under King Fuad, but retained control over the conduct of foreign affairs, defense, security of communications, and the Anglo-Egyptian Sudan. Militant nationalism was represented by the Wafd Party, led by Sa'ad Zaghlul Pasha and, after his death, by Nahas Pasha. The conditions of association were revised in the 1936 Anglo-Egyptian Treaty, under which Britain maintained armed forces only in specified areas and especially along the Suez Canal. In that year, Faruk ascended the throne.

Egyptian nationalism gathered further momentum in World War II, during which Egypt was used as an Allied base of operations, and in 1951 the government in Cairo abrogated the 1936 treaty. Royal extravagance, government corruption, the unsuccessful Palestine campaign against Israel in 1948, and delays in long-expected social and political reforms motivated a successful coup on 23 July 1952 by a group called the Society of the Free Officers. Faruk was dethroned and replaced by his seven-month-old son. A republic was proclaimed on 18 June 1953, with Gen. Muhammad Naguib (Najib), the nominal leader of the officers, as its first president. He, in turn, was forced out of power in 1954 by a younger man, Lt. Col. Gamal Abdel Nasser (Jamal 'Abd al-Nasir), leader of the revolution.

To increase the productive capacity of his country, Nasser entered into preliminary agreements with the US, the UK, and the UN to finance in part a new high dam at Aswan. At the same time, he also negotiated economic aid and arms shipments from the Soviet Bloc when he was unable to obtain what Egypt needed from the West. Financial backing for the dam was subsequently withheld by the US, whereupon, on 26 July 1956, President Nasser proclaimed the nationalization of the Suez Canal and announced that profits derived from its operations would be used for the building of the dam. (The last British occupation troops had been evacuated from their Suez Canal bases a month earlier.) The dam was completed with aid and technical assistance from the USSR.

Simultaneously, a crisis erupted between Egypt and Israel. Incidents involving Egyptian and Palestinian guerrillas (fadayin) and Israeli border patrols multiplied. On 29 October 1956, as part of a three-nation plot to bring down Nasser and reassert control over the Canal, Israeli armed forces swept into Egypt's Sinai Peninsula. The UK and France then issued an ultimatum to the belligerents to cease fire. When Egypt rejected the ultimatum, Britain and France took military action in the Port Sa'id area, at the northern end of the canal, landing troops and bombing Egyptian cities from the air. However, the intervention of the US and the USSR, acting through the UN, led to the withdrawal of the British, French, and Israeli forces by March 1957.

On 1 February 1958, Egypt and Syria proclaimed their union in the United Arab Republic (UAR), under one head of state, one flag, a common legislature, and a unified army. The proclamation was approved by a plebiscite vote of 99.9% in Egypt and 99.98% in Syria. Nasser became president of the UAR, and a new cabinet was formed in March 1958, consisting of 2 Egyptian and 2 Syrian vice-presidents, as well as 22 Egyptian and 12 Syrian ministers. Differing economic and political conditions prevented a complete fusion of the two regions, however. Nasser's economic measures were generally accepted, but his program of socialism and nationalization of banks and other commercial establishments were resented and opposed by Syrian businessmen. Syrian opposition to the union was crystallized when Nasser eliminated the separate regional cabinets and set up a unified cabinet in August 1961. On 28 September, the Syrian army revolted, and two days later it proclaimed Syrian independence. Even after the failure of the merger with Syria, Egypt, consistent with its Arab unity ideology, persisted in its attempts to form a union with other Arab states. Cooperation agreements were signed with Iraq, Yemen, Syria again, and Libya during the 1960s and early 1970s. None of these agreements produced a lasting, meaningful political union.

One reason for these political maneuverings was the continuing tension with Israel, which again erupted into open warfare on 5 June 1967, after the UN Emergency Force had on 19 May been withdrawn from the Egyptian-Israeli border at Egypt's demand; on 23 May, Egypt closed the Gulf of Aqaba to Israeli shipping. Israel quickly crippled the Egyptian air force and occupied the Gaza Strip and the Sinai to the Suez Canal, which was blocked and remained so until June 1975. A cease-fire was established on 8 June 1967. On 22 November 1967, the Security Council passed a resolution calling on Israel to withdraw from occupied Arab territories and for the recognition by the Arab states of Israel's right to independent existence within peaceful and secured frontiers. But neither side would agree to peace terms, and Israel continued to occupy the Gaza Strip and the Sinai. During the years after 1967, a "War of Attrition" was fought along the Canal with each side shelling the other and Israeli planes bombing Egyptian cities.

When Nasser died on 28 September 1970, his vice-president, Anwar al-Sadat, became president. After a political crisis that resulted in the dismissal from office in May 1971 of 'Ali Sabri and other left-wing leaders who had been close to Nasser (they were subsequently convicted of treason), President Sadat firmly established his hold on the government and began to implement pragmatic economic and social policies. Beginning in July 1971 with the announcement of a 10-year development program, he quickly followed with the introduction in September of a permanent constitution and a series of financial measures designed to give more freedom to the banking system and to encourage investment of foreign and domestic capital. In a surprise move on 18 July 1972, Sadat ordered the expulsion of the 15,000 Soviet military advisers and 25,000 dependents who had come to Egypt after the 1967 war. After the ouster of the Russians, Egypt was able to improve relations with the US, Europe, and the more conservative Arab states, which provided substantial financial assistance under the Khartoum Agreement to replace Suez Canal revenues (which had ceased when the Canal was closed by the 1967 war with Israel).

Frustrated in his ambition to recover the Sinai, President Sadat broke the 1967 cease-fire agreement on 6 October 1973 by attacking Israeli forces in the Sinai Peninsula; this assault was coordinated with a Syrian attack on Israeli forces occupying the Syrian Golan Heights. After initial successes, the Egyptian strike forces were defeated by the rapidly mobilized Israeli troops, who then crossed the Canal south of Isma'iliyah, destroyed Egypt's

surface-to-air missile sites, and cut off the Egyptian 3d Army. A cease-fire that came into effect on 24 October left Egyptian troops in the Sinai and Israeli troops on the west bank of the Canal. A series of disengagement agreements negotiated by US Secretary of State Henry Kissinger left Egypt in full control of the Canal and established a UN-supervised buffer zone in the Sinai between the Egyptian and Israeli forces. In November 1975, the Sinai oil fields at Abu Rudeis and Ra's Sudr were returned to Egypt.

President Sadat took a bold step toward establishing peace with Israel by going to Jerusalem in November 1977 and by receiving Israeli Prime Minister Menachem Begin at Isma'iliyah the following month. In September 1978, he entered into negotiations with Begin, mediated by US President Carter, at Camp David, Md., where the two Middle East leaders agreed to a framework for a comprehensive settlement of the conflict. Following further negotiations, Sadat signed the Egyptian-Israeli Peace Treaty in Washington, D.C., on 26 March 1979. The treaty provided for the staged withdrawal of Israeli forces from the Sinai, which was completed on schedule by 25 April 1982; set limits on forces and armaments for both sides; established a UN force to supervise the terms of the treaty; and called for full normalization of relations. However, the two nations were unable to agree on the question of autonomy for the Palestinians of the West Bank of the Jordan and in Gaza, as provided for in the Camp David framework. For their roles as peacemakers, Sadat and Begin were jointly awarded the 1978 Nobel Peace Prize. But other Arab leaders denounced the accords and sought to isolate Egypt within the Arab world. Domestically, Sadat encouraged a shift from Nasser's socialism to greater free-market conditions and some political liberalization, one result of which was an upsurge of activity by religious extremists. In early September 1981, Sadat ordered the arrest of 1,536 Muslims, Christian Copts, leftists, and other persons accused of fomenting violent acts. One month later, on 6 October, Sadat was assassinated in Cairo by four Muslim fundamentalists. The vice-president, Muhammad Hosni (Husni) Mubarak, who had been Sadat's closest adviser, succeeded him as president and immediately pledged to continue Sadat's policies, particularly the terms of the peace treaty with Israel. Relations with Israel cooled during 1982, however, especially after Israeli troops moved into Lebanon. In 1986, renewed efforts at normalization of diplomatic relations with Israel led to the resolution in Egypt's favor of a dispute over Taba, a tiny sliver of land which had not been returned with the rest of the Sinai.

As a result of Arab fears of an Iranian victory over Iraq in the Persian Gulf war, Egypt, which has the largest army in the Arab world as well as an increasingly important arms industry, was welcomed back into the Arab fold following the Amman Arab summit conference in November 1987. Egypt quickly renewed diplomatic relations with a number of Arab states and in May 1989 ended its isolation by rejoining the Arab League, the headquarters of which returned to Cairo. Mubarak continued Sadat's policies of moderation and peacemaking abroad and gradual political liberalization and movement towards the free market at home. In July 1989, he became chairman of the Organization of Africa Unity for one year. In 1990, Egypt played a key role in the coalition to expel Iraq from Kuwait and in 1993 and 1994 was active in promoting the Israeli-Palestinian peace accord.

Mubarak was reelected president in 1987 and 1993. Parliamentary elections in 1987 were termed the fairest since 1952; 100 members of the opposition were elected to the 458-seat chamber. The most serious opposition to the Mubarak government, however, is from outside the political system. Religious parties are banned and, as a consequence, Islamic militants have resorted to violence against the regime, threatening Christian Copts and tourism, a major source of foreign exchange earnings. Security forces have cracked down hard, but the movement has gathered strength, fueled by discontent with poor economic conditions, political autocracy, corruption, secularism, and Egypt's ties with the US and Israel. By April 1994, an estimated 350 persons had been killed; courts had passed death sentences on 50 militants.

13GOVERNMENT

On 25 March 1964, President Nasser proclaimed an interim constitution; it remained in effect until a permanent constitution, drafted by the National Assembly, was approved by the electorate in a plebiscite on 11 September 1971. The 1971 constitution declares Egypt to be a democratic socialist state and an integral part of the Arab nation. The state of emergency, in effect since the Sadat assassination in 1981, and tough new anti-terrorism laws against Islamists have given the government sweeping powers of repression, reminiscent of the Nasser era.

The president of the republic is the head of state and supreme commander of the armed forces. He appoints and retires as many vice-presidents and cabinet members as he wishes; he also appoints the prime minister. In addition, he appoints and retires civil, military, and diplomatic personnel in accordance with the law. The president's power to declare war and conclude treaties with foreign countries is subject to the approval of the People's Assembly, a unicameral legislative body consisting in 1988 of 444 elected and 10 appointed members serving five-year terms. A 210-member advisory body, the Shura Council, was formed in 1980. The People's Assembly nominates the president, who must then be confirmed by plebiscite for a six-year term. The constitution was amended by popular referendum in 1980 to permit Sadat to serve more than two terms. Vice-President Mubarak, who became president upon Sadat's assassination, was confirmed in that office in national referendums in October 1981, 1987, and 1993. Suffrage is universal at age 21.

14POLITICAL PARTIES

Since the founding of the republic in 1953, the president and his army colleagues have dominated Egyptian politics. The Arab Socialist Union (ASU; founded by President Nasser as the Egyptian National Union in 1957) was the sole legal political party until 1976, when President Sadat allowed three minor parties to participate in parliamentary elections. In 1978, Sadat replaced the ASU with his own organization, the National Democratic Party (NDP), of which he became chairman. In elections held in June 1979, the NDP won 342 seats in the People's Assembly; the Socialist Labor Party (SLP), 29 seats; the Liberal Socialist Party, 3; and independents, 8. In 1980, however, Sadat denounced the SLP as the "agent of a foreign power," and 13 of the party's deputies defected either to join the NDP or to become independent members of the legislature, thus reducing the number of SLP seats to 16.

In January 1982, President Mubarak was elected without opposition as chairman of the NDP. In elections held in May 1984, the NDP won 390 seats in the National Assembly. The New Wafd (Delegation) Party, the middle class successor of the dominant party of the pre-Nasser period now allied with the Moslem Brotherhood, won 58. In the 1987 Assembly elections, the ruling NDP again won about 70% of the vote. Seventeen percent voted for an alliance of Socialist Labor, Liberal Socialist and, under their banner (religious parties are banned), the Moslem Brotherhood; 11% voted for the New Wafd. Elections in 1990 drew only some 25% of eligible voters when the opposition boycotted the poll, charging unfair and undemocratic procedures.

Egypt's relatively free press allows parties to criticize the government (but not the president personally) and lively campaigns are conducted. The government, however, controls access to radio and TV and few believe that any opposition can overturn NDP control.

15LOCAL GOVERNMENT

Egypt has traditionally been divided into two regions: Lower Egypt (Wagh al-Bahari), north of Cairo, and Upper Egypt (As-Sa'id), south of the capital. Under the local government system established in 1960, Egypt is organized into 26 governorates, each headed by an appointed governor. The governorates are responsible for social, health, welfare, and educational services and for the social and economic development of their region. They are also required to supervise the city and village councils, which are constituted in a similar manner. Real authority resides in Cairo in a highly centralized regime, heavily burdened by bureaucracy.

16JUDICIAL SYSTEM

Simple police offenses, misdemeanors, and civil cases involving small amounts are subject to the jurisdiction of single-judge summary tribunals. The trial courts of the central tribunals, consisting of three justices each, sit in cases exceeding the jurisdiction of summary courts and also consider appeals. Traffic in narcotics and press offenses, considered serious crimes, are tried by the courts of appeals of the central tribunals in the first instance, sitting as assize courts. There are courts of appeals at Cairo, Alexandria, Tanta, Al-Mansurah, and Asyut. The highest tribunal is the Court of Cassation. The religious (Shari'ah) courts dealing with matters of personal status—marriage, divorce, inheritance, charitable funds—were abolished on 1 January 1956.

The 1971 constitution declares that the judiciary is independent of other state powers and that judges are independent and not subject to enforced retirement. The Supreme Constitutional Court is responsible for enforcing adherence to laws and regulations and for interpreting legislation and the constitution. The Office of the Socialist Public Prosecutor is responsible to the People's Assembly for the security of the people's rights, the integrity of the political system, and other matters.

The president appoints all civilian judges, from nominations by the Supreme Judicial Council, a body designed to assure the independence of the judiciary and composed of senior judges, lawyers, law professors, and the President of the Court of Cassation. The judiciary has demonstrated a good degree of independence from the executive branch; for example, it handed down recent decisions invalidating bans on political parties.

There exists a tension between the civil law derived from French heritage and the competition from Muslim political activists to advance the role of Islamic law. Recently, Islamic activists succeeded in amending the constitution to state that the Shari'a (Islamic law) is in principle the sole source of legislation.

The State of Emergency in place since the assassination of President Anwar Sadat has led to detention without due process for many persons. Emergency security courts try suspected terrorists whose only recourse upon conviction is an appeal for clemency to the president or prime minister.

17ARMED FORCES

Military service is compulsory for all males over 18. In 1993, the armed forces consisted of 410,000 men. The army had 290,000 men, organized into 12 combined arms divisions and 39 special brigades; the army reserves totaled about 500,000 men. The air force had 30,000 men and 492 combat aircraft and 74 armed helicopters, plus 70,000 personnel in the air defense command. The navy had 20,000 men, 4 submarines, 1 destroyer, 4 frigates, and about 39 other armed vessels for coast defense. Paramilitary forces numbered 400,000, including a national guard of 60,000, a central security force of 300,000, 2,000 coast guards, and 12,000 frontier forces.

The USSR was Egypt's principal arms supplier until 1972, when President Sadat expelled all Soviet military advisers, but Egypt retains its Russian weapons, supplemented by American and European arms. Since 1973, Egypt has obtained military assistance from the US, France, and other Western nations as well as from China. During the 1980s, Egypt imported around $14 billion in arms. Total US military assistance to Egypt during 1988–92 was $2.8 billion. Egypt spends about $1.7 billion a year on defense or 5% of gross domestic product.

18INTERNATIONAL COOPERATION

Egypt joined the UN as a charter member on 24 October 1945 and participates in ECA, ESCWA, and all the nonregional specialized agencies. Egypt became the first Arab state to normalize relations with Israel following the conclusion of the 1979 peace treaty. As a result of this act, however, Egypt's membership in the League of Arab States was suspended; Egypt did not rejoin the League until 1989. The country is a signatory to GATT and the Law of the Sea. It belongs to the African Development Bank, G-77, and OAU, and is a permanent observer at the OAS. Egypt's relations with the US have improved since 1973; relations with the former USSR continued to deteriorate until 1984, when diplomatic relations were restored, with an economic cooperation agreement announced between the two countries in 1986.

Between 1958 and 1973, Egypt made several attempts to establish united or federated states with its Arab neighbors. Egypt and Syria formed the United Arab Republic from February 1958 to September 1961, when Syria broke away; the United Arab States, consisting of Egypt, Syria, and Yemen, survived formally from March 1958 through December 1961, although never a political reality; and a federation between Egypt, Syria, and Iraq, officially established in April 1963, was never implemented. On 1 January 1972, Egypt, Syria, and Libya established the Federation of Arab Republics, but to little practical effect. A formal merger attempt between Egypt and Libya, nominally consummated on 1 September 1973, dissolved in practice when relations between the two countries soured. An Egyptian-Sudanese Charter of Integration was signed in October 1982 but never implemented.

19ECONOMY

Historically, the Egyptian economy was predominantly agricultural, with cotton as the mainstay. Land prices are extremely high because of the shortage of arable land, and output of food is not sufficient to meet the needs of a rapidly growing population. In 1986, more than 50% of the country's food was imported. Although Egypt has expanded its private sector in recent years, industry remains centrally controlled and for the most part government owned; since the 1950s, the government has developed the petroleum, services, and construction sectors, largely at the expense of agriculture. Egypt's significant economic growth rate of 8–10% annually from 1975 to 1981, made possible in large measure by the receipt of foreign aid and credits, had declined by 1985 to 5.4%; 1986 growth was estimated at 4.9%. Revenues for 1985/86 from petroleum exports, Suez Canal traffic, tourism, and remittances from Egyptians working abroad were eroded in the wake of sharp declines in international oil prices and developments in the Iran-Iraq war. In 1992–93 tourism plunged an estimated 20% because of sporadic attacks by Islamic extremists on tourist groups. The inflation rate grew from less than 5% annually in the 1960s to nearly 23% by 1986, reflecting worldwide price increases and the government's deficit spending. Recently published IMF figures for the period 1986/87–1991/92 show that real GDP growth averaged 4.7%.

In early 1993, Egypt embarked on a comprehensive economic reform and structural adjustment program, under the aegis of the IMF and the World Bank. Law 203 of 1991 established the legal basis for reform and privatization of the large public sector. Under an IMF stand-by program, Egypt implemented a range of monetary reforms in early 1991.

Gulf states rewarded Egypt with an infusion of $2 billion in cash and elimination of $7 billion debt for its role in forming the Arab anti-Iraq coalition. The US forgave another $7.1 billion in high-interest pre-1985 debt; these actions reduced Egypt's total external debt to about $40 billion in 1990. In 1991, total debt service amounted to $2.4 billion, down from $3.4 in 1990. The ratio of debt service to exports of goods and services has declined from more than 45% in the latter half of the 1980s to about 18% in fiscal 1992.

20INCOME

In 1992, Egypt's GNP was $34,514 million at current prices, or $630 per capita. For the period 1985–92 the average inflation rate was 17.1%, resulting in a real growth rate in per capita GNP of 0.8%.

In 1992 the GDP was $35,559 million in current US dollars. It is estimated that in 1989 agriculture, hunting, forestry, and fishing contributed 18% to GDP; mining and quarrying, 4%; manufacturing, 17%; electricity, gas, and water, 1%; construction, 5%; wholesale and retail trade, 9%; services, 17%; and other sources, 29%.

21LABOR

Egypt's civilian labor force (15–64 years) increased from 14.8 million in 1990 to 15.3 million in 1991, when 33.1% of the work force was employed in agriculture, 46% in services, and 20.9% in industry. Labor has tended to move from services to more productive occupations, except in the case of government employment, where the government's guarantee of jobs for all university graduates has led to serious underemployment. In the mid-1980s, the waiting period was lengthened for graduates seeking public sector employment, so that new government employees in 1992 were chosen from the class of 1984. Rapid growth in population and the creation of such guaranteed jobs have resulted in declining rates of labor productivity. Unemployment was estimated at 12% in 1992. In 1992, most of Egypt's state-owned companies were transferred to 27 new holding companies, which had the authority to buy, sell, merge, or liquidate any subsidiaries.

Egyptian workers obtained the legal right to organize into trade unions in 1942. A law of 1952 authorized the formation of trade union federations and permitted the formation of a national confederation to which unions having 1,000 or more members may belong. The most important trade union is the Egyptian Trade Union Federation, which opposes the privatization of profitable state-owned companies, an important part of reforms initiated in 1991 to stabilize the economy.

Conciliation and arbitration procedures for the settlement of labor disputes are compulsory, and strikes are prohibited while these procedures are in effect. The government and some labor contractors operate employment agencies. Semiskilled technical workers are in short supply, but there is an overabundance of unskilled industrial labor and of white-collar workers.

As of 1992, about 1 million Egyptians worked in Libya, 850,000 in Saudi Arabia, 150,000 in Iraq, 120,000 in Kuwait, and 112,000 in Jordan. Expatriate Egyptians remitted over $5.2 billion in 1991/92.

22AGRICULTURE

During the 1970s, despite substantial investment in land reclamation, agriculture lost its position as the dominant economic sector. Agricultural exports, which accounted for 87% of all merchandise export value in 1960, fell to 35% in 1974 and to 13% by 1992.

Cotton has been the staple crop, but its importance as an export is declining. Although production in 1992 (324,000 tons) was up 7% from 1991 (302,000 tons), receipts from exported cotton only accounted for 1% of total exports in 1992, down from 7% in 1990 and 11% in 1985. Egypt is also a substantial producer of wheat, corn, sugarcane, fruit and vegetables, fodder, and rice; substantial quantities of wheat are also imported despite increases in yield since 1970, and significant quantities of rice are exported. Agricultural output in tons in 1992 included corn, 5,226,000; wheat, 4,618,000; rice, 3,908,000; potatoes, 1,800,000; and oranges, 1,690,000. The government exercises a substantial degree of control over agriculture, not only to ensure the best use of irrigation water but also to limit the planting of cotton in favor of food grains. However, the government's ability to achieve this objective is limited by crop rotational constraints.

Egypt's arable area totals about 2.6 million hectares (6.5 million acres), about one-quarter of which is land reclaimed from the desert. However, the reclaimed lands only add 7% to the total value of agricultural production. Even though only 3% of the land is arable, it is extremely productive and can be cropped two or even three times per year. Most land is cropped at least twice a year, but agricultural productivity is limited by salinity, which afflicts an estimated 35% of cultivated land, and drainage problems.

Irrigation plays a major role in a country the very livelihood of which depends upon a single river. Most ambitious of all the irrigation projects is that of the Aswan High Dam, completed in 1971. A report published in March 1975 by the National Council for Production and Economic Affairs indicated that the dam had proved successful in controlling floodwaters and ensuring continuous water supplies, but that water consumption had been excessive and would have to be controlled. Some valuable land was lost below the dam because the flow of Nile silt was stopped, and increased salinity remains a problem. Further, five years of drought in the Ethiopian highlands—the source of the Nile River's water—caused the water level of Lake Nasser, the Aswan High Dam's reservoir, to drop to the lowest level ever in 1987. Another spectacular project designed to meet the water scarcity problem is the New Valley (the "second Nile"), aimed at development of the large artesian water supplies underlying the oases of the Western Desert. Total investment in agriculture and land reclamation for the government's Third Plan (1993–1997) was estimated at e£9,599 million.

The agrarian reform law of 1952 provided that no one might hold more than 190 feddans for farming and that each landholder must either farm the land himself or rent it under specified conditions. Up to 95 additional feddans might be held if the owner had children, and additional land had to be sold to the government. In 1961, the upper limit of landholding was reduced to 100 feddans, and no person was allowed to lease more than 50 feddans. Compensation to the former owners was in bonds bearing a low rate of interest, redeemable within 40 years. A law enacted in 1969 reduced landholdings by one person to 50 feddans. By the mid-1980s, 90% of all land titles were for holdings of less than 5 feddans, and about 300,000 families, or 8% of the rural population, had received land under the agrarian reform program. According to a 1990 agricultural census, there were some 3 million small land holdings, almost 96% of which were under 5 feddans (2.1 hectares/5.2 acres). Since the late 1980s, manmy reforms attempting to deregulate agriculture by liberalizing input and output prices and by eliminating crop area controls have been initiated. As a result, the gap between world and domestic prices for Egyptian agricultural commodities has been closed.

23 ANIMAL HUSBANDRY

Because of the very intensive cultivation of the soil, little land is available for animal husbandry, but efforts were made in the 1980s to increase the output of fodder per land unit and the productivity of livestock raising. In 1992, the estimated livestock population included 36,000,000 chickens, 4,800,000 goats, 4,350,000 sheep, 3,036,000 head of buffalo, 3,016,000 head of cattle, and 115,000 hogs. Livestock products in that year included 2,021,000 tons of cow and buffalo milk, 726,000 tons of meat, and 127,440 tons of eggs.

24 FISHING

Fishing is concentrated in the Nile Delta and River and in the Mediterranean and Red seas. The catch of sea, lake, and river fish amounted to 298,913 tons in 1992. Mullet and eels are caught in the Delta and sardines in the Mediterranean. There is a small-scale freezing and canning industry. Nevertheless, Egypt has been a net importer of fish. In the early 1980s, new fish-farming facilities were established at Maryut in the Delta.

25 FORESTRY

There are no forests in Egypt. The construction and furniture-making industries rely on wood imports. Softwood products come from Scandinavia and Russia; hardwood products from Western Europe.

26 MINING

Egypt's mineral resources include phosphates (around the Red Sea, along the Nile, and in the Western Desert), coal (in the Sinai), salt, iron oxides, gold, ocher, sulfate of magnesia, talc, building stone, and nitrate of soda. Extraction of limestone, clay, and gypsum during World War II rose in response to the Allied armies' urgent demand. Even though the mineral resources of Egypt have been exploited since antiquity, some regions of the country remain geologically unexplored.

An estimated 900,000 tons of salt and 1,100,000 tons of natural phosphate were produced in 1991. Iron ore deposits have been developed at Aswan to supply the steel plant at Helwan; production was about 2,400,000 tons in 1991. However, higher-quality deposits are also being exploited in the Western Desert. Gold and copper deposits exist, but are not of sufficient grade to justify profitable extraction.

27 ENERGY AND POWER

The brightest spot in Egypt's economic picture in the early 1980s was the development of the petroleum industry. With the return of the Sinai oil fields to Egypt, recoverable crude oil reserves were estimated at 6.2 billion barrels as of 1 January 1993. The industry's share of GDP rose from less than 5% in 1974 to nearly 20% in 1981, but declined to 15% in 1983/84 with the slump in world oil prices; however, in 1992, petroleum accounted for more than 25% of total export revenues. Oil production in 1992 averaged 925,000 barrels per day, up 38% from 1992. Recoverable reserves of natural gas were estimated at 15.4 trillion cu ft (436 billion cu m) in January 1993. Natural gas production totaled 350 billion cu ft (9.9 billion cu m).

Commercial quantities of oil were first found in 1908, and more petroleum was found in the late 1930s along the Gulf of Suez. Later, large oil fields were discovered in the Sinai Peninsula, the Gulf of Suez, and the Western Desert. The Abu Rudeis and Ra's Sudr oil fields in the Sinai, captured by Israel in 1967, were returned to Egyptian control in November 1975, and the remaining Sinai oil fields reverted to Egyptian control by the end of April 1982. Belayim, El Morgan, and Octoben (all in the Gulf of Suez area) are the major oil fields.

The General Petroleum Authority, established in 1956 to supervise the oil industry, was converted as part of the nationalization program of the 1960s into the Egyptian General Petroleum Corporation (EGPC). Most Egyptian production is handled by the Gulf of Suez Petroleum Company, a production-sharing arrangement between Amoco and EGPC, and by the International Egyptian Oil Company, the local branch of Italy's Agip. Royal Dutch/Shell and British Gas also operate in Egypt.

The Egyptian electric power system is almost entirely integrated, with thermal stations in Cairo and Alexandria and generators at Aswan. In 1992, output totaled 9.7 billion kwh. Hydroelectric power provides Egypt with 25% of its electricity production. A limited amount of additional capacity was obtained from generators in the barrages constructed downstream of the Aswan High Dam to reduce erosion; these supply electricity to rural communities.

Egypt's energy needs are estimated to triple by the end of the century; Egypt was the second largest consumer of energy on the African continent in 1992, after South Africa. To begin an ambitious program of nuclear power development, Egypt signed nuclear cooperation agreements with the US, UK, France, and the Federal Republic of Germany (FRG) in 1981. As of September 1992, a $60 million contract was awarded to Argentina to build a 22-Mw research reactor to replace an antiquated 2-Mw plant outside of Cairo.

28INDUSTRY

Egypt at the time of the 1952 revolution was much further advanced industrially than any other Arab country or indeed any country in Africa except South Africa. The value of industrial output (at constant 1975 prices) increased from E£825 million in 1974 to E£1,307 million in 1980/81. In 1986/87 industry and mining amounted to E£8,137 million or 16.7% of GDP. By 1991/92 the industrial sector accounted for about 18% of GDP.

Achievements in industrial development have gone far beyond what most observers considered possible. Cement, glass, iron and steel products, fertilizers, paper, petroleum refining, electric power, spinning, and sugar were among the industries that increased production. Newer industries include a wide variety of consumer durables and light producer goods such as tires, refrigerators, air conditioners, sewing machines, bicycles, electric meters, batteries, wire, and cable. Assembly-line operations for trucks, buses, radios, and television receivers were introduced. The Helwan iron and steel plant, 29 km (18 mi) south of Cairo, using imported coke, processes iron ore mined near Aswan into sheets, bars, billets, plates, and blooms. Industrial products in 1991/92 included 5,524,000 tons of nitrogenous fertilizers, 1,345,000 tons of phosphoric fertilizers, 395,000 refrigerators, 324,000 tons of cotton yarn, 17,300 tons of cement, 10,500 trucks, 7,700 buses, and 7,700 automobiles. Egypt and the Republic of South Africa are the largest producers of petroleum refinery products in Africa. Egypt is currently undertaking a large expansion program aimed at raising capacity to 775,000 barrels per day by the end of the decade.

The organization of government for the development of industry has gone through several stages since 1952, including the establishment of the Ministry of Industry as a separate entity in 1956, with licensing and other control powers. In 1957, the Economic Development Organization was formed to implement priority projects not taken up by private investors. In 1964, contracting companies in the public sector were fully nationalized: 119 firms and companies were merged into 3 joint-stock companies. A reorganization of public-sector enterprises was undertaken in 1967, and new industrial projects were begun in 1969 with assistancefrom the then-Soviet Union. Following the 1973 war, the government greatly increased its allocations to stimulate local private investment and attract foreign capital. The major characteristic of the investment plans was the heavy emphasis given to metallurgical industries. Increased investment in public-sector industries resulted in rapid rates of growth from 1973 to 1978. As of the mid-1980s, 35% of industrial production originated in the private sector, and this share was growing.

Egypt's industrial sector is currently undergoing major reforms. A $300-million World Bank adjustment agreement in place since July 1991 emphasizes a greater role for the private sector in addition to privatization and restructuring of state owned enterprises. Thus, in 1994, the private sector's share of industrial output has

risen to 50%. Private sector investment in industry amounted to E£1.6 billion in 1989/90 compared with E£1.3 billion in 1988/89 and E£900 million in 1987/88. The decision in 1991 to break the public sector's monopoly on the production of passenger cars has led to renewed growth in this sector with Suzuki General Motors, and Peugeot starting local manufacturing.

The arms industry is currently one of Egypt's most productive sectors. From 1983–88 arms exports averaged $300 million—$500 million a year.

29SCIENCE AND TECHNOLOGY

While Egypt's basic industries are of the traditional "smokestack" type, the government has begun to introduce high-technology enterprises. In 1977, the private sector was permitted to enter into production of computers and data-processing equipment, and several US and other foreign companies in this field established branches in Egypt. In 1983, Egypt imported about E£104 million worth of business machines and computer equipment, of which 10% was supplied by the US.

The Academy of Scientific Research and Technology, in Cairo, is the national body responsible for science and technology. The National Research Center, also in Cairo, carries out research in pure and applied sciences. The Ministry of Agriculture has 20 research centers in Cairo and Giza. The 1982/83–1986/87 five-year plan placed emphasis on the training of additional skilled personnel. In 1982, research and development expenditures totaled E£40 million pounds; 7,532 technicians and 20,893 scientists and engineers were engaged in research and development.

30DOMESTIC TRADE

Cairo and Alexandria are the most important commercial centers. Virtually all importers, exporters, and wholesalers have offices in one or both of these cities. The export-import business was entirely nationalized in 1961 and 1962. The principal retail centers have general and specialized stores as well as large bazaars. Smaller bazaars and open markets are found in the towns and villages. In recent years, the government has fostered the development of retail cooperative stores.

Usual business hours are from 9 AM to 2 PM and from 5 to 8 PM; Friday is the weekly day of rest. While the official language is Arabic, commercial firms frequently employ English or French for business correspondence.

31FOREIGN TRADE

Petroleum replaced cotton and cotton products as Egypt's principal export in 1976. Together they accounted for 81% of merchandise export value in 1983/84. Leading imports are wheat, chemical and pharmaceutical products, raw materials for industry, machinery, and motor vehicles. Egypt suffers from chronic trade deficits, which have steadily increased from E£8,311.8 million in 1987 to E£17,482.2 million in 1992.

Exports in 1991/92 (in millions of E£) were as follows:

Agricultural goods	245.9
Industrial goods	3,054.1
TOTAL INCLUDING OTHERS	3,636.4

The principal imports in 1991/92 (in millions of E£) were as follows:

Livestock, food, and drink	1,912.3
Transportation equipment and machines	2,355.8
Fats, oils, fuels, and minerals	955.6
Wood, cork, paper, and textiles	967.3
Chemicals, rubber, and leather	1,114.7
TOTAL INCLUDING OTHERS	10,039.5

Egypt's shift in political alliances has affected its trade patterns. Before 1973, when Egypt was linked to the then-Soviet Union, 55% of its exports went to COMECON countries, which supplied 30% of its imports. Today, the OECD countries supply more than 50% of Egypt's imports,with the US providing some 25% of all imports. Trade with Libya and Saudi Arabia has increased in recent years.

Imports and exports to Egypt's main trading partners include (% of total):

	1990	1991	1992
EXPORTS TO:			
Italy	12.3	14.8	20.6
US	14.2	16.1	25.4
Germany	10.6	10.4	10.1
Spain	1.4	4.8	6.9
Italy	6.5	6.8	8.7
France	4.0	5.9	6.2
Singapore	4.6	6.8	5.3
Greece	1.5	3.8	5.2
USSR (former)	15.8	6.3	4.9
Germany (combined)	4.8	3.7	4.7
IMPORTS FROM:			
US	8.6	7.6	8.2
France	9.4	6.9	7.0
Japan	3.7	4.1	4.8
UK	4.0	4.5	3.6
Netherlands	3.1	3.4	2.4
Australia	4.2	3.4	1.8

32BALANCE OF PAYMENTS

Egypt's chronic trade deficit is at least partially offset by remittances from Egyptians working overseas, Suez Canal tolls, and earnings from tourism. Bilateral and multilateral aid has also helped to keep balance-of-payments deficits within manageable limits. In 1992 merchandise exports totaled $3,400 million and imports $8,901 million. The merchandise trade balance was $-5,501 million.

The following table summarizes Egypt's balance of payments for 1991 and 1992 (in millions of US dollars):

	1991	1992
CURRENT ACCOUNT		
Goods, services, and income	−3,531	−4,264
Unrequited transfers	6,908	7,534
TOTALS	3,377	3,270
CAPITAL ACCOUNT		
Direct investment	191	455
Portfolio investment	21	6
Other long-term capital	−1,987	−1,546
Other short-term capital	−2,567	917
Exceptional financing	4,485	2,889
Reserves	−2,776	−6,249
TOTALS	−4,107	−3,986
Errors and omissions	730	716
Total change in reserves	2,639	−5,409

33BANKING AND SECURITIES

The National Bank of Egypt, founded in 1898, had as a private institution the exclusive right to issue currency and act as the government's banker. In January 1961, although permitted to retain its commercial banking business, it was divested of its central banking function, which was given to the newly established Central Bank of Egypt. Central Bank reserves declined from $1,528 in 1983 to $1,370 in 1985. As of 1993 central bank reserves were E£42,554 million The money supply rose from E£1,261 million

in 1974 to E£4,554 million in 1984. In 1992, the money supply, as measured by M2, was E£92,333 million.

In addition to the Central Bank, there were, until 1962, 25 other Arab and foreign banks and branches. In 1957, when foreign banks refused to finance Egypt's cotton crop after the Suez Canal was nationalized, the government took over British and French banks and insurance companies; those of other countries were taken over by January 1962. By the end of 1962, all banks, domestic and foreign, had been nationalized. The number of registered banks dwindled to only four by 1971.

In 1975, the public sector was allowed to transact freely with all banks, which became largely free to exercise all banking functions. The government's "open door" policy toward banking permitted international banks of good standing to establish branches in Egypt and exempted those banks from regulations governing the control of foreign exchange. There were over 200 financial institutions in Egypt in 1993, of which 35 were commercial banks.

Egypt subscribed 50.29% of the stock of the Arab Institution for Economic Development, established in January 1959 for the purpose of assisting member states to carry out development projects for which private funds were unavailable. The Arab Development Bank, under which name it became known, had an initial capitalization of E£20 million. It was modeled on the IBRD, whose staff collaborated in drawing up its charter. In 1971, the Arab International Bank was established to finance investments with foreign currencies and to promote Egypt's foreign trade.

Egyptians habitually have invested their funds in real estate, in foreign countries, or in gold. Although the Cairo and Alexandria stock exchanges were permitted to reopen in September 1961 after the massive nationalization decrees of July of that year, the volume of transactions was limited largely to government securities. In the 1970s, the exchanges resumed full operations, but volume is small.

34INSURANCE

Until the 1950s, insurance companies operating in Egypt were mostly branches of foreign institutions. In July 1961, Egypt promulgated laws nationalizing all insurance companies. In 1987, insurance premiums totaled US$660 million, US$2.3 per capita in life and US$10.7 per capita in non-life insurance. Total premiums amounted to 1.05% of the GDP. Life insurance in force in 1992 totaled E£14.4 billion.

35PUBLIC FINANCE

The government's current budget covers revenues and expenses of government agencies rendering services free of charge. The capital budget includes investments by state and local governments and by servicing authorities, plus capital investment transfers. From the mid-1970s through the 1980s, the budget deficit annually averaged about 20% of GDP. As a result of increased deficit spending, government expenditures rose to a peak of 63% of GDP in 1982. In 1990, a reform program was implemented, which has decreased the overall fiscal deficit from 20% of GDP in the 1980s to 6.4% of GDP in 1992. In 1991/92, revenues amounted to $12.6 billion, while expenditures came to $15.2 billion, including capital expenditures of $4 billion.

The following table shows actual revenues and expenditures for 1988 and 1989 in millions of pounds.

	1988	1989
REVENUE AND GRANTS		
Tax revenue	11,485	13,692
Non-tax revenue	7,426	7,633
Capital revenue	1,005	1,276
Grants	548	1,023
TOTAL	20,464	23,624

EXPENDITURES & LENDING MINUS REPAYMENTS	1988	1989
General public service	595	699
Defense	3,208	3,027
Public order and safety	827	986
Education	2,640	3,201
Health	549	664
Social security and welfare	2,918	2,869
Housing and community amenities	1,322	1,377
Recreation, cultural, and religious affairs	1,562	1,913
Economic affairs and services	2,010	1,951
Other expenditures	6,916	7,226
Lending minus repayments	2,632	3,837
TOTAL	25,180	27,750
Deficit/Surplus	–4,716	–4,126

In 1992 Egypt's total debt stood at US$38.2 billion.

36TAXATION

In the past, taxes were regressive, tax administration ineffective, and tax evasion frequent. Low taxes on the wealthy allowed extravagant consumption and hoarding of gold and foreign exchange. Since the revolution of 1952, the tax system has been made less regressive. As of 1993, the basic salary tax was E£447 on the first E£3,840 of taxable income and 22% on the excess. In addition, a general income tax was levied with a top marginal rate of 65%. Corporate profits are taxable at a rate of 40%. Double taxation agreements are in effect with numerous countries, including the US. Taxes on land and buildings are also levied, as well as stamp duties and fees.

37CUSTOMS AND DUTIES

Customs duties in Egypt serve not merely for protection but also for revenue. Imports are mostly unrestricted, although as of August 1992, 78 items were banned because of competition with domestic goods. Duties vary from 5–160% for most goods.

Free zones have been established in Alexandria, Cairo, Port Sa'id, Ismailia, and Suez; these are exempt from customs duties, but a tax of 1% is levied on the value of all goods entering or leaving free zones.

38FOREIGN INVESTMENT

Egypt has declared that foreign private capital is both desired and welcome and that foreign capital investment has a place in the country's economic development. Investors in approved specific enterprises are assured of facilities for transfer of profits, withdrawal of capital, and employment of necessary foreign personnel.

Under Law No. 65, enacted in September 1971, the government placed special emphasis on attracting Arab capital. In 1974, however, Egypt sought specifically to encourage capital investments from multinational corporations in the West; Law No. 65 was thus superseded by Law No. 43, enacted in June 1974. The latter specifies that new projects financed with foreign capital will not be nationalized or confiscated, that invested capital may be reexported within five years of its investment in Egypt, and that (within certain limitations) investment profits earned within Egypt may be transferred abroad.

Depending on their size, location, and other characteristics, new projects financed with foreign capital are exempt from taxation for five to eight years; in addition, payments of interest on foreign loans are not taxable, and investors are exempt from certain customs duties. There are two basic conditions for the approval of projects: (1) the project must be on an approved list in the fields of industrialization, mining, energy, tourism, transportation, reclamation and cultivation of barren land, or animal husbandry; and (2) projects must be established jointly with Egyptian public or private capital, although no strict percentage requirements are imposed, and in certain cases (for example, a branch of a foreign bank dealing exclusively with foreign currency) this requirement may be waived. Applications must be made to the General Authority for Arab Investment and the Free Zones, which consists of the minister of state for Arab and foreign economic cooperation and seven other members. In general, investments must be in the free zones of Alexandria, Cairo, Port Sa'id, and Suez. Law No. 159, passed in 1982, gives Egyptian investors most of the privileges enjoyed by foreign investors.

Since 1991, Egypt has liberalized its foreign trade by reducing the number of items on its list of banned imports. In 1990, the list covered 37% of all imports; in 1992, 11%; and in 1993, about 5%. The use of other non-tariff barriers on imports and export restrictions has also been reduced. (Between 1955 and 1973 the former USSR provided some $4.22 billion in loans.)

Credits came mostly from the former USSR and CMEA in the 1960s, but in the early 1970s Egypt declared an "open door" policy for Western investments. US investment and aid had increased to more than $2 billion annually by 1984/85. For its role in forming the Arab anti-Iraq coalition, the Gulf states rewarded Egypt with $2 billion in cash injections and a $7 billion debt write-off, while the US forgave $7.1 billion in high-interest pre-1985 military debt and agreed to reschedule Egypt's remaining debt of $5.1 billion on generous terms. Egypt also received significant grants from the EC and other Western nations. Thus gross official development assistance reached $10 billion in 1991 compared with $1.8 billion in 1989, making Egypt the world's largest recipient of foreign assistance.

39ECONOMIC DEVELOPMENT

At the time of the 1952 revolution, Egypt presented the familiar picture of a dual economy, having a small modern sector developed within a tradition-bound society. A rapidly expanding population was pressing hard on limited agricultural resources; there were severe problems of poverty, unemployment, unequal distribution of income and wealth, disease, political corruption, and illiteracy. Rapid industrialization was viewed as essential to economic improvement. The revolution was both a national revolution, Egyptianizing the economy by ridding it of foreign influence, and a social revolution, developing a "democratic, cooperative, socialist" society. The promised "socialism" was not at that time doctrinaire; it was pragmatically selective in its application.

First among the economic measures were the agrarian reform laws of 1952, equalizing holdings but retaining private ownership of land. A major objective was the diversion of private investment from land into industry. In this earlier period, industrialization also was fostered through government creation and expansion of industrial firms, and plans for the Aswan High Dam were developed.

In July 1961, in a major policy shift, socialist decrees brought virtually all economic activity under government ownership or control. The Charter for National Action, which elaborated the philosophy of Arab socialism, was approved by the National Congress of Popular Forces on 1 July 1962. It is clear that the Egyptian government had decided that industrialization and improvement of living standards could come only through central planning and direct government ownership and control of virtually the entire system of production and foreign trade. Private enterprise was allowed a minor role within the overall development plan. A few industrialists were allowed to take over the management of their enterprises.

Egypt inaugurated its first five-year development program in 1960, with a total investment of E£1,697 million. By the end of 1965, national income had increased in the five-year period by

39.6%; 171,000 new jobs had been created; and wages and salaries had increased by 54%. A second five-year development plan (1966–70) was canceled in 1967 because of the Arab-Israeli war, and annual plans were instituted. Shortly after the 1973 war, President Sadat introduced an "open door" economic development program that confirmed Egypt's socialist policy but decentralized decision making in the public sector, removed government constraints on the private sector, and attracted foreign private capital by liberalizing financial and trade regulations. As a result, most public-sector industries developed rapidly during the 1973–79 period. A five-year development plan (1980–84) was replaced in 1982 by the new plan for 1982–87, which projected total investments estimated at E£34,100 million; the public sector was allocated 76.5% of the total. Of fixed investments in development projects, the industrial and mining sector was to receive 26%, transport and communications 16%, agriculture 12%, housing 11%, and electric power 8%. Development expenditures for 1986/87 totaled E£5,320 million, with the expectation of a GDP of E£31,305 million, compared with E£20,727 million in 1981/82. By 1987/88–1991/92 investment allocation for the public sector dropped to 62% and to 42% in the current plan (1992/93–1996/97). The current plan aims at the privatization of several sectors by encouraging the private sector to invest more capital. GDP is expected to grow by 4% in real terms in 1992/93 to E£131 billion and by 5.1% in 1993/94 to E£161 billion. Total investment is planned to reach E£154 billion, of which E£89.5 billion is provided by the private sector.

During the 1962–86 period, US nonmilitary loans and grants to Egypt totaled $13 billion; another $4.7 billion came from multilateral organizations, including $2.9 billion from the IBRD and $980 million from IDA. Substantial assistance has also been received from Germany, Japan, the UK, former Czechoslovakia, and France, as well as from Arab countries. In 1978, however, President Sadat's peacemaking efforts with Israel led to a cessation of Arab funding.

By the end of 1985, Egypt had accumulated a foreign debt of some $51 billion (144% of GDP) becoming one of the developing world's largest debtors. Vast cash infusions and debt cancellation reduced Egypt's total external debt to about $40 billion in 1990. In 1991, total debt service amounted to $2.4 billion, down from $3.4 in 1990. The ratio of debt service to exports of goods and services has declined from more than 45% in the latter half of the 1980s to about 18% in fiscal 1992.

40SOCIAL DEVELOPMENT
Social programs focus on services including health care and family planning. Employers pay a percentage of their total wage bills to the government's social insurance organization for various forms of social insurance: 2% for workers' compensation and 24–26% for old age pensions and death and disability benefits. Companies with satisfactory medical facilities may obtain a reduction of up to 75% in the payments for the first of these. Employees pay 11–14% of their wages toward old age, disability, and survivor pensions. Unemployment insurance began in 1962; unemployed workers receive 60% of their last monthly wage.

Under Egyptian law, only males can transmit citizenship. A 1979 revision of the family status law liberalized divorce and custody provisions, but was repealed in 1985 because of conflicts with Islamic law. Women have won employment opportunities in a number of fields, but Egyptian feminists fear these gains will be halted by resurgent Islamic fundamentalism.

41HEALTH
Between 1982 and 1987 (during the first five-year plan), the government established 14 public and central hospitals, 115 rural health units, and 39 rural hospitals. The total number of beds increased by 9,257 during this period (to a total in 1985 of 96,700). In 1987, 190 general and central hospitals were established (26,200 beds), as well as 2,082 rural health units, and 78 village hospitals.

The Egyptian government formulated its second five-year plan from 1988 to 1992, in which it planned to complete 22 public/central hospitals, replace 81 public/central hospitals, and complete 25 health units in rural hospitals. It also wanted to establish 25 urban health centers (each serving around 150,000 people) and 100 rural health units (each serving about 5,000 people). From 1985 to 1990, there were 1.9 hospital beds per 1,000 people. Between 1988 and 1992, there was 1 physicians per 1,320 people, with a nurse to doctor ratio of 1.2.

Serious diseases in Egypt include schistosomiasis, malaria, hookworm, trachoma, tuberculosis, dysentery, beriberi, and typhus. In 1990, there were 78 per 100,000 reported cases of tuberculosis. Of children under 5 years of age, 13% were considered malnourished. Between 1990 and 1992, Egypt vaccinated children up to one year old against tuberculosis (92%); diphtheria, pertussis, and tetanus (89%); polio (89%); and measles (89%). The country's fertility rate was 4.5 in 1985-90, 10.5% below the previous 5-year period. In 1992, 47% of reproductive-age couples practiced contraception. Abortion is legal only for medical reasons. The overall death rate in 1992 was 9 per 1,000 inhabitants, and the infant mortality rate was 43 per 1,000 live births. Life expectancy in 1992 was 61 years.

Egypt would like to expand its health insurance, with the target of covering 75% of the population. Health care expenditures in 1990 amounted to $921 million.

42HOUSING
Prior to 1952, most Egyptians lived in mud huts. Postrevolutionary governments, however, have actively concerned themselves with housing. In order to encourage rural housing activities on nonfertile soil, "extension areas" have been allocated for villages. Efforts have been made to provide low-rent housing in towns; the units were constructed in cooperation with the Reconstruction and Popular Dwellings Co., in which the government held a share. Assisted by the state, which grants long-term and low-interest loans, cooperative societies also engage in housing construction. The state affords facilities for cooperatives to acquire land from the religious foundations.

Despite these efforts, Egypt's housing shortage remains acute, with about 1 million units needed in urban areas. Housing construction was a major priority of the 1982–87 development plan, but it seems unlikely that the current deficit can be met for many years. The greatest shortage is of low-cost housing. In 1982–87, the government allocated E£4,213 million for housing construction. As of June 1987, 78.7% of housing units were apartments, 11.5% were categorized as "separate room," and 8.4% were traditional rural dwellings. Renters occupied 44.6% of all units, and 30.9% were owner occupied.

43EDUCATION
In 1966, literacy in Egypt was estimated at less than 30%; in 1990, it was 48.4% (males, 62.9% and females, 33.8%). In 1952, primary schools had space for only about half the school-age children. However, marked progress has been achieved since then. By 1991 there were 6,541,725 students in 15,861 primary schools and 5,300,881 students in secondary schools. Teaching personnel at all levels totaled 566,112 in 1990.

The Education Act of 1953 provided free and compulsory education for all children between the ages of 6 and 12. Entry to preparatory schools is by competitive examination, which children take at the age of 10. Preparatory schools offer four-year courses leading to a certificate, which is the entrance requirement for three-year courses in secondary schools. Here there are a domestic science program for girls, a technical curriculum, and a general curriculum with emphasis on academic studies. The general secondary education certificate entitles the holder to enter a university. A majority of primary-school graduates continue their education in preparatory, secondary, or vocational schools.

A decree of 23 July 1962 provided free tuition at all Egyptian universities. The traditional center for religious education in the Muslim world is Al-Azhar in Cairo, which in 1983 celebrated 1,000 years of teaching as the oldest continuously operating school in the world. Al-Azhar offers instruction in 3 faculties and 14 affiliated institutes and maintains its own primary and secondary schools. All universities and higher level institutions had a total of 708,417 students in 1990. Universities and equivalent institutions had a faculty strength of 34,553 personnel.

There is also the American University in Cairo, which offers a wide range of undergraduate and graduate courses, as well as an American school in Cairo and one in Alexandria. The American Research Center in Cairo is supported by US universities and museums. It was established in 1948 to encourage the exchange of archaeologists and other researchers in almost all fields of interest.

Adult education, under the Ministry of Education, is increasingly important. The Institute of Popular Culture, with centers in Cairo and Alexandria, offers practical courses in vocational guidance, domestic science, the arts, commerce, languages, and industry. Business firms are under obligation, enjoined upon them by the government, to combat illiteracy among their labor staff members.

44LIBRARIES AND MUSEUMS

Egypt's largest libraries are the Egyptian National Library (2,117,000 volumes), Alexandria University Library (with over 1 million volumes), and the University of Cairo Library (more than 1 million volumes). The National Library also functions as the main public library for the nation's capital and supervises 11 branch libraries located in various Cairo districts. The Municipal Library in Alexandria contains one of the country's largest public library collections, with 23,390 Arabic and 35,400 European volumes. One of the most important special libraries is the Scientific and Technical Documentation Division of the National Research Center at Cairo, which has the best collection of scientific and technical material in the Arab world.

The Egyptian National Museum, founded in 1902, contains unique exhibits from prehistoric times up to the 3rd century AD, and it also has a notable Department of Antiquities, established in 1835, which supervises excavations and administers archaeological museums. There are many specialized museums, including the Coptic Museum, devoted to the history of the old Christian Monophysites; the Museum of Islamic Art; the Greco-Roman Museum; the Agricultural Museum; the Museum of Modern Art; the Railway Museum; and the Cotton Museum. Several former royal palaces have been transformed into museums: the Al-Gawhara Palace in Cairo, Ras at-Tin Palace in Alexandria, and Al-Montazah Palace in Montazah-Alexandria.

In 1969, after the original site was flooded as a result of the building of the Aswan High Dam, two of the most famous monuments of ancient Egypt at Abu Simbel were removed and re-created on a different site. In 1976, the Temple of Isis and other monuments on Philae, an island flooded by the dammed waters, were similarly relocated.

45MEDIA

The two leading newspapers, with their estimated 1991 daily circulations, were *Al-Ahram (The Pyramid;* 984,800) and *Al-Akhbar (The News;* 741,700). *Al-Jumhuriyah (The Republic;* 850,000) is the official organ of the government; *Al-Ahram* is the unofficial organ. The leading evening paper is *Al-Misa'a (105,000).* There is also an English-language newspaper, the *Egyptian Gazette* (32,000). On 23 May 1960, all Egyptian newspapers were nationalized and subjected to censorship. President Sadat ended formal press censorship in 1974, but the following year he set up a government council to supervise the newspapers. In 1981, President Mubarak revoked the ban on opposition newspapers, but the press remains sensitive to the wishes of the government. The Middle East News Agency is under the supervision of the information section of the Ministry of National Guidance.

Telephone, telegraph, radio, and television services are operated by the state-owned Telecommunication Organization. There are three television channels, broadcasting mostly in Arabic. In 1991 there were 3.9 million licensed television sets. Radios were estimated at 17,500,000 that year. There were an estimated 6,200,000 telephones in use in the same year.

46ORGANIZATIONS

Most organizations in Egypt serve occupational and professional (particularly agricultural) goals. The land reform law makes it compulsory for landholders who have obtained land under it to join cooperative societies to help supply them with tested seeds, tools if available, and possibly markets. There are many chambers of commerce, representing various cities and various economic groups. There are scholastic and archaeological, accounting, economic, historical, and other learned organizations.

47TOURISM, TRAVEL, AND RECREATION

Passports and visas are required of foreign visitors except nationals of certain Middle Eastern countries. However, transit passengers by ship or plane need no visas. Tourists arriving from many African countries must have proof of cholera and yellow fever vaccination.

Tourism has been a major foreign exchange earner. It grew steadily after the end of the Iran-Iraq war. In 1991, there were 2,214,277 foreign visitor arrivals, of whom 40% came from European countries and 42% from Arab countries. However, sporadic attacks by Islamic extremists on tourist groups caused tourism to decline by about 20% in 1992–93. In 1991, there were 53,959 rooms in hotels and other facilities, with 105,830 beds and a 43% occupancy rate, and tourism receipts totaled US$2.03 billion. Principal tourist attractions include the pyramids and Great Sphinx at Giza, the Abu Simbel temples south of Aswan, the Valley of the Kings at Luxor, and the Muhammad 'Ali Mosque in Cairo. Rides are available on *fellucas,* traditional sailing boats of the Nile. Popular pastimes among Egyptians include card playing, moviegoing, and sports such as soccer, swimming, tennis, and horse racing.

48FAMOUS EGYPTIANS

Egypt's first recorded ruler, or pharaoh, was Menes (or Narmer, fl.3100? BC), who united the southern and northern kingdoms and founded the capital at Memphis. Notable successor pharaohs included Cheops (Khufu, fl.26th cent. BC), who built the Great Pyramid at Giza; Thutmose III (r.1504?–1450 BC), who greatly extended the empire through conquest; Amenhotep III (r.1417–1379 BC), who ruled at the summit of ancient Egyptian civilization and built extensive monuments; his son Amenhotep IV (Akhenaten, or Ikhnaton, r.1379–1362 BC), who, with his queen, Nefertiti, instituted a brief period of monotheism; and Tutankhamen (r.1361–1352 BC), whose tomb containing valuable treasures was found practically intact in 1922. Cleopatra VII (69–30 BC) was involved in the political conflicts of the Romans.

Philo Judaeus (13? BC–AD 50?) attempted to combine Greek philosophy with Judaism. Ptolemy (Claudius Ptolemaeus, fl.2d cent. AD) was the foremost astronomer of ancient times. Egyptian-born Plotinus (AD 205?–270) was a neoplatonic philosopher in Rome.

The most notable of Egypt's rulers under the Muslim caliphate was Saladin (Salah ad-Din, 1138–93), sultan of Egypt and Syria and founder of the Ayyubid dynasty. The founder of Egypt as a part of the Ottoman Empire was Muhammad 'Ali (1769–1849), of Albanian origin, the first of a dynasty that ended with the deposition of Faruk in 1952. 'Arabi Pasha (Ahmad 'Arabi, 1841?–1911) led a popular uprising against British intervention in 1882 but was defeated. Later, the fiery political fight against British rule was waged by Sa'ad Zaghlul Pasha (1860?–1927), a founder of the Nationalist Party, Wafd.

No one had greater influence on Egypt during the 1950s and 1960s than Gamal Abdel Nasser (Jamal 'Abd al-Nasir, 1918–70), the moving spirit of the army's revolt against the monarchy in 1952. As prime minister (1954–56) and president (1956–70), Nasser set Egypt on its socialist course and attempted to unify the Arab world through confederation. His successor as president, Anwar al-Sadat (as-Sadat, 1918–81), continued Nasser's policies but with important modifications, especially in relation to Israel; with Menachem Begin he shared the Nobel Peace Prize in 1978 and negotiated the Egypt-Israel Peace Treaty of 1979. Upon Sadat's assassination, Muhammad Hosni (Husni) Mubarak (b. 1928), who had been air force chief of staff (1969–72) and vice-president (1975–81), became president of Egypt.

The poet Sami al-Barudi (1839–1904) wrote popular and highly regarded verses about Islam's heroic early age. 'Abbas al-Aqqad (1889–1964) has been called the greatest contemporary Arab poet and the most original Arab writer. Involved in a political plot, he was jailed and composed an Arab "De Profundis" about his life in prison. Taha Husayn (1889–1973), the most widely known modern Egyptian intellectual leader, was minister of education from 1950 to 1952. The poet and essayist Malak Hifni Nasif (1886–1918) sought an improvement in the status of women. Ahmad Zaki Abu Shadi (1892–1955) was a renowned poet, essayist, and dramatist. Mahmud Taymur (1894–1973), a leading dramatist, wrote popular social satires and comedies. Um Kalthum (Fatma al-Zahraa Ibrahim, 1898?–1975) was the most famous singer of the Arab world. Mohammed Hassanein Heikal (b. 1923), journalist and author, was the outspoken editor of the influential newspaper *Al-Ahram* (1957–74) until he was forced by the government to resign. In 1988, Naguib Mahfouz (b. 1912) won the Nobel Prize for Literature.

49DEPENDENCIES
Egypt has no territories or colonies.

50BIBLIOGRAPHY

Aftandilian, Gregory L. *Egypt's Bid for Arab Leadership: Implications for US Policy.* New York: Council on Foreign Relations Press, 1993.

Baker, Raymond W. *Egypt's Uncertain Revolution under Nasser and Sadat.* Cambridge, Mass.: Harvard University Press, 1978.

Baker, Raymond William. *Sadat and After: Struggles for Egypt's Political Soul.* Cambridge, Mass.: Harvard University Press, 1990.

Botman, Selma. *Egypt from Independence to Revolution, 1919–1952.* Syracuse, N.Y.: Syracuse University Press, 1991.

Briggs, Martin Shaw. *Muhammadan Architecture in Egypt and Palestine.* Oxford: Clarendon, 1924.

Budge, Sir Ernest Alfred Thompson Wallis. *Egyptian Religion.* New York: Universe Books, 1959.

Carlton, David. *Britain and the Suez Crisis.* New York: Blackwell, 1989, 1988.

Carter, Barbara. *The Copts in Egyptian Politics, 1918–1952.* Dover, N.H.: Longwood, 1985.

Cottrell, Leonard. *Life under the Pharaohs.* London: Evans, 1953.

Feinstein, Steve. *Egypt in Pictures.* Minneapolis: Lerner, 1988.

Handoussa, Beha and Gillian Potter (eds.). *Employment and Structural Adjustment: Egypt in the 1990s.* Cairo, Egypt: American University in Cairo Press, 1991.

Hansen, Bent. *Egypt and Turkey.* New York: Oxford University Press, 1991.

Hopkins, Nicholas S. *Agrarian Transformation in Egypt.* Boulder, Colo.: Westview Press, 1987.

Hopwood, Derek. *Egypt, Politics and Society, 1945–1990.* 3rd ed. New York: Harper Collins Academic, 1991.

Ismael, Taraq Y. *The U.A.R. in Africa: Egypt's Policy under Nasser.* Evanston, Ill.: Northwestern University Press, 1971.

Issawi, Charles. *Egypt in Revolution.* London: Oxford University Press, 1963.

Kees, Hermann. *Ancient Egypt: A Cultural Topography.* Chicago: University of Chicago Press, 1961.

King, W. J. *Historical Dictionary of Egypt.* Metuchen, N.J.: Scarecrow, 1984.

Kunz, Diane B. *The Economic Diplomacy of the Suez Crisis.* Chapel Hill: University of North Carolina Press, 1991.

Lorenz, Joseph P. *Egypt and the Arabs: Foreign Policy and the Search for National Identity.* Boulder, Colo.: Westview Press, 1990.

Mansfield, Peter. *The Arabs.* New York, Penguin, 1990.

———. *A History of the Middle East.* New York: Viking, 1991.

Metz, Helen Chapin. *Egypt, a Country Study.* 5th ed. Washington, D.C.: Library of Congress, 1991.

Oweiss, Ibrahim M. (ed.). *The Political Economy of Contemporary Egypt.* Washington, D.C.: Georgetown University, 1990.

Palmer, Monte. *The Egyptian Bureaucracy.* Syracuse, N.Y.: Syracuse University Press, 1988.

Posener, Georges (ed.). *Dictionary of Egyptian Civilization.* London: Methuen, 1962.

Rubin, Barry M. *Islamic Fundamentalism in Egyptian Politics.* New York: St. Martin's Press, 1990.

Springborg, Robert. *Mubarak's Egypt: Fragmentation of the Political Order.* Boulder, Colo.: Westview Press, 1989.

Toledano, Ehud R. *State and Society in Mid-nineteenth-century Egypt.* New York: Cambridge University Press, 1990.

Tripp, Charles and Roger Owen, (eds.) *Egypt under Mubarak.* New York: Routledge, 1989.

Vatikiotis, Peter J. *The History of Egypt.* Baltimore: Johns Hopkins University Press, 1986.

Waterbury, John. The Egypt of Nasser and Sadat. Princeton, N.J.,: Princeton University Press, 1983.

EQUATORIAL GUINEA

Republic of Equatorial Guinea
República de Guinea Ecuatorial

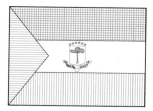

CAPITAL: Malabo (formerly Santa Isabel).

FLAG: The flag is a tricolor of green, white, and red horizontal stripes; a blue triangle joins them at the hoist. The arms in the center of the white stripe hold a cotton tree (the national symbol), six stars—one for each physical division of the country—and the motto "Unidad, Justicia, Paz."

ANTHEM: *Himno Nacional*, beginning "Caminemos pisando la senda de nuestra inmensa felicidad" ("Let us walk on the path of our immense happiness").

MONETARY UNIT: Communauté Financière Africaine franc (CFA Fr), introduced in 1985, is a paper currency tied to the French franc at the rate of CFA Fr 100 = Fr 1. CFA Fr 1 = $0.0018 (or $1 = CFA Fr571). There are coins of 1, 2, 5, 10, 25, 50, 100, and 500 CFA francs and notes of 50, 100, 500, 1,000, 5,000, and 10,000 francs.

WEIGHTS AND MEASURES: The metric system is the legal standard.

HOLIDAYS: New Year's Day, 1 January; Independence Day, 5 March; Labor Day, 1 May; OAU Day, 25 May; President's Birthday, 5 June; Armed Forces Day, 3 August; Human Rights Day, 10 December; Christmas, 25 December. Movable Christian holidays include Good Friday and Easter Monday.

TIME: 1 PM = noon GMT.

¹LOCATION, SIZE, AND EXTENT

Located on the west coast of Africa, Equatorial Guinea consists of a mainland enclave, Río Muni, and five inhabited islands: Bioko (between 1973 and 1979, Macías Nguema Biyogo, and before that Fernando Póo), Annobón (Pagalu during the 1970s), Corisco, Elobey Chico, and Elobey Grande. The total area is 28,050 sq km (10,830 sq mi), of which Río Muni, along with Corisco and the Elobeys, accounts for 26,017 sq km (10,045 sq mi) and Bioko, along with Annobón, 2,034 sq km (785 sq mi). Comparatively, the area occupied by Equatorial Guinea is slightly larger than the state of Maryland. Río Muni is bounded on the N by Cameroon, on the E and S by Gabon, and on the W by the Gulf of Guinea (Atlantic Ocean), with a length of 248 km (154 mi) ENE–WSW and 167 km (104 mi) SSE–NNW. Bioko, situated 56 km (35 mi) W of Cameroon and about 259 km (161 mi) NW of Río Muni, extends 74 km (46 mi) NE–SE and 37 km (23 mi) SE–NW. Annobón is 686 km (426 mi) SW of Bioko; Corisco and the Elobeys are off the SW coast of Bioko, within sight of Gabon. The total boundary length of Equatorial Guinea is 835 km (519 mi).

The capital city of Equatorial Guinea, Mbini, is located on the Gulf of Guinea coast.

²TOPOGRAPHY

Bioko and Annobón are volcanic islands that are part of the chain starting with the Cameroon Highlands and outcropping into the Atlantic as far as St. Helena. Río Muni is a fluvial mainland plateau, except for the sandy shore and the ridges of the Sierra Cristal range that separate the coast from the interior plateau. The Muni and Ntem rivers, on the south and north boundaries of Río Muni, are estuaries navigable for about 20 km (12 mi); the Mbini River, midway between them, is typical of the cascading streams that drain all of Río Muni. Bioko has short cascading streams; Annobón has only storm arroyos. Most of the country, including the islands, is tropical rain forest. On Annobón, volcanic deposits

restrict agriculture, and the Muni estuarial islands are sandy, but the rest of the country has tropical humus conducive to agriculture.

³CLIMATE

Equatorial Guinea has a tropical climate with distinct wet and dry seasons. From June to August, Río Muni is dry and Bioko wet; from December to February, the reverse obtains. In between there is gradual transition. Rain or mist occurs daily on Annobón, where a cloudless day has never been registered. The temperature at Malabo, Bioko, ranges from 16°C to 33°C (61–91°F), though on the southern Moka Plateau normal high temperatures are only 21°C (70°F). In Río Muni, the average temperature is about 27°C (80°F). Annual rainfall varies from 193 cm (76 in) at Malabo to 1,092 cm (430 in) at Ureka, Bioko, but Río Muni is somewhat drier.

⁴FLORA AND FAUNA

Dense tropical rain-forest vegetation prevails throughout Equatorial Guinea. There are 140 species of trees, especially palms and hardwoods. Yams and bananas were introduced by the early inhabitants and became staples. Monkeys, chimpanzees, elephants, and gray doves are common.

⁵ENVIRONMENT

In 1994, Equatorial Guinea's most significant environmental problems were deforestation, water pollution, and the preservation of wildlife. The forests are threatened by agricultural expansion, fires, and grazing. Sixty-three percent of people in the rural areas in Equatorial Guinea do not have pure water. The nation has 2.2 cubic miles of water with 82% used for farming purposes. As of 1994, the nation's wildlife is threatened by the expansion of the population centers and resulting damage to the living environment of plants and animals. Of 141 mammal species, 15 are endangered. Three species of birds in a total of 392, two types of reptiles, and one amphibian are also endangered. Seventeen species of plants are threatened with extinction. As of 1987, the drill (*Papio leucophaeus*) was probably extinct. Preuss's monkey and the green sea, hawksbill, and olive ridley turtles were listed as endangered.

6 POPULATION

A provisional census in 1983 recorded a population of 304,000; the population was estimated at 409,425 in 1994. A population of 452,000 was projected for the year 2000, assuming a crude birthrate of 40.8 per 1,000 population and a crude death rate of 16.2 during 1995–2000; for a net natural increase of 24.6. The population density in 1994 was about 16 persons per sq km (38 per sq mi). The principal town is Malabo, on Bioko, with about 31,000 people.

7 MIGRATION

As many as 45,000 Nigerian laborers served in Equatorial Guinea in the early 1970s, mostly working on Bioko cocoa plantations. In 1975, Nigeria began evacuating those contract laborers, charging the Equatorial Guinean government with a long history of mistreating them. These plantations are now short of labor.

About 100,000 people fled into exile during the regime of Francisco Macías Nguema. About 130,000 were abroad in 1993, including an estimated 80,000 in Gbon and 30,000 in Cameroon.

8 ETHNIC GROUPS

The largest single tribe is the Fang (Fon, or Pamúe), who entered Río Muni from the east largely between 1687 and 1926. The earlier Riomunians, who had probably arrived in the 14th century, were forced by the Fang to flee to the coast. The Bubi on Bioko are descendants of the indigenous African Bantu-speaking population that fled from the Cameroonian and Riomunian mainland in the 13th century. Fernandinos—descendants of mainland slaves liberated by the British navy in the 19th century—and Europeans, especially Spanish Asturians and Catalonians, have long dominated commerce and government. It is estimated that the 67 Fang clans represent 80% of the population.

9 LANGUAGES

Spanish is the official language of the government, commerce, and schools. The principal vernacular is Fang, which, like all the country's indigenous languages, is a Bantu tongue. Much petty commerce is conducted in pidgin English (Pichinglis). Annobón uses the fã d'Ambō, a pidgin form of Bantu speech with heavy 16th-century Portuguese inflection.

10 RELIGIONS

Although African traditional religion has left its vestiges among the indigenous tribes, by the mid-1980s about 96% of the population had been converted to Roman Catholicism. In 1975, many churches were closed, and the Roman Catholic Church was banned in 1978. After the 1979 coup, Catholic religious services were restored. As of 1993, Roman Catholics comprise some 98% of the population.

11 TRANSPORTATION

There are 300 km (185 mi) of highways in Bioko and 2,460 km (1,530 mi) in Río Muni. The chief ports are Bata and Mbini in Río Muni and Malabo and Luba on Bioko. Bata, modernized in the 1970s, can accommodate up to four vessels of 20,000 tons each. There is regular service between Malabo and Bata. In 1991, two merchant ships were in service with GRT of 6,000.

Bata's airport was the first major air transport facility. Malabo's airport was raised to jet standards in 1964 and became the focus of regional air services. A landing strip was built on Annobón in 1968. Air transport between Bata, Malabo, and Douala, Cameroon, is provided by Equatorial Guinea Air Lines (Algesa). There is international air service to Gabon, Nigeria, Morocco, and Spain.

12 HISTORY

Although numerous archaeological discoveries indicate a very early Sangoan (modified Acheulean) culture throughout Equatorial Guinea, the earliest traceable inhabitants were Pygmies, remnants of whom remain in northeastern Río Muni. Bioko was apparently uninhabited when the Bubi came by sea from the mainland in the 13th century. Río Muni seems to have been occupied by the Bantu in a series of waves that superseded the Pygmies—first by the Bubi, before 1200; then by the Benga, Bujeba, and Combe, perhaps about 1300; and, finally, by the Fang from the Congo Basin, after 1687. Although Annobón was uninhabited in 1471 when the Portuguese discovered it, it was the only one of the territories later incorporated into Equatorial Guinea that they attempted to develop. The proprietorship of Annobón was ill administered, however, and it was virtually self-governing for 250 years. In 1778, Portugal transferred its nominal claims over Annobón, Fernando Póo, and the entire coast from the Niger Delta to Cape López (in modern Gabon) to Spain, in return for Spain's renunciation of pirate claims in southern Brazil. Later that year, a Spanish expedition of occupation arrived from South America. The expedition withdrew in 1781 after disease and poor administration had cost the lives of 370 of the 547 Spaniards.

The primary Spanish mainland explorations were undertaken between 1875 and 1885. Catholic missionary efforts by the Claretians extended Spanish influence to Annobón (1884), completed the exploration of Fernando Póo (1883–1924), and began the penetration of Río Muni (1886–1925). The first effective efforts to penetrate the interior were undertaken in 1926–27 by Governor Ángel Barrera, who reportedly employed considerable force to subjugate the Fang. The administrative procedure for the colony was defined as the process of *reducción* (conquest), *repartimiento* (resettlement), and *encomienda* (placing in trust) of the indigenous people—the policy followed in Mexico and Peru 400 years earlier—but this time, the people were *encomendado* (entrusted) not to private masters but to the Claretians. After World War II, the Franco government initiated a policy of heavy investment to turn Spanish Guinea into a model colony.

Spanish Guinea became a province of Spain in 1958. In 1964, two provinces (Fernando Póo and Río Muni) were created under an autonomous regional government. Political opposition and Protestant missions, both banned in Spain, were tolerated, and the regional regime of Bonifacio Ondó Edú was virtually self-governing internally. In 1966, independence was promised. Two years later, an opposition faction under Francisco Macías Nguema won the preindependence elections and organized a sovereign government on 12 October 1968, when the colony became the independent Republic of Equatorial Guinea. Within six months, hostility between Riomunians and Fernandinos had sharpened. The continued presence of Spanish civil servants, troops, and ships and the unchanged influence of Spanish plantation management provoked a crisis in 1969. Two coups failed, the Spanish were evacuated, medical services were suspended (until WHO restaffed them), and fiscal transactions ceased. However, within six weeks a new understanding was reached with Spain, under UN auspices, and Spanish subsidies were restored.

On 23 August 1972, Francisco Macías Nguema was proclaimed president for life; subsequently he assumed ministerial posts of defense, foreign affairs, and trade. In 1973, many place names were Africanized by presidential decree. An exile group, the Equatorial Guinean Liberation Front, and others charged in December 1974 that more than two-thirds of the National Assembly elected in 1968 had disappeared, and that many prominent persons, especially political opponents of the president, had been assassinated. It was estimated that a quarter of the country's population was in exile in Cameroon, Gabon, and Europe. On 3 August 1979, Macías Nguema was overthrown in a military coup led by his Spanish-trained nephew, Lt.-Col. Teodoro Obiang

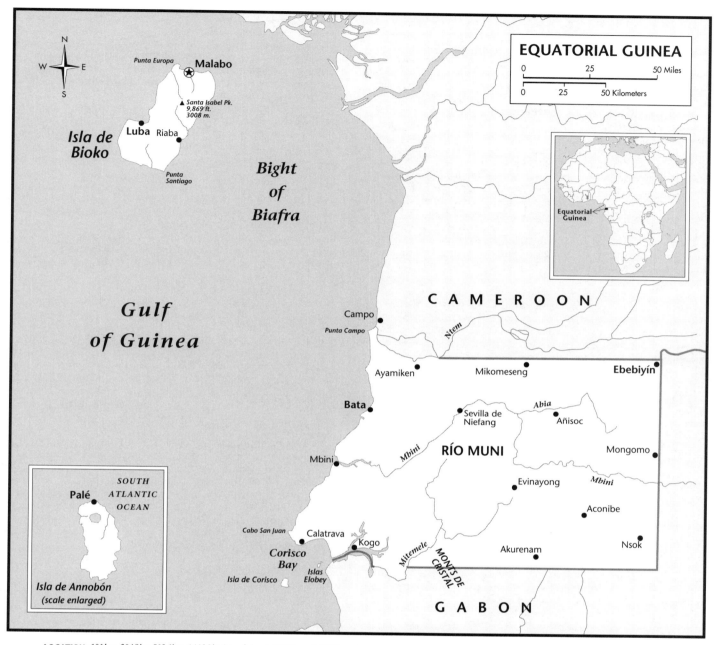

LOCATION: 1°1′ to 3°48′N; 8°26′ to 11°20′E Annobón at 1°25′s and 5°36′E. **BOUNDARY LENGTHS:** Cameroon, 183 km (114 mi); Gabon, 386 km (240 mi); Río Muni coastline, 167 km (104 mi); Bioko coastline, 174 km (108 mi). **TERRITORIAL SEA LIMIT:** 12 mi.

Nguema Mbasogo; the former president was tried shortly after the coup and executed on 29 September. International human rights organizations estimated that during his 11-year rule at least 50,000 people had been killed and 40,000 had been enslaved on state-owned plantations.

Under Obiang Nguema's leadership, the Supreme Military Council became the highest power in the country. The country continued to decay as corruption flourished and political opponents and others were imprisoned or put to death. Soviet influence was reduced, and economic and military cooperation with Spain was restored. A new constitution, approved in a referendum on 15 August 1982, provided that Obiang Nguema would remain head of state until 1989, when direct popular elections would take place. He was elected without opposition on 25 June 1989.

Nominally, since 17 November 1991, Equatorial Guinea has had a constitutional democracy with judicial integrity and multi-party elections. In reality, Obiang's Democratic Party of Equatorial Guinea (PDGE) controls everything. At least a fifth of the population lives in exile, mostly in Cameroon and Gabon.

13 GOVERNMENT

By referendum on 11 August 1968, Equatorial Guineans approved a constitution that became effective on Independence Day, 12 October 1968. The constitution required the country to join the UN and to coordinate Spanish financial, technical, and administrative assistance until total "Africanization" was achieved. Separatist activities on Bioko led to the suspension of the 1968 constitution in May 1971. The president assumed all powers and ruled by decree until a second constitution was approved by referendum in July 1973. Under this constitution, the only legal party, the United National Workers Party, designated deputies to the National Assembly and had the power to remove them. An article requiring election of the president by direct, secret, universal suffrage was suspended for President Francisco Macías Nguema, who had been proclaimed president for life on 23 August 1972.

After the 1979 coup, a new constitution was drafted with UN assistance. Approved by 95% of the voters in a referendum on 15 August 1982, this document provided for elections every five years to a National Assembly and for establishment of a Council of State. It also guaranteed civil rights and sets out the foundations of a free-market economy, while reserving for the public sector such key enterprises as energy and broadcasting. It was a sham. Lt.-Col. Obiang Nguema was inaugurated as president in Bata on 12 October 1982, and parliamentary elections (based on a single list, with no political parties permitted) were held on 28 August 1983. The PDGE won all 41 seats in the Chamber of People's Representatives in 10 July 1988 elections. Obiang was elected president unopposed on 25 June 1989, for a fourth seven-year term.

On 17 November 1991, a new constitution was adopted. Opposition parties began to be organized and sought official recognition in 1992. Eventually an election was held on 21 November 1993 and the PDGE won 68 of 80 seats. But the major opposition parties boycotted the election and as many as 80% of the eligible voters refused to participate. The new cabinet was expanded from 34 to 42 members.

14POLITICAL PARTIES

Following an abortive coup in March 1969, all existing political parties were merged into the United National Party (Partido Único Nacional) under the leadership of President Macías Nguema. Political activity outside this party was made illegal. The name of the party was later modified to United National Workers Party (Partido Único Nacional de los Trabajadores—PUNT). After the 1979 coup, all political parties were banned and the ruling Democratic Party for Equatorial Guinea (PDGE) monopolized power. Among the opposition parties in exile in the mid-1980s were the National Alliance for the Restoration of Democracy and the Democratic Movement for the Liberation of Equatorial Guinea. A source of opposition is resentment by Biokans of mainland domination.

The 1991 constitution legalized political parties and a January 1992 law on party formation initiated the process of party organization. But it restricted party membership and activity to those who had lived continuously in Equatorial Guinea for a number of years. Since most opposition politicians had been in exile since independence, the effect was to prohibit serious opposition. Small parties—the Liberal Democrat Convention, the Popular Union, and the Progressive Democratic Alliance—were recognized in 1992. The Equatorial Guinea Progress Party (PPGE) was legalized after a long delay and, in 1993, the Socialist Party of Equatorial Guinea (PSGE) was approved. By mid-1993, 13 legal opposition parties stood prepared to contest elections, scheduled for 12 September. A number of opposition leaders were even granted amnesty. Yet by May, several leaders were arrested and, in August, one died in jail. The September elections were postponed until 21 November, but opposition parties boycotted them. The PDGE won easily (68 out of 80 seats) amid a low voter turnout. The Joint Opposition Platform (POC), an alliance of eight opposition parties, had called for the boycott.

15LOCAL GOVERNMENT

The country is divided into seven provinces, each headed by a governor appointed by the president. The provinces are divided into districts and municipalities.

16JUDICIAL SYSTEM

The court system includes a Supreme Court, military courts, and customary (traditional) courts. The courts apply a blend of traditional law, military law, and Franco-era Spanish law which leads to some unpredictability in results. Appeals from courts of first instance are rare. A 5-member Constitutional Council established in 1993 decides constitutional issues.

Under the 1991 constitution, the judiciary is not independent from the executive branch. In fact, all judges and clerks and other judicial personnel are appointed and dismissed at the will of the President. In addition, corruption is a problem because of low wages for judicial personnel.

17ARMED FORCES

As of 1993, military personnel numbered 1,300—army, 1,100; navy, 120; and air force, 100. President Obiang Nguema's personal guard consists of a Moroccan battalion of 360 men. Paramilitary forces, including the Guardia Civil, number 2,000. The only combat capability comes from 16 Russian armed vehicles and 3–4 patrol craft. No reliable spending figures are available.

18INTERNATIONAL COOPERATION

Equatorial Guinea joined the UN on 12 November 1969; it participates in ECA and all the nonregional specialized agencies except IAEA, IFC, WIPO, and WMO. The nation is also a member of the African Development Bank, G-77, and OAU, and is a de facto participant in GATT. In December 1983, it joined the Central African Republic, the Congo, Chad, Cameroon, and Gabon in the Central African Customs and Economic Union. (Union Douanière et Économique de l'Afrique Centrale—UDEAC). In 1984, the nation signed the Law of the Sea treaty.

19ECONOMY

The agricultural sector supports 50% of the population. The country exports cocoa, coffee, and timber, and imports large quantities of foodstuffs. Production of oil began in 1991, and the exploration for additional reserves continues. Trace deposits of a few minerals have been located. Industry is limited to a few processing facilities for agricultural products. In spite of its recent compliance difficulties with the IMF structural adjustment program, the arrival of significant oil revenues has caused the economy to be viewed with guarded optimism.

The economy continues to rely to a considerable degree on its ties with Spain, a major aid contributor. With Equatorial Guinea's adherence to the French-sponsored Central African monetary union, the level of French aid has risen sharply.

In January 1994 France suddenly devalued the CFA franc, causing its value to drop in half overnight. Immediately, prices for almost all imported goods soared, including prices for food and essential drugs. Since 1948 France had guaranteed a fixed parity of one French franc to 50 African francs. The resulting stability in the currency had generally kept inflation low and helped to maintain a steady rate of growth. However, in the 1980s, the economies of the CFA countries began to stagnate in relation to other African nations, and France came under increased pressure from the World Bank, the IMF, and western countries to stop subsidizing the CFA franc. The devaluation, long expected in the investment community, was designed to encourage new investment, particularly in the export sectors of the economy, and discourage the use of hard currency reserves to buy products that could be grown domestically.

20INCOME

In 1992 Equatorial Guinea's GNP was $146 million at current prices, or $330 per capita. For the period 1985–92 the average inflation rate was −0.4%, resulting in a real growth rate in per capita GNP of −0.3%.

In 1992 the GDP was $159 million in current US dollars. Agriculture, hunting, forestry, and fishing contributed 50% to GDP; manufacturing, 1%; electricity, gas, and water, 3%; construction, 3%; wholesale and retail trade, 7%; transport, storage, and communication, 2%; finance, insurance, real estate, and business services, 2%; community, social, and personal services, 13%; and other sources 19%.

21LABOR

Most of the labor force of about 177,000 was employed in subsistence agriculture. The 1982 constitution denies state employees and workers in essential public services the right to strike, but as of 1992, a new law governing unions was under consideration. Workers currently do not have the right to free association and wages are set by the government and employers, with little or no input by workers. There was a statutory, monthly minimum wage of about $34 in 1986.

22AGRICULTURE

Agriculture is the main economic activity, involving about 50% of the population. An estimated 8% of the land is engaged in crop production. The island of Bioko has year-round rainfall, and the prevailing economic activity is cocoa cultivation. In Río Muni (on mainland Africa), where 80% of the population lives, food crops are the dominant economic activity, and cash crop cultivation is secondary. Agriculture (including forestry and fishing) accounts for 53% of GDP and 60% of exports. The main food crop is cassava, of which 47,000 tons were produced in 1992. Sweet potatoes are the second-largest food crop, with 35,000 tons in 1992, followed by bananas (17,000 tons).

Before independence, the main cash crops were cocoa, coffee, and palm kernels for palm oil. Guinean cocoa, of excellent quality, had an annual production of 38,000 tons in 1967. However, production experienced a sharp drop in the 1970s, falling to 4,512 tons in 1980. In 1992, production was estimated at 5,000 tons, and cocoa exports were valued at $5 million, contributing almost 10% to total exports. Coffee of comparatively poor quality is grown in northern Río Muni, along the Cameroon border. The preindependence production of 8,959 tons in 1967 fell to 500 tons in 1978; the decline was mainly caused by forcible transfer of coffee farmers to the Bioko cocoa plantations. Coffee production was an estimated 7,000 tons in 1992. Actual cocoa and coffee production is higher, but official figures do not take into account quantities smuggled abroad rather than delivered to state marketing agencies.

23ANIMAL HUSBANDRY

Cattle and poultry production is rapidly reaching its pre-independence levels of self-sufficiency with the financial help of the African Development Bank. However, production of domesticated animals is hindered by the presence of trypanosomiasis and other tropical deterrents. In 1992 there were 36,000 sheep, 8,000 goats, 5,000 hogs, and 5,000 cattle.

24FISHING

The fishing industry gained strength through the 1980s and is now almost entirely modernized; a tuna processing plant went into operation in 1990; shellfish account for roughly half the catch. Annobón subsists almost entirely on fishing and retains its traditional preeminence in offshore whaling and turtle gathering. Bioko is also a major fishing center, the chief catches being perch, tuna, mackerel, cod, pike, shark, and crayfish. The country's own catch was about 3,500 tons in 1991.

25FORESTRY

Timber from Rio Muni is Equatorial Guinea's leading export. Forests and woodlands cover over 45% of the land area. The Rio Muni area on the mainland produces okoumé and akoga from rainforests of considerable age. Even though the government has given permission to foreign firms, exploitation is difficult due to infrastructural problems. The government enacted a new forestry action plan in 1990 in an effort to strengthen the sector's development. In 1991, roundwood production was estimated at 607,000 m^3. In 1992, timber exports amounted to $18 million (34% of total exports), up from $15 million in 1991 (42% of that year's exports).

26MINING

Geological surveys indicate some uranium, iron, gold, manganese, tantalum, and uranium in Río Muni, but there has been no significant exploitation. A 1981 law stipulates that all mineral deposits are state property.

27ENERGY AND POWER

Installed power capacity in 1991 was 5,000 kw; production totaled 18 million kwh. In 1983, China completed a hydroelectric plant near Bata, with installed capacity of 3,200 kw. The 3.6 MW Riaba River hydroelectric plant opened in 1989. A second hydroelectric facility, funded by the Chinese, is planned for completion in the 1990s.

The first exploratory offshore petroleum well was drilled in early 1982. In 1991, production was initiated from the offshore Alba gas condensate field in the Gulf of Guinea; production is scheduled to increase to 4,000–5,000 barrels per day by the mid-1990s and Equatorial Guinea anticipates revenues of $25 million. Exports of oil began in April 1992.

28INDUSTRY

Equatorial Guinea's manufacturing sector is small, contributing 1.3% of GDP (1989). Two sawmills lead industrial production, followed by cement, bleach, and tuna canning plants. Small-scale soap manufacturing and food processing operations round out the industrial sector.

29SCIENCE AND TECHNOLOGY

Spain, China, the former USSR, and several other countries have provided Equatorial Guinea with technological assistance.

30DOMESTIC TRADE

Most interior wholesale and retail trade has been maintained through *factorías* (small general agencies) managed by individual Spanish owners or the representatives of small firms. Normal business hours are 8 AM to 12 noon and 4 to 6:30 PM, Monday through Friday, and 9 AM to 2 PM on Saturday.

31FOREIGN TRADE

Spain is Equatorial Guinea's principal trading partner. Exports to Spain represent 86.7% of the total. Cocoa and timber represented 93% of total exports in 1985. Major imports were foodstuffs and oil products, with most imports coming from France and Spain.

32BALANCE OF PAYMENTS

Equatorial Guinea depends on international assistance to finance its annual current-accounts deficit. Modest gains in timber and cocoa exports, along with important oil exports are expected to reduce the external account deficit from 23% of GDP in 1992 to 10% in 1995.

In 1991 merchandise exports totaled $35.75 million and imports $59.56 million. The merchandise trade balance was $–23.81 million.

33BANKING AND SECURITIES

The Bank of Issue of Equatorial Guinea was established on 12 October 1969 as the central bank. In January 1985, the country joined the franc zone, and the Bank of the Central African States

(Banque des États de l'Afrique Centrale—BEAC) became its central bank. Other banks are the Bank of Credit and Development and the Foreign Bank of Equatorial Guinea and Spain. In 1993, money in circulation amounted to CFA Fr32.4 billion. There are no securities exchanges.

34INSURANCE
No information is available.

35PUBLIC FINANCE
Equatorial Guinea made its first standby loan agreement with the IMF in 1985 and negotiated a structural adjustment agreement in 1988. Government problems with budget overruns and a continuing, structural imbalance of trade have frustrated IMF technicians, who stopped payments in 1990. Nonetheless, the government reduced the 1990 budget and enacted key portions of the structural adjustment program—import price liberalization, economic diversification, utility rate increases, clarification of property rights, and private sector stimulus. With these steps taken and with petroleum revenues increasing, the IMF restarted the blocked structural adjustment program in December 1991. Since then, the government has continued to work with the IMF on an enhanced structural adjustment agreement and on rescheduling Equatorial Guinea's external debt.

36TAXATION
The primary tax sources are customs duties, real and personal property, personal incomes, and estate levies.

37CUSTOMS AND DUTIES
Equatorial Guinea joined the UDEAC in 1983, allowing goods to move freely to and from its franc-zone neighbors. Nevertheless, customs levies remain the principal source of government income. Goods valued at over CFA Fr50,000 require an import license.

38FOREIGN INVESTMENT
Spain and France are the major aid donor countries working with the Equatorial Guinea government. Spain has recently conditioned aid, however, on improvements in the human rights record and progress in the democratization effort. Other donors include China, Nigeria, and several other Western and Middle Eastern countries.

39ECONOMIC DEVELOPMENT
In the 1990s, in conjunction with Spain, Equatorial Guinea is focusing on education, health, administrative reform, and economic infrastructures.

40SOCIAL DEVELOPMENT
There is little provision for social welfare. The great majority of the population goes without potable water, electricity, basic education, or even minimal health care. Human rights violations are commonplace.

41HEALTH
The national health system of Equatorial Guinea consists of four levels: health posts in each village of 600 people; dispensaries in health centers with a qualified nurse at the intermediate level; district level hospitals; and two referral hospitals at the most centralized level. In 1992, there were 1,026 hospital beds nationwide; of these, 910 were in hospitals, 8 were in health centers, and 108 were in health posts. In addition, 11 observation beds were in dispensaries. In 1990, Equatorial Guinea had 99 physicians as well as 154 nurses and 55 midwives.

There were 16,200 births in 1992 and an infant mortality rate of 118 per 1,000 live births. Life expectancy in 1992 was 48 years, with an overall death rate of 18 per 1,000 people.

Major health problems (1992 data) are preventable diseases, mainly malaria (increasingly chloroquine resistant), parasitic disease, upper respiratory infections, gastroenteritis, and complications of pregnancy. In the continental zone, sickle cell anemia is common. Approximately 66% of the country's children have been immunized against measles.

42HOUSING
No recent information is available.

43EDUCATION
Education is free and compulsory from 6 to 14 years of age. Primary education is for six years followed by four years of secondary in the first stage and two subsequent years of secondary education in the second stage. In 1986, 65,000 pupils attended primary and secondary schools. Literacy in 1990 was estimated at 50.2% (males, 64.1% and females 37.0%).

44LIBRARIES AND MUSEUMS
The Malabo Public Library contains some 17,000 volumes. The Claretian Mission at Malabo has about 4,000 volumes of Africana and Guineana, and an archaeological-ethnographic museum.

45MEDIA
A radiotelephone system connects the manual exchanges of Malabo, Luba, and Bata; it also serves outposts in other major towns and offers connections to the Canary Islands (and thence by cable to Europe). There were about 2,000 telephones in use in the late 1980s. The central radio transmissions from Malabo and Bata are augmented by a television transmitter on Santa Isabel Peak installed in 1968. Equatorial Guinea has three government-owned radio stations broadcasting in Spanish, French, and local languages, including Fang, Bubi, and Combe. There is one television station. There were an estimated 153,000 radios and 3,000 television sets in 1991.

The nation's two newspapers are *Poto Poto* in Bata (in Spanish and Fang) and *Ebano* (Spanish, circulation 1,500) in Malabo.

46ORGANIZATIONS
Apart from official and semiofficial organizations, there are only religious societies and sports clubs.

47TOURISM, TRAVEL, AND RECREATION
Because Equatorial Guinea has undergone many years of international isolation, its tourism industry is very undeveloped, with limited hotel space available in Malabo and Bata. Visitors from all countries require valid passports, visas, and onward tickets. Antimalarial precautions are recommended. Yellow-fever, smallpox, and cholera inoculations are generally required.

48FAMOUS EQUATORIAL GUINEANS
Francisco Macías Nguema (1924–79) was president until his overthrow and execution. His successor, Lt.-Col. Teodoro Obiang Nguema Mbasogo (b.1946), has ruled Equatorial Guinea since 1979.

49DEPENDENCIES
Equatorial Guinea has no territories or colonies.

50BIBLIOGRAPHY
Fegley, Randall. *Equatorial Guinea*. Santa Barbara, Calif.: Clio, 1991.
Liniger-Goumaz, Max. *Historical Dictionary of Equatorial Guinea*. 2d ed. Metuchen, N.J.: Scarecrow Press, 1988.
Sundiata, I. K. *Equatorial Guinea: Colonialism, State Terror, and the Search for Stability*. Boulder, Colo.: Westview Press, 1990.

ERITREA

State of Eritrea

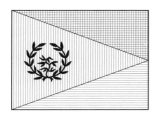

CAPITAL: Asmara (Asmera)

FLAG: A red triangle divides the flag into two right triangles; the upper triangle is green, the lower one is blue. A gold wreath encircling a gold olive branch is centered on the hoist side of the red triangle.

ANTHEM: *Eritrea National Anthem* beginning "Eritrea, Eritrea, Eritrea."

MONETARY UNIT: The birr is the official currency of Eritrea. One birr = US$0.20 as of fall 1994, but the exchange rate is expected to fluctuate.

WEIGHTS AND MEASURES: The metric system is used.

HOLIDAYS: New Year's Day, 1 January; Independence Day, 24 May; Martyrs' Day, 20 June; Anniversary of the Start of the Armed Struggle, 1 September. Movable holidays include 'Id al-Fitr, 'Id al-Adha, and 'Id Milad al-Nabi. Movable Orthodox Christian holidays include Fasika and Meskel.

TIME: 3 PM = noon GMT.

1 LOCATION, SIZE, AND EXTENT

Eritrea is located in eastern Africa. The area occupied by Eritrea is slightly larger than the state of Pennsylvania with a total area of 121,320 sq km (46,842 sq mi). Eritrea shares boundaries with the Red Sea on the NE, Djibouti on the SE, Ethiopia on the S, and Sudan on the W, and has a total boundary length of 2,781 km (1,728 mi).

2 TOPOGRAPHY

The topography of Eritrea is dominated by the extension of the Ethiopian north-south trending highlands, descending on the east to a coastal desert plain and on the northeast to hills and on the southwest to flat-to-rolling plains. Approximately 3% of the land is arable. Natural resources include gold, potash, zinc, copper, salt, and fish. Frequent droughts, soil erosion, deforestation, and overgrazing all present environmental challenges.

3 CLIMATE

Highs of 60°C (140°F) are not uncommon in the Danakil Depression in Eritrea's southernmost province, Denkalia. This is reportedly the hottest spot in the world. It is cooler and wetter in the central highlands. The western hills and lowlands are semi-arid. Heavy rainfall occurs during June, July, and August, except in the coastal desert.

4 FLORA AND FAUNA

Although the giraffe and babboon are extinct in Eritrea, there are populations of lion, leopard, zebra, species of monkey, gazelle, antelope, and elephant. The coastal areas are home to many species of turtle, lobster, and shrimp. Plant life includes acacia, cactus, aloe vera, prickly pear, and olive trees.

5 ENVIRONMENT

No information is available.

6 POPULATION

The population of Eritrea was 2,621,566 in 1984. Asmara, the capital, had a population of 275,385 according to non-governmental statistics, but the government of Eritrea reported the population of Asmara at 400,000. Non-governmental estimates of the total population in 1992 were 2,650,000 or 2,700,000, excluding refugees abroad; however, the government of Eritrea reported 3.5 million. Estimates of average population density ranges from about 22–28 per sq km (58–73 per sq mi).

7 MIGRATION

There were believed to be about 750,000 Eritrean refugees, or 20–30% of the total population, abroad in early 1994. Of these, 430,000 were in the Sudan and the rest principally in Ethiopia, Somalia, and Djibouti. Since 1989, some refugess have been returning to Eritrea. The Government of Eritrea had established a Commission for Eritrean Refugee Affairs (CERA) that has worked with the UN to develop a plan for repatriation and reintegration of refugees.

The Programme for Refugee Reintegration and Rehabilitation of Resettlement Areas in Eritrea (PROFERI) was finalized in June 1993. In three phases, PROFERI expects to repatriate 430,000 Eritrean refugees. PROFERI is designed to operate from 1 July 1993–31 January 1997. Its budget is reportedly US$262 billion, which will be raised through support of the international community. The refugees are 53.5% female, and 46.5% male, and 52% are under 15 years of age, with about 40% between 16 and 50 years of age. The average refugee family has 3.4 members. About 20% of the refugees were originally from urban areas, and another 54% were formerly farmers.

8 ETHNIC GROUPS

Ethnologists classify Eritreans into nine language groups. The Afar live in the southeast, the Tigrinya in south central Eritrea, and the Tigre in the north. The Saho live in the couth central/southeast. The Bilen live in central Eritrea, the Hadareb in the northwest, and the Kunama and Nara in the southwest. The ninth group, the Rashaida, inhabit the nothwest. The Tigrinya, Tigre, and Afar are believed to be the most populous ethnic groups.

9 LANGUAGES

No official language has been proclaimed. Arabic and Tigrinya are the working languages of the Eritrean government. Tigre is also widely spoken in the western lowlands, on the northern coas,t and in parts of the Sahel.

10 RELIGIONS

The population of Eritrea is equally divided between Christians and Muslims, and both Christian and Muslim holidays are observed. The Christian population is Orthodox Christian. A small percentage of the population practices animism.

11 TRANSPORTATION

The infrastructure suffered some damage during the war for independence with Ethiopia. Massawa, the principal port, serves Eritrea and northern Ethiopia. The port, which has a 7-m (24-ft) channel and pier facilities capable of accommodating five or six large vessels, was damaged by bombing raids from February 1990 to May 1991. In early 1992, agreements were concluded between the Eritrean and Ethiopean governments to make Assab a free port for Ethiopia, and Ethiopia will be dependent on Eritrean ports for its foreign trade. Assab has an oil refinery and facilities capable of handling more than one million tons of goods annually. A railway, which was almost completely destroyed during the war, once extended 308 km (191 mi) from Massawa on the Red Sea to Asmara, terminating near the Sudanese border. Reconstruction work on this railway starting from Massawa began in summer 1994. The airport at Asmara handles international jet transportation. Repair of the railroad and highway network is necessary for the revival of agriculture and industry. The government of Eritrea has established a budget for transport rehabilitation, two-thirds of which is allocated for road repair to ensure that all parts of the country have access to modern roads.

12 HISTORY

Turks, Egyptians, Italians, British, and Ethiopians have all colonized Eritrea over the years. In the modern scramble for Africa, Italy had occupied Eritrea since 1889. Sustained resistance to Italian rule developed into a unified sense of Eritrean nationalism among the various ethnic groups in the country. In April, 1941, British Commonwealth forces captured Eritrea from its Italian colonizers. With its defeat in World War II, Italy relinquished its legal right to its colonies in a 1947 treaty. The four main Allied powers (US, France, UK and USSR) agreed to try to dispose of the former Italian colonies through negotiation. If unsuccessful, they were to submit the matter to the UN General Assembly. Eritrea proved difficult. Ethiopian Emperor Haile Selassie was interested in acquiring it. US strategic interests in the Red Sea and US ties to Selassie led logically to US pressure to have Ethiopia administer Eritrea, under "the Sovereignty of the Ethiopian Crown." Ultimately, the US prevailed.

After a decade of British rule that began during World War II, Eritrea was federated with neighboring Ethiopia in 1952, following a vote in the UN. The US had lobbied for this decision. The Four Power Commission and the UN sent teams to Eritrea to estimate popular opinion based on meeting with various local leaders. These meetings provided support for the decision to federate Eritrea with Ethiopia; there was no popular vote or referendum. From 1952 until 1962, Ethiopia began to impose more direct rule. Eritrean protests were ignored by the UN.

Ethiopia formally annexed Eritrea in 1962. A year earlier, in September 1961, the Eritrean Liberation Front (ELF) launched the armed struggle for independence. By 1970, when the Eritrean People's Liberation Front (EPLF) was created, Eritrea had become Selassie's preoccupation. After Selassie was overthrown in 1974, the self-styled Marxist military dictatorship in Addis Ababa stepped up its campaign against Eritreans. "The Eritrean Problem" led the Dergue to vow "to liquidate the secessionist rebels."

The bitter war dragged on. At no time did the Eritrean forces number more than 100,000. Toward the end of the war, the Ethiopian Dergue government had one million troops under arms, a quarter of them in Eritrea. The Dergue also had used $12 billion in military supplies, training, and advisers from the Soviet Union and its bloc. In 30 years of war, more than 60,000 Eritrean fighters and 40,000 civilians were killed, and hundreds of thousands were forced into exile.

Between 1978 and 1981, the Eritrean People's Liberation Front (EPLF) fought and defeated the Eritrean Liberation Front (ELF) in a civil war marked by high EPLF morale, brilliant improvisation, and execution. The EPLF also proved adept at feeding and training its large army, servicing sophisticated military material—most of it captured from the Ethiopians—and in administering a government in liberated territories and developing social reforms in education, health and land reform. From 1981 until the end of the war in 1991, the EPLF continued to fight for Eritrean self-determination. The EPLF represented a united front, but included people with very diverse political views who shared the common goal of obtaining the right of self-determination for Eritreans. At the EPLF's Congress in 1987, they removed most of the Marxist rhetoric from their programs. EPLF also committed itself to greater democratization within its own organization.

In May 1991, the EPLF captured the last Ethiopian outposts in Eritrea; however, it made no attempt and had no desire to take over the Ethiopian government. President Mengistu Haile Mariam fled Addis Ababa and the Tigrean People's Liberation Front (TPLF) which had also been fighting against the Dergue since 1975 took over the Ethiopian government.

The EPLF occupied Asmara, Eritrea's capital, and created a provisional government for Eritrea, which functioned as an autonomous region until May 1993. Although Eritrea had been absorbed into the Ethiopian state in 1962, Eritreans did not regard their struggle as one of secession. They never recognized Ethiopian legitimacy over their territory; rather, they viewed their struggle as an anticolonial one, merely seeking to gain the independence that had been denied them by the UN in 1952.

From 1–5 July 1991, a major conference was held in Addis Ababa, where the EPLF and the transitional Ethiopian government issued a charter with a framework for the principles of self-determination, democracy, and mutual accommodation. A referendum on the question of independence was scheduled for April 1993.

During the peiod between the end of the war in May 1991 and the celebration of Independence Day in May 1993, the EPLF Central Committee was the National Assembly and the APLF formed a provisional government to run the country. The provisional government organized elections at the village, district, and provincial level throughout the country. In May 1991, a National Assembly was formed, including the EPLF Central Committee members; the chairman, secretary and one female member of each of the ten provincial councils; ten additional women (nominated by the National Union of Eritrean Women); and twenty others (prominent individuals who were not EPLF members, including former ELF leaders). The National Assembly then elected Isaias Afwerki president of the Provisional Government.

On 23–25 April 1993, 98.5% of the 1,173,000 registered voters voted in a referendum on independence from Ethiopia. The "yes" and "no" ballots were of different colors on one side to separate the votes. Approximately 80% of the population is illiterate, and the colors were used to assist those who could not read. The reverse of the ballot was a single color, and voters were instructed to detach the side that represented their choice and to fold the ballot in half before depositing it in the ballot box. The polling stations were set up with separate booths so that voters could make their choice and fold the ballot in privacy. However, the use of color-coded ballots prompted a few to argue that the principle of secret ballot was ignored. Nevertheless, the UN certified the results and on 24 May 1993, Eritrea became Africa's 52nd

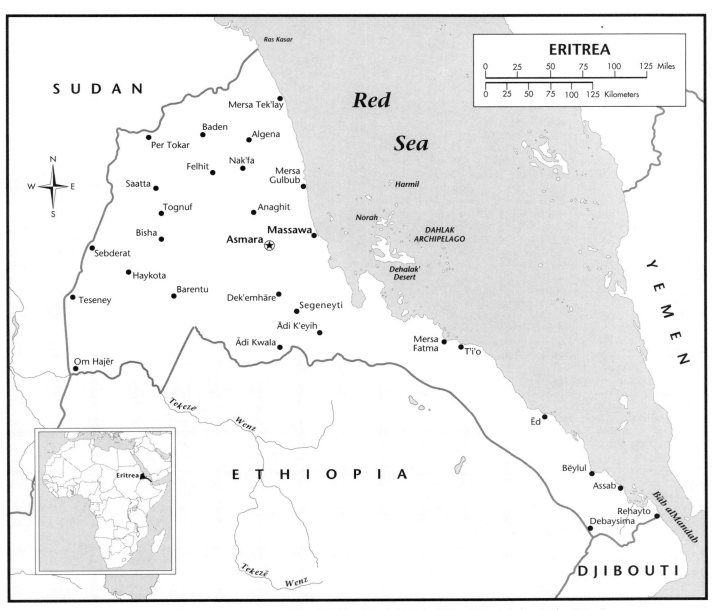

LOCATION: 15°N; 39°E. **BOUNDARY LENGTHS:** Djibouti, 113 km (70 mi); Ethiopia, 912 km (566 mi); Sudan, 605 km (375 mi); coastline, 1,151 km (715 mi); land and island coastline, 2,234 km (1,388 mi). **TERRITORIAL SEA LIMIT:** 12 mi.

independent state and four days later it was admitted to the UN and the OAU.

Relations with the new Ethiopian government remain good. The Eritrean ports of Assab and Masawa are duty-free ports for Ethiopian goods. A Joint High Ministerial Commission meets regularly and Afewarki and President Meles Zenawi have good personal ties. Links with the Sudan, however, are fraying. During the war against the Dergue, EPLF maintained bases in the Sudan. In 1994, clashes sprang up on the border between Eritrean troops and the Jihad, a group created by the Sudanese National Islamic Front and that had tried to infiltrate into Eritrea.

13 GOVERNMENT

After the defeat of the Dergue government, Eritrea functioned as a distinct political unit. Its provisional government was comprised of a 28-member executive council. After the formal acquisition of sovereignty, an interim administration was created to govern for four years.

Upon official independence, a National Assembly was formed, consisting of the Central Committee of the EPLF and 60 other individuals. Ten seats are reserved for women. The Assembly elected Isaias Afwerki president. He also serves as commander-in-chief of the armed forces and chairs the executive branch, the State Council, whose members he nominates. The National Assembly so far has ratified all of his nominations. It also began the process of drafting a constitution by setting up a constitution committee to study and debate the alternatives.

At its February 1994 Congress, the EPLF was reformed as the People's Front for Democracy and Justice (PFDJ). The PFDJ elected an Executive Council of 75 members, and called on the government to increase the number of non-PFDJ members in the National Assembly to 75.

The Constitutional Commission, appointed by the National Assembly in March 1994, has a two-year mandate (until March 1996) to develop a draft constitution. This process will include addressing the issues of political parties, and laws to govern their operation. The new constitution will then be submitted for ratification, and political parties will form and election will be held for a new government. At the time of independence, the Ntaional Assembly set a deadline of May 1998 for election of a new government.

14POLITICAL PARTIES

The Eritrean Liberation Front (ELF) launched the modern phase of Eritrea's war of self-determination in September 1961. In 1970, the Eritrean People's Liberation Front (EPLF) joined the war against Ethiopia. Both the ELF and the EPLF were mixed Muslim-Christian groups. The two groups differed in the way they dealt with religious, ethnic, and regional differences inside their organizations. For example, the ELF organized itself into relatively autonomous separate units by regional, and therefore typically religious and ethnic, divisions. The EPLF organization was comprised of units of mixed religious, ethnic, and regional composition. By 1977, the two parties controlled most of the countryside. But in 1978, they fought against one another and by 1981 the EPLF had prevailed. From 1981 to 1991, only the EPLF was operating in Eritrea.

One of the issues still unsettled is the nature and role of political parties. The President has opposed the creation of parties based on race, religion, region, or ethnicity. A split between Christian and Muslim-based parties would be disastrous because about half of the Eritreans are Sunni Muslim and the rest belong mainly to the Eritrean Orthodox Church, along with substantial numbers of Roman Catholics, Protestants and animists. But a multiparty system seems likely.

After the ELF's defeat in 1981, its leadership broke up into more than a dozen different factions. Some ELF members joined the EPLF; others fled to Sudan as refugees. After the end of the war in 1991, most of the former ELF leaders returned to Eritrea, to accept positions in the government or to become active in private business.

At its third Congress on 10–17 February 1994, the EPLF adopted a new name, the People's Front for Democracy and Justice (PFDJ) and committed themselves to widening their popular appeal beyond their predominantly Christian roots. Its 18-member Executive Committee includes only three former EPLF Executive Committee members and is chaired by the president.

15LOCAL GOVERNMENT

Since independence, the transitional government has developed a decentralized system of government with 10 semi-autonomous provinces. Elected committees and councils operate in villages. During the years since independence in 1991, Eritreans have been participating in a continuing process of electing governing councils for their villages, districts, and provinces. In areas which had been under control of the EPLF, residents are familiar with election procedures. In other areas formerly controlled by the Durgue, citizens had little experience with democratic elections. During the four-year reorganization of the government begun in 1993, every citizen will have the opportunity to participate in elections at local and national levels.

16JUDICIAL SYSTEM

The court system consists of courts of first instance, courts of appeals composed of 5 judges, and military courts which handle crimes committed by members of the military. The legal system is a civil law system, a borrowed version of Ethiopia's adaptation of the Napoleonic Code. Traditional courts play a major role in rural areas, where village elders determine property and family disputes under customary law or in the case of Muslims, the Koran.

Although the judiciary appears to function independently of the executive branch, it suffers from lack of resources and training.

Work on a new constitution began in spring 1994, and it may bring change to some aspects of the current judicial system.

17ARMED FORCES

During the struggle for independence, it is estimated that 3% of the total population was participating in the army. The process to demobilize about 50–60% of the army began in July 1993. The first phase was completed, demobilizing about 26,000 combatants, representing a reported 24% of the army. During the second phase of demobilization which began in spring 1994, another 21,000 fighters will be demobilized. Upon release from the army, demobilized troops receive food rations, a lump sum end-of-service payment, and assistance in finding employment or in starting a business. Of those demobilized during the second phase, about 4,000 will be employed in the civil service.

18INTERNATIONAL COOPERATION

Eritrea won its independence from Ethiopia 24 May 1993 and joined the UN later that year. Eritrea is a member of the Organization of African Unity (OAU) and the UN. It is also a member of the Horn of Africa regional organization known as AGADD (Inter-Governmental Authority of Drought and Development) and the East African regional organizations known as the PTA (Preferential Trade Agreement) and COMESA (Common Market of Eastern and Southern Africa). The country is in the process of establishing diplomatic relations with other nations of the world.

19ECONOMY

The Eritrean economy has yet to take form after years of armed struggle against the Ethiopian government. The population is still largely dependent on food aid. Agriculture and raising of livestock takes place throughout the country, in both the highlands and lowlands. Long term prospects for agricultural development appear to be strongest for in the western lowlands.

The natural resource profile of Eritrea is not yet known with certainty. Known mineral resources include copper, zinc, lead, gold, silver, marble, granite, barite, feldspar, kaolin, talc asbestos, salt, gypsum and potash.

The military regime which ruled Ethiopia from 1874 to 1991 nationalized all housing and all large and medium sized businesses and services, including banks, in Eritrea. The post-independence government has denationalized housing, and is committed to denationalization of business and services.

20INCOME

In 1992 Eritrea's GDP was $120–150 per capita. In 1992 the GDP was $544 million.

21LABOR

Agriculture is the most important sector and engages an estimated 80% of the population. Unemployment is expected to increase, as an estimated 500,000 refugees return from Sudan.

22AGRICULTURE

Three-quarters of Eritrea's people are subsistence farmers dependent on unreliable rainfall to feed families which average seven children. Although these farmers have experienced relative peace and good harvests since May 1991, food production has not been able to keep pace with a rapidly expanding population. Harvests have been variable due to rainfall variations and pest infestations. The present government dissolved the former Ethiopian military regime's marketing board and reinstituted private markets for agricultural products. However, as of late 1994, food distribution was not proceeding smoothly. Principal crops include sorghum, wheat, barley, teff, millet, legumes, vegetables, fruits, sesame, and linseed. War, drought, deforestation, and erosion have caused about 70–80% of the population to be dependent on food aid. In

1994, 280,000 tons of food were needed. Agricultural output, however, is reported to have increased slightly since 1991, due to the ending of the war, favorable weather, and a newly developed seed and fertilizer distribution system. The army is involved in agricultural restoration, evidence of the government's commitment to agricultural reform.

²³ANIMAL HUSBANDRY

Cattle (especially zebu), sheep, goats, and camels make up the majority of Eritrea's livestock. The government is emphasizing development of agriculture and animal husbandry are being emphasized by the government in order to decrease the reliance on international relief, caused by war and drought.

²⁴FISHING

With Eritrea's independence from Ethiopia, access to about 1,011 km (628 mi) of Red Sea coastline was obtained, making Ethiopia a landlocked nation. Because Eritrea now controls the coastline, long-term prospects for development of offshore fishing and oil are good. Since the end of the war, the Eritrean navy has begun patrolling Eritrea's coastal waters to limit poaching by unauthorized non-nationals. The development of local fishing will decrease the dependence on foreign food aid, even though fish has not been a major source of Eritreans' protein intake.

²⁵FORESTRY

As of late 1993, the Eritrean People's Liberation Front army was involved in tree planting; deforestation has long been a significant problem.

²⁶MINING

Marine salt is produced at Massawa and Assab. Mineral resources include copper, zinc, lead, gold, silver, marble, granite, barite, feldspar, kaolin, talc, asbestos, and potassium.

²⁷ENERGY AND POWER

The government is currently constructing additional electrical distribution lines. There is a petroleum refinery at Assab. Operations were shut down during the civil war, but have resumed based on an agreement between the Eritrean and Ethiopian governments. Production will be distributed to both countries, with service charges paid by Ethiopia. The refinery produced 3.3 million barrels of refined petroleum products in 1991. Natural gas was discovered in the Red Sea in 1969, but no commercially exploitable finds have been developed.

²⁸INDUSTRY

Ethiopia systematically dismantled the Eritrean industrial sector during the protracted civil war. The government of Eritrea is currently managing industries previously owned by the Mengistu regime. Most of these industries, including commercial agriculture, will require significant innvestment to achieve productivity. The government is seeking privatization of these industries, and has issued incentives such as exemptions from income tax, preferential treament in allocation of foreign exchange for imports, and provisions for remittance of foreign exchange abroad.

²⁹SCIENCE AND TECHNOLOGY

No information is available.

³⁰DOMESTIC TRADE

No information is available.

³¹FOREIGN TRADE

Because Eritrea now controls the total coastline that was formerly Ethiopia, long-term prospects for development of offshore fishing and oil are good. Main exports are raw materials, especially salt,

beverages, tobacco, food, and manufactured goods. Imports are mainly manufactured goods, food, and chemicals.

³²BALANCE OF PAYMENTS

No information is available.

³³BANKING AND SECURITIES

After the end of the war in 1991, the Bank of Eritrea (central bank) and the Commercial Bank of Eritrea were re-established, having been nationalized by the Ethiopian military junta in 1984. As of late 1994, Eritrea was in the process of establishing the Development Bank of Eritrea and a Housing and Savings Bank.

³⁴INSURANCE

The National Insurance Corporation of Eritrea was established after the end of the war. It engages in all classes of insurance except life insurance, and was the only insurance provide operating in Eritrea as of late 1994.

³⁵PUBLIC FINANCE

After independence, the state retained control over land, mineral resources, and infrastructure. Massive infusions of foreign aid and investment are needed to restore the infrastructure and services and to develop private sector growth. Membership into the IBRD and IMF were to have been approved in 1994.

³⁶TAXATION

Customs duty and import and export taxes are 33.6% of government revenue; direct domestic tax (business and personal income taxes) are 27.8% of government revenue; domestic sales tax and taxes on services are 26.1% of government revenue.

³⁷CUSTOMS AND DUTIES

Customs and duties vary depending upon the type of goods.

³⁸FOREIGN INVESTMENT

Investment in Eritrea has come primarily from contributions of Eritrean exiles. Foreign agency donations have amounted to some $140 million in the year ending June 1993. International aid was restricted by the lack of international recognition of the Eritrean government's sovereignty, a problem resolved in the UN in April 1993. The government issued an investment code in December 1991 to encourage investment in the Eritrean economy. Incentives for investments in certain areas include exemption from customs and duties, exemptions from income tax, and special treatment regarding foreign currency exchange.

³⁹ECONOMIC DEVELOPMENT

The development priorities of the Eritrean government are food security, the development of a market-style economy, and the privatization of formerly nationalized enterprises. Encouraging the return of Eritrean exiles abroad is also a government goal in the reconstruction effort. The Emergency and Recovery Action Program was launched in late 1991 to focus of recovery of the transportation system (roads, railroads, and port and airport facilities), agriculture (including reliable water sources), and industry.

⁴⁰SOCIAL DEVELOPMENT

During its struggle for independence, the EPLF created an elaborate and amazingly effective system of social services. It launched a literacy program, a health care system (including hospitals), and a food distribution network. Government estimates report that there is one doctor for every 28,000 people; other estimates are as high as one doctor for every 48,000 people. Adult literacy is 20%, with literacy for females estimated to be 10–15%. PFDJ stresses women's rights, especially important since women made up one-third of its members.

ELF supporters complain of human rights violations and perceived government resistance to the return to Eritrea of up to 500,000 refugees, about half of whom are Muslim, in the Sudan.

Because tens of thousands of refugees remain homeless when they return to Eritrea, the government has allocated a significant budget for construction of housing, schools, and clinics.

41HEALTH

The 1992 births in Eritrea totaled 140,000 (47 per 1,000 people). Infant mortality was estimated to be 135 per 1,000 live births, and the mortality rate for children under five was 203 per 1,000. From 1974 to 1991, Eritrea was at war with Ethiopia, with no figures on war-related deaths available at the time of publication. Average life expectancy in 1992 was 46 years. According to estimates by non-government sources, there is one doctor for every 48,000 Eritreans, and one nurse for every 1,750; however, the government estimates that there is one doctor for every 28,000 people, and one hospital bend for every 8,400 people.

42HOUSING

Returning refugees are experiencing a severe housing shortage. Thousands remain homeless aftern returning to Eritrea, and the government has placed a high priority on providing funding for housing construction.

43EDUCATION

The adult literacy rate is estimated to be 20%, with literacy for females lagging behind at 10–15%. In 1994, primary school enrollment was reported to be 42% of school-age children, with 68 pupils per textbook, and 37 pupils per teacher.

44LIBRARIES AND MUSEUMS

Asmara, the capital, has a city library and a library operated by the British Council. As of 1994, the US Information Agency planned to rehabilitate and reopen its library is Asmara. There is a National Museum in Asmara, located in the former palace, with exhibits on military history, art, and cultures.

45MEDIA

Television broadcasts are Monday, Wednesday, and Saturday evenings in Tigrinya and Arabic languages. *Dimtsi Hafash* radio broadcasts daily in various local languages. The bi-weekly newspaper, *Hadas Eritrea*, appears on Wednesday and Saturday in both a Tigrinya and an Arabic edition. An eight-page weekly newspaper, *Eritrea Profile*, is published on Saturday.

46ORGANIZATIONS

There are various religious humanitarian groups (Christian and Muslim), sports clubs, and art groups centering around music, theater, painting, and drawing. Professional organizations are operating, such as the Teachers Union, Association of Eritreans in Agricultural Sciences, Eritrean Nurses Association, Eritrean Pharmacists Association, and the Eritrean Medical Association. There is an Association of War Disabled Veteres. Various trade unions formed the National Confederation of Eritrean Workers in September 1994. There are National Unions of Eritrea Women and Eritrean Students and Youth, with branches throughout the country. Planned Parenthood Association, the Red Cross Society, a

Chamber of Commerce, and a Regional Centre for Human Rights and Development all operate in Eritrea.

47TOURISM, TRAVEL, AND RECREATION

Because Eritrea inherited the entire coastline of Ethiopia, there is long-term potential for development of tourism.

48FAMOUS ERITREANS

Isaias Afwarki has been president of Eritrea since its independence from Ethiopia 24 May 1993.

49DEPENDENCIES

Eritrea has no territories or colonies.

50BIBLIOGRAPHY

Abeba Tesfagiorgis. *A Painful Season and a Stubborn Hope.* Trenton, N.J.: Red Sea Press, 1992.

Birth of a Nation. Asmara, Eritrea: Government of Eritrea, 1993.

Cliffe, Lionel and Basil Davidson (eds.). *The Long Struggle of Eritrea for Independence and Constructive Peace.* Trenton, N.J.: Red Sea Press, 1988.

Connell, Dan. *Against All Odds.* Trenton, N.J.: Red Sea Press, 1993.

Doombos, Martin, et al., eds. *Beyond the Conflict in the Horn.* Trenton, N.J.: Red Sea Press, 1992.

Erlikh, Hagai. *Ethiopia and Eritrea During the Scramble for Africa: a Political Biography of Ras Alula, 1875–1897.* East Lansing, Mich.: African Studies Center, Michigan State University, 1982.

Farer, Tom J. *War Clouds on the Horn of Africa: the Widening Storm.* New York: Carnegie Endowment for International Peace, 1979.

Ghebre-ab, Habtu. *Ethiopia and Eritrea: A Documentary Study.* Trenton, N.J.: Red Sea Press, 1993.

Habte Selassie, Bereket. *Conflict and Intervention in the Horn of Africa.* New York: Montly Review Press, 1980.

Longrigg, Stephen Hemsley. *A Short History of Eritrea.* Westport, Conn.: Greenwood Press, 1974.

Nzongola-Ntalaja, Georges, ed. *Conflict in the Horn of Africa.* Atlanta: African Studies Association, 1991.

Okbazghi, Yohannes. *Eritrea: a Pawn in World Politics.* Gainesville: University of Florida Press, 1991.

Pankhurst, E. Sylvia. *Eritrea on the Eve.* London: Woodford Green, 1952.

Prouty, Chris. *Historical Dictionary of Ethiopia and Eritrea.* 2d ed. Metuchen, N.J.: Scarecrow Press, 1993.

Tesfagiorgis, Gebrehiwet, ed. *Emergent Eritrea: Challenges of Economic Development.* Washington, D.C.: Eritreans for Peace and Democracy (EPD), 1993.

Trevaskis, G. K. N. *Eritrea: A Colony in Transition: 1941–52.* New York: Oxford University Press, 1960.

Ullendorff, Edward. *The Two Zions.* New York: Oxford University Press, 1988.

Wilson, Amrit. *The Challeng Road: Women and the Eritrean Revolution.* Trenton, N.J.: Red Sea Press, 1991.

Yohannes, Okbazghi. *Eritrea: A Pawn in World Politics.* Gainesville: University of Florida Press, 1991.

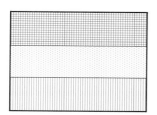

ETHIOPIA

People's Democratic Republic of Ethiopia

CAPITAL: Addis Ababa.

FLAG: The national flag is a tricolor of green, yellow, and red horizontal stripes.

ANTHEM: Traditional "Ityopia, Ityopia" is in use at the present time. A new anthem will be designated in the near future.

MONETARY UNIT: The birr (B) is a paper currency of 100 cents. There are coins of 1, 5, 10, 25, and 50 cents, and notes of 1, 5, 10, 50, and 100 birr. B1 = $0.2000 (or $1 = B5.00).

WEIGHTS AND MEASURES: The metric system is used, but some local weights and measures are also employed.

HOLIDAYS: Holidays generally follow the Old Style Coptic Church calendar. National holidays include Christmas, 7 January; Epiphany, 19 January; Victory of Adwa (1896), 2 March; Victory Day, 6 April; May Day, 1 May; New Year's Day, 11 September; Feast of the Holy Cross, 27 September. Movable Muslim holidays include 'Id al-Fitr and 'Id al-'Adha'.

TIME: 3 PM = noon GMT.

¹LOCATION, SIZE, AND EXTENT

Situated in eastern Africa, Ethiopia (formerly called Abyssinia) has an area of approximately 1,127,127 sq km (435,186 sq mi), with a length of 1,639 km (1,018 mi) E–W and a width of 1,577 km (980 mi) N–S. Comparatively, the area occupied by Ethiopia is slightly less than twice the size of the state of Texas. It is bounded on the N by Eritrea, on the NE by Djibouti, on the E and SE by Somalia, on the S by Kenya, and on the W by Sudan, with a total boundary length of 5,311 km (3,300 mi). The Ogaden region of eastern Ethiopia is claimed by Somalia and has been the subject of sporadic military conflict between the two nations since 1961; the southeastern boundary has never been demarcated. Ethiopia's capital city, Addis Ababa, is located near the center of the country.

²TOPOGRAPHY

Ethiopia contains a variety of distinct topographical zones. It is a country of geographical contrasts, varying from as much as 116 m (381 ft) below sea level in the Danakil depression to more than 4,600 m (15,000 ft) above in the mountainous regions. Ras Dashen, with an altitude of 4,617 m (15,148 ft), is the fourth-highest peak in Africa. The most distinctive feature is the northern part of the Great Rift Valley, which runs through the entire length of the country in a northeast-southwest direction, at a general elevation of 1,500 to 3,000 m (4,900–9,800 ft). Immediately to the west is the High Plateau region; this rugged tableland is marked by mountain ranges. East of the Great Rift Valley is the Somali Plateau—arid and rocky semidesert, extending to the Ogaden, which covers the entire southeastern section of the country. In the north, the Denakil Desert reaches to the Red Sea and the coastal foothills of Eritrea. The western boundary of Ethiopia follows roughly the western escarpment of the High Plateau, although in some regions the Sudan plains extend into Ethiopian territory. Also part of Ethiopia is the Dahlak Archipelago in the Red Sea.

Ethiopia's largest lake, Lake T'ana, is the source of the Blue Nile River. This river, which winds around in a great arc before merging with the White Nile in the Sudan, travels through great canyons, which reach depths of more than 1,200 m (4,000 ft). Several rivers in the southwest also make up a system of tributaries to the White Nile.

³CLIMATE

Ethiopian climate varies according to the different topographical regions. The central plateau has a moderate climate with minimal seasonal temperature variation. The mean minimum during the coldest season is 6°C (43°F), while the mean maximum rarely exceeds 26°C (79°F). Temperature variations in the lowlands are much greater, and the heat in the desert and Red Sea coastal areas is extreme, with occasional highs of 60°C (140°F). Heavy rainfall occurs in most of the country during June, July, and August. The High Plateau also experiences a second, though much milder, rainy season between December and February. Average annual precipitation on the central plateau is roughly 122 cm (48 in). The northern provinces receive less rainfall, and the average annual precipitation in the Ogaden is less than 10 cm (4 in). The westernmost region of Ethiopia receives an annual rainfall of nearly 200 cm (80 in). Severe droughts affected the country in 1982–84,1987–88, and 1991.

⁴FLORA AND FAUNA

Ethiopia has a large variety of indigenous plant and animal species. In some areas, the mountains are covered with shrubs such as pyracantha, jasmine, poinsettia, and a varied assortment of evergreens. Caraway, carcade, cardamom, chat, coriander, incense, myrrh, and red pepper are common. The lakes in the Great Rift Valley region abound with numerous species of birds, and wild animals are found in every region. Among the latter are the lion, civet and serval cats, elephant, bush pig, gazelle, antelope, ibex, kudu, dik-dik, oribi, reed buck, wild ass, zebra, hyena, baboon, and numerous species of monkey.

5ENVIRONMENT

Overgrazing, deforestation, and poor agricultural practices have contributed to soil erosion so severe, particularly in the Tigray and Eritrea regions, that substantial areas of farmland have been lost to cultivation. As of 1994, 600,000 acres of arable land are washed away each year. The combined effects of severe drought and a 17-year civil war have also added to Ethiopia's environmental problems. In 1991, the drought and resulting famine affected 8.7 million people. Ethiopia's forests are also endangered. Each year, the nation loses 340 square miles of forest land. The government did not begin afforestation and soil conservation programs until the early 1970s. Agencies responsible for environmental matters include the Ministry of Agriculture, the Forestry and Wildlife Development Authority, and the Ministry of National Water Resources. The nation's water supply is also at risk. Eighty-nine percent of people living in rural areas and 20% of all urban dwellers have impure water. Ethiopia has 26.4 cubic miles of water with 86% used in agriculture. The nation's cities produce 1.3 million tons of solid waste per year.

The damage to Ethiopia's natural environment has created problems for plants and animals. In 1994, twenty-five of Ethiopia's 265 mammal species are threatened. Of 836 bird species, 14 are endangered. One type of reptile in a total of six species and 44 plants in a total of 6,283 are also threatened with extinction. Endangered species in Ethiopia include the simian fox, African wild ass, Tora hartebeest, Swayne's hartebeest, Waliaibex (found only in Ethiopia), waldrapp, green sea turtle, and hawksbill turtle.

6POPULATION

The 1984 census put the population at 42,169,203; the population (including the population of recently independent Eritrea) was estimated at 58,359,664 in 1994. A population of 67,173,000 was projected for the year 2000, assuming a crude birthrate of 45.8 per 1,000 population, a crude death rate of 16.6, and a net natural increase of 29.2 during 1995–2000. The average population density in 1994 was 47.8 per sq km (123.7 per sq mi). The area of greatest density is the High Plateau, with more than 70% of the population.

About 12% of the people lived in urban areas in 1990. The population of Addis Ababa, the capital and chief city, was estimated at 1,808,000 in 1990. Other urban centers include Dire Dawa, Dese, Harer, Jima, Nazret, and Gonder.

7MIGRATION

Somalia has more than 1 million refugees from Ethiopia of Somali ethnic background. As of 1990, some 586,000 were in refugee camps. At the end of 1992 Ethiopia was harboring 406,100 Somali refugees. About 135,000 Ethiopians left Eritrea in 1991 when a new separatist government took power. There were 25,600 Sudanese refugees in Ethiopia.

Internal migration is from rural to urban areas. By 1982, up to 4.5 million people had been displaced as a result of occasional drought, past civil strife, and border fighting. In 1984–85, over 600,000 northern peasants were resettled, forcibly if necessary, in 77 sites in the more fertile west and south. Meanwhile, over 2.8 million rural inhabitants, mostly Oromo, were moved to collective villages. As the war for control of Ethiopia intensified between 1989 and 1991, more people were displaced.

8ETHNIC GROUPS

Ethiopia is a composite of more than 70 ethnic groups. The Amhara-Tigray group constitutes approximately 45% of the population and has traditionally been dominant politically. The Oromo (Galla) group represents approximately 40% of the population and is concentrated primarily in the southern half of the nation. The Shangalla make up about 6% of the population and reside on the western frontier. The Danakil (Afar) and Somali inhabit the arid regions of the east and southeast. Nilotic peoples live in the west and southwest along the Sudan border. The Falasha (who call themselves Beta Israel, and are popularly known as "black Jews") live in the mountains of Simen; they were reportedly the victims of economic discrimination before the 1974 revolution and of religious and cultural persecution after that time. Some 14,000 were secretly flown to Israel via the Sudan in 1984–85. About 14,000 more were flown out of Addis Ababa in 1991. Another 4,500 are believed to remain. The Beja of the northernmost region, the Agau of the central plateaus, and the Sidamo of the southern foothills and savanna regions are the remnants of the earliest known groups to have occupied Ethiopia.

9LANGUAGES

At least 70 different languages are spoken in Ethiopia. Most of these belong to the Semitic, Cushitic, and Omotic divisions of the Afro-Asiatic linguistic family. Amharic, the official national language, is a Semitic tongue, the native language of perhaps 30% of the people. Tigrinya and Tigray, also Semitic, are spoken in the north. Oromo, a Cushitic tongue, is widely spoken in the south, perhaps by 40% of all Ethiopians. Somali and Afar, also Cushitic languages, are spoken in the east. Omotic tongues are spoken in the southwest. Nilo-Saharan language speakers live in the far southwest and along the western border. English is the principal second language taught in schools.

10RELIGIONS

Until 1974, the Ethiopian Orthodox Church, a Christian confession associated with the Coptic Church and incorporating elements of Monophysite Christianity, was the established church, with the emperor as its titular leader. After the deposition of the emperor, the church lost most of its property (including an estimated 20% of all arable land) and political influence. In 1993 about 40% of Ethiopians were Ethiopian Orthodox Christians. More numerous are the Muslim peoples who inhabit the southwestern, northwestern, and eastern reaches of Ethiopia, amounting to some 45% of the population. The number of followers of African traditional religions is estimated at 5–15%, located mainly in the far south and west. Although of Afro-Asiatic stock, the Falasha practice a form of Judaism that is of great antiquity and is traditionally attributed to ancient Arabian-Jewish or Egyptian-Jewish immigration. Few Falasha remain after massive immigration and evacuation to Israel in 1984–85 and 1991.

11TRANSPORTATION

It is estimated that more than half of Ethiopia's produce is transported by pack animals, reflecting the inadequacy of the country's road network and the rugged terrain. About 75% of Ethiopian farms are more than a one-day walk to the nearest road. The road system in 1991 (before Eritrean independence), which included an all-weather road to Kenya, comprised 44,300 km (27,500 mi), of which 8% was paved. The number of passenger cars in use in 1992 was 37,799, and the number of commercial vehicles 20,939. As of 1992, there was only one vehicle registered for every 869 inhabitants, fewer vehicles per capita than any other African nation. Bus services link provincial centers to the capital.

Railways consist of a line from Djibouti to Addis Ababa that is 880 km (547 mi) long, of which 781 km (485 mi) are in Ethiopia, and is owned jointly by Djibouti and Ethiopia. Ethiopia's merchant fleet of 12 ships had a gross weight of 63,000 tons at the end of 1991. Neighboring Djibouti also serves as a depot for Ethiopian trade. Only one river, the Baro, is used for transport.

The Addis Ababa airport handles international jet transportation. Before the civil war, the national carrier, Ethiopian Airlines, flew to numerous African, Asian, and European cities, and has sole rights on domestic air traffic. This service operated before 1991 out of airfields in more than 40 cities and towns, many in

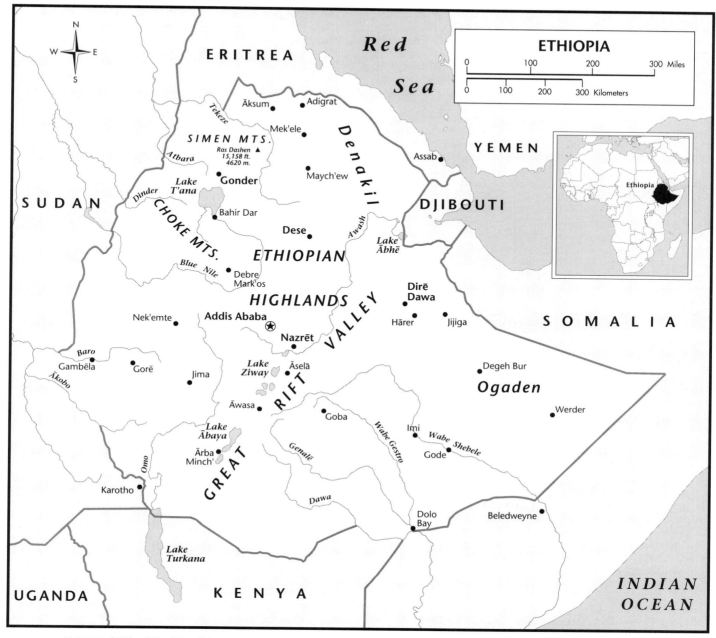

LOCATION: 3°30′ to 18°N; 33° to 48°E. **BOUNDARY LENGTHS:** Eritrea 912 km (566 mi); Djibouti, 313 km (194 mi); Somalia, 1,645 km (1,022 mi); Kenya, 785 km (488 mi); Sudan, 1,661 km (1,030 mi). **TERRITORIAL SEA LIMIT:** 12 mi.

isolated and otherwise inaccessible locations; it carried 635,600 passengers in 1991.

¹²HISTORY

Humanlike fossils have been found in the Denakil depression dating back 3.5 million years; in 1981, the 4-million-year-old fossil bones of a direct ancestor of *Homo sapiens* were discovered in the Awash River Valley. Evidence of cereal agriculture dates back to about 5000 BC. Homer refers to the Ethiopians as a "blameless race," and Herodotus claims that they were known in his time as the "most just men"; to the Greeks, however, Ethiopia was a vague and semimythical area that did not exactly correspond to the modern country. Ethiopia first appears in written history as the Aksumite (or Axumite) Empire, which was probably established around the beginning of the Christian era, although

national tradition attributes the foundation of the empire to Menelik I, the son of King Solomon and the Queen of Sheba. Christianity was introduced in the 4th century by Frumentius of Tyre, who was appointed bishop of the Ethiopian diocese by Patriarch Athanasius of Alexandria. The rise of Islam in the 7th century and the subsequent conquest of Egypt created a crisis for the Coptic Christian communities of northeast Africa. Ethiopia alone met the challenge, surviving until the 1970s as a Christian island in a Muslim sea.

The Aksumite dynasty suffered a slow decline. In 1137, the ruler of Lasta (now Lalibela), Tékla Haimanot, overthrew the Aksumite emperor, Del-Naad, and established the Zagwe dynasty. In 1270, the throne was again restored to the Solomonic dynasty, with the accession of Yekuno Amlak in the province of Shewa. Subsequently, Emperor Amda-Seyon 1 (r.1314–44) reestablished the Ethiopian suzerainty over the Muslim principalities along the Horn of Africa. The Muslim penetration of the highland regions resumed in the early 16th century and, from 1527 to 1543, the Muslims threatened to overrun the entire empire. In 1541, Ethiopia enlisted the assistance of several hundred Portuguese musketmen against a jihad led by Imam Ahmad (known as Gragn, or "the left-handed"). With these superior weapons, Ahmad was defeated and killed in battle in 1543.

The 18th and 19th centuries formed a period of political decentralization and incessant civil war; this period is called the Zamana Masafint ("Era of the Princes"). A young general named Lij Kassa Haylu established a powerful army which defeated the forces of his rivals. He was crowned Emperor Tewodros (Theodore II) in 1855 and succeeded in reunifying the empire, but he was defeated and killed by a British expeditionary force under Gen. Robert Napier in 1868. Italy occupied the Eritrean ports of Aseb (1869) and Mits'iwa (1885) and annexed Eritrea in 1890. The Italian advance was stopped by the defeat and total rout of a large Italian army by the Emperor Menelik II at Adwa in 1896, an Ethiopian victory that is still commemorated as a national holiday. Italy, however, maintained control of Eritrea and also occupied the coastal region of Banadir (Italian Somaliland) in 1900. Meanwhile, France and the UK had obtained Somali coastal enclaves through purchase and a series of protectorate treaties concluded in the past with local tribal chieftains.

Menelik died in 1913. Three years later, his grandson and successor, Lij Yasu, was deposed in favor of his aunt, Empress Zauditu (Judith). Ras Tafari Mekonnen of Shewa was selected as heir apparent and head of government. On 2 November 1930, he was crowned Emperor Haile Selassie I. Italy invaded and conquered Ethiopia in 1935–36. Forced to flee the country, the emperor returned in 1941 with the aid of British forces. By a UN decision, Eritrea, which had been under British administration since 1941, was federated to Ethiopia in 1952 and was incorporated into the empire 10 years later. By this time, an Eritrean secessionist movement was already stirring.

After an abortive coup in 1960, the emperor's political power began to lessen as political opposition increased. Guerrilla activity in Eritrea increased noticeably between 1970 and 1973; student and labor unrest also grew. After an official cover-up of catastrophic drought and famine conditions in Welo and Tigray provinces was uncovered in 1974, the armed forces overthrew the government. From 28 June to 12 September 1974, the emperor was systematically isolated and finally deposed. The monarchy was officially abolished in March 1975. Haile Selassie died 27 August 1975, while still in custody.

The new Provisional Military Administrative Council, also called the Derguedergue, came under the leadership of Maj. (later Lt. Col.) Mengistu Haile Mariam. The economy was extensively nationalized in 1975. Mengistu declared himself a Marxist-Leninist in 1976 and established close relations with Moscow. Perhaps 10,000 Ethiopians were killed in 1976–78, as the Dergue suppressed a revolt by civilian leftists that involved urban terrorism.

The war with Eritrean secessionists continued inconclusively until 1991. In mid-1977, Somalia invaded the Ogaden area to support the claims of ethnic Somalis there for self-determination. The assault was repulsed with the assistance of Soviet arms and Cuban soldiers in early 1978, when a 20-year treaty with the USSR was signed. Close links with Libya and the People's Democratic Republic of Yemen were established in 1981. In 1982, Ethiopian troops attempted without success to topple the Somali government by mounting an invasion of some 10,000 Ethiopian troops in support of the insurgent Somali Salvation Democratic Front. Hostilities with Somalia later eased and diplomatic relations were reestablished in 1988. But relations with the Sudan soured, as each country supported insurgent movements in the other.

A devastating drought and famine struck northern Ethiopia during 1982–84, taking an unknown toll in lives. Between November 1984 and October 1985 an international relief effort distributed 900,000 tons of food to nearly 8 million people. Food aid continued on a reduced scale, while the government launched massive resettlement programs that critics said were really intended to hamper the operations of armed insurgents and to collectivize agriculture.

The Worker's Party of Ethiopia (WPE) was established as the sole legal political party in 1984, on the tenth anniversary of the revolution. Two years later, a constitutional document was unveiled for discussion; after minor changes it was approved by 81% of the voters in a referendum held on 1 February 1987. Later that year, another devastating drought struck northern Ethiopia, continuing into 1988.

Despite mobilizing one million troops and receiving massive Soviet bloc military aid, the government was not able to defeat the Eritrean and Tigrayan insurgencies. Led by the Eritrean People's Liberation Front (EPLF) and the Tigre People's Liberation Front (TPLF), which is part of a larger coalition, the Ethiopian People's Revolutionary Democratic Front (EPRDF) triumphed.

On 21 May 1991, Mengistu was forced to resign as president, and he fled to Zimbabwe. His vice president surrendered to EPRDF forces on May 27. The next day, Meles Zenawi, leader of the FPRDF, established an interim government. In July, delegates from the three victorious guerrilla groups agreed on a structure of an interim government and to grant Eritrea the right to hold an internationally supervised referendum on independence.

Meanwhile, the remains of Haile Selassie I, who was murdered in 1974, were recovered and, on 23 July 1992, he was reburied in Trinity Cathedral, Addis Ababa.

The transitional government pledged to oversee the establishment of Ethiopia's first multiparty democracy. During 1993, a new constitution was being drafted. Elections are projected for 1994 for a constituent assembly and a national government. For the transitional government, a 65-member Council of Representatives is dominated by the four constituent parties of the EPRDF, itself dominated by the TPLF. The accession of Tigrayans and their policy of promoting ethnic identity and regionalism engender animosity from Amharas who traditionally held centralized power in Ethiopia.

In 1992, the multiparty government split sharply. The Oromo Liberation Front (OLF), the second largest partner, withdrew from the coalition on 23 June 1992. It claimed that the regional elections held on June 21 had been rigged by the EPRDF. The OLF and five other political groups had boycotted the elections. Some OLF forces took up arms against the government but they were put down. The OLF remains outside the government and much of its senior leadership is abroad.

Although there have been complaints about the government's human rights record, there is a marked improvement over the Mengistu years. Nonetheless, several thousand detainees have been held without trial for crimes committed under the previous regime. Academic and press freedom are weak, as is protection for opposition parties.

¹³GOVERNMENT

Although Ethiopia was, in theory, a constitutional monarchy between 1931 and 1974, sovereignty was vested solely in the emperor, a hereditary monarch. The ruler appointed the prime minister, senators, judges, governors, and mayors. The emperor was assisted by the Council of Ministers and the Crown Council, whose members he appointed.

After the military takeover in 1974, the parliament was dissolved and the Provisional Military Government (PMG) established. The PMG assumed full control of the government and continued to rule through its Provisional Military Administrative

Council, also called the Dergue, whose chairmanship Mengistu seized in February 1977. Government decisions were made by Mengistu on an ad hoc basis, sometimes in consultation with members of the Dergue's Standing Committee. Control over government ministries was maintained by assigning Dergue representatives to oversee their operations. The Commission for Organizing the Party of the Working People of Ethiopia acted as the Dergue's political arm.

The constitution approved by referendum on 1 February 1987 declared Ethiopia to be a people's democratic republic. A National Assembly (Shengo), with 835 members chosen by proportional representation for the various nationalities, theoretically had supreme power. The president, who was elected to a five-year term by the Assembly, acted as chief executive and commander-in-chief of the armed forces and nominated and presided over the cabinet and the state council, which had legislative power when the Assembly was not in session. The president also appointed top officials of the WPE, which was called the leading force in the state and society. The Assembly held its first meeting on 9 September; the next day, it elected Mengistu president. It also redrew the political map, creating five "autonomous regions" in order to weaken the appeal of the independence movements. It failed. Despite the trappings of representative government, all power remained in Mengistu's hands. He was head of state and government, leader of the only party and commander of the armed forces.

After Mengistu's defeat in May 1991, a transitional government was established, under the leadership of the Ethiopian People's Revolutionary Democratic Front, a coalition of parties opposed to the Dergue. Its leader is President Meles Zenawi. It and the Council of Representatives, 87 members, serve as a quasi-legislature. It oversees the drafting of a constitution, which would appear to be favoring strong regional governments in a federal structure, along ethnic lines, multiparty elections, and an independent judiciary. Elections for a constituent assembly were scheduled for June 1994.

In December 1993, 47 parties were said to have registered for an all-inclusive conference on Ethiopia's future. But the transitional government rejected the conference's demand that the opposition be included in a new transitional government. A number of opposition leaders who had returned from exile for the conference were arrested.

14POLITICAL PARTIES
In the past, there were no established political parties in Ethiopia. Political factions did exist, however, on the basis of religion, ethnicity, regionalism, or common economic interests. In the 1970s, a number of illegal separatist groups became active militarily. They included the Eritrean People's Liberation Front (EPLF), Eritrean Liberation Front (ELF), the Oromo People's Democratic Organization (OPDO), Tigray People's Liberation Front (TPLF), Oromo Liberation Front (OLF), and Western Somali Liberation Front (WSLF). Eventually, EPLF defeated the ELF in Eritrea.

Two civilian left-wing parties, the Ethiopian People's Revolutionary Party and the All-Ethiopian Socialist Movement, were crushed by the Dergue in 1976 and 1977, respectively. In 1979, the Dergue established the Commission for Organizing the Party of the Working People of Ethiopia (COPWE), in order to lay the groundwork for a Marxist-Leninist party along Soviet lines. The Worker's Party of Ethiopia (WPE) was established in 1984 as the sole legal political party. Its 11-man Politburo was headed by Mengistu.

The separatists successfully defeated Mengistu's forces and after Mengistu fled in May 1991, they established a transitional government under their coalition banner, the Ethiopian People's Revolutionary Democratic Front (EPRDF). The TPLF is the most prominent in the EPRDF, which also includes the Ethiopian

People's Democratic Movement (EPDM) and the Afar Democratic Union. The OLF is not part of the coalition. There are also numerous small, ethnic-based groups and several Islamic militant groups.

15LOCAL GOVERNMENT
Until 1987, Ethiopia was divided into 15 administrative regions, which in turn were subdivided into 103 subregions and 505 districts. In 1976, peasant associations were empowered to collect taxes and form women's associations, cooperatives, and militias. In the mid-1980s, an estimated 25,000 such peasant groups were in existence. Urban dwellers' associations were established for a variety of functions, including law and order.

In 1987, at its first sitting, the Shengo redrew the political map. It created five "autonomous regions" (Eritrea, Assab, Dire Dawa, Ogaden, and Tigre). The remaining provinces were further subdivided into 24 administrative zones.

The establishment of regions was altered with the creation of the transitional government in 1991. At that point, Eritrea was administered independently. The new regime called for 14 regional governments, but the June 1992 elections for 11 of the 14 regional assemblies was challenged and widespread fraud was alleged.

16JUDICIAL SYSTEM
The Transitional Government of Ethiopia is now putting into place a system of courts consisting of regional and central courts. Each region will have local (Woreda), district and Supreme Courts. There are also local Shari'a courts which hear religion and family cases involving Muslims. A federal high and federal Supreme Court will have jurisdiction over cases involving federal laws and issues of national import. The current judiciary suffers from a lack of trained personnel and financial constraints.

The judiciary now operates under the terms of a National Charter which functions as a transition constitution while the official new constitution is being drafted.

17ARMED FORCES
A new post–civil war military establishment is not yet formed. The two major rebel factions have perhaps 200,000 men armed with Russian weapons and vehicles captured from the Mengistu government in 1991. Soviet aviation and naval equipment also remains, but no Ethiopian air force or navy. Material and bases are quickly deteriorating. No defense spending estimates are available. All Russian and Cuban troops have departed.

18INTERNATIONAL COOPERATION
Ethiopia is a charter member of the UN, having joined on 13 November 1945; it belongs to the ECA and all the nonregional specialized agencies except WIPO. A participant in the African Development Bank and G-77, Ethiopia also is a member of the OAU, whose secretariat is located in Addis Ababa. The late Emperor Haile Selassie I was extremely active in inter-African affairs and was considered by many as Africa's leading statesman. Ethiopian troops fought under UN command in the Korean conflict and served in the Congo (now Zaire) in the early 1960s.

Ethiopia has received UN technical assistance in the fields of public administration, telecommunications, vocational training, agriculture, animal husbandry, education, civil aviation, and health. The nation is a signatory to the Law of the Sea.

19ECONOMY
Ethiopia's economy has been undergoing major reforms since May 1991, when a market-oriented government came to power. Three major droughts in the past twenty years, civil war, and cross-border conflicts have devastated the economy as much as did socialist-style totalitarianism.

Agriculture, hunting, forestry, and fishing engage 88.6% of the Ethiopian population (1984 census). The agricultural sector is diverse, producing maize, sorghum, millet, other cereals (barley, wheat, and teff), tubers, and sugarcane. Livestock production is also important, responsible for 18% of export earnings.

Ethiopia produces gold and has additional undeveloped deposits of platinum, marble, tantalite, copper, potash, salt, soda ash, zinc, nickel, and iron. Natural gas is found in the Ogaden.

20 INCOME

In 1992 Ethiopia's GNP was $6,206 million at current prices, or $110 per capita. For the period 1985–92 the average inflation rate was 3.2%, resulting in a real growth rate in per capita GNP of –2.0%.

In 1992 the GDP was $6,723 million in current US dollars. It was estimated in 1989 that agriculture, hunting, forestry, and fishing contributed 37% to GDP; manufacturing, 10%; electricity, gas, and water, 1%; construction, 4%; wholesale and retail trade, 9%; transport, storage, and communication, 6%; finance, insurance, real estate, and business services, 5%; community, social, and personal services, 6%; and other sources, 22%.

21 LABOR

Government estimates in 1992 indicated that 23,518,000 Ethiopians were economically active. This figure is subject to fluctuation because of the seasonal nature of much of the activity. About 80% of the total were engaged in agriculture and livestock raising. In 1992, about 70,860 persons were classified as unemployed.

Slavery and slave labor were a traditional part of Ethiopian life until the Italian occupation in 1935. Previously, the government ignored pressure from countries abroad that slavery be made illegal, and Ethiopia was admitted to the League of Nations in 1923 only after subscribing to the Convention of St. Germain, which bound its adherents to the suppression of slavery and the slave trade. In 1942, the emperor issued a proclamation for the abolition of the legal status of slavery, calling for severe penalties and possible death sentences for any transgression of the law.

Current working conditions vary according to occupation and region. In January 1977, the government-backed All-Ethiopia Trade Union was established, but was dissolved at the national level by the transitional government in 1991. The 1975 Labor Code, which was still in effect in 1992, established an 8-hour workday and a 48-hour workweek. Collective bargaining is permitted, but there were no known instances occurring in 1992.

22 AGRICULTURE

It has been estimated that nearly 70% of Ethiopia's land mass is cultivable, yet only 12.7% of the land is under cultivation and permanent crops. Agricultural and pastoral pursuits support over 80% of the population and form 47% of the GDP. Subsistence farming and livestock grazing, both inefficient, are the rule. Field crops account for 40% of gross agricultural output, cash crops for 20% and livestock for the rest.

The coffee variety known as arabica may have originated in Ethiopia, and the word *coffee* is derived from Kaffa (Kefa), the region in the southwest that is still the largest coffee-producing area of the country. Coffee is by far the most valuable cash export crop, accounting for 60% of foreign exchange earnings. Coffee production was an estimated at 216,000 tons in 1992, second in Africa; 36,000 tons were exported in 1992. Qat, the leaves from a shrub that are used to make tea and which have a mild narcotic effect, is another important cash export crop.

The most commonly produced cereal is teff (*Eragrostis abyssinica*), which is used to make the Ethiopian unleavened bread called injera. Corn and barley are the next most important grains, with an annual gross production of at least 1 million tons each. Sorghum, wheat, millet, peas, beans, lentils, and oilseeds are produced in substantial quantities; sugarcane and cotton are also grown. Production in 1992 included corn, 1,650,000 tons; barley, 1,000,000 tons; sorghum, 1,100,000 tons; wheat, 900,000 tons; broad beans, 282,000 tons; yams, 262,000 tons; potatoes, 388,000 tons; millet, 280,000 tons; and raw sugar, 163,000 tons.

The agricultural sector suffered severe damage from the civil war and its aftermath. Forced recruitment into the military led to a shortage of farm labor. Reforms aimed at introducing market-based incentives have been implemented, including freeing agricultural marketing and farm labor hiring practices. Emergency provisions of seeds, fertilizer, and other inputs have also been vital in rebuilding Ethiopia's agriculture.

23 ANIMAL HUSBANDRY

Ethiopia has the largest livestock population in Africa, and this subsector accounts for 40% of gross agricultural output. In normal years, animal husbandry provides a living for 75% of the population. The number of cattle (zebu type) was estimated at 31 million in 1992, about three-fifths of them primarily work animals. The country lacks facilities for fattening cattle brought in to slaughter, an adequate veterinary service, and breeding herds. Meat production was estimated at 571,000 tons in 1992; milk production was an estimated 774,000 tons. The number of sheep and goats was estimated at 23.2 million and 18.1 million, respectively, but periodic drought may have made the actual number much lower. The number of horses was estimated at 2,750,000, mules at 630,000, donkeys at 5,200,000, and camels at 1,070,000. These were primarily pack animals.

Hides and skins constitute the country's second-largest export item and generally command high prices on the world market. In 1991, exports of hides totaled $45 million, or 16% of total exports. In 1992, Ethiopia produced 23,700 tons of honey, more than any other nation in Africa.

24 FISHING

With the secession of Eritrea, Ethiopia lost access to an estimated 1,011 km (628 mi) of Red Sea coastline. In 1992, the Ethiopian and provisional Eritrean governments agreed to make Assab a free port for Ethiopia. Most Ethiopians do not eat seafood; hunting and fishing accounts for only a tiny fraction of the GDP. The catch was about 4,500 tons in 1991.

25 FORESTRY

In the 1930s, more than 30% of Ethiopia consisted of forests, but that total has fallen to 24%. *Boswellia* and species of commiphora produce gums used as the basis for frankincense and myrrh, respectively. A species of acacia is a source of gum arabic. Eucalyptus stands, introduced in the 19th century, are a valuable source of firewood, furniture, and poles. Roundwood production was an estimated 43.6 million m^3 in 1991; all but an estimated 1.7 million m^3 was for fuel.

26 MINING

Little of Ethiopia's expected mineral potential has been exploited. Mining and quarrying came to only $6.5 billion in 1991. Construction materials, including cement, are the most significant mineral commodity both in value and quantity. Gold is the principal export mineral for revenue; production amounted to 2,000 kg in 1991, up from 848 kg in 1990. Platinum, limestone, marble, pumice, and quartz sand are mined in limited quantities. Substantial iron ore deposits were discovered in the Welega region in 1985. Other undeveloped resources include tungsten, mercury, nickel, columbium, and tantalum.

27 ENERGY AND POWER

The Finchaa River Dam at the head of Lake T'ana, the largest hydroelectric scheme in the country, was officially inaugurated in

November 1974. This plant was built at a cost of about $40 million and has an installed generating capacity of 84 Mw and a potential annual output of approximately 532 million kwh. A 152-Mw station at Malka Wekana on the Wabi Shebelle River, built with в500 million from the former USSR and Czechoslovakia was constructed in the 1980s. Three hydroelectric plants in the Awash River Basin date from the 1960s. By 1980, most public power-generating sources, including all major hydroelectric plants, were part of three regional power grids. Ethiopia has vast untapped geothermal power sources. Production of electricity totaled 973 million kwh in 1991, of which the majority was hydroelectric.

About 91% of Ethiopia's energy comes from fuel wood and animal wastes, the rest from petroleum products and electricity. In 1991, International Petroleum Corporation was exploring an area for oil along the Sudanese border, some 500 km (310 mi) west of Addis Ababa.

28INDUSTRY

While Ethiopia's industrial sector engages primarily in food processing, it also produces sugar, alcohol and soft drinks, cigarettes, cotton and textiles, footwear, soap, ethyl alcohol, quicklime, and cement. In addition, Ethiopia's petroleum refinery produces some 800,000 tons of petroleum products annually.

Since 1991, privatization of Ethiopia's industry has been a major objective of the new government. This policy has reversed the aggressive nationalization program of the preceding government which had, by the mid-1980s, acquired ownership of about 80% of all industry.

29SCIENCE AND TECHNOLOGY

Scientific societies and research institutes in Addis Ababa include the Association for the Advancement of Agricultural Sciences in Africa, the Desert Locust Control Organization for Eastern Africa, the Ethiopian Medical Association, the Ethiopian Institute of Geological Surveys, the Geophysical Observatory, the Institute of Agricultural Research, and the International Livestock Center for Africa. Both the University of Addis Ababa and the University of Asmara maintain faculties of science, agriculture, and technology, and the former has a faculty of medicine, a college of agriculture, and a school of pharmacy. Also in Ethiopia are the Jimma Junior College of Agriculture and the Polytechnic Institute at Bahir-Dar.

30DOMESTIC TRADE

Addis Ababa is the paramount commercial and distribution center. Most of the economy is monetary, but transactions are still conducted by barter in some of the more isolated rural sectors. In general, office hours are from 9 AM to 1 PM and from 3 PM to 6 PM, Mondays through Fridays, and 9 AM to 1 PM on Saturdays. Shops are open until 8 PM.

31FOREIGN TRADE

Coffee, tea, cocoa, and spices led exports in 1988, accounting for 65% of the total. Livestock and livestock products accounted for an additional 18.2% of exports. Principal exports in 1988 (in thousands of US dollars) were as follows:

Live animals	14,409
Vegetables and fruit	16,633
Coffee, cocoa, tea, spices	273,683
Hides and skins	62,093
Oil seeds	7,657
Vegetable pharmacy materials	4 259
Petroleum and petroleum products	2,701
Other goods	33,659
TOTAL	421,098

Ethiopia is heavily dependent on imported manufactures. Machinery, petroleum, and petroleum products represent the leading import items. Large trade deficits were chronic in the late 1970s and the 1980s. Principal imports in 1988 (in thousands of birr) were as follows:

Food and live animals	149,658
Crude materials, not fuels	24,616
Mineral fuels, lubricants	107,575
Animal and vegetable oils	22,378
Chemicals	96,306
Machinery, transport equipment	80,915
Miscellaneous manufactures	41,030
Other goods	162,523
TOTAL	1,085,001

In 1988, Ethiopia exported 24% of its total exports to Germany; 9.8% were sent to the US. Of Ethiopia's imports, 17.3% came from Italy, 11.4% came from Germany, 11.0% came from the former Soviet Union, and 10.9% came from the US.

32BALANCE OF PAYMENTS

Ethiopia's balance of payments has been significantly affected by weather conditions, terms of trade, and emergency drought relief efforts provided by the international community. From 1961 to 1963, Ethiopia registered a balance-of-payments surplus, as the current deficit was offset by the inflow of foreign capital. From 1964 to 1971, the current accounts deficit exceeded the inflow of foreign funds. During the first half of the 1970s, Ethiopia's dependence on foreign capital decreased; the value of its agricultural commodities rose, with a consequent increase in foreign exchange reserves. Drought and political instability led to payments deficits during the second half of the decade. In 1981, Ethiopia registered its first payments surplus since 1976, but the following three years were in deficit. The current account deficit widened between 1985–86 and 1989–90 to nearly 10% of GDP. By 1990–91, the trade deficit stood at $779.6 million, due mainly to the collapse in world coffee prices.

In 1991 merchandise exports totaled $167.6 million and imports $470.8 million. The merchandise trade balance was $–303.2 million. The following table summarizes Ethiopia's balance of payments for 1990 and 1991 (in millions of US dollars):

	1990	1991
CURRENT ACCOUNT		
Goods, services, and income	−742.9	−401.4
Unrequited transfers	440.4	575.5
TOTALS	−302.5	174.0
CAPITAL ACCOUNT		
Other long-term capital	131.9	6.1
Other short-term capital	98.1	−210.2
Exceptional financing	188.8	328.8
Reserves	9.5	−43.7
TOTALS	428.2	81.0
Errors and omissions	−125.9	−255.0
Total change in reserves	13.8	−46.4

33BANKING AND SECURITIES

All banking institutions were nationalized after the government's formal Declaration of Socialism on 20 December 1974. The country's three private commercial banks were placed under the management of the National Bank of Ethiopia and, in 1981, under the state-owned Commercial Bank of Ethiopia (established in 1963), which had 151 branches in 1993. Other banks include the Agricultural and Industrial Development Bank and the

Housing and Savings Bank. In 1993, currency in circulation totaled B7,651 million. Commercial bank reserves were B1,635 million. Demand deposits of the Commercial Bank of Ethiopia in 1993 were B2,674million, and time and savings deposits B3,252 million. There are no securities exchanges, and Ethiopians are legally barred from acquiring or dealing in foreign securities.

34INSURANCE
In January 1975, the 13 insurance companies operating in Ethiopia were nationalized and fused into an inclusive national insurance organization, the Ethiopian Insurance Corp. Gross premium income in 1984 was B133.4 million. In 1985–86, 97.2% of all premiums were for non-life and 2.8% for life insurance.

35PUBLIC FINANCE
The Ethiopian fiscal year begins 8 July, in the Ethiopian month of Hamle. The following table shows actual revenues and expenditures for 1988 and 1989 in millions of birr.

	1988	1989
REVENUE AND GRANTS		
Tax revenue	2,325.2	2,386.8
Non-tax revenue	1,084.8	1,477.8
Capital revenue	22.3	17.4
Grants	46.4	190.9
TOTAL	3,478.7	4,072.9
EXPENDITURES & LENDING MINUS REPAYMENTS		
General public services	—	186.6
Defense	—	1,674.0
Public order and safety	158.1	140.1
Education	438.2	474.9
Health	142.2	145.3
Social security and welfare	193.8	224.0
Housing and community amenities	241.8	255.0
Recreation, cultural, and religious affairs	46.6	41.8
Economic affairs and services	1,086.6	1,246.0
Other expenditures	354.2	397.9
Lending minus repayments	101.4	315.2
TOTAL	4,262.9	5,100.9
Deficit/Surplus	−784.2	−1,028.0

In 1989 Ethiopia's total public debt stood at B9,517.1 million, of which B4,526.5 million was financed abroad. By 1992, the external debt amounted to B7.2 billion. Most of Ethiopia's debt is on concessionary noncommercial terms at low rates of interest. In 1992–93, Ethiopia's budget deficit (excluding grants) was estimated to have dropped to 10.2% of GDP. Ethiopia's public finances are under great budgetary pressure, as years of war and poverty have taken a heavy toll on the countryside, population, and infrastructure.

36TAXATION
Many business and personal income tax rates from the former government were still in effect as of 1993, ranging from 10% of monthly incomes from B50 to B250, to 85% of incomes over B3,750. A 40% income tax was levied on royalties, and a 2% ad valorem turnover tax on domestic sales. Tax rates were expected to be lowered in the near future.

37CUSTOMS AND DUTIES
The primary purpose of the tariff system is to provide revenues rather than to protect Ethiopian industry or to prohibit the importation of certain commodities. However, there are restrictions on importing certain goods that compete with domestically produced goods. Duty rates range up to 125%. Imports of certain agricultural and industrial tools and parts and many raw materials are duty-free. There are no free-trade zones, but a transshipment port is available in Djibouti.

38FOREIGN INVESTMENT
Since May 1991, the climate for foreign investment has improved dramatically. Private investment policies are more liberal, commercial performance standards have been applied to public enterprises, tax and tariffs have been reformed, and the currency has been devalued by 58%. The devaluation was the policy action required for the rescheduling of Ethiopia's foreign debt in 1992. Foreign exchange is now auctioned.

39ECONOMIC DEVELOPMENT
The policy of the Ethiopian government is to create the conditions necessary for sustained economic growth. Farmers have reacquired the economic freedom of price, of production, and of settlement. The government aspires to an agriculture-led industrialization and focuses its attention on food security, rural savings, and labor formation issues.

40SOCIAL DEVELOPMENT
Other than modest government allocations for pensions (B36.6 million in 1984), labor and social welfare (B18.3 million), and housing and community services (B .4 million), Ethiopia has no public welfare or social security programs. Government current spending on social services averaged less than B5 (below $3) per capita during 1984.

Women have traditionally been restricted to circumscribed roles, but a major effort is being made to achieve widespread literacy among women. There are high fertility, birth, and infant mortality rates. Abortion is available on broad health grounds.

41HEALTH
The availability of modern health services has been greatly extended since 1960, but these services still reach only a small portion of the population. Free medical care for the needy was introduced in 1977; however, between 1985 and 1992, only 46% of the population had access to health care services. Ethiopia built a new hospital at Gore, and a 500-bed hospital in Harer was completed. The tuberculosis center in Addis Ababa was expanded, and five new leprosariums were built in the provinces. Mental hospitals were built in Harer and Asmera, and the one in Addis Ababa was renovated.

From 1985 to 1990, Ethiopia had 3 hospital beds per 100,000 people. Records in 1992 show that there was only 1 physician for every 32,650 people. The nurse-to-doctor ratio was 2.4.

The wars, drought, political turmoil, and population pressures of the 1970s and early 1980s left their mark on the Ethiopian health situation. Between 1974 and 1992, there were 575,000 war-related deaths. Hundreds of thousands of Ethiopians died during a famine in 1973, and as many as 1 million may have died between 1983 and 1985. There were 2,627,000 births in 1992 (49.1 per 1,000 people), with only 2% of married women (ages 15 to 49) using contraception. Average life expectancy in 1992 was estimated at only 47 years; infant mortality was estimated at 123 per 1,000 live births.

Widespread diseases include malaria, tuberculosis, syphilis, gonorrhea, leprosy, dysentery, and schistosomiasis. In 1990, there were 155 reported cases of tuberculosis per 100,000 people. Between 1990 and 1992, Ethiopia made an effort to vaccinate children up to one year old against tuberculosis (21%); diphtheria, pertussis, and tetanus (13%); polio (13%); and measles (10%). In 1991 only 25% of the population had access to safe water, and only 19% had adequate sanitation. Total health care expenditures in 1990 were $229 million.

[42]HOUSING

Except in Addis Ababa, Harer, Dire Dawa, and a few other urban centers, most houses are built of mud or mortar and have thatched or tin roofs. In the rural areas the traditional thatched hut (tukul) is still the most common dwelling. As of 1984, 73% of all housing units were constructed with wood and mud, and 16% with wood and thatch. In urban areas, 38% of the units had private kitchens, 38% had no kitchens, and 18% had shared kitchens; 90% had no bath or shower facilities, and 50% had no toilet facilities. Government plans called for three million people to be resettled in 930,000 homes in 5,146 villages in 1987; earlier, according to official figures, over 1 million houses were built for 5.4 million people. Only about 6% of the population has access to safe water.

Housing development and finance are the joint responsibility of the Ministry of Housing and Urban Development and the Housing and Savings Bank, which was established in November 1975.

[43]EDUCATION

Ethiopia had an estimated 45% adult illiteracy rate in 1983 and compared poorly with the rest of Africa in the provision of schools and universities. Education received roughly 5% of the national budget in 1984. After the 1974 revolution, heavy emphasis was put on increasing literacy in rural areas. Practical subjects were stressed, as was the teaching of socialism.

Compulsory and free public education exists at the primary level. In 1991, elementary schools had a total enrollment of 2,063,636 pupils in 8,434 schools with 68,399 teachers, Junior and senior secondary schools had 775,211 pupils with 22,721 teachers. Addis Ababa University (formerly Haile Selassie I University) has extension centers in Alemaya, Gonder, Awasa, Bahir-Dar, and Debre Zeyit. The University of Asmera, a Roman Catholic institution, had 3,430 students. In 1991, the universities and equivalent institutions had 20,948 pupils with 1,440 teachers.

[44]LIBRARIES AND MUSEUMS

The Addis Ababa University Library contains 550,000 volumes. The National Library, established in 1944, holds 125,000 volumes.

Addis Ababa is home to the National Museum, which houses a general collection of regional archaeology, history, and art; the Museum of the Institute of Ethiopian Studies, which includes collections of religious art, musical instruments, and ancient coins; the Musée Archéologique; and the Natural History Museum. Many provincial monasteries and churches, as well as municipal authorities, maintain collections of documents, art, and antiquities.

[45]MEDIA

All telephone and telegraph facilities are owned by the government and operated by the National Board of Telecommunications. The principal population centers are connected with Addis Ababa by telephone and radio circuits, and there is an earth-satellite station. In 1991 there were 153,010 telephones in use. Radio and television stations are run by the government. The Voice of Ethiopia radio service broadcasts mostly on AM in Amharic, but also in English, French, Arabic, and local languages. Ethiopian Television broadcasts about four hours daily. In 1991 there were an estimated 9.7 million radios and 130,000 television sets in use.

All newspapers are strictly censored by the Ministry of Information and National Guidance. The two daily newspapers (with estimated 1991 circulations) are *Addis Zeman* (30,000; Amharic) and the *Ethiopian Herald* (6,500; English), both published at Addis Ababa.

[46]ORGANIZATIONS

Since the 1974 revolution, peasants' and urban dwellers' associations, encouraged by the government, have been the chief voluntary societies. Women's and youth groups are affiliated with the WPE. Ethiopia has a national chamber of commerce and eight regional and local ones.

[47]TOURISM, TRAVEL, AND RECREATION

All visitors except Kenyan nationals must have a visa. Travelers arriving from an infected area must have proof of yellow fever and cholera vaccinations; antimalarial precautions are recommended. The chief tourist attractions are big-game hunting, early Christian monuments and monasteries, and the ancient capitals of Gonder and Aksum. There are seven national parks. In 1991 there were 81,581 international tourist arrivals, 30% from Africa and 26% from Europe. Receipts from international tourism came to US$20 million. There were 2,783 hotel rooms with 4,931 beds.

Distance running is an Ethiopian specialty. Ethiopians won the 1960, 1964, and 1968 Olympic marathons, and the 1980 5,000-m and 10,000-m events.

[48]FAMOUS ETHIOPIANS

The most famous Ethiopian in national legend is Menelik I, the son of the Queen of Sheba and King Solomon, regarded as the founder of the Aksumite Empire. This tradition is contained in the *Kebra Negast*, or *Book of the Glory of Kings*. The most famous Christian saint of Ethiopia is Frumentius of Tyre (b.Phoenicia, d.380?), the founder of the Ethiopian Church. The 15th-century composer Yared established the Deggua, or liturgical music, of the Ethiopian Church. A 13th-century monarch, Lalibela, is renowned for the construction of the great monolithic churches of Lasta (now called Lalibela). Emperor Amda-Seyon I (r.1313–44) reestablished suzerainty over the Muslim kingdoms of the coastal lowland regions. During the reign of King Zar' a-Ya'qob (1434–68), a ruler renowned for his excellent administration and deep religious faith, Ethiopian literature attained its greatest heights. Emperor Menelik II (1844–1913) is considered the founder of modern Ethiopia. Emperor Haile Selassie I (1891–1975) was noted for his statesmanship and his introduction of many political, economic, and social reforms. Lt. Col. Mengistu Haile Mariam (b.1937) led the 1974 coup and has been head of state from 1977 to 1991.

[49]DEPENDENCIES

Ethiopia has no territories or colonies.

[50]BIBLIOGRAPHY

Abebe, Daniel. *Ethiopia in Pictures*. Minneapolis: Lerner, 1988.

Bailey, Glen. *An Analysis of the Ethiopian Revolution*. Athens: Ohio University Press, 1980.

Brietzke, Paul H. *Law, Development, and the Ethiopian Revolution*. Lewisburg, Pa.: Bucknell University Press, 1981.

Erlich, Haggai. *Ethiopia and the Challenge of Independence*. Boulder, Colo.: Lynne Rienner, 1986.

Gaitachew Bekele. *The Emperor's Clothes: A Personal Viewpoint on Politics and Administration in the Imperial Ethiopian Government, 1941–1974*. East Lansing: Michigan State University Press, 1993.

Griffin, Keith (ed.). *The Economy of Ethiopia*. New York: St. Martin's Press, 1992.

Halliday, Fred, and Maxine Molyneux. *The Ethiopian Revolution*. New York: Schocken, 1982.

Kaplan, Robert D. *Surrender or Starve: The Wars Behind the Famine*. Boulder, Colo.: Westview Press, 1988.

Kapuscinski, Ryszard. *The Emperor*. New York: Harcourt Brace Jovanovich, 1983.

Kebbede, Girma. *The State and Development in Ethiopia*. Atlantic Highlands, N.J.: Humanities Press, 1992.

Keller, Edmond J. *Revolutionary Ethiopia: From Empire to People's Republic*. Bloomington: Indiana University Press, 1988.

Lockot, Hans Wilhelm. *The Mission: The Life, Reign, and Character of Haile Sellassie I.* New York: St. Martin's Press, 1989.

Longrigg, Stephen H. *A Short History of Eritrea.* Westport, Conn.: Greenwood, 1975.

Marcus, Harold G. *Ethiopia, Great Britain, and the United States, 1971–74: The Politics of Empire.* Berkeley: University of California Press, 1983.

———. *Haile Sellassie I: The Formative Years, 1892–1936.* Berkeley: University of California Press, 1987.

Milkias, Paulos. *Ethiopia: A Comprehensive Bibliography.* Boston: G.K. Hall, 1989.

Ofcansky, Thomas P. and LaVerle Berry (eds.). *Ethiopia, a Country Study.* 4th ed. Washington, D.C.: Library of Congress, 1993.

Pankhurst, Richard K. P. *Economic History of Ethiopia, 1800–1935.* Evanston, Ill.: Northwestern University Press, 1974.

Prouty, Chris and Eugene Rosenfeld. *Historical Dictionary of Ethiopia and Eritrea.* 2d ed. Metuchen, N.J.: Scarecrow, 1993.

Schwab, Peter. *Ethiopia: Politics, Economics, and Society.* Boulder, Colo.: Lynne Rienner, 1985.

Sergew, H. Selassie. *Ethiopia: Ancient and Medieval History until 1270.* Addis Ababa: Haile Selassie I University Press, 1971.

Sorenson, John. *Imagining Ethiopia: Struggles for History and Identity in the Horn of Africa.* New Brunswick, N.J.: Rutgers University Press, 1993.

Tamrat, Tadessa. *Church and State in Ethiopia, 1270–1522.* Oxford: Clarendon, 1972.

Tiruneh, Andargachew. *The Ethiopian Revolution, 1974–1987: A Transformation from an Aristocratic to a Totalitarian Autocracy.* New York: Cambridge University Press, 1993.

Wubneh, Mulatu, and Yohannis Abate. *Ethiopia: Transition and Development in the Horn of Africa.* Boulder, Colo.: Westview, 1988.

FRENCH AFRICAN DEPENDENCIES

MAYOTTE

Mayotte, the southernmost of four main islands in the Comoros Archipelago, with an area of 374 sq km (144 sq mi), lies in the Mozambique Channel about 480 km (300 mi) NW of Madagascar, at 12°49′S and 45°17′E. Mayotte is surrounded by a coral reef, which encloses the islets of M'Zambourou (Grand Terre) and Pamanzi. Beyond the island's coastal plain, a plateau reaches heights of 660 m (2,165 ft). The average daily high is 32°C (90°F); the average low is 17°C (63°F). Average annual precipitation is about 124 cm (49 in). The population was estimated at 89,983 in 1993; a majority of the population was Muslim. Vanilla, ylang-ylang, coffee, and rice are among the leading agricultural products.

The island of Mayotte was originally ceded to France by its Malagasy ruler in 1843. Together with the other Comoro Islands, which became French colonies in 1912, it was attached to the French overseas territory of Madagascar until 1946, when the islands were given separate status within the French Republic. Mayotte is the only island in the Comoro chain that, by popular vote, chose to retain its link with France instead of joining an independent Comoro Islands state. This choice, indicated in the referendum of 22 December 1974, was confirmed in a separate referendum for Mayotte, conducted on 8 February 1976, when 99.4% favored remaining within France. The French vetoed a UN Security Council resolution of 7 February 1976 declaring the referendum "aggression" against the sovereignty and territorial integrity of the Comoros, which continues to claim the island. On 11 April, in a further referendum, 97.5% of those casting valid ballots (80% of the ballots were blank or declared invalid) voted for abandonment of the status of overseas territory; the vote was interpreted as indicating that Mayotte wished to become a French overseas department. The UN General Assembly called for incorporation of Mayotte within the Comoros on 21 October. Special status as a French "territorial collectivity," allowing for Mayotte eventually to become either an overseas department or independent, was conferred by the French government on 1 December 1976 and extended for five years on 6 December 1979. France maintains a naval base at Dzaoudzi. In elections held in 1991, the Mayotte Popular Movement (Mouvement Populaire Mahorais—MPM), which favors French departmental status, won 12 of the available 17 seats in the local assembly. Mayotte is represented by one deputy in the French National Assembly and one member in the Senate.

RÉUNION

Réunion, about 675 km (420 mi) E of Madagascar in the Indian Ocean, is the largest island in the Mascarene Archipelago. Réunion lies between 20°52′ and 21°22′S and between 55°13′ and 55°50′E, is 55 km (34 mi) long and 53 km (33 mi) wide, and has a coastline of 207 km (129 mi). It has an area of 2,510 sq km (969 sq mi).

Volcanic in origin, Réunion is mountainous, with 10 peaks—one of them, Piton de la Fournaise, still an active volcano—rising above 2,600 km (8,500 ft). The highest, Piton des Neiges, has an altitude of 3,069 m (10,066 ft). Rosewood, ebony, ironwood, and other tropical hardwoods are represented in the forests near the coast. Torrential rivers are numerous. The mean annual

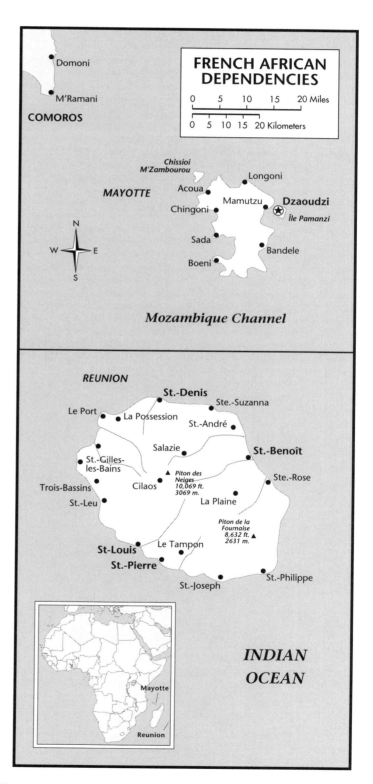

FRENCH AFRICAN DEPENDENCIES

0   5   10   15   20 Miles

0 5 10 15 20 Kilometers

COMOROS

Domoni

M'Ramani

Chissioi M'Zambourou

MAYOTTE

Acoua

Chingoni

Longoni

Mamutzu

Dzaoudzi

Île Pamanzi

Sada

Boeni

Bandele

Mozambique Channel

REUNION

St.-Denis

Le Port

La Possession

Ste.-Suzanna

St.-André

Salazie

St.-Gilles-les-Bains

Trois-Bassins

St.-Leu

Cilaos

Piton des Neiges 10,069 ft. 3069 m.

St.-Benoît

Ste.-Rose

La Plaine

Piton de la Fournaise 8,632 ft. 2631 m.

St-Louis

Le Tampon

St.-Pierre

St.-Joseph

St.-Philippe

Mayotte

Reunion

INDIAN OCEAN

temperature is 23°C (73°F) at sea level, but the climate, generally tropical, varies with orientation and altitude. The east coast receives almost daily precipitation, totaling some 350 cm (140 in) annually, but on the north coast, annual rainfall is only about half that. Cyclones, which threaten from December to April, have devastated Réunion several times. Sea fauna is rich and varied.

The population was estimated to be 639,622 in 1993. One-fourth of the islanders are of French origin, including those in the military; Réunion is the headquarters for French military forces in the Indian Ocean area. About 87% of the people are Roman Catholic, and most of the rest are Muslim.

There are about 2,800 km (1,740 mi) of roads, more than one-third of which are hard surfaced. Only the sugar plantations have functioning rail service. Pointe des Galets is the chief port, Saint-Pierre the main fishing port. Air France maintains a service from Gillot-Sud Airfield, near Saint-Denis, to Madagascar, and there are regular steamer services.

Réunion has telephone and telegraph connections with Mauritius, Madagascar, and France. Except for one private television channel, radio and television services are administered by the French broadcasting system. The newspapers *Journal de l'Île de la Réunion, Quotidien de la Réunion,* and *Témoignages* are published daily.

At the time of its discovery on 9 February 1513 by the Portuguese explorer Pedro de Mascarenhas, Réunion was uninhabited. A few French colonists came in the 16th century to Bourbon Island, as it was then known. It was settled by the French as a penal colony in the early 17th century, and in 1665, it became an outpost of the French East India Company. Coffee, and after 1800 sugarcane, helped make the colony relatively prosperous. French immigration continued from the 17th to the 19th century, supplemented by influxes of Negroes, Malays, Indochinese, Chinese, and Malabar Indians. The island received its present name in 1793. With the mid-19th century came a decline in Réunion's prosperity: slavery was abolished in 1848, and the opening of the Suez Canal in 1869 cost the island its importance as a stopover on the East Indies route.

An overseas department of France since 1946, and elevated to regional status in 1973, Réunion is represented in the French parliament by five deputies and three senators. Local administration is patterned on that of metropolitan France. There are a regional council of 45 elected members and a general council of 36.

The GDP was estimated at us$3.37 billion in 1987, or us$6,000 per capita. Agriculture employed about 30% of the economically active population in 1993. Geranium, vetiver, vanilla, and other plants used in the perfume industry also are important. Coffee, tobacco, and corn are also grown, as well as large quantities of tropical fruit. Foodstuffs are a main import.

The monetary unit is the French franc; Fr1 = $0.1824 (or $1 = Fr5.4812). Main imports include rice and petroleum products; chief exports are sugar and rum. Almost two-thirds of foreign trade is with France. Imports totaled us$1.7 billion in 1988; exports totaled $us166 million.

The infant mortality rate was 8.1 per 1,000 live births in 1993, down from 13 per 1,000 live births in the mid-1980s. The Université de la Réunion is in Saint-Denis.

In 1968, certain islands that had previously been administered from Madagascar, and later by the French Southern and Antarctic Territories, were placed under the direct administration of the commissioner residing in Saint-Denis. Europe Island (22°21′s and 40°21′E), in the Mozambique Channel about 340 km (210 mi) west of Madagascar, is heavily wooded and has a meteorological station and airstrip. Bassas da India (21°27′s and 39°45′E), in the Mozambique Channel, is a volcanic rock 2.4 m (8 ft) high, surrounded by reefs, which disappears under the waves at high tide. Juan de Nova (also known as Saint-Christophe, at 17°3′s and 42°43′E), also in the Mozambique Channel, about 145 km (90 mi) west of Madagascar, is exploited for its guano and other fertilizers. The Glorioso Islands (Îles Glorieuses), in the Indian Ocean 213 km (132 mi) northwest of Madagascar, at about 11°34′s and 47°17′E, consist of Grande Glorieuse, the Île du Lyse, and three tiny islets, the Roches Vertes; principal products are coconuts, corn, turtles, and guano. Tromelin Island (15°53′s and 54°31′E) has an important meteorological station.

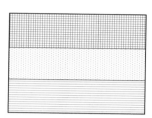

GABON

Gabonese Republic
République Gabonaise

CAPITAL: Libreville.

FLAG: The flag is a tricolor of green, golden yellow, and royal blue horizontal stripes.

ANTHEM: *La Concorde (Harmony).*

MONETARY UNIT: The Communauté Financière Africaine franc (CFA Fr) is a paper currency. There are coins of 1, 2, 5, 10, 25, 50, 100, and 500 CFA francs, and notes of 50, 100, 500, 1,000, 5,000, and 10,000 CFA francs. CFA Fr1 = $0.0018 (or $1 = CFA Fr571).

WEIGHTS AND MEASURES: The metric system is the legal standard.

HOLIDAYS: New Year's Day, 1 January; Day of Renewal, 12 March; Labor Day, 1 May; Africa Freedom Day, 25 May; Assumption, 15 August; Independence Day, 17 August; All Saints' Day, 1 November; Christmas, 25 December. Movable religious holidays include Easter Monday, Ascension, Pentecost Monday, 'Id al-Fitr, and 'Id al-'Adha'.

TIME: 1 PM = noon GMT.

¹LOCATION, SIZE, AND EXTENT

Situated on the west coast of Africa and straddling the Equator, Gabon has an area of 267,670 sq km (103,348 sq mi), extending 717 km (446 mi) NNE–SSW and 644 km (400 mi) ESE–WNW. Comparatively, the area occupied by Gabon is slightly smaller than the state of Colorado. It is bordered on the N by Cameroon, on the E and S by the Congo, on the W by the Atlantic Ocean, and on the NW by Equatorial Guinea, with a total boundary length of 3,436 km (2,135 mi).

Gabon's capital city, Libreville, is located on the country's northwestern coast.

²TOPOGRAPHY

Rising from the coastal lowlands, which range in width from 30 to 200 km (20 to 125 mi), is a band more than 96 km (60 mi) wide forming a rocky escarpment, which ranges in height from 450 to 600 m (1,480 to 1,970 ft). This plateau covers the north and east and most of the south. Rivers descending from the interior have carved deep channels in the face of the escarpment, dividing it into distinct blocks, such as the Crystal Mountains (Monts de Cristal) and the Chaillu Massif. There are mountains in various parts of Gabon, the highest peak being Mt. Iboundji (1,575 m/5,167 ft). The northern coastline is deeply indented with bays, estuaries, and deltas as far south as the mouth of the Ogooué River, forming excellent natural shelters. Farther south, the coast becomes more precipitous, but there are also coastal areas bordered by lagoons and mangrove swamps. Virtually the entire territory is contained in the basin of the Ogooué River, which is about 1,100 km (690 mi) long and navigable for about 400 km (250 mi). Its two major tributaries are the Ivindo and the Ngounié, which are navigable for 80–160 km (50–100 mi) into the interior.

³CLIMATE

Gabon has the moist, hot climate typical of tropical regions. The hottest month is January, with an average high at Libreville of 31°C (88°F) and an average low of 23°C (73°F). Average July temperatures in the capital range between 20° and 28°C (68° and

82°F). From June to September there is virtually no rain but high humidity; there is occasional rain in December and January. During the remaining months, rainfall is heavy. The excessive rainfall is caused by the condensation of moist air resulting from the meeting, directly off the coast, of the cold Benguela Current from the south and the warm Guinea Current from the north. At Libreville, the average annual rainfall is more than 254 cm (100 in). Farther north on the coast, it is 381 cm (150 in).

⁴FLORA AND FAUNA

Plant growth is rapid and dense. About 85% of the country is covered by heavy rain forest. The dense green of the vegetation never changes, since the more than 3,000 species of plants flower and lose their leaves continuously throughout the year according to species. Tree growth is especially rapid; in the more sparsely forested areas, the trees tower as high as 60 m (200 ft), and the trunks are thickly entwined with vines. There are about 300 species of trees. In the coastal regions, marine plants abound, and wide expanses are covered with tall papyrus grass.

Most tropical fauna species are found in Gabon. Wildlife includes elephants, buffalo, antelope, situtungas, lions, panthers, crocodiles, and gorillas. There are hundreds of species of birds.

⁵ENVIRONMENT

Gabon's environmental problems include deforestation, pollution and wildlife preservation. The forests that cover 85% of the country are threatened by excessive logging activities.

Gabon's coastal forests have been depleted, but there is a reforestation program, and most of the interior remains under dense forest cover. There are two national parks and four wildlife reserves in which hunting is banned. Pollution of the land is a problem in Gabon's growing urban centers due to industrial and domestic contaminants. Gabon's cities produce 0.1 million tons of solid waste annually. The nation's water is affected by pollutants from the oil industry. As of 1994, Gabon had 39.4 cubic miles of water. Seventy-two percent is used in domestic and urban areas. Fifty percent of the country's rural people do not have pure water. The expansion of Gabon's urban population is accompanied by a greater demand for meat. As a result, the nation's wildlife suffer from poaching. As of 1994, 17 of Gabon's 190 species of mammals are endangered. Four bird species in a total of 617 are also endangered along with two types of reptiles. Eighty of Gabon's 8,000 plant species are threatened with extinction.

6POPULATION

The population of Gabon was estimated at 1,375,000 in 1995 by the UN. This figure, however, was far higher than the US Census Bureau estimate of 1,126,808 for 1994. On the basis of the latter figure, the average population density was 4.2 per sq km (10.9 per sq mi). Most of the people live on the coast or are concentrated along rivers and roads; large areas of the interior are sparsely inhabited. About 46% of the population is urban. Major centers are Libreville, the capital and principal city, with about 289,000 inhabitants in 1990, and Port-Gentil, with about 164,000 in 1988.

7MIGRATION

Because of its limited population and booming economy, Gabon relies heavily on laborers from other African nations, including Benin, Cameroon, Equatorial Guinea, Mali, and Senegal. About 100,000–200,000 non-Gabonese Africans are believed to be in Gabon, many of them from Equatorial Guinea or Cameroon. There are about 30,000 Europeans, mostly French. About 122,000 Gabonese live abroad, according to a 1981 government paper.

8ETHNIC GROUPS

There are at least 40 distinct tribal groups in Gabon. The Pygmies are said to be the original inhabitants. Only about 3,000 of them remain, scattered in small groups in the heart of the forest. The largest tribal group, the Fang (about 30% of the population), came from the north in the 18th century and settled in northern Gabon. In the Woleu-Ntem part of Gabon, their direct descendants may be found almost unmixed with other Bantu ethnic strains. The Mbédé, Eshira, Bapounou, Batéké, and Bakèlè are other major groups. Smaller groups include the Omyènè, a linguistic group that includes the Mpongwe, Galoa, Nkomi, Orungu, and Enenga; these peoples live along the lower Ogooué, from Lambaréné to Port-Gentil. The Kota, or Bakota, are located mainly in the northeast, but several tribes have spread southward; they are well known for their carved wooden figures. Other groups include Vili and the Séké.

9LANGUAGES

French is the official language of the republic. The Fang language is spoken in northern Gabon, and other Bantu languages are spoken elsewhere in the country.

10RELIGIONS

Christians in Gabon number perhaps 60% of the total population, with 52.7% of the country being Roman Catholic in 1993. There are about 10,000 Muslims. Much of the population practices African indigenous religions, both exclusively and in addition to Christianity.

11TRANSPORTATION

Until the 1970s, Gabon had no railroads. A 936-km (582-mi) railroad construction program, the Trans-Gabon Railway, began in October 1974. In its first stage, completed in 1983, the project linked the port of Owendo with the interior city of Booué (332 km/206 mi) at a cost of CFA Fr227 billion, plus CFA Fr98 billion for related infrastructure. The second stage, completed in December 1986, links Booué with Franceville (357 km/222 mi) via Moanda, thus facilitating exports of manganese from the southeast and forestry exploitation in the same region. The proposed third stage would continue the line from Booué to Belinga in the northeast, where there are iron ore deposits. The project was on hold pending an improvement in world market conditions for iron ore.

Main roads connect virtually all major communities, but maintenance work is difficult because of heavy rainfall. In 1991, the road network comprised 7,500 km (4,660 mi), of which 560 km (348 mi) were tarred. A north–south road runs the length of the country, from Bitam to Ndendé. This main north–south link continues into Cameroon in the north and the Congo in the south. An east–west road connects Libreville and Mékambo. Farther south, another road runs from Mayumba to Lastoursville and Franceville. In 1991 there were about 23,000 automobiles and 17,000 commercial vehicles in use.

The busiest ports are Port-Gentil, the center for exports of petroleum products and imports of mining equipment, and Owendo, a new port that opened in 1974 on the Ogooué estuary, 10 km (6 mi) north of Libreville. Owendo's capacity, initially 300,000 tons, reached 1.5 million tons in 1979, when the port was enlarged to include timber-handling facilities. The smaller port at Mayumba also handles timber, and a deepwater port is planned for the city. In 1991, Gabon owned two oceangoing vessels totaling 18,000 GRT. The government also owned four river transport ships. River transportation is used especially to float logs.

Gabon has three international airports—at Libreville, Port-Gentil, and Franceville. There are another 56 usable airports, for a total of ten with permanent-surface runways. Air Gabon is the national airline, serving European, West and Central African, and domestic destinations. Traffic handled in 1991 at the Leon Mba airport at Libreville came to 611,000 passengers and about 10,900 tons of freight. Numerous other airlines also provide international flights. Air Affaires Gabon handles scheduled domestic service.

12HISTORY

Bantu peoples began to migrate to what is now Gabon from Cameroon and eastern Nigeria at least 2,000 years ago. The Portuguese sighted the coast as early as 1470 and gave Gabon its name because the shape of the Rio de Como estuary reminded them of a "gabao," a Portuguese hooded cloak. The Portuguese founded permanent outposts, notably at the mouth of the Ogooué River, and their missionaries followed shortly. After the Portuguese, the region was visited by the English, Dutch, and French. During the 17th century, the great French trading companies entered the slave trade. French Jesuit missionaries were active along the coast during this period, and their influence eventually extended to the powerful native kingdoms inland.

The abolition of the slave trade by France in 1815 ruined many merchants but did not end French interest in the Gabon coast. French vessels were entrusted to prevent the illegal slave trade, and the search for new products for trade led to French occupation of the coastal ports. In 1839, the French concluded a treaty with Denis, the African king whose authority extended over the northern Gabon coast, by which the kingdom was ceded to France in return for French protection. A similar treaty gained much of the southern coast below the Ogooué, and gradually other coastal chiefs accepted French control. The present capital, Libreville ("place of freedom"), was founded in 1849 by slaves who had been freed from a contraband-slave runner.

French explorers gradually penetrated the interior after 1847. During 1855–59, Paul du Chaillu went up the Ogooué River, where he became the first European to see a live gorilla. He was followed by the Marquis de Compiègne, Alfred Marche, and other explorers, who mapped out its tributaries. Pierre Savorgnan de Brazza explored almost the entire course of the river during 1876–78. In 1880, he founded Franceville. In 1885, the Congress of Berlin recognized French rights over the right bank of the

Congo, an area that Brazza had explored extensively. In 1890, Gabon formally became a part of French Congo. It was separated into a district administrative region in 1903 and in 1910 was organized as a separate colony, part of French Equatorial Africa. In 1940, Free French forces ousted the Vichy government from Gabon.

Léon Mba and Jean-Hilaire Aubame were the early leaders of the independence movement in Gabon, but their political inclinations were different. Mba led the Gabon Democratic Bloc; Aubame led the Gabonese branch of the Party of African Reunion. The latter actively sought the formation of federal, supranational groupings in Africa, whereas the former was strongly opposed to such associations. Underlying the attitude of Mba was the belief that Gabon, having the richest economic potential in the region, would end up supporting its poorer neighbors in any federal system.

In a referendum on 28 September 1958, the territory of Gabon voted to become an autonomous republic within the French Community. On 19 February 1959, a constitution was adopted, and a provisional government headed by Mba became the first official government of Gabon. Independence was formally proclaimed on 17 August 1960.

On 12 February 1961, Mba was elected president of the republic, heading a government of national union in which Aubame served as foreign minister. Friction continued between Mba and Aubame, however, and after several years of political maneuvering, Aubame led a successful coup d'état on 18 February 1964. Mba was reinstated on the very next day through French military intervention, as provided for by a treaty signed between the Mba government and the French in 1960.

Mba created the post of vice-president in February 1967, and at his death on 28 November of that year, power was transferred peacefully to his vice-president, Albert-Bernard Bongo. On 12 March 1968, Bongo announced the formal institution of a one-party system and the creation of the Gabon Democratic Party (PDG) as the country's sole legal political organization. He was reelected without opposition in 1973, 1979, and 1986. (It was announced in 1973 that Bongo had taken the name of Omar and converted to Islam.)

During the 1970s and early to mid-1980s, the exploitation of Gabon's valuable natural resources progressed rapidly, and in 1975, the country became a full member of OPEC. In 1986, depressed oil prices caused a sharp decline in oil earnings, resulting in severe austerity measures in 1986 and 1987.

These austerities in the face of Bongo's ostentations led to internal pressures for reform in the late 1980s. In 1989, Bongo began talks with some elements of the underground Movement for National Recovery (MORENA). This divided MORENA, but it failed to stem the emergence of new movements calling for the establishment of multiparty democracy.

After months of prodemocracy rallies and strikes, in 1990 Bongo ended 22 years of one-party rule. He began to talk about the legalization of opposition parties and called for elections in September. But the killing of an opposition leader on 23 May 1990 led to riots in Port-Gentil and Libreville. France sent in troops to protect its expatriates and corporate property. France also pressured Bongo to reform.

The multiparty legislative elections were held in September–October 1990, but they were filled with violence and suspected fraud. Opposition parties had not yet been declared formally legal.

In January 1991, the Assembly passed by unanimous vote a law legalizing opposition parties. Throughout 1991 and 1992, there was endemic unrest, government clamp downs and economic disruption. Still, the PDG reaffirmed its commitment to multiparty democracy. On 5 December 1993, multiparty presidential elections confirmed Bongo, running as an independent, as

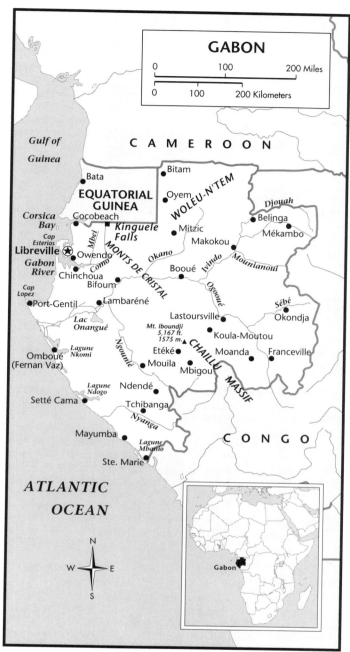

LOCATION: 2°19′N to 3°55′S; 9°18′ to 14°32′E. **BOUNDARY LENGTHS:** Cameroon, 302 km (188 mi); Congo, 1,656 km (1,029 mi); Atlantic coastline, 739 km (459 mi); Equatorial Guinea, 386 km (240 mi). **TERRITORIAL SEA LIMIT:** 12 mi.

president with 51% of the vote, against Paul Mba Abessole. Opposition parties protested the result and forced a postponement of the 26 December 1993 legislative elections. International observers complained of widespread procedural irregularities but found no evidence of deliberate fraud. Independent observers, however, have reported a governmental policy of limitations on freedoms of speech, press, association and assembly, and the harassment of its critics.

Mba Abessole, angry at the outcome, announced the formation of a rival government, dedicated to new presidential elections, restore peace, and maintain national unity. The rival administration was later supported by a High Council of the Republic, composed mostly of defeated presidential candidates.

13GOVERNMENT

According to the constitution promulgated on 19 February 1961 and subsequently amended, Gabon is a parliamentary democracy with a presidential form of government. Elected for a seven-year term by direct universal suffrage, the president, who is chief of state, selects and may dismiss members of the Council of Ministers, appoints government officials, and is chief of the armed forces. In 1967, the constitution was modified to provide for the election of a vice-president, but in 1975, the office was abolished and replaced by that of a prime minister. In 1983, the constitution was amended officially to declare Gabon a one-party state. Opposition parties were legalized in 1991.

Legislative power resides in the National Assembly, a unicameral body that is elected for five years by direct universal adult suffrage. In 1987, membership in the National Assembly was 120, of whom 111 were elected and 9 appointed by the president for five-year terms. Legislation may be initiated by the president or by members of the Assembly. The president may dissolve the Assembly and call for new elections within 40 days and may also prorogue the body for up to 18 months. Legislation is subject to presidential veto and must then be passed by a two-thirds vote to become law. The voting age is 18.

In March–April 1990, a national political conference discussed the political system. The PDG and 74 other organizations attended, essentially dividing into two loose coalitions, the ruling PDG and its allies, and the United Front of Opposition Associations and Parties. The conference approved sweeping reforms, including the creation of a national senate, decentralization of the budgetary process, and freedom of assembly and press.

Bongo resigned as PDG chairman and created a transitional government headed by a new prime minister, Casimir Oye-Mba. The Gabonese Social Democratic Grouping (GSDG), as the resulting government was called, included representatives from opposition parties. The GSDG drafted a new constitution that was eventually approved by the National Assembly, still controlled by the PDG. It came into force in March 1991. It provided for a basic bill of rights and an independent judiciary, but retained a strong presidency, to which Bongo was elected on 5 December 1993, by a 51.18% vote. That result was challenged in the Constitutional Court, which confirmed his victory.

Opposition parties declared Paul Mba Abessole, head of the National Rally of Woodcutters (RNB), the real winners and they set up a rival government.

14POLITICAL PARTIES

When Gabon became independent in 1960, there were two major political parties. The Gabon Democratic Bloc (Bloc Démocratique Gabonais—BDG), led by Léon Mba, was an offshoot of the African Democratic Rally (Rassemblement Démocratique Africain), created by Félix Houphouet-Boigny of Côte d'Ivoire. The Gabon Democratic and Social Union (Union Démocratique et Sociale Gabonaise—UDSG), led by Jean-Hilaire Aubame, was affiliated with the Party of African Reunion (Parti de Regroupement Africain), an international movement created by Léopold-Sédar Senghor of Senegal. In the first elections after independence, neither party won a majority in the Assembly, and in the elections held in 1961, the leaders of the two parties agreed upon a single list of candidates; this joint list polled 99% of the votes. Mba became president and Aubame became minister of foreign affairs in a "government of national amity." This government lasted until February 1963, when the BDG element forced the UDSG members to choose between a merger of the parties and resignation from the government. The UDSG ministers all resigned, but Aubame was later appointed president of the newly created Supreme Court. He resigned from this post in December 1963 and resumed his seat in the National Assembly.

In January 1964, Mba dissolved the Assembly and called for new elections on 23 February 1964. The UDSG was unable to present a list of candidates that would meet the electoral law, and when it seemed that the BDG list would be elected by default, the Gabonese military revolted and toppled the Mba government in a bloodless coup led by Aubame on 18 February 1964. French military forces intervened and reestablished the Mba government on 19 February. In the parliamentary elections held on 12 April 1964, the BDG list won 31 seats; the reorganized opposition gained 16 seats.

Another election was held in March 1967, in which Mba was reelected president and Albert-Bernard Bongo was elected vice-president. Mba died on 28 November 1967, and Bongo became president on 2 December of that year. On 12 March 1968, the Democratic Party of Gabon (Parti Démocratique Gabonais—PDG), headed by Bongo, became the sole political party. On 25 February 1973, President Bongo was elected to his first full seven-year term. On 30 December 1979, Bongo was reelected with 99.85% of the more than 700,000 votes cast, a total that exceeded by far the number of registered voters. He was reelected again on 9 November 1986, reportedly receiving all but 260 of 904,039 votes cast. The single list of PDG National Assembly candidates was elected in February 1980, although independents were also allowed to run. In 1985, the list consisted of all PDG members, chosen by party activists from 268 nominated; only 35 incumbent deputies were retained. Thirteen women were elected. In 1983, three generals were elected to the central committee of the PDG, the first such admission of the military into high party ranks.

The Movement for National Reform (Mouvement de Redressement National—MORENA), an opposition group, emerged in 1981 and formed a government in exile in 1985. A number of persons were sentenced to long jail terms in 1982 for alleged participation in MORENA. All had been released by mid-1986. In 1989, Bongo began talks with elements within MORENA, playing on division within their ranks. The resulting split ushered in the Rassemblement National des Bûcherons, National Rally of Woodcutters (RNB) and the MORENA-Original or Fundamental.

Emerging from the legalization of opposition party activity in March 1991 is the Association for Socialism in Gabon (APSG), the Gabonese Socialist Union (USG), the Circle for Renewal and Progress (CRP), and the Union for Democracy and Development (UDD).

15LOCAL GOVERNMENT

Gabon is divided into 9 provinces, administered by governors, which are subdivided into 37 prefectures, headed by prefects. There are eight separate subprefectures, governed by subprefects. These officers are directly responsible to the government at Libreville and are appointed by the president. In some areas, the traditional chiefs still retain power, but their position has grown less secure. Local elections for assemblies at all levels, including 12 municipal councils, were held in 1987; more than one list was allowed, but all candidates were screened by the PDG.

16JUDICIAL SYSTEM

The civil court system consists of three tiers: the trial court, the appellate court, and the Supreme Court. The 1991 constitution, which established many basic freedoms and fundamental rights, also created a Constitutional Court, a body which considers only constitutional issues, and which has demonstrated a good degree of independence in decisionmaking. Some of its decisions on election freedoms were integrated into the Electoral Code of 1993, which formed the framework for the first multi-party presidential election held that year.

The judiciary also consists of a military tribunal which handles offenses under military law, a state security court (a civilian tribunal), and a special criminal court for cases of fraud and corruption involving government officials. There is no longer recognition of traditional or customary courts, although village chiefs continue to engage in informal dispute resolution. The independence of the judiciary is less certain in state security trials where the influence of the executive may be of some import.

17ARMED FORCES
In 1993, Gabon had an army of 3,250 personnel; a navy of 500, with 7 vessels; and an air force of 1,000, with 20 combat aircraft and 7 armed helicopters. Paramilitary forces of coast guards and police totaled 4,800. France maintains a battalion of 500 marines in Gabon. Defense spending is $102 million (1990) or 3.2 percent of gross domestic product.

18INTERNATIONAL COOPERATION
Gabon was admitted to UN membership on 20 September 1960, and it has become a member of ECA and all the nonregional specialized agencies. Gabon is also a member of the African Development Bank, the French Community, G-77, the OAU, and OPEC and a signatory to GATT and the Law of the Sea. The OAU summit conference was held in Libreville in 1977. Together with the Central African Republic, the Congo, Chad, and Cameroon, it forms the UDEAC, a customs union in which merchandise, property, and capital circulate freely. As a party to the Lomé Convention, Gabon is also associated with the EEC. Libreville is the headquarters for the 12-member African Timber Organization of timber exporters and for the Economic Community of Central African States, consisting of the UDEAC countries and five others.

19ECONOMY
Rich in resources, Gabon is a country that, for a period of 15 years, realized growth rate of 9.5% before succumbing to oil-price instability and the laws of international borrowing; GDP growth in 1991 stood at 1.4%. Gabon found itself obliged to request a standby IMF credit as early as 1978.

Gabon is not self-sufficient in food; it is densely forested and only a fraction of the arable land is cultivated. Yet, 75.5% of its population (mid 1980s) gain their livelihood in the agricultural sector, where the staple food crops are cassava, plantains, and yams.

Gabon's cash crops are palm oil, cocoa, coffee, and sugar. Palm oil is the most important of the four, with production increasing 14.4% between 1988 and 1989. Cocoa has never regained its 1970s production highs. The coffee sector has been hard hit in recent years by low world prices and lower producer prices. Gabon is self-sufficient in sugar, which it exports to the US and the Central African Republic. Rubber production has been promoted in recent years, and Gabon now has four rubber plantations.

In January 1994 France suddenly devalued the CFA franc, causing its value to drop in half overnight. Immediately, prices for almost all imported goods soared, including prices for food and essential drugs. Since 1948 France had guaranteed a fixed parity of one French franc to 50 African francs. The resulting stability in the currency had generally kept inflation low and helped to maintain a steady rate of growth. However, in the 1980s, the economies of the CFA countries began to stagnate in relation to other African nations, and France came under increased pressure from the World Bank, the IMF, and western countries to stop subsidizing the CFA franc. The devaluation, long expected in the investment community, is designed to enourage new investment, particularly in the export sectors of the economy, and discourage the use of hard currency reserves to buy products that could be grown domestically.

In the face of dramatically escalating prices, uncertainty and anger led petroleum workers to strike for a doubling of their wages. The government reacted by imposing a national "state of alert." Lootings and burnings were reported as government troops tried to silence opposition parties. France has said it will nearly halve Gabon's debt, a move that has encouraged the international financial community. The long-term impact on Gabon's economy, however, is far from certain.

20INCOME
In 1992 Gabon's GNP was $5,341 million at current prices, or $4,450 per capita. For the period 1985–92 the average inflation rate was 1.6%, resulting in a real growth rate in per capita GNP of –2.1%. In 1992 the GDP was $5,913 million in current US dollars. Petroleum makes up 31.1% of that total, while agriculture and forestry account for 9.8%. Mining adds 4.6% to GDP and timber less than 1%. Refining and processing industries add 6.7% to GDP, trade 8.9%, and transport 4.9%.

21LABOR
Owing to a domestic labor shortage, Gabon had employed migrant workers (especially from Burkina Faso) to complete the Trans-Gabon Railway. In 1992 there were 87,000 persons in the labor force, down from 105,000 in 1990.

In 1992, the former monopoly of the Gabonese Labor Confederation (COSYGA) was abolished and disassociated with the ruling Democratic Party of Gabon, and two new labor federations have been started to compete with COSYGA. Since the 1990 National Conference, many small company-based unions have been started, resulting in sporadic and often disruptive strikes. Unions in each sector of the economy negotiate with employers over pay scales, working conditions, and benefits. Agreements between labor and management in each sector apply also to non-union and foreign national labor.

22AGRICULTURE
Since independence, the dominant position of the petroleum sector has greatly reduced the role of agriculture. Only 1.7% of the total land area is estimated to be under cultivation, and agriculture contributes only about 8% of the GDP on the average. In 1992, agricultural imports by Gabon accounted for nearly 14% of all imports. Gabon relies heavily on other African states and Europe for much of its food and other agricultural needs. Until World War II, agriculture was confined primarily to subsistence farming and the cultivation of such crops as manioc, bananas, corn, rice, taro, and yams. Since independence there has been an intensive effort to diversify and increase agricultural production. Experimental stations and demonstration farms have been set up, and cooperatives have been established by consolidating rural communities. However, agriculture received low priority until the 1976–81 development plan, and laborers prefer to seek employment in urban areas. Another problem is lack of transportation to markets.

In 1992, Gabon produced about 260,000 tons of cassava, 115,000 tons of yams, 72,000 tons of other roots and tubers, 245,000 tons of plantains, 31,000 tons of vegetables, and 24,000 tons of corn. Sugarcane production was about 160,000 tons. Cocoa is the most important cash crop; production in 1992 was 2,000 tons. Coffee production totaled 2,000 tons in 1992.

A state-owned 7,500-hectare (18,500-acre) palm oil plantation near Lambaréné began production in 1986. Palm oil production was 5,000 tons in 1992. A 4,300-hectare (10,600-acre) rubber project was being developed.

23ANIMAL HUSBANDRY
Animal husbandry is limited by the presence of the tsetse fly, though tsetse-resistant cattle have recently been imported from Senegal to a cattle project. In 1992 there were an estimated 164,000 hogs, 252,000 sheep and goats, 29,000 head of cattle, and 2 million chickens. In an effort to reduce Gabon's reliance on

meat imports, the government set aside 200,000 hectares (494,000 acres) in Gabon's unpopulated Savannah region for three ranches at Ngounie, Nyanga, and Lekabi. These ranches' herds numbered about 25,000 head as of 1993, with plans for increasing to 50,000 by 1998. Currently, however, frozen imports are the most important source of beef, costing four times less than locally produced beef. Poultry production satisfies about one-half of Gabon's consumption demand. Typical annual production of poultry amounts to 3,000 tons.

24FISHING

While there have been recent improvements in the fishing industry, it is still relatively undeveloped. Traditional fishing accounts for two-thirds of total catch. The waters off the Gabonese coast contain large quantities of fish. Gabonese waters are estimated to be able to support an annual catch of 15,000 tons of tuna and 12,000 tons of sardines. The fishing fleet was formerly based chiefly in Libreville. A new fishing port, however, was built at Port-Gentil in 1979. Port-Gentil is now the center of operations for the industrial fleet. Plans for a cannery, fish meal factory, and refrigerated storage facilities are underway. The total catch in 1991 was 22,000 tons, almost all from the Atlantic. By international agreement and Gabonese law, an exclusive economic zone extends 200 mi off the coast, which prohibits any foreign fishing company to fish in this zone without governmental authorization. However, since Gabon has no patrol boats, foreign trawlers (especially French and Spanish) often illegally capture tuna in Gabonese waters.

25FORESTRY

Gabon's forests, which cover an estimated 77% of its land surface, have always supplied many of the necessities of life, especially fuel and shelter. The forests contain over 400 species of trees, with about 100 species suitable for industrial use. Commercial exploitation began as early as 1892, but only in 1913 was okoumé, Gabon's most valuable wood, introduced to the international market. Forestry was the primary source of economic activity in the country until 1968, when the industry was supplanted by crude oil as an earner of foreign exchange. Gabon is the largest exporter of raw wood in the region, and its sales represent 20% of Africa's raw wood exports. Forestry is second only to the petroleum sector in export earnings, at $205 million in 1992 (8.8% of total exports). Gabon's reserves of exploitable timber in 1992 included: okoumé, 100 million cu m; ozigo, 25–35 million cu m; ilomba, 20–30 million cu m; azobe, 15–25 million cu m; and padouk, 10–20 million cu m.

Gabon supplies 90% of the world's okoumé, which makes excellent plywood, and also produces hardwoods, such as mahogany, kevazingo, and ebony. Other woods are dibetou (tigerwood or African walnut), movingui (Nigerian satinwood), and zingana (zebrano or zebrawood). Roundwood removals were estimated at 4,286,000 cu m in 1991, of which 1,633,000 was industrial wood and 2,653,000 fuel wood.

Exploitation had been hampered, to some extent, by the inadequacy of transportation infrastructure, a deficiency now alleviated by the Trans-Gabon Railway and Ndjole-Bitam highway. Reforestation has been continuously promoted, and selective thinning and clearing have prevented the okoumé from being forced out by other species. Over 50 firms are engaged in exploitation of Gabon's forests. Logging concessions covering about 5 million hectares (12.3 million acres) have been granted by the government, with the development of the least accessible areas largely carried out by foreign firms. Traditional demand in Europe for African lumber products has declined in recent years; during the 1980s, European demand for okoumé dropped by almost one-third. Markets in Japan, Morocco, and Israel, however, have become more receptive to African imports.

26MINING

Gabon is the richest of the former French Equatorial African colonies in known mineral deposits. Oil, potash, uranium, manganese, iron, lead, zinc, diamonds, marble, and phosphate have been discovered, and several deposits are being exploited commercially. The government has successfully increased its share of the profits accruing to foreign companies under development contracts. However, mining, other than petroleum or natural gas, constituted 7% of GDP and 10% of total exports in 1991.

After petroleum, manganese is Gabon's second most important mineral product; the country is the world's fourth leading producer of manganese. The high-grade deposits at Moanda, near Franceville, are among the richest in the world. Reserves are estimated at 200 million tons of ore, with a metal content of up to 48%. Production had been limited to a ceiling of 2.8 million tons a year, corresponding closely to the capacity of the cableway—at 76 km (47 mi), Africa's longest overhead cable—used to transport the mineral to the Congo border, from which it was carried by rail to the port of Pointe Noire. The Trans-Gabon Railway now provides an export outlet through the Gabonese port of Owendo. Shipping costs have been cut by $20 million per year with the new railroad, although ore shipments fell by 16.9% in 1991 to 1,833,000 tons. Manganese is exploited by the Mining Co. of L'Ougoué (Comilog), which ranks among the world's lowest-cost manganese producers. Comilog is an international consortium in which US Steel holds a 15.1% interest, and the government of Gabon maintains a 29.23% interest in the enterprise. In 1989, 2,592,407 tons of manganese were extracted, a record; annual production capacity in 1991 was 2,700,000 tons.

Uranium was discovered in 1956 at Mounana, in the Franceville area. Exploitation was begun in 1961 by the Uranium Mining Co. of Franceville, an international consortium in which the government has taken a 25% share. Until 1978, all production was sold to the French Atomic Energy Commission by agreement between the governments of France and Gabon. As of 1991, most sales were to Italy, Japan, and France. The ore is processed on site into "yellowcake," having a 74% concentration of uranium. In 1991, 700 tons of uranium were produced, as compared with a high of 1,033.4 tons in 1980. Gold deposits in the Etéké region of southern Gabon yielded 50 kg in 1991.

The Mékambo and Belinga iron fields in the northeastern corner of Gabon are ranked among the world's richest; reserves are estimated as high as a billion tons of ore of 60–65% iron content, and production could reach as much as 20 million tons a year. Although iron was discovered there in 1895, it was not until 1955 that a full-scale commercial license was issued. An exploitation syndicate of 45% French and other European capital and 55% US capital was formed, and in 1957, the syndicate established the Iron Mining Co. of Mékambo. In 1974, the government took 60% of the company shares in a move to speed up production. Exploitation still awaits the establishment of a 225 km (140 mi) extension of the Trans-Gabon Railroad from Booué to Belinga. This construction, however, has been considered unprofitable due to current market conditions.

27ENERGY AND POWER

Oil prospecting began in 1931. Deposits were found on the coast or offshore in the vicinity of Libreville and Port-Gentil, in the northwestern part of the country. Later, large deposits were found in the south. Oil exploited from the northwest is channeled by pipeline to Cape Lopez, where there are loading facilities for export. Huge additional deposits were found on Mandji Island in 1962 and are exported from Cape Lopez. The massive Rabi Kounga oil field was discovered in 1985; by 1990, it was producing 150,000 barrels per day. The field contains about 400–600 million barrels of recoverable crude oil. Important deposits at Gamba and at Lucinda (near Mayumba) in the south are exported from terminals at the production fields. Some 80–85% of production is offshore. Gabon's proven petroleum reserves were estimated at 172 million tons in 1973, but by 1992 had fallen to an estimated 100 million tons. A national petroleum distribution company, known as PIZO, was established in May 1975, with 50% government participation. In 1979, it was replaced by 100% state-owned PETROGAB, which was entitled to market 25% of production. As of 1991, ELF-Gabon, a subsidiary of the French state oil enterprise ELF-Aquitaine, and Shell-Gabon, a subsidiary of Royal Dutch/Shell, accounted for most of the petroleum output. The government's equity in each subsidiary was 25%. Numerous companies held exploration rights under agreements that would give the state 75–95% of the oil, with the companies being paid for services. Total production of crude oil fell from 11,600,000 tons in 1975 to 7,600,000 tons in 1984, but rose to 10,600,000 tons in 1989 and 14,700,000 tons in 1992. Gabon's production goes primarily to Argentina, Brazil, France, the US, and, more recently, Taiwan.

Natural gas reserves were estimated at 184.1 billion cu m in 1973 but had dwindled to an estimated 11.3 billion cu m by 1993. Gross production of natural gas in 1991 totaled 2 million cu m, almost all of which was flared. Recoverable reserves of uranium were estimated between 12,000 and 15,000 tons at the end of 1991; that year, Gabon produced 700 tons of uranium concentrate.

In 1991 there were hydroelectric stations at the Kinguélé and Tchimbélé dams on the Mbei River and at the Petite Poubara Dam, near Makokou on the Ogooué; thermal installations numbered 24. Production and distribution of electricity are maintained by the Energy and Water Co. of Gabon, which was formed in 1963 and is a 64% government-owned company also incorporating a number of smaller private and quasi-public entities. Production increased from 114 million kwh in 1971 to 914 million kwh (77% hydroelectric) in 1991, when installed capacity was about 279,000 kw (73% hydroelectric). Additional hydroelectric expansion is being planned. Natural gas is the principal fuel for the thermal plants.

28INDUSTRY

Gabon's industry is centered on petroleum, mining, and timber processing. Most industrial establishments are located near Libreville and Port-Gentil. Generally, they are owned by French private interests. In addition, there is an asphalt plant with an annual capacity of 10,000 tons, but no figures on production have been available since 1978, when 7,000 tons were produced. Timber-related concerns include five veneer plants and one of the world's largest plywood factories (capacity 85,000 cu m), located in Port-Gentil. A large wood pulp factory is being planned at Kango. In 1984, Gabon produced an estimated 97,000 cu m of veneers and 74,800 cu m of plywood. Other industries include textile plants, cement factories, breweries, shipyards, and cigarette factories. Industrial output in 1985 included 244,678 tons of cement and 1,216,893 hectoliters of beer. In 1990, Gabon had an installed electrical generating capacity of 279,000 kw, 73% from hydro-electric sources.

29SCIENCE AND TECHNOLOGY

Gabon has a shortage of trained scientists and technicians and relies heavily on foreign—mostly French—technical assistance. In Libreville there are a French bureau of geological and mineral research, a technical center for tropical forestry, a research institute for agriculture and forestry, and a center for technical and scientific research. A laboratory of primatology and tropical forest ecology is at Makokou, and an international center of medical research, concentrating on infectious diseases and fertility, is at Franceville. The University Omar Bongo has a faculty of sciences, schools of engineering and forestry and hydraulics, and a health science center. The African Institute of Information, at Libreville,

trains computer programmers and analysts. In 1986, research and development expenditures totaled CFA Fr380 million; 18 technicians and 199 scientists and engineers were engaged in research and development.

30DOMESTIC TRADE

Most local produce is sold directly to consumers or to intermediaries at local markets in villages and towns, while imported goods are disposed of at the same time. Company agents and independent middlemen buy export crops at local markets or directly from the producers for sale to large companies. Both French and domestic companies carry on wholesale and retail trade in the larger cities. Gabonese have been trained in retailing in newly built stores. Those who qualify after training have been encouraged to buy the stores with government-sponsored loans. Advertising is carried by local newspapers, company publications, handbills, billboards, and radio and television stations.

Business hours are 8 AM–noon and 3–6 PM, Monday through Friday, and 8 AM–1 PM, Saturday. Banks are open 7:30–11:30 AM and 2:30–4:30 PM, Monday through Friday.

31FOREIGN TRADE

Gabon has a record of trade surpluses. Until the late 1960s, timber was Gabon's main export. By 1969, however, crude petroleum had become the leader, accounting for 34% of total exports. Petroleum's share increased to 40.7% in 1972 and to 81.9% in 1974; it stood at 82.5% in 1985 but fell to 65% in 1986. Gabon is also a leading exporter of manganese. The principal exports in 1989 (estimated in billions of CFA francs) were as follows:

Petroleum	61.0
Timber	48.1
Manganese	59.3
Uranium	21.1
Other exports	20.1
TOTAL	209.6

The principal imports in 1989 (estimated, in billions of CFA francs) were as follows:

Machinery and apparatus	0.6
Transport equipment	4.2
Food products	31.8
Metal and metal products	7.2
Chemicals	13.1
Vegetable and animal products	0.5
Precision instruments	4.4
Textiles	4.3
Hygiene products	10.5
Vehicles	6.0
Mineral products	3.8
Other imports	32.4
TOTAL	41.8

France is Gabon's leading trade partner, accounting for 42.7% of exports, 53.1% of imports, and 49.6% of total trade in 1986. Trade with other European Economic Community members made up 19.7% of Gabon's total trade. The US was Gabon's second leading export customer, taking in 16.9% of exports. Other major trade partners included Spain, the UK, Italy, Germany, and Japan.

32BALANCE OF PAYMENTS

Gabon's traditionally favorable trade balance does not always result in a favorable balance on current accounts, largely because of dividend payments and other remittances by foreign enterprises but also because of payments on large debts accumulated in the 1970s. Generally, however, an increasingly strong export performance and rising inflows of private and government capital have made Gabon's payments position one of the strongest of any African country.

In 1992 merchandise exports totaled $2,297.4 million and imports $885.9 million. The merchandise trade balance was $1,411.5 million. The following table summarizes Gabon's balance of payments for 1991 and 1992 (in millions of US dollars):

	1991	1992
CURRENT ACCOUNT		
Goods, services, and income	303.1	6.8
Unrequited transfers	−119.8	−142.1
TOTALS	183.3	−135.3
CAPITAL ACCOUNT		
Direct investment	−116.3	−62.0
Other long-term capital	−257.3	−511.2
Other short-term capital	−80.1	−204.8
Exceptional financing	266.9	698.2
Other liabilities	3.9	1.5
Reserves	−73.4	208.9
TOTALS	−256.4	130.6
Errors and omissions	73.1	4.6

33BANKING AND SECURITIES

The bank of issue is the Bank of the Central African States (Banque des Etats de l'Afrique Centrale—BEAC), the central bank for UDEAC members.

Commercial banking in Gabon is largely controlled by French and other foreign interests. At the end of 1993 there were 5 commercial banks, including the International Bank of Commerce and Industry of Gabon, the Gabonese Union of Banks, and the International Bank for Gabon. The Gabonese Bank of Development, 69% Gabonese-owned, is the nation's development bank. Other institutions concerned with development are the National Fund of Rural Credit, the Gabonese Society of Participation and Development, and the Society of Gabonese National Investments.

As of 1993, commercial and development banks held combined net reserves of CFA Fr7.85 billion, demand deposits of CFA Fr86.9 billion, and time and savings deposits of CFA Fr99.85 billion; claims on the private sector totaled CFA Fr157.90 billion. There is no securities market in Gabon.

34INSURANCE

In 1986 there were four French insurance companies represented in Gabon. In 1974, a national company known as SONAGAR was created, 36% owned by the government. Only three other insurance companies now operate independently in Gabon. In 1984, 97.3% of all premiums were for non-life and 2.7% for life insurance.

35PUBLIC FINANCE

Gabon negotiated its first standby credit arrangement with the IMF in 1982 after Gabon debt-service ratio reached 17% in 1980. A second agreement was reached in 1986. Gabon's debt was rescheduled in 1987. Negotiation with the IMF came to a halt in November 1988 but resumed the following year and a new funding facility was negotiated. In 1990, political instability caused the suspension of the funding program, though the government continued to adhere to the agreed-upon adjustment criteria. Improvements were realized, and in 1990 the debt-service ratio had dropped to 7.1%. A similar IMF suspension occurred in 1992 with a renewed standby agreement.

The oil sector brings in 40% of government revenues. The fall of crude oil prices on world markets in 1986 caused government revenues to drop by 58% and public debt to double to $2 billion. In 1992, public expenditures exceeded revenue by CFA Fr 29.3 billion. The medium- and long-term external debt amounted to $3.2 billion at the end of 1992, representing about 55% of GDP.

The following table shows actual revenues and expenditures for 1990 and 1991 in billions of francs.

	1990	1991
REVENUE AND GRANTS		
Tax revenue	226.4	311.19
Non-tax revenue	107.0	129.0
Capital revenue	39.9	0.8
Grants	5.0	6.0
TOTAL	378.3	447.7
EXPENDITURES & LENDING MINUS REPAYMENTS	328.1	480.3
Deficit/Surplus	51.0	−25.2

Expenditures exceeded revenue by CFA Fr29.3 billion in 1992, because of a lack of revenue. In 1992, Gabon was unable to service its medium- and long-term external debt of $3.2 billion.

36TAXATION

A graduated income tax ranging from 5% to 60% is imposed on civil servants and others who are paid fixed salaries or who have sufficient income. A complementary tax is levied at 2% for incomes up to CFA Fr100,000 per month and 5% on incomes over that figure. Additional taxes are levied on business transactions and on real property. There is a value-added tax on all goods and services and a 2.6% payroll tax.

The corporate profits tax rate is 40% after deduction for business expenses. There is a 20% withholding tax on dividends. Government oil revenues are derived from royalty payments, a tax on petroleum company profits, a tax on exploration permits, and dividends paid by the petroleum companies.

37CUSTOMS AND DUTIES

Gabon, Cameroon, the Central African Republic, and the Congo are joined in a customs union, the UDEAC. Gabon is a part of the franc zone, within which goods and capital flow without obstruction.

Import duties consist of a fiscal duty applied to all goods entering the UDEAC area, whatever their origin. It averages 10–40%, although it may be as high as 90% on certain luxury items. There is also a customs duty, ranging from 2.5–30%, applied to all imported goods. In addition, there are an entry fee, a turnover tax of 10% on imports, a complementary import tax, and a special fee on postal and border imports. Imports from outside the franc zone and the EC are subject to licensing fees, and prior authorization is required. Export duties and taxes are levied on specific commodities.

38FOREIGN INVESTMENT

Gabon has benefited from considerable private investment centered on the development of petroleum resources. Prior to independence, French investments predominated. Since independence, however, Gabon has sought additional sources of investment. US companies have invested in the lumber industry, oil exploration, and mining; in 1987, US investment totaled about $700 million.

Gabon's investment code was enacted on 8 November 1961 (amended in 1967) to replace the more general code of the UDEAC. The code gives preferential treatment with regard to taxation, duties, importation of certain equipment and raw materials, and royalties to all enterprises considered important for the development of Gabon's economy. The code makes no distinction between foreign and locally owned firms. Free transfer of capital is guaranteed, and there are no restrictions on area of activity. All new industrial, mining, farming, or forestry operations are exempt from income tax for the first two years.

The government has moved toward more public participation in business while seeking not to discourage foreign investors. A 1974 directive required that all new foreign firms operating in Gabon have their headquarters there and accept at least a 10% state partnership. Foreign-owned companies must invest 10% of their profits in local industry. State participation in petroleum enterprises is at least 25%.

39ECONOMIC DEVELOPMENT

Economic liberalism tempered by planning is the basic policy of the Gabonese government, which seeks to make the most of the country's rich natural resources. Priority is being given to the agricultural sector, to reduce imports, and to diversify the economy. Limiting migration to the cities is also an important element in this strategy. Industrial development efforts are centered on resource processing industries. Building the infrastructure is also an identifiable priority. The devaluation of the CFA franc in 1994 should stimulate local production and discourage imports.

France remains Gabon's "privileged" partner in external economic policy. Foreign aid has fallen because of Gabon's prosperity. Assistance totaled $73.5 million in 1984. French aid totaled about $69 million in 1986. Relations with the Arab countries improved temporarily in the early 1970s, leading to the conversion of President Bongo to Islam. Although relations have cooled somewhat, Gabon remains a full member of OPEC and cooperates with the Arab world on oil price policy.

40SOCIAL DEVELOPMENT

Social services based on the French model have been introduced slowly. Since 1 July 1956, family allowances have been paid to all salaried workers. Other benefits include workers' compensation, old age insurance, medicine and hospitalization, and housing assistance. Contributions are made by employers and employees at a fixed percentage of the employee's wage. The funds are administered jointly by a council consisting of employers, employees, and the government.

41HEALTH

Most of the health services are public, but there are some private institutions, of which the best known is the hospital established in 1913 in Lambaréné by Albert Schweitzer. The hospital is now partially subsidized by the Gabonese government.

Gabon's medical infrastructure is considered one of the best in West Africa. By 1985 there were 28 hospitals, 87 medical centers, and 312 infirmaries and dispensaries. There were a total of 5,156 hospital beds. Records indicate that from 1985 to 1992, 90% of the population had access to health care services.

A comprehensive government health program treats such diseases as leprosy, sleeping sickness, malaria, filariasis, intestinal worms, and tuberculosis. From 1990 to 1992, the country made admirable efforts to immunize children up to one year old against tuberculosis (96%); diphtheria, pertussis, and tetanus (78%); polio (78%); and measles (76%). In 1990, there were approximately 220 reported cases of tuberculosis per 100,000 people. Gabon has a domestic supply of pharmaceuticals from a large, modern factory in Libreville.

There were 53,000 births in 1992 (a rate of 42 per 1,000 people). The fertility rate is about 4.0 children for the average woman who has lived through her childbearing years. The infant mortality rate is 97.3 per 1,000 live births and life expectancy is 51.5 years for males and 57 years for females. In 1993, the overall mortality rate was 16 per 1,000 inhabitants.

42HOUSING

Credit institutions make small loans for the repair of existing houses and larger loans (amounting to almost the total cost of the house) for the construction of new houses. Because of their higher credit rating, salaried civil servants and employees of trading companies receive most of the loans. The government has established a national habitation fund, and there have been a number of urban renewal projects. As of 1990, 90% of urban and 50% of rural dwellers had access to a public water supply.

43EDUCATION

The educational system is patterned on that of France, but changes are being introduced gradually to adapt the curriculum to local needs and traditions. The government gives high priority to education, especially the construction of rural schools. Education is free and compulsory between the ages of 6 and 16. In 1991 there were 1,024 primary schools with 210,000 pupils and 4,782 teachers. At the secondary level, general schools had 42,871 pupils and vocational schools had 8,477 pupils. There is also an adult literacy program. The adult literacy rate was estimated at 60.7% in 1990. About one-half of all schools are private or church-supported.

Omar Bongo University, at Libreville, includes faculties of law, sciences, and letters; teachers' training schools; and schools of law, engineering, forestry and hydraulics, administration, and management. At the university and other equivalent institutions, there were 3,000 students in 1991.

44LIBRARIES AND MUSEUMS

The National Library (founded in 1969), National Archives (1969), and Documentation Center (1980) together form a collection of 25,000 volumes. The Information Center Library in Libreville has 6,000 volumes. The Museum of Arts and Traditions at Libreville is the national museum.

45MEDIA

The Ministry of Information, Posts, and Telecommunications provides domestic services for Gabon and participates in international services. There are direct radiotelephone communications with Paris and other overseas points. Radio-Diffusion Télévision Gabonaise (RTG), which is owned and operated by the government, broadcasts in French and indigenous languages. Color television broadcasts have been introduced in major cities. In 1981, a commercial radio station, Africa No. 1, began operations. The most powerful radio station on the continent, it has participation from the French and Gabonese governments and private European media. In 1991 there were 13,800 telephones, 171,000 radios, and 45,000 television sets.

The national press service is the Gabonese Press Agency, which publishes a daily bulletin. L'Union in Libreville is the only daily newspaper. It is government-controlled and had an average daily circulation of 15,000 in 1991.

46ORGANIZATIONS

There is a chamber of commerce at Libreville and a Rotary Club at Port-Gentil. UNIGABON, a national organization established in October 1959, conducts liaison work among mining companies, labor unions, public works societies, and transportation companies. Church organizations are active in the country and have a sizable following. They operate several mission schools and health centers. In rural areas, cooperatives promote the production and marketing of agricultural products. Among the tribes, self-help societies have grown rapidly, particularly in the larger towns, where tribal members act together as mutual-aid societies. There are youth and women's organizations affiliated with the PDG.

47TOURISM, TRAVEL, AND RECREATION

Gabon's tourist attractions include fine beaches, ocean and inland fishing facilities, and scenic sites, such as the falls on the Ogooué River and the Crystal Mountains. Many visitors come to see the hospital founded by Albert Schweitzer at Lambaréné. In addition, there are two national parks and four wildlife reserves. Hunting is allowed in certain areas except during October and November.

Tourism facilities are limited. Hotel room capacity in 1990 was about 2,799 with a 28% occupancy rate. In 1991, an estimated 128,000 tourists arrived in Gabon, 76% from Europe and 15% from Africa. Tourism receipts totaled US$8 million. A visitor must have a passport and visa, except if from France, Germany, or certain African countries. Evidence of yellow fever immunization is also required.

48FAMOUS GABONESE

The best-known Gabonese are Léon Mba (1902–67), the president of the republic from 1960 to 1967, and Omar Bongo (Albert-Bernard Bongo, b.1935), the president of the republic since Mba's death. Born in Alsace (then part of Germany but now in France), Albert Schweitzer (1875–1965), a world-famous clergyman, physician, philosopher, and musicologist and the 1952 winner of the Nobel Prize for peace, administered a hospital that he established in Lambaréné in 1913.

49DEPENDENCIES

Gabon has no territories or colonies.

50BIBLIOGRAPHY

Aicardi de Saint-Paul, Marc. *Gabon: The Development of a Nation.* New York: Routledge, 1989.

Barnes, James F. *Gabon.* Boulder, Colo.: Westview, 1986.

Barnes, James Franklin. *Gabon: Beyond the Colonial Legacy.* Boulder, Colo.: Westview Press, 1992.

Brabazon, James. *Albert Schweitzer: A Biography.* London: Gollancz, 1976.

Cousins, Norman. *Dr. Schweitzer of Lambaréné.* Westport, Conn.: Greenwood, 1973.

Gardinier, David E. *Gabon.* Santa Barbara, Calif.: Clio Press, 1992.

Gardinier, David E. *Historical Dictionary of Gabon.* 2d ed. Metuchen, N.J.: Scarecrow Press, 1994.

Patterson, K. David. *The Northern Gabon Coast to 1875.* London: Oxford University Press, 1975.

Weinstein, Brian. *Gabon: Nation Building on the Ogooué.* Cambridge, Mass.: MIT Press, 1966.

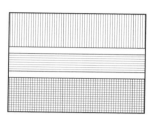

GAMBIA

Republic of the Gambia

CAPITAL: Banjul (formerly Bathurst).

FLAG: The flag is a tricolor of red, blue, and green horizontal bands, separated by narrow white stripes.

ANTHEM: *For the Gambia, Our Homeland.*

MONETARY UNIT: In 1971, the dalasi (D), a paper currency of 100 butut, replaced the Gambian pound. There are coins of 1, 5, 10, 25, and 50 butut and 1 dalasi, and notes of 1, 5, 10, 25, and 50 dalasi. D1 = $0.1031 (or $1 = D9.701).

WEIGHTS AND MEASURES: Both British and metric weights and measures are in use.

HOLIDAYS: New Year's Day, 1 January; Confederation Day, 1 February; Independence Day, 18 February; Labor Day, 1 May; Assumption, 15 August; Christmas, 25 December. Movable religious holidays include Good Friday, Easter Monday, 'Id al-Fitr, 'Id al-'Adha', and Milad an-Nabi.

TIME: GMT.

¹LOCATION, SIZE, AND EXTENT

Located on the west coast of Africa, the Gambia has an area of 11,300 sq km (4,363 sq mi), extending 320 km (199 mi) E–W and 48 km (30 mi) N–S. Comparatively, the area occupied by the Gambia is slightly more than twice the size of the state of Delaware. Bounded on the N, E, and S by Senegal (with which it is joined in the Confederation of Senegambia) and on the W by the Atlantic Ocean, the Gambia has a total boundary length of 820 km (510 mi).

Gambia's capital city, Banjul, is located on the Atlantic coast.

²TOPOGRAPHY

The Gambia River, the country's major waterway, rises in Guinea and follows a twisting path for about 1,600 km (1,000 mi) to the sea. In its last 470 km (292 mi), the river flows through the Republic of the Gambia, narrowing to a width of 5 km (3 mi) at Banjul; during the dry season, tidal saltwater intrudes as far as 250 km (155 mi) upstream. Brown mangrove swamps line both sides of the river for the first 145 km (90 mi) from the sea; the mangroves then give way to more open country and, in places, to red ironstone cliffs. The land on either side of the river is generally open savanna with wooded areas along the drainage channels. Elevation reaches a maximum of 73 m (240 ft).

³CLIMATE

The Gambia has a subtropical climate with distinct cool and hot seasons. From November to mid-May there is uninterrupted dry weather, with temperatures as low as 16°C (61°F) in Banjul and surrounding areas. Hot, humid weather predominates the rest of the year, with a rainy season from June to October; during this period, temperatures may rise as high as 43°C (109°F) but are usually lower near the sea. Mean temperatures range from 23°C (73°F) in January to 27°C (81°F) in June along the coast, and from 24°C (75°F) in January to 32°C (90°F) in May inland. The average annual rainfall ranges from 92 cm (36 in) in the interior to 145 cm (57 in) along the coast.

⁴FLORA AND FAUNA

The countryside contains many flowers, including yellow cassias and scarlet combretum. The tropical shrub area contains bougainvillea, oleander, and a dozen varieties of hibiscus. Distinctive fauna includes several varieties of monkeys.

⁵ENVIRONMENT

The Gambia's environmental concerns include deforestation, desertification, and water pollution. Deforestation is the most serious problem, with slash-and-burn agriculture the principal cause. In the 1950s, 34,000 hectares (84,000 acres) were set aside as forest parks, but by 1972, 11% of these reserves had been totally cleared. During 1981–85, deforestation averaged 2,000 hectares (5,000 acres) per year. Only 9% of the forests in the Gambia have survived the expansion of agricultural land and the use of trees for fuel. A 30% decrease in rainfall over the last 30 years has increased the rate of desertification for the Gambia's agricultural lands. Water pollution is a significant problem due to lack of adequate sanitation facilities. Impure water is responsible for life-threatening diseases which contribute to high infant mortality rates. The Gambia has 0.7 cubic miles of water with 91% used for farming activity. Fifty-two percent of the people in rural areas do not have pure water. As of 1994, the Gambia's wildlife is threatened by changes in their habitat and poaching. Seven of the nation's 108 mammal species, and 1 in a total of 489 bird species is threatened. One type of reptile is also endangered. As of 1987, the western giant eland was listed as an endangered species.

⁶POPULATION

The population of the Gambia at the time of the 1993 census was 1,025,867, up 47% from the 1983 census total of 695,886. The UN population projection for the year 2000 was 1,105,000, assuming a crude birthrate of 41.5 per 1,000 population, a crude death rate of 17.6, and a net natural increase of 23.9 during 1995–2000. The estimated population density in 1993 was 91 per sq km (235 per sq mi). About 75% of the population is rural. Banjul, the capital, had about 195,000 residents in 1990.

⁷MIGRATION

Each year, some 20,000–30,000 migrants from Senegal, Mali, and Guinea come to the Gambia to help harvest the peanut crop.

Gambians, in turn, move freely over national borders, which are poorly marked and difficult to police in West Africa. Gambia was home to 3,300 Senegalese and 300 Liberian refugees at the end of 1992.

8 ETHNIC GROUPS

The Mandingo (Malinké), who made up an estimated 42% of the population in 1993, came to the Gambia by the 13th century. Fulani (16%) predominate in the eastern part of the country; other major groups include the Wolof (15%), Jola (9%), and Serahuli (8%). About 1,200 non-Africans, including Syrians, Lebanese, and British, live in the Gambia.

9 LANGUAGES

English is the official language, but there are 21 distinct languages spoken. The principal vernaculars are Wolof and Mandinka, the latter spoken by the Mandingo.

10 RELIGIONS

Islam was introduced in the 12th century; about 85% of the population is now Muslim. Christians (3%), mostly Roman Catholics (2%), are concentrated in the Banjul area. Some Gambians also practice traditional African animist religions.

11 TRANSPORTATION

The Gambia River not only provides important internal transport but also is an international commercial link; oceangoing vessels can travel 240 km (150 mi) upstream. Banjul, the principal port, receives about 300 ships annually. Ferries operate across the river and between Banjul and Barra.

With the construction of major all-weather roads on both sides of the Gambia River, the waterway has become less significant for passenger traffic. As of 1991 there were 3,083 km (1,916 mi) of roads, including 431 km (268 mi) of paved roads; about 6,000 passenger cars and 2,500 commercial vehicles were in use. The Gambia has no railroads. There is an international airport at Yundum, 26 km (16 mi) from Banjul. Air Gambia, 60% state owned, acts as an agent only; foreign air carriers provide international service.

12 HISTORY

Small groups of Mandingos had settled in the Gambia by the 12th or 13th century AD, and a Mali-based Mandingo empire was dominant in the 13th and 14th centuries. Portuguese sailors discovered the Gambia River in 1455; its navigability made it uniquely important for European traders seeking to penetrate the interior. In 1587, English merchants began to trade in the area. The Royal African Company acquired a charter in 1678 and established a fort on James Island, a small island in the river estuary. In 1765, the forts and settlements in the Gambia were placed under the control of the crown, and for the next 18 years the Gambia formed part of the British colony of Senegambia, with headquarters at Saint-Louis. In 1783, the greater part of Senegambia was handed back to France; the Gambia section ceased to be a British colony and was returned to the Royal African Company.

In 1816, Capt. Alexander Grant entered into a treaty with the chief of Kombo for the cession of Banjul Island. He renamed it St. Mary's Island and established on it a settlement that he called Bathurst (now Banjul). In 1821, the British settlements in the Gambia were placed under the administration of the government of Sierra Leone. This arrangement continued until 1888, except for the period 1843–66, when the Gambia had its own colonial administration. In 1888, the Gambia again became a separate colony. Its boundaries were defined following an agreement with France in 1889.

After 1888, the Gambia was administered by a governor assisted by an Executive Council and a Legislative Council. In 1902, St. Mary's Island was established as a crown colony, while the rest of the territory became a protectorate. In 1960, universal adult suffrage was introduced in the protectorate, and a 34-member House of Representatives replaced the Legislative Council. The office of prime minister was created in 1962, and the Executive Council was reconstituted to include the governor as chairman, the prime minister, and eight other ministers. Dr. (later Sir) Dawda Kairaba Jawara, the leader of the Progressive People's Party (PPP), became the first prime minister. The Gambia attained full internal self-government on 4 October 1963, with Jawara as prime minister. An independence constitution, which came into force in February 1965, established the Gambia as a constitutional monarchy within the Commonwealth.

On 23 April 1970, after a referendum, the Gambia became a republic with Jawara as the first president. He and the ruling PPP remained in power into the 1980s, weathering an attempted left-wing coup and paramilitary rebellion in July 1981, which was quashed by Senegalese troops under a mutual defense pact signed in 1965; an estimated 500–800 people died in the uprising, and there was much property damage. In February 1982, the Confederation of Senegambia was formally constituted. Jawara was reelected to a new term as president that May, receiving 72.4% of the vote. He was reelected in March 1987, defeating two opponents with 59.2% of the vote, and again in April, 1992. He gained 59% of the vote to 22% for Sheriff Mustapha Dibba, his nearest of four rivals. His PPP was also returned to legislative power but with a reduced majority. It fell from 31 to 25 of the elected seats, in the 36-seat House of Representatives.

In March 1992 Jawara accused Libya of arming a force led by Samba Samyang, the leader of the 1981 coup attempt. Libya denied involvement. He also made similar accusations against Libya and Burkino Faso in 1988. In May 1992 Jawara announced an amnesty for most members of the Movement for Justice in Africa (MOJA) which had been linked to the failed 1981 coup. And in April 1993, two of MOJA's leaders returned from exile to organize as a political party.

Jawara was expected to retire in mid-term, but on 22 July 1994 he was overthrown in a bloodless military coup led by Lt. Yahya Jammeh. President Jawara took shelter in an American warship which, at the time, had been on a courtesy call. The junta of junior officers and a few civilians suspended the constitution, banned all political activity, detained its superior officers, and placed ministers of the former government under house arrest. The European Union and the United States suspended aid and pressed for a quick return to civilian rule.

13 GOVERNMENT

Under the republican constitution of 24 April 1970, as amended, the president, popularly elected for a five-year term, was the head of state. Presidential powers included designating a vice-president, who exercised the functions of a prime minister, and appointing cabinet members. The House of Representatives had 36 members elected by universal adult suffrage (at age 18), five chiefs elected by the Chiefs in Assembly, and eight appointed nonvoting members; the Attorney General is also a member ex officio. The military junta suspended the constitution on 22 July 1994.

14 POLITICAL PARTIES

The first Gambian political party, the Democratic Party, was formed in 1951 by Rev. John C. Faye. The Muslim Congress Party (CP) and the United Party (UP), led by Pierre S. N'Jie, were formed in 1952. The People's Progressive Party (PPP), under the leadership of Dawda Kairaba Jawara, was formed in 1958 and has governed the country since independence. The CP and the PPP merged in 1968. Two other parties were formed to compete

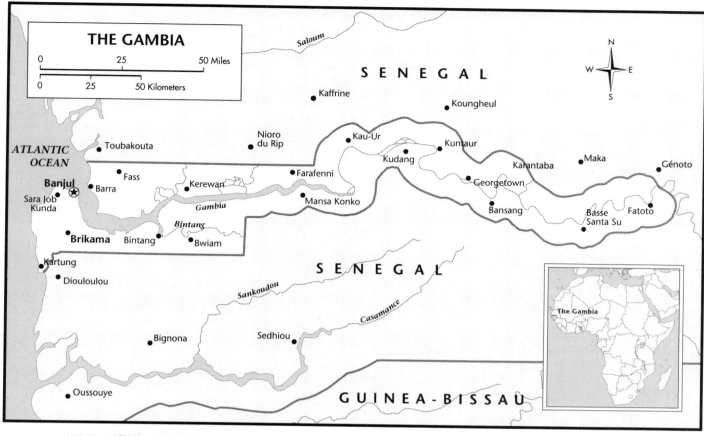

THE GAMBIA

0 25 50 Miles
0 25 50 Kilometers

LOCATION: 13°10′ to 13°35′36″N; 13°43′5″ to 16°49′31″W. **BOUNDARY LENGTHS:** Senegal, 756 km (470 mi); Atlantic coastline, 71 km (44 mi). **TERRITORIAL SEA LIMIT:** 12 mi.

in the 1977 elections, the National Liberation Party and the National Convention Party (NCP). In the elections of May 1982, the PPP won 27 seats (the same as in 1977), the NCP 3, and independents 5; in March 1987, the PPP won 31 seats and the NCP 5; and in April, 1992, PPP won 25 seats and the NCP 6.

Other parties include the Gambia People's Party (GPP), the People's Democratic Organization for Independence and Socialism (PDOIS), the Gambian People's Democratic Party (PDP), and the Movement for Justice in Africa (MOJA). After the 1994 coup all political parties were barred.

15LOCAL GOVERNMENT
There are five rural areas, not including Banjul, each with a council, the majority of whose members are elected. These areas are subdivided into 35 districts administered by chiefs with the help of village mayors and councillors. Banjul has a city council.

16JUDICIAL SYSTEM
Based on English common law, but including subsidiary legislative instruments enacted locally, the judicial system comprises the Supreme Court, the Court of Appeals, and subordinate courts. The Supreme Court, presided over by a chief justice, has both civil and criminal jurisdiction. Appeals from any decision of the Supreme Court go before the Court of Appeals, whose judgments may then be taken to the UK Privy Council. Muslim courts apply Shari'ah law in certain cases involving Muslim citizens. Magistrate's courts are courts of first instance in criminal and civil matters, while the district tribunals serve as appeals courts in cases of tribal law and custom. In traditional areas, chiefs retain power in relation to customary law and local affairs, while administrative officers function as magistrates.

Judges are appointed by the government, but generally operate free from influence of the executive or legislative branches.

17ARMED FORCES
The Gambia's armed forces had 800 members in 1993, of which the largest contingent was one infantry battalion. The 50-member naval patrol had 3 coastal patrol boats. Nigeria provides a 50-man training team, and about 100 Gambian soldiers are serving in a peacekeeping force in Liberia. Gambia spends perhaps $1 million on defense or less than 1% of its gross domestic product.

18INTERNATIONAL COOPERATION
The Gambia was admitted to the UN on 21 September 1965 and is a member of ECA and all the nonregional specialized agencies except IAEA, ILO, and UNIDO. It also belongs to the African Development Bank, Commonwealth of Nations, ECOWAS, G-77, and OAU. The nation is an adherent of GATT and a signatory to the Law of the Sea.

An agreement of confederation with Senegal, signed on 17 December 1981 and effective 1 February 1982, called for integration of the security services and armed forces of the two countries. The presidents of Senegal and the Gambia became president and vice-president of Senegambia, respectively. Each country remains sovereign and independent, however, and legislation must be ratified by the respective national parliaments.

19ECONOMY
The Gambia's light sandy soil is well suited to the cultivation of groundnuts, which is Gambia's principal agricultural export. However, groundnut production has fallen in recent years, and in 1990, tourism overtook groundnut exports as the nation's

number one export earner. Significant export revenues are earned from fishing and re-export trade. Though the Gambian economy is small, its management has been successful in stabilizing external debt and reining in inflation.

Trade is the largest contributor to GDP, with revenues of over D1.06 billion. Trade employs an estimated 50.8% of the Gambian population.

20INCOME
In 1992 Gambia's GNP was $367 million at current prices, or $390 per capita. For the period 1985–92 the average inflation rate was 14.4%, resulting in a real growth rate in per capita GNP of 1.8%. In 1992 the GDP was $357 million in current US dollars. It is estimated that in 1990 agriculture, hunting, forestry, and fishing contributed 24% to GDP; manufacturing, 6%; electricity, gas, and water, 1%; construction, 5%; wholesale and retail trade, 40%; transport, storage, and communication, 9%; finance, insurance, real estate, and business services, 9%; community, social, and personal services, 3%; and other sources, 4%.

21LABOR
Most of the population of 1 million engages in agriculture. Less than 20% of the work force consists of wage earners. In 1992, the wage labor force in the modern sector of the economy accounted for less than 20% of the total work force.

The Labor Act of 1990 allows all workers (except civil servants, police, and military personnel) to form associations and trade unions; strikes also are permitted with 14 days' notice (21 days for essential services) from the Commissioner of Labor. Collective bargaining occurs even though unions are small and fragmented. Minimum wages and hours of employment are set by six joint industrial councils (commerce, artisans, transport, the port industry, agriculture, and fisheries), but only 20% of the labor force is covered by minimum wage legislation.

22AGRICULTURE
The soil is mostly poor and sandy, except in the riverine swamps. On upland soils the main food crops, besides peanuts, are millet, manioc, corn, and beans. Most landholdings range between 5 and 9 hectares (12 and 22 acres). Agriculture supports about three-quarters of the active population, and contributed about 20% of value added in 1991–92. Irregular and inadequate rainfall has adversely affected crop production in recent years.

The principal cash crop is peanuts, grown on some 80,000 hectares (198,000 acres). Production totaled 80,000 tons in 1992. That year, the paddy rice crop was estimated at 22,000 tons. Other food crops in 1992 included an estimated 24,000 tons of corn and 65,000 tons of millet. Mangos, bananas, oranges, pawpaws, and limes are grown mainly in the Western Division. Oil palms provide oil for local consumption and kernels for export; palm oil production was estimated at 2,500 tons in 1992, and kernels at 2,000 tons.

23ANIMAL HUSBANDRY
The livestock population in 1992 was estimated at 400,000 head of cattle, 150,000 goats, 121,000 sheep, and 11,000 hogs.

24FISHING
In 1991, the catch was 23,743 tons, as compared with 4,100 tons in 1967. A 1982 agreement with Senegal allows nationals of each country to operate fishing companies in the other's waters.

25FORESTRY
Portions of the Gambia are covered by mangrove forest, open woodland, or savanna with woodland or bush. Wood resources are used for fuel (98%), poles, and rural housing construction. Roundwood removals were estimated at 940,000 cu m in 1991.

26MINING
Large deposits of ilmenite were discovered along the coast in 1953; they were exploited by UK interests from 1956 to 1959, but then operations ceased. The Gambia has significant glass sand deposits, which remain unexploited.

27ENERGY AND POWER
All electric power is produced at thermal stations. Installed capacity in 1985 totaled 13,000 kw, of which about 85% was public; production amounted to 68 million kwh. The government plans to expand electricity output by 15% annually.

28INDUSTRY
Industries include groundnut processing, building and repair of river craft, village handicrafts, and clothing manufacture. There are candle factories, two oil mills, a soft drink factory, a distillery, and a shoe factory; a soap and detergent plant opened in 1982. Although the government provides incentives for industrial development, manufacturing contributes only about 5.8% of the annual GDP.

29SCIENCE AND TECHNOLOGY
The Medical Research Council, a field station of the Dunn Nutrition Unit Laboratory in Cambridge, has a research laboratory on tropical diseases at Fajara, near Banjul. Gambia College has schools of agriculture, nursing and midwifery, and public health.

30DOMESTIC TRADE
The marketing of the peanut crop for export is handled by the Gambia Produce Marketing Board. Cooperative banking and marketing unions finance the activities of a network of cooperatives in the peanut-growing areas. Normal business hours are from 8 AM to noon and 2 to 5 PM, Monday through Thursday, 8 AM to noon and 3 to 5 PM on Friday, and 8 or 9 AM to noon on Saturday.

31FOREIGN TRADE
Groundnut products are by far the Gambia's leading export. However, groundnut exports were depressed in the early 1980s, first by drought and then by low world prices. The leading imports are manufactured goods, machinery, transport equipment, and food.

The principal exports in 1986 (in thousands of dalasi) were as follows:

Groundnuts, shelled	37,029
Groundnut meal	4,746
Fish and fish preparations	2,559
Groundnut oil	21,760
Other exports and reexports	170,254
TOTAL	236,348

The principal imports in 1986 (in thousands of dalasi) were as follows:

Food	228,393
Manufactures	162,022
Machinery and transportation equipment	137,985
Fuels	59,819
Chemicals	47,448
Beverages and tobacco	19,951
Animal and vegetable oils	5,253
Crude materials	7,772
Other imports	64,735
TOTAL	733,378

The UK accounted for 57.2% of the Gambia's imports in 1985–86, and Switzerland bought 59.2% of its exports.

32BALANCE OF PAYMENTS

In 1985, the government adopted a plan to minimize trade imbalances. By 1990–91, the current account deficit (not including grants) fell to 13% of GDP, caused by increased exports of horticultural products and growth in tourism.

In 1992 merchandise exports totaled $146.95 million and imports $177.76 million. The merchandise trade balance was $–30.81 million. The following table summarizes the Gambia's balance of payments for 1991 and 1992 (in millions of US dollars):

	1991	1992
CURRENT ACCOUNT		
Goods, services, and income	–41.35	–19.35
Unrequited transfers	58.11	59.39
TOTALS	16.77	40.04
CAPITAL ACCOUNT		
Direct investment	10.20	6.16
Other long-term capital	11.49	13.60
Other short-term capital	–0.93	–1.05
Exceptional financing	6.67	18.74
Reserves	–27.36	–35.06
TOTALS	0.07	–3.39
Errors and omissions	–16.70	–36.65

33BANKING AND SECURITIES

Government financial institutions include the Central Bank, the Agricultural Development Bank, and the Gambia Commercial and Development Bank. There are two private commercial banks. The money supply, as measured by M2, at the end of 1993 totaled D738.32 million.

34INSURANCE

Three insurance companies are represented in the Gambia, along with French and British underwriters.

35PUBLIC FINANCE

The fiscal year extends from 1 July to 30 June. The following table shows actual revenues and expenditures for 1990 in millions of dalasis.

	1990
REVENUE AND GRANTS	
Tax revenue	454.81
Non-tax revenue	30.96
Capital revenue	0.40
Grants	155.79
TOTAL	641.96
EXPENDITURES & LENDING MINUS REPAYMENTS	
General public services	99.44
Defense	23.58
Public order and safety	24.83
Education	67.47
Health	38.18
Social security and welfare	16.32
Housing and community amenities	25.47
Recreation, cultural, and religious affairs	8.05
Economic affairs and services	173.82
Other expenditures	112.44
Lending minus repayments	71.66
TOTAL	661.26
Deficit/Surplus	–19.30

In 1990 the Gambia's total domestic debt stood at D273.32 million.

In the 1980s, expansionary fiscal policies exacerbated a weakening economy; by 1985, the budget deficit reached 30% of GDP. An economic recovery program was initiated to reduce public expenditures, diversify the agricultural sector, and privatize the parastatal sector. This step preceded the 1988 agreement with the IMF for a structural adjustment program. Macroeconomic reforms begun in 1989 helped reduce the budget deficit to 4% of GDP by 1991.

36TAXATION

Direct taxes provide only a small proportion of revenues, the greater proportion being derived from customs and excise duties and from foreign loans and grants-in-aid. Individuals are taxed on the basis of a graduated scale; companies are taxed at a flat rate on undistributed profits. The government revised the income tax system in March 1988 and enacted new sales taxes in April 1988 to broaden the tax base, improve tax collection, and rationalize the tax system.

37CUSTOMS AND DUTIES

Customs duties are assessed by c.i.f. value, as is the 10% national sales tax, from which some imports are exempt. Some commodities may be subject to excise taxes.

38FOREIGN INVESTMENT

Joint ventures are encouraged, but a portion of the profits must be reinvested. Under an ordinance passed in 1964, developing industries are exempt from profits tax for five years.

39ECONOMIC DEVELOPMENT

Development goals have been focused on transport and communications improvements, increases in rice and groundnut yields, and production diversity.

The historical importance of Great Britain to the Gambia has declined, as Gambia has turned increasingly to the IDA and the European Development Fund, France, Germany, Switzerland, Japan, and Arab donors for aid.

40SOCIAL DEVELOPMENT

Social welfare is largely an extension of medical aid. Under tribal organization, the individual's basic welfare needs are traditionally met by the group. Women play little part in the public life of this conservative Islamic country.

41HEALTH

Health conditions are poor: in 1992, average life expectancy was estimated at only 45 years for women and men. Nearly half of all children die by age five, primarily because of malaria and diarrheal diseases. Malaria, tuberculosis, trypanosomiasis, and schistosomiasis are widespread. In 1990, there were approximately 220 reported cases of tuberculosis per 100,000 people. However, between 1991 and 1992, the country did vaccinate 83% of its children against measles.

The fertility rate is 6.4 and the infant mortality is 126.3 deaths per 1,000 live births. In 1994, the overall death rate was 19.4 per 1,000 people. In 1992 there were 12 doctors per 100,000 inhabitants, with a nurse to doctor ratio of 5.1. In 1990, there were 1.4 hospital beds per 1,000 people. Total health care expenditures for 1990 were $12,080 million.

42HOUSING

A Housing Finance Fund provides low-cost housing and related assistance. As of 1990, 92% of urban and 73% of rural dwellers had access to a public water supply.

⁴³EDUCATION

Primary school is free but not compulsory and lasts for six years. Secondary schooling is in two stages of five plus two years. In 1991, primary schools had an enrollment of 90,645 students and 2,876 teachers, while secondary schools had 21,786 students. There were nine higher-level schools, including a teachers' training college. The overall adult literacy rate has been estimated at 27.2% in 1990 with males estimated at 39% and females at 16%.

⁴⁴LIBRARIES AND MUSEUMS

The national library in Banjul contains 100,898 volumes. The Gambia National Museum, founded in 1982, is also in Banjul.

⁴⁵MEDIA

The *Gambia Weekly* (formerly, *The Gambia News Bulletin*) is issued by the government three times a week. The *Gambia Onward* is also published three times a week, and *The Gambia Times* (1991 circulation 1,000) appears fortnightly. All are published in English. In 1991 there were 9,312 telephones. Radio Gambia is the government noncommercial broadcasting station; there is also a commercial station, Radio Syd. Gambia has no television stations. In 1991 there were 150,000 radios.

⁴⁶ORGANIZATIONS

The Gambia Chamber of Commerce and Industry represents many of the principal Gambian, British, and French firms. A network of cooperative societies functions within the peanut-growing region.

⁴⁷TOURISM, TRAVEL, AND RECREATION

Tourism has experienced significant growth in recent years and is expected to be a major focus of investment in the 1990s. It now contributes about 10% of GDP and employs about 2.3% of the total labor force. Growth in the industry has been important, though recently (1992–1993) has been adversely affected by the recession in Europe. In 1990, 101,419 foreign tourists arrived in Gambia, 60% from Europe and 38% from Africa. There were 2,553 hotel rooms and 5,070 beds, and tourism payments reached US$26 million. All visitors need a valid passport and a yellow-fever vaccination certificate.

⁴⁸FAMOUS GAMBIANS

The first prime minister of the independent Gambia and the first president of the republic was Alhaji Sir Dawda Kairaba Jawara (b.1924), most recently reelected in 1992.

⁴⁹DEPENDENCIES

The Gambia has no territories or colonies.

⁵⁰BIBLIOGRAPHY

Gailey, Harry A. *A History of the Gambia.* New York: Irvington, 1982.

Gailey, Harry A. *Historical Dictionary of the Gambia.* 2d ed. Metuchen, N.J.: Scarecrow Press, 1987.

Gamble, David P. *The Gambia.* Santa Barbara, Calif.: Clio Press, 1988.

Gray, John M. *A History of the Gambia.* London: Frank Cass, 1966.

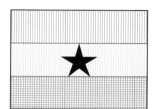

GHANA

Republic of Ghana

CAPITAL: Accra.

FLAG: The national flag is a tricolor of red, yellow, and green horizontal stripes, with a five-pointed black star in the center of the yellow stripe.

ANTHEM: *Hail the Name of Ghana.*

MONETARY UNIT: The cedi (₵) is a paper currency of 100 pesewas. There are coins of ½, 1, 2½, 5, 10, 20, and 50 pesewas and 1, 5, 10, 20, 50, and 100 cedis, and notes of 1, 2, 5, 10, 20, 50, 100, 200, 500, and 1,000 cedis. ₵1 = $0.0057 (or $1 = ₵176).

WEIGHTS AND MEASURES: The metric system is the legal standard.

HOLIDAYS: New Year's Day, 1 January; Anniversary of the Inauguration of the Fourth Republic, 7 January; Independence Day, 6 March; Labor Day, 1 May; Republic Day, 1 July; Christmas, 25 December; Boxing Day, 26 December; Movable religious holidays include Good Friday and Easter Monday.

TIME: GMT.

¹LOCATION, SIZE, AND EXTENT

Situated on the southern coast of the West African bulge, Ghana has an area of 238,540 sq km (92,100 sq mi), extending 672 km (418 mi) N–S and 536 km (333 mi) E–W. Bordered on the E by Togo, on the S by the Atlantic Ocean (Gulf of Guinea), on the W by Côte d'Ivoire, and on the NW and N by Burkina Faso, Ghana has a total boundary length of 2,632 km (1,635mi). Comparatively, the area occupied by Ghana is slightly smaller than the state of Oregon. Ghana's capital city, Accra, is located on the Gulf of Guinea coast.

²TOPOGRAPHY

The coastline consists mostly of a low sandy shore behind which stretches the coastal plain, except in the west, where the forest comes down to the sea. The forest belt, which extends northward from the western coast about 320 km (200 mi) and eastward for a maximum of about 270 km (170 mi), is broken up into heavily wooded hills and steep ridges. North of the forest is undulating savanna drained by the Black Volta and White Volta rivers, which join and flow south to the sea through a narrow gap in the hills. Ghana's highest point is Mount Afadjato at 885 m (2,903 ft) in a range of hills on the eastern border. Apart from the Volta, only the Pra and the Ankobra rivers permanently pierce the sand dunes, most of the other rivers terminating in brackish lagoons. There are no natural harbors. Lake Volta, formed by the impoundment of the Volta behind Akosombo Dam, is the world's largest manmade lake (8,485 sq km/3,276 sq mi).

³CLIMATE

The climate is tropical but relatively mild for the latitude. Climatic differences between various parts of the country are affected by the sun's journey north or south of the equator and the corresponding position of the intertropical convergence zone, the boundary between the moist southwesterly winds and the dry northeasterly winds. Except in the north, there are two rainy seasons, from April through June and from September to November. Squalls occur in the north during March and April, followed by

occasional rain until August and September, when the rainfall reaches its peak. Average temperatures range between 21° and 32°C (70–90°F), with relative humidity between 50% and 80%. Rainfall ranges from 83 to 220 cm (33–87 in) a year.

The harmattan, a dry desert wind, blows from the northeast from December to March, lowering the humidity and causing hot days and cool nights in the north; the effect of this wind is felt in the south during January. In most areas, temperatures are highest in March and lowest in August. Variation between day and night temperatures is relatively small, but greater in the north, especially in January, because of the harmattan. No temperature lower than 10°C (50°F) has ever been recorded in Ghana.

⁴FLORA AND FAUNA

Plants and animals are mainly those common to tropical regions, but because of human encroachment, Ghana has fewer large and wild mammals than in other parts of Africa. Most of the forest is in the south and in a strip along the border with Togo. Except for coastal scrub and grassland, the rest of Ghana is savanna.

⁵ENVIRONMENT

Slash-and-burn agriculture and overcultivation of cleared land have resulted in widespread soil erosion and exhaustion. Overgrazing, heavy logging, overcutting of firewood, and mining have taken a toll on forests and woodland, with deforestation proceeding at an annual rate of 278 square miles. One-third of Ghana's land area is threatened by desertification. Industrial pollutants include arsenic from gold mining and noxious fumes from smelters. Water pollution results from a combination of industrial sources, agricultural chemicals, and inadequate waste treatment facilities. Ghana's cities produce 0.5 million tons of solid waste annually. The nation has 12.7 cubic miles of water with 52% used for farming activity and 13% used for industrial purposes; 37% of all urban dwellers and 61% of the rural people do not have pure water.

In 1986, Ghana had five national parks and four other protected areas, with a total area of 1,182,845 ha (2,922,857 acres);

the ban on hunting in closed reserves is only sporadically enforced. Of the country's 222 mammal species, 13 are threatened, as well as 8 of the nation's 721 bird species and 1 type of reptile. In addition, 34 of 3,600 plant species are endangered.

6POPULATION

The population in 1994 was estimated at 17,156,376, an increase of some 40% over the 1984 census figure of 12,205,275. A population of 20,172,000 was projected for the year 2000, assuming a crude birthrate of 39.4 per 1,000 population, a crude death rate of 10.5, and a net natural increase of 28.9 during 1995–2000. Children under 15 constitute about 45% of all Ghanaians. Overall population density in 1986 was estimated at 72 per sq km (186 per sq mi), but at least 80% of the inhabitants resides in the south or in the far northeast and northwest. Approximately 36% of the population was urban in 1995. Accra, the capital and principal city, had a population of about 1,405,000 in 1990. The other large cities, with their estimated 1988 populations, were Kumasi (440,000) and Tema (206,000).

7MIGRATION

For generations, immigrants from Burkina Faso and Togo have done much of the manual work, including mining, in Ghana; immigrant traders from Nigeria have conducted much of the petty trade; and Lebanese and Syrians have been important as intermediaries. In 1969, when many foreigners were expelled, Ghana's alien community was about 2,000,000 out of a population of about 8,400,000. In 1986, the government estimated that at least 500,000 aliens were residing in Ghana, mostly engaged in trading.

Ghanaians also work abroad, some as fishermen in neighboring coastal countries. Many Ghanaians were welcomed in the 1970s by Nigeria, which was in the midst of an oil boom and in need of cheap labor. In early 1983, as the oil boom faded, up to 700,000 Ghanaians were expelled from Nigeria; soon after, however, many deportees were reportedly being invited back by Nigerian employers unable to fill the vacant posts with indigenous labor. But in May 1985, an estimated 100,000 Ghanaians again were expelled from Nigeria. At the end of 1992 Ghana was home to 12,000 Liberian refugees. Some 3,200 Ghanaians were refugees in Togo and 200 in Nigeria.

8ETHNIC GROUPS

It is fairly certain that Ghana has been occupied by peoples of Negroid stock since prehistoric times. Members of the Akan family, who make up more than 40% of the population, include the Twi, or Ashanti, inhabiting the Ashanti Region and central Ghana, and the Fanti, inhabiting the coastal areas. In the southwest, the Nzima, Ahanta, Evalue, and other tribes speak languages related to Twi and Fanti. The Accra plains are inhabited by tribes speaking variants of Ga, while east of the Volta River are the Ewe living in what used to be British-mandated Togoland. All these tribes are fairly recent arrivals in Ghana, the Akan having come between the 12th and 15th centuries, the Ga-Adangbe in the 16th century, and the Ewe in the 17th century. Most of the inhabitants of the Northern Region belong to the Mole-Dagbani group of Voltaic peoples or to the Gonja, who appear to bear some relation to the Akan.

9LANGUAGES

Of the 56 indigenous languages and dialects spoken in Ghana, 31 are used mainly in the northern part of the country. The languages follow the tribal divisions, with the related languages of Twi and Fanti being most prominent. English is the official language and is the universal medium of instruction in schools. It is officially supplemented by five local languages.

10RELIGIONS

In 1993, an estimated 38% of Ghanaians followed traditional African religions. Of the remainder, about 43% belonged to various Christian denominations, principally Roman Catholic (12.6%), Methodist, and Presbyterian. Approximately 12% were Muslim. Although there is no state religion, religious bodies are required to register with the government's Religious Affairs Committee.

11TRANSPORTATION

The government's development program has been largely devoted to improving internal communications; nevertheless, both road and rail systems deteriorated in the 1980s. Rehabilitation began in the late 1980s, with priority being given to the western route, which is the export route for Ghana's manganese and bauxite production and also serves the major gold-producing area. Rail lines are also the main means of transportation for such products as cocoa, logs, and sawn timber; they are also widely used for passenger service. There were 953 km (592 mi) of railway in 1991, with the main line linking Sekondi-Takoradi with Accra and Kumasi. In 1990, the railways carried 850,000 tons of freight, mostly ore and cement.

Ghana had about 36,000 km (22,370 mi) of roads in 1991, of which about 18% were paved. Good roads link Accra with Tema, Kumasi, Takoradi, and Akosombo. In 1991, Ghana had 82,000 private automobiles and 43,000 commercial vehicles. The government transport department operates a cross-country bus service; municipal transport facilities are available in all main towns.

The Black Star Line, owned by the government, operates a cargo-passenger service to Canada, the US, the UK, Italy, and West Africa. In 1991, Ghana had a merchant shipping fleet comprising 8 vessels and 61,000 GRT. Lake transport service between Akosombo and Yapei is operated by Volta Lake Transport Co.

Ghana has no natural harbors. An artificial deepwater port was built at Sekondi-Takoradi in the 1920s and expanded after World War II. A second deepwater port, at Tema, was opened in 1962, and in 1963 further extensions were made. At a few smaller ports, freight is moved by surfboats and lighters. The major rivers and Lake Volta provide about 1,400 km (870 mi) of navigable waterways.

Accra's international airport serves intercontinental as well as local West African traffic and served 762,000 passengers as of 1990. Smaller airports are located at Sekondi-Takoradi, Kumasi, Tamale, and Sunyani. Ghana Airways, owned by the government, operates domestic air services and flights to other African countries and to the Federal Republic of Germany (FRG), London, and Rome.

12HISTORY

Oral traditions indicate that the tribes presently occupying the country migrated southward roughly over the period 1200–1600. The origins of the peoples of Ghana are still conjectural, although the name "Ghana" was adopted on independence in the belief that Ghanaians are descendants of the inhabitants of the empire of Ghana, which flourished in western Sudan (present-day Mali), hundreds of miles to the northwest, more than a thousand years ago.

The recorded history of Ghana begins in 1471, when Portuguese traders landed on the coast in search of gold, ivory, and spices. Following the Portuguese came the Dutch, the Danes, the Swedes, the Prussians, and the British. Commerce in gold gave way to the slave trade until the latter was outlawed by Great Britain in 1807. The 19th century brought a gradual adjustment to legitimate trade, the withdrawal of all European powers except the British, and many wars involving the Ashanti, who had welded themselves into a powerful military confederacy; their position as the principal captors of slaves for European traders

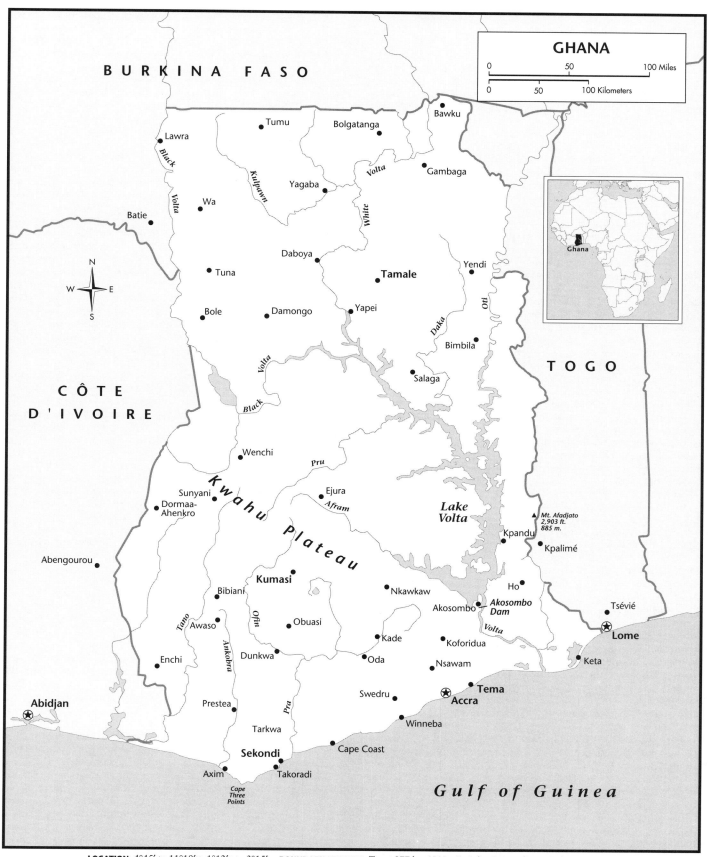

LOCATION: 4°45′ to 11°10′N; 1°12′E to 3°15′w. **BOUNDARY LENGTHS:** Togo, 877 km (545 mi); Atlantic coastline, 539 km (335 mi); Côte d'Ivoire, 668 km (415 mi); Burkina Faso, 544 km (338 mi). **TERRITORIAL SEA LIMIT:** 12 mi.

had brought them into conflict with the coastal tribes. British troops fought seven wars with the Ashanti from 1806 to 1901, when their kingdom was annexed by the British crown.

In 1874, the coastal area settlements had become a crown colony—the Gold Coast Colony—and in 1901 the Northern Territories were declared a British protectorate. In 1922, part of the former German colony of Togoland was placed under British mandate by the League of Nations, and it passed to British trusteeship under the UN after World War II. Throughout this period, Togoland was administered as part of the Gold Coast.

After a measure of local participation in government was first granted in 1946, the growing demand for self-government led in 1949 to the appointment of an all-African committee to inquire into constitutional reform. Under the new constitution introduced as a result of the findings of this committee, elections were held in 1951, and for the first time an African majority was granted a considerable measure of governmental responsibility. In 1954, further constitutional amendments were adopted under which the Gold Coast became, for practical purposes, self-governing. Two years later, the newly elected legislature passed a resolution calling for independence, and on 6 March 1957 the Gold Coast, including Ashanti, the Northern Territories Protectorate, and the Trust Territory of British Togoland, attained full independent membership in the Commonwealth of Nations under the name of Ghana. The Gold Coast thus became the first country in colonial Africa to gain independence. The nation became a republic on 1 July 1960.

During the period 1960–65, Ghana's first president, Kwame Nkrumah, steadily gained control over all aspects of Ghana's economic, political, cultural, and military affairs. His autocratic rule led to mounting but disorganized opposition. Following attempts on Nkrumah's life in August and September 1962, the political climate began to disintegrate, as government leaders accused of complicity in the assassination plots were executed or removed from office. A referendum in January 1964 established a one-party state and empowered the president to dismiss Supreme Court and High Court judges. Another attempt to assassinate Nkrumah occurred that month.

In February 1966, Nkrumah was overthrown. A military regime calling itself the National Liberation Council (NLC) established rule by decree, dismissing the civilian government and suspending the constitution. A three-year ban on political activities was lifted 1 May 1969, and after elections held in August, the Progressive Party, headed by Kofi A. Busia, formed a civilian government under a new constitution. During his two years in office, Busia lost much of his public following, and Ghana's worsening economic condition was the pretext in January 1972 for a military takeover led by Lt. Col. Ignatius Kutu Acheampong, who formed the National Redemption Council (NRC). Unlike the military rulers who came to power in 1966, however, the NRC made no plans for a rapid return to civilian rule. The NRC immediately repudiated part of the foreign debt remaining from the Nkrumah era and instituted an agricultural self-help program dubbed Operation Feed Yourself. By July 1973, the last 23 of some 2,000 persons arrested during the coup that brought the NRC to power had been released.

The NRC was restructured as the Supreme Military Council in 1976. A military coup on 5 July 1978 ousted Acheampong, who was replaced by Lt. Gen. Frederick Akuffo. Less than a year later, on 4 June 1979, a coup by enlisted men and junior officers brought the Armed Forces Revolutionary Council to power, led by a young flight lieutenant, Jerry Rawlings. Acheampong, Akuffo, and another former chief of state, A. A. Afrifa (who had engineered Nkrumah's overthrow in 1966), plus five others, were found guilty of corruption and executed in summary proceedings. Dozens of others were sentenced to long prison terms by secret courts. The new regime did, however, fulfill the pledge of the

Akuffa government by handing over power to civilians on 24 September 1979, following nationwide elections. The Nkrumah-style People's National Party (PNP) won 71 of 140 parliamentary seats in the balloting, and PNP candidate Hilla Limann was elected president.

Ghana's economic condition continued to deteriorate, and on 31 December 1981 a new coup led by Rawlings overthrew the civilian regime. The constitution was suspended, all political parties were banned, and about 100 business leaders and government officials, including Limann, were arrested. Rawlings became chairman of the ruling Provisional National Defense Council. In the following 27 months there were at least five more real or alleged coup attempts. Nine persons were executed in 1986 for attempting to overthrow the regime, and as of 1987 there remained concern over the activities of exile groups and military personnel.

Toward the end of the 1980s, an Economic Recovery Plan supported by the IMF began to reduce the size and economic role of the state and to spur economic recovery. The human costs have contributed to criticism of these austerity measures. Nevertheless, the ERP enjoys support among diverse political factions and may encourage Rawlings to move ahead with democratic reform.

A new constitution was approved by referendum on 28 April 1992 and Rawlings was elected in a sharply contested multiparty election on 3 November 1993. The legislative elections in December, however, were boycotted by the opposition, and the ruling National Democratic Congress (NDC) was able to capture 190 of the 200 seats.

On 4 January 1993, the Fourth Republic was proclaimed and Rawlings was inaugurated as president. Opposition parties, assembled as the Inter-Party Coordinating Committee (ICC), issued a joint statement announcing their acceptance of the "present institutional arrangements" on 7 January. Yet, the ICC still refused to accept the election results.

13GOVERNMENT

The military ruled Ghana by decree from 1972 to 1979, when an elected constituent assembly adopted a new constitution establishing a unicameral parliament and an executive branch headed by a president. On 31 December 1981, a military coup installed the Provisional National Defense Council (PNDC) as the supreme power; the constitution was suspended and the National Assembly dissolved. As of late 1987, Jerry Rawlings continued to function as chairman of the PNDC and its defense chief.

A Consultative Assembly, convened late in 1991 to draw up a new constitution, completed its work in March 1992. The government inserted a controversial amendment indemnifying officials of the PNDC from future prosecution for all acts of commission and omission during their term in office. In an April 1992 referendum, the constitution was approved by 92.5% of voters in a low turnout (58% of those eligible). It provides for a presidential system and a legislature (National Assembly) of 200 members. The Cabinet has over 90 officials of ministerial rank, a major contribution to popular disenchantment with government.

14POLITICAL PARTIES

The United Gold Coast Convention (UGCC) was established in 1947 with the declared aim of working for self-government at the earliest possible date. In 1949, as most of the UGCC leadership came to accept constitutional reform as an alternative to immediate self-government, the party secretary, Kwame Nkrumah, broke away and formed his own group, the Convention People's Party (CPP). In January 1950, Nkrumah announced a program of "positive action" for which he and the main leaders of the party were prosecuted and sentenced for sedition. At the first elections held in 1951 under a new constitution, the CPP obtained 71 of the 104 seats, and Nkrumah and his colleagues were released from prison to enter the new government. In May 1952, Kofi A. Busia, of the University College, founded the Ghana Congress Party (GCP), which continued the UGCC position of trying to form alliances with traditional chiefs. The GCP's leadership was a mixture of dissatisfied former CPP members and the professional-oriented leadership of the UGCC. In 1953, Nkrumah was elected life chairman and leader of the CPP.

In 1954, the assembly and cabinet became all-African. A new party, the Ashanti-based National Liberation Movement (NLM), was formed to fight the general centralizing tendencies of the CPP and also to maintain the position of the traditional rulers; the NLM leadership, except for Busia, consisted of former CPP members. In the elections held in 1956, however, the CPP retained its predominant position, winning 72 of 108 seats in the Legislative Assembly.

One of the first acts of independent Ghana under Nkrumah was the Avoidance of Discrimination Act (1957), prohibiting sectional parties based on racial, regional, or religious differences. This led the opposition parties to amalgamate into the new United Party (UP), opposing the government's centralization policies and the declining power of the traditional rulers. The effectiveness of the opposition was reduced following the 1960 election by the withdrawal of official recognition of the opposition as such and by the detention of several leading opposition members under the Preventive Detention Act (1958). In September 1962, the National Assembly passed by an overwhelming majority a resolution calling for the creation of a one-party state; this was approved by referendum in January 1964.

After the military takeover of February 1966, the National Liberation Council outlawed the CPP along with all other political organizations. The ban on political activities was lifted on 1 May 1969, and several parties participated in the August 1969 balloting. The two major parties contesting the election were the Progress Party (PP), led by Busia, which was perceived as an Akan-dominated party composed of former members of the opposition UP; and the National Alliance of Liberals (NAL), a Ewe- and CPP-dominated group under the leadership of the former CPP minister Komla Gbedemah. The PP won 105 seats in the 140-member National Assembly; 29 seats were captured by the NAL, and 6 by the five minor parties. In October 1970, the NAL merged with two of the smaller groups to form the Justice Party.

All political parties in Ghana were again disbanded following the January 1972 military coup led by Col. Acheampong. When political activities resumed in 1979, five parties contested the elections. The People's National Party (PNP), which won 71 of 140 seats at stake, claimed to represent the Nkrumah heritage; the Popular Front Party (PFP) and the United National Convention (UNC), which traced their lineage back to Busia's Progress Party, won 43 and 13, respectively. The Action Congress Party (ACP), drawing primary support from the Fanti tribe, won 10 seats, while the leftist Social Democratic Front won 3. After the elections, the PNP formed an alliance with the UNC. In October 1980, however, the UNC left the governing coalition, and in June joined with three other parties to form the All People's Party. The coup of December 1981 brought yet another dissolution of Ghana's political party structure. Opposition to the PNDC has been carried on by the Ghana Democratic Movement (organized in London in 1983) and a number of other groups.

With adoption of a new constitution in April 1992, the long-standing ban on political activity was lifted on 18 May 1992. Ghanaians prepared for the presidential and legislative elections to be held in November and December. The parties that emerged could be grouped into three clusters. The center-right group was the most cohesive and it consisted of followers of Kofi Busia. They formed the New Patriotic Party (NPP) and chose Adu Boaheu as their presidential candidate. The center-

left group was Nkrumahists. Ideological and leadership differences kept them divided into 5 separate parties, of which the People's National Convention, a party led by ex-President Limann, was best organized. PNDC supporters comprised the third grouping. They favored continuity and, after forming the National Democratic Congress (NDC), were able to draft Rawlings as their candidate.

Rawlings eventually defeated Boaheu (58% to 30%) for the presidency. Opposition parties boycotted the December 1992 legislation elections, and the NDC carried 190 of the 200 seats. But the fear of one-party control prompted a split in the NDC. So the official opposition in parliament is a faction of the ruling NDC.

Meanwhile, the NPP seems to provide the most serious challenge to the NDC. It sees itself as defender of the new constitution. The NPP broke away from the opposition, the Inter-Party Coordinating Committee, by announcing in August 1993 its recognition of the 1992 election results, which the ICC had refused to accept.

15 LOCAL GOVERNMENT

As of 1994, Ghana was divided into 10 regions: Eastern, Western, Ashanti, Northern, Volta, Central, Upper East, Upper West, Brong-Ahafo, and Greater Accra. The 10 regions are further subdivided into 58 districts and 267 local administrative units. In late 1982, the government announced that town and village councils, which had been dissolved after the 1981 coup, would be run by people's and workers' defense committees. They were replaced by Committees for the Defense of the Revolution in 1984. Elections for 103 district assemblies, 4 municipal assemblies, and 3 metropolitan assemblies were conducted in March 1994.

16 JUDICIAL SYSTEM

The 1993 Constitution established an independent judiciary and a number of autonomous institutions such as the Commission for Human Rights to investigate and take actions to remedy alleged violations of human rights. The new system is based largely on British legal procedures. The new court system consists of two levels: superior courts and lower courts. The superior courts include the Supreme Court, the Appeals Court, the High Court, and regional tribunals. Parliament has the authority to create a system of lower courts. The old public tribunals are being phased out as they clear their dockets.

Traditional courts in which village chiefs enforce customary tribal laws in resolving local divorce, child custody, and property disputes will continue to operate alongside the new courts.

17 ARMED FORCES

In 1993, Ghana's defense forces (7,200) consisted of units of the army (5,000), navy (1,000), and air force (1,200) as well as a presidential guard of 500 men and the People's Militia (5,000 part-time police). About one-third of the Ghanaian army (2,700) is serving in Liberia and four non-African states on peacekeeping duties. The remaining forces are organized for internal security duties. Ghana spends about $30 million (1989 estimate) on defense, or less than 1% of gross domestic product.

18 INTERNATIONAL COOPERATION

On 8 March 1957, Ghana was admitted to UN membership; the nation belongs to ECA and all the nonregional specialized agencies. Ghana is also a member of the African Development Bank, Commonwealth of Nations, G-77, and OAU. In November 1974, Ghana was admitted as a member of the International Bauxite Association, and in June 1975 it ratified the treaty creating ECOWAS. The nation is an adherent of GATT and a signatory of the Law of the Sea. In 1986, Ghana and Burkina Faso agreed to consider a political union, setting a 10-year timetable.

19ECONOMY

Ghana's economic history is one of the most intriguing of the post-independence period. In a modern-day riches-to-rags story, the cocoa wealth of 1958 became, inexorably, the food crisis of 1983 before Ghanaian leaders turned to the IMF for advice and fiscal relief. Since 1983, the economy has made measured progress toward recovery.

Ghana's economy is led by the agricultural sector, which employs two-thirds of the labor force. Its key crops are cassava, coco-yams (taro), plantains, and yams. Maize, millet, sorghum, rice, and groundnuts are also important staple crops. Agricultural crops which are sold for export include coffee, bananas, palm nuts, copra, limes, kola nuts, shea nuts, rubber, cotton, and kenaf. Recent production levels of maize, rice, cassava, and yams indicate that the food shortages of the early 1980s are a memory.

Cocoa, however, is the dominant export crop. In the late 1950s, Ghana was the world's premier producer of cocoa, which accounted for 45–70% of export earnings over the next 25 years. In 1986 cocoa accounted for 46% of export earnings. Since 1983, the cocoa sector has been revitalized through economic reforms and incentives to farmers. However, 1992 production of 243,000 tons was still well below government targets.

Ghana produces meat, but not enough to satisfy local demand. The fishing industry, likewise, produces only about 50% of local demand.

Ghana has significant deposits of gold, and important new investments were made in this sector in 1992. In that year, earnings from gold exports exceeded those of cocoa for the first time. Production currently exceeds 1 million oz. annually and that amount could double by 1996. Industrial diamonds are also produced, with an estimated output of 500,000 carats in 1992. Ghana is a modest oil producer and refines petroleum products. Bauxite deposits are substantial but largely unexploited: the aluminum smelter at Tema uses bauxite imported from Jamaica. Significant manganese production (319,000 tons in 1991) occurs at Nsuta.

20INCOME

In 1992 Ghana's GNP was $7,066 million at current prices, or $450 per capita. For the period 1985–92 the average inflation rate was 31.2%, resulting in a real growth rate in per capita GNP of 1.2%. In 1992 the GDP was $6,884 million in current US dollars. Of that GDP, agriculture made up 42.3%, forestry 4.2%, and fishing 1.3%. Mining contributed 1.8%, while manufacturing added 9.2%.

21LABOR

In 1989, an estimated 6.5 million Ghanaians were in the labor force, about 55% of them in agriculture. The Ghana Trades Union Congress (TUC), with a total membership of almost 600,000 covers workers and salaried employees in the public and private sectors. Seventeen unions are affiliated with TUC, whose constitution was suspended in 1982, when leaders of all member unions were ousted by the government. The minimum daily wage was raised from ₵218 to ₵460 in 1991.

22AGRICULTURE

Agriculture, especially cocoa, forms the basis of Ghana's economy, accounting for 50% of GDP. Cocoa exports in 1992 contributed 31% ($304 million) to total exports, down from 35% ($347 million) in 1991. A 50,000 ton shortfall in the 1992 cocoa harvest exacerbated budget deficits.

Cocoa beans were first introduced to Ghana in 1878 by Tettah Quarshie. Thereafter, the cultivation of cocoa increased steadily until Ghana became the world's largest cocoa producer, supplying more than one-third of world production by the mid-1960s. By the early 1980s, production was less than half that of two decades before; market conditions were aggravated by a drop of

nearly 75% in world cocoa prices between 1977 and 1982. In 1983/84, cocoa production totaled 158,000 tons, the lowest since independence; by 1992, production had recovered to about 280,000 tons (second highest after Côte d'Ivoire). The Ghana Cocoa Marketing Board purchases and (at least in theory) exports the entire cocoa crop, as well as coffee and shea nuts. Cocoa smuggling was made punishable by death in 1982.

Ghana continues to be a net food importer. The grain harvest in 1992 included corn, 580,000 tons; paddy rice, 100,000 tons; sorghum, 210,000 tons; and millet, 80,000 tons. Other crops were cassava, 400,000 tons; plantains, 1,200,000 tons; coco-yams (taro), 1,200,000 tons; yams, 1,000,000 tons; tomatoes, 100,000 tons; peanuts, 100,000 tons; sugarcane, 110,000 tons; coconuts, 220,000 tons; chilies and peppers, 160,000 tons; oranges, 50,000 tons; palm kernels, 34,000 tons; and palm oil, 100,000 tons. Considerable potential exists for the development of agricultural exports including pineapples, tomatoes, soybeans, and cut flowers.

23ANIMAL HUSBANDRY

Livestock can be raised only in the tsetse-free areas, mainly in the Northern Region and along the coastal plains from Accra to the eastern frontier. Ghana's indigenous West African shorthorn is one of the oldest cattle breeds in Africa. The elimination of deadly epizootic diseases by prophylactic inoculation of cattle (especially with the help of mobile immunization centers) resulted in a rise of the cattle population from 100,000 head in 1930 to 662,000 in 1968 and 1,400,000 in 1992. There were also about 2,600,000 goats, 2,500,000 sheep, 500,000 hogs, and 12,000,000 poultry. Many live animals and much meat are imported (mainly from Nigeria) to satisfy local demand. A serious problem for the livestock industry continues to be the provision of adequate feed for animals during the dry season.

24FISHING

In 1991, the total marine fish catch was 364,959 tons, and the freshwater catch (not including subsistence fishing) about 57,000 tons. In 1973, an industrial fishing complex at Tema began production of canned pilchards and sardines. Lake Volta accounts for about half the freshwater catch. Considerable potential exists for the development of shrimp and fish exports.

25FORESTRY

The forest area (primarily in the south) covers about 35% of the country. Since October 1972, the government has acquired a majority share in a number of foreign-owned timber companies. The Timber Marketing Board has a monopoly on the export of timber and timber products.

Among the roughly 300 timber-producing species are the warwa obech, mahogany, utile, baku, and kokrodua; species such as avodire, sapale, and makuri are considered the best in Africa. A ban on the export of 21 species was established in 1979 in order to encourage the production of sawn timber and timber products. The total production of roundwood in 1991 was 17,122,000 cu m; sawn wood production was 400,000 cu m. Roundwood exports amounted to 198,000 cu m in 1990, and 215,000 cu m in 1991. Exports of forest products in 1991 totaled $93.4 million, or 9.4% of total exports. After cocoa and minerals, sawn timber and logs constitute the third-largest export item. About 90% of the timber cut is used for fuel. The government is encouraging a shift to value-added timber exports in order to strengthen Ghana's position in the global market, create more employment, and bring in more foreign revenue.

26MINING

Gold, the first export of the Gold Coast, is still the most valuable mineral export, although extensive smuggling of gold and diamonds through the years has cut into revenues. During the 1950s, the low-grade mines found themselves in increasing difficulties and threatened to abandon operations. To prevent this, the government set up the Ghana State Mining Corp., which in 1961 acquired, by negotiation, the share capital of the five companies involved. In 1985, a Canadian company took over the management of the GSMC's three mines. In 1973, the government acquired 55% of the equity of Ashanti Goldfields and Ghana Consolidated Diamonds, the chief gold producer. Gold production in 1991 was a reported 26,311 kg, the highest level since 1964–65. This dramatic production increase was largely the result of the rehabilitation and expansion of the Ashanti mine, as well as the opening of the Bogosu and Teberebie Mines in 1990.

Production of manganese, begun in 1916, was almost completely controlled by the US-owned African Manganese Co. until that firm was taken over by the government-owned National Manganese Corp. in 1975. Although production prior to the early 1970s frequently exceeded 600,000 tons, only 319,000 tons were produced in 1991.

Diamonds, mostly of the industrial variety, are extracted both by African diggers using primitive methods and by a joint UK- and Ghanaian government-owned company. Total formal-sector production peaked in the 1970s, when production exceeded 2.5 million carats. Only the Akwatia Mine remained open for formal production in 1990. Diamond production has steadily increased since the early 1980s. In 1991, production amounted to 700,000 carats. Only one relatively small bauxite deposit is worked, at Bui, near Awaso, by Ghana Bauxite Company; reserves have been estimated at 30 years in the present ore being exploited at the Awaso Mine, and other ore reserves nearby are adequate to support mine life for a century. In 1991, production amounted to 380,000 tons; mining plans call for an increase in annual production to 500,000 tons. The US-owned Volta Aluminum Co. (Valco) smelts aluminum at Tema, but the bauxite from Ghana is first converted into alumina in Jamaica.

27ENERGY AND POWER

Output of electricity reached 6,152 million kwh in 1991, of which a portion was exported to Togo and Benin; at the end of 1991, total installed capacity was 1,187 Mw. The greatest single source of power is the Volta River Project, begun in 1962 and based on a hydroelectric installation at Akosombo, about 100 km (60 mi) northeast of Accra. Work on the Akosombo (or Volta River) Dam was finished in 1965. The first stage of the electrification project was completed in mid-1967 and had a capacity of 512,000 kw; by 1990, the plant's capacity had been expanded to 912,000 kw. The Volta River Authority supplies 99% of the total national electricity consumption, 50–60% of which is absorbed by aluminum refining. Excess electricity is sold to Togo, Benin, and Côte d'Ivoire. A $150-million project to extend the main grid to northern Ghana was completed in 1991.

In the 1980s, oil exploration was conducted offshore and in the Volta River Basin. In 1979, an offshore field developed by Agri-Petco, a US company, began operations; it was later taken over by Primary Fuel, also a US company. Production was 90,000 metric tons in 1985, only a small fraction of domestic requirements, and production ceased in 1986. The Ghana National Petroleum Corporation, which was established in 1984, reported production of oil at the rate of 6,000 barrels per day at the South Tano Basin in 1991. Nigerian oil accounts for the bulk of petroleum imports.

28INDUSTRY

Manufacturing represents a small part of the economy (9.3% in 1990). The excessively rapid industrialization of the 1960s laid the foundation for the eventual collapse of the urban economy. Food, cocoa, and timber processing plants led a list of industries

that included an oil refinery, textiles, vehicles, cement, paper, chemicals, soap, beverages, and shoes. Much of Ghana's industrial base was nationalized over the years. Encouraged by the IMF, however, Ghana has largely ended its parastatal era.

The Tema industrial estate includes the Tema Food Complex, comprised of a fish cannery, flour and feed mills, a tin-can factory, and other facilities. The aluminum smelter at Tema is owned by Kaiser Aluminum and is Ghana's largest manufacturing enterprise. Recent industrial activity has included a reopened glass factory, a new palm oil mill, a locally supplied cement plant, and facilities for milling rice, distilling citronella, and producing alcohol.

With the output of the Akosombo hydroelectric plant (912 MW) and the newer Kpong facility (160 MW), Ghana is largely self-sufficient in electric power and is able to export to Togo and Benin. The facilities are, however, drought-prone, as was demonstrated in the early 1980s when electrical shortages forced reduced aluminum production.

29SCIENCE AND TECHNOLOGY

The Council for Scientific and Industrial Research, in Accra, advises the government on scientific matters, coordinates the national research effort, and disseminates research results. Attached to the council are 17 research institutes, many of which deal with land and water resources. Other learned societies and research institutions in Ghana include the West African Science Association and the Cocoa Research Institute. The Ghana Academy of Arts and Sciences was founded in 1959.

The University of Ghana, at Legon, has faculties of agriculture, science, and a medical school, as well as institutes for medical research and for Volta River Basin studies. The University of Cape Coast has a faculty of science and a school of agriculture. The University of Science and Technology is at Kumasi.

30DOMESTIC TRADE

The overseas marketing of primary agricultural products is effected through governmental marketing boards, which use trading companies and cooperatives as agents to purchase commodities from the producers. Although there are retail stores in all towns and main trading centers, most retail trade is still carried on in markets, mainly by women. Many consumer goods are sold on the black market.

Normal business hours are from 8 AM to noon and 2 to 4:30 or 5 PM, Monday through Friday; some companies also open on Saturday morning. Banks are open from 8:30 AM to 2 PM, Monday through Thursday, and to 3 PM on Friday.

31FOREIGN TRADE

Although Ghana has historically enjoyed a surplus trade balance, deficits were recorded in 1983, 1984, and 1985. Exports again exceeded imports in 1986 and 1987, but turned negative in the years 1989 to 1991. Leading exports in 1987 (in millions of cedis) were as follows:

Cocoa	67,872.7
Gold	24,205.6
Manganese	1,205.7
Diamonds	697.0
Bauxite	851.4
Other exports	52,442.6
TOTAL	147,275,000

Imports came to ₵93,358.0 million in 1987. Principal imports included machinery and transport equipment (30.7%), basic manufactures (11.7%), chemicals (11.8%), mineral fuels/crude oil (15.4%), and food and live animals (5.4%).

The United Kingdom is Ghana's largest single trade partner, accounting for 26.9% of Ghana's exports and 41.4% of Ghana's imports. The United States (18.6%) and Germany (13.5%) are key export partners. Imports come from Nigeria (13.2%), Germany (11.5%), and the United States (11.1%).

32BALANCE OF PAYMENTS

Ghana has long had balance-of-payments difficulties. Ghana's overall trade account stood in deficit in 1991 as exports failed to keep pace with imports. Remittances from Ghanaians abroad plus donor aid helped the supply of hard currency.

In 1992 merchandise exports totaled $986.4 million and imports $1,456.7 million. The merchandise trade balance was $–470.3 million. The following table summarizes Ghana's balance of payments for 1991 and 1992 (in millions of US dollars):

	1991	1992
CURRENT ACCOUNT		
Goods, services, and income	–673.6	–846.5
Unrequited transfers	420.9	468.7
TOTALS	–252.7	–377.8
CAPITAL ACCOUNT		
Direct investment	20.0	22.5
Other long-term capital	353.5	370.4
Other short-term capital	–35.4	–71.3
Exceptional financing	27.5	–46.3
Reserves	–136.7	102.9
TOTALS	228.9	378.2
Errors and omissions	23.8	–0.4

33BANKING AND SECURITIES

The Bank of Ghana, established in 1957, is the central bank. Commercial banking services are rendered mainly by the government-owned Commercial Bank of Ghana; the government-owned Agricultural Development Bank, which is concerned with agricultural credit and cooperatives; and two British banks, Barclays Bank of Ghana Ltd. and the Standard Chartered Bank of Ghana Africa Ltd. (both 40% state-owned), which together had 67 branches in 1993. The Merchant Bank (Ghana) Ltd. is 30% state-owned.

Following a survey by the IDA, a National Investment Bank was established in 1963 to finance capital investment in private and state-owned industries and corporations. The Rawlings government sought to have it specialize in mining, manufacturing, and transport. The Bank for Housing and Construction, the Ghana Cooperative Bank, the Social Security Bank, Bank of Credit and Commerce (Ghana), National Trust Holding Co., and the National Savings and Credit Bank are other government banks. The money supply at the end of 1993 stood at ₵664.7 billion. A stock exchange was opened in Accra in 1987.

34INSURANCE

In 1962, the government set up the State Insurance Corp. (SIC) with the primary aims of tightening control over the activities of insurance companies (including their investment policies) and providing insurance coverage for the government and governmental bodies. In 1972, the SIC started a new subsidiary, the Ghana Reinsurance Organization, to curb the outflow of reinsurance premiums from the country. Insurance services were available in the early 1980s through 16 companies, 5 of them classified as foreign (although a 1976 law required the latter to distribute 20% of equity to the government and 40% to Ghanaian partners).

35PUBLIC FINANCE

Ghana turned to the IMF as the economy approached bankruptcy in 1983. The IMF-sponsored stabilization program, known as the ERP (Economic Recovery Program), has been pursued vigorously through its several phases, and borrowing from the IMF came to an end in 1992. Many changes took place in the ten years of the program. The currency was devalued repeatedly; foreign exchange was auctioned. The cocoa sector was revamped, starting with higher producer prices, and privatized. The number of civil service employees was reduced and the state unburdened itself of its parastatals. A systematic program removed government subsidies, and tax collection procedures were strengthened.

Ghana's budgets have habitually been in deficit, financed mainly through the domestic banking system, with consequent rapid increases in the money supply and the rate of inflation. In 1992, the fiscal deficit steeply increased due to increased wage demands from civil servants. Ghana's civil service is one of Africa's largest.

The following table shows actual revenues and expenditures for 1987 and 1988 in millions of cedis.

	1987	1988
REVENUE AND GRANTS		
Tax revenue	93,917	131,199
Non-tax revenue	11,092	11,039
Grants	6,037	11,553
TOTAL	111,046	153,791
EXPENDITURES & LENDING MINUS REPAYMENTS		
General public services	19,314	28,155
Defense	6,659	4,603
Education	24,930	36,995
Health	8,457	12,880
Social security and welfare	5,464	9,9144
Housing and community amenities	1,971	7,197
Recreation, cultural, and religious affairs	1,726	—
Economic affairs and services	16,045	27,563
Other expenditures	16,108	16,700
Adjustments	1,961	—
Lending minus repayments	4,852	5,983
TOTAL	106,987	149,880
Deficit/Surplus	4,059	3,911

In 1985 Ghana's total public debt stood at 47,605 million cedis of which 9,839 million cedis was financed abroad.

36TAXATION

The basic corporate tax rate is 35–45%; the concessional rate for Valco is 40%. The capital-gains tax rate is about 55% and the tax rate on dividends is 35–55%. A personal income tax ranging from 5–35% is also levied. A salary tax of 5% on employees and 12.5% on employers finances the Social Security and National Insurance Trust pension program. There are also property, sales, and excise taxes.

37CUSTOMS AND DUTIES

Ghana employs customs duties. Duty on most raw materials and capital goods was 15% in 1993, and duty on most consumer goods was 25%. There are import restrictions on ale/stout, cigarettes, cement pipes, roofing sheets, and asbestos/fibers. The acute shortage of foreign exchange often makes it difficult to secure import licenses or to obtain the foreign exchange needed to pay for imports. Export duties are a major source of government revenue.

In June 1975, Ghana ratified the Treaty of Lagos, thus becoming a member of ECOWAS. The principal objectives of ECOWAS are to end customs duties and other restrictions on trade between member states, to establish a common external customs tariff and commercial policy, and to eliminate disparities in the level of development among member states.

38FOREIGN INVESTMENT

Until recently, nationalized enterprise was the cornerstone of Ghanaian investment policy. Ghanaian leaders at times acknowledged the need for foreign capital and welcomed investment in new enterprises while seeking to retain government control over the economy. The economic crisis of the early 1980s led to some relaxation of state controls. The 1985 investment code offers tax concessions, guarantees against nationalization, free repatriation of dividends, and international arbitration of disputes. In 1993, it was announced that the investment code would be further liberalized. The government is styling itself on the model of a number of Asian countries where a dynamic private sector and healthy investment environment are essential. Ghana has announced its intention to draft a national private sector development plan.

The largest firm operating in Ghana is Valco, operated by the American company Kaiser Aluminum, whose guaranteed use of electric power for aluminum refining made possible the building of the Volta Dam and hydroelectric generating plant. Other American companies operating in Ghana include Star-Kist, Union Carbide, Amoco, Texaco, and Mobil.

39ECONOMIC DEVELOPMENT

Recent economic policy has aimed at correcting basic problems in every phase of the economy: unemployment, low productivity, high production costs, the large foreign debt, low savings and investing, inflation, and high private and government consumption.

Ghanaian development efforts are focused on the maintenance of high levels of increasingly productive commercial investment. Pledges from donors in 1984–87, came to over $2.2 billion (exclusive of IMF support), but disbursements lagged considerably behind pledges. Cumulative United States economic assistance totaled $506.4 million through 1986, with $24.2 million authorized for the 1986 fiscal year. Ghana had received a total of $1,155.6 million from multilateral sources through 1986, most of it from the World Bank, IDA, and African Development Bank.

40SOCIAL DEVELOPMENT

The Social Security and National Insurance Trust, established in 1972, covers wage employees. The secretariat of Mobilization and Productivity and the secretariat of Local Government and Rural Development deal with both urban and rural problems, including literacy, child welfare, and occupational safety. A rural training center in each region offers courses in methods of improving village life to departmental staff and voluntary leaders from rural areas. Social welfare work in urban areas ranges from the establishment of youth clubs and neighborhood centers to casework and court work.

Women play a prominent role in agriculture and domestic trade, and are represented at the highest levels of political life. The fertility rate in 1993 was estimated at 6.2; abortion is available on broad health grounds. The infant mortality rate is 103 deaths per 1,000 live births. Life expectancy is 53 years for males and 57 years for females.

41HEALTH

Waterborne parasitic diseases are a widespread health hazard, and the creation of Lake Volta and related irrigation systems has led to an increase in malaria, sleeping sickness, and schistosomiasis. The upper reaches of the Volta basin are seriously afflicted with onchocerciasis, a filarial worm disease transmitted by biting flies. In 1990, there were 222 reported cases of tuberculosis per 100,000 people. Between 1990 and 1992, efforts were made to vaccinate children up to one year old against tuberculosis (57%); diphtheria, pertussis, and tetanus (34%); polio (36%); and measles (40%). In 1990, a total of $204 million was spent on health care. Roughly one-third of children under 5 were considered malnourished. In 1992, 52% of the population had access to safe water and 42% had adequate sanitation.

In 1989, Ghana had 628 physicians, 67 pharmacists, 39 dentists, 3,998 nurses, and 1,736 midwives. In 1992, there were 4 doctors per 100,000 people, with a nurse to doctor ratio of 9:1. In 1990 there were 1.5 hospital beds per 1,000 inhabitants. In 1992, 60% of the population had access to health care services.

In 1993, Ghana's birth rate was 42 per 1,000 people, and about 13% of Ghana's married women (ages 15 to 49) used contraception. In 1992, the infant mortality rate was 103 per 1,000 live births, and the 1993 overall death rate was 12 per 1,000 people. The average life expectancy is 56 years.

42HOUSING

Ghana's housing needs have been increasing as the main towns grow in population. In 1982, the government established the State Housing Construction Co. to help supply new low-cost dwelling units. The Bank for Housing and Construction finances private housing schemes on a mortgage basis. Under another housing ownership scheme, civil servants may acquire accommodations on purchase-lease terms. The Cocoa Marketing Board, the Social Security and National Insurance Trust, and other organizations have also invested in housing projects; nevertheless, most houses continue to be built without government assistance. Foreign mining companies provide housing for all their overseas employees and many of their African workers. According to the latest available information for 1980–88, housing units numbered 2,458,000, with 5.2 people per dwelling.

43EDUCATION

Most of the older schools, started by Christian missions, have received substantial financial help from the government, but the state is increasingly responsible for the construction and maintenance of new schools. By 1990, an estimated 70% of Ghanaian men and 51% of the women were literate.

Primary education has been free since 1952 and compulsory since 1961. Lasting 6 years, it is followed by 7 years of secondary schooling. In 1990, Ghana had 11,165 primary schools with 66,946 teachers and 1,945,422 pupils. General secondary schools had 768,603 pupils and 39,903 teachers. The supply of teachers continues to fall far short of the number needed to keep pace with increasing student enrollment. Ghana has three universities with a combined 1990 enrollment of 9,609: the University of Ghana, in Legon, outside Accra; the University of Science and Technology in Kumasi; and the University of Cape Coast.

44LIBRARIES AND MUSEUMS

The Ghana Library Board maintains the Accra Central Library, 13 regional libraries, 47 branch libraries, mobile units, and children's libraries, with combined holdings of 1,576,000 volumes in 1989. The University of Ghana (Balme Library) in Legon has holdings of more than 350,000 volumes and is the largest research library in Ghana. The University of Science and Technology Library has 150,000 volumes. The Research Library on African Affairs (formerly the George Padmore Memorial Library), which opened in Accra in 1961, maintains a collection of publications on various aspects of Africa.

The Ghana National Museum, in Accra, founded by the University College of Ghana and now operated by the Museum and Monuments Board, contains hundreds of exhibits illustrating the culture, history, and arts and crafts of Ghana and West Africa. The West African Historical Museum at Cape Coast, sponsored by the Museum and Monuments Board and the University of Cape Coast, opened in 1971. The Ghana National Museum of Science and Technology is at Accra. There are regional museums at Ho and Kumasi, which is also home to the Ghana Military Museum. The University of Ghana has museums maintained by the departments of geology and archaeology and by the Institute of African Studies.

45 MEDIA

Telephone, telegraph, radio, and television services are owned and operated by the government. The government-owned Ghana Broadcasting Corp. makes radio services available throughout the country in English and six other languages; an international radio service beams programs in English, French, and Hausa to all parts of Africa. An international telex system was inaugurated in 1962, and a government-owned television service was established in 1965. There were about 4,150,000 radios, 235,000 television sets and 77,105 telephones in 1991.

The principal government-owned newspapers in Accra, with their daily 1991 circulations, are the *Daily Graphic* (100,000) and the *Ghanaian Times* (50,000). The *Pioneer* (100,000) is published in Kumasi.

46 ORGANIZATIONS

Cooperatives have played an important role in marketing agricultural produce, especially cocoa. In 1986, Ghana had 8,387 cooperative societies. The National Chamber of Commerce, with headquarters in Accra, has 13 district chambers. National cultural associations—including associations of writers, musicians, artists, dancers, and dramatists—have been established.

47 TOURISM, TRAVEL, AND RECREATION

Ghana has sought to develop a tourist trade. Attractions include casinos, fine beaches, game reserves, and old British, Dutch, and Portuguese trading forts and castles. Indigenous dance forms and folk music thrive in rural areas, and there are many cultural festivals. The National Cultural Center is in Kumasi, the capital of the Ashanti region, an area rich in traditional Ghanaian crafts. There is an Arts Center in Accra, as well as the National Museum, the Alwri Botanical Gardens, and the burial place of W.E.B. Du Bois. Visas or entry permits are required of all visitors. In 1991, about 172,000 visitors came to Ghana. In 1990, there were 6,330 hotel rooms with 9,086 beds and a 72% occupancy rate.

48 FAMOUS GHANAIANS

J. E. Casely Hayford (1867–1930), for 13 years a member of the Legislative Assembly, is remembered as a leading public-spirited citizen. Dr. J. E. K. Wegyir Aggrey (1875–1927), noted educational reformer, played a large part in the development of secondary education. Sir Henley Coussey (1891–1958) and Sir Emmanuel Quist (1882–1959) were distinguished jurists.

Persons from overseas who played a great part in the progress of Ghana were the Rev. Alexander Gordon Fraser (1873–1962), the first principal of Achimota School; Sir (Frederick) Gordon Guggisberg (1869–1930), who took the first steps toward Africanization of the public service and was instrumental in founding Achimota School; and Sir Charles Noble Arden-Clarke (1898–1962), who was governor of the Gold Coast during the preparatory years of independence (1948–57) and the first governor-general of Ghana. The writer, sociologist, and civil rights leader W(illiam) E(dward) B(urghardt) Du Bois (b.US, 1868–1963) settled in Ghana in 1961 and is buried in Accra.

Kwame Nkrumah (1909–72), the first president of the republic, served in that capacity until the military coup of February 1966; he died in exile in Guinea. J. B. Danquah (1895–1965), a lawyer, was named vice-president of the UGCC at the time of its founding in 1947. Detained along with Nkrumah after the Accra riots in 1948, he later helped to found the GCP. Arrested by Nkrumah in 1961, and again in 1964, he died in prison in 1965. Kofi Abrefa Busia (1913–78), a noted sociologist, was prime minister from October 1969 to January 1972. Flight-Lieut. Jerry (John) Rawlings (b.1947), the son of a Scottish father and a Ghanaian mother, led successful military coups in 1979 and 1981.

49 DEPENDENCIES

Ghana has no territories or colonies.

50 BIBLIOGRAPHY

Allman, Jean Marie. *The Quills of the Porcupine: Asante Nationalism in an Emergent Ghana.* Madison: University of Wisconsin Press, 1993.

American University. *Area Handbook for Ghana.* Washington, D.C.: Government Printing Office, 1979.

Anquandah, James. *Rediscovering Ghana's Past.* London: Longman, 1982.

Baynham, Simon. *The Military and Politics in Nkrumah's Ghana.* Boulder, Colo.: Westview Press, 1988.

Bourret, F. M. *Ghana: The Road to Independence.* Stanford, Calif.: Stanford University Press, 1960.

Davidson, Basil. *Black Star: A View of the Life and Times of Kwame Nkrumah.* Boulder, Colo.: Westview Press, 1989.

Ghana in Pictures. Minneapolis: Lerner, 1988.

Herbst, Jeffrey Ira. *The Politics of Reform in Ghana, 1982–1991.* Berkeley: University of California Press, 1993.

Huq, M. M. *The Economy of Ghana: The First 25 Years since Independence.* New York: St. Martin's Press, 1989.

McFarland, Daniel M. *Historical Dictionary of Ghana.* Metuchen, N.J.: Scarecrow, 1983.

Mendonsa, Eugene L. *The Politics of Divination.* Berkeley: University of California Press, 1982.

Myers, Robert A. *Ghana.* Santa Barbara, Calif.: Clio Press, 1991.

Nkrumah, Kwame. *Ghana: The Autobiography of Kwame Nkrumah.* New York: International Publications Service, 1970.

Rimmer, Douglas. *Staying Poor: Ghana's Political Economy, 1950–1990.* New York: Pergamon, 1992.

Rooney, David. *Kwame Nkrumah: The Political Kingdom in the Third World.* New York: St. Martin's Press, 1989, 1988.

Shillington, Kevin. *Ghana and the Rawlings Factor.* New York: St. Martin's Press, 1992.

Vogt, John. *Portuguese Rule on the Gold Coast, 1469–1862.* Athens: University of Georgia Press, 1978.

GUINEA

Republic of Guinea
République de Guinée

CAPITAL: Conakry.

FLAG: The national flag is a tricolor of red, yellow, and green vertical stripes.

ANTHEM: *Liberté (Liberty)*.

MONETARY UNIT: A new currency, the syli (s), of 100 cauris, was introduced in October 1972; s1 = 10 old Guinea francs. The Guinea franc (GFr) of 100 centimes was restored in January 1986 on a one-to-one basis with the syli. There are notes of 25, 50, 100, 500, 1,000, and 5,000 GFr. GFr1 = $0.0023 (or $1 = GFr440).

WEIGHTS AND MEASURES: The metric system is the legal standard.

HOLIDAYS: New Year's Day, 1 January; Labor Day, 1 May; Anniversary of Women's Revolt, 27 August; Referendum Day, 28 September; Independence Day, 2 October; Armed Forces Day, 1 November; Day of 1970 Invasion, 22 November; Christmas, 25 December. Movable religious holidays include 'Id al-Fitr, 'Id al-'Adha', and Easter Monday.

TIME: GMT.

¹LOCATION, SIZE, AND EXTENT

Guinea, on the west coast of Africa, has an area of 245,860 sq km (94,927 sq mi), extending 831 km (516 mi) SE–NW and 493 km (306 mi) NE–SW. Comparatively, the area occupied by Guinea is slightly smaller than the state of Oregon. Bordered on the N by Senegal, on the N and NE by Mali, on the E by Côte d'Ivoire, on the S by Liberia and Sierra Leone, on the W by the Atlantic Ocean, and on the NW by Guinea-Bissau, Guinea has a total boundary length of 3,719 km (2,311 mi).

Guinea's capital city, Conakry, is located on the country's Atlantic coast.

²TOPOGRAPHY

Guinea owes its frontiers mainly to the accidents of the late 19th-century partition of Africa and has no geographic unity. The country can be divided into four regions: Lower Guinea (Guinée Maritime), the alluvial coastal plain; Middle Guinea, the plateau region of the Futa Jallon (Fouta Djalon), deeply cut in many places by narrow valleys; Upper Guinea (Haute Guinée), a gently undulating plain with an average elevation of about 300 m (1,000 ft), savanna country broken by occasional rocky outcrops; and the forested Guinea Highlands (Guinée Forestière), composed of granites, schists, and quartzites, including Mt. Nimba (1,752 m/5,747 ft), the highest peak in the country, at the juncture of Guinea, Liberia, and Côte d'Ivoire. The Niger River and its important tributary the Milo have their source in the Guinea Highlands; the Gambia River and Senegal River (whose upper course is called the Bafing in Guinea) rise in the Futa Jallon.

³CLIMATE

The coastal region and much of the inland area have a tropical climate with a long rainy season of six months, a relatively high and uniform annual temperature, and high humidity. Conakry's year-round average high is 29°C (84°F), and the low is 23°C (73°F); its average rainfall is 430 cm (169 in) per year. April is the hottest month; July and August are the wettest. Rainfall in the Futa Jallon is much less (about 150–200 cm/60–80 in) and more

irregular, and temperatures are lower; moreover, the daily temperature range is much greater, especially during the dry season. In Upper Guinea, rainfall is lower than in the Futa Jallon; the average daily temperature range is as great as 14°C (25°F), and greater in the dry season. Rainfall in the highlands averages about 280 cm (110 in) annually; temperatures are relatively equable owing to the altitude, although with an average daily range of 18°C (32°F).

⁴FLORA AND FAUNA

Dense mangrove forests grow along the river mouths. Farther inland, the typical vegetation of Lower Guinea is woodland dominated by parinari, with many woody climbers and bushes below. Gum copal is common near streams. The Futa Jallon has been subject to excessive burning, and the lower slopes are characterized by secondary woodland, much sedge (catagyna pilosa), and expanses of laterite; the higher plateaus and peaks have dense forest, and some plants found nowhere else in the world have been reported on them. Savanna woodland characterizes Upper Guinea, with only tall grass in large areas; trees include the shea nut, tamarind, and locust bean. There is rain forest along the border with Liberia.

The elephant, hippopotamus, buffalo, lion, leopard, and many kinds of antelope and monkey are to be found in Guinea, as well as crocodiles and several species of venomous snakes. Birds are plentiful and diverse.

⁵ENVIRONMENT

Centuries of slash-and-burn agriculture have caused forested areas to be replaced by savanna woodland, grassland, or brush. During 1981–85, some 36,000 ha (89,000 acres) of land were deforested each year. Mining, the expansion of hydroelectric facilities, and pollution contribute to the erosion of the country's soils and desertification. Water pollution and improper waste disposal are significant environmental problems in Guinea. In 1994, water-borne diseases contributed to an infant mortality rate of 145 per 1,000 children. The nation has 54.2 cubic miles of water with 87% used in farming activity. Nearly two-thirds of the people living in rural areas do not have pure water. Guinea's cities produce 0.3 million tons of solid waste per year. As of 1994, 17 of Guinea's 188 mammal species and 6 of its 529 bird species were endangered, as well as 1 type of reptile and 1 amphibian, and 36 of the nation's plant species. Human encroachment and hunting have reduced Guinea's wildlife, especially its large mammals. A nature reserve has been established on Mt. Nimba.

6 POPULATION

A 1992 census reported the population at about 5,040,000. This was admittedly an undercount and did not include refugees, either. The population was estimated by the US Census Bureau in 1994 at 8,028,828, giving an average density of 32.7 per sq km (84.6 per sq mi). A 1995 population of 6,700,000 was estimated by the UN, which has projected a population of 7,759,000 for the year 2000, assuming a crude birthrate of 47.6 per 1,000 population, a crude death rate of 18.3, and a net natural increase of 29.3 during 1985–2000. The annual growth rate was about 3% in 1995, when 30% of the population was living in urban areas. Conakry, the capital and largest city, had an estimated population of 1,127,000 in 1990. Other large towns include Kankan (70,000), Labé, Nzérékoré, Boké, and Siguiri.

7 MIGRATION

After independence, Guineans left the country in increasing numbers, mostly for Senegal and Côte d'Ivoire. In the early and mid 1980s, probably 2 million Guineans were living abroad, perhaps half of them in Senegal and Côte d'Ivoire. Many of them returned after the end of the Sékou Touré regime in 1984. At the end of 1992, Guinea was accommodating 478,500 refugees fleeing the Liberian civil war. There were also about 120,000 refugees from Sierra Leone who were escaping the spillover from the Liberian fighting.

8 ETHNIC GROUPS

Of Guinea's two dozen ethnic groups, three predominate: the Fulani, Malinké, and Susu. The Fulani (sometimes called Peul), perhaps the largest single group, live mainly in the Futa Jallon. The Malinké (referred to in other parts of West Africa as Mandingo) and related peoples of the so-called Nuclear Mandé group live in eastern Guinea and are concentrated around Kankan, Beyla, and Kouroussa. The Susu, with related groups, are centered farther west and along the coast in the areas around Conakry, Forécariah, and Kindia. Related to them are the Dialonké, living farther east in Middle Guinea and western Upper Guinea. Toward the southeast, in the Guinea Highlands near the borders of Liberia and Côte d'Ivoire, are various Kru or peripheral Mandé groups; among them are the Kissi around Quéckédou, the Toma around Macenta, and the Koranko near Kissidougou. Notable among the 3,500 or so non-Africans in the mid-1980s were Lebanese and Syrians.

9 LANGUAGES

French is the official language and the language of administration. In 1967, a cultural revolution was announced for the purpose of "de-Westernizing" Guinean education. A literacy program begun in 1968 sought eventually to teach all citizens to speak and write one of the eight principal local languages: Malinké (Maninkakan), Fulani (Poular), Susu, Kpelle (Guerzé), Loma (Toma), Kissi, Coniagui, and Bassari, all of which belong to the Niger-Congo language group. After the fall of the Touré regime in 1984, French was again emphasized.

10 RELIGIONS

More than 90% of all Guineans, particularly the Fulani and Malinké, are Muslims; most of the remainder practice traditional African religions. Muslim practices, particularly public prayers and the prescribed fasts, are often combined with animist beliefs and ceremonies. Christian missions were established in the 19th century, but converts have been few; less than 2% of the population is Christian. In May 1967, President Sékou Touré ordered that only Guinean nationals be allowed to serve in the country's Roman Catholic priesthood. The Catholic archbishop in Conakry was sentenced to life imprisonment at hard labor in 1971 for allegedly plotting against the state; he was released in August 1979. In 1984 private education, long prohibited by the government, was again permitted.

11 TRANSPORTATION

Lack of an adequate transportation network has hindered the country's development. The state-owned, meter-gauge, single-track railroad from Conakry to Kankan (663 km/412 mi) was built between 1900 and 1914; it is in disrepair and no longer able to carry heavy traffic. As of 1991, the railway was being rehabilitated with French assistance. A standard-gauge track of about 112 km (70 mi) along this line, between Conakry and Debélé, near Kindia, links the port and the OBK bauxite mine. The Friguia Mining Co. built and maintains 144 km (89 mi) of railway between the Fria mines and alumina works and the port of Conakry; the Boké mining operation constructed a 135-km (84-mi) railroad linking its deposits at Sangarédi with the port of Kamsar. Of 30,100 km (18,700 mi) of roads, only some 1,145 km (711 mi) were tarred in 1987. There were 23,155 automobiles and 13,000 commercial vehicles in 1992.

Conakry has a natural deepwater harbor that handles foreign cargo (mostly bauxite and alumina). Port modernization is scheduled with aid from the IDA, the African Development Bank, and the Federal Republic of Germany (FRG). A deepwater port at Kamsar, completed in 1973, handles the output of the Boké bauxite mine, as much as 9 million tons a year. There are lesser ports at Kassa, Benty, and Kakande. Most rivers are of little value for navigation. A national shipping line is jointly owned with a Norwegian company.

Conakry's airport handles international jet traffic. It, three smaller airfields at Labé, Kankan, and Faranah, and a number of airstrips are served by the national carrier, Air Guinée, which also flies to other West African cities.

12 HISTORY

Archaeological evidence indicates that at least some stone tools found in Guinea were the work of peoples who had come there from the Sahara, perhaps because of the desiccation that had occurred in the Saharan region by 2000 BC. Agriculture was practiced along the coast of Guinea by AD 1000, with rice the staple crop.

Most of Upper Guinea fell within the area influenced by the medieval empire of Ghana at the height of its power, but none of present-day Guinea was actually within the empire. The northern half of present-day Guinea was, however, within the later Mali and Songhai empires.

Malinké did not begin arriving in Guinea until the 13th century, nor did the Fulani come in considerable numbers until the 17th century. In 1725, a holy war (jihad) was declared in Futa Jallon by Muslim Fulani. The onslaught, directed against the Malinké, was ultimately successful in establishing the independence of the Fulani of Futa Jallon and effecting their unity under the Almany (or paramount chief) Alfa of Timbo.

Meanwhile, European exploration of the Guinea coast was begun by the Portuguese in the middle of the 15th century. By the 17th century, French, British, and Portuguese traders and slavers were competing with one another. When the slave trade was prohibited during the first half of the 19th century, the Guinea creeks afforded secluded hiding places for slavers harried by the ships of

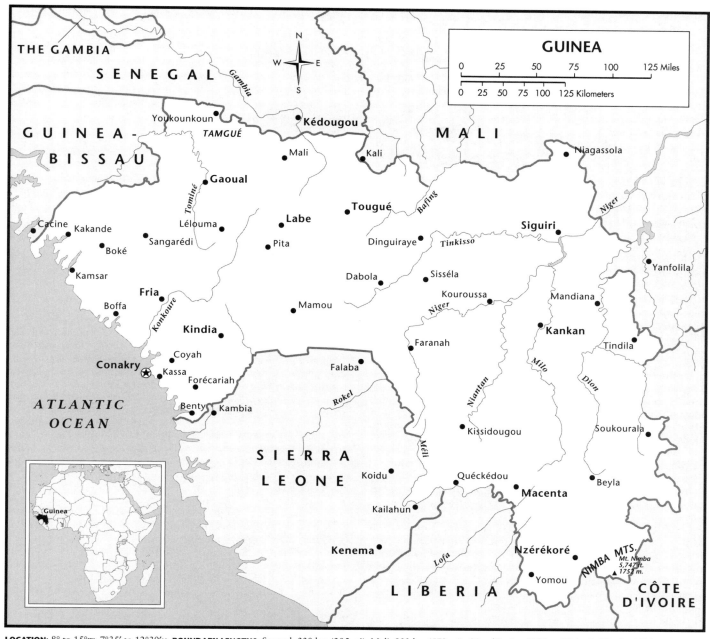

LOCATION: 8° to 15°w; 7°35′ to 12°30′N. **BOUNDARY LENGTHS:** Senegal, 330 km (205 mi); Mali, 932 km (579 mi); Côte d'Ivoire, 605 km (376 mi); Liberia, 563 km (350 mi); Sierra Leone, 652 km (405 mi); Atlantic coastline, 352 km (219 mi); Guinea-Bissau, 386 km (240 mi). **TERRITORIAL SEA LIMIT:** 12 mi.

the Royal Navy. French rights along the coast were expressly preserved by the Peace of Paris (1814), and French—as well as British and Portuguese—trading activities expanded in the middle years of the 19th century, when trade in peanuts, palm oil, hides, and rubber replaced that in slaves. The French established a protectorate over Boké in 1849 and consolidated their rule over the coastal areas in the 1860s. This inevitably led to attempts to secure a more satisfactory arrangement with the Fulani chiefs of Futa Jallon. A protectorate was established over the region in 1881, but effective sovereignty was not secured for another 15 years.

Resistance to the consolidation of the French advance up the Senegal and the Niger, toward Lake Chad, was made by Samory Touré, a Malinké born in Upper Guinea. He had seized Kankan in 1879 and established his authority in the area southeast of Siguiri, but his attacks on the area led the inhabitants to seek aid

from the French troops already established at Kita in the French Sudan (Soudan Français, now Mali) in 1882. Samory made treaties with the French in 1886 and again in 1890, but on various pretexts both he and the French later renounced them, and hostilities resumed. His capture in 1898 marked the end of any concerted local resistance to the French occupation of Guinea, Ivory Coast (now Côte d'Ivoire), and southern Mali.

In 1891, Guinea was constituted as a French territory separate from Senegal, of which it had hitherto been a part. Four years later, the French territories in West Africa were federated under a governor-general. The federation structure remained substantially unchanged until Guinea attained independence. In 1946, Africans in Guinea became French citizens, but the franchise was at first restricted to certain groups and was not replaced by universal adult suffrage until 1957.

The End of Colonial Rule

In September 1958, Guinea participated in the referendum on the new French constitution. On acceptance of the new constitution, French overseas territories had the option of choosing to continue their existing status, to move toward full integration into metropolitan France, or to acquire the status of an autonomous republic in the new quasi-federal French Community. If, however, they rejected the new constitution, they would become independent forthwith. French President Charles de Gaulle made it clear that a country pursuing the independent course would no longer receive French economic and financial aid or retain French technical and administrative officers. The electorate of Guinea rejected the new constitution overwhelmingly, and Guinea accordingly became an independent state on 2 October 1958, with Ahmed Sékou Touré, leader of Guinea's strongest labor union, as president.

During its first three decades of independence, Guinea developed into a militantly Socialist state, with nearly complete government control over the country's economic and political life. Guinea expelled the US Peace Corps in 1966 because of alleged involvement in a plot to overthrow President Touré. Similar charges were directed against France; diplomatic relations were severed in 1965 and did not resume until 1975. An ongoing source of contention between Guinea and its French-speaking neighbors was the estimated half-million expatriates in Senegal and Côte d'Ivoire; some were active dissidents who, in 1966, formed the National Liberation Front of Guinea (Front de Libération Nationale de Guinée—FLNG).

International tensions erupted again in 1970 when some 350 men, including FLNG partisans and Africans in the Portuguese army, invaded Guinea under the leadership of white Portuguese officers from Portuguese Guinea (now Guinea-Bissau). Waves of arrests, detentions, and some executions followed this invasion, which was repulsed after one day. Between 1969 and 1976, according to Amnesty International, 4,000 persons were detained for political reasons, with the fate of 2,900 unknown. After an alleged Fulani plot to assassinate Touré was disclosed in May 1976, Diallo Telli, a cabinet minister and formerly the first secretary-general of the OAU, was arrested and sent to prison, where he died without trial in November.

In 1977, protests against the regime's economic policy, which dealt harshly with unauthorized trading, led to riots in which three regional governors were killed. Touré responded by relaxing restrictions, offering amnesty to exiles (thousands of whom returned), and releasing hundreds of political prisoners. Ties were loosened with the Soviet bloc, as Touré sought increased Western aid and private investment for Guinea's sagging economy.

Single-list elections for an expanded National Assembly were held in 1980. Touré was elected unopposed to a fourth seven-year term as president on 9 May 1982; according to the government radio, he received 100% of the vote. A new constitution was adopted that month, and during the summer Touré visited the US as part of an economic policy reversal that found Guinea seeking Western investment to develop its huge mineral reserves. Measures announced in 1983 brought further economic liberalization, including the relegation of produce marketing to private traders.

Touré died on 26 March 1984 while undergoing cardiac treatment at The Cleveland Clinic; he had been rushed to the US after being stricken in Sa'udi Arabia the previous day. Prime Minister Louis Lansana Béavogui then became acting president, pending elections that were to be held within 45 days. On 3 April, however, just as the Political Bureau of the ruling Guinea Democratic Party (PDG) was about to name its choice as Touré's successor, the armed forces seized power, denouncing the last years of Touré's rule as a "bloody and ruthless dictatorship." The constitution was suspended, the National Assembly dissolved, and the PDG abolished. The leader of the coup, Col. Lansana Conté, assumed the presidency on 5 April, heading the Military Committee for National Recovery (Comité Militaire de Redressement National—CMRN). About 1,000 political prisoners were freed.

Conté suppressed an attempted military coup led by Col. Diarra Traoré on 4 July 1985. Almost two years later, it was announced that 58 persons, including both coup leaders and members of Touré's government, had been sentenced to death; however, it was believed that many of them, as well as Traoré, had actually been shot days after the coup attempt. All were identified with the Malinké, who were closely identified with the Touré regime. The military regime adopted free-market policies in an effort to revive the economy.

Under pressure locally and from abroad, Guinea embarked on a transition to multiparty democracy. The military-dominated government has not been entirely supportive of the process. It legalized parties in April 1992, but did not really allow them to function freely. It postponed presidential elections for over a year (until 19 December 1993) and then verified the results (Conté was elected by a narrow margin) after international monitors had rejected them as fraudulent. The legislative elections were delayed even longer. The result is that the military regime continues to govern in the face of its growing unpopularity.

13 GOVERNMENT

Guinea's first constitution took effect on 12 November 1958 and was substantially amended in 1963 and 1974. Under the new constitution promulgated in May 1982 (but suspended in the military coup of April 1984), sovereignty is declared to rest with the people and to be exercised by their representatives in the Guinea Democratic Party (PDG), the only legal political party. Party and state are declared to be one and indivisible. The head of state is the president, elected for a seven-year term by universal adult suffrage (at age 18). A National Assembly of 210 members was elected in 1980 from a single national list presented by the PDG; the announced term was five years, although the 1982 constitution and its precursors stipulated a term of seven (the Assembly was dissolved after four years, in 1984). The constitution gives Assembly members control of the budget and, with the president, the responsibility to initiate and formulate laws.

In practice, under the Touré regime there was no separation of functions or powers. The legislature, the cabinet, and the national administration were subordinate to the PDG in the direction and control of the nation. The Assembly served mainly to ratify the decisions of the PDG's Political Bureau, headed by Touré, who was also president of the republic and secretary-general of the PDG; the Assembly and the cabinet (appointed by Touré) implemented the decisions and orders of the party arrived at by the party congress, national conference, and the Political Bureau. Locally, PDG and government authority were synonymous.

The armed forces leaders who seized power after Touré's death ruled Guinea through the Military Committee for National Recovery (CMRN). Following the adoption by referendum of a new constitution on 21 December 1990, the CMRN was dissolved and a transitional Committee of National Recovery (CTRN) was set up in February 1991 as the country's legislative body. Two-thirds of the cabinet members are civilians, however. Military leaders still control the government process, even after the introduction of legal political parties and the start of an electoral process in which it is virtually impossible for opposition candidates to campaign.

14 POLITICAL PARTIES

From 1945, when political activity began in Guinea, until about 1953, the political scene was one of loose electoral alliances that relied more on the support of traditional chiefs and of the French administration than on political programs or organized memberships. After 1953, however, these alliances rapidly lost ground to the Guinea section of the African Democratic Rally (Rassemblement Démocratique Africain—RDA), an interterritorial organization founded in 1946. This section, known as the Guinea Democratic Party (Parti Démocratique de Guinée—PDG), was formed by Marxists determined to develop an organized mass political movement that cut across ethnic differences and had a strongly nationalist outlook. Their leader was Ahmed Sékou Touré, a prominent trade union leader in French West Africa. The alleged great-grandson of the warrior-chief Samory who had fought the French in the late 19th century, Touré had much support in areas where Samory had fought his last battles, although his strongest backers were the Susu in Lower Guinea. In 1957, the PDG won 57 of 60 seats in Territorial Assembly elections.

Convinced that the French Community proposed by De Gaulle would not result in real independence for the people of French West Africa, Touré called for a vote against joining the Community in the referendum of 28 September 1958. Some 95% of those voting in Guinea supported Touré in opting for Guinea's complete independence. In December 1958, the opposition parties fused with Touré's PDG, making it the only political party in the country. The precipitous withdrawal of the French bureaucracy in 1958 led, almost of necessity, to the PDG's inheritance of much of the structure of government.

During the 1960s, the PDG's party machinery was organized down to the grassroots level, with local committees replacing tribal authorities, and sectional, regional, and national conferences ensuring coordination and control. In 1968, a new local unit within the PDG, the Local Revolutionary Command (Pouvoir Révolutionnaire Local—PRL) was organized. By 1973, the PRL had assumed complete responsibility for local economic, social, and political affairs. There were 2,441 PRLs in 1981, each directed by a committee of seven members and headed by a mayor. Each of the 35 regions had a party decision-making body called a Federal Congress, headed by a secretary. A 13-member Federal Committee, headed by the regional governor, was the executive body. The 170 districts had similar bodies, called sections, congresses, and committees.

The Political Bureau, nominally responsible to a Central Committee, was the PDG's chief executive body. Until the military coup that abolished the PDG in April 1984, the Political Bureau was the focus of party and national power, and its members were the most important government ministers and officials, with Touré as chairman. The PDG and its mass organizations were outlawed after the 1984 coup.

Political parties were legalized in April 1992. Within a month, more than 30 parties had been formed, a number by government ministers who helped themselves to state funds and used the state agencies to promote their campaigns. The use of government vehicles for partisan activities and the disbursement of state monies to supporters were commonplace.

By July 1992, government had banned all political demonstrations. This hampered opposition parties preparing for National Assembly elections then scheduled for late-1992 and presidential elections scheduled for early 1993. Elections were delayed. Eventually, in December 1993, Gen. Conté officially got 51.7% in a widely and violently contested presidential election. International observers declared the campaigning and balloting unsatisfactory.

By late 1993, over 40 political parties were legally registered. Some were allied with the military government (e.g., the Party for Unity and Progress) and others were identifiably ethnic based. The most significant national opposition parties are the Rally for the Guinean People (RPG), the Union for a New Republic (UNR), and the Party for Renewal and Progress. Legislative elections were scheduled for 1994.

15 LOCAL GOVERNMENT

Under the Touré regime, the local units of the PDG, the Local Revolutionary Commands (PRLs), were responsible for the political and economic administration of rural areas. In principle, the PRLs regulated all commerce, farming, distribution of land, public works, and communications, as well as civil life and the people's courts in communities under their authority. Each PRL had, in principle, a company of militia of 101 members, subdivided into 4 platoons and 12 groups.

There are 33 regions or provinces, each headed by a presidentially appointed governor. The regions are subdivided into prefectures and subprefectures, and finally districts (known as quarters in cities), of which there are 175. Village and city neighborhood governing bodies were developed in 1986, sometimes by election. Under Touré, Africanization of the bureaucracy proceeded further in Guinea than in any other African country. Foreign experts were retained only in education and a few technical fields.

16 JUDICIAL SYSTEM

In 1958 and 1965, the government introduced some customary law but retained French law as the basic framework for the court system. The courts includes courts of first instance, two Courts of Appeal (in Kankan and in Conakry) and the Supreme Court. There is also a State Security Court, which last met to try those charged with plotting the 1985 coup attempt, and a military tribunal, which handles criminal cases involving military personnel.

A traditional system of dispute resolution exists alongside the court system at the village and neighborhood level in which a village chief or council of wise men attempt to render justice. These cases, if not resolved to the satisfaction of all parties involved, may be referred to the courts for further consideration.

Although the 1990 Constitution declares the independence of the judiciary, magistrates have no tenure and remain susceptible to influence by the executive branch.

17 ARMED FORCES

The armed forces numbered about 9,700 in 1993, including 8,500 in the army, 400 in the navy, and 800 in the air force. The army had 11 battalions with 53 T-34 and T-54 tanks among its predominantly Soviet-made equipment. The navy had 9 craft, and the air force 12 combat aircraft, including 8 Soviet-made MiG-21 fighters. There was a People's Militia of 7,000 and 2,600 in the gendarmerie and Republican Guard. Defense spending in 1989 was estimated at $27 million or 1% of GDP. Arms imports totaled $20 million in 1990 and $5 million in 1991.

18 INTERNATIONAL COOPERATION

Guinea was admitted to the UN on 12 December 1958 and is a member of ECA and all the nonregional specialized agencies except IAEA. It is a signatory of the Law of the Sea. Guinea also belongs to the African Development Bank, ECOWAS, G-77, and OAU; the nation hosted the ECOWAS summit conference in 1983. Guinea became a partner with Sierra Leone and Liberia in the Mano River Union in 1980, when it also joined Gambia and Senegal as a member of the Gambia River Development Organization. In addition, Guinea belongs to the Niger Basin Authority and the Organization of the Islamic Conference.

The International Bauxite Association was established in Conakry in 1974 with Guinea as a charter member. In 1975, Guinea signed the Lomé Convention, providing for aid and trade relations with the EC.

19 ECONOMY

Guinea has extensive mineral deposits, primarily bauxite, and hydroelectric resources, along with soils and climate favorable for producing a diverse array of food and export crops. The mining sector has shown continued growth since the 1960s, but agricultural production has stagnated and agricultural exports have declined. The small industrial sector has not produced to capacity. Consumer goods and foodstuffs have been in short supply, and a large portion of the earnings from mineral exports have been used for food imports.

After two decades of socialist-style economic management, a major reform movement gained political power in 1984. Of the more than 100 state enterprises, most were closed. Food prices were decontrolled, private trade reestablished, and the government began actively to seek foreign investment for sectors other than mining and energy.

Monetary reform was enacted in early 1986, with the 93% devaluation of currency foreshadowing Guinea's eventual return to the CFA franc zone. The "Paris Club" countries rescheduled Guinea's debt in early 1989, but foreign obligations mounted further and the debt-service ratio climbed to 19.3% by 1990. By mid-1990, further credit deliveries were suspended. The 1991 budget was agreed to by the IMF with some misgivings, but negotiations were suspended after the government announced its intention to double civil servants' salaries. By November 1991, an enhanced structural adjustment package had been agreed to.

[20]INCOME

In 1992 Guinea's GNP was $3,103 million at current prices, or $510 per capita. For the period 1985–92 the average inflation rate was 23.1%, resulting in a real growth rate in per capita GNP of 0.8%. In 1992 the GDP was $3,233 million in current US dollars. Of that total, agriculture accounted for 29.9% of economic activity while mining added 9.5%. Manufacturing contributed 5.6%, and trade an estimated 2.8%.

[21]LABOR

Over 80% of Guinea's population of about 7.2 million in 1992 relied on subsistence agriculture and livestock raising. Most of the wage and salary earners work in the public sector; mining is the other major source of salaried employment. Guinea's 1988 Labor Code permits all workers (except military and paramilitary) to create and participate in labor organizations. The General Workers Union of Guinea (UGTG) and the Free Union of Teachers and Researchers of Guinea (SLECG) have emerged since the new code ended the previously existing trade union monopoly system.

Collective bargaining is protected by law; the workweek for industry is 40 hours. Salaried workers, including public sector civilian employees, have the right to strike.

[22]AGRICULTURE

Only 2.6% of Guinea's arable land area is cultivated. Agriculture accounts for 20% of GDP and engages 80% of the active populaiton. The agricultural sector of the economy has stagnated since independence. The precipitate withdrawal of the French planters and removal of French tariff preference hurt Guinean agriculture, and drought conditions during the 1970s also hindered production. Since 1985, however, the free market policies of the Second Republic have encouraged growth in agricultural production, with slow but steady increases in output. Guinea is a net food importer, however, importing some 30% of its food needs.

Price controls have also had a dampening effect on output. In theory, until the reforms of the early 1980s, the state controlled the marketing of farm produce. However, even during the late 1970s, when all private trade in agricultural commodities was illegal, only a small amount of agricultural production actually passed through the state distribution system; some 500,000 private smallholders reportedly achieved yields twice as high as government collectives, despite having little or no access to government credit or research and extension facilities. During the 1970s and early 1980s, agricultural exports fell markedly, and

food production decreased, necessitating rice imports of at least 70,000 tons a year. (In 1984, a drought year, 186,000 tons of cereal had to be imported.) However, some restrictions on marketing were removed in 1979 and 1981; more recently, prices were decontrolled and many state farms and plantations dissolved. These steps appeared to bring improvements.

Guinea publishes no production statistics, so hard data on agricultural output are unavailable. The principal subsistence crops (with estimated 1992 production) are manioc, 660,000 tons; rice, 757,000 tons; sweet potatoes, 100,000 tons; yams, 100,000 tons; and corn, 94,000 tons. Cash crops are peanuts, palm kernels, bananas, pineapples, coffee, coconuts, sugarcane, and citrus fruits. In 1992, an estimated 420,000 tons of plantains, 225,000 tons of sugarcane, 230,000 tons of citrus fruits, 170,000 tons of bananas, 78,000 tons of peanuts, 40,000 tons of palm kernels, and 18,000 tons of coconuts were produced. That same year, coffee production was estimated at 30,000 tons, compared to 14,000 tons on average annually from 1979 to 1981. Prior to the reforms, a large portion of the coffee crop was smuggled out of the country.

[23]ANIMAL HUSBANDRY

In 1992 there were an estimated 1,900,000 head of cattle, 510,000 sheep, 460,000 goats, 33,000 hogs, and 13,000,000 chickens. Almost all the cattle are the small humpless Ndama variety kept by the Fulani in Futa Jallon and Upper Guinea, where sheep and goats also are herded. The Ndama cattle are not susceptible to animal trypanosomiasis and, although very small, their yield in meat is good.

[24]FISHING

Guinea's annual ocean fisheries potential exceeds 200,000 tons, according to World Bank estimates. Tuna is the most important catch. Many species found in Guinean waters are among the richest in West Africa and command high value. Domestic artisanal fisherman only catch about 13% of the estimated annual yield. Fishing contributes about 1.5% to GDP. A 1990 agreement with the European Community reflected a growing investment interest in the fishing sector. Since then, several small scale fishing ventures have been established, including a shrimp farming project financed by the African Development Bank, and development of private cold storage facilities in 14 different prefectures.

[25]FORESTRY

Forests and woodland make up almost two-thirds of Guinea's land area. The nation's forest resources offer great promise, the major constraint on development being lack of adequate transportation. Logging and sawmill facilities have been built in the Nzérékoré area. No timber is exported, and exploitation is subject to government control. Removal of roundwood was estimated at 3,988,000 cu m in 1991; about 89% of the harvest was used for fuel.

[26]MINING

Mining is the most dynamic sector of the Guinean economy, accounting for about 25% of the GDP and over 90% of exports. Rapid expansion, particularly of bauxite (aluminum ore) and alumina (aluminum oxide) production, occurred during the 1970s, but production subsequently declined. Although production of bauxite has remained somewhat constant, declining prices have led the Guinean mineral industry to diversify into gold and diamond production.

Estimates of bauxite deposits vary: the government has claimed that Guinea has 20 billion tons, with proven reserves amounting to 18 billion tons. As of 1991, Guinea was second only to Australia in the production of bauxite. Peak production was 17.5 million tons in 1990, up from 9 million tons in 1986.

Bauxite mining began in 1952 at Kassa, but these deposits were exhausted by 1962. A major deposit was subsequently developed at Fria, north of Conakry; beginning in 1960, the Fria International Co. for the Production of Aluminum, an international consortium of several Western aluminum producers, undertook construction of a major mining and processing complex there. In 1972, the company was renamed Friguia; it was 49% government owned, and the government took 65% of the profits, as it did from the other bauxite producers. Friguia's alumina production should improve as loans and technical assistance are received from financial institutions and foreign donors.

In 1966, the Guinea Bauxite Co. (CBG) was formed—49% owned by the government and 51% by an international consortium including US, West German, and Italian interests—to develop the Boké reserves at Sangarédi. Some $339 million was spent on development of the site, including a railroad to the port of Kamsar. The company began exporting bauxite in 1973 and produced about 10.6 million tons in 1991. A third bauxite mine, at Debélé, near Kindia, developed with a $100-million investment from the former USSR, is owned by the Kindia Office of Bauxite (OBK) and has an annual production capacity of 3 million tons.

Iron ore was mined at Kaloum until 1967. Larger, richer deposits have been found in the Mt. Nimba and Simandou mountain areas of eastern Guinea, along the Liberian border. In April 1974, the Mifergui-Simandou and Mifergui-Nimba mining companies were formed to exploit the deposits, with the government retaining half interest in the firms. Reserves are estimated at 300–600 million tons; producers hope political stability will be rapidly restored to Liberia, so that shipments can be made through that country to the port of Buchanan.

The Société Aurifère de Guinée (SAG), 49% owned by the state and 51% by the multinational Chevaning Mining Co., was established in 1985, and operates a placer mine near Siguiri. Artisanal gold production from the Siguiri and Dinguiraye areas was estimated at 3,000 kg, most of which gets smuggled out of the country since the government offers less than the market price for gold mined by individuals.

Diamond production totals by artisanal miners were unknown as of 1991. These small-scale diggers were allowed to lease plots from the government, turning over production to the central bank for export; in reality, a considerable share of production was smuggled out of the country, and for this reason such production was banned in 1985, but continued illegally in 1991, with all of it smuggled out of the country. The Aredor diamond project, 50% owned by the state and 50% by foreign investors (mainly Bridge Oil Co. of Australia), opened in 1984; production was boosted substantially, to 203,788 carats in 1986, over 90% of gem quality. Production for 1991 was 91,364 carats; the decline was attributed to widespread disruptions caused by illicit miners at the end of 1991.

27 ENERGY AND POWER

In 1991, installed capacity was 176,000 kw, 73% hydroelectric and 27% thermal. A total of about 521 million kwh was produced, much of it consumed by the Fria-Boké bauxite-processing complex. A proposed 100-Mw dam on the Bafing River would serve the proposed Tougué-Dabola processing plant. Another proposed dam would be built on the Konkouré River to provide power for the proposed aluminum plant at Ayé-Koé.

In 1991, wood accounted for 70% of the total energy requirement. In 1992, imported fuel and energy were valued at $117 million, or 15% of total imports. A 35,300-sq-km (13,600-sq-mi) offshore tract was being explored for oil deposits by the state corporation Société Guinéenne des Hydrocarbons (SGH) in partnership with Mobil Oil.

28 INDUSTRY

Manufacturing accounts for 6.3% of GDP and engages 0.6% of the labor force. Unfortunately, shortages of raw materials, technical expertise, and adequate markets are common. While the alumina smelter at Fria operates at over 90% capacity, other industrial plants operate at closer to 10% capacity. Among Guinea's other plants are a fruit cannery at Mamou; a fruit juice factory at Kankan; a tea factory at Macenta; a palm oil works at Kassa; a small tobacco factor at Beyla; two peanut oil works, at Dabola and at Agola; a textile complex at Sanoyah; and cement and plastics factories at Conakry. There are also a number of construction material plants, rice mills, and a sugar complex consisting of two dams, a plantation, and a refinery. During the socialist years, a sizeable parastatal industrial sector emerged. Guinea had 135 state-run industries in 1985. All but 24 had been sold or dissolved by mid-1992. It is hoped that the liberalized investment code will stimulate substantial increases in private and foreign investment.

Guinea has considerable hydroelectric power resources, with an estimated potential of 63,000 GWh. Mining enterprises operate 36 MW of the 176 MW of net installed capacity.

29 SCIENCE AND TECHNOLOGY

The National Directorate for Scientific and Technical Research is in Conakry. The Center for Rice Research is in Kankan, and the Institute for Fruit Research is in Kindia.

Five colleges and universities, including the University Gamal Abdel Nasser, offer degrees in basic and applied sciences. In 1984, 611 technicians and 1,282 scientists and engineers were engaged in research and development.

30 DOMESTIC TRADE

Until Guinea became independent, Europeans handled virtually all of the country's commercial trade, but the new government soon set up state trading enterprises. The establishment of a Guinean currency in March 1960 resulted in the elimination of most of the few remaining European traders. In 1965, President Touré signed decrees that effectively excluded foreigners from local trade.

In 1975, all private trade of agricultural goods was abolished, daily markets were banned, the frontiers were closed to all trade except bauxite, and the local units of the PDG were given full responsibility for the production and sale of agricultural commodities. In 1979, however, the government opened retail and wholesale trade to private business interests for all products except essential foodstuffs. In 1981, private marketing of foodstuffs within regions (but subject to official prices) was authorized, and two years later produce marketing was turned over to the private sector. A "parallel" market not officially recognized dealt both in goods and in foreign exchange, since the syli (at official rates) was considered greatly overvalued. The devaluation of currency in early 1986 reduced black marketeering. Prices have also been decontrolled.

Business hours are 7:30 AM to 3 PM, Monday through Thursday, 7:30 AM to 1 PM on Friday, and 7:30 AM to 1 PM on Saturday. Banks are normally open from 8 AM to 12:30 PM, Monday through Saturday.

31 FOREIGN TRADE

Export estimates for 1988 show bauxite and alumina as the export leaders, at 78.1% of total earnings. Diamonds and gold accounted for an additional 15.3%. Coffee represented another 3.1% of the total.

Semi-manufactured goods topped the list of imports at 43.9% of the total. Making up the other 56.1% were food products (12.8%), consumer goods (12.6%), petroleum products (13.7%), and capital goods (17.0%).

Guinea's exports (1986) went primarily to the United States (22.9%), Germany (13.6%), and Spain (12.7%). The biggest share of imports came from France (36.9%). Countertrade arrangements are not represented in the above figures.

32 BALANCE OF PAYMENTS

Before independence, Guinea's foreign exchange shortages were covered by the franc-zone stabilization fund. Although Guinea remained a member of the franc zone for 17 months until 1 March 1960, it did not apply to the fund for its foreign exchange needs, and therefore soon lacked the exchange to cover its trade gaps. Guinea runs a habitual deficit on current accounts, despite an annual trade surplus. In 1992, Guinea remained extremely dependent on mining for foreign exchange earnings. As a result of the decline in export earnings and shortfalls in projected revenues, Guinea had a $436 million current account deficit in 1992, representing 13.5% of GDP.

33 BANKING AND SECURITIES

At independence, central banking functions were carried out by the Central Bank of the West African States (Banque Centrale des États de l'Afrique de l'Ouest—BCEAO), and commercial banking by branches of five French banks. On 1 March 1960, Guinea withdrew from the franc zone. The Guinean branch of the BCEAO was abolished, and the Central Bank of Guinea was established. Later that year, four of the five private banks were closed down, and the fifth was nationalized in 1961. All banking activities were taken over by the Central Bank, but by 1962 its functions were decentralized and three new state-owned banks were added.

The National Credit Bank for Commerce, Industry, and Housing, with branches throughout Guinea, handled all commercial banking and made loans to finance commerce, industry, and housing. The Guinean Foreign Trade Bank performed functions related to foreign trade and the administration of import and export licensing controls. The National Agricultural Development Bank granted medium- and long-term loans for agricultural development. There was also a National Savings Bank. All these institutions except the Central Bank were abolished in late 1985 and were replaced by commercial banks.

There are 6 commercial banks in Guinea, including the International Bank for Africa in Guinea, the International Bank for Commerce and Industry in Guinea, and the General Association of Banking in Guinea. All involve French participation.

Local currency may not be exported or imported. There are no securities exchanges in Guinea.

34 INSURANCE

All insurance companies were nationalized in January 1962. There is a national insurance company, the National Society of Insurance and Reinsurance.

35 PUBLIC FINANCE

Government deficits have traditionally been large, particularly because of wages and salaries paid to Guinea's large contingent of public employees (which, however was cut back in the late 1980s). In the 1980s, tax receipts and transfers from state enterprises fell as the informal sector came into dominance. Simultaneously, subsidies to public companies intensified. As a result, debt service obligations rapidly increased. Since 1985, the government has sought to reduce public expenditures and promote private sector growth.

36 TAXATION

Personal income and capital gains are taxed at 35%, which is also the corporate tax rate. A 20% withholding tax is levied on dividends. Both employees and employers contribute to Social Security.

37 CUSTOMS AND DUTIES

Both import and export duties are levied. Import licenses are required for all imports regardless of country of origin, and import duties are levied uniformly. Rates in 1993 started at 2% on agricultural machinery and varied upward, with a 30% surtax on luxury goods. There was also a 10% sales tax on all imported and domestically produced products.

38 FOREIGN INVESTMENT

The only sectors of the economy in which private foreign investment was originally allowed after independence were mining and energy, but in the early 1980s agricultural investment was being sought to develop some of Guinea's large tracts of arable land not in use. Another sector now open to foreign investment is fishing, and in 1986, three commercial banks opened with foreign participation.

During 1983–85, direct foreign investment was $2.2 million. An investment code following the 1984 coup indicated a new emphasis on private investment and incentives. It was replaced by a new code in 1987 that pledged free repatriation of capital, tax relief for investment in four areas, and special incentives for small and medium-size enterprises, nonmining exports, enterprises using over 70% local inputs, and those locating outside Conakry. The chief barrier to foreign investment is the shortage of foreign exchange, which makes it difficult for companies to obtain needed imports.

39 ECONOMIC DEVELOPMENT

After independence, French-held financial, commercial, industrial, and distributive organizations were expropriated, and the national economy was divided into three sectors: a state sector, a mixed sector, and a sector for guaranteed private investment. By the mid-1970s, the private sector had become insignificant, and government policy increasingly leaned toward greater government control of the mixed enterprises and the state-sector companies.

In 1975, President Touré created the National Economic Council, over which he presided, with the aim of gaining more direct control of the economy. The council monitored import/export plans, output levels, wages, salaries, loans, agreements with foreign investors, and other major facets of economic activity. In June 1975, several holding companies were created to manage the whole gamut of state-sector companies. From the late 1970s until his death, however, Touré partially reversed course, increasing the scope of private trading within the centralized framework of the Guinean economy.

The 1981–85 development plan entailed spending of s32 billion and gave priority to rural development. The 1987–91 recovery program called for $670 million in spending through 1989, with 42% for infrastructure and 24% for rural development. A major aim was to diversify the economy and reduce the heavy reliance on bauxite.

Foreign aid averaged $50 million a year during 1980–85, excluding the former Soviet bloc; aid from Western and Arab sources had risen to $67.1 million in1985. France was the leading bilateral donor, providing FFr520 million in 1985 and FFr1,248 million during 1982–86. In February 1986, the IMF extended a 13-month, $39-million line of credit. A World Bank loan of $46 million followed. In March 1987, an economic consultative group approved Guinea's recovery strategies and extended $870 million in aid and balance-of-payments support through 1989. Further debt rescheduling by the "Paris Club" will be required to maintain stability and forward movement in Guinea's restructuring program.

40 SOCIAL DEVELOPMENT

There was a retrogression of social services during the Touré years. Although government sought to establish extensive social programs, they were badly organized and managed and, in the end, the treasury was empty. The fertility rate in 1993 was estimated to be 5.9; abortion is available for broadly defined health reasons. Free medical treatment is available, as well as free care for pregnant women and for infants. In reality, health service is poor. Life expectancy is 41 years for males and 46 years for females, among the lowest in the world.

41 HEALTH

In 1992 there were 6 hospital beds per 10,000 people, and a total of 773 physicians, or 13 per 100,000 people. It is estimated that 75% of the population had access to health care services.

Malaria, yaws, leprosy, and sleeping sickness (in the forest areas in the Guinea Highlands) have been the major tropical diseases; also endemic are tuberculosis and venereal diseases. In 1990, there were 166 reported cases of tuberculosis per 100,000 people. Yellow fever and smallpox have been brought under control, but schistosomiasis remains widespread. Data from 1991 show that only 53% of the population had access to safe water, and a mere 21% had access to adequate sanitation. From 1990 to 1992, children up to one year old were vaccinated against tuberculosis (65%); diphtheria, pertussis, and tetanus (52%); polio (52%); and measles (50%). Total health care expenditures in 1990 were $106 million.

In 1993 Guinea had a birth rate of 51 per 1,000 people. Birth control is virtually nonexistent in Guinea. Infant mortality in 1992 was 135 per 1,000 live births (among the highest in the world), and the overall mortality rate in 1993 was 20 per 1,000 people. Average estimated life expectancy during is 44 years.

42 HOUSING

The most common rural dwelling is round, windowless, and made of wattle and daub or sun-dried mud bricks, with a floor of packed earth and a conical thatched roof. Urban dwellings are usually one-story rectangular frame or mud-brick buildings, generally without electricity or indoor plumbing. Only 17% of the population had access to safe water in 1983. Conakry has a serious housing shortage. According to the latest available information for 1980–88, the total housing stock numbered 1,050,000, with 5.4 people per dwelling.

43 EDUCATION

Before Guinea became independent, its educational system was patterned on that of France. All schools were nationalized in 1961. French remains the language of instruction, ostensibly as an interim measure. In 1968, a "cultural revolution," aimed at de-Westernizing Guinean life, was inaugurated; since then, eight vernaculars have been added to the school curriculum, and village-level programs have been set up to assist in the implementation of the plan. Although the French educational structure and its traditional degrees have been retained, African history and geography are now stressed.

Education is free and compulsory between the ages of 7 and 13. In 1990, the estimated adult literacy rate was 24.0%, for males 34.9% and 13.4% for females. Children go through 6 years of primary and 7 years of secondary school.

In 1991 there were 359,406 primary-level pupils; secondary schools, general, vocational and teachers' training served 768,603 pupils. The Gamal Abdel Nasser Polytechnic Institute, established at Conakry in 1963, enrolled about 120 students in 1986. The Valéry Giscard d'Estaing Institute of Agro-Zootechnical Sciences, founded in 1978 at Faranah, had 1,003 students in 1986. The University of Conakry, founded in 1984, was in process of formation in 1987.

44 LIBRARIES AND MUSEUMS

The chief book collection and main exhibition center are in the National Institute of Research and Documentation at Conakry.

The National Library (40,000 volumes) and the National Archives are located in Conakry.

The National Museum, at Conakry, has displays of the ethnography and prehistory of Guinea, as well as a collection of art, fetishes, and masks of the Sacred Forest. The capital also has two natural history museums, covering botany and geology. There are regional museums in Kissidougou, Nzérékoré, and Youkounkoun.

45 MEDIA

The constitution proclaims the freedom of the press, subject to the law, but censorship is rigid, and all media are owned or controlled by the government. The official Guinean Press Agency publishes *Horoya* six times a week, with an estimated daily circulation of 13,000 in 1991.

Telephone, telegraph, and postal services are government-owned. Submarine cables connect Conakry with Dakar, Freetown, and Monrovia; telecommunication links by satellite are also available. Radiodiffusion-Télévision Guinéenne broadcasts in French, English, Portuguese, Arabic, Creole, and local languages. In 1991 there were about 248,000 radio receivers and 42,000 television sets in use.

46 ORGANIZATIONS

Regional farm organizations are leagued in a national union of planters' cooperatives. Mass organizations associated with the RDA include the Youth of the Democratic African Revolution and the Revolutionary Union of Guinean Women. The Guinea Chamber of Commerce, Industry, and Agriculture has 70 affiliates.

47 TOURISM, TRAVEL, AND RECREATION

Visitors to Guinea must have a valid passport and a visa. Precautions against cholera, tetanus, typhoid, typhus, and malaria are recommended. An annual cultural festival that includes theatrical and dance groups is held in October.

48 FAMOUS GUINEANS

A revered figure of the 19th century is Samory Touré (1830?–1900), a Malinké born in Upper Guinea, who conquered large areas and resisted French military forces until 1898. The founder of modern Guinea was his alleged great-grandson Ahmed Sékou Touré (1922–84), a prominent labor leader and political figure who became Guinea's first president in 1958. Guinea's best-known writer, Camara Laye (1928–80), wrote the novel *The Dark Child* (1953). Col. Lansana Conté (b.1944) became president in 1984.

49 DEPENDENCIES

Guinea has no territories or colonies.

50 BIBLIOGRAPHY

Adamolekun, Lapido. *Sékou Touré's Guinea: An Exercise in Nation Building.* New York: Methuen, 1976.

American University. *Area Handbook for Guinea.* 2d ed. Washington, D.C.: Government Printing Office, 1975.

Attwood, Wiulliam. *The Reds and the Blacks.* New York: Harper & Row, 1967.

Charles, Bernard. *La République de Guinée.* Paris: Berger-Levrault, 1972.

Derman, William and Louise. *Serfs, Peasants, and Socialists: A Former Serf Village in the Republic of Guinea.* Berkeley: University of California Press, 1973.

Nkrumah, Kwame. *Kwame Nkrumah: The Conakry Years, His Life and Letters.* Atlantic Highlands, N.J.: PANAF, 1990.

O'Toole, Thomas. *Historical Dictionary of Guinea (Republic of Guinea/Conakry).* 2d ed. Metuchen, N.J.: Scarecrow Press, 1987.

Rivière, Claude. *Guinea: The Mobilization of a People.* Ithaca, N.Y.: Cornell University Press, 1977.

Suret-Canale, Jean. *La République de Guinée.* Paris: Editions Sociales, 1970.

Yansane, Aguibou Y. *Decolonization in West African States, With French Colonial Legacy—Comparison and Contrast: Development in Gjinea, the Ivory Coast and Senegal, 1945–80.* Cambridge, Mass.: Schenkman Publishing Co., 1984.

Young, H. Crawford. *Ideology and National Development.* New Haven, Conn.: Yale University Press.

GUINEA-BISSAU

Republic of Guinea-Bissau
República da Guiné-Bissau

CAPITAL: Bissau.

FLAG: The flag has equal horizontal stripes of yellow over green in the fly, and a red vertical stripe at the hoist bearing a black star.

ANTHEM: *Esta é a Nossa Pátria Bem Amada (This Is Our Well-Beloved Land).*

MONETARY UNIT: The Guinean peso (PG) of 100 centavos replaced the Guinean escudo (GE) on 2 February 1976. There are coins of 50 centavos and 1, 2½, 5, and 20 pesos, and notes of 50, 100, 500, and 1,000 pesos. PG1 = $0.0808 (or $1 = PG12.369).

WEIGHTS AND MEASURES: The metric system is used.

HOLIDAYS: New Year's Day, 1 January; Death of Amilcar Cabral, 20 January; Labor Day, 1 May; Anniversary of the Killing of Pidjiguiti, 3 August; National Day, 24 September; Anniversary of the Movement of Readjustment, 14 November; Christmas Day, 25 December. Movable religious holidays include Korité (end of Ramadan) and Tabaski (Feast of the Sacrifice).

TIME: 11 AM = noon GMT.

¹LOCATION, SIZE, AND EXTENT
Situated on the west coast of Africa, Guinea-Bissau, formerly Portuguese Guinea, has a total area of 36,120 sq km (13,946 sq mi), about 10% of which is periodically submerged by tidal waters. Comparatively, the area occupied by Guinea-Bissau is slightly less than three times the size of the state of Connecticut. Besides its mainland territory, it includes the Bijagós Archipelago and various coastal islands—Jeta, Pecixe, Bolama, and Melo, among others. Extending 336 km (209 mi) N–S and 203 km (126 mi) E–W, Guinea-Bissau is bordered on the N by Senegal, on the E and SE by Guinea, and on the SW and W by the Atlantic Ocean, with a total boundary length of 1,074 km (667 mi).

Guinea-Bissau's capital city, Bissau, is located on the country's Atlantic coast.

²TOPOGRAPHY
The country is swampy at the coast and low-lying inland, except in the northeast. There are no significant mountains. The most important rivers include the Cacheu, Mansoa, Geba, and Corubal.

³CLIMATE
Guinea-Bissau has a hot, humid, typically tropical climate, with a rainy season that lasts from mid-May to mid-November and a cooler dry season occupying the rest of the year. The average temperature in the rainy season ranges from 26°C to 28°C (79–82°F). Rainfall generally exceeds 198 cm (78 in), but droughts occurred in 1977, 1979, 1980, and 1983. The rainiest months are July and August. During the dry season, when the harmattan (dust-laden wind) blows from the Sahara, average temperatures do not exceed 24°C (75°F). The coolest months are December and January.

⁴FLORA AND FAUNA
Guinea-Bissau has a variety of vegetation, with thick jungle in the interior plains, rice and mangrove fields along the coastal plains and swamps, and savanna in the north. Parts of Guinea-Bissau are rich in game, big and small. Several species of antelope, buffalo, monkeys, and snakes are found.

⁵ENVIRONMENT
One of the most significant environmental problems in Guinea-Bissau is fire, which destroys 40,000 ha of land per year and accelerates the loss of the nation's forests at a yearly rate of 220 sq mi. Over 80% of city dwellers and 73% of the people living in rural areas do not have pure water. The nation has 7.4 cu mi of water, with 63% used for farming activity. Only 30% of city dwellers have adequate sanitation. Another environmental issue is soil damage, caused by drought and erosion, as well as acidification and salinization. The Ministry of Natural Resources, created in January 1979, is responsible for making and enforcing environmental policy. Of Guinea-Bissau's 109 species of mammals, 5 are endangered, together with 2 of 376 bird species and 2 types of reptiles.

⁶POPULATION
The population of Guinea-Bissau was 767,739 according to the 1979 census, and was estimated at 1,099,676 in 1994, giving a population density of 30.4 per sq km (78.8 per sq mi). Bissau, the capital city, had an estimated population of 71,000 in 1990.

⁷MIGRATION
Centuries ago, the largely Muslim pastoral tribesmen to the east tended to migrate toward coastal regions, but this movement was inhibited to some degree by Portuguese colonization. In 1975, after the settlement of the guerrilla war against the Portuguese colonial administration, approximately 100,000 refugees returned from neighboring Senegal and Guinea. At the end of 1992, there were still 5,000 in Senegal, and Guinea-Bissau was harboring 12,200 Senegalese refugees.

⁸ETHNIC GROUPS
The principal African ethnic groups are the Balante (an estimated 30% of the African population), living mainly in the central

region; the Fulani (20%), in the north; the Malinké (13%), in the north-central area; and the Mandyako (14%) and Pepel (7%), in the coastal areas. Other ethnic groups constitute the remaining 16% of the African population.

Of the nonindigenous people, the Cape Verdean mulatto community, which originated in the Cape Verde Islands, is the largest group, accounting for about 2% of the total population of Guinea-Bissau. Resentment over the disproportionate political and commercial influence held by this group played a role in the 1980 coup. There is also a small foreign community, consisting mainly of Portuguese and of Lebanese and Syrian merchants.

⁹LANGUAGES

Wide differences prevail in languages, since each tribe has its own vernacular, subdivided into numerous dialects. A Guinean "crioulo," or Africanized Portuguese patois, is the lingua franca, while Portuguese is the official language.

¹⁰RELIGIONS

Most of the population (54%) has retained traditional religious beliefs, even the minority who have formally adopted Islam or Christianity. As of 1993, an estimated 38% of the population adhered to the Islamic faith, most to the Qadiriyyah or the Tijaniyyah order. The Fulani and Malinké are Muslim for the most part. In 1993, only about 8% of the population was Christian (almost entirely Roman Catholic).

¹¹TRANSPORTATION

Transportation facilities remain undeveloped, a factor that has hampered economic development as a whole, especially the exploitation of mineral deposits in the interior. There is no rail line in Guinea-Bissau. In 1991, the country had an estimated 3,218 km (2,000 mi) of roads, of which 2,698 km (1,676 mi) were tarred (these, however, consisted mostly of military penetration roads unfit for regular passenger and commercial traffic). In 1991 there were some 5,700 motorized vehicles, mostly in the city of Bissau.

Bissau is the main port; expansion and modernization projects costing at least $48 million were undertaken there in the early 1980s. The city is also the site of a modern international airport, while several aerodromes and landing strips serve the interior. Linhas Aéreas da Guiné-Bissau (LIA), the national airline, also has service to Dakar, Senegal. Transportes Aéreos Portuguéses (TAP), Air Guinea, Aeroflot, Air Senegal, Cape Verde Airlines, and Air Algérie provide international service.

¹²HISTORY

The earliest inhabitants, hunters and fishermen, were replaced by the Baga and other peoples who came from the east. The Portuguese explorer Nuno Tristão arrived in the region in June 1446 and established the first trading posts. The slave trade developed during the 17th century, centering around the port of Bissau, from which thousands of captive Africans were sent across the Atlantic to Latin America. Portugal retained at least nominal control of the area, and British claims to coastal regions were dismissed by arbitration in 1870. Nine years later, the area was made a separate Portuguese dependency, administratively subordinate to the Cape Verde Islands. Portuguese Guinea's boundaries with neighboring French possessions were delimited in an 1886 treaty, and formal borders were demarcated by a joint commission in 1905. The interior was not effectively occupied until about 1920, however, and Portuguese never settled in large numbers in the colony. In 1951, together with other Portuguese holdings in Africa, Guinea was made a Portuguese overseas province.

In September 1956, a group of dissatisfied Cape Verdeans founded an underground movement aimed at achieving independence from Portugal. It was named the African Party for the Independence of Guinea and Cape Verde (Partido Africano de Independência da Guiné e Cabo Verde—PAIGC), and Amilcar Cabral became its secretary-general. On 19 September 1959, after more than 50 Africans had been killed during a dock strike that erupted into a violent clash with police, Cabral called for an all-out struggle "by all possible means, including war." By 1963, large-scale guerrilla warfare had broken out in the territory.

During the ensuing years, PAIGC guerrillas, fighting a Portuguese force of about 30,000, increased their hold on the countryside. When Cabral was assassinated on 20 January 1973, reportedly by a PAIGC naval officer, Aristides Pereira took over the leadership of the movement, which on 24 September 1973 unilaterally proclaimed the independence of the Republic of Guinea-Bissau.

Prospects for a PAIGC victory improved dramatically after 25 April 1974, when the Lisbon government was overthrown in a coup and a new regime took over, under the mantle of Gen. António de Spínola, a former governor-general and military commander in Portuguese Guinea who had become an advocate of peaceful settlement of the war. On 26 August 1974, the Portuguese government and the PAIGC signed an agreement in Algiers providing for the independence of Guinea-Bissau effective 10 September, removal of all Portuguese troops by 31 October, and a referendum to determine the future status of the Cape Verde Islands.

The new government, under President Luis de Almeida Cabral, had to deal with extensive economic dislocations brought about by the war. On 27 September 1974, the government announced its intention to control all foreign trade, and in May 1975, the legislature approved a program to nationalize all land and to confiscate property belonging to persons who had "collaborated with the enemy" during the war.

In the first postindependence elections, held December 1976–January 1977, 80% of the population approved the PAIGC list of candidates for Regional Council membership. The 150-member National Assembly, selected by these representatives, convened on 13 March 1977. Luis Cabral was reelected president of Guinea-Bissau and of the 15-member Council of State, and Major João Bernardo Vieira was confirmed as the nation's vice-president and as president of the National Assembly.

On 14 November 1980, President Cabral, a mestiço with close ties to Cape Verde, was overthrown by a group of Guinean blacks under Vieira's command. Severe food shortages and tensions in the alliance between Guinea-Bissau and Cape Verde had precipitated the bloody military coup, which led to the dissolution of the National Assembly and Executive Council, suspension of the constitution, arrest of the president, and temporary abandonment of the goal of unification with Cape Verde. A Revolutionary Council composed of nine military officers and four civilian advisers was named on 19 November, and a provisional government was appointed the following day. Diplomatic relations with Cape Verde, suspended at the time of the coup, were resumed in June 1982.

The National People's Assembly, reestablished in April 1984, adopted a new constitution in May. It also elected a 15-member Council of State to serve as the nation's executive body; as president of this council, Vieira served as both head of state and head of government. In July 1986, following an abortive military coup in November 1985, six persons were executed and another five died during detention. Vieira and the PAIGC ruled Guinea-Bissau as a one-party state for ten years. But in 1990, Vieira denounced single-party rule as elitist, inherently undemocratic, and repressive. In April 1991, Guinea-Bissau formally embraced multipartyism and adopted a new constitution. The four major opposition parties formed the Democratic Forum in January 1992 and sought to unseat PAIGC.

Elections, originally scheduled for November 1992, were postponed until March 1993, giving the 11 opposition parties time to campaign and the multiparty electoral commission time to work out electoral procedures. They were again postponed until March 1994.

An attempted coup on 17 March 1993 led to the allegation that the leader of the Party for Renovation and Development (PRD), João da Costa, was implicated. On 4 February 1994, the supreme military court acquitted him of charges.

¹³GOVERNMENT

The constitution adopted in 1973, after the issuance of a declaration of independence on 24 September, was suspended following the 1980 coup. A new constitution was ratified on 16 May 1984 by the reestablished National People's Assembly; the Assembly and the regional councils are the nation's representative bodies. The popularly elected councils elect the 150-member Assembly from their own ranks, and the Assembly in turn elects a 15-member Council of State as the nation's executive body. The president of this council, whom the Assembly also elects, automatically becomes head of state, head of government, and commander in chief of the armed forces. All Assembly members must be members of the ruling African Party for the Independence of Guinea and Cape Verde (PAIGC).

A new constitution was adopted in April 1991, and opposition political parties were permitted. Government continues to control the pace of political reform which remains very slow. In 1993, it formed a National Elections Commission charged with organizing legislative and presidential elections for March 1994. The armed forces and the national police force are controlled by the PAIGC government and are responsible for human rights abuses, for which they are rarely tried or punished. In March 1993, a failed coup attempt led to the arrest of dozens of soldiers and opposition politicians. Many of the politicians were released in June.

¹⁴POLITICAL PARTIES

The ruling African Party for the Independence of Guinea and Cape Verde (Partido Africano de Independência da Guiné e Cabo Verde—-PAIGC) is the sole legal party in the Republic of Guinea-Bissau. During the presidency of Luis Cabral, several hundred political opponents of the regime were reportedly murdered and buried in mass graves.

The 1980 coup was condemned by Cape Verdean leaders of the PAIGC, and in January 1981 they broke with the Guinea-Bissau branch to form the African Party for the Independence of Cape Verde. The following November, Guinean party officials decided to retain the name PAIGC for their branch and to expel Cape Verdean founder-members from the party.

Opposition parties were legalized by a new constitution adopted in April 1991. A dozen parties were recognized. Among them are: the Party for Renewal and Development (PRD), which is composed of educated dissidents who quit the PAIGC because of its authoritarianism; the Social Democratic Front (FDS), led by one of the founders of the PAIGC, Raphael Barbosa; the Front for the Struggle for Guinea-Bissau's National Independence, which predates PAIGC and is led by Mindy Kankoila, an early independence leader who had been in exile for 40 years; the National Convention Party (mainly Muslims and FDS dissidents); and the League for the Protection of the Ecology (LPE). The most important opposition party is Bafata, the Guinea-Bissau Resistance-Bafata Movement. Many parties prior to the general elections of 1994 formed a coalition, including the PRD, the FDS, the LPE, the Movement for Unity and Democracy (MUD), and the Democratic Party for Progress (PDP).

¹⁵LOCAL GOVERNMENT

Guinea-Bissau has 8 regions, not including the capital, and 37 sectors. Each region has a regional council, as does the capital,

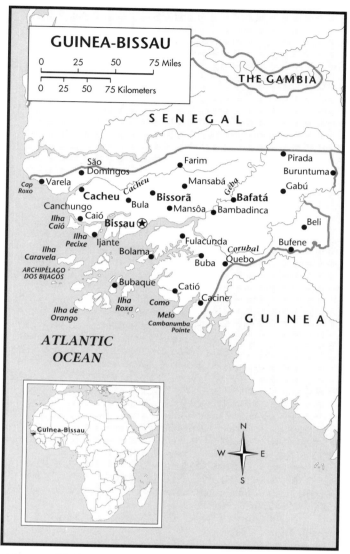

LOCATION: 10°52′ to 12°42′N; 13°38′ to 16°43′W. **BOUNDARY LENGTHS:** Senegal, 338 km (210 mi); Guinea, 386 km (240 mi); Atlantic coastline, 398 km (247 mi). **TERRITORIAL SEA LIMIT:** 12 mi.

with membership consisting of elected representatives from the various sectors. Party committees have been organized at both levels, and all council candidates must be approved by the PAIGC.

¹⁶JUDICIAL SYSTEM

The civilian court system is essentially a continuation of the Portuguese colonial system. Supreme Court judges are appointed by the president. The Supreme Court has jurisdiction over serious crimes and serves as an appeals court for the regional military courts. In rural areas, persons are often tried outside the formal system by traditional law. Dispute resolution before traditional counselors avoids the costs and congestion of the official courts.

The 1991 Constitution guarantees many civil rights and fundamental freedoms, including freedom of speech and freedom of religion.

¹⁷ARMED FORCES

The People's Revolutionary Armed Forces (FARP) in 1993 numbered 9,200, of whom 6,800 were soldiers, 300 sailors, and 100 airmen, all administratively in the single service army. FARP is armed with outdated Russian and Chinese equipment. There is a 2,000-man gendarmerie. The defense budget in 1987 was $9.3 million, but fell to $4.43 million in 1989 with the collapse of Russian support.

18INTERNATIONAL COOPERATION

Guinea-Bissau was admitted to the UN on 17 February 1974 and is a member of ECA and all the nonregional specialized agencies except IAEA and WIPO. The nation is a de facto party to GATT and a signatory to the Law of the Sea. It also participates in the African Development Bank, ECOWAS, G-77, and OAU. In June 1982, Guinea-Bissau and Cape Verde resumed full diplomatic relations (severed after the November 1980 coup) and reaffirmed the goal of eventual reunification.

19ECONOMY

Guinea-Bissau's economy is predominantly agricultural. The industrial sector is small, and mining is undeveloped. Average GDP growth over the 1980–91 period averaged 3.3% per annum, declining to 2.5% in 1992. The government is firmly committed to market-style economic policies after an initial decade of socialist central planning.

Livestock produces adequate supplies of meat, and hides are among Bissau's exports. Fishing prospects are excellent; the nation earned $2.2 million from the industry in 1991. Illegal fishing prevents a fuller realization of potential in this sector. Production and trade in forest products have been halted while implementation of reforestation policies occurs.

20INCOME

In 1992 Guinea-Bissau's GNP was $217 million at current prices, or $210 per capita. Inflation jumped from 17% in 1988 to 110% in 1992. For the period 1985–92 the average inflation rate was 71.1%, resulting in a real growth rate in per capita GNP of 0.4%.

In 1992 the GDP was $220 million in current US dollars. Of that, 45.6% was produced by the agricultural sector, 23.9% by the trade, restaurants, and hotels sector, 6.8% by manufacturing, and 6.4% by construction.

21LABOR

Subsistence agriculture sustained about 90% of the population of 1 million in 1992. The Constitution grants workers the freedom to join and form trade unions, with 1991 legislation enumerating the rights and obligations of new unions. The National Trade Union Confederation (UNTG), previously the nation's sole labor entity, reorganized itself in 1992 in order to more effectively represent workers. That year, two unions disassociated themselves with the UNTG and held direct negotiations with government employers.

22AGRICULTURE

The agricultural sector employs 80% of the labor force and contributed 46% of the 1992 GDP. Only 12% of the total land area was under permanent or seasonal cultivation in 1991. The country is divided into three major regions according to the water requirements of the major crops. On the coast and in river estuaries is the palm-tree (coconut) zone; rice is the predominant crop of the intermediary marshy areas; and peanuts are grown in the sandy areas of the interior. Rice is the major staple crop; corn, millet, and sorghum are also produced and consumed very widely. In the 1950s, Guinea-Bissau exported about 40,000 tons of rice per year; since 1962, rice has been imported, as frequent droughts often cause crop failure. In 1992, Guinea-Bissau produced 123,000 tons of rice, 25,000 tons of millet, 20,000 tons of peanuts, 25,000 tons of coconuts, 30,000 tons of cashew nuts, and 8,000 tons of palm kernels. Palm kernels, cashew nuts, and peanuts are the most important export crops. The war which culminated with independence in 1974 left the economy in shambles, reducing crop output by over one-third. Public investment, financed heavily by external borrowing, neglected agriculture to focus on the manufacturing sector. Agricultural recovery was hampered by inappropriate pricing policies, an overvalued exchange rate, and an inefficient marketing system. This policy has now been changed through price liberalization, so that some important goods like rice are now traded informally with neighboring countries.

23ANIMAL HUSBANDRY

Despite the damage wrought by the tsetse fly, cattle raising occupies many Guineans, especially among the Balante in the interior. In 1992, there were an estimated 450,000 head of cattle and 300,000 hogs, as well as 250,000 sheep and 250,000 goats.

24FISHING

Fishing is slowly growing into a viable industry. Agreements allow the EC countries to fish in national waters. Guinea-Bissau's own catch was an estimated 5,000 tons in 1991.

25FORESTRY

Guinean forests and savanna woodland, covering about 38% of the country, primarily supply wood and timber for domestic consumption and fuel and construction material. Roundwood production was about 569,000 cu m in 1991. Timber has become a leading export.

26MINING

Large deposits of bauxite, amounting to about 200 million tons, were found in the Boé area in 1972; lack of capital and transportation has hindered exploitation, however. Phosphate deposits, also unexploited, are estimated at 100 million tons. Mineral production in 1991 was limited to crude construciton materials, worth about $6 million. The lack of adequate infrastructure is the chief impediment to the development of the country's mineral resources.

27ENERGY AND POWER

Guinea-Bissau has great potential resources for hydroelectric power development for the domestic market and even for export. The potential production capacity of the Corubal and Geba rivers alone exceeds the country's estimated future need. Installed capacity in 1991 was 1,000 kw; production totaled 41 million kwh. In 1991, production of crude oil totaled 4,000 barrels, down from 20,000 barrels in 1988. Imports of fuel and energy accounted for almost 13% ($10 million) of total imports in 1991.

28INDUSTRY

Manufacturing constitutes a very minor part of Guinea-Bissau's economy, contributing approximately 6.8% a year to the GDP (1988). In 1986, a vehicle assembly plant reopened after a two-year hiatus. A sugar refinery and a rice and groundnut processing plant are in operation. Brewing and urban construction are also represented in the industrial sector.

In the late 1980s, Bissau attempted to attract foreign interest in several enterprises—a fish-processing plant, a plywood and furniture factory, and a plastics factory. The government has moved to raise producer prices and to partially privatize parastatal trading companies. Work is underway on the planning and financing of an electricity generating facility to increase total capacity to 15.4 Mw.

29SCIENCE AND TECHNOLOGY

No information is available.

[30]DOMESTIC TRADE

Under Portuguese rule, commercial activities were significant only in the cities. The PAIGC introduced chains of all-purpose "people's stores," communally owned and managed; some of these were handed over to private traders in 1985. A price control system for all retail commodities and farm produce has been established. As a result of overregulation, mismanagement, and corruption, essential goods were in short supply in the mid-1980s, while black marketeering and smuggling of farm produce abroad were rampant. Normal business hours in the capital are 8 AM to 12 noon and 3 to 6 PM, Monday–Friday.

[31]FOREIGN TRADE

Persistent imbalances have characterized Bissau's foreign trade. Cashew nuts have led all exports in terms of revenue, followed by groundnuts, shrimp and fish, sawn wood, cotton and palm kernels. Exports in 1986 (in millions of US dollars) were:

Cashew nuts	5.1
Fish	1.1
Palm kernels	1.0
Timber	1.0
Groundnuts	0.7
Cotton	0.5
Other	0.2
TOTAL	9.6

Imports, which were estimated at $54.9 million in 1988, include industrial and commercial supplies, fuels and lubricants, and transport equipment. Imported foods, beverages, and tobacco, which accounted for 21.7% of total imports, surpassed in value that of all of Guinea-Bissau's exports.

In 1985, most of Guinea-Bissau's exports went to Romania (44.6%) and France (18.3%). Of Bissau's imports, 20.1% came from Portugal, while 6.0% came from France and 5.8% came from the Netherlands.

[32]BALANCE OF PAYMENTS

Like Portuguese Guinea, Guinea-Bissau has had chronic balance-of-payments problems because of its huge annual trade deficit, which has persisted despite efforts to restructure trade by diversifying the range of commodities available for export and by establishing new trading partners and more favorable trade agreements. Foreign assistance is an essential element in meeting payments needs. The current account deficit grew from 25% of GDP in 1990 to 48% of GDP in 1992, but was expected to fall back to around 28%$ in 1993.

In 1992 merchandise exports totaled $6.47 million and imports $83.51 million. The merchandise trade balance was $–77.04 million. The following table summarizes Guinea-Bissau's balance of payments for 1991 and 1992 (in millions of US dollars):

	1991	1992
CURRENT ACCOUNT		
Goods, services, and income	–94.29	–120.63
Unrequited transfers	49.31	48.55
TOTALS	–44.98	–72.08
CAPITAL ACCOUNT		
Other long-term capital	–8.75	2.21
Exceptional financing	58.76	49.02
Reserves	9.86	–12.85
TOTALS	58.87	38.38
Errors and omissions	–13.89	33.70
Total change in reserves	9.89	–13.06

[33]BANKING AND SECURITIES

The National Bank of Guinea-Bissau is the central bank and bank of issue. A savings and loan bank and a postal savings bank, both domestically owned, operate in Bissau. In 1993, the money supply, as measured by M2, amounted to PG355.4 billion. There are no securities exchanges in Guinea-Bissau.

[34]INSURANCE

No recent information is available.

[35]PUBLIC FINANCE

The IMF-sponsored structural adjustment program in Bissau began in 1987 and projected the achievement of a 3.5% growth rate, reforms to the economy and public administration. Petroleum subsidies were reduced in 1988. In January 1989, customs duties and taxes on imports were lowered to reduce inflation. At the end of that year, the debt-service ratio stood at 43% of exports. The foreign debt was rescheduled by all major donors that fall.

The currency was devalued in May 1987. In January 1990, Guinea-Bissau agreed with Portugal to adopt the escudo. Reform of the national banking system has been underway since 1989.

Failure to meet IMF targets translated into a suspension of international financing when the IMF decided not to renew the structural adjustment program. Negotiations resumed with the World Bank and led to a resumption of World Bank funding in July 1993.

The following table shows actual revenues and expenditures for 1987 and 1989 in millions of pesos.

	1987	1989
REVENUE AND GRANTS		
Tax revenue	7,818	15,371
Non-tax revenue	4,322	27,311
Capital revenue	13	58
Grants	22,443	105,427
TOTAL	34,596	148,167
EXPENDITURES & LENDING MINUS REPAYMENTS		
General public services	12,456	—
Defense	2,168	8,027
Public order and safety	958	4,380
Education	2,541	5,051
Health	2,638	2,473
Social security and welfare	4,273	—
Housing and community amenities	4,067	—
Recreation, cultural, and religious affairs	198	—
Economic affairs and services	19,523	—
Lending minus repayments	3,667	—
TOTAL	52,489	201,725
Deficit/Surplus	–17,893	–53,558

[36]TAXATION

Current information is unavailable.

[37]CUSTOMS AND DUTIES

Import licenses are freely issued for most goods. Most imports are taxed, but luxury goods are more heavily taxed, while capital goods enjoy special treatment. Duties are applied ad valorem; some common ones are: rice (10%), gasoline (55%), diesel (15%), automobiles (40–95%), auto parts (36%), furniture (30%), and household appliances (25%).

[38]FOREIGN INVESTMENT

As of June 1990, the government of Guinea-Bissau took new steps to encourage additional domestic and foreign investment.

While key telecommunications, electricity, and infrastructure sectors remained under state control, others were to be privatized, including the brewery, the fishing industry, and the "people's shops" for retail trade. Bilateral and multilateral investment programs continue in each of the key productive sectors.

39ECONOMIC DEVELOPMENT

A main objective of the Guinea-Bissau government is the development of agriculture and infrastructure. Foreign aid averaged $64.3 million per year from 1982–85. Multilateral aid accounted for almost half this sum, chiefly from the IDA. The first development plan (1983–88) called for self-sufficiency in food supplies, with 25% of a $403.3 million investment going for construction and public works, 18% for rural development, and 14% for transport.

The second development plan (1988–91) was to be totally financed by foreign aid. Numerous countries and intergovernmental organizations have provided food aid, technical assistance, and balance-of-payments support.

40SOCIAL DEVELOPMENT

Provision of health services, including maternal and child care, nutrition programs, environmental sanitation, safe water distribution, and basic education, is the principal social goal of the Guinea-Bissau government. Women play an active part in government at all levels, and polygamy is prohibited for PAIGC members. Contraception is virtually nonexistent.

41HEALTH

The health care system is inadequate. The emphasis is on preventive medicine, with small mobile units serving the rural areas. In 1992 children were vaccinated against tuberculosis (100%); diphtheria, pertussis, and tetanus (66%); polio (65%); and measles (60%). In 1991, only 41% of the population had access to safe water, and only 31% had adequate sanitation. In 1992, there were an estimated 12 physicians per 100,000 population, with a nurse to doctor ratio of 5:1. There were an estimated 1.4 hospital beds per 1,000 people in 1990. The 1993 birth rate was 42.7 per 1,000 people, infant mortality was estimated at 122 deaths per 1,000 live births, and the general mortality rate was 21.3 per 1,000 people. Life expectancy is 45 years for males and 49 years for females.

42HOUSING

As of 1979, 44% of all housing units were adobe, 32% were mud, and 20% were mud and/or quirinton, a combination of woven branches and straw. In 81% of all units, lighting was by petrol lamps; 75% had no sewage system or septic tank, and 96% used either well or spring water.

43EDUCATION

During the war, the PAIGC claimed it had established 160 schools in areas under its control, with about 350 teachers and 15,000 pupils. In 1988 there were 79,035 primary pupils; 6,630 students were enrolled in secondary schools; of these, 5,505 were in general school, 176 were in teachers' training and 649 were in vocational programs.

Education is compulsory between the ages of 7 and 13, but only about 55% of all children in this age group actually attend school. In 1990, 36.5% of the adult population was estimated to be literate (males: 50.2% and females: 24.0%).

44LIBRARIES AND MUSEUMS

The Museum of Guinea-Bissau, in Bissau, has a library of 14,000 volumes and maintains collections of interest in the fields of ethnography, history, natural science, and economics. There are municipal libraries in major cities.

45MEDIA

The Guinea-Bissau's government-owned newspaper, *No Pintcha*, had an estimated circulation of 1,500 in 1991. The two radio networks are the government's Radiodifusão Nacional de Guiné-Bissau and Radio Libertad, which resumed broadcasting in 1990 after a 16-year hiatus. Televisao Experimental has been on the air since 1989. In 1991 there were 39,000 radios in the country. Both press and radio are government owned and controlled. An estimated 3,000 telephones were in use in the late 1980s.

46ORGANIZATIONS

No recent data are available.

47TOURISM, TRAVEL, AND RECREATION

Game shooting, a major attraction for many travelers in Africa, is popular in Guinea-Bissau. Game is abundant in the open country, as well as in the more hazardous forest and jungle areas. The traditional practices of various ethnic groups also interest and attracts tourists. The island of Bubaque and the town of Bolama are cited for their charm and beauty. All visitors need a valid passport and a visa secured in advance. Yellow fever and cholera vaccinations are required of many travelers, and typhoid, typhus, and tetanus inoculations and malaria suppressants are recommended.

48FAMOUS GUINEANS

The best-known Guinean of recent years was Amilcar Cabral (1921–73), a founder of PAIGC, its first secretary-general, and a key figure in the war for independence until he was assassinated. Luis de Almeida Cabral (b.1931), a cofounder of the liberation movement in September 1956, and the younger brother of Amilcar Cabral, subsequently became the first president of Guinea-Bissau; after release from detention by the Revolutionary Council in December 1981, he left the country. João Bernardo Vieira (b.1939), leader of the Revolutionary Council, came to power in the 1980 coup.

49DEPENDENCIES

Guinea-Bissau has no territories or colonies.

50BIBLIOGRAPHY

Dhada, Mustafah. *Warriors at Work: How Guinea Was Really Set Free*. Niwot, Colo.: University Press of Colorado, 1993.

Forrest, Joshua. *Guinea-Bissau: Power, Conflict, and Renewal in a West African Nation*. Boulder, Colo.: Westview Press, 1992.

Galli, Rosemary. *Guinea-Bissau*. Santa Barbara, Calif.: Clio, 1990.

Lobban, Richard. *Historical Dictionary of the Republic of Cape Verde*. 2d ed. Metuchen, N.J.: Scarecrow Press, 1988.

Lopes, Carlos. *Guinea Bissau, from Liberation Struggle to Independent Statehood*. Boulder, Colo.: Westview, 1987.

KENYA

Republic of Kenya
Jamhuri ya Kenya

CAPITAL: Nairobi.

FLAG: The flag is a horizontal tricolor of black, red, and green stripes separated by narrow white bars. At the center is a red shield with black and white markings superimposed on two crossed white spears.

ANTHEM: *Wimbo Wa Taifa (National Anthem),* beginning "Ee Mungu nguvu yetu, ilete baraka Kwetu" ("O God of all creation, bless this our land and nation").

MONETARY UNIT: The Kenya shilling (Sh) is a paper currency of 100 cents; the Kenya pound (к£) is a unit of account equivalent to 20 shillings. There are coins of 5, 10, and 50 cents and 1 and 5 shillings, and notes of 5, 10, 20, 50, 100, and 200 shillings. Sh1 = $0.0154 (or $1 = Sh64.858).

WEIGHTS AND MEASURES: The metric system is used.

HOLIDAYS: New Year's Day, 1 January; Labor Day, 1 May; Madaraka Day, 1 June; Kenyatta Day, 20 October; Uhuru (Independence) Day, 12 December; Christmas, 25 December; Boxing Day, 26 December. Movable holidays include Good Friday, Easter Monday, 'Id al-Fitr, and 'Id al-'Adha'.

TIME: 3 PM = noon GMT.

¹LOCATION, SIZE, AND EXTENT

Situated on the eastern coast of Africa, Kenya lies astride the equator. Its total area, including 11,230 sq km (4,336 sq mi) of water, is 582,650 sq km (224,962 sq mi), with a maximum length of 1,131 km (703 mi) SSE–NNW and a maximum width of 1,025 km (637 mi) ENE–WSW. Comparatively, the area occupied by Kenya is slightly more than twice the size of the state of Nevada. Kenya is bounded on the N by the Sudan and Ethiopia, on the E by Somalia, on the SE by the Indian Ocean, on the S by Tanzania, and on the W by Lake Victoria and Uganda, with a total boundary length of 3,982 km (2,474 mi).

Kenya's capital city, Nairobi, is located in the southcentral part of the country.

²TOPOGRAPHY

Kenya is notable for its topographical variety. The low-lying, fertile coastal region, fringed with coral reefs and islands, is backed by a gradually rising coastal plain, a dry region covered with savanna and thornbush. At an altitude of over 1,500 m (5,000 ft) and about 480 km (300 mi) inland, the plain gives way in the southwest to a high plateau, rising in parts to more than 3,050 m (10,000 ft), on which most of the population and the majority of economic activities are concentrated. The northern section of Kenya, forming three-fifths of the whole territory, is arid and of semidesert character, as is the bulk of the southeastern quarter. In the high plateau area, known as the Kenya Highlands, lie Mt. Kenya (5,199 m/17,057 ft), Mt. Elgon (4,310 m/14,140 ft), and the Aberdare Range (rising to 3,999 m/13,120 ft). The plateau is bisected from north to south by the Great Rift Valley, part of the geological fracture that can be traced from Syria through the Red Sea and East Africa to Mozambique. In the north of Kenya the valley is broad and shallow, embracing Lake Rudolf (Lake Turkana), which is 257 km (160 mi) long; farther south the valley narrows and deepens and is walled by escarpments 600–900 m (2,000–3,000 ft) high. West of the Great Rift Valley, the plateau descends to the plains that border Lake Victoria. The principal rivers are the Tana and the Athi, both flowing southeastward to the Indian Ocean, and the Ewaso Ngiro, which flows in a north-easterly direction to the swamps of the Lorian Plain.

³CLIMATE

The climate of Kenya is as varied as its topography. Climatic conditions range from the tropical humidity of the coast through the dry heat of the hinterland and northern plains to the coolness of the plateau and mountains; despite Kenya's equatorial position, Mt. Kenya is perpetually snow-capped. The coastal temperature averages 27°C (81°F), and the temperature decreases by slightly less than 2 degrees Celsius (about 3 degrees Fahrenheit) with each 300-m (1,000-ft) increase in altitude. The capital, Nairobi, at 1,661 m (5,449 ft), has a mean annual temperature of 19°C (66°F); at 2,740 m (9,000 ft) the average is 13°C (55°F). The arid northern plains range from 21° to 27°C (70–81°F).

Seasonal variations are distinguished by duration of rainfall rather than by changes of temperature. Most regions of the country have two rainy seasons, the long rains falling between April and June and the short rains between October and December. Average annual rainfall varies from 13 cm (5 in) a year in the most arid regions of the northern plains to 193 cm (76 in) near Lake Victoria. The coast and highland areas receive an annual average of 102 cm (40 in).

⁴FLORA AND FAUNA

The vegetation and animal life of Kenya reflect the variety of its topography and climate. In the coastal region coconut trees flourish, with occasional mangrove swamps and rain forest. The vast plains of the hinterland and the northern regions are covered with grass, low bush, and scrub, giving way in the high-lying plains to typical savanna country of open grass dotted with thorn trees, and in the more arid regions to bare earth and stunted scrub. The highland areas are in parts densely forested with bamboo and valuable timber, the predominant trees being African camphor, African olive, podo, and pencil cedar.

Wildlife of great variety is to be found in Kenya, both in the sparsely populated areas and in the national parks and reserves

197

that have been created for its protection. Elephant, rhinoceros, lion, zebra, giraffe, buffalo, hippopotamus, wildebeest, and many kinds of buck are among the large mammals that abound on the plains and along the rivers. Kenya's diverse bird species include cranes, flamingos, ostriches, and vultures.

5ENVIRONMENT

Deforestation and soil erosion are attributable to growing population pressure, which creates demands for increased food production and firewood. Drought and desertification (to which 83% of Kenya's land area is vulnerable) also threaten potential productive agricultural lands. Kenya has 3.6 cubic miles of water with 62% used in farming activity and 11% used for industrial purposes. The majority of people living in rural areas (85%) as well as 15% of city dwellers do not have pure water. In addition to pollutants from industry, the nation's cities produce 1.1 million tons of solid wastes. In an effort to preserve wildlife, the government has set aside more than 2.5 million ha (6.2 million acres) as national parks and game preserves. Game hunting and trade in ivory and skins have been banned, but poaching threatens leopards, cheetahs, lions, elephants, rhinoceroses, and other species. It is illegal to kill an animal even if it attacks. As of 1994, 17 species of mammals and 18 bird species are endangered, and 144 plant species are threatened with extinction. Endangered species include the Sokoke scops owl, Taita blue-banded papilio, Tana River mangabey, Tana River red colobus, green sea turtle, and hawksbill turtle.

6POPULATION

Kenya's population has increased with remarkable rapidity in recent decades. According to UN estimates, the national total rose by 28% from 6,416,000 in 1950 to 8,189,000 in 1960; by 37% to 11,253,000 in 1970; by 46% to 16,466,000 in 1980; by 36% to 22,400,000 in 1987; and by 24% to an estimated 27,885,000 in 1995. The crude death rate declined from 25.3 per 1,000 population during 1950–55 to 10.3 during 1990–95, while the crude birthrate increased to a peak of 53.6 for 1975–80, among the highest in the world. From 1975 through 1980, Kenya registered an average annual population increase of 3.82%, not only the highest of any nation in the world during that period but also the highest ever recorded for a single country; the estimated annual growth rate was 3.35% during 1990–95. The UN projected a population of 32,818,000 in the year 2000—more than five times the 1950 total—assuming a crude birthrate of 41.7 per 1,000 population, a crude death rate of 9.2, and a net natural increase of 325 during 1995–2000. Moreover, Kenya's population was expected to increase by at least 3% annually until about 2005. It is estimated that 47.4% of the population will be under 15 years of age in 1995; projections indicate that figure will drop to 46.2% in 2000.

For 1995, it was estimated that 27.7% of the population would be urban and 72.3% rural; during 1990–95, the urban population rose by an annual average of 6.55%. In 1990, Nairobi, the capital and principal city, had an estimated population of 1,518,000; Mombasa, the chief seaport, an estimated 442,369 in 1985. Other cities and their 1989 estimated populations were Kisumu, 185,100; Nakuru, 162,800; Machakos, 116,100; Meru, 78,100; Eldoret, 104,900; and Nyeri, 88,600. For 1995, the population density of Kenya was estimated at approximately 48 per sq km (124 per sq mi), up from 11 per sq km (29 per sq mi) in 1950. About 75% of the population lives on only 10% of the land. Northeast Province occupies 22% of the country but only has about 2.5% of the population.

7MIGRATION

Throughout Kenya there is a slow but steady movement of the rural population to the cities in search of employment. Some Kenyans have emigrated to Uganda, and ethnic Somalis are present in significant numbers in Kenya's North-Eastern Province.

Far-reaching migratory changes took place in the years immediately preceding and following independence. By 1961, the post-1945 trend of net European immigration was reversed, and in the three years that followed, approximately 29,000 Europeans left Kenya. Permanent emigration in 1964 reached 9,860, while permanent immigration totaled 5,406. In the first year of independence, some 6,000 Britons renounced their citizenship and applied for Kenyan citizenship; during the same period, approximately 70,000 persons living in Kenya—the majority of them Asians—were granted British passports. After the UK limited immigration by Asians in 1967, a crisis situation developed in Kenya. Work permits, without which Asians could not stay in the country beyond a limited period, were not issued, and the UK denied entry to Asians from Kenya who wanted to work in the UK. In 1973, the Kenya government served 1,500 notices of termination to Asian employees (there were 300 in 1972) and announced that by the end of 1974 it aimed to completely Kenyanize the country's retail and wholesale trade. In 1975, the Ministry of Commerce and Industry ordered the closing of 436 businesses, most of which belonged to Asians. Some 80,000 Asians were still living in Kenya at the time of the 1979 census, down from an estimated 180,000 in 1968.

At the end of 1992 there were 401,900 documented refugees in Kenya. Some 285,600 were Somalis, 68,600 Ethiopians, 21,800 Sudanese, and 3,600 Ugandans.

8ETHNIC GROUPS

African peoples indigenous to Kenya, who now form 98% of the population, fall into three major cultural and linguistic groups: Bantu, Nilotic, and Cushitic. Although most of the land area is occupied by Cushitic and Nilotic peoples, over 70% of the population is Bantu. The Luo, a Nilotic people, live in an area adjacent to Lake Victoria. Other Nilotes—Turkana, Maasai, Pokot, Nandi, Kipsigis, and Tugen—occupy a broad area in the west from Lake Rudolf to the Tanzania border. Cushites such as the Galla and Somali live in the eastern and northeastern parts of the country. The Bantu reside mainly in the coastal areas and the southwestern uplands; the most significant Bantu peoples are the Kikuyu, Kamba, and Luhya. The Kikuyu, who constitute the largest single ethnic group in Kenya, live for the most part north of Nairobi and have played a major role in the nation's political and social development. The estimated proportions of the major groups are Kikuyu 21%, Luhya 14%, Luo 13%, Kamba 11%, Kalenjin 11%, Kisii 6%, and Meru 5%.

The Arab population is centered on the Indian Ocean coast. The Swahili, a group of mixed Arab-Africans with a cultural affinity to the Arabs, also live in the coastal region. Most Asians in Kenya have origins traceable to the Indian subcontinent; living primarily in urban centers, they consist of at least 31 culturally separate groups but make up less than 0.4% of the nation's population. The European community, which has rebounded since the 1960s and stood at 40,000 in 1979, is primarily of British origin. About 12% of the Europeans hold Kenyan citizenship. A 1984 law provides that people born in Kenya of non-Kenyan parents can no longer claim Kenyan citizenship.

9LANGUAGES

Although there are linguistic groupings of very similar dialects, nearly all the African ethnic groups have their own distinct languages. Swahili, however, has become increasingly an East African lingua franca, and in 1974 it became Kenya's official language, along with English. English remains in wide use in business and government, and parliamentary bills must be drafted and presented in that language. Both Gujarati and Punjabi are widely used among the Asian community.

KENYA

0	50	100	150		200 Miles
0	50	100	150	200 Kilometers	

LOCATION: 4°30′N to 4°30′S; 34° to 42°E. **BOUNDARY LENGTHS:** Sudan, 306 km (190 mi); Ethiopia, 779 km (484 mi); Somalia, 682 km (424 mi); Indian Ocean, 523 km (325 mi); Tanzania, 769 km (478 mi); Lake Victoria, 138 km (86 mi); Uganda, 772 km (480 mi). **TERRITORIAL SEA LIMIT:** 12 mi.

¹⁰RELIGIONS

The pluralistic character of Kenya's society is evident in its religious affiliations. As of 1987, an estimated 73% of the population was Christian: 27% was Roman Catholic; and 46% belonged to traditional Protestant groups. Tribal religionists accounted for another 19% of the total population, and Muslims 6%. As in other African states with complex religious histories and some renewal of cultural self-consciousness, it is likely that a majority of ethnic Kenyans also hold traditional African beliefs.

11TRANSPORTATION

The Kenya Railways Corp. maintains 2,040 km (1,260 mi) of rail, of which over half make up the main line between the Ugandan border and Mombasa, the chief port.

A modern installation, the port at Mombasa serves Uganda, Tanzania, Rwanda, Burundi, Zaire, and the Sudan as well as Kenya. A national shipping line, 70% state owned, was created in 1987. There is steamer service on Lake Victoria.

In 1991, the road system comprised some 64,950 km (40,340 mi), of which 11% was bituminized. The major road from Nairobi to Mombasa is well paved, and the government has undertaken a campaign to widen and resurface secondary roads. All-weather roads linking Kenya with the Sudan and Ethiopia have been completed. In 1992 there were 291,134 motor vehicles, including 157,166 private passenger automobiles.

There are major international airports at Nairobi and Mombasa. The Nairobi air terminal, opened in 1958 and expanded in 1972 to receive jumbo jets, is a continental terminus for international services from Europe, Asia, and other parts of Africa. Air travel and air freight also are accommodated at Malindi, Kisumu, and numerous smaller airstrips. Kenya Airways flies to other nations of East Africa, the Middle East, Europe, and the Indian subcontinent; it carried 759,900 passengers in 1991. That year, Nairobi handled 1,516,000 passengers and 52,200 tons of freight; Mombasa, 704,000 passengers and 1,400 tons of freight.

12HISTORY

Fossil remains show that humanlike creatures lived in the area of Lake Rudolf perhaps 2 million years ago. As early as the third millennium BC, cattle were being herded in what is now northern Kenya. Sometime in the first millennium BC, food-producing Cushitic-speaking peoples, possibly from the Ethiopian highlands, appeared in Kenya. During the Iron Age (c.AD 1000), the first Bantu speakers arrived, probably from points south and west, resulting in the retreat of Cushitic speakers. The Nilotic speakers entered at the end of the 16th century from the north or northwest, from southern Sudan, and perhaps from the western Ethiopian borderland.

After their arrival, most groups settled into a pattern of slow and gradual movement highlighted by spurts of expansionist activity. For example, the Eastern Bantu (Kikuyu, Meru, Kamba, Pokomo, Teita, and Bajuni), possibly after settling in the area between Lamu and the Juba River, dispersed throughout southern and coastal Kenya. By 1400, the Kikuyu had reached the area near Mt. Kenya; they were joined there by the Meru in the 1750s. The Western Bantu (Luhya and Gusii) developed from an influx of Kalenjin (1598–1625) and Bantu (1598–1733) migrants. Other peoples, including the Luo, developed a strong ethnic identity and protected themselves from intruders. But as their population increased between 1750 and 1800, conflict arose, clans broke down, and another wave of migration ensued.

The Cushitic and Nilotic peoples (represented by Kalenjin ancestors of the Pokot, Nandi, Kipsigis, Kony, and Tugen) and others (such as the Turkana, Teso, and Galla) participated in independent movements beginning in the 16th century and lasting into the 18th. By 1800, the Kamba, acting as the chief carriers and go-betweens, dominated an extensive intergroup long-distance trade network that linked the interior to the East African coast. The last migrants into the country were the Somali, who did not enter northeastern Kenya in great numbers until the late 19th and early 20th centuries.

Meanwhile, another set of migrants settled on the Indian Ocean coast. As in the interior, the newcomers replaced the original hunter-gatherer inhabitants. In the period prior to the birth of Christ, Egyptians, Phoenicians, Persians, and possibly even Indonesians visited the coast. By the 10th century the Bantu had settled the coastal region in what the Arabs called the Land of the Zenj (blacks). As the area flourished, a mixed population of Arabs and Africans combined in creating the Swahili culture, a culture marked by its own language, a devotion to Islam, and the development of numerous coastal trade centers. Swahili cities such as Kilwa, Mombasa, and Pate remained independent of one another and of foreign control and, although they had little contact with the interior, grew wealthy from their mercantile contacts with India and Arabia.

Throughout the 16th century, following Vasco da Gama's landing at Malindi in 1498, the coastal cities struggled to remain independent of the external threats posed first by the Portuguese and then by the Omani Arabs. Although the Portuguese established posts and gained a monopoly of the trade along the Kenya coast, the Arabs, with help from their kinsmen in Oman, succeeded after a long period of conflict in driving out the Portuguese and reestablishing Arab authority in 1740. Independent Arab settlements persisted for a century until, during the rule (1806–56) of Sayyid Sa'id, a kind of unity was established. Arab control even in the 19th century continued to be confined to the coastal belt, however. In 1840, Sayyid Sa'id moved the capital of his sultanate to Zanzibar.

Just as the Arabs were vying for control of the coast in the decades before and after the turn of the 19th century, Europeans began to assert their influence in East Africa. After jostling with the Germans and the Italians for Zanzibari favors, the British emerged with a concession for the Kenya coast in 1887. European penetration of the interior had begun decades earlier with the explorations of two German missionaries, Johannes Rebmann and Johann Ludwig Krapf, in 1847–49, and with the arrival at Lake Victoria of the English explorer John Hanning Speke in 1858. In 1886, the UK and Germany reached agreement on their respective spheres of influence in East Africa, and the Imperial British East African Company, a private concern, began establishing its authority in the interior two years later. In 1890, a definitive Anglo-German agreement was signed, and arrangements were made with the sultan of Zanzibar for protection to be extended to his mainland holdings. When the company failed in 1895, the UK assumed direct control over what was then known as the East African Protectorate. In December 1901, the railway linking Mombasa with Lake Victoria was completed, and in the following year the boundary between Kenya and Uganda was shifted some 320 km (200 mi) westward to its present position. European and Asian settlement followed the building of the railway, and by World War I the modern development of Kenya was clearly evident. In 1920, following a series of military expeditions against the Nandi, Embu, Gusii, Kipsigis, and Somali, the protectorate, with the exception of the coastal strip (later ceded by Zanzibar), was declared a crown colony.

The political and constitutional development of Kenya reflected a continued conflict between the interests of Europeans, Asians, and Africans. British policy sought to find a balance between these interests, and constitutional progress reflected the changing power relationships. In the interwar years, the major challenge to European political power came from Asians who wanted equality with Europeans in governmental representative institutions. This challenge was successfully resisted, but in the postwar period a more dynamic threat came from African nationalism.

The Struggle for Independence

Africans made use of both legal and nonlegal methods in their struggle for power with the Europeans. The first efforts ended in the eruption of the Mau Mau movement, and a state of emergency was declared in October 1952. Supported primarily by the Kikuyu, Embu, and Meru tribes of Central Province, Mau Mau was a secretive insurrectionary movement that rejected the European-dominated social and political orders of Kenya. The emergency lasted until late 1959, and its cost in money was estimated at over UK£55 million. At one time, more than 79,000 Africans were detained, and an estimated 13,000 civilians (almost all African) were killed.

During the initial period of the emergency in 1954, the "Lyttelton" multiracial constitution was imposed on Kenyan political groups unable to agree among themselves. While providing for African and Asian participation in a council of ministers with Europeans, it continued the long-established system of communal representation for each racial group, with a formula of equality of representation in legislative and executive institutions between Europeans and non-Europeans. While nominated African representation in the central government councils had gradually increased since their inception in 1944, the introduction of direct elections for Africans to the Legislative Council in 1957 was their first outstanding political gain. The 1960 "Macleod" constitution permitted the coming into being of an African-elected majority in the Legislative Council; this represented a decisive shift in the direction of an African-controlled state of Kenya. Rapid advancement toward self-government and independence under African leadership was delayed, however, because of conflicts between the two major African political parties over the future constitutional structure of the country. A constitutional conference in London in early 1962 was able to achieve an agreement on a "framework" constitution, which included formation of a national government representing both political parties. Following new national elections under this constitution in May 1963, Kenya became internally self-governing on 1 June. On 12 December 1963, Kenya became independent, and exactly one year later it became a republic within the Commonwealth of Nations, with Jomo Kenyatta as the country's first president. His political party, the Kenya African National Union (KANU), dominated the government, and leaders of a rival party, banned in 1969, were detained. On the other hand, some electoral choice was permitted: although all parliamentary candidates in 1969, 1974, and 1979 were KANU members, more than half the incumbents were unseated in the balloting. An East African Community united Kenya, Tanzania, and Uganda in a common market and customs union until it was dissolved in 1977. Tanzania responded by closing its border with Kenya until November 1983.

Kenyatta died on 22 August 1978 and was succeeded by his vice-president, Daniel arap Moi, who was elected president without opposition a month later. In June 1982, the National Assembly voted unanimously to make Kenya formally a one-party state. Shortly thereafter, on 1 August 1982, a group of junior air force officers, supported by university students and urban workers, attempted a military coup. Looting in Nairobi, particularly of Asian-owned stores, continued for days, and more than 500 people were reportedly killed. The entire 2,100-member air force was dissolved, and Nairobi University was closed. Almost 1,000 persons received jail sentences in the following months, and 12 convicted conspirators were sentenced to death and reportedly executed in 1985. President Moi ran unopposed in the elections of September 1983; in the National Assembly voting during the same month, five cabinet ministers and 40% of all incumbents went down to defeat.

In 1986, Moi declared that KANU was above government, the parliament and the judiciary. Critics of Moi, even within KANU, were expelled from the party and government repression widened. In July 1990, opposition leaders were detained and clashes between pro-democracy demonstrators and police left five dead. Again in 1991, riot police dispersed thousands of protesters. A dozen opposition leaders, including former vice president, Oginga Odinga, were jailed.

As pressures mounted for political reform, the US and 11 other donor nations pressed Moi to reduce government corruption, to improve its poor human rights record, and to institute economic reforms. In December 1991, at a meeting of the governing council of KANU, Moi proposed dropping the 1982 amendment to the constitution that legalized one-party rule. KANU agreed to it, but opposition to Moi and civil unrest continued. Ethnic violence from 1991 to 1994 in the Rift Valley has left over 3,000 Kikuyu and Luo dead, allegedly the work of "trained warriors" from Moi's ethnic group.

In Nairobi in January 1992, more than 100,000 attended the first legal antigovernment rally in 22 years. Through the years, the Forum for the Restoration of Democracy (FORD) had emerged as the main opposition. But a conflict between Kenneth Matiba and Odinga signaled ethnic divisions in the run-up to elections required by 21 March 1993. Moi, exploiting those weaknesses, delayed the elections until November, then again until December. The opposition, divided into eight parties, saw its initial support fade away. Although the late December elections were generally peaceful, Matiba, Odinga, and Mwai Kibaki, of the Democratic Party of Kenya, refused to accept the results. Moi was reelected with 37% of the vote; Matiba had 26%, Kibaki 19%, and Odinga 17%. For the National Assembly, KANU won 100 of the 188 seats; FORD-Kenya, 31; FORD-Asili, 31; and DP, 23. However, many of Moi's cabinet ministers were defeated in their parliamentary contests. Foreign assistance has been reduced as Moi continues to pressure the opposition in and out of parliament.

In 1993, Africa Watch, a US-based human rights group, reported that as many as 1,500 Kenyans have been killed and over 300,000 displaced as a result of ethnic violence instigated by Moi's regime.

13GOVERNMENT

According to the constitution of 1963, as subsequently amended, the government of Kenya is led by a president who is chief of state, head of government, and commander-in-chief of the armed forces. The president is elected to serve a five-year term; he may, however, dissolve the National Assembly during his term, or the National Assembly may dissolve itself by a vote of no confidence, in which case a new presidential election must also be held. The president appoints the members of the cabinet (the vice-president and the heads of the various ministries) from among members of the Assembly. The cabinet is carefully balanced to maintain a multi-ethnic image, and the allocation of assistant ministerships is part of the communally arranged patronage system.

The unicameral National Assembly—established when the Senate and House of Representatives were merged by constitutional amendment in 1967—consisted in 1986 of 158 members elected for a maximum term of five years, plus 12 national members nominated by the president. A constitutional amendment in 1986 increased the number of elected seats (beginning with the next election) to 188. The speaker of the Assembly and the attorney general are ex-officio members. Suffrage is universal at age 21.

The constitution recognizes the principle of maximum allocation of governmental powers to local authorities, and provision is made for the establishment of provincial assemblies with local administrative powers. The central government may abridge or extend the powers of local government in the national interest.

14POLITICAL PARTIES

Following a constitutional conference at Lancaster House in London in February 1960, two national African parties were formed, the Kenya African National Union (KANU) and the Kenya African Democratic Union (KADU). The fundamental difference between the two parties resided in the fact that KANU tended to represent those persons and tribes that were most closely associated with an urban-oriented nationalism and sought a highly centralized political system for Kenya, while KADU represented the more rural and pastoral tribes, who feared a concentration of power by any central government. The political conflicts between these two parties tended to become identified with tribalism, since each party had a core group of tribes committed to it. In the national elections of May 1963, KANU won a majority of seats in both houses of parliament, and its leader, Jomo Kenyatta, assumed power. KADU dissolved itself voluntarily in 1964 and joined KANU.

Since 1964, KANU has dominated Kenyan politics. In March 1966, 30 KANU members of the House announced that they had formed an opposition party, later named the Kenya People's Union (KPU), led by Oginga Odinga, a Luo, who had resigned his post as vice-president. By-elections for the 30 seats, held in June 1966, resulted in the KPU's retention of only 9. In July 1969, Tom Mboya, the minister of economic planning, was assassinated. His death touched off old animosities between his tribe, the Luo, and the politically dominant Kikuyu, to which Kenyatta belonged. The government used the pretext of the assassination to ban the KPU and jail Odinga and other opposition leaders. In the 1969 elections, Kenyatta—who ran unopposed—and the KANU slate were returned to power. All parliamentary candidates also were KANU members in 1974 and 1979; however, there were many more candidates than constituencies, and in all three elections a majority of incumbents were unseated.

Following reports that Odinga, who had been freed in 1971, was planning to form a new, Socialist-oriented party, the National Assembly on 9 June 1982 declared Kenya a one-party state. In the wake of the attempted coup that August, Odinga was again detained, and treason charges were brought against his son, Raila Odinga, dean of the engineering school of the University of Nairobi. The treason charges were later dropped, but Oginga Odinga remained under house arrest from November 1982 to October 1983. By that time, presidential and parliamentary elections had been held, with some 900 KANU members vying for the 158 elective seats.

A clandestine dissident group known as Mwakenya was founded in 1981. In 1986, 44 persons were being held in connection with this group, 37 of whom were convicted of sedition. Other underground opposition groups emerged in the 1980s and in 1987 many joined to form the United Movement for Democracy (UMOJA, Swahili for unity).

In December 1991, the Moi government decided to end KANU's monopoly on legal political activity. A grand coalition known as the Forum for the Restoration of Democracy (FORD) was formed, but, before the December 1992 election, it fragmented into two factions—FORD-Kenya, headed by Oginga Odinga and FORD-Asili, led by Kenneth Matiba. The Democratic Party of Kenya (DP) is fronted by Mwai Kibaki and the Kenya National Congress (KNC) by Chilube wa Tsuma. Three other parties are active, even in the face of continued persecution by Moi's police. In particular, government has prevented opposition MPs, domestic and international human rights figures, and journalists from entering the security zones of the Rift Valley. In brief, the KANU-led government has not reconciled itself to the new era of multiparty politics; in 1993 alone, it arrested 36 of the 85 opposition MPs.

15LOCAL GOVERNMENT
Kenya is divided into seven provinces: Coast, North-Eastern, Eastern, Central, Rift Valley, Nyanza, and Western. (The Nairobi area is separate and has special status.) These are subdivided into 40 districts, each headed by a presidentially appointed commissioner; provincial administration is closely supervised by the central government. There are two types of upper local authorities (municipalities and county councils) and four types of lower authorities (urban councils, township authorities, area councils, and local councils). The Nairobi area, administered by a city council, is the direct responsibility of the central government. Many of the councils raise their own revenues by taxes, construct and maintain roads, carry out public health schemes, construct and improve housing, support education, and provide agricultural and social welfare services.

16JUDICIAL SYSTEM
The legal system is based on the 1963 Constitution, the Judicature Act of 1967, and common law court precedent. Customary law, to the extent it does not conflict with statutory law, is used as a guide in civil matters concerning persons of the same ethnic group.

The judicial system consists of the Court of Appeal, which has final appellate jurisdiction, and subordinate courts. The High Court, sitting continuously at Nairobi, Mombasa, Nakuru, and Kisumu, and periodically at Eldoret, Kakamega, Nyeri, Kitale, Kisii, and Meru, consists of a chief justice and 24 associate judges, who are appointed by the president of the republic. The High Court has both civil and criminal jurisdiction, serving as an appellate tribunal in some cases and as a court of first instance in others. Lower courts are presided over by resident magistrates and district magistrates. Questions of Islamic law are determined by qadis' courts. Military courts handle court martials of military personnel.

Although the constitution provides for an independent judiciary, the President has considerable influence over the judiciary. The President appoints the High Court Judges with the advice of the Judicial Service Commission. The President also has authority to dismiss judges, the Attorney General, and other officials upon recommendation of a tribunal appointed by the President.

17ARMED FORCES
Until 1963, Kenya's defense was the responsibility of the UK. On 10 December 1963, the withdrawal of British armed forces from Kenya was completed.

Military service is voluntary. In 1993 the army had 20,500 men in 16 specialized battalions; the navy had 650 men and 10 patrol craft. The air force had 40 combat aircraft and 38 armed helicopters. The 5,000-member national police has general service, air, and naval paramilitary units. In 1989 Kenya spent $100 million on defense or 1% of gross domestic product.

18INTERNATIONAL COOPERATION
On 16 December 1963, Kenya became a member of the UN; the nation participates in ECA and all the nonregional specialized agencies, and is a signatory to GATT and the Law of the Sea. Kenya is also a member of the African Development Bank, Commonwealth of Nations, G-77, and OAU; President Daniel arap Moi was OAU chairman during 1981/82 and 1982/83. In February 1975, Kenya signed the Lomé Convention, thereby acquiring preferential access to the EC for certain products. On 26 June 1980, Kenya signed an agreement with the US allowing the latter access to air and naval facilities at Mombasa.

Nairobi has become increasingly important as a headquarters for international agences (including the secretariat of the UN Environment Program) and as a convention center for world organizations.

19ECONOMY
Kenya's is an agricultural economy supported by a manufacturing sector, much of which dates from the preindependence period, and a tourism sector, which is an important foreign exchange earner. Financial difficulties and disagreements over the direction of future investments led to a suspension of foreign aid in 1992.

Kenya has a drought-prone agricultural sector in which maize is a principal staple crop, along with tubers—cassava, potatoes, and sweet potatoes. There is a shortage of arable land—only 7%

is first-quality farm land—and little irrigation. Even so, sector growth rates varied between 4.8% and 3.2% in the years prior to the 1992 drought (1986–91). The Kenyan state cereals marketing board was restructured in 1986 to allow more private-sector involvement.

[20]INCOME

In 1992 Kenya's GNP was $8,453 million at current prices, or $330 per capita. For the period 1985–92 the average inflation rate was 10.4%, resulting in a real growth rate in per capita GNP of 0.6%.

In 1992 the GDP was $8,011 million in current US dollars. It is estimated that in 1991 agriculture, hunting, forestry, and fishing contributed 25% to GDP; manufacturing, 10%; electricity, gas, and water, 1%; construction, 7%; wholesale and retail trade, 10%; transport, storage, and communication, 6%; finance, insurance, real estate, and business services, 13%; community, social, and personal services, 3%; and other sources, 25%.

[21]LABOR

In 1992, the monetary sector of the economy employed 1,441,800 workers, 19% of whom engaged in agriculture and forestry. Of public-sector employment, more than half (and 43% of all wage employment) was in community, social, and personal services; manufacturing employed 13% of all wage workers. Although employment has increased in manufacturing and transport, unemployment, estimated in 1992 at over 25% of the work force, remains a problem. Poverty is widespread, and the working poor, who put in long hours of labor for little return, greatly outnumber the unemployed. Women constituted 60% of the work force in 1992.

The trade union movement is strong in Kenya and continues to pressure the government for better wages and improved living standards. Complex rules, however, severely limit the right to strike. In 1980, the government formally disbanded the Kenyan Civil Servants Union, which at that time was the nation's largest single labor organization; in 1991, however, it was reinstated by President Moi. The principal labor federation is the Central Organization of Trade Unions (COTU). Except for the 150,000–200,000 teachers believed to be members of Kenya National Union of Teachers and four other smaller unions, all unions are affiliated with the COTU. There were some 33 unions in Kenya with approximately 350,000–385,000 workers in 1992, or about 25% of the country's industrialized work force.

[22]AGRICULTURE

Agriculture remains the most important economic activity in Kenya, although less than 5% of the land is used for crop and feed production. About 80% of the work force engages in subsistance agriculture. Although there are still important European-owned coffee, tea, and sisal plantations, an increasing number of peasant farmers grow cash crops.

From independence in 1963 to the oil crisis in 1973, the agricultural sector expanded by undergoing two basic changes: first, widespread acceptance of private ownership (replacing tribal ownership) and cash crop farming; second, the success of intensive nationwide efforts to expand and upgrade the production of African smallholders. Before World War II ended, agricultural development occurred almost exclusively in the "White Highlands," an area of some 31,000 sq km (12,000 sq mi) allocated to immigrant white settlers and plantation companies. Since independence, as part of a land consolidation and resettlement policy, the Kenya government, with financial aid from the UK, has gradually transferred large areas to African ownership. About 54% of all smallholdings are under 1 ha (2.5 acres). European-owned agriculture remains generally large-scale and almost entirely commercial.

After the 1973 oil crisis, agricultural growth slowed as less untapped land became available. Government involvement in marketing coupled with inefficient trade and exchange rate policies discouraged production during the 1970s. Coffee production booms in the late 1970s and in 1986 have in the past temporarily helped the economy in its struggle away from deficit spending and monetary expansion. Although the expansion of agricultural export crops has been the most important factor in stimulating economic development, much agricultural activity is also directed toward providing food for domestic consumption. Kenya's agriculture is sufficiently diversified to produce nearly all of the nation's basic foodstuffs. To some extent, Kenya also helps feed neighboring countries.

Coffee is Kenya's leading cash crop, earning $195 million in export income in 1991 and $163 million in 1992. Production in 1992 amounted to 70,000 tons. The suspension of the economic provisions of the International Coffee Agreement in July 1989 disrupted markets temporarily, driving coffee prices to historical lows. To compensate, Kenya increased export volume and decreased its inventory. Coffee is unlikely to be such a dominant export again in the near future. Tea ranks second to coffee among agricultural exports, and production for sale was 188,000 tons in 1992. Kenya is Africa's leading tea producer, and was third in the world in 1992, behind India and China. Other important crops in 1992 were sugarcane, 4,430,000 tons; corn, 2,561,000 tons; wheat, 200,000 tons; sisal, 35,000 tons; rice, 58,000 tons; and seed cotton, 28,000 tons.

Smallholders grow most of the corn and also produce significant quantities of potatoes, beans, peas, sorghum, sweet potatoes, cassava, bananas, and oilseeds. Other grain crops in 1992 included 55,000 tons of millet and 107,000 tons of sorghum. During the same year, Kenya harvested an estimated 240,000 tons of potatoes, 770,000 tons of cassava, and 600,000 tons of sweet potatoes. Production of fruits and vegetables included plantains, 360,000 tons; pineapples, 270,000 tons; and bananas, 220,000 tons.

[23]ANIMAL HUSBANDRY

In 1992 there were an estimated 11 million head of cattle, 6 million sheep, and 7.5 million goats. Milk production is adequate for domestic needs; in 1992, fresh whole cow milk production amounted to 1,810,000 tons. Some 1,600,000 cattle were delivered for slaughter in 1992. The number of chickens was estimated at 25 million.

[24]FISHING

Commercial fishing takes place on the coast of the Indian Ocean and on the shores of lakes Baringo, Naivasha, Rudolf, and Victoria. In the Victoria region, commercial companies process and package filleted and frozen lake fish, which are sold throughout East Africa. Fish farms have been established in various parts of Kenya. Sportsmen who fish in the highland lakes and streams provide a small amount of government revenue in the form of licenses and fees. The total fish catch for 1991 was 198,637 tons. Freshwater fish, particularly from Lake Victoria, predominated; the inland catch was 191,218 tons.

[25]FORESTRY

Both hardwoods and softwoods are produced in Kenya. The chief hardwoods are musheragi, muiri, mukeo, camphor, and musaise. The chief softwoods are podo, cedar, and cypress. The supply of softwoods is adequate for local needs, both for building and other purposes. Wattle, grown mainly on small African plantations, provides the base of an important industry. Kenya maintains some 2,320,000 ha (5,733,000 acres) in indigenous forests, mangroves, and forest plantations, about 4% of the total land area. Roundwood production in 1991 was an estimated 36.8 nnsmillion cu m, of which 95% went for fuel. Recorded exports of forest products were $3.6 million in 1992. In 1975, production of the first Kenya-made paper began at the Pan-African Paper Mills in Webuye.

26MINING
Although mining has declined steadily in importance since the end of World War II, it still contributes to the economy. The main products are soda ash, limestone, soapstone, fluorspar, salt, and gemstones. A soda works at Magadi produced 245,000 tons in 1991. Fluorspar production was 100,000 tons; limestone products, 20,000 tons; and salt, 102,000 tons.

27ENERGY AND POWER
In the years immediately following World War II, Kenya met the increased demand for electricity mainly through the use of fuel oil to provide thermal power. Since 1950, hydroelectric capacity has been dramatically increased, and new hydroelectric schemes have been developed. Nevertheless, the power supply is still insufficient to meet demand, and about 5% of Kenya's electricity was imported in 1991 from Uganda's Owen Falls Dam project. Kenya's geothermal resources along the Great Rift Valley have been tapped by a plant near Lake Naivasha with a capacity in 1993 of 45 Mw. National generation of electricity in 1991 totaled 3,227 million kwh; installed capacity was 829 Mw, of which 73% was hydroelectric. From 1986 to 1990, Kenya's consumption of electricity rose by 23%. The 140-Mw Kiambere Dam on the Tana River was completed in 1987. The 110-Mw Turkwell Gorge project, also hydroelectric, was scheduled for completion in 1990.

Wood accounts for about 90% of total energy consumption. All of Kenya's crude petroleum is imported; petroleum products are refined at Mombasa both for export and for domestic use. Oil prospecting continues along the Indian Ocean coast and offshore, but prospects of a commercially viable strike seem remote after nearly 40 years of exploration.

28INDUSTRY
The manufacturing sector accounted for 10.9% of GDP in 1992 and had benefited from growth at between 3.7% and 6% in the nine preceding years. Import controls had hampered industry growth in the 1970s and 1980s, but in 1990 these were lifted for manufactured goods destined for export.

The manufactures Kenya produces are relatively diverse. Petroleum refining accounted for 10.9% of export earnings in 1990. The transformation of agricultural raw materials, particularly of coffee and tea, remains the principal industrial activity. Meat and fruit canning, wheat flour and cornmeal milling, and sugar refining are also important. Electronics production, vehicle assembly, publishing, and soda ash processing are all significant parts of the sector. Assembly of computer components began in 1987. Kenya also manufactures chemicals, textiles, ceramics, shoes, beer and soft drinks, cigarettes, soap, machinery, metal products, cement, aluminum, steel, glass, rubber, wood, cork, and leather goods. One quarter of Kenya's industrial sector is owned by UK investors; American investors are the next largest group.

The oil refinery in Mombasa, jointly owned by the government and major oil companies, has a capacity of 4.2 million tons a year and serves Kenya, Uganda, Rwanda, Burundi, and offshore islands. Refinery products include gasoline, jet/turbo fuel, light diesel oil and fuel oil.

Electrical power is drawn from five hydroelectric facilities in the Tama River Basin, from the Olkaria geothermal plant, and from oil-burning plants on the coast. The most recent of the Tama hydroelectric plants was inaugurated in 1988 and increased the Tama generating capacity to 715 Mw. Demand for electricity is expected to grow by 6% annually until the year 2000, according to the Kenya Power and Lighting Co.

29SCIENCE AND TECHNOLOGY
Notable scientific institutions in Kenya include the UNESCO Regional Office for Science and Technology for Africa, in Nairobi; coffee and tea research foundations; cotton, grasslands, and plant-breeding research stations; and numerous centers for veterinary research. Medical research focuses on the study of leprosy and tuberculosis. The National Council for Science and Technology, at Nairobi, advises the government on scientific matters. The University of Nairobi has colleges of agriculture and veterinary sciences, medicine, engineering, and biological and physical sciences, and Kenyatta University has a science faculty. Kenya Polytechnic, also in Nairobi, offers courses in mechanical, electrical, and electronic engineering and other technical fields. Moi University, in Eldoret, has faculties of forest resources and wildlife administration, science, and technology. Other institutions are Egerton University and Jomo Kenyatta University College of Agriculture and Technology, in Nairobi.

30DOMESTIC TRADE
Mombasa and Nairobi, the two principal distribution centers for imported goods, are linked by rail or highway to the towns in their immediate areas. The head offices of all the leading import and export firms, mining companies, and banks, not only for Kenya but also for East Africa as a whole, are in one or the other of these two cities. Warehousing facilities are extensive in both cities. Credit is supplied by commercial credit companies and commercial banks. Many consumer goods are price controlled.

Office and shop hours are generally from 8:30 AM to 5 PM, Monday–Friday, with lunchtime closing from 1 to 2 PM, and from 8:30 AM to 12:30 PM on Saturday. Normal banking hours are 9 AM to 2 PM, Monday–Friday, and 9 to 11 AM on the first and last Saturday of each month. The languages of business correspondence are English, Gujarati, and Swahili.

There are a number of advertising firms. Newspapers and trade magazines are the principal advertising media, but radio and cinema advertising are increasingly used.

31FOREIGN TRADE
Tea (26.4%) and coffee (18.1%) were Kenya's leading exports in 1990; petroleum products (10.9%) have emerged as the main industrial export in recent years. Trade balances have been unfavorable since 1970. Principal exports in 1988 (in millions of Kenya pounds) were as follows:

Unroasted coffee	244
Tea	185
Petroleum products	110
Canned pineapple	25
Cement	10
Sisal	11
Soda ash	18
Pyrethrum	11
Beans, peas, etc.	12
Hides and skins	26
Other exports	265
TOTAL	917

In 1988, the UK took 19.6% of Kenya's exports, while Germany purchased 12.1%. Of Kenya's imports, 18.9% came from the UK, 12.3% from Japan, and 11.4% from the United Arab Emirates.

Principal imports in 1988 (in millions of Kenya pounds) were as follows:

Crude petroleum	210.43
Industrial machinery	395.45
Iron and steel	120.64
Motor vehicles and chassis	138.06
Refined petroleum	30.02
Plastics	80.92
Pharmaceuticals	43.73
Fertilizers	49.18
Agricultural machinery	29.48
Wheat	10.00
Paper and paper products	36.22
Rice	2.71
Other imports	618.30
TOTAL	1,765.14

32 BALANCE OF PAYMENTS

Kenya registered net deficits on current accounts in every year from 1968 through 1985, with the sole exception of 1977. These shortfalls, caused by the nation's chronic trade imbalance, were generally covered by foreign capital inflows. In the past few years, Kenya has been extremely reliant on foreign assistance, its major source of foreign exchange. In 1990, the balance of payments deficit was $147 million, the largest in recent years, with a debt-service ratio of 34.6%. The donor community suspended aid to Kenya in December 1991, concerned that a proposed media complex would raise the debt service ratio and discourage more productive investments. The US cancelled Kenya's debt on condition that Kenya abandon the project. In 1991, tourism earnings stagnated due to the Gulf War, and unfavorable weather conditions damaged agricultural exports. In November 1991, the government began issuing foreign exchange certificates as a means of encouraging repatriation of foreign exchange held abroad by Kenyan residents.

In 1992 merchandise exports totaled $1,004 million and imports $1,594.5 million. The merchandise trade balance was $−590.5 million. The following table summarizes Kenya's balance of payments for 1991 and 1992 (in millions of US dollars):

	1991	1992
CURRENT ACCOUNT		
Goods, services, and income	−563.7	−380.2
Unrequited transfers	348.9	282.5
TOTALS	−214.8	−97.7
CAPITAL ACCOUNT		
Direct investment	18.8	6.4
Other long-term capital	117.9	−168.5
Other short-term capital	−40.2	−108.0
Reserves	43.9	256.9
TOTALS	140.4	−13.2
Errors and omissions	74.4	110.9
Total change in reserves	79.2	−232.0

33 BANKING AND SECURITIES

Kenya acquired its first separate currency on 14 September 1966, when the initial par value for the Kenya shilling was announced by the IMF. The new coin replaced, at par value, the East African shilling, previously issued for Kenya, Tanzania, and Uganda by the East African Currency Board, whose assets were divided by those nations following a June 1965 agreement.

The Central Bank of Kenya was established in May 1966, taking over the administration of exchange control. Because the Kenya shilling soon became the strongest currency in East Africa, a black market for it developed. A complete ban on the export or import of Kenyan currency was imposed in 1971 to discourage

speculation. The money supply in December 1993 as measured by M2, was Sh123,654 million.

Of the 29 commercial banks operating in Kenya in 1985, several folded during a banking crisis in 1986. In 1992 there were 15 commercial banks operating in Kenya. Three banks—the Kenya Commercial Bank, Barclays Bank of Kenya, and the Standard Bank—have branches in Nairobi and Mombasa and at least 25 other locales throughout the country. The Kenya Commercial Bank and the National Bank of Kenya are government owned. As of 31 December 1993, commercial banks held Sh20,870 million in reserves and Sh23,783 million in foreign currency.

Although they depend largely on the commercial sector for credit outlay, banks have started to turn to agriculture as an outlet. Land and agricultural banks provide financial assistance to farmers in the form of long-term loans for the discharge of onerous mortgages and the purchase of livestock, implements, fertilizer, and so forth. Short-term loans are granted for seasonal expenses.

The Nairobi Stock Exchange was founded in 1965 with six members.

34 INSURANCE

Insurance companies must be registered and licensed. Gross premiums in 1990 were US$8.4 or 2.5% of the GDP. Categories of compulsory insurance include motor third-party liability for bodily injuries and cargo insurance for imports.

35 PUBLIC FINANCE

The fiscal year extends from 1 July to 30 June. Increased public sector employment widened the budget deficit to 71% of GDP in fiscal 1991, but was limited to 2.9% of GDP in fiscal 1992.

The following table shows actual revenues and expenditures for 1990 and 1991 in millions of shillings.

	1990	1991
REVENUE AND GRANTS		
Tax revenue	39,518	48,682
Non-tax revenue	4,226	5,899
Capital revenue	14	10
Grants	3,761	5,060
TOTAL	47,519	59,651
EXPENDITURES & LENDING MINUS REPAYMENTS		
General public services	6,292	7,168
Defense	5,385	5,910
Public order and safety	3,246	3,692
Education	10,680	12,873
Health	2,886	3,458
Social security and welfare	52	70
Housing and community amenities	2,037	2,098
Recreation, cultural, and religious affairs	1,220	1,168
Economic affairs and services	11,134	11,542
Other expenditures	10,769	15,934
Adjustments	—	—
Lending minus repayments	1,230	1,493
TOTAL	54,931	65,406
Deficit/Surplus	−7,412	−5,755

36 TAXATION

Income tax rates on individuals are graduated, rising to a top marginal rate (in 1993) of 40%. The corporate tax rate was 35% for locally incorporated companies and 42.5% for branches of foreign companies. Intercompany dividends are taxed at 12.5%. The sales tax was increased in the 1980s to a general rate of 18%, with a levy of 75% on some items and up to 100% on color television sets and other items.

37CUSTOMS AND DUTIES

All imports require licenses. Priority items such as raw materials, capital goods, spare parts, agricultural equipment, and medicines are freely importable. Other goods receive specific allocations to limit the drain on foreign exchange; luxury goods and items already produced domestically have the lowest priority. Tariffs vary from 10–60% of c.i.f. value. Imports are also subject to a 5–75% value-added tax, and there are excise-taxes on alcohol and tobacco. In addition to the normal import duties, suspended duties may be imposed by proclamation, generally as a means of assisting local industries producing a particular commodity. There are export duties on coffee and tea, and all exports require licenses. Proceeds must be surrendered for local currency.

38FOREIGN INVESTMENT

In 1964, in the wake of independence, foreign investment in Kenya totaled к£29.2 million, down considerably from the 1955 level of к£54.5 million. In a move to reverse this trend, the government issued a white paper in 1965 welcoming foreign investment and encouraging joint ventures. Foreign investments in 1965 totaled $29,835,000, rising to $51,000,000 in 1966, and $52,440,000 in 1971.

The pace of investment accelerated during the 1970s, and by 1984 it was estimated that US investment alone had a value of $350 million. Private firms in the UK and US are important sources of investment, and they have been joined by companies of other nations. In 1987, tax treaties with the UK, Germany, Zambia, Denmark, Norway, and Sweden were in force. In the mid-1980s, however, private foreign investment became stagnant. Although every government-approved investment is guaranteed ultimate repatriation, delays in remittances of interest and dividends abroad have occurred because of Kenya's payments problems.

39ECONOMIC DEVELOPMENT

Central to Kenyan government planning is a continuing expansion of the level of exports and diversification of cash crops. Moreover, Kenya has sought the orderly introduction of large numbers of African farmers into former European agricultural areas.

With the goal of full economic independence, the government continues to pursue Africanization of the private sector, particularly in commerce.

Kenya continues to assist private industry by tariff structures that permit the import of raw materials duty-free or at low rates; allow rebates or suspension of customs duties under certain conditions; and establish protective customs barriers. The 1979-83 development plan, Kenya's fourth, had as its main objective the alleviation of rural poverty; a total expenditure of Sh80 billion was envisaged. The 1984–88 development plan also emphasized the rural sector in calling for an annual real GDP growth of 4.9%.

Kenya has long depended on external assistance for development financing, but the extent of that dependence has varied with domestic conditions. Whereas in the mid-1960s Kenya depended on external sources for 82% of its total development resources, by the early 1970s the proportion had fallen to only 45%. The late 1970s and 1980s brought renewed reliance on external loans, as the proportion of foreign financing needed to cover the annual government budget deficit rose from 28% in 1978/79 to 67% in 1981/82 and an estimated 89% in 1985/86.

Development in Kenya now depends on the private sector and on foreign and domestic investment as the parastatal sector is dismantled. Foreign exchange earnings are key to the sixth development plan (1989–1993). Increased agricultural and industrial productivity, job creation, and diversification are also goals of current development policy.

40SOCIAL DEVELOPMENT

Facilities for social welfare have been largely in the hands of private and voluntary organizations. There is no nationwide social insurance system, but in 1978 two-thirds of wage workers were enrolled in a new national pension scheme. The government assists many of the voluntary organizations financially.

The private and voluntary agencies are highly developed. There are societies that care for the blind, the deaf and mute, and the physically disabled, and voluntary organizations that care for the poor and destitute. Homes and hostels have been established throughout the country for the care of orphans, young offenders, and juvenile prostitutes.

In the mid-1980s there were more than 10,000 community development self-help projects. The National Youth Service, which engages in these activities, had 7,000 enrollees in 1985. A government Women's Bureau assists women's development programs.

In 1967, Kenya became the first sub-Saharan African country to launch a national family planning program. By 1985, 798 maternal and child health and family planning clinics had been established; attendance was 464,590 in 1984. In 1985, President Daniel arap Moi called on married couples to have no more than four children. Nevertheless, the birthrate and fertility rate remain extremely high, largely because of what surveys have revealed is the strong desire of Kenyan women to have large families; according to one detailed sampling, currently married Kenyan women in 1984 wanted at least six children, a fertility preference far above that of women in most other developing nations. The estimated fertility rate of 8.1—the average number of children a woman will bear—is the highest in the world. Women in Kenya are traditionally responsible for planting, harvesting, and weeding food crops, and for this purpose children (at least in the short run) constitute an economic asset. Other factors influencing Kenya's rapid population growth are the traditional view of children as a prestige asset, useful for the cementing of familial alliances through advantageous marriages; tribal rivalries that have made members of each group fearful that population limitation will result in a diminution of its relative power and prestige; restriction of women's economic horizons and legal rights within marriage; and the widespread practice of polygamy. In addition, nearly 500,000 refugees from Ethiopia, Somalia and Sudam burden the welfare services of the state and add to the lawlessness of the border regions. Abortion is available for broadly defined health reasons.

41HEALTH

The National Hospital Insurance Fund is the most important health insurance program in Kenya. Membership is compulsory for all civil servants. As of 1990, contribution levels proved insufficient to meet hospital costs, and the government is planning to broker private health insurance policies. The government is continually improving and upgrading existing health facilities and opening new ones. Kenya produces cotton wadding domestically, but all other medical equipment and supplies are imported. High quality private practitioners require sophisticated medical equipment, but the public sector requires less expensive equipment. Private health institutions account for 60% of total medical equipment and supplies (import value). Kenya also has a well-developed pharmaceutical industry that can produce most medicaitons recommended by the WHO.

The government is attempting to reduce malnutrition and combat deficiency diseases. Among Kenya's major health problems are tuberculosis and protein deficiency, the latter especially among young children. In 1990, there were approximately 140 reported cases of tuberculosis per 100,000 people. Although the incidence of malaria has been reduced, it still accounted for over 20% of outpatient deaths in 1990. Water supply, sanitation, bilharzia, and sleeping sickness also pose major problems.

Schistosomiasis is endemic to some areas. In 1991, only 49% of the population had access to safe water, and only 43% had adequate sanitation. Immunization rates for 1992 for children up to one year old were high: tuberculosis (93%); diphtheria, pertussis, and tetanus (85%); polio (85%); and measles (81%).

There was a birth rate of 43.7 per 1,000 people in 1993, with only 27% of married women (ages 15 to 49) using contraception. There were 1,111,000 births in 1992, with an average life expectancy of 59 years. Infant mortality in 1992 was 51 per 1,000 live births, and the general mortality rate was 10.3 per 1,000 people in 1993. In 1991 and 1992, there were about 1,000 war-related deaths due to ethnic violence.

In 1990, about 77% of the population had access to health care services. In that year, Kenya had 1,063 physicians (1 for 10,130 people), 134 dentists, 118 pharmacists, and 2,692 nurses. In 1987, there were 254 hospitals, 294 health centers, and 1,553 health subcenters. There are 32,534 hospital beds (1.7 hospital beds per 1,000 people). Each government hospital has an independent budget. Public funding accounts for half the total health care expenditures ($375 million in 1990). The government is also encouraging the development of the private health care sector through tax incentives as well as other plans.

42HOUSING

Housing in rural areas is privately owned. Most of these homes, built with traditional materials, deteriorate in a relatively short time; an increasing number of people now build their homes with more permanent materials. The central government is responsible for all housing projects and works closely with local authorities. Many new housing projects have been undertaken with the financial aid of the National Housing Corp., which completed 1,009 units in 1985. According to the latest information for 1980–88, total housing stock stood at 3,470,000, with 6.1 people per dwelling.

43EDUCATION

Although education is not compulsory, primary education is free. Children start school at the age of five or six and spend eight years at primary school; five years at secondary school; and a further four years at the university. In 1990, there were 15,196 primary schools with 5,392,319 students. In general secondary schools, there were 614,161 students and teacher training programs had 17,914 students the same year. In 1990, there were 15,196 primary schools with 5,392,319 students. In general secondary schools, there were 614,161 students, and teacher training programs had 17,914 students. In the same year, adult literacy rate was 69%, an estimated 79.8% for men and 58.5% for women.

There are four main universities in Kenya. Kenyatta University was founded in 1972 and is located at Nairobi. The University of Nairobi was founded in 1956 as the Royal Technical College of East Africa. The Moi University was founded in 1984 at Eldoret. The Egerton University, located at Njoro, was founded in 1939. The language of instruction in all the universities is English. There were 4,392 teaching staff and 35,421 students at universities and equivalent institutions in 1990,

44LIBRARIES AND MUSEUMS

The Kenya National Library Service, founded in 1967 and located in Nairobi, maintains 15 branches and has 603,000 volumes. The largest public library is the McMillan Memorial Library, formerly a private institution, which was taken over by the Nairobi City Council in 1962; it contained 165,000 volumes in 1986, including a collection of Africana, and had two branches. The libraries of the University of Nairobi, with 400,000 volumes, are the best supported in Kenya.

The National Museum in Nairobi and the Ft. Jesus Museum in Mombasa are the largest in Kenya. There are numerous local museums.

45MEDIA

The Ministry of Transport and Communications is responsible for telecommunications. There were 357,251 telephones in 1991. The Voice of Kenya, broadcasting in English, Swahili, and local languages, operates one radio station and one television channel. In 1990, Channel 62, an independently owned television station, made its debut. It was estimated in 1991 that Kenya had 2.1 million radio receivers and 234,000 television sets.

In 1991, Kenya had five daily newspapers, all published in Nairobi. *The Nation*, founded in 1960, had a daily circulation of 178,700; the *Taifa Leo*, a Swahili newspaper, 48,600; the *Standard* (established in 1902), 55,000; the *Kenya Times*, 30,000; and the *Kenya Leo*, 40,000. While there is no formal censorship, the press is sometimes subject to harassment from public officials who have been treated unfavorably.

46ORGANIZATIONS

Voluntary societies are numerous. Some are affiliated with parent bodies in the UK; a few, such as the Rotary Club, the Round Table, and the Lions Club, are affiliated internationally. African women's clubs, called Maendeleo ya Wanawake, have been organized throughout Kenya. The Kenya National Chamber of Commerce and Industry, founded in 1965, had 46 local branches in 1993; its headquarters are in Nairobi.

47TOURISM, TRAVEL, AND RECREATION

Since Kenya attained independence, tourism has become the leading source of foreign exchange revenue. In 1991, 817,550 tourists visited Kenya, 57% from Europe and 27% from Africa. There were 26,466 hotel beds with a 59% occupancy rate, and tourism receipts amounted to US$424 million.

Accommodation in the form of lodges and campsites is available in the more remote areas. Photo safaris to the 19 national parks and game preserves are the chief attraction. The largest game preserve is Tsavo National Park, home of the world's greatest concentration of elephants; covering an area of about 21,343 sq km (8,241 sq mi), it is one of the world's largest wildlife sanctuaries. Nairobi has a professional repertory theater and a National Theater; the capital hosts a Festival of African music in July. Other attractions include the mosques of Mombasa, the spectacular scenery of the Great Rift Valley, the coffee plantations at Thika, the world-renowned Tree Hotels, and the view of snowcapped Mt. Kilimanjaro, across the border in Tanzania.

Kenyan track stars have excelled in international competition, especially distance running. Kenyans won a total of six gold medals in track at the 1968, 1972, and 1984 Olympic Games.

Tourists from most countries must have both a passport and a visa, but the visa requirement is waived for citizens of most Commonwealth countries (other than British citizens of Asian origin) and certain other nations. On arrival, those without visas must apply for a tourist permit from an immigration officer at the port of entry. Precautions against malaria, yellow fever, poliomyelitis, typhoid, and hepatitis are advisable for those traveling in the hinterland.

48FAMOUS KENYANS

The leading African figure in the modern history of Kenya was Jomo Kenyatta (1893?–1978). From the 1920s to the 1970s he was in the forefront of African nationalism. Imprisoned and restricted during the Mau Mau revolt for his alleged role in its organization, he was released in August 1961 and was president of independent Kenya from 1964 until his death. Another dominant African personality was Tom Mboya (1930–69), who commanded an international reputation as a political and labor leader. Oginga Odinga (b.1911), usually at odds with the ruling establishment, was vice-president from 1964 to 1966. Daniel arap Moi (b.1924), a son of poor farmers, was vice-president for 11 years before succeeding Kenyatta as president in 1978.

Sir Michael Blundell (b.1907), a leader of the European community after World War II, came to be identified with those who sought to create a nonracial political society; he was a director of Barclays Bank of Kenya from 1968 to 1981. Richard Leakey (b.1944) is a leading paleoanthropologist.

[49] DEPENDENCIES
Kenya has no territories or colonies.

[50] BIBLIOGRAPHY

American University. *Area Handbook for Kenya.* 3d ed. Washington D.C.: Government Printing Office, 1983.

Arnold, Gay. *Modern Kenya.* New York: Longman, 1981.

Barkan, Joel D., and John J. Okumu. *Politics and Public Policy in Kenya and Tanzania.* Rev. ed. New York: Praeger, 1984.

Brett, E. A. *Colonialism and Underdevelopment in East Africa, 1919–1939.* New York: Nok Press, 1973.

Chenevix Trench, Charles. *Men who Ruled Kenya: The Kenya Administration, 1892–1963.* New York: Radcliffe Press, 1993.

Clough, Marshall S. *Fighting Two Sides: Kenyan Chiefs and Politicians, 1918–1940.* Niwot, Colo.: University Press of Colorado, 1990.

Cole, Sonia. *The Prehistory of East Africa.* New York: Macmillan, 1963.

Collier, Paul, and Lal Deepak. *Labour and Poverty in Kenya, 1900–80.* New York: Oxford University Press, 1985.

Dinesen, Isak. *Out of Africa.* New York: Random House, 1972.

Gertzel, Cherry. *The Politics of Independent Kenya, 1963–68.* Evanston, Ill.: Northwestern University Press, 1970.

Harbeson, John W. *Nation-Building in Kenya: The Role of Land Reform.* Evanston, Ill.: Northwestern University Press, 1973.

Hazlewood, Arthur. *Education, Work, and Pay in East Africa.* New York: Oxford University Press, 1989.

Hazlewood, Arthur. *The Economy of Kenya: The Kenyatta Era.* New York: Oxford University Press, 1979.

Heyer, Judith. *Agricultural Development in Kenya.* New York: Oxford University Press, 1977.

Kenya in Pictures. Minneapolis: Lerner, 1988.

Kenyatta, Jomo. *Suffering without Bitterness: The Founding of the Kenya Nation.* Nairobi: East African Publishing House, 1968.

Langdon, Steven W. *Multinational Corporations in the Political Economy of Kenya.* New York: St. Martin's, 1981.

Lee, Christopher. *Land and Class in Kenya.* Toronto: University of Toronto Press, 1984.

Miller, Norman N. and Roger Yeager. *Kenya: The Quest for Prosperity.* 2d ed. Boulder, Colo.: Westview Press, 1994.

Murray-Brown, Jeremy. *Kenyatta.* London: Allen & Unwin, 1979.

Ogot, Bethwell. *Historical Dictionary of Kenya.* Metuchen, N.J.: Scarecrow, 1981.

Pavitt, Nigel. *Kenya, the First Explorers.* New York: St. Martin's, 1989.

Spear, T. *Kenya's Past: An Introduction to Historical Materials in Africa.* New York: Longman, 1981.

Swainson, Nicola. *The Development of Corporate Capitalism in Kenya, 1918–1977.* Berkeley: University of California Press, 1980.

Themes in Kenyan History. Athens: Ohio University Press, 1990.

Throup, David. *Economic & Social Origins of Mau Mau 1945–53.* Athens: Ohio University Press, 1988.

Widner, Jennifer A. *The Rise of a Party-state in Kenya: From "Harambee" to "Nyayo!".* Berkeley: University of California, 1992.

Zwanenberg, R. M. van, and Anne King. *An Economic History of Kenya and Uganda, 1800–1970.* Atlantic Highlands, N.J.: Humanities Press, 1975.

LESOTHO

Kingdom of Lesotho
Muso oa Lesotho

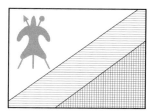

CAPITAL: Maseru.

FLAG: The flag is divided diagonally from the lower hoist side corner; the upper half is white bearing the brown silhouette of a large shield with crossed spear and club; the lower half is a diagonal blue band with a green triangle in the corner.

ANTHEM: *Lesotho Fatse La Bo-nata Rona (Lesotho, the Country of Our Fathers).*

MONETARY UNIT: Lesotho is part of the South African monetary area; the maloti of 100 lisente, introduced in 1980, is on a par with the South African rand (R), which is also legal tender. There are coins of 1, 2, 5, 10, 25, and 50 lisente, and notes of 2, 5, 10, 20, and 50 maloti (M). M1 = $0.2874 (or $1 = 3.4795).

WEIGHTS AND MEASURES: British and metric weights and measures are in general use.

HOLIDAYS: New Year's Day, 1 January; Moshoeshoe's Day, 12 March; Family Day, 1st Monday in July; King's Birthday, 17 July; Independence Day, 4 October; National Sports Day, 6 October; Christmas, 25 December; Boxing Day, 26 December. Movable Christian holidays include Good Friday, Easter Monday, and Ascension.

TIME: 2 PM = noon GMT.

¹LOCATION, SIZE, AND EXTENT

Lesotho is an enclave within the Republic of South Africa, with an area of 30,350 sq km (11,718 sq mi), extending 248 km (154 mi) NNE–SSW and 181 km (112 mi) ESE–WNW. Comparatively, the area occupied by Lesotho is slightly larger than the state of Maryland.

It is bordered on the E by Natal, on the S by Cape Province, and on the W and N by the Orange Free State, with a total boundary length of 909 km (565 mi). Lesotho claims that Basotho lands now part of South Africa were unjustly taken by force in the 19th century.

Lesotho's capital city, Maseru, is located on the country's northwest border.

²TOPOGRAPHY

Three distinct geographical regions, demarcated by ascending altitude, extend approximately north-south across Lesotho. The western quarter of the country is a plateau averaging 1,500 to 1,850 m (4,900–6,100 ft). The soil of this zone is derived from sandstone and, particularly in the westernmost region, is poor and badly eroded. The remainder of the country is highland. A zone of rolling foothills, ranging from 1,800 to 2,100 m (5,900–6,900 ft), forms the border between the lowlands and the mountains in the east.

The Drakensberg Range forms the entire eastern and southeastern border. A spur of this range, the Maluti Mountains, runs north and south. Where it joins the Drakensberg Range there is a high plateau between 2,700 and 3,200 m (8,900–10,500 ft) in elevation. The highest point is Thabana Ntlenyana, 3,482 m (11,425 ft), in the east. The rich volcanic soils of the foothills and mountains are some of the best in the country.

The sources of two of the principal rivers of South Africa, the Orange and the Tugela, are in these mountains. Tributaries of the Caledon River, which forms the country's western border, also rise here. The Orange and Caledon rivers, together with their tributaries, drain more than 90% of the country.

³CLIMATE

Temperatures vary widely from one geographical zone to another, and frequently within zones, depending on the altitude. In the lowlands, temperatures reach 32°C(90°F) or more in the summer and rarely fall below −7°C (19°F) in the winter. The range in the highlands is greater; temperatures sometimes fall below -18°C (0°F), and frost and hail are frequent hazards. Rainfall, which is mostly concentrated in the months from October to April, averages 71 cm (28 in) annually, varying from 191 cm (75 in) in parts of the mountains to as little as 60 cm (24 in) in the lowlands. Most of the rainwater is lost through runoff, and droughts are common.

⁴FLORA AND FAUNA

Grass is the natural vegetation in this virtually treeless country. The high plateau is covered with montane or subalpine grassland. Red oat grass forms a dry carpet in much of the Drakensberg foothill region. The country's small size, high elevation, and limited range of habitats restrict the variety of fauna, of which, as of 1982, no comprehensive survey had been taken. The African lammergeier, a bird common in the mountains of Ethiopia but nowhere else in Africa, and the bald ibis, both of which are near extinction, are found in small numbers in the Drakensberg Range.

⁵ENVIRONMENT

Much of the country has become denuded of its natural grass cover through uncontrolled grazing and rushing surface water. More than 3.5 million trees, mostly eucalyptus, have been planted as part of a gully control program, and for production of fuel and poles.

Unlike neighboring South Africa, Lesotho is not rich in game and other wildlife. The famous Basuto pony, of almost pure Arabian stock, reached its peak of quality and quantity around the turn of the century. After suffering a decline because of ruinous trading practices, overstocking, overgrazing, disease, and drought, the pony has begun to make a comeback through a selective breeding program and improved feeding methods. Other vanishing species, like the wildebeest and blesbok, have been reintroduced in areas where they formerly were numerous. Among the agencies with environmental responsibility is the National Environmental Secretariat of the Prime Minister's Office.

⁶POPULATION

In 1994, the population of Lesotho was estimated at 1,943,736. A population of 2,233,000 was projected for the year 2000, assuming a crude birthrate of 32.9 per 1,000 population, a crude death rate of 8.5, and a net natural increase of 24.4 during 1995–2000. Some 70% of the total population lives in the fertile lowlands, where the land can be most readily cultivated; the rest is scattered in the foothills and the mountains. The population density in 1994 was 64 per sq km (166 per sq mi). Maseru, the capital city, has an estimated population of 170,000 in 1990; other large towns are Teyateyaneng and Leribe.

⁷MIGRATION

In 1992 about 38% of the Lesothan male labor force of some 450,000 were working in the mines, homes, and farms in the Republic of South Africa. In 1991 there were 153,460 people living in South Africa who had been born in Lesotho. At the end of 1992, Lesotho had an estimated 100 registered South African exiles.

⁸ETHNIC GROUPS

Lesotho is ethnically homogeneous. At least 93% of the people are of Basotho origin, and 6% are Nguni. In 1984 there were about 1,600 whites and 800 Asians in Lesotho.

⁹LANGUAGES

The Sesotho language is spoken by virtually all the indigenous population. English shares with Sesotho the position of official language.

¹⁰RELIGIONS

Christian missions have long been active in Lesotho. As a result, according to 1993 estimates, some 90% of the population is Christian—about 37.8% Roman Catholic. Church membership was estimated earlier (1980) at 29.8% Lesotho Evangelical, 8% Anglican, and 7% other denominations. The remainder of the indigenous population, and probably many of its Christians as well, follow African traditional religions.

¹¹TRANSPORTATION

In 1991 there were 572 km (355 mi) of tarred roads linking Maseru with Leribe and Butha-buthe to the northeast, and Mafeteng and Mohales Hoek to the southwest. There were also 2,337 km (1,452 mi) of gravel, crushed stone, or stabilized soil roads. There were 5,129 passenger cars and 11,962 trucks and buses in 1982. A 1.6-km (1-mi) South African railway connects Maseru's industrial park to the Bloemfontein-Natal line, providing a valuable freight link to the Republic.

Lesotho Airways and South African Airways maintain scheduled passenger service between Johannesburg and a new international airport 19 km (12 mi) outside of Maseru. Lesotho Airways also has regular service to Swaziland, Zimbabwe, and Mozambique, and to 28 domestic airstrips. It carried an estimated 34,300 passengers in 1991/92. Air taxis and chartered planes serve airstrips at Maseru and other centers.

¹²HISTORY

What is now Lesotho was inhabited by hunter-gatherers, called the San Bushmen by the whites, until about 1600, when refugees from Bantu tribal wars began arriving. In 1818, Moshoeshoe, a minor chief of a northern tribe in what was to become Basutoland, brought together the survivors of the devastating Zulu and Matabele raids and founded the Basotho nation. During the early days of its existence, the Basotho also had to contend with incursions by Boers from the Orange Free State. Moshoeshoe sought UK protection, but not before much land had been lost to white settlers. His urgent appeals for assistance went unheeded until 1868, when Basutoland became a crown protectorate. Moshoeshoe died in 1870. The following year, Basutoland was annexed to the Cape Colony, over the protests of both Basotho and Boer leaders. In 1880, the so-called Gun War broke out between the Basotho and the Boers over the attempt to disarm the Basotho in accordance with the provisions of the Cape Peace Preservation Act of 1878. A high point in Basotho history was the successful resistance waged against the Cape's forces.

In 1884, Basutoland was returned to UK administration under a policy of indirect rule. Local government was introduced in 1910 with the creation of the Basutoland Council, an advisory body composed of the British resident commissioner, the paramount chief, and 99 appointed Basotho members. In effect, for the next 50 years the chiefs were allowed to govern. Under a new constitution that became effective in 1960, an indirectly elected legislative body, the Basutoland National Council, was created.

A constitutional conference held in London in 1964 approved the recommendations for a preindependence constitution that had been made by a constitutional commission. The new constitution went into effect on 30 April 1965, following the general election. The resident commissioner became the British government representative, retaining powers for defense, external affairs, internal security, and the public service.

In April 1966, a conflict arose in parliament between the government and the opposition over Prime Minister Leabua Jonathan's motion requesting Britain to set a date for independence. To forestall passage of the motion, Paramount Chief Moshoeshoe II replaced 5 of his 11 senatorial appointees with 5 opponents of the government. The High Court subsequently invalidated that action, declaring that his right to appoint 11 senators did not entail the right of dismissal. The Senate and National Assembly eventually passed the independence motion, the latter by a vote of 32 to 28, but the dispute foreshadowed a constitutional crisis that was not conclusively resolved at independence. The final independence conference was held in June 1966. Charging that the UK was granting independence to a minority government, and demanding a more significant role for the paramount chief, delegates representing the opposition withdrew. Moshoeshoe II himself declined to sign the final accord.

Independence

The UK granted independence to the newly named Kingdom of Lesotho on 4 October 1966; Moshoeshoe II was proclaimed king on that date. The first general election following the attainment of independence was held in January 1970. When it appeared that the ruling party, the Basotho National Party (BNP), would be defeated, Prime Minister Jonathan, its leader, declared a state of emergency and suspended the constitution. The Basotho Congress Party (BCP), led by Ntsu Mokhehle, claimed that it had won 33 seats to the BNP's 23. Leabua Jonathan admitted he had lost the election but nevertheless arrested the opposition leaders. The unrest, he said, was due to Communist influence, and since the majority of the people were behind him he would suspend the constitution and hold new elections later. King Moshoeshoe II was placed under house arrest, and in April 1970 the Netherlands gave him asylum. He was permitted to return in December.

Scattered attacks on police posts occurred in January 1974 in an alleged attempt by supporters of the BCP to overthrow the government of the ruling BNP. The abortive coup d'etat resulted in the arrest, killing, imprisonment, or exile of many people. In

March 1975, 15 BCP followers were found guilty of high treason. The struggle against the Jonathan government continued through the late 1970s and early 1980s, with the Lesotho Liberation Army (LLA), the military arm of the BCP in exile, claiming responsibility for periodic bombings in Maseru, ambushes of government officials, and attacks on police stations. The Lesotho government charged that South Africa was allowing the LLA to use its territory as a base of operations.

Relations with South Africa deteriorated after that nation granted independence in 1976 to the Bantu homeland of Transkei, on Lesotho's southeastern border. When Lesotho (like all other nations except South Africa) declined to recognize Transkei, the Transkeian authorities closed the border with Lesotho, which also angered South Africa by harboring members of the banned African National Congress (ANC), an exiled South African insurgent group. On 9 December 1982, South African troops raided private residences of alleged ANC members in Maseru; 42 persons were killed, including at least 12 Lesotho citizens. In the early 1980s, South Africa used economic pressures against Lesotho.

Parliamentary elections scheduled for August 1985 by the Jonathan government were called off because all five opposition parties refused to take part, charging that the voters' roll was fraudulent. Later that year, South Africa stepped up its destabilization activities, conducting a commando raid and aiding anti-government elements. On 1 January 1986, South Africa imposed a near-total blockade of Lesotho that resulted in severe shortages of food and essential supplies. On 20 January, a military coup led by Maj. Gen. Justin Metsing Lekhanya overthrew the government. All executive and legislative powers were vested in the king, acting on the advice of a six-man military council. On 25 January, a number of ANC members and sympathizers were flown from Lesotho to Zambia, whereupon South Africa ended its blockade of the country. All political activity was banned on 27 March.

There was widespread skepticism about the military government and its links to Pretoria, and agitation to return to civilian rule. In 1990, Lekhanya had Moshoeshoe II exiled (for a second time) after the king refused to agree to the dismissal of several senior officers. In November 1990, a new law was announced providing for a constitutional monarchy but barring Moshoeshoe from the throne. Later that month, Moshoeshoe's son (King Letsie III), was elected king by an assembly of chiefs.

In April 1991, rebel army officers staged a bloodless coup, forcing Lekhanya to resign. He was succeeded by Colonel Elias Ramaema as leader of a military junta. In July, 1992, the king was allowed to return to a hero's welcome.

Multiparty elections were scheduled for 28 November 1992, but they were postponed until 1993 because of delays in delimiting parliamentary constituencies. Finally, on 27 March 1993, in the first democratic elections in 23 years, the Basotho Congress Party, the major opposition party, won all 65 seats in the Assembly. The BCP formed a government under Prime Minister Dr. Ntsu Mokhehle. The upper house of the legislature, the Senate, is composed of the 22 principal chiefs and 11 appointed members chosen by the Council of State. The BCP offered to nominate four BNP members but only one opposition politician accepted. Several cabinet memebers were appointed from opposition ranks.

On 25 January 1994, army troops mutinied in Maseru after the government refused their demands for a 100% pay increase. Prime Minister Mokhehle requested military assistance from South Africa, but that request was denied. After three weeks of sporadic fighting, the two factions within the military agreed to a Commonwealth-brokered deal for negotiations with the government.

13 GOVERNMENT

According to the 1965 constitution and its 1993 replacement, the Kingdom of Lesotho is a monarchy with a bicameral parliament

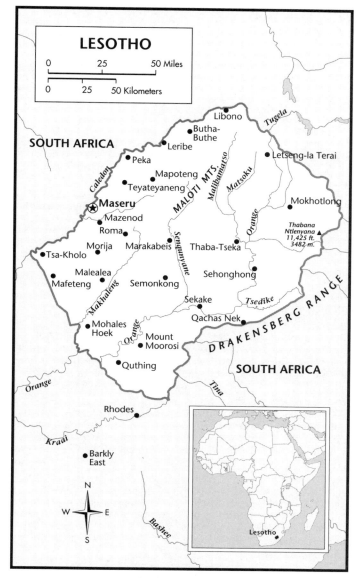

LOCATION: 28°35' to 30°40's; 27° to 29°30'E.

consisting of a National Assembly of 65 members elected for three-year terms, and a Senate with 33 members, including 22 chiefs and 11 others appointed by the chief of state.

Until 1993 the king was official chief of state (motlotlehi), and was designated by the College of Chiefs, according to Basotho custom. The prime minister (head of government) was appointed by the king and was a member of the majority party in the National Assembly. The cabinet was also appointed by the king, in accordance with advice of the prime minister, from among members of both houses of parliament. The 1993 constitution however, clearly defines the king's role as ceremonial.

Prime Minister Leabua Jonathan ruled by decree after he suspended the constitution in 1970. An appointive Interim National Assembly, established in 1973, included representatives of Lesotho's political parties but was largely the instrument of the BNP. A six-man military council assumed governmental powers in January 1986, to be superseded by the elected government in April 1993. Today the Cabinet is apointed by the prime minister who is also the leader of the majority party in the National Assembly.

[14]POLITICAL PARTIES

Lesotho's government party, the Basotho National Party (BNP), formerly the Basutoland National Party, was founded in 1959 and was in the forefront of Lesotho's independence drive. The BNP long stood for maintaining diplomatic relations with South Africa and for a cautious approach to cooperation with other African states, in an attitude of "choose our friends but live with our neighbors." However, in the 1970s and early 1980s, the BNP played a more active role in opposing apartheid.

The Basotho Congress Party (BCP), founded in 1952 and formerly known as the Basutoland African Congress, is an outspoken Pan-Africanist party. The first party to demand independence, it subsequently opposed the "premature" granting of independence to a minority government. The third major party is the Marematlou Freedom Party (MFP). This party was formed in 1965 by the merger of two parties that had supported the chieftaincy.

In the general election held on 29 April 1965, the BNP won 31 seats, the BCP 25 seats, and the MFP 4 seats in the National Assembly. Chief Jonathan was himself defeated in the election, and Sekhonyana Maseribane was appointed prime minister. Chief Jonathan won a by-election on 1 June and assumed the office of prime minister. The two opposition parties, which together had polled 56.2% of the vote to 41.6% for the BNP (with 2.2% of the vote going to others), in an election in which only 62% of those eligible had voted, joined forces to protest Britain's granting of independence to a minority government. They also called for a more even distribution of executive power between the prime minister and the chief of state, and appealed to the UN, the Commonwealth, and the OAU in an unsuccessful bid to have the independence agreement rescinded.

The BCP claimed it had won 33 seats in the 60-seat National Assembly in the January 1970 general elections; the BNP won 23 seats, and the ballots for 4 seats had not been counted. Confusion over the outcome of the 1970 election (in which the United Democratic Party and the Communist Party participated but won no seats) resulted in suspension of the constitution by Prime Minister Jonathan, and political activities of opposition parties were subsequently restricted. Prime Minister Jonathan appointed two members of opposition parties to his cabinet in November 1975. The BCP then split into two factions: members of one accepted government posts, while leaders of the other organized an armed insurgency in exile.

The March 1993 election was contested by more than a dozen parties, but the chief vote getters were the BCP, still headed by Dr. Mokhehle, and the BNP, led by Evaristus Sekhonyana. Among the others are the Marematlou Freedom Party (MFP), the United Democratic Party (UDP), and the Communist Party of Lesotho (CPL). The BCP holds all elected seats in the National Assembly.

[15]LOCAL GOVERNMENT

There are 10 districts, each headed by a centrally appointed district administrator. District councils, established in 1944, were abolished in 1966. Each district is subdivided into wards, most of them presided over by hereditary chiefs allied to the royal family. During the period of military rule, each district was headed by a district secretary and a district military officer appointed by the central government and the defense force, respectively.

[16]JUDICIAL SYSTEM

The judicial system consists of the High Court, the Court of Appeal, subordinate courts, and the Judicial Service Commission (JSC). The members of the High Court are the chief justice, who is appointed by the chief of state, acting on the advice of the prime minister, and an unspecified number of puisne judges appointed by the chief of state, acting on the advice of the JSC. The Court of Appeal is headed by a president, appointed by the chief of state, acting on the advice of the prime minister, and includes an unspecified number of justices of appeal, appointed by the chief of state, acting on the advice of the JSC. Parliament has the power of establishing subordinate courts and courts-martial. The High Court has unlimited original jurisdiction over civil and criminal matters, as well as appellate jurisdiction from subordinate courts. These subordinate courts, comprising resident magistrate's courts, judicial commissioner's courts, and central and local courts, administer statute laws, while chiefs administer customary and tribal laws. Roman-Dutch law applies. There is no trial by jury.

The Parliament is now considering the establishment of a law reform commission to review all laws for consistency with the 1993 Constitution.

[17]ARMED FORCES

A 2000-member army has 8 combat companies with US and UK weapons and one air squadron.

[18]INTERNATIONAL COOPERATION

Lesotho became a UN member on 17 October 1966 and participates in ECA and all the nonregional specialized agencies except IAEA, IMO, and WIPO. A Commonwealth member, Lesotho also takes part in the African Development Bank, G-77, and OAU. The nation is a de facto participant in GATT, as well as a signatory to the Law of the Sea. Lesotho is joined in a customs union with South Africa, Botswana, and Swaziland. The country's close relationship with South Africa is a major factor in its economic survival. Lesotho is a signatory to the Lomé Convention and a member of the nine-nation Southern African Development Coordinating Conference.

[19]ECONOMY

Lesotho is an agricultural country, with modest industrial, tourism and labor-remittance incomes. Its economic policy is closely tied to that of South Africa. Political reforms in South Africa and the involvement of the IMF have created new opportunities for the Lesotho economy.

[20]INCOME

In 1992 Lesotho's GNP was $1,090 million at current prices, or $590 per capita. For the period 1985–92 the average inflation rate was 13.5%, resulting in a real growth rate in per capita GNP of 0.8%.

Remittances from Lesotho's migrant labor force working in South Africa constitute a key source of Lesotho's income. In 1992, 40% of Lesotho's male work force worked in South African coal and gold mines, and their remittances represented 40% of GDP (1990).

The Lesotho government has a forced-savings program built around these remittances: 15% is inaccessible to the worker's family until the worker's return from the mines. Lesotho's dependence on South African labor policy has forced renewed interest in alternative labor in Lesotho itself.

In 1992 the GDP was $677 million in current US dollars. Agriculture, hunting, forestry, and fishing contributed 17% to GDP; manufacturing, 11%; electricity, gas, and water, 2%; construction, 19%; wholesale and retail trade, 8%; transport, storage, and communication, 3%; finance, insurance, real estate, and business services, 11%; community, social, and personal services, 1%; and other sources 28%.

[21]LABOR

About 70% of the entire Basotho population dwelling in Lesotho is engaged in agriculture and livestock raising. About 39% of the male labor force works in South Africa. The estimated unemployment rate in 1992 was 35%.

Trade unions are highly organized in the small sector of the work force that they cover. The Lesotho Labor Congress is the dominant labor association.

22AGRICULTURE

In 1992, about 11% of GDP came from agriculture. Crop production in Lesotho is a high-risk, low-yield activity due to poor soil quality and a harsh climate. All land is held in trust for the Basotho nation by the king and may not be alienated. The local chiefs allocate farmland to individuals, and user rights are generally available to married males; nevertheless, one out of seven households is landless. A 1979 act increases security of tenure by recording rights of inheritance and allowing mortgaging and subletting of land. The average landholding per family head is 1.9 ha (4.7 acres).

Only 11.2% of Lesotho's land area is arable, but less than 1% has high potential. Most cultivated land is in the western lowlands. The principal food crop is corn. Main agricultural production in 1992 included (in tons) corn, 61,000; sorghum, 10,000; wheat, 15,000; peas, 4,000; and beans, 3,000. The country suffered from recurrent drought conditions in the 1980s. Droughts in 1991 and 1992 reduced agricultural outputs by 26% and 21%, respectively.

Lesotho has one of the most advanced soil conservation programs in Africa. Terracing, grass stripping, and the construction of dams and irrigation canals are widely employed to cope with the severe erosion problems.

23ANIMAL HUSBANDRY

The raising of livestock is the principal economic undertaking in Lesotho. Grazing rights on all noncultivated land are communal, and no limits are placed on the number of livestock permitted to graze an area. Lesotho's main exports are wool and mohair; in general, however, the quality of the livestock is poor and yields are low. In 1992 there were an estimated 1.4 million sheep, 1 million goats, 536,000 head of cattle, 130,000 donkeys and mules, 122,000 horses, 75,000 hogs, and 1 million chickens.

A number of livestock improvement centers have been established, and Merino rams and Angora bucks have been imported from South Africa for breeding purposes. Cattle, sheep, and goats are exported on the hoof. Hides and skins, usually from animals that have died of starvation or disease or have been slaughtered for human consumption, are also exported.

24FISHING

Fishing has not yet been popularized, although the Malutsenyane River is one of the best natural trout-fishing grounds in Africa. There is virtually no commercial fishing. In 1991, four-fifths of the total catch consisted of 20 tons of carp.

25FORESTRY

Lesotho is almost devoid of natural woodland. Trees have been planted in conjunction with soil conservation programs. Roundwood production in 1991 was estimated at 631,000 cu m, all nonconiferous logs for fuel.

26MINING

Geological surveys have revealed a limited variety of exploitable mineral resources. Some alluvial diamonds have been found north of Mokhotlong, where individual and syndicate concession holders are prospecting. In 1968, the government awarded a concession to De Beers Consolidated Mines to mine fields in the Leribe District, and the government later received a 25% equity share. A diamond mine at Letseng-la-Terai, developed at a cost of R23 million, opened in 1977; in 1980, 53,714 carats were produced, but the mine was closed two years later. Exploration for other minerals, such as iron, coal, and uranium, continues. Mineral

production in 1991 was limited to small amounts of crushed stone, sand and gravel, clay, and diamonds.

27ENERGY AND POWER

About 80% of Lesotho's electrical power is imported from South Africa, at an annual cost of $8 million. On 24 October 1986, an agreement was signed with South Africa to undertake the jointly financed Lesotho Highlands Water Project. The project, which could cost M4 billion, calls for two 34-km (21-mi) tunnels to transport water from Lesotho's rivers to South Africa, with the first delivery by 1996 and maximum operation by 2020. Plans call for construction of seven dams, as well as a hydroelectric plant which could meet almost all of Lesotho's power needs. The new plant will generate 26 million kwh annually. Lesotho produces no petroleum and imports virtually all petroleum products from South Africa.

28INDUSTRY

Lesotho has a wide variety of light industries, which include, among others, tire retreading, tapestry weaving, diamond processing, and production of textiles, electric lighting, candles, ceramics, explosives, furniture, and fertilizers. In the 1980s, the Lesotho National Development Corporation promoted industrial development in the production of fruits and vegetables, tires, beer and soft drinks, parachutes, steel, and wire. In 1991 Lesotho inaugurated a television assembly plant. Average annual industrial growth between 1980 and 1991 was 12.8%, with its GDP contribution weighing in at 15.1% (1991).

29SCIENCE AND TECHNOLOGY

The government maintains an agricultural research station at Maseru, along with several experimental stations in the field. The National University of Lesotho has faculties of science and agriculture. Lesotho Agricultural College is located in Maseru.

30DOMESTIC TRADE

Except for the northern regions, where Indians generally monopolized trading activities, domestic trade traditionally has been largely in the hands of Europeans. Taiwanese also play a role. Nevertheless, more and more Basotho are taking out trading licenses. Traders play a central role in wool and mohair marketing, often acting as wool classers as well. The expertise of the traders varies widely. Some have regular suppliers and customers and maintain high quality, while others are prone to careless handling practices, lowering the market value of wool.

Normal business hours in urban areas are from 8 AM to 1 PM and from 2 to 5 PM, Monday through Friday, and from 8 AM to 1 PM on Saturday. Banks are open from 8:30 AM to 1 PM Monday–Friday, and 9:30 to 11 AM on Saturday.

31FOREIGN TRADE

Lesotho has suffered from a severe trade imbalance. Its chief exports are wool, mohair, and livestock. South Africa and Swaziland provide almost all of Lesotho's imports. Principal exports in 1985 came to M49.7 million and were estimated at M55 million in 1986. Imports in 1985 totaled M796.6 million.

32BALANCE OF PAYMENTS

Lesotho's chronic balance-of-payments deficit is partially offset by the flow of cash and material goods from Basotho workers in South Africa. Unrequited transfers related to the Highlands water project were largely responsible for the balance of pyaments surpluses of 1990 and 1991, and were sufficient to compensate for declining remittances, which are expected to dwindle further as problems in the South African mining sector result in layoffs.

In 1992 merchandise exports totaled $109.2 million and imports $972.6 million. The merchandise trade balance was

$823.4 million. The following table summarizes Lesotho's balance of payments for 1991 and 1992 (in millions of US dollars):

	1991	1992
CURRENT ACCOUNT		
Goods, services, and income	−323.1	−401.1
Unrequited transfers	406.2	478.8
TOTALS	83.1	37.6
CAPITAL ACCOUNT		
Direct investment	7.5	2.7
Other long-term capital	35.3	40.8
Other short-term capital	−103.6	−106.0
Reserves	−42.4	−49.9
TOTALS	−103.2	−112.4
Errors and omissions	20.1	74.8
Total change in reserves	−39.4	−35.9

33BANKING AND SECURITIES

Lesotho belongs to the South African monetary area. Under an agreement signed by Lesotho, Swaziland, and South Africa in December 1974, Lesotho and Swaziland have access to South African money and capital markets and are allowed to use the South African Reserve Bank as a lender of last resort. Lesotho is now responsible for its own monetary policy and controls its own financial institutions, but management of the rand currency and the gold and foreign exchange reserves of the rand area remains the sole responsibility of South Africa.

In 1980, the newly established Lesotho Monetary Authority (now the Central Bank of Lesotho) began issuing maloti as the national currency, but the South African rand remained legal tender and the loti was pegged at par with the rand. The money supply, as measured by M2, in Lesotho at the end of 1992 was M722.7 million. Net foreign assets of the banking sector were M773.92 million, of which the Central Bank of Lesotho held M483.1 million.

Other government financial institutions are the Lesotho Building Finance Corp. and the Lesotho Agricultural Development Bank. Standard Chartered Bank Africa and Barclays Bank were the commercial banks in 1993.

No securities exchange was in operation in Lesotho as of the mid-1990s.

34INSURANCE

Basotho recruited to work in the mines of South Africa can, with a small payment, obtain a life insurance policy for the duration of the contract period. In 1986, there was 1 life insurance company in operation and 1 composite company.

35PUBLIC FINANCE

During the late 1980's, the fiscal deficit (including grants) increased from 6.2% to 9.2% of GNP. Fiscal restraint and increased revenues have helped decrease the fiscal deficit to 0.3% of GNP in 1991–92, with a small surplus in 1992–93. The following table shows actual revenues and expenditures for 1990 and 1991 in thousands of maloti.

	1990	1991
REVENUE AND GRANTS		
Tax revenue	558,033	700,721
Non-tax revenue	69,531	118,934
Capital revenue	115	300
Grants	188,000	149,200
TOTAL	815,679	969,155

	1990	1991
EXPENDITURES & LENDING MINUS REPAYMENTS		
General public services	63,097	91,400
Defense	61,262	62,770
Public order and safety	35,409	44,950
Education	144,168	212,671
Health	88,266	111,173
Social Security and Welfare	13,411	14,965
Housing and community amenities	39,856	37,916
Recreation, cultural, and religious affairs	4,906	6,528
Economic affairs and services	278,846	306,620
Other expenditures	94,305	80,965
Lending minus repayments	8,950	9,050
TOTAL	832,476	979,008
Deficit/Surplus	−16,797	−9,853

In 1991 Lesotho's total public debt stood at 1,216,050 maloti of which 1,070,550 maloti was financed abroad.

36TAXATION

In 1960, a review of the tax structure was undertaken with a view toward ending the dual tax system, which made a distinction between Basotho and non-Basotho. It was decided that a basic tax, previously paid only by Basotho, would be paid by all male residents. A graded tax and a scaled income tax, both payable by all persons irrespective of race or sex, were subsequently imposed. The maximum tax rate for individuals is 35%, and corporations are taxed at a flat rate of 35%. There was a sales tax of 15% in 1993.

37CUSTOMS AND DUTIES

Customs and duties constitute the predominant source of ordinary revenue. Lesotho, together with Swaziland and Botswana, and Namibia, is a member of a customs union with South Africa; consequently, no tariffs exist on most goods moving among them. South Africa levies and collects the bulk of the customs, sales, and excise duties for the five countries, paying a share determined by an established formula of total customs collections to the other four. Imports from outside the customs union, regardless of ultimate destination, are subject to the same tariff rates.

38FOREIGN INVESTMENT

The government actively encourages foreign investment, particularly investment in manufacturing plants and agricultural projects. The Lesotho National Development Corp. promotes industrial estates, with such attractions as a 15-year discretionary tax holiday or accelerated depreciation allowances, plus LNDC capital participation of up to 25%.

39ECONOMIC DEVELOPMENT

The Lesotho government's development objectives are based on a food-security policy approach, built around small-scale irrigated agriculture projects and improved rural water supplies. Donors supported the fourth five-year plan (1988–91) with pledges of $390 million. Lesotho receives development assistance from the United Kingdom, South Africa, Canada, Taiwan, the World Bank, and various United Nations agencies. Political reforms in South Africa in 1994 should have a beneficial impact on the Lesotho economy.

40SOCIAL DEVELOPMENT

In the past, many social welfare programs were organized on the local level or by missions. But the need for concerted action to alleviate hardships brought about by the severe droughts led to the creation in 1965 of a Social Welfare Department under the Ministry of Health (later the Ministry of Health and Social Welfare). Community development teams stimulate local initiative by conducting courses and forming voluntary community development committees. The Homemakers' Association, an organization long active in social welfare, has given family-management courses in remote areas under a grant from the Oxford Committee for Famine Relief (Oxfam).

A few women hold important government posts, and some rural development programs are aimed at women. The fertility rate is 5.8, somewhat lower than that in Botswana or Swaziland, presumably because many men are working in South Africa. Abortion is legal only to save the woman's life.

41HEALTH

Lesotho's major health problems, such as pellagra and kwashiorkor, stem from poor nutrition and inadequate hygiene. In 1990, 27% of children under 5 years of age were considered malnourished. In 1991, 47% of the population had access to safe water, while 22% had adequate sanitation. Famines have resulted from periodic droughts. Tuberculosis and venereal diseases are also serious problems. There were an estimated 220 cases of tuberculosis per 100,000 people in 1990. In 1993 children up to one year old were vaccinated against tuberculosis (59%); diphtheria, pertussis, and tetanus (58%); polio (58%); and measles (80%).

The government of Lesotho is working to rehabilitate 2 hospitals and is making an overall effort to strengthen health care services. In 1990, there were 74 doctors, 60 pharmacists, and 874 nurses. In 1992, there were 0.12 doctors per 1,000 people, with a nurse to doctor ratio of 5:1. In 1990, there were 1.4 hospital beds per 1,000 inhabitants. In 1992 approximately 80% of the population had access to health care services

The 1993 birth rate was 34.4 per 1,000 people. In that year, the infant mortality rate per 1,000 live births was 108. Estimated life expectancy in 1992 was 60 years. The overall death rate in 1993 was 9.7 per 1,000 people.

42HOUSING

The Lesotho Housing Corp. builds new housing for sale and rent, and a government-supported development program is building low-cost housing. As of 1990, 59% of urban and 45% of rural dwellers had access to a public water supply.

43EDUCATION

A by-product of the long history of missionary activity in Lesotho was the relatively comprehensive development of education. In 1991, Lesotho had 1,198 primary schools. As of 1991, there were 361,144 primary school pupils taught by 6,685 teachers, and 46,572 general secondary school students taught by 2,407 teachers. In the same year, 1,600 students were enrolled in vocational training, under 140 teachers. Education is compulsory between the ages of 6 and 13. Primary schools were attended by an estimated 60% of eligible boys and 81% of girls; secondary schools, by 8% of boys and 17% of girls. Adult literacy is presently estimated to be over 75%.

The University of Lesotho, Botswana, and Swaziland (formerly known as Pius XII College), founded in 1964 at Roma, was unilaterally dissolved in October 1975 by Prime Minister Leabua Jonathan, who then renamed it the National University of Lesotho. Lesotho Agricultural College, at Maseru, was founded in 1955. In 1991, all higher level institutions has 4,164 pupils and 469 teaching staff: of these, 297 teachers and 3,060 pupils were at universities and equivalent institutions.

44LIBRARIES AND MUSEUMS

The Government Archive in Maseru has records dating from 1869. The library at the National University of Lesotho in Roma has more than 80,000 volumes. The British Council maintains a library in Maseru, with 7,405 volumes. The Lesotho National Museum, at Maseru, has collections on archaeology, ethnography, and geology. The Morija Museum has collections in the same fields.

45MEDIA

The government operates postal and telephone services; the exchange at Maseru has been automatic since 1963. An earth-satellite station was opened in 1986. There were 19,161 telephones in 1991. Government-owned Radio Lesotho broadcasts in English and Sesotho, and there is no television station. There were an estimated 58,000 radios and 11,000 television sets in use in 1991. The *Mochochonono* is a weekly government paper, printed in Sesotho and English. The *Leselinyana la Lesotho* and the *Moeletsi oa Basotho* are weeklies published by the Lesotho Evangelical Church and the Roman Catholic Church, respectively, with 1992 circulations of 15,000 and 12,000.

46ORGANIZATIONS

Youth-oriented organizations include the Boy Scouts, the Girl Guides, and the Association of Youth Clubs. Cooperative unions, partly government-financed and government-sponsored, consumer cooperatives, artisan cooperatives, and the Progressive Farmers play an important part in economic and social development. There are also more than 100 active agricultural marketing and credit societies.

47TOURISM, TRAVEL, AND RECREATION

The Lesotho National Tourist Board promotes tourism, which is increasing but still underdeveloped. In 1990 there were 171,000 overnight tourists. The country had 838 hotel rooms with 1,699 beds, and tourism receipts totaled US$18 million.

Visas are not required for stays of under 30 days. Permanent tourist camps are established in remote scenic areas for pony-trekking parties. The first such camp, consisting of bath- and kitchen-equipped grass huts, was built at Marakabeis, near the end of the Mountain Road. Although lacking in game, Lesotho has spectacular natural attractions in its mountains and in Malutsenyane Falls, as well as excellent trout-fishing grounds. The rock paintings near Teyateyaneng are also a potentially important tourist site. The country's first national park, Sehlabathebe Mountain National Park, was established in 1970 in the Qacha's Nek District. There is a gambling casino in Maseru.

48FAMOUS BASOTHO

Moshoeshoe (or Moshesh, 1786–1870), a chief of the Bakoena tribe in what was then northern Basutoland, is acclaimed as the founder of the Basotho nation. Moshoeshoe II (b. 1938) was proclaimed king of Lesotho on Independence Day, 4 October 1966. Chief Leabua Jonathan (1914–87), prime minister of Lesotho from its inception until 1986, was a leader in the drive for independence. Maj. Gen. Justin Metsing Lekhanya became head of the ruling military council and prime minister in 1986.

49DEPENDENCIES

Lesotho has no territories or colonies.

50BIBLIOGRAPHY

Bardill, John E., and James H. Cobbe. *Lesotho*. Boulder, Colo.: Westview, 1985.

Black, David R. *Foreign Policy in Small States: Botswana, Lesotho, Swaziland and Southern Africa*. Halifax, N.S.: Centre for Foreign Policy Studies, Dalhousie University, 1988.

Eldredge, Elizabeth A. *A South African Kingdom: The Pursuit of Security in Nineteenth-century Lesotho*. New York: Cambridge University Press, 1993.

Ferguson, James. *The Anti-politics Machine: "development," Depoliticization, and Bureaucratic Power in Lesotho*. New

York: Cambridge University Press, 1990.

Haliburton, Gordon. *Historical Dictionary of Lesotho.* Metuchen, N.J.: Scarecrow, 1977.

Khaletla, B. M. *Lesotho 1970: An African Coup under the Microscope.* Berkeley: University of California Press, 1972.

Machobane, L. B. B. J. *Government and Change in Lesotho, 1800–1966: A Study of Political Institutions.* New York: St. Martin's, 1990.

Thompson, Leonard. *Survival in Two Worlds: Moshoeshoe of Lesotho, 1786–1870.* London: Oxford University Press, 1975.

Willet, Shelagh M., and David Ambrose. *Lesotho: A Comprehensive Bibliography.* Santa Barbara, Calif.: ABC-Clio, 1980.

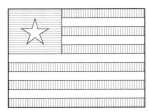

LIBERIA

Republic of Liberia

CAPITAL: Monrovia.

FLAG: The national flag, dating from 1847, consists of 11 horizontal stripes, alternately red (6) and white (5), with a single five-pointed white star on a square blue field 5 stripes deep in the upper left corner.

ANTHEM: *All Hail, Liberia, Hail.*

MONETARY UNIT: The Liberian dollar (L$) of 100 cents is established by law as equivalent to the US dollar. There are no Liberian notes. US notes in the denominations of 5, 10, 20, 50, and 100 dollars are in circulation and are legal tender. Both US and Liberian coins of 1, 5, 10, 25, and 50 cents, and 1 dollar are in circulation; in 1982, a $5 Liberian coin was issued.

WEIGHTS AND MEASURES: US and UK weights and measures are used.

HOLIDAYS: New Year's Day, 1 January; Armed Forces Day, 11 February; Decoration Day, 2d Wednesday in March; Birthday of J. J. Roberts (first president), 15 March; Fast and Prayer Day, 2d Friday in April; National Redemption Day, 12 April; Unification Day, 14 May; Independence Day, 26 July; Flag Day, 24 August; Thanksgiving Day, 1st Thursday in November; Anniversary of 1985 Coup Attempt, 12 November; President Tubman's Birthday, 29 November; Christmas, 25 December. Good Friday and Easter Monday are movable religious holidays.

TIME: GMT.

¹LOCATION, SIZE, AND EXTENT

Located on the west coast of Africa, Liberia has an area of about 111,370 sq km (43,000 sq mi), with a length of 548 km (341 mi) ESE–WNW and a width of 274 km (170 mi) NNE–SSW. Comparatively, the area occupied by Liberia is slightly larger than the state of Tennessee. On the N it is bounded by Guinea, on the E by Côte d'Ivoire, on the S and SW by the Atlantic Ocean, and on the NW by Sierra Leone, with a total boundary length of 2,123 km (1,345 mi).

Liberia's capital city, Monrovia, is located on the Atlantic coast.

²TOPOGRAPHY

There are three distinct belts lying parallel to the coast. The low coastal belt is about 40 km (25 mi) wide, with tidal creeks, shallow lagoons, and mangrove marshes. The land then rises to rolling hills, with elevations of 60–150 m (200–500 ft). The third belt, comprising the bulk of Liberia, is marked by abrupt changes of elevation in a series of low mountains and plateaus, less densely forested than the hilly region. The Nimba Mountains, near the Guinea frontier, rise to 1,384 m (4,540 ft) at Guest House Hill, the nation's highest point; the Wologizi Mountains reach a maximum of about 1,356 m (4,450 ft) with Mt. Wutuvi. Of the six principal rivers, all of which are at right angles to the coast and flow into the Atlantic Ocean, only the Farmington is of much commercial importance. Sandbars obstruct the mouths of all rivers, making entrance hazardous, and upstream there are rocky rapids.

³CLIMATE

The climate is tropical and humid, with little change in temperature throughout the year. The mean is 27°C (81°F), with temperatures rarely exceeding 36°C (97°F) or falling below 20°C (68°F). On the coast the heat is tempered by an almost constant breeze.

Yearly rainfall is as high as 510 cm (200 in) on the coast, decreasing to about 200 cm (80 in) in areas farthest inland. There are distinct wet and dry seasons, most of the rainfall occurring between late April and mid-November. Average relative humidity in the coastal area is about 82% during the rainy season and 78% in the dry, but it may drop to 50% or lower between December and March, when the dust-laden harmattan blows from the Sahara.

⁴FLORA AND FAUNA

Liberia, together with adjoining Sierra Leone and Côte d'Ivoire, includes the greatest of Africa's evergreen forests. There are about 235 species of trees; 90 varieties are present in potentially marketable quantities, including mahogany and ironwood. The bombex (cotton tree), the oil palm, and the kola tree are common. The wild rubber tree (*Funtumia elastica*) is indigenous, but the cultivated *Hevea brasiliensis* is the source of Liberia's commercial rubber. A variety of coffee peculiar to Liberia, *Coffea liberica*, was formerly common but has given way to the preferred *Coffea robusta*. Fruit trees include citrus varieties, the alligator apple, papaya, mango, and avocado. Pineapples grow wild. Among the cultivated plants are cassava, cotton, cacao, indigo, and upland rice.

Elephant and buffalo, once common in Liberia, have largely disappeared, but several species of antelope are found in the interior; two of these, the white-shouldered duiker and the zebra antelope, are peculiar to Liberia. A lemur called Bosman's potto and several species of monkey, including the long-haired and the Diana, are found in the forests. Wild pigs and porcupines exist in sparsely settled areas, and several members of the leopard group are also found. Most of the 15 species of snakes are venomous. Termites build lofty nests throughout the country. In some areas the tsetse fly is found, and driver ants and mosquitoes are common. Several varieties of snail act as hosts in the propagation of certain enteric diseases. Among the birds are the hornbill, wild guinea fowl, cattle egret (cowbird), flamingo, woodpecker, and weaver.

5ENVIRONMENT

The nation lacks regulatory agencies to supervise the preservation of the environment. As the 1980s began, Liberia was one of the last West African countries with significant primary forest reserves, but recent estimates suggest that some 42,000 ha (104,000 acres) of primary forest are annually converted to degraded forest or transformed into bushland by shifting cultivation. Commercial logging, firewood cutting, and a government land-clearing program also threaten primary forestland. Hunting and loss of habitat have decimated wildlife along the coastal plain, and there are no longer any large herds of big game in the interior.

The water supply is usually limited to open sources such as streams, swamps, and shallow, uncovered wells; the result, especially during the rainy season, is that insects and parasites thrive, creating a major health hazard. Liberia cities produce 2 million tons of solid waste per year. The Mano and St. John rivers are becoming increasingly polluted from the dumping of iron ore tailings, and the coastal waters from oil residue and the dumping of untreated sewage and waste water.

Eighteen of the nations mammal species and ten of its bird species are endangered. One of its plant species is threatened with extinction. The Jentink's duiker is considered an endangered species in Liberia.

6POPULATION

The population consists of indigenous Africans and descendants of American black settlers, in the ratio of at least 30 to 1. The first national census, completed in 1962, accounted for a population of 1,016,443; the 1974 census gave a total of 1,503,368, for an increase of 47.9%; and the 1984 census gave a population of 2,101,628. The estimate for mid-1994 was 3,018,551; a population of 3,565,000 was projected for the year 2000, assuming a crude birthrate of 44.5 per 1,000 population and a crude death rate of 12.6 during 1995–2000.

The estimated density in 1994 was 27.1 per sq km (70.2 per sq mi); the urban population was estimated at 51% in 1995 and was heaviest along the coast and major interior roads. More than one-third of the population lives within an 80-km (50-mi) radius of Monrovia, the capital, which had an estimated metropolitan-area population of 668,000 in 1990. After Monrovia, Buchanan, Harper, and Greenville are the largest port cities; Gbarnga, Kakata, Sanniquellie, Zorzor, and Ghanpa are major interior towns.

7MIGRATION

The Liberian civil war caused a great amount of migration in the early 1990s. More than 800,000 Liberians were internally displaced or abroad in early 1993. Of these 478,500 were in Guinea, 173,700 in Côte d'Ivoire, 12,000 in Ghana, 5,900 in Sierra Leone, and 2,900 in Nigeria. Paradoxically, Liberia was harboring 100,000 Sierra Leone refugees fleeing the spillover from the war. Some Ghanians and Guineans also live in Liberia.

8ETHNIC GROUPS

Besides the descendants of the early settlers, Liberia is peopled by about 28 ethnic groups, each with its own language. They are believed to have migrated from the north and east between the 12th and 16th centuries AD, bringing with them elements of Egyptian and Arabian culture, such as the spinning and weaving of cotton and the smelting of iron. Linguistically, the tribes may be divided into three main groups: the Mande people in the north and far west, the Kru tribes (including the Krahn) in the east and

southeast, and the Mel in the northwest. The largest groups are the Kpellé, Bassa, Gio, Kru, Grebo, and Mano. About 3% of the population is of US descent. There are also two tribes not strictly Liberian: the Mandingo, who are itinerant Muslim traders, and the Fanti fishermen, who come from Ghana and stay a few years at a time in Liberia.

Because of intermarriage and an aggressive national unification program, tribal divisions are rapidly becoming less distinct, especially around the capital. Nevertheless, there is a strong tendency among the indigenous people to preserve their tribal identities. Of the non-African resident population, the biggest component consists of Lebanese and Syrians.

9LANGUAGES

English is the official language, but only a minority of the people can speak or write it. The tribal people use their own languages, of which there are about 28. Of these, Vai, Bassa, and Loma can be written and are being used in correspondence by these tribes. The international phonetic alphabet, introduced by missionaries, has facilitated the use of many of the other tribal languages for correspondence and publication of local newsletters.

10RELIGIONS

The early settlers, freed American slaves, brought with them the culture and religion of the US Deep South of the slavery era. Their descendants are adherents of the principal Protestant denominations, of which the largest is the Methodist Church. Liberia is officially a Christian state. In 1984, it was estimated that the population was 67% Christian and 14% Muslim; the remainder were adherents of indigenous faiths (animists). Veneration of ancestors forms the core of Liberian traditional religion. Mandingo traders have made many Muslim converts, and Egyptian and Pakistani Muslim missionaries have been active since 1956.

11TRANSPORTATION

In 1991 there were 10,087 km (6,268 mi) of public roads, of which 2,848 km (1,770 mi) were classified as all-weather (laterite). Only 603 km (375 mi) were paved. There were 2,323 km (1,443 mi) of private roads, mostly laterite-surfaced roads built by rubber and lumber companies. Important paved roads connect Monrovia to the interior as far as the Guinea, Sierra Leone, and Côte d'Ivoire borders. In 1991 there were 8,000 registered passenger autos, and 4,000 commercial vehicles. Except for short-line buses, virtually all of Liberia's common carriers are taxicabs.

Liberia's railways in 1991 were all owned by mining companies and used for transportation of iron ore from mines to the ports of Buchanan and Monrovia; including the line of the National Iron Ore Co., which closed operations in 1985, they covered a total of 480 km (298 mi). Passenger service was introduced in 1964 on the 266-km (165-mi) line connecting the Liberian American-Swedish Minerals Co. (LAMCO) mines at Mt. Nimba with Buchanan.

The Free Port of Monrovia, opened in 1948, underwent substantial improvements during the late 1960s, so that ships with a draft up to 14 m (45 ft) can now be handled. A port used primarily for iron ore export was opened at Buchanan in 1963. These two deepwater ports handle over 98% of all cargo. Smaller ports, located at Greenville and Harper, handle mainly log exports. Many foreign-owned ships are registered in Liberia because of low fees and lenient labor laws; as a result, Liberia's registered merchant fleet in 1991 was second only to Panama in terms of tonnage, totaling 1,550 vessels with 52,622,000 GRT.

Robertsfield, 58 km (36 mi) from Monrovia, is the site of the sole international airport. Before the civil war, there were 49 usable airstrips. Medium-sized jets and small aircraft, including those of Air Liberia, provide service from Spriggs Payne Airport on the outskirts of Monrovia to destinations within Liberia.

12HISTORY

It is believed that many of the peoples of Liberia migrated there from the north and east between the 12th and 16th centuries AD. Portuguese explorers first visited the coast in 1461, and Europeans traded with coastal tribes during the next three centuries. Modern Liberia was founded in 1822 by freed black slaves from the US, sent to Africa under the auspices of the American Colonization Society, a private organization whose purpose was "to promote and execute a plan for colonizing in Africa, with their own consent, the free people of color residing in the US." The first settlement was on Providence Island near where the present capital city, Monrovia, is located. Although the Society, with the help of the US government under President James Monroe (after whom Monrovia is named), had arranged with local chiefs for a settlement, the colonists were attacked by native tribes and barely maintained their foothold.

The first governors of the settlement were agents appointed by the Colonization Society, but in 1847 the Republic of Liberia was established under a constitution modeled after that of the US. Black emigration to Liberia continued until the close of the US Civil War, during which about 14,000 settlers went to Liberia under the auspices of the Society, and some 5,700 blacks, recaptured from slave ships on the high seas by the US Navy, were sent by the US government. Liberia was recognized by various European governments, but on one pretext or another, and by force of arms, the infant republic was pushed out of areas it had lawfully acquired by purchase or exploration. Particularly during the last quarter of the 19th century, Liberia lost to adjoining British and French colonies territory rich in natural resources. Pressure on Liberia's borders continued well into the 20th century.

Added to these dangers was Liberia's precarious economic position. In the 1870s, Liberia contracted for a $500,000 loan from European sources. Because of its inability to generate sufficient revenue from exports, Liberia defaulted on this loan and was forced into a series of ever larger loans. Liberians were further compelled to allow collection of customs revenues by Europeans and Americans. Eventually, Liberia was able to secure a $5-million loan from a US firm, the Firestone Tire & Rubber Co., which set up rubber plantations in the country in 1926. The depression of the 1930s brought Liberia to the verge of bankruptcy, and government revenues fell in 1933 to a low of $321,000. In the early 1930s, Liberia's political sovereignty was also severely threatened. Accusations had begun to circulate internationally that Liberian laborers, with the complicity of high government officials, were being recruited for shipment to the Spanish island of Fernando Póo (now Bioko, in Equatorial Guinea) under conditions that resembled slave trading. A commission of inquiry, set up by the League of Nations at the request of Liberia's President Charles D. B. King, found some basis for the charges and implicated the vice-president, who was forced to resign. President King, shocked at the findings, also resigned.

Exportation of rubber from the new Firestone plantations began in 1934. The establishment of a US air base in Liberia during World War II and the building of an artificial harbor at Monrovia further stimulated the country's development. William V. S. Tubman, elected president in 1944 and reelected for five additional terms, sought to unify the country by attempting to bridge the wide economic, political, and social gaps between the descendants of the original American ex-slaves and the tribal peoples of the interior. Upon Tubman's death in 1971, Vice-President William R. Tolbert, Jr., succeeded to the presidency. Tolbert was nominated by the True Whigs, Liberia's only legal political party, and, having been elected without opposition in October 1975, was inaugurated for an eight-year term in January 1976.

Dae Takes Power

A coup on 12 April 1980 by army enlisted men brought an end to

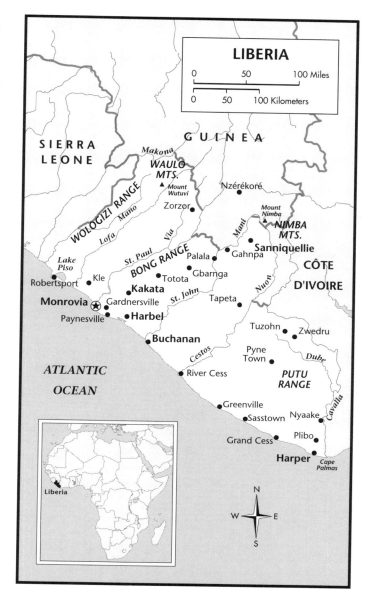

LOCATION: 4°20′ to 8°33′N; 7°22′ to 11°30′W. **BOUNDARY LENGTHS:** Guinea, 563 km (350 mi); Côte d'Ivoire, 716 km (445 mi); Atlantic coastline, 538 km (334 mi); Sierra Leone, 306 km (190 mi). **TERRITORIAL SEA LIMIT:** 200 mi.

rule by the True Whigs and by the Americo-Liberians that party largely represented. Tolbert and at least 26 supporters were killed in the fighting; 13 officials were publicly executed 10 days later. The People's Redemption Council (PRC), formed to rule the country, was led by Sgt. Samuel K. Doe, a Krahn tribesman, who became head of state. The constitution was suspended, but a return to civilian rule was promised for 1985. During 1981, the government, although beset by two separate coup attempts, declared an amnesty for all political prisoners and exiles; 40 political prisoners were released in September of that year; about 20 others were released in December. A draft constitution providing for a multiparty republic was issued in 1983 and approved by referendum in 1984.

In the elections held on 15 October 1985, nine political parties sought to challenge Doe's National Democratic Party of Liberia (NDPL), but only three were allowed to take part. Doe was elected president with 51% of the vote; the NDPL won 21 of the 26 Senate seats and 51 of the 64 seats in the House of Representatives.

Foreign observers called the elections fraudulent, and most of the opposition candidates who were elected refused to take their seats.

In November 1985, an estimated 500 to 600 people died in an unsuccessful coup attempt—the seventh since Doe took power. That was followed by retribution by loyalist Krahn troops. Thousands of Gio people were killed, since they were regarded as supporters of the coup leaders.

Since late December 1989, Liberia has fallen into chaos. A small group of insurgents, led by Charles Taylor, who had earlier fled Liberia amid charges of corruption, began a campaign to overthrow the dictatorial and ruthless Doe regime. Taylor's National Patriotic Front of Liberia (NPFL) entered the country from the Côte d'Ivoire in the east. The war developed into a vicious inter-ethnic bloodletting, between those associated with the regime (Krahn) and those victimized by it (Gio and Mano). Thousands of civilians were massacred by gunmen on both sides. Hundreds of thousands fled their homes.

By June 1990, Doe was besieged in Monrovia. A third force led by Prince Johnson, emerged as a breakaway from the NPFL. With military discipline absent and bloodshed throughout the capital region, members of the Economic Community of West Africa (ECOWAS) decided to establish a framework for peace. It created a regional peacekeeping force, ECOMOG, the ECOWAS Monitoring Group, and installed an interim government. ECOMOG was predominantly a Nigerian force, supplemented by contingents from Ghana, Guinea, Sierra Leone, the Gambia and, later, Senegal. It arrived in Monrovia in late August 1990. However, on 9 September 1990, Johnson's forces shot their way into ECOMOG's headquarters and captured Doe. His torture and execution were videotaped by his captors. ECOMOG was reinforced in order to protect the interim government headed by Dr. Amos Sawyer. Sawyer was able to establish his authority over most of Monrovia, but the rest of Liberia was in the hands of various factions of the NPFL or of local gangs.

Repeated attempts to get Taylor and Johnson to cooperate with Sawyer have been fruitless. Most West African states support ECOMOG and its mediation efforts but some, Burkino Faso in particular, back Taylor. Senegal pulled out of the ECOMOG forces in January 1993, Nigeria in 1994. Despite three major peace agreements since 1990, fighting has continued. Over half the population of Liberia resides within the Interim Government of National Unity's (IGNU's) area. The Taylor-led forces control several central and southern counties. The anti-NPFL United Liberation Movement for Democracy in Liberia (ULIMO), led by Alhaji Kromah, control three western counties and portions of two central counties. Remnants of Doe's Armed Forces of Liberia, nominally subordinate to IGNU but with ties to ULIMO, also are engaged in fighting. The Lofa Defense Force (LDF) challenges ULIMO in the northwest, and the Liberian Peace Council (LPC) fights against the NPFL in the southeast. On occasion, the fighting has spilled over the borders. The NPFL had been accused of invading Sierra Leone and of having destabilized its government and contributed to its fall in April 1992. In November 1992, Johnson surrendered to ECOMOG troops. ECOWAS, the UN and the OAU tried to establish ceasefires and to demobilize warring factions but to little avail. In September 1993, the UN established a small scale observer mission (UNOMIL) to help ECOMOG monitor a July ceasefire.

13GOVERNMENT

Under the constitution approved on 3 July 1984 and effective January 1986, Liberia is a republic modeled after the United States. Its constitution provides for a president and vice-president elected jointly by universal suffrage (at age 18) for a four-year term with a limit of two consecutive terms, although candidacy is again allowed after the lapse of at least one term. The president nominates judges from a list submitted by a commission, serves as commander-in-chief of the armed forces, and has the right to veto legislation; the veto can be overridden by a two-thirds vote of both legislative houses. The legislature is divided into a Senate, its 26 members elected by counties for nine years, and a House of Representatives, its 64 members elected by equally apportioned constituencies for six years.

The constitution outlaws the one-party state and stipulates that fundamental rights, such as free speech, press, and assembly, must be guaranteed. The president has the right to suspend certain rights by declaring a state of emergency in cases of war or serious civil unrest. This state of emergency, which must be confirmed by a two-thirds vote of both legislative houses, does not empower the president to suspend or abrogate the constitution, dissolve the legislature, suspend or dismiss the judiciary, or suspend the right of habeas corpus. Although the constitution guarantees fundamental freedoms to all persons irrespective of ethnic background, the document stipulates that "only persons who are Negro or of Negro descent shall qualify by birth or by naturalization to be citizens of Liberia." Only citizens may own land.

While all parties in the present civil war profess to honor the constitution, the document's provisions are selectively ignored and unevenly applied. Human rights are widely violated, especially in areas dominated by NPFL and ULIMO. Massacres and torture are commonplace.

At present, the interim government, headed by Dr. Amos Sawyer, is under a kind of receivership enforced by ECOMOG. The July 1993 ceasefire calls for the creation of a five-person Council of State and a 35-member transitional legislature, but little progress has been made in putting them in place and giving them authority to govern.

14POLITICAL PARTIES

The president and all members of the legislature were formerly members of the True Whig Party, which was organized in 1860 and held power continuously from 1878 to 1980. The Progressive People's Party (PPP), formed in 1979, claimed to represent the interests of Liberia's indigenous peoples, in contrast to the Americo-Liberian stance of the True Whigs.

In March 1980, several PPP members were arrested, a move that may have triggered the April coup. Although all political activity was banned, many True Whig members retained their government posts.

The National Democratic Party of Liberia (NDPL), established by former president Samuel K. Doe, was victorious in the 1985 elections. The newly formed Unity Party, Liberian Action Party, and Liberian Unification Party were allowed to take part in these elections.

The United People's Party (UPP), probably the largest opposition grouping, was founded by Gabriel Baccus Matthews, formerly head of the PPP. The UPP was not allowed to field candidates in 1985 but was legalized in 1986.

Charles Taylor's National Patriotic Front of Liberia (NPFL) currently operates outside of Monrovia. The United Liberation Movement of Liberia (ULIMO) has been identified with former Doe supporters. To say that these armed factions are political parties, however, distorts the meaning of political party.

15LOCAL GOVERNMENT

Liberia is divided into 13 counties, 2 territories, and the federal district of Monrovia. The counties are Grand Cape Mount, Sinoe, Grand Bassa, Maryland, River Cess, Bomi, Grand Kru, Margibi, Lofa, Borg, Grand Gedah, Nimba, and Montserrado. The territories are Marshall and Gibi.

The central government is supposed to appoint the county and territory superintendents. Counties are subdivided into districts headed by commissioners. There are also paramount, clan, and town chiefs. Cities elect their own mayors and councils.

[16]JUDICIAL SYSTEM

Most cases originate in magistrates' courts and may be taken for appeal to one of 10 circuit courts or to the highest court. More serious cases originate in the circuit courts. Traditional courts are presided over by tribal chiefs. A labor court was created in 1986.

The legal system is closely modeled on that of the United States. The 1984 constitution provides for the establishment of a Supreme Court consisting of a chief justice and four associate justices, to be appointed by the president from a panel recommended by a Judicial Service Commission; the consent of the Senate is required for these appointments and for the confirmation of lower court judges, to which a similar procedure applies.

Before the civil war, the judicial system was corrupt and dominated by the executive. By mid-1990 the system had collapsed and justice administration was co-opted by the military commanders of various factions. In 1991, the Interim Government of National Unity (IGNV), began to revive the court system in the Monrovia area. The National Patriotic Front of Liberia) (NPFL) has also begun to reopen the courts in the areas under its control.

[17]ARMED FORCES

The regular armed forces (5,000) and police garrison only parts of Monrovia. It no longer has air or naval capability. The rebel National Patriotic Forces of Liberia number 15,000. A six-nation African peacekeeping force numbers around 6,000.

[18]INTERNATIONAL COOPERATION

Liberia is a charter member of the UN, having joined on 2 November 1945; it takes part in ECA and all the nonregional specialized agencies except WIPO. It belongs to the African Development Bank, ECOWAS, G-77, and the OAU, and is a signatory to the Law of the Sea.

Liberia has participated in various African conferences and has advocated a cooperative association of African states to further such matters of mutual concern as public health, education, and trade. A customs bloc, the Mano River Union, was established in 1973 with Sierra Leone and Guinea. Leaders of the three countries signed a nonaggression and antisubversion pact in 1986.

Technical assistance activities of the UN in Liberia have emphasized agricultural development, teaching, vocational training, and control of yaws and malaria.

[19]ECONOMY

Liberia is an agricultural economy with 69.4% (1991) of the population earning its living in this sector. The principal crops are rice and manioc, yams, taro, sweet potatoes, okra, and groundnuts. However, Liberia's economy is in turmoil, the result of financial mismanagement and the effects of civil war which has divided the country into two economic zones, one centered in and around the major urban centers, the other comprising the bulk of the country's rural hinterland. From the start of hostilities in late 1989, the economy has been disabled with real-term GDP falling 9% in 1990 and 10% in 1991.

Even prior to the civil war, Liberia faced serious financial problems. Deficits created in the 1970s were deepened by a wave of higher expectations and by additional military spending resulting from the 1980 coup. To try to compensate, cuts in civil service salaries and currency manipulation were used as policy tools. A United States-led effort to bring better fiscal management to the Liberian economy failed, and in 1988 the World Bank closed its offices in Monrovia. In March of 1990, the IMF threatened to expel Liberia for nonpayment of its debt.

[20]INCOME

In 1992 Liberia's GNP was $400 per capita. For the period 1985–92 the average inflation rate was 12.0%. In 1992 the GDP was $980 million in current US dollars. It is estimated that in 1989 agriculture, hunting, forestry, and fishing contributed 34% to GDP; mining and quarrying, 10%; manufacturing, 7%; electricity, gas, and water, 2%; construction, 2%; wholesale and retail trade, 5%; transport, storage, and communication, 7%; finance, insurance, real estate, and business services, 12%; community, social, and personal services, 3%; and other sources, 18%.

[21]LABOR

Since the tribal people of the interior form the bulk of the population and engage primarily in subsistence agriculture, there were few skilled laborers in Liberia until recent years. Although there is still a dearth of highly skilled mechanics and technicians, an increasing number of Liberians are becoming able plant and machine operators. Since the beginning of the civil war in 1989, labor has not been a top priority for either the Monrovian interim government nor the National Patriotic Reconstruction Assembly government. The civil war shut down all business activity by mid-1990, and there has been only a gradual recovery.

Before the onslaught of civil war, the labor force totaled about 1,349,000 persons. In 1988 total civilian employment stood at 701,000 and unemployment at 43%. The principal private employer then was Firestone, with 9,000 employees in 1987. The policy of foreign-owned companies has been to employ Liberian labor in the first instance and to encourage the training of skilled workers, especially in mechanical pursuits. There are still shortages of middle- and higher-level technicians and managerial personnel. From time to time, labor shortages are reported in large agricultural enterprises. The government has enacted a minimum wage law, but the larger employers have generally paid wages in excess of the legal minimum.

The Labor Congress of Liberia (LCL), formed in 1951, was the first significant trade union. Following the first major strike in 1955, the LCL leadership was arrested and the union dissolved. In 1958, it was revived under the leadership of the Ministry for Social Affairs and functioned mainly as a government organ. As a protest against government interference in the LCL, the Congress of Industrial Organizations of Liberia (CIOL) was organized in 1960. The Liberian Federation of Labor Unions was formed in 1980 by a merger of the LCL and CIOL. The leading labor organization in the country is the Liberian Federation of Labor Unions (LFLU), with ten affiliated unions and a nominal membership of 15,000 in 1991–92.

[22]AGRICULTURE

Before the civil war, agriculture was the main source of livelihood for the great majority of Liberians. Except on plantations operated by foreign concessionaires and wealthy Liberians, farming techniques are primitive. The "bush rotation" system of shifting cultivation is followed, in which the farmer clears up to 2 ha (5 acres) of wild forest or low bush each year, lightly cultivates it with crude hand tools, and plants rice or cassava as the rainy season begins. In 1992, agriculture engaged about 71% of the labor force on 1% of the total land area. Estimated production of field crops in 1992 included cassava, 300,000 tons; rice, 110,000 tons; and sugarcane, 225,000 tons. The government maintains a retail price ceiling on rice. Rice and wheat productions are insufficient to meet local needs, however, and 128,000 tons of rice and 20,400 tons of wheat were imported in 1992.

The rain forest soils, while well drained, are strongly leached, making Liberia better adapted to tree-crop agriculture than to annual field-crop production. As of 1992, Charles Taylor's National Patriotic Reconstruction Assembly Government (NPRAG) controlled Liberia outside of Monrovia, which place the major rubber, rice, coffee, cocoa, vegetable, and fruit producing areas under its occupation. Rubber far outranks all other agricultural products in cash importance; rubber exports in 1992 were estimated at 32,000 tons, valued at $22 million. Exports increased significantly over 1991 (19,000 tons, valued at $15 million), due to a gradual recovery from the stoppage of all business activity in mid-1990 by the civil war. Rubber exports in 1990 (reflecting pre-war production) had amounted to 86,000 tons, valued at $68 million. Before the war, six foreign-owned concessions produced over two-thirds of the rubber crop, with Firestone's Harbel plantation as the biggest in the world. Firestone ended its long association with Liberian rubber production with the sale of its interests to the Japanese-owned Bridgestone in 1988. As of 1992, the Guthrie and LIBCO rubber plantations remained closed, but the US-owned LAC plantation was operating and exporting as the result of a working arrangement with the NPRAG.

The principal export crops produced by small farmers are coffee, cocoa, oil palm nuts, sugarcane, and fruits. Estimated production in 1992 was palm oil, 25,000 tons; palm kernels, 7,000 tons; and cocoa, 1,000 tons. Banana production came to 80,000 tons; plantains, 33,000 tons.

23 ANIMAL HUSBANDRY

The limited number of goats and sheep do not supply an adequate amount of protein for the Liberian diet, but poultry farming and marketing of eggs are on the increase; there were an estimated 4 million chickens in 1992. Experiments in crossing West African and Brahman cattle have not yet produced breeds resistant to the tsetse fly, but the potential remains for developing good beef animals. In 1992, Liberia had an estimated 220,000 sheep, 220,000 goats, 120,000 pigs, and 38,000 cattle.

24 FISHING

The fishing industry is dominated by the oceangoing trawlers of the Mesurado Fishing Co. The company also maintains a domestic distribution system that supplies a substantial amount of fish to the interior areas of the country. The total Liberian catch in 1991 was estimated at 9,620 tons.

25 FORESTRY

Although an estimated 44% of Liberia was covered by forest as the 1980s began, its use was confined to production of lumber for local needs. National forests constituted 18% of the land area in 1991. There were five major reforestation areas with a total of 4,260 ha (10,500 acres). There are about 235 timber species, of which 90 are potentially marketable, but natural stands of a single species are not common. This fact, plus difficulty of access and lack of practicable means of transportation, has tended to discourage commercial logging operations, despite the known existence of such valuable woods as African mahoganies and red ironwood. A number of foreign companies, mainly from the US, have been granted concessions. Roundwood and sawn-timber exports in 1991 totaled 701,000 cu m. Shipments of logs, sawn timber, and other forest products in 1991 were valued at $78.2 million. Roundwood production was estimated at 6,134,000 cu m in 1991.

26 MINING

Since December 1989, the mining sector has been severely damaged by civil war. Mining revenues, which had accounted for 22% of the GDP in 1989, came primarily from the export of iron ore with some revenue from legal gold and diamond exports. By 1991, a single iron ore mine, operated by the Iron Mining Company of Liberia (LIMCO) was one of only a few industrial operations functioning in the entire country. Liberia has significant reserves of moderate-grade iron ore, which may be exploited sometime after the limited reserves near Yekepa and Bong become exhausted. Some gold mining activity occurs, but much of the gold trafficked through Liberia was first smuggled from Guinea or Sierra Leone. Liberia's undeveloped resources include barite, chromium, kyanite, nickel, titaniferous sands, and uranium.

27 ENERGY AND POWER

The capacity of the country's electric generating plants was 332,000 kw in 1991, over half of which belongs to the Liberian Electricity Corp. Before the civil war, the Mt. Coffee Hydroelectric Plant, located on the St. Paul River, was the largest single source of electricity; a new 414-Mw facility on the St. Paul River was in the planning stage in 1987. Liberia's total production in 1991 was 450 million kwh, down from 834 million kwh in 1988. Liberia has no domestic petroleum resources. In 1991, wood accounted for 91% of the total energy requirement. The civil war has caused severe fuel distribution problems and shortages.

28 INDUSTRY

Liberia's industrial sector is dominated by processing plants associated with its key agricultural outputs: rubber, palm oil, and lumber. The Liberian-owned Mesurado Group manufactures detergent, soap, industrial gas and animal foods. Coca-Cola has a bottling plant in Liberia and leads the beverage industry. Liberia also produces cement, plastics, shoes, recycled steel, and refined petroleum products. In addition, Liberia's industrial base includes rice and sugar factories, cookies and candy, candles, foam rubber, hand tools and aluminum parts, umbrellas, and batteries. Of 849 enterprises operating in the Monrovia area in 1981, about half produced textiles.

In 1985, power production reached 904 million kwh, but it depended in large part on the Mt. Coffee hydroelectric plant, whose production capacity was destroyed in 1990 during the civil war.

Liberia is a leading "open registry" state for the world's merchant fleet, but its position has been slipping. In 1991, the Liberian fleet consisted of 1,605 vessels with a gross tonnage of 52.4 million tons. This represents a decline of 55.5% over the 1982 levels, due primarily a reduction in oil tanker numbers, competition from other registry states, and opposition to the open-registry system itself. In an effort to reverse this negative trend, the Liberian government (1989) shifted from a per-ton rate system to a flat-fee system of $2,500 per vessel.

29 SCIENCE AND TECHNOLOGY

Liberia has an agricultural experiment station in Suakoko; a geological, mining, and metallurgical society in Monrovia; and a research laboratory for the Mt. Nimba region, with headquarters in Robertsfield. The University of Liberia has colleges of agriculture and forestry, medicine, and science and technology. Cuttington University College has a science division, and the William V. S. Tubman College of Technology offers a three-year associate degree in engineering technology. The Liberian Institute for Biomedical Research, is at Monrovia. Booker Washington Institute offers agricultural and industrial courses.

30 DOMESTIC TRADE

Internal trade is carried on mainly by large firms, located in Monrovia, with branches in other principal towns. Most carry on import and export trade at wholesale and retail, and many act as sales agents for automobiles, industrial equipment, building materials, and electrical and household appliances. In general, the trading firms are foreign owned. Among tribal peoples, trade is often by barter.

Commercial credit is provided by the local banks in Monrovia. Credit and installment sales are not widely used.

Business hours are usually from 8 AM to noon and (except Saturdays) from 1 to 4 PM, but smaller stores are often open for longer hours. Sunday trading was banned in 1987. Government offices are open from 8 AM to noon and 2 to 4 PM weekdays and are closed on Saturdays. Normal banking hours are 8 AM to noon, Monday–Thursday, and 8 AM to 2 PM on Fridays.

31 FOREIGN TRADE

Liberia had a history of trade surpluses before the war. In 1985, for example, the surplus stood at L$149 million. Exports (1989) were led by iron ore sales, accounting for 51% of total exports, followed by rubber (26%) and timber (19.9%). Imports were led by machinery and transport equipment (33.6%), food and live animals (19.0%), basic manufactures (18.2%), and petroleum products (15.0%).

Leading purchasers of Liberian exports (1985) were Germany (32.3%) and the United States (19.1%). Liberia's imports came principally from the United States (25.8%), Japan (8.3%), and the United Kingdom (7.4%).

32 BALANCE OF PAYMENTS

Liberia has a chronic payments deficit, with its trade surplus offset by capital outflows and debt-service payments. Since civil war broke out in 1990, exports of foreign currency-earning raw materials (iron, rubber, timber, diamonds, and gold) have plummeted, and massive emergency aid operations have begun.

33 BANKING AND SECURITIES

In 1974, the government established the National Bank of Liberia. It became the exclusive banker and fiscal agent of the government, introduced reserve requirements for commercial banks, and undertook their supervision. As of 31 December 1993, the bank's foreign assets totaled $2.37 million. Claims on the government amounted to $1,271 million; on the commercial banks, $7.82 million.

Liberia's commercial banks have their main offices in Monrovia. They offer a normal range of commercial and international banking services. As of 31 December 1993, the total reserves of the commercial banking sector were $214.0 million; its foreign assets were $49.1 million. The banks' claims on the government were $8.8 million. Demand deposits totaled $150.0 million. The Liberian Bank for Development and Investment was established in November 1965 to provide additional medium- and long-term financial aid to worthwhile industrial projects. A National Housing and Savings Bank was established in 1972, with priority given to low-cost public housing. An Agricultural and Cooperative Development Bank provides credit to facilitate capital investment in agriculture.

In the 1980s, Liberia was plagued by the outflow and hoarding of US dollars, the only legal notes. The government minted a $5 coin to restore liquidity, but this action only led to more hoarding of US bills, which traded informally at a premium compared to similarly denominated Liberian coins.

34 INSURANCE

Liberia has no general insurance law. The nine insurance companies operating in Liberia in 1986 did a small-scale business.

35 PUBLIC FINANCE

Government budgets, roughly in balance up to the mid-1970s, have since run heavily into deficit. In 1988 Liberia's total public debt stood at $1,934.1 million, of which $1,427.1 million was financed abroad. Since civil war erupted in 1989, Liberia's fiscal management has collapsed.

36 TAXATION

Liberian tax laws apply equally to citizens and aliens. Concession agreements negotiated between foreign interests and the Liberian government often provide tax exemption or modification for periods of 5, 10, or more years after the start of operations.

A moderately progressive tax on net income earned from Liberian sources by individuals, partnerships, and corporations is the largest source of government revenue. Net income of both individuals and partnerships is subject to the same scheduled rates, with deductions similar to those allowed under US income tax laws. Net income is then taxed at rates ranging from 11% to a maximum of 65% on income over $99,000. Corporate tax rates range from 20% to 34% of taxable income with marginal rates of up to 50%. An additional national reconstruction tax of up to 8% on income over $1,000, imposed in 1981, was still in effect in 1991. Also levied are a sales tax of 0.5%–2%, inheritance and gift taxes, and social security payroll taxes.

37 CUSTOMS AND DUTIES

Imports are subject to tariff duties, which constitute a major source of government income. Import duties are specific (based on weight) for some commodities, ad valorem (based on c.i.f. value) for others. Specific duties apply to foodstuffs, beverages, petroleum products, and certain rubber and textile products. All exports and some imports require licenses. Customs duties are 75% on luxury items (plus import duty surcharges of up to 25% on cosmetics, perfumes, luxury jewelry, beer and malt beverages, alcoholic spirits, cigars, and cigarettes).

Goods may be landed, stored, sorted, manufactured, repacked, reforwarded, or transshipped within the area of the Free Port of Monrovia without payment of customs duties.

38 FOREIGN INVESTMENT

Liberia has historically maintained an "open door" policy toward foreign investment. It has allowed a limited period of exemption from certain types of taxes and permits an unrestricted flow of dividend payments. In the past, there were no foreign exchange restrictions, and remittance of profits is assured in principle.

Since 1985, however, investment in Liberia has become very precarious. The currency, once linked to the US dollar, has been inflated substantially, an inflation that seems likely to continue. Attempts to bring financial stability to the economy failed dramatically in the early 1990s with the failure of the US-sponsored oversight mission and the breakdown in relations between Liberia and the IMF. In 1989, interest on long term debt stood at 105% of exports.

In the past, most of Liberia's principal enterprises were foreign owned, with US investment—about $300 million in 1987—foremost. Substantial investments have also been made by the British, French, Swedish, Israelis, Swiss, Dutch, Italians, and Lebanese. More recently, there has been a tendency toward the formation of companies owned jointly by Liberians and foreigners.

39 ECONOMIC DEVELOPMENT

The civil war and international financial obligations dim the prospects of economic development. In spite of the record of financial mismanagement, the continued interest of the United States in Liberia's future is reflected in the increased levels of economic aid it has contributed during the civil war ($140 million in 1990–91).

The agricultural sector has sustained itself throughout these recent years, and much of the mining infrastructure is still in place. While refugee resettlement looms as an early postwar priority, future economic development depends on reestablishing international confidence in Liberia's financial management.

40 SOCIAL DEVELOPMENT

Before the civil war, welfare activities carried out by the Ministry of Health and Social Welfare; by US medical, economic, and agricultural missions (concentrated in AID); and by Christian missions. The Liberian Red Cross was active in child care and welfare, as were the Antoinette Tubman Welfare Foundation and the Catherine Mills Rehabilitation Center. In 1976, the National

Social Security and Welfare Corp. was established to administer pensions, sickness benefits, and welfare funds. Today, however, virtually no social services are functioning.

41 HEALTH

Liberia has one of Africa's highest fertility rates; in 1986 it averaged 6.9 children for every woman surviving through her childbearing years. There were 132,000 births in 1992, with an average life expectancy of only 55 years. In 1992 there were an estimated 12 doctors per 100,000 people, with a nurse to doctor ratio of 5:1. In the same year, only about 39% of the population had access to health care services.

The infant mortality rate was 146 per 1,000 live births in 1992 (up from 122 in 1985/86). The general mortality rate in 1993 was 14.2 per 1,000 people. The Liberian staple diet of rice or cassava (manioc) is deficient in protein, and children in particular suffer from the deficiency. The major causes of death are malaria and gastrointestinal disease, attributable in part to poor sanitation. The WHO estimates that about 1 million people in sub-Saharan Africa are HIV positive. Between 1990 and 1992, there were approximately 20,000 war-related deaths.

42 HOUSING

Many of the older corrugated-iron structures in Monrovia have been replaced with more modern dwellings, and houses of advanced design have been privately built to accommodate the growing urban population. There were 216,206 dwellings in 1981 and 500,000 as of 1988, with 4.8 people per dwelling.

The typical dwelling of the tribal people in the Liberian interior is the rondavel, a circular, one-room mud-and-wattle thatch-roofed hut, windowless and with a single low door. These rondavels are being replaced by large rectangular huts, also of mud and wattle, subdivided into two or more rooms and equipped with windows.

43 EDUCATION

Although education is compulsory from ages 6 to 16, probably fewer than half of all children aged 6–18 are in school. The adult literacy rate in 1990 was 39.5% (males: 49.8% and females: 28.8%). The largest secondary school is the Booker Washington Institute, a vocational school located at Kakata, with about 1,500 students.

There are three institutions of higher learning: the government-operated University of Liberia in Monrovia (established in 1862); Cuttington University College at Monrovia, an Episcopalian institution; and a three-year engineering school, the William V. S. Tubman College of Technology, founded at Monrovia in 1978.

44 LIBRARIES AND MUSEUMS

The government maintains a central public library in Monrovia, with 15,000 volumes. UNESCO also operates a library in Monrovia, and the Liberian Information Service has a research library in the same city. The University of Liberia's library contains 107,384 volumes. The National Museum of Liberia is housed in the renovated Supreme Court building in Monrovia, and the Tubman Center of African Cultures is located in Robertsport. Other museums include the National Cultural Center in Cape Mount, the Africana Museum at Monrovia, the W. V. S. Tubman Library-Museum at Harper, and the Biology Museum at the University of Liberia.

45 MEDIA

Many existing newspapers and magazines ceased publication when the Doe regime was overthrown in 1990. Since the following year, a number of new ones have been begun, including *The Inquirer*, *New Times*, and *The Patriot*.

The number of radio receivers increased from 152,000 in 1969 to 600,000 in 1991. The first television station was opened early in 1964; although government owned, it was partly commercial. In 1991 there were about 49,000 television sets.

46 ORGANIZATIONS

Civic groups in Monrovia include the YMCA and YWCA, the Antoinette Tubman Children's Welfare Foundation, the Liberia Evangelistic Women Workers, and the Red Cross, Boy Scouts, and Girl Guides. Liberia Chamber of Commerce has its headquarters in Monrovia. Numerous secret societies are found among all the ethnic groups. Cultural groups include the Society of Liberian Authors, Liberian Arts and Crafts Association, and Liberian Research Association.

47 TOURISM, TRAVEL, AND RECREATION

Continued civil unrest has had an adverse effect on tourism. Visitors, except for Guineans and Sierra Leoneans, must obtain a visa (permitting a 60-day stay). Several hotels in or near Monrovia are suitable for tourists, and although there are few hotels in the interior, several missionary organizations accommodate visitors.

48 FAMOUS LIBERIANS

Joseph Jenkins Roberts (1809–76), who was governor under the Colonization Society at the time the republic was established, became its first and later its sixth president (1848–56, 1872–76) and gained the respect of the European colonial powers by his able exposition of Liberia's rights as a free and independent nation. The national heroine is Matilda Newport, who helped to repel an attack on the first struggling settlement. Among white Americans who went to Liberia to assist the early black settlers were Jehudi Ashmun (1794–1828) and Ralph Randolph Gurley (1797–1872), who together reorganized the colonists in 1824. William Vacanarat Shadrach Tubman (1895–1971) was president of Liberia from 1944 until 1971. Angie E. Brooks-Randolph (b.1928) served as president of the 1969/70 UN General Assembly. William Richard Tolbert, Jr. (1913–80) succeeded Tubman as president. He was killed in the 1980 coup led by Samuel Kanyon Doe (b.1950), who subsequently assumed the titles of commander in chief of the armed forces and chairman of the PRC; he was elected president in 1985.

49 DEPENDENCIES

Liberia has no territories or colonies.

50 BIBLIOGRAPHY

American University. *Liberia: A Country Study.* 3d ed. Washington, D.C.: Government Printing Office, 1984.

Boley, G. E. *Liberia: The Rise and Fall of the First Republic.* New York: St. Martin's, 1985.

Dunn, D. Elwood, and Svend E. Holsoe. *Historical Dictionary of Liberia.* Metuchen, N.J.: Scarecrow, 1985.

Dunn, D. Elwood. *Liberia: A National Polity in Transition.* Metuchen, N.J.: Scarecrow Press, 1988.

Gershoni, Yekutiel. *Black Colonialism: The Americo-Liberian Struggle for the Hinterland.* Boulder, Colo.: Westview, 1984.

Gifford, Paul. *Christianity and Politics in Doe's Liberia.* New York: Cambridge University Press, 1993.

Kieh, George Klay. *Dependency and the Foreign Policy of a Small Power: The Liberian Case.* San Francisco: Mellen Research University Press, 1992.

Liebenow, J. Gus. *Liberia: The Quest for Democracy.* Bloomington: Indiana University Press, 1987.

Lowenkopf, Martin. *Politics in Liberia: The Conservative Road to Development.* Stanford, Calif.: Hoover Institution Press, 1976.

Wilson, Charles Morrow. *Liberia: Black Africa in Microcosm.* New York: Harper & Row, 1971.

LIBYA

Socialist People's Libyan Arab Jamahiriya
Al-Jamahiriyah al-ʿArabiyah al-Libiyah ash-Shaʿbiyah al-Ishtirakiyah

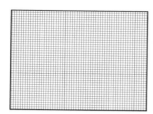

CAPITAL: Tripoli (Tarabulus).

FLAG: The national flag is plain green.

ANTHEM: *Almighty God.*

MONETARY UNIT: The Libyan dinar (LD) of 1,000 dirhams is a paper currency. There are coins of 1, 5, 10, 20, 50, and 100 dirhams, and notes of ¼, ½, 1, 5, and 10 dinars. LD1 = $3.1642 (or $1 = LD0.3160).

WEIGHTS AND MEASURES: The metric system is the legal standard, but some local weights and measures are used.

HOLIDAYS: UK Evacuation Day, 28 March; U.S. Evacuation Day, 11 June; Anniversary of the Revolution, 1 September; Constitution Day, 7 October. Muslim religious holidays include 'Id al-Fitr, 'Id al-'Adha', the 1st of Muharram, and Milad an-Nabi.

TIME: 2 PM = noon GMT.

¹LOCATION, SIZE, AND EXTENT

Situated on the coast of North Africa, Libya is the fourth-largest country on the continent, with an area of 1,759,540 sq km (679,362 sq mi), extending 1,989 km (1,236 mi) SE–NW and 1,502 km (933 mi) NE–SW. Comparatively, the area occupied by Libya is slightly larger than the state of Alaska. It is bounded on the N by the Mediterranean Sea, on the E by Egypt, on the SE by the Sudan, on the S by Chad and Niger, on the W by Algeria, and on the NW by Tunisia, with a total boundary length of 6,153 km (3,823 mi). The Aozou Strip (114,000 sq km/44,000 sq mi) in northern Chad was claimed and had been occupied by Libya since 1973; in a judgment of 3 February 1994, the UN International Court of Justice returned the Auzou strip to Chad. Monitored by an observer force deployed by the UN Security Council, Libyan forces withdrew on 31 May 1994.

Libya's capital city, Tripoli, is located on the Mediterranean coast.

²TOPOGRAPHY

Libya forms part of the North African plateau extending from the Atlantic Ocean to the Red Sea. The highest point is Bette, a 2,260-m (7,415-ft) peak in the extreme south. The chief geographical areas are Tripolitania, Cyrenaica, the Sirte Desert, and Fezzan. Tripolitania, in the northwest, consists of a series of terraces rising slowly from sea level along the coastal plain of Al-Jifara to a sharp escarpment. At the top of this escarpment is an upland plateau of sand, scrub, and scattered masses of stone, with elevations of up to 1,000 m (3,300 ft). Farther south are depressions extending from east to west. Here are found many oases and artesian wells.

The Sirte Desert is a barren area along the Gulf of Sidra separating Tripolitania and Cyrenaica. An upland plateau rising to about 600 m (2,000 ft) gives a rugged coastline to Cyrenaica. This plateau, the Jabal Akhdar, contains three of Libya's leading cities—Banghazi (or Benghazi), Al-Bayda, and Darnah. Farther south the desert is studded with oases such as Jalu and Jaghbub. The Fezzan, in the southwest, is largely a series of depressions with occasional oases. There are no perennial rivers in the country.

³CLIMATE

The climate has marked seasonal variations influenced by both the Mediterranean Sea and the desert. Along the Tripolitanian coast, summer temperatures reach between 40 and 46°C (104–115°F); farther south, temperatures are even higher. Summers in the north of Cyrenaica range from 27 to 32°C (81–90°F). In Tobruk (Tubruq), the average January temperature is 13°C (55°F); July, 26°C (79°F). The ghibli, a hot, dry desert wind, can change temperatures by 17–22°C (30–40°F) in both summer and winter.

Rainfall varies from region to region. Rain falls generally in a short winter period and frequently causes floods. Evaporation is high, and severe droughts are common. The Jabal Akhdar region of Cyrenaica receives a yearly average of 40 to 60 cm (16–24 in). Other regions have less than 20 cm (8 in), and the Sahara has less than 5 cm (2 in) a year.

⁴FLORA AND FAUNA

The primary plant is the deadly carrot (*Thapsia garganica*). Other flora are various cultivated fruit trees, date palms, junipers, and mastic trees. In 1986 there were approximately 3 million productive date palm trees and 3.4 million olive trees. Goats and cattle are found in the extreme north. In the south, sheep and camels are numerous.

⁵ENVIRONMENT

A major environmental concern is the depletion of underground water as a result of overuse in agricultural developments, causing salinity and sea-water penetration into the coastal aquifers. Another significant environmental problem in Libya is water pollution. The combined impact of sewage, oil byproducts, and industrial waste threatens the nation's coast and the Mediterranean Sea in general. Libya has 0.2 cu mi of water with 75% used in farming activity and 10% for industrial purposes. Twenty percent of the people living in rural areas do not have pure water. The nation's cities produce 0.6 million tons of solid waste per year. It contributes 0.1% to the world's total gas emissions. The desertification of existing fertile areas is being combated by the planting of trees as windbreaks. As of 1994, twelve of Libya's mammal species and 9 of its bird species are endangered.

225

Fifty-eight of its plant species are also endangered. In 1987, endangered species in Libya included the Mediterranean monk seal. The leopard and slender-horned gazelle are extinct.

6POPULATION

The population at the time of the 1984 census was 3,637,488, and the population in 1994 was estimated at 4,753,899 by the US Census Bureau. The UN, however, estimated the 1995 population at 5,407,000. A population of 6,386,000 was projected for the year 2000, assuming a crude birthrate of 39.9 per 1,000 population, a crude death rate of 6.9, and a net natural increase of 33 during 1995–2000. The population density for the whole country in 1994 was estimated at 2.7 per sq km (7 per sq mi), but 90% of Libya's inhabitants live in the narrow coastal regions of Cyrenaica and Tripolitania. Urbanization has increased rapidly in recent years; more than 85% of the population is now urban. The two chief cities, Tripoli and Banghazi, had populations of 1,650,000 and 850,000, respectively, in 1992.

7MIGRATION

The number of Italians was as high as 70,000 during the period of colonial rule. In 1964 there were 30,000. Most left after their land and property were nationalized in 1970. There were 30,000 Jews in Libya in 1948, but because of the Arab-Israeli conflict the community had virtually disappeared by 1973.

In 1984 there were officially 263,100 non-Libyans in the country, of whom more than 40% were Egyptians and 15% were Tunisians. The remainder came from a variety of other countries in Africa, the Mideast, and elsewhere. This figure was less than half the 569,000 foreigners in 1983, before new restrictions were placed on remittances abroad. In 1992, the foreign population was estimated at 2 million, half of them Egyptian, and 600,000 from South Korea, the Philippines, Thailand, and Vietnam. This higher figure probably reflects illegal immigration. About 100,000 Libyans were in exile in the mid-1980s.

The nomadic inhabitants of Libya follow regular patterns of migration; nomadic tribes in the south normally ignore international frontiers. Since the discovery of oil there has been significant internal migration from rural to urban regions.

8ETHNIC GROUPS

For thousands of years the inhabitants of Libya were Berbers. Arabs started arriving in the 7th century AD, displacing or assimilating their Berber predecessors. The Fezzan has a mixture of Arabs, Berbers, and black Africans from regions to the south. About 10,000 nomadic Tuareg live in the southwestern desert. Few Europeans remain permanently resident in Libya, but there were about 40,000 in the country in 1986.

9LANGUAGES

Arabic is the official language; since 1969, its use in daily life, even by foreigners, has been encouraged by government decree. English, which is also used in some government publications, has replaced Italian as the second language. Berber is spoken by small communities, especially in Tripolitania. Native speakers constitute about 5% of the population.

10RELIGIONS

In 1990, 97% of Libyans were estimated to be Sunni Muslims. Under the 1969 constitution, Islam is Libya's official religion, but freedom for other religions is guaranteed. There were about 48,000 Orthodox, Roman Catholic, and Protestant Christians in 1985, of whom some 40,000 were Roman Catholics.

11TRANSPORTATION

Transportation varies from dirt tracks suitable for camels and donkeys to a coastal highway extending for 1,822 km (1,132 mi) from the Tunisian to the Egyptian border. At the end of 1968, this highway was connected with a north–south road to Sabha; further extensions to Marzuq and Ghat were later completed, as well as a spur to Birak. In 1973, a 350-km (217-mi) road between Nalut and Ghadamis was completed. Roads also connect the Cyrenaica coastal centers with the interior. In all, there were 24,000 km (14,900 mi) of paved roads in 1991. That same year there were 450,000 private cars and 330,000 commercial vehicles registered in the country. Libya's two railway lines were closed down in the early 1960s.

The main ports are Tripoli, Banghazi, Qasr Ahmad (the port for Misratah), and Tobruk. Crude oil export terminals include Port Brega (Marsa al-Burayqah) and Ras Lanuf. Since 1973, Tripoli's harbor has been developed considerably. By the end of 1991, Libya's merchant fleet had 27 vessels totaling 665,000 GRT, including 12 tankers totaling 585,000 GRT.

Libya's two international airports are Tripoli Airport (34 km/21 mi south of Tripoli) and Benina Airport (19 km/12 mi from Banghazi). In 1968, a new airport at Sabha in the Fezzan was opened. Libyan Arab Airlines, established in 1965, operates to neighboring Arab countries, central and southern Africa, and Europe. Many major world airlines serve Libya. There is also regular domestic service, with airports at Tobruk, Port Brega, Ghat, Ghadamis, Misratah, and Al-Bayda.

12HISTORY

Archaeological evidence indicates that a Neolithic culture, skilled in the domestication of cattle and the cultivation of crops, existed as far back as 6000 BC along the Libyan coast. To the south, in what is now the Sahara, hunters and herdsmen roamed what was then a well-watered savanna. Increasing desiccation and the coming of the Berbers about 2000 BC, presumably from southwestern Asia, ended this period. The pharaohs of the so-called Libyan dynasties who ruled Egypt (c.950–720 BC) are thought to have been Berbers. Phoenician seafarers, who arrived early in the first millennium BC, founded settlements along the coast, including one that became Tripoli.

Around the 7th century BC, Greek colonists settled in Cyrenaica. In succeeding centuries, the western settlements fell under the sway of Carthage; the eastern settlements fell to the Egyptian dynasty of the Ptolemies in the 4th century BC. When the Romans defeated Carthage in the Punic Wars of the 3d and 2d centuries BC, they occupied the regions around Tripoli. In 96 BC, they forced Egypt to surrender Cyrenaica, and Roman influence later extended as far south as the Fezzan. Libya became very prosperous under Roman rule; with the decline of Rome, western Libya fell in the 5th century AD to Germanic Vandal invaders, who ruled from Carthage. In the 6th century, the Byzantines conquered the Vandals and ruled the coastal regions of Libya until the Arab conquest of the 7th century. The Arabs intermixed with the Berbers, who were gradually absorbed into the Muslim Arab culture.

Western Libya was administered by the Aghlabids of Tunisia in the 9th century, and by the Fatimids of Tunisia and then Egypt in the 10th. During the 11th century, invasions by two nomadic Arab peoples, the Bani Hilal and Bani Salim, destroyed many of the urban and agricultural areas. Normans from Sicily occupied Tripoli and surrounding regions in 1145 but were soon displaced by the Almohads of Morocco; during the 13th century, the Hafsids of Tunisia ruled western Libya. The eastern regions remained subject to Egyptian dynasties. In the 16th century, Spanish invaders seized parts of the coast, turning over control of Tripoli to the crusading Knights of the Order of St. John of Jerusalem. The Ottoman Turks occupied the coastal regions in 1551, ruling the country until 1711, when Ahmad Qaramanli, of Turkish origin, wrested semiautonomous status from Istanbul. Pirate captains, operating out of Tripoli, raided the Mediterranean and the Italian

LIBYA

0 50 100 150 250 Miles

0 50 100 150 250 Kilometers

LOCATION: 19°30′ to 33°N; 9°30′ to 25°E. **BOUNDARY LENGTHS:** Mediterranean coastline, 1,770 km (1,100 mi); Egypt, 1,115 km (693 mi); Sudan, 383 km (238 mi); Chad, 1,054 km (655 mi); Niger, 354 km (220 mi); Algeria, 982 km (610 mi); Tunisia, 459 km (285 mi). **TERRITORIAL SEA LIMIT:** 12 mi, but all of the Gulf of Sidra s of 32°30′ is claimed.

coasts. The Qaramanlis ruled until 1835, when the Ottomans again assumed control.

In September 1911, the Italians invaded Libya, meeting fierce resistance from both Turks and indigenous Libyans. A peace treaty of 17 October 1912 between Turkey and Italy placed Libya formally under Italian rule, but the Libyans continued

their resistance. Led by a Muslim religious brotherhood, the Sanusi, the Libyans (with some Turkish help) fought the Italians to a standstill during World War I. Following the war, and particularly after the accession of Benito Mussolini to power in Italy, the Italians continued their often brutal efforts to conquer Libya. In 1931, 'Umar al-Mukhtar, a leader of the Sanusi, was captured and executed, and in 1932 the Italian conquest was completed. In World War II, Libya became a main battleground for Allied and Axis forces, until it was occupied by victorious British and Free French troops. The Treaty of 1947 between Italy and the Allies ended Italian rule in Libya and, when the Allies could not decide upon the country's future, Libya's fate was left to the UN. On 21 November 1949, the UN General Assembly voted that Libya should become an independent state. On 24 December 1951, Libya gained independence, with Muhammad Idris al-Mahdi as-Sanusi as king. In 1959 significant oil discoveries were made.

On 1 September 1969, a secret army organization, the Free Unionist Officers, deposed the king and proclaimed a republican regime. On 8 September, the Revolutionary Command Council (RCC) announced the formation of a civilian government. This government resigned on 16 January 1970, and a new cabinet was formed under Col. Mu'ammar al-Qadhafi, chairman of the RCC. Later that year, the UK and US closed their military installations. On 15 April 1973, Qadhafi called for a "cultural revolution" based on Islamic principles. In subsequent months, hundreds of "people's committees" were established to oversee all sectors of the nation's political, cultural, and economic life. In April 1974, Qadhafi withdrew from the supervision of daily administrative functions (these were assumed by Maj. Abdul Salam Jallud), but he remained the effective head of state of Libya.

Qadhafi sought to make Libya the axis of a unified Arab nation. Union was achieved with Egypt, Tunisia, Morocco, Syria, and Sudan at various times, but only on paper. Subsequent relations with the many Arab nations, including Egypt and Tunisia, have often been tense. Libya itself, despite rhetorical support for radical Palestinians, has stayed on the sidelines in Arab-Israeli conflicts.

Qadhafi has been equally active in Africa. In 1973, he annexed from Chad the disputed Aouzou Strip, an area that may contain rich deposits of uranium. In 1979, his armed forces tried unsuccessfully to prop up the failing regime of Idi Amin in Uganda. Libya sent over 10,000 troops into Chad in 1980 in support of the regime of Goukouni Oueddei, and a union of the two nations was proposed. Intense international pressure, however, led to a Libyan withdrawal in November 1981. After the fall of Oueddei's regime in June 1982, Qadhafi provided military support for Oueddei's efforts to topple the new French-backed government in Chad. Libya's and Oueddei's forces were in control of much of northern Chad until 1987, when Chadian forces ousted them, capturing or destroying $1 billion in Libyan military equipment, and attacking bases inside Libya itself. In 1989, after acknowledging his error in moving into Chad, Qadhafi agreed to a cease-fire and the submission of the dispute over the Aouzou Strip to the Court of International Justice. The Court began consideration of the dispute in 1993.

Qadhafi has been accused of supporting subversive plots in such countries as Morocco, Niger, Sudan, Egypt, Tunisia, Ghana, Burkina Faso, Nigeria, Gambia, Somalia, Senegal, and Mali and of providing material support for a variety of insurgents, including the Irish Republican Army, Muslim rebels in the Philippines, and Japanese and German terrorists. Qadhafi did find some support in small, poor black African countries, eager for Libyan aid. In 1982, however, he suffered a setback when the annual OAU summit scheduled for Tripoli failed to convene because of disputes over Libya's policies in Chad and its support of Polisario guerrillas in Western Sahara. As a result, Qadhafi was denied his term as OAU chairman.

In 1981, two Libyan jets were shot down by US fighters over the Gulf of Sidra, an arm of the Mediterranean claimed by Qadhafi as Libya's territorial waters. In 1982, the US, charging Qadhafi with supporting international terrorism, banned oil imports from Libya and the export of US technology to Libya. In January 1986, the US, citing "irrefutable evidence" of Libyan involvement in Palestinian attacks on airports in Rome and Vienna in the previous month, ordered all Americans to leave Libya and cut off all economic ties as of mid-1986. In March, a US naval task force struck four Libyan vessels after US planes entering airspace over the Libyan-claimed Gulf of Sidra were fired upon. On 15 April, following a West Berlin bomb attack in which US servicemen were victims, US warplanes bombed targets in Tripoli and Banghazi. Libya said that Qadhafi's daughter was killed and two of his sons were wounded in the attack. Qadhafi has survived several reported assassination and coup attempts (1984 and 1993) and the opposition of Islamist groups which prompted him to crack down on militants in 1993. His most serious challenge has been the tough sanctions imposed in 1993 on Libya by the UN Security Council after he refused to surrender two men suspected in the terrorist bombing of a Pan American passenger jet over Lockerbie, Scotland, in 1988. The UN resolution prohibits sales of equipment and air travel to Libya and freezes its overseas bank deposits, but does not ban oil sales. Negotiations for the extradition and trial of the two suspects were continuing in 1994.

13 GOVERNMENT

The Libyan Arab Republic was established on 1 September 1969, and a new constitution was announced by the RCC on 11 December 1969. The constitution, which has been effectively superseded by the principles of Qadhafi's "Green Book," proclaimed Libya to be "an Arab, democratic, and free Republic which constitutes part of the Arab nation and whose objective is comprehensive Arab unity." Supreme authority rested with the 12-member RCC, which appointed both the prime minister and cabinet. Qadhafi, as chairman of the RCC, was the effective head of state and commander in chief of the armed forces. In March 1977, the nation's name was changed to the Socialist People's Libyan Arab Jamahiriya, and the "authority of the people" was proclaimed by a newly convened General People's Congress (GPC). The people theoretically exercise their authority through a system of people's congresses and committees. At the top of this system is the 1,112-member GPC, which replaced the RCC as the supreme instrument of government. All executive and legislative authority is vested in the GPC, but it meets for only two weeks a year and delegates most of its authority to its own Secretariat and to the General People's Committee, in effect the cabinet, which is appointed by the Secretariat. In 1979, Qadhafi gave up his official post as secretary-general of the GPC to become a "private citizen." As "Leader of the Revolution," however, he remains the de facto head of state. He also remains the commander of the armed forces and virtually all power is concentrated in him and his close advisers. In 1988, public discontent with shortages led Qadhafi to limit the authority of revolutionary committees, release many political prisoners, and remove restrictions on foreign travel and private enterprise.

14 POLITICAL PARTIES

Political parties have not played an effective role in Libya's history. All political parties were banned in 1947 by British administrators, but many groups soon emerged to debate their country's future. By 1949, the Tripolitanian National Congress Party, led by Bashir Sadawi, was the leading party. However, it was dissolved in 1952, following local disorders, after Libya's first election campaign.

In 1971, the RCC founded the Libyan Arab Socialist Union as an alternative to political parties. It was viewed as an organization to promote national unity but has functioned little since 1977. Seven exiled opposition groups agreed in Cairo in January 1987 to form a joint working group, but their work has had no discernible impact on political conditions in Libya.

15 LOCAL GOVERNMENT

Libya is divided into 10 administrative provinces and 46 municipalities, which are tightly controlled by the central government. A system of popular congresses has been formed to make recommendations to the GPC. There are basic congresses (2,236 in 1985), whose secretary and assistant secretary are delegates to the GPC, and municipal people's congresses, whose representatives are chosen from the basic congresses. The municipal people's congresses appoint people's committees to execute policy. Revolutionary committees, created in 1977, are nonofficial but send delegates to the GPC and were given the right by Qadhafi in 1979 to organize basic people's congress elections.

16 JUDICIAL SYSTEM

The Libyan legal system largely follows Egyptian codes and precedents. All cases relating to personal status are dealt with according to Muslim law. Minor civil and commercial cases may be heard by a sitting judge in each village and town. Other cases of the first instance are heard by courts of first instance, and appeals may be taken to provincial courts of appeal. There is also a Supreme Court, consisting of a president and judges appointed by the GPC. It may deal with constitutional and legislative questions referred to it and may hear administrative cases. There are also special people's and military courts that try purported crimes against the state. In 1981, the private practice of law was abolished and all lawyers became employees of the secretariat of justice. Since 1981, revolutionary committees have been encouraged to conduct public trials without legal safeguards.

17 ARMED FORCES

Compulsory military service for all males was introduced in 1975, but is selectively applied for two-to-four-year conscripts In theory, conscription also applies to females. In 1993, the army had 55,000 personnel organized into 28 brigades, about half armored, half infantry; armaments included 2,150 tanks, all made in the former Soviet Union. The navy had 8,000 personnel and 54 vessels, including 6 Russian submarines. The air force had 22,000 personnel, with 409 combat aircraft and 45 combat helicopters. There was also a paramilitary Pan-African Legion and Revolution Guard Corps of 6,000. The military budget was estimated at $1.7 billion or 7% of gross domestic product. During 1981–91, Libya imported $16.5 billion worth of arms, most of it from the USSR. Russian advisors number 1,000.

18 INTERNATIONAL COOPERATION

Libya is a member of the UN, having joined on 14 December 1955, and is a member of ECA and all the nonregional specialized agencies. It joined the Arab League in 1953, the OAU in 1963, and OPEC in 1962. In January 1968, it was a founding member of OAPEC, along with Sa'udi Arabia and Kuwait. Libya also belongs to the African Development Bank and G-77.

19 ECONOMY

Until the late 1950s, Libya was one of the poorest countries in the world. In 1950, per capita annual income was about $40, while Libya's most valuable source of foreign earnings was the revenue received for leasing bases to the UK and US (the bases were vacated in 1970). But with the discovery of the Zaltan oil field in 1959, the economic horizons of the country were dramatically enlarged. The first oil pipeline, from B'ir Zaltan to the coast, was opened in 1961. More oil fields were subsequently discovered, until in 1970 a peak oil output of 159.9 million tons was achieved. Production has fallen since then, but its value has increased, and Libya remains one of the world's leading oil producers. Petroleum, petroleum products, and natural gas accounted for more than 99% of the value of exports and for 40% of the GDP in 1985.

Until the late 1950s, about 80% of the population was engaged in agriculture and animal husbandry; in 1989, however, only 19% of the labor force was engaged in agricultural pursuits. Agriculture, forestry, and fishing represented only 5.5% of GDP in 1989. A massive water pipeline project, called the Great Man Made River (GMR) project was initiated in the early 1990s. The GMR will carry water in a 267-mile-long pipeline from 225 underground wells to an 880,000 gallon reservoir. This scheme envisages providing irrigation to 1.2 million acres which will be devoted to cereal cultivation. The government believes that this project will help Libya achieve self-sufficiency in grain. Total costs of the GMR are likely to exceed $25 billion.

The fall in oil prices and foreign oil demand that occurred in the early 1980s led to a severe drop in Libya's export earnings. Development plans were subsequently trimmed. The GDP was believed to have fallen 20% during 1984–86. After 1985, growth rates fluctuated sharply, reflecting changes in the oil market.

Since the 1992 UN-imposed air embargo, many large projects have been postponed because of budget restrictions. Libya's isolation has slowed the pace of oil exploration through the absence of major foreign oil companies. Lack of outlets is limiting the development of refineries, petrochemicals, and gas facilities.

20 INCOME

In 1992 Libya's GNP was $5,800 per capita. For the period 1985–92 the average inflation rate was 7.0%. In 1992 the GDP was $2,610 million in current US dollars.

21 LABOR

According to figures for 1992, the total labor force was 1,120,000, plus 1,750,000 non-Libyans. About 27% were employed in services; 31% in mining, manufacturing, construction, and utilities; 18% in agriculture, forestry, hunting and fishing, and 24% in government. Foreign workers, who do much of the blue-collar and technical work, are not treated with equality under Libyan labor law, and may only stay in the country for the duration of their employment contracts. The largest employer is the government, which operates public utilities, public works, several banks, the port and harbor organizations, and other enterprises. One of Qadhafi's goals has been guaranteed employment. Unemployment scarcely exists, and workers from foreign, especially Arab, countries, were recruited until development plans were scaled down in the 1980s. In early 1990, Qadhafi suddenly began deporting thousands of black African workers, claiming they were in Libya illegally. Chadian, Nigerian, Nigerien, Malian, and Ghanaian workers were rounded up at work or home and sent back with no warning to their respective governments.

A labor law issued by the government in May 1970 defines the rights of trade unions, provides for one trade union for each trade, and establishes arbitration and conciliation procedures. It prohibits strikes before the use of these procedures and provides for a 48-hour workweek, pension rights, and minimum rest periods. In the early 1990s, there had been no report of strikes for years, and presumably strikes were not permitted. A law promulgated in March 1970 provides that foreigners may be employed only if there are no Libyans available and that preference must be given to Arab nationals. A 1973 law provided for profit sharing in all firms, including state companies with more than 10 employees.

The General Federation of Producers' Trade Unions, created in 1972, is the official trade union organization. All Libyan workers are required to join a trade union (expatriates are banned from joining). Unions are administered through people's committees.

22 AGRICULTURE

Only about 1.2% of the country is cultivated. As of 1991, about 71% of the cultivated total was irrigated.

Agriculture is the only economic sector in which private ownership is still important. Cereals are grown in Tripolitania and Cyrenaica; agriculture in the Fezzan is concentrated in the oases. Virtually all crops are grown for domestic consumption. Nevertheless, most agricultural products must be imported; the cost, in 1992, was $1.1 billion. Estimated agricultural output in 1992, in tons, included tomatoes, 175,000; wheat, 150,000; potatoes, 150,000; barley, 145,000; and onions, 86,000. The 1992 production of fruits, in tons, included watermelons, 215,000; oranges, 98,000; dates, 76,000; and olives, 72,000.

Libya is investing a significant share of national revenues in agriculture in the hope of someday becoming agriculturally self-sufficient; cultivation has been changing from subsistence farming to highly mechanized operations. Development plans aim to increase irrigation and introduce and extend the use of advanced techniques; seeds and fertilizers have been subsidized. Areas singled out for development include the Al-Jifara Plain in Tripolitania; the Jabal Akhdar, east of Banghazi; part of the Fezzan; and the oases of Kufrah and Sarir. In the Kufrah oasis, large, untapped water reserves are being utilized to help provide fodder for sheep. In 1984, Libya embarked on a massive project to pipe water to the coast from underwater aquifers. The project was designed to transport 2 million cu m of water per day via 2,000 km (1,240 mi) of pipeline from 270 artesian wells in th east to connect Sirte and Benghazi. The first phase was inaugurated in 1991 at a cost of $5 billion; the total project is estimated to cost $25 billion. In all, the scheme would provide 50 years of irrigation to the coastal areas, where 80% of Libya's agriculture is located.

A government agency markets farm produce and has authority to operate cooperatives and farms. The Agricultural Bank has been provided with sufficient capital to make short- and long-term loans easily available.

23ANIMAL HUSBANDRY

Before the transformation of the economy by the discovery of oil, livestock was an important sector, providing transport, clothing, food, and skins for tents. South of the Jabal areas, a wide belt of drought-resistant vegetation extending across most of the country is still used by nomadic and seminomadic herdsmen for grazing. In the Fezzan, the nomads move about between oases or other places where vegetation is suitable for their animals. Libya's livestock are vulnerable to disease and drought, and in past years losses have reached as high as 60%.

The livestock population of Libya in 1992 included 5,600,000 sheep, 1,250,000 goats, 135,000 head of cattle, 155,000 camels, 28,000 horses, 63,000 donkeys, and 58 million chickens. Private dairy farms are allowed to operate, but their milk has to be sold to the state. The government maintains large poultry farms.

New strains of livestock and more efficient grazing practices are being encouraged. The government hopes its development plans will make Libya self-sufficient in meat supplies. Livestock products in 1992 included 179,000 tons of meat, 35,750 tons of eggs, 49,000 tons of sheep milk, and 150,000 tons of cow milk.

24FISHING

Fishing is of minor importance, but the government is actively supporting extension of fishing and related activities, including the construction of sardine canning factories and modern storage facilities in the principal ports and the creation of local fishing fleets. Libya's excellent fishing grounds contain tuna, sardines, and other fish, but the industry has failed to meet increasing domestic demand. The catch was 7,833 tons in 1991.

25FORESTRY

The only important forest areas in Libya are shrubby juniper growths in the Jabal Akhdar areas of Cyrenaica. A few conifers are found in more isolated districts. Tripolitania has some forest remnants in inaccessible regions. Encroaching sand dunes in the north create a need for afforestation, and many acacia, Aleppo pine, carob, cypress, eucalyptus, olive, and palm trees have been planted. As of 1991, some 695,000 hectares (1,717,000 acres) of Libyan territory were classified as "forest," but almost all of this land could more properly be called maquis. Dune fixation, both for reforestation and to preserve agricultural land, has been an important part of the forestry program.

Up to 1976, the government had planted 213 million seedlings, mostly in western Libya. By 1981, 165,405 hectares (408,722 acres) of forest and 63,443 hectares (156,770 acres) of windbreak had been planted. During the 1980s, reforestation was proceeding at the rate of 32,000 hectares (79,000 acres) per year. In 1991, roundwood removals were estimated at 645,000 cu m, of which 536,000 cu m were used for fuel.

26MINING

In addition to oil and natural gas, Libya has large reserves of iron ore in the Fezzan. There is also potash in the Sirte Desert, limestone (for cement), and marine salt. It is estimated that there are deposits of 7.5 million tons of magnesium salts and 1.6 million tons of potassium salts in Maradah, about 128 km (80 mi) south of the oil terminal at Port Brega. Estimated production in 1991 included lime, 260,000 tons; gypsum, 180,000 tons; and sulfur, 14,000 tons. Libya also possess gypsum, magnetite, phosphate rock, potash, salt, and sulfur reserves, but no reserve amounts have been officially reported.

27ENERGY AND POWER

In 1955, following the discovery of oil in Algeria, oil exploration began in Libya. Instead of creating an exclusive countrywide concession, the law divided all Libyan territory into lots: British, French, and US companies were granted concessions, beginning in November 1955. With the discovery of the Zaltan field by Esso interests in 1959, a new era in the economy of Libya opened. A pipeline was laid from Bi'r Zaltan to the coast at Port Brega and was opened in September 1961. Further discoveries led to the opening of additional oil ports. Among the main oil-producing fields are those at Gialo, Amal, Waha, Raguba, and Sarir. The Bouri offshore field, off the Tripolitania coast, was under development in the late 1980s.

In 1968, the Libyan government set new conditions that were to apply to concessionary agreements with petroleum companies. Under the new "partnership" agreements, the term of each contract was reduced from 50 to 25 years; Libyan participation was to begin at 25% when the company's average oil production reached 10 million tons per year and to increase gradually to a full 50% when production reached 27.5 million tons. In April 1968, the government established the Libyan General Petroleum Corp. (LIPETCO), whose functions included the negotiation and supervision of such agreements; LIPETCO negotiated four agreements during the next 2 years. By a decree of 5 March 1970, the RCC replaced LIPETCO with the Libyan National Oil Corp. (NOC), which was to oversee all phases of the oil industry. In 1971, all distributing companies were merged into the Brega Petroleum Marketing Co., which was to market, transport, and distribute oil within Libya. After the creation of NOC, an entire reorganization of the oil industry took place, marked by an increasing intervention of the Libyan government. By September 1970, agreements with the exploiting companies were reached, giving the Libyans a price for their oil similar to that paid in Middle Eastern countries. On 20 March 1971, the Tripoli Agreement further increased prices paid, as well as rates of taxation. During 1971, the government worked for new participation agreements with firms owned by Italian, US, French, German, Spanish, British, and Dutch nationals. When some of the companies refused to reduce their share to 49%, the British Petroleum (BP) affiliate was nationalized, becoming the Arab Gulf Exploration Co. In November 1974, BP agreed to accept £17.4 million in cash and a writeoff of £45 million in unpaid taxes and royalties as a full and final settlement of its claims. Other companies accepted the proposed system, with or without formal agreements.

In 1973, the remaining foreign oil companies had 51% of their assets nationalized; those not agreeing were taken over completely and received compensation in 1977. In 1991, the NOC had a 70% overall share in the oil industry, ranging from 51 to 81% in various foreign companies and consortiums.

Production fell after 1970, at first because of conservation and political decisions, and later because of falling demand for Libya's high-quality (but also high-cost) oil. From the 1970 peak of 157.4 million tons, production fell to 75.2 million tons by 1974. It rebounded to 99.6 million tons in 1979, but because of reduced world demand, production was only 47.9 million tons in 1987. The 1992 output was 73 million tons, second highest in Africa. Crude petroleum reserves were estimated at 3.1 billion tons in 1992. As of 1993, Libya could produce oil for 42 more years before depletion of reserves.

In 1993, Libya was receiving $17.55 a barrel for its low-sulfur oil, compared with $30.15 in 1985 and $2.09 in 1970. Its oil also earned a premium because of its proximity to European markets. However, with the high price and worldwide recession reducing demand, the price of world crude oil at times fell below $10 a barrel in 1986. Earnings from oil fell from a peak of $22.53 billion in 1980 to only $4.8 billion in 1986, before climbing back to $9.4 billion in 1992.

As of 1993, the UN sanctions imposed on 15 April 1992 did not include restrictions on petroleum exports. The US is trying to convince the UN to include an embargo of Libyan oil, which would devastate the economy. As of 1992, petroleum accounted for 98% of Libya's exports.

Reserves of natural gas were estimated at 1,300 billion cu m in 1992. Output increased from 465 million cu m in 1971 to a peak of 23,470 million cu m in 1979. Production was 6,900 million cu m in 1992. As of 1993, there were six natural gas plants in Libya; three at Intisar, two at Marsa al-Brega, and one at Zueitina.

Power production is a government enterprise. Total electric power generation in 1991 was estimated at 19,500 million kwh, compared with 256.6 million kwh in 1968; installed capacity was 4,100,000 kw. In 1991, all of Libya's power production was thermal and based on fossil fuels.

28 INDUSTRY

Libyan manufacturing industries had been developing significantly since the early 1960s, but have fallen far behind the petroleum sector of the economy. The total industrial contribution to GDP in 1962 was LD9 million; in 1972, it was LD28.3 million, or 1.3% of GDP; in 1980, LD265 million, or 2.6% of GDP; in 1984, LD360 million, or 4.8% of GDP, and in 1988 LD 487.5 million, or 7.3% of GDP. Among the many industries utilizing petroleum products is a natural gas liquefaction plant which went into operation in 1971 at Marsa al-Brega. There are refineries at Az-zawiyah (NOC) and Marsa al-Brega (ex-Esso/Noc) and a 2270,000 barrels per day export refinery at Ras Lanerf was completed in 1985. Total refinery capacity is now about 370,000 b/d, and actual refinery, throughput is thought to have risen to around 780,000 b/d in 1990.

A large methanol, ammonia, and urea plant is at Marsa al-Brega, and a major plant producing ethylene and other petrochemicals was opened at Ras Lanuf in 1987. The $6 billion iron and steel complex at Misratah began operations in 1990. A series of large cement plants was also being built, and production was 3.5 million tons in 1989. Ammonia production was 300,000 tons in 1989.

Libya's other manufacturing industries are small, lightly capitalized, and devoted primarily to the processing of local agricultural products (tanning, canning fruits and vegetables, milling flour, and processing olive oil), and to textiles, building materials, and basic consumer items. Handicraft products include carpets and rugs, silver jewelry, textiles, glassware, and leather goods.

29 SCIENCE AND TECHNOLOGY

There is a predominance of foreign labor in scientific and technical positions. Al-Fatah University, at Tripoli, has faculties of science, engineering, agriculture, medicine, pharmacy, veterinary medicine, nuclear engineering, and petroleum and mining engineering. The University of Garyounis at Banghazi has faculties of medicine, science, engineering, dentistry, and agriculture. Bright Star University of Technology, at Marsa al-Brega, was founded in 1981. Al-Arab Medical University has 2,209 students. Sebha University has faculties of science and agriculture, and schools of medicine and engineering. A postal and telecommunications institute is at Tripoli.

Despite its abundant oil and gas reserves, Libya is highly interested in nuclear power. A 10-Mw research reactor is located at Tajura.

30 DOMESTIC TRADE

Tripoli, the leading port and transportation center, is the focus of trading activities. Domestic trade is limited by the sparsity of population and transportation difficulties. In 1978, Qadhafi announced that individuals should cease engaging in trade or marketing, and in 1979 the private import-export trade was banned. In 1981, all shops were closed and replaced by huge supermarkets with stocks purchased by the state. About a dozen basic commodities are price-subsidized, and a rationing system was established in 1984. Because of an acute shortage of consumer goods, including food staples, some private stores were allowed to reopen by 1987. The sale of alcohol is prohibited.

An annual international trade fair is held in Tripoli each March. Normal business hours are 7 AM to 2 or 2:30 PM, Saturday through Thursday. Banks are open Saturday through Thursday from 8:30 AM to 12:30 PM in winter and from 8 AM to 12 PM in summer. Summer banking hours also include 4–5 PM, Saturday through Wednesday.

31 FOREIGN TRADE

Libya has long enjoyed a favorable trade balance because of exports of crude oil. However, lower world demand for Libya's high-priced oil reduced the country's usually hefty trade surplus to $192 million in 1981, but surpluses were again piled up in succeeding years by sharply cutting imports. By 1985 exports were $10 billion, less than half the 1980 level of $21.4 billion. In 1986, the crash in world oil prices resulted in total export earnings falling to $5.7 billion, of which crude oil accounted for $5.4 billion. A recovery in prices pushed crude oil export revenues up to $7.5 billion in 1989. The Persian Gulf crisis in 1990 led to a record-breaking $10 billion in export revenues. The most important imports are foodstuffs, machinery, transport equipment, iron and steel products, and basic manufactured goods.

The following table shows Libya's exports and imports (in millions of dollars):

FOREIGN TRADE	1988	1989	1990
Exports	5,374	7,750	10,005
Crude oil	5,169	7,500	9,700
Imports	−5,911	−5,497	−5,882
Balance	−537	2,253	4,123

Italy was the leading trade partner in 1986, with about 25% of total trade (28% of exports, 23% of imports). Germany accounted for about 13% (14% of exports, 12% of imports). Other leading trade partners were Spain, France, and the UK. In January 1986, the US halted all trade with Libya.

Exports to Italy rose 27.6% in 1983 and 54.1% in 1990. Total Libyan sales to Germany, Spain, France, and the UK registered year-on-year increases of 33%, 50%, 63%, and 57% respectively. The oil price decline in 1991 led to a 9% decrease in the value of exports to Italy. Libya's major suppliers in 1990 were Italy (taking 20.4% of the market share), Germany (14.2%), and the UK (8.1%). Trade with the USSR, which constituted mainly oil-for-arms barter deals, ended with the breakdown of the USSR in 1991.

32BALANCE OF PAYMENTS

Libya customarily registered balance-of-payments surpluses from 1962 until 1981, thanks to large trade surpluses derived from the export of oil. Declining oil production caused payments deficits from 1981 to 1984. The services and transfers accounts are in deficit because of travel by Libyans abroad, transportation costs, payments to foreign contractors, and remittances by foreign workers. The capital account is also usually in deficit because of Libyan aid and investment abroad. Foreign debt is difficult to calculate because trade debts are often settled by the barter supply of oil. In 1985, the total external debt (excluding most trade-released arrears) was put at $3.2 billion, but about $4 billion more was owed to foreign contractors, and an unspecified sum was owed to creditors from the former Soviet bloc countries.

Foreign exchange reserves, which reached $13,444 million at the end of June 1981, declined sharply to $5,936 million by 30 September 1982. As of 30 June 1987, they stood at $5,115 million.

33BANKING AND SECURITIES

The Central Bank of Libya, established in 1956, supervises the national banking system, regulates credit and interest, and issues bank notes. It also regulates the volume of currency in circulation, acts as a banker to the government, provides clearinghouse facilities for the country's commercial banks, and administers exchange control. Since 5 August 1962, the bank has been vested with a monopoly in the import of fine gold. As of 1992, Central Bank foreign assets were LD1,922.5 million.

Libya formerly had branches of many Arab, Italian, and British commercial banks; they were nationalized in 1969. The government ruled that 51% of the capital of each should be taken over by the government, which paid the value of this share. Thus, the Banco di Roma became Umma Bank, Barclays Bank eventually became Jamahiriya Bank, and the Banco di Sicilia became the Sahara Bank. The commercial department of the Central Bank was merged with two small banks to form the National Commercial Bank. In 1972, a reorganization of the commercial banks left the Jamahiriya and Umma banks owned by the Central Bank of Libya; two other institutions, the Sahara Bank and the Wahda Bank, were jointly owned by the Central Bank and private interests. As of 1992, commercial bank reserves totaled LD1,786.3 million; demand deposits were LD2,693 million.

The National Agricultural Bank, established in 1957, provides advice and guidance on agricultural problems, advances loans to farm cooperatives, and generally assists the agricultural community. The Industrial and Real Estate Bank, founded in 1965, made loans for building, food-processing, chemical, and traditional industries; later it was divided into the Savings and Real Estate Bank and the Development Bank. A decree in 1966 abolished interest on loans made by the government development banks. In 1972/73, the government created the Libyan Arab Foreign Bank, later renamed Jamahiriya Foreign Bank, owned by the Central

Bank of Libya, to invest in foreign countries. In 1981, its role in foreign investment was taken over by the Libyan Arab Foreign Investment Co.

There are no securities exchanges in Libya.

34INSURANCE

In 1986, all classes of insurance were available through the Libya Insurance Co. and Al-Mukhtar Insurance Co., both state enterprises. In the same year, 2% of all premiums paid were for life and 98% for non-life insurance. All licensed vehicles require third-party liability insurance, and all goods imported must be insured.

35PUBLIC FINANCE

Since 1974, the fiscal year has followed the calendar year. There are two budgets, one for ordinary expenses, the other (and larger one) for development. By law, 15% of oil revenues is put aside yearly into the country's reserves, while 70% of the remainder goes to development expenditures. All nonoil revenues are assigned to cover ordinary expenditures, and any shortfall is made up by transferring some of the petroleum revenues from the development budget.

If funds from petroleum revenues are not sufficient to cover development expenses, some planned projects are postponed. Although Libya has used part of its oil revenue to finance internal development (new schools, hospitals, roads) much has been wasted. Limited privatization continued in 1993, involving the sale of some parastatal assets. In 1989 revenues were $8.1 billion and expenditures were $9.8 billion, including capital expenditures of $3.1 billion.

36TAXATION

Individual income taxes are levied at different rates for income from real estate, agriculture, commerce, industry, and crafts, independent professions, and wages and salaries. Corporate taxes range from 20% to 60% on amounts over LD150,000. Also levied are a 16.667% royalty on petroleum production, a general income tax of up to 90% on amounts over LD100,000 and a Jihad tax.

37CUSTOMS AND DUTIES

As of 1977, 13 industries were exempt from taxation and customs to encourage domestic production, including plastics, footwear, and metal goods. In 1982, all import duties were eliminated.

Libya has a single-column tariff schedule. Goods from all countries are subject to the same duties. Also levied are customs surcharges totaling 15% of the application customs duties. Almost all customs duties are ad valorem.

38FOREIGN INVESTMENT

Outside of the oil industry, foreign investment in Libya is limited. No foreign investment is allowed in certain areas, including banking, insurance, domestic commerce, and foreign aid. A minimum of 51% of the capital of joint stock companies must be held by Libyans, and the chairman of the board of directors is required to be a Libyan national.

With the massive increase in oil revenues in the 1970s, Libya became a major exporter of capital. Economic cooperation agreements were signed with many African countries, and in 1976 Libya purchased 10% of the shares of the Italian auto company Fiat; it sold its Fiat holdings in 1986 for about $3 billion.

39ECONOMIC DEVELOPMENT

Under Libya's first five-year development plan (1963–68), several long-run measures were taken to raise industrial production and to expand and improve the quality of agriculture. Of the government's oil revenue, 70% was earmarked for the 1963–68 development plan. Of a total (for the five years) of $473,658,000, 23% was allocated for public works, 17.3% for agriculture, 16.4% for communications, 13.2% for education, 7.4% for public health, 4.1% for industry, and 18.6% for other areas.

The 1972–75 development plan had a total public development budget of LD1,165 million; the budget was subsequently increased to about LD2 billion. Its growth target was a 10.7% annual increase in the GDP. Investment was allocated as follows: industry and mineral resources, 15%; agriculture, 14.2%; communications, 14.1%; housing, 10.7%; petrochemicals, 10.5%; education, 9.3%; and other sectors, 26.2%.

The 1976–80 development plan projected an investment of LD7,500 million, but the actual investment was LD9,250 million, principally in agriculture, 20%; communications, 14%; industry, 13%; and housing, 12%.

The 1981–85 development plan called for investment of LD18.5 billion. It allocated funds principally to industry, 23%; agriculture, 18%; communications, 12%; and electricity, 12%. The average annual growth rate was projected at 9.4%. The drop in oil income caused a contraction in planned projects, however. A third five-year plan, which was due to run from 1986, never materialized.

In 1980, Libyan bilateral aid to developing countries totaled $281.9 million, or 0.92% of GNP. In 1981, however, the total was only $105.4 million, or 0.39% of GNP. In 1981, Libya also contributed $63.8 million to multilateral aid organizations, principally to the Arab agencies and the OPEC Fund. As of 1987, the investments of the Libyan Arab Foreign Investment Co. totaled LD310.2 million, including 30 companies in Arab countries. There are also significant Libyan holdings in African countries.

According to BIS, Libya increased its deposits in foreign banks in 1986, while at the same time reducing its outstanding debt. By 1989 Libya's net creditor position with BIS reporting banks had declined to $2.2 billion, from a high of $6.2 in 1987. Howeve, rising deposits in 1990 reflecting soaring oil revenues because of the Persian Gulf crisis, combined with reduced liabilities, led to a positive net balance of $5.2 billion. Due to the decline in oil export receipts in 1991, this surplus was reduced by 33%, to $3.5 billion.

40SOCIAL DEVELOPMENT

By law, all employees except domestic servants, home workers, and the immediate family of an employer are entitled to sickness, invalid, disability, death, and maternity benefits, unemployment payments, and pensions. Rehabilitation programs are provided for sick and disabled employees to provide them with new employment opportunities. Profit sharing, free medical care and education, and subsidized food are other social welfare benefits.

Although Qadhafi has encouraged broadened activities for women, customary Muslim restrictions still apply. In 1985–90, the average number of children born to women who had completed their childbearing years was 6.9, one of the highest fertility rates in the world. Abortion is legal only to save the mother's life.

There have been many reports of human rights violations, including torture, under the Qadhafi regime. Under Libyan law, persons may be detained incommunicado for unlimited periods, and the government has defended the imprisonment of political dissenters.

41HEALTH

In 1990, 100% of Libya's population had access to health care services; hospital beds were estimated at 1.4 per 1,000 people. In 1991, there were 4,749 doctors and 13,849 nurses, and in 1990, 686 dentists.

Endemic diseases include typhoid, venereal diseases, and infectious hepatitis. With the assistance of WHO, Libya has eradicated malaria, once a major problem. In 1990, there were an estimated 220 cases of tuberculosis per 100,000 people. In 1992, immunization rates for children up to one year old were: tuberculosis (91%); diphtheria, pertussis, and tetanus (62%); polio (62%); and measles (59%).

Libya had a birth rate in 1992 of 41.9 per 1,000 people, and there were 206,000 births, with an infant mortality rate of 70 per 1,000 live births. The maternal mortality rate was estimated at 70 per 100,000 live births in 1991. In 1993, the general mortality rate was 8.1 per 1,000 people. The average life expectancy was 63 years in 1992.

42HOUSING

Increasing urbanization has created slum conditions in the major cities. There have been slum clearance and building projects since 1954, but the housing deficit has not yet been met. Around 125,000 new homes were built between 1969 and 1977. Low-income families were allowed to buy ready-made houses from the state at 10% of cost or to build their own homes with interest-free loans. Spending on housing peaked in 1981 at LD296 million; in 1982 it fell to LD167 million. Real estate was the main area of private investment until 1978, when most tenants were made owners of their residences. The state paid full compensation to landlords for confiscated property and resold it to tenants at subsidized prices. According to the latest available information for 1980-88, total housing units numbered 700,000 with 5.6 people per dwelling.

43EDUCATION

When Libya attained independence, about 90% of its population was illiterate and there were few university graduates. Since then, the government has invested heavily in education, which is free at all levels. School is compulsory from the age of 6 until 15. Literacy was estimated at 63.8% in 1990 (males, 75.4% and females, 50.4%). In 1991, primary schools had 99,623 teachers and 1,238,986 pupils. Secondary schools had 18,501 teachers and 215,508 pupils. Of these, 39,491 were in teacher training schools and 37,157 were in vocational schools.

The University of Libya at Tripoli was renamed Al-Fatah University in 1976. It had about 24,000 students in 1986. The University of Libya at Banghazi was renamed the University of Garyounis in 1976. Student enrollment (including an agricultural campus at Al-Bayda) totaled about 1,000 students. The Bright Star University of Technology at Marsa al-Brega was founded in 1981. There were also two higher institutes of technology and one of mechanical and electrical engineering. Total enrollement at all higher level institutions was 72,899 in 1991.

44LIBRARIES AND MUSEUMS

The public library in Banghazi had 11,000 volumes in 1986. Libya's largest library, with 294,844 volumes in 1986, is at the University of Garyounis; at that time, the Government Library in Tripoli had 35,500 volumes. The National Archives, which have an extensive collection of documents relating to the history of Tripolitania under Ottoman rule, are in Tripoli. In addition, France and Italy maintain cultural centers with libraries in the national capital.

The museums exhibit mainly antiquities excavated from various Greek, Roman, Byzantine, and Arabic sites. The Department of Antiquities is responsible for all museums and archaeological sites in the country. The chief museums are at Tripoli, Banghazi, Shahhat, Leptis Magna (Labdah), and Sabratha (Sabratah).

45MEDIA

Postal, telephone, and wireless services are government-owned and -operated. Radiotelephone ties exist between Tripoli and

European centers. In 1992 there were 500,000 telephones. The Socialist People's Libyan Arab Jamahiriya Broadcasting Corp. broadcasts on radio in Arabic and English, and on television in Arabic, English, Italian, and French. In 1991 there were an estimated 1,060,000 radios and 467,000 television sets in use.

The major newspaper is *Al-Fajr al-Jadid,* a government-owned daily published in Tripoli, with circulation of about 40,000 in 1991. *Al-Zahf al-Akhdar,* published by the revolutionary committees, had a 1991 circulation of 35,000.

46ORGANIZATIONS

There are chambers of commerce in Tripoli and Banghazi. Except for these, Libya has few organizations. Membership in an illegal organization was made a capital offense in 1975.

47TOURISM, TRAVEL, AND RECREATION

Tourist attractions in Libya are its good climate, extensive beaches, and magnificent Greek and Roman ruins. However, tourist facilities are not widely available, because tourism has mostly been discouraged during the tenure of Qadhafi. It suffered a further blow with the 1992 imposition of UN sanctions related to the bombing of a Pan Am jet over Lockerbie, Scotland. However, the government has recently taken some steps to attract visitors, including plans to build a hotel on the island of Farwa near the Tunisian border and a string of motels along the coast. All visitors not from Arab countries need visas. Important passport information must appear in Arabic for a visa to be issued; the visa must also be completed in Arabic. Certificates of vaccination for yellow fever are required for those visitors arriving from infected areas.

48FAMOUS LIBYANS

As Roman emperor, Septimius Severus (r.193–211) was responsible for initiating an extensive building program at his native Leptis Magna. Muhammad bin 'Ali as-Sanusi (1780?–1859), the founder of the Sanusi order, established its headquarters in Cyrenaica in the 1840s. Muhammad Idris al-Mahdi as-Sanusi (1890–1983), his descendant, was Libya's first king, ruling the country from its independence until he was deposed in 1969. Col. Mu'ammar Muhammad al-Qadhafi (b.1942) has been the actual ruler of the country since that time. Omar al-Muntasser (b.1939) became secretary-general of the General People's Committee in 1987.

49DEPENDENCIES

Libya has no territories or colonies.

50BIBLIOGRAPHY

Ahmida, Ali Abdullatif. *The Making of Modern Libya: State Formation, Colonization, and Resistance, 1830–1932.* Albany: State University of New York Press, 1994.

Allan, J. A. *Libya Since Independence: Economic and Social Development.* London: Croon Helm, 1982.

Ayoub, Mahmoud. *Islam and the Third Universal Theory: The Religious Thought of Muammar al-Qadhdhafi.* New York: KPI, 1987.

Blundy, David. *Qaddafi and the Libyan Revolution.* Boston: Little, Brown, 1987.

Cooley, John K. *Libyan Sandstorm: The Complete Account of Qadhafi's Revolution.* New York: Holt, Rinehart & Winston, 1982.

Deeb, Mary Jane. *Libya's Foreign Policy in North Africa.* Boulder, Colo.: Westview Press, 1991.

ElWarfally, Mahmoud G. *Imagery and Ideology in U.S. Policy Toward Libya, 1969–1982.* Pittsburgh: University of Pittsburgh Press, 1988.

Haley, P. Edward. *Qadhafi and the United States Since 1969.* New York: Praeger, 1984.

Lawless, Richard I. *Libya.* Santa Barbara, Calif.: Clio Press, 1987.

Lemarchand, Rene (ed.). *The Green and the Black: Qadhafi's Policies in Africa.* Bloomington: Indiana University Press, 1988.

Metz, Helen Chapin (ed.). *Libya, a Country Study.* 4th ed. Washington, D.C.: Library of Congress, 1989.

Segre, Claudine G. *The Fourth Shore: The Italian Colonization of Libya.* Chicago: University of Chicago Press, 1975.

Sicker, Martin. *The Making of a Pariah State.* New York: Praeger, 1987.

Simons, G. L.. *Libya: The Struggle for Survival.* New York: St. Martin's, 1993.

St. John, Ronald Bruce. *Historical Dictionary of Libya.* 2d ed. Metuchen, N.J.: Scarecrow Press, 1991.

Waddams, Frank C. *The Libyan Oil Industry.* Baltimore: Johns Hopkins University Press, 1982.

Witherell, Julian W. *Libya, 1969–1989: An American Perspective: A Guide to U.S. Official Documents and Government-sponsored Publications.* Washington, D.C.: Library of Congress, 1990.

Wright, John. *Libya: A Modern History.* Baltimore: Johns Hopkins University Press, 1982.

MADAGASCAR

Democratic Republic of Madagascar
République Démocratique de Madagascar
Repoblika Demokratika n'i Madagaskar

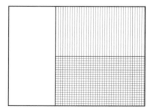

CAPITAL: Antananarivo.

FLAG: The flag consists of a white vertical stripe at the hoist flanked at the right by two horizontal stripes, the upper in red, the lower in green.

ANTHEM: *Ry Tanindrazanay Malala O (Our Beloved Country).*

MONETARY UNIT: The Malagasy franc (FMG) is a paper currency. There are coins of 1, 2, 5, 10, 20, 25, 50, 100, and 250 Malagasy francs and notes of 50, 100, 500, 1,000, 2,500 5,000, 10,000 and 25,000 Malagasy francs. FMG1 = $0.0081 (or $1 = FMG1,233).

WEIGHTS AND MEASURES: The metric system is generally used.

HOLIDAYS: New Year's Day, 1 January; Commemoration of 1947 Rebellion, 29 March; Labor Day, 1 May; Independence and National Day, 26 June; All Saints' Day, 1 November; Christmas, 25 December; Anniversary of the Democratic Republic of Madagascar, 30 December. Movable religious holidays include Good Friday, Easter Monday, Ascension, and Pentecost Monday.

TIME: 3 PM = noon GMT.

¹LOCATION, SIZE, AND EXTENT

Situated off the southeast coast of Africa, Madagascar is the fourth-largest island in the world, with an area of 587,040 sq km (226,657 sq mi), extending 1,570 km (976 mi) NNE–SSW and 569 km (354 mi) ESE–WNW. Comparatively, the area occupied by Madagascar is slightly less than twice the size of Arizona. It is separated from the coast of Africa by the Mozambique Channel, the least distance between the island and the coast being about 430 km (267 mi). The coastline of Madagascar is 4,828 km (3,000 mi). Madagascar claims a number of small islands in the Mozambique Channel—the Îles Glorieuses, Bassas da India, Juan de Nova, and Europa—covering about 28 sq km (11 sq mi), which are administered by France.

Madagascar's capital city, Antananarivo, is located near the center of the island.

²TOPOGRAPHY

Madagascar consists mainly of a block of crystalline rocks. It is generally described as a plateau, rising sharply from the narrow plain of the east coast and descending in a series of steps to the strip of sedimentary rocks along the west coast. The high plateau is much indented and, on the eastern edge, cut by deep gorges and waterfalls. There are numerous volcanic outcrops that produce heights over 1,800 m (6,000 ft); the highest point is Mount Maromokotro (2,876 m/9,436 ft) in the Tsaratanana Massif. The eastern coast is almost straight and has very few anchorages. Behind its coral beaches there is an almost continuous line of lagoons from Foulpointe to Farafangana. These are linked by manmade channels to form an inland waterway called the Pangalanes Canal. The island's major rivers flow westward and are navigable for about 160 km (100 mi) inland.

³CLIMATE

The climate of the eastern and northwestern coasts is dominated by the almost constant blowing of the southeasterly trade winds, which carry heavy rains during the austral winter (May to September). The central plateau and the western coast are sheltered from these winds but receive rain from the monsoon winds, which blow during the austral summer (October to April). Neither the trade winds nor the monsoons reach the southern part of the island, which consequently receives little rain and is, in places, a semidesert. The central plateau enjoys a tropical mountain climate with well-differentiated seasons. Generally speaking, the climate throughout the island is moderated by altitude, with the coast being hotter (average temperatures 21–27°C, or 70–80°F) and wetter than the plateau (average temperatures 13–19°C, or 55–67°F). Toamasina (Tamatave), on the east coast, has 284 cm (112 in) of rainfall annually, while Antananarivo, inland, has about 140 cm (55 in). In mid-April 1984, a cyclone struck the island, devastating the ports of Antsiranana and Mahajanga, and in mid-March 1986, another cyclone left about 20,000 people homeless.

⁴FLORA AND FAUNA

The flora and fauna of Madagascar have developed in isolation from those of Africa, and the flora is highly specialized.

Scientists hold that Madagascar was originally covered with evergreen forests in the wetter areas of the east and north, which gave place to savanna on the plateau and semiarid vegetation in the south. Much of the original vegetation was destroyed by burning, and the evergreen forest is now found only in a narrow strip along the steep eastern edge of the plateau, from north to south. Where the forest was destroyed, it was replaced by bush known as savoka, especially in the narrow east coast plain. There are a few small patches of deciduous forest in the northwest and west, and mangrove swamps are general along the northwest and west coasts. Most of Madagascar is covered with a rather bare savanna-steppe, green in the wet season but brown and red in the summer. The greater part of the plateau has a covering of laterite, and fertility is low. The extreme south is free of laterite, but lack of rainfall prevents the greater fertility from being of much practical use.

The fauna is remarkable chiefly because of the presence of 28 species of lemur, a lower primate largely confined to Madagascar. The island has 32 species of chameleon. Among the 238 species of birds, 106 are found nowhere else in the world. The same is true for 80% of the island's flowering plants and more than 95% of its reptiles. Madagascar is also unusual in its lack of poisonous snakes and, except for recent introductions, useful mammals.

5ENVIRONMENT

Erosion, caused by deforestation and overgrazing, is a serious problem in Madagascar. Many farmers burn off their old crops at the end of winter and damage surrounding forests. By 1994, 75% of Madagascar's forests had been eliminated. Water pollution caused mainly by sewage, is also a significant environmental problem in Madagascar: 90% of the people living in rural areas and 38% of all city dwellers are without pure water. The nation has 9.6 cubic miles of water with 99% used for farming activity and 1% used for domestic purposes. The nation's cities produce 0.6 million tons of solid waste per year. The Ministry of Animal Husbandry, Water, and Forests is the chief government agency with environmental responsibilities.

As of 1994, Madagascar was the home of over 200,000 species of flora and fauna. In addition to 50 of its mammal species and 28 of its bird species, 194 plant species are threatened with extinction. Endangered species in Madagascar include the Alaotra grebe, Madagascar pochard, Madagascar fish eagle, and seven species of lemur.

6POPULATION

In 1994, the estimated population of Madagascar was 13,406,672. A population of 16,579,000 was projected for the year 2000, assuming a crude birthrate of 42.7 per 1,000 population, a crude death rate of 11.2, and a net natural increase of 31.5 for 1995–2000. The rate of population growth is about 3.2% annually. The average population density in 1994 was estimated at 22.8 per sq km (59.1 per sq mi).

Madagascar's population was about 27% urban in 1995. Antananarivo (Tananarive), the capital and largest city, had about 687,000 inhabitants in 1990. The populations of the other important cities in 1988 were Fianarantsoa, 300,000; Antsiranana (Diégo-Suarez), 220,000; Toamasina, 230,000; Antsirabe, 220,000; and Mahajanga (Majunga), 200,000.

7MIGRATION

Since independence, government policy has been uniformly opposed to immigration in any form. The advent of independence led to some emigration of foreign nationals, but it was not until the early 1970s, when the government undertook policies of national control and nationalization of foreign businesses, that foreign residents began leaving in any appreciable numbers. Comorans numbered 60,000 in 1976, but after Comoran-Malagasy clashes in December of that year, about 16,000 were repatriated. About 15,000–20,000 remain. Rural-to-urban migration is nearly 6% a year.

8ETHNIC GROUPS

The Malagasy people are the result of the intermingling of immigrants. The original immigrants are believed to have been members of an Afro-Malagasy race that lived on the East African littoral. Later arrivals were Africans, Arabs, and, much more recently, immigrants from Europe, China, and India.

The 18–20 distinct African ethnic groups now recognized represent the political groupings forged before the arrival of the first Europeans. The major ethnic groups, according to 1974 numbers, are the Merina, Betsimisaraka, Betsileo, Tsimihety, Sakalava, Antandroy, Antaisaka, and Tanala. The Merina (about 25% of the population) and Betsileo (about 12%) live in the central high-

lands and show evidence of Asian origin, while the coastal peoples, such as the Betsimisaraka, Tsimihety, and Sakalava, are of predominantly African origin.

The Merina have been the ascendant group since the late 18th century. The course that colonialism took in Madagascar strengthened their domination of the political and intellectual life of the island. Resentment of the Merina and their dominant position by the other ethnic groups is still a source of social unrest.

In 1988 there were about 18,000 French in Madagascar. The number of Indians and Pakistanis was estimated at 17,000 and the number of Chinese at 9,000.

9LANGUAGES

The constitution does not name an official language. The principal languages are French and Malagasy. Malagasy is a Malayo-Polynesian language which has different but mutually intelligible dialects and is spoken throughout Madagascar. The Merina dialect has come to be considered the standard literary form of the language. Instruction in French is preferred by the coastal peoples, as it avoids connotations of Merina cultural dominance.

10RELIGIONS

Although there are many variations in detail, nearly all Malagasy share certain basic religious ideas, the central one being belief in the soul and its immortality. Besides the almighty (Andrianahary or Zanahary), secondary divinities are recognized, especially the earliest inhabitants of the island (Vazimba), legendary kings and queens, and other great ancestors. The burial places and other places of special significance in the lives of these secondary deities are objects of veneration and pilgrimages, during which special rites are performed.

Christianity was introduced to the Malagasy in the early 19th century, and it is influenced to a large extent by traditional beliefs. According to a 1993 estimate, some 43% of the population was Christian, with Roman Catholics slightly more numerous than Protestants. The Merina tend to be Protestant and the coastal peoples Catholic. Over half of the Malagasy are traditional tribal religionists, and about 1.7%, mostly on the northwest coast, follow Islam. There are small numbers of Baha'is, Hindus, Buddhists, and Jews.

11TRANSPORTATION

Although the terrain makes railway building difficult and expensive, there are four main railroads, all publicly operated, covering 1,020 km (634 mi). These run from Toamasina to Antananarivo, with a branch from Moramanga to Lake Alaotra; from Antananarivo to Antsirabe; and from Fianarantsoa to Manakara on the east coast.

There are about 40,000 km (24,860 mi) of motor roads on the island, of which 4,700 km (2,920 mi) were paved in 1991. The main roads radiate from Antananarivo to Mahajanga and Antsiranana, to Toamasina, to Fianarantsoa, and to Ihosy, from which one branch goes to Toliara (Tuléar) and another to Tolänaro (Fort Dauphin). The road from Antananarivo to Fianarantsoa is tarred, as are portions of the other main routes. In 1991 there were 46,359 passenger automobiles and 33,296 trucks and buses in use.

The three major ports are Toamasina, Nosy Be, and Mahajanga; Toliara and Antsiranana are also important. There are at least 13 other ports, engaged mainly in coastal trade. There was considerable freight traffic along the Pangalanes Canal, which runs parallel to the east coast from Toamasina to Farafangana for a distance of 700 km (435 mi). The canal was closed in 1979, however, because of silting; dredging had begun by 1985. The merchant fleet consisted of 12 vessels, with gross weight of 58,000 tons at the end of 1991.

The principal international airport, at Ivato, near Antananarivo, served some 340,000 embarking and disembarking passengers in 1990. Air Madagascar (the national airline), Air France, Alitalia, Aeroflot, Air Mauritius, and Air Tanzania also provide international service. Air Madagascar, which is owned partly by Air France, also services internal locations. In all there are 103 usable airports, 30 with permanent-surface runways.

12 HISTORY

Madagascar had no human inhabitants until about 2,500 years ago, when immigrants came, probably from Indonesia via the East African coast. This wave of immigration continued for at least 1,000 years, and there was also an influx of African peoples. Additional immigrants from Africa, Arabia, and the Persian Gulf and, much later, from Europe, India, and China did little more than supplement a fully settled population.

The earliest written histories of the Malagasy are the *sorabe*, in the Malagasy language using Arabic script. A Portuguese ship sighted the island and sailed along the coast in 1500. In 1502, the island was named Madagascar by the Portuguese, after the island of the same name originally reported by Marco Polo. During the 16th and 17th centuries, attempts were made by the Portuguese, British, Dutch, and French to establish settlements. All these efforts failed, and Madagascar became the lair of pirates who lived on Nosy Sainte Marie and intermarried with the Malagasy.

Among the Malagasy themselves, three main kingdoms appeared: that of the Merina in the central plateau, that of the Sakalava in the west, and that of the Betsimisaraka in the east. Under King Andrianampoinimerina (r.1787–1810), the foundations were laid for the primacy of the Merina kingdom.

Andrianampoinimerina was succeeded in 1810 by his son Radama I, under whose guidance the Merina kingdom extended its rule over the major portions of the island (especially over the Betsimisaraka kingdom and the south). Radama welcomed Europeans to assist in the modernization of the kingdom and to further his conquests. On Radama's death in 1828, he was succeeded by his wife, Ranavalona I, whose hostility to the innovations in her husband's reign led to a persecution of the Malagasy Christians and eventually to the expulsion of the Europeans after an Anglo-French bombardment of Toamasina in 1845.

Radama II, who succeeded his mother in 1861, was sympathetic to the French but was murdered in 1863. Shortly after this, Rainilaiarivony, who was to become prime minister and consort to three successive queens, took control of the government. The last three decades of Malagasy independence during the 19th century were marked by continued attempts of those opposed to innovation to undermine the prime minister's authority. He therefore slowed modernization and tried to retain independence by seeking British friendship against the French. The latter claimed a protectorate over parts of the Sakalava kingdom by virtue of treaties made in 1840, and disputes over this claim and over French properties on the island resulted in a war in 1883 which was ended in 1885 by a treaty giving the French control over Merina foreign policy.

The British recognized the French position under the terms of the Anglo-French Agreement of 1890, in exchange for French recognition of a British protectorate over Zanzibar. This exchange cleared the way for the French annexation of Madagascar in 1896. Malagasy resistance, especially in the south, was not finally overcome until 1904, however. Gen. Joseph Gallieni, governor-general from 1896 to 1905, opened the first government schools (hitherto all schools had been in the hands of the missions), established a free medical service for Malagasy, encouraged the study of Malagasy language and customs by the creation of the Malagasy Academy (Académie Malgache), and introduced new tropical crops in order to promote economic development. The impress of his policies remained substantial until the end of World War II. His successors, career colonial officials, struggled to promote economic growth, but World War I, subsequent

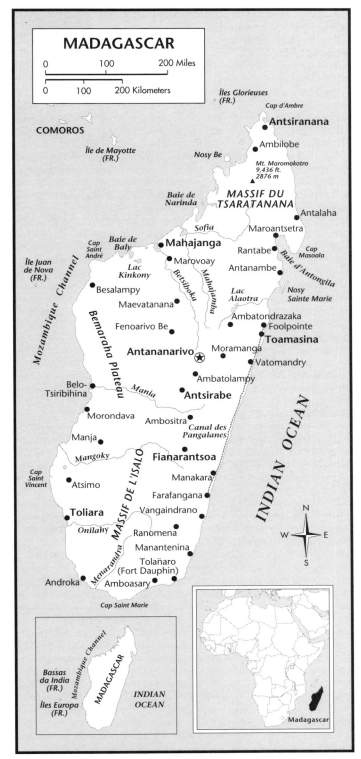

MADAGASCAR

0   100   200 Miles

0   100   200 Kilometers

LOCATION: 43°12′ to 50°17′E; 11°57′ to 25°38′S.
TERRITORIAL SEA LIMIT: 12 mi.

economic difficulties in France, and the prolonged depression of the 1930s, together with the absence of easily exploitable resources, the distance of Madagascar from its main markets, and the shortage of labor, combined to impede their efforts.

During World War II, the Vichy French retained control of Madagascar until it was occupied in 1942 by British troops to prevent its naval facilities from being used by the Japanese. In 1943, French administration was restored under Gen. de Gaulle's Free French government. Madagascar became a French overseas territory in 1946. All Malagasy thus became French citizens, but only a limited number were accorded the franchise (mainly those with some education or experience of European ways in the French civil services or armed forces). A Territorial Assembly was established, with some control of the budget. It was composed entirely of members indirectly elected by provincial assemblies. The latter were wholly elected bodies, but there were separate electorates (and separate seats) for the French citizens of metropolitan status (including Europeans, Réunionnais, and some Malagasy given such status) and for Malagasy citizens of local status. Although the latter had a majority of the seats in both provincial and territorial assemblies, the number of seats assigned to the metropolitan electorate was most disproportionate to its numerical strength. This system was denounced by the nationalists, who had secured a majority of the Malagasy seats in the Territorial Assembly as well as the three Malagasy seats in the French National Assembly.

In March 1947, a rebellion broke out, and for a time the French lost control of the east coast. Europeans and loyal Malagasy were murdered and roads cut. The suppression of the rebellion required substantial forces and took more than a year. Loss of life was estimated at 11,000. The nationalist movement was disrupted by the rebellion and subsequent repressions, but was not destroyed. A period of reform beginning in 1956 resulted in abolition of the dual electorate system, placed Malagasy in important government positions, and led to the rebirth of serious political activity.

The End of French Rule

In the referendum of 28 September 1958, Madagascar overwhelmingly voted for the new French constitution and became an autonomous republic in the new French Community. As the Malagasy Republic, it became a sovereign independent nation on 26 June 1960 and on 20 September 1960 was elected to UN membership.

The constitution that was adopted in October 1958 and amended in June 1960 provided Madagascar with a strong presidential form of government. The president, Philibert Tsiranana, remained in power until May 1972, when there were riots throughout Madagascar. The protests were led by a nationalist, leftist coalition of students, teachers, laborers, and urban unemployed. The repression that followed these demonstrations led to the fall of the Tsiranana government on 18 May. Gen. Gabriel Ramanantsoa was immediately asked to form a nonpolitical "government of national unity," which was composed of 11 ministers (5 military and 6 civilian). Ramanantsoa effectively destroyed the coalition by raising the minimum wages, providing strike pay, annulling the head and cattle taxes, prosecuting corrupt officials, and introducing price and currency controls. The new government also broke diplomatic ties with South Africa, established relations with the Communist bloc, withdrew from the franc zone, and arranged for the withdrawal of French military forces under new cooperation agreements with France.

On 5 February 1975, following a period of social and ethnic unrest, Ramanantsoa was replaced as head of state by Col. Richard Ratsimandrava, who was assassinated in an attempted coup six days later. A military Directorate composed of 18 officers was immediately formed and assumed all governmental authority. The Directorate was superseded on 13 June by the all-military Supreme Council of the Revolution, headed by Didier Ratsiraka, who had been minister of foreign affairs in the Ramanantsoa government.

In December 1975, a draft constitution was approved in a referendum by 95% of the voters and the Second Malagasy Republic,

to be called the Democratic Republic of Madagascar, was proclaimed. Ratsiraka was installed as president on 4 January 1976, thus remaining head of state.

The new regime accelerated growing state control of the economy, and Madagascar turned to the former USSR and the Democratic People's Republic of Korea for military aid. By 1979, however, growing economic difficulties forced Ratsiraka to develop closer ties with the West. Unemployment, inflation, and scarcities of basic foodstuffs caused serious rioting and social unrest in the early 1980s. Ratsiraka was elected to a new term as president on 7 November 1982. During 1986–87, the government was shaken by student protests against educational reforms, rioting in the port of Toamasina, attacks on Indo-Pakistani enterprises in four major urban centers, and famine in the south because of food-supply problems. By early 1987, the governing coalition appeared to be unraveling. On May Day, four of the parties called for the resignation of the government and early elections.

In July 1992, after seven weeks of pro-democracy protests, Ratsiraka finally agreed to dissolve the cabinet and begin talks with the opposition. He also offered to hold a referendum on a new constitution by the end of 1992. Although he rejected demonstrators' demands that he resign, Ratsiraka released Albert Zafy, a popular opponent, and offered to form a coalition government with opposition leaders. Protests continued and government troops fired on demonstrators in Antananarivo, killing as many as 50. In August, Ratsiraka asked his prime minister, Guy Willy Razanamasy, to form a new government and to "install democracy." By November, Ratsiraka agreed to share power with a transitional government headed by Zafy, his main rival. Ratsiraka's Revolutionary Supreme Council stepped down from power.

The democratization process survived an attempted coup on 29 July 1992, led by a faction of the Active Forces known as the Lifeblood Committee. On 19 August 1992, a new constitution was approved by national referendum. Ratsiraka's supporters interfered with the voting, seeking greater provincial autonomy. However the interior peoples, especially the Merina, strongly supported the new constitution. This was followed on 25 November by a presidential election, which a team of foreign observers deemed free and fair. Zafy defeated Ratsiraka, but without an absolute majority. In a run-off election on 10 February 1993, Zafy got 67% of the vote to Ratsiraka's 33%. In March and April 1993, there were violent confrontations between Ratsiraka's supporters and government forces.

Parliamentary elections were held in June to choose 184 deputies for the new National Assembly. Zafy's Forces Vives did well in the contest. Seats were allocated according to proportional representation. After delays due to charges of irregularities, it was announced that 25 groups had won seats, with Zafy supporters in the majority. The National Assembly, in turn, elected Francisque Ravony as prime minister — 55 votes to 45 for Roger Ralison and 35 for former Maoist leader, Manandagy Rakotonirina. (Ralison was the official candidate of the Active Forces, but he was rejected by a majority of pro-Zafy parliamentarians and replaced by Ravony.)

13GOVERNMENT

The constitution of 21 December 1975, like that of the First Republic, provided for a strong presidential system of government. The president was elected for a seven-year term and was both chief executive and head of state. The president was assisted by the Supreme Council of the Revolution (Conseil Suprême de la Révolution—CSR), which was to be "the guardian of the Malagasy Socialist Revolution." The president, as chairman of the CSR, named two-thirds of its members outright and chose the other third from a list submitted by the National People's

Assembly. The premier, the designated head of government, was appointed by the president and assisted by a cabinet.

A unicameral National People's Assembly was elected for a five-year term. Suffrage is universal at age 18.

The 19 August 1992 constitution of the Third Republic provides for a two-chamber legislature—a 184-deputy National Assembly and a Senate. The National Assembly alone has the authority to invest the prime minister. Two-thirds of the senators are chosen indirectly by electors representing territorial collectives and various economic and social sectors of the population, and one-third are appointed by the president.

The first government of the Third Republic was formed in late August 1993.

14POLITICAL PARTIES

Following World War II, the Democratic Movement for Malagasy Renewal (Mouvement Démocratique de la Rénouvation Malgache—MDRM), founded by several prominent nationalists, demanded that Madagascar be declared a free state within the French Union. The French, however, organized the island as an overseas territory, granting the vote to few Malagasy. In the wake of the 1947 rebellion, the leaders of the MDRM, whom the French accused of planning and leading the revolt, were convicted of treason and sentenced to death (later commuted to life imprisonment). Charges of French brutality in the suppression of the revolt, however, gained considerable sympathy for the nationalist cause.

After independence, the Social Democratic Party of Madagascar and the Comoros (Parti Social Démocrate de Madagascar et des Comores—PSD) became the dominant political organization in the Malagasy Republic. It was organized in 1957 under the leadership of Philibert Tsiranana, the son of a Tsimihety peasant, and advocated a gradual approach to independence. In the Assembly elections of September 1960, it won 75 seats out of 107. In the 1965 and 1970 elections, it increased its representation to 104 seats. The PSD was supported principally by peasants and other conservative elements, and favored strong ties with France. Tsiranana, who became president in 1960, was reelected in 1965 and again in 1972, just prior to his overthrow. The only real alternative during this period was the pro-Soviet Party of the Congress of Independence (Ankoton'ny Kongresi'ny Fahaleorantenan Madagaskara—AKFM), founded in 1958.

Other parties represented regions, provinces, tribes, or religious groups, but displayed little national strength. The most significant of the regional parties was the Movement for the Independence of Madagascar (Mouvement National pour l'Indépendance de Madagascar—MONIMA) which was led by Monja Jaona from Toliara. It represented the more radical intellectuals and landless peasants of the south. As a result of its armed opposition to the central government in April 1971, which was quickly and harshly suppressed, MONIMA became a truly left-wing opposition movement with support among students and urban radicals. Though MONIMA was banned, these elements led the series of demonstrations against the Tsiranana regime that resulted in its fall in May 1972. The ban on MONIMA was lifted in June.

After the assassination of the new head of state, Richard Ratsimandrava, in February 1975, all political parties were banned. The new constitution institutionalized the ban by providing for the creation of a sole party, to be called the National Front for the Defense of the Revolution (Front National pour la Defense de la Révolution—FNDR).

In effect, however, the FNDR became an umbrella group under which parties survived as "revolutionary associations." MONIMA withdrew from the FNDR in 1977 but returned in 1981, bringing to seven the number of parties in the FNDR. The chief party is Ratsiraka's Vanguard of the Malagasy Revolution (Avant-garde de la Révolution Malgache—AREMA). On 29 May 1977, it won control of almost all provincial and local bodies, and on 30 June 1977, in an election in which voters were presented with a single FNDR list, AREMA won 112 Assembly seats to 16 for the PCI and 9 for two other parties.

In the presidential election of 7 November 1982, President Ratsiraka won reelection with 80.17% of the vote. His sole opponent, Monja Jaona, leader of MONIMA, was removed from the CSR and temporarily placed under house arrest after he called for a general strike to protest the election results. In elections in August 1983, AREMA again won a commanding majority in the Assembly. MONIMA left the FNDR in 1987.

After the democratic changes of 1992 and 1993, some 30 parties operate in Madagascar. Zafy, the leader of the National Union for Democracy and Development (UNDD), heads a coalition of a dozen groups under the rubric Comité des Forces Vives. Following his defeat in the presidential elections of February 1993, Ratsiraka created a new party, the Vanguard Economic and Social Recovery (ARES—Avant Gardes pour le Redressement Économique et Social) to replace the defunct AREMA. It was a federalist party seeking to deny central government control of the provinces. Other functioning parties include MONIMA, the Congress Party for Malagasy Independence (AKFM), the Movement for National Unity (VONJY) and the PSD.

15LOCAL GOVERNMENT

The constitution of 1958 and its 1960 amendments provided that the Malagasy nation be divided into six provinces for administrative purposes. Madagascar is further subdivided into 18 regions and 92 districts. At the basic level are some 11,393 fokontany (village or urban neighborhood organizations). At the fokontany level, a president and council are elected; elections to the other councils are indirect, with the council at each level sending delegates to the council at the next highest level. All the divisions of the Malagasy state are directly responsible to the Ministry of the Interior. The 1992 constitution established a unitary state.

16JUDICIAL SYSTEM

The Malagasy judicial system is based on the French tradition. During the 1960s and 1970s the nation began a move from a bifurcated judicial system (customary courts for most Malagasy and local courts for foreign residents and urbanized Malagasy) to a single judicial system. At the top of the judicial system is the Supreme Court in Antananarivo. Other courts include the Court of Appeal, also in Antananarivo; courts of first instance for civil and criminal cases; ordinary and special criminal courts; and military courts. There are also a High Court of Justice to try high officials and a Constitutional Court. Military courts presided over by civilian magistrates hear cases involving national security.

The traditional courts (dina) continue to handle some civil disputes and recently have been used in criminal cases because of inconvenience and inadequacy of the formal court system. Decisions by dina are not appealable to the courts and lack the formal procedural protections of the formal court system. Their authority depends upon the mutual respect and consensus of the parties to abide by the ruling.

The 1992 Constitution guarantees an independent judiciary, and in practice the judiciary appears to be independent from the executive.

17ARMED FORCES

The armed forces of Madagascar were composed in 1993 of about 21,000 personnel, including an army of 20,000, a navy of 500 (100 marines), and an air force of 500. The navy had 2 ships and the air force 12 combat aircraft. The last French military forces stationed in Madagascar withdrew in 1975. Manpower is provided by conscription of all men from 20 to 50 for 18-month periods, but most servicemen are volunteers.

The paramilitary Gendarmerie National, which had a strength of 7,500 in 1993, is the main force for the maintenance of public order and internal security. Military spending was estimated at $37 million in 1989 or 2.2% of GDP.

[18]INTERNATIONAL COOPERATION

Madagascar was admitted to UN membership on 20 September 1960 and is a member of ECA and all the nonregional specialized agencies except WIPO. It is also a member of the African Development Bank, G-77, and OAU, and is associated with the EC through the Lomé Convention. Madagascar is a member of the nonaligned movement and a signatory to GATT and the Law of the Sea. In 1973, Madagascar left OCAM and the franc zone.

[19]ECONOMY

Madagascar has an agriculture-based economy that supports 76.1% of the country's labor force. There are substantial mineral deposits and industry, which accounts for 13% of GDP, is centered on food processing. Madagascar sponsors an Export Processing Zone and important investments have been made in tourism.

The agricultural sector, which accounted for 33% of GDP in 1991 and is prone to cyclone damage and drought. Average annual growth of the sector in the 1980s was about 2.4%. Rice is the staple crop although Madagascar has sought to diversify crop production by promoting maize and potatoes. Cassava, bananas, and sweet potatoes are also important. Export crops are coffee, vanilla, and cloves, with coffee the most important. The sugar sector has been revived with the help of French investments.

Though Madagascar has a considerable diversity of minerals, their remote locations have discouraged extraction. Chromite, graphite, and mica are exported along with gems such as topaz, garnets, and amethysts. Private mining interests have been invited to develop Madagascar's gold deposits, as well as ilmenite, zircon, rutile, nickel, platinum, and bauxite. There has also been renewed interest in Madagascar's oil potential.

Official government interest in tourism began in 1989, when a promotion project was launched. Madagascar has a wide variety of natural attractions, and tourist numbers increased by 50% over the first two years before declining slightly due to political turmoil.

[20]INCOME

In 1992 Madagascar's GNP was $2,809 million at current prices, or $230 per capita. For the period 1985–92 the average inflation rate was 15.6%, resulting in a real growth rate in per capita GNP of −1.7%.

In 1992 the GDP was $2,987 million in current US dollars. It was estimated that in 1985 agriculture, hunting, forestry, and fishing contributed 42% to GDP; mining and quarrying; manufacturing; electricity, gas, and water; and construction, 16%; wholesale and retail trade; transport, storage, and communication; finance, insurance, real estate, business services, community, social, and personal services; and other sources, 13%.

[21]LABOR

The labor force in 1992 was estimated at 4,900,000 persons. In 1992, agriculture (especially production of rice, vanilla, and coffee) employed 80% of the work force, with unionized labor making up less than 5% of the total. The number of registered unemployed was 15,733 in 1989, but real unemployment is much higher.

Workig conditions are regulated by the 1992 Constitution and by the labor code of 1952, which was revised in 1960 and again in 1975. The code provides for collective agreements between employers and trade unions, basic minimum wages fixed by the government on the advice of advisory committees, paid annual leave, maternity and children's allowances, and compensation for industrial injuries. Both public and private sector workers have the right to establish and join labor unions of their choice. In 1992, the transitional government exercised nominal control over organized labor. That same year, there were strikes by the railway workers' union, and Antananarivo bus drivers, as well as by workers at the state-owned power, petroleum, and air transport companies, two ministries, and the state fishing company.

The largest unions are the Christian Confederation of Malagasy Trade Unions, the Confederation of Malagasy Workers, the Union of Madagascar Workers' Syndicates, and the Union of Autonomous Syndicates of Madagascar.

[22]AGRICULTURE

Although Madagascar's economy is essentially agricultural, much of the land is unsuitable for cultivation because of its mountainous terrain, extensive laterization, and inadequate or irregular rainfall. Only about 5% of the land area is cultivated at any one time. Despite these figures, agriculture generates about 80% of export earnings and employs about 80% of the work force. Large-scale plantations dominate the production of sisal, sugarcane, tobacco, bananas, and cotton, but, overall, Malagasy agriculture is dependent mainly on small-scale subsistence farmers cultivating less than 1 ha (2.47 acres) of land.

A wide variety of food crops is grown. Rice is the staple of the Malagasy diet; production was an estimated 2,450,000 tons in 1992. Nevertheless, the yield is insufficient to meet the country's needs and in 1982, 1984, and 1990 cyclones severely damaged the rice crop. Cassava, bananas, and sweet potatoes are also important. In 1992, the gap between supply and demand necessitated the importation of 60,000 tons of rice, at a cost of about $24 million. Madagascar has sought to diversify staple crop production by promoting maize and potatoes. Other important food crops (with 1992 production figures) include cassava, 2,320,000 tons; sugarcane, 1,900,000 tons; sweet potatoes, 440,000 tons; potatoes, 276,000 tons; bananas, 220,000 tons; corn, 165,000 tons; and oranges, 85,000 tons.

The major Malagasy export is coffee. In the 1980s, coffee regularly earned about 24% of total export revenues. After the collapse of the International Coffee Organization in 1989, however, coffee exports accounted for only 8.6% of Malagasy foreign trade earnings in 1992 (down from 35% in 1985). Production was 85,000 tons in 1991 and about 87,000 tons in 1992. Vanilla is the second-ranking agricultural export, with exports of 698 tons of extract (for a value of $49.9 million) in 1992. International trade in natural vanilla is determined by agreements between producers (mainly Madagascar and the Comoros) and the principal importers by which export prices and traded volumes are fixed. The government does not encourage overproduction, since the international market demand is very sensitive because of competition from synthetic vanilla (vanillin). Madagascar is the world's major natural vanilla producer, accounting for about 73% of production in 1992. Cloves are the third main export corp, grown mostly by smallholders. Production follows a 4-year cycle with 2–3 years of high output followed by one year of low production. The clove export picture changed dramatically in 1987 with the entry of Indonesia into the market. Exports fell from 11,600 tons in 1985, to 8,000 tons in 1992. Other 1992 production figures for cash crops were seed cotton, 27,000 tons (compared to 32,000 in 1991); peanuts, 34,000 tons; sisal, 19,000 tons (20,000 in 1991); and cocoa, 4,000 tons. Pepper is another important export crop. Pepper exports in 1992 amounted to 1,789 tons, valued at $2.1 million. The sugar sector has been revived with the help of French investments. The needs of the domestic market are served by five sugar refineries.

Production of cash crops has been discouraged by the low prices paid by state agencies, which sometimes have failed to collect crops or pay for them on time.

23ANIMAL HUSBANDRY

More than half the land is used for raising livestock. Cattle occupy an important place in the Malagasy economy. They are, however, more important as evidence of wealth than as sources of meat and dairy products. Only since the end of World War I has the consumption of meat become widespread among Malagasy, and now beef consumption is relatively high compared with other African countries. Cattle are employed to trample the rice fields and to draw plows and small carts. Most cattle are of the humped zebu type. Madagascar has vast natural pastures (60% of total land area) and is free of cattle diseases; there is, therefore, considerable potential for increasing production.

Estimates of the size of livestock herds vary considerably. Estimates for 1992 were cattle, 10,276,000 head; hogs, 1,493,000; sheep, 770,000; and goats, 1,311,000. Total meat production was about 285,000 tons. Beef and live animals are exported. The population of cattle has remained steady because of a high young animal mortality rate resulting from traditional livestock-raising techniques.

24FISHING

Despite the island's long coastline, fishing is relatively undeveloped as an industry in Madagascar. On the east coast, with its stormy seas and absence of harbors, fishing is restricted mainly to the coastal lagoons and has been aptly characterized as virtually an extension of inland freshwater fishing. In the northwest, sardine and tuna are caught, and dried fish find a ready market. Dried fish also are prepared in the southwest. Lobsters, prawns, and shrimps are exported. Commercial maritime fishing is carried out by four joint-venture companies that operate along the northwest coast and account for most exports. The catch in 1991 was estimated at 101,020 tons, of which 27,730 tons were caught in inland waters. EC vessels are allowed to take up to 11,000 tons of tuna and prawns a year. French investment has helped establish a tuna cannery.

25FORESTRY

In 1991, the woodland area of Madagascar was estimated to cover more than 15.3 million ha (about 37.8 million acres), or about 26% of the land. The main objectives of forestry policy have been to arrest further destruction of the woodlands, to pursue a systematic reforestation program in the interests of soil conservation and the domestic demand for construction timber, and to continue to meet the domestic need for firewood, of great importance in view of the absence of petroleum or exploited coal deposits. Eucalyptus, introduced at the end of the 19th century, acacias (especially mimosa), and various kinds of pine have been extensively used in reforestation. Raffia is the only forest product exported in any quantity. Roundwood removals were estimated at 8,335,000 cu m in 1991; most was used for fuel.

26MINING

In 1975, the government nationalized all mineral resources (except graphite and mica) and brought prospecting and exploitation under state control. The exploitation of chromite and graphite is the principal mineral activity. In 1991, a reported 63,000 tons of chromite and 14,079 tons of graphite were extracted. Deposits of gem and ornamental stones, and stones for electrical geodes (quartz and celestine) have also been exploited. Marine-salt production was about 30,000 tons in 1991.

Extensive prospecting has led to the discovery of recoverable deposits of nickel (estimated at 70,000 tons) south of Ambositra, bauxite (100 million tons) at Manantenina, iron ore (350 million tons), 80 km (50 mi) southwest of Mahajanga, and coal (92 million tons) in the Sakoa Basin. These deposits have remained unexploited because Madagascar's poor internal transportation and power distribution systems have made it impossible to exploit them profitably.

27ENERGY AND POWER

There has been oil exploration since the early 20th century, but no important deposits had been found by the late 1980s. An estimated 80 million tons are thought to be extractable from bituminous sand deposits near Mahajanga, but in the early 1990s, it was not economically feasible. However, the Gulf War threat in 1991 to oil supplies sparked renewed interest in Madagascar's oil potential, and exploration efforts were redoubled. In 1992, the World Bank contributed $47 million to help Madagascar restructure its petroleum sector.

Installed electrical capacity in 1991 amounted to 220,000 kw, of which 85% was public. Annual output of power in 1991 was 569 million kwh, 56% of which was hydroelectrically produced. The first phase of the Andekaleta hydroelectric station, east of Antananarivo, came on line in 1982 with a capacity of 58 Mw, and plans were under way to double its capacity.

28INDUSTRY

By 1982, some 300 industrial companies, including all military and strategic industries, were state-owned or -controlled. The industrial centers are in the High Plateaux and near the Toamasina port. Industrialization has been severely hampered by inadequate internal transportation and a restricted local market. Industry's contribution to GDP declined at an average annual rate of 1.2% between 1980 and 1990, and most plants operate at less than one-third of full capacity.

The majority of industrial enterprises process agricultural products: rice, sugar, flour, tobacco, tapioca, and sisal. In addition, there are some meat-packing plants. Urea- and ammonia-based fertilizers are produced in a plant that opened in 1985. Other industrial enterprises include two cement plants, a paper pulp factory, cotton-spinning and -weaving mills, and three automobile assembly plants. The government-owned petroleum refinery at Toamasina has the capacity to handle at least 800,000 tons of imported crude oil a year, but it was closed during periods in the mid-1980s for rehabilitation. In 1990, it produced 25,000 tons of motor gasoline, 17,000 cu m of kerosene, 43,000 tons of gas-diesel oils, and 65,000 cu m of residual fuel oils.

Over two-thirds of Madagascar's electricity needs are supplied by the country's seven hydroelectric stations; thermal plants produce the remainder. Most of Madagascar's energy needs (80%) are supplied by wood and charcoal.

29SCIENCE AND TECHNOLOGY

France is the leading supplier of scientific and technical aid to Madagascar, and there are French research institutes in the country to study geology, hydrology, tropical forestry, and veterinary medicine.

The National Center of Applied Research in Rural Development is in Antananarivo. Also in the capital is a department of agronomical research, the National Institute of Geodesy and Cartography, and the Pasteur Institute, which is devoted to biological research. The Observatory of Antananarivo is affiliated with the University of Madagascar, which also has departments of sciences, agriculture, polytechnics, and health sciences. The University of Fianarantsoa has departments of mathematics, physics, chemistry, engineering, and computer science. In 1988, research and development expenditures totaled 14 billion francs; 956 technicians and 269 scientists and engineers were engaged in research and development.

30 DOMESTIC TRADE

Antananarivo, the capital and largest city, is the principal distribution center for the island. Toamasina, Mahajanga, Antsiranana, Toliara, and Tolänaro are the commercial centers for the provinces in which they are located. Distribution and packaging are being gradually modernized, and advertising in various media is assuming greater importance. Business hours vary, but generally are from about 8 AM to noon and 2 to 5:30 PM on weekdays and from 8 AM to noon on Saturdays. Banks are open 8 to 11 AM and 2 to 4 PM Monday–Friday.

Indians specialize in the retail sale of textiles, and Chinese in groceries. Most general merchants in the small eastern communities are Chinese; most on the west coast are Indian.

31 FOREIGN TRADE

Madagascar consistently runs a trade deficit. Exports consist mainly of unprocessed agricultural products and some extracted minerals. Imports are mainly manufactured goods: transport equipment, machinery, rice, and petroleum. Refined petroleum products were formerly imported in large quantities, but development of domestic refinery capacity altered this pattern. Madagascar now exports petroleum products to East Africa and to other Indian Ocean islands. Crude petroleum still must be imported.

Principal exports in 1991 (in millions of Malagasy francs) were as follows:

Coffee	51,920.0
Vanilla	84,887.0
Cloves and clove oil	46,025.6
Petroleum products	20,551.5
Sugar	19,125.2
Other exports	336,564.0
TOTAL	559,073.3

Imports in 1991 (in millions of Malagasy francs) were as follows:

Chemical products	88,345.8
Mineral products (excluding crude oil)	53,235.1
Crude petroleum	91,076.9
Textiles	12,743.2
Metal products	53,232.1
Machinery	132,212.0
Electrical equipment	43,995.0
Vehicles and parts	98,527.0
Other imports	212,322.4
TOTAL	785,689.5

France is by far Madagascar's leading trade partner, accounting for 25.7% of exports and 31.4% of imports in 1991. The United States accounted for 14.0% of exports and 6.8% of imports. Other export clients were Germany (10.0%) and Japan (8.5%). Imports likewise came from Germany (8.3%) and Japan (6.6%).

32 BALANCE OF PAYMENTS

Madagascar's payments balance is chronically negative. Since private investment has been limited, the deficits have been covered by foreign aid grants, official loans, and the use of central bank reserves from good years. In 1981 Madagascar was refused credit by its suppliers because of worsening deficits. The IMF provided a standby loan in 1982, conditional on devaluation of the currency, increased agricultural sector investments, producer price increases for rice and cotton, and the imposition of a ceiling on the minimum wage. These measures had a positive effect, although export production continued to decline. Consequently, further standby credits were negotiated and, in the late 1980s,

Madagascar's debt was periodically rescheduled conditional on further trade liberalization, tighter government spending controls, privatization of the state's banks, improvement of credit access, and the opening up of financial markets to foreigners. France and Germany canceled significant portions of Madagascar's debt at this time.

In 1992 merchandise exports totaled $328 million and imports $465 million. The merchandise trade balance was $–137 million. The following table summarizes Madagascar's balance of payments for 1991 and 1992 (in millions of US dollars):

	1991	1992
CURRENT ACCOUNT		
Goods, services, and income	–367	–371
Unrequited transfers	179	235
TOTALS	–188	–136
CAPITAL ACCOUNT		
Direct investment	14	21
Other long-term capital	–32	–93
Other short-term capital	–24	–16
Exceptional financing	251	292
Other liabilities	–4	–2
Reserves	–13	–15
TOTALS	192	187
Errors and omissions	–4	–52
Total change in reserves	–14	–20

33 BANKING AND SECURITIES

Upon leaving the franc zone in June 1973, the government established the Central Bank of the Malagasy Republic. Also organized at that time were the Malagasy National Development Bank, an agricultural credit institution, and the National Investment Co., an industrial investment bank. In June 1975, the Ratsiraka government nationalized all private financial institutions. In December 1976, Bankin'ny Tantsaha Mpamokatra (BTM) was established as the national rural development bank, Bankin'ny Indostria (BNI) as the national industrial development bank, and Banky Fampandrosoana ny Varotra (BFV) as the national bank for commerce. BTM and BFV have outlets in many communities. BNI closed in the late 1980s. There is also a savings bank and a postal checking account system. The money supply, as measured by M2, was FMG1,192.4 billion in December 1992. Economic reforms in 1988 allowed private foreign investment in the banking sector for the first time since the banks were nationalized. There are no securities exchanges in Madagascar.

34 INSURANCE

In June 1975, as part of the government's Malagasization program, all insurance companies were nationalized. Most of these had been French. Foreign companies now operate only as coinsurers. In 1985, there were 2 life and 2 composite insurance companies in operation; 8.4% of all premiums were for life and 91.6% for non-life insurance.

35 PUBLIC FINANCE

Madagascar's budget has been consistently in deficit. Wages and salaries are the largest component of government expenditure. In 1991, the budget deficit amounted to 11.8% of GDP, due to a lack of revenues caused by striking civil servants who were paid wages and salaries nonetheless. The following table shows actual revenues and expenditures for 1990 and 1991 in billions of francs.

Political instability in 1991 and 1992 has promoted a rise in the budget deficit and has slowed economic progress. Outstanding foreign debt represented 126% of GDP in 1992.

	1990	1991
REVENUE AND GRANTS		
Tax revenue	434.2	336.1
Non-tax revenue	112.8	81.5
Capital revenue	—	11.6
Grants	66.8	38.2
TOTAL	613.8	467.4
EXPENDITURES & LENDING MINUS REPAYMENTS		
General public services	142.0	147.8
Defense	53.5	55.8
Education	110.6	127.5
Health	45.1	48.7
Social security and welfare	17.5	10.9
Recreation, cultural, and religious affairs	1.4	1.6
Economic affairs and services	295.4	265.8
Other expenditures	14.1	6.9
TOTAL	648.7	739.8
Deficit/Surplus	−34.9	−272.4

36 TAXATION

Indirect taxes produce much more revenue than direct taxes. The most important indirect taxes are import duties, a value-added tax, a turnover tax, and consumption taxes. Export duties were suspended in 1985. Direct taxation consists of a graduated personal income tax with a maximum rate of 35%, a corporate profits tax at a flat rate of 35%, and a tax on income from transferable capital.

37 CUSTOMS AND DUTIES

Between 1960 and 1972, most Malagasy production went to France, where it was sold at subsidized prices. In return, preferential treatment was given to French imports. This reciprocal arrangement guaranteed the Malagasy a reliable return for their exports and enabled the French to pay low import duties and virtually monopolize the Malagasy market. Similar trade agreements were arranged with some EC countries. Beginning in 1972, however, the government restricted imports as much as possible and began the progressive cancellation of preferential arrangements to ensure greater diversity in supply sources. Import constraints were tightened in 1981, 1982, and 1983 because of a severe shortage of foreign exchange but were liberalized in 1986. In 1988, Madagascar began a three-stage comprehensive tariff reform to simplify and reduce rates. By the end of the third stage, imported goods will be divided into five categories, which will be taxed at rates of 10–50%.

38 FOREIGN INVESTMENT

Prior to independence, nearly all private investment was French. Since independence, there has been little private foreign investment due to restrictive policies toward private foreign investments and a history of expropriation without compensation. Nonetheless, public foreign investment is encouraged.

The investment code of 1973 requires that the Malagasy government own at least 51% of most new foreign projects, especially those involving strategic sectors of the economy. Import duties on equipment, excise on products, and taxes on profits may be reduced or waived. Priority may be given to an enterprise in the allocation of foreign exchange and in the sale of goods and services to the state and its enterprises. Arrangements must be negotiated on a case-by-case basis.

A new code that became operational in 1986 allows some exporters tax holidays of up to eight years, and there are special incentives for small enterprises. Foreign investors have the right to transfer dividends freely. The investment code of 1990 provides further incentives to foreign private investors and was opposed by local businesses for that reason. Rules covering foreign exchange and the number of foreign employees have been relaxed. Small- and medium-size companies are provided tax exemptions through the first ten years of operation.

A number of export processing zones have been set up in Madagascar. These have attracted investors from Asia, Mauritius, and France. Between 1990 and 1992, 69 new, foreign-financed businesses were established in Madagascar. The International Development Agency is providing support credits in this effort.

39 ECONOMIC DEVELOPMENT

The 1982–1984 development plan, more modest than the previous one owing to limited resources, called for a shift from social investments (especially education and health) to agriculture, industry, and infrastructure. The following 1984–87 plan called for spending centered mainly on transport improvements and agricultural development. The 1986–90 plan, which superseded the 1984–87 plan, had 30% of the budget coming from private sources and 40% from foreign sources. The plan called for investments of 47% in agriculture. in the ongoing effort to achieve food self-sufficiency and crop diversification.

Madagascar's main bilateral donors are France and Germany. Its main multilateral donors are the IDA and the EC. The United States, Japan, and the United Nations family of organizations are also aid contributors.

40 SOCIAL DEVELOPMENT

There is a National Social Security Fund that provides family allowances and workers' compensation for wage earners.

Women enjoy a highly visible and influential position in society, occupying many important posts in business and government. Abortion is legal only to save the woman's life. In the early 1990s, a woman who completed her childbearing years had borne an average of 6.75 children.

41 HEALTH

All medical services in Madagascar are free. Each province has a central hospital, and local clinics, dispensaries, and maternity-care centers are supplemented by mobile health units. Approximately 65% of the population has access to health care services. Total health care expenditure in 1990 was $79 million.

In 1990, there were 0.9 hospital beds per 1,000 people. In the same year, there were 1,392 doctors (1 per 8,130 people), 19 pharmacists, 89 dentists, 3,124 nurses, and 1,703 midwives.

The major endemic diseases are malaria, leprosy, schistosomiasis, and tuberculosis. Immunization rates for children up to one year old for 1992 were: tuberculosis (46%); diphtheria, pertussis, and tetanus (32%); polio (32%); and measles (27%). In 1990, 53% of children under 5 years of age were considered malnourished, and there were approximately 310 cases of tuberculosis reported per 100,000 people. In 1991, 23% of the population had access to safe water, and only 3% had adequate sanitation.

Madagascar has a birth rate of 45.4 per 1,000 inhabitants. Only 17% of married women (ages 15 to 49) use contraception. There were 589,000 births in 1992. The infant mortality rate in 1992 was 110 per 1,000 live births, and the overall mortality rate in 1993 was 12.7 per 1,000 people. The maternal mortality rate in 1991 was 570 per 100,000 live births. The average life expectancy is 55 years.

42 HOUSING

Malagasy houses, although constructed of varying materials in different parts of the island (brick and wood in the plateau, thatch and leaves in the west, and often on stilts in the east), are always rectangular, sited north–south, with the doorway opening to the west. In the central plateau, they are often two stories high and have outside terraces. The rapid growth of towns after World

War II created grave problems of housing and sanitation, especially in Antananarivo, whose situation on a rocky promontory aggravates the difficulties of overcrowding. According to the latest information available for 1980–88, the housing stock totaled 2,350,000 with 4.5 people per dwelling.

[43]EDUCATION

Although education is free and compulsory between the ages of 6 and 12, there is still a considerable degree of illiteracy. In 1990, illiteracy was estimated at 19.8% total (males: 12.3% and females: 27.1%). In the same year, there were 1,570,721 pupils attending 13,791 primary schools, secondary school enrollment was 340,191 pupils, and there were 35,824 students enrolled in higher education.

The University of Madagascar in Antananarivo, established in 1961, also has campuses at Antsiranana, Fianarantsoa, Mahajanga, Toamasina, and Toliara. Also in Antananarivo is the Rural College of Ambatobe and the National Institute of Telecommunications and Posts.

[44]LIBRARIES AND MUSEUMS

The principal libraries are the National Library in Antananarivo, with 205,000 volumes, and the university library, with 280,000 volumes. Other important libraries include the National Archives (10,000 volumes), the Antananarivo municipal library (22,600), and the Albert Camus Cultural Center Library (38,0000).

The palace of the queen in Antananarivo contains important art, archaeological, and historical exhibits, especially concerning the Merina kingdom. Other museums in the city are the Gallery of Fine Arts; the University of Madagascar's Museum of Art and Archaeology; the Folkore, Archaeology, Paleontology, and Animal Museum; the Historical Museum, and a natural history museum.

[45]MEDIA

The government owns and operates all major communications services. In 1991 there were 43,600 telephone subscribers. Radio-Télévision Malagasy broadcasts in French, Malagasy, and English, and telecasts in French and Malagasy; Radio Madgasi Kara, also state owned, broadcasts in French and Malagasy. In 1991 there were about 2.5 million radios and 248,000 television sets.

The principal daily newspapers are *Journal de Madagascar* (formerly *Madagascar-Matin*) (1991 circulation 5,000) and *Midi-Madagascar* (1991 circulation 23,000) in French; *Atrika* in French and Malagasy; and *Maresaka* and *Imongo Vaovao*, all published in Antananarivo. Despite prior censorship of all print media, the press is independent and quite outspoken.

[46]ORGANIZATIONS

There are hundreds of cooperatives, and the Ratsiraka government has been encouraging fokonolona, or village organizations, to stimulate planned agricultural undertakings.

There are numerous associations for sports. Chambers of commerce, originally established in 1902, are located in a dozen towns. There are also seven major employers' organizations. Tanora Tonga Saina is the government-sponsored youth movement.

[47]TOURISM, TRAVEL, AND RECREATION

Since the mid-1980s, the government has encouraged tourism as a source of foreign exchange, and the industry grew until 1991, when there was a decline due to civil unrest. In that year, there were 34,891 tourist arrivals (down 34% from 1990). Of these, nearly half were either French or German, with Swiss and Italians accounting for about 8% each and North Americans for about 7%. Public investment in the tourism infrastructure remains low, but there has been substantial private investment. In 1991, there were 4,119 hotel rooms with a 39.5% occupancy rate, and tourism receipts totaled US$26 million.

Visitors must have a passport and a visa issued by the Malagasy consular service. Certificates of vaccination against cholera and yellow fever are required of persons arriving from an infected area.

[48]FAMOUS MALAGASY

The poet Jean-Joseph Rabéarivelo (1901–37) published several volumes of poetry (*Volumes, Presques Songes, Sylves*). Jacques Rabémananjara (b.1914), a founder of the MDRM, is well known for his verse play, *Les Dieux malgaches*. Philibert Tsiranana (1910–78), a Tsimihety teacher, founded the PSD, and became Madagascar's first president in May 1959. Gen. Gabriel Ramanantsoa (1906–79) was head of state from May 1972 to February 1975. Adm. Didier Ratsiraka (b.1936) became head of state in June 1975 and president of the republic in January 1976.

[49]DEPENDENCIES

Two offshore islands, Nosy Boraha and Nosy Be, are considered by Madagascar as integral parts of the country.

[50]BIBLIOGRAPHY

American University. *Indian Ocean: Five Island Countries.* 2d ed. Washington, D.C.: Government Printing Office, 1982.

Bradt, Hilary. *Madagascar.* Santa Barbara, Calif.: Clio, 1993.

Brown, Mervyn. *Madagascar Rediscovered: A History from Early Times to Independence.* Hamden, Conn.: Shoe String, 1979.

Feeley-Harnik, Gillian. *A Green Estate: Restoring Independence in Madagascar.* Washington, D.C.: Smithsonian Institution Press, 1991.

Gow, Bonar A. *Madagascar and the Protestant Impact.* New York: Holmes & Meier, 1979.

Huntington, Richard. *Gender and Social Structure in Madagascar.* Bloomington: Indiana University Press, 1988.

Kottak, Conrad P. *The Past in the Present: History, Ecology, and Cultural Variation in Highland Madagascar.* Ann Arbor: University of Michigan Press, 1980.

Madagascar in Pictures. Minneapolis: Lerner Publications, 1988.

Preston-Mafham, Ken. *Madagascar: A Natural History.* New York: Facts on File, 1991.

MALAWI

Republic of Malawi

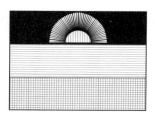

CAPITAL: Lilongwe.

FLAG: The national flag is a horizontal tricolor of black, red, and green, with a red rising sun in the center of the black stripe.

ANTHEM: Begins "O God, Bless Our Land of Malawi."

MONETARY UNIT: The kwacha (ĸ) of 100 tambala (t) is the national currency; it replaced the Malawi pound (m£) on 28 August 1970 and was linked with the pound sterling until November 1973. There are coins of 1, 2, 5, 10, and 20 tambala, and notes of 50 tambala and 1, 5, 10, 20, and 50 kwacha. ĸ1 = $0.1515 (or $1 = ĸ6.60).

WEIGHTS AND MEASURES: The metric system is the legal standard.

HOLIDAYS: New Year's Day, 1 January; Martyrs' Day, 3 March; Kamuzu Day, 14 May; Republic or National Day, 6 July; Mothers' Day, 17 October; National Tree Planting Day, 21 December; Christmas, 25 December; Boxing Day, 26 December. Movable holidays include Good Friday and Easter Monday.

TIME: 2 PM = noon GMT.

¹LOCATION, SIZE, AND EXTENT

A landlocked country in southeastern Africa, Malawi (formerly Nyasaland) has an area of 118,480 sq km (45,745 sq mi), of which 24,208 sq km (9,347 sq mi) consists of water, chiefly Lake Malawi (also known as Lake Niassa). Comparatively, the area occupied by Malawi is slightly larger than the state of Pennsylvania. Malawi extends 853 km (530 mi) N–S and 257 km (160 mi) E–W. It is bounded on the N and E by Tanzania, on the E, S, and SW by Mozambique, and on the W by Zambia, with a total boundary length of 2,881 km (1,790 mi).

Malawi's capital city, Lilongwe, is located in the southwestern part of the country.

²TOPOGRAPHY

Topographically, Malawi lies within the Great Rift Valley system. Lake Malawi, a body of water some 580 km (360 mi) long and about 460 m (1,500 ft) above sea level, is the country's most prominent physical feature. About 75% of the land surface is plateau between 750 m and 1,350 m (2,460 and 4,430 ft) above sea level. Highland elevations rise to over 2,440 m (8,000 ft) in the Nyika Plateau in the north and at Mt. Sapitwa (3,000 m/9,843 ft). The lowest point is on the southern border, where the Shire River approaches its confluence with the Zambezi at 37 m (121 ft) above sea level.

³CLIMATE

Variations in altitude in Malawi lead to wide differences in climate. The vast water surface of Lake Niassa has a cooling effect, but because of the low elevation, the margins of the lake have long hot seasons and high humidity, with a mean annual temperature of 24°C (75°F). Precipitation is heaviest along the northern coast of Lake Malawi, where the average is more than 163 cm (64 in) per year; about 70% of the country averages about 75–100 cm (30–40 in) annually. In general, the seasons may be divided into the cool (May to mid-August); the hot (mid-August to November); the rainy (November to April), with rains continuing longer in the northern and eastern mountains; and the post-rainy (April to May), with temperatures falling in May. Lilongwe, in central Malawi, at an elevation of 1,041 m (3,415 ft), has a moderately warm climate with adequate rainfall. The average daily minimum and maximum temperatures in November, the hottest month, are 17°C (63°F) and 29°C (84°F), respectively; those in July, the coolest month, are 7°C (45°F) and 23°C (73°F).

⁴FLORA AND FAUNA

About half of the land area is classified as forest or woodland, but some of this includes grassland, thicket, and scrub. There are indigenous softwoods in the better-watered areas, with bamboo and cedars on Mt. Sapitwa; evergreen conifers also grow in the highlands. Mopane, baobab, acacia, and mahogany trees are among those found at lower elevations.

There are many varieties of animal life. The elephant, giraffe, and buffalo are found in certain areas; hippopotamuses dwell on the shores of Lake Niassa. The kudu, duiker, bushbuck, tsessebe, wildebeest, and hartebeest are among the antelopes to be found. Other mammals in Malawi are the baboon, monkey, hyena, wolf, zebra, lion, nocturnal cat, badger, warthog, and porcupine.

There are at least 600 species of birds. Reptiles are plentiful and include freshwater turtle, crocodile, tortoise, marsh terrapin, chameleon, lizard, and many varieties of snakes; the Egyptian cobra has been found in the Shire Valley. Fish abound in the lakes and rivers; species include bream, bass, catfish, mudfish, perch, carp, and trout. Malawi is rich in insect life and has species in common with tropical West Africa and Tanzania.

⁵ENVIRONMENT

Almost all fertile land is already under cultivation, and continued population pressure raises the threat of soil erosion and exhaustion, as well as infringement on forest resources for agricultural purposes. The demand for firewood has significantly depleted the timber stock. Malawi has 2.2 cu mi of water with 49% used for farming and 17% used for industrial activity. One-third of city dwellers and about half of the rural population lack pure water.

The nation's cities produce 0.2 million tons of solid waste per year. Human encroachment has reduced wildlife habitats. The preservation of Malawi's wildlife is a significant environmental issue. Some of the nation's fish population is threatened with extinction due to pollution from sewage, industrial waste, and agricultural chemicals. As of 1994, 10 of the nation's mammal species and seven of its bird species were threatened, as well as 61 plant species. As of 1987 Malawi had four national parks and three game reserves; about 11% of the nation's total area was protected.

6 POPULATION

According to a 1994 estimate by the US Census Bureau, the population was 9,952,476. The UN projection for the year 2000 was 12,612,000, assuming a crude birthrate of 50.4 per 1,000 population (believed to be the highest in the world), a crude death rate of 20.5, and a net natural increase of 29.9 during 1995–2000. The estimated population density in 1994 was 84 per sq km (217.6 sq mi), one of the highest in Africa. The Southern Region had 50% of the population in 1987, the Central Region 40%, and the Northern Region 11%. The population of the largest city, Blantyre, was 331,588 in 1987; other towns are Mzuzu (44,238), and Zomba (42,878). Lilongwe, the capital, had about 310,000 people in 1990. About 13.5% of the population was urban in 1995.

7 MIGRATION

There has been considerable immigration into the south from Mozambique. At the end of 1992 there were 1,058,500 Mozambican refugees in Malawi. Accelerating migration from rural to urban areas contributed to an annual urban growth rate of about 6% in the early 1990s.

8 ETHNIC GROUPS

The people of Malawi belong mainly to various Central Bantu groups. About half belong to the Chewa and Nyanja groups, known collectively as Malawi (or Maravi) before the 19th century. About 15% are Lomwe (Alomwe), who live south of Lake Chilwa. Other indigenous Malawians include the Tumbuka and Tonga. The Ngoni and Yao arrived in the 19th century; together they constitute about 15% of the population. There are a few thousand Europeans, mainly of British origin, including descendants of Scottish missionaries. There are also small numbers of Portuguese, Asians (mainly Indians), and persons of mixed ancestry.

9 LANGUAGES

Numerous Bantu languages and dialects are spoken. Chichewa, the language of the Chewa and Nyanja, is spoken by more than half the population, but the Lomwe, Yao, and Tumbuka have their own widely spoken languages, respectively known as Chilomwe, Chiyao, and Chitumbuka. English and Chichewa are the official languages.

10 RELIGIONS

It was estimated in the early 1990s that about 50% of the population was Christian, including Protestants, Roman Catholics, and African Christian groups. Protestants include Baptists, Presbyterians, Adventists, and Lutherans. Tribal religionists account for as much as 15% of the population and Muslims 20%. The Jehovah's Witnesses were officially banned in 1967; about 3,500 of the estimated 24,000 members were arrested, and the remainder fled to Mozambique and Zambia. Repatriation to Malawi was completed by December 1972.

11 TRANSPORTATION

In the 1991, Malawi had 789 km (490 mi) of railways. The main line of the rail system consists of a single track of 3′6″ gauge running from Salima to Nsanje, a distance of 439 km (273 mi), and operated by Malawi Railways. The line was extended from Salima to Lilongwe in 1977 and was later extended to Mchinji, on the border with Zambia. At Chipoka, 32 km (20 mi) south of Salima, the railway connects with the Lake Malawi steamer service, also operated by Malawi Railways.

The railway line extends, in the south, from Nsanje to the port of Beira in Mozambique. The Central African Railway Co., a subsidiary of Malawi Railways, operates the 26 km (16 mi) span from Nsanje to the Mozambique border.

In 1991, Malawi had 13,300 km (8,265 mi) of roads. In the same year, there were 34,000 motor vehicles, of which about half were passenger cars.

Until 1982, about 95% of Malawi's foreign trade passed through Mozambican ports, mainly by rail connections, but by 1987, because of insurgent activity in Mozambique, over 95% of Malawi's exports were moving through South Africa's port of Durban. The use of this longer route, with only road transport through Malawi, was costing $50 million a year in extra transport expenses. Since 1990, when Mozambican rebels closed down the route, goods have been shipped through Zambia.

International and domestic air service is provided by Air Malawi, the national airline, established in 1967. Kamuzu International Airport, at Lilongwe, entered service in 1982; it handled 232,000 passengers in 1992. Air Malawi handled about 120,000 passengers in 1991.

12 HISTORY

Malawi has been inhabited for at least 12,000 years; its earliest peoples were nomadic hunter-gatherers. By the 13th century AD, Bantu-speaking migrants had entered the region. The Chewa peoples had become dominant by the early 16th century; their clans were consolidated under the leadership of a hereditary ruler called the karonga. Before the coming of the Europeans in the second half of the 19th century, Malawi was an important area of operations for Arab slave traders. The incursions of slaving took a heavy toll on the inhabitants, although the Chewa state never came under direct Arab rule. One of the major stated objectives of British intervention in the territory was to stamp out the slave trade.

The first European to explore the area extensively was David Livingstone, whose reports in the 1850s and 1860s were instrumental in the establishment of a series of mission stations in Nyasaland (as Malawi was then known) during the 1870s. In 1878, the African Lakes Company was formed by Scottish businessmen to supply the missions and provide a "legitimate" alternative to the slave trade. As the company extended its operations, it came into conflict with Yao tribesmen and Arab outposts toward the northern end of Lake Niassa. Fighting ensued in 1887–89, and pacification was completed only some years after the British government had annexed the whole of the territory in 1891. To Sir Harry Johnston, the first commissioner of the protectorate, fell the task of wiping out the remaining autonomous slave-trading groups. These antislavery operations were assisted by gunboats of the Royal Navy.

Nyasaland attracted a small group of European planters in the first decades of the 20th century. This group settled mainly in the Shire Highlands, and its numbers were never large. The territory was viewed by the imperial government as a tropical dependency, rather than as an area fit for widespread white settlement; many of the frictions that marred race relations in the Rhodesias were therefore minimized in Nyasaland. Missionaries and colonial civil servants consistently outnumbered planters in the European community, and lands occupied by European estates accounted for only a small part of the total land area.

Between World Wars I and II, the policy of the imperial government was built around the concept of "indirect rule"—that is, increasing the political responsibility of the African peoples by building on the foundations of their indigenous political institutions. Although this policy was not implemented at a rapid pace, it was generally assumed that Nyasaland would ultimately become an independent African-led state. In 1953, however, Nyasaland was joined with the two Rhodesias—Northern Rhodesia (now Zambia) and Southern Rhodesia (now Zimbabwe)—in the Central African Federation. The Africans' reaction to this political arrangement was hostile. Disturbances sparked by opposition to the federation in 1959 led to the declaration of a state of emergency, and some Africans, including Dr. Hastings Kamuzu Banda, were detained.

The African political leaders imprisoned in Southern Rhodesia were released in April 1960, and they gathered African support for the Malawi Congress Party (MCP). The MCP increased the campaign against federation rule and in the August 1961 elections polled more than 90% of the vote, winning all of the 20 lower-roll seats and 2 of 8 upper-roll places. An era of "responsible" government then began, with the MCP obtaining 5, and eventually 7, of the 10 available Executive Council positions. At a constitutional conference held in London in November 1962, it was agreed that Nyasaland should become fully self-governing early in 1963, and that Banda, who headed the MCP, should become prime minister. On 19 December 1962, the British government announced acceptance "in principle" of the right of Nyasaland to secede from the federation.

The Banda Era

In February 1963, as scheduled, Nyasaland became a self-governing republic. In July, at a conference held at Victoria Falls, it was decided that the Central African Federation would break up by the end of the year. In October, Banda visited the UK and successfully negotiated full independence, effective in mid-1964 after a general election based on universal adult suffrage. Accordingly, on 6 July 1964, Nyasaland became a fully independent Commonwealth country and adopted the name Malawi. On 6 July 1966, Malawi became a republic, and Banda assumed the presidency. After the constitution was amended in November 1970, Banda became president for life.

During the first decade of Banda's presidency, Malawi's relations with its black-ruled neighbors were sometimes stormy. At the opening session of the MCP convention in September 1968, President Banda made a claim to extensive territories outside the present boundaries of Malawi. The claim covered the whole of Lake Niassa and parts of Tanzania, Mozambique, and Zambia.

The Tanzanian government asserted that President Banda could make territorial claims only because he had the support of South Africa, Rhodesia (which at that time had a white minority government), and Portugal (which then still ruled Mozambique). In fact, in 1967, Malawi had become the first black African country to establish diplomatic relations with white-ruled South Africa; in August 1971, moreover, Banda became the first black African head of state to be officially received in South Africa, which supplied arms and development funds to Malawi.

The Banda government also faced some internal opposition. In October 1967, the Malawi government announced that a group of rebels, numbering about 25, wearing police uniforms and posing as insurgents from Mozambique, had entered Malawi with the intention of killing President Banda and his ministers. Eventually, eight of the rebels were convicted of treason and sentenced to death; five others, including Ledson Chidenge, a member of the National Assembly, were sentenced to death for the murder of a former official of the MCP.

The aging Banda continued to rule Malawi with an iron hand through the 1970s and into the late 1980s. Several thousand people were imprisoned for political offenses at one time or another during his rule. One of these was former Justice Minister Orton

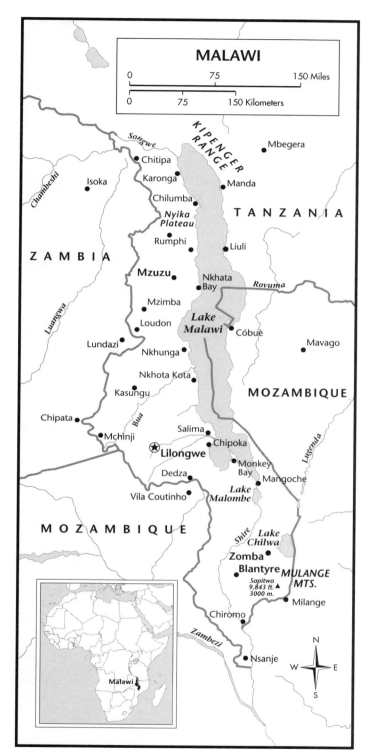

LOCATION: 9°27′ to 17°10′s; 32°20′ to 36°E. **BOUNDARY LENGTHS:** Tanzania, 451 km (280 mi); Mozambique, 1,497 km (930 mi); Zambia, 820 km (510 mi).

Chirwa, leader of an opposition group in exile, who in May 1983 was sentenced to death after having reportedly been abducted from a town across the Zambian border in late 1981. Chirwa's sentence was commuted to life imprisonment in 1984. He died in prison in October 1992. The leader of another dissident group, Attati Mpakati, was assassinated in Harare, Zimbabwe, in March 1983. Three government ministers and a member of parliament—

two of them key leaders of the MCP, with one of them, party secretary-general Dick Matenje, regarded as a possible successor to Banda—died in the middle of May 1983 in a mysterious car accident.

A serious problem in the 1980s concerned the activities of the Mozambique National Resistance (MNR), which, in its efforts (backed by South Africa) to bring down the government in Maputo, seriously disrupted Malawi's railway links with Mozambique ports. As a result, an increasing share of Malawi's trade had to be routed by road through Zambia and South Africa at great expense. In 1987, Malawi allowed Mozambican troops to patrol areas along their common border and sent several hundred troops into northeast Mozambique to help guard the railway leading to the port of Nacala. Other critical problems for Malawi are the nation's growing debt burden, severe draught, and the nearly 1 million refugees from Mozambique.

In 1992, Banda's grip began to weaken. In March, Malawi's eight Roman Catholic bishops issued a pastoral letter protesting detention without trial and harsh treatment of political prisoners. University students demonstrated. Wildcat strikes and rioting in Blantyre and Lilongwe followed the arrest of opposition trade unionist, Chakufwa Chihana in May. Nearly 40 were killed by police gunfire in the first significant antigovernment demonstrations since 1964. Chihana was released on bail in September and he formed a new group, the Alliance for Democracy (AFORD), that campaigned for multiparty elections. In December, Chihana was sentenced to two years for sedition.

Pressure mounted (including threats by aid donors abroad to suspend assistance), and in October Banda agreed to hold a referendum early in 1993 on whether Malawi should remain a one-party state. In the referendum, on 14 June 1993, 63% of those voting favored adopting multiparty democracy. Two opposition groups, AFORD and the United Democratic Front (UDF), both led by former MCP officials, held a massive rally in January 1993. Meanwhile, three opposition groups in exile merged to form the United Front for Multiparty Democracy, which then merged with the UDF inside Malawi. Chihana was released two days before the referendum.

Afterwards, Banda agreed to hold elections in 1994 and to draft a new constitution. Parliament adopted laws ending one-party rule and detention without trial and allowing dissidents to return home. Late in 1993, Banda underwent brain surgery in South Africa. Before that, Gwanda Chakuamba, a former government minister who had been jailed from 1980 until July 1993, was appointed as MCP secretary-general.

There were seven political parties legally registered to campaign for the 17 May 1994 elections. Bakili Muluzi of the UDF, a former cabinet minister, was elected president over Banda (MCP), Chihana (AFORD), and Kamlepo Kalua (Malaur Democratic Party). Of the 177 parliamentary seats contested, the UDF took 84 of them, the MCP took 55, and AFORD just 33. Muluzi immediately ordered the release of political prisoners and the closing of the most notorious jails. The transition was relatively smooth. Banda's paramilitary MCP Young Pioneers, were disarmed by the army and the police in December 1993, and an atmosphere of relative tolerance now prevails.

13GOVERNMENT

Malawi officially became a republic on 6 July 1966, and its constitution dates from that year. The president is the head of state and supreme executive authority. Legislative power is vested in the unicameral National Assembly, which consisted in 1987 of 112 elected members and 11 members nominated by the president; election is by universal adult suffrage. Parliamentary elections are to occur every five years unless the president dissolves the National Assembly before then. Until recent constitutional reforms, candidates, who had to be members of the ruling MCP,

were subject to approval by Hastings Kamuzu Banda, who assumed the presidency when Malawi became a republic; he was sworn in as president for life on 6 July 1971. Cabinet ministers were appointed by the president from among members of the National Assembly; there was no vice-president. Near the end of Banda's regime, the real powers of state were exercised by Cecilia "Mama" Kadzamira, his official hostess, and her uncle, John Tembo, the powerful minister of state.

In July and November 1993, parliament (still in MCP hands) passed bills eliminating from the constitution single-party clauses (such as Banda's life presidency), appending a bill of rights, establishing a multiparty electoral law, and repealing detention without trial provisions of the Public Security Act. Dialogue among various major parties resulted in the establishment of a National Consultative Council and a National Executive Committee, with representatives from all registered parties, to oversee changes in the constitution, laws, and election rules and procedures.

14POLITICAL PARTIES

Malawi was officially a one-party state from October 1973 until July 1993. The Malawi Congress Party (MCP) was the national party and Hastings Kamuzu Banda was its president for life. All candidates for the National Assembly had to be members of the MCP.

For years the opposition groups in exile achieved little success in their efforts to unseat the Banda government. The Socialist League of Malawi (LESOMA), with headquarters in Harare, was directed by Attati Mpakati until his assassination in March 1983. A second group, the Malawi Freedom Movement (MAFREMO), based in Tanzania, is led by Orton Chirwa, who was seized by Malawi authorities in late 1981 and imprisoned for life until his death in 1992. The Congress for the Second Republic, also based in Tanzania, is led by former External Affairs Minister Kanyama Chiume. The Save Malawi Committee (SAMACO) was formed in Lusaka, Zambia, in 1983.

In September 1992, trade unionist Chakufwa Chihana formed the Alliance for Democracy (AFORD) before being convicted of sedition. AFORD and others pushed successfully for a referendum on adopting a multiparty system, which was held on 14 June 1993. Voters rejected single-party rule by a margin of 63% to 35%, and opposition parties and coalition groups blossomed. The United Democratic Front (UDF) combined with a coalition in exile (the United Front for Multiparty Democracy) late in 1992.

Elections were held on 17 May 1994, with seven parties participating. The UDF won, trailed by the MCP, AFORD, and the Malawi Democratic Party.

15LOCAL GOVERNMENT

As of 1987, Malawi was divided into three regions—Northern, Central, and Southern—which were subdivided into 24 districts. District councilors are chosen by the district organizations of the MCP.

District councils provide markets, postal agencies, roads, and rural water supplies and exercise control over business premises and the brewing and sale of beer. More important, however, are the councils' responsibilities for primary education. Some of the councils run public health clinics. Council expenditures are mainly financed from direct government education grants, calculated to meet the salaries of teachers in most of the district schools. Other sources of revenue include annual taxes on all males over the age of 17 years who are residents in the district, and charges for services rendered.

Town councils have powers similar to those of the district councils, but with greater emphasis on the problems that arise in urban areas. Their main functions are sewerage, removal of refuse, the abatement of nuisances, construction and maintenance of roads, and, in some cases, the provision of fire-fighting services. Revenue for town councils comes mainly from direct taxes on property.

16JUDICIAL SYSTEM

Since 1969, Malawi has operated under two parallel court systems. In the first, essentially based on the UK legal system, there are numerous local courts throughout Malawi, with a local appeals court in each district. Formerly, these courts heard all cases of customary law and had wide statutory, criminal and civil jurisdiction.

In addition to the local court system, there are the Supreme Court of Appeal, the High Court, and magistrates' courts. The High Court consists of the chief justice, who is appointed by the president, and four puisne judges. There is a chain of appeals from the local courts up to the Supreme Court of Appeal.

A second system was established in November 1969, when the National Assembly empowered the president to authorize traditional African courts to try all types of criminal cases and to impose the death penalty; the president was also permitted to deny the right of appeal to the High Court against sentences passed by the traditional courts, a right formerly guaranteed by the constitution. Traditional court justices are all appointed by the president. Appeals from traditional courts go to the district traditional appeals courts and then to the National Traditional Appeal Court. Appeals from regional traditional courts, which are criminal courts of the first instance, go directly to the National Traditional Appeal Court.

In 1993, the Attorney General suspended the operation of regional and national level traditional courts in response to a report by the National Consultative Council on problems in the workings of the traditional court system. Since then the trend is toward moving serious criminal and political cases from traditional to modern courts. Education and training seminars have led to some improvements in the functioning of the local traditional courts. It appears that traditional courts at the local level may survive the recent reforms and continue to hear cases involving small claims and customary law.

The modern courts have begun to assert their independence in a number of decisions adverse to the executive and to the Malawi Congress Party (MCP). The government has not removed any judges in response to these decisions.

17ARMED FORCES

In 1993, Malawi had an army of 10,500 men, organized into 3 infantry battalions and 1 support battalion. The air force had 150 men, 4 armed helicopters, and 8 transports. A 100-member navy had 1 lake patrol craft. There was a paramilitary gendarmerie of 7,500. In 1989 Malawi spent $22 million on defense, or 1.6% of GDP. Malawi stations 1,500 soldiers in Mozambique.

18INTERNATIONAL COOPERATION

Malawi became a UN member on 1 December 1964; the nation participates in ECA and all the nonregional specialized agencies except IAEA and IMO. Malawi also belongs to the African Development Bank, Commonwealth of Nations, G-77, and OAU. It is a signatory of GATT and the Lomé Convention, and is a participant in the Southern African Development Coordinating Conference.

19ECONOMY

Malawi's is an agricultural economy which, in recent years, has been troubled by drought and financial instability. It is dependent for most of its income on the export sales of tobacco, tea, peanuts, coffee, and sugar. As a result of the 1992 drought, GDP declined by 7.9% after averaging 4.5% annual growth in 1989–91, and an impressive 6.7% annual growth rate during the 1970s. International aid donors, concerned about human rights

abuses in Malawi, have tied future support to human rights reforms.

Manufacturing is small-scale, directed mainly to the processing of export crops. In 1991, the agricultural sector employed 81.8% of Malawi's population and accounted for 33% of GDP. The sector experienced severe droughts in 1979–1981 and 1992. The mining sector in Malawi is undeveloped.

20INCOME

In 1992 Malawi's GNP was $1,896 million at current prices, or $210 per capita. For the period 1985–92 the average inflation rate was 17.6%, resulting in a real growth rate in per capita GNP of –0.3%.

In 1992 the GDP was $1,851 million in current US dollars. It is estimated that agriculture accounted for 28.1%, manufacturing 14.4%, and trade 13.5%.

21LABOR

At the end of 1990, the wage labor force totaled 473,370, including 211,080 in agriculture, forestry, and fishing; 63,870 in manufacturing; 80,930 in community and personal services; 26,690 in trade, restaurants and hotels; 25,650 in transport, storage, and communications; 43,710 in building and construction; and 21,440 in other sectors. The total labor force, according to the 1987 census, was 3,457,753. About 70% of all smallholder farms and over 50% of subsistence holdings were headed by women in 1992. Most Europeans employed in Malawi are in government administration; most of the Asians are employed in commerce.

The leading labor federation, the Trades Union Congress of Malawi, had some 6,500 members in the mid-1980s. The average monthly wage in 1990 was к175, with a low of к40 a month for agricultural workers.

22AGRICULTURE

The agricultural sector is drought-prone and experienced severe droughts in 1979–1981 and 1992. About 77% of the total land area of Malawi is under customary tenure—that is, subject to land allocation by village headmen based on traditional rights of succession by descent. Estate farming occupies about 23% of the cultivated land and provides about 90% of export earnings. In all, about 18% of Malawi's total land area is arable. Malawi is self-sufficient in food production (except during droughts), but the population increased more rapidly than the food supply in the 1980s.

Tea, a major export crop, is produced mostly on estates; about 16,000 ha (39,500 acres) are in tea plantations, mainly in the Mulanje and Thyolo districts. Production in 1992 was 28,000 tons. Production of tobacco, the chief export, amounted in 1992 to 139,000 tons, with exports totaling 8,300 tons for a value of $88.6 million. Sugarcane production was about 1,950,000 tons in 1992; the output of refined sugar reached 211,000 tons. Other cash crops produced in 1992 include peanuts, 23,000 tons, and seed cotton, 19,000 tons.

Although subsistence farmers participate in the production of export crops more extensively now than in the preindependence period, much customary agriculture is still devoted to cereal production. Pressure of population on the land is mounting and, in a few areas, expansion of acreage under export crops has been discouraged in favor of food production. Corn is the staple food crop; about 657,000 tons were produced in 1992. Late rains, floods, and an increasing Mozambican refugee population have kept corn production from meeting domestic demand. Other food crops, with 1992 estimated production figures, include cassava, 129,000 tons; potatoes, 330,000 tons; pulses, 258,000 tons; sorghum, 4,000 tons; plantains, 140,000 tons; bananas, 85,000 tons; and paddy rice, 20,000 tons.

23ANIMAL HUSBANDRY

Animal husbandry plays a minor role in the economy. Pressure on the land for cultivation is sufficiently intense in many areas to rule out stock-keeping on any scale. In 1992 there were an estimated 1,082,000 sheep and goats, 967,000 head of cattle, and 238,000 hogs. The number of poultry was estimated at 9 million in 1992. About 86,000 head of cattle were slaughtered in 1992. Milk production was estimated at 40,000 tons.

24FISHING

The growing commercial fishing industry is concentrated mainly in Lake Malawi, with small-scale activity in Lake Malombe, Lake Chilwa, and the Shire River. Fish farming is carried on in the south. The total catch in 1991 was estimated at 63,726 tons. Large employers of labor in the Southern Region are the major buyers, and much of the catch is sold directly to them. Fish from Lake Niassa contribute about 70% of animal protein consumption.

25FORESTRY

Natural forests are extensive, and in the high-altitude regions, the Forestry Department is engaged in a softwood afforestation program. Sizable plantations of pine, cypress, and cedar have been established. Roundwood removals in 1991 were estimated at 8.5 million cu m, of which 95% went for fuel.

26MINING

Quarrying for limestone and other building materials is the only current mining activity; in 1991, about 175,000 tons of limestone were quarried for the manufacture of cement. Small deposits of corundum, galena, gold, kyanite, asbestos, and mica have occasionally been exploited. Prospecting for other minerals has been undertaken, but no resources of commercial significance have been discovered except for coal, reserves of which are estimated at about 90 million tons, and bauxite (28.8 million tons). Coal production began in 1985 at the Kaziwiziwi mine in the Northern Region, near Livingstonia; production was 45,000 tons in 1991.

27ENERGY AND POWER

Both the consumption and the production of electric power are small, even by African standards. In 1991, 734 million kwh of power was sold by the Electric Supply Commission of Malawi; in addition, 16,000 kwh was produced privately. Installed capacity in 1991 totaled 185,000 kw. Almost 98% of power production was hydroelectric in 1991.

There are no known oil reserves, and all petroleum products are imported. Low-grade bituminous coal reserves were known about for many years, but have only recently been exploited, since imports from Mozambique are no longer reliable on account of civil war. As of 1991, two coal mines were operating near Livingstonia; production that year was estimated at 45,000 tons. In 1991, Malawi imported $58 million in fuel and energy, or 8% of total imports.

28INDUSTRY

After a decade of rapid expansion—11% average growth per year in the 1970s—the pace of manufacturing growth has slowed to a more modest 4–6% rate. Malawi's manufacturing sector is diverse. The processing of tea, tobacco, sugar, coffee, and cotton accounts for most of its output. Factories manufacture soap, detergents, cigarettes, furniture, cookies, bread, blankets and rugs, clothing, and mineral waters. Other installations include a gin distillery, a cotton mill, and two textile plants. Brick making is well established. Roofing tiles are also produced, and radios are assembled. Other products made in Malawi include agricultural implements, bicycle frames, polishes, edible oils and fats, cattle foodstuffs, flour, matches, fishing nets, rope, twine and yarns,

toiletries, and footwear. Two plants in Malawi retread tires, and its industries make a wide range of metal products.

29SCIENCE AND TECHNOLOGY

Research stations for tea, tobacco, and other aspects of agriculture conduct their activities under the auspices of the Ministry of Agriculture. The Ministry of Forestry and Natural Resources maintains forestry and fisheries research units. The University of Malawi includes Banda College of Agriculture and Kamuzu College of Nursing, both at Lilongwe Malawi Polytechnic at Blantyre; and Chancellor College at Zomba, which has a faculty of science.

30DOMESTIC TRADE

Domestic trade is concentrated in the larger towns. Licenses are required for all persons engaged in trading; fees vary with the nature of the business. Business hours are 7:30 or 8 AM to noon and 1 or 1:30 PM to 4:30 or 5 PM, Monday through Friday, and 7:30 or 8 AM to noon or 12:30 PM on Saturday. Banks are open weekdays from 8 to 12:30 PM (to 11:30 AM on Wednesday and 10:30 AM on Saturday).

31FOREIGN TRADE

Malawi's chief export crops are tobacco, tea, and sugar, followed by groundnuts, coffee, cassava, rice, cotton, and sunflower seeds. Tea is sold primarily to the United Kingdom while sugar exports go to the European Community and the United States. Principal imports are petroleum products, vehicles, piece goods, medicine, and agricultural machinery. Trade balances are generally negative, but there were surpluses in 1984 and 1988.

In 1989, Malawi's exports were sent primarily to the United Kingdom (21.0%), the United States (12.8%), Japan (12.8%), Germany (10.5%) and South Africa (9.7%). Imports came primarily from South Africa and other countries of the region (47.4%), the United Kingdom (17.1%), and Japan and Germany (each at 6.3%).

32BALANCE OF PAYMENTS

Malawi runs an annual deficit on current accounts, which is generally mitigated but not annulled by capital inflows, mostly in the form of development loans. During the first half of 1991, the balance of payments position deteriorated sharply compared to the same period in 1990, recording a deficit of $51.9 million for the first half of 1991 (up from $13.3 million for the same period of 1990). Lower capital inflows, coupled with increased exetrnal payments for imports and debt service were the causes of the rising deficit. The 1993 current account deficit was estimated at 15.4% of GDP.

33BANKING AND SECURITIES

The Reserve Bank of Malawi was established in Blantyre in 1964. It took over, by stages, the functions in Malawi of the former Bank of Rhodesia and Nyasaland until that bank wound up its affairs in June 1965. The main duties of the Reserve Bank are to maintain currency stability and to act as banker to the government and to the commercial banks. The Reserve Bank administers exchange control and acts as registrar for local registered stock. The Reserve Bank also handles the issue of treasury bills on behalf of the government. The money supply, as measured by M2, amounted to к1,945.5 million at the end of 1993.

Two commercial banks, the National Bank of Malawi and the Commercial Bank of Malawi, have branches or agencies throughout the country. In 1993, the former was 47% owned by Press Corp., 33% by ADMARC, and 20% by Standard Bank (UK); the latter was 40% owned by Press Corp., 30% by local interests, 20% by the Malawi Development Corp., and 10% by ADMARC. Commercial bank assets totaled $17.4 million at the end of 1986;

demand deposits amounted to ĸ560.15 million, and time and savings deposits totaled ĸ924.5 million. The Investment and Development Bank of Malawi provides medium- and long-term credit. The Post Office Savings Bank and New Building Society are savings institutions. There is no organized securities market.

34INSURANCE

Most insurance firms operating in Malawi are owned or sponsored by parent companies in the UK. However, the leading company, the National Insurance Co., is owned by Malawi interests. In 1985, insurance companies had gross premiums of ĸ24,552,000 and gross claims of ĸ14,754,000. Assets of all insurance companies were ĸ94,271,000. In 1986, there were 2 life, 5 non-life, and 3 composite insurance companies in operation; 31.9% of premiums were for life and 68.1% for non-life insurance. Motor vehicle insurance is compulsory.

35PUBLIC FINANCE

Government current revenues, 1,222 million kwacha in 1990, derive from import duties, income taxes on companies and individuals, income from government enterprises, excise duties, licenses, and sales tax. The fiscal year runs from 1 April to 31 March. The fiscal deficit was estimated at 15.7% of GDP for fiscal 1993.

In 1987 Malawi's foreign debt-service ratio reached 41%. Encouraged by the IMF, Malawi negotiated a rescheduling program in 1988 with both the "Paris Club" and the "London Club." By 1991, the debt-service ratio had declined to 27%.

36TAXATION

Individuals pay taxes on all income from Malawi, whether they are residents or non-residents, and tax rates range from 3–40%.

Companies are assessed 35% of net profits, (45% for branches of foreign companies). A 15% withholding tax is imposed on dividends or interest sent abroad. Municipal taxes are based on property valuations. A stamp tax, usually 3%, is payable on the open market value of property and securities transferred.

37CUSTOMS AND DUTIES

Tariff schedules are arranged to give preferential treatment to imports from the UK and other Commonwealth countries. Rebates are allowed on certain types of capital goods and on most materials used in local manufacturing industries.

The highest rates are charged on goods from countries not entitled to most-favored-nation treatment. Lower scales are applied to goods from non-Commonwealth members of GATT. Machinery, basic foodstuffs, and raw materials from the UK and the Commonwealth are generally admitted duty-free. Import licenses are required for purchases from non-GATT countries and of certain goods. Most tariffs range from zero to 45% of c.i.f. value, and there is also a 10% ad valorem surtax on all imports.

Luxury goods are assessed at higher rates than ordinary consumer items. Excise duties are levied for revenue purposes on spirits, beer, cigarettes and tobacco, petroleum products, and certain other items.

38FOREIGN INVESTMENT

The government actively encourages foreign investment, particularly in agriculture and in import-substitution and labor-intensive industries. Incentives such as exclusive licensing rights, tariff protection, and liberal depreciation allowances are among the incentives offered. Repatriation of dividends and profits are freely permitted.

Encouraged by the formation of the Malawi Development Corp. and the implementation of a development plan, foreign investment increased in the mid-1960s. A ĸ6-million sugar scheme on the lower Shire River was financed to a great extent by

foreign investment, as were a distillery and a brewery. In 1987, Lever Brothers, Portland Cement, and David Whitehouse & Sons had industrial plants in Malawi. The large plantation enterprises were originally established with capital largely from the United Kingdom.

39ECONOMIC DEVELOPMENT

Malawi's public investment program is revised annually to take account of changing needs and the expected availability of resources. The development program continues to be financed largely from external sources, and priority in the use of local resources is given to counterpart contributions to these external loans, grants, and investments.

During the first decades of independence, agricultural development were emphasized. The government sought to implement this policy by providing the family farmer with basic agricultural support facilities, such as extension services, training, irrigation, and research, and by increasing the output of fertile areas through farm credit, marketing, and processing facilities. During this period, four major agricultural developments were sponsored: the Shire Valley Agricultural Development Project in the south; the Lilongwe Land Development Program and the Central Region Lakeshore Development Project, both in the Central Region; and the Karonga Rural Development Project in the north.

More recently, improvements in the transportation infrastructure, especially in roads, have been emphasized. In the manufacturing sector, the government has stressed diversification. With major constraints on its foreign exchange, Malawi aims to reduce the trade gap, encourage exports, and reduce government expenditures.

The United Kingdom is Malawi's principal aid donor. South Africa has been a significant source of aid as well, especially in financing construction in the capital at Lilongwe and the railway extension from Lilongwe to Mchinji. Other significant aid donors have included the European Community, France, Canada, Germany, Japan, the United States, Denmark, the African Development Bank, and the WorldBank/IDA.

40SOCIAL DEVELOPMENT

The Ministry of Community Services is responsible for social welfare generally. Although the fertility rate is high (7 in the mid-1980s), and the birth rate is perhaps the world's highest, family planning services were officially discouraged until 1982, when a child-spacing program was officially approved. Abortion is legal only to save the woman's life. About 13% of married women (ages 15 to 49) use contraception.

A gradual improvement in Malawi's human rights record was evident beginning in 1992.

41HEALTH

Health services, which rank among the poorest in Africa, are under the jurisdiction and supervision of the Ministry of Health and are provided to Africans free of charge. In 1992, 80% of the population had access to health care services. The major health threats are malnutrition, malaria, and tuberculosis. In 1990, there were 173 reported cases of tuberculosis per 100,000 people, and an estimated 60% of children under 5 years old were considered malnourished. Hookworm and schistosomiasis are widespread. According to a Roman Catholic Church statement in 1987, there were thousands of AIDS cases in Malawi (1992 sub-Saharan estimates by the WHO show 1 million people who are HIV positive). In 1991, only 56% of the population had access to safe water; a surprising 84%, however, had adequate sanitation. Immunization rates in 1992 for children up to one year old were: tuberculosis (99%); diphtheria, pertussis, and tetanus (86%); polio (84%); and measles (82%).

In 1993, there were aproximately 567,000 births, resulting in a birth rate of 21.5 per 1,000 people. The infant mortality rate was 143 per 1,000 live births, one of the highest in Africa. The general mortality rate was 54.5 per 1,000 in 1993, and the maternal mortality rate was 400 per 100,000 live births in 1991. Life expectancy is 48 years (male) and 51 years (female).

In 1989, there were 186 doctors, 5 pharmacists, and 284 nurses. In 1992, there were 0.02 doctors per 1,000 inhabitants or about one physician for every 45,000 people and one nurse for every 1,800 persons. There were 1.6 hospital beds per 1,000 inhabitants in 1990, and total health care expenditures were $93 million.

42HOUSING

Government-built houses are either rented or sold. The Malawi Housing Corp. has also developed housing plots in order to relocate urban squatters. As of 1980, nearly half of all dwellings did not have flush toilets or private facilities. In the same year, 23% had a private shower or bath, while over half had no bathing facilities of any kind. Lighting was supplied by paraffin lamp (69%), electricity (23%), and pressure lamp (8%).

43EDUCATION

Control of education, including mission schools, is in the hands of the Ministry of Education. Attendance is compulsory for eight years at the primary level. Secondary education lasts for four years. Some 52% of adult males and 31% of females were literate in 1985.

In 1990, Malawi's 2,906 primary schools had 1,400,682 pupils; secondary schools had 32,275 students. Vocational schools had 780 pupils. The University of Malawi, inaugurated at Zomba on 6 October 1965, has four constituent colleges at Zomba, Lilongwe, and Blantyre. In 1989 there were 425 teachers and 5,594 pupils at the University and all other higher level institutions.

44LIBRARIES AND MUSEUMS

The Malawi National Library Service, founded in 1968, has more than 185,000 volumes and maintains a nationwide interloan system. The largest library is that of the University of Malawi (315,957 volumes). The US Information Agency maintains a small library in Lilongwe, and the British Council has libraries in Blantyre and in the capital. The National Archives are in Zomba. The Museum of Malawi Culture, in Blantyre, has a collection based on the nation's archaeology, history, and ethnography. Other museums include the Lake Malawi Museum in Mangochi and a regional museum in Mzuzu.

45MEDIA

Postal and telecommunications services are the responsibility of the government; there were 50,256 telephones in use in 1991. Radio broadcasting services are provided in English and Chichewa by the Malawi Broadcasting Corp. There are no television broadcast facilities. In 1991 there were 2.2 million radio sets in use.

The *Daily Times,* published in English in Blantyre, appears Monday through Friday and had a circulation of 25,000 in 1991. The *Malawi News,* published at Limbe on Sundays in English and Chichewa, had a circulation of 35,000. The press is strictly controlled.

46ORGANIZATIONS

A branch of the British Medical Association has been organized in Zomba. In the larger towns, musical societies and theater clubs have been established. Service clubs include the Rotary and the British Empire Service League. The League of Malawi Women and the League of Malawi Youth are active. The Malawi Chamber of Commerce and Industry has its headquarters at Blantyre.

47TOURISM, TRAVEL, AND RECREATION

The major tourist attraction in Malawi is Lake Niassa; the visitor is well served there by hotels and recreational facilities, and eight-day excursions around the lake are available. Game parks, Mt. Mulanje, and Mt. Zomba also attract the tourist trade. In 1990, 129,912 foreign tourists visited Malawi, 22% from Zambia, 17% from Mozambique, and 15% from Zimbabwe. There were 282 hotel rooms with 553 beds and a 42% occupancy rate. Receipts from tourism were estimated at US$11 million. Visitors from Commonwealth nations, the US, and many other countries do not need visas. Precautions against malaria are essential.

48FAMOUS MALAWIANS

The dominant political figure is Dr. Hastings Kamuzu Banda (b.1906). After a long period of medical practice in England, and a brief one in Ghana, he returned to Nyasaland in 1958 to lead the Malawi Congress Party. Following the declaration of a state of emergency, Banda was detained from March 1959 to April 1960. He became Malawi's first prime minister in 1963, and in 1966 he became Malawi's first president; he was named president for life in 1971 and ruled without interruption until ousted in a 1994 election mandated by constitutional reform.

49DEPENDENCIES

Malawi has no territories or colonies.

50BIBLIOGRAPHY

Agnew, Swanzie, and Michael Stubbs (eds.). *Malawi in Maps.* London: University of London Press, 1972.

American University. *Area Handbook for Malawi.* Washington, D.C.: Government Printing Office, 1975.

Boeder, Robert B. *Malawi.* Boulder, Colo.: Westview, 1986.

Chanock, Martin. *Law, Custom, and Social Order: The Colonial Experience in Malawi and Zambia.* New York: Cambridge University Press, 1985.

Crosby, C. A. *Historical Dictionary of Malawi.* 2d ed. Metuchen, N.J.: Scarecrow Press, 1993.

Heyneman, Stephen P. *The Evaluation of Human Capital in Malawi.* Washington, D.C.: World Bank, 1980.

Kalinga, Owen J. *A History of the Ngonde Kingdom of Malawi.* Hawthorn, N.Y.: Mouton, 1985.

McCracken, J. *Politics and Christianity in Malawi, 1875–1940.* London: Cambridge University Press, 1977.

McMaster, Carolyn. *Malawi: Foreign Policy and Development.* New York: St. Martin's, 1974.

Mtewa, Mekki. *Malawi: Democratic Theory and Public Policy.* Cambridge, Mass.: Schenkman, 1986.

O'Toole, Thomas. *Malawi in Pictures.* Minneapolis: Lerner Publications Co., 1988.

Pachai, Bridglal. *Land and Politics in Malawi.* Kingston, Ontario: Limestone, 1978.

Pachai, Bridglal. *The Early History of Malawi.* Evanston, Ill.: Northwestern University Press, 1972.

Pike, J. G. *Malawi: A Political and Economic History.* New York: Praeger, 1968.

Rotberg, Robert I. *The Rise of Nationalism in Central Africa: The Making of Malawi and Zambia, 1873–1964.* Cambridge, Mass.: Harvard University Press, 1965.

Vaughan, Megan. *The Story of an African Famine: Gender and Famine in Twentieth-Century Malawi.* New York: Cambridge University Press, 1987.

Williams, T. David. *Malawi: The Politics of Despair.* Ithaca, N.Y.: Cornell University Press, 1978.

Wills, A. J. *An Introduction to the History of Central Africa.* London: Oxford University Press, 1973.

MALI

Republic of Mali
République du Mali

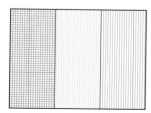

CAPITAL: Bamako.

FLAG: The flag is a tricolor of green, yellow, and red vertical stripes.

ANTHEM: National Anthem begins "At thy call, O Mali."

MONETARY UNIT: The Malian franc (MF), a paper currency that had been floating with the French franc, was replaced in June 1984 by the French Community Franc (CFA Fr) at a ratio of MF2 = CFA Fr1. There are coins of 1, 2, 5, 10, 25, 50, and 100 CFA francs and notes of 50, 100, 500, 1,000, 5,000, and 10,000 CFA francs. CFA Fr1 = $0.0018 (or $1 = CFA Fr571).

WEIGHTS AND MEASURES: The metric system is the legal standard.

HOLIDAYS: New Year's Day, 1 January; Armed Forces Day, 20 January; Labor Day, 1 May; Africa Day, 25 May; Independence Day, 22 September; Anniversary of 1968 coup, 19 November; Christmas, 25 December. Movable religious holidays include 'Id al-Fitr, 'Id al-'Adha', Milad an-Nabi, and Easter Monday.

TIME: GMT.

¹LOCATION, SIZE, AND EXTENT

A landlocked country in West Africa, Mali has an area of about 1,240,000 sq km (478,767 sq mi), extending 1,852 km (1,151 mi) ENE–WSW and 1,258 km (782 mi) NNW–SSE. Comparatively, the area occupied by Mali is slightly less than twice the size of the state of Texas. Bounded on the N and NE by Algeria, on the E and S by Niger, on the S by Burkina Faso and Côte d'Ivoire, and on the SW by Guinea, on the W by Senegal, and on the W and NW by Mauritania, Mali has a total boundary length of 7,243 km (4,661 mi). Mali's capital city, Bamako, is located in the southwestern part of the country.

²TOPOGRAPHY

There are few prominent surface features in Mali, which is crossed by two river systems–the Niger and the Senegal. In the southwest are low mountains deeply notched by valleys formed by the coursing of water. A second upland, in the circle formed by the Niger River, is virtually a plateau and contains Hombori Tondo, 1,155 m (3,789 ft), the highest point in Mali. In the northeast is Adrar des Iforas, an extension of Algeria's Ahaggar Mountains. The republic is divided into three natural zones: the Sudanese, an area of cultivation covering some 200,000 sq km (77,200 sq mi) in the south and in the inland delta (a pre-Tertiary lake bed into which the upper Niger once flowed); the Sahelian; and the Saharan.

³CLIMATE

Southern and western Mali have a Sudanese climate with a short rainy season from June to September. Rainfall averages 140 cm (55 in) at Sikasso in the far south. To the north is the Sahelian zone, a semiarid region along the southern border of the Sahara. At Gao, in Mali's northeast Sahel, rainfall is about 23 cm (9 in) a year. Actual year-to-year rainfall, however, is extremely erratic. In the Sahelian zone there are considerable variations of temperature, especially in April, May, and June, the period of maximum heat, and in December, when the hot, dry harmattan blows. Continuing north, one gradually enters into a Saharan climate, marked by the virtual absence of rain and an extremely dry atmosphere. Over 40% of the country is, in fact, desert, and unsuitable for agriculture. The year is divided into three main seasons varying in length according to latitude: November–February, a cool and dry season; March–May, a hot and dry season; and June–October, a season of rains characterized by lower temperatures and an increase in humidity. Between 1968 and 1974, Mali, with neighboring Sahel states, experienced the worst drought in 60 years. Drought returned during 1982–85, and there is continuing concern over the southward advance of the desert.

⁴FLORA AND FAUNA

The Saharan zone of Mali, an area of fixed dunes and false steppes, contains vegetation made up of thick-leaved and thorny plants (mimosas and gum trees). The vegetation of the Sahelian zone resembles that of the steppes, with thorny plants and shrubby savannas. The Sudanese zone is an area of herbaceous vegetation; its trees are bastard mahogany, kapok, baobab, and shea.

In the Saharan, or desert, zone, animal life includes dorcas, cheetah, and maned wild sheep, the latter in the mountains. In the Sahelian region are found oryx, gazelle, giraffe, wart hog, ostrich, bustard, red monkey, and cheetah, as well as lion, jackal, fox, hyena, and cynhyena. In the Sudanese zone there are large and small antelope, buffalo, elephant, lion, and monkey, plus such small game as hare, bustard, guinea fowl, quail, pigeon, and such water birds as duck, teal, sandpiper, peetweet, godwit, and woodcock. Other birds include pelican, marabou, ibis, egret, heron, eagle, and vulture.

⁵ENVIRONMENT

The major environmental problem in Mali is the increasing desertification of the country. The large numbers of people and livestock disrupted by the recent drought have increased the rate of soil erosion, deforestation, and loss of pastureland and have compounded the climatic problems. Mali also has an inadequate water supply: 59% of city dwellers and 96% of people living in rural areas do not have pure water. The country has 14.9 cu mi of water, of which 97% is used for farming and 1% is used for industrial purposes. Mali's cities produce 0.4 million tons of solid waste.

The nation's wildlife is threatened by drought, poaching, and the destruction of the environment. Mali has a national park and 4 animal reserves that cover a total of 808,600 ha (1,998,100 acres), as well as 6 forest reserves covering 229,400 ha (566,900 acres). In addition, the Sahel has an elephant reserve of 1,200,000 ha (2,965,000 acres) and a giraffe reserve of 1,750,000 ha (4,324,000 acres). However, the authorities lack the means to prevent poaching of protected animals or cutting down of trees for firewood. In 1994, 16 of Mali's mammal species and 4 bird species are endangered, and 15 species of plants were threatened with extinction. Endangered species included the waldrapp and western giant eland.

6 POPULATION

The population of Mali was estimated by the US Census Bureau at 8,997,507 in 1994, as compared with a census figure of 7,696,348 in 1987. The UN, however, gave a figure of 10,797,000 for 1995. Projected population by the UN for the year 2000 is 12,561,000, assuming a crude birthrate of 47.4 per 1,000 population, a crude death rate of 17.1, and a net natural increase of 30.3 over 1995–2000. In 1994 there were some 7 or so inhabitants per sq km (19 per sq mi), but the western quarter of the country has three-quarters of the population, and along the Niger River, population density exceeds 500 per sq km (1,300 per sq mi). By contrast fewer than 1.5 people per square km (4 per sq mi) live in the northern three-fifths of Mali. Population growth is estimated at 2.9% a year. About 10% of the inhabitants are nomadic, 27% urban, and the remainder rural. Bamako, the capital, had an estimated population of 738,000 in 1990. Other important towns are Ségou, Mopti, Sikasso, and Kayes.

7 MIGRATION

The Fulani, Tuareg, and other nomadic groups of northern Mali move freely across desert borders to and from neighboring countries. As many as 2 million Malians migrate seasonally to Côte d'Ivoire, Senegal, and Libya. In addition, desert nomads fled to Algeria, Burkina Faso and Mauritania in the early 1990s to escape government repression. At least 60,000 remained abroad as of 1994. There is also increasing migration from rural to urban areas. At the end of 1992, 13,000 Mauritanians were refugees in Mali.

8 ETHNIC GROUPS

The main ethnic groups of Mali are the Bambara (about 30–35%), Fulani (10–13%), Marka (Sarakolé or Soninké), Songhai, Malinké, Tuareg, Minianka, Sénoufo, and Dogon. The Bambara, mostly farmers, occupy all of central Mali bounded by the Côte d'Ivoire frontier in the south and Nara and Nioro in the north. The Fulani (or Peul), semisedentary herdsmen, are to be found throughout the republic, but mainly in the region of Mopti. The Marka, believed to be the founders of the ancient empire of Ghana, are mainly in the region of Ségou. The Songhai—farmers, fishermen, and merchants—live along the banks and islands of the Niger River, east of the inland delta. The Malinké live chiefly in the regions of Bafoulabé, Kita, and Bamako. The nomadic Tuareg, of Berber origin, are mainly in the north, in the Adrar des Iforas. The Minianka, largely farmers, populate the region of Koutiala, and the Senufo, also farmers, are found principally in the region of Sikasso. The Dogon, often considered to be the first occupants of Mali, are believed to have survived owing to the inaccessibility of their villages in the Hombori cliffs. The Dogon have won international esteem for their unique ceremonial artifacts. The majority of the peoples in Mali are Negroid; the Tuareg are classified as Caucasoid; and the Fulani are of mixed origin.

9 LANGUAGES

French, the official language, is the language of administration and of the schools and is the main unifying tongue for diverse elements. There are virtually as many languages as there are ethnic groups. The Semitic-speaking Arabs and Hamitic-speaking Tuareg are the only groups with a traditional written language, although in recent years other languages, most of which belong to the Niger-Congo group of African languages, have come to be written. Bambara is widely spoken in western, central, and southern Mali; Fulani in the Niger delta; and Songhai in the east and northeast.

10 RELIGIONS

The constitution provides for religious freedom. In the early 1990s, it was estimated that 80% of the people were Muslims; 18% animists; and 1.2% Roman Catholics and other Christians.

11 TRANSPORTATION

Transportation is controlled by the government's Malian Transport Authority. Mali has some 642 km (399 mi) of railroad, served by diesel electric locomotives. The main line, from Dakar in Senegal to Bamako, runs a twice-weekly passenger service. There is more frequent service between Bamako and Koulikoro, the last stop on the line, and between Bamako and Kayes. The IBRD has helped finance the modernization of the Malian rail system. Mali's road network includes about 15,700 km (9,750 mi) of highways of which some 1,700 km (1,050 mi) were paved as of 1991. A major project, completed in 1986, was the construction of a 558-km (347-mi) road between Gao and Sévare, near Mopti, to be part of a trans-Sahara highway linking Algeria and Nigeria. In 1991 there were about 31,000 vehicles in Mali.

Mali is landlocked; it is served by the port of Dakar in Senegal. The Niger River, which in Mali is 1,782 km (1,107 mi) long, is navigable except for a 59-km (37-mi) stretch between Bamako and Koulikoro (the main river port), where it is cut by rapids. The Bani River, a tributary of the Niger, is navigable for 224 km (139 mi) between San and Mopti. Regular service on the Niger is generally maintained from July through January. The Senegal is navigable between Kayes and Saint-Louis, Senegal, but only from August to October. In 1981, work began on a major dam at Manantali, on the Bafing tributary of the Senegal in Mali. When completed, this project will provide year-round navigation on the Senegal to Kayes. Mali, Senegal, and Mauritania make up the Senegal River Development Organization.

An international airport is at Senou, 14 km (9 mi) from Bamako. Air Mali, the state-owned airline, flies to Gao, Mopti, Kayes, Nioro, Tombouctou, Nara, Yelimané, and Goundam. There are also airports at Ségou, Tessalit, Bourem, and Kidal. In 1992, Mali joined the ten other signatories of the Yaounde Treaty and became a partner in Air Afrique.

12 HISTORY

The recorded history of the area now called Mali begins with the empire of Ghana, which is said to date from the 4th century AD. At its height in the 10th century, it occupied eastern Senegal, southwest Mali, and southern Mauritania and carried on a steady trade across the Sahara with Arab states. The Ghana Empire disintegrated by the 13th century and was succeeded by the Mali Empire, from which the independent republic takes its name.

The Mali Empire reached its peak in the 14th century under Mansa Musa (r.1312–37), who captured Tombouctou and made Mali a center of Muslim scholarship. Tombouctou and Djenné became key centers for trans-Sahara trade. By the 17th century,

MALI

| 0 | 100 | 200 | 300 Miles |
| 0 | 100 | 200 | 300 Kilometers |

LOCATION: 10°10′ to 25°N; 4°15′E to 12°15′W. **BOUNDARY LENGTHS:** Algeria, 1,376 km (855 mi); Niger, 821 km (510 mi); Burkina Faso, 1,202 km (747 mi); Côte d'Ivoire, 515 km (320 mi); Guinea, 932 km (579 mi); Senegal, 418 km (260 mi); Mauritania, 2,237 km (1,390 mi).

however, the empire had ceased to exist, and the Tuareg took much of the northern area.

Meanwhile, to the east, the Songhai Empire was founded around AD 700 on the middle Niger. Later centered at Gao, the empire was at its zenith after the capture of Tombouctou in 1468. The chief rulers in this period were Sonni 'Ali Ber (r.1464–92) and Askia Muhammad I (r.1492–1528). In 1591, the Songhai fell to an invading Moroccan army, which established secure bases at Gao, Tombouctou, and Djenné. Under Moroccan rule, a military caste known as the Arma developed, which controlled the countryside, but by 1780, the area had become fragmented into petty states.

In the 19th century, al-Hajj 'Umar, a member of the Tukulor tribe, waged a Muslim holy war against the pagans of the area. In 1862, he conquered Ségou and Macina, and the next year he plundered Tombouctou. He was killed in 1864 trying to put down a rebellion. Around 1880, the French began their advance into what was to become the Republic of Mali. They were

opposed from 1882 to 1898 by Samory Touré, a Malinké (Mandingo) leader who was ultimately captured and exiled. The capture of Sikasso in 1898 completed the French conquest.

Under French administration, the area became known as French Sudan (Soudan Français) and was a part of French West Africa. Achievements of French rule included the building of the Dakar-Bamako railway and a Niger Delta development scheme. In 1946, the Sudanese became French citizens, with representation in the French parliament. Under the constitution of 1946, the franchise was enlarged and a territorial assembly was established. Universal suffrage was established in 1957, when enlarged powers were conferred on the territorial assembly, which was also given the right to elect a council of ministers responsible for the administration of internal affairs. In 1958, under the constitution of the Fifth French Republic, French Sudan became an autonomous republic, called the Sudanese Republic, within the French Community.

Independence

In January 1959, in Dakar, representatives of the Sudanese Republic, Senegal, Dahomey (now Benin), and Upper Volta (now Burkina Faso) drafted a constitution of the Federation of Mali (named after the medieval African empire), but only the assemblies of the Sudanese Republic and Senegal ratified it and became members of the federation. Later that year the new Mali Federation asked the French Community to grant it complete sovereignty while permitting it to remaining a member of the Community. The Mali Federation became a sovereign state in June 1960.

Discord soon arose over external and internal policy, and on 20 August 1960, the federation was dissolved. On 22 September 1960, the Sudan declared itself independent as the Republic of Mali. Modibo Keita, a cofounder of the African Democratic Assembly and political secretary of the Mali Federation's African Federation Party, took control of the government. The break with Senegal was followed by the decision to leave the French Community. All ties between Senegal and Mali were severed, and Mali embargoed trade with or through Senegal until 1963, when an accord was reached.

The one-party dictatorship led by President Keita evolved into a socialist regime modeled on that of the People's Republic of China. However, by 1968, economic problems and discontent became severe. On 19 November, Keita was overthrown in a bloodless coup led by Lt. (later Gen.) Moussa Traoré. The 1960 constitution was abolished, and a 14-member Military Committee for National Liberation took command. The junta brought Mali back into the franc zone in 1968 and opened its doors to investment from nonsocialist as well as socialist countries.

Lt. Traoré became president in 1969, following an interim period of Yoro Diakité's presidency. (Diakité was expelled from the Military Committee in 1972 and died in the prison salt mines of Taoudenni in 1973.)

The military regime's efforts to improve the economic situation in Mali were frustrated by the prolonged period of drought that began in 1968 and peaked in 1972–73. It was estimated that, during that time, one-third of the population was rendered destitute. Severe drought conditions also prevailed in 1982–85.

In 1978, 29 army and police officers were convicted of plotting against the regime, and political unrest continued in later years. Traoré was elected president in 1979 under a new constitution, which also confirmed Mali as a one-party state. He was reelected in 1985. Fighting broke out between Mali and Burkina Faso on 25 December 1985 over possession of the Agacher Strip, an arid tract of land along their common border. About 65–70 men were killed before a cease-fire on 30 December. On 22 December 1986 the International Court of Justice, to which the dispute had been submitted in 1983, divided 2,952 sq km (1,140 sq mi) between the two countries in roughly equal parts.

On 26 March 1991, Lt. Col. Amadou Toumani Touré engineered a coup that toppled the Traoré government. following bloody confrontations between youth groups and the army in 1990 and 1991 in which more than 200 were killed. Touré immediately set up a National Reconciliation Council which appointed a broad-based Transitional Committee for Popular Salvation to oversee the transition to civilian democracy.

A National Conference which included 48 political parties and around 700 civic associations met from 29 July to 14 August 1991. It drafted new electoral rules, party statutes and a new constitution, which was adopted by referendum in January 1992, and established an agenda for the transition. There were elections for municipal councilors, National Assembly deputies, and, finally, presidential elections on 12 and 26 April 1992. Dr. Alpha Oumar Konaré, the leader of the Alliance for Democracy in Mali (ADEMA) became Mali's first democratically elected president with 69% of the vote. The Third Republic was launched. ADEMA also won 76 of the 116 National Assembly seats.

One of the last acts of the Touré transitional government was to negotiate (with Algerian mediation) a peace treaty in April 1992 with rebel Tuaregs in the north. Government acknowledged the northerners' special status and the Tuaregs renounced their claims to independence. Algeria agreed to guarantee the truce, which ended two years of fighting. In 1992 and 1993, between 60,000 and 100,000 Tuareg refugees returned from abroad. In February 1993, the government and the rebel group, the Unified Movements and Fronts of Azawad (MFUA) agreed to integrate MFUA guerrillas into the national army and, in May 1994, arrived at a further agreement to implement the 1992 National Pact.

Former President Touré and three associates were convicted of responsibility for the March 1991 massacres and sentenced to death on 12 February 1993. They await trial for their "economic crimes." However, student unrest continued and in April 1993, the government was forced to resign. Abdoulaye Sekou Sow replaced Younoussi Touré as prime minister on April 13, and the opposition party, the National Congress of Democratic Initiative (CNIT) was included in the government. Pressures mounted under the impact of the rigid IMF structural adjustment program, as violence continued among students and the unemployed, forcing the Sow government to fall from power in February 1994. The two opposition parties in cabinet also withdrew their support. The new government announced on 7 February 1994 contains 11 ADEMA members among its 16 ministers. The prime minister is Ibrahim Boubakar Keita.

¹³GOVERNMENT

After independence, Mali was governed by the 1960 constitution, which provided for a National Assembly. This body was abolished by the Keita regime in January 1968. Following the military coup of November 1968, the constitution itself was abolished and a provisional regime, the Military Committee for National Liberation, was established.

A long-awaited constitution was drawn up by the Military Committee in 1974 and endorsed in a public referendum on 2 June 1974. In this first national ballot since 1964, 99% of the electorate voted for acceptance. The constitution which took full effect in 1979 and was amended in 1981 provided for a president with a six-year term, an 82-member National Assembly, and a one-party system. The Assembly was elected for a three-year term. There is universal suffrage at age 21.

The 1979 constitution was replaced by a new constitution adopted by referendum in January 1992. The National Assembly now has 116 deputies with 10 parties represented. The president, elected by popular vote, chooses the prime minister who selects a cabinet (currently 22 ministers, including five from opposition parties).

¹⁴POLITICAL PARTIES

The first political party in Mali, the Sudan Progressive Party (Parti Soudanais Progressiste—PSP) was an affiliate of the French Socialist Party. It dominated political activity in French Sudan for 10 years. It was followed by the Sudanese Union, a revolutionary, anticolonial party, which had its main strength in the towns. In the two elections of autumn 1946, the Sudanese Union won 32% and 38% of the total votes.

The PSP continued to maintain its majority in the Territorial Assembly until the end of 1955, when a split in its ranks enabled the Union to capture a majority. By March 1957, the Sudanese Union won 60 of the 70 seats in the new Territorial Assembly, and in the Legislative Assembly election of March 1959 it obtained 76.3% of the votes and all the seats. After the break with Senegal, it emerged as the only party in the Republic of Mali, one with control that extended even to the smallest Muslim villages through its national political bureau. In the parliamentary elections of April 1964, the single list of 80 deputies presented by the Sudanese Union was elected by 99.5% of the voters. The party was disbanded at the time of the 1968 coup d'état.

The Democratic Union of Malian People (Union Démocratique de Peuple Malien—UDPM) was created as the sole legal political party in 1979. It chose the presidential candidate and the single list of candidates for the National Assembly. In National Assembly elections in 1979, UDPM candidates received 99.89% of the votes cast; in 1982, 99.82%; and in 1985, 99.47%; The party's general secretary since 1979 has been Gen. Moussa Traoré.

Shortly after the military coup in March 1991, some 48 parties were functioning, of which 23 contested the 1992 elections and ten elected deputies to the National Assembly. The Alliance for Democracy in Mali (ADEMA) is the majority party, but with the new prime minister and government formed on 12 April 1993, opposition parties were brought into cabinet. The National Committee for a Democratic Initiative (CNID) gained three cabinet posts. ADEMA has 76 seats in parliament, CNID has nine. Also in the National Assembly are the Sudanese Union/African Democratic Rally (US/RAD), eight seats; Popular Movement for the Development of the Republic of West Africa, six seats; Rally for Democracy and Progress (RDP) and the Union for Democracy and Development (UDD), four seats each; and four other parties. The UDPM, the former ruling party, relaunched itself in mid-1993.

15LOCAL GOVERNMENT

Mali is divided into seven regions and the capital district of Bamako. Each region is headed by an official appointed by the national government. The regions are subdivided into a total of 46 cercles, which are ruled by government-appointed commandants. The larger towns elect their own municipal councils and mayors. Only party-mandated single lists of candidates were allowed to run in 1981–82 and 1985. In 1992, elections were contested by some 23 parties. There are 279 arrondissements, each composed of several villages headed by chiefs.

16JUDICIAL SYSTEM

A Supreme Court was established in Bamako in 1969. It is made up of 19 members, nominated for five years. The judicial section has three civil chambers and one criminal chamber. The administrative section deals with appeals and fundamental rulings. The Court of Appeal is also in Bamako. There are two magistrate courts of first instance, courts for labor disputes, and a special court of state security. Customary courts have been abolished. The Supreme Court has both judicial and administrative powers. The 1992 Constitution established a separate constitutional court and a High Court of Justice charged with responsibility for trying senior government officials accused of treason.

The 1992 Constitution guarantees independence of the judiciary. In practice, however, the executive has considerable influence over the judiciary. The Ministry of Justice appoints judges and oversees law enforcement. The President heads the Superior Judicial, the body which supervises judicial activity.

Trials are public, defendants have the right to an attorney of their choice, and court-appointed attorneys are available to indigent defendants in criminal cases.

17ARMED FORCES

Armed forces strength was 7,350 in 1993, of whom 6,900 were in the ground forces, 50 in the marine forces, and 400 in the air forces, (all considered part of the army). Overall, the army consisted of 13 mixed battalions and an air defense missile battery. The air force was equipped with 39 aircraft and helicopters, and the navy possessed 3 river patrol boats. Paramilitary forces number 7,800. Mali has received military aid from the former USSR and Eastern Europe, including tanks and planes, and some Malian officers are Soviet trained. In 1989 Mali spent $41 million on defense, or 2% of GDP.

18INTERNATIONAL COOPERATION

Mali was admitted to the UN on 28 September 1960, and is a member of ECA and all the nonregional specialized agencies except IMO. It also belongs to the African Development Bank, ECOWAS, G-77, and OAU and is a de facto adherent to GATT. Mali is a member of the West African Economic Community (CEAO), which came into existence on 1 January 1974 as a formal economic community embracing the Côte d'Ivoire, Senegal, Mali, Niger, Burkina Faso, and Mauritania.

The nation is a signatory to the Lomé Convention, which covers aid and trade relations between developing countries and the EC. With Senegal and Mauritania, it comprises the Senegal River Development Organization, and it is also a partner in the Liptako-Gourma regional development scheme with Burkina Faso and Niger. Along with other Sahel states, Mali is a member of the Committee for the Control of the Drought.

19ECONOMY

Economic activity in Mali centers on domestic agricultural and livestock production. Vast stretches of Sahara desert limit Mali's agricultural potential and subject the country to severe, prolonged, recurrent drought (1968–74, 1982–85). In periods of adequate rainfall, Mali approaches food self-sufficiency. The GDP growth rates are affected by the rainfall as well. GDP has gone to a high of 12.5% in 1989 when rainfall was good to negative growth (−0.5%) in dry years.

The agricultural sector employs 85.5% of the population (mid-1980s). Irrigated lands along the Niger River have been the focus of recent infrastructure development loans designed to increase the production of rice. Historically, livestock production has been a mainstay of the Malian economy. The dry savannah plains are tsetse free, and production has been oriented to serve the growing market in Côte d'Ivoire to the south. Unfortunately, the severe drought in the 1980s is reported to have killed upwards of 80% of Malian herds.

State-centered policies pursued in the years following independence were largely unsuccessful and led to a reintegration of the Malian economy into the CFA franc zone. Subsequent economic plans imposed on Mali, first by the French and then by the IMF, sought to dismantle the parastatals, privatize industry, and disengage the government from manipulative agriculture policies and price controls. These measures were hindered by the influential Malian civil service, the drought in the early 1980s and, in 1986, the fall in cotton prices, which led the government to suspend its debt-servicing obligations and to a suspension of IMF and World Bank credits. However, deficits fell sharply in 1990 and 1991 as a result of higher taxes and reduced civil service and parastatal demands. Unfortunately, the political repercussions of the government's austerity measures led to its downfall in 1991. The new government, however, continued the structural adjustment process, and the effort to reduce the budget deficits was intensified.

In January 1994 France suddenly devalued the CFA franc, cutting its value in half overnight. Immediately, prices for almost all imported goods, including food and essential drugs, soared. Since 1948 France had guaranteed a fixed parity of one French franc to 50 African francs. The resulting stability in the currency had generally kept inflation low and helped to maintain a steady rate of growth. However, in the 1980s, the economies of the CFA countries began to stagnate in relation to other African nations, and France came under increased pressure from the World Bank, the IMF, and western countries to stop subsidizing the CFA franc. The devaluation, long expected in the investment community, is designed to enourage new investment, particularly in the export sectors of the economy, and discourage the use of hard currency reserves to buy products that could be grow domestically. Unlike exporting countries, however, Mali imports most of its food, has little to export, and therefore, may benefit little from the devaluation.

[20]INCOME

In 1992 Mali's GNP was $2,730 million at current prices, or $300 per capita. For the period 1985–92 the average inflation rate was 1.2%, resulting in a real growth rate in per capita GNP of −1.9%.

In 1992 the GDP was $2,827 million in current US dollars. It is estimated that in 1991 agriculture, hunting, forestry, and fishing contributed 44% to GDP; mining and quarrying, 2%; manufacturing, 7%; electricity, gas, water, and construction, 4%; wholesale and retail trade, 19%; transport, storage, and communication, 5%; finance, insurance, real estate, business services, community, social, and personal services, 9%; and other sources, 11%.

[21]LABOR

Of the total estimated work force of 2.9 million in 1991, 75% were engaged in agriculture or livestock raising. From 1985 to 1991, the labor force size increased by about 2.6% per year. Wage workers are given extensive protection under the labor laws, including a maximum workweek, a minimum wage, and a specified number of days of paid annual leave.

With the breakup of the Mali Federation in 1960, all the unions in the country joined together to form the National Union of Malian Workers (Union National des Travailleurs du Mali—UNTM). The UNTM was disbanded at the time of the 1968 coup, but was reestablished in 1970. The 1991 Constitution allows workers to form and join unions other than the UNTM, and provides for the right to strike.

[22]AGRICULTURE

Only the southern part of Mali is suited to farming, and less than 2% of Mali's area is cultivated. Agriculture (including forestry and fishing) accounts for half of GDP and 75% of the active labor force. Millet, rice, and corn are the basic food crops. Millet and sorghum are cultivated mainly in the areas around Ségou, Bandiagara, and Nioro. Paddy rice is cultivated on irrigated farms in the area around Mopti, Ségou, and Niafounké. Cereals are produced for subsistence by 90% of farmers. Peanuts are grown in the Sudanese zone, as are cotton, fruits, vegetables, and henna. The shea tree nut, which grows wild, is exploited by Malians for its oil.

Output fluctuates widely as a result of the amount and distribution of rainfall. The 1991/92 cereals harvest reached a record 2.25 million tons (a production surplus over the 1.6 million ton domestic requirement), thanks to favorable weather conditions, price liberalizations, and less government intervention in the cereals markets. Mali was the second-largest cotton fiber producer in Africa in 1992 (after Egypt), with a production of 114,000 tons. Production estimates in 1992 for principal agricultural crops grown for domestic use included millet and sorghum, 1,500,000 tons; sugarcane, 305,000 tons; corn, 219,000 tons; cassava, 73,000 tons; and sweet potatoes, 55,000 tons. The rice production figure was 405,000 tons. Production figures for export crops in 1992 included raw cotton, 180,000 tons, and groundnuts, 165,000 tons.

The Niger Office, now a state-controlled agency, was set up in 1932 to aid in improving cotton and rice production. It developed the irrigation and modern cultivation of some 81,000 ha (200,000 acres) in the dry inland delta of the Niger; in 1991, about 205,000 ha (506,500 acres) in Mali were irrigated. The infrastructure includes a dam (2.6 km wide/1.6 mi), irrigation canals, ditches and dikes, and such installations as housing stores,

warehouses, rice and oil mills, cotton-ginning factories, sugar refineries, soap factories, research stations, schools, and dispensaries. Growing cotton in irrigated fields did not succeed and was abandoned in 1970. All cotton is now grown in nonirrigated fields in the regions of Bamako, Ségou, and Sikasso.

[23]ANIMAL HUSBANDRY

In 1992 there were an estimated 13,316,000 sheep and goats, 5,373,000 head of cattle, 600,000 donkeys, 250,000 camels, 85,000 horses, 75,000 hogs, and 22,000,000 chickens in Mali.

Virtually all cattle are owned by nomads. Cattle herding is centered in the Sahel (Nioro-Nara), the central Niger Delta (Ségou-Mopti-Bandiagara-Niafounké-Goundam), and the curve of the Niger (Tombouctou-Gao). A significant portion of trade in live animals is clandestine, because of higher prices in neighboring countries. Principal clients for cattle are Côte d'Ivoire and Ghana, and for sheep and goats, Côte d'Ivoire and Algeria. Meat and cattle are also exported to other African neighbors, such as Guinea, Senegal, Niger, and Benin.

There are two modern slaughterhouses, in Bamako and Gao. Total meat production was estimated at 169,000 tons in 1992. Livestock exports are the second largest source of foreign exchange after cotton. Cattle exports alone earned $105 million in 1991. Milk production was estimated at 122,000 tons, and the production of hides and skins at 19,840 tons.

[24]FISHING

The Niger and its tributaries are extensively fished, and the Mopti region, where the Niger and Bani rivers flood the delta during the rainy season, accounts for 90% of the catch. The Senegal River accounts for most of the rest. Fishermen use nets, harpoons, and snares. About 90% of the fishing catch is dried or smoked for domestic consumption and export. River fishing was severely affected by the 1968–74 and 1982–85 droughts. The total catch was 60,031 tons in 1991.

[25]FORESTRY

Forest and woodland are estimated to cover some 6.9 million ha (17 million acres), or about 5.6% of the total land area. A total of 6 forest reserves cover 229,400 ha (566,900 acres). Mali's Water and Forests Service works to preserve and increase the amount and quality of general and classified forest domain and to assure reasonable exploitation. However, wood is Mali's primary energy source, and overcutting for fuel is a serious problem. Roundwood production in 1991 amounted to 5.7 million cu m, almost all for fuel.

[26]MINING

Mining activity at present includes a marble quarry at Sélinkégni, a limestone quarry at Diamou, a phosphate complex at Bourem, and small-scale extraction of salt near Taoudenni. Large-scale gold mining began in December 1984 at Kalana, southwest of Bougouni, with aid from the former USSR. Output in 1985 was 16,075 troy oz. (500 kg, or 1,100 lb). By 1991, total gold output from the mine since its opening amounted only to 2,600 kg, much less than had been expected. The Syama gold fields began production in 1990. Production of 6,200 kg per year is projected for 1994. A third field at Loulo is under development. Bauxite, iron, manganese, calcium, kaolin, copper, tin, zinc, lead, diamond, and lithium deposits have been located, but their exploitation depends, among other things, on improved transportation. All mines are owned by the state, but quarries may be privately owned.

Manganese reserves are estimated at 7.5 billion tons of 30–40% grade ore. Western Mali has numerous bauxite deposits, ranging from 10 to 580 million tons, with 2–48% aluminum content. Phosphate reserves are estimated at 10 million tons with anhydrous phosphate content of 31%. Estimated production of phosphate rock in 1991 was 10,000 tons.

Salt mining provides an evocative link between Mali's present and past. Two salt caravans, each including thousands of camels, annually transport salt in bars of 30 to 40 kg each from the famous salt city of Taoudenni, some 700 km (435 mi) north of Tombouctou, to Tombouctou and from there to Nioro and other distribution centers. Annual production is about 5,000 tons.

27ENERGY AND POWER

Petroleum exploration was conducted in the early 1980s, but without success. In 1992, energy and fuel imports accounted for almost 8% of total imports.

The Senegal River Development Organization's dam at Manantali, on which work began in 1981, is to provide power and irrigation water for Mali, Mauritania, and Senegal. In 1991, total production reached 276 million kwh (67% hydroelectric). Installed capacity was 87,000 kw (48% thermal). A 44.8-Mw hydroelectric facility at Selingué, southwest of Bamako on the Sankarani River, was completed in 1982.

28INDUSTRY

Mali has a very small industrial sector, mostly state enterprises producing textiles and consumer goods. Textiles account for about 50% of value added. In 1981, 29 state companies were responsible for over 75% of industrial output, including 9 of the 12 major plants in the food-processing sector. The 40 parastatals are inefficient producers and subsidized from state funds.

Processing industries have been given priority in industrial development; groundnut-oil, rice-polishing, fruit-preserving, sugar-distilling, tea, and cottonseed-oil and cottonseed-cake plants are in operation, as are three slaughterhouses. Other industrial facilities include a vinegar factory, a cigarette factory, a soft-drink plant, a flour mill, a shoe factory, a tannery, and two textile plants. Other plants make tiles, furniture, and farm implements and assemble radios, bicycles, and motorcycles. There are a few construction related facilities, including a cement works, a brick factory, and a ceramics factory.

In 1990, Mali generated 214 million kwh of power, 66% of it hydroelectric. Given Mali's drought-prone circumstances, hydroelectric production is unreliable, and production at the key 45-Mw Selingué hydroelectric plant is suspended when reservoir levels are low. However, the Manantali Dam on the Senegal River, inaugurated in 1992, is projected to add some 400 million kWh annually to the Malian grid.

29SCIENCE AND TECHNOLOGY

Mali has a shortage of trained scientists and technicians and relies heavily on foreign, chiefly French, assistance. A French tropical agronomy research center is located in Bamako. The National Directorship for Meteorology, also in Bamako, publishes bulletins on agrometeorology and climatology. A national association for mineral research and mining is located in Kati. The National Center of Scientific and Technological Research coordinates all research activity in Mali. National schools of engineering, medicine, and pharmacology are in Bamako. The Rural Polytechnic Institute of Katibougou has 12,000 students.

30DOMESTIC TRADE

Following independence, the government initiated an extensive program for the organization of rural cooperatives in the villages, with central purchasing organizations in the chief towns of the administrative districts.

Though trade at the retail level is privately organized, trade in export crops, import goods, and basic domestic commodities is controlled by a state marketing board, SOMIEX. The cereal market was opened to private enterprise in 1982. Normal business hours are from 8 AM to noon and from 3 to 5 PM, Monday–Saturday. On Fridays, most businesses close at noon. Banks are open from 8 AM to 2:30 PM, Monday–Thursday, and from 8 AM to 12:30 PM, Friday and Saturday.

31FOREIGN TRADE

Since independence, Mali has consistently maintained a trade deficit. Deficits have been exacerbated during drought years by emergency food imports. Cotton products and livestock are Mali's leading exports; in 1987, cotton made up 57.5% of total exports.

Mali's exports (in millions of CFA francs) in 1987 were:

Ginned cotton	30,955
Manufactured goods	16,445
Live animals	3,747
Processed foodstuffs	203
Mangoes	54
Fats and oils	10
Others	2,376
TOTAL	53,790

Mali's imports totaled 112,444 million CFA francs in 1987. Of those imports, industrial products accounted for 40.2%, petroleum products 14.8%, machinery 12.4%, transport equipment 9.7%, and dairy and sugar products 6.1%.

In 1987, Mali's leading export markets were Côte d'Ivoire (40.7%) and Senegal (26.2%). Mali's imports came principally from France (23.0%) and Côte d'Ivoire (18.2%).

Record trade deficits were recorded in 1986 (80,400 million CFA francs), but lower deficits occurred in the 1987–91 period (averaging 20,900 million CFA francs). Increased foreign aid and remittances to Mali from its citizens working in foreign countries contribute favorably to the current account balance.

32BALANCE OF PAYMENTS

Mali's chronic deficit in trade and other goods and services is largely offset by aid from other governments and international organizations. The balance of payments is sharply influenced by the volume in cotton exports and the world price of cotton, the volume of official livestock exports, and the value of government purchased imports.

In 1992 merchandise exports totaled $328.7 million and imports $191.5 million. The merchandise trade balance was $–148.4 million. The following table summarizes Mali's balance of payments for 1991 and 1992 (in millions of US dollars):

	1991	1992
CURRENT ACCOUNT		
Goods, services, and income	–428.2	–513.1
Unrequited transfers	406.2	424.3
TOTALS	–22.0	–88.8
CAPITAL ACCOUNT		
Direct investment	3.5	–7.6
Other long-term capital	58.1	5.3
Other short-term capital	4.5	9.9
Reserves	–129.0	0.8
TOTALS	25.4	133.5
Errors and omissions	–3.5	–44.7
Total change in reserves	–138.1	16.8

33BANKING AND SECURITIES

In 1959, the Central Bank of the West African States (Banque Centrale des États de l'Afrique de l'Ouest—BCEAO) succeeded the Currency Board of French West Africa and Togo as the bank of issue for the former French West African territories. Foreign exchange receipts of the member states went into the franc zone's exchange pool, which in turn covered their foreign exchange requirements. In July 1962, however, Mali withdrew from the BCEAO and West African Monetary Union and established a bank of its own, the Bank of the Republic of Mali, which issued a new currency, the Malian franc.

In 1967, Mali returned to the franc zone, with its franc set at half the value of the CFA franc. In March 1968, the banking system was reorganized, and the Central Bank of Mali was established as the central issuing bank. In December 1982, Mali's application to rejoin the West African Monetary Union was rejected, as Upper Volta (now Burkina Faso), which had a border dispute with Mali, continued to oppose Mali's re-admission until 1983. In 1984 it rejoined the BCEAO and the monetary union. Foreign assets came to CFA Fr97.99 billion in 1993, while the money supply, as measured by M2, was CFA Fr174.53 billion at the end of 1993.

In addition to the Central Bank, commercial banks in 1992 included: the Bank of Africa, Banque Commerciale de Sahel, Banque Malienne de Crédit et du Depots, and the Financial Bank Mali. Development banks in Mali include the Banque de Développement du Mali, and the Banque Nationale de Développment Agricole.

34INSURANCE

There were five non-life insurance companies in Mali in 1986, the largest being the National Fund of Insurance and Reinsurance, a state company. Third-party motor insurance is compulsory.

35PUBLIC FINANCE

Mali normally runs moderate budget deficits, when taking into account the road fund and a sinking fund, although both are considered accounts outside the general budget. Education is the largest area of expenditure; defense is second. Extraordinary receipts—in the form of foreign support—are an important source of revenue, although France ended budgetary support payments in 1980. The current government budget moved from a deficit of 0.3% of GDP in 1987 to a surplus of 2.1% fo GDP in 1991. The overall government budget deficit (including foreign-financed investment expenditure) dropped from 10.6% of GDP in 1987 to 8.5% of GDP in 1990, then climbed to 12% of GDP in 1991, due mainly to large expenditures from structural transition. The following table shows actual revenues and expenditures for 1987 and 1988 in billions of francs.

	1987	1988
REVENUE AND GRANTS		
Tax revenue	71.5	73.4
Non-tax revenue	8.1	15.4
Grants	37.8	35.5
TOTAL	127.2	149.8
EXPENDITURES & LENDING MINUS REPAYMENTS		
General public services	16.8	36.2
Defense	13.3	14.0
Public order and safety	0.6	0.6
Education	15.4	15.8
Health	4.1	3.6
Social security and welfare	5.2	4.6
Housing and community amenities	0.6	—
Recreation, cultural, and religious affairs	0.9	0.8
Economic affairs and services	29.1	9.3
Other expenditures	—	6.7
Lending minus repayments	0.2	2.6
TOTAL	158.1	177.4
Deficit/Surplus	–30.9	–27.6

36TAXATION

Elements of a progressive taxation system were introduced in 1992. There is a tax on business profits and a general income tax with a graduated rate. There is also sales tax, as well as an excise tax on alcoholic beverages, fuels and lubricants, cartridges and bullets, tobacco, and other goods. In addition, there are taxes on property, livestock, motor vehicles, and firearms and a head tax, among others. There are also registration and stamp fees.

37CUSTOMS AND DUTIES

Customs duties constitute the leading source of government income and are imposed on both imports and exports. Import policies have been liberalized, and import licensing eliminated, since 1988. However, imports from Israel and South Africa are banned.

Duties on most goods range from 5–30% for imports from non-CEAO countries, except for taxes on luxury goods, including cars and video cassette recorders, which vary from 80–100%. Duties for imports from CEAO members are approximately half the rate charged non-members.

38FOREIGN INVESTMENT

Foreign investment in Mali is relatively small and is mainly in retail trade or light industry. With independence and Mali's announcement of an economic policy aimed at "planned socialism," private foreign investment came to a standstill in 1961. By 1968, after seven years of almost no private foreign investment, the trend was reversed and Mali specifically requested private foreign investment to aid its development. The parastatal sector was to be dismantled, although it has remained a significant part of the economy. The investment code offers certain incentives, mostly in the form of tax-holidays of five to ten years to companies prepared to invest in certain areas.

39ECONOMIC DEVELOPMENT

Fiscal management reform and continued dependence on foreign aid into the foreseeable future are the hallmarks of the economic development effort in the coming years. The devaluation of the CFA franc should stimulate the livestock industry, as it has done in neighboring Burkina Faso. Gold sales should improve as the mining sector expands. The agricultural sector is still highly vulnerable to drought and, in spite of its natural potential, unlikely to produce at self-sufficiency levels.

40SOCIAL DEVELOPMENT

Social welfare is carried out mainly in urban areas, basically as an extension of labor benefits and medical aid under the labor code, which includes provisions for medical care workers' compensation, and retirement benefits. A system of family allowances for wage earners provides small maternity and children's allowances, along with classes in prenatal and infant care. These programs are administered by the National Social Insurance Institute. Under tribal organization, the individual's basic welfare needs are traditionally cared for by the group. This system, however, is breaking down as the country develops. In addition, the austerity measures imposed by the structural adjustment program has led to painful cutbacks in social services.

The government has made a special effort to improve the status of women, and a few women have entered government employment. Yet, social and cultural factors still sharply limit educational and economic opportunities for most women. The average woman who completed her childbearing years in the early 1980s had borne 6.8 children. Abortion is illegal.

41HEALTH

Most health care is provided by the public medical services.In 1980, there were 319 doctors, 250 nidwives, and 1,312 nurses, (more recent statistics are not available). In the same year, there were 3,200 hospital beds. At Bamako are the Institute of Tropical Ophthalmology and the Marchoux Institute for Leprosy, which, in addition to treating patients, carry out research. The number of private doctors and well-equipped medical institutions is small. In 1992, the population per physician was 19,450, and the population per nursing professional was 1,890. In 1990, only 35% of the population had access to health care services, and total health care expenditures amounted to $130 million.

The principal diseases are malaria, leprosy, tuberculosis, enteritis and other intestinal diseases, cholera, pneumonia, infectious and parasite-related diseases, such as schistosomiasis, onchocerciasis, and trypanosomiasis. Anemia, malnutrition, and tetanus are also widespread. In 1990, there were 289 reported cases of tuberculosis per 100,000 people. In 1991, only 41% of the population had access to safe water, 24% had adequate sanitation, and 31% of children under 5 years old were considered malnourished. In 1992, immunization rates for children up to one year old were: tuberculosis (70%); diphtheria, pertussis, and tetanus (34%); polio (34%); and measles (41%).

There were 504,000 births in 1992, for a national birth rate of 50.7 per 1,000 people. About 5% of married women (ages 15 to 49) use contraception. In 1992, the infant mortality rate was 122 per 1,000 live births; the maternal mortality rate in 1991 was a very high 2,000 per 100,000 live births; and the general mortality rate in 1993 was 19.1 per 1,000 people. The average life expectancy was 46 years.

42HOUSING

Housing structures in Bamako are mainly like those of a European city. Elsewhere, housing ranges from similar urban structures to the tents of Tuareg nomads, the circular mud huts with thatched roofs characteristic of the indigenous African villages, and traditional Sudanese architecture. The latter employs a common building material called banco, a mixture of wet mud and straw that dries into a hard, almost cementlike consistency. This is applied over wooden frames and can be used for buildings of several stories. The buildings resemble those in North Africa and the Middle East.

Since World War II, the growth of Bamako and other towns has been rapid, with government activity largely concentrated on improvement of urban housing and sanitation. The Real Estate Trust, a public corporation established in 1949, provides housing loans to persons wishing to build on their own land.

As of 1990, 100% of urban and 36% of rural dwellers had access to a public water supply, while 94% of urban and 5% of rural dwellers had access to sanitation services.

43EDUCATION

In 1990, 32% of the adult population of Mali was literate (40.8% of males and 23.9% of females). The Mali school system begins with an initial primary cycle of six years, followed by a six-year cycle of secondary schooling (divided into two three-year stages).

In 1991, there were 1,514 primary schools with 7,963 teachers and 375,131 pupils. In the general secondary schools, there were 4,854 teachers and 78,920 pupils. In addition, vocational schools had 8,715 pupils.

In Koulikoro is the Rural Polytechnic Institute of Katibougou. There are schools of business, administration, engineering, medicine and dentistry, and education in Bamako. All higher level institutions had a total of 701 teachers and 6,703 pupils in 1990.

44LIBRARIES AND MUSEUMS

In Bamako are located the National Library (18,000 volumes) and Archives, a municipal library, and the library of the Islamic Center, opened in 1987. In addition, the French Cultural Center, with 27,000 volumes, serves as a public library, and there is a US Information Service library. Tombouctou has a center of historic research with valuable Arabic manuscripts. Which also serves as a museum. The National Museum, which also has a library, is in Bamako, as is the Sudanese Museum. A regional museum is located in Gao with an ethnography collection.

45MEDIA

Virtually all media are owned by the state, and all journalists are employees of the state. Radio Mali, the government station, has several transmitters in various parts of the country. Broadcasts are made in French, English, and seven vernacular languages. There were 415,000 radios and 11,000 television sets in use in 1991. A television service financed by Libya began broadcasting for two hours a week in 1983. Telephone and telegraph services are publicly owned and operated, and there are direct telephone connections with Paris. In 1991 there were 15,000 telephones in Mali.

A daily newspaper, L'Essor, is published in Bamako; circulation was about 6,000 in 1991. Also published daily is the bulletin of the Chamber of Commerce and Industry of Mali. The government also publishes Sunjata (1991 circulation 3,000), a monthly journal of social and economic affairs, and Kibaru (13,500), which is distributed to rural areas.

46ORGANIZATIONS

There is a Chamber of Commerce and Industry in Bamako and a Chamber of Commerce in Kayes. There are youth and women's affiliates of the UDPM, and the government is hoping to increase food production through the formation of village cooperatives.

47TOURISM, TRAVEL, AND RECREATION

A government tourist organization was created in April 1974 to develop hunting, fishing, and sightseeing in Mali, particularly in the areas around Mopti, Tombouctou, and Gao. There are modern motels in Bamako and in Tombouctou, the ancient capital of Muslim learning and culture, previously forbidden to foreigners. Also of interest to the tourist are Mali's national park and game reserves. Football (soccer) is a popular sport.

A visa must be obtained for entry into Mali for all visitors except those from France or former French Africa. A vaccination certificate for yellow fever is also needed, except for travelers coming from noninfected areas and staying less than two weeks. In 1991 there were 37,962 tourist arrivals in hotels and other establishments, 44% from Africa, and 43% from Europe.

48FAMOUS MALIANS

Early figures associated with the area of present-day Mali include Mansa Musa (r.1312–37), ruler of the Mali Empire, and Sonni 'Ali Ber (r.1464–92) and Askia Muhammad I (r.1492–1528), rulers of the Songhai Empire. Later figures include al-Hajj 'Umar (1797–1864), who plunged the entire area into a bloody holy war before he was killed while trying to put down a rebellion, and Samory Touré, (1835–1900), who fought the French at the head of a Malinké (Mandingo) army for 16 years (1882–98). Modibo Keita (1915–77) was, until November 1968, a leading figure in the political life of the country. He became the first president of the Republic of Mali in 1960. Moussa Traoré (b.1936) was president of Mali from 1969 to 1991.

49DEPENDENCIES

Mali has no territories or colonies.

50BIBLIOGRAPHY

Bingen, James R. Food Production and Rural Development in the Sahel: Lessons from Mali's Operation Riz-Segou. Boulder, Colo.: Westview, 1985.

Bovill, Edward William. *The Golden Trade of the Moors*. London: Oxford University Press, 1958.

Davidson, Basil. *A History of West Africa to the Nineteenth Century*. New York: Doubleday Anchor, 1966.

Ernst, Klaus. *Tradition and Progress in the African Village: Non-Capitalist Reform of Rural Communities in Mali*. New York: St. Martin's, 1977.

Foltz, William J. *From French West Africa to the Mali Federation*. New Haven, Conn.: Yale University Press, 1965.

Imperato, Pascal J. (ed.). *Historical Dictionary of Mali*. Metuchen, N.J.: Scarecrow, 1977.

Imperato, Pascal J. and Eleanor M. *Mali: A Handbook of Historical Statistics*. Boston: G. K. Hall, 1982.

Imperato, Pascal James. *Mali: A Search for Direction*. Boulder, Colo.: Westview Press, 1989.

Jones, William I. *Planning an Economic Policy: Socialist Mali and Her Neighbors*. Washington, D.C.: Three Continents, 1976.

Levtzion, Nehemiah. *Ancient Ghana and Mali*. New York: Holmes & Meier, 1980.

Roberts, Richard L. *Warriors, Merchants, and Slaves: The State and the Economy in the Middle Niger Valley, 1700–1914*. Stanford, Calif.: Stanford University Press, 1987.

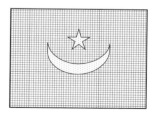

MAURITANIA

Mauritanian Islamic Republic
[French:] *République Islamique de Mauritanie*
[Arabic:] *Al-Jumhuriyah al-Islamiyah al-Muritaniyah*

CAPITAL: Nouakchott.

FLAG: The flag consists of a gold star and crescent on a light green field.

ANTHEM: *Mauritania* (no words).

MONETARY UNIT: The ouguiya (UM), a paper currency of 5 khoums, issued by the Central Bank of Mauritania, replaced the Communauté Financière Africaine franc on 29 June 1973. There are coins of 1 khoum and 1, 5, 10, and 20 ouguiyas, and notes of 100, 200, 500, and 1,000 ouguiyas. UM1 = $0.0082 (or $1 = UM122.530).

WEIGHTS AND MEASURES: The metric system is the legal standard.

HOLIDAYS: New Year's Day, 1 January; Labor Day, 1 May; African Liberation Day, 25 May; Anniversary of the Proclamation of the Republic, 28 November. Movable religious holidays include Laylat al-Miraj, 'Id al-Fitr, 'Id al-'Adha', 1st of Muharram (Muslim New Year), and Milad an-Nabi.

TIME: GMT.

¹LOCATION, SIZE, AND EXTENT

Situated in West Africa, Mauritania has an area of 1,030,700 sq km (397,955 sq mi). Mauritania extends 1,515 km (941 mi) NE–SW and 1,314 km (816 mi) SE–NW. Comparatively, the area occupied by Mauritania is slightly larger than three times the size of the state of New Mexico. It is bordered on the NE by Algeria, on the E and S by Mali, on the SW by Senegal, on the W by the Atlantic Ocean, and on the NW and N by the Western Sahara, with a total estimated boundary length of 5,828 km (3,621 mi).

Mauritania's capital city, Nouakchott, is located on the Atlantic Coast.

²TOPOGRAPHY

There are three distinct geographic regions in Mauritania: a narrow belt along the Senegal River valley in the south, where soil and climatic conditions permit settled agriculture; north of this valley, a broad east-west band characterized by vast sand plains and fixed dunes held in place by sparse grass and scrub trees; and a large northern arid region shading into the Sahara, advancing south several kilometers each year, and characterized by shifting sand dunes, rock outcroppings, and rugged mountainous plateaus that in a few places reach elevations of more than 500 m (1,640 ft). The high point, about 915 m (3,002 ft), is near Fdérik. The country is generally flat.

³CLIMATE

Although conditions are generally desertlike, three climatic regions can be distinguished. Southern Mauritania has a Sahelian climate; there is one rainy season from July to October. Annual rainfall averages 66 cm (26 in) in the far south; at Nouakchott the annual average is 14 cm (5.5 in).

Trade winds moderate the temperature in the coastal region, which is arid. The average maximum temperature at Nouadhibou for January is 26°C (79°F), and for October 32°C (90°F); average minimums are 13°C (55°F) for January and 19°C (66°F) for July.

Most of Mauritania north of Atar—about two-thirds of the country—has a Saharan climate. Daytime temperatures exceed 38°C (100°F) in most areas for over 6 months of the year, but the nights are cool. Average annual rainfall at Atar is 10 cm (4 in).

⁴FLORA AND FAUNA

In the desert there are some cacti and related species; oases support relatively luxuriant growth, notably date palms. In the south are grasses and trees common to the savanna regions, particularly the baobab tree, but also palms and acacias. The far south, in the Senegal River valley, has willows, jujube, and acacias. Lions, panthers, jackals, crocodiles, hippopotami, hyenas, cheetahs, otters, and monkeys survive in the south; in the north there are antelopes, wild sheep, ostriches and other large birds, and ducks.

⁵ENVIRONMENT

Deforestation is a severe problem because of the population's growing need for firewood and construction materials. Slash-and-burn agriculture has contributed to soil erosion, which is aggravated by drought. The expansion of the desert into agricultural lands is accelerated by limited rainfall, deforestation, the consumption of vegetation by livestock, and wind erosion. The expansion of domestic herds onto grazing land formerly restricted to wildlife has also taken a serious toll on the environment, both in erosion and in encroachment on wildlife species. The nation also has a problem with water pollution, resulting from the leakage of petroleum and industrial waste along with sewage into the nation's ports and rivers. A third of all urban dwellers and a slightly larger percentage of people in rural areas do not have pure water. The government plans to build a dam on the Senegal River to alleviate the country's water problems and stimulate agriculture.

In 1994, 14 of Mauritania's mammal species and five bird species were endangered, as well as three of its plant species.

⁶POPULATION

The total population in 1994 was estimated at 2,192,549, compared to a 1988 census figure of 1,864,236. The density averaged about 2.1 persons per sq km (5.5 per sq mi); the annual rate of increase was 2.9%. The UN projection for the year 2000 was 2,680,000, assuming a crude birthrate of 43.3 per 1,000 population, a crude death rate of 15.8, and a net natural increase of 27.5 during 1995–2000. Estimates in 1990 placed the population of Nouakchott, the capital, at 713,000. The urban population is about 54%; more than 90% of the population lives in the southern quarter of the country, including the Senegal River valley. Only 75,656 people lived in the northern half in 1988.

[7]MIGRATION

In seasonal grazing migrations, cattle are moved every year, and they are also led down to Senegal for sale. The droughts of the 1970s and early 1980s led to mass migrations to the towns. The population was 12% nomadic in 1988, compared to 83% in 1963. Some tribesmen of the Senegal River valley go to Dakar in Senegal for seasonal work or to engage in petty trade. A few thousand Mauritanians live in France. At the end of 1992 there were 66,500 Mauritanian refugees in Senegal and 13,100 in Mali. Mauritania was harboring about 18,000 Taureg and Maur refugees from Mali.

[8]ETHNIC GROUPS

Moors (Maures), the main ethnic group, constitute between three-fifths and four-fifths of the population. The Moors are a Caucasoid people of Berber and Arab stock, with some Negroid admixture. Other groups, all black, are the Tukulor, Sarakolé, Fulani (Fulbe), Wolof, and Bambara. The black population is found largely in southern Mauritania and in the cities. There are small numbers of Europeans, mainly French and Spanish (the latter from the Canary Islands), and a small colony of Lebanese traders.

[9]LANGUAGES

Arabic is the official language. The Arabic spoken in Mauritania is called Hassaniyah. Wolof, Peular, and Soninké are spoken in southern Mauritania and recognized as national languages. French is widely used, particularly in business, but its status as an official language was eliminated in the 1991 constitution.

[10]RELIGIONS

The state religion is Islam, and about 99% of the population is Sunni Muslim. The few thousand Christians are mostly foreigners. The Qadiriya and the Tijaniya are influential Islamic brotherhoods.

[11]TRANSPORTATION

Modern forms of transport are still undeveloped. There are few paved roads, only one freight railroad, two deep-water ports, and two airports that can handle international traffic.

In 1991, of some 7,525 km (4,676 mi) of roads, 22% were paved; there were only three paved highways, from Nouakchott north to Akjoujt and south to Rosso, continuing to Saint-Louis, Senegal. A 1,000-km (620-mi) east-west road between Nouakchott and Néma, started in 1975, was completed in 1985. A track continues north from Akjoujt to Bir Mogreïn, then branches northwest into Western Sahara and northeast into Algeria. Mauritania had about 15,000 motor vehicles in 1991.

The 652-km (405-mi) railway links the iron mines at Zouérate, near Fdérik, with the port at Point-Central, 10 km (6 mi) south of Nouadhibou. A 40-km (24-mi) spur was built in 1981 to accommodate the planned new mine at El-Rhein. There is a wharf at Nouakchott that handled 376,251 tons of freight in 1986; work on the construction of a deepwater port, financed by China, was completed in 1986. Nouadhibou, also a port, underwent extensive reconstruction, restoration, and equipment renewal in 1991. The Senegal River offers over 220 km (137 mi) of year-round transport.

The only airports that can handle long-distance jets are at Nouakchott and Nouadhibou. There are smaller airports at Ayoûn-el-'Atroûs, Akjoujt, Atar, Fdérik, Kaédi, Kifa, and Néma. Air Mauritanie (60% state owned) provides domestic flights as well as service to the Canary Islands and Senegal. The multinational Air Afrique also operates within Mauritania.

[12]HISTORY

Tens of thousands of years ago, the Sahara was verdant and filled with game. Desiccation eventually forced the inhabitants southward, a process that in the 3rd and 4th centuries AD was speeded by the Berbers, who had domesticated the camel. As the Berbers pressed down from the north toward the Senegal River valley, black Africans who lived in the path of the invaders were pushed southward. A Berber tribe, the Lemtouna, and two other Berber groups established a confederacy in the ninth century AD that carried on a thriving caravan trade in gold, slaves, and ivory from the south, in exchange for salt and other goods.

The Almoravids, a group of fervent Mauritanian Berbers, destroyed the great empire of Ghana in the 11th century, then turned northward, conquering North Africa and much of Spain. After the Almoravid empire was destroyed in the 12th century, the Mali kingdom, successor to Ghana, extended over southeastern Mauritania and dominated trade in the area. Later Mali was succeeded by the Songhai of Gao, whose empire fell to Moroccan invaders in 1591. Meanwhile, during the 14th and 15th centuries, Yemeni Bedouins who had been devastating North Africa moved into Mauritania; during the 17th century, they established complete dominance over the Berbers. The Arabs and Berbers in Mauritania have since thoroughly intermingled.

The Portuguese were the first Europeans to arrive, attracted in the 15th century by the trade in gold and slaves; later the gum arabic trade became important. Competition for control was keen among Portuguese, French, Dutch, and English traders. The issue was resolved in 1815, when Senegal was awarded to France in the post-Napoleonic war settlement. During the 19th century, the French explored the inland regions and signed treaties with Moorish chieftains. Penetration of the desert zone was accelerated around the turn of the century in attempts to thwart Moorish raids on the Senegal River tribes. A Frenchman, Xavier Coppolani, was responsible for the signing of many treaties, and played a key role in the extension of French influence in the area. By 1903, he was in control of Trarza, the Moors' main base for raids on the river tribes. Coppolani was killed in 1905, but his work was completed by Gen. Henri Gouraud, who gained effective control of the Adrar region by 1909. Mauritania was established as a colony in 1920, but its capital was located at Saint-Louis in Senegal. Mauritania thus became one of the eight territories that constituted the French West Africa federation.

In 1946, a Mauritanian Territorial Assembly was established, with some control over internal affairs. During the next 12 years, political power increasingly passed to local political leaders. Mauritania voted for the constitution of the Fifth French Republic at the referendum of 28 September 1958. It thus became a self-governing member of the French Community, and the Islamic Republic of Mauritania was proclaimed in November 1958. Complete independence was attained on 28 November 1960.

Since independence, the government of Mauritania has enjoyed considerable stability. Two problems that have dominated internal politics are regionalism and trade union pressures for more radical policies and higher wages. The black minority, located largely in the south, has staged antidiscrimination protests. In foreign affairs, the government has turned increasingly toward the Arab world. Mauritania joined the Arab League in 1973, and withdrew from the franc zone during the same year, but ties with Europe, especially France and the US, remain strong. The disastrous drought that struck Mauritania and the rest of the

MAURITANIA

0 75 150 225 300 Miles
0 75 150 225 300 Kilometers

ATLANTIC OCEAN

ALGERIA

Dayet el Khadra

Al Bir Lahlou

Erg Iguidi

Chegga

WESTERN SAHARA

Agmar

Bîr Mogreïn

'Ayoûn 'Abd el Mâlek

SAHARA DESERT

Fdérik

Zouérat

▲ Kediet ej Jill
3,002 ft.
915 m.

Awaday

El Moueïla

El Mrâyer

MALI

Bir Gandús

Cap Blanc

Nouadhibou

Ouadane

El Djouf

Baie de Lévrier

Tánoudert

Atar

Chinguetti

Île Tidra

Cap Timiris

Nouamrhar

Akjoujt

Tidjikdja

Tîchît

Nouakchott

Tijti

Boutilimit

Qualâta

Lac Rkiz

Aleg

'Ayoûn el 'Atroûs

Néma

Rosso

Bogué

Kîfa

Diadé

Lemoïlé

Senegal

Kaédi

Mbout

Médala

Maghama

Sélibaby

Nioro du Sahel

Bakel

Kayes

Niono

SENEGAL

Mauritania

MALI

N
W E
S

Bafoulabé

LOCATION: 14°42′ to 27°N; 4°30′ to 17°7′W. **BOUNDARY LENGTHS:** Algeria, 463 km (288 mi); Mali, 2,237 km (1,390 mi); Senegal, 813 km (505 mi); Atlantic coastline, 666 km (414 mi); Western Sahara, 1,561 km (970 mi). **TERRITORIAL SEA LIMIT:** 12 mi.

Sahel region during 1968–74 elicited substantial aid from the EC, the US, Spain, France, and the Arab countries.

Saharan War and Military Rule

On 14 November 1975, the governments of Spain, Morocco, and Mauritania reached an agreement whereby Spain agreed to abandon control of the Spanish Sahara by 28 February 1976 and to share administration of the territory until then with Morocco and Mauritania. On 14 April 1976, Morocco and Mauritania announced a border delimitation agreement under which Morocco received more than two-thirds of the region (including the richest phosphate deposits). The annexation of Western Sahara was opposed by the Popular Front for the Liberation of Saguia al-Hamra and Río de Oro (generally known as Polisario), which proclaimed the region as the Saharan Arab Democratic Republic. When Polisario forces, supported by Algeria, launched a war in Western Sahara, guerrilla raids on the Mauritanian railway, iron mines, and coastal settlements, including Nouakchott, forced Mauritania to call French and Moroccan troops to its defense. The effects of the war weakened the government both economically and politically, and in July 1978, Moktar Ould Daddah, Mauritania's president since 1961, was overthrown by a military coup. On 5 August 1979, Mauritania formally relinquished its portion of the disputed territory, except for the military base of LaGuera, near Nouadhibou; its share was occupied and annexed by Morocco. Mauritania thereafter pursued a policy of strict neutrality in the Morocco-Polisario conflict, a policy that strained relations with Morocco.

In the wake of the 1978 coup, the constitution was suspended and the National Assembly and the ruling Mauritanian People's Party (PPM) were dissolved. After a period of political uncertainty, Lt. Col. Khouna Ould Haydalla became chief of state and chairman of the ruling Military Committee for National Salvation as of 4 January 1980. There were unsuccessful attempts to overthrow his government in 1981 and 1982. Amnesty International claimed in 1983 that more than 100 political prisoners, including a former president and former prime minister, were being held in total darkness in underground cells in the desert. These prisoners were freed shortly after a military coup on 12 December 1984 brought Col. Moaouia Ould Sidi Mohamed Taya to power as chief of state.

As the economy faltered, however, racial and ethnic tensions increased. Since independence, the government has been dominated by Maurs, or Moors. The community has been divided between aristocrats and commoners, of Arab and Berber origin, and their black African slaves. The latter have adopted Moorish culture, but they remain socially segregated. Although the government refuses to release census data, it is estimated that Maurs account for between 30–60% of the population. The remainder are blacks, concentrated along the Senegal River border. Their growing oppression has been met with resistance from the underground Front for the Liberation of Africans in Mauritania (FLAM). Their grievances are linked with an unsuccessful coup attempt in 1987. Interethnic hostilities in 1989 exploded when a border dispute with Senegal led to race riots that left several hundred "Senegalese" dead in Nouackchott. The "Moorish" trading community in Senegal was targeted for retaliation in Senegal. Thousands of refugees streamed across the border in both directions. Mass deportation of "Mauritanians of Senegalese origin" fuel charges that Mauritania is trying to eliminate its non-Moorish population. Africa Watch estimates that at least 100,000 black slaves are held in Mauritania. Taya legalized opposition parties in July 1991, but he has also stepped up Arabization policies. There was a bloody purge conducted by the military from September 1990 through March 1991 during which some 500 mostly black soldiers were murdered. The PRDS parliament granted those responsible legal immunity in May 1993.

On 26 January 1992, Taya was elected in Mauritania's first multiparty presidential election, with 63% of the vote. Ahmed Ould Daddah, the strongest of the four rivals and half-brother of Mauritania's first president, gained 33% of the vote. However, the election was marked by fraud and six of the 14 opposition parties boycotted the March 1992 legislative elections. Taya's Democratic and Social Republican Party (PRDS) easily won 67 of 79 Assembly seats. The cabinet of Prime Minister Sidi Mohamed Ould Boubacar is composed of young technocrats. A new cabinet was formed in January 1993, and the Union of Democratic Forces (UDF), which had boycotted the legislative elections was offered three of the 21 ministries, including Finance.

13 GOVERNMENT

The constitution of 20 May 1961 declared Mauritania to be an Islamic republic. This constitution, which placed effective power in the hands of a president who was also head of the only legal political organization, the Mauritanian People's Party, was suspended in 1978 by the new military regime. Subsequently, executive and legislative powers were vested in the Military Committee for National Salvation. A draft constitution was published in 1980 but later abandoned; like the 1961 document, it called for a popularly elected president and National Assembly.

The July 1991 constitution delegates most powers to the executive. The president is to be elected by universal suffrage for a six-year term. The prime minister is appointed. Parliament, composed of a directly elected National Assembly and an indirectly elected Senate, poses no serious challenge and, moreover, is controlled by the president's party. Competing political parties were legalized in July 1991.

14 POLITICAL PARTIES

As elsewhere in French West Africa, formal political movements developed in Mauritania only after World War II. Horma Ould Babana, the leader of the first party to be established, the Mauritanian Entente, was elected to the French National Assembly in 1946. His party was considered too radical by the traditional chiefs, who organized a more conservative party, the Mauritanian Progressive Union (UPM). The UPM won 22 of 24 seats in the 1952 elections for the Territorial Assembly. In the 1957 elections, the first under universal adult suffrage, 33 of 34 persons elected to the Territorial Assembly were UPM members. In 1958, the UPM absorbed the weakened Entente into its organization, forming a single party, the Mauritanian Regroupment Party (PRM).

After independence, Prime Minister Moktar Ould Daddah in May 1961 set up a presidential system of government, and in the subsequent presidential election he was the only candidate. In December 1961, a new single party was formed, the Hizb Sha'b, or Mauritanian People's Party (Parti du Peuple Mauritanien—PPM). The PPM included minority parties as well as the PRM. By 1965, the single-party system had been established by law. President Ould Daddah was reelected in 1966, 1971, and 1976, but the PPM was dissolved after his ouster in 1978. No political parties functioned openly from 1978 until the 1991 military coup.

The Front for the Liberation of Africans in Mauritania (FLAM) was instrumental in stirring the 1989 unrest that ultimately led to multiparty elections. During this period of partisan organization, Taya formed the Democratic and Social Republican Party (Parti Republicain et Democratique Social—PRDS). Chief among 14 opposition parties has been the Union of Democratic Forces (UFD), which supported the runner-up in the January 1992 presidential election and boycotted the March parliamentary election. In May 1992, the UFD changed its name to UFD-New Era. In March 1993, it was weakened by the departure of eight centrist leaders to form a new political grouping. There are members of the UFD in the Cabinet. Also active are the Rally for Democratic and National Unity (RDUN), the

Union for Progress and Democracy (UPD), and the Mauritanian Renewal Party (PMR).

15 LOCAL GOVERNMENT

Mauritania is divided into the city of Nouakchott and 12 regions, each with a governor and a commission. The regions are subdivided into 49 departments. Elections to municipal councils were held in December 1986 and again in 1992. The January/February 1994 municipal elections led to PRDS control of around 170 of the 208 municipalities; the UFD won control of around 20, and independents won the rest. However, opposition parties alleged fraud.

16 JUDICIAL SYSTEM

The 1991 Constitution completely revised the judicial system, which had previously consisted of a lower court in Nouakchott, labor and military courts, a security court, and a Supreme Court in addition to qadi courts which handled family law cases.

The revised judicial system includes lower, middle, and upper level courts, each with specialized jurisdiction. The security court was abolished, and 43 department-level tribunals now bridge the traditional (qadi) and modern court systems. These courts are staffed by qadis or traditional magistrates trained in Koranic law. General civil caes are handled by 10 regional courts of first instance. Three regional courts of appeal hear challenges to decisions at the department level. A Supreme court, headed by a magistrate named by the President to a 5-year term, reviews appeals taken from decisions of the regional courts of appeal.

The 1991 Constitution also established a six-member Constitutional Court, three members of which are named by the President, two by the National Assembly President, and one by the Senate President.

While the judiciary is nominally independent, it is subject to pressure and influence by the executive, which controls the appointment and dismissal of judges. The system is strongly influenced by rulings and settlements of tribal elders based on Shari'a and tribal regulations.

The Codes of Civil and Criminal Procedure were revised in 1993 to bring them into line with the guarantees of the 1991 Constitution which provides for due process of law.

17 ARMED FORCES

The army had 9,000 men in 1993; the navy, 400 men and 5 patrol boats; and the air force, 200 men and 7 combat aircraft. Paramilitary personnel numbered 3,000. Mauritania has a bilateral defense agreement with France. There is a conscription law requiring 2 years service. Defense expenditures are $40 million or 4% of GDP.

18 INTERNATIONAL COOPERATION

Admitted to UN membership on 27 October 1961, Mauritania is a member of ECA and all the nonregional specialized agencies except IAEA. It is also a member of the African Development Bank, CEAO, ECOWAS, G-77, League of Arab States, OCAM, and OAU. Mauritania is a signatory to the Lomé Convention, GATT, and the Law of the Sea. In April 1975, it joined the Association of Iron Ore Exporting Countries. Mauritania has joined with Senegal and Mali to form the Organization for the Development of the Senegal River (Organisation pour la Mise en Valeur du Fleuve Sénégal—OMVS) and is a member, with neighboring Sahel states, of the Interstate Committee to Combat Sahel Drought.

19 ECONOMY

While Mauritania is an agricultural country, historically largely dependent on livestock production, its significant iron ore deposits have been the backbone of the export economy in recent years.

The droughts of the 1970s and 1980s transformed much of Mauritania, as the herds died off and the population shifted to urban areas. In 1965, 83% of the population lived as nomadic herders. By 1988, that percentage had fallen to 12%. As of 1989, 45% of the population was urban.

Most of Mauritania is desert or semiarid. Less than 1% of Mauritania receives sufficient rain for crop production, and that 1% is drought-prone. Leading staple crops are millet, sorghum, rice, corn, sweet potatoes and yams, pulses, and dates. The country is not agriculturally self-sufficient, and this situation has been aggravated by increasing urbanization. The government has raised its budgetary commitment to the rural sector from 10% (1981–85) to 35% (1985–88), focusing on the promotion of internationally funded irrigation projects.

The contribution of livestock herding to GDP is five times as great as that of agriculture. The droughts of the 1970s and 1980s devastated the herds, but the FAO estimates that they had attained pre-drought numbers by 1991. The recomposition of the Mauritanian herd and the development of water supplies have been a prime objective of the government.

20 INCOME

In 1992 Mauritania's GNP was $1,109 million at current prices, or $530 per capita. For the period 1985–92 the average inflation rate was 7.2%, resulting in a real growth rate in per capita GNP of –0.1%. The cost of living rose by 10.2% in the year 1991 to 1992.

In 1992 the GDP was $1,191 million in current US dollars. It is estimated that in 1989 agriculture, hunting, forestry, and fishing contributed 31% to GDP; mining and quarrying, 9%; manufacturing, electricity, gas, and water, 9%; construction, 6%; transport, storage, and communication, 4%; and other sources, 40%.

21 LABOR

Some 70% of Mauritania's inhabitants live within a subsistence economy. The estimated labor force numbered about 659,000 in 1992, with some 175,000 Mauritanians unemployed. Mining employed less than 1% of the labor force; fishing, 1.2%. All trade unions are grouped in a single federation, the Union of Mauritanian Workers (Union des Travailleurs de Mauritanie), which is affiliated with the ICFTU. The labor law of 1963 guarantees trade union rights, sets up a framework for collective bargaining, and provides for a 40-hour workweek. A guaranteed minimum wage has been established for nonagricultural workers, and was last raised in 1991.

22 AGRICULTURE

Settled agriculture is restricted to the strip of land along the Senegal River and to oases in the north; only 0.2% of Mauritania's total land area was classified as arable in 1991. In general, landholdings are small. Overall agricultural development has been hampered not only by unfavorable physical conditions but also by a complicated land-tenure system (modified in 1984) that traditionally rested on slavery, inadequate transportation, and the low priority placed on agriculture by most government developmental plans. The country's traditional dependence on food imports has been heightened by drought. Agriculture's share of GDP has been steadily falling; in 1991 it stood at 25.9%, down from 29% in 1987.

Millet and sorghum production reached 53,000 tons for 1992. Other crop production in 1992 included paddy rice, 18,000 tons; wheat and barley, 1,000 tons; and corn, 2,000 tons. Date production was 12,000 tons in 1992.

The Mauritanian government is encouraging agricultural development of the Senegal River valley. The OMVS began in 1981 to build a dam at Manantali, in Mali, for purposes of river transport, irrigation, and hydroelectric power. In conjunction with this OMVS project, Mauritania initiated an irrigation and development scheme in 1975 for the Gorgol River valley, involving construction of a dam; the scheme would increase arable land by over 3,600 ha (9,000 acres). This project was to be followed by other dams that together would add 30,000 ha (74,100 acres) for food production. Another OMVS project, begun in 1981, was designed to block salt water from entering the fertile Senegal River delta. From 1989 to 1991, a series of measures aimed at stimulation and rationalization of agricultural production were initiated, including producer price increases, marketing and distribution liberalization, and streamlining of government-owned agricultural organizations. Although the government allocated 35% of public investment in 1992 to the rural and agricultural sector, poor rains, overindebted farmers, and high produciton costs provided for meager harvests. The 1991 and 1992 harvests provided less than 20% of the domestic food requirement. Cereal imports rose form 95,336 tons in 1990 to 235,737 tons in 1992.

23 ANIMAL HUSBANDRY

Animal husbandry, a major activity in the traditional economy, grew rapidly during the 1960s because of a successful animal health campaign and, prior to 1968, favorable weather conditions. Indeed, cattle herds grew well beyond the number that could be supported by the natural vegetation. Thus, the land was already vulnerable when the drought years of 1968–74 reduced the cattle population from 2.6 million head in 1970 to 1.6 million in 1973. There were only 1,400,000 head in 1991, when sheep and goats numbered 9 million and camels 990,000.

The Moors tend to regard their cattle as symbols of wealth and prestige; this attitude discourages the herders from selling or slaughtering the animals. Reported figures are incomplete, however, since animal smuggling is common and much trade is unrecorded.

24 FISHING

With a potential catch of 600,000 tons, fishing employs 1.2% of the labor force and contributes about 5% to GDP. It is estimated that more than $1 billion worth of fish is netted each year within the 200-mi exclusive economic zone, but little of this sum benefits the treasury because the government lacks means of control and enforcement.

Since 1980, any foreigners wishing to fish in Mauritanian waters have been required by law to form a joint venture in which Mauritanian citizens or the government holds at least 51% of the capital. All of the catch must be landed in Mauritania for process and export, and each joint venture must establish an onshore processing facility. By 1987, over a dozen fishing companies had been established in Nouadhibou, including public and private interests from Algeria, France, Iraq, the Republic of Korea, Kuwait, Libya, Nigeria, Romania, Spain, and the former USSR. In May 1987, Mauritania signed a three-year fishing agreement with the EC, allowing all EC members to fish in Mauritanian waters; in return, Mauritania received approximately $23 million. Since the mid-1980s, however, depletion of the stocks has made Mauritanian fishing increasingly uneconomical. Fishing's contribution to GDP fell to 5% by 1991. Mauritania's boats have been in poor condition. In spite of the ship repair service in Nouadhibou, which opened in 1989, only about 50% of the fleet was up and running in 1992.

Traditional fishing is carried out along the Senegal River, and traditional sea fishing at Nouakchott and Nouadhibou. The national catch was estimated at 90,000 tons in 1991. Principal species caught included octopus, meagre, sardine, squid, and grouper.

25 FORESTRY

Sizable tree stands found in the southern regions are not fully exploited. The principal forest product is gum arabic, which is extracted from wild acacia trees that grow in the south. Until 1972, private traders collected and exported the gum; since 1972, it has officially been a monopoly of the state trading company, Société Nationale d'Importation et d'Exportation (SONIMEX). Nevertheless, much gum continues to be smuggled across the borders, particularly to Senegal. Roundwood removals were estimated at 13,000 cu m in 1991, 58% for fuel.

26 MINING

Iron deposits play a significant role in the economy. The Iron Mines Co. of Mauritania (MIFERMA), formed in 1951 and nationalized in 1974, began production at three mines in 1963, and since then iron has been a primary source of foreign exchange earnings. Port facilities and a rail link to the mine were constructed during the peak mining period 1960–74. Production declined from a peak of 11,860,000 tons in 1974 to 10,246,000 tons in 1991. In 1991 three mines near the Kédia d'Idjil region were active: Tazadit, Ruessa Sayala, and Azouazil. The El Rhein Mine operates in the Guelbs desert plains, and began production in 1984. The current focus is on the M'Haoudat fields near Zouérate.

Mauritania is also rich in copper, but hopes for significant commercial development did not fully materialize, and production ceased in 1978. The mine at Akjoujt was scheduled to reopen in 1984–85 with $100 million in financing from Arab countries; it is still closed but under consideration since the deposits were estimated to contain 100 million tons of ore averaging 2.25% copper with trace amounts of gold. Phosphate deposits have, however, been identified, and prospecting continues for petroleum, tungsten, and uranium.

Gypsum reserves are among the largest in the world, but technical problems brought a decline, and then a halt, to production in 1989 and 1990. Gypsum is exported mainly to Senegal; total production was 2,839 tons in 1991.

27 ENERGY AND POWER

The national utility company, SONELEC, manages the water and electricity supply for the urban areas of Nouakchott, Nouadhibou, Kaédi, Rosso, Akjoujt, Autres, and Atar. National installed capacity was 105,000 kw in 1991, 42% of it thermal; production increased from 49.9 million kwh in 1969 to 143 million kwh in 1991. Offshore oil exploration is being carried on by Texaco and Amoco in the southern and central coastal waters. In 1992, imports of fuels accounted for 18% of total imports.

28 INDUSTRY

Fish processing, the principal industrial activity, is carried out in Nouadhibou. By far the largest fish processor is Mauritanian Fish Industries (IMAPEC), a Spanish company in which the Mauritanian government acquired a 51% share in 1980. IMAPEC has facilities for salting, drying, canning, and freezing fish, and for producing fish flour; virtually all of its output is exported.

The first desalination plant in Africa was completed at Nouakchott in January 1969, with a capacity of 3,000 cu m a day. A rolling mill at Nouadhibou, built in 1977, produces small quantities of iron rods and steel. A petroleum refinery in Nouadhibou, with an annual capacity of 1 million tons, opened in 1982, shut down in 1983, and resumed operation in 1987 with help from Algeria. Algeria also helped revitalize a sugar refining plant. Similarly, Kuwaiti and Jordanian interests reopened the steel mill after a shutdown. Each of these operations represents a drain on state revenues, and the government has shifted policy toward the promotion of less ambitious industrial development.

In 1990 Mauritania has an electrical generating capacity of 140 million kwh (1990), most of which was thermally generated. Mauritania gains a portion of its power from dams built on the Senegal River in a joint venture with Senegal and Mali.

29SCIENCE AND TECHNOLOGY

A research institute for mining and industry is at Nouakchott. The Economic Community of West Africa has an institute in Nouadhibou-Cansado conducting research in the fisheries industry. The Higher Scientific Institute, founded in 1986, has departments of mathematics, physics, chemistry, biology, and geology.

30DOMESTIC TRADE

The government, through SONIMEX, holds a legal monopoly on imports of such consumer goods as rice, sugar, and tea, and on exports of gum arabic. Most established trading firms are based in France. Normal business hours are from 8 AM to noon and 2:30 to 7 PM, Monday through Saturday (except Friday). Banks are open weekdays from 8 to 11:15 AM and 2:30 to 4:00 PM.

31FOREIGN TRADE

Mauritania recorded trade surpluses from 1983 to 1989 ($98.6 million in 1989). Fish products were 58.6% of exports in 1989; iron ore 41.4%. In 1990, fish product exports increased by 23.8%, while iron ore exports declined by 2.4%.

Principal imports in 1986 (in millions of ouguiyas) were as follows:

Food products	4,553
Fuel	3,439
Investment goods	2,033
Transport vehicles and equipment	1,421
Other products	4,384
TOTALS	15,830

Mauritania's main trading partners in 1985 were Japan, the former USSR, Belgium, Italy, and France for exports, and Senegal, France, Spain, and Italy for imports.

32BALANCE OF PAYMENTS

The healthy trade surpluses (in excess of $50 million) that Mauritania had known in the late 1980s and in 1990 declined to $14 million in 1991 and $19 million in 1992, in spite of the rebound in fisheries exports. Lower iron ore exports (especially in 1992) and increased imports of food and mining equipment for the M'Haoudat project offset the good fish catch. Mauritania's potential of maintaining trade surpluses depends largely on the vagaries of the annual fish catch.

33BANKING AND SECURITIES

A national bank, the Central Bank of Mauritania (Banque Centrale de Mauritanie), was established in 1973. In addition there were four commercial banks in 1991 of which only one was private.

Banks in Mauritania in 1991 included Banque Arbe Libyene-Mauritanienne pour le Commerce Extérieur et le Développement (BNM). BALM, founded in 1990, is 51% owned by Libyans and 49% owned by the state. Other banks included Banque Al-Baraka Mauritanie Islamique (BAMIS), Banque Mauritanie pour le Commerce Interationale (BMCL), and Banque Nationale de Mauritania (BNM). BAMIS, established in 1990, is 50% Saudi owned and 10% BCM owned. BMCL, founded in 1990, is 10% BCM owned, and 90% of the bank is held by private interests. BNM, established in 1988, is 50% state owned.

34INSURANCE

Insurance was handled by 13 foreign companies until July 1974, when the Mauritanian government assumed full control of insurance and reinsurance. All insurance business is controlled by the Mauritanian Insurance and Reinsurance Co.

35PUBLIC FINANCE

Mauritania's budget is habitually in deficit. Mismanagement of public enterprises and an abundance of public sector employees led to large deficits in the early 1980s.

In 1985, the government began an IMF-sponsored adjustment program to stabilize the economy and diminish the role of the public sector. The overall fiscal cash deficit (excluding debt forgiveness) fell from 12% GDP in 1985 to 5.4% in 1989. From 1989 to 1992, however, due to the Persian Gulf Crisis and turmoil with Senegal, the adjustment effort was set back.

36TAXATION

The major indirect taxes are import duties, a turnover tax on exports and mining companies, excise levies on petroleum, alcoholic beverages, tea, and tobacco, a service tax, and a tax on vehicles. The major direct tax is an income tax on wages and salaries; a general income tax and a tax on the profits of industrial and commercial corporations are also imposed.

37CUSTOMS AND DUTIES

Along with other members of the CEAO, Mauritania imposes a revenue duty (droit fiscal) and a customs duty (droit de douane d'entrée) on most imported goods. Customs duty ranges from a minimum of 5% to a much higher rate for certain commodities. Fiscal duty ranges from 5–30% of c.i.f. value. Other taxes include a statistical tax, standard tax, and turnover tax. Material required for economic development is assessed at a lower rate. Exports and imports require licenses.

Since 1970, Mauritania has had a trade agreement with Senegal, allowing primary products to be traded between the two countries duty-free. Mauritania is an associate member of the EC.

38FOREIGN INVESTMENT

With the nationalization of the mining sector in 1974, private foreign investment dropped drastically. Extension of government control over imports and domestic trade has further curtailed the activity of foreign capital. The government's costly experience with parastatal investments has persuaded it to focus on private, small-scale capital investments. An industrial zone is under consideration for Nouackchott.

An investment code, approved in 1979, provides for tax holidays of up to 12 years on exports, imports of raw materials, and reinvested profits. Mineral and fish processing are priority areas. All direct investment by nonresidents is subject to prior approval, and liquidations of such investment also require approval. Similarly, capital transfers and large-scale foreign borrowings and repayments require prior authorization.

39ECONOMIC DEVELOPMENT

Until the export earning capacity of Mauritania improves, its economy will remain fragile. External deficit management dominates the public investment horizon.

40SOCIAL DEVELOPMENT

The National Social Insurance Fund administers family allowances, industrial accident benefits, insurance against occupational diseases, and old age pensions. Medical services are available free to those unable to pay. Opportunities for Mauritian women are severely limited by social and cultural factors. Female circumcision is widely practiced; abortion is illegal. The fertility rate was 6.9 in the mid-1980s.

A report by the Anti-Slavery Society of London in 1983 alleged that at least 100,000 blacks from southwestern Mauritania were being kept as slaves by Moors. Widespread rioting and the flight of refugees marked racial unrest in 1989 and 1990.

[41]HEALTH

Mauritania's public health system consists of administrative units and health facilities organized in pyramid style. According to 1992 data, there were 300 basic health units at the village level, 128 health posts, and 53 health centers. The health system is mostly public, but liberalization of private practice in the past several years has led to marked increase in the number of practitioners in the private sector—up to 8 clinics in 1990. Mauritania's only major hospital is in Nouakchott. In 1990, there were 127 doctors, 5 pharmacists, 15 dentists, 886 nurses, and 148 midwives. In 1992, only about 45% of the population had access to health care services. Private participation in the pharmaceutical sector has increased since 1987. There are 5 importers, 32 private pharmacies, and 130 commercial distribution points. Public facilities receive stocks from the Ministry of Health and Social Affairs. Drugs are distributed to patients at public facilities at no cost, but only 40% of demand can be met. Importation of narcotics is prohibited.

The main health problems include malaria, tuberculosis, measles, dysentery, and influenza. There were an estimated 220 cases of tuberculosis per 100,000 people in 1990. Pregnancy complications are common due to unhygienic conditions, and lack of medical care. In nondrought years the staple diet of milk and millet is nutritionally adequate, if somewhat deficient in vitamin C; in the 1980s, however, it was estimated that the calorie supply met only 86% of requirements. In 1992, immunization rates for children up to one year old were: tuberculosis (73%); diphtheria, pertussis, and tetanus (34%); polio (34%); and measles (39%).

The average life expectancy is among the lowest in the world—an estimated 48 years for both men and women. In 1992 there were 100,000 births for a birth rate of 17.5 per 1,000 people. The infant mortality rate was 118 per 1,000 live births, and the general mortality rate was 17.5 per 1,000 people (higher than average for low-income countries).

[42]HOUSING

Construction accounts for a small fraction of GDP. The chief construction company, the Building Society of Mauritania, is hampered by inadequate manpower and capitalization. To encourage housing development, the government introduced new regulations in 1975 to encourage builders and to compel civil servants to purchase their own property and thus relieve the demand for public housing. The phenomenal growth of Nouakchott and the effects of rural migration, impelled by drought, have strained housing resources. As of 1990, 67% of urban and 65% of rural dwellers had access to a public water supply, while 34% of urban dwellers had access to sanitation services.

[43]EDUCATION

In 1990, 35.7% of Mauritania's adult population was found to be literate. Of these, men were 45.9% and women 26.5% literate. Education is compulsory, but only a minority of school-age children attend school. In 1991, there were 188,580 students in primary schools and 39,821 in secondary schools. Of these, teacher training schools had 752 pupils and vocational schools had 1,030 pupils. In 1991, there were 4,039 teachers in primary schools and 2,184 in secondary schools. The National Institute of Higher Islamic Studies was established in Boutilimit in 1961, and the National School of Administration was founded in 1966 at Nouakchott. The University of Nouakchott, founded in 1981, has a faculty of letters and human sciences and a faculty of law and economics. All higher level institutions had a total of 250 teachers and 5,850 pupils in 1991.

[44]LIBRARIES AND MUSEUMS

The National Library at Nouakchott (10,000 volumes) and the National Archives (3,000) were both founded in 1955. The National Library is the depository for all the country's publications. The National Museum is also located in Nouakchott and has archaelogy and ethnography collections. There are several Arab libraries in the major towns.

[45]MEDIA

Many of Mauritania's post offices have telephone or telegraph services; by 1991 there were about 4,827 telephones in use. There are direct telephone communications from Nouakchott to Paris. Administrative contact within the country is maintained by radio-telephone. Two earth-satellite stations came into service in 1985–86. The government-owned national radio and television networks broadcast in French, Arabic, and several African languages. There were an estimated 300,000 radios and 49,000 television sets in 1991. Telecasts are in French and Arabic.

A government-operated daily, El Chaab, is published in French and Arabic.

[46]ORGANIZATIONS

The Chamber of Commerce, Industry, Agriculture, and Ranching is in Nouakchott.

[47]TOURISM, TRAVEL, AND RECREATION

There are few facilities for tourists, except in the capital, and travel is difficult outside of Nouakchott. Most visitors need a valid passport and visa; the visa requirement is waived for French and Italian nationals and citizens of Arab League countries and of the former French territories in Africa. Antimalarial precautions are recommended and a yellow-fever inoculation is required for travelers from infected areas.

Tourists are attracted to Atar, the ancient capital of the Almoravid kingdom, and Chinguetti, with houses and mosques dating back to the 13th century.

[48]FAMOUS MAURITANIANS

Abu Bakr ibn Omar (Boubakar), paramount chief of the Lemtouna, defeated Ghana in 1076. His lieutenant and cousin, Yusuf ibn Tashfin, conquered Morocco in 1082 and most of Spain in 1091. The best-known contemporary Mauritanian is Moktar Ould Daddah (b.1924), president from 1961 until 1978; after being ousted, he was eventually allowed to go to France. Lt. Col. Khouna Ould Haydalla (b. Spanish Sahara, 1940) became prime minister and chief of staff of the armed forces in 1978 and assumed the presidency in 1980. Col. Moaouia Ould Sidi Mohamed Taya, who had been prime minister (1981–84), became president in 1984.

[49]DEPENDENCIES

Since relinquishing its claim to Western Sahara, Mauritania has no territories or colonies.

[50]BIBLIOGRAPHY

Calderini, Simonetta. Mauritania. Santa Barbara, Calif.: Clio Press, 1992.

De Chassey, Claude. Mauritania 1900–1975. Paris: Harmattan, 1984.

Gerteiny, Alfred G. Historical Dictionary of Mauritania. Metuchen, N.J.: Scarecrow Press, 1981.

Handloff, Robert E. (ed.). Mauritania, a Country Study. 2nd ed. Washington, D.C.: Library of Congress, 1990.

Thompson, Virginia, and Richard Adloff. The Western Saharans. Totowa, N.J.: Barnes & Noble, 1980.

Toupet, Charles, and Jean-Robert Pitte. La Mauritanie. Paris: Presses Universitaires de France, 1977.

Westebbe, Richard M. The Economy of Mauritania. New York: Praeger, 1971.

MAURITIUS

Republic of Mauritius

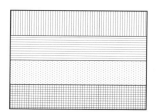

CAPITAL: Port Louis.

FLAG: The national flag consists of four horizontal stripes of red, blue, yellow, and green.

ANTHEM: *Glory to Thee, Motherland, O Motherland of Mine.*

MONETARY UNIT: The Mauritius rupee (R) is a currency of 100 cents. There are coins of 1, 2, 5, 10, 25, and 50 cents and 1 rupee, and notes of 5, 10, 20, 50, 100, 200, 500, and 1,000 rupees. R1 = $0.0550 (or $1 = R18.189).

WEIGHTS AND MEASURES: The metric system is in general use; traditional weights and measures are also employed.

HOLIDAYS: New Year, 1–2 January; National Day, 12 March; Labor Day, 1 May. Christian, Hindu, and Muslim holidays are also observed.

TIME: 4 PM = noon GMT.

¹LOCATION, SIZE, AND EXTENT

Mauritius is situated in the Indian Ocean, about 900 km (559 mi) E of Madagascar and 2,000 km (1,250 mi) off the nearest point of the African coast. The island of Rodrigues, an integral part of Mauritius, is located about 560 km (350 mi) off its northeastern coast. The two islands of Agalega lie 960 km (600 mi) to the north; also to the north is the St. Brandon Group (Cargados Carajos Shoals). Mauritius has a total area of 1,860 sq km (718 sq mi), of which the island of Mauritius occupies 1,865 sq km (720 sq mi); the island of Rodrigues, 104 sq km (40 sq mi); and the other offshore islands, 71 sq km (27 sq mi). Comparatively, the area occupied by Mauritius is slightly less than 10.5 times the size of Washington, D.C. Mauritius extends 61 km (38 mi) N–S and 47 km (29 mi) E–W, and has a coastline of 177 km (110 mi). The nation also claims Diego Garcia, a British dependency about 1,900 km (1,200 mi) to the northeast, and a French possession, Tromelin Island, about 555 km (345 mi) to the northwest. The OAU has supported Mauritius' claim to Diego Garcia.

The capital city of Mauritius, Port Louis, is located on the island's northwest coast.

²TOPOGRAPHY

Mauritius is mostly of volcanic formation and is almost entirely surrounded by coral reefs. A coastal plain rises sharply to a plateau 275 to 580 m (900–1,900 ft) high. Piton de la Rivière Noire, the highest peak, reaches 826 m (2,710 ft). The longest river is the Grand River South East, extending about 39 km (24 mi).

³CLIMATE

The subtropical maritime climate is humid, with prevailing southeast winds. The temperature ranges from 18° to 30°C (64–86°F) at sea level, and from 13° to 26°C (55–79°F) at an elevation of 460 m (1,500 ft); the warmest season lasts from October to April, the coolest from June to September. From October to March, southeast trade winds bring heavy rains to the central plateau and windward slopes, which have a yearly average rainfall of over 500 cm (200 in). On the coast, rainfall averages about 100 cm (40 in) annually. Daily showers occur from April to September and occasional tropical cyclones between December and April.

⁴FLORA AND FAUNA

Mauritius originally was covered by dense rain forest, which included heath and mossy forest at higher elevations and coastal palm savanna. Present vegetation consists chiefly of species brought by the settlers. Mauritius is the home of two indigenous snakes, the *Boleyria multicarinata* and *Casarea dussumieri*; also indigenous to Mauritius was the now extinct dodo bird, one of many exotic animal species that thrived in isolation from predators, including man. European settlers introduced dogs, cats, rats, monkeys, wild pigs, sambur deer, and mongoose.

⁵ENVIRONMENT

The main environmental problems facing Mauritius are water pollution, soil erosion, and preservation of its wildlife. The sources of water pollution are sewage and agricultural chemicals. Mauritius cities produce 0.1 million tons of solid waste annually. The erosion of the soil occurs through deforestation.

The Ministry of Housing, Lands, and the Environment has principal responsibility in environmental matters. According to UN reports in 1992, Mauritius ranks third in the world on the list of countries with the most endangered species. Of 30 species indigenous to the country, only 11 survive. As of 1994, three of Mauritius' mammal species and 10 of its bird species are endangered. 269 of its plant species are also endangered.

Endangered species on the island of Mauritius in 1987 included the pink pigeon, Round Island boa and keel-scaled boa, green sea turtle, and Mauritius varieties of kestrel, parakeet, and fody. Endangered species on Rodrigues included distinctive varieties of brush warbler, fody, flying fox, and day gecko.

⁶POPULATION

The 1990 census found the population of the island of Mauritius to be 1,024,571; 34,204 were on the island of Rodrigues. There were 167 people on other islands. In mid-1994, when the total estimated population was 1,106,593, the density was a very high 542 per sq km (1,406 per sq mi). A total population of 1,183,000 was projected for the year 2000, assuming a crude birthrate of 16.6 per 1,000 population, a crude death rate of 6.5, and a net natural increase of 10.1 during 1995–2000. Port Louis, the capital, had 142,505 inhabitants in 1991. Other cities and their 1991 populations were Beau Bassin/Rose Hill, 93,684; Quatre-Bornes, 70,997; Curepipe, 74,214; and Vacoas–Phoenix, 91,114. As of 1995, 40.7% of the population was urban.

7 MIGRATION

A small number of Mauritians emigrate each year, principally to Australia, Europe, and Canada.

8 ETHNIC GROUPS

The largest group on Mauritius—about 68%—is Indo-Mauritian, consisting of immigrants from India and their descendants. About 23% of the islanders are Creole (mixed European and African), 3% Chinese, and 2% French.

9 LANGUAGES

English is the official language; however, Creole, derived from French, is most widely spoken. On Rodrigues, virtually the entire population speaks Creole. In 1990 36% of Mauritius' population spoke Creole as their mother tongue. Some 33% spoke Bhojpuri as their first language and 16% spoke five other Indian languages—Hindi, Marathi, Tamil, Telegu, and Urdu. Another 2% were native French speakers. Only 888 people had English as a first language.

10 RELIGIONS

In 1990, Hindus constituted about 54% of the population, Roman Catholics 29%, and Muslims 17%. About 97% of those on the island of Rodrigues are Roman Catholics.

11 TRANSPORTATION

Mauritius had some 1,800 km (1,115 mi) of roads in 1991, more than 90% of which were paved. As of 1991, there were 59,263 civilian vehicles, including 50,016 private passenger cars trucks, and 2,021 buses. The five merchant ships in service had a combined capacity of 64,000 GRT. Air Mauritius provides about four flights weekly to Rodrigues from the main airport at Plaisance, as well as international flights.

12 HISTORY

Long uninhabited, Mauritius was probably visited by Arab and Malay seamen and later by Portuguese and other European voyagers. However, significant contact did not take place until the Dutch, under Admiral Wybrandt van Warwijck, arrived in 1598. They named the island after their stadtholder, Prince Maurice of Nassau. Settlers arrived in 1638; their settlements were abandoned in 1710, however, and the French took possession in 1715, sending settlers from Réunion in 1721. The island was governed by the French East India Company until 1767, and by the French government for the next 43 years, except for a brief period of independence during the French Revolution. During the Napoleonic wars, French-held Mauritius became a major threat to British shipping in the Indian Ocean, and Britain occupied it in 1810.

Under British rule, Mauritius became a sugar-producing island. The French community secured major control of the cane fields and sugar refineries; lacking any appreciable British settlement, the island remained French in culture. Abolition of slavery in the British Empire caused an acute labor problem as the former slaves, African in origin, left the sugar fields to go into other occupations. To offset this loss, the UK, from 1835, allowed the planters to import indentured laborers from India. The system continued until 1907, with 450,000 Indians migrating to Mauritius.

The constitution of 1831 provided for a Council of Government, in which representation was largely by Europeans, although a few Creoles won nomination. The constitution of 1886 provided for a council of 27 members, including 10 elected members. The electorate was limited by property qualifications, which denied the population of Indian descent elective representation until 1926. The constitution of 1947 abolished property qualifications and extended the franchise to both sexes. Since 1948, the Indian population has dominated the elective seats. As a result of a constitutional conference held in London in September 1965, Mauritius was granted full internal self-government.

Mauritius became independent on 12 March 1968, and a month later became a member of the UN. Disturbances at the time of independence between Muslims and Creoles forced declaration of a state of emergency, at which time UK troops from Singapore aided in restoring order. Sir Seewoosagur Ramgoolam, chief minister in the colonial government, became the first prime minister after independence. Ramgoolam's Mauritius Labor Party (MLP) held power alone, or in coalition with others, until June 1982, when an alliance of the Mauritian Militant Movement (MMM) and the Mauritian Socialist Party (PSM) captured all 60 directly elected seats on the island of Mauritius. This coalition, known as the Militant Socialist Movement (MSM) formed a government. MMM leader Aneerood Jugnauth became prime minister. In March 1983, however, 11 of the 19 ministers resigned, all MMM members, and new elections were called. The voting, in August of that year, produced a clear mandate for a new coalition forged by Jugnauth. The MMM-dominated coalition won another clear-cut victory in August 1987 Legislative Assembly elections.

Jugnauth's coalition received a mandate again in the September 1991 general elections, winning 59 of 62 directly elected seats. As promised, the MSM/MMM alliance amended the constitution making Mauritius a republic within the Commonwealth. Since March 12, 1992, Queen Elizabeth II has been replaced by a Mauritian chief of state.

13 GOVERNMENT

The Mauritian government is parliamentary, with executive power vested under the constitution in a president and a prime minister, who is leader of the majority party in parliament. The prime minister heads a Council of Ministers, which is responsible to a unicameral Legislative Assembly. Of its 70 members, 62 are elected by universal suffrage (age 18), and as many as eight "best losers" are chosen from runners-up by the Electoral Supervisory Commission by a formula designed to give at least minimal representation to all ethnic groups and underrepresented parties.

14 POLITICAL PARTIES

The Mauritius Labor Party (MLP), headed by Prime Minister Sir Seewoosagur Ramgoolam, received support during 35 continuous years in office (1947–82) from the Hindu and Creole communities and some Muslims; often sharing power in those years was the Muslim Committee of Action (MCA). The Mauritian Social Democratic Party (Parti Mauricien Social-Démocratique—PMSD) has long represented the Franco-Mauritian and Creole landowning class.

A new political party, the Mauritian Militant Movement (MMM), was formed in 1970. Its leaders were imprisoned in 1971 after the MMM called for a general strike to protest legislation banning strikes in industries controlled by MMM affiliates. The party leadership was later freed, and in the 1976 elections the MMM won more seats than the MLP, though not enough to achieve power. In the 1982 elections, the MMM captured 42 seats in parliament and joined the Mauritian Socialist Party (Parti Socialiste Mauricien—PSM) in a ruling coalition under Aneerood Jugnauth; unlike the MMM, which had strong Creole representation, the PSM was primarily Hindu.

Jugnauth's government fell apart in the early months of 1983, in the course of a power struggle within the MMM that led to the prime minister's expulsion from his own party. Jugnauth then formed the Mauritian Socialist Movement (Mouvement Socialiste Mauricien—MSM), which, in alliance with the MLP, captured 37 of 62 directly elected seats in the August balloting. The MMM won 19 seats, the PMSD 4, and a Rodrigues-based party, the Organisation du Peuple Rodriguais (OPR), 2. In August 1987 elections, the MSM, in alliance with the MLP and PMSD, won 39 of 62 directly elected seats; a three-party coalition including the MMM won 21 seats; and the OPR won 2 seats.

The legislative elections of 15 September 1991 resulted in the MSM/MMM alliance getting 59 seats (53% of the vote) and the MLP/PMSD alliance three seats (38%). By October 1993, however, the MMM had divided into two factions: one remained in the government and the other, headed by former Foreign Minister Paul Berenger, took opposition seats in parliament.

15 LOCAL GOVERNMENT

There are nine administrative divisions on the island of Mauritius. The lowest level of local government is the village council, composed of elected as well as nominated members; above the village councils are three district councils. Commissions govern the major towns. There are also three dependencies.

16 JUDICIAL SYSTEM

The statutes are based mainly on old French codes and on more recent laws with English precedents. The Supreme Court has a chief justice and six other judges who also serve on the Court of Criminal Appeal, the Court of Civil Appeal, the Intermediate Court, the Industrial Court, and 10 district courts. Final appeal can be made to the UK Privy Council.

The President, in consultation with the Prime Minister, nominates the Chief Justice, and then with the advice of the Chief Justice also appoints the associate judges. The President nominates other judges on the advice of the Judicial and Legal Service Commissions.

The legal system provides fair public trials for criminal defendants. Defendants have the right to counsel including court appointed counsel in case of indigency.

17 ARMED FORCES

The National Police Force, which includes a military Special Mobile Force, is responsible for defense. In 1993, it had some 4,000 members and a budjet of $5 million a year.

18 INTERNATIONAL COOPERATION

Mauritius joined the UN on 24 April 1968 and belongs to ECA and all the nonregional specialized agencies. The nation participates in the African Development Bank, Commonwealth of Nations, G-77, and OAU. Mauritius is a signatory both to GATT and to the Law of the Sea. In 1984, Mauritius joined Madagascar and Seychelles in establishing the Indian Ocean Commission; the Comoros and France (as the representative of Réunion) joined in 1985.

19 ECONOMY

The Mauritius economy, diverse and conservatively managed, is based on export-oriented manufactuing (mainly clothing), sugar, and tourism. Most of production is done by private enterprise, with the government largely limiting its role to providing institutional facilities and incentives for production. The economy grew at an impressive average rate of 6% over the last decade and reached full employment in the late 1980s. However, economic growth started to decline in 1988 as the economy started to experience some of the problems associated with success, including labor shortages, rising inflation, and capacity constraints. In 1990–91, the economy showed signs of a modest recovery and in

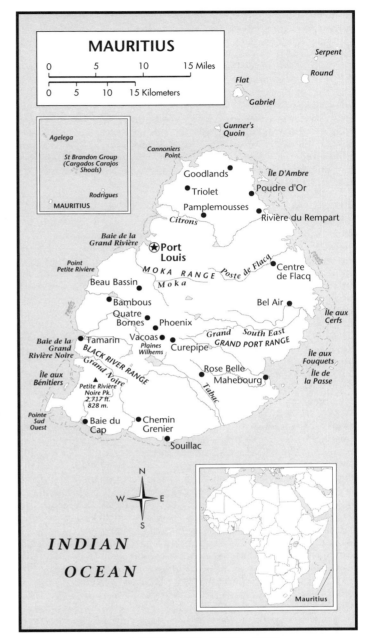

LOCATION: 19°50′ to 20°5′s; 57°18′ to 57°48′E.
TERRITORIAL SEA LIMIT: 12 mi.

1992 it was estimated to have grown at a rate of 4.4%.

Important to Mauritius' industrial development is the Export Processing Zone (EPZ) in which imported goods are processed for export. Legislation gives investors in EPZ enterprises tax relief, duty exemption on most imports, unlimited repatriation of capital and profits, and cut-rate electricity. However, the gradual erosion of the country's comparative advantage in labor-intensive exports has compelled the manufacturing industry to adopt more sophisticated and capital-intensive technologies in order to remain comptitive. In shifting to captital-intensive technologies, some large firms are moving their labor-intensive production to Madagascar.

To further enhance its competitive advantage, in June 1992 the government passed legislation for the creation of a commercial free port in Port Louis. The free port would provide warehousing as well as facilities for processing foods and materials for re-export to destinations around the world.

20INCOME

In 1992 Mauritius's GNP was $2,965 million at current prices, or $2,700 per capita. For the period 1985–92 the average inflation rate was 9.0%, resulting in a real growth rate in per capita GNP of 6.3%.

In 1992 the GDP was $3,035 million in current US dollars. Of that total, manufacturing was the leading sector at 23.0%, followed by trade, restaurants, and hotels at 17.2%. Transport accounted for 12.1%, as did financing and business services. Agriculture followed, contributing 10.4% to GDP. Annual inflation in 1991 was 7.0%.

21LABOR

There were 345,848 workers employed in major economic sectors as of July 1990. The principal employment sectors were services (mostly government), 19%; manufacturing, 30%; and agriculture and fishing, 16%. Unemployment (excluding Rodrigues) was 7,948 in 1992—down nearly ten-fold from 73,042 in 1983. Minimum wages are set by the government, and cost-of-living allowances are mandatory. In 1992, the Export Processing Zone (EPZ) employed 90,000 workers. In recent years, unions within the EPZ have been deregistered; less than 10% of EPZ workers are believed to be Unionized. In all, there were almost 300 labor unions at the end of 1992, with 110,000 members.

22AGRICULTURE

Sugarcane is the major crop. In 1991, 5,621,110 tons of cane were produced (third largest in Africa), from which the yield of raw and white sugar was 611,340 tons, and of molasses, 170,000 tons. In 1992, 6,400,000 tons of cane were produced. Sugarcane occupies 45% of Mauritius' total land area and 88% of its cultivated land. It is an estate economy, with 21 large estates accounting for 56.9 of the land cultivated. The 32,000 small operations account for 25% of the land cultivated and are grouped into cooperatives. Sugar's importance has diminished in recent years as manufacturing and tourism have grown; in 1991 it accounted for 7.8% of GDP and 30.1% of foreign earnings.

Tea production in Mauritius has been on the decline, disadvantaged by production cost increases, labor shortages, and low world prices. The area under tea cultivation declined from 2,905 ha in 1990 to 2,870 ha in 1991. Tobacco production, on the other hand, has increased steadily, from 799 tons in 1990 to 876 tons in 1991, and now provides the raw material for most locally produced cigarettes. In recent years, horticultural products have been successfully grown for export, including flowers (mainly anthuriums), tropical fruits, and vegetables. Exports of cut flowers in 1992 were estimated at $7 million.

Other crops and 1991 yields were: tea, green leaf processed, 30,635 tons; tea, black leaf, 5,934 tons; potatoes, 16,000 tons; tomatoes, 9,000 tons; bananas, 6,000 tons; corn, 2,000 tons; peanuts, 1,000 tons; tobacco, 876 tons; and coconuts, 3,000 tons. Almost any crop can be grown on Mauritius, but the shortage of land means almost all cereals must be imported, including rice, the staple food. Potatoes and other vegetables are grown in the sugar fields between rows of cane.

23ANIMAL HUSBANDRY

Cattle meat production recorded an increase of 5.3 per cent, from 2,049 tons in 1990 to 2,157 tons in 1991 while poultry production rose by 6% from 12,500 tons to 13,250 tons. In 1992, Mauritius had 34,000 head of cattle, 2 million chickens, 10,000 pigs, and 95,000 goats. That year, 25 tons of cow milk, 16 tons of meat, and 43 tons of hen eggs were produced.

24FISHING

The total catch in 1992 was 18,875 tons, up from only 9,763 tons in 1983. In 1991, nearly one-third of the catch consisted of skipjack tuna.

25FORESTRY

About 28% of the total land area of Mauritius is classified as forest. Roundwood removals were an estimated 17,000 cu m in 1991, and sawn wood production was about 5,000 cu m.

26MINING

There are few mineral resources in Mauritius. Small amounts of lime, salt, coral sand, and basalt construction stone are produced. Quarrying employed 170 persons in 1991.

27ENERGY AND POWER

The installed capacity of power plants in 1991 totaled 313,000 kw; production increased from 136 million kwh in 1970 to 813 million kwh in 1991, when hydroelectric plants supplied 9% of the total. About half of all primary energy consumed comes from bagasse, or sugarcane waste. Current energy growth is put at 12% per year.

28INDUSTRY

Manufacturing centers on the processing of agricultural products, sugar cane in particular. Each of the 21 large sugar-producing estates has its own factory. The closing of five of these and the remodeling of the others was one part of the recommendations of the Sugar Action Plan. Molasses and rum are among the sugar by-products produced in Mauritius. Local tobacco is made into cigarettes, and four factories are maintained to process tea. Other small industries produce goods for local consumption, such as beer and soft drinks, shoes, metal products, and paints.

Imortant to Mauritius' industrial development is the Export Processing Zone (EPZ) in which imported goods are processed for export. Legislation gives investors in EPZ enterprises tax relief, duty exemption on most imports, unlimited repatriation of capital and profits, and inexpensive electricity. Investors are primarily from Mauritius itself (60%) and Hong Kong (25%). The textile industry is the leading sector in the EPZ, generating 80% of exports. Other important industries include electronics, precision engineering, and skilled crafts. EPZ companies also produce toys, nails, razor blades, tires, and audio cassettes.

Since 1986, EPZ export earnings have led those of the sugar sector. These earnings are, however, in decline, as some industries relocate for tax reasons and others face a shortage of skilled labor. The labor problem has stimulated the emergence of suppliers of capital-intensive technologies and the establishment of advanced training and education programs.

29SCIENCE AND TECHNOLOGY

In 1989, 193 scientists and engineers and 172 technicians were engaged in research and experimental development, with expenditures totaling R104 million. The Mauritius Institute in Port Louis is a research center for the study of local fauna and flora. The French Ministry of Agriculture maintains a research office of pedology on the main island, which is also the home of the Mauritius Sugar Industry Research Institute. The University of Mauritius has schools of agriculture, engineering, and science. The Regional Sugarcane Training Center for Africa, located in Réduit, is sponsored by the United Nations Development Program.

30DOMESTIC TRADE

Port Louis is the commercial center and the chief port. Business hours are from 9 AM to 4 PM, Monday–Friday, and 9 AM to 1 PM on Saturday. Banks are open from 10 AM to 2 PM, Monday–Friday, and 9:30 to 11:30 AM on Saturday.

31FOREIGN TRADE

Mauritius suffers from a long-standing—and worsening—negative trade balance. Principal exports in 1992 (in millions of rupees) were as follows:

Export Processing Zone products	13,081
Sugar	5,668
Tea	95
Molasses	91
Other exports and reexports	578
TOTAL	19,513

Principal imports in 1992 (in millions of rupees) were as follows:

Petroleum products	1,766
Textile yarn and thread	1,825
Textile fabrics	3,174
Industrial machinery	1,770
Road motor vehicles	1,310
Other	12,548
TOTAL	25,313

In 1992, 34.8% of exports went to the United Kingdom, 21.0% to France, 12.5% to the United States, and 8.9% to Germany. The main sources of imports were France (13.3%), South Africa (12.9%), Japan (8.6%), and the United Kingdom (7.2%).

32BALANCE OF PAYMENTS

After a protracted period of deficits throughout the 1970s and first half of the 1980s, the current account shifted into surplus, equivalent to 1% of GDP in 1985/86. The surplus reached an apex of 7.3% of GDP in 1986/87, owing to an exceptionally high level of sugar exports and the rapid growth of products from the Export Processing Zone. More recently, however, the current account weakened to a deficit in 1989–1991, reflecting the consumption and investment booms. The deficit ws reduced to 0.4% of GDP in 1991/92 and was expected to have reached 0.7% in 1992/93. The overall balance of payments surplus which emerged in 1984/85 reached its zenith of $175 million in 1986/87, and remained high thereafter in spite of the deterioration of the current account. These repetitive surpluses were chiefly due to large capital infloiws, especially foreign direct investment and local investors' borrowing from abroad.

In 1992 merchandise exports totaled $1,291.5 million and imports $1,475.6 million. The merchandise trade balance was $–184.1 million. The following table summarizes Mauritius' balance of payments for 1991 and 1992 (in millions of US dollars):

	1991	1992
CURRENT ACCOUNT		
Goods, services, and income	–118.3	–102.0
Unrequited transfers	81.3	88.5
TOTALS	–37.0	–13.5
CAPITAL ACCOUNT		
Direct investment	8.1	–28.6
Portfolio investment	–0.4	—
Other long-term capital	70.6	–4.0
Other short-term capital	–39.8	.3
Reserves	–190.8	–43.3
TOTALS	–152.3	–75.6
Errors and omissions	189.3	89.1
Total change in reserves	–177.9	73.0

33BANKING AND SECURITIES

The Bank of Mauritius, the central bank, had total assets of R19,148 million on 30 June 1992. The Development Bank of Mauritius was established in March 1964 to provide loans for agricultural and industrial enterprises. The 13 commercial banks operating in the country had foreign assets of R14,194 million in 1993. There were seven offshore banking units operating in Mauritius in 1991. The country has a security exchange, the Stock Exchange of Mauritius, which listed 22 companies with a market capitalization of US$377 million in 1992.

34INSURANCE

In 1986 there were 13 domestic insurance companies.

35PUBLIC FINANCE

From the mid-1970s to 1981, the ratio of fiscal deficit to GDP increased from under 10% to 14%, due to deficit public spending. During the 1980s, an export-oriented economy caused the fiscal deficit to decline to 3% of GDP by 1989, and to 2% by 1991. The following table shows actual revenues and expenditures for 1992 and 1993 in millions of rupees.

	1992	1993
REVENUE AND GRANTS		
Tax revenue	9.957.1	10,812.4
Non-tax revenue	1,420.9	1,473.0
Grants	25.2	75.0
TOTAL	11,403.2	12,360.4
EXPENDITURES & LENDING MINUS REPAYMENTS		
General public services	1,226.1	1,346.7
Defense	175.6	196.8
Public order and safety	872.9	1,076.7
Education	1,684.0	1,821.9
Health	930.9	1,090.6
Social security and welfare	1,764.7	1,937.1
Housing and community amenities	480.4	790.9
Recreation, cultural, and religious affairs	335.3	194.3
Economic affairs and services	1,915.9	2,096.7
Other expenditures	2,131.9	1,813.1
Lending minus repayments	244.0	27.0
TOTAL	11,761.6	12,391.8
Deficit/Surplus	–358.4	–31.4

In 1992 Mauritius' total public debt stood at R16,035.5 million, of which R5,475.6 million was financed abroad.

36TAXATION

Income tax for individuals is levied on a progressive scale, ranging from 5% to 30% in 1992/93. Companies are taxed 35% of chargeable income, except for offshore firms or those in a free port zone, which pay no income tax. In addition, mutual funds, unit trusts, and certain other types of companies pay a reduced rate of 15%. A general sales tax averaging 5% was imposed in 1983. There are also local income taxes, a capital gains tax on certain landowners, and a land development tax.

37CUSTOMS AND DUTIES

A 17% c.i.f. value import duty is charged, as well as a 5–6% sales tax. Alcoholic beverages and cigarettes are subject to special import taxes.

38FOREIGN INVESTMENT

The government offers a variety of investment incentives, including, for industries in the Export Processing Zone, a corporate tax exemption of at least 10 years, an exemption from import duties on capital goods and most raw materials, free repatriation of profits, dividends, and invested capital, and a waiver of income taxes on dividends for 10 years. Foremost among foreign investors are those from Hong Kong, followed by French, South African, German, and Indian interests.

[39]ECONOMIC DEVELOPMENT

Mauritius had ambitious development plans (1988–90) which called for investments in agriculture (14.1%), telecommunications (11.6%), roads and general infrastructure (16.5%), and housing, water and the environment (14.6%). France has backed training for labor, a new stock exchange, and irrigation projects, while the EC is supporting efforts at diversifying agriculture. Mauritius' plan to become an international financial center advanced as liberalized currency rules were put into effect in 1986 and licenses granted.

[40]SOCIAL DEVELOPMENT

Under a family allowance program, 18,972 beneficiaries received a total of R12.5 million in 1984/85, when government retirement pensions totaling R176.78 million were paid to 82,064 persons. The government heavily subsidizes the prices of rice and wheat flour. Free medical care is generally available. A government-backed family planning program helped reduce the annual population growth rate from 3.5% in 1950 to 1% in 1985.

[41]HEALTH

In 1985, Mauritius had 7 general hospitals, 4 special hospitals, and 2 private hospitals. There were also 56 government dispensaries, 29 dispensaries on sugar estates, and 74 maternity, child health, and family planning centers. In 1990, there were 900 doctors (1 physician per 1,180 people); in 1989, there were 107 pharmacists, 134 dentists, and 2,673 nurses.

The average life expectancy in Mauritius in 1992 was 70 years, and the infant mortality rate was 20 per 1,000 live births. The general mortality rate in 1993 was 6.5 per 1,000 people, and the maternal mortality rate was 99 per 100,000 live births. In 1993 Mauritius had a birth rate of 18.1 per 1,000 people with 75% of married women (ages 15 to 49) using contraception.

In 1991, 96% of the population of Mauritius had access to safe water, and 94% had adequate sanitation, while 100% had access to health care services in 1992. However, in 1990, about 24% of children under 5 years old were considered malnourished, and there were an estimated 220 cases of tuberculosis per 100,000. Immunization rates for 1992 for children up to one year old were: tuberculosis (87%); diphtheria, pertussis, and tetanus (91%); and measles (87%).

[42]HOUSING

There are three basic types of houses: wattle and daub construction with thatched roofs; galvanized sheet-iron structures; and houses constructed of wood. As of 1983, 70% of all housing units were detached, 15% were semi-detached, and 14% were subdivided.

[43]EDUCATION

Education is free up to college level and is not compulsory between the ages of 5 and 12. The estimated adult literacy rate in 1990 was 77.9% (85.2% for males and 74.7% for females). In 1991, an estimated 290 primary schools had 135,233 pupils and 6,369 teachers, and about 125 secondary (general) schools had 78,110 pupils. Postsecondary institutions include the University of Mauritius, the Mauritius College of the Air, and the Mahatma Gandhi Institute. In 1990, universities and other equivalent institutions had 1,658 pupils and 274 teaching staff.

[44]LIBRARIES AND MUSEUMS

Government libraries include the Mauritius Institute Public Library (60,000 volumes), the Mauritius Archives, the University of Mauritius Library (93,000), and the Port Louis City Library (100,000). The 26 school libraries contained over 161,000 volumes in 1990. The Sugar Industry Research Institute Library maintains a unique collection of 26,000 volumes on all aspects of sugar cane cultivation and manufacture. The Mauritius Institute operates the Natural History Museum in Port Louis. The Historical Museum is in Mahébourg.

[45]MEDIA

All parts of the island are linked by telegraph, telephone, and postal services; in 1991 there were 74,118 telephones in use. The state-owned Mauritius Broadcasting Corp. provides radio and television service in French, English, Hindi, and Chinese; there were 390,000 radios and 236,000 television sets in 1991. Leading daily newspapers (with 1991 circulations) include *L'Express* (30,000), *Le Mauricien* (30,000), and *The New Nation* (9,000), each published in Port Louis in both French and English.

[46]ORGANIZATIONS

There are various commercial and scholarly organizations of the Western type, including the Mauritius Chamber of Commerce and Industry; the Indian Traders' Association; the Mauritius Employers' Federation; The Mauritius Cooperative Agricultural Federation (which had 209 member societies in 1993); and the Mauritius Cooperative Union.

[47]TOURISM, TRAVEL, AND RECREATION

The government has made efforts to promote upscale tourism and attract visitors from more countries. Tourism constitutes the country's third-largest earner of foreign exchange after sugar and apparel. In 1992, 330,880 tourists visited Mauritius, 19% from France, 8% from Germany, 7% from the UK, and 45% from other African nations, led by South Africa. There were 5,064 hotel rooms with 10,482 beds and a 66% occupancy rate, and tourist receipts totaled US$264 million. Total employment in the tourist industry went up from 10,000 at the end of March 1991 to 11,252 at the end of March 1992.

In addition to the nation's beaches, lagoons, and other scenic sites, tourist attractions include the colonial architecture of Port Louis, an extinct volcano in Curepipe, the fishing port and naval museum at Mahebourg, and the Botanical Gardens at Pamplemousses.

No visas are required for nationals of many European countries and the US, provided a return or onward ticket can be produced on arrival.

[48]FAMOUS MAURITIANS

Sir Seewoosagur Ramgoolam (1900–85), the first leader of independent Mauritius, was prime minister from 1968 to 1982, when Aneerood Jugnauth (b.1930) succeeded him.

[49]DEPENDENCIES

Dependencies are the Agalega Islands and the St. Brandon Group.

[50]BIBLIOGRAPHY

Bennett, Pramila Ramgulam. *Mauritius Collaboration of George John Bennett*. Santa Barbara, Calif.: Clio Press, 1992.

Bowman, Larry W. *Mauritius: Democracy and Development in the Indian Ocean*. Boulder, Colo.: Westview Press, 1991.

Mauritius: Expanding Horizons. Washington, D.C.: World Bank, 1992.

Ramdin, T. *Mauritius: A Geographical Survey*. New York: International Publications Service, 1969.

Selvon, Sydney. *Historical Dictionary of Mauritius*. 2d ed. Metuchen, N.J.: Scarecrow Press, 1991.

Simmons, Adele S. *Modern Mauritius: The Politics of Decolonization*. Bloomington: Indiana University Press, 1982.

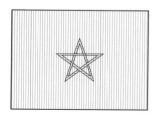

MOROCCO*

Kingdom of Morocco
Al-Mamlakah al-Maghribiyah

CAPITAL: Rabat.

FLAG: The national flag consists of a green five-pointed star at the center of a red field.

ANTHEM: The *Hymne Chérifien* is a 20th-century composition without words.

MONETARY UNIT: The dirham (DH) is a paper currency of 100 Moroccan centimes. There are coins of 1, 5, 10, and 20 Moroccan centimes and ½, 1, and 5 dirhams, and notes of 5, 10, 50, 100, and 200 dirhams. DH1 = $0.1064 (or $1 = DH9.396).

WEIGHTS AND MEASURES: The metric system is the legal standard.

HOLIDAYS: New Year's Day, 1 January; Anniversary of the King's Accession, 3 March; Labor Day, 1 May; National Day, 14 August; Anniversary of the Green March, 6 November; Independence Day, 18 November. Movable religious holidays include 'Id al-Fitr, 'Id al-Adha', 1st of Muharram (Muslim New Year), and Milad an-Nabi.

TIME: GMT.

1 LOCATION, SIZE, AND EXTENT

Situated at the northwestern corner of Africa, with its northern-most point only 29 km (18 mi) south of Gibraltar, Morocco claims a total area of 446,550 sq km (172,414 sq mi), of which the Western Sahara comprises 252,120 sq km (97,344 sq mi). The Western Sahara is claimed and administered by Morocco, but as of late 1994, sovereignty is unresolved. Comparatively, the area occupied by Morocco is slightly larger than the state of California. Morocco extends 1,809 km (1,124 mi) NE–SW and 525 km (326 mi) SE–NW. Morocco proper is bordered on the N by the Mediterranean Sea and the two Spanish enclaves of Ceuta and Melilla, on the E and SE by Algeria, on the S by Western Sahara, and on the W by the Atlantic Ocean, with a total boundary length of 3,837 km (2,384 mi).

Morocco's capital city, Rabat, is located on the Atlantic coast.

2 TOPOGRAPHY

Morocco proper is divided into three natural regions: (1) the fertile northern coastal plain along the Mediterranean, which also contains Er Rif, mountains varying in elevation up to about 2,400 m (8,000 ft); (2) the rich plateaus and lowlands lying between the three parallel ranges of the rugged Atlas Mountains, which extend from the Atlantic coast in the southwest to Algeria and the Mediterranean in the northeast; and (3) the semiarid area in southern and eastern Morocco, which merges into the Sahara Desert. The Atlas Mountains, with an average elevation of 3,350 m (11,000 ft), contain some of the highest peaks of North Africa, including Mt. Toubkal (4,165 m/13,665 ft), the highest of all. South of the Atlas are the Anti-Atlas Mountains, with volcanic Mt. Siroua (3,300 m/10,800 ft). The Western Sahara is rocky, sandy, and sparsely populated, unsuited for agriculture but rich in phosphate deposits.

Morocco has the most extensive river system in North Africa. Moroccan rivers generally flow northwestward to the Atlantic or southeastward toward the Sahara; the Moulouya (Muluya), an exception, flows 560 km (350 mi) northeastward from the Atlas to the Mediterranean. Principal rivers with outlets in the Atlantic are the Oumer, Rebia, Sebou (Sebu), Bou Regreg. Tensift, Draa, and Sous (Sus). The Ziz (Zis) and Rheris are the main rivers flowing southward into the Sahara.

3 CLIMATE

The rugged mountain ranges and the Atlantic Ocean moderate the tropical heat of Morocco. Temperatures in Casablanca range from an average minimum of 7°C (45°F) to a maximum of 17°C (63°F) in January and from a minimum of 18°C (64°F) to a maximum of 26°C (79°F) in July. Temperature variations are relatively small along the Atlantic coast, while the interior is characterized by extreme variations. The eastern slopes of the Atlas Mountains, which divert the moisture-laden Atlantic winds, have a rigorous pre-Saharan climate, while the western slopes are relatively cool and well watered. The rainy seasons are from October to November and from April to May. Maximum annual rainfall (75–100 cm/30–40 in) occurs in the northwest. Other parts of the country receive much less; half of all arable land receives no more than 35 cm (14 in) a year.

4 FLORA AND FAUNA

Extensive stands of cork oak exist in the Atlantic coastal region, while rich evergreen oak, cedar, and pine forests are found on the slopes of the Atlas. In the steppe region, shrubs, jujube trees, and the mastic abound, and along the wadis there are poplars, willows, and tamarisks. The olive tree is widely distributed, but the oil-yielding argan tree, unique to Morocco, grows only in the Sous Valley. The desert is void of vegetation except for occasional oases. Although the lion has disappeared, panthers, jackals, foxes, and gazelles are numerous. The surrounding waters abound in sardines, anchovies, and tuna.

5 ENVIRONMENT

Morocco's growing population has resulted in agricultural and pastoral expansion into forested and marginal areas. Livestock overgrazing, clearing of forests for fuel, and poor soil conservation

---

*All data includes Western Sahara unless otherwise noted.

practices have led to soil erosion and desertification. Pollution of Morocco's water and land resources is due to the dumping of 100,000 tons of industrial wastes into the ocean, 68,000 tons into the country's inland water sources and 58,000 tons into the soil. The nation has about 7.2 cubic miles of water. Ninety-one percent is used in farming and 3% for industrial activity. One hundred percent of the nation's cities have pure water. Eighty-two percent of the rural dwellers do not. Morocco's cities produce 2.4 million tons of solid waste per year. The nation's environment is further challenged by pesticides, insect infestation, and accidental oil spills. Destruction of wildlife has occurred on a large scale, despite strict laws regulating hunting and fishing. Moreover, the drainage of coastal marshlands to irrigate cultivated land has significantly reduced the numbers of crested coots, purple herons, and marbled and white-headed ducks. In 1994, the elimination of living areas for Morocco's wildlife threatens 9 of the nation's mammal species and 14 bird species. One-hundred and ninety-four plant species are also endangered. Endangered species in Morocco as of 1983 included the Barbary hyena, Barbary leopard, waldrapp, Spanish imperial eagle, Mediterranean monk seal, and Cuvier's gazelle. The Ministry of Housing Development and Environment considers environmental impact as an integral part of its development strategy.

6POPULATION

The population of Morocco in 1994 was estimated at 27,881,024. The UN projection for the year 2000 was 31,719,000, assuming a crude birthrate of 30.2 per 1,000 population, a crude death rate of 7.1, and a net natural increase of 23.1 during 1995–2000. For 1990–95, the annual population growth rate was 2.4%. The population density is highest in the plains and coastal areas of northwestern Morocco; the overall density in 1994 was 39 per sq km (102 per sq mi), including the sparsely populated Western Sahara. As of 1990, greater Casablanca had a population of about 3,210,000; greater Rabat, the capital (including Salé), had a population of 1,472,000. Other major cities (including suburbs) with 1990 estimates are Marrakech, 1,517,000; Fès (Fez), 1,012,000; Meknès, 750,000; Tangier, 554,000; Oujda, 962,000; Tétouan, 856,000; Safi, 845,000; and Kénitra, 905,000. The Western Sahara had an estimated population of 212,633 in 1994.

7MIGRATION

The Moroccan government encourages emigration because of the benefit to the balance of payments of remittances from about 1.7 Moroccans living and working abroad. Remittances came to 6.5% of GDP and 44% of exports in 1989. In 1990, 584,700 Moroccans lived in France, 141,600 in Belgium, 67,500 in Germany, 156,900 in the Netherlands, and 50,000 in Spain. There is some seasonal migration within Morocco, as workers move into cities and towns after planting and harvesting are finished. Over 200,000 people migrate permanently to the cities each year; the urban share of the total population increased from 29% to 48% between 1960 and 1994. The war in Western Sahara has been a cause of significant migration, both of settlers from Morocco proper and of refugees to Algeria, (165,000 of the latter at the end of 1992).

8ETHNIC GROUPS

Berbers, who comprise about 34% of the population, are concentrated largely in the northern regions of the Rif, the middle plains of the Atlas, and the Sous Valley. Arabs, who constitute nearly 66% of the population, are distributed principally along the Atlantic coastal plain and in the cities. The Berbers and Arabs are closely intermingled, and bilingualism is common. Formerly the Jewish community played a significant role in the economic life of the country, but its numbers decreased from about 227,000 in

1948 to an estimated 10,000 in 1989. In 1992, some 60,000 foreign citizens, mostly French, Spanish, Italian, and Algerian nationals, were living in Morocco.

9LANGUAGES

Although classical Arabic is the written and official language, Maghribi Arabic, a dialect peculiar to Morocco, is widely spoken; it can hardly be understood by Arabs of the Middle East. Berber dialects, principally Rifi, Tamazight, and Tashilhit, are spoken in more remote mountainous areas by less than one-third of the populace. French and Spanish also are used.

10RELIGIONS

More than 98% of Moroccans are Sunni Muslims of the Malerte school. The activity of other sects (chiefly Sufi) has diminished since independence. Islam was officially declared the state religion in 1961, but full religious freedom is accorded Christians and Jews. In 1993 there were about 69,000 Christians, of whom 28,000 were Roman Catholics. Tangier and Casablanca have small Protestant communities. There is also a diminishing Jewish minority.

11TRANSPORTATION

The road network in 1991 comprised 27,740 km (17,238 mi) of paved roads suitable for year-round traffic and 31,458 km (19,548 mi) of dry-season tracks. There were 811,896 passenger cars and 291,973 commercial vehicles in use in 1992.

The railroad system is administered by the National Railroad Office and consists of 1,893 km (1,176 mi) of standard-gauge railways, of which about 51% is electrified; diesel-operated trains are used on the remainder. The main lines run from Marrakech to Casablanca, Rabat, and Sidi Kacem and then branch north to Tangier and east to Meknès, Fès, and Oujda (on the Algerian border).

About 33.6 million tons of goods were handled by Moroccan ports in 1985. Casablanca is by far the most important port, accounting for more than 55% of goods loaded and unloaded. Tangier is the principal passenger and tourist port; Mohammedia handles most oil imports and can accommodate 100,000-ton tankers. There are also regional ports at Safi, Agadir, and Nador, as well as 10 minor ports. The Moroccan Navigation Co. (Compagnie Marocaine de Navigation—COMANAV), the largest shipping company, is 96% government owned; 49 merchant ships had combined gross tonnage of 316,000 at the end of 1991.

Morocco has eight international airports, at Casablanca, Rabat, Tangier, Marrakech, Agadir, Fès, Oujda, and Al-Hoceima. The government-controlled Royal Air Maroc was founded in 1953 and operates flights to the US, Latin America, Europe, Africa, and the Middle East; the airline also provides domestic service through a subsidiary, Royal Air Inter. In 1992, Morocco performed 3,273 million passenger-km and 70 million freight ton-km of air service.

12HISTORY

The Berbers, the earliest known inhabitants of Morocco, suffered successive waves of invaders in ancient times: the Phoenicians, Carthaginians, Romans (1st century BC), Vandals (5th century AD), and finally the Byzantines (6th century). In 682, when the Arabs swept through North Africa, Okba (Uqba ibn-Nefi) conquered Morocco. Under successive Moorish dynasties, beginning with Idris I (Idris bin 'Abdallah) in 788, the Berber tribes were united and the Islamic faith and Arabic language adopted. The Idrisid dynasty, an offshoot of the Umayyad dynasty, with its capital at Fès (founded in 800), lasted until 974, when it was overthrown by the Berbers. Rising in the Sahara in the early 11th century, the powerful Muslim sect of the Almoravids extended its conquests over North Africa and ultimately into Spain. 'Abdallah bin Yasin,

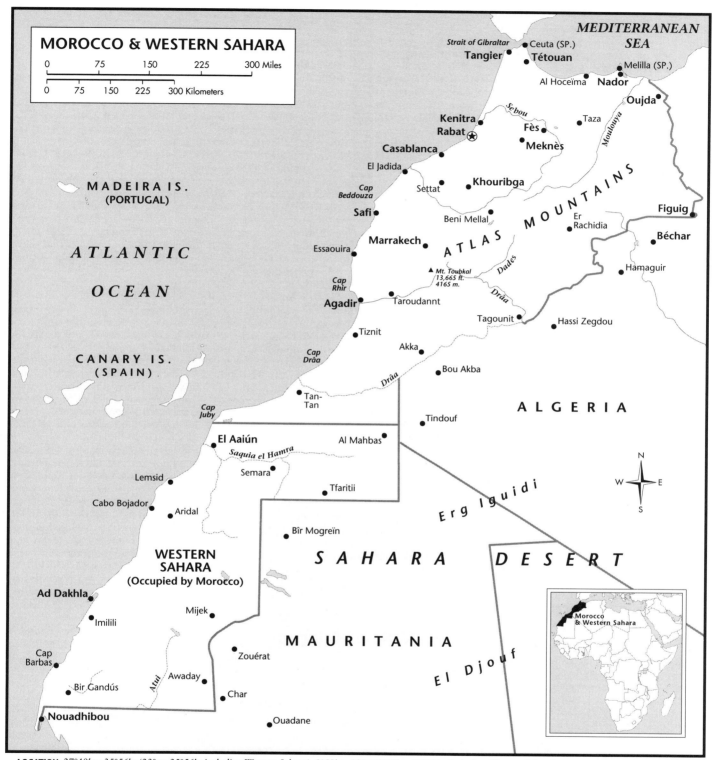

MOROCCO & WESTERN SAHARA

0   75   150   225   300 Miles

0   75   150   225   300 Kilometers

MADEIRA IS.
(PORTUGAL)

ATLANTIC

OCEAN

CANARY IS.
(SPAIN)

MEDITERRANEAN
SEA

Strait of Gibraltar
Tangier   Ceuta (SP.)
Tétouan
Melilla (SP.)
Al Hoceïma   Nador
Oujda
Kenitra   Sebou   Taza
Rabat
Casablanca   Fès
Meknès
El Jadida
Cap   Settat   Khouribga
Beddouza
Safi   Beni Mellal   Er
Rachidia   Figuig
Marrakech   ATLAS MOUNTAINS   Béchar
Essaouira
Mt. Toubkal   Dadès   Hamaguir
Cap   13,665 ft.
Rhir   4165 m.   Drâa
Agadir   Taroudannt
Tagounit   Hassi Zegdou
Tiznit
Akka
Cap   Bou Akba
Drâa   Drâa
Tan-   Tindouf   ALGERIA
Tan
Cap   El Aaiún   Al Mahbas
Juby   Saquia el Hamra
Lemsid   Semara   Erg Iguidi
Cabo Bojador   Tfaritii
Aridal
WESTERN   Bîr Mogreïn   SAHARA DESERT
SAHARA
(Occupied by Morocco)
Ad Dakhla   Mijek
Imilili   MAURITANIA
Cap   Zouérat
Barbas   Atui   Awaday
Bir Gandús   Char   El Djouf
Nouadhibou   Ouadane

Morocco
& Western Sahara

LOCATION: 27°40′ to 35°56′N (23° to 35°56′N including Western Sahara); 0°58′ to 13°W (0°58′ to 16°21′W including Western Sahara). **BOUNDARY LENGTHS:** (excluding Western Sahara): total coastline, 1,835 km (1,140 mi); Algeria, 1,637 km (1,017 mi); Western Sahara, 443 km (275 mi). **TERRITORIAL SEA LIMIT:** 12 mi.

its chief, was proclaimed ruler over Morocco in 1055. In 1147, the Almohad sect (Al-Muwahhidun), led by 'Abd al-Mumin bin 'Ali, conquered the Almoravids and ruled Morocco until 1269, when the Marinid (Beni Marin) dynasty came to power.

In the 16th century, the Sa'adi dynasty, the new monarchical line, began. Ahmad al-Mansur (called Ad-Dahabi, "the Golden"),

the greatest of the Sa'adi kings, ruled from 1578 to 1603 and inaugurated the golden age of Moroccan history. He protected Morocco from Turkish invasion, strengthened the country's defenses, reorganized the army, and adorned his magnificent capital at Marrakech with the vast booty captured in Timbuktu (1591). The decadence of the last Sa'adi kings brought Morocco under the control of the Filali dynasty, of mixed Arab and Berber descent, which continued to modern times.

Trade with France and other European countries became increasingly important in the 18th and 19th centuries, and when the French in 1844 defeated the combined Moroccan and Algerian forces at Isly, France became the ascendant power. Spain, under an agreement with France, invaded and occupied northern Morocco in 1860. There followed some 45 years of trade rivalry among the European nations in Morocco. The Act of Algeciras, signed on 7 April 1906 by representatives of the US, Germany, the UK, France, and Spain (among others), established the principle of commercial equality in Morocco and provided for a joint Spanish-French police force in Moroccan ports.

On 30 March 1912, after France had ceded some 260,000 sq km (100,000 sq mi) of the French Congo to Germany, the French imposed a protectorate in Morocco under Marshal Louis Lyautey. The Moroccans, led by 'Abd al-Karim, a guerrilla leader, fought for independence in the Rif War (1921–26) but were defeated by the combined French and Spanish forces, although sporadic fighting continued in Morocco until 1934.

A nationalist movement first took shape around the Plan of Reforms (1934) submitted to the French government by a group of young Moroccans. In 1934, the National Action Bloc was formed, and 'Alal al-Fasi became the uncontested nationalist leader. In December 1943, the Bloc was revived as the Istiqlal (Independence) Party which during and after World War II pressed for independence and reforms. It received support from the Sultan, Sidi Muhammad bin Yusuf, later King Muhammad V, who became the symbol of the independence struggle. He was exiled in late 1953, and two years of terrorism ensued. After lengthy negotiations, the Franco-Moroccan agreement of 2 March 1956 granted independence, and Muhammad V became king of Morocco. Incorporated into the new nation was Tangier, once British territory, which had come under the rule of a consortium of powers in 1906 and since 1923 had been the center of an international zone.

After the death of Muhammad V on 26 February 1961, his son was crowned King Hassan II and became head of government. Hassan II increased his political power throughout the 1960s. In 1962, a constitutional monarchy was established, with the king retaining extensive powers. In June 1965, after student riots and other disorders, Hassan II declared a state of emergency and assumed all legislative and executive powers. A revised constitution promulgated in 1970 and approved by popular referendum gave the king broad personal power but reestablished parliament and ended the state of emergency. An attempted coup d'etat by right-wing army officers in July 1971 forced the king to accept, at least in principle, the need for a more broadly based government. A third constitution, approved by referendum on 1 March 1972, transferred many of the king's executive and legislative powers to a parliament which was to have two-thirds of its members directly elected. However, a second coup attempt in August 1972 caused the king to renew the emergency decrees.

In 1975, after Spain announced its intention of withdrawing from sparsely populated, but phosphate-rich Spanish Sahara (now the Western Sahara), the king pressed Morocco's claim to most of the territory. Following the government's well-organized "Green March" of about 350,000 Moroccans into the territory in November, Spain ceded the northern two-thirds of the region to Morocco and the southern third to Mauritania. However, Algeria refused to recognize the annexation and supported the claim to the territory by guerrillas of the Popular Front for the Liberation of Saguia al-Hamra and Río de Oro, better known as Polisario; the movement, based in the Algerian border town of Tindouf, proclaimed Western Sahara as the Saharan Arab Democratic Republic (SADR). In 1979, Mauritania renounced its claim to the southern part of the territory, which Morocco then occupied and

annexed. By the early 1980s, Morocco had moved up to 100,000 soldiers into Western Sahara in a costly effort to put down the Polisario revolt. The army built a wall of earth and sand around the productive northwestern coastal region, containing about 20% of the total area, the towns of El Aaiún and Samara, and phosphate mines; later, three-quarters of the Western Sahara was enclosed. In the meantime, Polisario received not only military support, mainly from Algeria and Libya, but also diplomatic support from some 50 countries and from the OAU, which in 1982 seated a delegation from the SADR, provoking a walkout by Morocco and more than a dozen other members. In 1984, Morocco resigned from the OAU when it seated the SADR at its annual summit meeting. Earlier, in 1981, the King's agreement under African pressure for a referendum in the territory provoked strong criticism from Morocco's Socialist Party.

In 1988, UN Secretary General Perez de Cuellar persuaded Moroccan and Polisario representatives to accept a peace plan which included a cease-fire (effective in September 1991) and a referendum for the territory on independence or integration with Morocco. The vote was scheduled for 1992, but has been blocked by disagreement by the two sides on details, especially over voter eligibility.

On 13 August 1984, Morocco and Libya signed a treaty calling for a federation of the two countries. No concrete steps were taken, and Hassan II abrogated the pact following Libyan denunciation of the king for officially receiving Israeli Premier Shimon Peres in July 1986. Israeli Prime Minister Rabin made a public visit in 1993 as the King continued to play a moderate role in the search for an Arab-Israel settlement. In 1989, after a border agreement and restored relations with Algeria, Morocco promoted the formation of the Arab Maghreb Union of the states of North Africa. King Hassan's government maintains close relations with Sa'udi Arabia and the other Gulf states and was the first Arab nation to condemn the Iraqi invasion of Kuwait.

Austerity measures demanded by the IMF in return for new credits led to serious street riots in June 1984 in protest against an imminent price hike (subsequently canceled) for basic foodstuffs. In 1993, after pro-government parties won most local elections the previous year, parliamentary elections were held. The two largest opposition parties, the Istiqlal and USFP, won over 40% of the vote, but center-right parties of the ruling coalition gained a slim majority in the vote's second stage amid charges of election fraud. When the opposition refused to join in a new coalition, a cabinet of technocrats and independents was approved by the King under Prime Mohamed Karim Lamrani, who promised to accelerate the privatization of state-owned enterprises.

13 GOVERNMENT

The Moroccan crown is hereditary and is passed on to the oldest male descendant in direct line or to the closest collateral male relative. The king, claiming descent from the Prophet Mohammad, is commander of the faithful and the symbol of national unity. He makes all civil and military appointments and signs and ratifies treaties. He can dismiss the parliament (if in session) and bypass elected institutions by submitting a referendum to the people on any major issue or whenever parliament rejects a bill he favors. He presides over the cabinet, and if the integrity of the national territory is threatened or events liable to jeopardize the functioning of Morocco's national institutions occur, he may declare a state of emergency.

The constitution of 1992, approved by referendum, provides for a modified constitutional monarchy with a prime minister with increased authority appointed by the king. The document also expanded the limited powers of the Chamber of Representatives to include budget questions, votes on bills presented by the king, and investigative authority. The parliament's 333 members are elected to six-year terms. Two-thirds of the members are elected directly, and the remainder are chosen by electoral colleges representing provincial and prefectural assemblies and community, business, and labor groups. Suffrage is universal at age 20.

14 POLITICAL PARTIES

Morocco has a well-developed multiparty system with 16 official recognized parties and remarkably stable and long-lived leadership. The largest traditional party is the Istiqlal (Independence) Party, whose leader after its formation in 1943 was 'Alal al-Fasi. The Istiqlal, once a firm supporter of the throne, now follows a reformist program and backs the king on specific measures only; it had no representation in the government from 1963 to 1977.

The National Union of Popular Forces (Union Nationale des Forces Populaires—UNFP) was formed in September 1959, following a split in the ranks of the Istiqlal in January of that year. At that time, the UNFP was a coalition of left-wing ex-Istiqlalis, trade unionists, resistance fighters, and dissident members of minor political parties and drew support from the modern cities (Casablanca) and the Sous River Valley. Among its leaders were Mehdi bin Barka; Muhammad al-Basri, a leader of the Liberation Army in 1953–55; 'Abderrahim Bouabid; and Mahjub bin Sadiq, head of the Moroccan Labor Union (Union Marocaine du Travail—UMT). The party was handicapped by factionalism and further weakened by the political neutrality of the UMT after 1963, by the kidnapping and disappearance of Bin Barka in France in 1965, and by other apparent instances of government repression, including the imprisonment of Bin Sadiq in 1967.

In 1970, the UNFP and Istiqlal, having lost some popular support, formed the National Front to boycott the elections. The Front was dissolved in 1972, by which time the split between the political and trade union wings of the UNFP had become open, and in 1973 many UNFP leaders were arrested and tried for sedition in connection with civil disorders and guerrilla activities. The UNFP formally split into two parties in 1974, the more radical trade union wing calling itself the UNFP and the political wing forming the Socialist Union of Popular Forces (Union Socialiste des Forces Populaires—USFP).

The program of the Moroccan Communist Party has often been close to that of the UNFP. From 1969 to 1974, the Communist Party was banned, but since then it has appeared under various names, the latest being the Party for Progress and Socialism (Parti du Progrès et du Socialisme—PPS).

Other political groupings include the pro-royalist National Rally of Independents (Rassemblement National des Indépendents—RNI), formed in 1977 by Ahmed Osman, former prime minister; the National Democrats (Parti National Démocrate—PND), a splinter group of the RNI established in 1981 by Arsalane el-Jadidi; and the Constitutional Union (Union Constitutionnelle—UC), formed by Prime Minister Maati Bouabid in 1983. Thirteen known Islamic groups are banned.

King Hassan II has sometimes worked through the party system and sometimes ignored it. In 1963, royalist forces united into the Front for the Defense of Constitutional Institutions. A leading party in the Front was the Popular Movement (Mouvement Populaire—MP), the party of Berber mountaineers. Governments formed by Hassan II have consisted of MP members, followers of royalist front parties, and independents and technocrats loyal to the king.

15 LOCAL GOVERNMENT

Local administration still follows many French and Spanish procedural patterns, but final authority rests with the king through the Ministry of the Interior. Morocco proper has 39 provinces and 8 urban prefectures (including 2 at Rabat-Salé and 5 at Casablanca). Each province and prefecture has a governor appointed by the king. The provinces and prefectures select councils or

assemblies which hold public sessions in the spring and fall. The assemblies are largely restricted to social and economic questions.

The provinces are divided into administrative areas, called cercles, each headed by a superqaid (caidat). Each cercle is subdivided into rural and urban communes, each headed by a qaid or a pasha, respectively, and assisted by a council. Councillors are elected for six-year terms, and each council is composed of 9 to 51 members, depending on the size of the commune. The council president, chosen by secret ballot, presents the budget and applies the decisions of the council. Real power, however, is exercised by the qaid or pasha. The communes (859 in 1986) are supervised by the Ministry of the Interior, which retains final decision-making authority.

16 JUDICIAL SYSTEM

Morocco has a dual legal system consisting of secular courts based on French legal tradition and Islamic courts which adjudicate family and inheritance matters for Moroccan Muslims.

The secular system includes courts of first instance, appellate courts, and a Supreme Court. The Supreme Court is divided into five chambers: criminal correctional (civil) appeals, social, administrative, and constitutional. A special court may try officials on charges raised by a two-thirds majority of the full Majlis. The Supreme Council of the Judiciary regulates the judiciary and is presided over by the king. Judges are appointed on the advice of the council. Judges in the secular system are university trained lawyers. Since 1965 only Moroccans may be appointed as judges and Arabic is the official language of the courts.

The Islamic court system consists of only trial level courts from which no appeal is taken. Judges in this system were traditionally clerics with little legal training; more recently appointed judges have been formally educated in Islamic law. Cases are decided on the basis of the Koran and derivative Shari'a.

17 ARMED FORCES

Total Moroccan armed strength in 1993 was 195,000. The army had 75,000 men, the navy 7,000, and the air force 13,500. Military hardware included 284 main battle tanks and 105 light tanks; 1 frigate and 27 patrol and coastal combatant ships and boats; and 90 combat aircraft, including 3 jet squadrons. Paramilitary forces totaled 40,000. Some 60 Moroccan troops were stationed in Equatorial Guinea and 5,000 in the United Arab Emirates. Polisario, the Western Saharan insurgent force, had 10,000 men. The UN has 370 observers in Morocco.

The army is a professional organization with a high rate of reenlistment. In 1966, a royal decree instituted national conscription at age 18 for 18 months service, but there are few conscripts.

The 1992 budget called for defense expenditures of $1.1 billion or 4.2 percent of gross domestic product. During 1981–91, Morocco purchased weapons worth about $2.8 billion from Europe and the US.

18 INTERNATIONAL COOPERATION

Morocco became a UN member on 12 November 1956 and participates in ECA and all the nonregional specialized agencies. The nation is a member of the African Development Bank, G-77, and the League of Arab States and is a signatory to the Law of the Sea. In recent decades, Morocco has pursued a policy of nonalignment and has sought and received aid from the US, Western Europe, and the former USSR. Relations with Algeria and Libya have been tense, especially since Morocco's takeover of the Western Sahara. In 1988, UN Secretary General Perez de Cuellar negotiated with Moroccan and Polisario (a group seeking sovereignty for the Western Sahara as the Saharan Arab Democratic Republic) to accept a cease-fire and to hold a referendum for the territory to determine whether it will be independent of integrate with Morocco. Although the vote was scheduled for 1992, as of late

1994 it has been blocked by disagreements over voter eligibility. Committed to the Arab cause in the Arab-Israeli conflict, Morocco sent troops to Syria in 1973. In 1989, Morocco restored relations with Algeria; it maintains relations with Saudi Arabia and the other Gulf states, and condemned the Iraqi invasion of Kuwait.

19ECONOMY

The major resources of the Moroccan economy are agriculture, phosphates, and tourism. In recent years citrus fruit exports have remained below $200 million. Sales of fish and seafood are increasing rapidly. Industry and mining contribute about one-fourth of the annual GDP. Morocco is the world's third-largest producer of phosphates (after the US and the former USSR), and the price fluctuations of phosphates on the international market greatly influence Morocco's economy. Tourism and workers' remittances have played a critical role since independence.

The high cost of imports, especially of petroleum imports, is a major problem. Another chronic problem is unreliable rainfall, which produces drought or sudden floods; in the early 1980s, the country's worst drought of this century forced Morocco to import much grain and adversely affected the economy. Morocco suffers both from unemployment and from a shortage of managerial and administrative personnel. Since 1983, Morocco has rescheduled payments on its heavy foreign debt, which was about $17 billion in 1987, and increased to $23 billion in 1990. Rescheduling reduced anticipated debt payments in 1987 from $2.9 billion to $1.6 billion and to $1.7 billion in 1990. The IMF extended a 16-month, $280-million standby credit in December 1986; in return, Morocco was expected to cut public spending and reduce the government's role in the economy. In 1989, the Moroccan Parliament approved a privatization law calling for transfer from the public to the private sector before December 1995, of government-held equities in 112 companies. Negotiations with IMF concerning a standby credit to cover calendar year 1992 were underway. The World Bank approved a Structural Adjustment Loan (SAL) in 1988 and discussions on a second SAL are taking place.

20INCOME

In 1992 Morocco's GNP was $27,210 million at current prices, or $1,040 per capita. For the period 1985–92 the average inflation rate was 5.7%, resulting in a real growth rate in per capita GNP of 1.3%.

In 1992 the GDP was $28,401 million in current US dollars. It is estimated that in 1991 agriculture, hunting, forestry, and fishing contributed 19% to GDP; mining and quarrying, 2%; manufacturing, 18%; electricity, gas, and water, 6%; construction, 5%; wholesale and retail trade, 13%; transport, storage, and communication, 6%; finance, insurance, real estate, and business services, 4%; community, social, and personal services, 10%; and other sources 17%.

21LABOR

The employed work force was estimated in 1992 at 7.6 million, of whom 15% were in the agricultural sector, 26% in commerce and services, and 59% in services and other sectors. The unemployment rate in urban areas was estimated at more than 19%.

Moroccan trade unions have been called the most powerful pressure group in the country. The major trade union organization, the Moroccan Federation of Labor (Union Marocaine du Travail—UMT) was organized in 1955. The strongest unions within the UMT include the railroad, public works, mining, and transportation workers. Another major trade union federation, the General Union of Moroccan Workers (Union Générale des Travailleurs du Maroc—UGTM), was founded in 1960. Its main strength is among teachers and port workers. The Democratic

Confederation of Labor (CDT) was founded in 1978 and draws its strength from intellectuals, teachers, and public sector employees desirous of European-style liberal tenets. In December 1990, the CDT and UGTM called for a general strike in a campaign for social reforms and pay and benefit improvements for workers. In Fez, the strike erupted into rioting; army troops opened fire on unarmed civilians resulting in many fatalities. In 1991 there were 364 strikes, resulting in the loss of 381,637 working days.

The 48-hour workweek is established by law, and overtime pay rates apply to all work in excess of 48 hours. At least one day of rest must be granted per week. A minimum wage was established in 1958; as of 1992 the minimum was DH6.60 an hour for industry and commerce and DH34.18 a day in agriculture. Social security, effective since 1961, covers some 15% of the work force. There is also legislation covering health, sanitation, and safety standards for a small number of workers.

22AGRICULTURE

Excluding Western Sahara, 18% of the total area was arable in 1991. The bulk of the indigenous population carries out traditional subsistence farming on plots of less than 5 hectares (12 acres). A temperate climate and sufficient precipitation are especially conducive to agricultural development in the northwest. Morocco is essentially self-sufficient in food production. Recently, an irregularity in rainfall has necessitated the importation of grains. The government distributed some 500,000 hectares (1,235,500 acres) of farmland formerly owned by European settlers to Moroccan farmers in the late 1960s and the 1970s. To encourage Moroccans to modernize the traditional sector, the Agricultural Investment Code of 1969 required farmers in irrigated areas to meet the minimum standards of efficiency outlined by the government or lose their land. These standards applied to all farms of 5 hectares (12 acres) or more.

Dams and irrigation projects were begun under French rule and have continued since independence. In traditional areas, irrigation is by springs and wells, diversion of streams, and tunnels from the hills, as well as by modern dams and reservoirs. There are dams and irrigation projects on most of the country's major rivers, including the Sebou River in the northwest, which, along with its tributaries, accounts for some 45% of Morocco's water resources. Continued widespread variation in rainfall continues to produce serious droughts and occasional flash floods. In January 1994, the Kuwaiti Economic Development Fund agreed to lend $60 million to the Moroccan government to help finance an irrigation project in the Haouz and Tassaout region of southern Morocco, which will provide irrigation services for 200,000 small farmers.

The principal export crops are citrus fruits and vegetables. The following table shows the estimated output of principal crops (in thousands of tons) in 1991 and 1992:

	1991	1992
EXPORT		
Sugar beets	3,036	2,754
Wheat	4,939	1,562
Barley	3,253	1,081
Sugarcane	1,028	994
Potatoes	1,074	900
Tomatoes	806	900
Oranges	1,097	784
Olives	390	500
Corn	335	216
Dates	107	82
Beans, dry	5	5

23ANIMAL HUSBANDRY

Livestock raising contributes about one-third of agricultural income. Livestock fares poorly on the overgrazed pasture, and periods of drought reduce growth on an estimated 20.9 million hectares (51.6 million acres) of permanent pastureland as well as the output of fodder crops. There were some 17 million sheep, 5.5 million goats, 3.3 million cattle, 915,000 donkeys, 33,000 camels, and 42 million chickens in 1992. In that year, production of beef was estimated at 160,000 tons; mutton and lamb, 90,000 tons; goat meat, 18,000 tons; and poultry, 152,000 tons. Output of cow's milk was about 970,000 tons in 1992; output of eggs was 94,700 tons. Even though most of the import licensing system has been abolished, licenses are still required for imported livestock and animal genetic materials, in an effort to protect local production.

24FISHING

Fishing, which has been a major industry since the 1930s, is centered in Agadir, Safi, and Tan-Tan. In some years, Morocco is the world's largest producer of the European sardine (*Sardina pilchardus*). In 1991, the fish catch totaled 592,881 tons, with sardines accounting for 370,649 tons and cuttlefish 17,153. Other seafood included octopuses, 65,072 tons, and anchovies, 19,579 tons. Some 83,000 tons of canned sardines were produced in 1991. Much of the fish catch is processed into fish meal, fertilizer, and animal fodder. The government owns trawler companies jointly with foreigners and has sought to promote the fishing industry, which has a potential estimated at 3 million tons a year. The waters off Western Sahara are particularly rich in seafood.

25FORESTRY

Forests and woodland cover about 12% of the land area and provide subsistence for families engaged in cork gathering, wood cutting, and other forestry occupations. Cork, the principal forest product, is grown on 300,000 hectares (741,000 acres) of state-owned cork oak forests. Production was about 93,000 tons in 1985, virtually all of it exported. Other commercial trees are evergreen oak, thuja, argan, and cedar. Esparto grass and vegetable fiber are other important forest products. Artificial plantings of more than 45,000 hectares (111,000 acres) of eucalyptus trees furnish the raw materials for a rapidly expanding cellulose textile industry. Production of roundwood in 1991 totaled 2.5 million cu m.

Reforestation has become a major goal of the government; the 1981–85 development plan proposed to reforest about 25,000 hectares (62,000 acres) annually; actual reforestation was about 13,000 hectares (32,000 acres) per year.

26MINING

Morocco has about two-thirds of the world's proved reserves of phosphates and is the world's largest phosphate exporter, accounting for about 32% of world trade in that commodity. Reserves of high-grade phosphate rock have been estimated at 22 billion tons. The government owns the subsoil mineral rights for all minerals and exploits the phosphates under a state-owned company. Production of lime phosphate was 17,900,000 tons in 1991. The export value in 1991 of bulk phosphate rock amounted to $343 million, a significant drop from the previous year. The value of phosphates has declined sharply since 1974.

Under the 1981–85 plan, Morocco proposed to expand annual output of phosphate rock to 27 million tons. In addition, an estimated 1.5 billion tons of phosphates discovered at Bu Craa and Izic in the Western Sahara in 1963 were taken over by Morocco in 1976, and Spain sold to Morocco a 65% interest in Fosbucraa, the Saharan phosphate company. Plans called for increased domestic processing of the phosphate into phosphoric acid for export, but financial obstacles continue to impede the project's development.

Morocco also has significant deposits of copper ore. The nation produced an estimated 39,000 tons of copper concentrates in 1991; almost all was exported. Iron ore production decreased from 407,000 tons in 1977 to 97,000 tons in 1991. At Jerada, in the Oujda region, is the only anthracite mine in the Mediterranean area, producing 551,000 tons in 1991. Other minerals and 1991 estimated output include lead (102,000 tons), manganese (59,000 tons), zinc (71,000 tons), barites (433,000 tons), salt (130,000 tons), and fluorspar (75,000 tons).

27ENERGY AND POWER

Morocco is dependent on imported petroleum to satisfy almost 75% of its energy needs; fuel imports accounted for 14.5% of total import value in 1991. Although little oil has been found within Morocco itself, several foreign companies were exploring for oil in the late-1980s, both offshore and in the interior. As of 1991, there were 12 oil wells producing some 900 barrels per day. In 1991, Morocco's production of crude petroleum amounted to 15,500 tons. A large natural gas find at the Essaouira (Mogador) field, announced in January 1982, led the government to make ambitious plans for its exploitation. In 1991, 62 million cu m were produced. Morocco had an estimated 2.1 million barrels of proven oil reserves and 1.2 billion m3 of proven natural gas reserves in 1991.

Electricity production has grown rapidly, from 1,935 million kwh in 1970 to 9,834 million kwh in 1991. The National Electricity Authority controls 85% of Morocco's electricity-producing capacity, which totaled 2,434,000 kw (28% hydro) in 1991. Morocco has many hydroelectric plants and three major thermal generating stations.

28INDUSTRY

The manufacturing sector produces light consumer goods, especially foodstuffs, beverages, textiles, matches, and metal and leather products. Heavy industry is largely limited to petroleum refining, chemical fertilizers, automobile and tractor assembly, foundry work, asphalt, and cement. Many of the processed agricultural products and consumer goods are primarily for local consumption, but Morocco exports canned fish and fruit, wine, leather goods, and textiles, as well as such traditional Moroccan handicrafts as carpets and brass, copper, silver, and wood implements. There are currently thirteen sugar-beet-processing factories and five major sugar refineries. The textile industry employs over one-fourth of the industrial work force and exports 84% of its production.

There are three oil refineries, two at Mohammedia and one at Sidi Kacem, as well as several petrochemical plants, a polyvinyl chloride factory, and four phosphate-processing plants. Three phosphoric acid plants and fertilizer factories were under construction in 1986. There are four plants assembling cars and small utility vehicles: Renault Moroc, Sopriam, Somaca, and Smeia. Nine cement factories reached a total of 4.6 million tons in 1985.

The Safi industrial complex, opened in 1965, processes phosphates from Youssoufia, pyrrhotites from Kettara, and ammonia. The complex has a production capacity of 150,000 tons of ammonium phosphate a year and 200,000 tons of superphosphate. There are about 30 chemical and allied industries, including a paraffin refinery. Output of phosphate fertilizers was 924,000 tons in 1985; phosphoric acid production was about 1,250,000 tons in 1985; and sulfuric acid production was 758,000 tons in 1984. A phosphoric acid treatment plant at Iorf Lasfar, built in 1986, adds 400,000 tons to Morocco's phosphoric acid production capacity. Two planned units, Maroc-Phosphore V and VI, are intended to produce 4.55 million tons of sulphuric acid and 1.32 million tons of phosphoric acid annually.

Ownership in the manufacturing sector is largely private, but the government owns the phosphate-chemical fertilizer industry and much of the sugar-milling capacity, through either partnership or joint financing. It is also a major participant in the car and truck assembly industry and in tire manufacturing.

29SCIENCE AND TECHNOLOGY

Research institutions include the Scientific Institute (founded 1920), in Rabat, which does fundamental research in the natural sciences and the Scientific Institute of Maritime Fishing (founded 1948), in Casablanca, which studies oceanography, marine biology, and topics related to development of the fishing industry. Nine universities and colleges offer degrees in basic and applied sciences.

30DOMESTIC TRADE

Government intervenes directly in domestic trade through regulation of trade and commerce in various agricultural and other items, and through price controls on basic necessities. There are state coordinating agencies for agricultural commodities and fisheries, which fund development projects, seek increases in productivity and sales volume, and maintain price stability.

Casablanca, the chief port, is the commercial center of Morocco. Other principal distribution centers include Safi, Agadir, and Tangier. Retail establishments include department stores in the main cities and shops and specialty stores. Bazaars cater especially to the tourist trade.

Business hours are generally from 9 AM to noon and from 3 to 6 PM, but some shops stay open much later. Banks are open from 8:15 to 11:30 AM and 2:15 to 4:30 PM, Monday–Friday. Principal advertising media are newspapers, motion picture theaters, radio, television, and posters.

31FOREIGN TRADE

Morocco has a chronic trade deficit, which worsened with depressed phosphate prices in the late 1970s and the 1980s. The principal exports in 1985 were phosphates and phosphoric acid, which together constituted 37% of total exports. Next in importance were citrus fruits, clothing, fertilizers, preserved fish, and vegetables. In 1991 agriculture constituted 31% of total exports and phosphorus only 8%. Morocco's major imports are crude petroleum and foodstuffs.

France is by far Morocco's leading trade partner, providing 26% of imports and trading 32% of exports in 1990. Spain took 8.1% of Morocco's exports and supplied 10.2% of imports in 1990. Over 60% of Morocco's merchandise trade is with the EC. Morocco and the EC have begun discussions on an association agreement that may lead to the reduction of trade barriers between the two areas. Trade flows with other Maghieb countries, despite the creation of the Arab Maghieb Union (ATIU), remain negligible.

Exports and imports to Morocco's major trading partners for the period 1988–90 were (% of total):

	1988	1989	1990
EXPORTS TO:			
France	27.2	29.5	32.3
Spain	7.5	8.4	8.1
Germany	5.9	5.3	7.4
Italy	5.9	6.4	6.9
Belgium/Luxembourg	3.9	5.7	4.7
Japan	4.8	4.6	4.6
IMPORTS FROM:			
France	22.5	24.4	26.1
US	7.1	9.1	8.2
Germany	7.2	6.2	7.7
Italy	5.6	6.3	7.0
Iraq	5.0	7.0	3.8

32BALANCE OF PAYMENTS

Remittances from Moroccans working abroad, foreign aid, and a growing tourist trade have helped to offset chronic trade deficits. In recent years, Morocco has turned increasingly to foreign borrowing to meet its financial needs.

In 1992 merchandise exports totaled $3,956 million and imports $6,692 million. The merchandise trade balance was $–2,736 million. The following table summarizes Morocco's balance of payments for 1991 and 1992 (in millions of US dollars):

	1991	1992
CURRENT ACCOUNT		
Goods, services, and income	–2,689	–2,966
Unrequited transfers	2,293	2,539
TOTALS	396	427
CAPITAL ACCOUNT		
Direct investment	320	424
Other long-term capital	1,008	409
Other short-term capital	130	518
Other liabilities	1,167	946
Reserves	–1,167	–946
TOTALS	291	405
Errors and omissions	88	2
Total change in reserves	–1,209	–619

33BANKING AND SECURITIES

The Bank of Morocco (Banque du Maroc), the central bank, has the sole privilege of note issue. It required to maintain a gold or convertible-currency reserve equal to one-ninth of its note issue. The Ministry of Finance is responsible for the organization of banking and the money market. The money supply, as measured by M2, amounted to DH35,548 million as of December 1992.

Exchange control regulations are set and administered by an agency of the Ministry of Finance. Most exports are not licensed. An exporter must repatriate any exchange received, and according to 1971 regulations, foreign exchange brought into Morocco must be declared and exchanged for dirhams at authorized banks. There is no foreign exchange market in Morocco.

There were 18 commercial banks in 1993, all at least 51% Moroccan owned; some foreign banks were Moroccanized in 1975. Public sector financial organizations specializing in development finance include the National Bank for Economic Development, Moroccan Bank for Foreign Trade, National Agricultural Credit Bank, and Deposit and Investment Fund. Also instrumental in development finance is the Bureau of Mineral Exploration and Participation, which has participatory interests in the production of all coal, petroleum, lead, and manganese. The National Bank for Economic Development, established in 1959, has been particularly active in financing manufacturing. The Agricultural Credit Bank makes loans to credit organizations, public institutions, and cooperatives. Private individuals borrow from local agricultural credit banks or from the agricultural credit and provident societies. The stock exchange (Bourse des Valeurs) at Casablanca handles mostly European and a few North African issues.

34INSURANCE

Insurance is regulated by the Ministry of Finance. At the end of 1986 there were 40 insurance companies, 2 life, 17 non-life, and 21 composite. In the same year, 16.5% of all premiums were paid for life and 83.5% for non-life insurance. In 1990, total premiums amounted to $20.1 per capita, or 1.9% of the GDP.

35PUBLIC FINANCE

The budget year coincides with the calendar year. From 1983 to 1991, government expenditures fell from 32% of GDP to 26% of

GDP; the budget deficit (excluding grants) declined from 12% of GDP to 3% of GDP during that same period. By the late 1990s, the budget is expected to be balanced. Following several debt servicing agreements dating back to October 1983, the debt service to exports ratio was less than 28% in 1991.

The following table shows actual revenues and expenditures for 1989 and 1990 in millions of dirhams.

	1989	1990
REVENUES AND GRANTS		
Tax revenue	43,001	48,691
Non-tax revenue	5,711	7,521
Capital revenue	526	423
Grants	—	—
TOTAL	49,238	56,635
EXPENDITURES & LENDING MINUS REPAYMENTS		
General public services	9,375	12,005
Defense	7,193	7,873
Public order and safety	4,229	4,368
Education	10,135	11,161
Health	1,620	1,839
Social security and welfare	3,251	3,317
Housing and community amenities	275	262
Recreation, cultural, and religious affairs	310	347
Economic affairs and services	11,586	9,333
Other expenditures	11,147	10,838
Lending minus repayments	68	53
TOTAL	59,189	61,395
Deficit/Surplus	−9,951	−4,760

In 1990 Morocco's total public debt stood at DH216,905 million, of which DH159,404 million was financed abroad.

36TAXATION

All wage earners are liable to a progressive tax on salaries, remunerations, and allowances; as of 1993, income tax rates ranged from 14% to 48%. Collection and remittance of the tax on salaries, remunerations, and allowances are incumbent on the employer, who deducts them from the payroll. There are also social security taxes and supplementary taxes on professional and rental income.

The professional profits and gains tax, the most important tax in Morocco, can be assessed on annual turnover or on net annual profits. There is a value-added tax at a normal rate of 7–19%, but the tax rates vary according to the nature of the product or service. A national solidarity tax was introduced after the Agadir earthquake in 1960; its revenue was used to rebuild Agadir. In 1966, the solidarity tax was made permanent. In March 1984, King Hassan II announced that Moroccan farmers would be exempt from taxation until the year 2000, in order to help them recover from the effects of the drought of the early 1980s.

37CUSTOMS AND DUTIES

In June 1957, import duties were revised from the 12.5% ad valorem rates imposed by the Act of Algeciras. Under amended schedules, duties ranged from 2.5–60% and in some cases were raised as high as 200% ad valorem, with some commodities on the free list. The revised rates were designed to reduce imports of nonessential goods and to protect and encourage certain industries. To accomplish this second objective, rates on some raw materials were reduced and those on finished products increased. Export taxes were discontinued in 1971. In November 1985, maximum customs duties were reduced to 45% and stood at 40% as of 1993. Also levied are a 12.5% import tax and a value-added tax that ranges from 7–30%.

The policy of import liberalization begun in 1967 has continued, and new commodities have been added to the list of items not subject to quotas. In the 1970 general import program, items not subject to quotas accounted for 75% of the imports. As of 1993, most goods do not require import licenses. Duties are as high as 45%, with a 12.5% import tax. Value-added taxes are levied at rates of 7–30%.

Agreements between Morocco and the EC have provided for mutual tariff concessions. Citrus tariffs were cut 80% by the EC by the mid-1970s; tariffs on canned fruit and vegetables were reduced more than 50%; and fish products, wine, olive oil, and cereals were given special concessions. In return, Morocco reduced its minimum tariffs by 30% and adjusted quotas on imports to Morocco. The import tariff does not apply within the free zone of the Port of Tangier.

38FOREIGN INVESTMENT

Foreign investment declined somewhat during the 1960s and 1970s because of political uncertainty and because of the government's Moroccanization policy requiring majority Moroccan ownership of foreign banks, trading companies, insurance firms, and small manufacturing plants. Many foreign firms either sold out or closed down before 30 September 1974, the first deadline for compliance with Moroccanization policies. In an effort to attract foreign capital, the government passed a new investment code in August 1973 that offered substantial tax concessions to private investors. To encourage badly needed foreign investment, a revised code introduced in 1982 permitted foreign investors 100% ownership of local companies in certain sectors and unrestricted transfer of capital. The effective repent in 1990 of the Moroccanization law and regulatory changes, including tax breaks and streamlined approval procedures, have led to a more than three-fold increase in foreign investment inflows over the last 4 years.

While in 1985, foreign direct investment in Morocco totaled $27.4 million, nearly six times the figure for 1984, it soared to approximately $217 million in 1990, $375 million in 1991, and $500 million in 1992.

39ECONOMIC DEVELOPMENT

Government policy stresses expansion and development of the economy, essentially through private enterprise. Morocco decided to abide by the IMF's Article VIII, thus beginning the privatization of 112 public entities—mainly manufacturing enterprises, hotels, and financial institutions—slated for divestiture under the 1989 privatization law.

Morocco has instituted a series of development plans to modernize the economy and increase production. Net investment under the five-year plan for 1960–64 was DH6.6 billion (about $1.3 billion). The plan called for a growth rate of 6.2%, but by 1964 the growth rate had reached only 3%. A new three-year plan (1965–67) was inaugurated in 1965, with a revised annual growth target of 3.7%. The main emphasis of the plan was on the development and modernization of the agricultural sector. The five-year development plan for 1968–72 called for expenditures of DH998 million, of which DH460 million was for agriculture and irrigation. The development of the tourist industry also figured prominently in the plan. The objective was to attain an annual 5% growth rate in GDP; the real growth rate actually exceeded 6% a year.

The five-year plan for 1973–77 envisaged an investment of DH26.3 billion and a real economic growth of 7.5% annually. Industries singled out for development included chemicals (especially phosphoric acid), phosphate production, paper products, and metal fabrication. Tourist development was also stressed. In 1975, King Hassan II announced a 50% increase in investment targets to allow for the effects of inflation.

The 1978–80 plan was one of stabilization and retrenchment, designed to improve Morocco's balance-of-payments position, but the 4% annual growth rate achieved was disappointing. The ambitious five-year plan for 1981–85, estimated to cost more than $18 billion, aimed at achieving a growth rate of 6.5% annually. The plan's principal priority was to create some 900,000 new jobs and to train managers and workers in modern agricultural and industrial techniques. Other major goals were to increase production in agriculture and fisheries to make the country self-sufficient in food, and to develop energy (by building more hydroelectric installations and by finding more petroleum and other fossil fuels), industry, and tourism to enable Morocco to lessen its dependence on foreign loans. The plan called for significant expansion of irrigated land, for increased public works projects such as hospitals and schools, and for economic decentralization and regional development through the construction of 25 new industrial parks outside the crowded Casablanca-Kénitra coastal area. Proposed infrastructural improvements included the $2-billion rail line from Marrakech to El Aaiún; a new fishing port at Ad-Dakhla, near Argoub in the Western Sahara; and a bridge-tunnel complex across the Strait of Gibraltar to link Morocco directly with Spain. New large industrial projects include phosphoric acid plants, sugar refineries, mines to exploit cobalt, coal, silver, lead, and copper deposits, and oil-shale development. The drought and Morocco's growing debt problem held back some of these projects, however.

By 1991, US bilateral aid amounted to $137.8 million. Outstanding foreign debt commitments and their serving remain a significant obstacle to economic development. The 1992 financing requirements were mostly covered, largely because of grants and bilateral credit. Despite the cancellation by Sa'udi Arabia of $2.8 billion of debt, the total still exceeded $23 billion. Despite reschedulings through both the Paris Club of official creditors and the London Club of commercial creditors, servicing the debt accounted for 30% of exports of goods and services.

40 SOCIAL DEVELOPMENT

The social security system covers employees and apprentices in industrial and commercial fields and the professions, as well as agriculture and forestry. There is also voluntary coverage for persons leaving covered employment, and voluntary complementary insurance is available. Benefits include maternity allowances, disability pensions, old age pensions, death allowances, and allowances for illness. Employees contribute 1.68% of earnings, and employers contribute 3.36% of payroll contributions. Most of the country's voluntary social welfare societies are subsidized by the government and coordinated by the central and regional offices of the National Mutual Aid Society. Private groups include the Red Crescent, an affiliate of the International Red Cross.

Population control has been a government goal since 1966, but achievements have usually fallen short of targets. Under the 1968–72 development plan, 500,000 women of childbearing age were to be provided with contraceptive methods, but less than 20% of that number were reached. In 1979, in an effort to improve the efficiency and scope of the program, the government eliminated the requirement that a physician participate in family planning decisions and left that responsibility to nurses and paramedical personnel. By 1989, family planning programs reached 442,000 persons. In 1992, an estimated 42% of couples of childbearing age were using contraception, and the fertility rate had dropped to 4.8%.

Women comprise about 24% of the work force and are employed mostly in the industrial, service, and teaching sectors. They have the right to vote and run for office (in 1993 two women were elected to parliament). Women do not have equal status under Islamic family and estate laws.

41 HEALTH

Health conditions are relatively poor, but programs of mass education in child and parent hygiene, as well as government-supervised health services in schools and colleges, have helped to raise standards. Campaigns have been conducted against malaria, tuberculosis, venereal diseases, and cancer. However, gastrointestinal infections, malaria, typhoid, trachoma, and tuberculosis remain widespread. The WHO and UNICEF have cooperated in the government's campaigns against eye disorders and venereal diseases.

In 1992, 70% of the population had access to health care services. In 1992, children up to one year of age were vaccinated against tuberculosis (93%); diphtheria, pertussis, and tetanus (87%); polio (81%); and measles (81%). Total health care expenditures in 1990 were $661 million.

In 1990, there were 4,862 doctors and 26,174 hospital beds. In 1992, there were 2 physicians per 10,000 people. Of the 4,862 doctors, 2,619 were in the public sector and the remaining were in private practice. In 1989, there were 12 university hospitals, 20 regional hospitals, 45 provincial hospitals, 11 local hospitals, 14 diagnostic centers, and 377 health centers (164 urban and 213 rural).

The 1993 birth rate was 32.3 per 1,000 people, and about 42% of married women (ages 15 to 49) used contraception. There were 854,000 births in 1992, with infant mortality estimated at 50 per 1,000 live births. The general mortality rate was 8.3 per 1,000 inhabitants in 1993. Maternal mortality in 1991 was estimated at 300 per 100,000 live births. The average estimated life expectancy was 63 years.

42 HOUSING

Since the 1950s, significant numbers of Moroccans (estimated at over 4 million) have moved from the countryside to the urban centers to escape rural unemployment. Housing and sanitation, consequently, have become urban problems. The government is engaged in a low-cost housing program to reduce the slum areas, called bidonvilles, that have formed around the large urban centers, especially Casablanca and Rabat.

By 1965, only 13,000 low-cost housing units had been built by the government. After 1965, the focus of government development activities shifted from social programs to agricultural and industrial development, and public housing funds were substantially reduced. However, the government continued to develop government-owned lots for low-income families. The lots are equipped with water, electricity, and a sewer system, and the annual rental rate is a percentage of the retail price of the lot. Loans have been available for private home construction, and builders have also received financial and technical assistance from the government to build workers' housing. In the mid-1980s, an estimated 55% of Moroccans had access to safe water.

As of 1982, traditional dwellings accounted for 64% of the housing units and flats for 18%. Of all urban households, 43% were rented, 41% were owner occupied, and 12% were rent free. In the same year, 48% of all units were brick and stone, 26% were stone and mud, and 19% were adobe. Nearly three-fourths had private kitchens, 43% had private toilets, 30% had piped water, and 37% had electricity.

43 EDUCATION

In 1990, an estimated 61.3% of men and 38% of women were literate. The school system includes modern secular public institutions, traditional religious schools, and private schools. Nine years of compulsory primary education was made a law in 1962. In 1991, 2,578,566 pupils were in primary school and 1,168,918 in secondary school. In vocational schools, there were 17,147 students. Girls leave school younger than boys and are a minority in secondary as well as primary schools; they make up fewer than one-third of university students.

The language of instruction in primary schools is Arabic during the first two years, and both Arabic and French are used for the next three years. French is partly the language of instruction in secondary schools. The traditional religious schools are attended by only a small fraction of students. The government is committed to a unified public school system but has permitted private schools to continue because of the lack of alternative resources.

Morocco has six universities. Al-Qarawiyin University at Fès, founded in 859, is reputed to be the oldest university in the world; it was reorganized in 1962/63 as an Islamic university, supervised by the Ministry of Education. The first modern Moroccan university, the University of Rabat (now the Muhammad V University), was opened in 1957. Other universities are Muhammad bin 'Abdallah (founded 1974), in Fès; Hassan II (1975), Casablanca; Cadi Ayyad (1978), Marrakech; and Muhammad I (1978), Oujda. There are about two dozen colleges and conservatories. In 1990, enrollment at all higher level institutions was 221,217.

44LIBRARIES AND MUSEUMS

The General Library and Archives, located on the campus of Muhammad V University in Rabat, is the national library, with holdings of 600,000 volumes. Its notable collection of medieval books and manuscripts, of particular interest to Muslim scholars, contains 1,600 ancient manuscripts of famous Islamic writers, including an important treatise by Averroës and classical treatises on medicine and pharmacy. Of the 18 public libraries in Morocco, the largest is in Casablanca, with almost 360,000 volumes.

The Division of Museums, Sites, Archaeology, and Historic Monuments of the Ministry of Cultural Affairs administers 11 museums in major cities and at the ancient Roman site of Volubilis, northwest of Meknès. In some cities, such as Fès and Marrakech, small houses of historic and artistic interest have been preserved as museums.

45MEDIA

The postal, telephone, telegraph, radio, and television services are government operated. Telephone and telegraph services connect most towns, and cable service is available to France, Spain, and Gibraltar. In 1991 there were 361,800 telephones. Radiodiffusion Television Marocaine presents programs in Arabic, in Berber dialects, and in English, French, and Spanish. The television service, with studios in Casablanca and Rabat, presents daily programs in Arabic and French. A private television station, 2M International, began broadcasting in French and Arabic in 1989. In 1991 there were an estimated 5,385,000 radios and 1.9 million television sets.

Press freedom is guaranteed by the constitution, and censorship of domestic publications was lifted in 1977, but criticism of Islam, the King, the monarchical system, or Morocco's claim to the Western Sahara is not permitted. Leading daily newspapers published in Rabat include the Arabic-language *Al Anba'a* (1991 circulation 20,000) and the French-language *L'Opinion* (50,000) and *Al-Maghrib* (20,000). The French-language *Matin du Sahara* (50,000) and *Maroc Soir* (50,000) are published in Casablanca.

46ORGANIZATIONS

The Moroccan Trade, Industry, and Handicrafts Association encourages economic development. Chambers of commerce, industry, and agriculture function in most Moroccan cities. British, French, Spanish, and international chambers of commerce are active in Tangier. There are associations of primary- and secondary-school teachers, parents, older students, and alumni. There are at least two major student political groups: the National Union of Moroccan Students and the General Union of Moroccan Students.

Morocco has drama societies, music organizations (notably the Association for Andalusian Music), and artists' associations, the one in Rabat being particularly active. Professional organizations include societies of doctors, pharmacists, lawyers, and engineers. Societies have been formed to encourage the study of economics, geography, prehistory, sociology, and statistics.

The National Mutual Aid Society, a welfare organization with many subdivisions, is headed by Princess Lalla Aïcha, the king's sister. Other groups include the Red Crescent, Boy Scouts, Girl Scouts, and various women's associations.

47TOURISM, TRAVEL, AND RECREATION

Morocco's scenic variety and beauty, fascinating medieval cities, and favorable climate contribute to a steadily increasing flow of tourists. Tourism is one of the fastest-growing areas of the Moroccan economy and a valuable foreign exchange earner. There were 4,162,239 tourists in 1991, of whom 49% were Algerian, 7% French, and 5% Spanish. Expansion of tourist facilities continues; the number of rooms available in hotels, pensions, and holiday villages was 59,935 in 1991, with 116,171 beds. Income from tourism amounted to $1.05 billion in the same year.

Most visitors require passports but not visas for stays of less than three months. Coastal beach resorts offer excellent swimming and boating facilities. Sports associations are widespread, particularly for soccer, swimming, boxing, basketball, and tennis.

48FAMOUS MOROCCANS

Important leaders and rulers include Idris I (Idris bin 'Abdallah, r.788–91), of the Umayyad dynasty, who came to Morocco and was able to consolidate much of the area. His son Idris II (r.791–804) founded Fès, the early capital. Yusuf bin Tashfin (r.1061–1106), a religious reformer, conquered much of Spain and northern Africa. Muhammad bin Tumart (1078?–1130) founded the Almohad sect and developed a democratic form of government. The founder of the Almohad dynasty, 'Abd al-Mumin bin 'Ali (1094?–1163), conquered Morocco and parts of Spain. Yakub al-Mansur (r.1184–99), who controlled all of North Africa west of Egypt, encouraged architecture and scholarship. Ahmad al-Mansur (r.1578–1603) drove all foreign forces out of Morocco, conquered the western Sudan, and established commercial and other contacts with England and Europe. Mawlay Isma'il (r.1672–1727) reunited Morocco and organized a harsh but effective centralized government. A capable and strong ruler famous for his justice was Muhammad bin 'Abdallah (r.1757–90).

Morocco has attracted many great minds, and it has been said that none of the great names in western Arabic philosophy is unconnected with Morocco. Avicenna (Ibn Sina, or Abu 'Ali al-Husayn, 980?–1037), a great Persian physician and philosopher and an author of long-used textbooks on medicine, who was born near Bukhara, lived for a number of years in Morocco. So did Avenzoar (Ibn Zuhr, or Abu Marwan 'Abd al-Malik bin Abu-'l-'Ala' Zuhr, c.1090?–1162), physician and scholar, born in Sevilla, in Spain, and author of important medical treatises. Averroës (Ibn Rushd, or Abu al-Walid Muhammad ibn Ahmad ibn Rushd, 1126–98), greatest Arab philosopher of Spain, was born in Córdoba and lived in Morocco for many years. The doctor and philosopher Abubacer (Abu Bakr Muhammad bin 'Abd al-Malik bin Tufayl, d.1118) was likewise brought to the Moroccan court from Spain.

Among distinguished native-born Moroccans was Ahmad bin 'Ali al-Badawi (c.1200?–76), a Muslim saint who was active principally in Egypt. The great traveler Ibn Battutah (Abu 'Abdallah Muhammad bin Battutah, 1304–68?) visited and wrote about many countries of Africa, Asia, and Europe. The poetry of Muhammad bin Ibrahim (d.1955) is read throughout the Islamic world.

A famous fighter for Moroccan independence was 'Abd al-Karim (Muhammad 'Abd al-Karim al-Khattabi, 1882?–1963), who led a long campaign in the 1920s against French and Spanish forces. King Muhammad V (1909–61) gave up his throne as a gesture for independence, was arrested and exiled by the French, and returned in 1955 to become the first ruler of newly independent Morocco. He was succeeded by his son Hassan II (b.1929), who continued his father's modernization program and expanded Morocco's territory and mineral resources by annexing Western Sahara.

⁴⁹DEPENDENCIES

Morocco has no territories or colonies.

⁵⁰BIBLIOGRAPHY

American University. *Morocco: A Country study.* Washington, D.C.: Government Printing Office, 1985.

Cook, Weston F. *The Hundred Years War for Morocco: Gunpowder and the Military Revolution in the Early Modern Muslim world.* Boulder, Colo.: Westview Press, 1994.

Entelis, John P. *Culture and Counterculture in Moroccan Politics.* Boulder, Colo.: Westview Press, 1989.

Geertz, Clifford, et al. *Meaning and Order in Moroccan Society.* New York: Cambridge University Press, 1979.

Halstead, John P. *Rebirth of a Nation: The Origins and Rise of Moroccan Nationalism, 1912–1944.* Cambridge, Mass.: Harvard University Press, 1967.

Hodges, Tony. *Historical Dictionary of Western Sahara.* Metuchen, N.J.: Scarecrow, 1982.

Hoffman, Bernard G. *Structure of Traditional Moroccan Rural Society.* New York: Humanities, 1967.

Merat, Christian. *Morocco: Economic and Social Development Report.* Washington, D.C.: World Bank, 1981.

Morocco in pictures. Minneapolis: Lerner, 1988.

Munson, Henry. *Religion and Power in Morocco.* New Haven, Conn.: Yale University Press, 1993.

Porch, Douglas. *The Conquest of Morocco.* New York: Knopf, 1983.

Spencer, William. *Historical Dictionary of Morocco.* Metuchen, N.J.: Scarecrow, 1980.

Zartmann, I. William (ed.). *The Political Economy of Morocco.* New York: Praeger, 1987.

MOZAMBIQUE

Republic of Mozambique
República de Moçambique

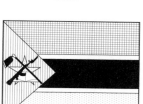

CAPITAL: Maputo (formerly Lourenço Marques).

FLAG: The flag consists of broad stripes of green, black, and yellow, separated by narrow bands of white. Extending from the hoist is a red triangle; centered on the triangle is a yellow five-pointed star upon which is a white book over which are crossed the black silhouettes of a hoe and an AK47 rifle.

ANTHEM: Begins "Viva viva FRELIMO."

MONETARY UNIT: The Mozambique escudo (ME), linked until 1977 with the Portuguese escudo, was in June 1980 renamed the metical (MT); it is a paper currency of 100 centavos. There are coins of ½, 1, 2½, 5, 10, and 20 meticais, and notes of 50, 100, 500, and 1,000 meticais. MT1=$0.0022 (or $1=MT454.5).

WEIGHTS AND MEASURES: The metric system is in use.

HOLIDAYS: New Year's Day, 1 January; Heroes' Day, 3 February; Women's Day, 7 April; Workers' Day, 1 May; Independence Day, 25 June; Anniversary of the End of Armed Struggle, 7 September; Anniversary of the Opening of Armed Struggle, 25 September; Family Day, 25 December.

TIME: 2 PM = noon GMT.

¹LOCATION, SIZE, AND EXTENT

Located on the southeastern coast of Africa, opposite the island of Madagascar, Mozambique (Moçambique), formerly known as Portuguese East Africa, has an area of 801,590 sq km (309,496 sq mi), of which land constitutes 786,380 sq km (303,621 sq mi) and inland water 13,000 sq km (5,020 sq mi). Comparatively, the area occupied by Mozambique is slightly less than twice the size of the state of California. The country extends 2,016 km (1,253 mi) NNE–SSW and 772 km (480 mi) ESE–WNW. It is bordered by Tanzania on the N, the Indian Ocean (Mozambique Channel) on the E, the Republic of South Africa on the S, Swaziland, South Africa, and Zimbabwe on the W, and Zambia and Malawi on the NW, with a total boundary length of 7,041 km (4,375 mi).

²TOPOGRAPHY

Mozambique is 44% coastal lowlands, rising toward the west to a plateau 150 to 610 m (500–2,000 ft) above sea level and on the western border to a higher plateau, 550 to 910 m (1,800–3,000 ft), with mountains reaching a height of nearly 2,440 m (8,000 ft). The highest mountains are Namuli (2,419 m/7,936 ft) in Zambézia Province and Binga (2,436 m/7,992 ft) in Manica Province on the Zimbabwean border. The most important rivers are the Zambezi (flowing southeast across the center of Mozambique into the Indian Ocean), the Limpopo in the south, the Save (Sabi) in the center, and the Lugenda in the north. The most important lake is the navigable Lake Malawi (Lake Niassa); Lake Cahora Bassa was formed by the impoundment of the Cahora Bassa Dam. In the river valleys and deltas, the soil is rich and fertile, but southern and central Mozambique have poor and sandy soil, and parts of the interior are dry.

³CLIMATE

Two main seasons, one wet and one dry, divide the climatic year. The wet season, from November through March, has monthly averages between 27°C and 29°C (81–84°F), with cooler temperatures in the interior uplands. The dry season lasts from April to October and has June and July temperatures averaging 18–20°C

(64–68°F). The average annual rainfall is greatest (about 142 cm/56 in) over the western hills and the central areas, and lowest (41–81 cm/16–32 in) in the southwest.

⁴FLORA AND FAUNA

Thick forest covers the wet regions, where there are fertile soils, but the drier interior, which has sandy or rocky soils, supports only a thin savanna vegetation. Extensive stands of hardwood, such as ebony, flourish throughout the country. Mozambique has elephants, buffalo, wildebeests, zebras, palapalas, hippopotamuses, lions, crocodiles, nyalas, and other southern African game species, as well as over 300 varieties of birds.

⁵ENVIRONMENT

One of Mozambique's most challenging environmental problems is the health of its citizens. The civil war combined with natural disasters from flooding and drought have created a life-threatening situation for the nation's people. According to a 1992 UN report, humans are the most endangered species in Mozambique. Other significant environmental problems include the loss of 70% of the nation's forests. Mozambique has already launched reforestation projects, mostly involving the planting of conifers and eucalyptus. The purity of the nation's water supply is also a significant issue. Mozambique has 13.9 cubic miles of water. Sixty-six percent is used in farming and 10% for industrial purposes. Fifty-six percent of the nation's city dwellers and 83% of the rural people do not have pure water. As of 1994, 10 of the nation's mammal species and 11 bird species are endangered. Eighty-nine plant species are threatened with extinction. Endangered species in Mozambique include the green sea, hawksbill, olive ridley, and leatherback turtles.

⁶POPULATION

The 1994 population was estimated at 17,276,496 by the US Census Bureau, but the UN estimated the 1995 population at 16,395,000. A population of 19,436,000 was projected for the year 2000, assuming a crude birthrate of 42.5 per 1,000 population, a crude death rate of 17.1, and a net natural increase of 25.4 during 1995–2000. The population in 1990–95 was growing at a rate of about 2.8% annually. The estimated density in 1994 was 22 per sq km (56 per sq mi). About 34% of the population was urban in 1995. Maputo (formerly Lourenço Marques), the capital, had an estimated 1990 population of 1,561,000. Beira had an estimated population of 299,300, and Nampula had 202,600, and Nocala had 104,300. About 60% of the population lives in the central and southern coastal provinces.

7 MIGRATION

Mozambicans have provided labor for South African mines in the past. Some remain there: in 1991 South Africa had 145,862 black people born in Mozambique, 72% of them male.

Between April 1974 and the end of 1976, an estimated 235,000 of the 250,000 Portuguese in Mozambique fled the country. Famine and war produced another exodus in the 1980s, but this time of blacks. On October 1992 peace agreement left 4.5 million internally displaced and 1.5 million refugees abroad. Of the latter at the end of 1992, 1,058,500 were in Malawi; about 200,000 in South Africa, 136,600 in Zimbabwe, 75,200 in Tanzania, 48,100 in Swaziland, and 26,300 in Zambia. By May 1993 about 750,000 people in both categories had returned home.

8 ETHNIC GROUPS

There are 10 major ethnic clusters. The largest, residing north of the Zambezi, is the Makua-Lomwé group, representing about 37% of the total population. The Yao (Ajawa) live in Niassa Province. The Makonde live mainly along the Rovuma River. Other northern groups are the Nguni (who also live in the far south) and the Maravi. South of the Zambezi, the main group is the Tsonga (about 23%), who have figured prominently as Mozambican mine laborers in South Africa. The Chopi are coastal people of Inhambane Province. The Shona or Karanga (about 9%) dwell in the central region. Also living in Mozambique in the mid-1980s were some 15,000 Indians, 10,000 Europeans, and 35,000 persons of mixed European and African ancestry.

9 LANGUAGES

Portuguese remains the official language. Different African ethnic groups speak their respective languages and dialects.

10 RELIGIONS

The People's Republic of Mozambique is a secular state. The government guarantees every citizen full freedom of conscience and the right to practice a religion or not. Church schools and hospitals were nationalized after independence. The population follows African traditional religions, the Christian faith (mainly Roman Catholicism), or Islam. Estimates of the proportions vary, but tribal religionists probably account for 60% of the population. In 1993, there were about 5 million Christians and 4 million Muslims. Roman Catholics made up some 12.5%.

11 TRANSPORTATION

Transport networks are of major importance to the economy. Mozambique's landlocked neighbors—Malawi, Zambia, Zimbabwe, and Swaziland—along with South Africa are the main users of the Mozambican transport system. An international effort was under way in 1987 to rehabilitate Mozambique's railways, roads, and ports and to defend them against Mozambique National Resistance (RENAMO) attacks so that landlocked southern African countries would have a workable alternative to using South African facilities for their foreign trade.

The railways are the best-developed sector, with three good rail links between major Mozambican ports and neighboring countries. By independence, almost the entire railway system was owned by the state and passed into the hands of the new government. The route system is 3,288 km (2,043 mi) long; the single largest user is South Africa. There are six routes which make up the majority of the country's railroads: the Nacala Corridor, connecting Nacala to Malawi (300 km/186 mi); the Sena Corridor, linking Beira, via Dondo, to the coalfields at Moatize (513 km/ 319 mi) and to Malawi (370 km/230 mi); the Beira Corridor, connecting Beira to Zimbabwe (315 km/196 mi); the Limpopo Corridor, linking Maputo with Zimbabwe (534 km/332 mi); the Resano Garcia line, connecting Maputo to South Africa (88 km/ 55 mi); and the Goba line, linking Maputo to Swaziland (68 km/ 42 mi). The road network totals some 26,498 km (16,466 mi), of which 4,593 km (2,854 mi) is paved, but few roads are suitable for trucks and passenger cars. In 1992 there were 70,000 vehicles, including 35,000 passenger cars.

Maputo, by far the leading port, has an excellent multipurpose harbor, with exceptional loading, unloading, and storage facilities; it is a major outlet for South Africa, Swaziland, Zimbabwe, Zambia, Malawi, and eastern Zaire. Other ports include Beira, Nacala, and Inhambane, which was reopened in 1980 after a 20-year closure. The Mozambican merchant fleet consisted of five freighters at the end of 1991.

Mozambique Air Lines (Linhas Aéreas de Moçambique—LAM), the state airline, operates both international and domestic services. It carried 44,900 passengers and 800,000 freight ton-km in 1992. The National Enterprise of Transport and Aerial Labor (Empresa Nacional de Transporte e Trabalho Aéreo—TTA) also provides domestic service. Maputo and Beira have international airports, which together accommodated 519,000 arriving and departing passengers in 1991.

12 HISTORY

Mozambique's earliest inhabitants were hunter-gatherers, often referred to as Bushmen. The land was occupied by Bantu peoples by about AD 1000. In the following centuries, trade developed with Arabs who came across the Indian Ocean to Sofala. The first Europeans in the area were the Portuguese, who began to settle and trade on the coast early in the 16th century. During the 17th century, the Portuguese competed with Arabs for the trade in slaves, gold, and ivory, and set up agricultural plantations and estates. The owners of these estates, the prazeiros, were Portuguese or of mixed African and Portuguese blood (mestiços); many had their own private armies. Mozambique was ruled as part of Goa until 1752, when it was given its own administration.

Until the late 1800s, Portuguese penetration was restricted to the coast and the Zambezi Valley. The African peoples strongly resisted further expansion, but they were ultimately subdued. By the end of the 19th century, the Portuguese had made boundary agreements with their colonial rivals, the UK and Germany, and had suppressed much of the African resistance. Authority was given to trading companies such as Mozambique Co., which forced local people to pay taxes and work on the plantations. After the Portuguese revolution of 1926, the government of Portugal took a more direct interest in Mozambique. The trading companies' influence declined, and Mozambique in 1951 became an overseas province of Portugal.

As in other Portuguese territories, African resistance to Portuguese rule grew stronger as the British and French colonies in Africa began to win their independence. Gradually, various liberation movements were formed. On 25 June 1962, these groups united to form the Mozambique Liberation Front (FRELIMO) and elected Eduardo C. Mondlane as its first president. The armed struggle began on 25 September 1964, when FRELIMO guerrillas trained in Algeria went into action for the first time in Cabo Delgado. By 1965, fighting had spread to Niassa, and by 1968, FRELIMO was able to open fronts in the Tete region. By that time, it claimed to control one-fifth of the country. In

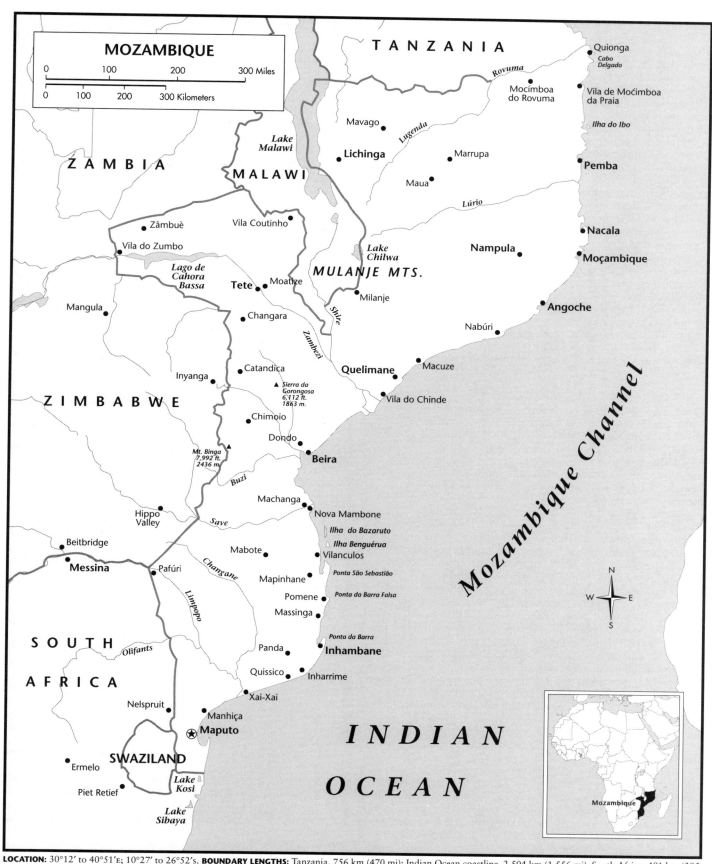

MOZAMBIQUE

0	100	200	300 Miles
0	100	200	300 Kilometers

TANZANIA

ZAMBIA

MALAWI

ZIMBABWE

SOUTH

AFRICA

SWAZILAND

INDIAN

OCEAN

Mozambique Channel

Lake Malawi

Lake Chilwa

Lake Kosi

Lake Sibaya

Lago de Cahora Bassa

MULANJE MTS.

Quionga
Cabo Delgado
Mocímboa do Rovuma
Vila de Moćímboa da Praia
Ilha do Ibo
Mavago
Lichinga
Marrupa
Pemba
Maua
Lúrio
Nacala
Nampula
Moçambique
Vila Coutinho
Zâmbuè
Vila do Zumbo
Angoche
Milanje
Nabúri
Tete
Moatize
Mangula
Changara
Macuze
Quelimane
Catandica
▲ *Sierra da Gorongosa 6,112 ft. 1863 m.*
Vila do Chinde
Inyanga
Chimoio
Dondo
Beira
Mt. Binga 7,992 ft. 2436 m. ▲
Machanga
Nova Mambone
Ilha do Bazaruto
Ilha Benguérua
Hippo Valley
Mabote
Vilanculos
Beitbridge
Ponta São Sebastião
Messina
Pafúri
Mapinhane
Pomene
Ponta da Barra Falsa
Massinga
Ponta da Barra
Panda
Inhambane
Quissico
Inharrime
Xai-Xai
Nelspruit
Manhiça
✪ Maputo
Ermelo
Piet Retief

Rovuma
Lugenda
Shire
Zambezi
Buzi
Save
Changane
Limpopo
Olifants

N
W E
S

Mozambique

LOCATION: 30°12′ to 40°51′E; 10°27′ to 26°52′S. **BOUNDARY LENGTHS:** Tanzania, 756 km (470 mi); Indian Ocean coastline, 2,504 km (1,556 mi); South Africa, 491 km (305 mi); Swaziland, 108 km (67 mi); Zimbabwe, 1,223 km (760 mi); Zambia, 424 km (263 mi); Malawi, 1,497 km (930 mi). **TERRITORIAL SEA LIMIT:** 12 mi.

response, the Portuguese committed more and more troops, military supplies, and military aid funds to the territory. On 3 February 1969, Mondlane was assassinated in Dar es Salaam, Tanzania; the acting leader of FRELIMO, Samora Machel, became president of the organization in December 1970.

The turning point in the struggle for independence came with the Portuguese revolution of 25 April 1974. Negotiations between Portuguese and FRELIMO representatives led to the conclusion of an independence agreement in Zambia in September. Mozambique became officially independent at midnight on 24–25 June 1975, and the People's Republic of Mozambique was proclaimed in ceremonies on 25 June. Machel, who had returned to Mozambique on 24 May after 13 years in exile, became the nation's first president. He quickly affirmed Mozambique's support of the liberation movement in Rhodesia, and guerrilla activity along the Rhodesian border increased. On 3 March 1976, Mozambique closed its border with Rhodesia, severed rail and communications links, and nationalized Rhodesian-owned property. Because the transit fees paid by Rhodesia had been a major source of foreign exchange revenue, the action aggravated Mozambique's economic ills. During this period, Rhodesian forces conducted land and air raids into Mozambique to punish black nationalist guerrillas based there. These raids ended and the border was reopened in 1980, following the agreement that transformed Rhodesia into Zimbabwe. However, South African airmen bombed Maputo in 1981 and 1983 in retaliation for Mozambique's granting refuge to members of the African National Congress (ANC), a South African black nationalist group.

The Mozambique National Resistance (RENAMO), created in 1976, allegedly by Portuguese settler and business interests with white Rhodesian (Central Intelligence Organization) backing, conducted extensive guerrilla operations in Mozambique during the 1980s. With an armed strength estimated as high as 12,000, RENAMO blew up bridges and cut rail and road links and pipelines. After the loss of its Rhodesian support, RENAMO received substantial aid from South Africa and also had bases in Malawi. Voluntary support for RENAMO within Mozambique was difficult to ascertain, but there was known to be considerable disaffection with the government because of food shortages and resistance by peasants to being resettled onto communal farms. In addition to these political problems, Mozambique experienced widespread floods in 1977–78 and recurrent drought from 1979 on, especially in 1992.

On 16 March 1984, Mozambique and South Africa signed a nonaggression pact at Nkomati whereby Mozambique agreed to keep the ANC from using Mozambican territory for guerrilla attacks on South Africa, while South Africa agreed to stop supporting RENAMO. Nevertheless, South Africa continued to aid RENAMO and, as a result, in 1985 Mozambique pulled out of the commission that monitored the nonaggression pact. On 19 October 1986, President Machel and 33 others were killed when their Soviet-built jetliner crashed inside South Africa while returning to Maputo. Mozambican officials accused South Africa of employing a radio beacon to lure the craft off course to its destruction, but an international commission found that the crash was caused by negligence on the part of the Soviet crew. On 3 November 1986, FRELIMO's Central Committee elected Foreign Minister Joaquim A. Chissano president. In 1987, despite the jetliner crash and despite Mozambican claims that RENAMO and South Africa were responsible for the massacre of 386 people in a village near Inhambane, Mozambique and South Africa revived their nonagression pact. Fighting intensified and hundreds of thousands of Mozambicans fled to Malawi and Zimbabwe.

In 1990, there was movement towards resolving the civil war. There were serious signs in the late 1980s that FRELIMO was moderating its views. At its 1989 Congress, FRELIMO formally abandoned its commitment to the primacy of Marxism-Leninism. The first peace talks in 13 years were scheduled for Blantyre, Malawi, but they broke down just before they were to open. In August, government and rebel leaders concluded three days of talks in Rome. That same month, Chissano announced that FRELIMO had agreed to allow opposition parties to compete openly and legally. Finally in November, government and RENAMO agreed to appoint the Italian government and the Catholic Church as mediators in peace talks.

It took until 4 October 1992 to sign a peace treaty ending the war, but sporadic fighting and new RENAMO demands slowed down the implementation process. Chissano and Afonso Dhlakama, RENAMO's leader, signed an agreement that called for the withdrawal of Zimbabwean and Malawian troops that had assisted government forces guarding transport routes and the regrouping of both government and RENAMO soldiers at assembly points. It called for the formation of a new national army composed of half government and half RENAMO troops. A joint commission of government and RENAMO, along with a small UN monitoring force, and other joint commissioners, the police, and intelligence services were to oversee the agreement's implementation. In addition, multiparty elections were to be held within a year.

Delays troubled the process practically from the start. RENAMO was slow to appoint its representatives to the joint commissions. The UN operation (UNOMOZ) was formally approved in December 1992, but no troops arrived until March 1993 and it was mid-year before 6,000 troops were deployed. RENAMO failed to implement the provision for demobilization and all of the provisions regarding freedom of movement and political organization in areas it controlled. New RENAMO demands were put forward almost monthly and, despite direct meetings between Dhlakama and Chissano and an October 1993 visit by UN Sec. Gen. Boutros Boutros-Ghali, the delays continued. In mid-1993, the national election was postponed until October 1994.

Political party activity has picked up. By the end of 1993, 16 parties were active, 11 of which met the registration criteria set by government. In March 1993, government presented a draft electoral law to opposition parties, but not until late July was a meeting convened to discuss it. The opposition parties demand a two-thirds majority on the National Electoral Commission. After Boutros-Ghali's visit, a compromise (10 out of 21 for the opposition parties) was agreed to. Delays also marked the effort to confine armed forces in designated areas.

13GOVERNMENT

The constitution of the People's Republic of Mozambique became effective at midnight on 24–25 June 1975. Under the constitution and its revision enacted during 1977–78, Mozambique was a republic in which FRELIMO was the sole legal party. The president was the chief of state; the president of FRELIMO had to be the president of the republic. He acted on the advice of the Council of State Ministers, which he appointed and over which he presided. He also appointed provincial governors. The position of prime minister was created in a 1986 constitutional revision. The National People's Assembly, with 226 members, was the supreme organ of the state. Elections to the Assembly were held in 1977 and 1986, with the candidates chosen from a single FRELIMO slate.

A revised constitution with a multiparty system of government came into force on 30 November 1990. The name of the country was changed from the People's Republic to the Republic of Mozambique. Governmental institutions remain otherwise unchanged. One can expect, however, a radical revision of the constitution before or after the October 1994 elections.

According to the 1990 constitution, the president is to be elected by universal adult suffrage for a five-year term and might be reelected on only two consecutive occasions. The Assembly of the Republic will replace the People's Assembly. Its deputies (between 200 and 250) are to be elected for five-year terms.

14 POLITICAL PARTIES

The Mozambique Liberation Front (Frente de Libertação de Moçambique—FRELIMO), the sole legal political party until 1991, was founded in 1962 by the merger of three existing nationalist parties. Formation of FRELIMO did not mean complete political unity. Splinter groups or organizations began to appear in Cairo, Nairobi, and elsewhere, but none of these splinter organizations ever received the support of the OAU, which gave official recognition only to FRELIMO.

In August 1973, five anti-FRELIMO groups formed the National Coalition Party (Partido de Coligação Nacional—PCN). The PCN program called for a referendum on the country's future and the restoration of peace and multiracialism. The organized opposition from the Portuguese community took the form of the Independent Front for the Continuation of Western Rule (Frente Independente de Continuidade Ocidental—FICO, or "I stay"). FICO called for Portugal to continue the war against FRELIMO. In fact, however, the Portuguese government chose to recognize FRELIMO. After the formation of a provisional FRELIMO government in September 1974, the PCN was dissolved and its leaders detained.

Two years after independence, in 1977, FRELIMO was transformed from a liberation movement into a Marxist-Leninist vanguard party dedicated to the creation of a Socialist state. It formally downgraded its ideological commitment at its July 1989 congress. Proposals to broaden party membership and decision making were also adopted. The new constitution in force in November 1990 legalized a multiparty system. Since then, activity has been vigorous. FRELIMO and RENAMO (created in 1987 as a dissident armed force) have been most popular, the latter especially in the central regions. The Mozambican National Union (UNAMO) registered early and there are several smaller parties, including the Democratic Party of Mozambique (PADEMO) and the Mozambique National Movement (MONAMO). They were gearing up for multiparty presidential and legislative elections in October 1994.

15 LOCAL GOVERNMENT

All of Mozambique outside the capital is organized into 10 provinces, subdivided into 112 districts, 12 municipalities, and 894 localities; the capital city of Maputo is considered an 11th province. Each provincial government is presided over by a governor, who is the representative of the president of the republic and is responsible to FRELIMO and the national government for his activities. Each province also has a provincial assembly, which legislates on matters exclusively bearing on that province. District, municipal, and local assemblies were established in 1977; local elections were held in that year and in 1986. Some 20,230 deputies for 894 local assemblies were elected by adult suffrage at age 18 from candidates chosen by local units of FRELIMO or, in their absence, by other local groups. Deputies of the provincial, district, and municipal assemblies were elected by the local bodies. No elections have been held since the legalization of opposition parties in 1990.

16 JUDICIAL SYSTEM

The formal justice system is bifurcated into a civil/criminal system under auspices of the Ministry of Justice and a military justice system under joint supervision of the Ministries of Defense and Justice. At the apex is the Supreme Court which hears appeals from both systems. Local customary courts, part of the civil/criminal system, handle estate, divorce, and other social and family issues.

Since abolition of the Revolutionary Military Tribunal and establishment of the Supreme Court in 1988, those accused of crimes against the state are tried in civilian courts under standard criminal procedural rules.

The 1990 constitution declares the establishment of an independent judiciary, with judges nominated by other jurists instead of designated by administrative appointment. It is the president, however, who continues to appoint the justices of the Supreme Court.

17 ARMED FORCES

The armed forces of Mozambique are responsible for the defense of national independence and for the political mobilization of the masses. Two years of military service are compulsory for African men and women over age 18, but is selectively enforced. The armed forces in 1993 included 45,000 army personnel (85% conscripts) equipped with 100 Soviet-made T-34, T-54, and T-55 tanks; a 1,200-member navy with 12 coastal patrol craft; and an air force of 4,000, with 43 MiG-21s and 6 armed helicopters. A border guard had 5,000 members. Some 65 advisers from Russia and North Korea were stationed in Mozambique, and about 3,000 Zimbabwean and 1,500 Malawian troops help maintain security. The resistance probably has 20,000 troops. Arms imports for 1981–85 were estimated at $850 million, then dropped to $700 million in 1986–91. Mozambique spent $107 million on defense (1989) or 6–7% of gross domestic product.

18 INTERNATIONAL COOPERATION

Mozambique was admitted to the UN on 16 September 1975 and takes part in ECA and all the nonregional specialized agencies except IAEA and WIPO. The country also belongs to the African Development Bank, G-77, and OAU, is a de facto adherent of GATT, and has signed the Law of the Sea. Mozambique plays a leading role in the Southern African Development Coordination Conference. A 20-year treaty of friendship and cooperation was signed with the former USSR in 1977. Mozambique joined the IMF and its sister organizations, the IBRD, IDA, and IFC, in 1985.

19 ECONOMY

Mozambique, with its agricultural economy and considerable mineral reserves, is a highly indebted, poverty-stricken country. Civil war, ineffective socialist economic policies, and severe droughts plagued Mozambique's economy throughout the 1980s, leaving it heavily dependent on foreign aid. Lack of security outside of major cities and the inability of relief organizations to find safe corridors for the transport of relief supplies only further depressed economic activity. Recent shifts in economic policy toward a market economy and a resolution of the civil war have laid the foundation for an economic recovery in the 1990s. However, during 1991, Mozambique's economy continued a downward slump. Growth targets of the World Bank/International Monetary Fund-guided Economic and Social Rehabilitation Program (ESRP) went unmet. The country continued to move toward a market economy in 1993, and although the GDP declined 2% in 1992, the IMF predicted 4% growth in 1993. The use of outdated data collection systems, geared more to a state-managed economy, means that the increasing vitality of the private sector tends to go unmeasured. The return of rain after the worst drought on record in 1992 and continuing peace meant that many Mozambicans were able to farm their lands again, making them less dependent on food aid. Approximately 80% of the population is employed in agriculture, mostly on a small-scale, subsistence level. Longer term prospects for growth are encouraging, but highly dependent on good weather and a stable political situation.

20INCOME

In 1992 Mozambique's GNP was $1,034 million at current prices, or $60 per capita, among the poorest in the world. Inflation was 35.2% in 1991, down from 47.0% the preceding year. For the period 1985–92 the average inflation rate was 48.1%, resulting in a real growth rate in per capita GNP of –1.3%. In 1992 the GDP was $1,052 million in current US dollars. In 1986, the last year for which statistics are available, agriculture accounted for 36.1% of GDP, manufacturing 19.6%, and transport 8.3%.

21LABOR

Nearly 80% of all economically active Mozambicans are engaged in agriculture. Under the FRELIMO government, industrial workers' organizations, created within factories, are intended to serve as the basis of new trade unions. The Mozambique Workers' Organization (Organização dos Trabalhadores Moçambicanos—OTM) was created in 1983 as the national labor federation. In December 1991 a new labor law was passed which gave existing unions the right to register independently. By the beginning of 1992, nine unions had officially registered, three of which renounced OTM affiliation. A national minimum wage for agricultural laborers was introduced in 1980. There is a constitutional right to strike, with the exception of government employees, police, military personnel, and employees of other essential services.

22AGRICULTURE

Since 1981 Mozambique's agricultural sector has been barely functional due to a combination of manmade and natural causes. The prolonged drought of 1981 to 1984 was followed by the floods and cyclone of 1984. By 1986, a famine emerged from renewed drought and civil war. Drought continued into 1987, followed by floods and locusts in 1988. Normal rainfall came in 1990, only to be followed by renewed drought in 1991 and 1992. In some regions food production declined by 80% and in 1992 the food deficit reached a record 1.3 million tons. Normal rains returned in 1993, but the ongoing food relief requirement, exclusive of war refugees, was put at 1 million tons through 1994.

Only about 4% of Mozambique is under cultivation at any one time, and more than two-thirds of the land is not exploited in any way. Nevertheless, agricultural pursuits support almost 80% of the population and provide nearly two-thirds of the GDP.

At the time of independence, about 1% of the farm population operated large-scale mechanized farms; these occupied 2,487,554 hectares (6,146,845 acres), divided into 4,626 farming units, and represented about 50% of all farmed land. These few farmers were concessionaries, virtually all of them expatriates, engaged in growing high-yield cash crops. The other 99% were subsistence farmers, tilling 2,493,504 hectares (6,161,548 acres) fragmented into 1,647,702 family plots. Although the FRELIMO government proclaimed a policy of land nationalization, some private plantations still existed in the mid-1980s. In addition, there were state-owned plantations and 1,147 communal villages. The latter represented about 20% of the rural population. Since independence, there has been a serious decline in agricultural production, attributed to the collapse of rural transport and marketing systems when Portuguese farmers and traders left the country. In the 1980s, state farms received the bulk of agricultural investment, but the yields were poor.

Mozambique's major cash crops are cashew nuts, cotton, copra, sugar, tea, and cassava, and its major food crops are corn and sorghum. Crop production in 1992 included cassava, 3,239,000 tons; sugarcane 320,000 tons; coconuts, 300,000 tons; sorghum, 66,000 tons; peanuts, 80,000 tons; corn, 133,000 tons; bananas, 80,000 tons; citrus fruits, 39,000 tons; cashew nuts, 40,000 tons; rice, 33,000 tons; copra, 72,000 tons; cotton fiber, 13,000 tons; sunflowers, 20,000 tons; and cottonseed, 30,000 tons. Mozambique is a net importer of food; in 1992, 1,164,200 tons of cereals were imported, valued at $1.9 billion. The 1991–92 drought over southern Africa caused near-complete crop failure in Mozambique's southern half. However, favorable weather in the north resulted in good localized harvests, although transportation and marketing bottlenecks still prevented intranational transport of surplus to food-deficit areas. Increased acreage used for cotton production resulted in the highest level of output (39,000 tons in 1991) since 1975. In 1991, an increased cashew harvest overwhelmed national processing capability so that 10% of the 1991 total 60,000 tons was sent to India for processing. About 60% of Mozambique's cashew production is exported to the US.

23ANIMAL HUSBANDRY

Animal husbandry, a very promising sector in the Mozambican economy, has nevertheless been systematically neglected. A total lack of credit, deadly epizootic diseases, and other diseases carried by the tsetse fly make a commercially viable animal husbandry industry almost impracticable for the African traditional farmers, who predominate in this sector. In 1992 there were an estimated 1,250,000 head of cattle, 385,000 goats, 170,000 hogs, and 118,000 sheep. The number of chickens was estimated at 22 million. Beef and veal production was estimated at 36,000 tons; cows' milk, 68,000 tons; and hen eggs, 12.8 million. Mozambique must import substantial quantities of meat and livestock products.

24FISHING

In 1991, commercial fishery production was 34,000 tons, of which lobsters and prawns were primarily for export. The potential catch is estimated at 500,000 tons of fish and 14,000 tons of prawns. South African trawlers are allowed to fish in Mozambican waters in return for providing a portion of their catch to Mozambique. In 1992, exports of shrimp and other seafood made up 46% ($64 million) of total exports. The European Community, Italy, and Japan have each entered into agreements designed to help develop the fishing industry.

25FORESTRY

Wood production is from natural forests and is almost entirely consumed by the local rural populations for fuel and construction. Forests and woodlands constituted about 14.1 million hectares (34.9 million acres) in 1991. The timber industry is centered along the Beira Railroad and in Zambézia Province, where sawn and construction timber are produced for the nearby South African market. About 16 million cu m of roundwood was produced in 1991, about 94% for fuel. Sawn wood production was 16,000 tons in 1991.

26MINING

Mozambique is rich in mineral deposits, but the industry remains largely undeveloped. Zambézia, Nampula, and Tete provinces have large deposits of columbite, tantalite, beryl, semiprecious stones, feldspar, kaolin, and coal. Manica Province produces copper and bauxite. In 1991, production included bauxite, 7,690 tons, and gold, 394 kg.

27ENERGY AND POWER

Coal has been mined in Mozambique since 1856, and exploitable reserves were said to be 2 billion tons in 1991. The output was estimated at 534,000 tons in 1981 but only 50,832 tons in 1991. The mines were nationalized in 1978. Surveys have indicated the strong possibility of offshore and onshore oil deposits. Natural gas reserves have been estimated at 40 billion cu m. As of 1991, the government was negotiating with several South African companies to build a 900 km (560 mi) natural gas pipeline from Pande to South Africa.

The Cahora Bassa Dam went into operation in the fall of 1975 in Tete Province. In 1977, Mozambique started selling substantial quantities of electricity to South Africa, but the transmission line has been sabotaged repeatedly by the Mozambique National Resistant (MNR) beginning in 1981. Work started on a national power grid in 1980, including plans to add to Cahora Bassa's generating capacity, which was 2,040,000 kw in 1991. In 1991, installed capacity was 2.3 million kw; electric power production totaled 490 million kwh, of which 10% was hydroelectric. Sabotage of the main power line pylons continued to prevent any export of electricity to South Africa in 1991.

Mozambique imports all of its petroleum supplies, though oil prospecting is pursued both on and off shore.

28 INDUSTRY

Mozambique's industrial sector is primarily centered on the processing of locally produced raw materials. Sugar, cashews, tea, and wheat lead in this regard. Brewing and textile production emerged in the 1980s, along with cement, fertilizer, and agricultural implement manufacturing. A petroleum refinery near Maputo is in operation, though producing at less than its 850,000-ton annual capacity. Other industries make glass, ceramics, paper, tires, railway equipment, radios, bicycles, and matches. Economic reforms of the early 1990s have promoted private ownership of industry and brought about a decline in the number of parastatals. Government policy now supports the development of small-scale industry which uses local materials to make import substitutes.

29 SCIENCE AND TECHNOLOGY

Eduardo Mondlane University, in Maputo, has faculties of agricultural sciences, biology, engineering, mathematics, medicine, veterinary sciences, and sciences. Maputo also has the National Institute of Geology, the Institute of Cotton Research, the National Institute of Health, and the Meteorological Service.

30 DOMESTIC TRADE

The cities of Maputo, Beira, and Nampula are the main centers of commercial life. Maputo and Beira are trading centers and ports of entry.

The 1978 nationalization of rented or abandoned property seriously shook business confidence. After 1980, however, many retail outlets, small firms, and restaurants were denationalized. Asians from the Indian subcontinent remain prominent in commerce. Price controls and acute shortages of consumer goods and industrial raw materials have fostered the growth of an extensive black market. Rationing of 11 basic commodities was introduced in 1981. Business hours are 8:30 AM to 12 noon and 2–5 PM, Mondays through Fridays, 8 AM to 12 noon on Saturdays.

31 FOREIGN TRADE

Agricultural products are Mozambique's leading exports. Principal exports in 1990 included shrimp, cashew nuts, sugar, and cotton.

The leading client for Mozambique's exports was Spain in 1990 (17.9%), followed by the US (11.5%), Japan (10.4%), and South Africa (7.0%). In 1986, the US (12.4%) and the USSR (12.1%) vied for first place as supplier of Mozambique's imports. They were followed by South Africa (10.3%).

32 BALANCE OF PAYMENTS

Mozambique has traditionally had a balance-of-payments deficit, and relies heavily on imported consumer and capital goods. Imports have risen steadily from 1987 to 1991, so that the current account deficit (excluding grants) increased form 52.9% of GDP in 1988 to 55.6% of GDP in 1991.

In 1992 merchandise exports totaled $139.3 million and imports $798.5 million. The merchandise trade balance was $–659.2 million.

33 BANKING AND SECURITIES

The Mozambican branch of the defunct Portuguese National Overseas Bank was nationalized without compensation. By a decree of 23 May 1975, it was reconstituted as the Bank of Mozambique. Functioning as a central bank, it serves as the government's banker and financial adviser, and as controller of monetary and credit policies. It is also an issuing bank, a commercial bank, and the state treasury; the bank manages Mozambique's external assets and acts as an intermediary in all international monetary transactions.

The bank has its headquarters at Maputo. In 1978, the government nationalized four of the five remaining private commercial banks (the Banco Standard Totta de Moçambique remains private). In that year, a second state bank, the People's Investment Bank, was created and given responsibility for supervising a building society, the Mozambique Credit Institute (the industrial bank), and the National Development Bank. In December 1991 the Bank of Mozambique was separated into the Bank of Mozambique and Banco Commercial de Mozambique. It is hoped the move will encourage foreign investment in the commercial banking sector. There are three commercial banks in Mozambique. All the commercial banks are at least partially owned by the state.

34 INSURANCE

In 1977, all insurance companies were nationalized and Empresa Moçambicana de Seguros was established as the sole state insurance enterprise. In 1986, 6.4% of all premiums were paid for life and 93.6% for non-life insurance.

35 PUBLIC FINANCE

The overall deficit (after grants) fell from 11.8% of GDP in 1987 to 6% in 1991, following the implementation of a market-oriented recovery program. In 1992, Mozambique's external debt stood at $4.9 billion, one of the world's highest.

36 TAXATION

Under Portuguese rule, taxation and tax collection were full of inequities and corruption at all levels of government. In 1978, after independence, much higher and more progressive taxes were introduced. These included an income tax on wages, salaries, and other benefits; a purchase tax applied to most consumer goods; and a tax levied on the sales of all enterprises. A tax of 15% on all oil produced in Mozambique was imposed in December 1982, in addition to the normal profits tax.

37 CUSTOMS AND DUTIES

Prior to independence, Portugal enjoyed most-favored-nation treatment and had imposed export quotas for certain products, such as wines and textiles, on Mozambique. With the introduction of new import restrictions in 1975, the list of luxury goods (which are heavily taxed) increased considerably. Some have a flat tax, others are taxed ad valorem. Import licenses are required for all goods. In 1993, a standard customs tariff of 7.5% ad valorem and a 7% surcharge were levied on most imports.

38 FOREIGN INVESTMENT

The liberalizing of Mozambique's economy began with the initiation of its economic recovery plan (ERP) in January 1987. Included in the program were measures to stimulate the private sector, an effort reinforced in 1990 by further legislation. In June 1993, the investment code was reformed to put foreign and local investors on an equal footing with respect to fiscal and customs regulations. The parastatal sector has been progressively privatized, with 180 enterprises transferred to the private sector by mid-1993.

39 ECONOMIC DEVELOPMENT

The government of Mozambique has abandoned its post-independence preference for a socialist organization of society, which it had tried to effect through the creation of cooperatives, state farms, and industries. In cooperation with the IMF, Mozambique is reforming its economy and preparing for a post-civil war period of economic growth.

40 SOCIAL DEVELOPMENT

After FRELIMO's takeover, large numbers of war-wounded were rehabilitated, and thousands of war orphans were cared for and educated. Equality for women was declared, and many were in the party or government. FRELIMO and its affiliate, the Organization of Mozambican Women, have actively sought to end gender discrimination. They have widened educational and occupational opportunities for women and have pushed for a family law protecting women against desertion, abuse, sexual harassment, and arbitrary divorce. In places it is enforced.

But the civil war and major droughts have hampered government's already stretched ability to make good on its social welfare promises. Moreover, there is evidence that both FRELIMO and RENAMO sought to use the distribution of relief supplies for partisan purposes.

41 HEALTH

Almost all health care services are provided by the government's National Health Service. The army maintains its own health posts and two hospitals. Traditional healers continue to play a significant role. All medical products must be registered with the Ministry of Health and, due to currency constraints, Mozambique is entirely dependent on bilateral and multilateral donors for its drug needs (estimated at $20 million annually). Mozambique spent $85 million on health care in 1990. In 1992, only 39% of the population had access to health care services.

In 1992, there were 2 doctors per 100,000 people, with a nurse to doctor ratio of 13.1. The shortage of medical supplies and trained personnel has remained severe throughout Mozambique.

The 1993 birth rate was 45.1 per 1,000 inhabitants. Only 4% of married women ages 15 to 49 years used contraception. There were 683,000 births in 1992.

In 1993, the infant mortality rate was estimated at 167 per 1,000 live births, and the general mortality rate was 18.2 per 1,000 people. The maternal mortality rate in 1991 was 300 per 100,000 live births. In addition, there were approximately 1.1 million civil war-related deaths between 1981 and 1992. Estimated average life expectancy was only 47 years in 1992.

42 HOUSING

As of 1980, 63% of housing units were constructed of woven straw, 14% of cane and woodsticks, and 8% of bricks and concrete. In the same year, 65% of all households used well water, 19% river and spring water, 8% piped outdoor water, and 4% piped indoor water. Nearly 96% were without electricity and over half had no toilet facilities.

43 EDUCATION

Education is compulsory for seven years. In 1992, there were 3,384 primary schools with 22,132 teachers and 1,199,847 pupils. General secondary schools had 3,614 teachers and 144,671 pupils; 4,020 pupils were also reported to be in teacher training programs. Students in vocational schools were 9,719. Eduardo Mondlane University is established at Maputo. The objective of the government is to promote the spread of education at all levels through democratization guided by the state. Since the country still had an estimated adult illiteracy rate of 67.1% in 1990 (males, 54.9% and females, 78.7%), literacy training is a high priority area.

44 LIBRARIES AND MUSEUMS

The National Library of Mozambique, founded in 1961, contains 110,000 volumes. The principal museums in Maputo are the Museum of Natural History, founded in 1911, specializing in natural history and ethnography; the Freire de Andrade Museum (minerals); and the Military History Museum. Beira and Nampula have general museums; Manica has a natural history museum; and Isla da Inhaca, near Maputo, has a museum of marine biology.

45 MEDIA

Postal and telecommunications services are government-operated. In the larger cities, telephones are automatic. There were 64,113 telephones in use in 1991. Radio Moçambique, the official radio service, broadcasts in Portuguese, English, Afrikaans, and local languages. Televisas Experimental is the government-owned television service. In 1991 there were an estimated 680,000 radios and 42,000 televisions.

Daily newspapers (with their estimated 1991 circulations) are *Notícias* (Maputo, mornings and Sundays, 65,000) and *Diario do Moçambique* (Beira, evenings, 16,000). Other publications include *Domingo*, a Sunday paper founded in 1981 (Maputo, 50,000).

46 ORGANIZATIONS

On 31 March 1976, the government banned 47 clubs and associations active under Portuguese rule. FRELIMO has emphasized mass organizations, such as the Organization of Mozambican Women and the Organization of Mozambican Youth.

47 TOURISM, TRAVEL, AND RECREATION

Prior to independence tourism, mostly from South Africa and the former Rhodesia, was a very important activity. However, concern for security in the late 1970s and throughout the 1980s due to the political situation left the tourist industry at a mere fraction of its previous levels. With civil stability and with economic prospects improving in recent years, hope is high that a renewed tourist industry will result. All foreign nationals need visas.

48 FAMOUS MOZAMBICANS

Eduardo C. Mondlane (1920–69) was the first president of FRELIMO. His successor, and later the first president of independent Mozambique, was Samora Moïsés Machel (1933–86). Joaquim Alberto Chissano (b.1939), foreign minister since independence, succeeded Machel as president.

49 DEPENDENCIES

Mozambique has no territories or colonies.

50 BIBLIOGRAPHY

Andersson, Hilary. *Mozambique: A War Against the People.* New York: St. Martin's, 1992.

Azevedo, Mario Joaquim. *Historical Dictionary of Mozambique.* Metuchen, N.J.: Scarecrow Press, 1991.

Christie, Iain. *Samora Machel, a Biography.* Atlantic Highlands, N.J.: Panaf, 1989.

Darch, Colin. *Mozambique.* Santa Barbara, Calif.: Clio Press, 1987.

Lord, Graham. *Ghosts of King Solomon's Mines: Mozambique and Zimbabwe: a Quest.* London: Sinclair-Stevenson, 1991.

Marshall, Judith. *Literacy, Power and Democracy in Mozambique: The Governance of Learning from Colonization to the Present.* Boulder, Colo.: Westview Press, 1993.

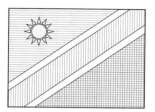

NAMIBIA

Republic of Namibia

CAPITAL: Windhoek.

FLAG: Top left triangle is blue, center diagonal band is red, and the bottom right triangle is green. Colors are separated by narrow white bands. On the blue triangle is a golden sun with twelve triangular rays.

ANTHEM: *Namibia Land of the Brave*, music and words by Axali Doeseb.

MONETARY UNIT: The South African rand (R) of 100 cents is in use; notes and coins are those of South Africa. R1 = $0.2874 (or $1 = R3.4795).

WEIGHTS AND MEASURES: The metric system is in use.

HOLIDAYS: New Year's Day, 1 January; Independence Day, 21 March; Easter, 1–4 April; Workers' Day, 1 May; Casinga Day, 4 May; Ascension Day, 12 May; Africa Day, 25 May; Heroes' Day, 26 August; Day of Goodwill, 7 October; Human Rights Day, 10 December; Christmas, 26–26 December.

TIME: 2 PM = noon GMT.

¹LOCATION, SIZE, AND EXTENT

A vast land of desert and semidesert along the southwestern coast of Africa, Namibia covers 824,290 sq km (318,260 sq mi). Comparatively, the area occupied by Namibia is slightly more than half the size of the state of Alaska. The maximum N–S extension is about 1,530 km (950 mi); the territory extends E–W some 560 km (350 mi), excluding a thin northern panhandle, the Caprivi Strip, which extends eastward another 435 km (270 mi) and measures 61 km (38 mi) at its widest point. Namibia is bordered by Angola and Zambia in the N, by Botswana in the E, by South Africa in the SE and S, and by the Atlantic Ocean to the W, with a total boundary length of 5,424 km (3,370 mi). The enclave of Walvis Bay (1,124 sq km/434 sq mi) was administered from 1977 to 1994 as part of South Africa's Cape Province, as were 13 offshore islands. Walvis Bay was reincorporated into Namibia on 1 March 1994. Namibia's capital city, Windhoek, is in the center of the country.

²TOPOGRAPHY

Namibia is largely an elevated, waterless plateau partly suitable for arid grazing. The average altitude is 1,080 m (3,543 ft) above sea level; the high point, near the coast, is Mt. Brandberg, at 2,606 m (8,550 ft). Along almost the entire range of the coast there are sandy wastes and high, reddish sand dunes. The coastal strip comprises the Namib Desert, and the eastern region is part of the Kalahari Desert. All four permanent rivers form borders: the Kunene and Okavango in the north, the Zambezi in the northeast, and the Orange (Oranje) in the south.

³CLIMATE

Namibia's climate is the driest in Africa, with sunny, warm days and cooler nights, especially during the winter months. The mean January temperature at Windhoek is 23°C (73°F); in winter, the mean temperature is 13°C (55°F). The fertile northern strip is always warmer, having a climate similar to that of southern Angola.

Much of Namibia is a land of perennial drought. The annual rainfall, which is concentrated in the December–March period, generally averages more than 50 cm (20 in) in the far north, 2.5–15 cm (1–6 in) in the south, and 20–40 cm (8–16 in) in the central plateau. But the rains often fail: some regions have gone 90 years without a drop of rain.

⁴FLORA AND FAUNA

Namibia is the home of a great variety of large fauna and avifauna. In the game parks and the neighboring grazing areas, there are the tallest elephants in the world, along with rhinoceroses; an abundance of lions, cheetahs, and leopards; ostriches; and a profusion of ungulates, including the giraffe, zebra, kudu, eland, black-faced impala, hartebeest, springbok, gemsbok, and wildebeest. Birds of prey are numerous, as are the Kori bustard and the Karroo korhaan. Among the unique flora are the desert welwitschia and many varieties of aloe.

⁵ENVIRONMENT

Namibia's environmental concerns include water pollution and insufficient water for its population. The nation has 2.2 cubic miles of water. Eighty-two percent is used in farming and 12% for industrial purposes. Ten percent of the nation's city dwellers and 63% of the people living in rural areas do not have pure water. The nation's cities produce 0.1 million tons of solid waste per year. Deforestation and soil erosion also threaten the nation's land. Agricultural chemicals, such as DDT, are also a threat to the environment due to excessive usage. The Namibian Wildlife Trust, organized in 1982, works closely with the Department of Nature Conservation to maintain the habitat and to prevent poaching of threatened fauna and avifauna. Twelve nature conservation areas cover 99,616 sq km (38,462 sq mi). Among these are the 22,270-sq-km (8,603-sq-mi) Etosha National Park, one of Africa's best-run and least-visited animal preserves; a smaller game park near Windhoek; and the Namib Desert Park (23,401 sq km/9,035 sq mi), east of Swakopmund. There is a seal reserve at Cape Cross, north of Swakopmund. In 1994, Namibia's wildlife is threatened due to environmental damage. Eleven mammal species and seven bird species are endangered. Seventeen species of plants are threatened with extinction. As of 1992, UN sources identified the black rhino, cave catfish, and the wild dog as endangered species.

6POPULATION

According to the 1991 census, the population of Namibia was 1,401,711. In 1994, the total population was estimated at 1,690,483. The projected population for the year 2000 is 1,964,000, assuming a crude birthrate of 39.5 per 1,000 population and a death rate of 9.2 for 1995–2000. Annual population growth was estimated at 2.7%. The population density in 1985 was 2 persons per sq km (4.4 per sq mi). Windhoek, the capital, had a 1991 population of 158,609. About 55% of the population lives in the northern part of the country. One-third of the population lived in urban localities in 1991.

7MIGRATION

Namibia's migrant labor force exceeds 100,000. Ovambo from northern Namibia have moved south since the 1920s to work in the diamond mines near the mouth of the Orange River, in the port of Walvis Bay, and in the cities and towns of the interior. Ovambo formerly migrated by the thousands to work in the gold mines of South Africa, but that traffic has diminished. Only 14,817 blacks of Namibian birth were resident in South Africa in 1991. Some Ovambo have gravitated from neighboring Angola into northern Namibia. As of 1986 there were 69,000 Namibian refugees in Angola and 7,000 in Zambia. A UN repatriation program ended in mid-1990, with 42,736 returned.

8ETHNIC GROUPS

The largest group is the Ovambo, numbering about 665,000 in 1991, who live mainly in the well-watered north. The second-largest group is the Kavango (124,000), residing along the Okavango River. The Damara (100,000) live east of the arid coast and to the south of the Ovambo, and the Herero (100,000), a herding people, range north of Windhoek. The whites, including about 25,000 speakers of German, 40,000 Afrikaners, and 5,000 English-speakers, totaled about 85,000 in 1991. Whites live predominantly in central and southern Namibia. The Caprivians, living in the easternmost portion of the strip, numbered 50,000, while the Nama (64,000) are herders in the deep south. The Coloureds (peoples of mixed descent, numbering 48,000 in 1985) live largely in Windhoek and other cities; the Basters of Rehoboth (28,000 in 1985) are a farming community of mixed origin. There were about 32,000 San (Bushmen) and 7,000 Tswana in 1985.

9LANGUAGES

The official language of Namibia is English. Afrikaans and German are also spoken. However, Ovambo, in any of several dialects, is the language spoken by more Namibians than any other, and Herero is widely spoken in Windhoek. The Coloureds and the Basters favor Afrikaans, which is also the first tongue of the majority of whites.

10RELIGIONS

Perhaps 90% of Namibians are Christians; the rest practice traditional African religions. It is estimated that two-thirds of all Namibians attend Western-style religious services weekly. The first missionaries to proselytize in Namibia were British Congregationalists and Methodists; German and Finnish Lutherans and German-speaking Roman Catholics followed. The Lutheran community (three churches), under an elected leader in Windhoek, numbers about 528,000. The two Roman Catholic dioceses of northern and southern Namibia together claimed a membership of 195,000 in 1993. The Anglican (Episcopal) Church of Namibia also has missionary origins; its membership is about 57,000. The Dutch Reformed Churches have a largely white membership of 63,000, and there are several charismatic and independent church groups.

11TRANSPORTATION

Namibia is traversed by 2,341 km (1,455 mi) of railway, with a main line from South Africa connecting east of Karasburg and continuing to Keetmanshoop (with a side branch to Lüderitz), Mariental, and Windhoek before heading eastward to the ranching area of Gobabis and north to the copper-mining area of Tsumeb. Westward from Windhoek and also southwestward from Tsumeb, the main rail lines link the interior with Swakopmund and Walvis Bay. Of Namibia's 54,500 km (33,867 mi) of road, 4,079 km (2,535 mi) were paved in 1991. There were 109,940 registered vehicles in 1992.

Walvis Bay, a South African enclave from 1977 to 1994, has been the main handler of Namibia's imports and exports and the home of the territory's once-vital fishing fleet since the 1920s; about 95% of all Namibian seaborne trade is transshipped there. Lüderitz, the site of the first German entry in 1883, has lost its status as a port because of harbor silting and poor transport links; however, it remains a center of the territory's crayfish industry.

The territory's international airport is near Windhoek, with other modern facilities at Rundu, Grootfontein, Walvis Bay, Lüderitz, Keetmanshoop, and Oranjemund. Other towns have dirt airstrips, and many white Namibians fly their own aircraft from their farms to the urban centers. Air Namibia flew 149,200 international and domestic passengers in 1991. South African Airways links Windhoek to Europe and to the principal cities in South Africa.

12HISTORY

Paintings of animal figures on rock slabs in Namibia testify to at least 25,000 years of human habitation in the territory. The San (Bushmen) may have been Namibia's earliest inhabitants. The Damara also claim to be the true indigenous Namibians, who were compelled to welcome waves of Herero and Ovambo from the north. By the 19th century, the Damara, Ovambo, and Herero were the largest indigenous ethnic groups, with the Kavango and the Caprivians also settled in the areas where they now reside. There was competition for land, mostly between the Ovambo and the Herero, and the Herero may have established some primacy. But then the invaders arrived. First came the Hottentots (now called Nama), brown-skinned peoples of mixed parentage from South Africa. They had guns and conquered a large swath of southern and central Namibia from the Herero and the Damara. The Germans came in 1883, initially as commercial colonizers and missionaries and then as soldiers. With military might (largely cannon and machine guns), the Germans in the 1890s moved inland across the desert from Walvis Bay (which had been annexed by the British in 1878 and incorporated into Cape Colony in 1884) to Windhoek, establishing forts and subjugating the Herero and Damara. This colonization was bloody: the Germans forcibly took land and cattle from the Herero, whose revolt was suppressed by the Germans at a cost of about 65,000 Herero lives. A Nama revolt met a similar fate in 1904.

When World War I broke out, the South Africans invaded Süd-West Afrika, as the German colony was then known. The South Africans wished to annex the territory, but the new League of Nations granted South Africa a mandate instead. From 1920 to 1946, South Africa administered the mandatory territory as if it were an integral part of the Union. However, it spent little money on social services and largely neglected (as had the Germans) the Ovambo-Kavango sphere in the north.

After World War II, South Africa refused to acknowledge the jurisdiction of the UN over Namibia as a successor organization

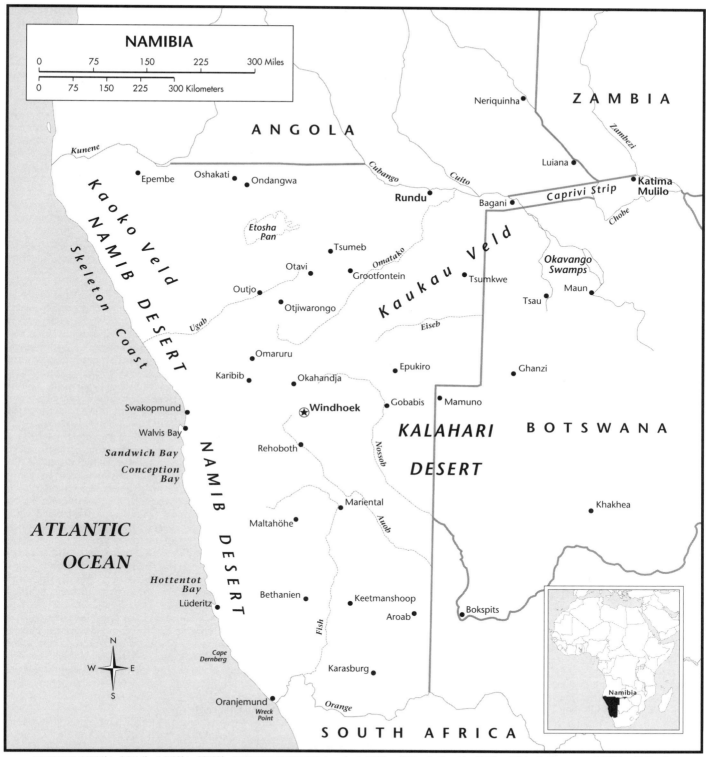

LOCATION: 11°44′ to 25°16′E; 16°58′ to 28°58′s. **BOUNDARY LENGTHS:** Angola, 1,376 km (855 mi); Zambia, 203 km (126 mi); Botswana, 1,397 km (868 mi); South Africa, 1,078 km (670 mi); Atlantic Ocean, including Walvis Bay, 1,507 km (936 mi). **TERRITORIAL SEA LIMIT:** 12 mi.

to the League of Nations. Instead, it progressively integrated Namibia into the Union as what amounted to a fifth province. In the 1950s, senators from South West Africa sat in the South African parliament, and Windhoek was reduced to the status of a provincial capital. The UN took South Africa before the International Court of Justice, but the first verdicts in 1962 and 1966

were ambiguous. Only in 1971 did the Court take definitive issue with South Africa, declaring its occupation of Namibia illegal. In 1978, the UN Security Council rejected South Africa's annexation of Walvis Bay.

Meanwhile, in 1960, representatives of the indigenous majority had formed the South-West Africa People's Organization

(SWAPO) to seek independence and black majority rule. Beginning in 1966, but especially after 1977, SWAPO used guerrilla tactics with varying success. South Africa countered by building up its armed forces along Namibia's borders with Zambia and Angola, where SWAPO had established bases and from where it launched raids.

In 1978, South Africa ostensibly accepted a Western-sponsored plan for an independent Namibia, but at the same time sponsored elections for a constituent assembly (opposed by the UN) that resulted in the victory of a white-dominated multi-ethnic party, the Democratic Turnhalle Alliance. Representatives of the US, the UK, the Federal Republic of Germany (FRG), France, and Canada—the Contact Group—then attempted to devise a formula acceptable to South Africa that would permit Namibia to proceed to independence in accordance with the transfer framework embodied in UN Security Council Resolution 435 of 1978. South Africa's demand that Cuban forces leave neighboring Angola as part of a settlement was rejected by black African countries, however.

A "transitional government of national unity," composed of South African-appointed members of six parties, was installed in 1985. The South African administrator-general retained the right to veto legislation, and South Africa continued to exercise authority over foreign affairs and defense. As the war heated up, so did international efforts to arrive at a lasting resolution. In May 1988, a US mediation team, headed by Assistant Secretary of State for African Affairs Chester A. Crocker, brought negotiators from Angola, Cuba, and South Africa (and observers from the Soviet Union) together in London. For seven months, negotiators worked intensely to arrive at an agreement to bring peace to the region, in the context of UN Resolution 435. On 13 December 1988, representatives of Angola, Cuba, and South Africa signed the Protocol of Brazzaville by which South Africa agreed to implement the UN Plan for Namibia and Cuba and Angola ageed to a phased, total withdrawal of Cuban troops from Angola. Further agreeements on details were signed in New York on 22 December 1988.

The date chosen to implement UN Resolution 435 was 1 April 1989. South African Louis Pienaar was named Administrator-General to supervise the transition to independence and the UN Special Representative, Martti Ahtisaari, headed the UN Transition Assistance Group (UNTAG).

The process got off to a shaky start on 1 April. In contravention of SWAPO President Sam Nujoma's assurances to the UN to abide by a ceasefire and repatriate only unarmed insurgents, around 2,000 armed members of the People's Liberation Army (PLAN), SWAPO's military wing, crossed from Angola to establish a military presence in northern Namibia. South African forces were authorized to oppose them and 375 PLAN fighters were killed. This misunderstanding was overcome by negotiations and peace was restored.

Elections were held 7–11 November 1989, and were certified as free and fair by the UN special representative. This transitional period involved the return of 42,000 or more refugees and the return of SWAPO politicians and PLAN fighters in exile. SWAPO took 57% of the vote, just short of the two-thirds necessary to enable it to have a free hand in drafting a constitution. The Democratic Turnahalle Alliance (DTA) received 29% and a variety of ethnic-based parties the rest. The constituent assembly met on 21 November 1989 and drafted and adopted a constitution by 9 February 1990 based on the 1982 constituitonal principles. Namibia became independent on 21 March 1990. Nujoma was sworn in as president by UN Sec. Gen. Javier Pérez de Cuéllar.

Since indepence, the SWAPO government (whose support comes chiefly from the Ovambo people of the north and from urban areas) has pursued a policy of "reconciliation" with the white inhabitants. It is a vibrant multiparty, nonracial democracy.

In 1993, agreement was reached with South Africa to reincorporate Walvis Bay into Namibia, an act completed on 1 March 1994.

13 GOVERNMENT

The Namibia constitution adopted on 21 March 1990 is considered a model of democratic government. Universal suffrage and a strong emphasis on human rights and political freedom are prominent. An independent judiciary and legal obligations to improve the disadvantaged sectors of the population are written into the government. Namibia has a bicameral legislature. It consists of a National Assembly of 72 elected deputies and up to six members appointed by the president and a National Council comprised of two members from each of 13 regions. The president is elected by direct, popular vote and serves as head of state and government and commander-in-chief of the Defense Force for no more than two five-year terms. There is also an independent ombudsman to investigate complaints and take action in defense of the interests of individuals and organization in their dealings with the state.

14 POLITICAL PARTIES

The South-West Africa People's Organization (SWAPO) is the largest political party, and during the struggle for independence, it was recognized by the OAU and the UN General Assembly as the sole legitimate representative of the Namibian people. It was at the time divided between an exile wing and an internal wing and it was difficult to maintain links between the two. SWAPO leaders within the territory were subject to harassment and detention and the external wing was engaged in war with the South Africans. There are a number of ethnic parties, including the South-West African National Union (SWANU), largely representing the Herero; the Democratic Turnhalle Alliance (DTA), a white-led amalgam of constituent ethnic parties and former clients of South Africa; the Christian Democratic Action, which draws on the Ovambo; the SWAPO-Democrats, a small Ovambo-based group; the Damara Council; the Namibia Christian Democratic Party (a Kavango group); the small Namibia Independence Party (based in Windhoek); the National Party, a white group; the Labour Party, with Coloured support; and the Rehoboth Free Democratic Party, drawn from the Baster community of the Rehoboth area. All but SWAPO, Christian Democratic Action, and the Damara Council were represented in the bodies appointed in 1985.

In the 1989 elections to the constituent assembly, SWAPO gained 41 seats (57.3%); the DTA 21 seats (28.6%); the United Democratic Front, four seats (5.6%); and the Action Christian National, three seats (3.5%). The other parties collectively gained three seats on 5% of the vote.

SWAPO did even better in local and regional elections. In December 1992, SWAPO gained control of nine regional councils while DTA took only three. The new constituency boundaries served to reduce the impact of ethnic voting blocs. DTA also suffered from revelations of covert South African funding for its 1989 campaign.

15 LOCAL GOVERNMENT

There are 13 regions in Namibia. The most populous is Ohangwena (178,000), followed by Oshikoto (176,000), Khomas (161,000), Oshana (159,000), Omusati (158,000), Okavango (136,000), Erongo (98,500), Caprivi (92,000), Otjozondjupa (85,000), Hardap (80,000), Karas (73,000), Kunene (58,500) and Omaheke (55,600). They are governed by elected councils. Local governments (municipalities, towns and villages) have elected councils.

16 JUDICIAL SYSTEM

The court system retains Roman-Dutch elements inherited from South Africa along with elements of the traditional court system.

The formal court system is arranged in three tiers: magistrates' courts, the High Court, and the Supreme Court. The Supreme Court serves as the highest court of appeals and also exercises constitutional review of legislation.

The traditional courts handle minor criminal offenses such as petty theft and violations of local customs. In 1991 a presidential commission recommended that the traditional courts be maintained provided they act consistently with the constitution and laws. Legislation enacted in 1993 was intended to bridge the gap between traditional and magistrates' courts by creation of a system of "community courts."

The constitution calls for an independent judiciary as well as an extensive bill of rights protecting freedom of speech, press, assembly, association, and religion and a guarantee of redress for those whose fundamental rights have been violated. It provides for an ombudsman to deliver free legal advice upon request.

Because of a shortage of trained magistrates and lack of legal counsel, courts typically face a significant backlog of cases awaiting trial. The government appointed the first public defender in 1993 and renewed funding for representation for indigent defendants.

Although the constitution prohibits racial discrimination, some apartheid-based laws dating from before independence have not yet been repealed.

[17] ARMED FORCES

Postwar national forces number 7,400 men in 8 mixed battalions and 100 men in naval patrol forces. There is a small national police force. Defense spending is $66 million or 3.4 percent of gross domestic product (1992).

[18] INTERNATIONAL COOPERATION

Namibia is a member of five UN agencies—the FAO, IAEA, ILO, ITU, and UNESCO—and is an associate member of WHO.

[19] ECONOMY

Namibia's economy is dependent on a few primary commodity exports, including minerals (diamonds, uranium, copper, lead, silver), livestock (both meat and hides), and fishing. These three sectors account for 43% of GDP and nearly 90% of exports. Led by the diamond industry, the GDP grew 5.1% in 1991. The economy is highly integrated with that of South Africa. Three-fourths of Namibia's imports originate there, and transport and communications infrastructure are strongly linked with South Africa. Years of white rule have resulted in one of the most unequal income distributions on the African continent. However, a democratically elected government is following pragmatic economic policies committed to the development of previously neglected regions of the country.

The economy has a superior transport and communications infrastructure, an extensive natural resouce base, a small population, and a stable government committed to competitiveness in attracting investment. For these reasons analysts believe that Namibia's economy holds enormous potential for long-term economic growth.

[20] INCOME

In 1992 Namibia's GNP was $2,502 million at current prices, or $1,610 per capita. Although the per capita GNP is relatively high for Africa, it obscures a tremendous income inequality between the black and minority white populations. For the period 1985–92 the average inflation rate was 10.2%, resulting in a real growth rate in per capita GNP of 1.1%. In 1992 the GDP was $2,464 million in current US dollars. Mining accounted for 28.8% of GDP, followed by community, social, and personal services at 18.6%, agriculture and fishing, at 15.0%, and trade, at 10.7%. Manufacturing accounted for 6.2%, while finance accounted for 6.4%.

[21] LABOR

Commercial and subsistence agriculture supported 70% of the population in 1992, but only 16% of the labor force is employed in commercial farming. The unemployment rate was about 25% in 1992.

The constitution provides freedom of association, including the right to form and join trade unions, which was extended to public servants, farm workers, and domestic employees under the Labor Act of March 1992. The principal trade union organization is the National Union of Namibian Workers (NUNW), a SWAPO-aligned federation of 7 industrial unions with 70,000 members. The main public service and construction unions are affiliates of the Namibia People's Social Movement (NPSM), formerly known as the Namibian Christian Social Trade Unions.

[22] AGRICULTURE

Less than 1% of Namibia is arable. About 70% of the active population depends on agriculture directly or indirectly for their living. Agriculture consists of two sectors: a commercial sector with some 50,000 workers (producing 80% of annual yields), and a subsistence sector situated largely in communal areas. Colonialism left Namibia with a three-tier agricultural production system: 4,000 commercial ranches; 20,000 stock-raising households; and 120,000 mixed-farming operations. The ranches displaced local farmers on 66% of the viable farmland and left only 5% of the land to the 120,000 mixed-farming operations.

Corn is grown primarily in the area known as the Grootfontein–Otavi–Tsumeb triangle, where farms are much smaller than in other parts of the country. Corn production in 1992 amounted only to 13,000 tons (down from 50,000 tons in 1991). Recent droughts have created a dependency on grain imports; in 1992, 53,800 tons of corn were imported. Namibia is dependent on South Africa for corn, sugar, fruit, and vegetables.

Caprivi and Kavango in the northeast have potential for extensive crop development. Communal farms there are estimated to produce 60% of their staple food, such as mahango (which is also used to brew beer). Cotton, groundnut, rice, sorghum, and vegetable production have begun on an experimental basis in Kavango. An irrigation project at Hardap Dam near Mariental produces corn, alfalfa, feed corn, and grapes.

[23] ANIMAL HUSBANDRY

Namibia is an arid country with very little arable land. Livestock production is the major agricultural activity, making up more than 90% of that sector's output. In 1992, there were an estimated 2,100,000 head of cattle, 3 million sheep, and 1,972,000 goats. About 200,000 cattle and 1,208,000 sheep and goats were slaughtered in 1992. Karakul pelts have been a leading export, but the world market is currently depressed. Namibia has ideal conditions for commercial breeding of ostriches, and of other African game animals for meat, hide, trophy, and tourism purposes.

[24] FISHING

The fish stocks of the rich Benguela current system were seriously depleted in the late 1970s and throughout the 1980s. Most species, however, are expected to recover by the late 1990s as a result of conservation programs. Fishing and fish processing are among the nation's best prospects for employment and economic growth. The government has predicted that by 2000, production could increase eight-fold, driving a $900 million industry which could constitute 30% of GDP. In early 1992, a new fisheries code was presented to Parliament, which stressed employment and training opportunities for Namibian citizens, profit reinvestment, and revenue gain for the nation. The total catch in 1991 was 204,517 tons. After independence in 1990, the volume of the nominal catch skyrocketed nearly ten-fold.

25 FORESTRY

About 22% of Namibia consists of forests and woodland, including woodland savanna, all in the north and northeast. Most of the timber is used locally.

26 MINING

The most valuable minerals produced in 1991 included diamonds, uranium, copper, silver, lead, zinc, gold, pyrite, and salt. In 1991, the Namibian mining industry accounted for 29% of the GDP, and was the largest private sector area of employment. Namibia is among the world's premier producers of gem diamonds, which are mainly recovered from a 96-km (60-mi) stretch along the coastline north of the Orange River. Consolidated Diamond Mines, Ltd. (CDM), a subsidiary of De Beers Consolidated Mines of South Africa, produced 1.2 million carats in 1991, their best year since 1981.

Rössing Uranium, owned by Rio Tinto-Zinc of the UK, produced about 3,185 tons of uranium oxide in 1991 at the world's largest opencast uranium mine, at Swakopmund. CDM and Rössing Uranium together account for 75% of the mining sector's production value. CDM is the sixth largest producer of near-gem and gem quality diamonds in the world, and Rössing ranks fifth among occidental nations in uranium production. In all, Namibia during 1991 produced an estimated 30,000 tons of mined copper, 11,800 tons of mined lead, 33,133 tons of zinc concentrates, and 67 tons of refined cadmium. Small amounts of tin, gold, columbium, and tantalum were also produced. Salt production was 98,222 tons. Coal has been discovered in southeastern Namibia.

27 ENERGY AND POWER

The South-West Africa Water and Electricity Corp. (SWADEC) draws power from a partially completed hydroelectric facility on the Angola-Namibian border and from thermal plants near Walvis Bay and Windhoek. It also has a link to South Africa's power grid. Installed capacity was 490 Mw in 1991; production totaled 1,290 million kwh. All coal and petroleum products come from South Africa.

Three Norwegian oil companies were exploring an offshore area of 11,000 sq km in the early 1990s. Seven more oil concessions were to have been awarded in 1992.

28 INDUSTRY

Namibia's small industrial sector is centered on meat and fish processing, with some production of basic consumer goods. There are furniture and clothing factories, metal and engineering works, assembly plants for imported components, and a cement plant. In 1991, output increased by 5%. Historically, Namibia has been dependent on South Africa's manufacturing sector.

Largely due to the influence of the mining sector, Namibia has considerable electrical power generating facilities. The 120-Mw Van Eck power station, the 320-Mw Ruacana hydroelectric station, and the 45-Mw Paratus facility form a local generating capacity that is linked not only to the South African grid but to the Zambian grid as well. Fighting in Angola has delayed the Epupa hydroelectric project which would give Namibia the potential to export electric power.

29 SCIENCE AND TECHNOLOGY

The Namibia Department of Agriculture and Nature Conservation, in Windhoek, supports extensive research on natural resources and ecology. The Desert Ecological Research Unit of Namibia carries out exploration and research in the Namib Desert and semi-arid Namibia. The University of Namibia has a faculty of science.

30 DOMESTIC TRADE

Windhoek is the country's commercial center.

31 FOREIGN TRADE

In 1991, minerals made up 33% of Namibia's exports. The level of both exports and imports increased over the year ending 1992, leaving Namibia with a $30 million trade surplus. Key trading partners are South Africa, Switzerland, Germany, Japan, and the US.

32 BALANCE OF PAYMENTS

Traditionally, Namibia has maintained a trade surplus resulting from its valuable mineral exports. However, over 95% of Namibia's consumption and investment goods are imported, resulting in wide fluctuations in the merchandise trade surplus due to the constant changes in world mineral prices. Namibia joined the IMF in September 1990.

In 1992 merchandise exports totaled $1,288 million and imports $1,177 million. The merchandise trade balance was $111 million. The following table summarizes Namibia's balance of payments for 1991 and 1992 (in millions of US dollars):

	1991	1992
CURRENT ACCOUNT		
Goods, services, and income	−83	−162
Unrequited transfers	335	304
TOTALS	252	142
CAPITAL ACCOUNT		
Direct investment	100	53
Portfolio investment	−26	4
Other long-term capital	−262	−227
Other short-term capital	−23	81
Exceptional financing	—	—
Other liabilities	—	—
Reserves	14	7
TOTALS	−197	−82
Errors and omissions	−54	−33
Total change in reserves	20	13

33 BANKING AND SECURITIES

Namibia uses the South African rand as currency, and its banking system is integrated with that of South Africa. There were five registered commercial banks in 1993. The Namibian Stock Exchange is located in Windhoek.

34 INSURANCE

South African-based firms provide insurance coverage.

35 PUBLIC FINANCE

Namibia inherited a relatively strong financial position at independence in 1990, with a budget essentially in balance. Public indebtedness fell from 32% of GDP in 1985 to 16% in 1990. The annual budget consumed some 57% of GDP in 1991–92. Namibia's civil service wage expenditures are high, as the new government promised to retain all willing civil servants at the time of independence.

The following table shows actual revenues and expenditures for 1990 and 1991 in millions of rands.

	1990	1991
REVENUE AND GRANTS		
Tax revenue	1,538.0	1,985.1
Non-tax revenue	196.8	310.1
Capital revenue	0.1	3.7
Grants	100	105.0
TOTAL	1,834.9	2,403.9

EXPENDITURES & LENDING MINUS REPAYMENT	1990	1991
General public services	323.3	460.0
Defense	113.0	184.0
Public order and safety	159.1	210.9
Education	423.6	628.2
Health	225.9	275.2
Social security and welfare	131.5	192.9
Housing and community amenities	175.3	225.4
Recreation, cultural, and religious affairs	68.5	83.5
Economic affairs and services	294.1	491.0
Other expenditures	126.5	79.2
Lending minus repayments	3.2	17.7
TOTAL	2,044.0	2,848.0

36 TAXATION

There is a progressive personal income tax with a top rate of 40%. The basic tax on corporate profits is 40%, but diamond producers pay 50%. A 10% surcharge has been imposed on these taxes since 1981. A general sales tax of 11%, a tax on nonresident shareholders, and a tax on undistributed profits are also levied.

37 CUSTOMS AND DUTIES

Namibia is part of the Southern African Customs Union; no tariffs exist on most goods moving between members. Imports from outside the union are subject to a common tariff rate; most imports need licenses. South Africa levies and collects most of the customs and excise duties for the other members and then pays each a share, based on an established formula.

38 FOREIGN INVESTMENT

International investment, mostly South African, has historically played an important role in Namibia. In addition, there is significant UK and US investment in mining. Otherwise, foreign investment is negligible. In December 1990, foreign investment legislation was liberalized. In April 1993, Namibia announced a program of private-sector investment incentives which included lower taxes, grants, and development loans. The creation of an Export Processing Zone is also under consideration.

39 ECONOMIC DEVELOPMENT

Namibia's government will continue to build and diversify its economy around its mineral reserves. Priorities include expanding the manufacturing sector, land reform, agricultural development in the populous north, and improved education and health opportunities. Transfer of Walvis Bay and 12 offshore islands to Namibia has returned to Namibia its deep-water port and 20% of its offshore rights.

40 SOCIAL DEVELOPMENT

By many economic and social indicators, including population per physician, per hospital bed, and per telephone, Namibia is statistically better off than many black African countries. However, such figures are skewed by Namibia's relatively large white population (6.8% in 1985). Such comparisons also mask the huge disparities between rural and urban Namibia.

Because of this, government is committed to and obliged by the constitution to promote actively the welfare of the people, including gender, racial and regional equality.

41 HEALTH

In 1985 there were 64 hospitals and 130 clinics, with about 7,500 beds. Medical personnel in 1991 included 321 doctors, 91 pharmacists, 51 dentists, and a nursing staff of 4,385. In 1990, the population per physician was 4,620. Most facilities are in the towns, where most whites live. Since health services are provided by the ethnically based second-tier authorities, the system is effectively segregated. In 1992, average life expectancy was 58 years; infant mortality was 62 per 1,000 live births. The general mortality rate was 10.7 per 1,000 inhabitants in 1993, and the maternal mortality rate was estimated at 370 per 100,000 live births in 1991.

In 1993 Namibia had a birth rate of 42.5 per 1,000 people; 26% of married women ages 15 to 49 years used some form of contraception. There were 66,000 births in 1992.

In 1992, 72% of the population had access to health care services. Immunization rates in 1992 were very good for children up to one year old: tuberculosis (90%); diphtheria, pertussis, and tetanus (65%); polio (65%); and measles (63%).

42 HOUSING

There is a sharp contrast in housing standards between white and black Namibians. Most rural dwellings are self-constructed from local materials. Regional and town governments build and rent housing to migrants, but the demand has overwhelmed the supply. In 1992 the backlog in housing units was estimated at 45,000 units.

43 EDUCATION

Education is compulsory for nine years between the ages of 7 and 16. Primary education is for seven years, and secondary for five years. In 1990, 313,528 Namibians were in primary and 62,976 pupils were in secondary schools. Of these, 61,801 were in general schools and 1,175 were in vocational schools. There is an Academy for Tertiary Education for adult students. In 1983, adult literacy was nearly 100% for whites and 28% for blacks. In 1991, there were 4,157 pupils and 331 teachers in all higher level institutions. Of these, 141 teachers and 1,496 pupils were in universities and equivalent institutions.

44 LIBRARIES AND MUSEUMS

Libraries serve most cities and towns. The National Archives and a public library (75,000 volumes) are both located in Windhoek. There is a national museum in Windhoek, with an emphasis on the natural and human sciences, and local museums in Lüderitz and Swakopmund.

45 MEDIA

The five daily newspapers are published in Windhoek. The leading ones (with 1991 circulation) are: *The Times of Namibia* (16,200); *The Namibian* (15,000); *The Windhoek Advertiser* (10,000); and *Die Republikein* (12,000). The Namibian Broadcasting Corp. transmits radio programs in English, German, Afrikaans, and African languages. Television relays from South Africa began in the Windhoek and Oshakati areas in 1981. In 1991 there were 188,000 radios and 31,000 television sets.

Namibia has good quality telephone service, with 18 automatic telephone exchanges that can put callers in touch with 63 countries. Communication with rural areas is provided by 65 fixed radio stations and 500 mobile stations. Fax machines and telex services are readily available.

46 ORGANIZATIONS

There are two chambers of commerce in Windhoek.

47 TOURISM, TRAVEL, AND RECREATION

Namibia's prime tourist attractions are game viewing, trophy hunting, and the scenic beauty of its deserts. In the west, Swakopmund is a Hanseatic-style resort town populated by Namibians of German descent. It is the center for tours of the nearby Namib dunes, and for visits to the wild Skeleton Coast to the north. In the south, the Fish River Canyon, 85 km (53 mi) long and 700 m (2,300 ft) deep, ranks second in size to the Grand Canyon. European tourism is well developed, but the North American and Far Eastern markets are only now starting to grow.

[48]FAMOUS NAMIBIANS

Herman Toivo ja Toivo (b.1915?), the founder of SWAPO and the leader of Namibian nationalism, languished in a South African prison from 1966, when he was convicted of treason, until his release in March 1984. Sam Nujoma (b.1929) has been leader of SWAPO since 1966.

[49]DEPENDENCIES

Namibia has no territories or colonies.

[50]BIBLIOGRAPHY

Berat, Lynn. *Walvis Bay: Decolonization and International Law.* New Haven: Yale University Press, 1990.

Cliffe, Lionel et al., *The Transition to Independence in Namibia.* Boulder: Lynne Rienner, 1994.

Cooper, Allan D. (ed.). *Allies in Apartheid: Western Capitalism in Occupied Namibia.* New York: St. Martin's Press, 1988.

Dore, Isaak I. *The International Mandate System and Namibia.* Boulder, Colo.: Westview, 1985.

Green, Reginald O., et al. (eds.). *Namibia: The Last Colony.* London: Longman, 1981.

Jaster, Robert S. *The 1988 Peace Accords and the Future of South-western Africa.* London: Brassey's for the International Institute for Strategic Studies, 1990.

Katjavivi, Peter H. *A History of Resistance in Namibia.* Trenton, N.J.: Africa World Press, 1990, 1988.

Rotberg, Robert I. (ed.). *Namibia: Political and Economic Prospects.* Lexington, Mass.: D. C. Heath, 1982.

Sparks, Donald L. *Namibia: The Nation After Independence.* Boulder, Colo.: Westview Press, 1992.

Tötemeyer, Gerhard. *Namibia Old and New.* New York: St. Martin's, 1978.

NIGER

Republic of Niger
République du Niger

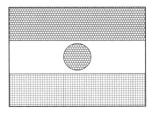

CAPITAL: Niamey.

FLAG: The flag is a tricolor of orange, white, and green horizontal stripes, with an orange orb at the center of the white stripe.

ANTHEM: *La Nigérienne.*

MONETARY UNIT: The Communauté Financière Africaine franc (CFA Fr) is a paper currency with one basic official rate based on the French franc (CFA Fr = 1 French franc). There are coins of 1, 2, 5, 10, 25, 50, 100, and 500 CFA francs, and notes of 50, 100, 500, 1,000, 5,000, and 10,000 CFA francs. CFA Fr1 = $0.0018 (or $1 = CFA Fr571).

WEIGHTS AND MEASURES: The metric system is the legal standard.

HOLIDAYS: New Year's Day, 1 January; Anniversary of 1974 military coup, 15 April; Labor Day, 1 May; Independence Day, 3 August; Proclamation of the Republic, 18 December; Christmas, 25 December. Movable religious holidays include 'Id al-Fitr, 'Id al-'Adha', and Milad an-Nabi.

TIME: 1 PM = noon GMT.

¹LOCATION, SIZE, AND EXTENT

A landlocked country, the Republic of the Niger is the largest state in West Africa, with an area of 1,267,000 sq km (489,191 sq mi), extending 1,845 km (1,146 mi) ENE-WSW and 1,025 km (637 mi) NNW-SSE. Comparatively, the area occupied by Niger is slightly less than twice the size of the state of Texas. Bordered on the N by Libya, on the E by Chad, on the S by Nigeria, on the SW by Benin and Burkina Faso, on the W by Mali, and on the NW by Algeria, Niger has a total boundary length of 5,697 km (3,540 mi). Niger's capital city, Niamey, is located in the southwestern part of the country.

²TOPOGRAPHY

Niger is four-fifths desert, and most of the northeast is uninhabitable. The southern fifth of the country is savanna, suitable mainly for livestock raising and limited agriculture. In the north-central region is the volcanic Aïr Massif, reaching a height of 1,944 m (6,376 ft) on Mt. Gréboun, the nation's highest point. Massifs along the Libyan border average about 800 m (2,600 ft). The southern plateau is at an elevation of 300–500 m (1,000–1,650 ft). The Niger River flows for about 550 km (342 mi) through southwestern Niger. To the north of the Niger are many ancient stream channels that flow periodically during wet weather. A portion of Lake Chad is situated in the southeastern corner of the country.

³CLIMATE

Niger, one of the hottest countries in the world, has three basic climatic zones: the Saharan desert in the north, the Sahel to the south of the desert, and the Sudan in the southwest corner. The intense heat of the Saharan zone often causes the scant rainfall to evaporate before it hits the ground; at Bilma, in the east, annual rainfall is only 2 cm (0.79 in). On the average, rainfall in the Aïr Massif is limited to a maximum of 25 cm (10 in) annually, and most of it comes during a single two-month period. At Agadez, in the northern Sahel, annual rainfall averages 16.5 cm (6.5 in), but yearly totals often vary greatly. Between 1968 and 1975, the Sahel suffered a catastrophic drought. In the south, rainfall is higher. It averages 59 cm (23 in) at Niamey, in the southern Sahel, and 87 cm (34 in) at Gaya, in the Sudanese zone. The rainy season is from June through September, with most rain in July and August. At Niamey, the average maximum daily temperature fluctuates from 31°C (88°F) in August to 41°C (106°F) in April. Nights are cool (below 20°C /68°F) from November to February.

⁴FLORA AND FAUNA

The northern desert has vegetation only after rare rainfalls. The savanna includes a vast variety of herbaceous vegetation, with such trees as bastard mahogany, kapok, baobab, and the shea tree (karité). There are antelope, lion, waterbuck, leopard, hyena, monkey, warthog, and countless varieties of bird and insect life. In the Niger River are crocodiles, hippopotamuses, and sometimes manatee. Turtles, lizards, pythons, horned vipers, and other varieties of snakes abound.

⁵ENVIRONMENT

In Niger, serious depletion of vegetation has been caused by the burning of brush and grass to prepare for the planting of crops, often on marginal land; by overgrazing of range lands; and by tree cutting for fuel and construction. Niger loses 70,000-80,000 hectores of forest land annually. The result has been soil erosion and increasing desertification. An estimated 200,000–800,000 hectares (500,000–2,000,000 acres) is lost to the desert annually. The nation has 3.4 cubic miles of water. Seventy-four percent is used in farming activity and 5% for industrial activity. Ninety-eight percent of the people living in cities have pure water. Twenty-nine percent of the nation's city dwellers do not have adequate waste disposal.

With Benin and Burkina Faso, Niger administers "W" National Park, of which 334,375 hectares (826,254 acres) are in Niger. There are also several game reserves, but resources for safeguarding protected fauna are insufficient. In 1994, the nation's wildlife was endangered by unlawful hunting and poaching. Fifteen of Niger's mammal species and one of its bird species are endangered. As of 1987, the scimitar-horned oryx was an endangered species.

6POPULATION

According to the 1988 census, the population of Niger was 7,250,383; by 1994, it had risen to an estimated 9,031,163. The annual growth rate is about 3.2%. A population of 10,640,000 is projected for the year 2000, based on a crude birthrate of 48 per 1,000 population, a crude death rate of 16.8, and a net natural increase of 31.2 during 1995–2000. Only about 200,000 people live in the northern half. Average population density in 1994 was 7.1 per sq km (18.5 per sq mi). In 1990, Niamey, the capital, had about 580,000 people. Other major cities, with their 1988 populations, are Zinder, 120,900; Maradi, 113,000; Tahoua, 51,600; and Agadez, 50,200. About 77% of the population is rural; about 48% is under 15 years of age. About 20% of the population consists of nomads.

7MIGRATION

Most of the northern area of Niger is inhabited by migratory peoples who follow their flocks and herds through the mountainous countryside. During the 1968–75 Sahelian drought, however, these people were forced to leave the north. Many nomads migrated to urban areas in order to keep from starving, but some have since returned. As many as 500,000 people may have moved to Nigeria since the drought. About 100,000 returned in early 1983, when many foreigners were expelled from Nigeria. Thousands more Nigeriens were expelled from Nigeria in 1985, and in 1986, Algeria expelled about 2,000 of the 50,000 Nigerien nomads in southern Algeria. The migration from rural to urban areas has continued. At the end of 1992 there were 3,400 Chadian refugees in Niger.

8ETHNIC GROUPS

The Hausa are the largest ethnic group, forming 53% of the total population. The Djerma-Songhai, the second-largest group, constitute 22% of the population. They, like the Hausa, are sedentary farmers living on the arable southern tier. The Djerma-Songhai are concentrated in the southwest; the Hausa, in south-central and southeast Niger. Many of Niger's inhabitants are nomadic or seminomadic livestock-raising peoples, including the Fulani, or Peul (10%), the Tuareg (10%), and the Kanuri (4%).

9LANGUAGES

French is the national and official language, but it is spoken by only a small minority of the people. The various ethnic groups use their own local languages, and Hausa is spoken all over the country as the language of trade. Djerma is also used extensively.

10RELIGIONS

An estimated 88% of the population is Muslim, 11.5% belongs to traditional animist tribal religions, and 0.5% is Christian. The most influential Muslim groups are the Tijaniyya, Senussi, and Hamalists.

11TRANSPORTATION

Landlocked Niger relies heavily on road and air transportation. As of 1991 there were 39,970 km (24,840 mi) of roads, of which 8% were bituminously paved. The principal road runs from west to east, beginning at Ayorou, going through Niamey, Dosso, Maradi, and Zinder, and ending at Nguigmi. A 902-km (560-mi) all-weather stretch between Niamey and Zinder was opened in 1980. Extending from the main route are roads from Niamey to Burkina Faso (not paved), from Zinder to Algeria through Agadez (with tough desert driving on dirt tracks), from Dosso to Benin, and from Birni Nkonni and Maradi to Nigeria. A 602-km (385-mi) highway between Tahoua and the uranium mines at Arlit was completed in 1981. SNTN, a government joint venture with a private French company, is the most important road hauler and has a monopoly over certain routes. In 1991 there were 36,000 registered motor vehicles.

Niger's most important international transport route is by road to the rail terminus at Parakou, Benin. From there, OCBN, a joint Benin-Niger railway, operates service to the Benin port of Cotonou. As of 1991, plans were under discussion to extend the Cotonou-Parakou line to Niamey. In 1973, a direct sea link was opened, with Canadian and US funding, along the Niger River from Gaya to Port Harcourt, Nigeria, on the Atlantic. This route is navigable between September and March.

There are 31 airports of which 7 have permanent-surface runways. The international airport is at Niamey. It handled 85,000 passengers and 6,200 tons of freight in 1991. There are domestic airports at Agadez, Maradi, Zinder, Arlit, and Tahoua. Niger is a participant in the transnational Air Afrique, which provides international service, along with several other airlines.

12HISTORY

Through extensive archaeological research, much evidence has been uncovered indicating that man has been present in northern Niger for over 600,000 years. By at least 4000 BC, a mixed population of Libyan, Berber, and Negroid peoples had evolved an agricultural and cattle-herding economy in the Sahara. Written history begins only with Arab chronicles of the 10th century AD. By the 14th century, the Hausa had founded several city-states along the southern border of what is today the Republic of the Niger. About 1515, an army of the Songhai Empire of Gao (now in Mali), led by Askia Muhammad I, subjugated the Hausa states and captured the Berber city of Agadez, whose sultanate had existed for many generations. The city had been important largely because of its position on the caravan trade routes from Tripoli and Egypt into the Lake Chad area. The fall of the Songhai Empire to Moroccan invaders in 1591 led to expansion of the Bornu Empire, which was centered in northeast Nigeria, into the eastern and central sections of the region. The Hausa states and the Tuareg also remained important. It was probably during the 17th century that the Djerma settled in the southwest. Between 1804 and 1810, a devout Fulani Muslim named 'Uthman dan Fodio waged a holy war against the Hausa states, which he subjugated along with a part of the Bornu Empire, west of Lake Chad. About that time, European explorers began to enter the area, starting with a Scot, Mungo Park, in 1805–6.

Bornu, Hausa, and Fulani entities vied for power during the 19th century, a period during which political control was fragmented. The first French military expeditions into the Niger area, at the close of the 19th century, were stiffly resisted. Despite this opposition, French forces pushed steadily eastward and by 1900 had succeeded in encircling Lake Chad with military outposts. In 1901, the military district of Niger was created as part of a larger unit known as Haut-Sénégal et Niger. Rebellions plagued the French forces on a minor scale until World War I, when a major uprising took place. Some 1,000 Tuareg warriors attacked Zinder in a move promoted by pro-German elements intent on creating unrest in French and British African holdings. British troops were dispatched from Nigeria to assist the French in putting down the disturbance. Although this combined operation broke the Tuareg resistance, not until 1922 was peace fully restored. In that year, the French made Niger a colony.

Niger's colonial history is similar to that of other former French West African territories. It had a governor but was administered from Paris through the governor-general in Dakar, Senegal. From 1932 to 1947, Niger was administered jointly with Upper Volta (now Burkina Faso) for budgetary reasons. World War II barely touched Niger, since the country was too isolated and undeveloped to offer anything of use to the Free French forces.

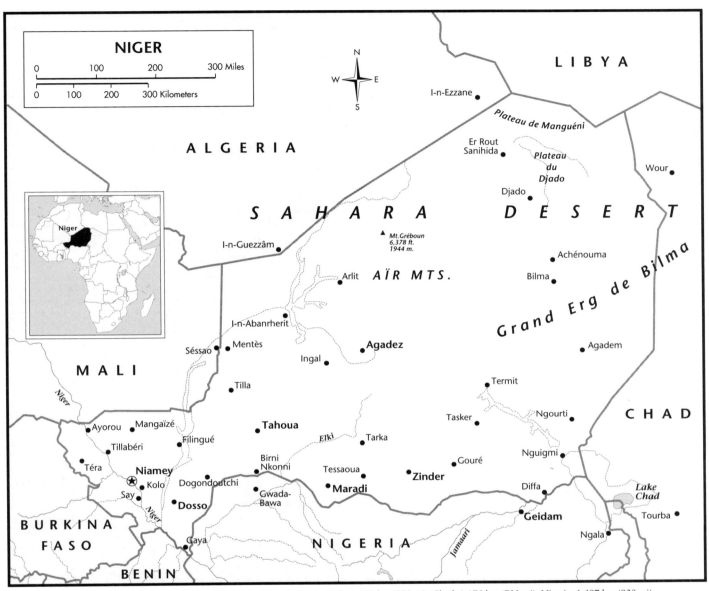

NIGER

| 0 | 100 | 200 | 300 Miles |
| 0 | 100 | 200 | 300 Kilometers |

LIBYA

ALGERIA

I-n-Ezzane

Plateau de Manguéni

Er Rout
Sanihida

Plateau
du
Djado

Wour

Djado

S A H A R A   D E S E R T

I-n-Guezzâm

▲ Mt.Gréboun
6,378 ft.
1944 m.

Achénouma

Arlit   AÏR MTS.   Bilma

Grand Erg de Bilma

I-n-Abanrherit

Séssao   Mentès   Agadez   Agadem

MALI

Ingal

Tilla

Niger

Mangaïzé

Ayorou

Tillabéri

Birni
Nkonni

Tahoua

Elki   Tarka

Termit

Tasker

Ngourti

CHAD

Nguigmi

Filingué

Téra

Niamey

Kolo

Say

Dogondoutchi

Gwada-
Bawa

Tessaoua

Maradi

Gouré

Zinder

Diffa

Lake
Chad

Niger

Dosso

BURKINA
FASO

Gaya

N I G E R I A

Jamaari

Geidam

Tourba

Ngala

BENIN

LOCATION: 12° to 23°30′N; 0°30′ to 15°30′E. **BOUNDARY LENGTHS:** Libya, 354 km (220 mi); Chad, 1,175 km (730 mi); Nigeria, 1,497 km (930 mi); Benin, 190 km (118 mi); Burkina Faso 628 km (390 mi); Mali, 821 km (510 mi); Algeria, 956 km (594 mi).

In 1946, the French constitution conferred French citizenship on the inhabitants of all the French territories and provided for a gradual decentralization of power and limited participation in indigenous political life. On 28 September 1958, voters in Niger approved the constitution of the Fifth French Republic, and on 19 December 1958, Niger's Territorial Assembly voted to become an autonomous state, the Republic of the Niger, within the French Community. A ministerial government was formed by Hamani Diori, a deputy to the French National Assembly and secretary-general to the Niger branch of the African Democratic Rally (Rassemblement Démocratique Africaine—RDA). On 11 July 1960, agreements on national sovereignty were signed by Niger and France, and on 3 August 1960, the Republic of the Niger proclaimed its independence. Diori, who had been able to consolidate his political dominance with the help of the French colonial administration, became Niger's first president. His principal opponent was Djibo Bakary, whose party, known as the Sawaba, had been banned in 1959 for advocating a "no" vote in the 1958 French constitutional referendum. The Sawaba was

allegedly responsible for a number of unsuccessful attempts to assassinate Diori after 1959.

Diori was able to stay in power throughout the 1960s and early 1970s. His amicable relations with the French enabled him to obtain considerable technical, military, and financial aid from the French government. In 1968, following a dispute between the ruling Niger Progressive Party (Parti Progressiste Nigérien—PPN) and the civil service over alleged corruption of civil service personnel, the PPN was given a larger role in the national administration. Over the years, Diori developed a reputation as an African statesman and was able to settle several disputes between other African nations. However, unrest developed at home as Niger, together with its Sahel neighbors, suffered widespread devastation from the drought of the early 1970s.

On 15 April 1974, the Diori government was overthrown by a military coup led by Lt. Col. Seyni Kountché, the former chief of staff who subsequently assumed the presidency. Madame Diori was killed in the rebellion, as were approximately 100 others, and the former president was detained (1974–80) under house arrest. Soon after the coup, French troops stationed in Niger left at Kountché's request.

The economy grew markedly in the late 1970s, chiefly because of a uranium boom that ended in 1980. The Kountché regime, which is generally pro-Western, broke diplomatic relations with Libya in January 1981 in alarm and anger over Libya's military intervention in Chad. Relations with Libya slowly improved, and diplomatic ties resumed in 1982. Nevertheless, Niger continued to fear Libyan efforts at subversion, particularly among the Tuareg of northern Niger. In October 1983, an attempted coup in Niamey was suppressed by forces loyal to President Kountché. Kountché died of a brain tumor in November 1987, and (then) Col. 'Ali Seybou (now Brig. Gen.), the army chief of staff, was appointed president.

The National Movement for the Development of Society (MNSD) was created in 1989 as Niger's sole political party. Since then, however, there has been a ground swell for multiparty democracy, spearheaded by the labor confederation, which organized a widely-observed, two-day-long general strike. The president acceded to the calling of a National Conference (July–October 1991) to prepare a new constitution. It appointed an interim government, headed by Amadou Cheiffou. It worked, along with the Seybou government, to prepare Niger for multiparty elections. The transition was difficult with widespread fighting in the north and a military mutiny in February 1992 and again in July 1993. The elections were postponed several times. After the adoption of a new constitution in a December 1992 referendum, a series of elections were held. In the first round of balloting for the presidency on 27 February 1993, Tandja Mamadou, Seybou's successor as leader of the MNSD, gained 34% of the votes cast. Mahamane Ousmane got 27%. In a March runoff voters for the five other candidates switched to Ousmane, and he was elected with 54% of the vote.

The legislative elections in February brought similar results. The MNSD won the largest number of the seats (29), but a coalition of nine opposition parties, the Alliance of Forces of Change (AFC) dominates the National Assembly with 50 of the 83 seats. The AFC is led by Prime Minister Mohamadou Issoufou.

The new government moved quickly to deal with the Tuareg insurgency in the north. In March, it reached a three-month truce with the major Tuareg group, the Liberation Front of Air and Azaouak (FLAA). In June 1993, it was extended for three more months. By September, however, the Tuaregs split into three factions and only one, the Front for the Liberation of Tamoust (FLT), agreed to renew the truce for three more months. Some Tuaregs, chiefly under the Armée Revolutionnaire de la Libération du Norde Niger (ARLNN) continue the rebellion as talks continue. Government reprisals for Tuareg raids are frequent. Government accuses Libya of inciting Tuaregs. Others accuse the Niger regime of showing favoritism for members of the Zarma (or Djerma), one of the five major ethnolinguistic groups in Niger. High level talks, under the joint mediation of Algeria, Burkina Faso, and France, were resumed in February 1994.

13 GOVERNMENT

The constitution of 8 November 1960 established the president of the republic, elected for a five-year term by direct universal suffrage, as chief of state and head of the executive branch. Legislative power was invested in a 50-member unicameral National Assembly. This constitution was suspended following the military coup of 15 April 1974, when the National Assembly was also dissolved. All executive and legislative power was taken over by the Supreme Military Council, composed of army officers. The president of the Supreme Military Council is president of the council of ministers (cabinet) and head of state. This office was held by Seyni Kountché from 1974 to 1987. Most cabinet officers were civilians in 1987.

In 1987, a national development council was established to serve as a constituent assembly on a nonparty basis. It drafted the constitution of the Second Republic that came into force on 24 September 1989.

A national conference from July to October 1991, drafted a new, multiparty democratic constitution that was approved by national referendum on 26 December 1992. It established the Third Republic with a National Assembly of 83 deputies chosen by popular and competitive elections, a president likewise elected, and a prime minister elected by the Assembly. That new government was sworn in on 23 April 1993.

14 POLITICAL PARTIES

In Niger, party politics came into being only after World War II. In 1946, the African Democratic Rally (Rassemblement Démocratique Africain—RDA) gained a foothold in Niger, largely with the help of its several labor unions. By 1948, however, this initial gain had dwindled, and the PPN, the local branch of the RDA, was unable to reelect its candidate to the French National Assembly. Meanwhile, other parties, based on regional interests, gained in strength.

In 1957, Djibo Bakary, the leader of a dissident RDA group, helped form a socialist party that became known as the PRA. Branches were quickly established in most of the other French-African territories.

Shortly before the voting on the new French constitution in September 1958, the PPN joined with chiefs and dissident PRA members to form a coalition, the Union for the Franco-African Community (Union pour la Communauté Franco-Africaine), led by Hamani Diori, leader of the PPN. In general elections on 14 December 1958, the PRA group (known as the Sawaba), led by Djibo Bakary, was defeated by the new coalition, which won 54 of the 60 seats in the Assembly. The new Assembly quickly voted that the territory should become the autonomous Republic of the Niger within the French Community. Diori became president of the General Council, and with the achievement of full independence, he became president of the republic. Diori proceeded to consolidate the position of the PPN by allying himself with Niger's powerful Muslim traditional chiefs, exiling Bakary, and banning the Sawaba in 1959. In 1964 and 1965, Bakary organized attacks from abroad on Diori's life.

The PPN became the only legal party under the Diori regime. In the October 1970 elections, Diori won 99.98% of the votes cast, and the PPN won 97.09% of the votes cast for the National Assembly. After the coup of 15 April 1974, the military government suppressed all political organizations in the country. Both Diori and Bakary (who returned from exile) were imprisoned until 1980.

Seybou's military government created the National Movement for the Development of Society (MNSD) in 1989 as the sole political party. But it failed to maintain control. After the constitutional referendum of December 1992 ushered in multiparty democracy, several new parties were formed. Although the MNSD is the largest party in the legislature (29 of 83 seats), it did not form the government. A coalition of nine parties known as the Alliance of the Forces of Change (AFC) now controls the National Assembly and the presidency. The AFC includes the Social Democratic Convention (CDS); the Nigerien Party for Democracy and Socialism (PNDS); the Nigerien Alliance for Democracy and Progress (ANDP); the Nigerien Progressive Party-Reunion for Democracy in Africa (PPN-RDA); the Nigerien Democratic Social Party (PSDN); and the Union for Democracy and Social Progress (UPS).

15 LOCAL GOVERNMENT

There are 7 departments, subdivided into 38 arrondissements, in Niger. These units are administered by prefects and subprefects, respectively, who are appointed by the central government. There are 150 communes (urban centers), of which 4 are fully autonomous. Although mayors are appointed by the central government, they also come under the aegis of the prefects and subprefects. There is a pyramidal system of councils at the village, arrondissement, departmental, and national levels with advisory powers only. Only at the village level are members directly elected, under the supervision of the Supreme Military Council. Some members of the higher councils are elected by the council below; other members are appointed. Village chiefs have an important role in rural local government.

16JUDICIAL SYSTEM

The legal system is basically French in civil law, with important customary-law modifications. Before the coup of April 1974, the Supreme Court consisted of constitutional, juridical, and accounting sections and the High Court of Justice. The High Court of Justice, which was appointed by the National Assembly from among its own membership, was empowered to try the president and members of the government for crimes or offenses committed in performance of their official duties. The 1992 constitution calls for an independent judiciary. The Supreme Court is now the final court of appeals. Special courts deal with civil service corruption. There are also magistrates' courts, assize courts in three cities, eight labor courts, and justices of the peace in 19 administrative districts.

Traditional and customary courts hear cases involving divorce or inheritance. There are no religious courts. Customary courts, located in larger towns and cities, are presided over by a legal practitioner with basic legal training who is advised about local tradition by a local assessor. The actions of chiefs in traditional courts and of the presiding practitioner in customary courts are not regulated by the code provisions. Appeals can be taken from both customary and traditional courts to the formal court system.

The government has authority to establish a state security court to try crimes against the state.

17ARMED FORCES

Niger's army numbered 3,200 in 1993. There were 100 personnel in the air force with 13 administrative aircraft. Paramilitary forces numbered 4,500. France provides military advisers and is the chief source of military equipment. Niger spends $27 million on defense (1989) or 1.3 percent of gross domestic product.

18INTERNATIONAL COOPERATION

Niger was admitted to UN membership on 20 September 1960, and is a member of ECA and all the other nonregional specialized agencies except IMO. Niger is also a member of the African Development Bank, ECOWAS, G-77, OCAM, and OAU and a signatory to GATT and the Law of the Sea. It has joined with Benin, Côte d'Ivoire, and Burkina Faso in the Council of the Entente, a customs union with a common solidarity fund.

19ECONOMY

Niger is an arid, landlocked country with much of its territory forming a portion of the Sahara. Most of its people live in a marginally productive and highly drought-prone band of arable land along Niger's southern border with Nigeria. The mainstays of the economy are uranium mining, foreign assistance, herding, and subsistence agriculture. Less than 3% of the country is under cultivation. Agriculture and livestock production employed an estimated 90% of the labor force and in 1991 the sector accounted for 35% of GDP. Niger's mining sector is based on uranium; proven reserves are put at 360,000 tons. The development of uranium resources boosted export earnings until the decline in international demand for the mineral in the early 1980s. Export earnings to the sector declined from 13% of GDP in 1980 to 5%

of GDP in 1990. By mid-1993, uranium prices had been reduced to CFA Fr 14,450/kg.

In January 1994 France suddenly devalued the CFA franc, causing its value to drop in half overnight. Since 1948 France had guaranteed a fixed parity of one French franc to 50 African francs. The devaluation of the CFA franc should help in making Niger's uranium cost competitive. In the short term, however, the devaluation has caused prices for almost all imported goods to soar, including prices for food and essential drugs.

Oil and gold may contribute to the economy by the middle of the 1990s. In the meantime, foreign businesses are leaving and the service industry supporting uranium mining continues to shrink.

20INCOME

In 1992 Niger's GNP was $2,466 million at current prices, or $300 per capita. For the period 1985–92 the average inflation rate was −1.6%, resulting in a real growth rate in per capita GNP of −1.5%.

In 1992 the GDP was $2,345 million in current US dollars. It is estimated that the agricultural sector contributed 34.9% of that amount, followed by market and non-market services (22.4%). Trade was a substantial 20.2% of GDP. Mining (5.1%) and manufacturing (6.5%) were less significant.

21LABOR

About 90% of the population in 1990 was engaged in agriculture and livestock raising. Salaried employment was about 60,000 in 1992. Those in government service (not including government-owned corporations) numbered 24,131 in 1991, mostly in public utilities (18.4%) and social services (16.6%).

The Union of Workers' Syndicates of Niger (Union des Syndicats des Travailleurs du Niger—USTN) is the only trade union. It was founded in Niamey in 1960 and is affiliated with the African Trade Union Confederation. USTN has about 18,000 members. Its head is appointed by the government. There are also three employers' organizations.

22AGRICULTURE

Although only 2.8% of Niger's area is cultivated, farmers increased their production following the 1968–75 drought, and in 1980, the country became self-sufficient in food crops. The most plentiful rains in 30 years fell during the 1992–1993 season, pushing agricultural production up by 64%. Irrigation and off-season farming projects are of keen interest to the government and foreign donors. Over 90% of the active population is engaged in crop cultivation or animal husbandry. Agricultural techniques are still rudimentary; there are a few tractors in use (only 178 in 1991), and most farmers do not keep draft animals. Very little fertilizer is used. Irrigated land in 1991 totaled about 40,000 hectares (98,800 acres). Only 12% of Niger's total land area, located along the southern border, is potentially useful for rainfed cultivation. Over 95% of agriculture is on farms of less than 5 hectares (12 acres), with the average about 3 hectares (7.5 acres). Production of millet, the staple food of most of the people, depends heavily on rainfall. In 1992, millet production was 1,784,000 tons, sorghum was 393,000 tons, and rice was 70,000 tons. Other crops (with their estimated output) include cassava (218,000 tons), sugarcane (140,000 tons), onions (170,000 tons), and sweet potatoes and yams (35,000 tons). Cowpeas are an important crop, but are only competitive as an export in neighboring Nigeria's market due to transportation costs. The government of Niger is encouraging crop diversification and the raising of export crops like onions, garlic, peppers, and potatoes, in addition to cowpeas.

Peanuts, formerly the main source of agricultural export revenue, are planted mainly in the Zinder area. Production increased from 8,980 tons in 1945 to a high of 298,000 tons in 1967.

Because of a lack of producer incentives, production declined to only 87,000 tons in 1982, and only a fraction of that total was delivered to the government marketing agency, SOMARA, which had a monopoly on pricing and marketing peanut products until 1986. Production was reported at 40,000 tons for 1992.

Cotton, introduced in 1956 to reduce Niger's dependence on peanuts, has also suffered from lack of grower incentives. Production of seed cotton rose from 218 tons in 1956 to 6,682 tons in 1967 but was only ground 3,000 tons in 1991; production was reported to be 2,000 tons in 1992.

[23]ANIMAL HUSBANDRY

Almost half the land area of Niger is classified as pasture, but, like agriculture, animal husbandry has suffered greatly from insufficient rainfall. In 1992, there were an estimated 1,800,000 head of cattle, 8,800,000 sheep and goats, and 363,000 camels. About 12% of Niger's GDP comes from livestock production, which engages 29% of the population. Official statistics of Niger seriously underrepresent total exports—most animals are herded across borders without documentation.

Meat production, which had dropped to 38,000 tons in 1973, was an estimated 110,000 tons in 1992. Production of milk from goats and cows came to 87,000 and 152,000 tons, respectively. Cattle hides came to about 4,360 tons in 1992; sheepskins, 1,500 tons; and goatskins, 3,340 tons. There is a tannery at Maradi. Sandals, briefcases, and fine ladies handbags of high quality are produced in small numbers but seldom exported.

Meat exports are inspected and controlled by the customs service before leaving the country. Only inspected, tuberculin-tested cattle are used in export meat production. The Niger River valley south of Say is infested by the tsetse fly, and trypanosomiasis is, therefore, a major cattle disease.

[24]FISHING

There is no commercial fishing on a wide scale, but fishing is an appreciable source of revenue for the Sorko on the Niger River and the Boudouma on Lake Chad. The fishermen on Lake Chad consume most of their catch. Most of the total annual catch of 3,150 tons in 1991 was from the Niger River and its tributaries; a small amount is from the Lake Chad region.

[25]FORESTRY

The forest domain is only about 1.5% of Niger's surface. Roundwood production was estimated at 5,116,000 cu m in 1991, almost all for fuel. Small amounts of gum arabic are extracted from acacia trees. Some tree planting has been undertaken, mainly with acacia species, but deforestation remains a serious problem. About 5,500 hectares (13,600 acres) are reforested annually and hundreds of thousands of trees are planted, but these are highly vulnerable to drought.

[26]MINING

Niger ranked seventh in the world in uranium production in 1991 and had proven reserves, at several sites, estimated at 360,000 tons, the fifth largest uranium reserves in the world. High-grade uranium ore was discovered in substantial quantities by the French in 1967, in the Aïr mountain range, about 250 km (150 mi) northwest of Agadez. Processing of ore began in 1971, in a plant at the Arlit uranium mines, owned by the Aïr Society of Mines (Société des Mines de l'Aïr—SOMAIR). The French Atomic Energy Commission owns 27% of SOMAIR, a private international consortium owns another 40%, and the Niger government controls 33%. A second mine was opened nearby at Akouta in 1978 by the Mineral Company of Akouta (Compagnie Minière d'Akouta—COMINAK), which is 31% owned by the Niger government, 34% by an affiliate of the French Atomic Energy Commission, 25% by private Japanese interests, and 10%

by private Spanish interests. Combined production from the two plants was 3,330 tons in 1991. A third mine, jointly owned by the Niger government, the French Atomic Energy Commission, and Kuwaiti interests, opened at Tassa in 1986 and was leased to SOMAIR for operation. A uranium boom occurred in the late 1970s, but with the reduction in world demand for uranium ore in nuclear power plants during the 1980s, prices fell. Government revenues from uranium ore have fallen, despite the fact that Niger is partly protected by contracts negotiated earlier; France, which takes in over one-half of production, was paying triple over the spot price in 1991.

Although uranium is the only mineral resource to be significantly developed, other minerals have also been mined. Salt is found near Bilma and elsewhere, and there are some natron and sodium sulfate deposits. Salt production was about 3,000 tons in 1991. There are an estimated 650 million tons of iron ore deposits at Say, 60 km (37 mi) from Niamey. Cassiterite (tin ore) is mined near Agadez; production was 20 tons in 1991. Phosphates are located at Akker, 60 km (37 mi) northeast of Tahoua; about 1,000 tons were produced in 1985. At least 400 million tons of phosphate deposits lie in "W" National Park, in the Niger River Valley. Molybdenum is extracted by COMINAK in connection with uranium ore; production was 10 tons in 1991. Tungsten and columbite are extracted in connection with cassiterite. There are unexploited deposits of manganese, lithium, copper, zinc, lead, silver, cobalt, kaolin, feldspar, gypsum, limestone, marble, and clay.

[27]ENERGY AND POWER

Niger depends on petroleum imports for most of its production of electrical energy. Coal is mined at Anou Araren by the Nigerien Society of Anou Araren Coal (Société Nigérienne de Charbon d'Anou Araren—SONICHAR), 61.4% state owned. Production was 156,542 tons in 1991. The coal is used as fuel in a 37.7-Mw thermal power station that serves Agadez and the uranium mines. Proved reserves of coal at Anou Araren are 6 million tons. The production of electricity comes totally from thermal stations. Their combined installed capacity was 63,000 kw in 1991. In 1991, 168 million kwh of electricity was produced, while an estimated 188 million kwh was imported from Nigeria. A 125-Mw hydroelectric complex has been proposed near Ayorou, on the Niger River.

Oil exploration has been taking place in the Agadem Basin, north of Lake Chad, since 1975. Elf Aquitaine of France and Exxon have a joint exploration permit, with Elf controlling 62.5% of the venture and doing the actual exploration. As of 1992, petroleum of a significant quantity had been found to justify further exploration.

Niger is also the third largest exporter of uranium in the world. Two mines produced 3,330 tons of concentrate in 1991. As of 1992, with global demand for uranium down, sales accounted for only 12% of government revenue.

[28]INDUSTRY

Manufacturing provides about 6.5% of Niger's total GDP (1990) and consists mainly of the processing of domestic agricultural commodities. Agricultural products are processed at a groundnut oil plant, rice mills, flour mills, cotton gins, and tanneries. A textile mill and cement plant are in operation, and light industries produce beer and soft drinks, processed meats, noodle products, baked goods, soaps and detergents, perfume, plastic and metal goods, farm equipment, canned vegetables, pasta, and construction materials.

[29]SCIENCE AND TECHNOLOGY

Niger relies heavily on foreign sources for technical expertise, and French agencies are especially active; the Bureau of Geological and Mineral Research, the French Company for the Development of Textile Fibers, the Institute of Fruit and Citrus Fruit Research, and the French Institute of Scientific Research for Development and Cooperation all have offices in Niamey.

The National Institute of Agronomical Research of Niger, in Niamey, maintains two soil-science stations, at Tarka and Kolo. There is also a national office of solar energy and a veterinary laboratory in Niamey. The Livestock Service of Niger has a Sahelian experimental station at Filingué for breeding zebu cattle and a center for goat breeding and poultry raising at Maradi. The University of Niamey includes schools of science and health services.

30DOMESTIC TRADE

There are three domestic commercial sectors in Niger. Merchants and peddlers in the small villages sell such items as beverages, cigarettes, soap, cloth, perfume, and batteries. Large foreign concerns (usually French-owned) import products to be sold in stores in Niamey and in the secondary cities. The government is a major partner in large commercial societies, many of which enjoy monopolies. The National Society of Commerce and of Production of Niger, an 81% state-owned company, has organized stores throughout the interior and maintains a monopoly on the importation of certain essential products, such as sugar, wheat, and salt. Rice imports have been banned in order to promote self-sufficiency. There is a thriving private trade in foodstuffs.

31FOREIGN TRADE

Niger's chronic negative trade balance turned positive in 1991, recording a $10.6 million surplus. Trade figures show that uranium accounts for 78.9% of exports by value. Exports of live animals and hides represent 13.8% of exports. Vegetable exports contribute 2.2% of export earnings. Imports are led by cereals (23.3%) and miscellaneous manufactured goods (18.2%).

France takes the majority of Niger's exports, followed by Nigeria. Of Niger's imports, 30% come from France, and 11% from the US.

32BALANCE OF PAYMENTS

Niger's visible trade balance is usually negative. Its deficit in goods and services is offset by infusions of public and private capital, as well as substantial amounts of direct foreign aid. In the early 1980s, the nation suffered particularly from declining uranium export earnings. The overall balance of payments deficit grew sharply in 1992, as exports continued to decline.

In 1992 merchandise exports totaled $283.0 million and imports $331.0 million. The merchandise trade balance was $–48 million.

33BANKING AND SECURITIES

The Central Bank of the West African States (Banque Centrale des États de l'Afrique de l'Ouest—BCEAO) is the bank of issue for Niger and other West African states. Niger has a monetary committee that reports to the BCEAO and works under BCEAO general rules but possesses autonomy in internal credit matters.

The other major development banks in Niger are the Development Bank of the Republic of the Niger (59% state owned in 1987), Crédit du Niger (45% state owned), and the Niger Credit and Cooperation Union (100% state owned). There are five commercial banks in Niger: the Banque Arabe Libyenne-Nigerienne pour le Commerce, Exterieur et le Developpment (Belinex), Baio-Niger, Nigerie International Bank Niamey, and the Nigerian Trust Bank. Belinex, founded in 1989, is 50% Libyan-owned and 50% owned by the state. Baio-Niger, founded in 1980, is 84% owned by Meridien BIAO SA (Luxemburg). The Nigerie International Bank Niamey, founded in 1991, is 40% owned by Citibank NA (US). The Nigerian Trust Bank, founded in 1990, absorbed the assets of the former Bank of Credit and Commerce upon its formation.

34INSURANCE

As of 1986, four insurance companies were registered in Niger. Third-party automobile liability was compulsory, and no life insurance was being written. In 1987, automobile insurance accounted for 45% of all premium revenues.

35PUBLIC FINANCE

Budgets are nominally balanced but only through the infusion of foreign loan funds and grants. Expenditures have been severely constrained, especially for development, since 1982–83 because of the fall in receipts from the sale of uranium ore. The end of the uranium boom left the public sector poorly equipped to adapt, as public expenditures had focused on intrastructure and construction projects at the expense of agricultural development. Consequently, heavy foreign debts were incurred. Following a 29% drop in tax revenues in 1991, the 1992 fiscal deficit came to 2.5% of GDP.

36TAXATION

Although both a proportional and a general income tax of 60% are levied, few citizens of Niger are more than marginally taxed, since their incomes are too low. The most important sources of revenue are the taxes on industrial and commercial profits and the turnover tax on domestic goods and imports. Other significant sources of revenue from taxes are social security contributions, the registration tax, and excises on petroleum products, alcohol, and cigarettes. The corporate tax rate is 45%.

37CUSTOMS AND DUTIES

In general, two main taxes make up the tariff system. A fiscal import duty is applied to all incoming goods, regardless of origin, and serves as a source of revenue. A customs duty is levied on all goods from other than franc-zone countries and serves as a protection for goods of French or franc-zone origin. Goods imported from countries that have trade agreements with Niger pay a minimum customs duty, while those from other countries are subject to a higher general tariff. Goods from EC countries other than France are dutiable at less than the minimum.

38FOREIGN INVESTMENT

Except for uranium mining, foreign private capital has not been easy to attract to Niger. Prospective investors are often discouraged by Niger's small markets, inadequate infrastructure, bureaucratic delays, shortage of local capital, lack of skilled labor, and exorbitant transportation costs.

Niger's investment codes are liberal, with tax relief and tariff protection depending on the level of investment. Further advantages accrue to those investing in small-scale enterprise. The government seeks foreign investment in most sectors, and private-sector investment in parastatal enterprise is welcome.

39ECONOMIC DEVELOPMENT

Government development programs have had three basic aims: first, to diversify production of foodstuffs; second, to develop underground water resources; and third, to develop and improve the country's infrastructure. France is the leading bilateral aid donor.

40SOCIAL DEVELOPMENT

The National Fund of Social Security provides pensions, family allowances, and workers' compensation for employees in the private sector. Civil servants participate in a national provident fund and also receive family allowances from the national government budget.

Polygamy is legal. In cases of divorce, the husband receives custody of all children under eight years of age. The fertility rate in the mid-1980s was an average of 7.1 children for each woman completing her childbearing years, one of the highest in Africa. The government sponsors an office of women's affairs and a women's association, but that does little to improve the status of women, who are denied educational and employment opportunities and who are legally and socially disadvantaged.

[41]HEALTH

In 1990, there were 142 physicians, 29 pharmacists, 5 dentists, 2,036 nurses, and 456 midwives. In 1992, there were 3 physicians per 100,000 people. In addition there were 38 medical centers and 198 dispensaries throughout the country. Health care expenditures in 1990 were $126 million. Only 41% of the population had access to health care services in 1992.

In 1993, immunization rates for children up to one year old were as follows: tuberculosis (40%); diphtheria, pertussis, and tetanus (21%); polio (21%); and measles (28%). In 1990, there were 144 reported cases of tuberculosis per 100,000 inhabitants. Almost 50% of children under 5 years are considered malnourished.

In 1993 the birth rate was 51.3 per 1,000 people with only 4% of married women (ages 15 to 49) using contraception. There were 428,000 births in 1992. The average life expectancy in Niger in 1992 was 46 years. The infant mortality rate was 191 per 1,000 live births, an increase of about 50 since 1985. General mortality was 18.7 per 1,000 people in 1993, and maternal mortality was 700 per 100,000 live births.

[42]HOUSING

Most government buildings and many houses in the metropolitan centers are essentially French in style. The Crédit du Niger offers housing loans.

The Tuareg nomads live in covered tents, while the Fulani live in small collapsible huts made of straw mats. The villagers in the east live in round straw huts. In the center of the country, villagers construct houses of "banco," a mixture of mud and straw that has, when dried, a hard, cementlike consistency. According to the latest available information, for 1980–88 Niger's housing stock totaled 1,400,000 with 4.6 people per dwelling.

[43]EDUCATION

The educational system is patterned on that of France, but changes are gradually being introduced to adapt the curriculum to local needs and traditions. Programs aim at expanding the educational system in order to improve the adult literacy rate, which stood at 28.4% in 1990 (males: 40.4% and females: 16.8%).

Schooling is compulsory for children aged 7–15. In 1990, there were 2,807 primary schools with 8,759 teachers and 368,732 pupils. While primary schooling lasts for six years, secondary lasts for seven years. In 1990, there were 76,758 pupils in secondary schools. Of these, 74,337 were in general secondary; 1,578 in teacher training courses, and 843 were in vocational schools.

In 1989, 4,506 students were enrolled in higher institutions. In 1963, the National School of Administration was founded in Niamey. The University of Niamey, founded in 1973, has schools of the sciences, letters, education, mathematics, agriculture, health, economics, and social sciences. The Islamic University of West Africa at Say, mostly financed by the Organization of the Islamic Conference, was inaugurated in 1987. A faculty of medicine and polytechnic attached to the university was under construction.

[44]LIBRARIES AND MUSEUMS

There are state-run libraries in the large municipalities, as well as libraries maintained by religious orders, the military, and professional and other groups. The Regional Center of Research and of Documentation for the Oral Tradition, in Niamey, was founded in cooperation with UNESCO in 1968; it preserves the oral history of West Africa and had a library of 5,000. Also in Niamey are the Archives of the Republic of Niger, which contain many colonial documents; a government document center; and the National Museum of Niger, which has ethnographic and paleontological exhibits, as well as a zoo, botanical gardens, craft workshops, and youth training centers.

[45]MEDIA

The Voice of the Sahel and Télé-Sahel, the government's radio and television broadcasting units, respectively, broadcast in French, Djerma, Hausa, Tamachek, Kanuri, Fulfuldé, Toubou, Gourmantché, and Arabic. There were an estimated 480,000 radios and 37,000 television sets in 1991, and there were 11,824 telephones in use. Major publications include the daily *Le Sahel*, with a circulation of about 5,000, and the weekly *Sahel Dimanche;* a monthly, the *Journal Officiel de la République du Niger,* is also published. All are government publications.

[46]ORGANIZATIONS

The Chamber of Commerce, Agriculture, and Industry, with headquarters at Niamey, has 80 full members and 40 dependent members. There are also chambers of commerce in Agadez, Maradi, Tahoua, and Zinder. A women's association and the government-sponsored Samaraya youth movement are also active.

[47]TOURISM, TRAVEL, AND RECREATION

The government has promoted both domestic and international tourism since 1984. The "W" National Park along the Niger River offers views of a variety of fauna, including lions and elephants. Other tourist attractions include Agadez's 16th-century mosque, one of the oldest in West Africa; villages built on piles in Lake Chad; the annual six-week gathering of nomads near Ingal; the Great Market and Great Mosque in Niamey, and the Sahara desert.

There were about 16,000 tourist arrivals in 1991, 43% from Africa and 42% from Europe. Tourist receipts were estimated at US $16 million. There were 1,524 hotel rooms with 3,048 beds and a 33% occupancy rate. Nigeriens engage in fishing, swimming, and a variety of team sports.

[48]FAMOUS NIGERIENS

Hamani Diori (b.1916), a former schoolteacher, became leader of the local section of the PPN in 1946, became president of the General Council of the Republic of Niger in 1958, and was president of the Republic of the Niger until April 1974, when he was deposed by a military coup. Seyni Kountché (1931–87) became head of state after the coup of 1974 and ruled the country until his death.

[49]DEPENDENCIES

The Republic of the Niger has no territories or colonies.

[50]BIBLIOGRAPHY

Decalo, Samuel. *Historical Dictionary of Niger.* 2d ed. Metuchen, N.J.: Scarecrow Press, 1989.

Fugelstad, F. *A History of Niger, 1850–1960.* London: Oxford University Press, 1984.

Miles, William F. S. *Hausaland Divided: Colonialism and Independence in Nigeria and Niger.* Ithaca: Cornell University Press, 1994.

Roberts, Richard L. *Warriors, Merchants, and Slaves: the State and the Economy in the Middle Niger Valley, 1700–1914.* Stanford, Calif.: Stanford University Press, 1987.

Van Offelen, Marion, and Carol Beckwith. *Nomads of Niger.* New York: Harry Abrams, 1983.

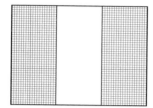

UNITY AND FAITH

NIGERIA

Federal Republic of Nigeria
Nigeria

CAPITAL: Abuja

FLAG: The national flag consists of three vertical stripes; the green outer stripes represent Nigerian agriculture; the white center stripe represents unity and peace.

ANTHEM: *Arise, All Compatriots.*

MONETARY UNIT: On 1 January 1973, the Nigerian pound (N£) was replaced by the naira (N) of 100 kobo at a rate of N2 = N£1. There are coins of ½, 1, 5, 10, 25, and 50 kobo and 1 naira, and notes of 5, 10, 20, and 50 naira. N1 = $0.24 (or $1 = N4.141).

WEIGHTS AND MEASURES: As of May 1975, the metric system is the official standard, replacing the imperial measures.

HOLIDAYS: New Year's Day, 1 January; National Day, 1 October; Christmas, 25 December; Boxing Day, 26 December. Movable Christian religious holidays include Good Friday and Easter Monday; movable Muslim religious holidays include 'Id al-Fitr, 'Id al-'Adha', and Milad an-Nabi.

TIME: 1 PM = noon GMT.

¹LOCATION, SIZE, AND EXTENT

Located at the extreme inner corner of the Gulf of Guinea on the west coast of Africa, Nigeria occupies an area of 923,770 sq. km (356,670 sq mi), extending 1,130 km (700 mi) E–W and 1,050 km (650 mi) N–S. Comparatively, the area occupied by Nigeria is slightly more than twice the size of the state of California. It is bordered by Chad on the NE, by Cameroon on the E, by the Atlantic Ocean (Gulf of Guinea) on the S, by Benin (formerly Dahomey) on the W, and by Niger on the NW and N, with a total boundary length of 4,900 km (3,045 mi). The borders between Nigeria and Chad and Nigeria and Cameroon are disputed, and there have been occasional border clashes.

Nigeria's capital city, Abuja, is located in the center of the country.

²TOPOGRAPHY

Along the entire coastline of Nigeria lies a belt of mangrove swamp forest from 16 to 96 km (10–60 mi) in width, which is intersected by branches of the Niger and innumerable other smaller rivers and creeks. Beyond the swamp forest is a zone, from 80 to 160 km (50–100 mi) wide, of undulating tropical rain forest. The country then rises to a plateau at a general elevation of about 600 m (2,000 ft) but reaches a maximum of 2,042 m (6,700 ft) on the eastern border in the Shebshi Mountains, and the vegetation changes from woodland to savanna, with thick forest in the mountains. In the extreme north, the country approaches the southern part of the Sahara.

The Niger, the third-largest river of Africa, enters Nigeria from the northwest and runs in a southeasterly direction, meeting its principal tributary, the Benue, at Lokoja, about 550 km (340 mi) from the sea. It then flows south to the delta, through which it empties into the Gulf of Guinea via numerous channels. Other main tributaries of the Niger are the Sokoto and Kaduna rivers. The second great drainage system of Nigeria flows north and east from the central plateau and empties into Lake Chad. Kainji Lake, in the northwest, was created by construction of a dam on the Niger above Jebba.

³CLIMATE

Although Nigeria lies wholly within the tropical zone, there are wide climatic variations in different regions of the country. Near the coast, the seasons are not sharply defined. Temperatures rarely exceed 32°C (90°F), but humidity is very high and nights are hot. Inland, there are two distinct seasons: a wet season from April to October, with generally lower temperatures, and a dry season from November to March, with midday temperatures that surpass 38°C (100°F) but relatively cool nights, dropping as low as 12°C (54°F). On the Jos Plateau, temperatures are more moderate.

Average rainfall along the coast varies from about 180 cm (70 in) in the west to about 430 cm (170 in) in certain parts of the east. Inland, it decreases to around 130 cm (50 in) over most of central Nigeria and only 50 cm (20 in) in the extreme north.

Two principal wind currents affect Nigeria. The harmattan, from the northeast, is hot and dry and carries a reddish dust from the desert; it causes high temperatures during the day and cool nights. The southwest wind brings cloudy and rainy weather.

⁴FLORA AND FAUNA

The natural vegetation is divisible into two main sections, directly related to the chief climatic regions of the country: (1) high forest, including both swamp and rain forests, and (2) savanna. Along the coastal area, the mangrove tree predominates, while immediately inland is freshwater swamp forest, which is somewhat more diversified, including varieties of palms, the abura, and mahogany. North of the swamp forest lies the rain forest, which forms a belt with an average width of some 130 km (80 mi). Here, trees reach as much as 60 m (200 ft) in height. Principal trees include the African mahogany, iroko, African walnut, and the most popular export wood, the obeche. Farther inland, the rain forest becomes displaced by tall grass and deciduous trees of small stature, characteristic of the savanna.

Few large animals are found in the rain forest; gorillas and chimpanzees in decreasing numbers are present, as well as baboons and monkeys. Reptiles abound, including crocodiles, lizards, and snakes of many species. Although many kinds of mam-

313

mals can be found inland from the rain forest, these are not nearly so plentiful as in East or South Africa. Nigeria possesses two dozen species of antelope, but large concentrations of animals, even the common antelope, are rarely observed. The hippopotamus, elephant, giraffe, leopard, and lion now remain only in scattered localities and in diminishing number. Wildcats, however, are more common and widely distributed. Wildlife in the savanna includes antelope, lions, leopards, gazelles, and desert hyenas. Nigeria also abounds in bird life, a great number of species being represented.

⁵ENVIRONMENT

Nigeria's environmental problems are typical of developing states. Excessive cultivation has resulted in loss of soil fertility. In 1992, UN reports identified soil erosion as Nigeria's most pressing environmental concern. The problem affects 50 million people. Increased cutting of timber has made inroads into forest resources, exceeding replantings. By 1985, deforestation claimed 1,544 square miles of the nation's forest land, an average of 5% per year. Large towns in the northern savanna areas have experienced shortages of fuel wood. In addition, oil spills, the burning of toxic wastes, and urban air pollution are problems in more developed areas. Water pollution is also a problem due to improper handling of sewage. It has 62.6 cubic miles of water. Fifty-four percent is used for farming activity and 15% for industrial purposes. One percent of federal revenue is allocated to environmental protection and conservation. The principal environmental agencies are the Environmental Planning and Protection Division of the Federal Ministry of Works and Housing, and the analogous division within the federal Ministry of Industry.

In 1994, twenty-five of Nigeria's mammal species are threatened. Ten types of birds and nine plant species are also endangered. Endangered species include the drill, Presuu's red colobus, and the Ibadan malimbe.

⁶POPULATION

Although Nigeria is known to be the most populous nation in Africa, uncertainty has clouded the question of how many inhabitants the country actually has. The 1991 census reported a total of 88,514,501 people. This has been accepted as reasonably accurate by the US Census Bureau, which had estimated a population 34 million higher for 1991. Accordigly, its estimate for 1995 was revised downward to 101,232,251. Projected earlier, the UN estimate for 1995 was 126,929,000; a population of 147,709,000 was projected for the year 2000, assuming a crude birthrate of 42.7 per 1,000 population, a crude death rate of 12.5, and a net natural increase of 30.2 during 1995–2000.

Similar uncertainties apply to other demographic factors. Although the urban population is believed to be growing more rapidly than the rural, only about 39% of all Nigerians live in urban areas. Regional differences are significant; population is densest in the south and sparsest in the north. The principal cities are Lagos, the former capital and still the largest city, with a population 7,998,000 in 1991 and the highest population density of any major African urban conglomeration. Ibadan is believed to have about 2 million people and Kano over 1 million.

⁷MIGRATION

Immigrants are drawn from neighboring nations by economic opportunity. On 17 January 1983, Nigeria, suffering from an economic crisis brought about by decreased earnings from oil, ordered all resident aliens to leave the country. Some 700,000 Ghanaians departed during the following weeks, as did smaller numbers from Benin, Cameroon, Chad, Mali, Niger, Togo, and Burkina Faso. In 1985, about 200,000 to 250,000 aliens were expelled, including about 100,000 from Ghana and 50,000 from

Niger. There were small numbers of refugees at the end of 1992, including 2,900 Liberians and 1,400 Chadians.

⁸ETHNIC GROUPS

The predominant racial group is West African Negroid. The purest lineage is now found in the southeastern forest belt, but Negroid stock forms the basic substratum throughout most of Nigeria. Non-Negroid racial types include the Fulani (Fulbe), of Mediterranean extraction, who are widely dispersed throughout the north but who have become largely assimilated to the predominant Negroid type, and the Semitic Shuwa Arabs, who are confined to the Lake Chad area in the extreme northeast.

There are three dominant ethnolinguistic groups. The Yoruba predominate in Ogun, Ondo, Oyo, and Osun states. The Ibo (Igbo) predominate in Anambra, Imo, Abia, and Enugu states. The Hausa and Fulani constitute the largest single groups in Sokoto, Kaduna, Jigawa, Katsina, and Kano states. Other important groups include the Kanuri in Borno and Yobe states; the Edo (Bini) in Edo State; the Ibibio in Akwa Ibam State; the Ijaw (Ijo) in Rivers State; the Tiv in Benue and Plateau states; and the Nupe in Niger State. The Hausa in the past have been officially estimated to constitute 21% of the population; Yoruba, 20%; Ibo, 16.1%; Fulani, 12%; Kanuri, 4.1%; Ibibio, 3.6%; Tiv, 2.5%; Ijaw, 2%; and others, 18.7%.

⁹LANGUAGES

The official language is English, although there are over 300 distinct indigenous tongues. Hausa is the mother tongue of more than 40% of the inhabitants of the northern states. Yoruba is commonly used in southwestern urban centers, including Lagos. Ethnic divisions roughly reflect the distribution of other vernaculars.

¹⁰RELIGIONS

Religious composition varies greatly according to region. The northern states are predominantly Muslim; the southern states are predominantly Christian. According to 1993 estimates, about 48% of the total population is Muslim, and 34% Christian; 10% belonged to traditional African religions. Religious unrest in the north, sometimes directed at Christians, periodically erupts; violence among Muslim sects has political overtones as well. Christians are divided relatively evenly among Roman Catholics, Anglicans, other Protestants, and adherents of indigenous African churches. The government's decision in 1986 to accept full membership in the international Organization of the Islamic Conference aroused some disquiet among non-Muslims.

¹¹TRANSPORTATION

The main waterways are the Niger and Benue rivers and a system of navigable creeks and lagoons in the southern part of the country. The Niger is navigable to Onitsha by large riverboat and to Lokoja by barge throughout the year. Ports farther upstream on the Niger and Benue can be reached in the high-water season. Inland waterways total about 9,000 km (5,580 mi). Lagos remains Nigeria's principal port, handling more than 75% of the country's general cargo. Other ports are Port Harcourt, Calabar, and the delta port complex of Warri, Sapele, Koko, Burutu, Bonny, and Alesa Eleme. The Nigerian National Shipping Line, government-owned since 1961, operated a fleet of 28 ships of 418,000 gross tons between West Africa and Europe in 1991. A 1987 decree requires 40% of total cargo generated by trade with Nigeria to be carried on Nigerian shipping.

The Nigerian railway system, operated by the statutory Nigerian Railway Corp., consists of 3,510 km (2,181 mi) of single track, and is the fifth largest in Africa. The greater part of the 3'6"-gauge system consists of two generally north–south lines, originating in Lagos and Port Harcourt. The western line runs northeast from Lagos through Ibadan, Ilorin, and Kaduna to

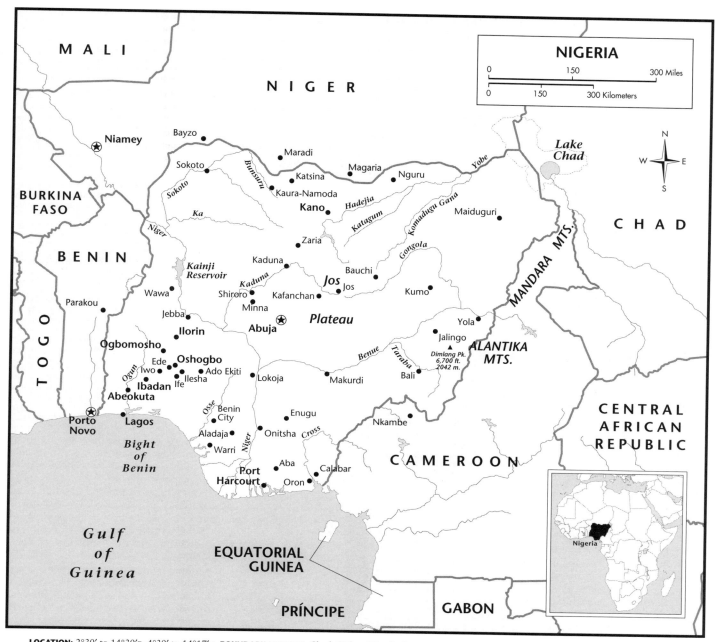

LOCATION: 2°30′ to 14°30′E; 4°30′ to 14°17′N. **BOUNDARY LENGTHS:** Chad, 88 km (55 mi); Cameroon, 1,690 km (1,050 mi); Atlantic coastline, 774 km (481 mi); Benin, 772 km (480 mi); Niger, 1,497 km (930 mi). **TERRITORIAL SEA LIMIT:** 30 mi.

Kano; the eastern line runs from Port Harcourt through Enugu and Makurdi, and joins the western line at Kaduna. Extensions carry the former north to Nguru and the latter north to Kaura-Namoda. Three branch lines connect other industrial and commercial centers to the main system. A 645-km (400-mi) extension of the Port Harcourt line from Kafanchan to Maiduguri, linking the main system with the northeastern corner of the country, was completed in 1964.

Nigeria in 1991 had about 120,000 km (74,570 mi) of roads, of which 35,000 km (21,750 mi) were paved. In 1991, some 1.4 million vehicles were registered, including 785,000 passenger cars.

Air traffic has been growing steadily. International service is provided from Lagos, Port Harcourt, and Kano airports by more than two dozen international airlines; a new cargo-oriented international airport in Abuja was operational in 1987. Nigeria Airways, which operates internal Nigerian services and participates in international services, became a wholly Nigerian-owned company in 1961. Its regularly scheduled flights link Lagos and 15 of the 19 state capitals. Nigeria Airways also flies to many West African destinations, to Nairobi, Kenya, and Jiddah, Sa'udi Arabia, and to New York, London, Amsterdam, and Rome. In 1991, 555,700 domestic passengers and 374,300 international passengers were carried. In 1993, Nigeria Airways began discussing the sale of its international operations to a foreign airline after incurring unacceptable losses as a parastatal. Domestic operations are to remain in state hands.

12 HISTORY

The history of Nigeria prior to the beginnings of British administration is sparsely documented, but archaeological evidence indicates that an Iron Age culture was present sometime between 500 BC and AD 200, and agriculture and livestock raising long before then. About the 11th century AD, Yoruba city-states developed in western Nigeria, and some, such as Benin, became powerful kingdoms in later centuries. During medieval times, northern Nigeria had contact with the large kingdoms of the western Sudan (Ghana, Mali, and Songhai) and with countries of the Mediterranean across the Sahara. Islamic influence was firmly established by the end of the 15th century, and Kano was famous not only as a center of Islamic studies but also as a great commercial entrepôt of the western Sudan. Until the arrival of the British, northern Nigeria was economically oriented toward the north and east, and woven cloth and leatherwork were exported as far as the North African ports of the Mediterranean. At the beginning of the 19th century, a jihad, or holy war, led by a Fulani sheikh, Uthman dan Fodio, established Fulani rule over the surviving Hausa kingdoms, until the British conquest at the end of the century.

In the south, the Portuguese were the first Europeans to establish close relations with the coastal people. In the late 15th century, they established a depot to handle trade goods and slaves from Benin. The Portuguese monopoly was broken after a century, and other European nations participated in the burgeoning slave trade. The British abolished slave trading in 1807, and thereafter British policy was directed at enforcing that ban on other nations. Interest in legitimate commerce developed slowly, but the discovery of the mouth of the Niger in 1830 provided an important impetus. The extension of British influence over Nigeria was gradual and, initially at least, unplanned. In 1861, the British annexed the island of Lagos, an important center of palm oil trade, and thereafter, they gradually extended their influence over the adjacent mainland of Yorubaland.

In 1887, British influence over the eastern coast, which had been promoted since 1849 by consular agents, was regularized by the establishment of the Oil Rivers Protectorate. This too was gradually extended inland and became the Niger Coast Protectorate in 1894. The acquisition of the interior of Nigeria, however, was accomplished largely by Sir George Goldie, founder of the Royal Niger Company, who by 1885 had eliminated commercial competition on the Niger and, by claiming treaties with responsible African authorities, had secured recognition of British influence over the Niger Basin by the European powers at the Berlin Conference. This influence was more fancied than real, but it provided the basis for British rule over northern Nigeria, which was consolidated by a series of punitive expeditions culminating in the establishment of the Protectorate of Northern Nigeria in 1900.

The separate administrative units were finally amalgamated in 1914 into the Colony and Protectorate of Nigeria, with Sir Frederick Lugard as governor-general. Despite the ostensible unification, the administrative individuality of the three separate regions—North, East, and West—was maintained. The chief characteristic of British rule in Nigeria was its system of local administration, known as indirect rule. The success of the system depended on fairly centralized hierarchical political units. It functioned well in the North, with variable success in the West, and poorly in the East.

After World War II, increasing pressures for self-government resulted in a succession of short-lived constitutions. The constitution of 1954 established a federal form of government, greatly extending the functions of the regional governments. A constitutional conference of May and June 1957 decided upon immediate self-government for the Eastern and Western regions, the Northern to follow in 1959. The step from self-government to independence was quickly taken. On 1 October 1960, Nigeria became a fully independent member of the British Commonwealth, and on 1 October 1963 it became a republic. Nnamdi Azikiwe was elected the first president of the Federal Republic of Nigeria.

Internal disorders, which began in 1962 and were caused mainly by regional resentment over the domination of the federal government by Northern elements, culminated in a military coup on 15 January 1966. Organized by a group of Eastern junior army officers, the coup led to the deaths of the federal prime minister, Sir Abubakar Tafawa Balewa; the prime minister of the Northern Region, Sir Ahmadu Bello; and the prime minister of the Western Region, Chief S. L. Akintola. By 17 January, Maj. Gen. Johnson Aguiyi-Ironsi, commander-in-chief of the army, had suppressed the revolt and assumed supreme power. He suspended the constitution and dissolved the legislature, established a military government, and appointed military governors to replace the popularly elected civilian governors in the regions. On 29 July 1966, mutinous elements in the army, largely Northern army officers, staged a countercoup, killed Gen. Ironsi, and replaced him with Lt. Col. Yakubu Gowon as head of the military government. The July coup led to the massacre of thousands of Easterners residing in the Northern Region and to the exodus of more than 1 million persons (mostly Ibos) to the Eastern Region.

On 28 May 1967, Col. Gowon assumed emergency powers as head of the Federal Military Government and announced the division of the country into 12 states; 6 states were formed from the Northern Region; 3 states from the Eastern Region; and the Mid-West, Western, and Lagos areas became separate states. Rejecting the realignment, Eastern Region leaders announced on 30 May the independent Republic of Biafra, with Lt. Col. Odumegwu Ojukwu as head of state. On 6 July, the federal government declared war on the fledgling republic. By the time the war ended, on 12 January 1970, Biafra had been reduced to about one-tenth of its original 78,000-sq-km (30,000-sq-mi) area, and a million or more persons had perished, many of disease and starvation. Following the surrender, many Ibos returned to their former positions in Lagos, and Gen. Gowon's military regime sought to rehabilitate the three Eastern states as quickly as possible.

In October 1970, with the civil war behind him, Gen. Gowon set 1976 as the target date for Nigeria's return to civilian rule. Political change came slowly, however, and in October 1974, Gowon announced an indefinite postponement in plans for the transfer of power. The regime's recalcitrance in this and other areas, including its failure to check the power of the state governors and to reduce the general level of corruption, led to Gowon's overthrow on 29 July 1975. His successor, Brig. Murtala Ramat Muhammad, moved vigorously in dismissing inefficient and corrupt officials and in establishing an ombudsman commission. One of his plans was to establish a new capital territory in the center of the country, at Abuja. On 13 February 1976, Muhammad was assassinated in the course of an abortive insurgency. He was replaced as head of the government by the former chief of staff of the armed forces, Lt. Gen. Olusegun Obasanjo, who pledged to carry on his predecessor's program. In March 1976, a decree established a 19-state federation. Political party activity was again permitted in late 1978, and a new constitution took effect on 1 October 1979, the day Alhaji Shehu Shagari took office as president. Leader of the conservative National Party of Nigeria, he also had the support of the Nigerian People's Party (NPP), led by former president Azikiwe. The NPP withdrew its support in 1981, leaving Shagari at the head of a minority government. In August 1983, Shagari won reelection to a second term as president; in late December, however, he was ousted in a military coup.

The new military regime, led by Maj.-Gen. Muhammadu Buhari, provoked growing public dissatisfaction because of its increasingly authoritarian character, and a military coup on 27 August 1985 brought Maj.-Gen. Ibrahim Badamasi Babangida to power. Assuming the title of president, Babangida banned Second Republic (1979–83) officials from participation in politics for 10 years. A return to full civilian rule was pledged by 1992, with local elections on a nonparty basis, the creation of a constituent assembly, the establishment of no more than two political parties, state elections, a national census, and finally presidential elections. The first step in the process—local elections on 12 December 1987—were marred by irregularities. To deal with Nigeria's economic troubles, stemming from the fall of world oil prices in the 1980s, Babangida inaugurated a "home-grown" Structural Adjustment Program (SAP) prompted by the IMF but not directed by them. It involved cuts in public spending, decreased state control over the economy, stimulation of exports, devaluation of the currency, and rescheduling of debt. Yet, government's own budgetary excesses undermined the SAP.

A mostly elected Constituent Assembly met in 1988 and approved modifications in the 1979 constitution. The process of party formation proved awkward in a society as heterogeneous as Nigeria's. None of the 13 potential parties gained Babangida's approval. Instead, he decided to create two new parties, one "a little to the right" of center, another "a little to the left." Neither challenged government effectively.

Babangida's guided transitional program from military to a democratic civilian Third Republic was scheduled to be completed in 1992. But, despite growing prodemocracy demands, it was marked by crisis after crisis. Clashes between Muslims and Christians in 1991 and 1992 spread through northern cities. Hundreds were killed in the rioting itself and then by the army seeking to contain the riots.

In elections for state governors and assemblies, the National Republican Convention (NRC) won 13 of 30 assemblies and 16 governships. The Social Democratic Party (SDP) carried 17 and 14, respectively. But voter indifference and fear of intimidation was high. When state governments took office, intraparty wrangling and political violence marred their performance.

Nonetheless, by January 1992, Nigerians geared up for the national presidential and legislative elections scheduled for later in the year. Nigeria's first successful census since independence (results announced in March 1992) indicated a population of 88.5 million, some 20 million fewer than estimated. The election register had to be revised downward, from 70 million to 39 million voters. On 20 May 20 1992, government banned all political, religious and ethnic organizations other than the two approved political parties.

Legislative elections were conducted on 4 July and the SDP won 47 of the 91 Senate seats and 310 of the 593 seats in the House of Representatives. The NRC won 37 and 267 seats, respectively. The ruling military council pushed back the transition date until January 1993 and postponed the inauguration of the National Assembly to coincide with the establishment of the Third Republic.

In August and September, the country began the process of narrowing the field of presidential candidates from 20 to 2 in preparation for the December elections. But on 17 November 1992, Babargida announced a third delay in the transfer of power from 2 January until 27 August 1993. Political violence and charges of electoral fraud disrupted the first round of presidential primaries. The second round in September was flawed, too. Faced with a virtual breakdown of the electoral machinery, the military council suspended the primary results in October. All 23 of the presidential aspirants were banned from future political competition. These disruptions were compounded by high levels of student and labor unrest, detentions of dissidents, and ethnic and religious fighting. Nonetheless, the military council had promised civilian government in 1993.

A new round of presidential nominations took place in March 1993. Chief M.K.O. Abiola (SDP) and Alhaji Bashir Tofay (NRC), both Muslim businessmen with ties to Babangida, won nomination. The presidential election of 12 June took place amid a flurry of legal efforts to halt it and great voter confusion. Abiola apparently defeated Tofa handily, 58.4% to 41.6% according to unofficial results.

But the National Electoral Commission set aside the results on 16 June and Babangida annulled the election a week later citing irregularities, poor turnout, and legal complications. Abiola, backed largely by the Yoruba people, demanded to be certified as president-elect. Civil unrest, especially in Lagos, followed.

After weeks of uncertainty and tension, Babangida resigned the presidency and his military commission on 26 August 1993. He handpicked a transitional council headed by Chief Ernest Shonekan. By mid-November, Gen. Sani Abacha forced Shonekan to resign and he installed himself as head of state. On 18 November 1993, he abolished all state and local governments and the national legislature. He replaced many civilian officials with military commanders. He banned political parties and all political activity and ordered strikers to return to work. The following week, he named an 11-member Provisional Ruling Council composed mainly of generals and police officials. He also created a 32-member Federal Executive Council to head government ministries. It included prominent civilians and some prodemocracy and human rights activists.

In 1994, Abiola proclaimed himself president on 11 June and then went into hiding. He was arrested later that month.

13 GOVERNMENT

The 1979 constitution, promulgated by the outgoing military government, established a federal system resembling that of the US, with a directly elected president and vice-president (whose names appear on the same ballot) and separate executive, legislative, and judicial branches.

The military government that took command after the December 1983 coup suspended the 1979 constitution. The president held executive and legislative authority, in consultation with the 28-member Armed Forces Ruling Council, and appointed the cabinet.

After the Abacha seizure of power on 17 November 1993, the 1979 constitution was still suspended. A military-dominated Provisional Ruling Council (PRC) rules by decree. A 32-member Federal Executive Council manages government departments, the PRC dissolved the elected national and state legislatures and the local councils. They replaced elected civilian governors with military administrators. The PRC also announced that it would hold a constitutional conference to plan for the future and to establish a timetable for a return to democracy. On 21 November 1993, Abacha signed a decree restoring the 1979 constitution (Second Republic). Nonetheless, legal experts cannot agree on which documents form the basis for Nigerian government and law.

14 POLITICAL PARTIES

The uneven awakening of political consciousness among the larger tribal and nationality groups in Nigeria hindered the formation of a truly national Nigerian political party; tribal or regional consciousness remained the main determinant of political affiliation. Before 1966, the major parties in Nigeria were the Northern People's Congress (NPC), overwhelmingly dominant in the Northern Region and possessing a plurality in the federal House of Representatives; the National Council of Nigerian Citizens (NCNC), dominant in the Eastern Region and junior partner in coalition with the NPC in the federal House of Representatives; and the Action Group, majority party in the Western Region and the leading opposition group in the federal legislature. There was little difference in the policies and platforms of the major parties. All tended to support welfare and development programs, although the NPC program was somewhat more modest than that of the others. Following the 1959 elections, the NCNC joined in a coalition with the NPC in the federal government.

The first national elections in independent Nigeria, held on 30 December 1964, were contested by two political alliances: the

Nigerian National Alliance (NNA), led by Sir Ahmadu Bello, premier of the Northern Region, and the United Progressive Grand Alliance (UPGA), led by Michael Okpara, premier of the Eastern Region. The NNA comprised the NPC, the Western-based Nigerian National Democratic Party, and opposition parties representing ethnic minorities in the Eastern and Mid-Western regions. The UPGA included the NCNC, the Action Group, the Northern Elements Progressive Union (the main opposition party in the Northern Region), and the United Middle Belt Congress (a non-Muslim party strongly opposed to the NPC).

Tribal and regional antagonisms formed the main issue in the election. The Northerners feared Ibo domination of the federal government and sought support from the Yoruba, while the UPGA accused the Muslim Northerners of anti-Southern, anti-democratic, and anti-Christian attitudes. The election results, announced on 6 January 1965, gave a large majority to the NNA (198 of 267 constituencies). Before the balloting began, the UPGA charged that unconstitutional practices were taking place and announced that it would boycott the elections, in which only 4 million of the 15 million eligible voters actually cast ballots. On 4 January 1965, President Azikiwe called on Prime Minister Balewa to form a new government. In the supplementary elections held on 18 March 1965, the UPGA won all 51 seats in the Eastern Region and 3 seats in Lagos. This was followed by announcement of an enlarged and reorganized cabinet on 31 March. Ten months later the Balewa government was overthrown, the military assumed power, and on 24 May 1966 all political parties were banned.

When legal political activity resumed in 1978, five parties emerged: the National Party of Nigeria (NPN), representing chiefly the North and an educated, wealthy elite; the Nigerian People's Party (NPP), strong among the Ibos and slightly to the left of the NPN; the Unity Party of Nigeria (UPN), Yoruba-led and Socialist-oriented; the People's Redemption Party, advocating radical social change; and the Great Nigeria People's Party, espousing welfare capitalism. Shagari, the NPN presidential candidate, received the most votes (33.9%) in the 11 August 1979 presidential election, with Obafemi Awolowo of the UPN a close second (29.2%). In National Assembly elections held on 7 and 14 July 1979, the NPN won 36 of the 95 Senate seats and 168 of 440 House of Representatives seats. The UPN was second with 28 and 111, respectively; the NPP third with 16 and 78. Each of the five parties won control of at least two state governments in elections held 21 and 28 July 1979. In the presidential election of August 1983, incumbent President Shagari of the NPN won reelection to a second 4-year term, polling 12,047,638 votes (47%). Obafemi Awolowo of the UPN placed second with 7,885,434 votes (31%). That same month, Shagari's NPN posted victories in Senate and House elections. However, there were widespread charges of irregularities in the balloting. All existing political parties were dissolved after the December 1983 coup.

During the period of partisan activity during which a transfer of power from military to civilian rule had been plotted, two parties were permitted. A right-of-center National Republican Convention (NRC) and a left-of-center Social Democratic Party (SDP) were kept on a tight leash. The two-chamber National Assembly to which they were elected never was granted genuine power. The results of the much postponed presidential elections of June 1993 were annulled by Babangida. In November 1993, the new military rulers suspended all partisan and political activity.

15LOCAL GOVERNMENT

In March 1976, a reorganization of Nigeria's major administrative divisions was undertaken. The 12 preexisting states were reconstituted into 19 states as follows: Ogun, Ondo, and Oyo states were created out of the former Western State; Imo and Anambra states from East-Central State; Niger and Sokoto states

from North-Western State; Benue and Plateau states from Benue-Plateau State; and Bauchi, Borno, and Gongola from North-Eastern State. Seven other states remained basically unchanged except for minor boundary adjustments and some name changes; these are (with original names where applicable, in parentheses) Lagos, Kaduna (North-Central), Kano, Bendel (Mid-West), Cross River (South-Eastern), Rivers, and Kwara. In addition, plans were announced for establishment of a Federal Capital Territory of 7,315 sq km (2,824 sq mi) as the new national capital. The new district was carved from the central part of the country between Kaduna, Plateau, and Niger states. Under the military regime established in 1983, all state governors were appointed by the ruling council; in 1987, all but one governor was a military officer. The governor of each state served as chairman of an appointed state executive council.

Under Nigeria's federal system, a fixed amount of most federal revenue is allotted to the states and localities. By the fall of the Babangida regime in August 1993, there were 30 states and one territory (the Abuja Capital Territory). They had been governed by elected state legislatures and governors. On 18 November 1993, these governments were abolished and the civilian governors were replaced by military commanders.

16JUDICIAL SYSTEM

The Supreme Court, its members appointed by the president, is the highest court in Nigeria. It hears appeals from the Federal Court of Appeals, which in turn hears appeals from the Federal High Court and state high courts. The Supreme Court also has original jurisdiction over constitutional disputes between the federal government and the states or between states.

Customary and area courts exist to administer local laws and customs. Their jurisdiction varies according to the warrant under which they were established. In the northern states, Muslim law (Shari'ah) is administered in most courts. Decisions can be appealed to state courts.

Each state has magisterial court districts. These courts have original jurisdiction for both criminal and civil matters in the south, but only criminal matters in the north. Each state also has a high court that hears appeals from magistrates' courts and has original jurisdiction over the more serious crimes.

Decree One, which suspended the constitution in 1984, remains in force. Although the then-existing framework of the judiciary remains undisturbed, Decree One established a parallel system of military tribunals which have exclusive jurisdiction over certain offenses such as corruption, armed robbery, coup plotting, and illegal sales of petroleum.

The continued governmental reliance on tribunals operating outside the framework of constitutional protections seriously compromises the independence of the judiciary and sacrifices any semblance of due process. The role of the judiciary is also undercut by frequent governmental refusal to respect court rulings.

17ARMED FORCES

The Nigerian armed forces are the largest in sub-Saharan Africa after South Africa, with 76,000 personnel in 1993. The army, with 62,000 personnel, was divided into 10 brigades (infantry, armor, air borne, mechanized) with brigades or battalions attached for reconnaissance, artillery, and engineering. Equipment was largely of European or Soviet origin. The navy, with a total strength of 4,500, possessed 2 frigates, 3 corvettes, and 51 smaller craft. The air force, composed of 9,500 personnel, had 95 combat aircraft.

The Nigerian police are the responsibility of the federal government. The force is under a federal inspector-general, but each state contingent is under a commissioner who takes directions from the state governor; nevertheless, he is not responsible to the governor but rather to the Ministry of Internal Affairs.

During 1981–85, $1.8 billion worth of arms was imported. The UK, France, Germany, and Italy provided about 75% of the total. Arms imports dropped to $410 million (1986–91). Nigeria contributes about 5,000 troops to 7 different peacekeeping operations, the majority in Liberia.

Nigeria spent $300 million on defense in 1990 or 1% of gross domestic product.

18 INTERNATIONAL COOPERATION

Nigeria, a Commonwealth member, was admitted to the UN on 7 October 1960, and since that time has become affiliated with ECA and all the nonregional specialized agencies except WIPO. It is also a member of G-77 and the OAU, and is a signatory of GATT and the Law of the Sea.

Nigeria joined OPEC in June 1971 and became a signatory to the Lomé Convention among African, Caribbean, and Pacific countries. Nigeria signed an agreement with the EEC in February 1975, giving Nigeria free access to the EEC markets and concessionary loan and industrial cooperation privileges in exchange for most-favored-nation status for EEC members. In May 1975, Nigeria signed an agreement setting up ECOWAS. Among the regional organizations of which Nigeria is a member are the Niger Basin Authority and the Lake Chad Basin Commission.

19 ECONOMY

The Nigerian economy, with an enterprising population and a wealth of natural resources, offers tremendous potential for economic growth. However, poor economic policy, political instability, and an overreliance on oil exports has created severe structural problems in the economy. When the oil boom of the 1970s came to an end in the early 1980s, Nigeria's failure to bring domestic and foreign expenditures in line with its lower income led to a rapid buildup of internal and external deficits. Nigeria deferred payments on its large foreign debt, adopted austerity measures, scaled back ambitious development plans, and introduced a foreign exchange auction system that devalued the naira. These policies had a positive effect and from 1986 to 1990 real GDP grew at a 5.4% average annual rate. However, in 1992, real GDP grew at only 4.1%, while the large government deficits, 10% of GDP in 1992, continued to expand. A crippling blow to the economy came in mid-1994 when oil workers in the southeast, unhappy with the way the central government collects oil revenue without giving any back, went on strike. Crude oil accounts for over 90% of exports and over 80% of government revenue. With daily output down 25% because of the strike, the government's lack of revenue forced it to stop servicing most of its $28 billion external debt. In the meantime the budget deficit reached $1 billion, over 12% of GDP. Fuel has become scarce. With the economy in a shambles, primary agricultural production remains the basic economic activity for the great majority of Nigerians.

20 INCOME

In 1992 Nigeria's GNP was $32,944 million at current prices, or $320 per capita. For the period 1985–92 the average inflation rate was 28%, resulting in a real growth rate in per capita GNP of 3.4%.

In 1992 the GDP was $30,612 million in current US dollars. It is estimated that agriculture, hunting, forestry, and fishing contributed 30% to GDP; mining and quarrying, 37%; manufacturing, 6%; construction, 2%; wholesale and retail trade, 13%; transport, storage, and communication, 2%; finance, insurance, real estate, and business services, 6%; and other sources, 4%.

21 LABOR

The total labor force in Nigeria was 30.6 million in 1992, and civilian employment amounted to 8.4 million. The unemployment rate was officially estimated at 4.2%, but that amount is believed to be greatly underestimated. Of those gainfully employed, 71% are in agriculture, with about 15% in manufacturing and about 13% in services.

The four labor federations were merged in 1978 into the Nigerian Labour Congress (NLC), which was strengthened by legislation establishing a compulsory dues checkoff system. As of 1992, NLC had 3.5 million members, for a total unionization of 11.5%. As of 1992, the minimum wage was equivalent to approximately $26 per month. In January 1991, the government abolished the uniform wage structure for all government agencies, allowing workers to negotiate their own employment conditions, wages, and benefits.

22 AGRICULTURE

In terms of employment, agriculture is by far the most important sector of Nigeria's economy, engaging a majority of the working population. Agricultural holdings are generally small and scattered; farming is often of the subsistence variety, characterized by simple tools and shifting cultivation. About 32 million hectares (79 million acres), or 36% of Nigeria's land area, were under cultivation in 1991. The economic benefits of large-scale agriculture are recognized, and the government favors the formation of cooperative societies and settlements to encourage production on a large scale. Large-scale agriculture, however, is not common. Despite an abundant water supply, a favorable climate, and wide areas of arable land, productivity is restricted owing to low soil fertility in many areas and inefficient methods of cultivation.

The agricultural products of Nigeria can be divided into two main groups: food crops, produced for home consumption, and export products. Prior to the civil war, the country was self-sufficient in food, but imports of food increased substantially after 1973. Bread, made primarily from US wheat, replaced domestic crops as the cheapest staple food for much of the urban population. The most important food crops are yams and manioc (cassava) in the south and sorghum (Guinea corn) and millet in the north. In 1992, production of yams was 20 million tons; manioc, 20 million tons; sorghum, 4.1 million tons; and millet, 3.2 million tons. Other crops were cocoyams and sweet potatoes, 1.5 million tons; maize, 1.7 million tons; and bananas and plantains, 1.3 million tons. Rice, grown in several areas, yielded over 3.4 million tons. Production of peanuts (unshelled) was 1,214,000 tons (highest in Africa), and of raw sugar 75,000 tons. Many fruits and vegetables are also grown by Nigerian farmers.

Production of nonfood crops in 1992 included palm oil, 900,000 tons; palm kernels, 385,000 tons; cocoa beans, 130,000 tons; rubber, 110,000 tons; cotton, 63,000 tons; and tobacco, 9,000 tons. Agricultural exports (including manufactured food and agricultural products) decreased in quantity after 1970, partly because of the discouraging effect of low world prices.

In 1979, the importing of many foods was banned, including fresh milk, vegetables, roots and tubers, fruits, and poultry. The exporting of milk, sugar, flour, and hides and skins was also banned. During 1985–87, imports of wheat, corn, rice, and vegetable oil were banned as declining income from oil encouraged greater attention to the agricultural sector. In 1986, government marketing boards were closed down, and a free market in all agricultural products was established. Uneven rains and fertilizer shortages caused below average harvests of most staple and cash crops in 1992. In October 1992, the government lifted the ban on wheat imports temporarily for eight months. Import bans on rice, corn, vegetable oils, and malting barley remain in effect. As of May 1993, the government was considering importing food to alleviate shortages and extraordinarily high prices for food staples.

23 ANIMAL HUSBANDRY

In 1992 there were an estimated 15,700,000 head of cattle in Nigeria, over 90% of them in the north, owned mostly by nomadic Fulani. The prevalence of the tsetse fly in other areas restricts the majority of cattle to the fly-free dry savanna areas. The cattle owned by the Fulani and Hausa consist mainly of zebu breeds; cattle in the south are mainly Shorthorns. There were also an estimated 24 million goats, 13,500,000 sheep, 1,205,000 horses and donkeys, 5,328,000 pigs, and 160 million chickens.

Improvements in stock, slaughterhouse, cold storage, and transport facilities have made parts of Nigeria almost self-sufficient in meat production, but many Nigerians outside the north suffer protein deficiency in their diet. In 1992, 837,000 tons of meat and 370,000 tons of cow's milk were produced. The Livestock and Meat Authority controls operations in transport and slaughtering in the north. An estimated 13.8 million sheep and goats and 2.57 million head of cattle were slaughtered in 1992.

24FISHING

Fish is an important dietary element and one of the few sources of animal protein available to many Nigerians. Fishing is carried on in Nigeria's many rivers, creeks, and lagoons, and in Lake Chad; trawlers operate along the coast. The total fishing catch was 266,552 tons in 1991, not enough to meet national requirements. In 1991, imports of fresh, chilled, or frozen fish totaled 462,880 tons.

Both federal and state governments are encouraging the development of local fisheries, inland and at sea, by sponsoring research, stocking reservoirs, and offering training in improved fish culture and fishing gear. Fish ponds have been established in the southern part of the country. Although the fishing industry output has increased 42% over its 1986 level, it has yet to regain its 538,000-ton high of 1983.

25FORESTRY

About 13% of Nigeria, or roughly 11,600 hectares (28,664,000 acres) is classified as forest or woodland. High forest reserves occur mostly in Ogun, Ondo, and Oyo states; savanna forest reserves, chiefly in the northern states, are limited in value, yielding only firewood and local building materials. In 1991, 111,059,000 cu m of roundwood were produced, over 92% for fuel. Exports of timber and finished wood products were banned in 1976 in order to preserve domestic supplies. The ban was subsequently lifted and the forestry sector recorded gains. However, the country suffers from desertification, anemic reforestation efforts, and high levels of domestic wood consumption.

26MINING

Nigeria produced more than 246 tons of tin concentrates in 1991. A smelter at Jos produces refined tin for export. In 1991, production of columbite totaled 36 tons.

Nigeria is the only West African producer of coal, for the railroads, electric power, and cement manufacturing, mainly from mines around Enugu. Output in 1991 was 138,000 tons. Total reserves were estimated at 1.5 billion tons in 1991. Nigeria has plentiful supplies of limestone, and its production totaled 1,436,000 tons in 1991, supplying cement plants.

Extensive iron deposits include reserves of 2.5 billion tons with an average content of 37%. Small quantities of gold are mined in Oyo State.

27ENERGY AND POWER

Coal has been superseded as the chief source of Nigeria's electric power by oil, natural gas, and newly developed hydroelectric facilities. In 1969, the 11,500-Mw Kainji Dam, 100 km (62 mi) north of Jebba, was inaugurated. The N£87.6-million dam was built with loans from the IBRD (N£34.5 million) and from the UK, US, Canada, Italy, and the Netherlands. The 560-Mw Jebba plant on the Niger, the 600-Mw Shiroro plant on the Kaduna, and a 1,320-Mw thermal station at Igbin, near Lagos, will further add to

hydroelectric capacity. Hydroelectric production accounted for 22% of total power generation during 1991, thermal for the rest, almost entirely with oil or gas for fuel. Installed capacity in 1991 totaled almost 4,040,000 kw; electricity produced totaled an estimated 9,955 million kwh.

Within four decades, oil has grown to a position of dominance in the Nigerian economy. A Dutch-UK consortium made the first commercial strike of oil in 1956 and began to export in 1958. A number of other companies, mainly US and French, subsequently began exploration, and large reserves were discovered. Production was reduced substantially by the civil war, but by 1973 output was up to 2 million barrels a day—making Nigeria the largest producer in Africa, a position it retains. Proved reserves in 1993 amounted to about 17.9 billion barrels. Crude oil production rose from 1,285,000 barrels per day in 1982 to 1,635,000 barrels per day in 1989 to 1,895,000 barrels daily in 1991. Production in 1992 was 91.6 million tons, or an average of 1,850,000 barrels per day, down 2.1% from 1991. Oil export revenues in 1992 rose to $10.8 billion from $6.5 billion in 1986, even though the average price plunged from $28.65 per barrel in 1986 to $18.20 per barrel in 1992. In 1993, oil revenues accounted for 96% of total export revenues.

The main fields are located mostly in Rivers, Imo, and Bendel states of the delta region, both onshore and in the Gulf of Guinea. In May 1974, the Nigerian National Oil (later Petroleum) Co. (NNPC) acquired a 55% share in all the petroleum companies in Nigeria, with effect from April 1974. Compensation was made by granting "buy-back" rights to 50% of production with an option on a further 25% at $12.50 per barrel until 1976. This buy-back price was reduced to $11.60 on 1 April 1975. In 1979, the NNPC raised its equity share to 60% and also took over British Petroleum's remaining 20% share in the Shell/BP Consortium. There were seven main oil consortiums in 1992; the largest was Shell/NNPC.

Crude oil production has resulted in the joint production of natural gas, most of which is wasted through flaring. In May 1993, Chevron and NNPC began the first major project to reduce offshore gas flaring in Nigeria. When complete, the project will reduce flaring by 80%. In 1992, Nigeria produced 4.9 billion cu m of natural gas; reserves were estimated at 3.4 trillion cu m.

28INDUSTRY

In 1989, the manufacturing sector accounted for 8.5% of GDP, down from its 1986–90 average of 10%. Capacity utilization was as low as 25% in 1987, though it is thought to have rebounded to 34.5% by 1992.

The textile industry has shown the greatest growth since independence, and the country is virtually self-sufficient in printed fabrics, blankets, and towels. Other areas of expansion include cement production (3,500,000 tons in 1990), tire production, and furniture assembly. The Delta Steel Plant at Aladja, built by a German-Austrian consortium, began production in 1982 and supplies three steel rolling mills at Oshogbo, Katsina and Jos. The steel complex at Abeokuta began producing in 1983 and its third-stage construction, raising its total capacity to 5.3 million tons per year, was near completion in 1993.

Other important industries include sawmills, cigarette factories, breweries, sugar refining, rubber, paper, soap and detergent factories, footwear factories, pharmaceutical plants, tire factory, paint factories, and assembly plants for radios, record players, and television sets. Nigeria has six state-owned motor-vehicle assembly plants for Volkswagen, Peugeot, and Mercedes products.

29SCIENCE AND TECHNOLOGY

Learned societies include ones for ecology, entomology, fisheries, forestry, genetics, geology, medicine, veterinary medicine, microbiology, nutrition, and engineering; research institutes focus on cereals, cocoa, lake ecology, horticulture, forestry, livestock, root crops, veterinary medicine, oceanography and marine sciences, oil palms, rubber, and tropical agriculture, among other areas. In the mid-1980s, roughly 60% of all university places for entering students were reserved for programs of study in such fields as agriculture, engineering, and medicine. The Nigerian Academy of Science, founded in 1977, promotes and coordinates scientific and technological activities, trains scientists, advises the government on scientific matters, and organizes symposia and lectures. The Federal Ministry of Science and Technology has 25 attached research institutes. In 1987, research and development expenditures totaled N86 million; 6,042 technicians and 1,338 scientists and engineers were engaged in research and development.

30 DOMESTIC TRADE

The distribution of consumer goods is effected largely through a complex network of intermediary traders, who extend the area of distribution and often break down products into very small units for delivery to the ultimate consumer. A few trading companies, especially those with European equity and management, carry full product lines. Village markets are universal but tend to be more highly organized in the densely populated areas of the south. The great market centers such as Ibadan and Kano are daily attended by many thousands.

Advertising has increased markedly since independence. Newspapers, magazines, radio, television, billboards, and movies are all utilized.

31 FOREIGN TRADE

Exports in 1992 totaled N205,613 million, 97.9% of which was accounted for by petroleum. Cocoa was the largest agricultural export. Imports in 1992 reached the N143,151 million level, resulting in a trade surplus of N62,462 million. Primary imports (1987) are machinery and manufactured goods (38.2%), basic manufactures (25.1%), chemicals (16.9%), and food (10.5%).

Positive trade balances had been common since the early 1960s, but in 1981 the trade balance fell into deficit as imports continued to climb while petroleum exports fell. Trade recovered in 1984 and has remained positive since, reaching a high in 1990 of $8.6 billion.

The direction of Nigeria's trade has changed during the last two decades. In 1965, five countries (led by the UK, with 42% of the total, followed by the Netherlands, the US, Germany, and Italy) bought 80% of Nigeria's predominantly agricultural exports. In 1987, the US (47%) was the largest market (principally for petroleum), followed by the Netherlands (11.3%), Spain (7.9%), and France (7.2%). The UK remained Nigeria's largest supplier of imports (16.8%), followed by Germany (13.4%), France (10.0%), Japan (9.0%), and the US (8.3%).

32 BALANCE OF PAYMENTS

The key elements in Nigeria's balance of payments are the volume and value of oil exports. Despite slightly higher production, oil exports earned about $1 billion less in 1992 than in the previous year due to a fall in realized prices for Nigerian crude oil. In spite of a surplus in traded goods and services, Nigeria saw a large deficit in its overall balance of payments in 1992 due to debt servicing and the London Club debt buy-back in January 1992. Reserves plummeted so that by early 1993, they could only cover no more than one or tow months of imports. In 1992 merchandise ecports totaled $11,791 million and imports $7,181 million. The merchandise trade balance was $4,610 million.

The following table summarizes Nigeria's balance of payments for 1991 and 1992 (in millions of US dollars):

	1991	1992
CURRENT ACCOUNT		
Goods services and income	958	1,515
Unrequited transfers	744	753
TOTALS	1202	2268
CAPITAL ACCOUNT		
Direct investment	712	897
Portfolio investment	−61	1,884
Other long-term capital	−3,088	−5,180
Other short-term capital	−196	−5,385
Exceptional financing	2,163	1,911
Reserves	−640	3,727
TOTALS	−1,110	2,146
Errors and omissions	−92	−122
Total change in reserves	−571	3468

33 BANKING AND SECURITIES

Before World War II, two large British banks, the Bank of British West Africa and Barclays Bank, virtually monopolized Nigerian banking. After 1945, a number of African-owned banks entered the field; between 1946 and 1952, however, more than 20 such banks either failed or went into voluntary liquidation, primarily because of undercapitalization and rash loan policies. Banking ordinances have since been issued to correct this situation: in 1969, for example, the Banking Decree established minimum capital requirements for licensed banks, based on the total deposits. Licenses are mandatory.

The bank of issue is the Central Bank of Nigeria, established in 1958. The Central Bank regulates most commercial banking operations in Nigeria, but the federal Ministry of Finance has retained control of most international activities of the financial sector. As of 1991, foreign assets of the Central Bank stood at N44,267 million.

In 1991, Nigeria had 120 commercial banks, with total foreign assets estimated at N10,663 million at the end of 1991. The 1969 Banking Decree requires that all banking institutions be incorporated in Nigeria, and a 1976 law gives the government 60% ownership of all foreign banks. Important additional sources of credit are provided by thrift and loan societies and by the branches of the National Development Corp. The Nigerian Industrial Development Bank (NIDB), established in 1964 in collaboration with the IFC and European, Japanese, and US investment institutions, provides long- and medium-term financing to concerns in the industrial nonpetroleum, mining, and tourist sectors. The National Bank for Commerce and Industry helps finance smaller enterprises. Merchant banking has expanded rapidly since 1973, when the Union Dominican Trust Co. began operations. Other US, UK, and Japanese financial institutions have since set up merchant facilities in the country. In July 1990 the state banks were privatized. Beginning in 1990 the country allowed the establishment of foreign banks. Sixty percent of the foreign banks that are established in Nigeria must be held by Nigerian interests. In the same year the government began a program to establish 500 community banks. In 1991 demand deposits in the commercial banks totaled N20,180 million. The money supply at the end of 1991 was N79,068.

The Nigerian (formerly Lagos) Stock Exchange began operations on 1 July 1961, following passage of the Lagos Stock Exchange Act; the government promulgated regulations for the exchange and provided that all dealings in stock on behalf of principals be carried out only by members of the exchange. The government encourages public issues of shares by Nigerian companies in an effort to mobilize local capital for the country's development. The exchange, in Lagos, with branches in Kaduna and Port Harcourt, deals in government stocks and in shares of public companies registered in Nigeria. The stock exchange is managed by the Investment Co. of Nigeria. Since the provision of new investment incentives under the Nigerian Enterprises Promotion Decree of April 1974, activity on the stock exchange has increased.

34INSURANCE

The Nigerian Reinsurance Corp. requires foreign insurance companies to reinsure 20% through the corporation. There were 87 registered insurance companies in operation at the end of 1986, of which 69 were fully Nigerian. Included were 3 life insurance companies, 60 non-life companies, and 24 composite firms. In the same year, 29.3% of all premiums were for life and 70.7% for non-life insurance. In 1976, the government took a 60% interest in foreign-owned insurance companies. The only compulsory insurance is that for motor vehicles. Laws of 1976 and 1977 regulate insurance firms, particularly those in the life insurance field, and provide for their registration, investigation, and minimum capitalization. Total premiums amounted to US$1.8 per capita in 1990.

35PUBLIC FINANCE

The federal government is responsible for collecting taxes on income, profits, and property, as well as import and export taxes and excise duties. The petroleum sector provides about 70% of budgetary revenues. A large share of these revenues is redistributed to state governments. The budget is consistently in deficit.

Public investment flourished during the oil boom years of the 1970s. When the oil market prices collapsed in the 1980s however, the Nigerian government maintained its high level of spending, thus acquiring substantial foreign debt. Although privatization efforts began in 1986, increased government spending outside the official budget since 1990 has damaged public finance reform. As a result, the federal deficit increased from 2.8% of GDP in 1990 to 9% in 1992. Nigeria's medium- and long-term debt rose from US$14.6 billion in 1985 to US$31 billion in 1992.

36TAXATION

By far the most important direct tax is the petroleum profits tax. The rate on taxable profits of petroleum companies since 1975 has been 85%, but a guaranteed profit of US$2.30 per barrel was established in 1986.

Despite the heavy dependence on petroleum and mining revenues, other direct taxes remain relatively high. The corporate tax rate was 35% in 1993. However, income from the export of Nigerian goods by foreign companies was not subject to the tax. There was also a capital gains tax of 20% and a tax of 5% on dividends. Personal income tax rates ranged from 10% on the first N10,000 to 35% on taxable incomes over N100,000. Excise duties on beer, tobacco, textiles, and other goods are also levied.

37CUSTOMS AND DUTIES

The federal government levies customs duties on most imports, but these duties were substantially reduced in 1986. The average import duty is about 20%, although rates vary from 5% to as high as 300%. All imports are also subject to a 6% surcharge.

Most goods produced in Nigeria may be freely exported.

38FOREIGN INVESTMENT

Nigeria is one of West Africa's most populous and developed countries. Most investors are from Europe, Japan, or the US. In the petroleum industry, most investment is from the UK, the US, and France. Federal and state governments welcome foreign investment and provide incentives that include financial assistance, help in locating sites, tax holidays, protection from imports, export rebates, customs duty relief, and, in some cases, duty-free raw materials. Exemption from income tax may be provided for entry into a "pioneer" industry; interest on certain foreign loans is tax-exempt. There is also an accelerated depreciation program. Foreign investment is particularly welcome in certain areas, including agribusiness, export and import-substitution industries, automotive assembly, and petrochemicals.

Investment in the petroleum industry was carried out on a very large scale in the 1970s, including funds devoted to production, refining, and petrochemicals. By 1975, private US and UK investments were estimated at more than $1 billion each, mostly in the oil industry.

Investments in other areas have been made by the former Soviet Union, Austria, Germany (iron and steel), and by Japanese firms (petroleum and synthetic fabrics).

The Nigerian Enterprises Decree of 1972, strengthened and extended in 1977, placed limitations on the share of foreign equity permitted in Nigerian firms in certain industries. Certain areas of activity, including some manufacturing and many service industries, are also reserved exclusively for Nigerian ownership. Others require 40–60% Nigerian control. These decrees were relaxed in March 1988; in December 1989, a new decree was issued, permitting 100% foreign ownership in any new venture except those in banking, oil, insurance, and mining.

39ECONOMIC DEVELOPMENT

The agriculture sector has been the focus of intense development interest in recent years, with food self-sufficiency the goal. In 1990, agriculture received 28% of the federal budget and was the subject of a separate three-year development plan involving public and private spending targets concentrating on the family farmer. The program includes price stabilization plans and schemes to revitalize the palm oil, cocoa, and rubber subsectors.

An integrated petrochemical industry is a priority. Using the output of the nation's refineries, Nigeria produces benzene, carbon black, and polypropylene. The development of liquid natural gas facilities is expected to lead to the production of methanol, fertilizer, and domestic gas.

In the manufacturing sector, the government is backing a policy of local sourcing whereby locally produced raw materials are converted into finished products. The rehabilitation of the nation's transportation infrastructure is part of a three-year rolling investment plan begun in 1990.

40SOCIAL DEVELOPMENT

There are two kinds of welfare services in Nigeria—those provided by voluntary agencies and those provided by the government. Voluntary agencies comprise those fully or partially subsidized by the government, those financed by a parent body such as a church or mosque, and those financed from subscriptions of their members. Workers are protected under the Labor Code Act (1958) and the Workmen's Compensation Act, which provides protection for workers in case of industrial accidents. A national provident fund scheme, inaugurated in 1961, was the first broad social security measure in Nigeria. The scheme is contributory and is designed to make systematic financial provisions for workers when unemployment occurs due to old age or illness. Most companies also provide pension plans for their employees.

Despite recent gains in the workplace, women have only a minor role in politics. Abortion is legal only to save the woman's life.

Nigeria's human rights record, slowly improving in the run-up to a transfer of power to a civilian government, worsened in 1993. Arbitrary arrest and detention are commonly used to silence the government's critics. Press freedom is limited. The army regularly acts to intimidate and put down protests. Prodemocracy and human rights groups, student activists, journalists, and trade unionists are in retreat.

41HEALTH

Nigeria's health care delivery system consists of a network of primary, secondary, and tertiary facilities. According to 1992 data, primary care is largely provided through approximately 4,000 health clinics and dispensaries scattered throughout the country. As for secondary care, there are about 700 health care centers and 1,670 maternity centers; tertiary care is handled through 12 university teaching hospitals with about 6,500 beds. In 1990, there were 1.4 hospital beds per 1,000 inhabitants. The target areas for mass procurement of medical equipment are the teaching hospitals. The lack of proper infrastructural facilities and inadequate remuneration of public sector health care workers have also spurred the development of a limited number of privately owned hospitals which cater to those who can afford them. The country is in need of medical supplies and equipment. Some pharmaceuticals are manufactured in Nigeria.

In 1989, there were 17,954 physicians, 5,318 pharmacists, 1,088 dentists, 64,503 nurses, and 52,378 midwives in Nigeria. In 1992, there were 15 physicians per 100,000 people, with a nurse to doctor ratio of 6.0. In 1992, 66% of the population had access to health care services and, in 1990, total health care expenditures were $906 million.

Despite the receding influence of such endemic diseases as yellow fever as a result of improving and more widespread medical facilities, health problems in Nigeria remain acute. Malaria and pulmonary tuberculosis are the diseases of most frequent incidence, but serious outbreaks of cerebrospinal meningitis still occur in the north. Just under half of all deaths are thought to be among children, who are especially vulnerable to malaria and account for 75% of registered malaria deaths. In 1990, there were about 222 cases of tuberculosis per 100,000 people.

Schistosomiasis, Guinea worm, trachoma, river blindness, and yaws are other diseases of high frequency. Progress, however, has been made in the treatment of sleeping sickness (trypanosomiasis) and leprosy. The former has been nearly eliminated by the introduction of new drugs, while the introduction of sulfone therapy has nearly halted the incidence of new cases of leprosy in the eastern states.

A program for the eradication of river blindness and malaria has been undertaken in cooperation with WHO. The government is also working on the control of sexually transmitted diseases, including HIV/AIDS, which is growing, through public education and behavior change. Immunization rates for 1992 for children up to one year old were as follows: tuberculosis (50%); diphtheria, pertussis, and tetanus (31%); polio (30%); and measles (36%).

42HOUSING

Housing generally has not ranked high on the scale of priorities for social spending, and state governments have tended to rely upon local authorities to meet the problem. Efforts at providing low-cost rural housing have been minimal, despite the creation of the Federal Mortgage Bank of Nigeria in 1977, and shantytowns and slums are common in urban areas. As of 1979, 37% of all housing units were cement or brick roofed with asbestos or corrugated iron; 34% were mud plastered with cement and roofed with corrugated iron. In the same year, 44% of urban dwellings were rented, 37% were owner occupied, 17% were rent free, and 2% were "quasi-rented" at below-average rates. The total number of housing units in 1992 was 25,661,000.

43EDUCATION

The 1979 constitution made primary education the responsibility of the states and local councils. State and federal authorities have concurrent powers over postprimary education. The first six years of primary education were made compulsory in 1976. Recent years have seen a marked growth in educational facilities, but the overall adult literacy rate for the country was only about 50.7% (males, 62.3% and females, 39.5%) in 1990.

The advancement in education in the southern states, compared with the relative lag in the northern states, reflects the contribution of Christian missions to the Nigerian educational system. Teacher-training colleges are operated by missions or voluntary societies; their schools, however, are regulated and largely supported by the government.

Primary education begins in the local language but introduces English in the third year. In 1991 there were 13,776,854 students in 35,446 primary schools and 3,123,277 and 141,491 teachers in secondary schools.

In 1990, an estimated 113,556 students were in vocational institutes. Technical education is provided by technical institutes, trade centers, and handicraft centers. There were an estimated 103,170 students in teacher training secondary schools in 1990.

There are also 13 polytechnic colleges and 4 colleges of technology. A major obstacle to the further advancement of education in Nigeria is the shortage of qualified teachers; large numbers of foreigners are employed, particularly by the universities. In 1989, all higher level institutions had 19,601 teaching staff and 335,824 pupils.

44LIBRARIES AND MUSEUMS

The National Library of Nigeria was founded in Lagos in 1962 and had about 158,000 volumes in 1986. State governments have libraries in their respective capitals and in all the local government headquarters. Almost all of the 20 universities have libraries. In 1989 the public libraries had a combined total of over 1.1 million volumes. The chief university library is that of the University of Ibadan, which contains 370,000 volumes. Other sizable university collections are at the University of Lagos (250,000 volumes), the University of Ife (348,187), and the University of Nigeria at Nsukka and Enugu (589,512).

The National Museum in Lagos contains many specimens of Nigerian art, mostly pieces of statuary and carvings, remarkable for their variety and quality. It also has archaeological and ethnographic exhibits. Other museums represent more specialized interests: the museum at Ife opened in 1955 in response to halt the looting of national art treasures, contains world-renowned bronze and terra cotta heads; the museum at Benin City has a collection of bronzes; and that at Oron has a valuable collection of ancestor carvings. The museum at Jos, opened in 1952 originally as the National Museum, is a center of research into the prehistoric culture of Nigeria. The Esie Museum, at Ilorin in Kwara State, has stone antiquities, and the National Museum at Kaduna has archaeological and ethnographic exhibits, including a "craft village." The Owo Museum, in Ondo State, displays arts, crafts, and ethnographic relics. There are also museums in Kano, Argungu, and Oshogbo.

45MEDIA

The press is highly developed, although there have been frequent attempts by military leaders to limit its freedom. In 1991 there were 31 daily newspapers in Nigeria, some of them published by the federal or state governments.

Leading Nigerian daily newspapers (with their 1991 estimated circulations) are:

	CIRCULATION
Daily Times (Lagos)	300,000
Concord (Lagos)	200,000
Guardian (Lagos)	150,000
Punch (Lagos)	150,000
Nigerian Tribune (Ibadan)	109,000
New Nigerian (Lagos and Kaduna)	80,000

Telephone and telegraph communications are the responsibility of the Federal Ministry of Communications through its parastatal

NITEL. In 1991 there were 259,626 telephones in service. Trunk lines and UHF links connect all the major towns, and all of these have exchange units, including automatic exchanges at Lagos, Ibadan, Kaduna, Kano, Jos, and Port Harcourt. Postal services are provided by another parastatal—NIPOST. There are post offices in all 305 local-government headquarters and other major towns.

Radio broadcasting is the joint responsibility of the federal and state governments, operating under the Federal Radio Corp. of Nigeria, created in 1978; state radio stations broadcast in English and local languages. Television, introduced in 1959, now operates throughout the country under the direction of the Nigerian Television Authority, with stations in all state capitals and channels set aside for the state governments. Several states also run their own stations. There is no private radio or television service. In 1991, the country had 19,350,000 radios and 3,650,000 television sets.

46ORGANIZATIONS

Cooperatives are very important in Nigerian economic life, numbering over 25,000 in 1993. Many different societies are included in this category—consumers' societies, thrift and credit societies, and others—but the most important are the marketing societies, which play a significant role in handling export produce, and sometimes in the production of both food and cash crops. However, the Structural Adjustment Program is gradually replacing cooperatives with farmers' societies and export societies.

Red Cross societies, the Girl Guides, the Boy Scouts, YWCA organizations, Muslim societies, Jamat Aid groups, and other community, social, and service groups are active in all towns and villages. Literary and art associations meet regularly in Lagos, Kaduna, Enugu, and other major cities. There are sports clubs in Lagos and all the state capitals. In 1993 there were chambers of commerce in all 19 state capitals and Abuja, and a National Association of Chambers of Commerce, Industry, Mines, and Agriculture in Lagos and Abuja.

47TOURISM, TRAVEL, AND RECREATION

Persons entering Nigeria must have a passport and visa, except for nationals of Commonwealth nations or the Republic of Ireland, who need a passport and an entry permit. Moreover, all travelers must be in possession of a valid yellow fever inoculation certificate; antimalaria precautions are recommended. There are five-star hotels in Lagos, Abuja, and Kaduna, and first-class hotels in all the state capitals, but demand still outstrips the supply, with occupancy rates in quality hotels at 80%. A 250-room addition is planned for the Federal Palace Hotel in Lagos. Sports and social clubs offer facilities for swimming, sailing, tennis, squash, golf, and polo. Receipts from tourism amounted to US$25 million in 1990, when 190,000 foreign tourists visited Nigeria.

48FAMOUS NIGERIANS

Famous Nigerians of the 19th century include 'Uthman dan Fodio (d.1817), who founded the Fulani empire at the beginning of the century, and Samuel Ajayi Crowther (1809–92), a Yoruba missionary of the Church of England who was consecrated first bishop of the Niger Territories in 1864.

The Palm Wine Drinkard and other stories by Amos Tutuola (b.1920) exploit the rich resources of traditional Nigerian folk tales. Benedict Chuka Enwonu (b.1921), Nigeria's leading painter and sculptor, has gained international fame, as has Wole Soyinka (b.1934), a prominent playwright who was awarded the 1986 Nobel Prize for Literature, the first African so honored. Novelists of note include Chinua Achebe (b.1930) and Cyprian Ekwensi (b.1921). Sports figures include Dick Tiger (1929–71), twice world middleweight champion and once light-heavyweight champion.

Herbert Macaulay (1864–1946) is regarded as the father of Nigerian nationalism. Among contemporary political figures, Dr. (Benjamin) Nnamdi Azikiwe (b.1904), long one of the leading West African nationalists and formerly premier of the Eastern Region, was a founder of the NCNC and first governor-general and president of independent Nigeria. Former chief rival of Azikiwe and founder of the Action Group, Chief Obafemi Awolowo (1909–87) resigned as premier of the Western Region to lead the opposition in the federal House of Assembly. He was named commissioner for finance in the Federal Military Government. The hereditary leader of the Hausa-Fulani ruling class in northern Nigeria and leader of the NPC until his assassination in January 1966 was Alhaji Sir Ahmadu Bello, sardauna of Sokoto (1909–66), who became prime minister of the Northern Region in 1954. The first prime minister of the Federation was Alhaji Sir Abubakar Tafawa Balewa (1912–66), who also was assassinated in the 1966 coup. Chief Simeon Olaosebikan Adebo (b.1913), a leading Nigerian diplomat, has held several UN posts. Maj. Gen. Yakubu Gowon (b.1934) headed the Federal Military Government from July 1966 to July 1975, when he was deposed in a bloodless coup during his absence from Nigeria at an OAU meeting. Gowon is credited with formulating the post–civil war policy of reconciliation with the Ibos that resulted in the country's rapid recovery. Alhaji Shehu Shagari (b.1925) served in several high government posts before being elected president in 1979. Reelected in 1983, he was subsequently deposed in a military coup from which Maj. Gen. Muhammadu Buhari (b.1942) emerged as leader of the Supreme Military Council and head of state but was ousted in 1985 by Maj. Gen. Ibrahim Badamasi Babangida (b.1940 or 1941), who assumed the presidency.

49DEPENDENCIES

Nigeria has no territories or colonies.

50BIBLIOGRAPHY

Ate, Bassey E. *Decolonization and Dependence: The Development of Nigerian-US Relations, 1960–1984.* Boulder, Colo.: Westview, 1985.

Biersteker, Thomas J. *Multinationals, the State, and Control of the Nigerian Economy.* Princeton, N.J.: Princeton University Press, 1987.

Ekundare, R. Olufemi. *Economic History of Nigeria, 1860–1960.* New York: Holmes & Meier, 1973.

Forrest, Tom. *Politics and Economic Development in Nigeria.* Boulder, Colo.: Westview Press, 1993.

Ikein, Augustine. *The Impact of Oil on a Developing Country: The Case of Nigeria.* New York: Praeger, 1990.

Isichei, Elizabeth. *A History of Nigeria.* London: Longman, 1983.

Koehn, Peter H. *Public Policy and Administration in Africa: Lessons from Nigeria.* Boulder, Colo.: Westview Press, 1990.

Metz, Helen Chapin (ed.). *Nigeria, a Country Study.* 5th ed. Washington, D.C.: Library of Congress, 1992.

Myers, Robert A. *Nigeria.* Santa Barbara, Calif.: Clio Press, 1989.

Nafziger, E. Wayne. *The Economics of Political Instability: The Nigerian-Biafran War.* Boulder, Colo:. Westview, 1982.

Nigeria in Pictures. Minneapolis: Lerner Publications Co., 1988.

Oyediran, Oyeleye (ed.). *Nigerian Government and Politics Under Military Rule, 1966–79.* New York: St. Martin's, 1979.

Oyewole, A. *Historical Dictionary of Nigeria.* Metuchen, N.J.: Scarecrow Press, 1987.

Shepard, Robert Bruce. *Nigeria, Africa, and the United States: from Kennedy to Reagan.* Bloomington: Indiana University Press, 1991.

Thompson, Joseph E. *American Policy and African Famine: the Nigeria-Biafra War, 1966–1970.* New York: Greenwood Press, 1990.

Watts, Michael (ed.). *State, Oil, and Agriculture in Nigeria.* Berkeley: Institute of International Studies, University of California, 1987.

RWANDA

Republic of Rwanda
Republika y'u Rwanda

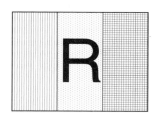

CAPITAL: Kigali.

FLAG: The national flag is a tricolor of red, yellow, and green vertical stripes. The letter "R" in black, appears in the center of the yellow stripe.

ANTHEM: Rwanda Rwacu (Our Rwanda).

MONETARY UNIT: The Rwanda franc (RFr) is a paper currency. There are coins of 1, 5, 10, 20, and 50 francs and notes of 100, 500, 1,000, and 5,000 francs. RFr1 = $0.0135 (or $1 = RFr74.086).

WEIGHTS AND MEASURES: The metric system is the legal standard.

HOLIDAYS: New Year's Day, 1 January; Democracy Day, 28 January; Labor Day, 1 May; Independence Day, 1 July; Peace and National Unity Day, 5 July; Assumption, 15 August; Anniversary of 1961 Referendum, 25 September; Armed Forces' Day, 26 October; All Saints' Day, 1 November; Christmas, 25 December. Movable religious holidays include Easter Monday, Ascension, and Pentecost Monday.

TIME: 2 PM = noon GMT.

¹LOCATION, SIZE, AND EXTENT

Rwanda, a landlocked country in east-central Africa, has an area of 26,340 sq km (10,170 sq mi), extending 248 km (154 mi) NE–SW and 166 km (103 mi) SE–NW. Comparatively, the area occupied by Rwanda is slightly smaller than the state of Maryland. It is bordered on the N by Uganda, on the E by Tanzania, on the S by Burundi, and on the W and NW by Zaire, with a total boundary length of 893 km (555 mi).

Rwanda's capital city, Kigali, is located near the center of the country.

²TOPOGRAPHY

Rwanda lies on the great East African plateau, with the divide between the water systems of the Nile and Congo rivers passing in a north–south direction through the western part of the country. To the west of the divide, the land drops sharply to Lake Kivu in the Great Rift Valley; to the east, the land falls gradually across the central plateau—its grassy highlands are the core areas of settlement of Rwanda's peoples—to the swamps and lakes on the country's eastern border. Almost all of Rwanda is at least 1,000 m (3,300 ft) above sea level; the central plateau is between 1,500 and 2,000 m (4,950–6,600 ft) high. In the northwest on the border with Zaire are the volcanic Virunga Mountains; the highest peak, Mt. Karisimbi (4,519 m/14,826 ft), is snowcapped. Lake Kivu, 1,460 m (4,790 ft) above sea level, drains into Lake Tanganyika through the sharply descending Ruzizi River. The Kagera River, which forms much of Rwanda's eastern border, flows into Lake Victoria.

³CLIMATE

The high altitude of Rwanda provides the country with a pleasant tropical highland climate, with a mean daily temperature range of less than 2°C (4°F). Temperatures vary considerably from region to region because of the variations in altitude. At Kigali, on the central plateau, the average temperature is 20°C (68°F). Rainfall is heaviest in the southwest and lightest in the east. A long rainy season lasts from February to May and a short one from November through December. At Gisovu, in the west, near Kibuye, annual rainfall averages 160 cm (63 in); at Gabiro, in the northeast, 78 cm (31 in); and at Butare, in the south, 115 cm (45 in).

⁴FLORA AND FAUNA

Most of Rwanda is a region of savanna grassland. There is little forest left; the country is one of the most eroded and deforested in all of tropical Africa. Remaining woodlands are small areas of tropical forests along the western border, north and south of Lake Kivu. The most common trees are eucalyptus—imported from the south in the 1890s—acacias, and oil palms.

Wildlife was abundant before the region became agricultural. There are still elephants, hippopotamuses, buffalo, cheetahs, lions, zebras, leopards, monkeys, gorillas, jackals, hyena, wild boar, antelope, flying lemurs, crocodiles, guinea hens, partridges, ducks, geese, quail, and snipe. Because the region is densely populated, these are becoming fewer, and some species are disappearing.

⁵ENVIRONMENT

The war in Rwanda, beginning in 1990, has damaged the environment. The ability of the nation's agricultural sector to meet the demands of its large population are complicated by the overuse and infertility of the soil. Soil erosion and overgrazing are also serious. The remaining forested area is under intense pressure from uncontrolled cutting for fuel. During 1981–85, deforestation averaged 3,000 hectares (7,400 acres) per year. Malaria and sleeping sickness have spread because forest clearing and irrigation have increased the breeding areas for disease-carrying insects. Rwanda has 1.5 cubic miles of water with 68% used for farming and 8% used for industrial activity. Sixteen percent of the nation's city dwellers and 33% of the rural people do not have safe water. The nation's cities produce 0.1 million tons of solid waste per year.

In northeastern Rwanda the beautiful Kagera National Park is a game reserve, sheltering many types of wildlife. Volcano National Park, which surrounds Mt. Karisimbi and was Africa's first wildlife park, is one of the last existing homes of the mountain gorilla, which numbered 280 in 1986, up from 250 five years earlier. The national parks suffered from uncontrolled poaching and unauthorized cultivation until recent years. As a result of government and conservationist efforts, no gorilla was killed between 1983 and 1987. As of 1994, 11 of the nation's mammal species and seven of its bird species are threatened with extinction.

6POPULATION

Rwanda is the most densely populated country on the African continent. In 1994, it had an estimated population of 8,846,620, according to the US Census Bureau, compared with a census population of 7,164,994 on 15 August 1991. However, the UN estimate for 1995 was 8,330,000. The estimated population density in 1994 was 336 persons per sq km (870 per sq mi). A population of 9,766,000 was projected by the UN for the year 2000 assuming a crude birthrate of 49.3 per 1,000 population, a crude death rate of 17.6, and a net natural increase of 31.7 during 1995–2000. The estimated growth rate is 3.4% annually. Kigali, the capital and largest city, has grown rapidly, from 15,000 in 1969 to 219,000 in 1990. But only 6% of Rwanda's inhabitants lived in urban areas in 1990.

7MIGRATION

Before independence, many Rwandans, compelled by famine and underemployment, migrated to neighboring Zaire, Uganda, and Tanzania. The Hutu and Tutsi political quarrels have caused numerous Tutsi to flee their homeland, many of them going to Burundi, where there were 245,600 refugees at the end of 1992. Renewed violence in 1994 spawned a new exodus from Rwanda. In a single day (30 April) more than 250,000 people—generally Hutu—streamed into Tanzania. About 1.8 million were internally displaced. In the mid-1960s, nearly 400,000 Rwandans were listed as permanent residents of Uganda. Some 85,800 Rwandan refugees were in Uganda at the end of 1992. There were 50,900 in Zaire and 50,000 in Tanzania. These were mostly Tutsis. At the same time Rwanda was harboring 25,200 refugees from Burundi, mainly Hutus. In late 1993 hundreds of thousands more Hutus fled to Rwanda to escape ethnic violence by the Tutsi-dominated Burundi army.

8ETHNIC GROUPS

The population is about 85% Hutu, a Bantu people, traditionally farmers. The Tutsi, a warrior people, once constituted about 14% of the total population, but many have fled into neighboring territories for refuge, especially since civil strife began in 1959. The Tutsi migrated to Rwanda sometime before the 15th century. There are also some Twa, a Pygmy tribe of hunters related to the Pygmies of Zaire; the earliest known inhabitants of the region, they now constitute about 1% of the population of Rwanda. There are also small numbers of Asians and Europeans.

9LANGUAGES

The main language is Kinyarwanda, a member of the Bantu language family. The official languages are Kinyarwanda and French.

10RELIGIONS

European missionaries, notably the White Fathers, introduced Christianity to Rwanda in the late 19th century. In 1988, an estimated 74% of Rwandans were Christian, and in 1993 an estimated 44% were Roman Catholic. As much as one-half the population follows traditional African religion, believing in living spirits and a distant and impersonal creator, Imana. Muslims made up around 8%, and there were also small groups of Baha'is and Hindus. In October 1986, 295 members of religious sects not recognized by the state were sentenced to prison for inciting rebellion.

11TRANSPORTATION

In 1991, 4,885 km (3,036 mi) of road, one of the most intensive systems in all of Africa, radiated through Rwanda, but only about 9% was paved. Five principal roads connect Kigali to other Rwandan cities, and an asphalted road connects Butare and Cyangugu. Most roads become impassable during the rainy season, and there are few bridges. In 1992, there were 7,868 automobiles, and 2,048 commercial vehicles in use. Bus service connects Kigali to the 10 prefectures. The most important roads for landlocked Rwanda's external trade run from Kigali to Kibungo and from Kigali to Kakitumba, thence connecting by road and rail with Indian Ocean ports in Tanzania and Kenya. About 90% of foreign trade is via the Kakitumba route, which leads to the Kenyan ports via Uganda. Rwanda has no railroads. There is traffic on Lake Kivu to Zaire from Gisenyi, Kibuye, and Cyangugu.

There are international airports at Kigali-Kanombe and at Kamembe, served by Air Rwanda, Sabena, Air Zaïre, Aeroflot, Air Burundi, Kenya Airways, Air Tanzania, Ethiopian Airlines, and Air France. Direct flights from Europe are available from Brussels, Paris, and Athens. Internal air traffic is provided by Air Rwanda to six domestic airfields. In 1991, Air Rwanda flew 10,100 passengers some 900,000 km (559,000 mi).

12HISTORY

Stone Age habitation, as far back as 35,000 years, has been reported in the region now called Rwanda. The first known inhabitants of the area were the Twa, a pygmoid group following hunting and gathering subsistence patterns. Later, between the 7th and 10th centuries AD, the Bantu-speaking Hutu people, who followed a settled, agricultural way of life, arrived, probably from the region of the Congo River basin. Between the 14th and 15th centuries, the Tutsi, a pastoral people of Nilotic origin, arrived from the north and formed numbers of small and independent chieftaincies. At the end of the 15th century, a few of these chieftaincies merged to form a state, near Kigali, under the leadership of Ruganzu I Bwimba. In the 16th century, the Tutsi dynasty began a process of expansion that continued into the late 19th century under the prominent Tutsi leader Kigeri IV Rwabugiri (d.1895).

The Tutsi conquest initiated a process of political integration. The ownership of land was gradually transferred from the Hutu tribes to the mwami, the king of the Tutsi, who became the supreme head and, in theory, absolute master of the country. He was the incarnation of the state and enjoyed an almost divine prestige. A feudal social system based on caste—the conquering Tutsi and the subject Hutu—was the dominant feature of social relations, and especially of economic and political relations. The ownership of cattle, a vital element in the social system, was controlled by the Tutsi, who in turn parceled out their use to the Hutu. The Hutu did the farming and grew the food, but had no part in government. The Tutsi did no manual labor. To a certain extent, however, the castes were open to each other, and the northwest remained Hutu-controlled. Intermarriage, especially between Tutsi males and Hutu females, was common. The Hutu language, Kinyarwanda, was eventually adopted by the Tutsi.

The first European known to have explored the region was John Hanning Speke, who traveled with Richard Burton to Lake Tanganyika in 1858, where he turned north in his search for the headwaters of the Nile. In 1871, Stanley and Livingstone landed at Bujumbura (now the capital of neighboring Burundi) and explored the Ruzizi River region. After the Berlin Conference of 1884–85, the German zone of influence in East Africa was extended to include Rwanda and Burundi, and in 1894, a German lieutenant, Count von Götzen, discovered Lake Kivu. Roman Catholic missionaries soon followed. After the mwami submitted to German rule without resistance in 1899, the Germans administered the territory through the traditional authorities in accordance with the laws and customs of the region. Belgium occupied the territory in 1916 during World War I, and was awarded a mandate that was known as Ruanda-Urundi (present-day Rwanda and Burundi) by the League of Nations in 1923. In 1925, an administrative union was formed between the Ruanda-Urundi mandate and the Belgian Congo (now Zaire). A key policy of Belgian rule was the strengthening of the effective control of the Tutsi dynasty—under Belgian supervision—throughout Rwanda.

In 1946, Ruanda-Urundi became a UN trust territory under Belgian administration. Events in Africa after World War II aroused Hutu political consciousness and led the Hutu to demand the abolition of social and political inequalities. In November 1959, a Hutu revolution began, continuing sporadically for the next few years. Many Tutsi either were killed or fled to neighboring territories. The Belgian authorities, along with the Roman Catholic missionaries, provided crucial support to the Hutu during this troubled period. A provisional government, republican in tendency and composed predominantly of members of the Parmehutu Party, was set up in Ruanda in October 1960. In the following January, the leaders of the Parmehutu proclaimed the deposition of the mwami and the creation of a republican regime. The new regime was recognized de facto by the administering authority, but the UN declared it to have been established by irregular and unlawful means.

On 25 September 1961, legislative elections and a referendum on retaining the institution and person of the mwami were held in Ruanda at the insistence of the UN General Assembly and under the supervision of the UN Commission for Ruanda-Urundi. The elections gave the Parmehutu, led by Grégoire Kayibanda, an overwhelming majority. In the referendum, about 95% of the electorate took part, voting 4 to 1 to abolish the monarchy. The UN strongly urged both Ruanda and Urundi to come to independence united, but reluctantly agreed that neither country wished to do so. On 27 June 1962, the UN General Assembly passed a resolution providing for the independent states of Rwanda and Burundi, and on 1 July, Rwanda became an independent country.

In December 1963, following an abortive invasion by Tutsi refugees from Burundi, a massive repression launched against the remaining resident Tutsi population caused the death of an estimated 12,000 Tutsi. The massacre was the signal for a renewed exodus of Tutsi elements into the neighboring territories of Uganda, Tanzania, the Congo (later Zaire), and Burundi. In all, 150,000 Tutsi fled between 1959 and 1964.

In January 1964, the monetary and economic union that had existed between Burundi and Rwanda was terminated. Despite severe economic difficulties, Grégoire Kayibanda was reelected to a third four-year term as president in 1969. However, continuing internal unrest led the Rwandan army to overthrow the Kayibanda government in July 1973, and Maj. Gen. Juvénal Habyarimana assumed the presidency. His regime, dominated by officers from the north, took a more moderate stand on the issue of Hutu-Tutsi relationships than had the previous administration.

In 1975, he institutionalized his military regime, creating a one-party state under his National Revolutionary Movement for Development (MRND). A system of ethnic quotas was introduced that formally limited the Tutsi minority to 14% of the positions in the workplace and in the schools.

The regime was corrupt and authoritarian, and popular discontent grew through the 1980s. The MRND agreed to allow partisan competition and several new parties emerged in 1990 and 1991. But the greatest threat to the regime came in October 1990, when over 1,000 Tutsi refugees invaded Rwanda from Uganda. This group, called the Rwanda Patriotic Front (RPF) had considerable success, considering that around 1,000 French, Belgian, and Zairian paratroopers helped defend the government in Kigali. Government forces retaliated by massacring Tutsi. A ceasefire was worked

LOCATION: 1°4′ to 2°50′s; 28°51′ to 30°55′E. **BOUNDARY LENGTHS:** Uganda, 169 km (105 mi); Tanzania, 217 km (135 mi); Burundi, 290 km (180 mi); Zaire, 217 km (135 mi).

out later in October and Uganda, Burundi, and Zaire agreed to send in peacekeeping forces to supervise it. But fighting broke out again in January, 1991. Further ceasefires were negotiated between government and Tutsi rebels in Brussels in March 1991 and in Arusha, Tanzania in July 1992, but fighting continued to smolder.

On the political front, in November 1990, Habyarimana announced that political parties would be permitted in 1991 and that tribal names would be abolished from national identity cards. In April 1992, Habyarimana appointed an opposition politician, Dismos Nsengiyaremye, as prime minister. The new cabinet included nine members of the MRND and 10 opposition party members. Their supporters fought in the streets. Hardliners around Habyarimana were accused of trying to sidetrack the democratization process. By June, government had officially recognized 15 opposition parties. Talks with Tutsi leaders continued on power sharing, but the Hutu-Tutsi division appears to be beyond reconciliation. A power sharing agreement was signed in Tanzania in January 1993, but this failed to end fighting. Another peace agreement was signed on 4 August 1993. The UN Security Council authorized on 5 October 1993 a peacekeeping force to assist in implementing the agreement. Unrest continued and no transitional government, which the agreement called for, was established.

In 1994, a total breakdown occurred. In February, the minister of public works was assassinated. His supporters, in turn, murdered an opposition politician. In April, a rocket downed an airplane carrying the presidents of Rwanda and Burundi. All aboard were killed. They had been returning to Kigali from regional peace talks in Tanzania. From that point on, Rwanda became a killing field as members of the Rwandan army and other bands of armed Hutu set out to murder all the Tutsi they could find and many moderate Hutu politicians, including Prime Minister Agathe Uwilingiyimana. The extremist coalition, the Coalition for the Defense of the Republic (CDR) provoked and, sometimes, directed the killing. In response, the RPF stepped up its efforts in order to liberate as much territory and as many Tutsi as it could before the armed gangs killed them.

By July 1994, several hundred thousand, mostly Tutsi, had been killed, several hundred thousand had fled their homes and the country (to Burundi, Tanzania, and Zaire) and the RPF occupied over half the country. Kigali was seized. UN forces have been unable to stem the tide or to broker a workable ceasefire agreement. In late June, French troops entered Rwanda from Zaire. They claimed their effort was purely humanitarian, but, before long, they were squared off against RPF forces trying to occupy the southwest part of the country.

13 GOVERNMENT

The constitution of December 1978 provided for a unitary republic with executive, legislative, and judicial branches. The executive was headed by a president elected for a five-year term who presided over the council of ministers and was commander in chief of the armed forces. The secretary-general of the National Revolutionary Movement for Development, the sole legal political party, was empowered to act in the president's stead in the case of incapacity. The president shared legislative power with the country's unicameral legislature, the National Development Council, which consisted of 70 members.

A new constitution was adopted on 18 June 1991. It legalized independent parties. The executive branch consisted of an elected president and a prime minister and a Council of Ministers chosen from the legislature. The unicameral legislature continued the name, National Development Council.

The 4 August 1993 Peace Accord signed with the RPF called for a 22-month transition period leading to multiparty elections and the establishment of several new institutions. That accord became a casualty in the anarchy of 1994.

14 POLITICAL PARTIES

In the last years of Belgian administration many political organizations were formed. In March 1957, Grégoire Kayibanda and other young Hutu leaders issued a public manifesto demanding a continuation of Belgian rule until the Hutu were better prepared to assume a role in political affairs. In June 1957, they formed the Hutu Social Movement, which, in 1959, became the Party of the Hutu Emancipation Movement (Parti du Mouvement de l'Emancipation Hutu—Parmehutu). Parmehutu thereupon set a policy of ending Tutsi rule and abolishing the feudal system.

The Rwanda National Union Party (Union Nationale Rwandaise—UNAR), founded in September 1959 by Prosper Bwanakweli and backed by the mwami, was the leading monarchist party, calling for immediate self-government and independence under a hereditary (Tutsi) constitutional monarchy.

In the 1961 elections, Parmehutu received 77.7% of the votes cast; UNAR won 16.8%, and other minority parties 5.5%. Under a system of proportional representation, 35 of the 44 seats in the National Assembly went to Parmehutu. Parmehutu extended its control in the 1969 elections, and thereafter became the only political party in Rwanda until its disbanding by the military in 1973.

In 1975, President Habyarimana founded and became party president of the National Revolutionary Movement for Development (Mouvement Revolutionnaire Nationale pour le Développement—MRND), which became the nation's only legal party.

Party membership is automatic at birth. The president of the MRND was the sole candidate in national presidential elections and appointed the party's secretary-general and central committee. In December 1981, the 64 deputies to the National Development Council were elected from 128 candidates chosen by the MRND. In the elections of December 1983, 140 MRND candidates vied for 70 seats in an enlarged Council; 17 former deputies were defeated.

In November 1990, the president announced that opposition political parties would be permitted to organize in 1991. Several new parties emerged, including the Democratic Republican Movement (MDR), the Liberal Party (LP), the Democratic and Socialist Party (PSD), and the Coalition for the Defense of the Republic (CDR). The latter, headed by Martin Bucyana, is sometimes charged with provoking the 1994 massacres. The Tutsi-based Rwandan Patriotic Front (RPF), as an army once in exile and, after April 1994, firmly entrenched within Rwanda, had been outside the legitimate process of coalition government. Partisan activity, per se, has been on hold as survival and coercion preoccupy the politicians.

15 LOCAL GOVERNMENT

Rwanda is divided into 10 prefectures, or provinces, which coincide with former Belgian administrative divisions. The prefectures are supposed to be administered by prefects appointed by the president. The former subchiefdoms and extratribal divisions were reorganized into 143 communes or municipalities. The commune, now the basic political and administrative unit in Rwanda, is administered by an elected communal council presided over by a mayor. The communes have always had limited scope, since most major decisions were made by the central government. But the disorder of 1994 leaves direction of local affairs uncertain.

16 JUDICIAL SYSTEM

The Rwandan legal system is based on Belgian and German civil codes and customary law. There are courts of the first instance, provincial courts, courts of appeal, and a court of cassation. Also functioning are a constitutional court composed of the court of cassation and a council of state; a court of accounts, which examines public accounts; and a court of state security for treason and national security cases.

Although the constitution provides for an independent judiciary, certain provisions also give the executive branch and the president authority to appoint and dismiss judges. In practice, the courts are susceptible to government influence and manipulation.

The constitution guarantees defendants the right to counsel. A shortage of attorneys, however, leaves many criminal defendants unrepresented. In many regions the chaos resulting from the recent civil war has disrupted the normal functioning of the judicial system.

17 ARMED FORCES

Rwanda's armed forces, established in 1960, totaled 5,200 in 1993, including an army of 5,000, mostly infantry. An air corps, with 200 personnel and a total of 15 aircraft, is administered by the army. The national police numbers 1,200. Most equipment comes from Europe along with instructors, advisors, and one air borne company. In 1991, expenditures for defense may have been $36 million. The civil war of 1994 has probably destroyed the government armed forces, who could not stop the Hutu–Tutsi tribal conflict.

18 INTERNATIONAL COOPERATION

Rwanda was admitted to UN membership on 18 September 1962, and is a member of ECA and all of the nonregional specialized agencies except IAEA and IMO. It is also a member of the

African Development Bank, G-77, OAU, and OCAM and is an associate member of the EEC. Rwanda is a signatory of GATT and the Law of the Sea.

In 1976, Rwanda joined Burundi and Zaire in the Economic Community of the Great Lakes Countries, formed to develop the economic potential of the basin of Lakes Kivu and Tanganyika; its headquarters are in Gisenyi. In 1977, Rwanda joined Burundi and Tanzania in forming an economic community for the management and development of the Kagera River Basin. Uganda became a part of the community in 1980. Its headquarters are in Kigali.

¹⁹ECONOMY

Rwanda has an agricultural economy with relatively few mineral resources. The country has a high population density, intensified by a 3.3% annual population growth rate, which puts pressure on the land and the economy. The Rwandan economy, which contracted in real terms by 1.7% in 1991, was estimated to grow by 1.3% in 1992. However, prospects for 1993 were dim. The budget deficit was expected to reach roughly $170 million in 1993, about 9.3% of GDP, while the trade deficit in 1992 widened by about 45% as exports continued to fall. The manufacturing base is limited to a few basic products. Soil erosion has limited growth in the agricultural sector. Poor markets, lack of natural resources, underdeveloped entrepreneurial and managerial skills, and difficult transportation problems all painted a discouraging picture for the economy. However, these problems pale in comparison to those brought about in 1994 by the civil war.

²⁰INCOME

In 1992 Rwanda's GNP was $1,813 million at current prices, or $250 per capita. For the period 1985–92 the average inflation rate was 2.4%, resulting in a real growth rate in per capita GNP of –2.8%.

In 1992 the GDP was $1,552 million in current US dollars. It is estimated that in 1989, the last year for which statistics are available, agriculture, hunting, forestry, and fishing contributed 40% to GDP; manufacturing, 13%; construction, 7%; wholesale and retail trade, 13%; transport, storage, and communication, 7%; finance, insurance, real estate, and business services, 8%; community, social, and personal services, 8%; and other sources, 3%.

²¹LABOR

According to official 1989 estimates, about 3,143,000 persons were economically active. About 90% were engaged in agriculture, forestry, hunting and fishing; 3% in mining, manufacturing, construction, and utilities; and 4% in services. The government is the largest single employer of wage laborers. The Central Union of Rwandan Workers (CESTRAR), Rwanda's largest and formerly sole authorized trade union organization, separated from the government and the MRND in 1991 as part of the political reforms under the new constitution. Four new independent unions were recognized by the government in 1991–92: the Union Association of Health Personnel in Rwanda; the Interprofessional Union of Workers of Rwanda; the Union of Secondary School Teachers; and the Association of Christian Unions, which represents public and private sector workers, small businessmen, and subsistence farmers. These new unions compete with CESTRAR for members. About 75% of the small industrial work force is unionized, but few are covered by collective bargaining agreements.

²²AGRICULTURE

Before the onslaught of civil war in April 1994, about 93% of Rwanda's inhabitants earned their living, directly or indirectly, from agriculture. Except for heavily eroded regions, the soil has a good humus content and is fertile, especially in the alluvial valleys and in the volcanic soils of the northwest. In 1991, about 1.1 million hectares (2.8 million acres) were under cultivation. Subsistence agriculture predominates, and the basic agricultural unit is the small family farm of about 1 hectare (2.5 acres).

In 1992, the principal food crops (in tons) were plantains, 2,900,000; sweet potatoes, 770,000; cassava, 400,000; potatoes, 280,000; dry beans, 200,000; and sorghum, 175,000. The corn crop came to 100,000 tons and the sugarcane crop to 52,000 tons. The plantain crop is used principally for making beer and wine. Coffee, grown by some 600,000 smallholders, is the chief cash crop; in 1990, 45,579 tons, with a cash value of $671.2 million, were exported, and in 1992 exports decreased to 33,851 tons (worth $351.6 million). Tea production came to about 14,000 tons in 1992. In 1991, tea accounted for 23% of export earnings. Coffee and tea together generally contribute 80% to export earnigns. Rwanda also exports quinine and pyrethrum.

Rwanda has had devastating periods of famine. In 1928–29, more than 400,000 Rwandans died or were forced to migrate; in 1943–44, the figure was 300,000. Government planning has aimed at mitigating such catastrophes by striving for annual increases of food-crop production. Included in the government effort has been the introduction of rice cultivation by agronomists from Taiwan and China. Export diversification has been encouraged by the government, including production of alternatives such as sunflowers, and fruits and vegetables for the European winter market.

²³ANIMAL HUSBANDRY

Most farmers also raise livestock. In 1992 there were 610,000 head of cattle, 1,100,000 goats, 395,000 sheep, and 142,000 pigs. Chickens were also widely raised; in 1992 there were an estimated 1 million. Beekeeping is another important activity, with 15 tons of honey produced in 1992. About 135,000 cattle were slaughtered in 1992, providing 14,000 tons of meat.

The number of cattle owned by an individual has traditionally been a key indicator of status in Rwanda's social system. This factor has resulted in the accumulation of large herds of poor-quality stock. The government is striving to eliminate excess cattle and to improve the remainder by the introduction of modern stock-raising methods.

²⁴FISHING

Fishing in the lakes and rivers is principally for local consumption. In 1991, Rwanda produced an estimated catch of 3,551 tons. The presence of methane-producing organisms in Lake Kivu limits the development of aquatic life.

²⁵FORESTRY

There are no commercially exploitable woodlands; existing growths are too inaccessible for profitable development, although they are used locally for fuel and building. Erosion and cutting (due to farming and stock raising) have almost entirely eliminated Rwanda's original forests. Remaining growths are concentrated along the top of the Nile-Zaire divide and on the volcanic mountains of the northwest. There are scattered savanna woodlands in the eastern prefectures. In 1991, woodlands and forests covered an estimated 551,000 hectares (1,361,000 acres) Roundwood removals came to an estimated 5,620,000 cu m in 1991, almost all for fuel.

²⁶MINING

Mining and quarrying accounted for 6% of total exports, or about $6.1 million, in 1990. There are many difficulties blocking full utilization of existing resources, including the absence of high-grade ores and the lack of sufficient capital. Many mines have been closed, and those that have remained open often operate at less than full capacity. In 1991, estimated mineral production included 730 tons of cassiterite (tin ore), 175 tons of tungsten ore, 60,000 tons of cement, and 150 tons of columbite and tantalite. Gold mine output was 700 kg. Some lava beds of the west and northwest contain potassium compounds useful for fertilizers. In 1990, 897 tons of tin ore and 196 tons of tungsten ore were exported to Belgium and Luxembourg, and 108 tons of tin ore were shipped to Singapore. Neighboring Zaire imported 51 tons of Rwandan cement in 1990.

27ENERGY AND POWER

Rwanda imports all of its petroleum products from Kenya. The parastatal PETRORWANDA controls 40-45% of the market for petroleum imports. These included, in 1990, 301,000 barrels of gasoline, 92,000 barrels of kerosene, and 176,000 barrels of gas-diesel oils. Before the civil war, about 1 million cu m of methane gas was extracted from Lake Kivu each year; the gas was either used by the brewery in Gisenyi or converted into compressed fuel for trucks. Rwanda has an estimated 60 billion cu m of natural gas reserves and 6 billion cu m of peat reserves, which could also be used as a domestic energy resource.

Rwanda's electrical energy derives chiefly from hydroelectric sources. Electricity production in 1991 totaled 179 million kwh. Most of the electric power comes from four hydroelectric stations. An additional 10 million kwh was imported from Zaire. Total installed capacity in 1991 was 60,000 kw, almost all of it hydroelectric. In 1983, a $63-million hydroelectric station was constructed on the Ruzizi River, on the border with Zaire.

28INDUSTRY

Manufacturing ordinarily contributes about 20% of Rwanda's GDP (1991), though only about 2% of the labor force is engaged in industrial occupations. Most manufacturing and processing establishments have been at the artisan level, turning out items such as pottery, wicker baskets, bricks, shoes, tile, and insecticide. Rwanda has light industry which produces sugar, coffee, tea, flour, cigars, beer, wine, soft drinks, metal products, and assembled radios. Rwanda also has textile mills, soap factories, auto repair shops, a match factory, a pyrethrum refinery, and plants for producing paint, pharmaceuticals, and furniture. As of 1987, a sugar mill, financed by Arab development funds, was being built, and a new pyrethrum plant at Ruhengeri was planned. A cement factory at Cyangugu, financed and managed by China, opened in 1985. Industrial production in 1990 included soap, 9,000 metric tons; cement, 57,000 tons; radios, 2,000; cigarettes, 331 million; beer, 915,000 hectoliters; soft drinks, 101,000 hectoliters; and plastic shoes, 24,000 pairs.

Rwanda has a considerable hydroelectric power potential of some 200 Mw, of which only 20 Mw have been harnessed. As of 1990, Rwanda produced 46% of its power needs, with the remainder imported primarily from Zaire.

29SCIENCE AND TECHNOLOGY

The Institute of Agronomical Sciences of Rwanda and the National Institute of Scientific Research have their headquarters in Butare, and the Geological Service of Rwanda is in Kigali. The National University of Rwanda, in Butare, has faculties of sciences, medicine, agriculture, and applied sciences. In 1985, research and development expenditures totaled RFr919 million; 67 technicians and 71 scientists and engineers were engaged in research and development.

30DOMESTIC TRADE

Kigali is the main commercial center in Rwanda and has a small outdoor market. Business hours are from 8 AM to noon and from 2 to 5 PM, Monday through Friday. Banks are open from 8:30 AM to noon and from 2 to 5 PM, Monday–Friday.

31FOREIGN TRADE

Rwanda has maintained a negative trade balance for many years. The major exports are coffee and tea. Principal exports in 1991 (in millions of Rwanda francs) were as follows:

Coffee	7,209.8
Tea	2,796.6
Cassiterite	319.7
Pyrethrum	279.3
Quinquina	24.1
Other exports	1,341.7
TOTAL	11,971.2

Imports consist chiefly of food and clothing (13.7%), manufactured goods (41.6%), transportation equipment, machinery, and tools (17.5%), and petroleum products (12.8%). Imports in 1991 came to RFr38,474.5 million.

Germany took 21.3% of Rwanda's exports in 1991, followed by the Netherlands (18.8%) and Belgium (11.8%). Imports came from Belgium (17.1%), Kenya (13.4%), France (6.8%), and Germany (6.0%).

32BALANCE OF PAYMENTS

The outbreak of war in 1990 had a serious negative impact on Rwanda's balance of payments. In 1992, the trade deficit was estimated to have increased by 45% over 1991; exports were estimated to have fallen by 30% during the same period (due to low coffee prices and depleted stocks). With the renewed civil war, the 1994 trade deficit can be expected to be even worse.

In 1992 merchandise exports totaled $68.5 million and imports $240.4 million. The merchandise trade balance was $–171.9 million. The following table summarizes Rwanda's balance of payments for 1991 and 1992 (in millions of US dollars):

	1991	1992
CURRENT ACCOUNT		
Goods, services, and income	–214.8	–267.8
Unrequited transfers	180.7	183.2
TOTALS	–34.1	–84.6
CAPITAL ACCOUNT		
Direct investment	4.6	2.2
Portfolio investment	–0.1	—
Other long-term capital	75.3	34.6
Other short-term capital	19.3	25.6
Exceptional financing	—	—
Other liabilities	—	—
Reserves	–65.2	9.0
TOTALS	33.8	66.4
Errors and omissions	0.2	18.2
Total change in reserves	–66.2	19.4

33BANKING AND SECURITIES

From 1922 until the independence of Zaire (Belgian Congo) in 1960, the monetary and banking systems of Rwanda and Burundi were integrated with those of the Congo. In July 1962, upon becoming independent, Rwanda and Burundi formed a joint monetary union administered by a common central bank. This bank was dissolved, and its functions as a central banking institution were transferred, in April 1964, to the National Bank of the Republic of Rwanda. The Bank imposes foreign exchange controls and administers the import licensing system. As of 1993, the money supply, as measured by M2, totaled RFr38,742 million.

The Commercial Bank of Rwanda and the Bank of Kigali (51% and 50% owned by the state, respectively) provide complete banking facilities. Demand deposits in commercial banks amounted to RFr12,876 million at the end of 1993; time and savings accounts totaled RFr13,356 million. Rwanda also has a savings bank and a postal savings bank. The Rwandese Bank of Development and the People's Bank of Rwanda are the nation's development banks. There is no stock exchange in Rwanda.

34INSURANCE

The Rwandan National Insurance Co., formed in 1975, is 90% state owned. The Rwandan Insurance Society was founded in 1984. Insurance companies wishing to do business in Rwanda must be at least 51% Rwandan owned. In 1986, 99.2% of premium payments were for non-life insurance, including 55.9% for automotive coverage.

35PUBLIC FINANCE

Rwanda has both an ordinary budget for recurrent operations and a development budget for controlling development projects. In the 1960s and 1970s, prudent public finance management and generous foreign aid helped keep deficits and inflation low. With the fall of coffee prices during the 1980s, however, the government increased its control over the economy, and raised annual budget deficits to the equivalent of 11% of GDP by 1990. The overall fiscal deficit stood at 13.9% of GDP in 1992. Because of the recent widespread civil conflict of 1994, the Rwandan government expects to be totally reliant on foreign aid for several years.

The following table shows actual revenues and expenditures for 1991 and 1992 in millions of francs.

	1991	1992
REVENUE AND GRANTS		
Tax revenue	23,349	25,274
Non-tax revenue	2,707	3,449
Capital revenue	—	—
Grants	13,738	10,796
TOTAL	39,738	39,519
Expenditures & lending minus repayments	47,289	54,553
Deficit/Surplus	−7,551	−15,034

In 1991 Rwanda's total public debt stood at RFr131,613 million, of which MFr95,817 million was financed abroad.

36TAXATION

Direct taxation includes a tax on industrial and commercial profits. Taxes on dividends and a turnover (sales) tax are also levied. Indirect taxation, forming the bulk of government tax revenue, is derived largely from import and export duties.

37CUSTOMS AND DUTIES

Import duties have been the most important source of tax revenues since independence. There are two kinds of duties, both levied ad valorem: customs duties, averaging 15–30%, and revenue duties, averaging 5–15% (up to 60% for some goods). A 1% handling fee is also levied. All imports valued over RFr100,000 require a license.

38FOREIGN INVESTMENT

Rwanda has attempted to attract foreign investment. The investment code of 1 July 1962, modified in 1977, offers preferential treatment to foreign companies judged to be of primary importance. These advantages include reduction of or exemption from import duties and exemption from the tax on dividends for the first five years. Profits may be repatriated at the official exchange rate. There are no restrictions on personnel recruitment and no

demands for Africanization. Nevertheless, foreign investment is small because of Rwanda's small domestic market and inadequate infrastructure. Net direct foreign investment in 1991 was $4.6 million.

39ECONOMIC DEVELOPMENT

Rwanda's attempt to establish food self-sufficiency has delayed many of its development plans in other sectors. A water supply project jointly financed by the World Bank, the European Community and the Arab Bank BADEA was given priority in 1986 and 1987. Various infrastructure projects were continued, including the Kigali airport, the satellite ground station and road rebuilding. International financing was acquired to improve the government's planning capacity.

40SOCIAL DEVELOPMENT

Social security programs aimed at meeting the individual's basic welfare needs have been established in law since independence. Old age pensions for workers, family allowances, and payments for those injured on the job are provided for all wage earners. There are government- and missionary-sponsored mutual aid societies, which increasingly supply the many social services once provided by the clan and family under Rwanda's traditional social structure.

Although sex discrimination is outlawed by the constitution, women have only limited property rights and are not treated equally in employment, education, and other areas. Abortion is illegal. In the early 1980s, the fertility rate was 7.6, high even for Africa. Family planning services were introduced in 1986. In 1994, there was a total breakdown of all governmental services throughout the country.

41HEALTH

In normal times, malnutrition is the greatest health problem in Rwanda. Animal proteins and fats are scarce. Kwashiorkor, a protein-calorie deficiency, is common, contributing to the death of many children and to liver trouble in older individuals; it also increases the severity of other prevalent diseases, among them pneumonia, tuberculosis, measles, whooping cough, and dysentery. Malaria and trypanosomiasis (sleeping sickness) are endemic. In 1987, Kigali was reported to have one of the world's highest rates of infection with the AIDS virus; Rwandan Red Cross figures showed that between 10 and 15% of blood collected was contaminated with the virus.

Poor sanitation measures and water pollution also cause serious health problems; in 1991, 66% of the population had access to safe water, and 58% had adequate sanitation. In 1990, there were about 260 cases of tuberculosis per 100,000 people, and 33% of children under 5 years old were considered malnourished. Immunization rates for 1992 for children up to one year of age were: tuberculosis (94%); diphtheria, pertussis, and tetanus (85%); polio (85%); and measles (81%).

In 1985, there were 397 hospitals, dispensaries, and other health establishments, with a total of 9,069 beds. In 1990, there were 1.7 hospital beds per 1,000 inhabitants. In 1992, there were 2 doctors per 100,000 people, with a nurse to doctor ratio of 1.7. Total health care expenditures were $74 million in 1990 and, in 1992, 80% of the population had access to health care services. WHO, FAO, and UNICEF provide aid in public health services. Since the late 1960s, the UN, Belgium, France, and the US have been assisting Rwanda in specific health-related projects.

There were 396,000 births in 1992, a birth rate of 52.1 per 1,000 people. Average life expectancy in 1992 was 46 years (unchanged since 1985). In 1992, the infant mortality rate was estimated at 131 per 1,000 live births (a slight increase from 1985). The overall death rate in 1993 was 18.2 per 1,000 people, and maternal mortality was 210 per 100,000 live births in 1991.

These rates do not include the war-related deaths between 1991 and 1992 (about 2,000—Tutsi and Hutu conflict); and in 1994 (over 500,000 deaths, mostly of Tutsi civilians by Hutu militias). Due to the intensity of this civil war, the country of Rwanda has been devastated.

⁴²HOUSING

The basic type of housing in the rural areas is an edifice, most commonly beehive-shaped, made of mud bricks and poles, and covered with thatch. These residences are dispersed in the collines, farms organized on a family basis, and they accounted for 89% of Rwanda's housing units in 1978. In that year, 95% of all housing was owner occupied. In Kigali, the capital, modern construction has been under way to house its rapidly growing population.

⁴³EDUCATION

There were no public schools in Rwanda until the 1950s, and secondary education was attainable only at a school founded in 1929 at Butare by Roman Catholic missionaries. With independence, Rwanda began a major expansion of its educational programs; in 1983, expenditure for education was RFr4,491.3 million, the largest item in the national budget. However, the Catholic Church continues to play the leading role in education. In 1990, adult literacy was estimated at 50.2% (males, 63.9% and females, 37.1%).

Education is free and compulsory for all children aged 7 to 15, but the law is not widely enforced. Primary school is for eight years followed by six years of secondary education. Most primary and secondary schools are under the direction of religious missions, but many receive state subsidies. In 1990, there were 1,671 primary schools, with 19,183 teachers and 1,100,437 pupils attending. In 1990 there were 70,400 pupils and 2,802 teachers in secondary schools. Of these, nearly 39,849 pupils were in vocational schools, 14,378 were in teacher training programs, and 16,173 were in general secondary schools.

The National University of Rwanda at Butare was founded in 1963 by the government and a Canadian Roman Catholic order. Other known institutions are the African and Mauritian Institute of Statistics and Applied Economics in Kigali. In 1989, all higher level institutions had 3,389 pupils and 646 teaching staff.

⁴⁴LIBRARIES AND MUSEUMS

At the time of publishing it was not possible to identify what, if any, impact the current civil strife has had on libraries or museums. The largest library collection was at the National University, which had 138,000 volumes. There is a public library in Kigali, with 10,000 volumes, and smaller collections are found in the administrative centers of the other prefectures. A National Library was founded in 1989 and had a beginning collection of 6,000 volumes.

The National Museum in Butare contains an important collection for the study of the cultural evolution of the country and is housed in a new building inaugurated in January 1989. An ethnological museum is maintained in Kabgayi and a geological museum in Ruhengeri.

⁴⁵MEDIA

Telephone and telegraphic communications are the responsibility of the Ministry of Posts, Telecommunications, and Transport. Telephone service is limited to Kigali and a few other important centers; there were 12,593 telephones in 1991. The government-operated Radio of the Rwandan Republic provides domestic broadcasting service in French, Swahili, and Kinyarwanda; Deutsche Welle provides broadcasts in German, English, French, Hausa, Swahili, and Amharic. In 1991 there were about 467,000 radios. There is no television in Rwanda. A French-language daily press bulletin containing news of government activities is the only regular source of information on current developments for those who do not understand Kinyarwanda.

⁴⁶ORGANIZATIONS

Under the Belgian administration, various commercial, agricultural, and welfare organizations were founded, and many have continued in operation since independence. There is a chamber of commerce and industry in Kigali. The government has supported the growth of agricultural cooperatives.

⁴⁷TOURISM, TRAVEL, AND RECREATION

Tourism declined after 1990 due to war and economic factors, but showed some improvement in 1992. Tourists are drawn by Rwanda's mountain gorillas, wild game preserve, and by hiking opportunities in the Volcano National Park.

A valid passport is required of all tourists, and a visa is necessary for all but the nationals of Tanzania, Uganda, and Germany. A certificate of vaccination against yellow fever is required of persons arriving from an infected area.

⁴⁸FAMOUS RWANDANS

Kigeri IV Rwabugiri (d.1895) was one of the most famous rulers of the precolonial Rwanda kingdom. Grégoire Kayibanda (1924–76), the first president of independent Rwanda, studied for the priesthood and became a teacher. He founded Parmehutu, the party that led the move to independence. Juvénal Habyarimana (b.1937) became president in July 1973.

⁴⁹DEPENDENCIES

The Republic of Rwanda has no territories or colonies.

⁵⁰BIBLIOGRAPHY

Lemarchand, René. *Rwanda and Burundi.* New York: Praeger, 1970.

Linden, Ian and Jane. *Church and Revolution in Rwanda.* New York: Holmes & Meier, 1977.

Louis, William Roger. *Ruanda-Urundi, 1884–1919.* Oxford: Clarendon Press, 1963.

Maquet, Jacques J. *The Premise of Inequality in Ruanda: A Study of Political Relations in a Central African Kingdom.* London: Oxford University Press, 1961.

Nyrop, Richard F. *Rwanda: A Country Study.* Washington, D.C.: The American University, 1982.

Witherell, Julian W. *French-speaking Central Africa; a Guide to Official Publications in American Libraries.* Washington, D.C.: Library of Congress, 1973.

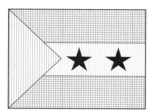

SÃO TOMÉ AND PRÍNCIPE

Democratic Republic of São Tomé and Príncipe
República Democrática de São Tomé e Príncipe

CAPITAL: São Tomé.

FLAG: The flag consists of three unequal horizontal stripes of green, yellow, and green; there is a red triangle at the hoist, and two black stars on the yellow stripe.

ANTHEM: *Independéncia Total (Total Independence).*

MONETARY UNIT: The dobra (Db) of 100 centimos replaced the São Tomé and Príncipe escudo (E) on a one-to-one basis in September 1977. There are coins of 50 centimos and 1, 2, 5, 10, and 20 dobras, and notes of 50, 100, 500, and 1,000 dobras. Db 1 = $0.0306 (or $1 = Db32.6394)

WEIGHTS AND MEASURES: The metric system is used.

HOLIDAYS: New Year's Day, 1 January; Martyrs' Day, 4 February; Labor Day, 1 May; Independence Day, 12 July; Armed Forces Day, first week in September; Farmers' Day, 30 September. The principal Christian holidays are also observed.

TIME: GMT.

¹LOCATION, SIZE, AND EXTENT

São Tomé and Príncipe, the smallest country in Africa, lies in the Gulf of Guinea, about 360 km (225 mi) off the west coast of Gabon. The nation has an area of 960 sq km (371 sq mi), of which São Tomé comprises 855 sq km (330 sq mi) and Príncipe 109 sq km (42 sq mi). Comparatively, the area occupied by São Tomé and Príncipe is slightly less than 5.5 times the size of Washington, D.C. São Tomé extends about 49 km (30 mi) NNE–SSW and 29 km (18 mi) ESE–WNW; it has a coastline of 141 km (88 mi). Príncipe has a length of approximately 21 km (13 mi) SSE–NNW and a width of 15 km (9 mi) ENE–WSW; its shoreline is 209 km (130 mi).

São Tomé and Príncipe's capital city, São Tomé, is located on the northeast coast of the island of São Tomé.

²TOPOGRAPHY

The islands form part of a chain of extinct volcanoes and are both quite mountainous. Pico de São Tomé, the highest peak on São Tomé, is 2,024 m (6,640 ft) above sea level. Most other peaks rise to only a little more than half that height. Príncipe's plateau area, extending along the northwestern coast, is larger than that of São Tomé. Pico de Príncipe is Príncipe's tallest mountain, reaching 948 m (3,109 ft) above sea level.

³CLIMATE

The islands are tropical, but temperature varies a good deal with altitude. Coastal temperatures average around 27°C (81°F), but the mountain regions average only 20°C (68°F). Seasons are distinguished more by a change in precipitation than by a change in temperature. From October to May, São Tomé and Príncipe receive between 380 and 510 cm (150–200 in) of rain, most of it falling on the southern portions. The northern areas receive only about 100–150 cm (40–60 in) of rain.

⁴FLORA AND FAUNA

Except for the coastal flatlands, where cocoa and coffee plantations predominate, São Tomé and Príncipe are dominated by forestland. Above 1,370 m (4,500 ft), the tropical rain forest

changes to cloud-mountain forest. There is little livestock, but domestic fowl are abundant.

⁵ENVIRONMENT

Water and land pollution are the most significant problems in São Tomé and Príncipe. The purity of the nation's water supply is questionable due to the lack of adequate water treatment systems. The nation's forests are also threatened due to overuse. There is currently no regulatory policy to regulate the preservation of the forests. The nation's cities are threatened by inadequate sewage treatment. Soil erosion and soil exhaustion are other major environmental problems. According to a UN report in 1992, the government of São Tomé and Príncipe recognized the need for environmental regulation.

⁶POPULATION

In 1994, the estimated population of São Tomé and Príncipe was 140,321, of whom all but about 9,000 lived on São Tomé. The population is growing at an annual rate of about 2.8%. In 1994, the estimated population density was 146 per sq km (377 per sq mi). The capital city, São Tomé, and its environs had an estimated 50,000 inhabitants in 1990. Santo António, is the largest town on Príncipe.

⁷MIGRATION

Historically, São Tomé and Príncipe received a substantial flow of what was allegedly temporary immigration in the form of contract labor. The *serviçais*, as they were called, came largely from Angola and Mozambique to work on the cocoa plantations; many were never repatriated. More recently, plantation labor has come from drought-stricken Cape Verde. Before 1974, Cape Verdeans were subsidized by the Portuguese government to settle on São Tomé and Príncipe in an effort to boost the islands' plantation economy. After the April 1974 revolution in Portugal and the coming of independence to the Portuguese territories, almost all the 3,000–4,000 European settlers left, while several hundred Angolans fled to São Tomé. Subsequently, more than 10,000 São Tomean exiles returned from Angola, and most Cape Verdeans left São Tomé.

8ETHNIC GROUPS

Most of the island's permanent residents are Fôrros, descendants of the Portuguese colonists and their African slaves, who came from Gabon and the Guinea coast. Along the southeast coast of São Tomé lives a group called the Angolares, the descendants of Angolan slaves, shipwrecked in the 16th century, who established independent fishing communities. Almost all of the few thousand Portuguese expatriates on the islands left in 1974–75.

9LANGUAGES

Portuguese, the official language, is spoken in a Creole dialect that reveals the heavy influence of African Bantu languages.

10RELIGIONS

Roman Catholicism is the dominant religion, with professing Catholics estimated at 82.5% in 1993. Traditional African religions are also practiced, and there is a small Protestant minority, including Seventh-Day Adventists and an indigenous Protestant church.

11TRANSPORTATION

Transportation networks on São Tomé and Príncipe reflect the plantation economy. Surfaced roads, about 200 km (125 mi), serve principally to bring export crops to the port towns; schooners are the main means of transportation for people living far from town. São Tomé and Santo António are the main ports; large freighters must be unloaded from their anchorage by barge because the ports are not deep enough to accommodate them.

São Tomé was an important link in the Atlantic marine and air network of the Portuguese overseas territories. The international airport at São Tomé, which serviced an estimated 23,000 passengers in 1991, is serviced principally by the Angolan airline Transportes Aéreos de Angola, although Transportes Aéreos Portugueses and Aeroflot make occasional stops. Equatorial Airline of São Tomé and Príncipe, a government joint venture with a private European airline, flies to Príncipe and Libreville, Gabon.

12HISTORY

São Tomé and Príncipe were probably uninhabited volcanic islands when the Portuguese landed there in 1471. In 1485, São Tomé was made a *donatário* (concession) of João de Paiva; the *donatário* provided for de Paiva to administer and profit by his administration of São Tomé according to Portuguese law. Subsequently, São Tomé served as a slave station.

The islands were settled by a group of Europeans and their African slaves. In 1493, 2,000 Jewish children were taken to São Tomé in an effort to populate the islands and raise the children as Christians, but by 1532 only 50 or 60 were left. It was Portuguese policy to deport its criminals, *degradados*, and orphans to remote colonial areas, and many of São Tomé's earliest male settlers came in this fashion. Female settlers were more often African slave women, and from the ensuing marriages a large mestiço population developed. A third group, separate from the European and mestiço populations, consisted of Angolares, descendants of shipwrecked Angolan slaves.

By the mid-16th century, the islands were Africa's leading exporter of sugar. São Tomé and Príncipe were taken over by the Portuguese crown in 1522 and 1573, respectively. Eventually, sugar lost its commercial importance, but in the early 19th century, two new cash crops, coffee and cocoa, were introduced, and by 1908 São Tomé had become the world's largest producer of cocoa. Plantation slavery or slavelike contract labor remained the basis of island labor for hundreds of years, and even when slavery formally ended, in 1869, the plantations employed laborers "recruited" on "contract" from other areas of Portuguese-speaking Africa. In 1906, Henry Nevinson published his book *A Modern Slavery,* which exposed the use of involuntary recruits,

unacceptably high labor mortality, and poor work conditions on the islands. The outcry resulted in a boycott of São Tomé cocoa. The scandal occasioned some reforms, but oppressive conditions continued. As late as 1953, the governor of São Tomé ordered Portuguese troops to open fire on striking plantation workers, leaving nearly 1,000 people dead, an action that aroused nationalist feeling.

A liberation group formed in the islands in 1960, but Portuguese control made it impossible to wage an effective guerrilla war. The organization, the Committee for the Liberation of São Tomé and Príncipe (later renamed the Movement for the Liberation of São Tomé and Príncipe—MLSTP), remained in exile in Gabon until it was recognized by Portugal in 1974 as the sole legitimate representative of the people of São Tomé and Príncipe.

An independence agreement was concluded between Portuguese and MLSTP negotiators on 26 November 1974, and a transitional government was installed on 21 December. On 12 July 1975, São Tomé and Príncipe achieved full independence. On the same day, Manuel Pinto da Costa, the secretary-general of the MLSTP, was inaugurated as the country's first president.

Following an alleged plot to overthrow the government, about 1,500 troops from Angola and Guinea-Bissau were stationed on the islands in 1978 at Pinto da Costa's request. Soviet, East European, and Cuban personnel were also reportedly on the islands. In 1979, Prime Minister Miguel dos Anjos da Cunha Lisboa Trouvoada was arrested and charged with attempting to seize power. His post was assumed by Pinto da Costa, and the MLSTP was reported to be seriously split. In the early 1980s there was unrest on Príncipe, apparently provoked by separatists. By 1985, São Tomé and Príncipe had begun to establish closer ties with the West.

In 1990, a new policy of *abertura,* or political and economic "opening," was adopted. It led to the legalization of opposition parties and direct elections with secret balloting. The secret police were purged and freedom of association and press were encouraged. A number of groups, many led by politicians in exile, united as the Party of Democratic Convergence-Group of Reflection (PDC-GR) and were led by Miguel Trovoada. An independent labor movement was launched and strikes were legalized. Abertura was also reflected in the evolution of a market economy and the privatization of state farms and enterprises.

On 20 January 1991, the nation held its first multiparty legislative elections. The former ruling party (MLSTP) was defeated by the PDC-GR. PDC-GR got 54.4% (33 seats) of the vote, the MLSTP 30.5% (21 seats), and the Democratic Opposition Coalition (CODO) 5.2% (1 seat). In the presidential election on 3 March 1991, Trovoada was elected unopposed.

In 1993, the PDC-GR continued to dominate the central government, but partisan activity has accelerated. The president and the prime minister, both PDC-GR, also became involved in a dispute over interpretation of the constitution on the separation of powers. In November, a joint communique by four opposition parties accused government of "leading the country towards a social explosion" and denounced its "authoritarian and repressive attitude."

13GOVERNMENT

On 12 July 1975, São Tomé and Príncipe, formerly considered overseas territories of Portugal, became an independent democratic republic. The constitution, drafted by a constituent assembly, took effect on 12 December 1975. The president was chief of state, elected by the 40-member People's Assembly for a term of four years. The prime minister, who was elected to a five-year term by the People's Assembly on the recommendation of the MLSTP, appointed and headed the cabinet. District popular assemblies elected in August 1985 chose the members of the People's Assembly, which elected Pinto da Costa to a third term as president on 30 September 1985. The MLSTP had been the sole legal political party until 1990. A new constitution was announced by da Costa in 1989 and adopted by the People's Assembly in April, 1990 and approved in an August referendum and went into force in September, 1990. The president is chosen by a muliparty election for a maximum of two five-year terms. The People's Assembly, now composed of 55 members, is elected to four-year terms in multiparty elections. Suffrage is universal at age 18.

¹⁴POLITICAL PARTIES

On 15 October 1974, the government of Portugal recognized the Movement for the Liberation of São Tomé and Príncipe (Movimento de Libertação de São Tomé e Príncipe—MLSTP) as the sole legitimate representative for the islands. The party, formed in exile in 1960, at a Pan-African conference in Ghana, originally called itself the Committee for the Liberation of São Tomé and Príncipe (Comité de Libertação de São Tomé e Príncipe—CLSTP). In 1965, CLSTP publicly demanded independence and economic reforms for the islands. At a conference in Guinea in 1972, the CLSTP changed its name to the MLSTP and moved its headquarters to Gabon. Until the declaration of 15 October 1974, the MLSTP remained partially underground and in exile, expressing itself through a legal party, the Pro-Liberation Movement Association, led by the poet Alda de Espírito Santo. After independence, the MLSTP became the only political party. Until 1991, Manuel Pinto da Costa was secretary-general of MLSTP and president of the republic.

With the legalization of opposition party activity, several politicians returned from exile to organize their followers. Miguel Trovoada, an MLSTP founder who had been exiled after challenging da Costa's leadership, formed the Democratic Convergence Party-Group of Reflection (PCD-GR) and, in the 1991 elections, it captured control of the People's Assembly and the presidency. The Democratic Opposition Coalition (CODO) and the Christian Democratic Front (FDC), and other parties together captured 15% of the vote for the legislature.

In December 1992, the MLSTP came back to score a series of landslide victories in municipal and regional elections. It took control of six of the eight regional governing bodies.

¹⁵LOCAL GOVERNMENT

São Tomé and Príncipe is divided into two provinces, corresponding to the two islands, and 7 counties, of which 6 are on São Tomé.

¹⁶JUDICIAL SYSTEM

The accord signed on 26 November 1974 between the Portuguese government and the MLSTP served as the legal code in the islands until 12 December 1975, when the new constitution was formally implemented. The highest court is the Supreme Tribunal, which is named by and responsible to the People's Assembly.

The constitution affords litigants in civil cases the right to a fair public trial and a right to appeal. It affords criminal defendants a public trail before a judge as well as legal representation. A shortage of trained lawyers, however, makes implementing this right difficult.

¹⁷ARMED FORCES

A small citizen's army was formed by the MLSTP government after Portuguese troops were withdrawn. There are also several hundred Angolan troops.

¹⁸INTERNATIONAL COOPERATION

São Tomé and Príncipe, admitted to UN membership on 16 September 1975, takes part in ECA, FAO, IBRD, ICAO, IDA, IFAD, ILO, IMF, ITU, UNESCO, UPU, WHO, and WMO. The nation is

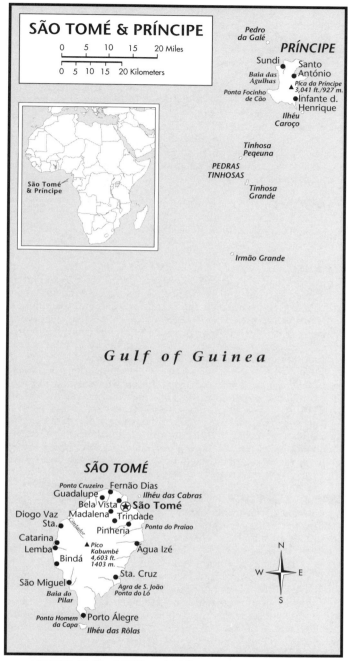

LOCATION: São Tomé: 0°13′N and 6°37′E. Príncipe: 1°37′N and 7°24′E.
TERRITORIAL SEA LIMIT: 12 mi.

also a member of the African Development Bank, G-77, and OAU. A signatory of the Lomé Convention, the nation is also a de facto participant in GATT and has signed the Law of the Sea.

¹⁹ECONOMY

São Tomé and Príncipe is one of the poorest countries in the world. It is not self-sufficient in food, and imports 45% of its supply (1991). The economy is based on cocoa-producing plantation agriculture, but the fall of cocoa prices since the early 1980s has created serious problems for the government. One consequence of the price decline was the abandonment of post-independence socialist-style economic policies in favor of market-style policies. Since 1987, economic policy has been driven by a World Bank and IMF-sponsored structural adjustment program with the objective of weaning the economy of its dependence on cocoa exports and foodstuff imports. Since 1991, the government has imposed fiscal and economic austerity measures, continued to devalue the currency, reformed the banking sector, raised electricity and fuel prices, and continued to privatize the non-agricultural sector. Although the economy contracted in real terms in 1990 and 1991, slow growth resumed in 1992. An unfortunate byproduct of the reforms was a 50% rise in consumer prices in 1992, a trend which stabilized in 1993. However, by the end of 1993 only a handful of plantations had managed even the first small steps away from state control, and the structural adjustment program tended to exacerbate economic hardship.

[20]INCOME

In 1992, GDP was estimated at US$41.4 million. Of that, the agricultural sector accounted for 28.9%, trade 16.9%, and transport 3.7%.

[21]LABOR

Agriculture and fishing supported over half the population in 1991. Laborers for the plantation sector come from mainland Africa and Cape Verde on a contract basis; Angola, Mozambique, and Nigeria are the major sources of contract labor. Plantation laborers gained a 400% wage increase on the eve of independence. Soon after, labor disruptions and the reorganization of production reduced the output of plantation crops.

Unemployment can reach up to 50% of the work force, largely because of the unpopularity of plantation work among the Fôrros. Unrelated to the former sole union (an affiliate of the MLSTP), or any political party, the Independent Union Federation (IUF) formed in 1992 to take advantage of freedom of association provisions now in the constitution. Workers may organize and bargain collectively. The government remains the primary mediator for labor, even though privatization has reduced the relative role of the government as an employer.

[22]AGRICULTURE

Plantation agriculture has long dominated the economy of the islands. Before nationalization in 1975, private companies owned more than 80% of the arable land. Their plantations were managed by São Tomé mestiços, Cape Verdeans, and São Tomé Europeans. The rest of the arable land was owned by about 11,000 small proprietors. The nationalization law limited the private holdings to 100 hectares (247 acres) and reorganized 29 plantations into 15 state companies. In 1985, however, the government began legally recognizing the right of individual families to cultivate land within the state plantations. The two largest plantations were leased to European management in 1986.

A variety of microclimates enables the cultivation of diverse tropical crops, but soils are especially suited for cocoa (introduced from Brazil in the late 19th century), which is the major export crop. About half of all cultivated land is used for cocoa production. Labor disruptions, a reduced workweek, inadequate investment in repair and maintenance, and the use of worktime to conduct management and cooperative training programs combined to lower the cocoa output from 10,000 tons in 1975 to 3,900 tons in 1987. Production of cocoa was believed to be about 2,000 tons in 1992. Cocoa exports accounted for 80% of export earnings in 1992. Copra is the second most important crop; production in 1992 totaled about 3,000 tons. Other agricultural products in 1992 were palm kernels, 500 tons; bananas, 3,000 tons; cassava, 5,000 tons; and coconuts, 42,000 tons.

Since 1990, economic policy has been driven by a World Bank and IMF-sponsored structural adjustment program aimed at diminishing the dependence on cocoa exports and food imports.

The program called for fundamental land reform and accompanying measures to stimulate cultivation of food crops for local consumption.

[23]ANIMAL HUSBANDRY

The livestock sector, largely pigs, was plagued by African swine fever once in 1979 and again in 1992, necessitating the destruction of the entire herd of some 30,000 animals. Disease severely affected chicken and egg production in 1993. There is no tsetse-borne disease in São Tomé, but production is limited by tuberculosis. In 1992 there were an estimated 4,000 head of cattle, 2,000 sheep, 4,000 goats, and 3,000 pigs.

[24]FISHING

The Angolare community of São Tomé supplies fish to the domestic market. In 1991, the catch was 3,500 tons. Between 1976 and 1983, substantial investments were made in fishing by the government, but the investment has not significantly contributed to GDP; rather, it has exacerbated a nearly unsustainable debt service burden. European Economic Community (EEC) vessels catch tuna in island waters under license. There are also fishing agreements with Angola and Portugal. Foreign assistance has focused more recently on artisanal fishing.

[25]FORESTRY

Twenty-nine percent of São Tomé and Príncipe is covered with primary, though inaccessible, forest. Wood is used on the plantations for fuel to dry cocoa beans and elsewhere as a building material. Unrestricted cutting has been the rule in spite of the legal sanctions against it. In 1993, new forest regulations were issued and guards were trained to enforce them. Reforestation and scientific foresting have been enforced to avoid further loss. Roundwood removals are estimated at 9,000 cu m a year.

[26]MINING

Little mining activity takes place on the islands. Mineral wealth remains largely unexplored, although lime deposits are exploited for the local market. A British-American joint venture contracted in 1970 for exploration rights for gas and oil on the islands and in their adjacent waters, but the presence of volcanic rock was a major technical handicap, and exploration ceased in 1974.

[27]ENERGY AND POWER

Hydroelectric facilities are on the Contador River on São Tomé. About 8 million of São Tomé's 15 million kwh of electric power in 1991 were produced by hydroelectricity; the rest was thermal. Total installed capacity in the islands was 6,000 kw in 1991. Most of São Tomé is electrified, but only a quarter of the nation's households has electricity. Imported fuel and energy made up 13% of total imports in 1992, at a cost of $4 million. As of 1992, only 10% of Sao Tome's abundant hydroelectric potential had been harnessed.

[28]INDUSTRY

São Tomé has very little industry; the industrial sector constitutes only 9.8% of the GDP. Soap, beverages, finished wood and furniture, bread, textiles, bricks and ceramics, garments, and palm oil are produced on the islands.

Electrical power was produced by diesel generators (53%) and hydroelectric sources (47%) in 1989. Reliance on fuel oil has translated into periodic blackouts as the price of oil rises. A project to increase storage capacity and the new private-sector management should reduce the number of blackouts in the future.

[29]SCIENCE AND TECHNOLOGY

The Ministry of Agriculture maintains a library in São Tomé.

³⁰DOMESTIC TRADE

The landholding population of São Tomé and Príncipe grows some produce for the local market, but not on a large scale. Similarly, the Angolare population of São Tomé supplies fish to the local market. The port towns of São Tomé and Santo António are the principal commercial and distribution centers.

³¹FOREIGN TRADE

São Tomé and Príncipe's trade balance depends on price levels for cocoa, which accounts for about 85% of export earnings. Copra is also exported. In 1986, exports were estimated at $6.3 million and imports at $14.8 million. The leading imports are foodstuffs, fuels, textiles, and machinery. The leading purchasers of exports are the Netherlands and Germany.

³²BALANCE OF PAYMENTS

Since the country cannot supply enough food and clothing for its own people, imports remain high, while export revenues vary according to world agricultural prices. In 1991, the trade deficit of $19 million was nearly 60% of GDP, when the value of imports exceeded that of exports by a factor of five. There is also an outflow of remittances for workers employed under contract from abroad.

³³BANKING AND SECURITIES

The Banco Nacional de São Tomé e Príncipe is the central bank and also handles commercial banking. The Caixa de Crédito is a government savings and loan institution serving industry, agriculture, and housing. There is also a postal savings bank. There is no stock exchange.

³⁴INSURANCE

A national insurance and reinsurance company was founded in 1980. There is also an insurance fund for civil servants.

³⁵PUBLIC FINANCE

The budget of São Tomé and Príncipe is habitually in deficit, with foreign loans making up part of the difference and borrowing from the central bank most of the rest. The current fiscal deficit averaged over 20% of GDP during 1975–86. Since 1987, the government has sought to correct fiscal imbalances by tax reforms and public expenditure reductions. From 1987 to 1992, the current fiscal deficit (excluding interest on foreign debt) shifted from a deficit of 6.5% of GDP to a surplus of 2% of GDP.

³⁶TAXATION

Export and import taxes, customs duties, and sales tax are the main sources of revenue from taxation. Income tax accounted for 7% of revenue from taxes in 1985.

³⁷CUSTOMS AND DUTIES

All imports require a license. Customs duties are levied, but recent information on rates and dutiable items is not available. In 1987, a state enterprise marketed all exports and imports of 12 basic commodities.

³⁸FOREIGN INVESTMENT

Since independence, investments have been minimal. An investment code adopted in 1986 allows free transfer of profits, dividends, and liquidated assets, as well as exemption from export duties. Some investors may qualify for tax and import-duty exemptions.

³⁹ECONOMIC DEVELOPMENT

With the help of the United Nations Development Programme, the government hopes to stabilize cocoa production through long-lease arrangements with private-sector management companies. A shift to black pepper and arabica coffee could revitalize the coffee sector. Food self-sufficiency depends on the success of the government's policy of turning fringe cocoa land over to mixed-agriculture family farmers. Projects to export plantains, cocoyam, and citrus fruits to Gabon are under study. The pork herds are to be reestablished. The fishing, forestry, and tourist industries are being revitalized. The government plans to promote the development of additional food-processing and construction material industries, as well as to improve the paved road network.

⁴⁰SOCIAL DEVELOPMENT

Before independence, social welfare was handled largely by private agencies and companies in the islands. The plantation corporations were responsible for the social welfare of their laborers. Missionary endeavors associated with the Catholic Church also played a part in fostering community well-being. After independence, the government assumed these roles.

Women enjoy constitutional equality with men, and some have been government ministers, but in general they are limited to a subordinate role by the traditional culture.

⁴¹HEALTH

The government hopes that crop diversification will help alleviate malnutrition, which continues to plague the country. There were an estimated 220 cases of tuberculosis per 100,000 people reported in 1990. In 1992, 61% of the country's children had been vaccinated against measles.

In 1983 there were 16 hospitals and dispensaries, with 651 beds. By 1989, there were 61 doctors, 1 pharmacist, 5 dentists, 233 nurses, and 54 midwives.

There were 4,500 births in 1992. The infant mortality rate was 65 per 1,000 live births, and the mortality rate for children under 5 years old was 85 per 1,000 live births (about 400 deaths). Life expectancy in 1992 was 68 years.

⁴²HOUSING

Housing on the islands varies greatly, from the estate houses of the plantation headquarters to the thatch huts of the plantation laborers. Some town buildings are wooden; others are mud block with timber, as are plantation-labor dormitories. As of 1981, 87% of all housing was wood and 26% was brick. In the same year, 62% of all dwellings were detached and 37% were apartments. Of existing housing units, 84% were principal residences, 22% had electricity, 9% had toilets, 9% had a bath or shower, and 9% had a sewage system.

⁴³EDUCATION

The school system before independence was basically that of Portugal. Schooling is compulsory for three years only. Primary education is for four years and secondary has two stages: the first four years are followed by three years. In 1989 there were 19,822 pupils in 64 primary schools with 559 teachers; in general secondary schools, there were 318 teachers and 7,446 pupils. In vocational schools, 101 pupils were enrolled the same year.

The MLSTP government has declared universal primary education to be a priority. In the mid-1980s, adult illiteracy was 43%.

⁴⁴LIBRARIES AND MUSEUMS

São Tomé maintains a public library and a general National Museum, founded in 1976 and located in the Fortress of Saint Sebastian constructed in 1585.

⁴⁵MEDIA

The *Diario da Republica* (1991 circulation: 500) is published weekly by the government. *Noticias Sao Tome e Principe* is a quarterly, with a 1991 circulation of 2,000. The national radio station broadcasts in Portuguese; there were an estimated 32,000 radios in 1991. A television station broadcasts two days a week. In 1991 there were 2,800 telephones in use.

46 ORGANIZATIONS

Cooperative movements sponsored by the MLSTP function as part of the government's economic development program.

47 TOURISM, TRAVEL, AND RECREATION

São Tomé and Príncipe's scenic beauty, wildlife, and unique historic architecture have the potential to attract tourists, but even though the islands have been a port of call for voyagers for centuries, tourist facilities are minimal and restricted largely to the port towns and their environs. The first tourist hotel opened in 1986 and the government is encouraging greater private investment in the tourist sector. Two sports facilities opened in 1992. All visitors must have visas. A yellow-fever vaccination certificate is required for stays of over two weeks.

48 FAMOUS SÃO TOMÉANS

Rei Amador (d.1596), who rebelled against the Portuguese and almost overran the island in 1595, is a national hero. Alda de Espírito Santo (b.1926) is a poet and nationalist leader. Manuel Pinto da Costa (b.1937), the secretary-general of the MLSTP, became the country's first president on 12 July 1975.

49 DEPENDENCIES

São Tomé and Príncipe has no territories or colonies.

50 BIBLIOGRAPHY

A Educacao na Republica Democratica de S. Tome e Principe: analise sectorial. Lisboa: Fundacao Calouste Gulbenkian, 1986.

Abshire, David M., and Michael A. Samuels (eds.). Portuguese Africa: A Handbook. New York: Praeger, 1969.

Chilcote, Ronald H. Emerging Nationalism in Portuguese Africa: Documents. Stanford, Calif.: Hoover Institution Press, 1972.

Gibson, Richard. African Liberation Movements. Oxford: Oxford University Press, 1972.

Hodges, Tony. Sao Tome and Principe: from Plantation Colony to Microstate. Boulder, Colo.: Westview Press, 1988.

Nevinson, Henry Wood. A Modern Slavery. With an intorduction by Basil Davidson. London: Daimon Press, 1963 (orig. 1906).

SENEGAL

Republic of Senegal
République du Sénégal

CAPITAL: Dakar.

FLAG: The flag is a tricolor of green, yellow, and red vertical stripes; at the center of the yellow stripe is a green star.

ANTHEM: Begins "Pincez, tous, vos koras, frappez les balafons" ("Pluck your koras, strike the balafons").

MONETARY UNIT: The Communauté Financière Africaine franc (CFA Fr) is the national currency. There are coins of 1, 2, 5, 10, 25, 50, 100, and 500 CFA francs, and notes of 50, 100, 500, 1,000, 5,000, and 10,000 CFA francs. CFA Fr1 = $0.0018 (or $1 = CFA Fr571).

WEIGHTS AND MEASURES: The metric system is the legal standard.

HOLIDAYS: New Year's Day, 1 January; Independence Day, 4 April; Labor Day, 1 May; Day of Association, 14 July; Assumption, 15 August; All Saints' Day, 1 November; Christmas, 25 December. Movable religious holidays include 'Id al-Fitr, 'Id al-'Adha', Milad an-Nabi, Good Friday, Easter Monday, Ascension, and Pentecost Monday.

TIME: GMT.

¹LOCATION, SIZE, AND EXTENT

Situated on the western bulge of Africa, Senegal has a land area of 196,190 sq km (75,749 sq mi), extending 690 km (429 mi) SE–NW and 406 km (252 mi) NE–SW. Comparatively, the area occupied by Senegal is slightly smaller than the state of South Dakota. It is bordered on the N and NE by Mauritania, on the E by Mali, on the S by Guinea and Guinea-Bissau, and on the W by the Atlantic Ocean. Its westernmost point is also that of the African mainland. On the NE the boundary is set by the Senegal River, and on the E by the Falémé River. Senegal surrounds the long, narrow republic of the Gambia on three sides and is joined with it in the Confederation of Senegambia. The total boundary length of Senegal is 3,171 km (1,970 mi).

Senegal's capital city, Dakar, is located on the Atlantic coast.

²TOPOGRAPHY

The northern part of the Senegal coast has dunes from Cap Vert to Saint-Louis, but to the south are muddy estuaries. Behind the coast is a sandy plain, which extends north to the floodplain of the Senegal River. The Casamance region in the south, isolated from the rest of Senegal by the Republic of the Gambia, is low but more varied in relief, while to the southeast lie the Tamgué foothills, which rise to a maximum altitude of 581 m (1,906 ft). Much of the northwest of Senegal (known as the Ferlo) is semidesert, but the center and most of the south, except for the forest of Casamance, are open savanna country. The major rivers—the Senegal, Saloum, Gambie, and Casamance—flow from east to west.

³CLIMATE

Temperatures are lowest along the coast and highest inland; rainfall is highest in the south and lowest in the north. The wet season, which lasts from June to October, is shorter in the north and longer in the south, especially near the southwest coast. The average annual rainfall ranges from 34 cm (13 in) at Podor in the extreme north to 155 cm (61 in) at Ziguinchor, in the southwest. At Dakar, the average is 57 cm (22 in); at Tambacounda, in the interior, it is 94 cm (37 in). Temperatures vary according to the season, with the highest temperatures registered in the northeast. At Dakar, during the cool season (December–April), the average daily maximum is 26°C (79°F) and the average minimum 17°C (63°F); during the hot season (May–November), the averages are 30°C (86°F) and 20°C (68°F).

⁴FLORA AND FAUNA

Vegetation varies in different areas of Senegal, depending on the average rainfall. The most tropical part of southern Casamance has mangrove swamps and remnants of high forest, including oil palms, bamboo, African teak, and the silk-cotton tree. The dry thornland of the northeast has spiny shrubs, especially acacia, including the gum-bearing species. Most of Senegal is savanna. Trees, which are widely spaced in this region, include the African locust bean, tallow tree, and gingerbread plum, along with cassias and acacias. The lion and leopard are occasionally found in the northeast, as are chimpanzees, elephants, hippopotamuses, and buffalo. The wild pig, hare, guinea fowl, quail, and bustard are widely distributed. Insects and birds are abundant, and there are numerous lizards, snakes, and other reptiles.

⁵ENVIRONMENT

Approximately 25% of Senegal is classified as arid, and another 70% is semiarid. Much of the land is threatened with desertification because of overgrazing, inadequately controlled cutting of forests for fuel, and soil erosion from overcultivation. According to a UN report, 4.5% of Senegal's forests have been eliminated. By 1985, the total amount of land subject to deforestation was 193 square miles. Dakar suffers from such typical urban problems as improper sanitation (especially during the rainy season, when sewers overflow) and air pollution from motor vehicles. The nation contributes 0.1% of the global total of gas emissions. The nation has 5.6 cubic miles of water with 92% used for farming activity and 3% used for industrial purposes. Thirty-five percent of the nation's city dwellers and 74% of the people living in rural areas do not have pure water. Senegal's cities produce

0.6 million tons of solid waste per year. Important environmental agencies include the Ministry of Scientific and Technical Research, which is responsible for coordinating all research and development in Senegal.

Senegal has six national parks, comprising about 4% of the total area; game in forest reserves is classified by law as partially or completely protected, but poaching remains a problem. In 1994, 11 mammal species and five bird species are endangered. Thirty-two types of plants are threatened with extinction. Endangered species include the western giant eland and four species of turtle (green sea, olive ridley, hawksbill, and leatherback).

6 POPULATION

Senegal's estimated 1994 population was 8,718,693, 26% above the 1988 census total of 6,928,405. This estimate by the US Census Bureau was somewhat higher than the UN's projected figure of 8,387,000 for 1995. A population of 9,581,000 was projected by the UN for the year 2000, assuming a crude birthrate of 41.1 per 1,000 population, a crude death rate of 14.5, and a net natural increase of 26.6 during 1995–2000. The estimated growth rate during 1990–95 was 2.7%. The average estimated population density in 1994 was 44.4 per sq km (115.1 per sq mi). About 42% of the population is urban.

Dakar, the capital and principal city, had a population of about 1,613,000 in 1990. Other important towns with their estimated 1992 populations are Thiès, 319,000; Kaolack, the peanut export center, 181,000; and Saint-Louis, 179,000.

7 MIGRATION

There is considerable seasonal migration between the Gambia and Senegal in connection with cultivation and harvesting of peanuts. Estimates of the number of Guineans who had fled to Senegal for political reasons ranged from 40,000 to more than 500,000, but all apparently returned after a 1984 military coup in Guinea. Also living in Senegal are perhaps 20,000 French and more than 18,000 Lebanese, about a third of whom have Senegalese nationality. Some Senegalese work in France; others have moved to other African countries in search of work, especially to Côte d'Ivoire. Senegal was home to 66,500 Mauritanian refugees at the end of 1992 and 5,000 from Guinea–Bissau. There were 12,200 Senegalese refugees in Guinea-Bissau.

8 ETHNIC GROUPS

The largest ethnic group is the Wolof, who made up 44% of the total population in 1988; they live mainly in the northwest. Closely related are the Sérer (15%), in west-central Senegal, who are skilled peanut cultivators, and the Lebu, mostly fishermen and farmers, concentrated in the Dakar area.

Other important groups are the Tukulor, who live predominantly in the northeast; the Fulani (Peul) and Bambara, scattered throughout the country; the Maelinkó or Mandingo (5%), in the southeast and in Casamance; and the Diola of Casamance. A total of 122,340 persons (1.8%) of the 1988 population were foreigners.

9 LANGUAGES

French, the official language, is the language of administration and of the schools. Wolof was spoken by 71% of the people in Senegal in 1988; Poular, 21%; Serer, 14%; Mandingue, 6%; Diola, 6%; and Sarakhole/Sohinke, 1.4%.

10 RELIGIONS

The constitution provides for religious freedom. In 1989, 93% of the people professed Islam; the Tijaniya and Muridiya brotherhoods have great social, political, and economic influence. About 6% of Senegalese are Christians, mainly Roman Catholics, with the rest (4%) observing African traditional religions.

11 TRANSPORTATION

Senegal has 1,034 km (642 mi) of railroads, all owned by the government. The main lines run from Dakar to Thiès and thence to Kidira on the Mali border, and from Thiès to Saint-Louis. There are also branch lines from Guinguineo to Kaolack, from Louga to Linguère, and from Diourbel to Touba, serving the peanut-growing areas. Of Senegal's 14,007 km (8,705 mi) of classified roads in 1991, some 3,777 km (2,347 mi) were tarred, and 10,230 km (6,358 mi) were laterite or improved earth. There are modern roads from Dakar to Thiès, Saint-Louis, and Matam, and from Dakar to Kaolack and on through the Gambia to Ziguinchor in Casamance. In 1991 there were 137,000 vehicles.

Favorably located at the westernmost point of the continent and possessing up-to-date equipment, Dakar is one of the great ports of Africa, a major import-export center and a port of call for freight and passenger ships. The port, which can accommodate ships of up to 100,000 tons, handled 5 million tons of cargo in 1988, when mineral commodities accounted for 15% of total import tonnage. The Senegalese Maritime Navigation Co. (Compagnie Sénégalaise de Navigation Maritime—COSENAM), a river and ocean freight transport line in which the government has an 84% share, was founded in 1979. Gross weight of the 3 ships of the merchant fleet came to 10,000 tons in 1991.

The Senegal River, which has a sandbar across its mouth, is navigable by shallow-draft vessels all year round from Saint-Louis to Podor (225 km/140 mi), and between August and October as far as Kayes in Mali (924 km/574 mi). It is closed to foreign ships. The Saloum is navigable by oceangoing vessels to the important peanut port of Kaolack, 114 km (71 mi) upriver. The Casamance River is navigable to Ziguinchor, although not without difficulty.

Dakar's Yoff International Airport, a West African air center, is served by many foreign airlines. Air France, Air Senegal, and Air Afrique maintain routes connecting Saint-Louis, Thiès, Ziguinchor, Kédougou, Tambacounda, and 10 other towns with secondary air fields. Air Senegal is 50% owned by the government and 40% by Air Afrique, in which Senegal also holds a 7% share.

12 HISTORY

Knowledge of the history of Senegal before the 16th century is fragmentary. The major feature seems to have been the gradual movement into Senegal of the Wolof and Sérer peoples from the northeast, who reached their present positions between the 10th and 15th centuries AD. At various times parts of Senegal were included in the empires of Tekrur, Ghana, and Mali. At the height of its power at the beginning of the 14th century, Mali controlled the Falémé and Upper Senegal. That century saw the emergence of the Jolof empire, controlling the six Wolof states of Jolof, Kayor, Baol, Walo, Sine, and Salum. In the middle of the 16th century, Kayor revolted and conquered Baol, but the other Wolof states continued to admit a shadowy suzerainty of Jolof. As the power of Kayor and Baol increased toward the end of the 17th century, however, Jolof power declined, probably because it was cut off by those states from access to the sea and European trading. The 18th and early 19th centuries were marked by struggles among the northernmost Wolof states and by sporadic Mauritanian attacks on them.

European activities in Senegal began with the Portuguese arrival at the Cap Vert Peninsula and the mouth of the Senegal River in 1444–45. The Portuguese enjoyed a monopoly on trade in slaves and gold until the 17th century, when they were succeeded by the Dutch, who virtually dominated all trade by 1650. The later 17th century brought the beginnings of the Anglo-French rivalry, which dominated the 18th century in Senegal as elsewhere. Throughout the 17th and 18th centuries, the main trading activities were the export of slaves and of gum arabic.

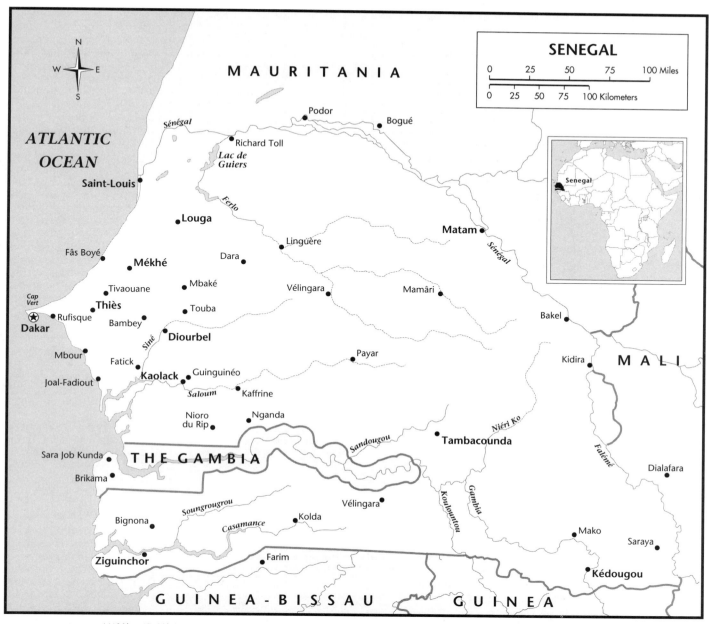

LOCATION: 11°30′ to 17°30′w; 12° to 17°n. **BOUNDARY LENGTHS:** Mauritania, 813 km (505 mi); Mali, 418 km (260 mi); Guinea, 330 km (205 mi); Guinea-Bissau, 338 km (210 mi); Atlantic coastline, 446 km (277 mi); Gambia, 756 km (470 mi). **TERRITORIAL SEA LIMIT:** 12 mi.

Peanut cultivation by African peasants, the foundation of Senegal's modern economy, began in the mid-19th century.

French rule was confined to the old trading posts of Saint-Louis (founded in 1659), Gorée, and Rufisque until its expansion under the Second Empire, during the governorship of Gen. Louis Faidherbe (1854–65). The French occupation of Senegal was consolidated and extended under the Third Republic during the last 30 years of the 19th century. In 1871, Senegal was again allowed to send a deputy to the French parliament, a right that had been abolished under the Second Empire. In the following decade, municipalities on the French model were established in Saint-Louis, Gorée, Dakar, and Rufisque, and only the inhabitants of these towns took part in the elections of the deputy.

Between 1895 and 1904, a series of decrees consolidated eight territories into a French West Africa federation, of which Dakar became the capital. In 1920, a Colonial Council, partly elected by the citizens of the old towns and partly consisting of chiefs from the rest of Senegal, replaced the elected General Council previously established for the four towns. All the elected bodies were suppressed in 1940 but restored at the end of the war, and in 1946 Senegal was given two deputies in the French parliament. Under the constitution of 1946, the franchise was extended and a Territorial Assembly was established in Senegal. Universal suffrage was established in 1957. In 1958, Senegal accepted the new French constitution and became an autonomous republic within the French Community.

On 17 January 1959, in Dakar, representatives of French Sudan (now Mali), Senegal, Dahomey (now Benin), and Upper Volta (now Burkina Faso) drafted a constitution for a Federation of Mali, but only the assemblies of French Sudan and Senegal ratified it and became members of the federation. The Mali Federation became a sovereign state on 20 June 1960, but conflicting views soon led to its breakup. On 20 August, the Legislative Assembly of Senegal proclaimed Senegal's national independence and announced its withdrawal from the federation. A new republican constitution was adopted on 25 August, and on 5 September, Léopold-Sédar Senghor was elected president and Mamadou Dia became prime minister, in effect retaining a position he had held since 1957.

After an attempt by Dia to avoid a vote of no-confidence in the National Assembly by calling out the national police, the legislature met in special session on 17 December 1962 and overthrew Dia's government by a motion of censure. Dia was arrested, and Senghor was elected by unanimous vote of the deputies as head of government. Less than three months later, the electorate approved a new constitution that abolished the post of prime minister and made the president both chief of state and head of the executive branch. A constitutional amendment in 1970 reestablished the office of prime minister, and Abdou Diouf, former minister of planning and industry, was appointed to the post on 26 February 1970. Dia, in detention since 1962, was released in March 1974 as part of an independence celebration.

Having been reelected president in 1968, 1973, and 1978, Senghor resigned as president at the end of 1980 and was succeeded by Diouf. In the summer of 1981, 2,000 Senegalese troops were sent to the Gambia to put down an attempted military coup there. The Confederation of Senegambia was constituted in February 1982 with Diouf as president. Under the terms of confederation, the two countries pledged to integrate their armed and security forces, form an economic and monetary union, and coordinate foreign policy, communications, and possibly other endeavors. Diouf was elected to a full term as president on 27 February 1983, receiving 83.5% of the vote in a five-candidate contest. All parties were guaranteed equal access to the media, but the secret ballot was optional, and independent observers reported widespread electoral irregularities. The office of prime minister—constitutionally regarded as the president's successor—was once again abolished in April 1983.

The ruling Parti Socialiste Sénégalais (PS) was victorious in municipal and rural elections held in November 1984, although 12 of the 15 registered parties boycotted the polls. Diouf has liberalized the political process and restructured his administration, making it less corrupt and more efficient. It advocates modulated reform in the face of reactionary elements in the PS.

In the 1988 national elections, Diouf carried 77% of the vote and the PS took 103 of the 120 seats in the National Assembly. Despite a generally fair election, opposition protests escalated into rioting in Dakar. The city was placed under a three-month state of emergency. Diouf's principal opponent, Maitre Abdoulaye Wade of the Democratic Party, was among those arrested and tried for incitement. Afterwards, Diouf met with Wade and tensions were eased. In April 1991, Wade accepted the post of Minister of State in Diouf's cabinet.

Diouf and PS again won reelection in February 1993. His margin of victory, however, shrank to 58% versus 32% for Wade. The PS took only 84 seats in the May legislative elections and the PDS increased its representation from 17 to 27 seats. The Jappoo Leggeeyal Senegalese Party and the Democratic League won three seats each. Two other parties took the other three seats.

Opposition parties charged fraud, but the Constitutional Court certified the results as official. International observers noted irregularities but declared the election generally "free and fair." At that time, the vice president of the Constitutional Court was assassinated. Government detained and in October charged Wade and other PDS members with complicity in the murder. MPs were later released, being subject to parliamentary immunity.

In April 1989, a nationwide state of emergency was declared and a curfew imposed in Dakar after rioters killed dozens of Mauritanians. Protesters had been enraged by reports of the killing of hundreds of Senegalese in Maruitania.

Relations with Mauritania were broken and armed clashes along the border and internal rioting led to the expulsion of most Mauritanians residing in Senegal. Diplomatic relations were reestablished in April, 1992 and the northern border along the Senegal River was reopened.

In the southernmost province of Casamance, a separatist group, the Movement of Democratic Forces of the Casamance (MFDC), has challenged the armed forces for years. A 1991 ceasefire failed to prevent further fighting. A joint peace commission, mediated by Guinea-Bissau, met in 1992, but still the dispute continued. Another ceasefire agreement, signed in July 1993, however, appears to be holding, although there are numerous charges of human rights abuses by both sides. Hundreds have been killed.

In foreign affairs, the government followed a conservative pro-French and anti-Libyan policy. Diouf was secretary-general of the OAU from 1985 to 1986. From 1990 to 1993, Senegalese armed forces played a major role in the ECOMOG peacekeeping effort in Liberia.

¹³GOVERNMENT

Under the 1963 constitution, as amended, the president of the republic determines national policy and has the power to dissolve the National Assembly. The president (who is elected for a five-year term by direct universal suffrage) may not veto legislation, but if the president asks the National Assembly to reconsider a measure it has enacted, the bill must be passed again by a three-fifths majority before it becomes law. The president also may ask the Supreme Court to rule on the constitutionality of a proposed law. With the consent of the president of the National Assembly and the Supreme Court, the president of the republic may submit any proposed law to national referendum.

Legislative power is exercised by the 120-member National Assembly, elected for five years simultaneously with the president. The Assembly elects the 16 members of the High Court of Justice from among its ranks. Members of the Council of Ministers may not be Assembly members.

¹⁴POLITICAL PARTIES

The Senegal branch of the French Socialist Party (SFIO) won the first postwar elections largely because its leaders constituted the only organized party that had contacts in all parts of the colony. It sought to establish political and juridical equality between French and Senegalese citizens. In 1948, however, its leaders, Ahmadou Lamine-Guèye and Léopold-Sédar Senghor, quarreled. Senghor left the SFIO and founded a new party, the Senegalese Democratic Bloc (Bloc Démocratique Sénégalais—BDS), which was based more in the rural areas than in the old communes, from which Lamine-Guèye derived his political support. The new party emphasized social and economic rather than juridical issues and geared its program closely to peasant interests and grievances. In 1951, it won both Senegalese seats in the French National Assembly and, in 1952, 43 of the 50 seats in Senegal's Territorial Assembly.

In the French National Assembly, Senghor had meanwhile taken a leading part in creating a new parliamentary group, the Overseas Independents (Indépendants d'Outre-Mer—IOM), emphasizing African and colonial problems. It was, however, confronted by another African party, the African Democratic Rally (Rassemblement Démocratique Africain—RDA), founded in October 1946 by African deputies hostile to the provisions of the constitution of 1946 regarding the overseas territories. Although the RDA substantially reduced the number of seats held by the IOM in the French parliament, in Senegal it made no inroads on the two established parties, the BDS and the SFIO.

Senghor and his associate Mamadou Dia secured overwhelming majorities at the parliamentary elections in 1956 and launched a campaign to unite all Senegalese parties. They faced the opposition of Lamine-Guèye, who sponsored a first attempt to create an African Socialist movement loosely associated with the SFIO, and of the RDA leadership, which aimed at bringing about the unity of all parties within the RDA.

In 1956, Senghor's party, the BDS, was reorganized to become the Popular Senegalese Bloc (Bloc Popular Sénégalais), which took a strongly nationalistic stance. In the Territorial Assembly elections in 1957, the first held under complete universal suffrage, it won 47 seats, while the SFIO won only 12. Lamine-Guèye and Senghor were reconciled in 1958, and their respective parties fused in April 1958 to form the Senegalese Progressive Union (Union Progressiste Sénégalaise—UPS). The UPS supported the new French constitution in the referendum of September 1958, and in the elections to the Senegal legislature in 1959 it won all 80 seats. After independence in 1960, the UPS remained the dominant political party. President Senghor was its secretary-general, and the party's National Council was responsible for major national policy decisions. In 1976, the UPS changed its name to the Senegalese Socialist Party (Parti Socialiste Sénégalais—PS), after joining the Socialist International.

There was no legal opposition party from 1966 until 1974, when the Senegalese Democratic Party (Parti Démocratique Sénégalais—PDS) was formed in order to meet the constitutional requirement for a responsible opposition. The PDS won 17 Assembly seats in 1978, compared with 83 for the PS.

In 1981, the constitution, which had restricted the number of political parties to four, was amended to end all restrictions. Seven parties contested the National Assembly elections of 9 May 1993. The PS won 84 seats; the PDS won 27; the Jappoo Leggeeyal ("Let Us Unite") Party and the Democratic League won three seats each; the Independence and Labor Party (PIT) won two seats; and the Senegalese Democratic Union/Renewal party got one.

There has been a steady increase in PDS representation (it won only eight seats in 1983) and decline in PS support (down from 111 seats in 1983). The separatist Movement of Democratic Forces of Sasamance (MFDC) in the south has taken up arms and refused to contest elections. Several hundred of their supporters were killed in clashes with Senegalese army in 1992 and 1993.

15LOCAL GOVERNMENT

Senegal's local administrative organization consists of ten regions—Fatick, Kaolack, Kolda, Ziguinchor, Tambacounda, Saint-Louis, Thiès, Diourbel, Louga, and Dakar—each headed by an appointed governor and an elected local assembly. The regions are divided into 28 departments, each headed by a prefect, who is assisted by two special secretaries. The departments in turn are divided into 99 districts (arrondissements), each headed by a subprefect. In rural areas the basic administrative unit is the rural community, usually made up of a group of villages with a total population of about 10,000.

16JUDICIAL SYSTEM

The High Council of the Magistrature, founded in 1960 and headed by the president, determines the constitutionality of laws and international commitments and decides when members of the legislature and the executive have exceeded their authority. A 16-member High Court of Justice, founded in 1962 and elected by the National Assembly from among its own members, presides over impeachment proceedings. The Supreme Court, founded in 1960, is made up of members appointed by the president of the republic on the advice of the High Council of the Magistrature. In June 1973, a Court of State Security was set up to deal with political offenses. Criminal cases are essentially subject to French criminal law. Petty offenses are dealt with by justices of the peace in each department; ranked next in the judicial system are courts

of first instance in each region. There are assize courts in Dakar, Kaolack, Saint-Louis, and Ziguinchor and a Court of Appeal in Dakar. There is also a military court system and a special Court for the Repression of the Unlawful Accumulation of Wealth.

The constitution declares the independence of the judiciary, from the executive, the legislature and the armed forces. Judges are appointed by the president after nomination by the minister of justice. In practice, low pay and political ties make magistrates vulnerable to outside pressures.

Criminal defendants are presumed innocent until proven guilty and are afforded public trials, and the right to legal counsel, among other procedural rights.

17ARMED FORCES

Senegal's armed forces totaled about 9,700 men in 1993. The army of 8,500 men included 9 infantry or armored battalions, 1 artillery battalion, and 1 engineering battalion. The navy of 700 had 10 patrol craft and small landing craft, and the air force of 500 had 9 aircraft. There was also a paramilitary force of some 6,800 men. Military outlays in 1993 were about $100 million or 2% of gross domestic product. Senegal supplied a battalion for service in Liberia and UN observers in three other nations. France maintains a reinforced marine regiment of 1,200 in Senegal.

18INTERNATIONAL COOPERATION

Senegal was admitted to UN membership on 28 September 1960 and is a member of ECA and all the nonregional specialized agencies. Senegal belongs to ADB, ECOWAS, G-77, and OAU, as well as BCEAO, the Organization for the Development of the Senegal River (founded in 1975), and the Organization for the Development of the Gambia River (founded in 1978), among other groups. Senegal remains in the franc zone and is a signatory to GATT and the Law of the Sea.

In accordance with an agreement approved by the legislatures of Senegal and the Gambia in December 1981, the Confederation of Senegambia came into existence on 1 February 1982. There is a Council of Ministers with 9 members and a Confederal Assembly of 60 members. Although Senegal holds majority representation in both bodies, as well as the confederal presidency, there are substantial minority guarantees; moreover, the confederation is to function without prejudice to the independence and sovereignty of each country.

19ECONOMY

Senegal's economy is based on its agricultural sector, primarily peanut production, and a modest industrial sector. Agriculture is highly vulnerable to declining rainfall, desertification, and changes in world commodity prices. When the first of a series of droughts struck in the latter part of the 1960s, the economy deteriorated rapidly. Today, 30 years after achieving independence, Senegal's resource-poor economy remains fragile and dependent upon foreign donors for continued viability.

In 1979 Senegal began a long term structural adjustment program under the direction of the World Bank, the IMF, and bilateral donors. The program was aimed at reducing government deficits, the rate of inflation, and the negative trade balance. The government carried out a major program of privatization of the parastatal enterprises, reducing or eliminating its holdings in 30 of the approximately 40 institutions targeted. Some success was realized and from 1991 to 1992 the economy grew 2.5% on average in real terms. However, due to depressed economic conditions, low world prices for its exports, and its lack of international competitiveness, Senegal failed to meet most of its 1992 structural adjustment targets. Consequently, the country sank deeper into debt and low or no growth was predicted for 1993. In February 1993 President Diouf was re-elected for a new 7-year term, and his socialist party won a large majority of the legislative seats in May 1993. In deference to the labor unions and a possibility of political unrest, the new government's 1993 budget failed to cut civil service wages. In addition, implementation of legislation to allow employers more flexiblity in making layoffs was postponed.

In January 1994 France suddenly devalued the CFA franc, causing its value to drop in half overnight. Immediately, prices for almost all imported goods soared, including prices for food and essential drugs. Since 1948 France had guaranteed a fixed parity of one French franc to 50 African francs. The resulting stability in the currency had generally kept inflation low and helped to maintain a steady rate of growth. However, in the 1980s, the economies of the CFA countries began to stagnate in relation to other African nations, and France came under increased pressure from the World Bank, the IMF, and Western countries to stop subsidizing the CFA franc. The devaluation, long expected in the investment community, is designed to encourage new investment, particularly in the export sectors of the economy, and discourage the use of hard currency reserves to buy products that could be grown domestically.

In the face of raising prices, thousands demonstrated against the government. The government imposed temporary price controls in an effort to prevent price-gouging by local merchants and halt the sharp rise in inflation.

20INCOME

In 1992 Senegal's GNP was $6,124 million at current prices, or $780 per capita. For the period 1985–92 the average inflation rate was 1.7%, resulting in a real growth rate in per capita GNP of 0.3%.

In 1992 the GDP was $6,277 million in current US dollars. It is estimated that in 1989, the last year for which statistics are available, agriculture, hunting, forestry, and fishing contributed 19% to GDP; mining and quarrying, 1%; manufacturing, 13%; electricity, gas, and water, 2%; construction, 3%; wholesale and retail trade, transport, storage, communication, finance, insurance, real estate, business services, community, social, and personal services 50%; and other sources, 12%.

21LABOR

The total work force was estimated at 3,900,000 in 1992, of whom 70% were in agriculture. There were some 130,130 wage earners in 1991, of whom about half worked in the public sector. The unemployment rate in Dakar was 12% in 1992. An estimated 900,000 persons worked in the informal sector.

Senegal's fundamental labor legislation is based on the French overseas labor code of 1952, which provides for collective agreements between employers and trade unions, for the fixing of basic minimum wages by the government on recommendation of advisory committees, and for a 40- to 48-hour workweek (except for agricultural workers, who may work longer hours subject to an annual maximum of 2,400 hours). The code also provides for paid annual leave and for child allowances. The right to strike is recognized by law, and there are special labor courts. In 1992 there were 19 strikes involving 3,954 workers. The major trade union is the National Confederation of Senegalese Workers, which since 1970 has been the official union affiliated with the ruling PS.

22AGRICULTURE

Senegal is predominantly an agricultural country, with about 70% of its working population involved in farming. Most Senegalese farms are small (1.5–2.4 hectares/3.7–5.9 acres), and about 60% are in the so-called Peanut Basin, east of Dakar. Much of the agricultural land is still tribally owned. Only about 12% of Senegal's total land area is cultivated; peanuts took up 39% of the cultivated land in 1992.

Since independence, the Senegalese government has developed a system of generally small cooperatives to rationalize agricultural production and marketing and to free the farmers from chronic indebtedness to private traders; these were replaced in 1984 by a network of "village sections" with financial autonomy. As of 1985 there were 4,472 such sections. Parastatal agencies guarantee minimum prices of major agricultural crops, including peanuts, millet, sorghum, rice, and cotton.

In theory all peanuts are processed locally, and prices of processed peanut oil and other peanut products are set by parastatal agencies. Production of unshelled peanuts varies widely because of periodic drought, and production is frequently underreported because of unauthorized sales to processors in neighboring countries. In 1992, the reported production was 578,000 tons, down from 754,000 tons in 1991. Cotton, Senegal's other major export crop, is produced and marketed under the direction of the Society for the Development of Textile Fibers (Société de Développement des Fibres Textiles—SODEFITEX). Seed cotton production was 52,000 tons in 1991 and 51,000 tons in 1992; lint cotton output was an estimated 20,000 tons during 1992.

Production of food crops, some of which are grown in rotation with peanuts, does not meet Senegal's needs. In 1992, over 350,000 tons of rice were imported. Millet and sorghum production was 671,000 tons in 1991 and 563,000 tons in 1992; output of paddy rice during the same period fell from 194,000 to 177,000 tons but corn increased from 103,000 to 115,000 tons. Cassava output was about 46,000 tons in 1992, when the vegetable harvest totaled an estimated 134,000 tons and fruits an estimated 110,000 tons. Market gardening takes place largely in the Dakar region and to a lesser extent around Thiès. Sugarcane, grown on about 8,000 hectares (19,700 acres), yielded 837,000 tons of sugarcane in 1992.

23ANIMAL HUSBANDRY

Raising livestock is a primary activity in the northern section of Senegal and a secondary one for farmers in the southern and central regions. Cattle are raised mainly by the Sérer and by nomadic Fulani. Sheep and goats are important in parts of the southwest. Cattle imported from Mauritania meet part of the nation's meat requirements, but livestock are also exported to neighboring countries.

In 1992, the estimated livestock population included 2,800,000 head of cattle, 3,600,000 sheep, 2,400,000 goats, 730,000 horses and donkeys, 310,000 hogs, 15,000 camels, and 19 million poultry. The slaughter in 1992 yielded an estimated 43,000 tons of beef and veal and 20,000 tons of sheep and goat meat. Hides are exported or used in local shoe production and handicrafts. Substantial quantities of cheese, butter, and canned and powdered milk are imported.

24FISHING

Senegal has a flourishing fishing industry, and Dakar is one of the most important Atlantic tuna ports. In 1990, fish exports accounted for 22.4% ($200 million) of total exports. The total catch in 1991 was 319,693 tons, half of which was sardines.

25FORESTRY

Senegal has about 10.5 million hectares (25.9 million acres) of classified woodland and forest, most of it in the Casamance region. Timber production is small, with firewood and charcoal being the most important forest products. About 5,098,000 cu m of roundwood was cut in 1991, of which about 88% went for fuel. Senegal is highly vulnerable to declining rainfall and desertification.

26MINING

Mining, especially of phosphates at a deposit some 80 km (50 mi) northeast of Dakar, has taken on added importance for Senegal's economy in the postindependence era. Production of aluminum phosphate increased from 160,400 tons in 1968 to 405,400 tons in 1974, before falling to 191,000 tons in 1987. It stood at 92,000 tons in 1991. Calcium phosphate output increased from 1,100,000 tons in 1968 to 1,472,000 tons in 1974; in 1991, production reached 1,741,000 tons. Mining of sea salt rose from 80,000 tons in 1968 to 150,000 tons in 1974; in 1991, it came to about 102,000 tons. Iron ore deposits, estimated at 600 million tons, have been identified in southeastern Senegal, but their development would not yet justify the cost of creating the extensive port shipping and rail infrastructure needed to exploit the deposits. Eastern Senegal also has about 350,000 tons of marble, as well as deposits of uranium, titanium, serpentine, and other minerals.

27ENERGY AND POWER

Electric power generation is almost entirely thermal. Installed capacity was 231,000 kw in 1991; production in 1991 totaled 756 million kwh, 98% of it in public plants.

At the end of 1991, Unocal received a 3-year oil concession for the Oôme Flore area, some 60 km (37 mi) offshore of Casamance. Senegal's oil and natural gas reserves, despite sporadic exploration for the last 40 years, are not well known. About 150 wells have been drilled, but the only commercial discoveries are limited to small natural gas fields east of Dakar. There are also extensive reserves of peat along the coast between Dakar and Saint-Louis. An oil refinery near Dakar, with an annual capacity of 1,200,000 tons, produces petroleum products from imported crude oil. Production was 773,900 tons in 1991. In 1990, Senegal imported 769,900 tons of crude oil from Nigeria and Gabon.

28INDUSTRY

In francophone West Africa, Senegal's manufacturing sector is second only to that of the Côte d'Ivoire (Ivory Coast), producing some 13.1% of GDP (1989). Agroindustry (oil mills, sugar refineries, fish canneries, flour mills, bakeries, beverage and dairy processing, and tobacco manufacturing) plays a key role and accounts for some 40% of value added. Especially important are the four groundnut-processing mills, which produced 108,100 tons of groundnut oil in 1985. Textiles, leather goods, chemicals, paper, wood products, and building materials are also important manufactures. The textile industry includes four cotton-ginning mills, factories for weaving, dyeing, and printing cloth, and plants that produce mattresses, thread, and hats. In 1988, an integrated textile complex was inaugurated at Kaolack, enhancing Senegal's textile capabilities considerably. Other industrial products include plywood, boats, bicycles, soap, paints, acetylene, sulfuric acid, phosphoric acid, phosphate fertilizer, and cigarettes. The petroleum refinery has a 1.4 million-ton annual capacity. Privatization of government parastatal companies began several years ago with 16 either sold or liquidated by mid-1991.

Senegal has an installed capacity of 216 Mw from six thermal power stations. The Manantali hydroelectric plant has added 800 million kwh a year, and plans have been prepared for further developing the hydroelectric potential of the Senegal River.

29SCIENCE AND TECHNOLOGY

The African Regional Center for Technology, with 30 member states, has its headquarters in Dakar. Most research facilities in Senegal deal with agricultural subjects. Dakar has centers for mining, biology, and medical research and a research institute on African food and nutrition problems. An institute of research for oils and oilseeds is at Bambey. The Senegalese National Center of Agricultural Research, with headquarters at Dakar, operates a national center of agronomical research at Bambey, a national laboratory of livestock and veterinary research at Dakar, an oceanographic center at Dakar, and numerous other technical facilities throughout the country.

The University Cheikh Anta Diop of Dakar has faculties of medicine and sciences, and research institutes in psychopathology, leprosy, pediatrics, renewable energy, applied tropical medicine, applied mathematics, health, environmental science and applied nuclear technology. The University of Saint Louis has an applied mathematics unit. Other facilities for scientific training include a polytechnic school at Thiès, an international school of sciences and veterinary medicine, representing 13 French-speaking countries, at Dakar, and an institute of nutritional technology at Dakar. In 1981, 2,662 technicians and 1,948 scientists and engineers were engaged in research and development.

30DOMESTIC TRADE

Domestic trade is to a large extent controlled by the government through marketing agencies, which buy groundnuts from the cooperatives at a fixed price and sell them to the processing plants. In 1985–86, however, groundnut marketing was opened up to private traders. Many staple foods are price controlled and subsidized by the government.

Dakar is not only the capital and largest city of Senegal but also the major commercial and industrial center of West Africa. Many large trading firms have headquarters in France. Lebanese residents also play an important role in trade. Smuggling of goods from the Gambia is a serious problem, since such illicit imports undercut Senegalese products in price.

Normal business hours are usually from 8 or 9 AM to noon and 3 to 6 PM, Monday–Friday, and 8 or 9 AM to noon on Saturday. Banks are usually open 8 to 11:15 AM and 2:30 to 4:30 PM, Monday–Friday.

31FOREIGN TRADE

Food products were Senegal's leading exports (37.8%) in 1988, followed by groundnut oil and cakes. Petroleum refinery products, phosphates, and chemicals were also important exports. Senegal's exports in 1988 (in millions of CFA francs) were the following:

Seafood	31,274
Groundnut and groundnut products	23,412
Other food products	33,999
Petroleum products	19,373
Phosphates	21,361
Other raw materials	10,740
Machinery and transport equipment	6,012
Fertilizers	3,828
Chemicals	17,835
Cotton and cotton goods	2,129
Other manufactures	5,013
Other exports	1,107
TOTAL	176,083

The leading imports are industrial products, machinery and transport equipment, and food products. Senegal's imports in 1988 (in millions of CFA francs) were as follow:

Food products, beverages, tobacco	82,631
Petroleum products	49,274
Other raw materials	14,143
Fats and oils	4,986
Machinery and transport equipment	72,903
Chemicals and pharmaceuticals	36,352
Miscellaneous manufactures	61,282
TOTAL	321,571

France is Senegal's principal trading partner, accounting for 37.6% of exports and 31.5% of imports in 1988. Senegal sent

9.7% of its exports to India. It bought 6.4% of its imports from the US and lesser amounts (between 5.7% and 3.9%) from Côte d'Ivoire, Spain, Nigeria, Japan, Italy, and Germany.

32BALANCE OF PAYMENTS

Since independence, as in colonial times, Senegal's balance of payments has generally run a deficit on current accounts, mainly covered by foreign aid from France (and, in recent decades, from other EEC members). Remittances from Senegalese working in France, together with small inflows of private capital, have also helped cover the shortfalls. Excluding government transfers, Senegal's current account deficit was 7.4% of GDP in 1992. A reduction of imports and increased private savings have caused the external balance to decline since the mid-1980s.

In 1991 merchandise exports totaled $903.2 million and imports $1,187.1 million. The merchandise trade balance was $–283.6 million. The following table summarizes Senegal's balance of payments for 1990 and 1991 (in millions of US dollars):

	1990	1991
CURRENT ACCOUNT		
Goods, services, and income	−510.2	−531.4
Unrequited transfers	294.6	293.5
TOTALS	−215.6	−237.9
CAPITAL ACCOUNT		
Direct investment	—	—
Portfolio investment	—	—
Other long-term capital	92.9	−8.9
Other short-term capital	−88.7	−46.0
Exceptional financing	246.1	273.3
Reserves	−18.0	8.5
TOTALS	232.3	226.9
Errors and omissions	−16.9	10.9
Total change in reserves	6.4	10.8

33BANKING AND SECURITIES

In 1959, the Central Bank of the West African States (Banque Centrale des États de l'Afrique de l'Ouest—BCEAO) succeeded the Currency Board of French West Africa and Togo as the bank of issue for the former French West African territories. In 1962, it was reorganized as the joint note-issue bank of Benin, Côte d'Ivoire, Mauritania (which left in 1973), Niger, Senegal, Togo, and Upper Volta (now Burkina Faso), members of the West African Monetary Union. BCEAO notes, known as CFA francs, are guaranteed by France without limitation. Foreign exchange receipts of the member states go into the franc area's exchange pool, which in turn covers their foreign exchange requirements. In 1973, the member states of the BCEAO signed new statutes that, among other things, provided for increased Africanization of bank personnel, transfer of headquarters from Paris to Dakar, and greater participation of the bank in the development activities of member states. As of 30 October 1986, central bank reserves credited to Senegal totaled CFA Fr15.7 billion.

Commercial banks operating in Senegal include the International Bank for Occidental Africa (French-owned) and the General Association of Banks of Senegal. As of 1993, deposit money banks in Senegal had CFA Fr101.4 billion in demand deposits and CFA Fr139.2 billion in time and savings deposits.

The most significant development bank is the government-controlled National Development Bank of Senegal, which participates in development projects and provides credit for government organizations, mixed societies, and cooperatives. Another development financing institution is the Housing Bank of Senegal. A new credit institution, the National Fund for Agricultural Credit, was created in 1984. There are no securities exchanges in Senegal.

34INSURANCE

As of 1986, 6 domestic companies provided insurance in Senegal. In 1984, premiums amounted to CFA Fr2,517.7 million for life insurance and CFA Fr13,060 million for non-life. Third-party motor insurance is compulsory. In 1987, 54.9% of premium payments were for life and 45.1% for non-life insurance (of which 46.7% was accounted for by automobile insurance).

35PUBLIC FINANCE

Although Senegal's finances are recorded as being in balance each year, in fact the country has run persistent deficits since 1976, generally covered by foreign aid. From 1987 to 1990, Senegal's fiscal deficit grew from 2.6% of GDP to 4.3% of GDP. In spite of an austere surplus of 0.2% of GDP in 1991, Senegal still was highly reliant on debt relief to cover public finances. An unsustainably high civil service wage bill of CFA Fr132.9 billion in 1992 represented 54% of recurrent expenditures.

36TAXATION

Senegal's tax structure includes a salary tax on the employer (3–6%) and a general income tax with rates ranging up to 50%. The rate of the tax on industrial and commercial profits is 33.3% for incorporated enterprises.

Indirect taxes have long been the mainstay of Senegal's tax system, with import duties by far the most important. Other indirect taxes include the business license tax, export taxes, a real estate tax, and registration and stamp taxes. The value-added tax has a basic rate of 20% but can range as high as 50% on luxury items.

37CUSTOMS AND DUTIES

Imports are subject to a customs duty of 15% and a fiscal tax that varies from 10–50% based on the type of good. A value-added tax of 7–30% and a petroleum product tax (CFA Fr15.5–24.5 per liter) are levied as well.

In 1982, Senegal abolished its import licensing system, opening the market to all countries on an equal basis; previously, only products from the franc zone and the EC could be imported without a license.

38FOREIGN INVESTMENT

Following independence, Senegal's economic policy shifted from a largely laissez-faire, noninterventionist stance to a policy of increasing government participation in economic affairs. By 1975, the government had effectively nationalized groundnut trade and processing, assumed majority control of the two main phosphate companies, and nationalized water distribution and electricity production. Half a generation later, in 1991, a slow privatization of the parastatal sector was underway.

In spite of its parastatal tradition, Senegal encourages private investment, which remains substantial. The investment code, enacted in 1962 and significantly revised in 1972, 1978, and 1981, encourages both domestic and foreign private investment in industrial, agricultural, mineral, transport, tourist, and other enterprises that conform to the goals of the national development program. Incentives include tax advantages and exemptions from customs and duties. Most private investment in Senegal comes from France.

An industrial free trade zone located outside Dakar offers preferential access to West African Economic Community, ECOWAS, and European Economic Community countries. Aside from exchange-control regulations, there are no restrictions on the repatriation of capital and earnings for amounts up to CFA Fr200,000; above this amount, prior government approval is required. By the beginning of 1992, 15 firms had begun operations in the zone. In December 1983, Senegal signed a bilateral investment treaty with the US, becoming the first sub-Saharan African nation to do so.

39ECONOMIC DEVELOPMENT

Senegal's development program addresses the basic problems encountered by Senegal's economy: lack of diversified output, the inefficiency of investments, the role of state in economic activity, and the excessive expansion of domestic consumer demand. These problems have been partly addressed by programs focusing on food self-sufficiency, fishing, and tourism, and by strengthening high-return activities. Projects such as the Manantali irrigation project, the phosphate-to-fertilizer recovery project, and the trawler modernization program are examples of what Senegal is doing within this policy framework. In the area of manufacturing, capacity utilization improvement, equipment modernization, and low-capital production are emphasized.

40SOCIAL DEVELOPMENT

Since 1956, a system of family allowances for wage earners has provided small maternity and child benefits. The system is financed by employer contributions at the rate of 6% of gross salary; another 1–5% contribution finances a fund for occupational health and accident coverage. Shared equally by employer and employee is a 6% contribution to a fund for general medical and hospital expenses. In addition, employers contribute 4.8% of gross salary to a retirement fund and employees 3.2%; the retirement age is 65.

More than half of all women between the ages of 15 and 64 participate in the work force. The fertility rate in the mid-1980s was 7.1; abortion is legal only to save the woman's life. Discrimination against women is widespread. Despite the vigorous multiparty political activity, there have been charges of human rights violations, as well as restrictions on freedom of press and association. The violators seldom are punished.

41HEALTH

In 1993, Senegal had a birth rate of 43 per 1,000 people, and 11% of married women (ages 15 to 49) used contraception. In 1992, there were 334,000 births. In the same year, life expectancy was 49 years.

In 1990, there were 407 doctors, 200 pharmacists, 58 dentists, 474 midwives, and 562 nurses; in 1992, there were 5 doctors per 100,000 people, with a nurse to doctor ratio of 2:6. In 1985, there were 63 hospitals and health centers; and, in 1990, there were 0.8 hospital beds per 1,000 people. Still, in 1992, only 40% of the population had access to health care services.

Major health problems include measles and, to a lesser extent, meningitis, along with such water-related diseases as malaria, trypanosomiasis, onchocerciasis, and schistosomiasis. There were approximately 166 cases of tuberculosis per 100,000 people in 1990 and, in the same year, 22% of children under 5 years old were considered malnourished. In 1991, only 48% of the population had access to safe water and only 55% had adequate sanitation. Immunization rates for children up to one year old in 1992 were: tuberculosis (65%); diphtheria, pertussis, and tetanus (47%); polio (47%); and measles (43%). Total health care expenditures in 1990 were $214 million.

Infant mortality was 90 per 1,000 live births in 1992; maternal mortality was 600 per 100,000 live births; and the general mortality rate was 16 per 1,000 people in 1993.

42HOUSING

Most housing in Dakar is like that of a European city. Elsewhere, housing ranges from European-type structures to the circular mud huts with thatched roofs common in villages.

Since World War II, the growth of Dakar and other towns has been rapid, with government activity largely concentrated on improvement of urban housing and sanitation. Low-cost housing is being erected in Dakar by the Office of Moderate-Rent Housing, but the pace slowed in the 1970s because of the economic strain caused by poor peanut crops. Only 43% of Senegal's population was estimated to have access to safe water in 1983. According to the latest available information for 1980–88, the total housing stock numbered 1,350,000 with 4.9 people per dwelling.

43EDUCATION

Education is compulsory at the primary level between ages 6 and 12; however, because of a lack of facilities, just over half the children in this age group attend school. In 1990, there were 2,640 primary schools in which 708,448 students were enrolled. At the secondary level, 181,170 students were attending schools the same year. The University of Dakar has two graduate schools and numerous research centers. A polytechnic college opened at Thiès in 1973. Other colleges include a national school of administration at Dakar and a school of sciences and veterinary medicine for French-speaking Africa. Universities and equivalent institutions had 16,764 students in 1989. Literacy rates are low: in 1990, 38.3% of adults were literate. The estimated figures were 51.9% for men and 25.1% for women.

44LIBRARIES AND MUSEUMS

There are four major libraries in Senegal, all located in Dakar. The oldest is the Archives of Senegal, founded in 1913, which has a collection of more than 26,000 volumes. The largest is the Central Library of the University of Dakar, founded in 1952, which has over 325,000 volumes. The Basic Institute of Black Africa (Institut Fondamental d'Afrique Noire—IFAN) and the Alliance Française maintain libraries of over 70,000 and 10,000 volumes, respectively. In addition to these major facilities, there are specialized libraries attached to various research institutes.

The Museum of African Art in Dakar and the History Museum and the Museum of the Sea on Gorée Island are operated by IFAN. There are natural history museums in Dakar and Saint-Louis.

45MEDIA

Telephone and telegraph services, publicly owned and operated, are good by African standards, particularly in the coastal area and in the main centers of peanut production. In 1985 there were 53,765 telephones in use, of which 38,707 were in Dakar. French submarine cables connect Dakar with Paris, Casablanca, Conakry (Guinea), and Recife (Brazil), and radiotelephone facilities are also in operation. The postal system provides international telephone facilities.

The government-operated radio and television service has transmitters throughout the country. The two national radio networks based in Dakar broadcast mostly in French, while the regional stations in Rufisque, Saint-Louis, Tambacounda, Kaolack, and Ziguinchor, which originate their own programs, broadcast primarily in six local languages. There were 860,000 radios in 1991. Transmission of educational television programs began in 1973, and by 1991 there were 273,000 television sets in use.

The constitution guarantees freedom of opinion, which the press is generally free to exercise. There was one daily newspaper in 1991, Le Soleil du Sénégal, the PS party newspaper, with an estimated 19,000 circulation.

46ORGANIZATIONS

The Alliance Française sponsors lectures and concerts. The Daniel Boitier Center in Dakar is a Roman Catholic organization for the study of social and economic problems. Of the many sport and social associations in the towns, those for soccer are especially popular, but racing clubs, aero clubs, and automobile clubs are also active. There are chambers of commerce, industry, and agriculture in the principal cities.

47TOURISM, TRAVEL, AND RECREATION

Since the early 1970s, tourism has become a foreign exchange earner, 3% of GDP in 1990. The comfortable climate, variety of cultural attractions, attractive physical features such as the coastal beaches and the 5,996-sq-km (2,315-sq-mi) Niokolo-Koba National Park, and the relative proximity to Europe have combined to make Senegal an increasingly popular vacation area, and international conference center. Gorée Island, near Dakar, has many former slave houses, where perhaps 20 million slaves were kept before being shipped to America between 1536 and 1848. Fishing is popular, and hunting is allowed from December to May on an 80,000-hectare (198,000-acre) reserve.

All visitors must have valid yellow fever inoculation certificates; nationals of some European and African countries do not need visas. In 1991, 233,512 foreign tourists arrived at hotels and other facilities, 56% from France, 21% from other European countries, and 16% from Africa. There were 6,826 hotel rooms with 13,652 beds and a 34% occupancy rate, and tourism receipts were estimated at US$171 million.

48FAMOUS SENEGALESE

Blaise Diagne (1872–1934) was the first African to be elected to the French parliament and to hold office in the French government as an undersecretary of state. Léopold-Sédar Senghor (b.1906), president of Senegal from 1960 until his retirement in 1980, is a French-language poet of distinction; in 1984, he became a life member of the French Academy, the first black African to receive that honor. Abdou Diouf (b.1935) became president of Senegal in 1981 after serving as Senghor's prime minister from 1970 through 1980. Senegalese writers include Birago Diop (b.1906), author of short stories, and David Diop (1927–60), an internationally known poet. Ousmane Sembene (b.1923) is a film director and writer of international repute. Cheikh Anta Diop (1923–86), RND leader, wrote many works of distinction on African history.

49DEPENDENCIES

Senegal has no territories or colonies.

50BIBLIOGRAPHY

Behrman, Lucy C. *Muslim Brotherhood and Politics in Senegal.* Cambridge, Mass.: Harvard University Press, 1970.

Boone, Catherine. *Merchant Capital and the Roots of State Power in Senegal, 1930–1985.* New York: Cambridge University Press, 1992.

Colvin, Lucie G. *Historical Dictionary of Senegal.* Metuchen, N.J.: Scarecrow Press, 1981.

Delgado, Christopher L. and Sidi Jammeh (eds.). *The Political Economy of Senegal under Structural Adjustment.* New York: Praeger, 1991.

Fatton, Robert. *The Making of a Liberal Democracy: Senegal's Passive Revolution, 1975–1985.* Boulder, Colo.: Lynne Rienner Publishers, 1987.

Foltz, William J. *From French West Africa to the Mali Federation.* New Haven, Conn.: Yale University Press, 1965.

Gellar, Sheldon. *Senegal: An African Nation between Islam and the West.* London: Gower, 1983.

Gersovitz, Mark and John Waterbury (eds.). *The Political Economy of Risk and Choice in Senegal.* Totowa, N.J.: F. Cass, 1987.

Johnson, G. Wesley, Jr. *The Emergence of Black Politics in Senegal.* Stanford, Calif.: Stanford University Press, 1971.

Markovitz, Irving Leonard. *Léopold-Sédar Senghor and the Politics of Négritude.* New York: Atheneum, 1969.

Schumacher, Edward J. *Politics, Bureaucracy, and Rural Development in Senegal.* Berkeley: University of California Press, 1975.

Senegal in pictures. Minneapolis: Lerner, 1988.

Terrell, Katherine D. *The Industrial Labor Market and Economic Performance in Senegal: A Study in Enterprise Ownership, Export Orientation, and Government Regulation.* Boulder, Colo.: Westview Press, 1989.

Thompson, Virginia, and Richard Adloff. *French West Africa.* Stanford, Calif.: Stanford University Press, 1958.

Vaillant, Janet G. *Black, French, and African: A Life of Leopold Sedar Senghor.* Cambridge, Mass.: Harvard University Press, 1990.

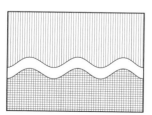

SEYCHELLES

Republic of Seychelles

CAPITAL: Victoria.

FLAG: The flag is red above and green below, divided horizontally by a white wave pattern.

ANTHEM: Begins "Seychellois both staunch and true."

MONETARY UNIT: The Seychelles rupee (R) is a paper currency of 100 cents. There are coins of 5, 10, and 25 cents and 1, 5, 10, 20, 25, 50, 100, 1,000, and 1,500 rupees and notes of 10, 25, 50, and 100 rupees. R1 = $0.1940 (or $1 = R5.1318).

WEIGHTS AND MEASURES: The metric system is the legal standard.

HOLIDAYS: New Year's, 1–2 January; Labor Day, 1 May; National Day, 5 June; Independence Day, 29 June; Assumption, 15 August; All Saints' Day, 1 November; Immaculate Conception, 8 December; Christmas, 25 December. Movable religious holidays include Good Friday, Easter Monday, Corpus Christi, and Ascension.

TIME: 4 PM = noon GMT.

¹LOCATION, SIZE, AND EXTENT

Seychelles, an archipelago in the Indian Ocean, consists of an estimated 115 islands, most of which are not permanently inhabited. The second-smallest country in Africa, Seychelles has an area of 455 sq km (176 sq mi), of which Mahé, the principal island, comprises 142 sq km (55 sq mi). Comparatively, the area occupied by Seychelles is slightly more than 2.5 times the size of Washington, D.C. There are two main clusters: one is a granitic group, centering around Mahé; the other, to the SW, includes the coralline Aldabra Islands and the Farquhar group. Situated about 1,600 km (1,000 mi) off the east coast of Africa, Mahé extends 27 km (17 mi) N–S and 11 km (7 mi) E–W and has a coastline of 491 km (305 mi).

The capital city of Seychelles, Victoria, is located on the island of Mahé.

²TOPOGRAPHY

The Seychelles Islands are the highest points of the Mascarene Ridge, an Indian Ocean ridge running in a generally north-south direction. The granitic islands rise above the sea surface to form a peak or ridge which, in the case of Mahé, attains an elevation of 912 m (2,992 ft) at Morne Seychellois, the highest point. Rugged crests, towering cliffs, boulders, and domes contribute to the islands' great natural beauty. Here and there, in the hollows in the rock relief, are pockets of lateritic soil, often very thin and easily eroded. Mahé possesses white, sandy beaches behind which are flats of coral and shell known locally as plateaus. Small streams descending the mountain slopes deposit alluvial material, creating the most fertile soils on the island.

The coralline Seychelles are, in contrast, low lying, rising only a few feet above the surface of the sea. Many have the typical Indian Ocean lagoon. Soils tend to be thin, with poor moisture retention. These islands are suited only to the coconut palm and a few other species.

³CLIMATE

Although the Seychelles Islands lie close to the Equator, their maritime situation results in coastal temperatures that are fairly constant at about 27°C (81°F) throughout the year. At higher altitudes, temperatures are lower, especially at night. Mean annual rainfall at sea level on Mahé is 236 cm (93 in); in the mountains there may be as much as 356 cm (140 in) a year. On the southwestern coral islands, rainfall is much lower, averaging about 50 cm (20 in) a year on Aldabra. May to October is the relatively dry sunny season; in this period, the southeast monsoon winds bring brief showers every two or three days. The northwest monsoon arrives in December and continues until March, bringing frequent and heavy rain. Humidity is high, especially in the coastal areas.

⁴FLORA AND FAUNA

Only on Praslin and Curieuse islands, northeast of Mahé, can any of the primary forest be seen. On both islands the native forests of coco-de-mer have been protected in small reserves; its fruit, a huge coconut weighing up to 18 kg (40 lb), is the largest seed in the world. Virtually all the broadleaf evergreen rain forest has been cut down. In its place are the coconut plantations, with occasional patches of vanilla. Other existing trees are native to the islands and have adapted to the local conditions. Underplanting is quite usual and includes avocado, breadfruit, banana, cinnamon, mango, papaya, patchouli, and pineapple.

Sharks abound in the surrounding oceans, but on land there are no reptiles or mammals that present a threat to human life. The most noteworthy animal is the giant tortoise; once very plentiful, the species is now sorely depleted. There is a great variety of bird life including dozens of the world's rarest species, but very few insects.

⁵ENVIRONMENT

Seychelles does not have the resources to maintain a comprehensive program of environmental regulation. The monitoring of the environment is complicated by the fact that the nation consists of 15 islands distributed over a 1.3 million km2 area. The nation has a water pollution problem due to industrial by-products and sewage. Fires, landslides, and oil leakage also affect the environment in Seychelles. The government has undertaken the Environmental Management Plan of Seychelles 1990–2000 which proposes 12 areas of environmental regulation. The Ministry of Planning and External Relations and the Ministry of National Development hold principal environmental responsibility. The Aldabra atoll is a native preserve. The olive ridley, hawksbill, and green sea turtles and the Seychelles black parrot, Seychelles magpie robin, and Aldabra brush warbler are endangered species.

6POPULATION
The population was 68,598 in 1987 and was estimated at 70,671 in mid-1994. At the census in 1977, 88% of the total population lived on the island of Mahé. Most of the remaining population lived on Praslin (7%) and La Digue (3%). A total of 24,324 people lived in Victoria, the capital and principal city (including its suburbs), at the time of the 1987 census The estimated average population density in 1985 was 159 per sq km (413 per sq mi), and the annual growth rate is about 1%.

7MIGRATION
Entry for the purpose of employment is strictly controlled. Since the 1950s, some retirees from the UK have settled in Seychelles. In 1990, 371 new immigrants arrived, and 664 Seychellois departed permanently.

8ETHNIC GROUPS
There are no distinct ethnic divisions, apart from small Indian and Chinese groups constituting about 1% of the total population. The bulk of the population is Seychellois, a mixture of African, French, and Asian strains.

9LANGUAGES
Creole, a simplified form of French with borrowings from African languages, has been the first language since 1981 and is the initial language in public schools. English is second and French third. All are official languages. English is the official language of the National Assembly.

10RELIGIONS
The bulk of the population in 1993, some 90%, was Roman Catholic with 6% Anglicans, and Hindus, Muslims, and Seventh-day Adventists each numbering a few hundred. There are also small numbers of Buddhists and Baha'is.

11TRANSPORTATION
Until the opening of the international airport on Mahé in 1971, the Seychelles Islands were entirely dependent on the sea for their links with the rest of the world. Until 1970, passenger and cargo service by ship was irregular; in the early 1970s, however, new deepwater facilities were dredged at Victoria Harbour. Private ferries connect Mahé to Praslin and La Digue.

The road network totaled 260 km (162 mi) in 1991, of which 160 km (99 mi) was tarmac surfaced, all on Mahé. One road encircles the island, and another runs across the island by way of the central mountain ridge. There were 4,563 automobiles, and 1,860 commercial vehicles in 1992.

Seychelles International Airport is at Pointe Larue on Mahé. Flights to London, Zurich, Frankfurt, and Rome are in service via Air Seychelles, the national carrier. Air France's scheduled flights connect Seychelles with Europe. Air Seychelles, which also runs domestic flights, carried about 181,000 passengers over the course of nine months in 1992. Ligne Aérienne Seychelles (LAS), a private line, ran charter flights to Australia, Singapore, Botswana, and Malawi.

12HISTORY
The Seychelles Islands (then uninhabited) were discovered by the Portuguese explorer Vasco da Gama in 1502, and an English expedition visited the islands in 1609. The name Seychelles derives from the Vicomte des Séchelles, Louis XV's finance minister. The French first claimed the islands in 1756, but colonization did not begin until 1768, when a party of 22 Frenchmen arrived, bringing with them a number of slaves. As competition grew among European nations for the lucrative trade with India and the Indies, more and more seamen called at the islands to provision their vessels and to pick up commodities useful for trade.

The French and British warred for control of the islands between 1793 and 1813. French bases were blockaded in 1794 and again in 1804; on each occasion, the French capitulated. Under the Treaty of Paris (1814), the islands, together with Mauritius, were ceded to Britain. Both before and after the cession, the islands were administered from Mauritius as dependent territories. When the British made clear that they would enforce the ban on slavery throughout the Empire, many of the French landowners who had continued to import African slaves, largely from Mauritius and Réunion, departed for Africa and elsewhere, taking their slaves with them. However, with slavery ended, thousands of liberated slaves and others came into the islands. Indian labor was introduced to work on the plantations, and some Chinese were brought in as shopkeepers.

In 1872, a Board of Civil Governors was created, giving the islands a greater degree of political autonomy; a Legislative Council and an Executive Council were established in 1888. On 31 August 1903, the islands became a crown colony, no longer subordinate to Mauritius. By this date, the cosmopolitan character of Seychelles had been established. Intermarriage between the descendants of the French settlers and the African and Asian populations produced the Seychellois of today.

In 1948, the first elections were held, filling four seats on the Legislative Council. A new constitution was written in 1966, effective from 1967, vesting authority in a governor and a Governing Council. General elections, the first based on the principle of universal adult suffrage, were held in December 1967 for the new Legislative Assembly. Further amendments to the constitution in March 1970 gave the Seychellois greater autonomy over affairs of internal government.

Seychelles achieved independence at 12:05 AM on 29 June 1976. Upon independence, the UK government recommended the transfer from the British Indian Ocean Territory to Seychelles of the island groups of Aldabra and Farquhar and the island of Desroches. These islands, which had been detached from Seychelles in 1965, were duly returned to the new republic.

James Richard Marie Mancham, leader of the conservative Seychelles Democratic Party, became president on independence, heading a coalition government that included Seychelles People's United Party (SPUP) leader France Albert René as prime minister. Mancham was overthrown by a coup on 5 June 1977 and went into exile; René became president. He suspended the constitution, dismissed the legislature, and ruled by decree.

In 1978, a new political party, the Seychelles People's Progressive Front (SPPF), absorbed the SPUP. The constitution of March 1979, adopted by referendum, established a one-party state. In November 1981, about 50 mercenaries recruited in South Africa landed in Mahé, briefly seized the airport, and apparently planned to return Mancham to power; however, Seychellois troops forced them to flee. Tanzanian troops, airlifted to Seychelles following this incident, also played a part in restoring order after an abortive army mutiny of 17–18 August 1982 took at least nine lives. All Tanzanian troops had left the country by the end of 1984. A number of other plots have been alleged since then.

René was reelected president without opposition in June 1984. Since then, the Seychelles has made progress economically and socially. Under rising pressure to democratize, in December 1991, René agreed to reform the system. Multiparty elections were held in July 1992 (the first since 1974), and the prospect of reconciliation between René and Mancham supporters has been raised.

Many dissidents, including Mancham, returned from exile. René's SPPF won 58% of the vote for a commission to rewrite the constitution but in November, voters rejected the revised constitution the René supporters proposed. It needed a 60% majority to pass. It carried only 53% favorable vote.

Finally, in June 1993, 73% of the voters approved a new constitution providing for multiparty government. Both the SPPF and Mancham's Democratic Party (DP) campaigned for its adoption. "Free and fair" presidential and National Assembly elections were held 23 July 1993. The SPPF won all but one of the directly elected legislative seats (DP won it), but an additional number of seats are distributed on the basis of the proportion of total vote. Composition of the National Assembly is 25 SPPF members and eight opposition members.

13GOVERNMENT

Under the constitution of 5 June 1979, the president was the head of state. Nominated by a congress of the Seychelles People's Progressive Front (SPPF), the only legal political party, the president ran for election unopposed. Legislative power was vested in the People's Assembly, which consisted of 25 members, 23 representing constituencies and 2 nominated by the president. Electoral candidates were chosen in primaries by SPPF members from up to three in each constituency nominated by the SPPF Central Executive Committee of each constituency. The cabinet was chosen by the president.

In June 1993, 73.6% of the voters approved a new constitution drafted by a bipartisan commission. It called for multiparty elections of a president and a National Assembly of 33 members, 22 directly elected and 11 allocated on a proportional basis. The new constitution guarantees extensive political and civil liberties. But it also allows the curtailment of freedom of expression in order to protect "the reputation, rights, and freedoms of private lives of persons." This is a thinly veiled limitation on the freedom of the press.

14POLITICAL PARTIES

Before 1978 there were two political parties, the Seychelles Democratic Party (SDP) and the Seychelles People's United Party (SPUP), both founded in 1964. In the last legislative elections prior to independence, on 25 April 1974, the SDP won 13 of 15 elective seats and the SPUP 2. Appointments in June 1975 brought total party strength to 18 for the SDP and 7 for the SPUP. The successor to the SPUP, the Seychelles People's Progressive Front (SPPF), was established in 1979 as the sole legal party, with the avowed objective of creating a Socialist state; the SDP was declared to have "disappeared." There were at least three opposition groups in exile. In the 1979 parliamentary elections, 55 candidates sanctioned by the SPPF competed for 23 elective seats in the People's Assembly. In the 1983 parliamentary elections, 17 of the 23 elected candidates ran unopposed; and in the December 1987 elections, 36 candidates, all of them members of the SPPF, competed for the 23 seats in the People's Assembly.

After René's announcement of a return to multiparty democracy, parties began to organize in preparation for an election to a constituent assembly in July 1992. Many dissidents returned from exile and the Democratic Party (DP) was reestablished. Also established were the Seychelles Party (PS), the Seychelles Democratic Movement (MSPD), and the Seychelles Liberal Party (SLP). There were eight opposition members in the 33-seat National Assembly after the 23 July 1993 elections. René's SPPF easily captured the presidency. The DP, the Parti Seselwa, the Seychellois National Movement and the National Alliance Party opposed the adoption of the new constitution in 1993 and contested the July 1993 elections as the United Opposition (UO) coalition.

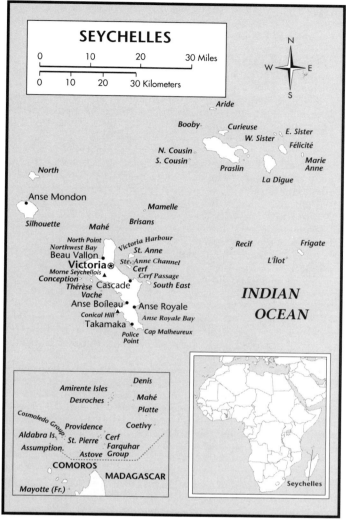

LOCATION: 3°41′ to 10°13′s; 46°12′ to 56°17′E. **TERRITORIAL SEA LIMIT:** 12 mi.

15LOCAL GOVERNMENT

The People's Assembly serves as the organ of local government. According to the 1979 constitution, there were 23 administrative districts.

16JUDICIAL SYSTEM

Magistrates' courts are normally the courts of the first instance. The Supreme Court hears appeals and takes original jurisdiction of some cases. The Court of Appeal hears appeals from the Supreme Court. Appointment to the post of chief justice is made by the president of Seychelles, and in consultation with the chief justice, the president appoints all other judges. Civil law is based on the French Napoleonic Code, while criminal law follows the British model. Members of the armed forces accused of serious offenses are tried by court-martial unless the President decrees otherwise.

A Constitutional Commission has called for an independent judiciary. The current procedure provides for judicial appointments to be made by a Constitutional Appointments Authority, which has at times allowed the ruling party to influence appointments.

17ARMED FORCES

The Seychelles People's Liberation Army (SPLA) was created in 1977, along with a People's Militia. They were merged in 1981 into the Seychelles People's Defense Force of 1,300 men equipped with 6 naval craft, 7 aircraft, and infantry weapons. In 1991 the SPLA spent $15 million on defense.

[18]INTERNATIONAL COOPERATION
Admitted to UN membership on 21 September 1976, Seychelles participates in ECA and all the nonregional specialized agencies except IAEA, IDA, ITU, and WIPO. The nation belongs to the African Development Bank, the Indian Ocean Commission, the Commonwealth of Nations, G-77, and OAU, is a de facto adherent of GATT, and signed the Law of the Sea.

[19]ECONOMY
With the opening of the international airport in 1971, the Seychelles economy began to move away from cash crops to the development of tourism, which now accounts for over 10% of GDP. Seychelles is heavily dependent on imports and financial aid. Although private enterprise and private property are permitted, the public and quasi-public sectors drive the economy. The government controls the importation, licensing, and distribution of virtually all goods and services, and exercises significant control over all phases of the economy.

[20]INCOME
In 1992 Seychelles' GNP was $378 million at current prices, or $5,480 per capita. For the period 1985–92 the average inflation rate was 3.4%, resulting in a real growth rate in per capita GNP of 4.1%.

In 1992 the GDP was $393 million in current US dollars. It is estimated that agriculture, hunting, forestry, and fishing contributed 5% to GDP; manufacturing, 10%; electricity, gas, and water, 1%; construction, 5%; wholesale and retail trade, 27%; transport, storage, and communication, 12%; finance, insurance, real estate, and business services, 11%; community, social, and personal services, 2%; and other sources, 28%.

[21]LABOR
In 1990, formal employment was 23,510, about 70% in the public sector, including parastatals. In addition, there are self-employed people, casual workers, domestic servants, and agricultural workers on smallholdings. A trade union federation, the National Workers' Union, was created in 1978 as an integral part of the SPPF and is the sole union. All job vacancies are filled through the government labor office, with preference for the unemployed.

[22]AGRICULTURE
Although agriculture has long been the basis of the Seychelles economy, it contributed only 5.1% of GDP in 1992. Production in 1992 included coconuts, 7,000 tons; bananas, about 2,000 tons; and 1,000 tons of copra. Other crops produced for export are cinnamon bark, vanilla, cloves, and patchouli (an essence used in soap and perfume). Sweet potatoes, yams, breadfruit, and cassava are grown in small quantities but are not sufficient to satisfy the local demand. Oranges, lemons, grapefruit, bananas, and mangoes meet the local requirement only in season. Tea planting began in the early 1960s; 1991 exports totaled 1,000 tons.

[23]ANIMAL HUSBANDRY
Seychelles is self-sufficient in the production of pork, poultry, and eggs. In 1992 there were about 19,000 hogs, 5,000 goats, and 2,000 head of cattle. Cattle of improved strains are imported and maintained on an intensive feedlot system.

[24]FISHING
Per-capita fish consumption in the Seychelles is very high, yet the development of industrial fishing is at its early stages. The development of port services for foreign tuna fishing fleets since the early 1980s has raised incomes and living standards, while diminishing the role of artisanal fishing. Fishing accounts for about 1% of GDP and about 8% of exports. Foreign vessels fishing in Seychelles waters must be licensed to operate within the 200-mi economic zone, which encompassed one of the world's richest tuna-fishing grounds. French investments have focused on tuna fishing and canning. The European Community, Korea, and Japan hold the key licenses to Seychelles coastal fishing. Fish landings by the domestic fleet totaled 1,501 tons of snapper and 423 tons of mackerel in 1991. The total catch that year was 5,913 tons.

[25]FORESTRY
Little natural forest remains. Coconut plantations are the main source of timber, aside from imports. A reforestation program, which projects the planting of 100 ha each year, will allow Seychelles to emerge self-sufficient in timber by the year 2000.

[26]MINING
Mineral production consists of small quantities of rock, coral, and sand for construction. Production of small quantities of guano, extracted from Assumption, ceased in the mid-1980s. Experimental granite quarrying was begun in 1981.

[27]ENERGY AND POWER
Practically the whole of Mahé is now supplied with electricity produced by diesel power in Victoria. The total installed capacity increased from 3,400 kw in 1972 to 29,000 kw in 1991, while the output reached 102 million kwh. Petroleum tar balls from underground seeps were known to occur for many years on the beaches of Coetivy Island, Mahé, and some other islands. Exploration began in 1969 and was continued by Texaco in the 1970s and Amoco in the 1980s. In 1984, the Seychelles National Oil Company (SNOC) was formed as a parastatal company. In late 1992, SNOC reported that studies on the tar balls continued to show an inclination for a significant oil potential.

[28]INDUSTRY
Light industry contributes about 10% of the GDP. The largest plant is the tuna cannery, opened in 1987. The rest are small and process local agricultural products. A tea factory handles locally grown tea. Others process copra and vanilla pods and extract coconut oil. There is a plastics factory, a brewery and soft drink bottler, and a cinnamon distiller. Salt, cigarettes, boats, furniture, steel products, publications, animal feeds, processed meats, dairy products, paints, and assembled televisions are also produced.

Electrical power needs are rising rapidly; demand jumped 20% between 1988 and 1989, to 94.3 million kwh. Power is generated entirely from imported petroleum. The Seychelles has made a priority the modernization and expansion of its Victoria port and linking it to the airport. Water system development is ongoing to relieve the problem of water shortages.

[29]SCIENCE AND TECHNOLOGY
In 1983 there were 24 scientists, engineers, and technicians engaged in research and experimental development, and research and development expenditures totaled r13 million. Seychelles Polytechnic has schools of agriculture, engineering, health studies, science, and maritime studies.

[30]DOMESTIC TRADE
The Seychelles Marketing Board, with wide powers over imports, distribution, and quality of goods, was established in 1984, but its monopoly on the sale of fruits and vegetables was abandoned in 1987. The small Chinese merchant class plays an important part in the retail trade. The variety of goods for sale is very

limited. There are price controls on most foodstuffs. Normal business hours are 8 AM to noon and 1:30 to 5 PM, Monday–Friday.

31 FOREIGN TRADE

Foreign trade is habitually in deficit. The principal exports (95.5% of the total in 1988) are copra, cinnamon bark, and frozen fish. Guano, tortoise shells, cloves, patchouli leaves, and seashells are also exported (4.0% of the 1988 total). Machinery and transport equipment comprised 30.8% of total imports in 1988. Basic manufactures followed at 26.5%, food, beverages, and tobacco at 20.4%; and petroleum products at 14.1%

In 1988, 56.2% of Seychelles exports went to France and another 11.2% to the UK. The leading import suppliers were Kuwait (16.7%), the UK (14.8%), South Africa (13.1%), and Singapore (10.0%).

32 BALANCE OF PAYMENTS

Development aid, income from tourism, and earnings from reexports have generally been sufficient to offset Seychelles' persistent visible trade deficit. As of 31 May 1987, foreign exchange reserves totaled $14 million. The foreign debt was estimated at $111 million at the end of 1985.

33 BANKING AND SECURITIES

The Seychelles Monetary Authority, established in 1978 as the bank of issue, became the Central Bank of Seychelles in 1983. Other government banks are the Seychelles Savings Bank and the Development Bank of Seychelles. There were branches of five private foreign-owned commercial banks in 1993. As of 1993 commercial banks held foreign assets totaling R40.3 million. The money supply amounted to R1,104.3 million at the end of 1986. There is no stock exchange in Seychelles.

34 INSURANCE

All private insurance companies were nationalized in 1983 and their business transferred to the State Assurance Corp. In 1985–86, non-life insurance accounted for 99.4% of all premium payments.

35 PUBLIC FINANCE

Annual budgets of increasing deficits were common in the 1980s. The public sector is responsible for two-thirds of Seychelles' employment, and the budget amounts to about 50% of GDP. Public investment focuses on social and physical infrastructure, tourism, and export activities. In 1990, the budget deficit of recent years transformed into a surplus of 2% of GDP (including transfers). The decline in tourism (largely due to the Persian Gulf Crisis) in 1991 helped cause a budget deficit of 2.5% of GDP, which increased to 4.5% in 1992 and an estimated 6% in 1993.

The following table shows actual revenues and expenditures for 1988 and 1989 in millions of rupees.

	1988	1989
REVENUE AND GRANTS		
Tax revenue	613.4	770.8
Non-tax revenue	170.6	191.5
Capital revenue	0.2	0.8
Grants	24.0	26.4
TOTAL	808.2	989.5
EXPENDITURES & LENDING MINUS REPAYMENTS	864.4	1,109.3
Deficit/Surplus	−56.2	−119.8

In 1988 Seychelles's total public debt stood at R1,408.3 million, of which R618.3 million was financed abroad.

36 TAXATION

Income tax is levied on net income at progressive rates. Profits of foreign enterprises are taxed at a flat rate. The principal indirect taxes are customs duties and a turnover tax. In 1982, a tax on gross gaming revenue was added on top of the normal profits tax.

37 CUSTOMS AND DUTIES

All imports are controlled by the Seychelles Marketing Board (SMB), which places quotas on certain imports (such as motor vehicles) and other types of restrictions on other items. Prohibited goods include arms and ammunition, dangerous drugs, pornographic materials, and spearguns. Import tariffs are 30% of c.i.f. value.

38 FOREIGN INVESTMENT

The government offers full repatriation of after-tax profits; normal exemption from import duties for machinery, spare parts, and raw materials; and possible tariff protection. While parastatals are common in Seychelles, there is no policy of nationalization, though joint ventures are preferred when foreign capital is involved. Public and private investment is sought for the tourist, fishing, agriculture, and manufacturing sectors.

39 ECONOMIC DEVELOPMENT

The 1985–89 plan sought to create jobs and emphasized developing cash crops, tourism, and the fishing industry. The 1990–94 plan emphasized the need to attract foreign investment. Of considerable interest to donors in the 1990s is the 10-year plan to improve the Seychelles environment.

40 SOCIAL DEVELOPMENT

The Seychelles are sometimes called a model welfare state. The National Provident Fund makes payments for marriage, emigration, invalidity, survivors, and old age. Employees and employers are required to make monthly contributions (5% of salary and 10% of payroll, respectively). There is also a workers' compensation scheme. Health services are free for all residents.

41 HEALTH

In 1984 there were 5 hospitals, as well as 19 clinics and a number of health centers throughout the islands; in all there were 331 hospital beds in 1985. In 1990, the Seychelles had 90 doctors, 1 pharmacist, 9 dentists, and 279 nurses. In 1992 there were 1,600 births. The infant mortality rate in 1992 was 16 per 1,000 live births, and average life expectancy was 71 years. In the same year, 92% of the country's children were vaccinated against measles and, in 1990, an estimated 220 cases of tuberculosis were reported.

42 HOUSING

As of the 1981–82 census update, most homes were wood (53%) or stone (44%) with corrugated iron roofs; many rural houses were thatched. Owners occupied 62% of dwellings, 19% were rented privately, 9% were provided by an employer, and 8% were rented from the government. Of all housing units, 45% had flush toilets and 57% had electricity. The Home Ownership Scheme lends money for building costs to low-income families, and the Housing Loan Fund provides loans for families who want to purchase or build their own homes. Concrete-block housing developments have been constructed.

43 EDUCATION

Since 1980, public education has been free and compulsory for the nine-year period of primary schooling for children between the ages of 6 and 15. Secondary education, which was originally for two years, was reduced to one year in 1991. In 1989, there were 25 primary schools with 781 teachers. In 1991 the students in primary schools totaled 14,669. In secondary schools, there were 4,396 students in 1990 and 4,495 in 1991. Of the 1991 figure, 302 were in teacher training programs and 1,302 were in vocational courses in 1991. Seychelles does not provide education at university level, but there is a teacher-training college and a polytechnic institute. Only members of the National Youth Service can apply to the teacher-training college. Adult literacy was estimated at 85% in 1990. In the absence of higher education facilities, many students study abroad, especially the UK.

44LIBRARIES AND MUSEUMS

The National Archives and Museum and a National Library (43,000 volumes) are both located in Victoria (Mahé Island).

45MEDIA

The number of telephones in use was 13,937 in 1991. Radio-Television Seychelles, which is government owned, broadcasts in English, French, and Creole; a Protestant missionary group also broadcasts. There were about 33,000 radios in 1991. Television service began in 1983; there were about 6,000 receivers in 1991.

There is one daily newspaper—*Seychelles Nation* (1991 circulation about 3,200)—published by the government in English, French, and Creole. The president has the authority to censor publications.

46ORGANIZATIONS

Trade groups include the Seychelles Chamber of Commerce and Industry and the Seychelles Farmers' Association. The Women's Association and the Youth Organization are arms of the SPPF.

47TOURISM, TRAVEL, AND RECREATION

The prosperity of Seychelles depends on tourism. Visitors can enjoy coral beaches, water sports including scuba diving, water skiing, and windsurfing, and boat or yacht tours of the islands. The archipelago's wildlife is also a popular tourist attraction. There were 98,000 visitor arrivals in 1991, largely from Italy, France, the UK, and South Africa; income from tourism was US$99 million. The 1,840 hotel rooms and 3,680 beds were filled to 56% of capacity. Visas are not normally required.

48FAMOUS SEYCHELLOIS

The leader of the SDP, Sir James Richard Marie Mancham (b.1939), became Seychelles' first president in 1976. He was deposed in 1977 by France Albert René (b.1935).

49DEPENDENCIES

Seychelles has no territories or colonies.

50BIBLIOGRAPHY

Benedict, Marion and Burton. *Women and Money in Seychelles.* Berkeley: University of California Press, 1982.

Bennett, George. *Seychelles Pramila Ramgulam Bennett.* Oxford, England; Santa Barbara, Calif.: Clio Press, 1993.

Franda, Marcus. *The Seychelles: Unquiet Islands.* Boulder, Colo.: Westview, 1982.

Lionnot, Guy. *The Seychelles.* Harrisburg, Pa.: Stackpole, 1972.

McAteer, William. *Rivals in Eden: A History of the French Settlement and British Conquest of the Seychelles Islands, 1742–1818.* Sussex, Eng.: Book Guild, 1990.

Vine, Peter. *Seychelles.* London, Eng.: Immel Pub. Co., 1989.

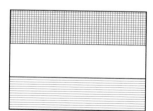

SIERRA LEONE

Republic of Sierra Leone

CAPITAL: Freetown.

FLAG: The national flag is a tricolor of green, white, and blue horizontal stripes.

ANTHEM: Begins "High we exalt thee, realm of the free, Great is the love we have for thee."

MONETARY UNIT: The leone (Le) is a paper currency of 100 cents. There are coins of 1/2, 1, 5, 10, 20, and 50 cents, and notes of 1, 2, 5, 10, 20, 50, 100, and 500 leones. Le1 = $0.0017 (or $1 = Le577.23).

WEIGHTS AND MEASURES: The metric system is employed.

HOLIDAYS: New Year's Day, 1 January; Independence Day, 27 April; Bank Holiday, August; Christmas, 24–25 December; Boxing Day, 26 December. Movable religious holidays include Good Friday, Easter Monday, Whitmonday, 'Id al-Fitr, 'Id-al-'Adha', and Milad an-Nabi.

TIME: GMT.

¹LOCATION, SIZE, AND EXTENT

Situated on the west coast of Africa, Sierra Leone has an area of 71,740 sq km (27,699 sq mi), extending 338 km (210 mi) N–S and 304 km (189 mi) E–W. Comparatively, the area occupied by Sierra Leone is slightly smaller than the state of South Carolina. It is bounded on the N and E by Guinea, on the SE by Liberia, and on the S and W by the Atlantic Ocean, with a total boundary length of 1,360 km (845 mi). In addition to the mainland proper, Sierra Leone also includes the offshore Banana and Turtle islands and Sherbro Island, as well as other small islets.

Sierra Leone's capital city, Freetown, is located on the Atlantic Coast.

²TOPOGRAPHY

The Sierra Leone Peninsula in the extreme west is mostly mountainous, rising to about 884 m (2,900 ft). The western part of the country, excluding the Peninsula, consists of coastal mangrove swamps. Farther east, a coastal plain extends inland for about 100–160 km (60–100 mi); many rivers in this area are navigable for short distances. Stretches of wooded hill country lead east and northeast to a plateau region generally ranging in elevation from 300 to 610 m (1,000 to 2,000 ft). There are peaks of over 1,830 m (6,000 ft), reaching a maximum of 1,948 m (6,390 ft) at Bintimani in the Loma Mountains.

³CLIMATE

Temperatures and humidity are high, and rainfall is heavy. The mean temperature is about 27°C (81°F) on the coast and almost as high on the eastern plateau. There are two distinct seasons: the dry season, from November to April, and the wet season, over the rest of the year, with the heaviest precipitation in July, August, and September. Rainfall is greatest along the coast, especially in the mountains, where there is more than 580 cm (230 in) annually, but it averages more than 315 cm (125 in) a year in most of the country, with 366 cm (144 in) at Freetown. The relative humidity ranges from an average of 80% during the wet season to about 50% during the dry season.

⁴FLORA AND FAUNA

About 25–35% of the land area, mostly in the north, consists of savanna or grasslands; 20–25%, mostly in the south-center, is low bush; another 20–25%, in the southeast, is secondary forest or high bush; 10–20% is swampland; and 3–5% is primary rain forest.

The emerald cuckoo, which has been described as the most beautiful bird in Africa, is found in Sierra Leone, although it has disappeared from the rest of West Africa. Other species include the Senegal firefinch, common bulbul, little African swift, Didric cuckoo, bronze manakin, cattle egret (or "tickbird"), and many birds that breed in Europe but winter in Sierra Leone. Crocodiles and hippopotamuses are indigenous to the river regions of the coastal plain.

⁵ENVIRONMENT

Water pollution is a significant problem in Sierra Leone due to mining by-products and sewage. The nation has 38.4 cubic miles of water. Eighty-nine percent is used for farming and 4% for industrial purposes. Twenty percent of the nation's city dwellers and 80% of those living in rural areas do not have pure water. The nation's cities produce 0.3 million tons of solid waste per year.

Population pressure, leading to an intensification of agriculture, has resulted in soil depletion, while lumbering, cattle grazing, and slash-and-burn farming have decimated the primary forest. By 1985, deforestation had progressed to a total of 23 square miles. Agricultural lands are gradually replacing forestlands due to the need for food by a population that increased by 80% during the period between 1963 and 1990. Hunting for food has reduced the stock of wild mammals, and Cutamba Killimi National Park, which has some wildlife species found only in this part of West Africa, is exploited by poachers.

Government agencies with environmental responsibilities include the Ministry of Agriculture, Natural Resources, and Forestry, Ministry of Mines, Ministry of Lands and Human Development, Ministry of Energy and Power, and Ministry of Economic Planning and National Development. In 1994, 13 of Sierra Leone's mammal species and seven bird species are endangered. Twelve of the nation's plant species are also threatened. Endangered species in Sierra Leone include the white-breasted Guinea fowl.

6 POPULATION

The population of Sierra Leone was 4,619,433, according to a 1994 estimate, with an average density of 64 per sq km (167 per sq mi). A population of 5,395,000 was projected for the year 2000, assuming a crude birthrate of 45.5 per 1,000 population, a crude death rate of 19.6, and a net natural increase of 25.9 during 1995–2000. Freetown, the capital, had an estimated population of 669,000 in 1990, when about 32% of all Sierra Leoneans lived in urban areas. Other main towns are Koindu, Bo, Kenema, and Makeni.

7 MIGRATION

Historically, there has been considerable movement over the borders to and from Guinea and Liberia. In the mid-1980s, the number of nonnative Africans was estimated at 30,000. At the end of 1992, 5,900 Africans were refugees in Sierra Leona. At the end of 1991, 236,000 people in Sierra Leone had been displaced by the spillover of the Liberian civil war. Many of them fled to Guinea, which had more than 120,000 refugees from Sierra Leone at the end of 1992.

8 ETHNIC GROUPS

The African population is composed of some 18 ethnic groups, the 2 largest being the Mende (about 34% of the population) and Temne (about 31%). Other peoples are the Bullom, Fulani, Gola, Kissi, Kono, Koranko, Krim, Kru, Limba, Loko, Malinké, Sherbro, Susu, Vai, Yalunka, and Creole. Most of the 40,000–80,000 Creoles, descendants of settlers from Europe, the West Indies, North America, and other parts of West Africa, live on the Peninsula. Perhaps 8,000 Asians (mostly Lebanese) and Europeans live in Sierra Leone, mainly in the towns.

9 LANGUAGES

The Mende and Temne languages are widely spoken in the south and north, respectively. The lingua franca is Krio, the mother tongue of the Creoles, derived largely from English, with words added from various West African languages. English is the official language.

10 RELIGIONS

Approximately one-half of the population followed African traditional religions in the early 1990s. Earlier (1980), about 40% were Muslims (primarily in the north and west). About 10% were Christians (primarily in the Western Area) including, in 1993, 2.1% Roman Catholic. Christian missions are active throughout the country, and Muslim missions, chiefly Ahmadi, are active mainly in the Western Area.

11 TRANSPORTATION

In 1970 there were more than 580 km (360 mi) of railway, but by the end of 1975, following an IBRD recommendation, Sierra Leone had dismantled most of its rail system and replaced it with new roadways; in the mid-1980s, only 84 km (52 mi) of narrow-gauge railway remained, connecting the closed iron mines at Marampa with the port of Pepel, on the Sierra Leone River. The line remains operable but is in limited use. Sierra Leone has about 7,400 km (4,600 mi) of roads, of which some 15.5% were paved. A 43-km (28-mi) road link between Waterloo and Masiaka is to be rebuilt at a cost of $13.9 million. In 1991 there were 47,659 registered motor vehicles, including 35,870 automobiles, and 11,789 commercial vehicles.

Freetown has one of the finest natural harbors in the world, with an excellent deepwater quay, built in 1953. In 1970, work was completed on an extension that provides the port with berth facilities for six to eight ships and about 24 hectares (60 acres) of storage area. Pepel specializes in the export of iron ore, and Point Sam, the Sherbro River terminal, handles bauxite and rutile.

Bonthe and Sulima are other ports. Sierra Leone has many rivers, but most are navigable only over short distances for about three months of the year, during the rainy season.

An international airport at Lungi is connected by ferry to Freetown, across the bay. Extension of the runway was completed in 1968, bringing the airport to top-class international airport standard. It is served by about a dozen international airlines with regular flights to Europe, North and South America, and the rest of West Africa. Domestic service operates from Hastings Airfield, 22 km (14 mi) from Freetown, linking the capital to nearly all the large provincial towns.

The national air carrier, founded in 1961 as Sierra Leone Airways, was reconstituted in 1982 as Sierra Leone Airlines, under the management of Alia-Royal Jordanian Airline, which holds a 20% share.

12 HISTORY

Archaeological research indicates that by AD 800 the use of iron had been introduced into what is now Sierra Leone and that by AD 1000 the coastal peoples were practicing agriculture. Beginning perhaps in the 13th century, migrants arrived from the more advanced savanna lands to the north and east.

European contact began in 1462 with the Portuguese explorer Pedro da Cintra, who gave the mountainous Peninsula the name Sierra Leone ("Lion Mountains"). From the 16th to the early 19th century, the region was raided for slaves for the Atlantic trade, and later in the 19th century, it was ravaged by African war leaders and slavers.

The colony of Sierra Leone was founded by British philanthropists to relieve the horrors of this slave trade. Granville Sharp, a leader in the movement to abolish slavery, planned it as a home for African slaves freed in England. In 1787, he sent out the first settlers to what he called "The Province of Freedom." In the following year, one of the Temne kings and his subordinate chiefs sold and ceded a strip of land on the north shore of the Sierra Leone Peninsula to Capt. John Taylor on behalf of the "free community of settlers, their heirs and successors, lately arrived from England, and under the protection of the British Government." A few years later, they were joined by settlers of African origin from England, Nova Scotia (freed slaves who, as loyalists, had fled the American Revolution), and Jamaica.

The Sierra Leone Company, of which Sharp was a director, was formed in 1791 to administer the settlement. The land did not prove as fertile as described, and the settlement was the victim of attacks by neighboring tribes and by a French squadron. The burden of defense and settlement proved too heavy for the company, and Sierra Leone was transferred to the crown in 1808. The colony received additions of land up to 1861 through various treaties of friendship and cession from the local chiefs.

After 1807, when the British Parliament passed an act making the slave trade illegal, the new colony was used as a base from which the act could be enforced. Beginning in 1808, hundreds, and sometimes thousands, of slaves were freed each year, most of them remaining in Sierra Leone. In 1896, a British protectorate was declared over the hinterland of Sierra Leone, which was separate from the colony. Revolts in 1898 were provoked mainly by attempts to extend British colonial jurisdiction into the protectorate.

A 1924 constitution provided for the election of three members to a Legislative Council on a restricted franchise, and the constitution of 1951 provided for an elected majority, resulting in African rule. In 1957, the Legislative Council was replaced by a House of Representatives, most members of which were elected, and the literacy requirement for voters was dropped. In 1958, Milton Margai became Sierra Leone's first prime minister; in 1960, he led a delegation to London to establish conditions for full independence.

Independence

Sierra Leone became an independent country within the Commonwealth of Nations on 27 April 1961. Milton Margai continued as prime minister until his death in 1964, when he was succeeded by his half-brother, Albert Margai, who held office until the national elections in March 1967. The outcome of the elections was disputed, but the All-People's Congress (APC) claimed a plurality of the seats in the House of Representatives. Before Siaka Stevens, chairman of the APC, could take office as prime minister, he was ousted in a bloodless coup led by the army chief, Brig. David Lansana. Martial law was declared, and a National Reformation Council remained in control for 13 months, until 18 April 1968, when it was overthrown by the Anti-Corruption Revolutionary Movement, a military group that formed the National Interim Council. On 26 April 1968, Stevens was installed as prime minister of a civilian government. Continuing political unrest prompted the declaration of a state of emergency in 1970 and a ban on the newly created United Democratic Party, an opposition group whose leaders were arrested.

In 1971, after an abortive military coup which was suppressed with aid from Guinea, a new constitution was adopted. The country was declared a republic on 19 April 1971. Two days later, Siaka Stevens, then prime minister, became the nation's first president. National elections were held in May 1973, and the APC won a nearly unanimous victory following the decision of the opposition Sierra Leone People's Party to withdraw its candidates because of alleged electoral irregularities. An alleged plot to overthrow Stevens failed in 1974, and in March 1976, he was elected without opposition for a second five-year term as president. In 1978, a new constitution was adopted, making the country a one-party state.

An economic slowdown, coupled with revelations of government corruption, led to a general strike in September 1981, called by the Sierra Leone Labour Congress; some labor leaders and other government critics were temporarily detained under emergency regulations, but the government met a key demand of the strikers by moving to reduce the prices of basic commodities. Violence and irregularities marked the parliamentary elections held in 1982, which were limited to the APC.

Stevens did not run for reelection as president in 1985, yielding power to his handpicked successor, Maj. Gen. Joseph Saidu Momoh, the armed forces commander, whose nomination by the APC was ratified in his unopposed election in October 1985. Parliamentary elections were held in May 1986. Following an alleged attempt to assassinate Momoh in March 1987, over 60 persons were arrested, including First Vice-President Francis Minah, who was removed from office. An extensive reshuffling of the cabinet followed. Further reports of alleged coup attempts followed.

In April 1991, Sierra Leone was invaded from Liberia by forces commanded by Liberian rebel, Charles Taylor. Domestic support within Sierra Leone mounted and by 29 April 1992, Momoh was overthrown in a military coup. Momoh fled to Guinea. A National Provisional Ruling Council (NPRC) was created but, shortly afterward, on 2 May, the head of the five-member junta, Lt. Col. Yahya, was arrested by his colleagues and replaced by Capt. Valentine Strasser, who was formally designated head of state.

The Strasser government soon limited the status of the 1991 constitution by a series of decrees and public notices. It also imposed a number of laws limiting political freedoms. The NPRC dissolved parliament and political parties. They ruled by decree. Strasser talked of returning Sierra Leone to multiparty democracy. His main goal was to end the fighting in the southeast where the forces of the National Patriot Front of Liberia and Sierra Leone dissidents were engaging a less-than-committed Sierra Leone armed force. Forces from the ECOWAS Monitoring Group sought to create a buffer along the boundary between the two

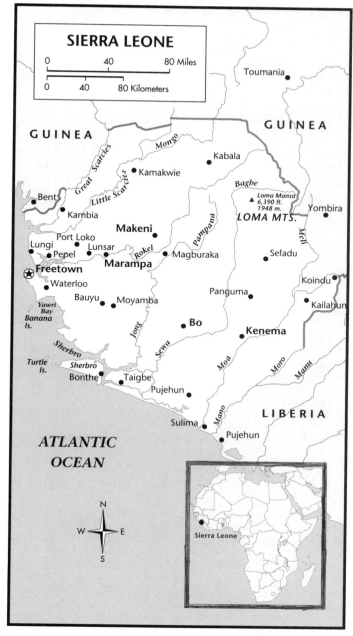

LOCATION: 6°55′ to 10°N; 10°16′ to 13°18′w. **BOUNDARY LENGTHS:** Guinea, 652 km (405 mi); Liberia, 306 km (190 mi); Atlantic coastline, 406 km (252 mi). **TERRITORIAL SEA LIMIT:** 12 mi.

countries. The rebellion led by Foday Sankoh of the Revolutionary United Front (RUF) simmered throughout 1993, although it seemed to falter as the Liberian rebels across the border lost ground. Still the military situation became stalemated. In November 1993, Strasser announced a unilateral ceasefire and an amnesty for rebels.

Through 1992 and 1993, Strasser used the security situation to consolidate his power. In December 1992, government executed 26 alleged coup plotters from the Momoh government. In mid-1993, Strasser arrested his vice-president, Capt. Solomon Musa.

The NPRC established a Supreme Council of State, including NPRC members, other military officers and one civilian. Both bodies formulate government policy. Day-by-day operations are overseen by department secretaries who together comprise the cabinet.

In November 1993, Strasser issued a timetable for a transition to democracy to culminate in general elections in late 1995. A month later, the NPRC released a "Working Document on the Constitution" to serve as the basis for public debates leading to a constitutional referendum in May 1995.

13GOVERNMENT

Under the constitution adopted in June 1978, Sierra Leone had a republican form of government. Executive authority was exercised by the president and cabinet. The president was the leader of the sole recognized, constitutionally permitted party, the APC, and was chosen by a conference of delegates; he then became the only eligible presidential candidate, assuming office for seven years if he received a majority of valid votes in a national election. The president appointed cabinet ministers and two vice-presidents from among the members of the legislature.

The legislature, a unicameral House of Representatives presided over by a speaker, consisted (as of 1986) of 127 members, of whom 105 were popularly elected, 12 were paramount chiefs elected by chiefdom councils in their respective districts, and 10 were appointed by the president. The representatives were elected for a five-year term, but elections could be called earlier. Any citizen 25 years of age or older who is able to speak and read English was qualified for election to the House, but candidates first had to be approved by APC officials. Suffrage was universal at age 21.

A new constitution came into force on 1 October 1991, but it was superseded by the military junta established after the 29 April 1992 coup. Shortly thereafter, the parliament and political parties were dissolved and the NPRC now rules by decree through a Supreme Council of State (SCS) and a Council of State Secretaries (CSS-Cabinet). In November 1993 they announced a timetable leading to multiparty democracy and general elections in 1995.

14POLITICAL PARTIES

The sole parliamentary party, the APC, which had been in power from 1967 until April 1992, was formed in 1960 by Siaka Stevens, who was president of Sierra Leone from 1971 to 1985. The Sierra Leone People's Party (SLPP), formed in 1951, ruled the country from its inception until 1967, when the APC claimed to have won a plurality of the seats in a disputed parliamentary election. The APC continued to gain parliamentary power and in the 1973 elections won all but 1 of the 85 elective seats, the SLPP having withdrawn its candidates as a protest against alleged electoral irregularities. In 1978, a new constitution made the APC the sole legal party; the SLPP was formally dissolved, and all members of parliament were required to declare themselves members of the APC on penalty of losing their seats.

The history of the APC arises out of that of the SLPP. The SLPP was formed in 1951 by uniting the Sierra Leone Organization Society, founded in the protectorate in 1946, and the Freetown People's Party, founded in the colony by the Rev. Etheldred Jones, also known as Lamina Sankoh. Although the SLPP won only 2 seats of the 7 open to election in 1951, it was given recognition when the indirectly elected protectorate members and eight paramount chiefs joined with it. In 1953, Milton Margai became chief minister, and in 1957, the SLPP won 26 of the 39 seats being contested.

During this pre-APC period, the National Council of Sierra Leone (NCSL), founded in 1951, was the principal opposition group. It was influential only in the colony and favored a federal constitution with separate assemblies for the colony and the protectorate. When universal adult suffrage was introduced in 1957, the NCSL lost all its seats in the legislature. The United People's Party (UPP) was founded in 1956 by Cyril Rogers-Wright and Wallace Johnson to unite the interests of the colony and the protectorate. In the 1957 general elections, it won 1 seat in the legislature and gained 3 more after election petitions to the courts, so that it then constituted the principal legislative opposition.

In September 1958, Siaka Stevens and Milton Margai's half-brother, Albert Margai, withdrew from the SLPP and formed the People's National Party (PNP) to pursue a more militant policy. In 1960, the PNP and UPP joined the United National Front of all parties for the April constitutional talks in London. A national coalition government was formed, and Albert Margai became a cabinet minister.

Stevens then left the United Front to form a new opposition group, the Elections Before Independence Movement (EBIM). Expelled from the PNP, he transformed the EBIM into the APC and, with support from younger radicals and much of the trade union movement, campaigned for a neutralist foreign policy and the need for a general election before independence. In March 1961, Stevens and some of his supporters were charged with sedition, libel, and incitement and were jailed just before independence under emergency regulations. They were later released and acquitted of the charges.

In the election of 25 May 1962, the SLPP won 28 of 62 seats for ordinary members of the House of Representatives, the APC 16, the Sierra Leone Progressive Movement 4, and independents 14. After the election returns were announced, 12 of the independents declared themselves members of the SLPP, and Milton Margai was able to form a new government. Upon his death on 28 April 1964, Albert Margai became prime minister. Thirteen months of military rule followed the disputed 1967 elections, after which Siaka Stevens, leader of the APC, assumed the prime ministership.

In September 1970, another opposition group, the United Democratic Party, was formed. Shortly afterward, a state of emergency was declared, and on 8 October, the party was banned. The SLPP won 15 seats in the 1977 elections, the last in which an opposition party was allowed to participate. In the 1983 balloting, 173 candidates competed for 66 seats, and the remaining 19 elective seats (mostly held by members of the outgoing government) were uncontested. In the 1986 balloting, 335 candidates competed for the 105 popularly elected seats. Over half the sitting members, including three cabinet ministers, were defeated, and over 60% of those elected were newcomers to the House.

After the April 1992 military coup, all political parties were banned and parliament was dissolved. Currently the NPRC, the military junta that rules by decree, is planning to turn power over to a civilian government after multiparty elections in late 1995.

15LOCAL GOVERNMENT

Sierra Leone is divided into the Western Area (the former colony) and the Northern, Eastern, and Southern provinces (formerly the protectorate). The three provinces are divided into a total of 12 districts with 148 chiefdoms. Local government in the Western Area is administered by municipalities. Rural areas are governed by village committees, which send members to district councils, which in turn are represented in a rural area council.

Each province has a resident minister as administrative head. Local units within the provinces are, in ascending order of importance, villages, extended villages or sections, chiefdoms, and district councils. The 12 district councils, which contain elected members as well as paramount chiefs, are responsible for primary education, health centers, agricultural extension work, social welfare, community development, and transportation services (roads, bridges, and ferries).

16JUDICIAL SYSTEM

Local courts apply traditional law and customs in the chiefdoms. Magistrates hold court in the various districts and in Freetown, administering the English-based code of law. Appeals from magistrates' courts are heard by the High Court, which also has unlimited original civil and criminal jurisdiction. Appeals from High Court decisions may be made to the Court of Appeal and finally to the Supreme Court, consisting of a chief justice and not fewer than three other justices. The attorney-general is a cabinet minister and head of the state law office, which is administered by the solicitor-general. Many of the justices, magistrates, and other lawyers are Sierra Leoneans trained in British universities or at Inns of Court in London.

The National Provisional Ruling Council (NPRC) formed after the 1992 military coup has not altered the previously existing judicial system, but it has set up special commissions of inquiry to handle some cases. A 1992 decree authorizes the government to create a Special Military Tribunal to try persons involved in "rebellion" against the NPRC or who commit serious crimes. In 1993, the decree was amended to permit appeal from the Tribunal to the courts.

The judiciary is not independent in practice and remains subject to manipulation.

[17]ARMED FORCES

In 1993, the Sierra Leone armed services had about 6,150 members, including 6,000 ground troops in one brigade group and 150 naval (coast guard) personnel, in addition to an 800-member state security force. Military service is voluntary. Sierra Leone sent 400 men to Liberia and hosts 800 Nigerian soldiers.

[18]INTERNATIONAL COOPERATION

Admitted as the 100th member of the UN on 27 September 1961, Sierra Leone participates in ECA and all the nonregional specialized agencies. The country belongs to the African Development Bank, Commonwealth of Nations, ECOWAS, G-77, and OAU. During 1980–81, President Siaka Stevens served as Chairman of the OAU, and Freetown hosted the organization's summit conference in July 1980; high-level ECA and ECOWAS meetings took place in Freetown in the following year. Sierra Leone is a signatory to GATT, the Lomé Convention, and the Law of the Sea.

Sierra Leone signed a defense pact with Guinea in 1971 allowing for the exchange of some army personnel. In October 1973, Sierra Leone and Liberia concluded the Mano River Union agreement, aimed at establishing an economic union of the two countries; Guinea joined the union in 1980. Trade restrictions among the three nations were abolished in 1981, and a common external tariff was established for most items of trade.

[19]ECONOMY

Although Sierra Leone is a potentially rich country with diverse resources, which include diamonds, gold, rutile, bauxite, and a variety of agricultural products, the economy has been severely depressed over the past two decades. Currently, agriculture employs 70% of the labor force.

The country has a chronic balance-of-payments deficit aggravated by a rebellion in the export-producing diamond regions of the country. The economy suffered from low production, poor export performance, large budget deficits, shortage of essential goods, deterioration of infrastructural facilities, inability to service external debts, a prevasive parallel market, and inflation. Despite all, the government has adhered to a structural adjustment program established in 1991–92 that called for a reduction in the number of civil service employees, increased privatization of the economy, increased taxation, and fiscal discipline. The program has produced major improvements in the stability of the exchange rate and reduced inflation. Consequently, Sierra Leone is gaining the support of the World Bank, IMF, and other international agencies, a step critical to any chance for economic improvement.

[20]INCOME

In 1992 Sierra Leone's GNP was $726 million at current prices, or $170 per capita. For the period 1985–92 the average inflation rate was 75.3%, resulting in a real growth rate in per capita GNP of 0.0%.

In 1992 the GDP was $696 million in current US dollars. It is estimated that agriculture, hunting, forestry, and fishing contributed 35% to GDP; mining and quarrying, 9%; manufacturing, 9%; construction, 1%; wholesale and retail trade, 20%; transport, storage, and communication, 9%; finance, insurance, real estate, and business services, 12%; and other sources, 4%.

[21]LABOR

Agriculture is the occupation of at least two-thirds of the population; manufacturing engages only 2% of the labor force. Only 70,200 Sierra Leoneans were wage earners as of 1988 (in establishments with six or more workers). Registered unemployment was 2,432 in 1986.

The 1991 constitution provides for the right of association, and all workers (including civil servants) have the right to join trade unions of their choice. The trade union movement in Sierra Leone, one of the oldest in West Africa, dates back to 1913, when Wallace Johnson organized the Customs Employees Union. Under his influence, other unions developed, and in 1943, the first Sierra Leone Trade Union Council (TUC) was formed. The Sierra Leone Council of Labour, which replaced the TUC in 1946, merged in May 1966 with the Sierra Leone Federation of Labour to form the Sierra Leone Labour Congress (SLLC). All unions are members of the SLLC, although membership is voluntary. In the mid-1980s, the SLLC had over a dozen constituent unions totaling about 40,000 members.

[22]AGRICULTURE

Agriculture is the primary occupation in Sierra Leone, employing two-thirds of the labor force and accounting for 40% of GDP. Most Sierra Leoneans live on small, scattered farms, following a scheme of bush-fallow rotation, slash-and-burn field preparation, and limited use of fertilizer.

Rice, grown by 80% of farmers, is the most important subsistence crop and, along with millet in the northeast, is a food staple; an estimated 420,000 tons were produced in 1992. A rice exporter in the past, Sierra Leone imported 107,200 tons at a cost of $35 million in 1992. The Rice Research Institute, located in the Northern Province, breeds high-yielding varieties for seed. Other domestic food crops include cassava, yams, peanuts, corn, pineapples, coconuts, tomatoes, and pepper.

Agricultural exports, which in 1992 amounted to a little under 8% of the total export value, include coffee, cocoa, palm kernels, piassava, kola nuts, and ginger.

Coffee is grown in the Eastern and Southern provinces. Coffee exports, which started with 3 tons in 1890, rose to about 8,200 tons in 1990, with a value of us$80.7 million. Cocoa is grown in the Kenema and Kailahun districts of the Eastern Province and in the Pujehun District of the Southern Province, mainly on small-holdings of about 0.4–1.2 hectares (1–3 acres). In 1992, exports of cocoa totaled 3,900 tons, valued at $4 million.

Palm produce is derived from stands of wild palms, mainly in the northeast and southeast. Although there is substantial local consumption of palm kernels, they are a major agricultural export, averaging 75,000 tons a year in the 1930s but only 100 tons, valued at $20,000, in 1991.

Piassava, a raffia palm fiber used for broom and brush bristles, is grown in the swampy areas of the extreme south. Small amounts of kola nuts were also exported, and modest crops of bananas, pineapples, and sugarcane were grown.

The monopoly of Sierra Leone Produce Marketing as the sole exporter of agricultural commodities was recently abolished. The

March 1991 invasion of rebels from Liberia in the eastern and southeastern provinces severely damaged agricultural production and exports; it could take several years to rehabilitate production.

23ANIMAL HUSBANDRY

Estimates of livestock in 1992 were 333,000 head of cattle, 275,000 sheep, 152,000 goats, and 50,000 hogs. Large numbers of Ndama cattle are kept, mainly by nomads in the savanna area of the northeast. Poultry farmers had an estimated 6 million chickens in 1992.

24FISHING

Fresh fish is not a staple for the country as a whole but is much prized in Freetown and other parts of the Peninsula. The fishing industry, which once was confined to inshore waters, has spread into the middle waters and includes canoe, industrial, freshwater, and shellfish fisheries. Total fish and shellfish production in 1991 was 50,000 tons. Shrimp is the main export. The government has a joint venture agreement with Maritime Protection Services Sierra Leone Ltd., the purpose of which is to prevent poaching, protect artisanal fishing, increase revenue, and conserve maritime resources.

25FORESTRY

Although much of Sierra Leone was once forested, intensive farming gradually eliminated most of the forest area. There are still about 2 million hectares (5 million acres) of forests and woodland, with most of the prime forestland in the government estate in the mountainous eastern half of the country and in the Western Area hills. In 1991, an estimated total of 3.1 million cu m of roundwood was harvested, 96% of it for fuel.

26MINING

Alluvial diamonds, first discovered in Kono District in 1930, are widely scattered over a large area but particularly along the upper Sewa River. Officially recorded production fell from 466,000 carats in 1948 to 18,000 carats in 1988, but production was reported at 243,000 carats in 1991, of which 160,000 carats were of gem quality. It is believed that a substantial portion of the diamonds close to the earth's surface is smuggled out of the country.

For 25 years, the Sierra Leone Selection Trust (SLST), a subsidiary of the Consolidated African Selection Trust, had exclusive diamond prospecting rights and gave the government 27.5% of its annual net profit. However, this monopoly, plus numerous finds of gem diamonds at or close to the surface, encouraged so much illicit mining and illicit exportation that in 1955, the government renegotiated the SLST's concession, limiting it to two areas, Yengema in Kono District and Tongo in Kenema District, and compensated the company for surrendering its rights in other areas. In 1956, the government introduced the Alluvial Diamond Mining Scheme, in which Sierra Leoneans were issued licenses to dig in declared areas totaling more than 23,300 sq km (9,000 sq mi). In addition to a licensing fee, each licensee had to pay land rental to the local chiefdom authorities and could employ up to 20 diggers. A buying organization, the Government Diamond Office (the Government Gold and Diamond Office since 1985), was set up in agreement with the Diamond Corp. in London. Foreigners, who had figured significantly in illicit diamond dealing, were removed from the diamond-mining areas. In 1962, the government ordered the SLST to sell all its diamonds through the Government Diamond Office. In 1970, the government acquired a 51% interest in the SLST and formed the National Diamond Mining Co. In early 1991, the government started acquiescing control of diamond and gold export activities back to the private sector in order to curtail illicit trading and maximize revenues.

International diamond miners and dealers are now being sought by the government.

The main iron ore deposits are near Marampa in the Port Loko District and between the Sokoya and Waka hills in the Tonkolili District. Mining began in 1933, and the Sierra Leone Development Co. embarked on a program of expansion of its mine at Marampa in 1961. Exports increased from 952,000 tons in 1960 to 2,404,866 tons in 1973, but in 1975 the mine was closed. It reopened in December 1982 under government ownership and Austrian management, and shipment of iron ore resumed in February 1983; in 1985, however, the mine was closed once again.

Bauxite mining in the Mokanji Hills area of the Southern Province was begun by the Sierra Leone Ore and Metal Co. in 1963. Production of 1,288,000 tons was reported in 1991. A second bauxite operation and alumina plant are to be developed at Port Loko.

Mining of rutile, a titanium oxide used in paints and metal alloys, began in the Southern Province near Bonthe in 1967; because of technical difficulties, mining operations were stopped in 1971. A prospecting license was granted in 1972 to a new company, Sierra Rutile, owned, in 1987, by a US corporation, Nord Resources. A pilot plant was in operation in 1973, and production resumed in December 1979. Output rose from 46,000 tons in 1980–81 to a record 154,000 tons in 1991.

A zircon recovery plant opened in April 1991, using old tailings and new mine output from the rutile mines; in 1991, zircon production was a reported 1,119 tons. Production of alluvial gold was 26 kg in 1991. Other known minerals are antimony, cassiterite, columbite, corundum, fluorspar, ilmenite, lead, lignite, magnetite, molybdenum, monazite, platinum, silver, tantalite, tin, titanium, tungsten, and zinc.

27ENERGY AND POWER

Total national production increased from 42.6 million kwh in 1960 to 230 million kwh in 1991, of which about 60% was generated by public utilities. Installed capacity in 1991 was 126,000 kw. As of 1993, the World Bank approved a rehabilitation plan for the National Power Authority (NPA) to provide generation, transmission, and distribution facilities in the western area, and to establish the possibility of making the NPA into a commercially viable utility. Apart from wood, lignite is the only natural fuel found, but known deposits are not being economically exploited. Several companies prospected for offshore oil in the late 1970s and the 1980s. As of October 1991, Nigeria was supplying Sierra Leone with 260,000 barrels of oil per month, primarily for the refinery at Freetown.

28INDUSTRY

Manufacturing accounted for 8.6% of GDP in 1991. The sector has suffered from a lack of foreign exchange, high import costs, and unreliable local services. The Wellington Industrial Estate, covering 46 hectares just east of Freetown, was developed in the 1960s by the government to encourage investments. Its factories produce a variety of products, including cement, nails, shoes, oxygen, cigarettes, beer and soft drinks, paint, and knitted goods. Timber for prefabricated buildings is milled, and another factory produces modern furniture. Small factories in the Freetown area process tuna and palm oil. In 1990, an oil refinery in Freetown, 50% government owned, produced 259,000 metric tons of distilled petroleum products. Village craft products include a popular cloth, rope, sail canvas, boats, wood carvings, baskets, and leather goods.

29SCIENCE AND TECHNOLOGY

The Institute of Marine Biology and Oceanography and the Sierra Leone Science Association are affiliated with Fourah Bay College of the University of Sierra Leone at Freetown. The college itself has faculties of engineering and pure and applied sciences. A paramedical school in Bo operates with funds from the government and the European community. The Ministry of Mines has a geological survey division to locate mineral deposits and advise on all matters relating to the earth. The Sierra Leone Medical and Dental Association has 220 members.

30 DOMESTIC TRADE

Freetown is the principal commercial and distribution center. Internal trade is carried on mainly by trading firms that deal in a variety of merchandise. A substantial part of domestic trade is in the hands of Syrian and Lebanese merchants, although in 1969 the government restricted foreigners from engaging in many categories of business without the prior permission of the Ministry of Trade and Industry. Normal business hours are from 8 AM to 12:30 PM and 2 to 4:30 or 5 PM, Monday through Friday, with a half day on Saturday. Banks are open from 8 AM to 1:30 PM, Monday through Thursday, and 8 to 2 PM on Friday.

31 FOREIGN TRADE

Sierra Leone exports primary minerals and agricultural commodities and imports food and machinery. The trade balance recovered in 1992 after repeated deficits in recent years. The principal exports in 1992 (in thousands of leones) were as follows:

Rutile	32,878,622
Bauxite	19,408,339
Diamonds	15,359,990
Coffee	1,350,959
Cocoa	1,053,099
Palm kernels	6,864
Piassava	50,130
Other exports	8,764,408
TOTAL	78,872,411

The principal imports in 1992 (in thousands of leones) were as follows:

Foodstuffs	22,341,246
Beverages and tobacco	734,914
Crude materials	1,423,360
Animal and vegetable oils and fats	1,801,560
Mineral fuels	6,787,278
Chemicals	7,122,618
Basic manufactures	9,199,174
Machinery and transport equipment	12,313,716
Miscellaneous manufactures	3,452,733
TOTAL	65,176,599

Sierra Leone's leading export partner in 1992 were the US (30.6%), followed by Germany (12.2%) and the UK (8.8%). Imports to Sierra Leone came from the UK (14.2%), Germany (10.9%), and China (10.1%).

32 BALANCE OF PAYMENTS

Sierra Leone's frequently negative balance of trade and habitual deficit in current accounts are somewhat counterbalanced by capital inflows, generally from foreign governments. Foreign exchange reserves averaged less than one month of imports throughout the 1980s, and the balance of payments deficit was mainly financed by accumulating areas. In 1991, the current account deficit stood at over 18% of GDP, but was reduced to under 14% of GDP in 1992 by currency devaluation, expanding export growth and a drop in imports.

In 1991 merchandise exports totaled $149.5 million and imports $138.3 million. The merchandise trade balance was $11.2 million. The following table summarizes Sierra Leone's balance of payments for 1990 and 1991 (in millions of US dollars):

	1990	1991
CURRENT ACCOUNT		
Goods, services, and income	−76.3	0.9
Unrequited transfers	6.9	9.8
TOTALS	−69.4	10.7
CAPITAL ACCOUNT		
Direct investment	32.4	7.5
Portfolio investment	—	—
Other long-term capital	−48.5	−33.2
Other short-term capital	15.4	35.1
Exceptional financing	30.6	−1.3
Other liabilities	—	—
Reserves	−9.6	−18.1
TOTALS	20.3	−10.0
Errors and omissions	49.2	−0.7
Total change in reserves	2.1	11.4

33 BANKING AND SECURITIES

The Bank of Sierra Leone, established in 1963, is the central bank and bank of issue. The Banking Act of 1964 provides for the regulation of commercial banks by the central bank, including the control of money supply. As of 31 January 1987, total monetary reserves of the central bank were Le1,540.7 million. Currency in circulation as of 31 January 1987 was Le1,062.3 million.

In the 1990s, there were six commercial banks operating in the country. Standard Chartered Bank Sierra Leone and Barclays Bank of Sierra Leone are both foreign banks that are locally incorporated, with Sierra Leonean staff. The International Bank of Trade and Industry opened in 1982, with funds from Lebanese and Sierra Leonean investors. In 1993, commercial banks held demand deposits totaling Le12,753 million and time and savings deposits of Le15,951 million.

The National Development Bank was established in 1968 to finance agricultural and industrial projects. The National Cooperative Development Bank, established in 1971, serves as a central bank for all cooperatives and makes modest loans to individual farmers and cooperatives for agricultural improvements. Sierra Leone also has a Post Office Savings Bank.

There is no securities exchange in Sierra Leone.

34 INSURANCE

Branches and agencies of nine foreign (principally British) insurance companies operated in Sierra Leone in 1982. The National Insurance Co. is government owned.

All insurance companies in Sierra Leone are supervised by the Ministry of Finance.

35 PUBLIC FINANCE

Dwindling budgetary revenues in the 1980s from an eroding tax base and public sector mismanagement caused public investment in infrastructure and maintenance to all but stop. An IMF-sponsored standby agreement which began in 1986 was halted the next year because of poor fiscal and monetary policies. By 1989, the central government was even unable to buy the paper needed to print more money. Efforts to stabilize the economy through public finance reform were disrupted in 1990 by the civil war in Liberia and the Persian Gulf crisis. These reforms nevertheless resulted in an increase of revenues from 9.2% of GDP in 1989 to 12.4% of GDP in 1992.

The following table shows actual revenues and expenditures for 1990 in millions of leones.

	1990
REVENUE AND GRANTS	
Tax revenue	5,231
Non-tax revenue	252
Capital revenue	15
Grants	322
TOTAL	5,821

EXPENDITURES & LENDING MINUS REPAYMENTS IN 1990	1990
General public services	896
Defense	808
Public order and safety	289
Education	1,088
Health	786
Social security and welfare	185
Housing and community amenities	68
Recreation, cultural, and religious affairs	4
Economic affairs and services	2,373
Other expenditures	1,695
Adjustments	
Lending minus repayments	43
TOTAL	8,233
Deficit/Surplus	–2,413

In 1991 the Sierra Leone's public debt stood at Le354,800 million of which Le337,768 million was financed abroad.

36 TAXATION

The main items of taxation are customs duties and direct taxes, which include income taxes. A 1963 amendment to the income tax act abolished all personal deductions except medical and dental expenses and the costs of passage to and from Sierra Leone. A husband and wife are now assessed separately for income tax on their individual incomes. Income tax is charged at a flat rate, with one rate for citizens and a higher rate for noncitizens. Also levied are a 55% corporate tax, property tax, payroll tax, social security contributions, and taxes on goods and services.

37 CUSTOMS AND DUTIES

All import licensing requirements were eliminated in 1989, and all other restrictions, including those on cigarettes, ended in early 1992. Imports from other Manu River Union (MRU) members enter duty free. Most duties for non-MRU imports average 20% but range from 0 to 100% on luxury goods. There is an additional 12.5% sales tax levied on all imports.

38 FOREIGN INVESTMENT

The government encourages the development of plantations and the investment of foreign private capital in agriculture and worthwhile new enterprises. Safeguards are provided against nationalization, and repatriation of capital, profits, and interest is permitted. Legislation in 1983 offered tax relief for up to five years, preferential access to import licenses, exemption from customs and duties on capital equipment and new materials, and special bonuses for companies setting up outside Freetown.

39 ECONOMIC DEVELOPMENT

The Sierra Leone government, in addition to stabilizing its balance-of-payment and budgetary deficits and meeting its debt obligations, seeks investors in its mining sector. As of 1992, the IMF was prepared to release funds to the government in support of programs in the agricultural, health, and education sectors.

40 SOCIAL DEVELOPMENT

A community center, opened in 1946 in Freetown, enabled the Welfare Department to sponsor women's institutes and other groups interested in child welfare and domestic affairs; promote

youth groups; set up programs for the care of the aged, the blind, and the mentally handicapped; and train staff and voluntary workers. In 1955, these allied services were reorganized into a new government department, now known as the Ministry of Social Welfare. A National Coordinating Committee concerned with community development and social services has also been set up, and there is a National Training Center for social workers. In 1972, the National Council of Social Services was established as a central body for coordinating and channeling the work of voluntary organizations.

The government allows the Planned Parenthood Association to provide services but does not actively encourage family planning and population limitation. The fertility rate was estimated at 6 in 1993. Abortion is available for broadly defined health purposes. Women are guaranteed equal rights under the constitution, and a number of women have held prominent posts, including that of Supreme Court justice. Even so, discrimination and violence against women are frequent.

41 HEALTH

In 1985, Sierra Leone had 52 hospitals and 263 dispensaries and health-treatment centers. In 1986, Sa'udi Arabia was building hospitals in Freetown and Makeni, and health centers in Bo and Kenema. In 1992, there were 7 doctors per 100,000 people, with a nurse to doctor ratio of 5.0. In 1990, there was 1 hospital bed per 1,000 inhabitants. In 1992, only 38% of the population had access to health care services.

With WHO and UNICEF technical assistance, an endemic diseases control unit reduced the incidence of sleeping sickness and yaws and began a leprosy-control campaign. Malaria, tuberculosis, and schistosomiasis remain serious health hazards, however, as is malnutrition, with the calorie supply meeting only 83% of minimum requirements in 1992. In 1990, there were 167 reported cases of tuberculosis per 100,000 people. Immunization rates for children up to one year old in 1992 were quite high: tuberculosis (89%); diphtheria, pertussis, and tetanus (72%); polio (72%); and measles (65%). The country spent $22 million on health care in 1990.

Sierra Leone's population in 1993 was 4.5 million, with a birth rate of 48.2 per 1,000 people, with about 4% of married women (ages 15 to 49) using contraception. There were 213,000 births in 1992.

The infant mortality rate was 144 per 1,000 live births in 1992, and maternal mortality was 450 per 100,000 live births in 1991. The overall death rate in 1993 was 21.6 per 1,000 inhabitants. Life expectancy for males in 1992 was only 43 years, one of the lowest in the world.

42 HOUSING

Many of the older two-story wooden houses in Freetown are being replaced by structures built largely of concrete blocks, with corrugated iron or cement-asbestos roofs. Building is controlled in the major towns, and designs are subject to approval.

Village houses in the provinces are traditionally made of sticks, with mud walls and thatch or grass roofs; they may be circular or rectangular in shape. In some villages, wattle-and-daub construction is being replaced by sun-dried mud blocks, and roofs of grass, palm thatch, or palm tiles are giving way to corrugated iron sheeting. In 1981, 40% of all households had piped water, 15% had flush toilets, and 40% had electric lighting.

In 1987, Israel agreed to build 1,000 low-cost houses near Freetown, providing the financing and receiving a 51% share in the project.

43 EDUCATION

In 1990 Sierra Leone's 1,795 primary schools had 10,850 teachers and a total enrollment of 367,426 pupils, and secondary schools had 102,474 pupils and 5,969 teachers. Primary education is neither wholly free nor compulsory, but the ultimate goal of the government is to provide free primary school facilities for every child. In 1990 the adult literacy rate was estimated to be 20.7% (males: 30.7% and females: 11.3%).

Fourah Bay College, the oldest institution of higher learning in West Africa, was founded in 1827 by the Church Missionary Society, primarily to provide theological training. It was affiliated with the University of Durham in England in 1876 and received a royal charter in 1959 as the University College of Sierra Leone. In 1967, the University of Sierra Leone was chartered with two constituent colleges, Fourah Bay (in Freetown) and Njala University College (in Moyamba District). In 1990, all higher level institutions were reported to have had 4,742 pupils and 600 teaching personnel.

44LIBRARIES AND MUSEUMS

The library of Fourah Bay College, founded in 1827 had 140,000 volumes. The public collections maintained in 10 cities and towns by the Sierra Leone Library Board have a combined total of about 100,000 volumes. The Sierra Leone National Museum contains documents concerning Sierra Leone and its history and various works of sculpture, especially Nomolis stone fetishes representing seated figures of unknown origin that have been found in the Mende areas.

45MEDIA

The Sierra Leone Broadcasting Service manages radio and television transmissions. Radio Sierra Leone, the oldest broadcasting service in English-speaking West Africa, broadcasts mainly in English, with regular news and discussion programs in several indigenous languages and a weekly program in French. The Sierra Leone Television Service was inaugurated in 1963. In 1991 there were 4 radio transmitters and about 950,000 radio receivers, as well as 2 television transmitters and about 43,000 television receivers. International cablegram, telex, and telephone services are provided by Sierra Leone External Telecommunications.

The only daily newspaper is the government-owned *Daily Mail* (with a 1986 circulation of about 10,000), but there were several privately owned weekly newspapers in 1991. Under legislation enacted in 1980, all newspapers must register with the Ministry of Information and pay a sizable registration fee.

46ORGANIZATIONS

There is a chamber of commerce in Freetown. Several voluntary associations exist, mostly in the Freetown area; most of these are women's religious, cultural, political, or economic groups. Coordinating bodies include the Federation of Sierra Leone Women's Organizations and the United Church Women. The cooperative movement has grown rapidly since the 1960s.

47TOURISM, TRAVEL, AND RECREATION

Sierra Leone has magnificent beaches, including Lumley Beach on the outskirts of Freetown, perhaps the finest in West Africa. Natural scenic wonders include Bintimani and the Loma Mountains, Lake Sonfon, and the Bumbuna Falls. There are several modern hotels in Freetown, as well as a luxury hotel and casino at Lumley Beach. The main provincial towns have smaller hotels, and a number of government rest houses are located throughout the country. International tourist arrivals numbered about 118,000 in 1991, and tourist receipts were about US$19 million in 1990.

Visas are not required for nationals of the UK, other Commonwealth countries, and many Western European nations, but a valid passport and an entry permit are essential. Certification of yellow fever vaccination is required for those arriving from infected areas, and tourists are advised to take precautions against malaria.

48FAMOUS SIERRA LEONEANS

Sir Samuel Lewis (1843–1903) was a member of the Legislative Council for more than 20 years and the first mayor of Freetown. Sir Milton Augustus Strieby Margai (1895–1964), the grandson of a Mende warrior chief, was the founder of the SLPP and the first prime minister of Sierra Leone, a post he held until his death. Sir Albert Michael Margai (1910–80) succeeded his half-brother as prime minister from 1964 to 1967. Siaka Probyn Stevens (b.1905), the founder of the APC, was prime minister from 1968 to 1971 and became the republic's first president from 1971 to 1985. John Musselman Karefa-Smart (b.1915) served as minister of lands, mines, and labor, in which capacity he organized Sierra Leone's diamond industry, and also served as assistant director-general of WHO from 1965 to 1970. Davidson Nicol (b.1924) was his country's permanent representative to the UN from 1969 to 1971, served as president of the Security Council in 1970, and became executive director of UNITAR in 1972. Maj. Gen. Joseph Saidu Momoh (b.1937) succeeded Stevens as president in 1985.

49DEPENDENCIES

Sierra Leone has no territories or colonies.

50BIBLIOGRAPHY

Alie, Joe A. D. *A New History of Sierra Leone*. New York: St. Martin's, 1990.

Alldridge, Thomas J. *Sierra Leone As It was and Is: Its Progress, People, Native Customs and Undeveloped Wealth*. Gordon Press, 1976

American University. *Area Handbook for Sierra Leone*. Washington, D.C.: Government Printing Office, 1976.

Binns, Margaret. *Sierra Leone*. Oxford, England; Santa Barbara, Calif.: Clio Press, 1992.

Cartwright, John R. *Political Leadership in Sierra Leone*. Toronto: University of Toronto Press, 1978.

Clarke, J. I., ed. *Sierra Leone in Maps*. New York: Holmes and Meier, 1972

Clifford, Mary L. *The Land and People of Sierra Leone*. Lippincott, 1974

Collier, Gershon B. *Sierra Leone: Experiment in Democracy in an African Nation*. New York: New York University Press, 1970.

Cox, Thomas M. *Civil-Military Relations in Sierra Leone*. Cambridge, Mass.: Harvard University Press, 1976.

Foray, Cyril P. *Historical Dictionary of Sierra Leone*. Metuchen, N.J.: Scarecrow, 1977.

Fyfe, Christopher. *A Short History of Sierra Leone*. New York: Longman, 1979.

Greene, Graham. *The Heart of the Matter*. New York: Viking, 1948.

Hayward, Fred M. "*The Development of a Radical Political Organization in the Bush*: A Case Study in Sierra Leone." *Canadian Journal of African Sutdies*. Vol. 6:1 (1972), pp. 1-28.

Kilson, Martin L. *Political Change in a West Affrican State*. Cambridge: Harvard University Peress, 1966.

Kup, A. Peter. *Sierra Leone: A Concise History*. New York: St. Martin's, 1975.

Riddell, Barry J. *Spatial Dynamics of Modernization in Sierra Leone*. Evanston, Ill.: Northwestern University Press, 1978.

Saylor, Ralph G. *Economic System of Sierra Leone*. Durham (Commonwealth Studies Center, No. 31): Duke University Press, 1968.

Simpson, Dick. "Ethnic Conflict in Sierra Leone." *The Politics of Cultural Sub-Nationalism in Africa*. Victor A. Olorunsola, ed. Garden City, N.Y.: Anchor Books, 1972.

Spitzer, Leo. *The Creoles of Sierra Leone*. Madison: University of Wisconsin Press, 1974.

White, E. Frances. *Sierra Leone's Settler Women Traders: Women on the Afro-European Frontier.* Ann Arbor: University of Michigan Press, 1987.

Wyse, Akintola J. G. *H.C. Bankole-Bright and Politics in Colonial Sierra Leone, 1919–1958.* New York: Cambridge University Press, 1990.

SOMALIA

CAPITAL: Mogadishu (Muqdisho).

FLAG: The national flag is light blue with a five-pointed white star in the center.

ANTHEM: *Somalia Hanolato (Long Live Somalia).*

MONETARY UNIT: The Somali shilling (SH) of 100 cents is a paper currency. There are coins of 1, 5, 10, and 50 cents and 1 shilling, and notes of 5, 10, 20, 100, 500, and 1,000 shillings. SH1 = $0.01 (or $1 = SH100).

WEIGHTS AND MEASURES: The metric system is in use.

HOLIDAYS: New Year's Day, 1 January; Labor Day, 1 May; National Independence Day, 26 June; Foundation of the Republic, 1 July. Muslim religious holidays include 'Id al-Fitr, 'Id al-Adha', 'Ashura, and Milad an-Nabi.

TIME: 3 PM = noon GMT.

¹LOCATION, SIZE, AND EXTENT

Situated on the horn of East Africa, Somalia has an area of 637,660 sq km (246,202 sq mi), extending 1,847 km (1,148 mi) NNE–SSW and 835 km (519 mi) ESE–WNW. Comparatively, the area occupied by Somalia is slightly smaller than the state of Texas. It is bounded on the N by the Gulf of Aden, on the E and S by the Indian Ocean, on the SW by Kenya, on the W and NW by Ethiopia, and on the NW by Djibouti, with a total boundary length of 5,391 km (3,350 mi). The boundary with Djibouti has been fixed by international agreement, but the western border with Ethiopia remains in dispute. Somalia is committed to supporting the right of self-determination for ethnic Somalis in all adjacent countries, including their right to join in a greater Somalia that would include the Ogaden, now part of Ethiopia.

Somalia's capital city, Mogadishu, is located on the Indian Ocean coast.

²TOPOGRAPHY

The northern region is somewhat mountainous, with plateaus reaching between 900 and 2,100 m (3,000–7,000 ft). To the northeast there is an extremely dry dissected plateau that reaches a maximum elevation of nearly 2,450 m (8,000 ft). South and west of this area, extending to the Shabeelle River, lies a plateau whose maximum elevation is 685 m (2,250 ft). The region between the Juba and Shabeelle rivers is low agricultural land, and the area that extends southwest of the Jubba River to Kenya is low pastureland.

The Jubba and Shabeelle rivers originate in Ethiopia and flow toward the Indian Ocean. They provide water for irrigation but are not navigable by commercial vessels. The Shabeelle dries up before reaching the ocean. Despite its lengthy shoreline, Somalia has only one natural harbor, Berbera.

³CLIMATE

Somalia has a tropical but not torrid climate, and there is little seasonal change in temperature. In the low areas, the mean temperature ranges from about 24°C to 31°C (75° to 88°F). The plateau region is cooler, the southwest warmer. The periodic winds, the southwest monsoon (June–September), and the northeast monsoon (December–March) influence temperature and rainfall. Rain falls in two seasons of the year: heavy rains from March to May, and light rains from September to December. Average annual rainfall is estimated at less than 28 cm (11 in). Droughts are not infrequent.

⁴FLORA AND FAUNA

Acacia thorntrees, aloes, baobab, candelabra, and incense trees are native to the semiarid regions. Mangrove, kapok, and papaya grow along the rivers. Coconut, dune palm, pine, juniper, cactus, and flowering trees such as the flamboyant were imported and have become widespread in the populated areas.

Animal life includes the elephant, lion, wildcat, giraffe, zebra, hyena, hippopotamus, waterbuck, gazelle, dik-dik, lizard, crocodile, turtle, porcupine, baboon, and boar. There is a large variety of snakes, the best known being the puff adder, the spitting cobra, and the krait. Domestic animals are camels, sheep, goats, and cattle. The most common birds are the ostrich, duck, guinea fowl, bustard, partridge, green pigeon, sand grouse, and heron.

⁵ENVIRONMENT

The increasing aridity of the Somali climate, coupled with excessive timber cutting and overgrazing, has led to deforestation and extension of the desert area. In a five-year period, Somalis can anticipate two years of drought. In 1985, deforestation had affected 52 square miles of land in Somalia. Overgrazing between Mogadishu and Chisimayu has resulted in the gradual movement of coastal sand dunes inland, posing a serious threat to agricultural areas and human habitation. The three-year plan for 1979–81 called for a continuation of efforts to plant trees and stabilize dunes. Somalia has 2.8 cubic miles of water. Ninety-seven percent is used for farming. Three percent is for urban and domestic use. Fifty percent of the nation's city dwellers and 71% of the people living in rural areas do not have pure water. The nation's cities produce 0.5 million tons of solid waste per year.

Along with its large livestock herd, Somalia in the early 1980s still had one of the most abundant and varied stocks of savanna and other wildlife in Africa. The hunting and trapping of antelopes and gazelles for their skins was banned in 1969. However, many species continued to be adversely affected by growing numbers of livestock, exclusion from watering spots by human settlement, and the cutting of bush vegetation and tree cover.

In 1994, 17 of the country's mammal species and seven bird species were endangered. Fifty-two types of plants were threatened with extinction. Endangered species in Somalia include the black rhinoceros, Pelzeln's dorcas gazelle, Swayne's hartebeest, and the green sea, hawksbill, and leatherback turtle.

6POPULATION

In 1994, Somalia had a population estimated by the US Census Bureau at 7,400,107. But the UN, which apparently included refugees in its count while the Census Bureau did not, estimated the 1995 population at 10,173,000. A population of 11,864,000 was projected by the UN for the year 2000, based on an estimated crude birthrate of 47.3 per 1,000 population and a crude death rate of 16.6 for 1985. The average population density in 1994 was 11.6 per sq km (30 per sq mi), according to the Census Bureau estimate. The largest city and its estimated 1990 population is Mogadishu, the capital, 779,000; Hargeysa (the former capital of British Somaliland), had about 150,000 in 1991. Other cities included Chisimayu; Berbera, and Merca.

7MIGRATION

Since about half of all Somalis are nomadic or seminomadic, there are substantial movements back and forth across the frontiers in the normal range of grazing activities. Within the country there has been a gradual migration toward the south and southwest, especially since the north was drought-stricken in the 1970s and early 1980s. A campaign of political terror began in 1986. So severe were the effects that it was estimated in 1993 that three-quarters of the population had been internally displaced since 1988.

The conflict with Ethiopia led to the influx of many refugees from the Ogaden, most of them ethnic Somalis. In 1990, an estimated 586,000 were being assisted by the UN High Commissioner for Refugees in refugee camps. The government claimed the total number in refugee camps was over 1.3 million. Yet the political violence in Somalia was so extreme that about 600,000 people fled the country between 1988 and 1991. At the end of 1992, there were 406,100 in Ethiopia, 285,600 in Kenya, 20,000 in Djibouti, and 4,900 in Egypt.

8ETHNIC GROUPS

The Somalis are classified as a Hamitic people with a Cushitic culture. It is believed that the Somalis descend from people who migrated from the equatorial lakes of Africa to settle in the area of Somalia's two rivers, there to intermix with pastoral groups from the north and migrants from the Arabian Peninsula, the Persian Gulf, and perhaps Southeast Asia.

Ethnic Somalis, who made up about 98.8% of the population in 1985, are divided into two main clan families: the Samaal, which includes the Darod, Isaaq, Hawiye, and Dir clan groups; and the Saab, which includes the Rahanweyn and Digil clans and other smaller clan groups. The Samaal, approximately 70% of the population, are principally nomadic or seminomadic pastoralists; the Digil and Rahanweyn, who constitute about 20% of the population, are primarily farmers and sedentary herders. There are also small Bantu-speaking groups who live along the Shabeelle and Jubba rivers.

The nonindigenous population consists primarily of Arabs, Italians, Pakistanis, and Indians. The Italians are mainly engaged in teaching, business, and banana production; the Arabs, Pakistanis, and Indians are primarily shopkeepers.

9LANGUAGES

Somali, classified as a lowland Eastern Cushitic language, is spoken by all Somalis, with dialectal differences that follow clan family divisions. Loanwords from Arabic, English, and Italian have been thoroughly assimilated by Somali phonetic rules. Until 1972, the official languages of Somalia were oral Somali, Arabic, English, and Italian. In 1973, a written form of Somali, with a script based on the Latin alphabet, was adopted as the nation's chief official language, with Arabic a secondary one. This official script largely replaced the use of English and Italian in newspapers and public documents. It is used in all schools.

10RELIGIONS

The Somalis are Sunni Muslims of the Shafi'i sect. According to their tradition, their ultimate ancestors were of the Qurayshitic lineage of the Prophet Muhammad. Except for a small number of urbanites influenced by higher education, all Somalis belong to one of the following brotherhoods: Qadiriyyah, Salihiyyah, Ahmadiyyah, and Rifaiyyah. As Muslims they adhere to the law of the Shari'ah whenever it does not conflict with local customary law. Pre-Islamic traditions are still strong in areas outside the major towns.

Islam is the religion of the state. Christian mission schools closed in 1972, and foreign Protestant missionaries were expelled in 1976. The 1960 constitution forbade proselytizing of any religion but Islam. Protestants and Catholics make up less than 1% of the population.

11TRANSPORTATION

Of 22,000 km (13,650 mi) of roads in Somalia in 1991, 12% were paved. A 1,054-km (655-mi) road constructed with Chinese financing and work crew participation, completed in 1978, tied together the northern and southern parts of the country for the first time. Motor vehicles in use in 1991 numbered 22,500. There are no railways and no commercial water transport facilities.

The ports of Mogadishu, Chisimayu, and Berbera are served by vessels from many parts of the world, as well as by Somali and Arab dhows. Mogadishu in recent years handled more than 70% of Somalia's export and import traffic. In 1991, the state-owned shipping line operated four oceangoing vessels.

The major airfields are in Mogadishu and Berbera. International air service has been provided by the state-owned Somali Airlines (among other carriers), which also has regular flights connecting Mogadishu with regional centers and with Kenya, Djibouti, Sa'udi Arabia, the Comoros, Yemen, the Persian Gulf states, Frankfurt, Cairo, and Rome.

12HISTORY

Somalia was known as the Land of Punt by ancient Egyptians, who came to Somalia's northern shores for incense and aromatic herbs. In the 9th or 10th century, Somalis began pushing south from the Gulf of Aden coast. About this time, Arabs and Persians established settlements along the Indian Ocean coast. During the 15th and 16th centuries, Portuguese explorers attempted without success to establish Portuguese sovereignty over the Somali coast. Meanwhile, the main coastal centers continued to be controlled by Arab merchant families under the nominal suzerainty of the sultanate of Oman, which transferred its seat to Zanzibar in the early 19th century.

After the British armed forces occupied Aden in 1839, they developed an interest in the northern Somali coast. By 1874, Egyptians occupied several points on the shore, but their occupation was short-lived. From 1884 to 1886, the British signed a number of "protectorate" treaties with Somali chiefs of the northern area. The protectorate was first administered by the resident in Aden and later (1907) by the Colonial Office. From 1899 to 1920, British rule was constantly disrupted by the "holy war" waged by 'Abdallah bin Hasan (generally known in English literature as the "Mad Mullah").

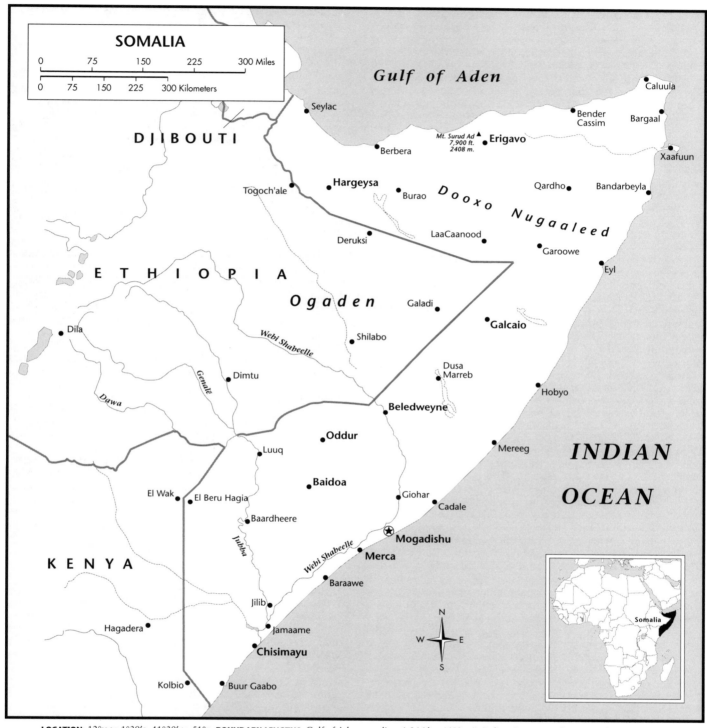

SOMALIA

0 75 150 225 300 Miles

0 75 150 225 300 Kilometers

Gulf of Aden

Caluula

Seylac

DJIBOUTI

Bender Cassim

Bargaal

Mt. Surud Ad 7,900 ft. 2408 m. ▲

Erigavo

Berbera

Xaafuun

Hargeysa

Qardho

Bandarbeyla

Togoch'ale

Burao

Dooxo Nugaaleed

Deruksi

LaaCaanood

Garoowe

ETHIOPIA

Ogaden

Eyl

Galadi

Dila

Shilabo

Galcaio

Webi Shabeelle

Dimtu

Dusa Marreb

Genale

Hobyo

Dawa

Beledweyne

Oddur

Mereeg

Luuq

INDIAN

Baidoa

OCEAN

El Wak

El Beru Hagia

Giohar

Cadale

Baardheere

Mogadishu ✪

Jubba

Merca

Webi Shabeelle

Baraawe

Jilib

Hagadera

Jamaame

N

Chisimayu

W E

Kolbio

Buur Gaabo

S

KENYA

Somalia

LOCATION: 12°N to 1°39′S; 41°30′ to 51°E. **BOUNDARY LENGTHS:** Gulf of Aden coastline, 1,046 km (650 mi); Indian Ocean coastline, 2,173 km (1,350 mi); Kenya, 682 km (424 mi); Ethiopia, 1,645 km (1,022 mi); Djibouti, 61 km (38 mi). **TERRITORIAL SEA LIMIT:** 200 mi.

Italian expansion in Somalia began in 1885, when Antonio Cecchi, an explorer, led an Italian expedition into the lower Juba region and concluded a commercial treaty with the sultan of Zanzibar. In 1889, Italy established protectorates over the eastern territories then under the nominal rule of the sultans of Obbia and of Alula; and in 1892, the sultan of Zanzibar leased concessions along the Indian Ocean coast to Italy. Direct administrative control of the territory known as Italian Somaliland was not established until 1905. The Fascist government increased Italian authority by its extensive military operations. In 1925, the British government, in line with secret agreements with Italy during World War I, transferred the Jubaland (an area south of the Jubba River) to Italian control. During the Italo-Ethiopian conflict (1934–36), Somalia was a staging area for Italy's invasion and conquest of Ethiopia. From 1936 to 1941, Somalia and the Somali-inhabited portion of Ethiopia, the Ogaden, were combined in an enlarged province of Italian East Africa.

In 1940–41, Italian troops briefly occupied British Somaliland but were soon defeated by the British, who conquered Italian Somaliland and reestablished their authority over British Somaliland. Although the Ogaden was returned to Ethiopia in 1948, British administration over the rest of Italian Somaliland continued until 1950, when Italy became the UN trusteeship authority. A significant impetus to the Somali nationalist movement was provided by the UN in 1949 when the General Assembly resolved that Italian Somaliland would receive its independence in 1960. By the end of 1956, Somalis were in almost complete charge of domestic affairs. Meanwhile, Somalis in British Somaliland were demanding self-government. As Italy agreed to grant independence on 1 July 1960 to its trust territory, the UK gave its protectorate independence on 26 June 1960, thus enabling the two Somali territories to join in a united Somali Republic on 1 July 1960. On 20 July 1961, the Somali people ratified a new constitution, drafted in 1960, and one month later confirmed Aden 'Abdullah Osman Daar as the nation's first president.

From the inception of independence, the Somali government supported the concept of self-determination for the people of the Somali-inhabited areas of Ethiopia (the Ogaden section), Kenya (most of the northeastern region), and French Somaliland (now the Republic of Djibouti), including the right to be united within a greater Somalia. Numerous border clashes occurred between Somalia and Ethiopia, and between Somalia and Kenya. Soviet influence in Somalia grew after Moscow agreed in 1962 to provide substantial military aid.

Abdirashid 'Ali Shermarke, who was elected president in 1967, was assassinated on 15 October 1969. Six days later, army commanders seized power with the support of the police. The military leaders dissolved parliament, suspended the constitution, arrested members of the cabinet, and changed the name of the country to the Somali Democratic Republic. Maj. Gen. Jalle Mohamed Siad Barre, commander of the army, was named chairman of a 25-member Supreme Revolutionary Council (SRC) that assumed the powers of the president, the Supreme Court, and the National Assembly. Siad Barre was later named president.

In 1970, President Siad Barre proclaimed "scientific socialism" as the republic's guiding ideology. This Marxist ideology stressed hard work and public service and was regarded by the SRC as fully compatible with Islam. A number of industries and large firms, especially foreign banks and oil companies, were nationalized. Self-help projects were instituted to clean up the towns and villages, construct roads and sidewalks, dig and maintain wells and irrigation canals, build infirmaries and schools, and stabilize sand dunes. In 1972, the SRC proclaimed the adoption of a Latin script for Somali; in 1973, it inaugurated widespread literacy campaigns. The drought that affected large areas of Africa from 1968 to 1973 became severe in Somalia in late 1974, and in November of that year, the SRC declared a state of emergency, set up relief camps, and initiated food rationing.

Controversy arose in 1975 over US charges that the USSR was developing a military installation at the port of Berbera. Somalia denied the charges and invited inspection by journalists and US congressmen, who reported that they had found evidence of Soviet missile-handling facilities there. Somali officials did acknowledge receipt of Soviet military and technical advisers. Meanwhile, Ethiopia claimed that a Soviet-equipped Somalia represented a threat to its security. That same year, Siad Barre extended formal recognition to the Western Somali Liberation Front in the Ogaden. Somali forces took part in the fighting but were defeated in 1977, soon after the USSR had swung its support to Ethiopia. Late in the year, Siad Barre expelled the Soviets. Relations with the US warmed, and in 1980, in return for military and economic aid (about $80 million in 1982), Siad Barre agreed to allow the US use of air and naval facilities at the northern port of Berbera, facilities that had been built by the USSR, and also at Mogadishu.

A new constitution was ratified in 1979. On 30 December 1979, an unopposed list of 171 candidates was elected to the People's Assembly, which, the following month, elected Siad Barre unanimously to a new term of office. (Unopposed elections were again held on 31 December 1984.) In October 1980, Siad Barre declared a state of emergency and reestablished the SRC, responding to the activities of an Ethiopian-backed opposition movement, the Somali Salvation Democratic Front (SSDF). The state of emergency was lifted in March 1982, but at midyear the insurgents, supported by a reported 10,000 Ethiopian troops, invaded Somalia. By December, however, only a small area was in insurgent or Ethiopian hands.

In January 1986, Siad Barre met with Lt. Col. Mengistu Haile Mariam, Ethiopia's head of state, in Djibouti, in an effort to improve relations between the two countries. Two other meetings of Somali and Ethiopian officials were held in May and August, but no agreement was reached. On 23 May 1986, Siad Barre was seriously injured in an automobile accident. After his unopposed reelection on 23 December 1986—the first direct presidential election in Somalia—Siad appointed a prime minister for the first time, Lt. Gen. Mohamed 'Ali Samater, the first vice-president and minister of defense. The SSDF had virtually crumbled by the end of 1986, but in 1987 another insurgent group, the Somali National Movement, was conducting operations in the north (the former British Somaliland). In February 1987, relations between Somalia and Ethiopia deteriorated following an Ethiopian attack on six settlements. Growing out of the Soviet shift to the Ethiopian side, American-Somali relations became closer during the administration of US president Ronald Reagan. This included a 10-year agreement providing US forces access to naval and air facilities at Berbera and increasing US military aid to Somalia.

In 1988, both the Ethiopian and Somalian governments, faced by growing internal resistance, pledged to respect their border. By 1990, the Somali regime was losing control. Armed resistance from the Somali Salvation Democratic Front (SSDF), the Somali Democratic Alliance (SDA), the Somali Democratic Movement (SDM), the Somali National Movement (SNM), the Somali Patriot Movement (SPM), and the United Somali Congress (USC) were turning the Somali territory into a death trap. Government forces were no less ruthless. Each was led by a clan leader or local warlord. Donor nations threatened to cut off aid unless the atrocities were ended.

In March 1990, Barre called for dialogue and, possibly, an end to single-party rule, but he was eventually ousted and, in January 1991, he fled Mogadishu. The USC seized the capital, but fighting continued. The SNM controlled much of the north and declared its territory the independent state of "Somaliland." By December, the USC had split in two. One faction was led by Ali Mahdi Muhammad, the interim president, the other by Gen. Muhammad Farrah Aideed. They were from different subclans of the Hawiye clan. The fighting continued and the warring factions prevented people from planting and harvesting crops. Several hundred thousand people died. Far more were threatened by starvation. Over a half-million fled to Kenya. Contagious disease spread through refugee camps inside the country. The starvation and total breakdown of public services was publicized in the western media. Calls for the UN to intervene mounted. Yet, the food relief that was sent was stolen by soldiers and armed looters. Private relief efforts were frustrated and subject to extortion. Late on 3 December 1992, the UN Security Council passed a resolution to deploy a massive US-led international military intervention (UNITAF-United Task Force) to safeguard relief operations. By the end of December, Aideed and Ali Maludi had pledged to stop fighting. The UNITAF spread throughout the country. Violence decreased dramatically. But later, gunmen began to appear again.

US forces seemed to have shifted their mandate toward the UN-Boutros-Ghali position of trying to confiscate arms and "technicals"—vehicles with mounted heavy weapons. Although the problem of relief distribution had largely been solved, there was no central government, few public institutions, and local warlords and their forces became increasing emboldened.

By early 1993, over 34,000 troops from 24 UN members—75% from the US—were deployed. Starvation was virtually ended, a modicum of order had been restored, and hope had returned. Yet, little was done to achieve a political solution or to disarm the factions. From January 1993 until 27 March, 15 armed factions met in Addis Ababa, Ethiopia, to haggle and finally reach agreement to end hostilities and to form a transitional National Council for a two-year period to serve as the political authority in Somalia.

On 4 May 1993, Operation Restore Hope, as the relief effort was labeled, was declared successful, and US force levels were sharply reduced. Command of relief, disarmament, and reconstruction work was assumed by the UN. This effort, UNOSOM II, featured Pakistani, US, Belgian, Italian, Moroccan, and French troops, commanded by a Turkish general. On 23 June 1993, however, 23 Pakistani solders were killed in an ambush, and the UN Security Council ordered the arrest of those responsible. Gen. Aideed's forces were blamed and a $25,000 bounty was placed on Aideed's head.

Mogadishu became a war zone. In early October 1993, 18 US Army Rangers were killed and 75 were wounded in a firefight. American public opinion and politicians pressured President Bill Clinton to withdraw US troops. He established a 31 March 1994 deadline and instructed his special envoy, Charles Oakley, to return to Somalia and begin a new diplomatic initiative. Efforts at inclusive UN-sponsored, and then Ethiopian-sponsored, talks failed. Later discussions in Kenya and in Mogadishu reached agreements that teetered on collapse as the factions jockeyed for advantage. By this time, Aideed's forces were called the Somali National Alliance (SNA) and Ali Mahdi led the "Group of Twelve." Kenya's President Moi mediated. After the US pullout, some 19,000 UN troops remained to try to maintain order. A 4 February 1994 Security Council Resolution (897) redefined the UNOSOM II mandate, emphasizing peacemaking and reconstruction. In effect, it was a recognition that the assertive, coercive strategy of the UN had failed and that a more neutral role was necessary. It sets a March 1995 deadline for the completion of its mission.

13GOVERNMENT

From July 1961 to October 1969, Somalia was a parliamentary democracy based on the principle of separation of powers. After the army's seizure of power in October 1969, Maj. Gen. Siad Barre was named chairman of the 25-member SRC, which then elected him president. A constitution, approved in January 1979 by the ruling Somali Revolutionary Socialist Party and ratified by popular referendum on 25 August, vested legislative authority in the People's Assembly of 177 members serving five-year terms. This assembly could be dissolved by a two-thirds vote of its members or by the president. The People's Assembly was given the right to elect the president to a six-year, renewable term. (This was changed in 1984 to a direct popular election for a seven-year term.) The president was authorized to appoint members of the cabinet and to act as its chairman. He was declared commander in chief of the armed forces, with the power to declare war and to appoint the president of the Supreme Court. An article of the document allowed him to invoke emergency rule. On 24 October 1980, Siad Barre issued a decree suspending those constitutional provisions that were incompatible with the state of emergency triggered by the conflict with Ethiopia.

Large-scale fighting among clan factions from 1989 to January 1991 brought about the collapse of the Barre regime and his flight from Mogadishu. An interim administration (based on the 1969 constitution) was created by the United Somali Congress, but it collapsed in November 1991 and its two warring factions plunged Somalia into total civil war. The northern province declared its independence on 18 May 1991 as the sovereign state of "Somaliland," the name it bore under British colonial rule. That independence, so far, has brought relatively orderly rule. On 5 May 1993, Mohammed Ibrahim Egal was elected president by members of the central committee.

Since Barre's overthrow in June 1991, Somalia has had no viable central government. Some 15 armed factions have been fighting, except for the relatively peaceful early months of UN-US administration from December 1992 until around June 1993. Currently, the UNOSOM II is technically in control, but the clan-based armed forces continue to fight one another, and occasionally, the UN and to "rule" in their own bailiwicks.

14POLITICAL PARTIES

Somalia had a multiparty system of government prior to October 1969; opposition in parliament came from within the majority party as well as from the opposition parties. The Somali Youth League (SYL), the largest party, was formed in 1943 as the Somali Youth Club. Its program included the unification of all Somalis (including those in Kenya, Ethiopia, and French Somaliland); social, political, and economic development; and nonalignment in international affairs. It represented almost all government personnel, entrepreneurs, and skilled and quasi-skilled workers of the southern area, formerly Italian Somaliland. In the first national elections after independence, held on 30 March 1964, the SYL won an absolute majority of 69 of the 123 parliamentary seats. The remaining seats were divided among 11 parties. In general elections held in March 1969, the ruling SYL, led by Mohammed Ibrahim Egal, was returned to power. A total of 64 political parties contested the elections. In October 1969, the Supreme Revolutionary Council (SRC) prohibited all political parties and announced that elections would be held in due course. In 1976, the SRC was abolished and its functions transferred to the leadership of the newly formed Somali Revolutionary Socialist Party (SRSP), which was led by the former SRC members. Siad Barre was general secretary of the SRSP, which remained the sole legal party until his overthrow in January 1991. The Somali National Movement (SNM) has seized control of the north and established the independent state of "Somaliland." Since then, armed factions largely identified with clans and subclans have divided up the territory as they fight and negotiate to expand their influence. Many of them bear the titles of political parties; e.g., the Somali Democratic Movement, the Somali National Union, the Somali Patriotic Movement, and the United Somali Congress (USC). In fact, their bases are not national. The USC controlled Mogadishu and much of central Somalia until late in 1991 when it split into two major factions. Aideed's Somali National Alliance (SNA) identified with the Habar Gadir subclan of the Hawiye clan and Ali Mahdi's Somali Salvation Alliance (Abgal subclan of the Hawiyes). Currently the latter exists as the "Group of Twelve" coalition and these are the two dominant claimants to national power.

15LOCAL GOVERNMENT

Somalia until 1973 was divided into eight regions, each headed by an official chosen by the central government. The regions were subdivided into 48 districts, headed by district commissioners also appointed by the government. There were 83 municipalities and submunicipalities. The powers of the municipal councils included local taxation, town planning, registry and census, public services, and approval of the local budget. The major educational, economic, and social services were financed and maintained by the central government, which also exerted supervisory control over the municipal councils through its power to remove mayors and to dissolve the councils.

In 1973, a local government reorganization raised the number of regions from 8 to 16 and the number of districts to 80. In 1986 there were 15 regions, each governed by a regional revolutionary council, the members of which were appointed by the president.

By 1990, this pattern of local government had collapsed. The UN and US sought to restructure local services and representative bodies, but this has been difficult to sustain without a convincing military presence. Until March 1995, UNOSOM-II is mandated to create the peace necessary to help reconstruct the country.

16JUDICIAL SYSTEM

Under the 1961 constitution, the Supreme Court was the highest juridical organ of the republic, having ultimate jurisdiction over all civil, penal, and administrative matters, and over all rights established by the constitution and by the laws of the state. Other judicial organs were qadi courts (Muslim courts), district courts, provincial courts, and courts of assize. Judicial organs of second instance were a tribunal of qadis, a court of appeals, and an appeals court of assize. Somali citizens participated as jurors in the courts of assize and the appeals court of assize. The Ministry of Justice administered the prison system and the offices and employees of the judicial organs. It prepared projects and regulations dealing with judicial matters and it supervised notaries, the bar, and the Office of State Attorney.

When the SRC assumed all judicial as well as executive and legislative powers in October 1969, it suspended the Supreme Court. However, the Court was reopened in December 1969, and the rest of the court system was left much as before. A new National Security Court was empowered to rule on cases involving persons accused of attempting to undermine the independence, unity, and security of the state. The 1979 constitution established the Constitutional Court (composed of the Supreme Court and delegates to the People's Assembly) to decide on the constitutionality of laws. It also empowered the Higher Judicial Council, chaired by the president and composed of high-ranking SRC members, to be responsible for the selection, promotion, and discipline of members of the judiciary.

As a result of the civil disorder in recent years, most of the structure for the administration of justice has collapsed. The UN operation in Somalia has overseen administration of the Somalia Penal Code in those areas under UN supervision. Islamic law and traditional mediation continue to be applied to settle disputes over property and criminal offenses. The fear of renewed anarchy interferes with impartial administration of justice. Prosecutions for war crimes is quite difficult.

In 1993, plans were released for a three-tier judicial system with courts of appeals, regional courts, and district courts. The Transitional National Council (TNC) also has plans for drafting a new constitution.

17ARMED FORCES

The regular armed forces disintegrated in the revolution of 1991, leaving the nation awash with Russian, Chinese, and European weapons. Clan gangs armed with these weapons terrorized relief workers during their humanitarian efforts sponsored by international and private organizations, and battled a UN and US expeditionary force to a standstill. Between December 1992 and March 1994 over 100,000 US military personnel served in Somalia. As of late 1994, the UN contingent—19,000 troops from 24 nations—remains. The number of armed Somalias eludes count, but numbers in the tens of thousands.

18INTERNATIONAL COOPERATION

Somalia, which joined the UN on 30 September 1960, participates in ECA and all the nonregional specialized agencies except IAEA.

It is also a member of the African Development Bank, G-77, League of Arab States, and OAU. Somalia signed the Law of the Sea in 1982.

19ECONOMY

Somalia's economy is an agricultural one based primarily on livestock and, to a lesser extent, on farming. There has been little exploitation of mineral resources. Since 1990, the economy has been a shambles, the consequence of drought and of protracted civil strife which has left the country without central authority. By early 1992, virtually all trade, industrial and agricultural activities had stopped, large numbers of people were forced from their homes, and more than 6 million people were at risk of starvation. In 1993, however, donors pledged $130 million toward Somalia's reconstruction, and good rains and increased stability eased the food situation.

20INCOME

In 1987, the last year for which the UN has statistics, Somalia's GDP in current prices was SH168,608 million. Agriculture, hunting, forestry, and fishing contributed 62% to GDP; manufacturing, 5%; electricity, gas, and water, –1%; construction, 3%; wholesale and retail trade, 10%; transport, storage, and communication, 7%; finance, insurance, real estate, and business services, 5%; community, social, and personal services, 3%; and other sources, 5%. Annual inflation was 81.7% in 1988.

21LABOR

In 1992, workers' rights vanished amid the civil chaos and fighting. Nomadic and seminomadic shepherds made up about 60% of the working population in the mid-1980s; some 22% were farmers. About 19% of the labor force was in government, trade, and services and 9% in industry in the late-1980s. Since the overwhelming majority of the population was engaged in stock herding or agriculture, the number of unemployed was not large, but there was considerable unemployment in the urban centers.

Labor codes were enacted in the early 1960s for minimum wages, hours of work, employment of women and children, vacations, and collective bargaining. After the 1969 revolution, the SRC dissolved the existing unions and took action to organize the General Federation of Somali Trade Unions along lines more in keeping with its plans for a Socialist state, but it was believed to have ceased functioning with the recent collapse of the government.

22AGRICULTURE

In 1991, only 1.6% of Somalia's total land area was cultivated, and 69% was permanent pasture. There are two main types of agriculture, one indigenous and the other introduced by European settlers. The Somalis have traditionally engaged in rain-fed dry-land farming or in dry-land farming complemented by irrigation from the waters of the Shabeelle and Jubba rivers or from collected rainwater. Corn, sorghum, beans, rice, vegetables, cotton, and sesame are grown by both methods. Somali and Italian farmers operating the banana farms practice more modern European-style techniques, as do some of the newly created Somali cooperatives. A system of state-administered farms grew rapidly during the early 1970s.

The commercial crops, bananas and sugarcane, are grown on irrigated land along the two rivers. Bananas constitute the nation's major commercial crop; output was 55,000 tons in 1992, down from 110,000 tons in 1990. Sugarcane is cultivated at Giohar and Jilib by a state-owned company. Sugarcane production in 1992 totaled some 50,000 tons, down from 290,000 tons in 1991 and 500,000 tons in 1985. Somalia is the world's leading producer of frankincense.

Between 1975 and 1991, all land was nationalized. Existing

customary rights were generally honored, but the state took over large areas of irrigable land in the river valleys. Plantations had to register to obtain a concession grant, with the value of the land itself excluded from the selling price. As of 1993, privatization and assistance from Italy (the main market for banana exports) were expected to help revitalize the agricultural sector.

23 ANIMAL HUSBANDRY
The majority of Somalis raise livestock; in some areas, particularly in the north, this is the only means of subsistence. The national livestock herd was estimated at 10 million head at the end of 1992. Live animals constituted 36% of the nation's exports in 1991, compared to 73% in 1983, partly because of drought, a ban imposed by Sa'udi Arabia on African cattle that were suspected to be infected with rinderpest, and political turmoil. Livestock exports included 40,000 sheep and goats, 20,000 cattle, and others, with a combined value of $31.5 million, down from $71.2 million in 1987. The export of hides and skins is also important.

24 FISHING
Approximately 1% of the population was engaged full-time in fishing in 1992. Fish-processing plants produced fish flour, inedible oil, and semirefined edible oil. In 1985, fish—tuna, sardines, mackerel, and lobster—and fish products accounted for 10.7% of exports. The catch in 1991 was 16,100 tons. Reconstruction will include the development of fisheries. As of 1993, the yearly potential catch was estimated at 200,000 tons, which could bring in $26 million in revenue each year. One of the government's aims has been to establish fishing cooperatives, and in 1975, thousands of nomads from the drought-affected area were resettled in fishing villages.

25 FORESTRY
Broadly defined, forests covered 14.4% of Somalia's land area in 1991, but only 3.9% of the land had dense tree stands. Somalia is one of the few areas in the world where frankincense is produced; incense trees of the genus Boswellia are found in the northeast. Gum arabic in small quantities is also produced. In the scant forests along the rivers of the Jubba region, *Euphorbia ruspoli* is milled and used for the production of banana crates. Roundwood production was estimated at 7,326,000 cu m.

26 MINING
In 1991, the only nonfuel minerals being exploited were materials quarried for construction—cement, gypsum, and limestone—and 5,000 tons of marine salt. Small amounts of sepiolite (meerschaum) were also reportedly extracted in 1991. There are unexploited deposits of uranium, bauxite, iron ore, quartz, gypsum, anhydrite, thorium, and columbite. Tin was mined by the British before World War II.

27 ENERGY AND POWER
Somalia relies on imported petroleum products for the production of its electric energy. Installed capacity in 1991 was 60,000 kw, almost entirely thermal; total production was 110 million kwh, only half of the 1990 total. On the Jubba River near Baardheere, a dam is scheduled to be built adding 10,000 kw to Somalia's installed capacity. In 1991, there were also four 200 kw windmills in operation.

As of 1991, Somalia was entirely dependent on imports to fill its oil needs. An oil refinery, built with Iraqi assistance, opened at Gesira, near Mogadishu, in 1978. In 1985, 240,000 tons of crude oil were imported for the refinery, 60,000 free from Sa'udi Arabia. In 1991, 53,000 tons of petroleum products were produced, down from 265,000 in 1989. The only immediately exploitable domestic sources of energy are firewood and charcoal.

28 INDUSTRY
Industries mainly serve the domestic market and, to a lesser extent, provide some of the needs of Somalia's agricultural exports, such as the manufacture of crates for packing bananas. The most important industries are the petroleum refinery, the state-owned sugar plants at Jowhar and Gelib, an oilseed-crushing mill, and a soap factory. Newer industries manufacture corrugated iron, paint, cigarettes and matches, aluminum utensils, cardboard boxes and polyethylene bags, and textiles. A cement plant at Berbera was completed in 1985.

The fish- and meat-canning export industries operate below capacity. The meat-packing industry was depressed in the mid-1970s, first by the drought and then by the cancellation of a meat-export contract with the former Soviet Union. Textiles are produced at the SOMALTEX plant, which supplies virtually the entire domestic market. Most major enterprises are government-owned, but private plants produce food, beverages, chemicals, clothing, and footwear. There are also plants for milk processing, vegetable and fruit canning, and wheat flour and pasta manufacturing, as well as several grain mills. The country's first pharmaceuticals factory, near Mogadishu, opened in 1986. Some private investment has also taken place in such areas as metal products, chemicals, and furniture assembly. Local craft industries produce sandals and other leather products, cotton cloth, pottery, baskets, and clay or meerschaum vessels.

29 SCIENCE AND TECHNOLOGY
In 1993, the Somali National University in Mogadishu had faculties of medicine, agriculture, veterinary medicine, engineering, geology, and industrial chemistry. Also located in Mogadishu were the Institute for the Preparation of Serums and Vaccines, the Laboratory of Hygiene and Prophylaxy, and the Society of Medicine and Tropical Hygiene. Mogadishu has a school of public health and a veterinary college. A technical college is located in Burao.

30 DOMESTIC TRADE
Small shops barter or sell a limited number of such imported and domestic items as tea and coffee, kerosene, sugar, cotton goods, spices, cereals, skins, hides, and ghee. Outside the urban centers, the barter system is often employed. In the urban centers, small traders deal essentially in a cash economy. Usual business hours are from 8 AM to 12:30 PM and from 4:30 PM to 7 PM, Saturday to Thursday. Advertising is not widely used, but there are small advertisements in the government newspapers and in periodicals.

31 FOREIGN TRADE
Somalia consistently registers a merchandise trade deficit. Bananas, followed closely by live animal sales, are the nation's leading export (1988), while petroleum is the leading import.

The single greatest purchaser of Somalia's exports in 1985 was Sa'udi Arabia, accounting for 34.2% of total exports. The leading import supplier was Italy, accounting for 25.8% of all imports. Remittances from Somalis working abroad constitute one of the Somalia's main sources of foreign exchange.

32 BALANCE OF PAYMENTS
Since independence, Somalia has consistently had an unfavorable balance of payments on current accounts, caused by deficits of trade and invisible transactions. In the 1980s, Somalia depended on direct transfers and capital assistance from other governments, and has become even more dependent since civil war and ensuing anarchy broke out in 1991.

33 BANKING AND SECURITIES
The Central Bank of Somalia, a government institution with branches in every region, controls the issue of currency and

performs the central banking functions of the state. In 1989, the Central Bank had sH20.6 billion in foreign assets and sH47.15 billion in claims on the commercial bank. At the same time, the government-owned Commercial and Savings Bank of Somalia, with offices in 33 cities and towns, had sH35.2 billion in reserves, sH64.0 billion in demand deposits, and sH18.0 billion in time and savings deposits. The Somali Development Bank promotes the development of productive enterprises, for which it makes both medium-term and long-term loans. The money supply, as measured by M2, in 1989 totaled sH158 billion. There are no securities exchanges in Somalia.

34INSURANCE

A small number of European agencies which had acted as agents for foreign insurance companies were replaced by a state-owned insurance company, the National Insurance Co. of Somalia, in 1972.

35PUBLIC FINANCE

The Somali budget has been in deficit since the early 1970s. Disintegration of the national economy since 1991 has led to relief and military intervention by the UN. No central government existed as of 1993, so there was no functioning system of civil administration to collect and disburse public finances.

36TAXATION

Direct taxes are imposed on income and profits. In 1986, tax rates on wages and salaries ranged from 0% on the first sH50 of income to 18.9%. Income from trade and the professions was taxed at rates of up to 35%. Indirect taxes are imposed on imports, exports, mortgages, vehicle registration, sugar, alcohol, and a number of other goods and services.

37CUSTOMS AND DUTIES

Customs and duties are levied primarily to provide income for the state and to offer protection to local industries. Most duties are ad valorem and range from zero to 100%. Unspecified goods are dutiable at 25% ad valorem. A general sales tax of 10% for imported goods is also levied.

38FOREIGN INVESTMENT

In May 1970, the government fully nationalized a number of industries and companies, including the National Company for Agriculture and Industry, the Italo-Somali Electric Co., all oil distributors, and all foreign banks. The government agreed to compensate investors for their losses.

A comprehensive foreign investment law provides favorable tax terms for foreign investors, protection of investments, and repatriation of profits and capital. After Somalia joined the League of Arab States in 1974, economic and trade agreements were reached with most of the Arab states. Iraq agreed to construct an oil refinery and to lend Somalia money to cover its 50% of the cost. Agreements with other Arab states covered construction of a power plant; improvement of the national insurance company; construction of dams, irrigation projects, and an abattoir and meat-canning factory; and formation of jointly owned companies in shipping and agriculture. In the late 1970s, the leading supplier of funds, through bilateral loans, was China. In the 1980s, Italy emerged as the leading bilateral donor; much of its economic aid was directed toward livestock raising, fisheries, and the development of communications in the northeast.

39ECONOMIC DEVELOPMENT

Successive Somali governments have sought to stimulate production in all sectors of agriculture, commerce, and industry. However, drought, inflation, civil strife, and the rise of oil prices have severely hampered these programs. Government priorities prior to the civil war included the expansion of the fishing fleet, food self-sufficiency based on the development of the Baardheere dam project, livestock breeding, and meat export programs, and transport and telecommunication improvements.

Clan warfare has left Somalia without a central government since 1991. Economic development in the latter part of the 1990s will be devoted in large part to the rebuilding of the Somali civil administration.

40SOCIAL DEVELOPMENT

To reduce unemployment and juvenile delinquency, the government has sponsored self-help schemes all over the country in such projects as the construction of roads, schools, and clinics. All health facilities have been nationalized. Although the government's aim was to provide universal free medical treatment, in the mid-1980s it still lacked the means to do so.

The internal fighting and widespread drought conditions between 1989 and late 1992 have totally destroyed government and its provision of social services. Private humanitarian agencies tried to fill the needs but fighting, extortion, and the activities of armed factions and looters chased many of them away. The UN is also trying to fill the needs but it, too, finds its operation difficult. Somalia simply has no national government.

41HEALTH

Somalia has a high incidence of tuberculosis (an estimated 222 cases per 100,000 people in 1990), schistosomiasis, and pulmonary disturbances. Malaria and intestinal parasites are endemic. Serious dietary deficiencies are found, particularly in the north. In 1991, only 37% of the population had access to pure drinking water, which is rarely available outside the larger cities. Water outside these centers should be filtered, boiled, or chemically treated. Somalis, however, take few of these precautions. A very low 18% of the population had adequate sanitation in 1991, and only 27% had access to health care services.

In 1972, all health facilities and the services of all private medical personnel were placed under state control. Government policy was eventually to provide free medical treatment for all. One of the self-help projects instituted by the SRC was the construction of local clinics. In 1982, there were 76 hospitals and 87 mother and child healthcare centers. In 1990, there were 0.8 hospital beds per 1000 people. In the same year, there were about 500 doctors; in 1992, there were 7 doctors per 100,000 people, with a nurse to doctor ratio of 7:1.

Somalia has a birth rate of 50.3 per 1,000 people with only 1% of married women (ages 15 to 49) using contraception. There were 469,000 births in 1992, and the average life expectancy was only 47 years. The general mortality rate in 1993 was 18.5 per 1,000 inhabitants; the infant mortality rate was 125 per 1,000 live births in 1992; and the maternal mortality rate was a very high 1,100 per 100,000 live births in 1991. These mortality rates do not include civil war-related deaths of about 355,000 from 1988 to 1992, or the thousands of deaths between 1993 and 1994.

Immunization rates for children up to one year old in 1992 were: tuberculosis (31%); diphtheria, pertussis, and tetanus (18%); polio (18%); and measles (30%). Total health care expenditures in 1990 were $60 million.

42HOUSING

Development schemes aided by UN and foreign assistance programs have helped alleviate housing shortages in Mogadishu and Hargeysa. Town planning and housing are under the jurisdiction of municipalities, and assistance is given by the central government only when it has approved a project submitted by the municipality. The typical Somali house is either a cylindrical hut with a conical thatched roof or a rectangular hut with an angular roof of thatch or metal. According to the latest available information for 1980–88, the total number of housing units was 710,000 with 6.8 people per dwelling.

43 EDUCATION

Private schools were closed or nationalized in 1972, and all education was put under the jurisdiction of the central government. In May 1975, primary education was made compulsory, and a minimum of six years of schooling was made mandatory; however, many prospective students, particularly among the nomadic population, could not be accommodated. Secondary education lasts for four years but is not compulsory. A mass literacy campaign was conducted in the mid-1970s, but there is some question of how lasting the effects were, particularly among the nomadic population. In the mid-1980s, literacy remained low, perhaps 18% among adult men and 6% among adult women. In 1990 UNESCO estimated the adult literacy rate to be 24.1% (males, 36.1% and females, 14.0%).

In 1985, there were 196,496 pupils and 10,338 teachers in 1,224 primary schools, and 45,686 students and 2,786 teachers in secondary schools. The same year, 5,933 secondary school children were in vocational courses. The Somali National University, located at Mogadishu, also had a technical college, a veterinary college, and schools of public health, industry, seamanship and fishing, and Islamic disciplines. All institutions at the higher level had 817 teachers and 15,672 students in 1986.

During 1992, Somalia was in a state of anarchy and not only did the country's economy collapse, but its educational system did as well. Few schools were operating and even the Somali National University was closed in 1991.

44 LIBRARIES AND MUSEUMS

The National Museum of Somalia in Mogadishu (30,000 volumes)maintains a highly specialized library with more than 3,000 volumes dealing primarily with African and Somali culture, government, and history. The National Library of Higher Education and Culture has 8,000 volumes, and the Somali Institute of Public Administration also has a book collection; both are in Mogadishu. The National Museum in Mogadishu is a restored residence of the viceroy of the sultan of Zanzibar. Besides its comprehensive collection of Somali ethnographic material, the museum has local art objects, fossils, and old coins. The Regional Museum of the Northern Province of Somalia is in Hargeysa.

45 MEDIA

As of 1992, the government published a daily newspaper in Somali, *Xiddigta Oktobar,* and a weekly newspaper in English, *Heegan.*

The Somali National News Agency (SONNA) in 1974 established regional offices in several major Somali towns. SONNA provides news information for radio and press, supplies information to foreign correspondents in Somalia, and publishes a daily news bulletin, *October Star,* in Somali and English.

Somalia had an estimated 6,000 telephones in 1985. In 1992, it had two radio stations—Radio Mogadishu and Radio Hargeisa—both government-owned, and an estimated 330,000 radio receivers. A television service, limited to the Mogadishu area, was inaugurated in 1983; it broadcasts in Somali and Arabic. There were 108,000 television sets in 1991.

46 ORGANIZATIONS

Private organizations that existed in the 1960s have largely been replaced by government-sponsored groups. Among party-controlled groups are the Union of Somali Cooperatives Movement, the Somali Women's Democratic Organization, and the Somali Revolutionary Youth Organization.

47 TOURISM, TRAVEL, AND RECREATION

Somalia's modest tourist industry has been stagnant since the civil war began. Every person entering Somalia is required to have a valid passport, a proper visa, and an official certificate showing immunization against cholera and yellow fever.

Before the war, Somalia offered lovely beaches, excellent skin diving, and numerous species of East African wildlife. About 39,000 tourists visited Somalia from abroad in 1985.

48 FAMOUS SOMALIS

The most important historical figure in Somali history is Muhammad 'Abdallah bin Hasan (known popularly in English literature as the "Mad Mullah"). He was born about 1860 and during his youth devoted himself to religious studies. In August 1899, with his followers of the Salihiyyah confraternity, he declared a holy war against the British, Italians, and Ethiopians. His resistance to the British lasted until his death in November 1920. Muhammad, also known as one of Somalia's greatest poets, was the first to call for Somali unity. Other important historical figures include Sharif Abu Bakr bin 'Abdallah al-'Aydarus (d.1503), who founded the Qadiriyyah confraternity in the Somali region; Sheikh 'Ali Maye Durogba of Marka (d.1917), who founded the Ahmadiyyah sect in Somalia; and Sheikh Muhammad Guled (d.1918), who started the Salihiyyah sect in Somalia.

'Abdullahi 'Issa Mohamud (b.1921) was prime minister during the Italian trusteeship administration (1956–60) and was Somalia's first foreign minister. Aden 'Abdullah Osman Daar (b.1908) is regarded as the Somali most responsible for bringing about the transition of the Somali territory from dependence to independence; he was the nation's first president. Abdirashid 'Ali Shermarke (1919–69) was Somalia's first prime minister after independence and the nation's second president. He was assassinated on 15 October 1969 by a member of his bodyguard. Maj. Gen. Jalle Mohamed Siad Barre (b.1921) was the leader of the bloodless coup that took over the government six days later and established the SRC. He subsequently became president of the Somali Democratic Republic. Mohamed 'Ali Samater (b.1931), first vice-president and minister of defense, became prime minister in 1986.

49 DEPENDENCIES

Somalia has no territories or colonies.

50 BIBLIOGRAPHY

Abdi Ismail Samatar. *The State and Rural Transformation in Northern Somalia, 1884–1986.* Madison, Wis.: University of Wisconsin Press, 1989.

Burton, Richard F. *First Footsteps in Eastern Africa.* London: Longman, Brown, Green and Longmans, 1856.

Cassanelli, Lee V. *The Shaping of Somali Society.* Philadelphia: University of Pennsylvania Press, 1982.

Castagno, Margaret. *Historical Dictionary of Somalia.* Metuchen, N.J.: Scarecrow, 1975.

Contini, Paolo. *The Somali Republic: An Experiment in Legal Integration.* London: Cass, 1969.

Delaney, Mark W. *Somalia.* Santa Barbara, Calif.: Clio, 1988.

Hess, Robert L. *Italian Colonialism in Somalia.* Chicago: University of Chicago Press, 1966.

Jardine, D. *The Mad Mullah of Somaliland.* Westport, Conn.: Negro Universities Press, 1969 (orig. 1924).

Karp, Mark. *The Economics of Trusteeship in Somalia.* Boston: Boston University Press, 1960.

Laitin, David D. and Said S. Samatar. *Somalia: Nation in Search of a State.* Boulder, Colo.: Westview Press; London, England: Gower, 1987.

Laitin, David D. *Politics, Language, and Thought: The Somali Experience.* Chicago: University of Chicago Press, 1977.

Lewis, I. M. *A Modern History of Somalia: Nation and State in the Horn of Africa.* Boulder, Colo.: Westview Press, 1988.

Loughran, Katheryne S., *et al.* (eds.). *Somalia in Word and Image.* Bloomington: Indiana University Press, 1986.

Massey, Garth. *Subsistence and Change: Lessons of Agropasto-ralism in Somalia.* Boulder, Colo.: Westview Press, 1987.

Metz, Helen Chapin (ed.). *Somalia: A Country Study.* 4th ed. Washington, D.C.: Library of Congress, 1993.

Thompson, Virginia, and Richard Adloff. *Djibouti and the Horn of Africa.* Stanford, Calif.: Stanford University Press, 1968.

SOUTH AFRICA

Republic of South Africa
Republiek van Suid-Afrika

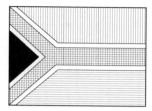

CAPITAL: Cape Town (legislative); Pretoria (administrative); Bloemfontein (judicial).

FLAG: The national flag, adopted in 1994, consists of a blue-black triangle placed vertical to the hoist and bordered in gold-yellow. Bands of red, white, green, white, and blue appear horizontally.

ANTHEM: Two anthems are currently in use; the official anthem, *Die Stem van Suid-Afrika (The Call of South Africa)*, and *Nkosi Sikelel' Afrika (God Bless Africa)*, a hymn adopted by most liberation groups.

MONETARY UNIT: The South African rand (R) is a paper currency of 100 cents. It is used throughout the South African monetary area, which includes all the black homelands. There are coins of 1, 2, 5, 10, 20, and 50 cents and 1 rand, and notes of 2, 5, 10, 20, and 50 rand. R1 = $0.2874 (or $1 = R3.4795).

WEIGHTS AND MEASURES: The metric system is in use.

HOLIDAYS: New Year's Day, 1 January; Republic Day, 31 May; Kruger Day, 10 October; Day of the Vow, 16 December; Christmas, 25 December; Goodwill Day, 26 December. Movable religious holidays include Good Friday and Ascension; Family Day is a movable secular holiday.

TIME: 2 PM = noon GMT.

¹LOCATION, SIZE, AND EXTENT

The area of South Africa is 1,321,219 sq km (510,125 sq mi). Comparatively, the area occupied by South Africa is slightly less than twice the size of the state of Texas. The achievement of independence, in the South African view, by the remaining homelands, with a combined area of 66,132 sq km (25,534 sq mi) in 1985, would further reduce the South African total to 1,057,094 sq km (408,144 sq mi).

Considered as a whole, South Africa extends 1,821 km (1,132 mi) NE–SW and 1,066 km (662 mi) SE–NW. It is bounded on the N by Botswana and Zimbabwe (formerly Rhodesia), on the NE by Mozambique and Swaziland, on the E by the Indian Ocean, on the S by the confluence of the Indian and Atlantic oceans, on the W by the Atlantic Ocean, and on the NW by Namibia. South Africa also controls two small islands, Prince Edward and Marion, which lie some 1,920 km (1,200 mi) southeast of Cape Town. South Africa's capital city, Pretoria, is located in the northeastern part of the country.

²TOPOGRAPHY

South Africa has a mean altitude of about 1,200 m (3,900 ft), and at least 40% of the surface is at a higher elevation. Parts of Johannesburg are more than 1,800 m (6,000 ft) above sea level. There are three major zones: the marginal regions, ranging in width from 80 to 240 km (50–150 mi) in the east to 60–80 km (35–50 mi) in the west, and including the eastern plateau slopes, Cape folded belt, and western plateau slopes; a vast saucer-shaped interior plateau, separated from the marginal zone by the Great Escarpment; and the Kalahari Basin, only the southern part of which projects into north-central South Africa. The land rises steadily from west to east to the Drakensberg Mountains (part of the Great Escarpment), the tallest of which is Mt. Injasuti (3,408 m/11,181 ft), on the border with Lesotho. The coastal belt of the west and south ranges between 150 and 180 m (500 and 600 ft) above sea level and is very fertile, producing citrus fruits and grapes, particularly in the western Cape. North of the coastal belt stretch the Little and the Great Karoo highlands, which are bounded by mountains, are semiarid to arid, and merge into sandy wastes that ultimately join the arid Kalahari. The high grass prairie, or veld, of the Orange Free State and the Transvaal is famous for its deposits of gold and silver; other minerals are found in the Transvaal's bush veld. From the Drakensberg, the land falls toward the Indian Ocean in the rolling hills and valleys of Natal, which are covered with rich vegetation and, near the coast, subtropical plants, including sugarcane.

The two most important rivers draining the interior plateau are the Orange (with its tributary the Vaal), which flows into the Atlantic Ocean, and the Limpopo, which empties into the Indian Ocean through Mozambique. Of the fast-flowing rivers with steeply graded courses that produce spectacular waterfalls, the largest is the Tugela, which rises in the Mont-aux-Sources and flows swiftly to the Indian Ocean.

³CLIMATE

South Africa lies almost wholly within the southern temperate zone, and its climate is more equable than that of corresponding northern latitudes because of its surrounding waters. Temperature differentials between east and west coasts stem from the influences, respectively, of the warm Mozambique (Agulhas) Current and the cold Benguela Current. The average daily minimum temperature at Durban, on the east coast, ranges from 11°C (52°F) in July to 21°C (70°F) in February; on the west coast, at Port Nolloth, the range is from 7°C (45°F) to 12°C (54°F) during the corresponding months. Temperatures are cooler in the highlands: at Johannesburg, the average daily minimum is 4°C (39°F) in June and July and 14°C (57°F) in January. On the high veld there are sharp differences of temperature between day and night, but there is less daily fluctuation nearer the coast. Rainfall is unpredictable in large parts of the country, and prolonged droughts are a serious restriction on farming in such areas. While the mean annual rainfall is 46 cm (18 in), 21% of the country receives less than 20 cm (8 in) and 31% gets more than 60 cm (24 in). Much of South

Africa gets its rain in the summer months, but the western coastal belt is a winter rain area. Along the Cape south coast, rain falls during both seasons.

⁴FLORA AND FAUNA

The variety of South Africa's climate and altitude accounts for its diversified flora and fauna. Major vegetation zones include the forest and palm belt of the east, south, and southwest coasts; the temperate grasslands (veld) of the eastern portion of the interior plateau; the desert and semidesert (Karoo) vegetation of the western interior; and the bushveld (savanna) of the Kalahari and the northeast. Of the 200 natural orders of plants in the world, over 140 are represented, and South Africa has over 25,000 species of flora, including a floral kingdom found nowhere else. There are 200 species of euphorbia, about 350 different kinds of heath in the Cape Province alone, and more than 500 species of grass. Wild flowers (including the protea, South Africa's national flower) grow in great profusion throughout the Cape region.

Aardvark, jackal, lion, elephant, wild buffalo, hippopotamus, and various kinds of antelope are still found in some parts of the country. In the great game parks, animals may be seen living in natural surroundings. So extensive is the variety both of smaller mammals and of plants that they have not yet all been identified. The number of different kinds of birds is approximately 900; that of snakes, 200. The number of species of insects is estimated at 40,000, and there are about 1,000 kinds of fish.

⁵ENVIRONMENT

Recent industrialization and urbanization have taken their toll on the South African environment, as have such agricultural practices as veld fires, overgrazing of livestock, and intensive use of pesticides. Soil erosion and desertification are two more significant environmental issues in South Africa. Three hundred to four hundred million tons of soil per year are lost. The country's limited water resources have been impaired by mineralization, eutrophication, and acidic mine drainage. South Africa has 12.0 cubic miles of water. Sixty-seven percent is used for farming and 17% for industrial activity. According to current estimates, South Africa's water resources will be improved and able to support the demand for water before the end of this century. The country's cities produce 4.2 million tons of solid waste per year. Air pollution in urban areas stems primarily from coal burning and motor vehicle exhausts. The nation contributes 1.1% of the world's total gas emissions. The level of emissions per person is twice the world average.

The principal environmental bodies are the Department of Water Affairs, the Department of Environmental Affairs, and the Department of National Health and Population Activities. Pursuant to a government "white paper" about environmental conservation policy, approved in 1980, a comprehensive environmental protection bill was given parliamentary approval in 1982. Steps to be taken include development of a comprehensive technology for treating sewage and industrial effluents, surveys of threatened natural habitats, research on marine pollution, monitoring of atmospheric pollutants, and a program of environmental education in the public schools.

As of 1994, 25 mammal species and 13 bird species were endangered. Plant species numbering 1,116 are also endangered. Endangered species in South Africa include the riverine rabbit, Cape Mountain zebra, Treur River barb, and several species of butterfly. About 3% of the total land area is allocated to wildlife preservation, and there are numerous nature and game reserves and national parks. Some 120 rare Addo elephants are protected in Addo Elephant National Park, 56 km (35 mi) north of Port Elizabeth; Bontebok National Park (near Swellendam, Cape Province) is a habitat for the last surviving herd of bontebok antelope; Mountain Zebra National Park (near Cradock, in Cape

Province) is a refuge for several hundred rare mountain zebras and springbok; and Kruger National Park, in northeastern Transvaal, has almost every species of South African wildlife in its natural habitat.

⁶POPULATION

South Africa's population was estimated by the US Census Bureau at 43,942,832 in 1994. Excluding the "sovereign" black homelands of Bophuthatswana, Ciskei, Transkei, and Venda, the 1991 population was 26,288,390 according to that year's census. This was considered an undercount, however, and the population (excluding the homelands) was estimated by the government ot 31,917,000 in 1992. It was projected by the UN at 47,912,000 for the year 2000 (including all homelands), assuming a crude birthrate of 29.6 per 1,000 population, a crude death rate of 7.6, and a net natural increase of 22 during 1995–2000. Estimated average population density for 1994 was 36 per sq km (93 per sq mi). However, more than a third of the people live on only 4% of the land area. According to the 1991 census, the total population was 60% urban.

The largest city, the commercial and industrial center of Johannesburg, had a 1991 census population of 1,907,229; the legislative capital, Cape Town, had 1,869,144; and Pretoria, the administrative capital, had 1,025,790. Other major cities (with their 1991 census populations) include Durban, 1,106,971; Port Elizabeth, 825,799; and Bloemfontein (the judicial capital), 300,150. Soweto, mainly inhabited by blacks, had 596,632.

At the 1991 census, 8,402,192 people lived in the Bahtu homelands (excluding Bophuthatswana, Ciskei, Transkei, and Venda); 9,584,250 blacks lived in "white" South Africa, of whom 73% lived in urban areas. The four formerly independent homelands had an estimated population of 6,700,000 in 1991.

⁷MIGRATION

Preference has been given in the past to immigrants from those countries from which South Africa's present white population is derived. Between 1963 and 1984, the number of immigrants averaged about 37,000 annually, and the number of emigrants about 12,000. Between 1980 and 1984, some 72,528 Zimbabwe residents emigrated to South Africa. Since then immigration has fallen, and, perhaps as a consequence, the white population actually dropped between 1980 and 1991. Of the 63,495 immigrants between 1986 and 1991, 16,815 came from other African countries, 16,056 from the UK, 16,512 from other European countries, and 14,112 from other parts of the world. Emigration came to 46,541 during these years.

In 1986, it was estimated that between 1.5 million and 2 million black Africans migrate temporarily to South Africa each year to fulfill work contracts, although only about 500,000 foreign male Africans are living and working in the country at any given time. South Africa was providing informal sanctuary to perhaps 200,000 refugees from Mozambique in 1992; about 8,700 South Africans had been granted refugee status in other African countries. Of these, 7,100 were in Swaziland.

⁸ETHNIC GROUPS

South Africa has one of the world's most complex ethnic patterns. Furthermore, legal separation of the racial communities was a cornerstone of government policy through most of the 20th century. This racial policy, often called apartheid but referred to in South African government circles as "separate development," created and maintained one of the most rigidly segregated societies in the world. During the 1970s and 1980s, enforcement of separatist policies eased, but the division of the population into four racial communities remained. As of the 1991 census, blacks formed the largest segment of the population, constituting 68.4% (17,973,320) of the total; this proportion, which excludes

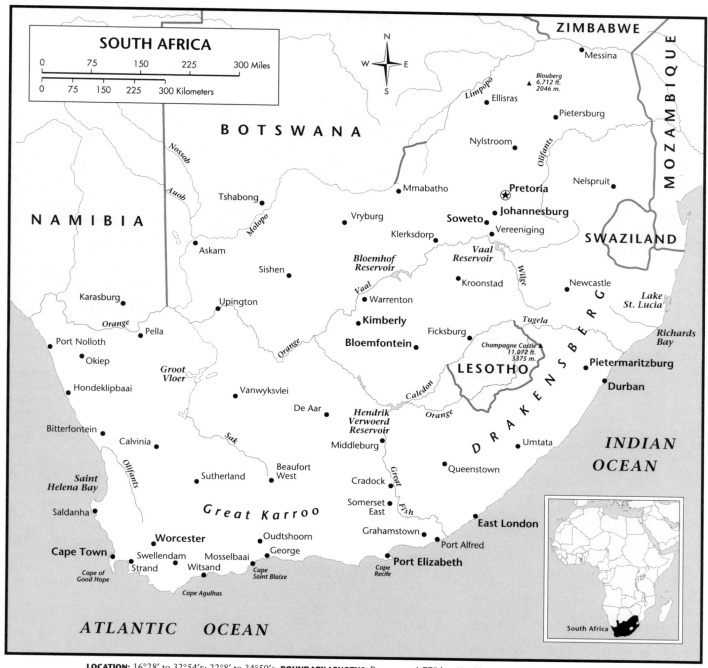

SOUTH AFRICA

0 75 150 225 300 Miles

0 75 150 225 300 Kilometers

LOCATION: 16°28′ to 32°54′E; 22°8′ to 34°50′S. BOUNDARY LENGTHS: Botswana, 1,778 km (1,105 mi); Zimbabwe, 225 km (140 mi); Mozambique, 491 km (305 mi); Swaziland, 449 km (279 mi); total coastline, 2,954 km (1,836 mi, including Transkei and Ciskei); Namibia (South West Africa), 1,078 km (670 mi); Lesotho, 909 km (565 mi). TERRITORIAL SEA LIMIT: 12 mi.

Bophuthatswana, Ciskei, Transkei, and Venda, whose populations are almost entirely black, would be 74.8% if those four homelands were included. As of 1991, whites accounted for 17.2% (4,521,873) with the homelands excluded, but only for 13.7% with the homelands included; Cape Coloureds, 11.1% (2,929,329); and Asians, 3.3% (863,874).

The black population includes a large number of peoples. According to a 1985 estimate, the largest groups were the Zulu, about 5.3 million; Xhosa, 2.1 million; Northern Sotho, 2.6 million; Southern Sotho, 1.6 million; Tswana, 1.1 million; Shangana-Tsongo, 1 million; and Swazi, 841,000. Bophuthatswana, Ciskei, Transkei, and Venda contained another 3.5 million Xhosa and 1.6 million Tswana.

About 60% of the whites are descendants of Dutch, French Huguenot, and German settlers, and about 40% are of British descent; South Africans of European, especially Dutch, descent are called Afrikaners. The Cape Coloureds are a long-established racial amalgam of white, Hottentot, and other African, Indian, and Malay lineage. Some 86% live in Cape Province.

The Asians include descendants of Indian, East Indian, and Chinese indentured laborers who were not repatriated after their brief period of service as miners.

9 LANGUAGES

The interim constitution adopted in 1993 recognized 11 languages as official at the national level. Afrikaans, English, isi

Ndebele, Sesotho sa Leboa, Sesotho, isi Swati, Xitsonga, Setswana, Tshivenda, isi Xhosa, and isi Zulu. The African languages spoken in South Africa are of the Niger-Congo family. In general, English is more commonly spoken in the cities, and Afrikaans in the rural areas.

Afrikaans is a variant of the Dutch spoken by the 17th-century colonists, and it includes lexical items, phrases, and syntactic structures from Malay, Portuguese, the Bantu group, Hottentot, and other African languages, as well as from English, French, and German. Afrikaans has borrowed from English words such as *gelling* (gallon), *jaart* (yard), *sjieling* (shilling), and *trippens* (three pence), while English has taken over *kraal, veld,* and other Afrikaans words. More than 70% of South African whites are bilingual. Afrikaans was the mother tongue of 58%, and English of 39% in 1991; the remaining 3% included speakers of German, Portuguese, and other languages. Some 83% of Coloureds spoke Afrikaans as their first language. Asians mostly (95%) spoke English as their first language. Zulu was the most comon language of the blacks; 39% spoke it as their first language (excluding blacks in the four "sovereign" homelands).

10 RELIGIONS

In the early 1990s, nearly 70% of the population was Christian, and about 28% followed indigenous tribal religions. Black Christians were found in substantial numbers in all the European denominations, as well as in some 3,000 separatist sects under their own leaders. Nearly half of white South Africans, including almost all the Afrikaans-speaking population, belonged to the Dutch Reformed churches. The next-largest denomination was the Anglican (Episcopal), with 10% of the white population. About 9% was Methodist, 8% Roman Catholic, and 3% Presbyterian. About 3% of the white population was Jewish. Most Christian nonwhites were members of the Dutch Reformed, Anglican, Roman Catholic, and other Christian churches. Most Asians retained their Asian religions, principally Hinduism (1.3%) and Islam (1.1%). In 1993 there were about 100,000 Jews in South Africa, and some 8,000 Baha'is.

11 TRANSPORTATION

South Africa's transportation network is among the most modern and extensive on the continent. In 1991 there were 188,309 km (117,015 mi) of national and provincial roads, of which 54,013 km (33,564 mi) were paved. There were 3,488,570 automobiles and 1,899,721 commercial vehicles in 1992.

The South African Transport Service, a government department under the minister of transport affairs, operates the railways, principal harbors, South African Airways, and some road transportation services. In 1991 there were 20,638 route-km (12,824 route-mi) of track. South African Railways wants to introduce 200-km/hr (120-mph) "bullet" trains between Pretoria and Johannesburg.

In 1991, the South African merchant fleet consisted of a total volume of 213,000 GRT. South Africa's seven ports, owned and operated by the government, include the deepwater ports of Durban, Port Elizabeth, and Table Bay (at Cape Town); other ports with good facilities are Richards Bay, Saldanha Bay, East London, and Mosselbaai (or Mossel Bay).

The government-owned South African Airways, which operates both international and domestic flights, carried 1,957,900 passengers and flew 78 million ton-km of freight during five months of activity in 1991. Jan Smuts Airport, near Johannesburg, is the major international airport; other international airports are located at Cape Town and Durban.

12 HISTORY

Fossil skulls suggest that South Africa may have been one of the earliest scenes of human evolution. Little is known of the original settlers, but when Europeans first arrived, there were two distinct groups of peoples—the Bushmen, primitive nomadic hunters of the western desert upland country, and the Hottentots, a pastoral people who occupied the southern and eastern coastal areas. Before AD 100, Bantu-speaking peoples entered the Transvaal from the north, settling territories in the north and east.

In 1488, the Portuguese sailor Bartholomeu Dias discovered the Cape of Good Hope, and on Christmas Day of 1497, Vasco da Gama discovered Natal. The first European settlement at the Cape was made in 1652 under Jan van Riebeeck on behalf of the Dutch East India Co., which needed a refreshment station on the route to the East. Because there was a shortage of farm labor, the Dutch imported slaves from West Africa, Madagascar, and the East Indies, and because of the scarcity of European women, mixed marriages took place, eventually producing the Cape Coloured people. Huguenot settlers joined the small Dutch settlement in 1688. Continued demands for meat and relatively poor agricultural production encouraged the development of cattle farming, which in turn led to the need for more grazing land. Settlements were established on the coastal plain, along the valleys, and on the Great Karoo. The European population multiplied, but the Bushmen and Hottentots declined in numbers. The first contacts with Bantu-speaking Africans were made along the Great Fish River, which, in 1778, the Cape authorities proclaimed the boundary between the colonists and the Africans. The first serious clash came in 1779, when invading Xhosa tribesmen were driven back across the river border. Three more frontier wars were fought by 1812.

In 1795, Britain occupied the Cape, and in 1814, the area was ceded to the UK by the Treaty of Vienna. The free Coloured inhabitants of the Cape were given the same legal and political status as whites, and in 1834, slavery was abolished. Because of severe droughts and in reaction to British policy and administration, about 6,000 Boers (Dutch farmers) undertook the Great Trek in 1834–36, migrating northward into the present Orange Free State and the Transvaal. Some crossed the Drakensberg Mountains into Natal. The British annexed Natal in 1843 and extended their rule over Kaffraria in 1847, Griqualand West in 1871, and Zululand and Tongaland in 1887. The Transvaal was annexed in 1877 but returned to independence after a revolt in 1880–81, culminating in a British defeat by the Boers at Majuba Hill. In 1881, Swaziland also was declared independent. After a war between the Boers and Basutos, the British proclaimed Basutoland (now Lesotho) a British territory, and in 1884, it became a British protectorate. The British granted local self-government to the Cape in 1872 and to Natal in 1897.

Meanwhile, the spread of European settlements into areas occupied by Africans led to the setting aside of large native reserves and to the development of separate white and black communities. In 1860, indentured Indians were brought into Natal to work on the sugarcane plantations; by 1911, when India halted the emigration because of what it called "poor working conditions," more than 150,000 Indians had come to South Africa as contract laborers. It was in South Africa, while pursuing the Indians' claims of injustice, that Mohandas (Mahatma) Gandhi, then a young lawyer, developed his philosophy of nonviolent resistance.

The discovery around 1870 of diamonds along the Orange and Vaal rivers and in the Kimberley district led to an influx of foreigners and brought prosperity to the Cape and the Orange Free State. Railways were built and trade increased. The discovery of gold on the Witwatersrand in 1886 brought in thousands of additional newcomers and made Transvaal potentially the wealthiest state. Tension between the Boers and outsiders attracted to Transvaal was accentuated by an unsuccessful attempt to capture Johannesburg by Dr. Leander Starr Jameson (Jameson Raid) in 1895–96 and culminated in the South African (or Boer) War in 1899–1902. After a desperate struggle against the larger British forces, the Boer republics of Transvaal and the Orange Free State gave up their independence by the Treaty of Vereeniging on 31 May 1902 but shortly thereafter were granted self-government by the British. In a convention during 1908–9, the leaders of the Afrikaners (as the Boers were now called), together with those from the Cape and Natal, drafted a constitution for a united South Africa that passed the British Parliament as the South Africa Act in 1909 and became effective on 31 May 1910. The constitution provided for a union of the four territories or provinces, to be known as the Union of South Africa. In 1913, the Union Parliament passed the Bantu Land Act, setting aside 8.9 million hectares (22 million acres) of land as black areas; an additional 6.3 million hectares (15.6 million acres) were added to the black homelands by another parliamentary act in 1936.

The Union of South Africa fought with the Allies in World War I, signed the Treaty of Versailles, and became a member of the League of Nations. In 1920, the League gave South Africa a mandate over the former German colony of South West Africa (now generally called Namibia), which lasted until 1946, when South Africa refused to recognize UN authority over the area and regarded it as an integral part of the country. In 1926, a British declaration granted South Africa national autonomy and equal legal status with the UK. Mining and industrialization advanced in the period between the two wars. More intensive exploitation of the wealth of the country led to better living standards. South Africa sent troops to fight the Nazis in World War II, although many Afrikaners favored neutrality. In 1948, the National Party (NP) took power, influencing the general character of life in South Africa and, in particular, enforcing its policies of apartheid, or racial separation (officially called "separate development" after 1960) of whites and nonwhites.

South Africa's white electorate approved a republican form of government in a 1960 referendum, and South Africa became a republic on 31 May 1961. The republican constitution did not deviate substantially from the former one, the only major change being the substitution of a president for the monarch as the head of state. As a result of objections from nonwhite members of the Commonwealth of Nations to South Africa's presence, South Africa withdrew its application for continued Commonwealth membership in 1961.

The immediate period surrounding the creation of the republic was one of mounting pressures applied to the government because of its apartheid policies. In 1960, black unrest swelled to the point where a state of emergency was declared. On 21 March 1960, a black demonstration was staged against the "pass laws," laws requiring blacks to carry "reference books," or internal passports, thus enabling the government to restrict their movement into urban areas. The demonstration resulted in the killing at Sharpeville of 69 black protesters by government troops and provided the touchstone for local black protests and for widespread expressions of outrage in international forums. During 1963–64, the government acted to stiffen its control over blacks living in white areas. After 1 May 1963, the General Law Amendment Act allowed the government to hold people for consecutive 90-day periods without trial (the length was decreased to 15 days in 1966). In 1965, the Suppression of Communism Amendment Bill renewed the government's authority to detain for security reasons persons who had completed prison sentences.

As the Portuguese colonial empire disbanded and blacks came to the fore in Mozambique and Angola during the mid-1970s, South African troops joined the Angolan civil conflict, in an unsuccessful attempt to prevent a Soviet-backed faction from coming to power, but then withdrew from Angola in March 1976. South Africa subsequently launched sporadic attacks on Angola (which supported insurgents seeking to end South African rule over Namibia) and Mozambique and aided insurgencies in the two former Portuguese territories; these operations (and other raids into Botswana, Lesotho, and Zimbabwe) were apparently in response to the aid and political support given by South Africa's neighbors to the African National Congress (ANC), a black nationalist group.

Beginning in June 1976, the worst domestic confrontation since Sharpeville took place in Soweto, on the outskirts of Johannesburg, where blacks violently protested the compulsory use of Afrikaans in schools; suppression of the riots by South African police left at least 174 blacks dead and 1,139 injured. The Afrikaans requirement was subsequently modified. During the late 1970s, new protest groups and leaders emerged among the young blacks. After one of these leaders, 30-year-old Steven Biko, died while in police custody on 12 September 1977, there were renewed protests. As a result, on 4 November, the UN Security Council approved a mandatory arms embargo against South Africa—the first ever imposed on a member nation.

As of 1981, the government had recognized four of the ten black homelands as "sovereign" states: Bophuthatswana, Ciskei, Transkei, and Venda. All members of the ethnic groups associated with these homelands automatically lost their South African citizenship; the government's stated intent to grant independence to the remaining six homelands meant that the vast majority of South Africa's blacks would eventually lose their South African citizenship. In an effort to conciliate nonwhites and international opinion, the government scrapped many aspects of apartheid in the mid-1980s, including the "pass laws" and the laws barring interracial sexual relations and marriage. A new constitution established legislative houses for Coloureds and Indians in 1984, although only 31% and 20% of the respective eligible voters went to the polls.

These measures failed to meet black aspirations, however, and as political violence mounted, in July 1985, the government imposed a state of emergency in 36 magisterial districts, embracing nearly all of the urban black population, which lasted over seven months. During this time, 7,996 persons were detained and 757 people died in political violence, by government count. A new, nationwide state of emergency was imposed in June 1986, with police and the military exercising extraordinary powers of arrest and detention. At least 4,000 and possibly as many as 10,000 were detained in 1986, including over 1,400 aged 18 or under.

In 1984, South Africa and Mozambique signed an agreement by which each country pledged not to aid the antigovernment forces in the other country; also in 1984, South Africa signed an agreement under which it withdrew forces that it had sent into southern Angola in an effort to forestall aid to guerrillas in Namibia. However, the government continued to hold its neighbors responsible for ANC violence, and South African raids into Botswana, Zambia, and Zimbabwe were conducted during 1985–86. In 1987, the government announced that it was withdrawing troops that it had sent into Angola to aid the rebels fighting against the Angolan government, which was supported by Cuban and Soviet troops.

In July 1987, the government cracked down on the United Democratic Front (UDF), an umbrella organization of over 600 civic, sports, church, trade union, women's, professional, youth and student bodies opposed to apartheid. Some 22 of its leaders were charged with treason and many more were forced to go underground. On 24 February 1988, government banned 17 anti-apartheid organizations, including the UDF and the largest trade union. Repression increased throughout 1987 and 1988, as did protest against state policies. Alternative newspapers, *New Nation* and *Weekly Mail,* were prohibited briefly from publishing. Various anti-apartheid leaders were assassinated by secret hit squads identified with the police and military intelligence. Others were detained and otherwise restricted; still others were served with banning orders. In retaliation, protest strikes and demonstrations mounted, as did organization efforts among anti-apartheid activists.

In 1989, President P.W. Botha resigned as head of the NP after a "mild stroke" in January. He was replaced by F. W. de Klerk who, on 15 August, was also named acting state president. After the 6 September general election, de Klerk was elected to a five-year term as president.

De Klerk launched a series of reforms in September 1989 that led speedily to the release of ANC leader Nelson Mandela and others on 10 February 1990. The ANC and other resistance militants, including the Communist Party, were legalized. Mandela had been in prison 27 years and had become a revered symbol of resistance to apartheid.

At that point, the ANC began to organize within South Africa. Government began "talks about talks" with the ANC and in August 1990, the ANC suspended its armed struggle. Most leaders of the ANC returned from exile. Still, fighting continued, largely between ANC activists and supporters of the Zulu-dominated Inkatha Freedom Party, strongest in Natal province. More than 6,000 people were killed in political violence in 1990 and 1991, many victims of fighting provoked by a "third force" of operatives employed by hardliners within the Defense Force and the police.

In 1991, de Klerk introduced and parliament passed measures to repeal laws that had institutionalized apartheid policies — the Land Act (1913 and 1936), the Group Areas Act (1950), and the Population Registration Act (1950). A number of repressive security acts were repealed as well.

In July, the ANC convened its first full conference in South Africa in 30 years. They elected Mandela president and Cyril Ramaphosa the secretary general. The ailing Oliver Tambo moved from president to a new post, National Chairman.

Meanwhile, negotiations continued over constitutional changes and plans for nonracial elections and the transition to majority rule. Numerous parties engaged in a Convention for a Democratic South Africa (CODESA) starting in December 1991. On 14 September 1991, government, the ANC and Inkatha signed a pact to end factional fighting. Other groups signed on, but it hardly stemmed the high levels of violence. The militant right wing refused to cooperate with any negotiations and agreements. In order to strengthen his negotiating hand, de Klerk called a whites-only referendum for 17 March 1992. Of the 85% turnout, 68.7% supported de Klerk's efforts to negotiate a settlement. By May, however, CODESA talks bogged down. The ANC mounted a series of mass protests against the stalemated CODESA talks. After 42 residents were horribly murdered at Boipatong Township by Zulu hostel dwellers allegedly assisted by police, the ANC withdrew from CODESA. On 7 September, 24 ANC supporters were killed by the Ciskei army troops as they marched in protest on the homeland's capital.

Later that month, negotiations began again between government and the ANC. A 26 September summit between Mandela and de Klerk produced a Record of Understanding that met several key ANC demands. But this angered KwaZulu Chief Mangosuthu G. Buthelezi, so he withdrew from the talks. In February 1993, government and the ANC reached agreement on plans for a transition to democracy. Multiparty negotiations followed in April. An interim parliament was to be elected for a five-year period after a general election in April 1994. All parties gaining over 5% of the vote would be represented in the new cabinet. The new parliament would also serve as a constituent assembly to iron out details of a new constitution. The broad guidelines were agreed upon by the government, the ANC, and other parties in late December 1993. A transitional Executive Council to oversee some aspects of government, including security, came into existence in December 1993. Inkatha, led by Buthelezi, and the right

wing Conservative Party refused to participate. The Conservative Party and Inkatha boycotted the talks on multiparty government. But just a few days before the scheduled elections, Inkatha agreed to participate. White conservatives tried to hold out for an Afrikaner homeland, yet the white right was divided on whether to participate in preelection talks, in the election itself, or whether to take up arms as a last resort. There were inefficiencies and some claims of electoral fraud and intimidation, especially by the ANC against Inkatha in Natal province. The elections proceeded relatively peacefully and with great enthusiasm. They were pronounced "free and fair" by international observers and the independent Electoral Commission.

The results left the ANC as the major vote getter with 62.5%. The NP gained 20.4%; the Inkatha Freedom Party, 10.5%; the Freedom Front, 2.2%; the Democratic Party, 1.7%; and the Pan-Africanist Congress, 1.2%. ANC, thus, was awarded 252 of 400 seats in parliament. It is the governing party in all but two of the nine regions. The IFP carried KwaZulu/Natal and the NP holds the Western Cape. Mandela is president and the ANC's Thabo Mbeki and the NP's de Klerk are deputy presidents. Even Buthelezi was persuaded to take a ministerial post in the cabinet.

13GOVERNMENT

Although the terms of a new constitution have yet to be finalized, the broad outlines were hammered out prior to the 27–29 April 1994 election. There is a 400-seat National Assembly chosen by proportional representation (200 nationally and 200 from regional lists). There is also a Senate of 90 members, 10 from each province or region and selected by each provincial assembly. They serve as both a legislature and a constituent assembly. They also elect the president and deputy presidents. The president names a cabinet, divided proportionally between parties that have gained at least 5% of the vote.

Although the degree of autonomy and the level of power given to the regions is a contentious and undecided issue, the nine provinces have assemblies based on the total number of votes cast in the general election. Thus, the number of members each provincial legislature has depends on the number of votes cast divided by 50,000. The executive branch of the provincial governments are, like the legislatures, allocated proportionally.

14POLITICAL PARTIES

The early division in the South African party system was between those who promoted Afrikaner nationalism and those Afrikaans-speaking and English-speaking persons who worked together toward goals on which both sides could agree. When General Louis Botha formed the first cabinet in 1910, he combined the moderate Afrikaners and English into the South African National Party, which confronted an English-speaking opposition. Soon afterward, however, General J.B.M. Hertzog formed the National Party (NP), dedicated to placing the interests of South Africa above those of the British Empire and to developing the Afrikaner group until it was as powerful as were English South Africans.

Hard-pressed by Hertzog's NP in 1920, General Jan Christiaan Smuts, who succeeded Botha, fused the South African National Party with the English-speaking Unionists, establishing the alignment of the English-speaking, except those in the Labour Party (LP), with moderate Afrikaners. The LP allied itself with Hertzog, who achieved office in 1924. Together they carried through the so-called civilized labor policy, designed to safeguard a wide area in the economy for white labor.

Economic crisis during the Depression forced a new alignment of parties that brought Hertzog and Smuts into coalition in 1933 and fusion in the United Party (UP) in 1934. Daniel F. Malan broke with Hertzog in 1934 to form the "purified" NP, dedicated to a more exclusive and radical Afrikaner nationalism than Hertzog had ever preached.

When World War II broke out, Hertzog wished to remain neutral. Smuts swung the House of Assembly in support of the Allies and became prime minister with the support of all English-speaking South Africans and a substantial group of moderate Afrikaners in the UP. Malan won the 1948 election, the first whose campaign was waged chiefly on the racial issue. The sharpest division between the two parties arose from NP efforts to remove the Coloureds from the common voting roll.

The basic division in the party system was between the NP, which favored the policy of apartheid, or totally separate development of the different races, and the UP, which favored social and residential segregation but economic integration. The members of the NP were mainly Afrikaans-speaking and those of the UP were English-speaking, but each party had a considerable number of members of the other language group. Beginning in 1950, the Nationalists implemented their program of apartheid. Between 1953 and 1987, the NP won nine successive parliamentary elections under four party leaders: Malan (in 1953); Hendrik Frensch Verwoerd (1958, 1961, 1966); Balthazar Johannes Vorster (1970, 1974, 1977); and Pieter W. Botha (1981–87). Vorster, who succeeded Verwoerd as prime minister after the assassination of Verwoerd in 1966, left the office in 1978 to become president. In the following year, however, he was forced to resign because of a political scandal involving the misappropriation of government funds to finance clandestine political and propaganda activities in the US, Norway, and other Western countries. The Nationalists' program met with little effective opposition from the UP, which formally disbanded in 1977. In that year, leaders of the UP and its splinter group, the Democratic Party, which had formed in 1973, established the New Republic Party (NRP), with support from English-speaking voters in Natal and the Eastern Cape. The NRP endorsed continuing white rule, but with a softening of apartheid. In the same year, another merger produced the Progressive Federal Party (PFP), which drew its main backing from English-speaking voters in urban areas and stood for universal suffrage within a federal system, with guarantees of minority rights. In the 1987 elections, the NP increased its representation from 116 (in 1981) to 123 seats. The PFP fell from 26 to 19 seats; the NRP lost 4 of its 5 seats. In 1989, the last national race-based parliamentary elections, the NP suffered a setback, winning just 48% of the vote and 93 seats. The PFP dissolved itself in favor of the Democratic Party, which took 33 seats.

The Conservative Party (CP) opposed any form of power sharing with nonwhites. It was led by a former cabinet minister, Andries Treurnicht. The CP became the official opposition party after winning 23 seats in the 1987 elections and 39 in 1989.

Several Coloured and Indian parties participated in the August 1984 elections for the houses of Parliament created for their respective ethnic groups. The Labour Party, a Coloured party headed by the Rev. Allan Hendrickse, won 76 of the 80 directly elected seats; it opposed the new constitution, advocated repeal of all discriminatory measures, and said that it was campaigning on behalf of all nonwhites but was vague on the question of whether it would accept a unitary state governed on the principle of one-person, one-vote. All five Indian parties participating in the elections favored protection of minority rights and rejected government in a unitary state on the basis of one-person, one-vote. The National People's Party won 18 and Solidarity 17 of the 40 directly elected seats; the two parties formed a governing alliance in January 1986.

In 1985, the government repealed a law that had prohibited people of different racial groups from belonging to the same political party.

Several extraparliamentary organizations of Africans and Asians have been formed on a national basis. The African National Congress (ANC) and the South African Indian Congress have cooperated with each other and have sought to cooperate with white liberal organizations. Banned in 1960, the ANC turned from its earlier tradition of nonviolence toward sabotage and other terrorist acts. In 1987, the government offered to legalize the group if it renounced violence. In 1987 and onward, talks were held outside the country between the ANC and diverse groups of white South Africans.

Notable among the more militant African groups is the Pan-Africanist Congress (PAC), which broke away from the ANC in 1959 and was banned in 1960. The ANC and PAC had been recognized by the UN General Assembly as "the authentic representatives" of the people of South Africa. During the 1970s, a loose coalition of African student groups known as the Black Consciousness Movement developed under the leadership of Steven Biko. The United Democratic Front (UDF) was founded in 1983, claiming at its peak to be a multiracial alliance of nearly 700 groups representing nearly 2 million people. It dissolved itself in August 1991, after having continued resistance to apartheid while the ANC was in exile. Considerable ferment occurred among political parties in the run-up to the 1994 elections. The Inkatha Freedom Party (IFP) headed by Zulu Chief Mangosuthu Buthelezi, at first had a cozy relationship with the NP, but that dissolved once the NP began negotiating in earnest with the ANC. Not until just days before the elections in 1994 did the IFP agree to run candidates. It captured over 10% of the national vote and managed to win the election for the provincial government in Natal. The Freedom Front (FF) became the electoral vehicle for Gen. Constand Viljoen, former head of the Defense Force. He contested the results (2.2% of the vote, nine seats) despite resistance from the CP and other right-wing bodies. The FF seeks to work within the system to achieve the creation of an autonomous Afrikaner state.

The South African Communist Party (SACP) has a long history of opposing racism and apartheid. It was made illegal between 1960 and 1990 and is now an important component of the ANC coalition. Several of its leaders are key cabinet members, although, technically, they also belong to the ANC. Whether they break away to run candidates of their own depends on their links to the trade unions and the ANC's commitment to radical economic policies.

15 LOCAL GOVERNMENT

The four provinces—Cape, Natal, Transvaal, and Orange Free State—dealt chiefly with local matters, such as hospitals, roads, municipal government, and educational matters that can be classified as general affairs (applying to all population groups). The provinces receive annual subsidies from the national government. Elected provincial councils were abolished in 1986 and replaced by regional services councils, with representation by local authorities. Executive power in each province is exercised by an administrator and executive committee appointed by the state president and responsible to the national government.

Under the 1984 constitution, local government was to be assigned to the three parliamentary houses, as applicable, or, in regard to general affairs, to the Department of Constitutional Development and Planning. However, residents in each (segregated) residential area, including blacks, elected primary local authorities, who rendered certain services as well as represented their constituents at the provincial level. As far as local government and administration for whites were concerned, elected municipal councils were retained. The local affairs of blacks living in the six black homelands within the Republic of South Africa were administered by the respective homeland governments.

Under the post-1994 election arrangements, nine provincial governments were established. Their legislatures were determined (in size and party representation) by proportional representation. The actual distribution of governmental powers and responsibilities has to be worked out by the constituent assembly.

A transitional local government arrangement prevails. Local elections are scheduled for late 1994. Meanwhile, city and town councils will be made up 40% by proportional representation, 30% from white, Indian and Coloured wards, and 30% from black wards.

16JUDICIAL SYSTEM

South Africa has a unified judicial system. The Supreme Court has a supreme appellate division and provincial and local divisions with both original and appellate jurisdictions. The Court of Appeals, with its seat in Bloemfontein, the judicial capital, normally consists of the chief justice and a variable number of appellate judges. Special superior courts may be constituted to try security cases, and there were, in 1986, 309 magistrates' offices vested with certain judicial as well as administrative powers. Judges are appointed by the state president. There were no nonwhite judges as of 1987.

The common law of the Republic of South Africa is Roman-Dutch law, which has evolved from the uncodified law of the Netherlands as it existed when the Cape of Good Hope was ceded to Great Britain. It has been influenced by English common law in procedures more than in substantive matters. Trial by jury was abolished in 1969.

Black tribal chiefs and headmen have limited jurisdiction to hear cases in traditional courts. There are appeals courts, divorce courts, and children's courts for blacks. In self-governing black homelands, lower courts have been established by the legislative assemblies.

The judiciary has moved in the direction of more independence from the other branches with instances of alleged political interference with courts on the decline. Prospects have considerably improved for nonwhite law school graduates to receive "Articles of Clerkship" which qualify them for admission to the bar.

17ARMED FORCES

In 1993 the South African defense force consisted of the permanent force, the citizen force, and the commandos, but may change with a new government and constitution in 1994. The permanent force is the regular professional nucleus. All medically fit white male citizens of South Africa are required to serve for 12 months in the armed forces; nonwhites serve on a voluntary basis. After fulfilling this service, conscripts are allotted to the citizen force, which consists of reservists who may be called up in case of war, training, internal disorders, or other national emergencies. The commandos are an armed civilian paramilitary force used to defend their home areas.

In 1993, South Africa had 72,400 personnel, of whom 36,400 were conscripts. The army had 50,000 troops, of whom 18,900 were with the permanent forces. The total strength of the navy was 4,500, of whom 3,300 were permanent force personnel. The air force, with 16,400 regulars and 3,000 conscripts, had 259 combat aircraft and 14–20 armed helicopters. There is also a medical corps of 8,000. In 1993 there were 135,000 active members of the citizen force and 140,000 commandos.

In 1993, South Africa spent $3.5 billion on defense, or about 3 percent of gross domestic product. The South African police numbers 100,000 officers and 37,000 reserves. As they do in the armed forces, African volunteers serve in the police. A special medical service corps of 8,000 supports the armed forces. Before the peace of 1992–94, African guerrillas under ANC direction numbered perhaps 10,000. Homeland self-defense forces had about 8,000 African members.

18INTERNATIONAL COOPERATION

South Africa became a charter member of the UN on 7 November 1945 and has technically remained a member, despite continued disputes with the world body over apartheid and the country's unwillingness to place its League of Nations mandate, Namibia, under UN international trusteeship. After the UN General Assembly put the apartheid issue on its agenda, South Africa retained only token representation at the UN from 1955 to 1958. In 1966, the Assembly terminated South Africa's mandate over Namibia; in 1971, the International Court of Justice issued an advisory opinion holding that South Africa's presence in Namibia was illegal. On separate occasions in 1974, 1979, and 1980, South Africa attempted to participate in the General Assembly's meetings, but each time the Assembly prevented the South African delegation from taking its seat; however, resolutions to expel South Africa from the UN have been vetoed in the Security Council by the UK, US, and France. South Africa agreed in principle in 1978 to permit elections in Namibia that would lead to the territory's independence, but the matter was unresolved until national elections in 1994. The nation adheres to GATT and the Law of the Sea.

South Africa is in the process of reestablishing membership in the ECA, IMF, and the World Bank. South Africa sent token forces to serve with the UN in Korea and has contributed funds to the Office of the High Commissioner for Refugees and to UNICEF. South Africa also belongs to the IAEA, ICAO, IDA, IFC, ITU, UPU, WHO, and WIPO.

A founding member of the Commonwealth of Nations, South Africa withdrew on 31 May 1961 as a result of objections by nonwhite members to its membership. South Africa is joined in a customs union with Botswana, Lesotho, and Swaziland. Originally, the three smaller lands were to have been transferred to South African control, but the plan was dropped by the British after South Africa left the Commonwealth, and the three subsequently became independent.

Despite the existence of certain economic relationships, occasionally covert, the nation has been diplomatically isolated from other states on the African continent since Angola, Mozambique, and Zimbabwe were constituted as black-ruled countries during 1975–80, leaving South Africa as the continent's only white-minority regime. A sports-minded people, white South Africans have shown themselves especially sensitive to the exclusion of South African teams from international competition, such as the Olympic Games (since 1960). Due to recent changes in South Africa's political situation, the country was reinstated to international competition by the International Olympic Committee. South Africa sent a team to the 1992 Winter and Summer Olympics.

19ECONOMY

The opening of the political process to all South Africans and the election of a new multiracial government in 1994 has marked a turning point in South Africa's economic history. With a modest agriculture sector, fabulous mineral wealth, and a diverse manufacturing sector, South Africa's influence extends well beyond its borders. It has a mixed economy, with substantial government intervention and a number of state-owned enterprises existing jointly with a strong private sector. A chief characteristic of the private sector is the high concentration of ownership by a small group of integrated conglomerate structures. For the past five years the economy has been in recession with recovery dependent on the world economy, continued growth in the country's exports, and greater access to foreign capital following the lifting of trade and financial sanctions.

20INCOME

In 1992 South Africa's GNP was $106,019 million at current prices, or $2,670 per capita. For the period 1985–92 the average inflation rate was 14.4%, resulting in a real growth rate in per capita GNP of –1.3%.

In 1992 the GDP was $114,680 million in current US dollars. It is estimated that agriculture, hunting, forestry, and fishing contributed 4% to GDP; mining and quarrying, 9%; manufacturing, 22%; electricity, gas, and water, 4%; construction, 3%; wholesale and retail trade, 12%; transport, storage, and communication, 8%; finance, insurance, real estate, and business services, 13%; community, social, and personal services, 2%; and other sources, 23%.

21 LABOR

Until 1979, the Industrial Conciliation Act authorized the minister of labor to reserve specified classes of work to each race; the more highly paid jobs are still held mainly by whites. In general, most skilled positions are held by whites, while all unskilled labor and more than half the semiskilled labor is nonwhite. Because of a shortage of skilled white labor, nonwhites have been moving up to skilled positions in several sectors. There is a preponderance of male workers over females, partly because black migratory laborers leave their families in the homelands while working in the white areas. As a direct result, most farm work in black areas is performed by women.

As of mid-1991, 11,624,000 persons were classified as economically active; the labor force is expected to grow by nearly 50% during the rest of the decade, reaching 18 million by 2000. In 1991 there were 1,417,127 workers in manufacturing, the majority of whom were nonwhite. In that year, of the 840,747 persons employed in mining, the great majority was black. In 1982, an estimated 2,168,000 blacks from the ten black homelands (including the formerly "independent" homelands) worked in South Africa as commuters or legal migratory workers, and in 1984, some 350,000 legal migrant black workers came from neighboring states, most of them from Lesotho, Malawi, and Mozambique. The number of foreign blacks living and working illegally in South Africa has been estimated at 1,200,000.

Black trade unions were not officially recognized until 1979, when the law was modified to allow blacks not assigned to black homelands to join black trade unions. At the end of 1992 there were 200 registered trade unions. In December 1985, 34 unions, with 450,000 members, formed the Confederation of South African Trade Unions. Other trade union confederations included the Council of Unions of South Africa (180,000 members), the Azanian Confederation of Trade Unions (70,000), the South African Confederation of Labour (127,000), and the Trade Union Council of South Africa (420,000). Since 1956, no union may be affiliated with a political party or candidate. The number of strikes increased with the growth of black participation in unions; in 1988 there were 1,025 strikes, involving 161,679 workers. In 1992, there were 789 strikes involving 137,946 workers.

Industrial councils representing organized labor and management in each industry devise and enforce agreements on working conditions and wages. A wage agreement negotiated by an industrial council has the force of law in the industry concerned if it is published in the *Government Gazette* (the legislative record) following approval by the Ministry of Labour. In industries and trades where employers and employees are not organized, the minister of labour, acting on the advice of the government-appointed wage board, may prescribe compulsory wages and conditions of employment. Average wage increases of 12% in 1992 were significantly below the 16.1% raise of 1991, and did not even exceed the pace of inflation (13.9%).

Hours of work vary from 40 to 46 per week. Some collective agreements provide for three weeks' annual leave, and many industries work a five-day week. Employers must provide satisfactory working conditions and accident-prevention measures. Workers' compensation, financed by employers, covers employees killed or injured at work, and compensation is payable in the case of occupational diseases. Unemployment insurance is paid to certain types of contributing employees. In 1992, unemployment reached an estimated 42%, with over 100,000 jobs lost in manufacturing, mining, and construction. The economy's inability to meet the booming employment demand has pushed many into the informal sector. The National Economic Forum, a tripartite structure representing labor, business, and government, is involved in nurturing job creation and job training.

22 AGRICULTURE

Over 80% of the total land area is available for farming, but only 12% is cultivated. Many areas suffer from erratic rainfall and soil erosion; cultivated land is not expected to exceed 15% in the future because of these adversities. Only 8.5% of cultivated land was irrigated in 1991. The worst drought of this century in southern Africa resulted in near to total crop failure in 1991–92. Many farmers subsequently abandoned the countryside for urban areas. During 1992, total agricultural production fell by 16.8%. Production levels for specific crops fell as much as 75%. Nevertheless, except for rice, tea, coffee, and cocoa, the country is typically self-sufficient in essential food production.

Farming by whites is becoming more diversified, and fertilizers, mechanization, and irrigation are used more widely. Price fluctuations are controlled through marketing boards. The lands farmed by blacks are generally less fertile and productive than white-held areas. The land is owned and worked communally, but since at least 35% of able-bodied males leave the land to work in the mines and in industry, much cultivation, apart from plowing, is done by women using hand hoes. Manure and compost are little used. Development has been handicapped by lack of money, initiative, technical equipment, and skill, as well as by poor transportation facilities. Crop yields are generally low.

The principal crop of both whites and blacks is corn ("mealies")—the staple diet of the blacks—which is grown mainly on the plateau of the Orange Free State and Transvaal. Some 28% of the sown area is planted in corn; output totaled 3,125,000 tons in 1992 (down from 8,709,000 tons in 1990). Wheat can be grown only in winter; production of wheat totaled 1,269,000 tons in 1992 (2,132,000 tons in 1991). An indigenous sorghum ("Kaffir corn") is used by the blacks to make beer and is an important source of protein in their diet. Less important, but planted in considerable quantities, are the other winter cereals—barley, oats, and rye. Because of the drought, in 1992 South Africa had to import 4.8 million tons of cereals—five times the 1990 amount. Potatoes are produced in large quantities on white-owned farms.

Sugarcane, indigenous to the Natal coastal belt, was grown before World War II in quantities sufficient to export. Increasing domestic demand after the war absorbed the total output, but with a rise in production and an expansion of the capacity of sugar mills, South Africa became a large sugar exporter. Sugarcane production totaled 18,500,000 tons in 1992. Deciduous and citrus fruits, some of them exported, are also profitable. Vegetables, peanuts, sunflower seeds, groundnuts, soy beans, coffee, ginger, tobacco, cotton, and various types of fodder plants are used domestically. Wine is an important product; over 90% of it is consumed locally. In 1992, 1,450,000 tons of grapes were produced.

23 ANIMAL HUSBANDRY

Until the end of the 19th century, cattle were kept mainly for draft purposes and bred for strength and endurance; meat and fat needs were provided by sheep. The cattle gave little milk and yielded poor-quality meat, while the sheep gave only fat mutton and no wool. The introduction of foreign breeds and crossbreeding gradually improved the stock, providing excellent meat, wool of fairly good quality, and good milk yields. The country's sheep breeds consist mainly of Merino for wool and Dorpes for mutton. Cattle breeds include the introduced Hereford and Aberdeen

Angus as well as the indigenous Afrikaner. Diary cows are mostly Fresian, forming a well-developed dairy industry.

The livestock in 1992 included 32,110,000 sheep, 13,585,000 head of cattle, 5,900,000 goats, 1,490,000 hogs, and 40 million chickens. Total estimated output of livestock products in 1992 was meat, 1,392,000 tons; milk, 2,390,000 tons; eggs, 221,200,000 tons; and wool, 145,500 tons.

24FISHING

South Africa is Africa's most important fishing nation. The Fisheries Development Corp., established in 1944, has helped modernize equipment, secure better conditions of life for fishermen, and stimulate the catching and canning of fish. In 1993, about 22,000 people were employed in the fishing industry. The fishing fleet is operated mainly from Cape Town harbor.

In 1991, the fish catch amounted to 498,884 tons, and was valued at nearly $38 million. Abalone, hake, kingklip, rock lobster, pilchard, anchovy, oysters, mussels, octopus, and shark were the main varieties caught. Hake accounts for 70% of all domestic white fish sales. One-third of the hake catch and nearly all of the abalone are exported. Major fishery products are fish meal, canned fish, and fish oil.

Rock lobster is caught mainly along the western and southern Cape coasts; about 1,835 tons of rock lobster were caught in 1991, with much of it processed into frozen lobster tails for export. About 75% of the lobster catch is exported. South Africa no longer engages in whaling.

25FORESTRY

South Africa is sparsely wooded, with a wooded and forested area of about 4.5 million hectares (11.1 million acres), or less than 4% of the land area. Cutting in indigenous forests is strictly controlled. Commercial forestry covers 1.2 million hectares (31 million acres), with pine and commercial softwoods, eucalyptus, and wattle the principal timbers produced. South Africa is an important producer of wattle and wattle extract, used in the tanning of leather. Domestic timber production satisfies 90% of domestic needs. Wood is imported for furniture manufacture, railroad ties, and high-quality paper.

26MINING

Since the latter part of the 19th century, the South African economy has been based on the production and export of minerals. Alluvial diamonds were discovered along the Orange River in 1867 and surface diamonds at Kimberly in 1870, and thereafter both types were discovered in other parts of South Africa. The wealth derived from the sale of diamonds provided the initial capital for the development of the Witwatersrand gold mines after gold was discovered in 1886. The market created by the gold mines in turn provided the impetus for coal mining and later for the development of the iron and steel industry, which in its turn required the development of other minerals. In the 20th century, other metallic and nonmetallic ores were discovered and exploited, yielding minerals of industrial importance. Taxation of mining enterprises has supported South African agriculture and financed many of the country's administrative and social needs. The railways were built mainly to transport mineral products, and minerals still form a major part of rail freight.

As of 1991, South Africa (excluding the independent homelands) produced 28% of the world's gold metal (averaging 31% annually from 1987 to 1991), 38% of its chrome ore, 36% of manganese, and 8% of diamonds. South Africa leads the world in the production of gem diamonds and ferrochromium. It is also a leading producer of platinum-group metals, uranium, vermiculite, antimony, industrial diamonds, and asbestos. Other minerals produced include corundum, nickel, talc, copper, tin, and silver. The country also has much coal and iron ore and all the materials

needed for alloying steel, a factor of great importance for its industrial development.

Iron ore production rose from 10,955,336 tons in 1973 to 28,958,000 tons in 1991. South Africa ranked eighth among world producers and seventh among exporters of iron ore in 1991. Coal output increased from 62.4 million tons in 1973 to 178 million tons in 1991. Production of gold rose steadily through the 1960s and 1970s, as the Republic drew not only on the older mines of Transvaal but also on the newer ones of the Orange Free State to keep pace with burgeoning world-market demands. In 1991, 83 gold mines were in production. Gold production averaged 791 tons annually during 1970–80 and totaled 601 tons in 1991. South Africa claims 75% of the world's chromite reserves; production in 1991 totaled 5,110,000 tons. De Beers, the South African mining giant, accounts for 95% of South Africa's production and controls about 80% of the world's uncut diamond trade. South Africa's diamond production in 1991 totaled 8,421,000 carats. In the early and mid-1980s, declining output of diamonds at the Kimberley mines was more than offset by expanded production at the Finsch mine in the northern Cape and at reopened works in Namaqualand. The new Venetia mine in northern Transvaal accounts for about 40% of total production. Dimension stone is also quarried and exported (500,000 tons in 1991). Granite, gabbro, syenite, diabase, tonalite and norite (a.k.a. "black granite") are supplied to Japan, Italy, Spain, and the Middle East. The value of all exported minerals in 1991 was $12.5 billion (down from $12.9 billion in 1990), representing more than 52% of total exports.

27ENERGY AND POWER

South Africa produces at least half of all electricity generated on the African continent. Coal supplies about 80% of the country's primary energy needs. Since 1980, the Department of Mineral and Energy Affairs has directed energy acquisition and distribution. A national high-voltage grid network was established in the 1970s. Electric generation totaled 163,500 million kwh in 1991.

South Africa's electricity consumption is 147 billion kwh (1990). The Electricity Supply Commission generates 93% of the total, primarily from locally mined coal. Peak electricity demand is provided by the hydro facilities of the Orange River Project and Mozambique's Cahora Bassa dam. The Koeberg nuclear power station has encountered serious technical difficulties, but is expected to provide 10% of South Africa's electricity needs when it is fully operational. The Eskom public utility supplied 98% of South Africa's electricity in 1991. Seventeen coal-fired plants accounted for 88.5% of installed capacity; nuclear power, 5.1%; and hydroelectric power, 1.5%. Net generating capacity totaled 26,500 Mw at the end of 1991. Eskom estimated in 1992 that only 30% of South African homes and 10% of the homes in the southern African region had electricity. By 1997, Eskom plans to electrify 3 million homes in South Africa under its "Electricity for All" program. Eskom also exports electricity to several neighboring countries.

In 1992, South Africa was the world's eight largest producer of coal, with an estimated production of 174 million tons. Proven reserves from 19 coal fields in 1992 totaled 55.3 billion tons of anthracite and bituminous coal. The Witbank Basin accounts for over 40% of yearly output. About 65% of annual production comes from underground mining operations. Eskom uses about 40% of annual production for power generation. The South African Coal, Oil, and Gas Corporation (SASOL) is a world leader in oil-from-coal technology. SASOL operates two coal gasification plants in Secunda and one in Sasalburg. SASOL uses about 32 million tons of coal annually in order to provide 4 million tons of fuel per year, mostly to the gasoline market. South Africa produces no crude oil, but does have four crude oil refineries whose current combined annual distillation capacity is about 21.5

million tons. The Mossgas Project plans to develop natural gas condensate deposits at Mossel Bay into synthetic fuel. In March 1992, the project delivered its first sea-to-shore gas to a synthetic fuel plant. The natural gas converted at the plant will be converted into gasoline, diesel oil, and kerosene. The Mossgas Project is a subject of national debate because of its extreme expense.

South Africa ranked seventh in 1991 among uranium-producing countries. Uranium production fell from 4,735 tons mined in 1987 to 1,974 tons in 1991, due to decreased world demand. Gold mines also produce uranium, which can be extracted from mine dumps as well as ore and oxide reserves. Uranium reserves were estimated at 305,000 tons in 1991. Ownership of uranium is vested in the Atomic Energy Corporation on behalf of the state. In 1975, a pilot plant for the manufacture of enriched uranium went into operation at Valindaba (Transvaal), and it was extended to a production plant, scheduled to open in 1987. Africa's only nuclear power station, at Koeburg near Cape Town, began operating in 1984. South Africa and the US are signatories to a 1957 bilateral atomic-power treaty.

28 INDUSTRY

The manufacturing sector is the largest contributor to GDP. It has evolved over the past 70 years, beginning with light consumer industry in the 1920s and expanding into heavy industry with the creation of ISCOR (Iron and Steel Corporation of South Africa) in 1928. Industrial growth expanded at a 10.2% average annual rate in the 1960s. This slowed to 2.9% in the 1970s. Industry is localized in the southern Transvaal, western Cape, Durban-Pinetown and Port Elizabeth-Uitenhage areas. Government attempts to decentralize industry were economically unsuccessful and the policy was reformed in 1991.

The largest industrial sector is the metal products and engineering sector dominated by ISCOR, now privatized. The steel industry feeds a substantial motor vehicle sector. The food, beverage, and tobacco industry is expanding, employing 16% of the manufacturing labor force, but contributes less to exports than previously. The clothing and textiles sector produces 90% of local needs. The chemical sector centers on sizeable fertilizer production and the Modderfontein explosives factory. The sector is also home to the synthetic fuels production industry which, with three plants in operation, serves 40% of the nation's motor fuels demand.

29 SCIENCE AND TECHNOLOGY

Among South Africa's earliest research ventures was the Royal Observatory at the Cape of Good Hope, established by the British Admiralty in 1820. Societies of leading engineers, architects, chemists, metallurgists, and geologists were organized in the 1890s, and the South African Association for the Advancement of Science was established in 1902. The Council for Scientific and Industrial Research (founded 1945) has 13 research divisions. The Atomic Energy Corporation established an experimental nuclear reactor in 1965 and has since directed the government's nuclear program; in 1970, it was announced that its researchers had devised a new uranium-enrichment process, subsequently developed by the national Uranium Enrichment Corp. The Scientific Advisory Council to the Minister of National Education (established in 1962) promotes the application of scientific knowledge and recommends national science policies and programs.

30 DOMESTIC TRADE

Although blacks in South Africa comprise 80% of the population, they only have 36% of the income, up from 26% in 1970. Until the late 1970s, discriminatory legislation severely reduced the rate of economic opportunities open to South African blacks.

Blacks were prohibited from forming corporations, owning manufacturing plants, or entering most skilled professions. With the recent changes in the government, some marketing experts envision a new integrated market developing as blacks take advantage of the freedom of mobility and spread over a wider geographic area. Nonwhite South Africans now account for approximately 60% of all consumer spending.

Business hours are from 8:30 AM to 5 PM, Monday through Friday, and from 8:30 AM until 12:30 PM on Saturday. Banks are usually open weekdays from 9 AM to 3:30 PM, but only to 1 PM on Wednesdays, and from 8:30 to 11 AM on Saturdays. There are many advertising agencies. Total expenditures on advertising were well over R1 billion in 1983. The Advertising Standards Authority of South Africa seeks to improve standards.

31 FOREIGN TRADE

Gold and other metals and minerals are the most valuable export commodities. In 1986, the US banned imports of South African coal, uranium, textiles, iron, steel, agricultural products, and foodstuffs. A Commonwealth Committee (except the UK) agreed to recommend banning the import of South African agricultural products, uranium, coal, and iron and steel to its member nations. The European Economic Community (EEC) banned iron and steel. International sanctions were lifted as progress was made toward the 1994 transition to a multiracial government.

The principal exports in 1992 (in millions of rand) were as follows:

Base metals and products	9,399.0
Precious stones and metals	7,570.8
Textiles	1,734.6
Chemicals	3,286.6
Mineral products	7,558.8
Food, beverages, tobacco	1,891.1
Vegetable products	2,208.6
Other exports	33,807.3
TOTAL	67,456.8

By far the largest expenditures on imports are for machinery (28.8%), chemicals, and motor vehicles. The principal imports in 1992 (in millions of rand) were as follows:

Chemicals	5,766.3
Artificial resins and plastics	2,226.6
Paper, paperboard, etc.	1,512.9
Textiles	2,475.0
Base metals	2,462.8
Machinery	14,965.9
Transport equipment	6,505.7
Scientific instruments	2,226.1
Other imports	13,775.9
TOTAL	51,917.2

The leading buyer of South African exports in 1991 was Switzerland (8.9%), followed by the UK (7.8%), Japan (6.3%), the US (6.2%) and Germany (5.3%). Imports came from Germany (17.6%), the US (13.7%), Japan (10.6%), and the UK (10.3%).

32 BALANCE OF PAYMENTS

Gold invariably represents the great majority of the country's international reserves. In 1992, major capital outflows and a decline from the 1991 record surplus on the current account resulted in the fall of R2.3 billion in net foreign reserves for the year, compared to increases of R2.9 billion and R1.4 billion in 1990 and 1991. At the end of 1992, the total gross gold and foreign reserves amounted to R11.2 billion (up R1.4 billion from 1991), equivalent to about two months of import cover.

In 1992 merchandise exports totaled US$23,645 million and imports US$18,216 million. The merchandise trade balance was US$5,429 million. The following table summarizes South Africa's balance of payments for 1991 and 1992 (in millions of US dollars):

	1991	1992
CURRENT ACCOUNT		
Goods, services, and income	2,595	1,282
Unrequited transfers	70	106
TOTALS	2,665	1,388
CAPITAL ACCOUNT		
Direct investment	−8	−5
Portfolio investment	−196	524
Other long-term capital	−768	−1,041
Other short-term capital	1,200	429
Exceptional financing	−388	282
Other liabilities	−6	−10
Reserves	−1,110	−402
TOTALS	−1,276	−223
Errors and omissions	−1,388	−1,163
Total change in reserves	−1,089	−476

33 BANKING AND SECURITIES

The South African Reserve Bank, the central bank of issue, began operations in 1921, and in 1924 assumed liability for the outstanding notes of the commercial banks. It purchases and disposes of the entire gold output. At the end of 1993, the Reserve Bank held 1,008 million troy ounces of gold. In September 1985, because of a net outflow of capital arising from South Africa's declaration of a state of emergency, a two-tier foreign-exchange system was adopted by the bank, involving a commercial rand for current transactions and a financial rand for investments or disinvestments by nonresidents. At the same time, certain debt payments, mainly to foreign banks, were frozen; limited payments were resumed in April 1986.

In 1993 there were 10 commercial banks, 8 merchant banks, and 3 discount houses. Each bank is required to maintain a reserve balance with the South African Reserve Bank equal to 8% of its short-term liabilities. Since the commercial banks have restricted themselves to traditional functions, many other institutions have been established to make loans or investments to stimulate economic growth and development. The government has sponsored financial institutions such as the Development Bank of South Africa, the Corporation for Public Deposits, the Industrial Development Corp. (IDC), the Fisheries Development Corp., and the Corporation for Economic Development.

The Johannesburg Stock Exchange ranks 10th in the world in market capitalization. As of February 1992, its total capitalization was R532,540 million, compared with R399,395 in 1991.

34 INSURANCE

Life insurance in force in 1992 totaled R720,000 million. Automobile third-party liability is compulsory; compulsory workers' compensation insurance is virtually a government monopoly. At the beginning of 1994, a consortium of black investors negotiated a deal to buy 51% of African Life, a life insurance company serving over 2 million customers, for R160 million from majority share holders.

35 PUBLIC FINANCE

The fiscal year runs from 1 April to 31 March. The minister of finance presents the budget to Parliament in March for authorization of expenditures and imposition of the necessary taxes. The following table shows actual revenues and expenditures for 1989 and 1990 in millions of rand.

	1989	1990
REVENUE AND GRANTS		
Tax revenue	67,055	70,435
Non-tax revenue	5,089	5,738
Capital revenue	899	168
Grants	334	646
TOTAL	73,377	76,987
EXPENDITURES & LENDING MINUS REPAYMENTS	73,942	88,762
Deficit/Surplus	−565	−11,775

In 1990 South Africa's total public debt stood at R98,210 million, of which R1,595 million was financed abroad.

Government spending in 1992–93 ran 18.2% over budget due to the unexpected addition of R3.4 billion in drought relief efforts. Meanwhile, revenues rose only 4% from the previous year but were still R9.6 billion short of anticipated income. As a result of the recession and tax structure and collection shortcomings, the government borrowing requirement rose to 8.6% of GDP.

36 TAXATION

The principal taxes are income tax, which accounts for more than half of total current receipts; customs and excise duties; and a 10% value-added tax started in 1993. Taxes fall into two categories: those levied by the government on all persons and companies deriving income from South African sources, and provincial taxes payable only by persons resident in the Republic. There is no tax on capital gains. Company tax for all enterprises except gold and diamond mines is 48% of taxable income. Gold mines are taxed according to the ratio of profits to gross sales; oil and gas companies pay 48% plus a 3% surcharge; other mining companies, 48% plus a surcharge (3% in 1993). Income tax is paid according to a progressive scale and varies with income, marital status, and gender. The pay-as-you-earn system of income tax payment was instituted in April 1963.

Other taxes include provincial and city taxes, transfer taxes, donations tax, stamp duties, and licenses.

37 CUSTOMS AND DUTIES

Although South Africa has signed GATT and has been liberalizing import controls with the intention of eventually removing them completely, some classes of imports are still subject to licenses and control regulations. Customs duties are levied on a wide variety of imports but commonly at moderate rates, although a surcharge of 5–40% is imposed on a number of goods. Excise taxes ranging from 10–35% are raised principally on liquor, wine, beer, cigarettes, petroleum products, and new automobiles. One of the heaviest duties is on petroleum products; a portion of this tax helps finance the extension of main roads.

South Africa maintains a common customs area with Botswana, Lesotho, Namibia, Swaziland, and the black homelands of Bophuthatswana, Ciskei, Transkei, and Venda, through the South African Customs Union. Common customs, excise, and sales duties are levied, but the other members may impose additional tariffs for protective purposes.

38 FOREIGN INVESTMENT

Despite a considerable increase in recent years in domestic savings available for investment, foreign capital investment plays a significant role in South African economic development, and a number of manufacturing and industrial concerns have been established by the UK, the US, and continental European companies since World War II. By 1987, gross domestic fixed investment totaled R29,025 million. UK capital has been invested primarily in manufacturing and in the development of new gold fields in Transvaal and the Orange Free State. Prominent British firms have established themselves in heavy engineering. American investments are mainly in mining and manufacturing, and in wholesale and retail trade. Some 250 American companies accounted for about one-fifth of total foreign investment in South Africa as of 1982. However, between 1984 and early 1987, the number of US companies with direct investments in South Africa dropped from 325 to 259; among the 29 US companies that pulled out in 1986 were IBM and General Motors, which sold their subsidiaries to local interests. In 1986, the US and the EEC banned new investment in South Africa. Restrictions imposed in September 1985 on the ability of nonresidents to repatriate capital, including dividend remittances, have also had a dampening effect on foreign investment. Investment was 15% in 1992 compared to an average 24% between 1982 and 1985. The establishment of multiracial government and the lifting of sanctions should lead to expanded foreign investment in South Africa.

39 ECONOMIC DEVELOPMENT

The recession of 1989 to 1993 was provoked by a drop in investment from 24% to 15%. With the inauguration of multiracial government, this investment is likely to be restored and is key to the economy's ability to create new jobs and to generate growth. Tremendous changes in the structure of the economy are required as well to relieve the pressures of poverty and inequality which have resulted from apartheid. A realistic strategy that attends to popular expectations and aspirations as well as to sound economic principles will look to reducing tariffs and other restrictive practices, linking wages and output, ending exchange controls, reforming taxes, and optimizing welfare allocations.

40 SOCIAL DEVELOPMENT

South Africa has a comprehensive system of social legislation, which includes unemployment insurance, industrial accident insurance, old age pensions, disability pensions, war veterans' pensions, pensions for the blind, maternity grants, and (for whites prior to 1990) allowances for large families of small means. The cost of most of these benefits is borne by the national government, but the cost of industrial accident insurance is borne by employers, while contributions to the unemployment insurance fund are made by employers, employees, and the government. These benefits are made available on a graduated scale related to the standard of living of the different racial groups. In addition, there are about 25 major private welfare organizations partly subsidized by government funds. A variety of pension and provident funds also have been established by railways, commercial and business firms, and the gold-mining industry for the protection of employees and their families.

Human-rights activists have long focused on South Africa's perpetuation of white-minority rule, its disfranchisement of the black majority, and its restrictions on the rights of Coloureds and Asians. The national government long claimed that black protest movements were Communist-instigated. It assumed broad powers under South African law to ban any organization suspected of communism or subversive activities, to prohibit its publications, to liquidate its assets, and to detain without court proceedings (for up to six months) or to strip of civil rights any of its members or known supporters. All outdoor gatherings, except sporting events or specially authorized meetings, were banned between 1976 and 1990. The state of emergency imposed regionally in 1985 and reimposed nationally in 1986 allowed any member of the police or military to arrest and detain, on his own authority, any person whom he believed to be a threat to public safety. Much of that security legislation was repealed in the final months of the de Klerk government. The current ANC "government of national unity" is seeking to provide more social services for its black constituents within the context of the constraints of a weakened economy. Its first priority is housing, health, education, and the creation of more jobs in the formal economic sector.

41 HEALTH

As of 1992, the South African government increased its spending in the public and private sectors of health care. Emphasis on better health care resulted in numerous projects to expand and modernize existing hospitals and clinics, as well as build new ones. There was also emphasis on preventive health care, as well as a greater demand for laboratory analysis and therapeutic equipment and disposables. Most electronic and high-tech equipment is imported.

South Africa's governmental policy has been directed toward a more streamlined and equitable public health service to bridge the country's social and ideological divisions. With apartheid dissolved and a new 1994 government in place, other new programs may come into being. Provincial administrations maintain most major hospitals and receive subsidies from the national government. Hospital care is free for those unable to bear the costs, including nonwhites, but medical treatment is generally conducted on a private basis.

In 1990, there were 684 hospitals, with Baragwanath Hospital near Johannesburg the largest in southern Africa (nearly 3,000 beds). In 1989, there were 143,519 hospital beds (4.8 per 1,000 people). Private health care equaled 35% of total health care expenditures in 1990 ($5,671 million) and was growing fast. Chains of independent hospitals were being established.

In 1989 there were 22,260 physicians and, in 1992, there were 0.61 doctors per 1,000 people with a nurse to doctor ratio of 4.5. In 1990, the population per physician was 1,750. About 80% of doctors take care of urban citizens (only 56% of the population). Large sectors of the population live in conditions nearer to those of a developing country.

There are medical schools at the universities of Cape Town, Stellenbosch, Witwatersrand, Pretoria, Natal, and the Orange Free State. Since 1959 (and prior to 1994), most nonwhite medical students attended the nonwhite medical school at the University of Natal. The Medical University of Southern Africa (near Pretoria) was opened for black students in 1978. The South African Institute for Medical Research in Johannesburg is well known for its studies of silicosis and other diseases to which mine workers are subject. The most prevalent infectious diseases reported in South Africa in 1984 were tuberculosis, measles, typhoid, malaria, and viral hepatitis. Circulatory disorders are the leading causes of death. By 1990, leprosy had been reduced to less than 1 per 100,000, but malaria and tuberculosis still cause serious problems. In 1990, there were 250 cases of tuberculosis per 100,000 people and 650 cases of AIDS.

The 1993 population of South Africa was 40.8 million, with a birth rate of 31.3 per 1,000 people and about 48% of married women (ages 15 to 49) using contraception. There were 1.3 million births in 1992. Children up to one year of age were immunized in 1992 against tuberculosis (85%); diphtheria, pertussis, and tetanus (67%); polio (69%); and measles (63%).

Infant mortality in 1992 was 53 per 1,000 live births, and the maternal mortality rate was estimated at 84 per 100,000 live births in 1991. The overall mortality rate was 8.6 per 1,000 people in 1993. Between 1983 and 1992, there were about 15,000 deaths due to political and ethnic violence. Average life expectancy was 63 years in 1992.

42 HOUSING

In 1994 the housing backlog was estimated to be 1.2 million homes for the black population, while there is a surplus of white housing units of 83,000. Experts in south Africa forecast that almost 3 million homes will have to be provided by the year 2000 in the urban areas of the country. Recently, there has been an explosive growth of shacks and shantytowns surrounding South Africa's major urban areas. This backlog and demand translate into the need to build 250,000 dwelling units a year until the end of the century, or roughly 1,000 units per working day. Presently, only 25,000 dwelling units are being built each year.

Most of the black townships and squatter settlements lack the basic infrastructure and services of water, sewage, and electricity. Efforts to solve South Africa's housing problem must focus not only on construction. but on servicing current and prospective sites by building roads and providing electricity, sanitation, and water. For example, an estimated 66% of the country's population have no access to electricity, and in most black townships there is only one water tap per several thousand people.

43 EDUCATION

Systems of primary, secondary, and university education are generally provided in separate English-language and Afrikaans-language institutions. Education for whites is free and compulsory between the ages of 7 and 16. In 1984, 988,369 white children attended 2,379 provincial and private schools. Education is also free for Coloureds and Asians between the ages of 7 and 16 (Coloureds) or 15 (Asians). School attendance is not generally compulsory for blacks. Adult literacy was close to 100% for whites and about 50% for blacks in the mid-1980s.

Since the Soweto riots of 1976, the national government has greatly increased expenditures for black education, and black student enrollment has risen sharply. The government reported in 1991 that primary and secondary schools combined had 1,021,442 white students, 5,794,100 blacks, 874,315 coloured, and 255,529 Asians.

Of the 11 universities mainly for whites, 5 are Afrikaans-language (Orange Free State at Bloemfontein, Potchefstroom, Pretoria, Rand Afrikaans University, and Stellenbosch); 4 are English-language (Cape Town, Natal at Durban and Pietermaritzburg, Rhodes at Grahamstown, and Witwatersrand at Johannesburg); the University of Port Elizabeth teaches in both Afrikaans and English; and the University of South Africa at Pretoria is for correspondence students. In 1991 there were 21 universities and even those universities which were not admitting students from other races prior to the 1980s, now started admitting them. In 1984 there were 198,675 students enrolled in these universities (excluding correspondence students), including about 7,500 non-whites. In that year, 19,231 students were enrolled in the four black universities. The University of the Western Cape is for Coloureds, and the University of Durban-Westville is for Indians. In 1984, 11,160 students were enrolled at the two universities. In 1991, all university-level students were estimated as follows: 157,432 white; 110,130 blacks; 19,575 Coloureds; and 21,035 Asians.

44 LIBRARIES AND MUSEUMS

The principal libraries include the Cape Town City Libraries, the Johannesburg Public Library, the South African Library (Cape Town), the University of Cape Town Libraries, the Library of Parliament (Cape Town), the University of Witwatersrand Library, the University of Pretoria Libraries, the State Library (Pretoria), and the University of the Orange Free State Library.

The Africana Museum in Johannesburg contains outstanding displays of black life. The Kaffrarian Museum in King William's Town has imposing collections of indigenous animals. The National Museum in Bloemfontein contains an ictidosaur skeleton and the Florisbad human fossil skull. The East London Museum houses the first coelacanth to be caught (the entire family had previously been thought to be extinct). Two important institutions in Cape Town are the South African Cultural History Museum and the South African National Gallery.

45 MEDIA

The government operates the postal, telegraph, and telephone services through the Department of Posts and Telecommunications. In 1992 there were over 4.5 million telephones. The South African Broadcasting Corp. (SABC), a semigovernmental organization, offers transmissions in English, Afrikaans, and nine Bantu languages. It derives its income from listeners' licenses and from its commercial services. External broadcasting services are operated by the Voice of South Africa. The country's first television service was begun in January 1976 under government auspices. In 1981 a separate channel began broadcasting to blacks in native languages. In 1986 there were 4 commercial broadcasting services, with transmissions in English, Afrikaans, and four Bantu languages. There were an estimated 3,800,000 television sets and 11,800,000 radios in 1991.

The English and Afrikaans populations have their own newspapers, distinguished not only by language but also by the variety and slant of news. Two Sunday newspapers are published in Johannesburg and two in Durban, one in Afrikaans and three in English. About 150 local newspapers appear weekly or biweekly. Magazines and general periodicals are divided equally between Afrikaans and English. The main daily newspaper for blacks, Johannesburg's *The World,* was banned in 1976.

Nearly all newspapers in South Africa are published by members of the Newspaper Press Union (NPU). Its main function is to hear and decide complaints against the press in cases where the complaints do not fall under the jurisdiction of the courts. The Media Council, established by the NPU, seeks to maintain editorial standards and to deal with infringements of the NPU press code. In 1974, the press code was amended to compel newspapers to exercise "due care and responsibility" in matters relating to racial, ethnic, religious, and cultural groups in South Africa. On political matters, such as the 1979 scandal that led Vorster to resign the presidency, the press is capable of acting with investigative freedom and vigor. Nevertheless, the government does have the power to prohibit subsequent editions of any South African periodical whose contents are considered undesirable. Stringent new government regulations in December 1986 imposed a broad range of news censorship, including prepublication censorship.

The largest English-language newspapers (with 1992 daily circulations) are the *Star* (206,991) and *The Citizen* (118,210), in Johannesburg; *Argus* (100,583) and *Cape Times* (60,318), in Cape Town; and the *Daily News* (96,933), in Durban. Important Afrikaans-language dailies include *Die Burger* (77,673), in Cape Town, and *Beeld* (97,894), in Johannesburg. The two largest-circulation Sunday newspapers are the English-language *Sunday Times* (506,114) and the Afrikaans-language *Rapport* (374,828), both in Johannesburg. *The Sowetan,* an English-language Johannesburg daily aimed at a black readership, had a circulation of 157,982 in 1992, and *Ilanga,* published in Zubu and English twice weekly in Durban, had a circulation of 236,910 in the same year.

46 ORGANIZATIONS

The cooperative movement began before the consummation of the Union, concentrating then as now on marketing agricultural produce. The movement's rapid advance, however, dates from 1922, when the first Cooperative Societies Act was passed. Every branch of farming has its own associations, to which about 75% of all farmers belong; these groups are affiliated with provincial organizations, which, in turn, are members of the South African Agricultural Union.

The South African Federated Chamber of Industries is the chief employers' organization. The Association of Chambers of Commerce (ASSOCOM) was formed in 1892 to promote commerce and industry in South Africa. In 1990 the South African Chamber of Business (SACOB) was formed by the merger of the

Association of Commerce and Industry and the South African Federated Chamber of Industries. One hundred and two chambers of commerce and industry are members of SACOB.

To provide special aid to Afrikaans-speaking businesspeople, the Afrikaanse Handelsinstituut was established in Pretoria in 1942. It now assists all Afrikaner businesses involved in commerce, finance, and mining. Membership is offered if at least half the capital of a firm is owned by Afrikaners.

The Royal Society of South Africa, founded in 1877, is the leading scholarly organization. The Geological Society of South Africa (founded in 1895) has published important research in its *Transactions,* and its influence extends beyond South Africa. The African Music Society, an international organization that specializes in the recording of music of all parts of Africa, has its headquarters near Johannesburg. Other organizations have been established for studies in Afrikaans, archaeology, economics, medicine, technology, and other fields.

47TOURISM, TRAVEL, AND RECREATION

Tourists must have valid passports and, in most cases, visas. The tourism industry is based on private enterprise, but the government oversees tourist facilities through the South African Tourist Corporation, which also promotes tourism abroad. In 1991, international sanctions against tourism were lifted with the support of the ANC, and tourist arrivals rose to 1.7 million, with receipts of US$1.05 billion. There were 45,215 hotel rooms with 88,670 beds and a 49.6% occupancy rate.

In addition to the principal cities and many ocean beaches, popular attractions include the Kruger National Park, situated in the northeast, on the Mozambique and Zimbabwe borders, and several game reserves; the Castle of Good Hope fortress at Cape Town (built during 1666–82); and the Kimberley Mine Museum at the site of the famous Big Hole diamond mine. Entertainment facilities include symphony halls, theaters, movies, nightclubs, and discos. Among popular pastimes are golf, tennis, bowls, hunting, horse racing, rugby, soccer, cricket, and water sports.

48FAMOUS SOUTH AFRICANS

Among the most famous tribal leaders in what is now South Africa were Shaka (1773–1828), who built the Zulu into a powerful nation, and Cetewayo (d.1884), who led the Zulu in an unsuccessful war against the British in 1879. Other outstanding figures of 19th-century South Africa were Stephanus Johannus Paulus (Oom Paul) Kruger (1825–1904), president of the Transvaal and leader of the Boers, and British-born Cecil John Rhodes (1853–1902), entrepreneur and empire builder, after whom the Rhodesias (now Zambia and Zimbabwe) were named. Jan Christiaan Smuts (1870–1950), statesman and military leader, was one of the great men of the first half of the 20th century. He and two other prime ministers of Boer descent—Louis Botha (1862–1919) and James Barry Munnik Hertzog (1866–1942)—attempted to merge the two white nationality groups in a common loyalty to the British Commonwealth. Daniel François Malan (1874–1959), an Afrikaner Nationalist leader, led his party to victory in 1948 and served as prime minister (1948–54) when South Africa's racial separation policies were codified. Hendrik Frensch Verwoerd (1901–66), Nationalist prime minister from 1958 until his assassination, vigorously enforced separate development of the races and created the black homelands. His successor, Balthazar Johannes Vorster (1915–83), served as prime minister from 1966 until his elevation to the presidency in 1978; he resigned in the following year because of a political scandal. Pieter Willem Botha (b.1916) became prime minister in 1978 and president in 1984.

Among the best-known South African writers in the English language was Olive (Emily Albertina) Schreiner (1855–1920),

whose *Story of an African Farm* has become a classic. A collection of short stories about Afrikaner farmers, *The Little Karoo,* by Pauline Smith (1882–1957), is regarded as a masterpiece. South African authors of novels and short stories such as Sarah Gertrude Millin (Liebson, b. Russia, 1889–1968), Alan Stewart Paton (1903–88), Sir Laurens Van der Post (b.1906), Peter Abrahams (b.1919), Ezekiel Mphahlele (b.1919), Nadine Gordimer (b.1923), Dan Jacobson (b.1929), and John M. Coetzee (b.1940) have won considerable attention in the UK and the US. Ignatius Roy Dunnachie Campbell (1901–57) was an eminent South African poet, and his friend William Charles Franklyn Plomer (1903–73) was a highly regarded novelist, poet, essayist, and critic. Athol Fugard (b.1932) has written internationally acclaimed plays about South African race relations.

Well-known authors and poets in the Afrikaans language are Cornelis Jacob Langenhoven (1873–1932), author of the national anthem; Christian Frederick Louis Leipoldt (1880–1947); N.P. van Wyk Louw (1906–70); the poet, playwright, and critic Uys Krige (1910–87), who also wrote in English; and André Brink (b.1935). Eugène Nielsen Marais (1871–1936), a journalist, lawyer, poet, and natural historian, was an outstanding student of animal and insect behavior. Breyten Breytenbach (b.1939) has earned international recognition as an important Afrikaans poet; he served seven years in prison (1975–82) after pleading guilty to a passport violation and to illegal contacts with an African political group.

V. (J.E.A.) Volschenck (1853–1935) is sometimes called the "father of South African art," and Anton Van Wouw (b.Netherlands, 1862–1945) is called the "doyen" of South African sculpture. Other artists include the painters Robert Gwelo Goodman (b.England, 1871–1939), Jacob Hendrik Pierneef (1886–1957), and Walter W. Battiss (b.England, 1906–82), also an authority on Bushman art; and the internationally recognized sculptor Coert Laurens Steynberg (1905–82).

Other noted South Africans are historian George McCall Theal (b.Canada, 1837–1919); the physical anthropologist Raymond Arthur Dart (b.Australia, 1893); Clement Martyn Doke (b.England, 1893–1983), an authority on Bantu philology; the social anthropologist Isaac Schapera (1905–86); Louis Franklin Freed (b.Lithuania, 1903), a specialist on tropical diseases; and the pioneer open-heart surgeon, Christiaan Neething Barnard (b.1922). Lord Henry de Villiers of Wynberg (1842–1914) was chief justice of Cape Colony and of the Union of South Africa.

South Africa's first Nobel Prize winner (for peace in 1961) was Chief Albert John Luthuli (1898–1967), a former president of the ANC, who maintained a policy of nonviolence and of cooperation between whites and blacks. Desmond Mpilo Tutu (b.1931), the secretary general of the South African Council of Churches during 1979–84 and an outspoken foe of apartheid, received the 1984 Nobel Prize for peace. As archbishop of Cape Town, he became the Anglican primate for southern Africa in 1986. Nelson R. Mandela (b.1918), a prominent leader of the ANC, was sentenced to life imprisonment in 1964; his release was a principal demand of antigovernment activists. Oliver Tambo (b.1919), the president of the ANC since 1977, directed the group from exile. Another outspoken critic of the government was the Rev. Allan Boesak (b.1947), a UDC founder and the president of the World Alliance of Reformed Churches since 1982. More conciliatory toward the regime was Gatsha Buthelezi (b.1928), the chief of the Zulu people, who heads the Inkatha movement; he favors a gradualist approach to black power sharing.

49DEPENDENCIES

South Africa has no territories or colonies. Until recently South Africa maintained a civil administration and a military presence in Namibia (South West Africa). Namibia, a sovereign state, is discussed under its own heading elsewhere in this volume.

50 BIBLIOGRAPHY

American University. *South Africa: A Country Study.* Washington, D.C.: Government Printing Office, 1981.

Barthorp, Michael. *The Anglo-Boer Wars: The British and the Afrikaners, 1815–1902.* New York: Blandford Press, 1987.

Brewer, John D. *After Soweto: An Unfinished Journey.* New York: Oxford University Press, 1986.

Buthelezi, Gatsha. *South Africa: My Vision of the Future.* London: Weidenfeld and Nicolson, 1990.

Carter, Gwendolen M. *Which Way Is South Africa Going?* Bloomington: Indiana University Press, 1980.

Danziger, Christopher. *South African History: 1910–1970.* New York: Oxford University Press, 1978.

Davenport, T. R. H. *South Africa: A Modern History.* 3rd ed. Toronto: University of Toronto Press, 1987.

Kalley, Jacqueline A. *South Africa under Apartheid: A Select and Annotated Bibliography.* Westport, Conn.: Meckler, 1989.

Kanfer, Stefan. *The Last Empire: De Beers, Diamonds and the World.* New York: Farrar Straus Giroux, 1993.

Leach, Graham. *The Afrikaners: Their Last Great Trek.* London, England: Macmillan London, 1989.

Mandela, Nelson. *The Struggle Is My Life.* Rev. ed. New York: Pathfinders, 1986.

Marx, Anthony W. *Lessons of Struggle: South African Internal Opposition, 1960–1990.* New York: Oxford University Press, 1992.

Meli, Francis. *A History of the ANC: South Africa Belongs to Us.* Bloomington: Indiana University Press, 1989, 1988.

Price, Robert M. *The Apartheid State in Crisis: Political Transformation in South Africa, 1975–1990.* New York: Oxford University Press, 1991.

Saunders, Christopher. *Historical Dictionary of South Africa.* Metuchen, N. J.: Scarecrow, 1983.

Smith, David Marshall. *Apartheid in South Africa, 3rd ed.* Cambridge; New York: Cambridge University Press, 1990.

Stadler, Alfred William. *The Political Economy of Modern South Africa.* New York: St. Martin's Press, 1987.

Thompson, Leonard Monteath. *A History of South Africa.* New Haven: Yale University Press, 1990.

Walker, Eric Anderson. *The Great Trek.* New York: Barnes & Noble, 1964.

Watson, R. L. *South Africa in Pictures.* Minneapolis: Lerner Publications Co., 1988.

Wepman, Dennis. *Desmond Tutu.* New York: F. Watts, 1989.

Wilson, Monica, and Leonard Thompson (eds.). *The Oxford History of South Africa.* New York: Oxford University Press, 1969–71.

Woods, Donald. *Biko.* 3rd rev. ed. New York: H. Holt, 1991.

SUDAN

Republic of Sudan
Jumhuriyat as-Sudan

CAPITAL: Khartoum.

FLAG: The national flag consists of a tricolor of red, white, and black horizontal stripes, with a green triangle at the hoist.

ANTHEM: *Jundi al-Allah (Soldiers of God).*

MONETARY UNIT: The Sudanese pound (£s) is a paper currency of 100 piasters (qurush) or 1,000 milliemes. There are coins of 1, 2, 5, and 10 milliemes and 2, 5, 10, and 50 piasters, and notes of 25 and 50 piasters and 1, 5, 10, 20, and 50 Sudanese pounds. £s1 = $0.2625 (or $1 = £s3.81).

WEIGHTS AND MEASURES: The metric system is the legal standard, but a highly diverse system based on Egyptian and British standards is in local use.

HOLIDAYS: Independence Day, 1 January; Unity Day, 3 March; Uprising Day, 6 April; Decentralization Day, 1 July; Christmas, 25 December. Movable Muslim religious holidays include the 1st of Muharram (Muslim New Year), 'Id al-Fitr, 'Id al-'Adha', and Milad an-Nabi.

TIME: 2 PM = noon GMT.

¹LOCATION, SIZE, AND EXTENT

Situated in northeast Africa, Sudan is the largest country on the continent, covering an area of 2,505,810 sq km (967,490 sq mi), with a length of 2,192 km (1,362 mi) SSE–NNW and a width of 1,880 km (1,168 mi) ENE–WSW. Comparatively, the area occupied by Sudan is slightly more than one-quarter the size of the US. It is bounded on the N by Egypt, on the NE by the Red Sea, on the E by Ethiopia, on the S by Kenya, Uganda, and Zaire, on the W by the Central African Republic and Chad, and on the NW by Libya.

The Anglo-Egyptian Agreement of 19 January 1899 established the parallel of 22°N as the international boundary between Egypt and Sudan. In 1902, however, a special administrative boundary was delineated between the Nile and the Red Sea, in order to facilitate the administration of nomadic tribes and to maintain the continuity of certain tribal areas in the border region. The Egypt-Sudan boundary west of the Nile runs 892 km (554 mi); east of the Nile, the international boundary is 383 km (238 mi), and the administrative boundary is 357 km (222 mi). Including this administrative line, Sudan's total boundary length is 8,550 km (5,313 mi).

Sudan's capital city, Khartoum, is located in the northeastern part of the country.

²TOPOGRAHY

The greatest part of Sudan is a vast plain traversed by the northward-flowing Nile River and its tributaries. Widely separated mountain chains and many hilly areas often reach altitudes of more than 2,000 m (6,500 ft). The northern area is mainly desert, with rock at or near the surface covered by thin soils of low fertility. The western undulating sandy wastes merge into the Red Sea Hills to the east.

The dominating geographic feature is the Nile River, formed near Khartoum by the confluence of the Blue Nile and White Nile rivers. There are natural harbors at Port Sudan (Bur Sudan) and Suakin on the Red Sea.

The highest elevation is at Mount Kinyeti 3187 m (10,456 ft) along the southern border with Uganda.

³CLIMATE

Maximum temperatures range from 32°C (90°F) in winter to 42°C (108°F) in summer; the hottest months are May and June. Rainfall decreases from south to north, the annual average varying from 120 cm (47 in) in the south to less than 10 cm (4 in) in the north; the rainy season is from July to September. Climatic hazards—sandstorms in the northern deserts and flooding rains in the central belt—often interfere with railroad traffic. The most temperate climate occurs in the Red Sea Hills.

⁴FLORA AND FAUNA

Acacia, desert shrub, and acacia short-grass shrub grow in the northern desert and the grasslands of the west. The broad-leafed tropical woodland and forest region is for the most part in the southwest, where areas of luxuriant growth and closed forests are found; grass covers much of the steppe area of the southeast. Date palms line the banks of the Nile. Wildlife includes most of the mammals, birds, and reptiles common to central Africa. Many varieties of fish are found in the rivers and in the coastal waters of the Red Sea.

⁵ENVIRONMENT

A shortage of potable water inhibits agriculture, animal husbandry, and human settlement in much of Sudan. Sudan has 7.2 cu mi of water, of which 99% is used for farming and the remaining 1% is used for domestic purposes. Serious health problems are caused by diseases carried in the water supply; 80% of the nation's rural dwellers do not have pure water. The water on the nation's coasts is also polluted by industrial by-products, oil, and sewage. Sudan's cities produce 1.1 million tons of solid waste per year. The nation's agricultural land is threatened by the advance of the desert. Current estimates show that the desert overtakes 2–6 miles of land each year. Government agencies vested with environmental responsibilities include the National Committee for Environment (within the National Council for Research) and the ministries of Agriculture, Natural Resources, Irrigation, Energy, and Health. Due to uncontrolled hunting, the nation's wildlife is threatened: 17 mammal species and 8 bird species are endangered as well as 9 types of plants. Endangered species include the waldrapp, northern white rhinoceros, Tora hartebeest, slender-horned gazelle, and hawksbill turtle.

6POPULATION

The estimated population in 1994 was 29,774,480; a population of 33,166 was projected for the year 2000, assuming a crude birthrate of 40 per 1,000 live births, a crude death rate of 12.9, and a net natural increase of 27.1 during 1995–2000. The population density in 1994 was 11.9 per sq km (30.8 per sq mi). As of 1995, about 25% of the population lived in urban centers, the largest of which was Khartoum, the political and economic capital; together with Khartoum North and Omdurman, it had a population exceeding 1,950,000 in 1990. Other major cities include Port Sudan, the only modern seaport, Wad Madani, Al Ubayyid, the principal city of central Sudan, and 'Atbarah.

7MIGRATION

Civil war and famine in southern Sudan were estimated to have displaced up to 3.5 million people by early 1990. Many fled abroad: there were 109,400 refugees in Zaire, 92,100 in Ugunda, 21,800 in Kenya, 25,600 in Ethiopia, and 17,700 in the Central African Republic, at the end of 1992.

As of the end of 1992, the Office of the UN High Commissioner of Refugees estimated that there were 725,600 refugees in Sudan; the refugees included 703,500 from Ethiopia, 3,800 from Uganda, and 16,000 from Chad. Many Sudanese were working abroad in the mid 1990s, chiefly in Sa'udi Arabia and other Persian Gulf countries but also in Libya. Although their remittances were significant for the Sudanese economy, the absence of these workers, many of them skilled, constituted a "brain drain" of serious proportions. Perhaps 200,000 were expelled from Persian Gulf countries in 1991 because Sudan supported Iraq in the Gulf war.

8ETHNIC GROUPS

Indigenous Sudanese include Arabs (an estimated 39% of the population); Nilotic or Negroid peoples, of whom the Dinka form the largest portion and constitute about 10% of the national population; and Beja (6%). In all, there are nearly 600 ethnic groups. Nearly a million people of West African origin were living in Sudan in 1990.

9LANGUAGES

Arabic, the official language, is the mother tongue of about half the population. Besides standard Arabic there are two major colloquial forms. There is also a pidgin used in the South. English is used widely, in many cases serving as a lingua franca among the southern tribes. In all, more than 400 languages and dialects are spoken.

10RELIGIONS

The state religion is Islam, whose adherents, primarily Sufi, are estimated to constitute up to 70% of the population; most of them live in the north. As an important transit station for Mecca-bound African pilgrims, Sudan remains intimately linked with the Islamic world. The blacks of southern Sudan are mainly traditionalists (5%). As a result of missionary work, over 8% of the population are Christians, mostly Roman Catholics. Greek Orthodox, Coptic, and Anglican Christians are found in small numbers in towns.

Among the Muslims, religious brotherhoods (tarigat) play an important role in sectarian and communal life. The 1973 constitution guaranteed unrestricted freedom of religion, but Islam was cited as the official religion. Christian mission schools in the south were nationalized in 1957, and foreign missionaries were expelled from the south in 1963–64; at present, Christian missionary activities are confined to non-Muslims. In 1984, Islamic penal codes were introduced by the government, and strengthened by additional legislation in 1992.

11TRANSPORTATION

With the exception of a few interurban bus lines and taxi systems, all land, sea, river, and air transportation facilities are owned by the state. The 5,500 km (3,418 mi) of railroad track links most of the main towns of Sudan. The principal terminals are Khartoum and Port Sudan in the east; Wadi Halfa' in the north (on the Egyptian border); Al Ubayyid in the center of the country; Nyala in the west; and Waw in the south; 'Atbarah on the Nile River (north of Khartoum) is an important junction and seat of the central administration, repair shops, and equipment-manufacturing plants of the Sudan Railways Corp.

In 1966, a bridge linking Khartoum North and Omdurman, and the enlargement of the bridge on the White Nile between Khartoum and Omdurman were completed, facilitating the circulation of traffic around these three towns. A major road (1,197 km/744 mi) linking Port Sudan with Khartoum was completed in 1980. In 1991, the overall road system, including earth tracks, totaled 20,000 km (12,400 mi), of which 8% was paved. There were 116,000 automobiles, and 57,000 commercial vehicles.

River transport services link many communities. The White Nile route between Kusti and Juba (1,436 km/892 mi) is of crucial importance. Port Sudan, on the Red Sea, is primarily a cargo port, handling all of Sudan's cotton exports as well as most food imports. Passenger traffic is insignificant except for Mecca-bound pilgrims. A small Sudanese merchant marine was founded with assistance from the former Yugoslavia. As of 1991, it had 5 vessels, with a gross tonnage of 42,277.

The international airport is at Khartoum. The state-owned Sudan Airways Corp., founded in 1947, links the main cities and provides extensive international service. Flights to the south were suspended in the mid-1980s because of the civil war.

12HISTORY

The salient events in recorded Sudanese history occurred in the northern half of the country. The kingdom of Kush (or Cush), rich in gold and iron and sustained by irrigation from the Nile floodwaters, broke away from Egyptian rule about 1000 BC, becoming a separate kingdom, with its capital at Napatan, and developing under the pervasive influence of Egyptian culture. It conquered Egypt for a time (736–657 BC), moved its capital to Meroe (now Merowe) in 538 BC, and was destroyed about AD 350 by the Aksumite (or Axumite) Empire in Ethiopia.

Following the fall of Kush, two successor kingdoms arose: Maqurra, in northern Sudan, with its capital at Old Dongola; and Alwa, in central Sudan, with its capital at Soba. Maqurra fell in the 15th century to an alliance of Arabs and Mamlukes from Egypt. Around the beginning of the 17th century, Alwa was conquered by an alliance of Arabs and a loose confederation of tribes ruled by the "Black Sultans" of the Funj dynasty, with their capital at Sennar. The inhabitants of the south, until the 20th century, lived in primitive tribal isolation, interrupted only by explorers and perennial slave raiding.

In the 1820s, the autonomous Ottoman viceroy of Egypt, Muhammad 'Ali, defeated the Funj sultan and brought Sudan under Turco-Egyptian rule, which lasted until 1885. By then, most of the Sudanese tribes had revolted against the harshness and corruption of the regime and rallied under the leadership of a northern shipwright, Muhammad Ahmad bin 'Abdallah. He proclaimed himself the Mahdi (Rightly Guided One), whose coming to achieve the complete victory of Islam had been prophesied in Muslim tradition. After decisively defeating a series of punitive expeditions, the Mahdi took possession of Khartoum in 1885,

LOCATION: 23° to 3°N; 22° to 38°E. **BOUNDARY LENGTHS:** Egypt 1,273 km (789 mi); Red Sea coastline, 853 km (529 mi); Ethiopia and Eritrea, 2,221 km (1,377 mi); Kenya, 232km (144 mi); Uganda, 435 km (270 mi); Zaire, 628 km (390 mi); Central African Republic, 1,167 km (725 mi); Chad, 1,360 km (845 mi); Libya, 383 km (238 mi). **TERRITORIAL SEA LIMIT:** 12 mi.

whereupon his troops captured and beheaded the governor, Gen. Charles Gordon, one of the British officers in the employ of Egypt. The Mahdi installed himself as head of a theocratic state, which survived until 1898, when an Anglo-Egyptian invasion force under Gen. Horatio Herbert Kitchener defeated the Mahdi's successor, the Khalifa ('Abdallah bin Muhammad), in the battle of Omdurman. British rule was set up under a nominal Anglo-Egyptian "condominium" following a French attempt to seize parts of Sudan, an effort thwarted by Kitchener at Fashoda (now Kodok) in an incident that almost provoked a war between

France and Great Britain. British administration did much to restore law and order, repress slave trading, and bring modern government and economic stability to Anglo-Egyptian Sudan, as it was then called.

Sudanese nationalism erupted after World War I with Egyptian support and received its decisive impetus during World War II, when British-led Sudanese troops distinguished themselves in repelling a vastly superior Italian force. An Egyptian scheme to join Egypt and Sudan in a dual monarchy under King Faruk miscarried, as did other proposals for the "unity of the Nile Valley."

Prolonged Anglo-Egyptian negotiations for agreement on a mutually acceptable form of Sudanese independence reached fruition in 1953, after Faruk was deposed.

The new Republic of the Sudan, under a parliamentary government, was proclaimed on 1 January 1956. On 17 November 1958, a military dictatorship was installed, headed by Lt. Gen. Ibrahim Abboud, commander-in-chief of the armed forces, after a bloodless coup that had the support of some party leaders. President Abboud's military regime was overthrown on 26 October 1964, and civilian politicians ruled for the next five years.

A revolutionary council led by Col. Gaafar Mohammed Nimeiri (Ja'far Muhammad Numayri) overthrew the government in a bloodless coup on 25 May 1969 and established the Democratic Republic of the Sudan. The new government suspended the constitution, the Supreme Council of State, the National Assembly, and all political parties; the ex-president and former ministers were arrested. Nimeiri became prime minister in October 1969. On 25 May 1971, he proclaimed that Sudan would become a one-party state, with the Sudanese Socialist Union the sole political organization. A provisional constitution was promulgated on 13 August 1971, and Nimeiri, running unopposed, was elected president in September, receiving 98.6% of the votes cast. One of Nimeiri's most significant acts was to bring an end to the sporadic civil war that had plagued Sudan since independence. A settlement with autonomist forces in the south was reached in February 1972, when negotiators for the Sudanese government and the South Sudan Liberation Front, the Anyanya rebels, agreed on a cease-fire and on autonomy for the southern provinces.

Nimeiri was reelected without opposition in 1977 and 1983, but his regime had to weather considerable turmoil both domestically and in relations with neighboring countries, especially Libya. An abortive left-wing coup attempt in July 1971 led to the execution of leading Sudanese Communists; the banning of the Trade Union Federation, the Public Servants Union, and the Teachers Union (all formerly Communist-dominated); and the expulsion of East German security advisers. Another alleged coup was foiled in January 1973, and an abortive, Libyan-inspired attempt on Nimeiri's life was disclosed by the Sudanese government in April 1974. Student riots and disclosure of yet another abortive coup came in October 1974, and during the following year the Nimeiri government faced and successfully suppressed at least two military rebellions.

In July 1976, an attempted coup by the Ansar brotherhood, allegedly with Libyan support, was crushed. In subsequent years, Nimeiri charged repeatedly that Libya was aiding Muslim dissidents in Sudan. On 16 March 1984, Omdurman was bombed by what Sudan, Egypt, and the US claimed (but Libya denied) was a Libyan air force TU-22. Nimeiri declared a state of emergency in April 1984 to cope with protests over rising prices and a new government Islamization program (in July of that year, the National People's Assembly rejected his attempt to make Sudan an official Islamic state). The state of emergency ended in September 1984, but by then a new rebellion was under way in the south, which had become alienated by Nimeiri's efforts to restrict its autonomy and apply Shari'ah (Muslim law). Many Sudanese were shocked by the execution of Mahmoud Mohammed Taha, a popular Muslim political and religious leader, for heresy (in criticizing the application of Shari'ah) in January 1985.

Riots broke out in the spring of 1985, when, in order to gain new loans from international creditors, Nimeiri removed subsidies on basic commodities, causing prices to rise. On 7 April 1985, Nimeiri was replaced by a military council headed by Gen. Abdel-Rahman Swar ad-Dhahab. The country was renamed the Republic of Sudan, the ruling Sudanese Socialist Union was abolished, political and press freedom was restored, and food prices were lowered. Sudan reverted to a policy of nonalignment in foreign policy, backing away from its close ties with Egypt and the US.

Unrest in the South

General elections held in April 1986 resulted in a moderate civilian coalition government headed by Prime Minister Sadiq al-Mahdi. The government's chief problem was the continuing rebellion by the Sudanese People's Liberation Army (SPLA), which controlled much of the south and prevented voting there. The SPLA halted air traffic (including food relief) to the south and opposed two major projects vital to the economy—oil exploration and a canal that would provide water to the parched north. The coalition government was headed by the northern-based Ummah. It began searching for a formula to unite the country with the SPLA which, unlike the earlier Anyanya, was also committed to unity. Divisions with government over meeting key SPLA demands, most especially the repeal of Islamic law, prolonged the civil war. In March 1989, a new government composed of Ummah Party and Democratic Unionist Party (DUP) ministers agreed to accommodate the SPLA.

However, on 30 June 1989, a group of army officers led by Brig. Omar Hassam al-Bashir overthrew the civilian government. Mahdi was arrested and fighting in the south escalated. The coup makers created a National Salvation Revolutionary Command Council (RCC), a junta composed of 15 military officers assisted by a civilian cabinet, suspending the 1985 transitional constitution, abrogating press freedoms, and dissolving all parties and trade unions. In September 1989 the government sponsored a "National Dialogue Conference on the Political System" which produced a proposal for a new federal system of government. On 22 March 1991, federalism was officially adopted but southern leaders still fear central government dominance.

On 23 April 1990, Bashir declared a state of emergency and dissolved parliament. An alleged coup attempt prompted that move. The following day, 28 officers were court martialed and executed. Yet none of these reforms seemed to placate southern leaders. Peace talks sponsored by ex-US president Jimmy Carter, Nigeria, and others broke down with few positive results.

Bashir's Islamic government is dominated by the fundamentalist National Islamic Front (NIF), under the leadership of Hassan al-Turabi. Bashir remains president, chief of state, prime minister and chief of the armed forces. Sudan has given sanctuary to Muslim rebels from Tunisia and Algeria, to the Hezbollah (Party of God), and to Abu Nidal's Palestinian rebels. Iran and Libya assist Sudan militarily. The regime has purged the civil service, the armed forces, the judiciary and the educational system of non-Muslims. It has also promulgated a Penal Code based on Islamic Law.

With the fall of Ethiopia's Marxist government in 1991, the SPLA lost its chief patron. A 1992 government offensive, coupled with a major political split in the SPLA, has reduced rebel-held territory but increased casualties and displaced persons (the latter numbering, at times, over two million). Sudan stands on the brink of famine. SPLA leader John Garang's idea of a secular Sudan (the "Torit" faction) is now challenged by militants (the "Nasir" faction of the SPLA) who see no future in combination with the Islamic north. They demand autonomy or complete independence for the south. Khartoum seeks to play on those SPLA divisions in its strategy for negotiation and war. Today, much of the fighting in the south is between southerners.

Because of its militant Islamic policies, Sudan's allies are limited to Afghanistan, Iran, Libya and Syria. The UN General Assembly condemned Sudan's human rights violations in March 1993. The US added Sudan to its list of countries spawning international terrorism in August 1993, and tensions with Egypt are growing as well.

As the fighting in the south grows, so does the famine. Private and UN relief efforts have been suspended from time to time after attacks by rebels. Fighting between factions of the SPLA adds to the unrest.

13 GOVERNMENT

A permanent constitution came into effect on 8 May 1973. Sudan's first permanent governing document since independence in 1956, it established a presidential system and a one-party state, with the Sudanese Socialist Union (SSU) as the only political party. Nominated by the SSU for a six-year renewable term, the president (after confirmation by national plebiscite) appointed vice-presidents, a prime minister, and cabinet ministers, who were answerable to him. The president was also supreme commander of the armed forces. Legislative power was vested in the 151-seat National People's Assembly. This constitution was suspended on 6 April 1985. A temporary constitution was established on 10 October 1985, pending a permanent one to be drawn up by the National Assembly elected in 1986. A six-member civilian Supreme Council, including a president, was established as the nation's executive body in 1986, replacing the military council that had seized power in 1985. A Council of Ministers, led by a prime minister and responsible to the National Assembly, was also established to carry out executive powers.

After the 1989 military coup, the 1985 transitional constitution was suspended. In January 1991, the RCC imposed Islamic law in the six northern provinces. Executive and legislative authority was vested in a 15-member Revolutionary Command Council (RCC). Its chairman, acting as prime minister, appointed a 300-member transitional National Assembly. In mid-October 1993, Bashir dissolved the RCC and officially declared himself president of a new civilian government. Elections are planned for 1994 and 1995.

14 POLITICAL PARTIES

The political groupings that emerged in Sudan's struggle for independence focused on personalities or specific interest groups rather than ideology or party machinery. The most powerful force before 1958 was the Ansar sect and the Ansar-sponsored Ummah Party. Other parties were closely affiliated with the Khatmiyah sect, led by Sayyid 'Ali al-Mirghani; the leftist-dominated labor unions; the Graduates Congress, an organization of college graduates; and leaders of the black tribes of the south. For the first three years of the country's independence, these parties were strongly divided on such issues as union with Egypt (opposed by the Ummah Party); alignment with the West in economic and foreign affairs (opposed by the Khatmiyah, the labor unions, and the Graduates); Communism (courted by elements in most parties and labor unions); political secularization (sought by leaders not aligned with the religious sects); federalism (demanded by southern spokesmen); and fear of the royal aspirations of the Mahdi family. These divisions helped bring about the downfall of several coalition cabinets and finally weakened the parliamentary system to the point where the army could successfully carry out a coup without encountering resistance. Political activity was banned in 1958 and was not resumed until the overthrow of the Abboud government in October 1964.

In 1966, the Ummah Party split into two groups, one conservative, the other progressive. The following year, the Democratic Unionist Party (DUP) was formed from the amalgamation of the National Unionist Party and the People's Democratic Party. In the May 1968 elections, the DUP won 101 of 218 parliamentary seats, while no other party captured more than 36.

After the 1969 military takeover, existing political parties were banned, and a special attempt was made, beginning in 1971, to suppress the powerful Communist Party. The 1973 constitution provided for a one-party state, with the Sudanese Socialist Union (SSU), established by Nimeiri in 1971, as the sole legal political organization. In elections for the National People's Assembly, only candidates approved by the SSU were allowed to run.

In April 1986, in the first free elections held since 1968, the Ummah Party won 99 of 301 parliamentary seats, the DUP won

63, and the fundamentalist National Islamic Front (NIF) won 51. The remaining seats went mainly to regional parties, but 37 seats from the south were unfilled because of the civil war and the boycott of the elections by the Sudanese People's Liberation Front. The Ummah Party, the DUP, and four southern parties formed a coalition government, with the NIF in opposition. In August 1987, the coalition fell apart when the DUP broke away from the Ummah Party after an election in which it lost one of its two seats on the Supreme Council to an Ummah candidate, reportedly because the DUP candidate had been a close aide of Nimeiri. Prime Minister Sadiq al-Mahdi, aligned with the Ummah Party, retained his position until his overthrow in June, 1989.

In the elections for the National Assembly, held (except in the south) from 21 April to 8 May 1965, the Ummah again emerged as the most important party, gaining 76 of the 173 contested seats. The National Unionist Party, a right-wing party favoring close relations with Egypt, won 53 seats and formed a coalition government with the Ummah Party. During the mid-1960s, two regional parties—the Southern Front, formed in 1964 by southerners living in the north, and the Sudan African National Union (SANU), formed in 1966 by Sudanese exiles in Uganda—advocated self-determination and independence for the south.

The RCC, which formed the latest military government, dissolved all parties in 1989. The NIF, however, continues to function openly and is the strength behind the government. NIF members and supporters hold most key positions and with the abolition of the RCC in October 1993, the NIF further tightened its grip on the state.

The main opposition to the central government is the Sudan's People's Liberation Army (SPLA) which, in 1993, split into two main groups, the "Torit" faction led by John Garang, and the SPLA-United led by Rick Machar and consisting of the Nasir faction and the "Forces of Unity".

15 LOCAL GOVERNMENT

Formerly, Sudan was divided for administrative purposes into 18 provinces, of which the 6 southern provinces constituted an autonomous region with its own 60-member assembly. Under a reorganization program completed in June 1983, Sudan was divided into 8 distinct regions, 5 northern and 3 southern, each with its own people's assembly and presidentially-appointed governor, plus the special province of Khartoum. The former southern regional assembly, elected in April 1982, was divided into three new people's assemblies, 1 for each of the newly created southern regions, but the total membership remained the same. The reorganization in the south was seen as the Nimeiri government's response to a recent resurgence of autonomist sentiment and the emergence of the SPLA. This reoganization was canceled after Nimeiri was overthrown, and regional assemblies were suspended. Sudan had 6 regions, each with a governor, and Khartoum was separately administered with a commission general.

After the 1989 military coup, Sudan was divided into nine "autonomous" states. A constitutional decree of 2 February 1994 redivided Sudan into 26 states. Bashir claimed that each state government would enjoy executive and legislative powers which citizens had "never experienced in remote areas". A governor would be responsible for each state. Southern states were expected to be exempted from Islamic laws.

16 JUDICIAL SYSTEM

According to the 1973 constitution, the judiciary is directly responsible to the president, through a council headed by him. For the Muslim population, justice in personal matters, such as domestic relations and probate, is administered by Muslim law courts, which form the Shari'ah Division of the Sudan judiciary. The Shari'ah Division includes a court of appeal, high courts, and qadis' courts. The president of the Shari'ah judiciary is the grand qadi. Civil justice is administered by the Supreme Court, courts of appeal, and lower courts. Criminal justice is administered by major courts, magistrates' courts, and local people's courts, which try civil cases as well. On 30 September 1983, nearly all of Sudan's 13,000 prisoners were reportedly freed.

The judiciary remains largely subservient to the government. In 1989 the National Salvation Revolution Command Council (RCC) assumed control and placed responsibility for supervision of the judiciary in the Ministry of Justice. The 1989 Special Courts Act created three-person security courts to deal with offenses involving violations of constitutional decrees, emergency regulations and some sections of the Penal Code. A 1993 decree dissolving the RCC placed power to issue constitutional decrees with the transitional National Assembly, which, at the time, was controlled by the National Islamic Front (NIF).

17ARMED FORCES

A three-year military conscription is legal, but in practice military service remained voluntary, sometimes coercive. The army has an estimated strength of 75,000, organized into 9 divisions and 29 brigades, all undermanned by western standards. The navy, established in 1962, has 1,500 personnel and 2 patrol craft; the air force has 6,000 personnel and 51 combat aircraft, plus air defense missile units. Paramilitary forces number 15–20,000. Estimated defense expenditures in 1989 were $610 million or 7.2% of GDP.

The Sudanese armed forces, largely Moslem, face an estimated 50,000 rebels, Christian or animist, of the Sudanese People's Liberation Army. The government forces employ a mix of US, European, and Russian arms. Sudan imports about $90 million in arms a year.

18INTERNATIONAL COOPERATION

Sudan, having joined the UN on 12 November 1956, participates in ECA and all the nonregional specialized agencies. The nation belongs to the African Development Bank, G-77, League of Arab States, and OAU. Sudan is a signatory to the Law of the Sea and has signed an agreement with Egypt, Uganda, and Ethiopia concerning the use and control of Nile waters. The headquarters of the Arab Bank for African Development are in Khartoum.

Under the provisions of the Egyptian-Sudanese Charter of Integration, signed by Nimeiri and Egyptian President Hosni (Husni) Mubarak in October 1982, the Nile Valley Parliament held its first meeting in May 1983 in Khartoum; the 60-member body was drawn equally from the two nations. In February 1983, the Higher Council for Integration, headed by Nimeiri and Mubarak, agreed to eliminate customs duties on most trade between the two countries. Sudan dissolved the institutions established under the charter of integration in 1986, although it claimed that the process would be revived.

19ECONOMY

Sudan has an agricultural economy with considerable potential for irrigated production. The livestock sector is sizable as well. However, droughts have led to recent famines, and civil war has led to the virtual collapse of the economy. It is estimated that in the south as many as 1 million civilians have died and more than 5 million have been uprooted.

Sudan's failure to service its international debt, together with a poor human rights record, led, in 1993, to the World Bank suspending financing of 15 development projects, and to the IMF suspending Sudan's voting rights in the organization. Until the political situation stabilizes, prospects are dim for improvement in the economy.

20INCOME

In 1992 Sudan's GNP was $184 per capita. For the period 1985–92 the average inflation rate was 150%.

In 1992 the GDP was $520 million in current US dollars. It is estimated that agriculture, hunting, forestry, and fishing contributed 29% to GDP; manufacturing, 8%; electricity, gas, and water, 2%; construction, 6%; wholesale and retail trade, 17%; transport, storage, and communication, 9%; finance, insurance, real estate, and business services, 12%; community, social, and personal services, 2%; and other sources, 15%.

21LABOR

About two-thirds of the population of 26 million relied on agriculture in 1991/92. Industry engages less than 10% of the labor force. Unemployment officially stood at 30% in 1990/91. The trade union movement was reconstituted after the 1971 coup attempt. Strikes, banned by the government in May 1969, were legalized in 1985. The 1989 coup, however, brought a swift end to the strong labor movement which had been growing under the Sadiq al-Mahdi administration. The National Salvation Revolution Command Council (RCC) abolished labor unions and prohibited strikes by decree on 30 June 1989. In September 1989, the Sudan Workers Trade Union Federation (with some 800,000 members) was restored with the same leadership but under tight government control.

22AGRICULTURE

About one-third of the total area of Africa's largest country is suitable for agricultural development. Abundant rainfall in the south permits both agriculture and grazing grounds for the large herds owned by nomadic tribes. In the north, along the banks of the Nile and other rivers, irrigation farming prevails. Of an estimated 12.9 million ha (31.8 million acres) of arable land, about 1.9 million ha (4.7 million acres) are irrigated. Principal cash crops are cotton, sesame, peanuts, sugarcane, dates, citrus fruits, mangoes, coffee, and tobacco; the principal subsistence crops are sorghum, millet, wheat, beans, cowpeas, pulses, corn, and barley. Cotton is the principal export crop and the lifeblood of the country's economy; in 1992, over 76,000 tons of cotton were exported, valued at $116 million (28% of total exports).

Government regional development schemes have played a decisive part in the economy since the 1920s. The Gezirah Scheme, located between the Blue and White Niles near their confluence at Khartoum, is the world's largest under a single management and provides a substantial portion of foreign exchange and government revenue. This storage irrigation project, which covers 840,000 ha (more than 2 million acres) but has an additional potential of 2 million ha (5 million acres), dates back to 1911 and was put into operation by a British firm. After the expiration of the firm's contract with the Sudanese government in 1950, the land was leased to tenant farmers, who numbered over 100,000 in 1987. They manage the scheme jointly with the government through the Gezirah Board. In July 1980, construction began on the 354-km (220-mi) Jonglei Canal, intended to drain the Sudd swamp and channel water from the White Nile to the arid northern Sudan and to Egypt. Built by a French consortium at a projected cost of $260 million and scheduled for completion in 1985, the canal could irrigate up to 243,000 ha (600,000 acres) of Sudanese land. By 1984, however, the project had been halted by SPLA opposition, with less than 100 km (62 mi) to be excavated. In 1992, the public and private agricultural sectors invested heavily in land preparations, pesticides, and related inputs. Agricultural funding for such projects comes from the World Bank, the African Development Bank, and the International Fund for Agricultural Development. However, completion of these projects has been complicated by debt-repayment problems.

In spite of efforts to improve Sudan's agricultural resources, famine conditions have existed in southern Sudan since 1986. Inadequate rains, a poor distribution infrastructure, and civil war have hampered relief efforts.

Among agricultural products in 1992 were sorghum, 4,320,000 tons; peanuts, 454,000 tons; sesame, 330,000 tons, (the highest in Africa); and wheat, 895,000 tons. Cotton fiber production in 1992 was 87,000 tons. Production in 1992 also included sugarcane, 4,600,000 tons; millet, 424,000 tons; cottonseed, 170,000 tons; tomatoes, 151,000 tons; cassava, 9,000 tons; dates, 142,000 tons; yams, 129,000 tons; and corn, 51,000 tons.

23 ANIMAL HUSBANDRY

In 1992, the livestock population was estimated at 21.6 million head of cattle, 22.6 million sheep, 18.7 million goats, 2.8 million camels, and 35 million chickens. The national livestock herd was second only to that of Ethiopia in Africa. Cattle, found mostly in the southern rainfall area, are of two types: the shorthorn zebu of Asian origin and the longhorn sanga. Nomadic or seminomadic pastoral tribes own the bulk of the cattle. Sudanese sheep have hairy coats and are grown for meat rather than wool. They are owned almost exclusively by nomadic or seminomadic tribes. The tsetse fly prevents livestock raising in an area of approximately 200,000 sq km (77,000 sq mi) in the south. Livestock products in 1992 included an estimated 3,193,000 tons of milk, 449,000 tons of meat, and 34,500 tons of eggs. Widespread smuggling also reduces income available to the government from livestock exports.

The value of livestock exports in 1992 was $72.8 million, a reduction from the $83.7 million in 1991.

24 FISHING

In the southern provinces and towns, fish, particularly the Nile perch, is a diet staple. The river yields some 110 varieties of fish, and the Red Sea is another valuable fishing ground. In 1991, the total catch was 33,303 tons.

25 FORESTRY

About 44 million ha (108 million acres) of Sudan are covered by woodlands and forests, half of which are dense stands of trees, mostly in the south. Sudan supplies over 80% of the world's needs of gum arabic, extracted from the acacia. Production of roundwood, which is almost entirely used for fuel, was estimated at 23.4 million cu m in 1991. Timber production, apart from cutting for local village needs, is confined to forests lying within reach of navigable rivers or areas served by roads and railways. The Ministry of Agriculture and Natural Resources maintains forests, administers public preserves, and operates sawmills. The forest preserves cover over 25,900 sq km (10,000 sq mi), or more than 1% of the total land area.

26 MINING

Sudan is not rich in mineral resources, although large iron ore reserves have been found near Port Sudan. Concessions are operated in the Red Sea Hills for the mining of mica, manganese, gold, and salt. Estimated mineral production in 1991 included salt, 75,000 tons; chromium ore, 10,000 tons; and crude gypsum and anhydrite, 7,000 tons. Commercial-scale gold mining in the Red Sea Hills began in late 1985; production in 1991 amounted to 50 kg, down 90% from 1989.

27 ENERGY AND POWER

In the absence of coal reserves, Sudan has come to rely mainly on waterpower to meet its commercial energy needs. In 1991, installed capacity was 500,000 kw, nearly half of it hydroelectric; production of electricity amounted to 1,329 million kwh. Power shortages are frequent, especially in summer, but capacity was increased in 1985 at power plants in Burri and Khartoum North. In 1991, the burning of wood fulfilled 82% of the total energy requirement.

Modest petroleum reserves, estimated at 219 million barrels, have been discovered. The government is strongly encouraging the development of crude oil production. International Petroleum (Canada), Rompetrol (Romania), and Chevron were involved in oil explorations as of 1992. Iraq and Iran also have agreed to assist Sudan in the development of its petroleum sector.

28 INDUSTRY

Sudan's industrial sector has been buffeted by a series of events leading to a significant contraction of output. Foreign exchange was very scarce in the early 1980s and led to shortages of raw materials, skilled labor, and energy. In February 1985, the granting of import licenses and letters of credit was suspended. Over 100 manufacturing enterprises shut down as a result. By 1989, many factories were thought to be operating at 5% of capacity.

Prior to this difficult period, Sudan's industries supplied many items that had formerly been imported—cotton textiles, sugar, hides and skins, cement, tires, flour, soap, shoes, cigarettes, batteries, sesame oil, biscuits, confectionery, household appliances, paints and varnishes, and plastics. Textiles, the largest industry, are part of a decade-long (1985–95) rehabilitation project. There are a number of cotton ginning plants of which one, the Gezira plant, is the largest in the world. Sudan has 25 spinning and weaving mills.

Other factories process cotton seed and groundnuts into oil and cake. The Kenana sugar complex, commissioned in 1980, is one of the largest sugar plantation and refining installations in the world, jointly owned by the government and Kuwaiti, Sa'udi, and Japanese private interests. Petroleum products are refined at Port Sudan refinery.

Sudan's public generating capacity was 1,000 Mw in 1985. Hydroelectric power from the Blue Nile grid nearly doubled in capacity in 1986 with the inauguration of the Power III project. Thermal stations were developed in 1986 at Khartoum and Burri. In 1988, work on the Khartoum North plant advanced and new turbines added 84 Mw of capacity at Roseires. Generating facilities at Kassala and Khashm el-Girba had a 1990 completion date, and the Power IV energy proposal has been presented to meet projected demand in the year 2000. Production difficulties, droughts, and maintenance problems have led to an increase in private generating capacity since 1982.

29 SCIENCE AND TECHNOLOGY

The National Council for Research is responsible for planning and directing national research programs in agriculture, atomic energy, peaceful uses of outer space, and other fields. The Agriculture Research Corporation of the Ministry of Agriculture has its headquarters in Wad Medani, and a forest research institute and the Geological Research Authority operate in Khartoum. The universities of Gezirah, Juba, and Khartoum all have faculties or colleges in scientific and technical fields, and Khartoum Polytechnic has colleges of agriculture and of engineering and science.

30 DOMESTIC TRADE

Sudan's mercantile community is well organized through the Sudan Chamber of Commerce, which supplies information and facilitates negotiations with the authorities. The major foreign-owned trading companies, which had controlled Sudanese trade, were nationalized in 1970.

Department stores are uncommon; the few modern shops feature imported products. Most retail trade is conducted in open-air markets or in stalls in buildings near market centers. Because of the low literacy rate, newspaper advertising is of limited significance. Window and sidewalk displays and outdoor advertising are the principal marketing aids. An international trade fair is held annually at Khartoum.

Markets usually function from 7 AM to 2 PM. Business hours are from 8:30 AM to 1:30 PM and 5 to 8 PM, Saturday through

Thursday, with Friday as the day of rest. Normal banking hours are 8:30 to noon, Saturday through Thursday.

31FOREIGN TRADE

Sudan's trade balance has been negative for many years, though the trade balance improved in 1992 from a us$–835.7 million to a us$–596.8 million. The main exports are agricultural products including cotton, gum arabic, sesame, and millet and sorghum.

The main imports are a broad range of industrial goods, petroleum products, and foodstuffs.

In 1987, 49.1% of Sudan's exports went to the countries of the EC, followed by Japan (6.3%) and the United States (4.7%). Sa'udi Arabia was Sudan's highest import supplier (14.9%, almost entirely petroleum) in 1986.

32BALANCE OF PAYMENTS

There is a habitual payments deficit, although a surplus was recorded in 1984. Inflows from export earnings and remittances were estimated at $2 million per day in mid-1992, which still only covered about one-half the amount needed to finance exports. Remittances from Sudanese nationals were disrupted by the Gulf War; by 1991/92 they had doubled to $106 million from the previous year, but were still only a fraction of the $445 million remitted in 1987/88.

In 1992 merchandise exports totaled $213.4 million and imports $810.2 million. The merchandise trade balance was $596.8 million. The following table summarizes Sudan's balance of payments for 1991 and 1992 (in millions of US dollars):

	1991	1992
CURRENT ACCOUNT		
Goods, services, and income	−1,085.5	−738.9
Unrequited transfers	127.7	232.7
TOTALS	957.8	506.2
CAPITAL ACCOUNT		
Direct investment	—	—
Portfolio investment	—	—
Other long-term capital	486.3	268.5
Other short-term capital	100.8	47.9
Exceptional financing	269.1	129.5
Other liabilities	—	—
Reserves	3.8	29.3
TOTALS	860	475.2
Errors and omissions	97.8	31.0
Total change in reserves	9.0	−7.9

33BANKING AND SECURITIES

The Bank of Sudan, the central bank, was founded in 1960. As of 1992 the money supply, as measured by M2, amounted to £s754.3 million. There are seven specialized state banks, for industry, agriculture, housing, savings, and development. The 11 commercial banks were nationalized in 1970; all foreign banks were nationalized at that time, but foreign ownership was again permitted in 1975. In December 1990 the government decided to adopt Islamic banking principles. In 1993 there were 7 commercial banks. No stock exchange or organized over-the-counter market exists in the Sudan.

34INSURANCE

All foreign insurance companies were nationalized in 1970; there were 13 Sudanese insurance companies in 1986 and a National Reinsurance Corp. In the same year, virtually all coverage was non-life, 45.6% for transport, 25% automobile, and 21.5% fire insurance.

35PUBLIC FINANCE

Sudan's budgets were in deficit throughout the 1960s, 1970s, and 1980s. The budget deficit soared to 22% of GDP in 1991/92, which aggravated inflation. Neither the budget deficit nor inflation shows signs of shrinking as civil war continues in the South, consuming precious budgetary resources. The budget deficit lowered to an estimated 5% of GDP in 1992/93, including grants.

36TAXATION

Direct taxes constituted about 14% of current receipts in 1985/86, and indirect taxes accounted for about 67%. Types of levies include a business profits tax, income tax on salaries, various consumption and production taxes, stamp duties, and miscellaneous fees and charges, including a development tax. The personal income tax was first imposed in July 1964, and an income tax on Sudanese working abroad was added later. Remittances from Sudanese working abroad doubled to us$106 million in 1991/92, but were still significantly down from the us$445 million figure of 1987/88, before the Gulf War. Income from property, hitherto exempt from any tax, became subject to the business profits tax on 1 January 1964.

37CUSTOMS AND DUTIES

The Sudan has a liberal trade policy, although it restricts imports of some goods considered competitive with those produced locally. The customs tariff applies to goods from all countries except Egypt and Jordan, which receive preferential treatment. Most tariff rates are ad valorem and range from zero to 1,100%. Specific rates are applied mostly to alcoholic beverages and tobacco. Commodities not specifically included in the tariff schedule are dutiable at 40% ad valorem. Also levied are guay dues, royalties, consumption taxes, and a 10% defense tax.

38FOREIGN INVESTMENT

In 1971, Sudan nationalized the holdings of foreign investors, mostly British. A privatization effort and a move toward a mixed economy began slowly in the early 1980s and picked up momentum via negotiations with the IMF in 1985. The 1980 Encouragement of Investment Act provided for repatriation of profits, tax incentives, customs relief, industrial rates for transport and electricity. However, the introduction of Shari'a law in 1983 (unenforced since 1985), along with foreign exchange shortages, discouraged investors through 1986. In 1990, the government invited foreign investors to purchase companies in the parastatal sector. Key properties in the agricultural, tourist, transportation and communications sectors were identified as candidates for privatization under the National Economic Salvation Program. In 1992, the creation of four free-trade zones was announced in an attempt to encourage additional foreign investment.

39ECONOMIC DEVELOPMENT

The suspension of foreign aid and balance-of-payment support by a growing list of countries has all but stopped economic development. In spite of this, Sudan's government retains food self-sufficiency as a priority goal and seeks to reallocate investment toward agriculture and other productive sectors. Private investment is welcome as the parastatal sector is privatized.

40SOCIAL DEVELOPMENT

Organized social welfare is administered by the central and local governments, labor unions, and fraternal organizations, including those of the larger foreign groups and ethnic minorities. Social legislation requires business firms to provide benefits for their employees.

Because of the largely rural character of the country, social welfare in the Western sense is generally confined to the small urban population or to the great agricultural schemes operated by the government. On the other hand, much private assistance is extended to the poor and afflicted because of religion and the strong sense of family solidarity that encompasses even remotely related kin. In many areas of the south, local officials provide informal guidance and assistance to individual families in need of help.

Since the military coup in 1989, the fundamentalist Islamic government has sought to redefine the place of women in society. Prior to that, the state sought to guarantee basic rights and freedoms to all women, both Muslim and non-Muslim. They were afforded opportunities in trade, the professions, and higher education. These freedoms are currently curtailed. Women have been removed from the civil service and tertiary education. They are no longer free to travel without a male escort.

Because of the civil war, starvation and malnutrition are rife. In addition, the human rights situation is dismal. Government and SPLA forces regularly commit abuses, including massacres, kidnapping, enslavement, forced conscription, and rape. Relief workers are also vulnerable. Freedom of speech, press, assembly, association, and political choice are repressed throughout the Sudan. The government's Arabization and Islamization policies are coercive.

41HEALTH
Despite the extension of medical services and supervision, such diseases as malaria, schistosomiasis, sleeping sickness, tuberculosis (about 211 cases per 100,000 people in 1990), and various forms of dysentery persist. Food aid was not reaching famine-stricken southern Sudan in the mid-1980s because of civil war. In 1990, 55% of children under 5 years old were considered malnourished.

The central government operates most research laboratories and dispensaries. Hospital facilities and medical and public health services are free, but only 51% of the population had access to them in 1992. In 1990, there were 9 hospital beds per 100,000 people and an estimated total of 2,400 doctors. In 1992, there were 9 doctors per 100,000 inhabitants, with a nurse to doctor ratio of 2.7. There are very few private practitioners.

There were 1,128,000 births in 1992. The 1993 the birth rate was 42 per 1,000 people, with about 9% of married women (ages 15 to 49) using contraception.

In 1992, average life expectancy was estimated at 52 years, and the infant mortality rate was 100 per 1,000 live births. In 1991, maternal mortality was 550 per 100,000 live births, and the general mortality rate was 14.3 per 1,000 people in 1993. Between 1984 and 1992, there were about 506,000 civil war-related deaths.

In 1991, only 48% of the population had access to safe water and 75% had adequate sanitation. Immunization rates in 1992 for children up to one year old were quite high: tuberculosis (75%); diphtheria, pertussis, and tetanus (67%); polio (67%); and measles (66%). Total health care expenditures in 1990 were $300 million.

42HOUSING
Most Sudanese live in simple houses of their own or rent from landlords or agricultural-scheme authorities. As of 1983, 60% of housing units were "gottias", single rooms with round mud walls and a conical straw roof; 36% were menzils, multi-room houses with toilet facilities. Of all dwellings, 86% were owned, 8% were rented, and 3% were occupied without cash rent. Water was piped to 29% of all households, while 49% relied on wells, and 21% on rivers or waterholes. Only 2% had private flush toilets. Almost every house, even in the cities, has a walled courtyard or garden. In the big cities, bungalows are provided for important government officials and high-level foreign employees. A national housing authority provides low-cost housing to government employees, rural schoolteachers, and persons in low-income groups. A town-planning ordinance provides for slum clearance and replanning of towns. Khartoum has a number of modern apartment buildings.

43EDUCATION
In 1990, 57.3% of the adult male and 88.3% of the adult female population were illiterate. In the mid-1980s, only 57% of school-age boys and 41% of eligible girls were actually attending primary school; the proportions for secondary school were 23% and 16%, respectively. Most schools are operated or subsidized by the central government through the Ministry of Education.

In 1990, 7,939 primary schools had 2,042,743 students and 60,047 teachers; secondary schools had 731,624 students and 33,628 teachers. Of the total number of secondary students, 5,328 were in teacher training schools and 30,332 were in vocational. The University of Khartoum was established in 1956; in 1986, its 10 faculties had about 14,000 students. A branch of Cairo University was opened at Khartoum in 1955; by 1986, it had about 20,000 students. Other institutions include the Islamic University of Omdurman and the universities of El-Gezirah (at Wad Madani) and Juba. In 1989, all higher level institutions had 2,522 teachers and 60,134 students.

44LIBRARIES AND MUSEUMS
The principal library is at Khartoum University, with over 209,000 volumes. There is also a public library in Omdurman. Minor library facilities are maintained by secondary schools, houses of worship, government agencies, and foreign community centers. The National Records Office, in Khartoum, serves as the national archives and contains over 20 million documents.

There are antiquities museums in Khartoum and Merowe. Merowe also is the site of excavations of buildings from the kingdom of Kush. The Khalifa's tomb in Omdurman contains relics of Mahdist and other recent history. The National Botanic Garden in Khartoum contains rare specimens of Sudanese flora. Khartoum also has an ethnographic museum, a natural history museum, and the general Sudan National Museum. There are also museums at Al Ubayyid, Port Sudan, Wadi Halfa', and Wad Madani.

45MEDIA
Postal, telegraph, and broadcasting services are state owned; in 1991 there were 77,920 telephones. The Sudan Broadcasting Service, the government-controlled radio network, transmits daily in Arabic, English, French, Amharic, Somali, and other languages; 5,375,000 radios were in use in 1991. Television service was inaugurated in 1963; by 1991 there were about 2 million sets in use. An earth satellite station was completed in November 1974.

When it came to power in June 1989, the al-Bashir government banned all newspapers and magazines except one pro-government military newspaper. Prior to this there had been several dailies, one weekly, and a quarterly, *Sudanow.*

46ORGANIZATIONS
The cooperative movement, which began in the 1930s, has achieved some importance, especially in the irrigation schemes. In the Gezirah Scheme, tenant farmers have formed many cultural, educational, and recreational groupings.

The Sudan Chamber of Commerce (Khartoum), comprising both local and foreign business interests, performs various functions for the government. There are several smaller chambers, most of them organized by resident European and Egyptian traders. More than 30 clubs serve foreign and minority groups and business firms. Clubs are the principal centers of social activity in Sudanese towns.

47TOURISM, TRAVEL, AND RECREATION
The main tourist attractions are big-game hunting in the jungles of the south, boat excursions down the Nile through the jungle and desert, deep-sea fishing, the Red Sea Hills, the underwater gardens at Port Sudan, and archaeological sites in the north. Since the civil war and the advent of Islamic rule, tourism in the

Sudan is virtually non-existent. There were 1,423 tourist arrivals in 1991, generating receipts of US$8 million. Visitors to the Sudan require a passport and a visa. Precautions against cholera, typhoid, tetanus, poliomyelitis, yellow fever, and malaria are recommended.

48 FAMOUS SUDANESE

The one Sudanese to achieve world renown in modern history was the Mahdi (Muhammad Ahmad bin 'Abdallah, 1843–85), who set out on a self-appointed mission to purify Islam, a mission he hoped would carry him ultimately to Istanbul and to the apex of the Muslim world. Under his banner, the people of Sudan rose against their Egyptian overlords and for over a decade kept most of their country free from foreign rule. The Mahdi died shortly after the seizure of Khartoum. His able but harsh successor, the Khalifa ('Abdallah bin Muhammad at-Ta'a'ishi, d.1899), organized an independent government, which lasted until 1898, when an Anglo-Egyptian expeditionary corps reconquered Sudan.

The Mahdist wars provided the background for the exploits of famous British soldiers and administrators, among them generals Charles George Gordon (1833–85), Horatio Herbert Kitchener (1850–1916), and Sir Francis Reginald Wingate (1861–1953), the first governor-general of the condominium, as well as other foreign officers and explorers in the service of Egypt, such as the Italian Romolo Gessi (1831–81), the German Emin Pasha (Eduard Carl Oscar Theodor Schnitzer, 1840–92), the American Charles Chaillé-Long (1842–1917), and the Austrian Sir Rudolf Carl von Slatin (1857–1932).

Osman Digna ('Uthnab Abu Bakr Digna, c. 1840–1926), an organizer and leader of the Mahdist armies, and Sayyid 'Abd ar-Rahman al-Mahdi (1885–1959), posthumous son of the Mahdi, are revered by Sudanese. The most influential figure in recent years was Gaafar Mohammed Nimeiri (Ja'far Muhammad Numayri, b.1930), leader of Sudan from the 1969 coup until 1985. Sadiq al-Mahdi (b. 1936) was prime minister during 1966–67 and 1985–87.

49 DEPENDENCIES

Sudan has no territories or colonies.

50 BIBLIOGRAPHY

Arkell, Anthony J. *A History of the Sudan, from the Earliest Times to 1821*. London: Athlone, 1961.

Bechtold, Peter. *Politics in the Sudan: Parliamentary and Military Rule in an Emerging African Nation*. New York: Praeger, 1976.

Beshir, Mohamed O. *The Southern Sudan: From Conflict to Peace*. New York: Barnes & Noble, 1976.

Collins, Robert O. *Land Beyond the Rivers*. New Haven, Conn.: Yale University Press, 1971.

Collins, Robert O. *Shadows in the Grass: Great Britain and the Southern Sudan, 1918–1956*. New Haven, Conn.: Yale University Press, 1983.

Daly, M. W. *Imperial Sudan: The Anglo-Egyptian Condominium, 1934–1956*. New York: Cambridge University Press, 1991.

———. *Sudan*. Santa Barbara, Calif.: Clio Press, 1992.

———, Ahmad Alawad Sikainga (eds.). *Civil War in the Sudan*. New York: British Academic Press, 1993.

Deng, Francis Mading. *Bonds of Silk: The Human Factor in the British Administration of the Sudan*. East Lansing, Mich.: Michigan State University Press, 1989.

Fluehr-Lobban, Carolyn, Richard A. Lobban Jr. and John Obert Voll (eds.). *Historical Dictionary of the Sudan*. 2d ed. Metuchen, N.J.: Scarecrow Press, 1992.

Gurdon, Charles. *Sudan at the Crossroads*. London: Menas, 1984.

Hill, Richard Leslie, *Egypt in the Sudan, 1820–1881*. London: Oxford University Press, 1959.

Holt, P. M. *The History of the Sudan, from the Coming of Islam to the Present Day*. 4th ed. New York: Longman, 1988.

Lees, Francis, and Hugh Brooks. *The Economic and Political Development of the Sudan*. Boulder, Colo.: Westview, 1977.

Malwal, Bona. *People and Power in Sudan*. London: Ithaca Press, 1981.

Metz, Helen Chapin (ed.). *Sudan: A Country Study*. 4th ed. Washington, D.C.: Library of Congress, 1992.

Niblock, Tim. *Class and Power in Sudan: The Dynamics of Sudanese Politics, 1898–1985*. Albany: State University of New York Press, 1987.

Sudan in Pictures. Minneapolis: Lerner Publications Co., 1988.

Trimingham, John Spencer. *Islam in the Sudan*. London: Oxford University Press, 1958.

Voll, John, and Sarah Voll. *The Sudan*. Boulder, Colo.: Westview, 1985.

Warburg, Gabriel. *Historical Discord in the Nile Valley*. Evanston, Ill.: Northwestern University Press, 1992.

SWAZILAND

Kingdom of Swaziland

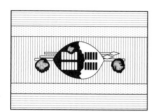

CAPITAL: Mbabane (administrative and judicial); Lobamba (royal and parliamentary).

FLAG: Blue, yellow, crimson, yellow, and blue stripes with the shield and spears of the Emasotsha regiment superimposed on the crimson stripe.

ANTHEM: National Anthem, beginning "O God, bestower of the blessings of the Swazi."

MONETARY UNIT: The lilangeni (pl. emalangeni; E) of 100 cents is a paper currency equal in value to the South African rand, which is also legal tender. There are coins of 1, 2, 5, 10, 20, and 50 cents, 1 lilangeni, and notes of 2, 5, 10, 20, and 50 emalangeni. E1 = $0.2874TK (or $1 = E3.4795).

WEIGHTS AND MEASURES: The metric system replaced imperial weights and measures in September 1969.

HOLIDAYS: New Year's Day, 1 January; Commonwealth Day, 2d Monday in March; National Flag Day, 25 April; Birthday of King Sobhuza II, 22 July; Umhlanga (Reed Dance) Day, last Monday in August; Somhlolo (Independence) Day, 6 September; UN Day, 24 October; Christmas Day, 25 December; Boxing Day, 26 December. Movable religious holidays include Good Friday, Holy Saturday, Easter Monday, Ascension, and the Incwala Ceremony.

TIME: 2 PM = noon GMT.

1LOCATION, SIZE, AND EXTENT
A landlocked country in southern Africa, Swaziland has an area of 17,360 sq km (6,703 sq mi), extending 176 km (109 mi) N–S and 135 km (84 mi) E–W. Comparatively, the area occupied by Swaziland is slightly smaller than the state of New Jersey. It is bounded by Mozambique on the NE and by the Republic of South Africa (including the homelands) on the SE, S, W, and N, with a total boundary length of 535 km (332 mi).

Swaziland's capital city, Mbabane, is located in the westcentral part of the country.

2TOPOGRAPHY
The country is divided west-to-east into four well defined regions, the first three being of roughly equal breadth. The four regions extend north and south and are known as the high-, middle-, and lowveld and the Lubombo plain and escarpment. The highveld on the west rises to a high point of 1,850 m (6,070 ft) and has an average altitude of over 1,070 m (3,510 ft). The middleveld averages about 610–760 m (2,000–2,500 ft), and the low- or bushveld less than 300 m (1,000 ft). The Lubombo plain, at an average height of 610 m (2,000 ft), extends to the Lubombo escarpment, which is part of the Lubombo Mountains in the east. The entire country is traversed by rivers or streams, making it one of the best watered areas in southern Africa.

3CLIMATE
The highveld has a humid near-temperate climate with about 140 cm (55 in) of mean annual rainfall. The middleveld and Lubombo are subtropical and somewhat drier, with about 85 cm (33 in) of annual rainfall; the lowveld, almost tropical, is subhumid, receiving about 60 cm (24 in) of rain in an average year. Rainfall tends to be concentrated in a few violent storms in the summer (October–March). Temperatures range from as low as -3°C (27°F) in winter in the highlands to as high as 42°C (108°F) in summer in the lowlands. At Mbabane, temperatures average 20°C (68°F) in January and 12°C (54°F) in July.

4FLORA AND FAUNA
Grassland, savanna, mixed bush, and scrub cover most of Swaziland. There is some forest in the highlands. Flora include aloes, orchids, and begonias. Large indigenous mammals include the blue wildebeest, kudu, impala, zebra, waterbuck, and hippopotamus; however, wildlife has become very scarce outside the protected areas. Crocodiles live in the lowland rivers. Bird life is plentiful and includes the European stork, sacred ibis, and gray heron.

5ENVIRONMENT
The chief environmental problem is soil erosion and degradation, particularly because of overgrazing. Population growth and the increased demand for fuel has threatened the country's forests. The resulting deforestation has contributed to the loss of valuable soil. Swaziland has 4 protected areas for wildlife—2 wildlife sanctuaries and 2 nature reserves—totaling 40,045 ha (98,953 acres), all in the northern half of the country. Another significant environmental problem in Swaziland is air pollution. The sources are transportation vehicles and pollution from other countries in the area. Water pollution from industrial and agricultural sources is also a problem. as well as contamination by untreated sewage, which contributes to the spread of life-threatening diseases. Swaziland has 1.7 cu mi of water, of which 93% is used for farming and 2% for industrial activity. Over 90% of the nation's rural people do not have pure water. As of 1994, none of Swaziland's 46 animal species were endangered, but 5 of the nation's bird species and 25 types of plants were threatened with extinction.

6POPULATION
According to the 1986 census, Swaziland's population was 681,059. A population of 984,000 was projected by the UN for the year 2000, assuming a crude birthrate of 36.2 per 1,000 population, a crude death rate of 9.2, and a net natural increase of 27 during 1995–2000. The estimated average density in 1994 was 53 persons per sq km (139 per sq mi). An estimated 31% of the

population was urban in 1995. Major towns were Mbabane, the capital, about 47,000 (1990), and Manzini, 18,048 in 1986.

7MIGRATION

Over the years, there has been a noticeable drift of educated Africans, many of whom have acquired British citizenship, from South Africa to Swaziland. At the end of 1992, Swaziland also harbored 55,600 refugees, about 7,400 of them South Africans, primarily Swazis fleeing the black homeland of KwaZulu. There were also 48,100 Mozambican refugees, and perhaps as many illegal immigrants. In 1991 there were 49,118 Swaziland-born blacks residing in South Africa.

8ETHNIC GROUPS

The indigenous African population is Swazi, comprising more than 70 clans, of which the Nkosi Dlamini, the royal clan, is dominant. Other Africans, mainly from Mozambique, numbered 14,468 in 1986. There were also 11,000 Europeans, 2,403 people of mixed race, and 228 Asiatics.

9LANGUAGES

English and Siswati, which is spoken by almost all Swazi, are the official languages.

10RELIGIONS

Of the adult Swazi population, about 20% practice traditional African religions. Except for a small Muslim community, the rest of the population is Christian, with about 30% belonging to independent African churches. In 1993, Roman Catholics comprised some 5.3% of the population, and there was a small Bahai presence.

11TRANSPORTATION

The country had 2,853 km (1,773 mi) of roads in 1991; 510 km (317 mi) were tarred. A highway runs between the southern boundary with South Africa and the eastern boundary with Mozambique. There were 21,287 passenger cars and 15,874 trucks and buses in use in 1991. The 224-km (139-mi) Swaziland Railway links iron mines at Ngwenya with the Mozambique Railway and the port of Maputo in Mozambique. In the 1970s, a 94-km (58-mi) southern spur was constructed to the South African border. A 115-km (71-mi) northern spur to the South African border was completed in 1986. Matsapa Airport, near Manzini, provides service, via Royal Swazi National Airways, to South Africa, Mozambique, Zambia, Malawi, Zimbabwe, Botswana, Kenya, and Tanzania. In all, 90,000 passengers were carried in 1991.

12HISTORY

Like other parts of southern Africa, Swaziland was originally occupied by hunting and gathering peoples known as Bushmen. In the 16th century, according to tradition, Bantu-speaking peoples advanced southwest to what is now Mozambique. During the migration, these groups disintegrated to form the various tribes of southern Africa. In fact, however, the Swazi do not appear to have broken away from the main body of the Bantu until the middle of the 18th century. The Swazi emerged as a distinct tribe at the beginning of the 19th century and were in constant conflict with the Zulu; they moved gradually northward and made their first formal contact with the British in the 1840s, when their ruler, Mswati II, applied to the British for help against the Zulu. The British succeeded in improving relations between the two tribes.

About this time, the first Europeans came to Swaziland to settle. The independence of Swaziland was guaranteed by the British and Transvaal governments in 1881 and 1884, but owing to the excessive number of concessions (including land, grazing, and mineral rights) granted to European entrepreneurs by Mbandzeni

(the king) during the 1880s, the UK decided some form of control was necessary. In 1890, a provisional government was established, representing the Swazi, the British, and the Transvaal. From 1894 to 1899, the Transvaal government undertook the protection and administration of Swaziland. After the South African (Boer) War of 1899–1902, the administration of Swaziland was transferred to the British governor of the Transvaal. An order in council established the relationship between the Swazi and the UK in 1903, providing the basic authority under which British administration was conducted for 60 years.

Independence

Responsibility for Swaziland was transferred in 1907 to the high commissioner for South Africa. An elected European Advisory Council was constituted in 1921. By the provisions of the Native Administration Proclamation of 1941, the position of the ngwenyama (paramount chief) as native authority was recognized. In 1963, constitutional discussions looking toward independence were opened in London. The following year, elections for a legislative council were held under the country's first constitution. After further constitutional talks, held in London in 1965, Swaziland became an independent nation within the Commonwealth on 6 September 1968.

On 12 April 1973, King Sobhuza II, who had been head of the Swazi nation since 1921, announced that the constitution had been repealed and that he had assumed supreme executive, legislative, and judicial powers. In 1979, a new parliament was chosen, partly through indirect elections and partly through royal appointment.

After Sobhuza died in 1982, a prolonged power struggle took place. At first his senior wife, Queen Mother Dzeliwe, became head of state and regent. Members of the Liqoqo, the king's advisory council, seized effective power and appointed a new "Queen Regent" in August, 1983 (Ntombi, one of Sobhuza's other wives). At that time it was announced that Makhosetive, the 15-year-old son of Ntombi and one of Sobhuza's 67 sons, would ascend the throne upon reaching adulthood. He was crowned King Mswati III on 25 April 1986. The intrigues continued until the new king approved the demotion of the Liqoqo back to its advisory status. He has ruled through his prime minister and cabinet.

In 1982, South Africa and Swaziland secretly signed a security agreement. Under pressure from South Africa, Swaziland arrested and deported members of the African National Congress, the leading black nationalist group in South Africa. On three different occasions in late 1985 and 1986, South African commando squads conducted raids in Swaziland, killing a number of ANC members and supporters. In November 1987, a new parliament was elected and a new cabinet appointed. Obed Dlamini was the prime minister from 1989 until 1993. In September and October, 1993, popular elections were held for parliament and a new prime minister, Prince Mbilini, took office, replacing Dlamini, who was defeated in the second round of voting.

13GOVERNMENT

Swaziland was a constitutional monarchy until King Sobhuza II repealed the constitution in 1973 and assumed absolute power. The king then ruled the country as king-in-council, on the advice of his former cabinet and two traditional Swazi councils, one consisting of all the chiefs and other notables, the other of the king, the queen mother, and (in theory) all adult males.

A new constitution was promulgated in 1978. In 1979, a new parliament was created, with a House of Assembly consisting of 50 members, 40 of whom were chosen by indirect election and 10 appointed by the crown; the 20-member Senate had 10 members chosen by indirect election and 10 appointed by the crown. To become law, legislation passed by parliament must be approved by the crown. The cabinet is presided over by a prime minister appointed by the crown from among the members of parliament.

In response to popular moves calling for reform, King Mswati III appointed several commissions to review the tinkhundla (local government) system. In July 1992, the second Tinkhundla Review Commission (popularly called Vusela II) reported to the king. Government accepted its main recommendations—increase tinkhundla centers, allow direct representation in parliament, and institute a secret ballot. Opposition parties complained that Vusela II did not consult a broad range of Swazis and that the reforms did not address the issue of the legality of political parties. The king followed the Vusela II recommendations, rejected the creation of a multiparty system and, on 21 August 1993, the electoral process got started with nomination of candidates. On 25 September primary elections selected 3 candidates for each district and in October, in runoff elections, voters chose 55 members for the House of Assembly. The king appointed 10 more. A Senate was chosen, 10 members elected by the House of Assembly, and 20 appointed by the king.

14POLITICAL PARTIES

All parties are banned under the 1978 constitution, but this ban is defied by the People's United Democratic Movement (Pudemo), the Swaziland United Front, the Swaziland Progressive Party, the Imbokodv National Movement, the Ngwane National Liberatory Congress, the Swaziland National Front, and the Swaziland United Party, which operate openly. The latter two were formed in 1992. Pudemo went so far as to declare itself legal in February 1992, and to demand a national convention of all political factions and a referendum on the constitution.

15LOCAL GOVERNMENT

Swaziland is divided into four districts: Hhohho, Manzini, Shiselweni, and Lubombo, the largest. District commissioners are appointed by the central government. Mbabane, Manzini, and two other towns have municipal governments. Paralleling statutory government structure is a traditional system consisting of the king and his traditional advisors, traditional courts, and 40 tinkhundla subregional districts in which traditional chiefs are grouped.

16JUDICIAL SYSTEM

The dual judicial system consists of a set of courts based on a western model and western law and a set of national courts which follows Swazi law and custom. The former consists of a Court of Appeals and a High Court, plus magistrate's courts in each of the four districts. The traditional courts deal with minor offenses and violations of traditional Swazi law and custom. Sentences in traditional courts are subject to appeal and review to the Court of Appeals and High Court. The king has authority to appoint a special tribunal with its own procedural rules in treason and sedition cases.

The courts are independent of executive and military control or influence.

17ARMED FORCES

The Umbutfo Swaziland Defense Force has fewer than 3,000 personnel and functions as a border patrol and an internal security force. A royal guard battalion was formed in 1982.

18INTERNATIONAL COOPERATION

Swaziland joined the UN on 24 September 1968 and participates in ECA and all the nonregional specialized agencies except IAEA, IMO, WIPO, and UNIDO. The country also belongs to the African Development Bank, Commonwealth of Nations, G-77, and OAU. Swaziland is a signatory to the Lomé Convention and the Law of the Sea and is a de facto adherent of GATT.

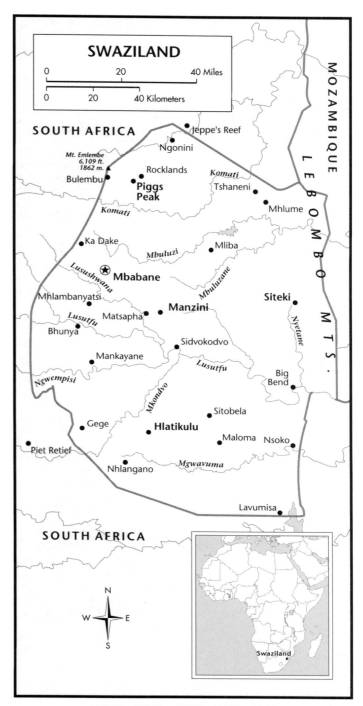

LOCATION: 25°43' to 27°20's; 30°48' to 32°8'E
BOUNDARY LENGTHS: Mozambique, 108 km (67 mi); South Africa (including homelands), 446 km (277 mi).

19ECONOMY

Swaziland's economy is based firmly on free market principles. The governments' monetary and fiscal policies are prudent and, as a result, the country's balance-of-payments position is strong and its debt burden light. The majority of Swazis are engaged in subsistence agriculture, though a relatively diversified industrial sector accounts for the largest component of the formal economy. Because of its small size, Swaziland relies heavily on the export sector, composed primarily of large firms with predominantly foreign ownership. Swaziland's economy benefited considerably from investments emigrating from South Africa during the sanctions period. Growth in sugar production has also made a solid contribution.

20 INCOME

In 1992 Swaziland's GNP was $930 million at current prices, or $1,080 per capita. Annual inflation in 1992 was 19.7% while for the period 1985–92 the average inflation rate was 12.7%, resulting in a real growth rate in per capita GNP of 6.4%.

In 1992 the GDP was $998 million in current US dollars. It is estimated that agriculture, hunting, forestry, and fishing contributed 14% to GDP; mining and quarrying, 1%; manufacturing, 20%; electricity, gas, and water, 3%; construction, 3%; wholesale and retail trade, 11%; transport, storage, and communication, 6%; finance, insurance, real estate, and business services, 12%; community, social, and personal services, 1%; and other sources 30%.

21 LABOR

The domestic wage labor force was about 91,333 in 1989; nearly one-seventh were engaged in sugar production. Agriculture employs about 26% of the wage labor force. The Swaziland Federation of Trade Unions is the major labor organization. There is also an employers' federation.

22 AGRICULTURE

Swazi nation land, which comprises over 60% of the total land area, is held in trust by the crown for the Swazi people and supports about 70% of the population. Nearly half of the remaining land, which is freehold title, is owned by Europeans; the rest is owned by government or parastatal bodies. Under the traditional land tenure system, farmers till small plots, averaging less than 3 ha (7.4 acres), but have no title or right to sell this land. The average freehold title farm, by contrast, is about 800 ha (2,000 acres), and over 60% of freehold title cropland is irrigated. In this modern sector, agriculture expanded considerably in the early 1970s, mainly because of improved irrigation, better strains, and widespread introduction and use of fertilizers. Sugar is the most important cash crop, and corn is the staple crop. Most of the sugar produced is exported to Western Europe and North America. Output in 1992 included sugarcane, 3.6 million tons, and corn, 54,000 tons. Much of the sugar is exported to the EC, in accordance with the Sugar Protocol of the Lomé Convention; increasing amounts, however, are sold and refined domestically. Citrus production in 1992 was about 87,000 tons; pineapple production, about 45,000 tons. Cotton fiber production in that year was 10,000 tons. Between 1970 and 1982, 17 Rural Development Areas were established to assist traditional farmers; the program was expected to extend eventually to all Swazi nation land. The 1991/92 drought caused corn and cotton production to seriously decline; as a result the government sought emergency food assistance.

23 ANIMAL HUSBANDRY

Livestock raising, like agriculture, is divided into two sectors: a traditional system of grazing on communal lands for subsistence needs, and modern, commercial ranches on freehold title land. Livestock numbers recovered in 1991 from a previous drought-related selloff. In 1992, Swaziland had about 753,000 head of cattle, 406,000 goats, 23,000 sheep, 31,000 hogs, 13,000 equines, and 1,000,000 poultry. The country slaughtered a total of 63,000 head of cattle in 1992. However, the meat processing industry has been unstable since 1988.

24 FISHING

By 1982, several commercial fish farms had been established and some Rural Development Areas had fish ponds. Annual production is estimated at 105 tons.

25 FORESTRY

Swaziland's forests (pine and eucalyptus) are among the world's largest planted forests, covering 104,000 ha (257,000 acres), or about 6% of the land area. Roundwood output totaled 2,223,000 cu m in 1991, about 70% coniferous. Sawn wood production was 103,000 cu m. Of Swaziland's planted forests, half supply the Usutu pulp mill, a large export earner producing unbleached wood pulp.

26 MINING

Iron ore was Swaziland's major mineral export, but production, after reaching 2,239,818 tons in 1975, ceased altogether by the end of the 1970s. Chrysolite asbestos, mined since 1939, yielded 13,888 tons in 1991; asbestos mining is 15% government owned. Coal production, also government owned, was 122,502 tons in 1991; coal reserves have been estimated at 1 billion tons. Diamonds, mainly of industrial quality, have been mined since 1984, with the mine jointly operated by the Swazi Nation (distinct from the government) and a South African company. Production was 57,420 carats in 1991.

27 ENERGY AND POWER

In 1991, the Swaziland Electricity Board had a total installed capacity of 60,000 kw, primarily by hydroelectric stations. In 1991, a total of 155 million kwh was generated. In 1991, fuel imports amounted to $95 million, or 73% of total imports. About $10 million of imported electricity came from South Africa in 1991. All petroleum products come from South Africa.

28 INDUSTRY

Sanctions against South Africa in 1988 and internal unrest inspired interest in the relocation of South African-based industry, such as Coca-Cola, in Swaziland. Reexports of South African manufactures with "Made in Swaziland" labels also became current at this time. The industrial sector growth of the 1980s slowed in the early 1990s. Textile manufacturing, which flourished when South African tariffs were high, began to wither when they were equalized. Light manufacturing of knits, footwear, gloves, office equipment, beverages, confectionery, furniture, glass, and bricks brought annual growth in the sector to the 5.5% level. Before 1986, manufacturing industries mainly processed agricultural, livestock, and forestry products, such as wood pulp, canned fruit and juices, and sugar. In 1971, the establishment of the Industrial Development Corporation (IDC) was instrumental in developing various projects, including an ethyl alcohol distillery and a radio and television assembly plant. The IDC was later renamed and restructured in 1986 with commercially viable enterprises transferred to a new agency, the Swaziland Industrial Development Corporation, 55% of which was held by foreign banks and development agencies. In addition, the Small Enterprise Development Corp. was established in 1970.

Most of Swaziland's energy—78% of 494 GWH in 1991—is imported from South Africa. The largest energy-generating capacity in Swaziland is the 50 Mw Luphohlo-Ezulwini hydroelectric station.

29 SCIENCE AND TECHNOLOGY

The University of Swaziland has faculties of agriculture and science. There is also a college of technology. The Geological Survey and Mines Department conducts mining research, and three other institutes conduct agricultural research.

30 DOMESTIC TRADE

Mbabane and Manzini are the principal commercial centers. Manufactured articles are generally available in all urban centers and are marketed mostly by Europeans. Business hours are from

8:15 or 8:30 AM to 1 PM and from 2 to 5 PM, Monday–Friday, and from 8:15 or 8:30 AM to 1 PM, Saturday. Banks are open weekdays from 8:30 AM to 1 PM and Saturdays from 8:30 to 11 AM.

31FOREIGN TRADE

Swaziland had a favorable balance of trade throughout the 1970s, but in the early 1980s, dramatic declines in market prices for sugar and wood pulp led to increasingly larger deficits. More than 95% of imports either originate in or transit through South Africa. Principal exports in 1990 (in millions of emalangeni) were as follows:

Sugar	441.9
Timber and wood pulp	174.1
Canned fruit	50.6
Asbestos, coal, diamonds	53.9
Edible concentrates	252.8

Principal imports in 1985 (in millions of emalangeni) were as follows:

Minerals, fuels, and lubricants	272.5
Machinery and transport equipment	490.0
Manufactured goods	272.8
Food and live animals	245.4
Chemicals and chemical products	171.4

32BALANCE OF PAYMENTS

Despite a deteriorating trade balance, Swaziland enjoys a favorable balance of payments. Net foreign reserves grew each year from 1986 to 1991, to $221.5 million by the end of 1991. Swaziland is aided in this regard by a Common Monetary Area (CMA) agreement, under which South African rands are informally considered legal tender in Swaziland and circulate freely and abundantly. Consequently, Swaziland can pay for approximately 90% of its imports, which come from or through South Africa in freely available rands, without having to spend valuable hard currency reserves. Meanwhile, exports go primarily to Europe and North America, where they earn foreign currency reserves, thus freeing Swaziland from the foreign exchange constraints faced by many other African countries.

In 1992 merchandise exports totaled $608.1 million and imports $698.2 million. The merchandise trade balance was $–90.1 million. The following table summarizes Swaziland's balance of payments for 1991 and 1992 (in millions of US dollars):

	1991	1992
CURRENT ACCOUNT		
Goods, services, and income	−94.5	−106.3
Unrequited transfers	97.7	131.7
TOTALS	3.2	25.4
CAPITAL ACCOUNT		
Direct investment	34.2	42.0
Portfolio investment	−0.5	0.1
Other long-term capital	6.2	4.1
Other short-term capital	−27.9	−24.5
Reserves	−13.5	−95.1
TOTALS	−1.5	−73.4
Errors and omissions	−1.8	48.2
Total change in reserves	44.5	−137.1

33BANKING AND SECURITIES

The Central Bank of Swaziland had foreign assets of E875.03 million in 1993. The total money supply, as measured by M2, was E754.31 million in the same year. The nation's commercial banks are subsidiaries of Barclays Bank and the Standard Chartered Bank. Other financial institutions are the Swaziland Development and Savings Bank and the Union Bank of Swaziland.

34INSURANCE

The Swaziland Royal Insurance Corp., 51% state owned, began operating in 1974; there were two other insurance brokers in 1987.

35PUBLIC FINANCE

The government maintains a prudent fiscal policy by avoiding large deficits and restricting public sector growth. From 1987 to 1991, large budgetary surpluses were registered, and the government began making repayments on the external debt as a net creditor to the bank. Budgetary deficits returned in 1992 and 1993.

The following table shows actual revenues and expenditures for 1988 and 1989 in millions of emalangeni.

	1988	1989
REVENUE AND GRANTS		
Tax revenue	380.44	503.74
Non-tax revenue	42.10	66.29
Capital revenue	0.10	0.03
Grants	5.55	14.24
TOTAL	428.19	584.30
EXPENDITURES & LENDING MINUS REPAYMENTS		
General public services	54.81	74.42
Defense	19.60	22.20
Public order and safety	33.81	44.40
Education	84.84	104.58
Health	30.44	35.28
Social Security and Welfare	—	1.72
Housing and community amenities	30.58	19.61
Recreation, cultural, and religious affairs	—	3.96
Economic affairs and services	78.52	96.76
Other expenditures	22.23	24.35
Lending minus repayments	14.16	61.56
TOTAL	368.99	488.84
Deficit/Surplus	59.20	95.46

In 1989 Swaziland's total public debt stood at E592.63 million, of which E555.40 million was financed abroad.

36TAXATION

All income earned in Swaziland is subject to a progressive personal income tax ranging from 4–50%. Companies are taxed at a flat rate of 37.5%.

37CUSTOMS AND DUTIES

Swaziland belongs to a customs union with South Africa, Lesotho, Botswana, and Namibia. South Africa levies and collects most of the customs, sales, and excise duties for the five member states, paying a share of the revenues to the other four. Local import duties are applied to wines, spirits, and beer.

38FOREIGN INVESTMENT

More than half of all enterprises are foreign owned or joint ventures. In 1985, foreign companies invested $1.1 million in Swaziland. Cognizant of its subordinate relationship to South Africa, Swaziland has fostered an investment climate agreeable to foreign businesses.

39ECONOMIC DEVELOPMENT

The growth experienced in recent years has left unaffected the 66% of Swazis who live on small family farms. While manufacturing employment has risen to 94,054 in 1991, another 50,351 Swazis are unemployed and actively seeking work. It is hoped that the inauguration of a multiracial government will prove beneficial to ongoing Swaziland-South African economic development.

40SOCIAL DEVELOPMENT

Social services have developed slowly. The government subsidizes workers whose wages fall below specified minimums, and workers' compensation is also provided. Women do not have full legal equality with men, and a married woman is virtually a legal minor. The Employment Act of 1980 forbade sex discrimination, however. Only 2 women are numbered among the 55 members elected to the House of Assembly.

41HEALTH

Major health problems include bilharzia, typhoid, tapeworm, gastroenteritis, malaria, kwashiorkor, and pellagra. In 1990, there were an estimated 220 cases of tuberculosis per 100,000 people, and only about 30% of the population had access to safe water.

In 1990, there were 83 doctors, 7 dentists, 13 pharmacists, and 1,264 nurses. Traditional healers are still consulted by over 80% of the population.

There were 29,600 births in 1992. The 1993 the birth rate was 37.2 per 1,000 people. In 1992, average life expectancy was 58 years. The infant mortality rate in 1992 was 74 per 1,000 live births, with 3,200 deaths of children under 5 years of age that year. General mortality was 10.4 per 1,000 people in 1993. About 55% of the population had access to health care services in 1990 and, in 1992, 85% of children were vaccinated against measles.

42HOUSING

The government aims to improve housing conditions for low-income groups through self-help schemes and by providing mortgage facilities. In 1985, 30 residential buildings worth E3,310,900 were completed; squatter settlements have developed, however, accounting for as much as half of annual shelter production in those cities. As of 1990, 100% of urban and 7% of rural dwellers had access to a public water supply, while 100% of urban and 10% of rural inhabitants had access to sanitation services.

43EDUCATION

There are government, mission, and private schools. The majority of primary and secondary schools are run by missions with grants from the government. In 1991 there were 514 primary schools with 172,908 pupils and 5,347 teachers. General secondary schools had 44,085 students and 2,430 teachers. Children go through seven years of primary and five years of secondary schooling. Higher education is provided by the University of Swaziland and the Swaziland College of Technology. In all higher level institutions there were 452 teaching staff and 3,224 students in 1991.

44LIBRARIES AND MUSEUMS

The Swaziland National Library Service was founded in 1971; with 80,000 volumes, it has 13 branches throughout the country and operates school libraries at secondary levels. A National Library was established in 1986. There is also a mobile library service. The Swaziland National Museum, in Lobamba, founded in 1972, with collections primarily of ethnographic material and cultural objects of South Africa Bantu groups.

45MEDIA

In 1991 there were 23,905 telephones in service. The government-operated Swaziland Broadcasting Service broadcasts radio programs in English and Siswati and television programs in English. In 1991 there were about 127,000 radios and 15,000 television sets. There are two daily English newspapers, the *Times of Swaziland* and the *Swaziland Observer*, with circulations in 1991 of 8,000 and 3,500, respectively, and a daily newspaper published in Siswati, *Tikhatsi Temaswati*.

46ORGANIZATIONS

There are more than 123 cooperative societies, including the Swaziland Central Cooperatives Union. The national chamber of commerce and industry is in Mbabane.

47TOURISM, TRAVEL, AND RECREATION

Tourism has been increasingly promoted and by the mid-1980s was a main source of foreign exchange revenue. Swaziland offers the tourist a magnificent variety of scenery and casinos at Mbabane, Nhlangano, and Pigg's Peak. In 1991 there were 279,000 tourists; 223,000 were Africans. Tourist expenditures totaled an estimated US$26 million. There were 1,210 hotel rooms and 2,494 beds, with an occupancy rate of 37.4%. Tourists come primarily from South Africa (60% in 1990). Visitors to Swaziland require valid passports.

48FAMOUS SWAZI

Sobhuza II (1899–1982) was king, or ngwenyama, of the Swazi nation from 1921 until his death. Mswati III (b.1968) became king in 1986.

49DEPENDENCIES

Swaziland has no territories or colonies.

50BIBLIOGRAPHY

Balima, Mildred Grimes. *Botswana, Lesotho, and Swaziland; a Guide to Official Publications, 1868–1968.* Washington, D.C.: Library of Congress, 1971.

Black, David R. *Foreign Policy in Small States: Botswana, Lesotho, Swaziland and Southern Africa.* Halifax, N.S.: Dalhousie University, 1988.

Bonner, Phillip. *Kings, Commoners and Concessionaires: The Evolution and Dissolution of the Nineteenth-Century Swazi State.* New York: Cambridge University Press, 1983.

Booth, Alan R. *Swaziland: Tradition and Change in a Southern African Kingdom.* Boulder, Colo.: Westview, 1984.

Grotpeter, John J. *Historical Dictionary of Swaziland.* Metuchen, N.J.: Scarecrow Press, 1975.

Kuper, Hilda. *An African Aristocracy.* New York: Holmes & Meier, 1980 (orig. 1965).

Kuper, Hilda. *Sobhuza II: Ngwenyama and King of Swaziland.* New York: Holmes & Meier, 1978.

TANZANIA

United Republic of Tanzania
Jamhuri Ya Muungano Wa Tanzania

CAPITAL: Dar es Salaam.

FLAG: The flag consists of a black diagonal stripe running from the lower corner of the hoist to the upper corner of the fly and flanked by yellow stripes. The diagonal stripes separate two triangular areas: green at the upper corner of the hoist and blue at the lower corner of the fly.

ANTHEM: The Tanzanian National Anthem is a setting to new words of the widely known hymn *Mungu Ibariki Afrika (God Bless Africa)*.

MONETARY UNIT: The Tanzanian shilling (Sh) of 100 cents is a paper currency. There are coins of 5, 10, 20, and 50 cents and 1, 5, 10, and 20 shillings, and notes of 10, 20, 50, 100, 200, 500, and 1,000 shillings. Sh1 = $0.0020 (or $1 = Sh494.41).

WEIGHTS AND MEASURES: The metric system is used.

HOLIDAYS: Zanzibar Revolution Day, 12 January; Chama Cha Mapinduzi Day, 5 February; Union Day, 26 April; International Workers' Day, 1 May; Farmers' Day, 7 July; Independence Day, 9 December; Christmas, 25 December. Movable religious holidays include 'Id al-Fitr, 'Id al-'Adha', Milad an-Nabi, Good Friday, and Easter Monday.

TIME: 3 PM = noon GMT.

1 LOCATION, SIZE, AND EXTENT

Situated in East Africa just south of the equator, mainland Tanzania lies between the area of the great lakes—Victoria, Tanganyika, and Malawi (Niassa)—and the Indian Ocean. It contains a total area of 945,090 sq km (364,901 sq mi), including 59,047 sq km (22,798 sq mi) of inland water. Comparatively, the area occupied by Tanzania is slightly larger than twice the size of the state of California. Tanzania extends 1,190 km (740 mi) N–S and 1,200 km (750 mi) E–W. It is bounded on the N by Uganda and Kenya, on the E by the Indian Ocean, on the S by Mozambique and Malawi, on the SW by Zambia, and on the W by Zaire, Burundi, and Rwanda, with a total boundary length of 4,826 km (2,999 mi). Tanzania claims part of Lake Malawi, although its internationally recognized boundary is the eastern shore.

The section of the United Republic known as Zanzibar comprises the islands of Zanzibar and Pemba and all islets within 19 km (12 mi) of their coasts, as well as uninhabited Latham Island, 58 km (36 mi) S of Zanzibar Island. Zanzibar Island lies 35 km (22 mi) off the coast, and Pemba Island is about 40 km (25 mi) to the NE. The former has an area of 1,657 sq km (640 sq mi), and the latter 984 sq km (380 sq mi).

Tanzania's capital city, Dar es Salaam, is located on the Indian Ocean coast.

2 TOPOGRAPHY

Except for the islands and a coastal strip varying in width from 16 to 64 km (10–40 mi), Tanzania lies at an altitude of over 200 m (660 ft). A plateau averaging 900–1,800 m (3,000–6,000 ft) in height makes up the greater part of the country. Mountains are grouped in various sections. The Pare range is in the northeast, and the Kipengere Range is in the southwest. Kilimanjaro (5,895 m/19,340 ft), in the north, is the highest mountain in Africa.

On the borders are three large lakes: Victoria, the second largest freshwater lake in the world, exceeded only by Lake Superior; Tanganyika, second only to Lake Baykal as the deepest in the

world; and Lake Malawi. Lakes within Tanzania include Natron, Eyasi, Manyara, and Rukwa.

Tanzania has few permanent rivers. During half the year, the central plateau has no running water, but in the rainy season, flooding presents a problem.

Two-thirds of Zanzibar Island, to the center and the east, consists of low-lying coral country covered by bush and grass plains and is largely uninhabited except for fishing settlements on the east coast. The western side of the island is fertile and has several ridges rising above 60 m (200 ft). Masingini Ridge, at 119 m (390 ft), is the highest point on the island. The west and center of Pemba Island consists of a flat-topped ridge about 9.5 km (6 mi) wide, deeply bisected by streams. Pemba is hilly, but its highest point is only 95 m (311 ft). Apart from the narrow belt of coral country in the east, the island is fertile and densely populated.

3 CLIMATE

There are four main climatic zones: (1) the coastal area and immediate hinterland, where conditions are tropical, with temperatures averaging about 27°C (81°F), rainfall varying from 100 to 193 cm (40 to 76 in), and high humidity; (2) the central plateau, which is hot and dry, with rainfall from 50 to 76 cm (20 to 30 in), although with considerable daily and seasonal temperature variations; (3) the semitemperate highland areas, where the climate is healthy and bracing; and (4) the high, moist lake regions. There is little seasonal variation in the Lake Victoria area, but the eastern sections average only 75–100 cm (30–40 in) of rain, while the western parts receive 200–230 cm (80–90 in). A small area north of Lake Niassa receives 250 cm (100 in) of rain. There are two rainy seasons in the north, from November to December and from March through May. In the south there is one rainy season, from November to March.

The climate on the islands is tropical, but the heat is tempered by sea breezes that are constant throughout the year, except during the rainy seasons. The seasons are well defined. From December to

March, when the northeast monsoon blows, it is hot and comparatively dry. The heavy rains fall in April and May, and the lesser in November and December. It is coolest and driest from June to October, during the southwest monsoon.

4FLORA AND FAUNA

Common savanna species cover most of the drier inland areas—amounting to about one-third of the country—between altitudes of 300 and 1,200 m (1,000 and 4,000 ft). Two main types of closed-forest trees—low-level hardwoods and mountain softwoods—are found in high-rainfall areas on the main mountain masses and in parts of the Lake Victoria Basin. Wooded grasslands are widely scattered throughout the country. The drier central areas include bushlands and thickets. Grasslands and heath are common in the highlands, while the coast has mangrove forest.

The 4 million wild mammals include representatives of 430 species and subspecies, notably antelope, zebra, elephant, hippopotamus, rhinoceros, giraffe, and lion. Various types of monkeys are plentiful.

There are about 1,000 species of birds, ranging in size from ostrich to warbler. Insect life, consisting of more than 60,000 species, includes injurious species and disease carriers. There are at least 25 species of reptiles and amphibians and 25 poisonous varieties among the 100 species of snakes. Fish are plentiful.

The flora and fauna of Zanzibar and Pemba are varied. Mammals common to both are galagos, fruit-eating and insectivorous bats, genets, mongooses, small shrews, rats, and mice. Zanzibar has the leopard, Syke's monkey, civet, and giant rat. Unique species of tree coney are found on Pemba and Tumbatu Islands. There are also 5 unique mammals—Kirk's colobus (monkey), 2 elephant shrews, duiker antelope, and squirrel.

5ENVIRONMENT

The Ministry of Natural Resources and Tourism, the Tanzania National Parks Department, and the Ministry of Lands, Housing, and Urban Development are the government agencies entrusted with environmental responsibilities in Tanzania. One of the nation's major concerns is soil degradation as a result of recent droughts. The nation's land is also affected by the related problems of desertification. The nation loses 1,350 square miles of its forestland annually. Tanzania has 18.2 cu mi of water with 74% used for farming and 5% for industrial activity. A fourth of the nation's city dwellers and 54% of the people living in rural areas do not have pure water. The nation's cities produce 1.8 million tons of solid waste per year. As of 1994, 30 of Tanzania's mammal species were in danger of extinction, 26 bird species and 158 plant species are also endangered. The nation's fish are also threatened by the use of dynamite by the fish industry. The dynamite damages reefs which provide a home for the fish. Endangered species include the Uluguru bush-shrike, green sea turtle, hawksbill turtle, olive ridley turtle, and Zanzibar suni are.

6POPULATION

The population of the entire country was estimated at 29,736,704 in mid 1994, compared with a 1988 census figure of 23,174,336. A population of 35,916,000 was projected for 2000, assuming a crude birthrate of 45.1 per 1,000 population, a crude death rate of 14.1, and a net natural increase of 31 during 1995–2000.

The overall population density in 1994 was estimated at 31.5 per sq km (81.5 per sq mi). The most densely populated regions are the well-watered or elevated areas, particularly in the Usambara Mountains, around Kilimanjaro and Meru, on the shores of Lake Victoria, in the Southern Highlands, and in the coastal areas around Tanga and Dar es Salaam. In 1995, an estimated 24% of the population was urban. The principal cities (with 1988 census populations) are Dar es Salaam, 1,360,850; Zanzibar, 157,634;

Mwanza, 223,013; Tanga, 187,634; and Dodoma, 203,853. The 1988 census established the population of the islands at 640,578.

7MIGRATION

Out of an estimated Asian population of 100,000 in 1967, almost half, most of them with British passports, had left the country by 1980. Arabs, who were the dominant group on Zanzibar before the 1964 revolution in spite of forming less than 20% of the population, fled after the event to the mainland or the Middle East. There is some emigration of laborers seeking work in neighboring countries, but Tanzanians who leave the country without authorization are subject to prosecution on return. During the clove harvest, labor moves from the towns to the clove plantations, from Zanzibar to Pemba, and from the mainland territories to Pemba. As a result of migration from rural areas to the cities, the urban population is estimated to be growing by 6.5% per year. Urban authorities are empowered to return the unemployed to their villages. At the end of 1992, Tanzania was host to some 292,100 refugees, including 149,500 from Burundi, 75,000 from Mozambique, 21,000 from Rwanda, and 16,000 from Zaire.

8ETHNIC GROUPS

About 120 peoples have been categorized into 5 ethnic groups distinguishable by their physical characteristics and languages. Approximately 95% of Tanzanians may be roughly classified as Bantu, a comparatively recent blend mainly of Hamitic and Negroid stocks. Tribes range in membership from only a few thousand to the Sukuma tribe, which numbers more than 2 million. Other major tribes include the Nyamwezi, Makonde, Haya, and Chagga. The Luo, east of Lake Victoria, are the only people of Nilotic origin; the Masai of the northern highlands are Nilo-Hamites. A very small number of Bushmen-like people are scattered throughout northern Tanzania, where small tribes of Cushitic origin also live. The inhabitants of Zanzibar and Pemba are chiefly descendants of mainland Africans or are of mixed African and Arab extraction. Among non-Africans, there are about 70,000 Arabs, 40,000 Asians, and 10,000 Europeans in Tanzania.

9LANGUAGES

Most Tanzanians speak variations of Bantu languages and dialects. Various languages also have Hamitic or Nilotic origins. Swahili (or Kiswahili) is the lingua franca and is understood in most parts of the country, although its usefulness declines toward the west. English and Kiunguja, the form of Swahili spoken in Zanzibar, are the official languages. Arabic is widely spoken in Zanzibar and Pemba.

10RELIGIONS

Many of the mainland peoples adhere to African traditional beliefs, and religious practices vary from tribe to tribe. Islam is the creed of many coastal inhabitants and is well established in the inland towns that were situated along the 19th-century slave caravan routes. Christianity has spread since the early 20th century and is predominant in some districts. About 35% of the population is Muslim and 30% Christian; of the latter, about two-thirds are Roman Catholic.

Almost all of the population (95% in 1993) of the islands is Muslim. Most are orthodox Sunnis of the Shafi school.

11TRANSPORTATION

The Tanzanian Railways Corporation operates domestic railway services on 3,555 km (2,209 mi) of track. The Central Line extends 1,255 km (780 mi) from Dar es Salaam to Kigoma; its main branch lines are Tabora to Mwanza (381 km/237 mi) and Kaliua to Mpanda (211 km/131 mi). The Northern Line, extending from Dar es Salaam and Tanga to Moshi and Arusha, is

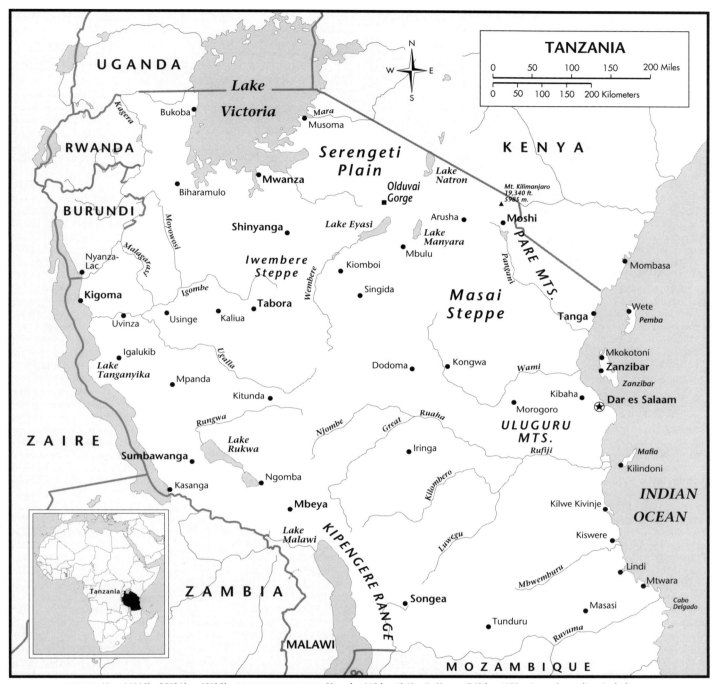

LOCATION: 1° to 11°45′s; 29°21′ to 40°25′E. **BOUNDARY LENGTHS:** Uganda, 418 km (260 mi); Kenya, 769 km (478 mi); total coastline (including coasts of Zanzibar and Pemba islands), 1,271 km (790 mi); Mozambique, 756 km (470 mi); Malawi, 451 km (280 mi); Zambia, 322 km (200 mi); Zaire, 459 km (285 mi); Burundi, 451 km (280 mi); Rwanda, 217 km (135 mi). **TERRITORIAL SEA LIMIT:** 50 mi.

linked to the railway systems of Kenya and Uganda. The 1,857-km (1,154-mi) Tazara railway, operated by the Tanzania-Zambia Railway Authority, links Dar es Salaam in Tanzania with Kpiri Mposhi in Zambia; 962 km (598 mi) of the line are in Tanzania. The Tazara railway is used mainly to transport goods for Zambia and Malawi. In 1991, Tanzania had 81,900 km (50,900 mi) of roads, including earth tracks, 4.3% of them paved. In 1991 there were 84,517 motor vehicles, including 46,552 passenger cars.

Tanzania has a small national merchant shipping line of three freighters and one tanker. The principal ports on the mainland are Dar es Salaam, Mtwara, Tanga, and Lindi, all of which are managed by the Tanzanian Harbours Authority. Tanzanian ports handle cargo for landlocked Zambia, Zaire, Uganda, Rwanda, and Burundi. Freight and passenger vessels serve Mwanza and other Lake Victoria ports, among them Bukoba and Musoma. A joint Burundian-Tanzanian shipping company operates on Lake Tanganyika, and the Tanzanian Railways Corporation operates vessels on lakes Tanganyika, Victoria, and Niassa.

Most internal air services are operated by Air Tanzania, which also flies internationally. Charter companies operate flights to some 94 government-maintained airports, landing fields, and privately owned airstrips. Foreign airlines provide service from international airports at Dar es Salaam and in the vicinity of Mt. Kilimanjaro (opened in 1971). There is also an international airport on Zanzibar, which maintains its own airline, Zanair. Air Tanzania carried 172,800 passengers in 1992.

12HISTORY

Paleontologists Louis and Mary Leakey, working at Olduvai Gorge and elsewhere in northern Tanzania, uncovered fossil evidence that humanlike creatures inhabited the area at least as early as 3.7 million years ago. Excavations of Stone Age sites have revealed that the hunter-gatherers of the late Stone Age, known as Bushmen, were gradually displaced by successive waves of Cushitic, Bantu, and Nilotic peoples. By the 1st millennium AD, the Iron Age Urewe culture had developed along the western shore of Lake Victoria.

Arabs from the Persian Gulf area were engaged in trade along the Indian Ocean coast by the 9th century AD and by the 12th century had established trading posts on the mainland and the offshore islands. Intermarriage between the Arabs and coastal Bantu-speaking peoples resulted in the creation of the Swahili people and language. (*Swahili* literally means "of the coast.")

The first contacts of European nations with the East African coast were incidental to their quest for spices. In 1498, Vasco da Gama rounded the Cape of Good Hope, and thereafter the Portuguese established posts on the East African coast for refreshment on the way to India. Eventually, the Portuguese lost control of the sea routes, and in 1698, the Ya'aruba imam of the Ibahdi Arabs of Oman, Sa'if bin Sultan, expelled the Portuguese from every position that they held north of Mozambique. The Ibahdis of Oman long remained in at least nominal control of East Africa, and there was a lucrative trade in slaves and ivory.

Sayyid Sa'id bin Sultan (the ruler of Oman during 1806–56), above all others, must be regarded as the founder of modern Zanzibar. Sa'id first visited Zanzibar in 1828, and in 1840, he made the island his capital. A believer in free trade, he encouraged foreign merchants, including Indians, broke up Arab monopolies, and made commercial treaties with the US and UK. Zanzibar is indebted to him most for his establishment of the clove tree. By the time he died in 1856, he had established a large, loosely held empire that included Oman and Zanzibar and the East African coast inland to the Great Lakes and the Congo. Zanzibar produced three-quarters of the world's clove supply on plantations worked by slaves from the mainland. British pressure forced the closing of the slave trade in 1876, although slavery itself was not abolished until 1897.

The first Europeans to explore the interior were the British Sir Richard Francis Burton and John Hanning Speke, who crossed the country in 1857 to search for the source of the Nile, which Speke discovered in 1858. In 1866, Sultan Majid of Zanzibar began building the coastal town of Dar es Salaam ("Haven of Peace"). In 1871, Scottish missionary and explorer David Livingstone had reached Ujiji when his whereabouts became unknown to the outside world; the Anglo-American explorer Henry Morton Stanley, commisioned by a US newspaper, located him there later in that year. Tanganyika (the name for the mainland prior to the 1964 union with Zanzibar) came under German influence in 1884–85, when Karl Peters concluded treaties with chiefs of the interior in order to secure a charter for his German East Africa Company.

In 1890, two treaties between Germany and Great Britain were signed: the first partitioned the territories on the mainland hitherto controlled by the sultan of Zanzibar; the second officially recognized Anglo-German spheres of influence, excluded Germany from the Upper Nile, and established a British protectorate over Zanzibar and Pemba. Tanganyika and Ruanda-Urundi (now Rwanda and Burundi) became recognized as German East Africa in 1891. As they occupied the interior, the German-led troops put down tribal opposition and uprisings. During World War I, a small German force led by General Paul von Lettow-Vorbeck fought a long defensive guerrilla war against British armies, and much of Tanganyika was laid waste.

Moving Toward Independence

Beginning in 1920, the UK administered Tanganyika as a mandate of the League of Nations. A customs union was established with Kenya and Uganda, the cultivation of export crops was encouraged, and a system of indirect rule was instituted. A Legislative Council for Tanganyika was created in 1926, but not until 1945 were seats reserved for Africans. In 1946, Tanganyika became a UN trust territory. After 1954, the Tanganyika African National Union (TANU) petitioned the UN Trusteeship Council to put pressure on the UK administration to establish a timetable for independence. TANU-supported candidates won the elections of 1958–60 for the Legislative Council, and Julius Nyerere became chief minister in September 1960. On 9 December 1961, Tanganyika became an independent nation, and a year later, on 9 December 1962, it was established as a republic, headed by Nyerere as president.

In Zanzibar, a Legislative Council with an elected element had been established in 1957. On 24 June 1963, Zanzibar attained internal self-government; it became completely independent on 10 December 1963. On 12 January 1964, however, the predominantly Arab government was overthrown by African nationalists. The sultan, who had fled, was deposed, and Abeid Karume was installed as president. On 26 April 1964, Tanganyika merged with Zanzibar and became the United Republic of Tanganyika and Zanzibar, with Nyerere as president; in October, the name was changed to Tanzania. Karume, still president of Zanzibar and a vice-president of Tanzania, was assassinated on 7 April 1972; his successor as head of the Zanzibar Revolutionary Council was Aboud Jumbe.

Under Nyerere, Tanzania became steadily more socialist. In international affairs, Tanzania became one of the strongest supporters of majority rule in southern Africa, backing liberation movements in Mozambique and Rhodesia (now Zimbabwe). Growing differences between the East African Community's three members—Kenya, Tanzania, and Uganda—led to the breakup of the 10-year-old group in 1977. Tanzania's border with Kenya remained closed until 1983. On 30 October 1978, Ugandan forces invaded Tanzania; Nyerere retaliated by sending 20,000 Tanzanian troops into Uganda. Ugandan President Idi Amin's forces were routed in April 1979, and former president Milton Obote, who had been living in exile in Tanzania, was returned to power. In 1982, Tanzanian troops helped put down an army mutiny in the Seychelles.

In 1980, Nyerere was reelected without opposition to a fifth term as president, which he said would be his last. During the early 1980s, Tanzania was plagued by poor economic performance, and there was a small, unsuccessful army mutiny against Nyerere in January 1983. There was also rising dissatisfaction in Zanzibar over the islands' political ties to the mainland; an attempt to overthrow Jumbe in June 1980 failed. As a result, Aboud Jumbe resigned his posts as vice-president of Tanzania and president of Zanzibar in January 1984. Ali Hassan Mwinyi, Jumbe's successor, was elected president of Zanzibar in April 1984. He was succeeded by Idris Abdul Wakil in October 1985. Mwinyi succeeded Nyerere as president of Tanzania in November 1985, following presidential and parliamentary elections, and was reelected in 1990. Mwinyi was identified with those in the ruling party, Chama Cha Mapinduzi (CCM), seeking greater political and economic liberalization, and in 1990 Nyerere resigned as chairman of the CCM.

Liberalization was not easy to attain. Except for religion, the CCM controlled almost all areas of social affairs. Party cells at work and in the community shadowed Tanzanians constantly. In February 1992, at an extraordinary national conference of CCM, delegates voted unanimously to introduce a multiparty system. On 17 June 1992, Mwinyi signed into law constitutional amendments that allowed new parties (with certain exceptions) to participate in elections.

Rifts between the mainland (Tanganyika) and Zanzibar grew in the 1990s, often linked to the ongoing Christian-Muslim division. In December 1992, in violation of the constitution, the government in heavily Muslim Zanzibar covertly joined the international Islamic Conference Organization (ICO). In August 1993, parliament passed a motion calling for constitutional revisions to create a separate government for Tanganyika, to parallel the Zanzibar government. At that point, Zanzibar agreed to withdraw from the ICO and to allow Tanzanians from the mainland to visit without passports. Further constitutional discussions were drifting toward Zanzibar's secession.

On the religious front, in April fundamentalist Muslims were arrested for attacking owners of pork butcheries in Dar es Salaam. Demonstrations at their trials led to more arrests and a government ban on the Council for the Propagation of the Koran. Government also arrested an evangelist pastor who had formed an alliance of Christian parties in April 1993. Mwinyi shuffled his cabinet several times in 1993 to balance Christian and Muslim interests.

13 GOVERNMENT

A new constitution, replacing the 1965 interim one, went into effect in April 1977 and was substantially amended in October 1984 and in 1992. The president, who is both chief of state and head of government, is elected for a five-year term by universal adult suffrage. Before 1992, the president was nominated by the sole legal party, the Chama Cha Mapinduzi (CCM). He is limited to two terms. The president is assisted by a prime minister and cabinet. There are two vice-presidents, appointed by the president: one is the prime minister; the other is the president of Zanzibar. If the president of Tanzania is from Zanzibar, the prime minister must be from the mainland. In 1993, however, it was agreed to have just one vice president, the running mate of the winning presidential nominee.

As of 1985, the unicameral National Assembly consisted of 216 members elected by universal adult suffrage for five-year terms and 75 appointed members, many of whom serve by virtue of holding other government posts. Presidential and legislative elections are held concurrently, and in each legislative constituency. The prime minister, who is chosen from the Assembly members, heads the Assembly. If the president withholds his assent from a bill passed by the Assembly, it does not become a law unless the Assembly passes it again by a two-thirds majority. The president may dissolve the Assembly and call for new presidential and legislative elections if he refuses to assent to a law passed by such a majority within 32 days of its passage.

The Revolutionary Council of Zanzibar, which has held power on the islands since 1964, adopted a separate constitution in October 1979; it was replaced by a new one in January 1985. The new constitution provides for a popularly elected president and a Council of Representatives of 75 members, 50 of whom are popularly elected and 25 appointed. The government of Zanzibar has exclusive jurisdiction over internal matters, including immigration, finances, and economic policy. In the 1990s, Zanzibar seems to be moving toward even greater autonomy, if not secession.

In August 1993, the National Assembly adopted a resolution which provided for the possibility of setting up a mainland or Tanganyikan government to parallel that of Zanzibar. The CCM favors such a third government (the Union government is the first government). Others favor scrapping the two component administrations and having just a single government for the entire Union.

14 POLITICAL PARTIES

The Tanganyika African National Union (TANU), established in 1954, was the overwhelmingly dominant political party in the preindependence period. TANU and the ruling Afro-Shirazi Party of Zanzibar were merged into the Chama Cha Mapinduzi (CCM) Revolutionary Party. It is the sole legal political party in Tanzania. All candidates must be approved by the CCM and are permitted to campaign only on the CCM platform. Elections are competitive, however. In the balloting on 13 and 27 October 1985, 328 candidates competed for 169 elective seats in the National Assembly. In 1987, former president Julius K. Nyerere was reelected chairman of the CCM. He stepped down in 1990, to be succeeded by Ali Hassam Mwinyi.

The CCM officially favors nonracism and African socialism. The basic aims, laid down in Nyerere's Arusha Declaration of 1967, are social equality, self-reliance, economic cooperation with other African states, and ujamaa (familyhood)—the development of forms of economic activity, particularly in rural areas, based on collective efforts. The party is divided into locally organized branches, which are grouped into districts, which in turn are grouped into regions. The 172-member National Executive Committee is the principal policymaking and directing body of the CCM. A central committee of 18 members is elected at periodic party congresses.

Although Tanzania amended its constitution in 1992 to become a multiparty state, the CCM still controls government, pending national elections in 1995. Other parties have tried to organize. Many complain of harassment by government and CCM activists. Before taking part in elections, the new parties undergo a six-month probation during which they can recruit and organize. Some 20 opposition groups had registered in the first four months of their legality. However, parties representing regional, racial, ethnic, or religious groups are explicitly prohibited. Among opposition groups are the Civil United Front/Chama Cha Wananchi (CUF/CCW), the National Committee for Constitutional Reform (NCCR), the Union for Multiparty Democracy (UMD), the Party for Democracy and Progress, and the Democratic Party (DP), led by a firebrand evangelist preacher, Christopher Mtikila.

15 LOCAL GOVERNMENT

Mainland Tanzania is divided into 20 administrative regions, which are subdivided into 86 districts. Zanzibar and Pemba are divided into 5 regions. Regional commissioners are appointed by the central government, as are area commissioners and development directors for the districts.

The units of local government are district development councils. Each district development council includes elected members, but these bodies are only advisory. In Zanzibar, revolutionary committees are responsible for regional administration. Under an agricultural resettlement program, more than 8,000 villages were established, including more than 14 million people. Each village has an elected council. In practice, however, no one is sure how many of these villages are really new. A small number of ujamaa villages have attempted to organize on a communal basis, with all capital goods held in common except for hand tools.

16 JUDICIAL SYSTEM

Mainland Tanzanian law is a combination of British and East African customary law. Local courts are presided over by appointed magistrates. They have limited jurisdiction, and there is a right of appeal to district courts, headed by either resident or district magistrates. Appeal can be made to the High Court, which consists of a chief justice and 17 judges appointed by the president. It has both civil and criminal jurisdiction over all persons and all matters. Appeals from the High Court can be made to the five-member Court of Appeal. Judges are appointed to the Court of Appeal and the High Court by the president on the advice of the chief justice and to courts at lower levels by the chief justice.

The judiciary in Zanzibar has substantial autonomy. It had people's courts presided over by elected magistrates, normally without lawyers for the accused, until 1985, when the court system was made parallel to that of the mainland. Islamic courts handle some matters.

Cases concerning the Zanzibar Constitution are heard only in Zanzibar courts. All other cases may be appealed to the Court of Appeal of the Republic.

Although declared independent by the Constitution, the judiciary is subject to executive branch influence and is criticized as inefficient and corrupt. Questions have been raised as to the availability of a fair trial in politically charged cases.

[17]ARMED FORCES

Tanzania's armed forces totaled 46,800 in 1993. The army had 45,000 personnel in 8 infantry brigades, 1 tank brigade, and 10 supporting arms battalions. The navy had 800 personnel and 20 craft, and the air force had 1,000 personnel and 24 combat aircraft. Police field forces, which include naval and air units, number 1,500. The citizens' militia totaled 100,000. The former USSR was Tanzania's principal weapons supplier. between 1987 and 1991. Tanzania has conscription (some 20,000 in the army) for 2 years. Reserves are 10,000. Defense spending is around $119 million (1989) or 2% of GDP.

[18]INTERNATIONAL COOPERATION

Tanganyika was admitted to UN membership on 14 December 1961, and Zanzibar on 16 December 1963; following their union into what was eventually called Tanzania, the two regions retained a single membership. Tanzania is a member of ECA and all the nonregional specialized agencies. It is also a member of the African Development Bank, Commonwealth of Nations, G-77, and OAU and is a signatory to GATT and the Law of the Sea.

On 1 December 1967, the heads of state of Kenya, Uganda, and Tanzania created the East African Community (EAC), with its headquarters at Arusha. The three countries maintained a common external tariff and corporations to run their airlines, railways, harbors, postal delivery, telecommunications, and other services. However, the EAC was dissolved in 1977. Tanzania is an associate member of the EC under the terms of the Lomé Convention and a member of the Southern African Development Coordinating Conference and the Preferential Trade Area for East and Southern Africa. Along with Rwanda, Burundi, and Uganda, it belongs to the Kagera Basin Organization.

[19]ECONOMY

Tanzania has an agricultural economy whose chief commercial crops are sisal, coffee, cotton, tea, tobacco, spices, and cashew nuts. The most important minerals are diamonds and coal. Industry is mainly concerned with the processing of raw materials for export and local consumption.

After 25 years of socialist experimentation achieved important advances in education and health, poor economic performance led the government, in 1986, to adopt market-style reforms in conjunction with the IMF structural adjustment program. Significant progress has been made in revitalizing the economy, though at a slower pace than many observers would like.

[20]INCOME

In 1992 Tanzania's GNP was $2,561 million at current prices, or $110 per capita. For the period 1985–92 the average inflation rate was 25.2%, resulting in a real growth rate in per capita GNP of 1.4%.

In 1992 the GDP was $2,712 million in current US dollars. It is estimated that agriculture, hunting, forestry, and fishing contributed 52% to GDP; mining and quarrying, 1%; manufacturing, 3%; electricity, gas, and water, 1%; construction, 2%; wholesale and retail trade, 12%; transport, storage, and communication, 7%; finance, insurance, real estate, and business services, 4%; community, social, and personal services, 5%; and other sources 13%.

[21]LABOR

Over 90% of Tanzania's working population (680 million in 1992) is engaged in agriculture, 1% in mining, and much of the remainder in public service.

A minimum wage is fixed by law; in mid-1987, it was raised to Sh1,260 (urban) and Sh1,060 (rural) a month. Strikes are illegal without preliminary attempts at settlement before a labor tribunal, which makes binding decisions. At Dar es Salaam, all workers are required to have work permits. The larger urban centers have both unemployed and underemployed workers.

In 1964, by legislation of the National Assembly, the existing 13 trade unions were dissolved and amalgamated into a single national institution, the National Union of Tanzanian Workers. This was reorganized in 1978 to take in Zanzibar trade union activity as the Organization of Tanzania Trade Unions (OTTU), which still is the only labor union organization. As of 1992, however, a subgrouping of Chakiwatan teachers began to demand the right to form their own trade union. The OTTU is currently restructuring to enable union workers the opportunity to elect leaders who are not necessarily affiliated with the ruling party.

[22]AGRICULTURE

In 1993, about 12% of the total land area was cultivated, with about two-thirds belonging to farmers owning or operating farms of 5 ha (12.4 acres) or less. A massive collectivization and cooperative agricultural program was begun in 1967; by the end of 1980, 8,167 self-help villages, involving more than 14 million people, had been established. The program was coupled with the takeover of large estates.

The principal food crops are corn, millet, rice, sorghum, and pulses. The chief cash crops are coffee, cotton, and cashew nuts; sisal, cloves, sugar, tea, pyrethrum, and tobacco are also important. Tanzania is one of Africa's leading producers of sisal; in 1992, production was 35,000 tons. Other estimated agricultural production in 1992 included manioc, 7,111,000 tons; corn, 2,226,000 tons; sorghum, 587,000 tons; rice, 392,000 tons; and millet, 263,000 tons. Production in 1992 also included coffee, 56,000 tons; cotton, 73,000 tons; cashew nuts, 40,150 tons; tea, 18,000 tons; tobacco, 17,000 tons; sweet potatoes, 257,000 tons; white potatoes, 200,000 tons; and 65,000 tons of peanuts. Sugarcane production in that year was an estimated 1,410,000 tons; bananas and plantains, 794,000 tons each; dry beans, 195,000 tons; seed cotton, 218,000 tons; and cottonseed, 142,000 tons.

Tanzania was once the leading producer of cloves, which are grown mostly on Pemba; it is also an important producer of coconuts (365,000 tons in 1992), mostly from the island of Zanzibar. Production of copra was around 34,000 tons in 1992.

There was a steady decline in agricultural production during the late 1970s and early 1980s because of drought and low prices paid by the state crop-marketing agencies. In addition, there was a shortage of farm implements; only 3,000 of the nation's 10,000 tractors were in working order in 1982, and even hand hoes and oxen plows were in acute shortage. By 1991, there were some 6,700 tractors in service (down from 6,900 in 1989). In 1992, Tanzania imported 44,000 tons of corn, 110,000 tons of rice, and 97,800 tons of wheat. Beginning in 1986, reforms of the cooperative unions and crop marketing boards have aided production. The purchase of crops (especially coffee, cotton, sisal, tea, and pyrethrum) has been opened to private traders.

23 ANIMAL HUSBANDRY

Although large areas are unsuitable for livestock because of the tsetse fly, considerable numbers of cattle, sheep, and goats are kept, and livestock raising makes a substantial contribution to the economy. The estimated livestock population in 1992 included 13.2 million head of cattle, 3.7 million sheep, and 25 million poultry. About 285,000 tons of meat were produced in 1992. Milk production was 460,000 tons in the same year.

24 FISHING

With over 6% of Tanzania's area consisting of open lake waters, inland fishing, especially on Lake Tanganyika, occupies an important place in the economy. There is also fishing in the Indian Ocean. The total catch was 400,300 tons in 1991, about 86% from inland waters.

25 FORESTRY

In 1991, 40,820,000 ha (100,866,000 acres), or 46% of Tanzania's total land area, was classified as forest and woodland. There are about 13,000,000 ha (32,000,000 acres) of permanent forest reserves. Small plantations for fast-growing trees have been established in these reserves. On the islands, remains of former forests are found only in two reserves.

Production in 1991 included about 35.5 million cu m of roundwood and about 156,000 cu m of sawn wood.

26 MINING

Tanzania's known mineral resources include diamonds, gold, mica, salt, tin, tungsten, coal, iron, phosphates, lead, copper, and uranium, but only diamonds were of major importance in the economy in the mid-1980s. Salt output was 64,419 tons in 1991. Gold production fell from 2,825 kg in 1965 to less than 10 kg in 1981 but rose to 1,629 kg in 1990 and to 2,779 kg in 1991; the 1991 increase was mostly due to gold bought by the Bank of Tanzania from private miners. Thre three main gold fields are at Musoma east of Lake Victoria, at Lupa southeast of Lake Rukwa, and at Mpanda east of Lake Tanganyika. Production of apatite, a phosphate mineral, was 22,419 tons in 1991.

Diamonds are mined at the Williamson field in Mwadui. The deposits are owned jointly by the Tanzanian government and Willcroft of Canada. Diamond production in recent years has fallen far short of the 1967 peak of 988,000 carats; output in 1991 was 99,763 carats, 30% of which was industrial quality, the remainder being gem or semi-gem quality. Lime production in 1991 was 870 tons, down from 3,000 tons in 1988; gypsum production was 35,263 tons.

The Tanzanian government operates three cement facilities at Tanga, Wazo Hill, and Mbeya. Estimated 1991 cement production amounted to 540,000 tons.

27 ENERGY AND POWER

Tanzania imports all of its crude oil; in 1991, about 65% of foreign exchange earnings were spent on crude oil imports. The refinery at Dar es Salaam refined about 600,000 tons in 1991 and exported petroleum products to Rwanda and Burundi. The Songo Songo gas field off Kilwa Kisiwani had proven reserves of 41 billion cu m, and a project was being planned, with Canadian interests, to build pipelines between 1992 and 1994 and to set up treatment plants. Another gas deposit of about 130 billion cu m has been found at Kimbiji, about 40 km (25 mi) south of Dar es Salaam.

Installed electrical capacity was 439,000 kw in 1991; of the total, 60% was hydroelectric. An 80,000-kw hydroelectric station at Mtera Dam on the Great Ruaha River was scheduled for completion in 1988. Electrical production was 901 million kwh in 1991. The Tanzanian Electric Supply Co., acquired by the government in 1964, provides about 89% of the output. Public power generation on the island is the responsibility of the Zanzibar State Fuel and Power Corp.

28 INDUSTRY

Tanzania's industrial sector accounted for 4.7% of GDP in 1991, though it had been in decline, averaging a negative 2.4% annually over the 1980–91 period. Fuel and import costs, lack of foreign exchange, and unreliable local services have tested the sector severely. Tanzanian industry is centered on the processing of local products and on import substitution. Some products are exported to neighboring countries: textiles and clothes, shoes, tires, batteries, transformers and switchgear, electric stoves, bottles, cement, and paper. Other industries include oil refining, fertilizers, rolling and casting mills, metal working, beer and soft drinks, vehicle assembly, bicycles, canning, industrial machine goods, glass and ceramics, agricultural implements, electrical goods, wood products, bricks and tiles, oxygen and carbon dioxide, and pharmaceutical products.

Since the economic reform program was introduced in 1986, progress has been slow in the industrial sector. Foreign exchange is more available, allowing some companies to reopen. Scandinavian investments have made Tanzania self-sufficient in cement after years of chronic shortages. Tanzania's biggest ever integrated industrial development project is a $260 million investment in paper manufacturing. The oil refinery was rehabilitated in an $18 million effort over the 1991–93 period. As part of an infrastructure redevelopment plan, a $104 million petroleum distribution project is underway.

Growth in Tanzania's electrical needs is estimated at 11–13% annually. Consequently, the development of the electrical grid is the focus of several major development efforts. Launched in 1991, an eight-year program includes the commissioning of the 200-Mw Jihansi power station, enlargement of the Pangani Falls station, and the construction of a power line from Singida to Arusha. With the addition of the 80-Mw Mtera hydroelectric station, the Kidatu complex now has a generating capacity of 519 Mw.

29 SCIENCE AND TECHNOLOGY

Much of the scientific and technical research in Tanzania is directed toward agriculture. Facilities include the Livestock Production Research Institute at Dodoma, the National Institute for Medical Research at Amani and Mwanza, a forestry research institute at Lushoto (100 km/60 mi northwest of Tanga), a sisal research station at Mlingano, and the Tropical Pesticides Research Institute at Arusha. The University of Dar es Salaam has faculties of science, medicine, and engineering and an institute of marine sciences; Sokoine University of Agriculture, in Morogoro, has faculties of agriculture, forestry, and veterinary medicine.

30 DOMESTIC TRADE

Dar es Salaam is Tanzania's main distribution center. Mombasa, in Kenya, and inland Tanzanian towns also serve as trade centers. Most wholesale and import-export trade has been nationalized. Many goods are price-controlled; however, many can be obtained only on the black market.

Normal business hours are 7:30 to 2:30 PM, Monday through Friday; firms that take a lunch break at noon may stay open to 4 or 4:30 PM. Banks are open from 8:30 to noon, Monday through Friday, and 8:30 to 11 AM on Saturday.

31 FOREIGN TRADE

Agricultural products are Tanzania's principal export items: coffee, cotton, cloves, sisal, cashew nuts, and pyrethrum. Diamonds, gemstones, textiles, hides, extracts, instant coffee, timber, fish and prawns, fresh fruit and vegetables, and honey are also exported. The principal exports in 1990 (in millions of shillings) were:

Coffee	16,074
Cotton	14,820
Cashew nuts	650
Tea	1,210
Diamonds	629
Sisal	638
Cloves	1,485
Tobacco	2,438
Other exports and reexports	41,111
TOTAL	79,055

The chief imports are transport equipment and intermediate and industrial goods machinery. Imports have led exports value, resulting in sizeable trade deficits (1988–1990). In 1988, Tanzania's leading export partner was Germany (14.2%) followed by the United Kingdom (10.1%), and India (6.4%). Imports came primarily from the United Kingdom (17.3%), Japan (12.5%), Germany (11.8%), and Italy (7.8%).

[32]BALANCE OF PAYMENTS

Tanzania typically runs a current account deficit, although long term capital investment from abroad resulted in surpluses for several years during the 1970s. Agricultural marketing reforms and flexible exchange policies are expected to provide export growth in upcoming years, as exports move from the underground to the official market because of the devaluation of the shilling.

In 1990 merchandise exports totaled $407.8 million and imports $1,186.3 million. The merchandise trade balance was $−778.5 million. The following table summarizes Tanzania's balance of payments for 1989 and 1990 (in millions of US dollars):

	1989	1990
CURRENT ACCOUNT		
Goods, services, and income	−1,011.0	−1,119.5
Unrequited transfers	652.2	693.5
TOTALS	−358.8	−426.0
CAPITAL ACCOUNT		
Other long-term capital	26.2	127.1
Other short-term capital	−4.5	−0.6
Exceptional financing	437.8	307.2
Reserves	14.2	−140.9
TOTALS	473.7	292.8
Errors and omissions	−114.9	133.1
Total change in reserves	10.6	−127.2

[33]BANKING AND SECURITIES

On 5 February 1967, Tanzania nationalized all banks. The Bank of Tanzania, the central bank and bank of issue, provides banking advice to the National Bank of Commerce, which took over the duties of the former private commercial banks. Other Tanzanian banks include the People's Bank of Zanzibar, the Tanzania Investment Bank, the Tanzania Housing Bank, the Rural Cooperative and Development Bank, and the Tanganyika Post Office Savings Bank.

At the end of 1988, money in circulation was Sh87.8 billion. There are no securities exchanges in Tanzania.

[34]INSURANCE

All insurance companies were nationalized in 1967. There is one national insurance company, the National Insurance Corporation of Tanzania, that covers life, fire, automobile, and general accident insurance. In 1982, the total net premium income amounted to Sh389.2 million.

[35]PUBLIC FINANCE

The Tanzanian budget covers cash expenditures and receipts for the mainland only, and does not include Zanzibar government revenues and expenditures. Total expenditures include a development budget. The fiscal year ends on 30 June. In the early 1980s, the annual budget deficit went over 10% of GDP, and payment arrears on external debts started to mount. Since 1986, the government has improved its fiscal and monetary policies, with mixed results. Tanzania's total debt of $6.4 billion in 1991 represented 256% of GNP.

[36]TAXATION

Sales tax is the main source of government revenue, followed by income taxes. Income taxes are levied on wages and salaries, profits, and rental income; rates vary from 5% to 30%. The standard corporate tax is 35% for local companies and 40% for foreign companies.

[37]CUSTOMS AND DUTIES

Tanzania has a single column tariff with many items dutiable ad valorem. The number of customs categories has been cut from 20 to 7. Tariff rates range mostly from 30% to 60% with a number of statutory exemptions. In 1992, the government abolished duties and taxes on raw materials for industry as part of an economic reform program. Most goods are subject to a sales tax of up to 50% of c.i.f. value. Zanzibar levies a wharfage surcharge of $0.30 on each imported package regardless of size or value.

[38]FOREIGN INVESTMENT

With the initiation of economic reforms in 1986, investment interest in Tanzania has grown considerably in all sectors. The investment code of 1990 was designed to encourage foreign and local investment. The banking industry has been substantially reformed to make it more competitive, and operations of foreign banks were authorized in 1991.

[39]ECONOMIC DEVELOPMENT

The Tanzanian government has focused in recent years on reorganizing and restructuring its economic institutions. Progress has been encouraging and private sector investors are increasingly interested in mining, transport, tourist, and fishing sector opportunities.

The fourth five-year development plan (1981–86) was not fully carried out because of Tanzania's economic crisis. Among the projects implemented were an industrial complex, a pulp and paper project, a machine-tool plant, a phosphate plant, and the development of natural gas deposits. The Economic and Social Action Plan of 1990 scaled back the government's ambitions and sought to continue moderate growth in the economy, improve foreign trade, and alleviate some of the social costs of economic reform. Development planning is now conducted on an annual basis, with recent development priorities set in the areas of transport infrastructure, health, and education.

[40]SOCIAL DEVELOPMENT

The government's Rural Development Division concentrates on community development (including health, labor, and literacy programs) rather than on welfare programs. Employees in state-owned enterprises are covered by the Parastatal Pension Fund. Workers not covered by any pension scheme are covered by the National Provident Fund. The elderly, widows, and the physically and mentally handicapped normally are provided for by the traditional tribal system. Orphaned and abandoned children usually are cared for similarly, but missions and voluntary agencies also are active in this field.

The regime emphasizes educational and cottage industry training for women and equal pay for equal work. In 1986, about

20% of village council membership was female, and there were two women cabinet members. There are 15 parliamentary seats reserved for women. A law on the mainland requires a first wife to register her approval in court before her husband can take a second wife. Abortion is legal on broad health grounds. Nevertheless, discrimination and violence against women are widespread. The fertility rate in the mid-1990s was estimated at 6.2. Life expectancy for males and females is 49 and 54 years, respectively. The government cooperates with the Family Planning Association of Tanzania, a private organization, to educate the population on birth control.

In the field of human rights, the Tanzanian government has detained persons indefinitely under the Preventive Detention Act of 1962, but the number of those detained has been small.

41HEALTH

In 1975, the government began to nationalize all hospitals, including those run by Christian missions; private medical practice was ended in 1980. Medical treatment is free or highly subsidized in company clinics as well as hospitals.

The pyramid struture of Tanzania's national health care system, stressing primary care at an affordable cost, makes it a pioneer in sub-Saharan Africa. As of 1992, however, there were severe budgetary constraints and the country had no plans to expand public health care until the budget improved. An estimated 76% of the population had access to health care services in 1992, and, in 1990, total health care expenditures were $109 million. Life expectancy was 51 years in 1992.

In 1992, there were 3,000 rural health facilities, 17 regional hospitals, and 3 national medical centers, in the same year, the ratio of nurses to doctors was 7:3. In 1990, there were 1.1 hospital beds per 1,000 people, and 1,200 physicians; data shows there was 1 doctor for every 24,880 inhabitants, and 1 nurse for every 5,470 people. Medical staff morale was low due to declining wages, and management and operational difficulties in the central medical stores and domestic pharmaceuticals industries. Imports of drugs are overseen by the Pharmaceutical Board; there are 4 local manufacturers.

Special programs of disease control have been carried out with the assistance of WHO and UNICEF for most major diseases, including malaria, tuberculosis, sleeping sickness, schistosomiasis, poliomyelitis, and yaws. In 1990, there were 140 cases of tuberculosis reported per 100,000. Twenty percent of children under 5 years old are considered malnourished. In 1991, only 49% of the population had access to safe water, and 64% had adequate sanitation. In 1992, children up to 1 year old were immunized against tuberculosis (99%); diphtheria, pertussis, and tetanus (84%); polio (83%); and measles (82%).

The 1993 population of Tanzania was 28.8 million, with a birth rate of 48.1 per 1,000 people, and about 10% of married women (ages 15 to 49) using contraception. There were 1.4 million births in 1992.

Infant mortality in 1992 was 111 per 1,000 live births, and maternal mortality was an estimated 340 per 100,000 live births in 1991. The general mortality rate was 14.6 per 1,000 people in 1993.

42HOUSING

Tanzania has developed a serious urban housing shortage as a result of the influx of people to the towns. All development planning has included considerable financial allocations for urban housing schemes. With private enterprise unable to meet the demand, the government in 1951 launched a low-cost housing program, which has been continued since that time. As of 1978, 41% of dwellings were constructed with mud and poles, 23% with mud bricks and blocks, 18% with concrete and stone, 9% with poles, and 7% with baked and burned bricks. In the same

year, 56% of all housing was owner occupied and 38% was rented. Piped indoor water was available to 26% of households, and 53% had private toilets.

43EDUCATION

Education is compulsory for children aged 7 to 14. In 1991, there were a total of 3,512,347 students and 98,174 teachers in the 10,437 primary schools; in the same year, there were 183,109 students and 9,904 teachers in the 193 secondary schools. The University College in Dar es Salaam opened in 1961 and achieved university status in 1970. The Sokoine University of Agriculture, at Morogoro, was founded in 1984. Other educational facilities in Tanzania include trade schools, the Dar es Salaam Technical College, a business college and a political science college in Dar es Salaam, the College of African Wildlife Management at Mweka, and the College of National Education in Korogwe. Literacy was estimated at 79% in 1987, a rate second only to Mauritius among African countries. In 1989, all higher level institutions had 5,254 students and 1,206 teaching staff.

44LIBRARIES AND MUSEUMS

The Tanzania Library Service was established in 1964. It maintains the National Central Library in Dar es Salaam, 16 public libraries, school library service, and a rural extension service. The other major library is the University of Dar es Salaam Library (600,000 volumes).

The National Museums of Tanzania, with branches in Dar es Salaam and Arusha, have ethnographical, archaeological, historical, geological, and natural history sections; the discoveries from Olduvai Gorge are located there. The Department of Geological Survey maintains a geological museum in Dodoma. There are also museums in Arusha, Bagamoyo, Mikumi, Mwanza, and Tabora.

In Zanzibar, the Government Museum has extensive exhibits illustrating the history, ethnography, industries, and natural history of Zanzibar and Pemba.

45MEDIA

Radio Tanzania, a government corporation, broadcasts internally in Swahili and English and abroad in English, Afrikaans, and several indigenous African languages. Radio Tanzania Zanzibar broadcasts in Swahili. Television is broadcast only from Zanzibar. In 1991 there were 660,000 radios and 42,000 television sets. In the same year, there were 130,504 telephones in use.

The press is government-controlled. The largest dailies, both published in Dar es Salaam, are the government-owned *Daily News* (in English), with a circulation of about 80,000 in 1992, and the CCM-owned *Uhuru* (in Swahili), with a circulation of 100,000. *Kipanga* (in Swahili) is published on Zanzibar by the government. *Mzalendo* (in Swahili) is published on Sunday and has a circulation of 115,000.

46ORGANIZATIONS

In most of the larger centers, chambers of commerce represent commercial, agricultural, and industrial interests. Rural cooperatives, dissolved in 1976, were reintroduced in 1982 to take over from state bodies the functions of crop purchasing and distribution of agricultural products.

The CCM has five principal affiliates: the Umoja Wa Wawawake Wa Tanzania, a women's organization; the Youth League; the Workers' Organization; the Union of Cooperative Societies; and the Tanzania Parents' Association.

47TOURISM, TRAVEL, AND RECREATION

Tanzania has great natural resources in its Indian Ocean coastline and 12 national parks, especially the 14,763 sq km (5,700 sq mi) Serengeti National Park, famed for its profusion of wildlife. Other attractions are the national dancing troupe and the ebony wood sculptures of the Makonde tribe. Several hotels have been built since independence, normally by the state in partnership with foreign private enterprise. There were 4,673 hotel beds in 1985. The Tanzania Tourist Corporation plans to spend US$55 million on hotel rehabilitation and attract foreign companies to manage more of the country's hotels. Tourist visits average 150,000 per year. All tourists are required to have a valid passport and visitor's pass; visas are required except for nationals of Commonwealth countries, Scandinavian countries, and Ireland.

48 FAMOUS TANZANIANS

The most famous 19th-century Zanzibari was Sayyid Sa'id bin Ahmad al-Albusa'idi (b.Oman, 1791–1856), who founded the Sultanate. Mkwawa, chief of the Hehe, carried on guerrilla warfare against the Germans for three years until he was betrayed for a reward in 1898. The Germans cut off his head and sent it to the anthropological museum in Bremen; in 1961, Mkwawa's skull was returned to the Hehe. The foremost present-day figure is Julius Kambarage Nyerere (b.1922), the founder and first president of independent Tanganyika (and later of Tanzania) from 1962 to 1985, when he stepped down. He was succeeded by 'Ali Hassan Mwinyi (b.1925), who had been president of Zanzibar during 1984–85. Abeid Karume (1905–72), a sailor of Congolese origin, was the first president of Zanzibar and first vice-president of Tanzania until his assassination. He was succeeded by Aboud Jumbe (b.1920), who resigned both posts in 1984. Since 1985, the president of Zanzibar has been Idris Abdul Wakil (b.1925). Edward Moringe Sokoine (1938–84), a prime minister during 1977–80 and 1983–84, was regarded as Nyerere's most likely successor until he died in a car crash. Salim Ahmed Salim (b.1942) was a president of the UN General Assembly during 1979–80, a foreign minister during 1980–84, and a prime minister during 1984–85. An internationally known Tanzanian runner is Filbert Bayi (b.1953), a former world record holder at 1,500 m.

49 DEPENDENCIES

Tanzania has no territorries or colonies.

50 BIBLIOGRAPHY

Bailey, Martin. *Union of Tanganyika and Zanzibar: A Study in Political Integration.* Syracuse, N.Y.: Syracuse University Foreign & Comparative Studies Program, 1973.

Bennett, Norman R. *A History of the Arab State of Zanzibar.* New York: Methuen, 1978.

Clark, W. Edmund. *Socialist Development and Public Investment in Tanzania, 1964–73.* Toronto: University of Toronto Press, 1978.

Collier, Paul. *Labour and Poverty in Rural Tanzania: Ujamaa and Rural Development in the United Republic of Tanzania.* New York: Oxford University Press, 1990.

Coulson, Andrew. *Tanzania: A Political Economy.* New York: Oxford University Press, 1982.

Hodd, Michael (ed.). *Tanzania after Nyerere.* New York: Pinter Publishers, 1988.

Hopkins, Raymond F. *Political Roles in a New State: Tanzania's First Decade.* New Haven, Conn.: Yale University Press, 1971.

Hyden, Goran. *Beyond Ujamaa in Tanzania: Underdevelopment and an Uncaptured Peasantry.* Berkeley: University of California Press, 1980.

Kaplan, Irving (ed.). *Tanzania: A Country Study.* 2d ed. Washington, D.C.: Dept. of the Army, 1987.

Kimambo, I. N., and A. J. Temu (eds.). *A History of Tanzania.* Evanston, Ill.: Northwestern University Press, 1969.

Kurtz, Laura S. *Historical Dictionary of Tanzania.* Metuchen, N.J.: Scarecrow, 1978.

Nyerere, Julius K. *Freedom and Socialism: Uhuru na Ujamaa. A Selection from Writings and Speeches, 1965–67.* London: Oxford University Press, 1968.

Pratt, C. *Critical Phase in Tanzania, 1945–68.* Cambridge: Cambridge University Press, 1976.

Resnick, Idrian. *The Long Transition: Building Socialism in Tanzania.* New York: Monthly Review Press, 1982.

Rigby, Peter. *Cattle, Capitalism, and Class: Ilparakuyo Maasai Transformations.* Philadelphia: Temple University Press, 1992.

Sender, John. *Poverty, Class, and Gender in Rural Africa: A Tanzanian Case Study.* New York: Routledge, 1990.

Yeager, Rodger. *Tanzania: An African Experiment.* 2d ed. Boulder, Colo.: Westview Press, 1989.

TOGO

Republic of Togo
République Togolaise

CAPITAL: Lomé.

FLAG: The national flag consists of five alternating horizontal stripes of green and yellow. A five-pointed white star is at the center of a red canton which spans the height of the top three stripes.

ANTHEM: *Terre de nos aïeux (Land of Our Fathers).*

MONETARY UNIT: The Communauté Financière Africaine franc (CFA Fr) is a paper currency of 100 centimes. There are coins of 1, 2, 5, 10, 25, 50, 100, and 500 CFA francs and notes of 50, 100, 500, 1,000, 5,000, and 10,000 CFA francs. CFA Fr1 = $0.0018 (or $1 = CFA Fr571).

WEIGHTS AND MEASURES: The metric system is the legal standard.

HOLIDAYS: New Year's Day, 1 January; National Liberation Day, 13 January; Economic Liberation Day, 24 January; Victory Day, 24 April; Independence Day, 27 April; Labor Day, 1 May; Martyrs' Day, 21 June; Assumption, 15 August; All Saints' Day, Anniversary of the failed attack on Lome, 24 September; 1 November; Christmas, 25 December. Movable religious holidays include Easter Monday, Ascension, Whitmonday, 'Id al-Fitr, and 'Id al-'Adha'.

TIME: GMT.

¹LOCATION, SIZE, AND EXTENT

Situated on the west coast of Africa, Togo has an area of 56,790 sq km (21,927 sq mi), extending 510 km (317 mi) N–S and 45 to 140 km (28–87 mi) E–W. Comparatively, the area occupied by Togo is slightly smaller than the state of West Virginia. Togo is bounded on the N by Burkina Faso, on the E by Benin, on the S by the Gulf of Guinea, and on the W by Ghana, with a total boundary length of 1,703 km (1,058 mi).

Togo's capital city, Lomé, is located on the Gulf of Guinea coast.

²TOPOGRAPHY

Togo is traversed in the center by a chain of hills, the Togo Mountains, extending roughly southwest into Ghana and northeastward into Benin and averaging about 700 m (2,300 ft) in height. The highest elevation is Mt. Agou (986 m/3,235 ft). To the north and west of these hills, the Oti River drains in a southwesterly direction into the Volta River, which constitutes a part of the upper boundary with Ghana. To the north of the Oti River Valley lies gently undulating savanna country. From the southern spurs of the central hills, a plateau stretches gradually southward to a coastal plain. The coastline consists of a flat sandy beach thickly planted with coconut trees and partially separated from the mainland by lagoons and lakes that are the former estuaries of several rivers.

³CLIMATE

Togo has a humid, tropical climate, but receives less rainfall than most of the other countries along the Gulf of Guinea. In the south there are two rainy seasons, from March to early July and in September and October. The heaviest rainfall occurs in the hills of the west, southwest, and center, where the precipitation averages about 150 cm (60 in) a year. North of the Togo Mountains there is one rainy season, lasting from April to early October. Rainfall in this region averages 100 cm (40 in) a year. The coast gets the least rainfall, about 78 cm (31 in) annually. The average maximum and minimum temperatures are 30°C (86°F) and 23°C (73°F) at Lomé, on the southern coast, and 35°C (95°F) and 15°C (59°F) at Mango, in the north.

⁴FLORA AND FAUNA

Natural vegetation is chiefly of the savanna type, luxuriant in the rainy season, brittle grass and shrub during the dry season. Dense belts of reeds are found along the coastal lagoons. Much of the largest wildlife has been exterminated in the southern area, but in the north, elephants and lions still can be found. Hippopotamuses and crocodiles live in and along the rivers, and monkeys are fairly common. The coastal swamps abound in snakes.

⁵ENVIRONMENT

The dense tropical rain forests that once covered much of the country are now found only along the river valleys and in isolated pockets of the Atakora Mountains. Slash-and-burn agriculture and the cutting of wood for fuel are the major causes of forest depletion. Soils are generally of poor quality, requiring intensive fertilization and cultivation to be productive. The soil and water supply are threatened by pesticides and fertilizers. The nation's land is also threatened by desertification. Water pollution is a significant problem in Togo where 51.5% of the people living in rural areas do not have pure water. The condition of the water supply contributes to the spread of disease. Responsibility in environmental matters is vested in the Ministry of Rural Development and the Ministry of Environment and Tourism. The government of Togo has tried to protect the nation's environment through a comprehensive legislative package, the Environmental Code of 1988. The nation's wildlife population is at risk due to poaching and the clearing of land for agricultural purposes. Attempts at strict regulation have failed and, in 1992, UN sources reported widespread destruction of wildlife in Togo.

⁶POPULATION

Togo is one of the more densely populated countries in tropical Africa. The population as of the 1981 census was 2,705,250; the estimated 1994 population was 4,246,187, with an average density of 75 persons per sq km (194 per sq mi). Density is greatest in the south, exceeding 200 per sq km (500 per sq mi) in some areas. A population of 4,818,000 was projected for the year 2000, assuming a crude birthrate of 41.8 per 1,000 population, a crude death rate of 11.4, and a net natural increase of 30.4 during 1995–2000.

As of 1995, the population was 31% urban and 69% rural; the urban population was increasing at a rate of 4.8% during the first half of the 1990s. The only city of major size is Lomé, the capital, with a 1990 population of 513,000. Other important centers are Sokodé, 60,000; Kpalimé, 33,000; Atakpamé, 30,000; and Aného, 24,000.

7MIGRATION
There is a steady migration of laborers from rural to urban areas. Members of the Ewe group migrate to and from Ghana. Formerly, an estimated 100,000 workers went to Ghana from Togo each year, but because of Ghana's declining economy, this number has probably decreased. There is also much movement of Ouatchi, Adja, Kabré, and Losso peoples to and from Benin. Some of the aliens expelled from Nigeria in 1983 were Togolese; moreover, Togo suffered the disruptive effect of the hundreds of thousands of Ghanaians who returned home from Nigeria via the Togolese coastal roads. Foreign refugees in Togo, including Ewe dissidents in exile from Ghana, are entitled to employment and free medical treatment, although they retain the status of aliens. About 7% of the population consists of noncitizens.

8ETHNIC GROUPS
Togo's heterogeneous population is a mosaic of at least 18 tribal groups possessing neither language nor history in common. The main ethnic group consists of the Ewe and such related peoples as the Ouatchi, Fon, and Adja; they live in the south and constitute at least 40% of the population. Next in size are the Kabrè and related Losso living in the north. As elsewhere in Africa, political and ethnic boundaries do not coincide. Thus, the Ewe are divided by the Togo-Ghana boundary, and large numbers of Ouatchi, Adja, Kabrè, and Losso live in adjacent Benin. Other significant groups are the Mina, Cotocoli, Moba, Gourma, Akposso, Ana, Lamba, Ehoué, and Bassari. Despite Togo's complex ethnic, linguistic, and racial makeup, a major distinction can be made between the tribes of Sudanic origin that inhabit the northern regions and those of the true Negroid Bantu type found in the south. There may be some 2,500 non-Africans in Togo, mostly French.

9LANGUAGES
French is the official language. Most newspapers are printed in French, and trade and commerce passing through Anécho and Lomé usually are conducted in that language; however, the public schools combine French with Ewe or Kabiyé, depending on the region. In southern Togo, Ewe is the dominant tongue, while pidgin English and French are used widely in the principal trading towns. In northern Togo, Kabiyé predominates, although Hausa is also widely spoken. In all, more than 44 different languages and dialects are spoken in Togo.

10RELIGIONS
As of 1993, an estimated one-half of Togolese followed African traditional religions. Up to 35% were Christian (about 23% Roman Catholic), and some 15% practiced Islam.

11TRANSPORTATION
Togo has a relatively well developed road system of about 6,462 km (4,015 mi), of which 1,762 km (1,095 mi) are paved. One main road, completely paved since 1980, runs north from Lomé to the border with Burkina Faso; another runs east along the coast from Lomé to Aného and onward to the Benin border; and a third runs west along the coast to the Ghana border. Because of extreme variations in weather, the roads that are not paved require constant attention; during the dry season, they are very dusty and crack easily, but during the rainy season they become extremely muddy and are frequently washed out. In 1991 there were 26,000 passenger cars and 16,000 commercial vehicles. Togo has 516 km (321 mi) of meter-gauge rail, including three major lines from Lomé: to Kpalimé (116 km/72 mi), to Aného (44 km/27 mi), and to Atakpamé and Blitta (276 km/171 mi). An 80-km (50-mi) spur goes to Tabligbo. The rail system is operated by Chemin de Fer Togolais.

Togo lacks a natural harbor, but in 1968 a major deepwater port east of central Lomé was completed with a loan from the Federal Republic of Germany (FRG). An autonomous free port at Lomé serves landlocked Burkina Faso, Niger, and Mali. There is also a phosphate-handling port at Kpémé. A small merchant-shipping fleet was created in 1974 as a joint venture with the FRG; in 1991 there were three oceangoing ships, with a combined gross weight of 21,000 tons.

The international airport at Lomé links Togo with other countries of West and Central Africa and with Europe; a second international airport, at Niamtougou, was completed in the early 1980s. International airlines serving Togo include Air Afrique, of which Togo owns a 7% share. Air Togo operates domestic service, flying to airstrips at Atakpamé, Sokodé, Sansanné-Mango, Lama-Kara, Niamtougou, and Dapaong.

12HISTORY
Between the 12th and the 18th century, the Ewe, Adja, and related peoples, who now constitute a majority of the population of southern Togo and adjoining Ghana, came to this area from the Niger River Valley as a result of pressure from the east. Portuguese sailors visited the coast in the 15th and 16th centuries. Slave shipments began from Grand Popo (now in Benin), Petit Popo (now Aného), and other coastal villages; traders introduced the growing of cassava, coconuts, corn, and other crops in order to provision their slave ships. The French established trading posts at Petit Popo in 1626 and again in 1767, but abandoned them each time. The French were again active there and at Porto-Séguro, east of Lomé, from 1865 to 1883.

German traders came to Grand Popo as early as 1856, but did not arrive in significant numbers until 1880. Germany finally established control over the area, its first African acquisition, on 5 July 1884, when Dr. Gustav Nachtigal made a treaty with the chief of Togo, a village on the north side of a lagoon behind Porto-Séguro. The treaty established a German protectorate over a small coastal enclave, and the village name eventually was given to the entire territory. The Germans established a capital first at Baguida, then at Zebe, and in 1897 at Lomé. Boundary delimitations with the British and French were made in 1897 and 1899. Although the Volta River formed a natural boundary between Togo and the Gold Coast (now Ghana), as a result of the negotiations, the frontier diverged from the river about 320 km (200 mi) north of Lomé and descended diagonally, so that the so-called Volta Triangle on the left bank became part of the Gold Coast. The boundary arrangements resulted in splitting the Ewe, Adja, Ouatchi, Fon, and other peoples between the Gold Coast, Togo, and Dahomey (now Benin). As the Germans extended their control to the north, they built roads and railroads and established administrative, legal, economic, educational, and other institutions.

Soon after the outbreak of World War I in August 1914, neighboring French and British units gained control of Togo. In a provisional arrangement, the British took the coastal area and the railways, and the French assumed control of the interior. League of Nations mandates were established in 1922.

Following World War II, both the UK and France placed their spheres of Togoland under UN trusteeship. Beginning in 1947, leaders of the Ewe people repeatedly petitioned the UN first for Ewe unification and subsequently for Togoland unification. At the time, the Ewe were under three different administrations: the Gold Coast, British Togoland, and French Togoland. For nine years thereafter, the Togoland question was before the UN. Its resolution was difficult not only because of the resistance of the British and French governments to the Ewe demands, but also because both the Ewe and non-Ewe of the two Togolands were deeply divided on the form self-determination should take. The problem was partially resolved by a plebiscite held in British Togoland on 9 May 1956 under UN supervision. A majority of the registered voters decided in favor of integration of British Togoland with an independent Gold Coast. Consequently, when the Gold Coast became the independent state of Ghana, British Togoland ceased to exist.

On 28 October 1956, in a referendum held in French Togoland, 72% of the registered voters chose to terminate French trusteeship and to accept the status of internal autonomy and continued association with France that had been proffered them by the French government. This unilateral effort to terminate French trusteeship was not accepted by the UN.

Independence

In April 1958, new elections were held under UN supervision. The Committee for Togolese Union, pledged to secure complete independence, won control of the Togo Assembly, and its leader, Sylvanus Olympio, subsequently became prime minister. On 13 October 1958, the French government announced that full independence would be granted, and on 27 April 1960, the Republic of Togo became a sovereign nation, with Olympio as president.

President Olympio was assassinated on 13 January 1963 by military insurgents. At the insurgents' behest, Nicolas Grunitzky, the exiled leader of the Togolese Party for Progress, returned to Togo and formed a provisional government. He abrogated the constitution, dissolved the National Assembly, and called new elections. In the May 1963 balloting, Grunitzky was elected president, a new 56-member National Assembly was chosen, and a new constitution was approved by national referendum.

Grunitzky held office through 1966. The final months of his presidency were marked by antigovernment demonstrations involving many of Olympio's former supporters and sympathizers. On 13 January 1967, the Grunitzky government was overthrown by a military coup led by Col. Kléber Dadjo, who was succeeded in April 1967 by Lt. Col. Étienne Éyadéma. The constitution was again suspended and the Assembly dissolved, and Éyadéma declared himself president.

In 1969, Éyadéma proposed the establishment of a national party of unification, the Togolese People's Rally (Rassemblement du Peuple Togolais—RPT). At its first party congress in November 1971, the RPT representatives opposed the idea of constitutional government and asked for a national referendum in support of the Éyadéma regime. This took place in January 1972, with 99% of the population voting for Éyadéma. Survivors of a 1970 plot to overthrow the regime were pardoned after the referendum, and several former members of Olympio's government joined the RPT. Others of Olympio's supporters went into exile or into business, and there was no coherent opposition to the government.

In 1974, Éyadéma began to advocate a "cultural authenticity" policy, stimulated at least in part by the crash of his private plane in January 1974, from which he escaped uninjured. The crash (the cause of which he believed suspicious) followed his nationalization of the phosphate industry and appeared to spur his drive for further Africanization in Togo. At this time, Éyadéma dropped his first name, Étienne, using instead his African second name, Gnassingbé.

Éyadéma was reelected as president without opposition on 30 December 1979, when the voters also approved a draft constitution

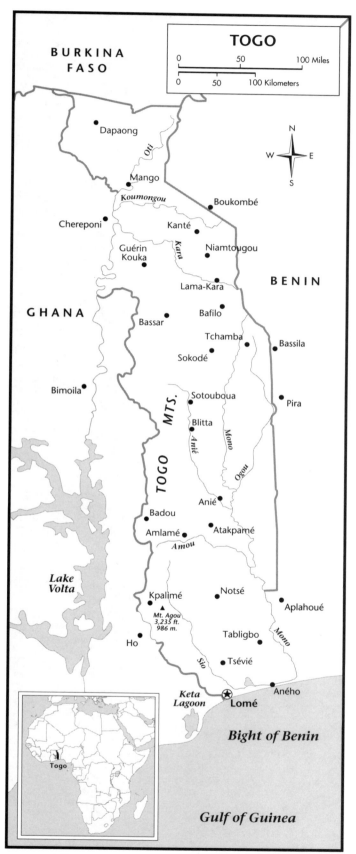

LOCATION: 6°5′ to 11°11′N; 0°5′ to 1°45′E. **BOUNDARY LENGTHS:** Burkina Faso, 126 km (78 mi); Benin, 620 km (385 mi); Gulf of Guinea coastline, 50 km (31 mi); Ghana, 877 km (545 mi). **TERRITORIAL SEA LIMIT:** 30 mi.

for what was called the Third Republic (succeeding the republics headed by Olympio and Grunitzky). A 67-member National Assembly was elected at the same time. Éyadéma remained firmly in control in the early 1980s, despite the disruptions caused by Nigeria's expulsion of illegal aliens and the economic decline attributable to falling phosphate prices. An alleged plot to assassinate Éyadéma on 13 January 1983, while French President François Mitterrand was visiting Togo, apparently misfired. Éyadéma reportedly blamed Gilchrist Olympio, the son of the former president, for the coup attempt.

On 23–24 September 1986, about 60 insurgents, mostly Togolese in exile, attempted to seize control of Lomé but were repulsed. About 150 French and 350 Zairian troops were flown in to help restore order. The official death toll was 26. The coup attempt was reportedly financed by Gilchrist Olympio, who was sentenced to death in absentia. Another 12 men were given death sentences, and 14 were sentenced to life imprisonment. Éyadéma accused Ghana and Burkina Faso of aiding the insurgents. In National Assembly elections on 24 March 1985, 216 candidates, all approved by the RPT, contested 77 seats; only 20 deputies were reelected. Éyadéma was elected unopposed to a new seven-year term as president on 21 December 1986.

Opposition to Éyadéma's rule came to a head in March 1991 when, after police clashes with thousands of anti-government demonstrators, the government agreed to institute a multiparty system and to grant amnesty to dissidents. On 28 August 1991, Éyadéma ended 24 years of military rule by surrendering authority to Joseph Kokou Koffigoh, an interim prime minister selected by a National Conference. The RPT was to be disbanded and Éyadéma barred from running for the presidency.

In October and November 1991, armed forces loyal to Éyadéma failed several times to overthrow Koffigoh. On 3 December 1991, however, they attacked the government palace and seized him. The French refused to help Koffigoh; instead, he was forced to compromise and he formed a coalition government with Éyadéma and legalized the RPT.

On 5 May 1992, opposition leader Gilchrist Olympio was severely wounded in an ambush, and in July another opposition figure was assassinated. The transitional government several times rescheduled the referendum on a new constitution. Finally, on 27 September 1992, it was approved. The legislative and presidential elections were postponed again and again until August 1993.

The Army, composed largely of Kabyé (Éyadéma's group) has never accepted Éyadéma's ouster, the National Conference, or Koffigoh. Eventually, Koffigoh's interim government was dissolved in 1992, and Éyadéma consolidated his powers. However, in January, 1993 he reappointed Koffigoh prime minister of a government which cooperated closely with Éyadéma, now president. On 25 August 1993, Éyadéma easily won reelection as president (97% of the vote). The electoral process, however, was marred by a low turnout (all major opposition candidates refused to participate) and serious irregularities.

Legislative elections were held in two rounds in February 1994. With the exception of Olympio's Union of the Forces of Change (UFC), the main opposition parties participated. The RPT reportedly took 33 of the 81 seats in the first round. The Action Committee for Renewal (CAR), won 19. Koffigoh's New Force Coordination failed to take a single seat. Nonetheless, the armed forces continued to attack opposition politicians. The second round voting was marred by violence, with armed gangs attacking voting stations and opposition supporters. Still, international observers declared the election satisfactory.

On February 24, 1994, the National Electoral Commission released results for 76 seats as follows: opposition, 38 seats; RPT, 37 seats; Koffigoh, 1 seat. The rest were to be sorted out by the Supreme Court. No one seemed satisfied, and the ongoing struggle between Éyadéma and the opposition-dominated High Council of the Republic continues to dominate politics in Togo.

13 GOVERNMENT

The constitution of 30 December 1979 provided for a president nominated by the RPT and elected for a seven-year term by universal adult suffrage at age 18. The president nominated and presided over the cabinet and may rule by decree after declaring a state of emergency. Members of the National Assembly were nominated by the RPT and directly elected for five years. The legislature, which may be dissolved by the president, met twice a year.

A new constitution mandating multiparty elections was approved in a referendum on 27 September 1992. Although opposition parties are permitted, they are not allowed to function without intimidation and coercion. Bloody confrontations mark each stage of an ostensibly civilian governing process.

Technically, the president is chosen in a direct, popular, multiparty election. The legislature, the 81-seat National Assembly, is likewise selected in national, multiparty elections.

14 POLITICAL PARTIES

Political parties in Togo were considerably more active and competitive before independence than after, and since 1969, the nation has been a one-party state. In the first Territorial Assembly elections in 1946, there were two parties, the Committee of Togolese Unity (Comité de l'Unité Togolaise—CUT) and the Togolese Party for Progress (Parti Togolais du Progrès—PTP). The CUT was overwhelmingly successful, and Sylvanus Olympio, the CUT leader and Assembly president, campaigned for Ewe reunification. The CUT controlled all Assembly seats from 1946 to 1952. In the 1952 elections, however, the CUT was defeated, and it refused to participate in further elections because it claimed that the PTP was receiving French support. In the territorial elections of 1955, the PTP won all 30 Assembly seats, and when Togo was given autonomy in 1956, Nicolas Grunitzky, PTP leader, became prime minister.

In the UN-supervised elections of April 1958, the CUT regained power with a demand for independence from France, while the PTP and the Union of Chiefs and Peoples of the North (Union des Chefs et des Populations du Nord—UCPN) advocated that Togo remain an autonomous republic within the French Union. The two defeated parties merged in October 1959 to form the Togolese People's Democratic Union (Union Démocratique des Populations Togolaises—UDPT), under Grunitzky's leadership.

In March 1961, the National Assembly enacted legislation that based elections to the Assembly on a party-list system, with a single ballot in which a majority would be decisive. In the April 1961 elections, which were held on this single-list system, candidates from the alliance of the UDPT and the Togolese Youth Movement (Mouvement de la Jeunesse Togolaise—Juvento) were prevented from registering and were not permitted on the ballot. Consequently, the new Assembly consisted entirely of CUT members.

After Olympio (who had become president in 1960) was assassinated by military insurgents, Grunitzky, who was living in exile in Benin (then Dahomey), was invited back to Togo to form a provisional government. Grunitzky announced that free elections would be held, but in fact the delegates of the four leading parties—UDPT, Juvento, the Togolese Unity Movement (Unité Togolaise, formed from the CUT after Olympio's assassination), and the Togolese Popular Movement (Mouvement Populaire Togolais)—as well as the insurgents' Committee of Vigilance, agreed on a single national union list of candidates. In the elections of 5 May 1963, Grunitzky became president and Antoine Meatchi vice-president; a new 56-member Assembly was elected; and a new constitution was approved by national referendum. In early

1967, however, Grunitzky was deposed, and a military regime took power, with no constitution and no legislature.

Organized political activity was suspended until 1969, when the Togolese People's Rally (Rassemblement du Peuple Togolais—RPT) was founded as the nation's sole legal political party. President Éyadéma heads the RPT, which has a Central Committee and a Political Bureau. In the 1979 and 1985 legislative elections, all candidates were nominated by the RPT. In the 1994 legislative elections, however, other parties participated.

Political opposition to Éyadéma has become bolder since late 1990. For years, an anti-Éyadéma group, the Togolese Movement for Democracy (Mouvement Togolais pour la Démocratie), functioned from exile in Paris. After opposition parties were legalized on 12 April 1991, and especially after the National Conference engineered a governmental change in August 1991, other parties began to function, albeit in an atmosphere of threat from the armed forces and pro-Éyadéma gangs. Among the new parties are the Togolese Union for Democracy (UTD), the Partí Démocratique Togolais (PTD), the Action Committee for Renewal (CAR), and Union of the Forces of Change (UFC). The CAR seems to be the strongest opposition group. The main opposition groups are allied in the Collective of Democratic Opposition (COD-2).

15 LOCAL GOVERNMENT

Togo is divided into five administrative regions—Maritime, Plateaux, Centrale, Kara, and Savanes—each supervised by an inspector. By a law enacted on 23 June 1981, the regions are subdivided into 21 prefectures. Inspectors and prefects are appointed by the president. The prefectures have elected councils. Togo's first direct local elections were held on 5 July 1987.

Each of the six fully established communes—Anécho, Atakpamé, Lomé, Palimé, Sokodé, and Tsévié—has a popularly elected municipal council and a mayor elected by the council. The urban center of Bassari is a commune with an elected municipal council and a mayor who is appointed by the central government.

16 JUDICIAL SYSTEM

Maintaining the independence of the judiciary is the responsibility of the Superior Council of Magistrates, which was set up in 1964 and includes the president of the republic as chairman, the minister of justice, the president and vice-president of the Supreme Court, and others. The Supreme Court, which sits in Lomé, consists of constitutional, judicial, administrative, and commercial chambers. Other judicial institutions include two Courts of Appeal (one civil, the other criminal); tribunals of first instance, divided into civil, commercial, and correctional chambers; labor and children's tribunals; and the Court of State Security, set up in September 1970 to judge crimes involving foreign or domestic subversion. A Tribunal for Recovery of Public Funds handles cases involving misuse of public funds and a Court of Assizes handles cases involving violent crimes.

The judicial system blends African traditional law and the Napoleonic Code in trying civil and criminal cases. In practice, the judiciary is subject to the influence and control of the executive branch.

Defendants in criminal cases are presumed innocent and are afforded the right to counsel. Village chiefs or a Council of Elders may try minor criminal cases in rural areas. Appeals from such rulings may be taken to the regular court system.

17 ARMED FORCES

In 1993, Togo's 4,800-man army consisted of 5 regiments armed with Russian, French, Chinese and US weapons. The 250-man air force had 16 combat aircraft, and the 200-member naval unit had 2 coastal patrol vessels. Paramilitary forces numbered 750. Defense spending in 1989 was $43 million or 3% of GDP.

18 INTERNATIONAL COOPERATION

Togo was admitted to UN membership on 29 September 1960. It is a member of ECA and all the nonregional specialized agencies except IAEA. Togo also belongs to the African Development Bank, ECOWAS, G-77, OAU, OCAM, and UMOA. The nation has signed GATT and the Law of the Sea.

One priority of Togo's foreign policy is development of regional cooperation. In pursuit of this goal, Togo was a prime mover in the founding of ECOWAS, which includes both English- and French-speaking countries. Togo has been an active member of the Conseil d'Entente, which includes Côte d'Ivoire, Niger, Burkina Faso, and Benin. Togo hosted the signing ceremony for the Lomé Convention (providing for preferential treatment by the EC for developing countries) in February 1975 and it is also an associate member of the EC.

19 ECONOMY

Togo has an agricultural economy with about 80% of its people engaged in subsistence agriculture. Togo is drought-prone but is food self-sufficient in years of ample rainfall. The nation also has an active commercial sector and significant phosphate deposits upon which it draws for foreign exchange.

Recent political instability has compounded the erratic economic performance of the late 1980s and early 1990s. International aid was suspended in 1992 as a means of pressuring the government into quicker action towards democratic reforms. Declining prices for Togo's principal exports (phosphates, coffee, cocoa, and cotton) continue to affect the economy adversely.

In January 1994 France suddenly devalued the CFA franc, cutting its value in half overnight. Immediately, prices for almost all imported goods soared, including prices for food and essential drugs. The devaluation, long expected in the investment community, is designed to enourage new investment, particularly in the export sectors of the economy, and discourage the use of hard currency reserves to buy products that could be grown domestically.

20 INCOME

In 1992 Togo's GNP was $1,575 million at current prices, or $400 per capita. For the period 1985–92 the average inflation rate was 2.3%, resulting in a real growth rate in per capita GNP of –1.5%.

In 1992 the GDP was $1,611 million in current US dollars. It is estimated that in 1983, the last year for which statistics are available, agriculture, hunting, forestry, and fishing contributed 33% to GDP; mining and quarrying, 1%; manufacturing, 7%; electricity, gas, and water, 1%; construction, 3%; wholesale and retail trade, 17%; transport, storage, and communication, 7%; finance, insurance, real estate, and business services, 6%; community, social, and personal services, 13%; and other sources 13%.

21 LABOR

About 80% of the 3.4 million inhabitants are engaged in agriculture. Of salaried employees (63,944 in 1987), 48% were in services, 13% in commerce, 8% in manufacturing, with the remainder in other sectors.

Trade unions in Togo, which once were the base for left-wing opposition to the military regime, have been incorporated into the one-party system. The Central Committee of the RPT dissolved the central bodies of all Togolese trade unions in December 1972, and the National Workers Confederation of Togo (Confédération Nationale des Travailleurs du Togo—CNTT) was established in 1973 as the sole national union. In 1991, the National Conference suspended the automatic withholding of CNTT dues for all workers, and it froze CNTT's assets. Several trade unions left the CNTT, some of which then affiliated with two new federations: the Labor Federation of Togolese Workers and the National Union of Independent Syndicates. Since 1991, all three labor federations have taken a more active role in independent collective bargaining.

[22]AGRICULTURE

Togo is predominantly an agricultural country, with about four-fifths of the work force engaged in farming. Approximately 12% of the land area is arable. Most food crops are produced by subsistence farmers who operate on family farms of less than 3 ha (7 acres). Peanuts and sorghum are grown in the extreme north; sorghum, yams, and cotton in the region around Niamtougou; sorghum, cotton, and corn in the central region; coffee, cocoa, and cotton in the southern plateau; and manioc, corn, and copra near the coast. Agriculture accounts for one-third of GDP.

In recent years, the government has emphasized food production. Main food crops in 1992 (in tons) included manioc, 480,000; yams, 393,000; corn, 239,000; and sorghum and millet, 191,000. Although Togo is basically self-sufficient in food, certain cereals—notably wheat, which cannot be grown in Togo—must be imported.

Leading cash crops are coffee and cocoa, followed by cotton, palm kernels, copra, peanuts, and shea nuts (karité). Coffee production decreased from 22,000 tons in 1991 to 13,000 tons in 1992. Cocoa production amounted to just 7,000 tons in 1992—half the amount produced a dozen years earlier. Since world prices for both coffee and cocoa have been falling, there has been a greater emphasis on cotton production, with cotton exports increasing by over 400% from 1984 to 1992. Cotton production averaged 7,000 tons annually from 1979 to 1981; production in 1992 totaled 41,000 tons of fiber. A new state organization, the Togolese Cotton Co., had been set up in 1974 to develop the industry. Production of palm kernels, historically erratic, increased from 14,500 tons in 1990 to 14,800 tons in 1991 to 15,900 tons in 1992. There are over 100,000 coconut trees in Togo; about 2,000 tons of copra are produced annually. The peanut crop in 1992 was 22,000 tons (shelled). Some attempts are being made to export pineapples, house plants, vegetables, and palm oil.

[23]ANIMAL HUSBANDRY

Alleviation of the tsetse fly in the savanna area north of the Atakora Mountains has permitted the development of small-scale cattle raising. Most of the cattle thus produced, principally the humpless West African shorthorn type, are either consumed locally or, when there are surpluses, driven south for consumption in the main cities and towns. Few cattle are exported. Grazing is communal, in the south on family group lands and in the north on tribal lands. Water supplies are short in certain areas.

Livestock in 1992 included an estimated 1,500,000 sheep, 2,000,000 goats, 800,000 hogs, 320,000 head of cattle, and 7,000,000 poultry. There are slaughterhouses at Lomé, Atakpamé, Sokodé, Lama-Kara, Sansanné-Mango, and Dapaong.

[24]FISHING

Fishing remains relatively unimportant, in part because of the country's limited territorial waters. Production, mostly by small operators employing pirogues, amounted to an estimated 12,524 tons in 1991; about 97% of that was caught in Atlantic waters and the rest inland. Almost all fish is sold smoked or dried. A new fishing quay has been constructed at Lomé, and a joint Libyan-Togolese fishing company has been established. Togo imports fish from Europe and its West African neighbors.

[25]FORESTRY

Although much of Togo once was forested, the country now must import wood. Production of roundwood in 1991 was estimated at 1,234,000 cu m, of which 85% was for fuel.

[26]MINING

Lime phosphate, found mostly in the coastal region, is Togo's principal mineral resource. In 1991, Togo was the world's tenth largest producer of phosphate rock. Production increased from 1,473,000 tons in 1969 to about 2,965,000 tons in 1991; virtually the entire output is exported. Canada, Mexico, and France were the three main importing nations of Togolese phosphate in 1991. The phosphate industry was nationalized in 1974, and production is now carried on by the Togolese Office of Phosphates (Office Togolais des Phosphates—OTP).

Exploitation of marble reserves in the region around Niamtougou was begun in 1970 by the Togolese Marble Co. In 1991, the state-run *Nouvelle Société Togolaise de Marbre et de Matériaux* (Nouvelle Sotoma) quarried 250 tons and 600 tons of block and crushed stone, respectively. By September 1991, however, Sotoma closed, leaving the government the job of finding private investors to lease or purchase the operation.

Iron ore reserves, in north-central Togo (east of Bassari), are 95 million tons, averaging more than 40% iron. Other mineral deposits include limestone, granite, chromite, bauxite, manganese, gold, copper, and nickel.

[27]ENERGY AND POWER

Togo receives about four-fifths of its electricity in the form of hydroelectric power from the Akosombo (or Volta River) Dam in Ghana. The transmission line, partly financed by an interest-free loan from the Canadian government, was formally inaugurated in July 1975. There is also a hydroelectric station at Kpimé, near Kpalimé, built with Yugoslav assistance. The 65-Mw Mono River hydroelectric plant, near Atakpamé, began operating in 1987. The project has an annual output of 150 million kwh, enough to meet 25% of the combined demand of Togo and the joint project's partner, Benin. A 15–20 Mw hydroelectric plant was proposed for Adjaralara, 75 km (47 mi) downstream on the Mono River. Togo's installed capacity in 1991 was 34,000 kw (89% conventional thermal, 11% hydroelectric), and its electrical output that year totaled 60 million kwh; consumption of electricity was 350 million kwh.

Petroleum exploration has been conducted, but no reserves have yet been located. An estimated 135,206 tons of petroleum products were imported in 1990.

[28]INDUSTRY

Industrial production represents a small part of the economy (10% of GDP in 1991), with textiles and the processing of agricultural products—palm oil extraction, coffee roasting, cassava flour milling, and cotton ginning and weaving—being the most important sectors. Other industries were developed to provide consumer goods—footwear, beverages, confectionery, salt, and tires. Until the mid-1980s, most industries were partly or totally government owned. Sales and leases reduced the parastatal sector by nearly half as of 1990.

Togo's cement clinker plant, with a capacity of 800,000 tons, has been reopened as a parastatal and supplies the cement required by the state-sponsored dam and urban construction programs. The textile complex at Kara, along with a second plant at Dadja, were bought by American and Korean interests in 1987. A new cotton ginning plant opened in 1991 in Talo. Togo's brewery is 40% state owned and 60% owned by private German interests. A plastics factory is 25% state owned and 75% owned by Danish and Swiss interests. A state-owned steel plant was leased to an American entrepreneur in 1984 and converted into a rerolling facility. The state-owned national oil refinery was leased to Shell Togo and converted into a storage facility.

A free-trade zone opened in Lomé in 1990. Though there is interest in this program, recent political instability has slowed its development.

The 537 kms of railway are outmoded. The volume of freight handled at the Lomé port has declined in spite of recent modernization. Togo's electrical power comes from the Akosombo hydroelectric plant in Ghana. Since the opening of the Nangbeto project on the Mono River, this joint Togo-Benin hydro facility has provided an extra 65 Mw to the regional grid.

29 SCIENCE AND TECHNOLOGY

The National Institute of Scientific Research, in Lomé, is the central scientific coordinating body. Several French research institutes have branches in the capital, and there are pilot farm projects throughout the country. The University of Benin at Lomé maintains schools of sciences, medicine, industrial engineering, and agriculture. Togo also has an agricultural school at Kpalimé and a technical college at Sokodé.

30 DOMESTIC TRADE

The Togolese are among the most active traders on the West African coast, with much of the domestic trade handled by women. The national trade organization, Société Nationale de Commerce (SONACOM), has a monopoly on importation and distribution of soaps, cereals, sugar, salt, and industrial products, but there is still a flourishing free market both within Togo and with neighboring countries.

Most wholesalers have their headquarters in Lomé, the principal commercial and financial center. In Lomé, some shops specialize in such lines as dry goods, foodstuffs, and hardware. Elsewhere, retailers deal in a wide variety of goods rather than specializing in a few products. In the smaller towns, individual merchants deal in locally grown products and items of the first necessity.

Business hours are from 7:30 to 11:30 AM and 2:30 to 6 PM, Monday through Friday, and from 7:30 AM to 12:30 PM on Saturday. Banks are normally open from 7:30 to 11:30 AM and 2:30 to 4 PM on weekdays only.

31 FOREIGN TRADE

Togo has maintained a trade deficit for many years, though the amount has varied depending in international prices for coffee and phosphates and the success of the ongoing austerity policies. The trade deficit narrowed to CFA Fr21,300 million in 1991.

The principal exports are phosphates, cocoa, cotton (ginned), and coffee.

The principal imports are cotton textiles; food, beverages, and tobacco; machinery and transport material; petroleum products; and chemical products.

China was Togo's leading export partner in 1989 (12.5%) followed by France (8.7%), the former USSR (7.7%), and Italy (7.5%). Togo's imports came primarily from France (29.6%), Netherlands (11.8%), and Germany (7.6%).

32 BALANCE OF PAYMENTS

Before independence, trade deficits were made up largely through capital credits provided by France. These have since been replaced by international loans and suppliers' credits.

In 1992 merchandise exports totaled $322.3 million and imports $418.2 million. The merchandise trade balance was $–95.9 million.

33 BANKING AND SECURITIES

The bank of issue is the Central Bank of the West African States (Banque Centrale des États de l'Afrique de l'Ouest—BCEAO), which also acts in that capacity for Benin, Côte d'Ivoire, Niger, Senegal, and Burkina Faso. Togo has a 10% share in the BCEAO, the development bank of which has its headquarters in Lomé.

In 1993, Togo had five commercial and savings banks, of which the most important were the International Bank for Occidental Africa, the Bank of Credit and Commerce International, the Libyan Arab-Togolese Bank of Foreign Commerce, the Togolese Bank for Credit and Industry, and the Union Bank of Togo (the latter two with a state share of 35%).

Development banks include the Togolese Development Bank, founded in 1967, with a 60% state share; the 36.4% state-owned National Farm Credit Fund; and the state-owned National Investment Co., which is intended to mobilize savings, guarantee loans to small- and medium-sized domestic enterprises, and amortize the public debt.

There are no securities exchanges in Togo.

34 INSURANCE

The Togolese Insurance Group is 63% state owned; about a half-dozen French companies were also operating in Togo in the mid-1980s.

35 PUBLIC FINANCE

By the late 1970's, public investment expenditures had reached an unsustainable level (exceeding 40% of GDP), touched off by an earlier rise of commodity prices. As a result, large payment arrears on the external debt began to mount. In the mid-1980s, the fiscal deficit was reduced largely through IMP credits and debt reschedulings. The civil unrest of 1991 resulted in decreased revenues and increased expenditures, and led to an overall budget deficit of 7.5% of GDP. In 1992, further civil unrest widened the budget deficit to 8.5% of GDP. As a result, payment arrears of CFA Fr9.6 billion and CFA Fr12 billion accumulated in 1991 and 1992 respectively.

36 TAXATION

Taxes are levied on individual incomes and on corporate profits and capital gains. A transactions tax, a tax on fuel consumption, and social security contributions are also paid. There are also registration and stamp taxes and a tax on income from securities. A 5% "solidarity" surtax on salaries was imposed in 1983 as an austerity measure.

37 CUSTOMS AND DUTIES

Togo requires an import license for all goods valued at 10,000 CFA francs or more imported from outside the franc zone. Tariffs are based on a non-discriminatory schedule ranging from 5% to 25% of c.i.f. value, and there is a customs stamp tax and a statistical tax. Restricted or prohibited goods include animals, arms, ammunition, distilling equipment, narcotics, and explosives.

38 FOREIGN INVESTMENT

Togo's liberal investment code offers tax holidays, exemption from customs duties, and guaranteed repatriation of capital and profits. Total foreign ownership is allowed, but not for investments of less than CFA Fr300 million, which must have 51% local capital participation and employ 70% local workers. Manufacturing operations in the port of Lomé are eligible for permanent customs exemptions on imported raw materials and exported finished products. The free-trade zone is an initiative the benefit of which awaits the return of political stability.

39 ECONOMIC DEVELOPMENT

The 1981–85 development plan called for spending roughly equal allocation levels for rural development (26.5%), industry (29.2%), and infrastructure (29.5%). In the 1986–90 development plan, principal allocations were for infrastructure and rural development.

Of the development funds for the 1986–90 plan, 90% were sought from foreign sources. Principal sources of development aid are France, Germany, the United States, China, the EC, the World Bank, and IDA. France ranked first among the bilateral donors, with Germany second. The government has been diverted from implementing the plan by international financial considerations and concerns over the process of democratization.

40 SOCIAL DEVELOPMENT

The government's social welfare program, established in 1973, includes family allowances and maternity benefits; old age, disability, and death benefits; and workers' compensation. The program supplements a continued strong sense of social obligation to one's family or clan, even among Africans in the urban centers.

The status of women is changing. Legally women are equal in the new Togolese society, but seldom are they treated as such. The Union of Togolese Women and a women's group affiliated with the RPT assist in the fight against illiteracy and disease and are involved in child welfare. Women continue to play an important role in Togo's economic life; some have become wealthy through their involvement in domestic and regional trade.

41 HEALTH

Medical services include permanent treatment centers and a mobile organization for preventive medicine. Special facilities treat leprosy, sleeping sickness, and mental illness. All services are free except at the clinic attached to the hospital in Lomé, where some patients pay a nominal fee. In 1991, the nation's medical personnel included 319 doctors and 1,187 nurses. In 1990, there were 22 dentists, 65 pharmacists, and 222 midwives. In 1992, there were 8 doctors per 100,000 people, with a nurse to doctor ratio of 6.2. About 61% of the population had access to health care services in 1992; total health care expenditures were $67 million for 1990.

The Mobile Service for Hygiene and Preventive Medicine performs mass inoculations, carries on pest control campaigns, and provides education in hygiene and basic preventive measures. Its activities have led to significant decreases in mortality caused by smallpox, yellow fever, and sleeping sickness. Yaws, malaria, and leprosy continue to be major medical problems, however. In 1990, there were 244 reported cases of tuberculosis per 100,000 people. Immunization rates for children up to one year old in 1992 were: tuberculosis (74%); diphtheria, pertussis, and tetanus (53%); polio (47%); and measles (29%).

There were 169,000 births in 1992. The birth rate is 44.5 per 1,000 people with about 34% of married women (ages 15 to 49) using contraception. The infant mortality rate was 86 per 1,000 live births in 1992, and the maternal mortality rate was 420 per 100,000 live births. The general mortality rate was 12.8 per 1,000 inhabitants in 1993. Average life expectancy is 55 years.

42 HOUSING

With the limited resources at its disposal, the government is endeavoring to solve the problem of urban overcrowding by promoting housing schemes and establishing sanitation facilities. By 1991, 60% of the population had access to safe water. According to the latest available information for 1980–88, total housing units numbered 470,000 with 6.2 people per dwelling.

43 EDUCATION

Literacy rates in 1990 were estimated at 56.4% for men and 30.7% for women. Primary education (ages 6–12) is compulsory and free of charge. Secondary education is for seven years. In 1990, there were 651,962 pupils in 2,494 primary schools, 125,545 pupils in secondary schools, and 8,392 students in technical schools. Mission schools play an important role in education.

The University of Benin is at Lomé. Lomé also has colleges of administration, architecture, and urban planning. In 1989, all higher level schools had 7,826 students.

44 LIBRARIES AND MUSEUMS

The National Library in Lomé has 13,600 volumes, and the University of Benin library has 70,000. The National Museum, founded in Lomé in 1975, has ethnography, history, and art exhibits.

45 MEDIA

All media are run by the government, and criticism of key government policies or officials is not permitted. The *Journal Official de la République du Togo* is published daily in Lomé; another Lomé daily, *La Nouvelle Marche,* published in French and Ewe, had a circulation of 10,000 in 1992. Telecommunications links are maintained with major African, European, and American cities. There is an automatic telephone exchange in Lomé, where most of the nation's 12,000 telephones (1991) are located. The radio network presents programs in French, English, and local languages; in 1991 there were an estimated 770,000 radios. Television service, broadcast in French and local languages, began in 1973; in 1991, Togo had about 23,000 television sets.

46 ORGANIZATIONS

The Chamber of Commerce, Agriculture, and Industry is active in Lomé. The CNTT and the major women's and youth groups are affiliated with the RPT. Cultural organizations, all located in Lomé, include the Alliance Française, American Cultural Center, Goethe-Institut, and Togolese Association for Cultural Exchanges with Foreign Countries.

47 TOURISM, TRAVEL, AND RECREATION

Tourist attractions include the Mandouri hunting reserve, in the northeast, and the beaches and deepsea fishing of the Gulf of Guinea coast. In 1990 there were about 103,246 tourist arrivals in hotels and other establishments, 44% from Europe and 48% from Africa. In 1991, Togo's tourist industry suffered a decline due to the Gulf War, and political instability has discouraged tourism as well. The occupancy rate in Lomé hotels dropped to 15% in 1991 but rebounded to 26% in 1992. Togo's 119 hotels had 2,372 rooms in 1992.

48 FAMOUS TOGOLESE

Togo's most prominent statesman was Sylvanus Olympio (1902–63), who led his country's fight for independence and was its first president. Gnassingbé Éyadéma (b.Étienne Éyadéma, 1937) has been president of Togo since 1967. Edem Kodjo (b.1938) was OAU secretary-general, 1978–84.

49 DEPENDENCIES

Togo has no territories or colonies.

50 BIBLIOGRAPHY

Calvert, Albert Frederick. *Togoland.* London: Laurie, 1918.

Coleman, James Smoot. *Togoland.* New York: Carnegie Endowment for International Peace, 1956.

Cornevin, Robert. *Histoire du Togo.* Paris: Berger-Levrault, 1969.

Curkeet, A. A. *Togo: Portrait of a West African Francophone Republic in the 1980s.* Jefferson, N.C.: McFarland & Co., 1993.

Debrunner, Hans W. *A Church between Colonial Powers.* London: Butterworth, 1965.

Decalo, Samuel. *Historical Dictionary of Togo.* 2d ed. Metuchen, N.J.: Scarecrow Press, 1987.

Knoll, Arthur J. *Togo under Imperial Germany, 1884–1914: A Case Study in Colonial Rule.* Stanford, Calif.: Hoover Institution Press, 1978.

Kuczynski, Robert René. *The Cameroons and Togoland: A Demographic Study.* London: Oxford University Press, 1939.

TUNISIA

Republic of Tunisia
Al-Jumhuriyah at-Tunisiyah

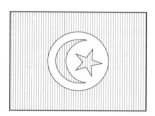

CAPITAL: Tunis.

FLAG: Centered on a red ground is a white disk bearing a red crescent and a red five-pointed star.

ANTHEM: *Al-Khaladi (The Glorious)*.

MONETARY UNIT: The Tunisian dinar (D) is a paper currency of 1,000 millimes. There are coins of 1, 2, 5, 10, 20, 50, and 100 millimes and of ½, 1, and 5 dinars, and notes of 1, 5, 10, and 20 dinars. D1 = $1.2763 (or $1 = D0.7835).

WEIGHTS AND MEASURES: The metric system is the legal standard.

HOLIDAYS: New Year's Day, 1 January; Independence Day, 20 March; Martyrs' Day, 9 April; Labor Day, 1 May; Victory Day, 1 June; Republic Day, 25 July; Women's Day, 13 August; Evacuation Day, 15 October; Accession of President Ben Ali, 7 November. Movable religious holidays include 'Id al-Fitr, 'Id al-'Adha', 1st of Muharram (Muslim New Year), and Milad an-Nabi.

TIME: 1 PM = noon GMT.

¹LOCATION, SIZE, AND EXTENT

Situated on the northern coast of Africa, Tunisia has an area of 163,610 sq km (63,170 sq mi), extending 792 km (492 mi) N–S and 350 km (217 mi) E–W. Comparatively, the area occupied by Tunisia is slightly larger than the state of Georgia. It is bounded on the N and E by the Mediterranean Sea, on the SE by Libya, and on the W by Algeria, with a total boundary length of 2,572 km (1,598 mi).

Tunisia's capital city, Tunis, is located on the Mediterranean Sea coast.

²TOPOGRAPHY

The Medjerda, Teboursouk, and Tebessa mountains—eastern extensions of the Atlas chain—divide the country into two distinct regions, the well-watered north and the semiarid south. The latter includes Tunisia's highest point, Jebel Chumbi, 1,544 m (5,064 ft), near Qasserine. The northern region is further divided into three subregions: the northwest, with extensive cork forests; the north-central, with its fertile grasslands; and the northeast, from Tunis to Cape el-Tib, noted for its livestock, citrus fruits, and garden produce. The southern region contains a central plateau and a desert area in the extreme south, which merges into the Sahara and is characterized by date palm oases and saline lakes, the largest of which is Shott el-Jerid. The Medjerda, the most important river system, rises in Algeria and drains into the Gulf of Tunis.

³CLIMATE

Tunisia consists of two climatic belts, with Mediterranean influences in the north and Saharan in the south. Temperatures are moderate along the coast, with an average annual reading of 18°C (64°F), and hot in the interior south. The summer season in the north, from May through September, is hot and dry; the winter, which extends from October to April, is mild and characterized by frequent rains. Temperatures at Tunis range from an average minimum of 6°C (43°F) and maximum of 14°C (57°F) in January, to an average minimum of 21°C (70°F) and maximum of 33°C (91°F) in August. Precipitation in the Kroumirie region reaches a high of 150 cm (59 in) annually, while rainfall in the extreme south averages less than 20 cm (8 in) a year.

⁴FLORA AND FAUNA

Tunisia has a great variety of trees, including cork oak, oak, pines, jujube, and gum. More than one-fourth of the country is covered by esparto grass, which is the characteristic vegetation of the steppe region. Jackal, wild boar, and several species of gazelle are numerous. Horned vipers and scorpions are common in the Sahara. The sleeved mouflon, a species of wild sheep, is found in the mountains.

⁵ENVIRONMENT

Loss of agricultural land to erosion, and degradation of range and forest lands because of overgrazing or overcutting of timber for fuel are major concerns. Erosion eliminates about 45,000 acres of land. Seventy-six percent of the nation's land area is threatened by erosion. Overcrowding and poor sanitation in urban centers are also major environmental problems. Pollution from industry and farming activities threatens the nation's limited water supply. Tunisia has 0.9 cubic miles of water with 80% used for farming and 7% for industrial purposes. Sixty-nine percent of the people living in rural areas do not have pure water. The nation's cities produce 0.9 million tons of solid waste. Tunisia contributes 0.1% of the world's total gas emissions. There are four national parks.

In 1994, six of the nation's mammal species and 14 bird species are endangered. Twenty-six types of plants are also endangered. As of 1987, endangered species in Tunisia included the Barbary hyena, Barbary leopard, two species of gazelle (Cuvier's and slender-horned), and the Mediterranean monk seal. A World Wildlife Fund project succeeded in rescuing the Atlas deer from near extinction. Extinct are the leopard, cheetah, scimitar-horned oryx, and Mococcan dorcas gazelle.

⁶POPULATION

According to the 1984 census, the population of Tunisia was 6,966,173. The 1994 estimate was 8,777,590. A total of 9,781,000 was projected for the year 2000, assuming a crude birthrate of 24 per 1,000 population, a crude death rate of 5.9, and a net natural increase of 18.1 during 1995–2000. The average density in 1994 was 54 persons per sq km (139 per sq mi), ranging from only about 4 per sq km (10 per sq mi) in the south to over 400 per sq km (1,000 per sq mi) in the thickly settled north. In 1994, 59% of Tunisians lived in urban areas, of which Tunis, with a metropolitan population of about 2,084,000, was the largest. Other cities are Sfax (Safaqis); Ariana (a suburb of Tunis); Bizerte (Binzart); Gabes; and Sousse (Susa).

7 MIGRATION

French and Italian migration to Tunisia dates from the French military occupation of 1881. There were 255,000 Europeans in Tunisia in 1956, but most have since left the country. With the conclusion of the Franco-Algerian war in 1962, 110,000 Algerian refugees returned to their homeland.

Internal migration constitutes a serious problem. Rural unemployment has caused significant population movement to urban centers, where conditions are often harsh. Since 1964, the government has sought to decentralize industry and to resettle nomads and seminomads in permanent villages. Many Tunisians seek employment abroad; in the early 1990s there were approximately 350,000 Tunisian workers in foreign countries, mostly Libya and France. Their remittances came to nearly 5% of the GDP in 1989. Some 207,500 Tunisians lived in France in 1990.

8 ETHNIC GROUPS

Tunisia has a highly homogeneous population, almost entirely of Arab and Berber descent. The number of Tunisian Jews, 71,500 in 1946, had declined to about 2,500 by 1989. The small European population consists mostly of French and Italians.

9 LANGUAGES

Arabic is the official language. French is taught to all schoolchildren and is commonly used in administration and commerce. Small numbers of people speak Berber.

10 RELIGIONS

Although Islam is the state religion, Tunisians traditionally are tolerant of other beliefs. Nearly all (99%) Tunisians are Sunni Muslims, following the Malikite school of legal interpretation. Small Muslim minorities belong to the Hanafite school or to the Ibadhi sect. The non-Muslims consist mainly of about 12,000 Roman Catholics and a declining number of Jews (the Jews of Jerba claim to have come there at the end of the Babylonian Captivity in the 6th century BC).

The early 1980s brought a government offensive against the growing Islamic fundamentalist movement. In 1981, two fundamentalist parties were banned, and some 100 members were brought to trial and sentenced to prison terms for offending the dignity of the head of state and belonging to an unauthorized organization. Another crackdown on Islamic fundamentalists began in 1986, with about 2,000 arrested in 1986 and 1987. Islamic militants continued to agitate into the 1990s, however.

11 TRANSPORTATION

As of 1991, 17,700 km (11,000 mi) of highway, 51% of it paved, connected the major cities and provided access to most regions of the country. In 1991 there were 330,000 passenger cars and 185,000 commercial vehicles. The Tunisian National Railway Co. (Société National des Chemins de Fer Tunisiens) operates over 2,000 km (1,200 mi) of standard- and narrow-gauge track, located mostly in the northern region and central plateau. A metro rail system for Tunis opened in 1985.

Tunisia has excellent shipping facilities at Tunis, the principal port, and at Sfax, Sousse, Bizerte, and Gabes; Sekhira is the port for oil exports. The free port terminal at Zarzis is scheduled for further development at an estimated cost of $20.8 million, in order to expand harbor and storage facilities. Tunisia's modest merchant fleet, established in 1958, operates a freighter service principally to French ports; as of 1991 there were 22 oceangoing ships, totaling 151,000 GRT. The Tunisian Navigation Co. is the principal shipping firm.

Tunis-Carthage Airport, about 14 km (9 mi) from the capital, provides direct connections to most of the major cities of Europe and the Middle East. There are four other international airports, at Monastir, Jerba, Tozeur, and Sfax. Tunis Air, the national airline, is owned by the Tunisian government (51%), Air France, and Tunisian citizens; in 1992, the line carried 1.2 million passengers.

12 HISTORY

The history of early Tunisia and its indigenous inhabitants, the Berbers, is obscure prior to the founding of Carthage by seafaring Phoenicians from Tyre (in present-day Lebanon) in the 9th century BC. A great mercantile state developed at Carthage (near modern-day Tunis), which proceeded to dominate the western Mediterranean world. The great Carthaginian general Hannibal engineered the monumental trans-Alpine assault on Rome in 211 BC and inflicted costly losses on the Roman Empire until choosing suicide rather than capture in 183 BC. Carthage was eventually burned to the ground by the Romans at the culmination of the Punic Wars in 146 BC. The Romans subsequently rebuilt the city, making it one of the great cities of the ancient world. With the decline of the Roman Empire, Tunisia fell successively to Vandal invaders during the 5th century AD, to the Byzantines in the 6th century, and finally to the Arabs in the 7th century. Thenceforth, Tunisia remained an integral part of the Muslim world.

In the 9th century, the governor of Tunisia, Ibrahim ibn Aghlab, founded a local dynasty nominally under the sovereignty of the 'Abbasid caliphs of Baghdad. The Aghlabids conquered Sicily and made Tunisia prosperous. In 909, the Fatimids ended Aghlabid rule, using Tunisia as a base for their subsequent conquest of Egypt. They left Tunisia in control of the subordinate Zirid dynasty until the 11th century, when the Zirids rebelled against Fatimid control. The Fatimids unleashed nomadic Arab tribes, the Banu Hilal and Banu Sulaym, to punish the Zirids, a move resulting in the destruction of the Zirid state and the general economic decline of Tunisia. In the 13th century, the Hafsids, a group subordinate to the Almohad dynasty based in Morocco, restored order to Tunisia. They founded a Tunisian dynasty that, from the 13th century to the 16th, made Tunisia one of the flourishing regions of North Africa. In the beginning of the 16th century, however, Spain's occupation of important coastal locations precipitated the demise of Hafsid rule.

In 1574, the Ottoman Turks occupied Tunisia, ruling it with a dey appointed by the Ottoman ruler. The dey's lieutenants, the beys, gradually became the effective rulers, in fact if not in name. Ultimately, in 1705, the bey Husayn ibn 'Ali established a dynasty. Successive Husaynids ruled Tunisia as vassals of the Ottomans until 1881 and under the French until 1956, the year of Tunisia's independence (the dynasty was abolished in 1957). During the 19th century, the Tunisian dynasts acted virtually as independent rulers, making vigorous efforts to utilize Western knowledge and technology to modernize the state. But these efforts led to fiscal bankruptcy and thus to the establishment of an international commission made up of British, French, and Italian representatives to supervise Tunisian finances. Continued rivalry between French and Italian interests culminated in a French invasion of Tunisia in May 1881. A protectorate was created in that year by the Treaty of Bardo; the Convention of La Marsa (1883) allowed the Tunisian dynasty to continue, although effective direction of affairs passed to the French. French interests invested heavily in Tunisia, and a process of modernization was vigorously pursued; at the same time, direct administration in the name of the dynasty was gradually expanded. The Tunisians, in turn, supported France in World War I.

The beginnings of modern nationalism in Tunisia emerged before the outbreak of the war, with hopes of greater Tunisian participation in government encouraged during the war by pronouncements such as the Fourteen Points (1918) of Woodrow Wilson. When these hopes were not realized, Tunisians formed a moderate nationalist grouping, the Destour ("Constitutional") Party. Dissatisfaction over the group's poor organization led, in 1934, to a split: the more active members, led by Habib Bourguiba, founded the Neo-Destour Party. France responded to demands for internal autonomy with repression, including the deposition and exile of the sovereign Munsif Bey. On 23 August 1945, the two Destour parties proclaimed that the will of the Tunisian people was independence. But the French still held firm. In December 1951, they again rejected a request by the Tunisian government for internal autonomy. The situation worsened when extremists among the French colonists launched a wave of terrorism. Finally, on 31 July 1954, French Premier Pierre Mendès-France promised the bey internal autonomy. After long negotiations accompanied by considerable local disorder, a French-Tunisian convention was signed on 3 June 1955 in Paris. On 20 March 1956, France recognized Tunisian independence.

In April 1956, Habib Bourguiba formed the first government of independent Tunisia, and on 25 July 1957, the Constituent Assembly, having established a republic and transformed itself into a legislative assembly, elected Bourguiba chief of state and deposed the bey. A new constitution came into effect on 1 June 1959. Bourguiba won the first presidential election in 1959 and was reelected in 1964, 1969, and 1974, when the National Assembly amended the constitution to make him president for life.

Economic malaise and political repression during the late 1970s led to student and labor unrest. A general strike called by the General Union of Tunisian Workers (UGTT) on 26 January 1978, in order to protest assaults on union offices and the harassment of labor leaders, brought confrontations with government troops in which at least 50 demonstrators and looters were killed and 200 trade union officials, including UGTT Secretary-General Habib Achour, were arrested. Prime Minister Hedi Nouira was succeeded by Mohamed Mzali in April 1980, marking the advent of a political liberalization. Trade union leaders were released from jails, and Achour ultimately received a full presidential pardon. In July 1981, the formation of opposition political parties was permitted. In elections that November, candidates of Bourguiba's ruling Destourian Socialist Party, aligned in a National Front with the UGTT, garnered all 136 National Assembly seats and 94.6% of the popular vote. An economic slump in 1982–83 brought a renewal of tensions; in January 1984, after five days of rioting in Tunis, the government was forced to rescind the doubling of bread prices that had been ordered as an austerity measure.

After independence, Tunisia pursued a nonaligned course in foreign affairs while maintaining close economic ties with the West. Tunisia's relations with Algeria, strained during the 1970s, improved markedly during the early 1980s, and on 19 March 1983 the two nations signed a 20-year treaty of peace and friendship. Relations with Libya have been stormy since the stillborn Treaty of Jerba (1974), a hastily drafted document that had been intended to merge the two countries into the Islamic Arab Republic; within weeks after signing the accord, Bourguiba, under pressure from Algeria and from members of his own government, retreated to a more gradualist approach toward Arab unity. A further irritant was the territorial dispute between Libya and Tunisia over partition of the oil-rich Gulf of Gabes, resolved by the international Court of Justice in Libya's favor in 1982.

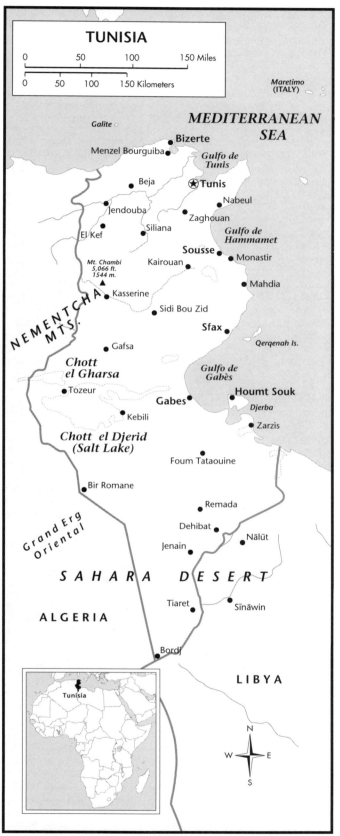

LOCATION: 7°33′ to 11°38′E; 29°54′ to 37°21′N. **BOUNDARY LENGTHS:** Mediterranean coastline, 1,028 km (639 mi); Libya, 459 km (285 mi); Algeria, 958 km (595 mi). **TERRITORIAL SEA LIMIT:** 12 mi.

Tunisian-Libyan relations reached a low point in January 1980, when some 30 commandos (entering from Algeria but apparently aided by Libya) briefly seized an army barracks and other buildings at Gafsa in an abortive attempt to inspire a popular uprising against Bourguiba. In 1981, Libya vetoed Tunisia's bid to join OAPEC and expelled several thousand Tunisian workers; more Tunisian workers were expelled in 1985.

Following the evacuation of the Palestine Liberation Organization (PLO) from Lebanon in August 1982, Tunisia admitted PLO Chairman Yasir Arafat and nearly 1,000 Palestinian fighters. An Israeli bombing raid on the PLO headquarters near Tunis killed about 70 persons. By 1987, the PLO presence was down to about 200, all civilians. In 1993, Tunisia welcomed an official Israeli delegation as part of the peace process.

In 1986 and 1987, Bourguiba dealt with labor agitation for wage increases by again jailing UGTT leader Achour and disbanding the confederation. He turned on many of his former political associates, including his wife and son, while blocking two legal opposition parties from taking part in elections. Reasserting his control of Tunisian politics, Bourguiba dismissed Prime Minister Mzali, who fled to Algeria and denounced the regime. A massive roundup of Islamic fundamentalists in 1987 was the president's answer to what he termed a terrorist conspiracy sponsored by Iran, and diplomatic relations with Tehran were broken. On 27 September 1987, a state security court found 76 defendants guilty of plotting against the government and planting bombs; seven (five in absentia) were sentenced to death.

The trusted Minister of Interior, who had conducted the crackdown, General Zine el-Abidine Ben Ali, was named Prime Minister in September 1987. Six weeks later, Ben Ali seized power, ousting Bourguiba, who he said was too ill and senile to govern any longer. He assumed the presidency himself, promising political liberalization. Almost 2,500 political prisoners were released and the special state security courts were abolished. The following year, Tunisia's constitution was revised, ending the presidency for life and permitting the chief executive three, five-year terms. Elections were advanced from 1991 to 1989 and Ben Ali ran unopposed. Candidates of the renamed Destour Party, the Constitutional Democratic Rally (RCD), won all of the 141 seats in the Chamber of Deputies, although the Islamist Party, An-Nahda, won an average of 18% of the vote where members contested as independents.

After an attack on RCD headquarters in 1990, the government moved decisively against its Islamist opposition. Thousands were arrested and in 1992 military trials, 265 were convicted. In March 1994 parliamentary elections, Ben Ali again was unopposed and the RCD took all 144 seats. Under a proportional system, opposition candidates were allowed to fill 19 seats set aside for them. Tunisia has continued to follow a moderate, nonaligned course in foreign relations, complicated by sporadic difficulties with its immediate neighbors. Relations with Libya remained tense after ties were resumed in 1987; Algeria signed a border agreement in 1993 and planned a gas pipeline through Tunisia to Italy. Although the US has provided economic and military aid, Tunisia opposed American support for Kuwait following Iraq's invasion in 1990.

13 GOVERNMENT

According to the constitution of 1959, Tunisia is an Islamic republic, although since independence it has been a thoroughly secular state. The president, who is chief of state, must be a Muslim and a Tunisian citizen, born of a Tunisian father and grandfather, and at least 40 years old. The president enjoys extensive powers, initiating and directing state policy and appointing judges, provincial governors, the mayor of Tunis, and other high officials, The cabinet, headed by a prime minister, varies in size and is under presidential domination.

The unicameral National Assembly (Majlis al-Ummah) was expanded in 1993 to 160 members, elected by general, free, direct, and secret ballot. All citizens 20 years of age or older may vote; candidates must be at least 30 years old and born of a Tunisian father. The Assembly sits twice a year for five years, but may be extended in the event that a national emergency prevents new elections. Presidential ratification is required before a bill passed by the legislature can become law, but the Assembly may override the president's veto by a two-thirds majority. The president may enact decrees in an emergency or when the Assembly is in recess.

14 POLITICAL PARTIES

The Constitutional Democratic Rally (RCD) dominates the country's political life. Its leader from its founding as the Neo-Destour Party in 1934 to 1987 was Habib Bourguiba. In the first national elections, in 1956, all 98 seats in the Constituent Assembly were won by the National Union, a united front of the Neo-Destour Party with the UGTT, the National Union of Tunisian Farmers, and the Tunisian Union of Craftsmen and Merchants. In the November 1959 elections for the National Assembly, the Communist Party (Parti Communiste Tunisien) presented a list of 13 candidates in Tunis and Gafsa; elsewhere, the PSD was unopposed, and the ruling party won all 90 seats at stake. From 1959 to 1994, the RCD (acting in 1981 as part of a National Front with the UGTT) held a monopoly of Assembly seats.

Banned in 1963, the Communist Party was the first opposition group to be fully legalized under the political liberalization of 1981. Two other parties, the Movement of Social Democrats (Mouvement des Démocrates Socialistes) and the Movement (or Party) of Popular Unity (Mouvement (Parti) de l'Unité Populaire), failed to retain their provisional authorization when each fell short of receiving a 5% share of the total vote in the November 1981 election but nevertheless were formally legalized in 1983. The principal Islamist part, An Nahda, has been outlawed. In 1992, it was hit hard by the jailing of many of its senior leaders.

15 LOCAL GOVERNMENT

Tunisia is divided into 23 provinces (wilayets, or governorates). Each province is headed by a governor appointed by the president through the secretary of interior. The governor is assisted by elected municipal councils and a governmental council, members of which are appointed for a three-year term by the central government on the governor's nomination. Each province is in turn divided into delegations (mutamadiyat), the number of which varies with the size and social and economic importance of the province. There were 199 in the mid-1980s. The number of communes, or municipalities, was 254. In local elections boycotted by the opposition in 1990, RCD candidates won control of all but one of the councils.

16 JUDICIAL SYSTEM

The constitution provides for an independent judiciary. Magistrates are appointed by the president upon recommendation of the Supreme Council of the Magistracy; its members are drawn from the Department of Justice and the courts of appeal and cassation. In the mid-1980s there were 51 cantonal courts, 13 courts of first instance, and 3 courts of appeal. A Court of Cassation in Tunis has three civil sections and one criminal section; it acts as the ultimate court of appeal. In addition, a High Court is constituted for the sole purpose of prosecuting a member of the government accused of high treason. The Council of State is an administrative tribunal empowered to resolve conflicts between citizens and the state and public authorities; as an accounting department, it is empowered to audit and examine government records.

Civil and criminal law generally follows French-influenced practices that evolved during the period of the protectorate. Since

1956 there has been a steady reform of existing Islamic legislation, including the abolition of polygamy.

A Military Tribunal consisting of a presiding civilian judge from the Court of Cassation and four military judges hears cases involving military personnel as well as cases concerning civilians when national security is deemed to be at stake. Decisions of the Military Tribunal may be appealed to the Court of Cassation.

[17]ARMED FORCES

As of 1993, Tunisia had an army of 27,000, all but 2,000 conscripts. The navy had 4,500 men, 1 frigate and 20 patrol and coastal combatants. The air force had 3,500 personnel and 38 combat aircraft. There is obligatory 12-month military service. The national police (Public Order Brigade) has 3,500 men, and the national guard 10,000. Arms come from the US, NATO countries, and China.

[18]INTERNATIONAL COOPERATION

Admitted to UN membership on 12 November 1956, Tunisia belongs to ECA and all the nonregional specialized agencies. The nation also participates in the African Development Bank, G-77, and OAU, and is a signatory of the Law of the Sea. Tunisia joined the Arab League on 1 October 1958 but boycotted its meetings from 1958 to 1961, and again in 1966; its headquarters were transferred from Cairo to Tunis in 1979. Tunisia is a member of the Maghreb Permanent Consultative Committee.

[19]ECONOMY

Agriculture, which engages about one-third of the labor force, is still the mainstay of the Tunisian economy, although minerals (especially crude oil and phosphates) and tourism are the leading sources of foreign exchange. Industrial development has increased rapidly since the 1960s. Nevertheless, unemployment and underemployment continue to plague the economy. The GDP grew by 4.7% annually during 1961–70 and by 7.3% during 1970–81, but by only 2.9% during 1982–87. In 1986, GDP fell by 1% because of drought and lower oil prices; in 1987, it increased by an estimated 3.5%. GDP grew by 6.5% in 1990, mainly because merchandise exports increased 11%, tourism receipts provided $1 billion, and agricultural production increased by 27%. However, petroleum production fell 10%, to 4.6 million tons, and the total value of phosphate and chemical exports dipped 10%. In 1991, GDP grew 2.8% despite the 27.5% drop in tourism revenues—a secondary effect of the Persian Gulf War. The growth is almost entirely due to a 12% expansion in the agricultural sector, which saw record crops in wheat and olive oil. Recovery cmae in 1992. Tourism rebounded to about its 1990 level and, with a third year of record food harvests, economic growth accelerated to 8.1%. Economic growth in 1993 and 1994 were predicted to be around 6% because of slower investment after the record levels of 1992.

Privatization began in 1987 but proceeds slowly; only 40 small enterprises have been privatized. Recently the Ministry of Planning and Regional Development has been given the responsibility of privatization. The private sector currently accounts for 53% of output and is expected to account for 60% by 1996.

[20]INCOME

In 1992 Tunisia's GNP was $14,615 million at current prices, or $1,740 per capita. For the period 1985–92 the average inflation rate was 6.6%, resulting in a real growth rate in per capita GNP of 2.1%.

In 1992 the GDP was $15,813 million in current US dollars. It is estimated that in 1989 agriculture, hunting, forestry, and fishing contributed 11% to GDP; mining and quarrying, 8%; manufacturing, 15%; electricity, gas, and water, 2%; construction, 4%; wholesale and retail trade, 20%; transport, storage, and communication, 5%; finance, insurance, real estate, and business services, 5%; community, social, and personal services, 5%; and other sources, 25%.

[21]LABOR

The labor force was estimated at 2,500,000 in 1992, including seasonal agricultural workers. Since 1958, regional workshops to combat underemployment have provided jobs in land development, reforestation, terracing, and drainage. Full employment has been a goal of successive development plans; however, unemployment still ranges from 15% to 25% (16% in 1992), and up to 30% of male workers between the ages of 18 and 25 years of age suffer from unemployment or underemployment. The largest and most powerful trade union is the General Union of Tunisian Workers (Union Générale des Travailleurs Tunisiens—UGTT). The UGTT, which claimed about 375,000 members in 1992, belongs to the ICFTU. In 1986, the UGTT was forced to merge with the pro-government National Union of Tunisian Workers (Union Nationale des Travailleurs Tunisien—UNTT, formed in 1984), and its leadership was purged.

The Labor Code of 1966 regulates working conditions. Minimum wage rates, which vary by occupation, are fixed by two commissions, one at Tunis for northern Tunisia and one at Sfax for the south. Disputes are settled by the secretary of state for social affairs. The Agricultural Labor Code grants farmworkers bonuses based on size of harvests, skill, and seniority; limited working hours, including a six-day week; severance pay; and wage increments. For other workers there are fixed five-day workweeks of 40 and 48 hours, varying according to occupation. If the workday exceeds 10 hours, overtime rates must be paid. All workers are entitled to annual paid leave of up to 18 working days; women receive maternity leave of 4 to 6 weeks. All nonagricultural employers with over 40 workers are required to have a medical facility available. Regional labor councils seek to foster cooperation between management and labor.

[22]AGRICULTURE

Fertile land is generally limited to the north, where cereals, olives, fruits, grapes, and vegetables are produced. In the southern desert and plateau, desert farming is precarious, but barley is produced in quantity. About 2,908,000 hectares (7,185,670 acres) were arable in 1991, and 69,000 hectares (170,500 acres) were given over to permanent crops. In 1991, 232,000 hectares (573,200 acres) were irrigated and accounted for perhaps 25% of output.

Harvests have traditionally yielded sizable surpluses for export, chiefly to France. Tunisia's early growing season allows the nation to profit from exporting fresh produce to Europe before European crops ripen. Crops fluctuate greatly in size, however, depending upon the weather. In very poor years, wheat and barley must be imported to satisfy local food requirements.

Chief grain crops in 1992 were wheat, 1,584,000 tons, and barley, 570,000 tons. Olive trees number some 55 million; output in 1992 comprised 121,000 tons of olive oil. Other important commodities (with 1992 production figures, in thousands of tons) were tomatoes, 550; citrus fruits, 185; sugar beets, 291; potatoes, 218; wine, 41; dates, 82; table grapes, 113; pears, 36; and cantaloupes and other melons, 82.

The government has undertaken irrigation and soil conservation projects to improve agricultural production and raise the living standard of rural areas. The 1962–71 plan aimed at constructing 40 dams, mostly in the Medjerda River system, plus opening over 1,000 new wells, particularly in the southern regions. In the period 1962–64, the government initiated a program to help the new cooperative farm system, with a total investment of D150.5 million; remaining European-owned farms were nationalized as part of the program. In 1969, however, the development of cooperatives was halted, and appropriated land was redistributed to individual Tunisian owners. Irrigation and flood-control projects, many undertaken with foreign aid, were under way in Bizerte, the Medjerda River basin, and other locales in the early 1980s. To increase and direct the flow of capital to this sector, the government has established the Agricultural Investment Promotion Agency and the National Agricultural Development Bank.

23ANIMAL HUSBANDRY

Although animal breeding is a major occupation in the central plateau and southern region, the largest herds are in the well-watered north. In 1985 there were an estimated 6.4 million sheep, 1.3 million goats, 636,000 head of cattle, 311,000 mules and asses, 230,000 camels, and 41 million poultry.

Since 1970, a great effort has been undertaken to develop the livestock sector to meet increased demands created by Tunisia's improved standard of living and expanding tourism. Poultry farming is being encouraged to provide farmers with an additional resource and to increase protein in the local diet.

24FISHING

Commercial fishing takes place along the Mediterranean coast and in the Lake of Tunis and Lake Achkel. Small quantities of tuna, sardines, shrimp, and lobsters are exported. Except for some trawler and sponge fishing, most activity is on a limited scale; the 1991 catch was 90,710 tons. In 1992, fish and fishery products exports totaled $72.9 million, slightly less than 2% of total exports. The National Fisheries Office owns part of the trawler fleet.

25FORESTRY

Forest and wooded lands covered about 668,000 hectares (1,651,000 acres) in 1991, a large proportion of which was state owned. The oak and pine forests of the northern highlands provide cork for export (some 7,500 tons produced annually) and firewood for local use. Estimated forestry output in 1991 included wood for fuel, 3,152,000 cu m; wood-based panels, 97,000 cu m; paper and paperboard, 78,000 tons; and sawn wood, 16,000 cu m.

26MINING

Although mineral production in Tunisia is not diverse, it is still an important source of revenue. Production of crude petroleum and phosphate rock, the two most important commodities, both increased in 1991 over 1990. In the south there are extensive deposits of phosphate rock, Tunisia's chief mineral resource, aside from petroleum; known reserves of phosphate are estimated at 3.5 to 4 billion tons, (5% of world reserves) and, as of 1991, Tunisia ranked fifth in the world in phosphate production. A new phosphate mining complex at Gafsa opened in 1986. High-grade iron ores are found in the north, while deposits of lead and zinc are widely dispersed. Small quantities of fluorspar are produced and high-quality marine salt is exploited along the coast. Barite, limestone, gypsum, and silver are also mined or quarried. Uranium was discovered in 1965. In 1991, mineral production included calcium phosphate, 6,400,000 tons; iron ore, 295,000 tons; zinc concentrates, 9,353 tons; and lead concentrates, 1,285 tons. Cement production was 3,300,000 tons and marine salt, 441,000 tons. In 1991, Tunisia also produced 322,366 tons of barite, 100,000 tons of gypsum, 37,580 tons of fluorspar, and 900 kg of silver.

27ENERGY AND POWER

Exploration for oil began in 1956, following the discovery of deposits in Algeria. In 1964, oil was discovered near the southern Algerian border by the Italian National Hydrocarbon Agency; subsequent discoveries have been made on the continental shelf east of Sfax, in the Gulf of Gabes, and at other sites. Petroleum

reserves were estimated at 1,700 million barrels in 1992; total production in 1992 was reported 5,189,000 tons. In 1992, petroleum products accounted for 15% of the total export value, 5.3% of the total value of imports, and about 10% of GDP. The Tunisian government retains approximately 50% control of the oil industry. In 1992, 22 new oil wells were drilled, 7 of which were offshore.

Natural gas plant liquids production totaled 5,000 barrels per day in 1992. The largest producing area for natural gas is offshore, north of Djerba Island, with a pipeline to Sfax. Four branch pipelines connect with the Italian-Algerian trans-Mediterranean natural gas pipeline (inaugurated in 1983), supplying imported Algerian gas for Tunisian industries.

Electrical service in Tunisia was nationalized in 1958; since 1962, the government-owned Tunisian Electric and Gas Co. has controlled all power concerns. Installed capacity was 1,414 Mw in 1991; electricity production was 5,555 million kwh, with 99% of the total supplied by conventional thermal plants.

28INDUSTRY

Tunisia has a relatively diversified economy, with agricultural, mining, energy, and manufacturing production. Food industries include flour milling; fish, fruit, and vegetable canning; olive oil processing; and sugar refining. In 1991, Tunisia produced 1.8 million tons of wheat, 225,000 tons of citrus fruit, and 650,000 tons of tomatoes. The manufacturing industry is dominated by textile and leathers operations and accounted for 15.8% of GDP and 38.5% of merchandise exports in 1993. The skills of the Tunisian work force and their relatively low wages have led an increasing number of European clothing firms to subcontract their work to Tunisian factories, thereby causing a sharp increase in Tunisia's exports of clothing.

Since Tunisia is one of the world's largest sources of phosphates, mineral-processing industries are dominated by the manufacture of phosphate fertilizers, expanded by the opening in 1985 of a new complex at Gafsa, (40% owned by Kuwaiti interests). In 1990, fertilizer production included triple superphosphate, 792,000 tons, and phosphoric acid, 777,000 tons. Production of diammonium phosphate was 552,000 tons in 1990. Other manufactured goods included cement, 3.12 million tons, and iron and steel, 291,000 tons. Several plants assemble vehicles; auto production was 860 units in 1988; pick-ups, 630; trucks, 430; and tractors, 290. Handicrafts industries produce clothing, rugs, pottery, and copper and leather goods for both local and export markets.

The tourist industry is Tunisia's leading net earner of foreign exchange. The Tunisian government plans to expand existing facilities over the next decade. In 1989, 3.2 million foreign visitors came to Tunisia compared with 3.5 million in 1988. In 1990, the tourist sector provided approximately $1 billion to the Tunisian economy. By the year 2000 the government hopes to increase hotel bed capacity from 112,000 to 200,000.

29SCIENCE AND TECHNOLOGY

The Pasteur Institute, founded in 1906, conducts medical research in Tunis; that city is also home to institutes for the study of veterinary science and geology. There are research centers for agronomy, irrigation, forestry, and livestock breeding in Ariana (a suburb of Tunis), and there is a fisheries research institute at Salammbo. The University of Tunis maintains a comprehensive science program, including colleges of engineering and mathematics, physics, and natural sciences. The University of Sfax has faculties of medicine and science.

30DOMESTIC TRADE

Tunis is the principal commercial, industrial, and distribution center; most of the import and export houses, banks, and mining firms have their central offices in the city. Other commercial and distribution centers are Sfax, noted for olive oil and phosphate shipments, and Bizerte, known for grain and olive oil. Fairs are held at various times of the year in Sfax, Sousse, Tunis, and other towns. An extensive system of price controls, although reduced in the mid-1980s, governs the cost of goods and services produced by state enterprises; in addition, the government exerts pressure on private firms to show restraint in price increases. A National Subsidy Fund, used to maintain artificially low prices for basic consumer goods, is slowly being dismantled, though not without public protest.

Normal business hours in winter are from 8:30 AM to noon or 1 PM and 3 to 5:45 PM, Monday–Thursday, and from 8AM to 1 or 1:30 PM on Friday and Saturday; summer hours are 7 AM to 1 PM, six days a week. Banks are open in winter from 8 to 11 AM and 2 to 4 PM, Monday–Thursday, and 8 to 11 AM and 1 to 3 PM on Friday; summer hours, on weekdays, are 8 to 11 AM. The chief advertising media are daily newspapers, outdoor displays, and motion picture theaters. Arabic is the language of sales promotion, French the language of commercial correspondence.

31 FOREIGN TRADE

Tunisia's foreign trade is based upon the export of mineral and agricultural products, textiles, and chemicals in exchange for consumer goods, raw and processed materials, and agricultural and industrial equipment. Textiles are now the largest component of both exports and imports. By 1991 its share of exports expanded to 35% and of imports to 21%. The oil industry's share in Tunisian foreign trade dropped from a peak of 44% of the total in 1984 to only 14% in 1991. Cereals have always been an important item. Trade balances remain negative: between 1974 and 1981, exports increased threefold in current prices, but the cost of imports rose by a factor of four. In the 1980s the trade deficit continued to widen, reaching $1.2 billion in 1991 and $2 billion in 1992.

Principal exports and imports (in millions of dinars) were as follows:

	1988	1989	1990
EXPORTS			
Textilesl	614.3	812.9	1,091.3
Petroleum, gas & derivatives	330.7	555.5	531.6
Fertilizer	237.4	276.0	228.9
Chemicals	182.0	225.1	185.9
Machinery (electrical)	89.6	121.9	169.5
Olive oil	70.7	81.5	106.9
Fish	90.9	84.5	101.1
Hides & leather	48.2	66.7	87.9
Fruit	48.2	54.0	56.8
Phosphates	32.5	39.3	22.9
TOTAL, INCLUDING OTHERS	2,055.4	2,782.0	3,086.5
IMPORTS			
Textiles	552.5	713.7	935.3
Machinery	356.4	529.6	690.8
Petroleum	146.3	266.4	328.9
Electrical equipment	163.9	216.3	305.9
Vehicles	167.0	242.6	289.9
Cereals	256.1	177.6	191.9
Plastics	111.8	124.4	138.5
Pharmaceutical goods	68.8	95.1	104.9
Wood	64.8	92.2	96.1
Scientific equipment	60.7	77.0	85.2
TOTAL, INCLUDING OTHERS	3,167.0	4,163.6	4,826.4

Western Europe is the focus of Tunisia's foreign trade, with France as largest trading partner. The improvement in relations between the countries of the Arab Maghreb Union (AMU) is beginning to have an effect on Tunisian trade, with sales to Libya

on the rise in 1989. Main trading partners were as follows (% of total trade by value):

	1989	1990	1991
EXPORTS TO:			
France	24.6	26.6	24.6
Italy	18.7	21.1	19.2
Germany	12.9	15.1	19.2
Belgium	6.1	6.9	6.1
Libya	4.1	4.6	5.8
Spain	2.7	2.6	3.6
IMPORTS FROM:			
France	26.4	27.8	26.0
Italy	13.7	15.9	17.2
Germany	11.7	12.4	14.2
US	5.1	5.2	5.0
Spain	3.8	3.0	5.3
Algeria	2.3	2.0	1.2

32 BALANCE OF PAYMENTS

Since 1960, Tunisia has experienced perennial trade deficits. These have been partly covered by tourist income, by remittances from Tunisian workers abroad, and by foreign investment and assistance, but heavy balance of payments deficits were recorded between 1984 and 1986. The 8th Development Plan (1992–96) aims at improving the balance of payments deficit from 4.2% of GDP in 1991 to 2% by 1996 by encouraging freer trade, foreign direct investments, and elimination of exchange restrictions.

In 1992 merchandise exports totaled $4,033 million and imports $6,077 million. The merchandise trade balance was $–2,044 million. The following table summarizes Tunisia's balance of payments for 1991 and 1992 (in millions of US dollars):

	1991	1992
CURRENT ACCOUNT		
Goods services and income	–1,177	–1,607
Unrequited transfers	709	661
TOTALS	–468	–946
CAPITAL ACCOUNT		
Direct investment	122	374
Portfolio investment	19	46
Other long-term capital	210	203
Other short-term capital	–15	361
Reserves	55	–97
TOTALS	391	887
Errors and omissions	77	59
Total change in reserves	86	–30

33 BANKING AND SECURITIES

The Central Bank of Tunisia (Banque Centrale de Tunisie—BCT), established in September 1958, is the sole bank of issue. The BCT's reserves at the end of 1990 totaled D42.6 million. The Tunisian Banking Co. (Société Tunisienne de Banque—STB) was established in 1957; it is the leading commercial and investment bank, with 69 branches in 1987; the state holds 52% of the STB's capital. At the end of 1993, demand deposits in Tunisian commercial banks totaled D1,676 million. The total money supply in 1993, as measured by M2, was D6,870 million.

Savings institutions in 1987 included 12 deposit banks, the postal savings system, the National Savings Bank, and the National Savings Bank for Housing. Among other financial institutions were 12 commercial banking units and six international development joint-venture banks. The National Bank of Agricultural Development was founded in 1983, and there are other state development banks for the manufacturing and tourism sectors.

A stock exchange began operations in Tunis in May 1970. While its activities have been expanding steadily, they remain limited to transactions in securities issued by the state and the stocks of a few private or government-owned firms.

34INSURANCE

In 1986, there were two life, two non-life, and 10 composite insurance companies operating in Tunisia. About half were privately owned; the rest were state owned, mutual, or cooperative. Per capita premium payments totaled $24.2 or 1.5% of the GDP, in 1990. Some of the major French insurance firms have offices in Tunis. Life insurance in force in 1992 totaled D739 million.

35PUBLIC FINANCE

Each year, an administrative budget and a development budget are submitted to the National Assembly. Oil revenues and levies on imports provide the major sources of current revenue. With the fall of oil prices in 1986, public sector investment and expenditures were cut back substantially. In the late 1980s, a structural adjustment program sponsored by the World Bank and IMF focused on reducing the role of public sector. From 1987–89, the budget deficit averaged 3.5%of GDP, as compared with 5.6% during 1980–86. In 1992, the budget deficit stood at 2.6% of GDP.

The following table shows actual revenues and expenditures for 1991 and 1992 in millions of dinars.

	1991	1992
REVENUE AND GRANTS		
Tax revenue	2,874.7	3,205.5
Non-tax revenue	604.9	721.7
Capital revenue	12.0	9.2
Grants	32.5	72.0
TOTAL	3,524.1	4,028.4
EXPENDITURES & LENDING MINUS REPAYMENTS		
General public services	736.7	852.0
Defense	224.2	236.7
Public order and safety	238.4	290.3
Education	702.3	770.7
Health	254.1	290.9
Social Security and Welfare	558.3	627.2
Housing and community amenities	176.4	191.7
Recreation, cultural, and religious affairs	92.3	114.6
Economic affairs and services	980.9	989.1
Other expenditures	416.0	451.0
Adjustments	−362.5	−422.5
Lending minus repayments	3.9	−14.3
TOTAL	4,021.1	4,377.4
Deficit/Surplus	−497.0	−349.0

In 1992 Tunisia's total public debt stood at D6,400.0 million, of which D4,435.0 million was financed abroad.

36TAXATION

Personal taxes include a progressive income tax (15–35% in 1993) and a benefits tax levied on gross salaries and paid quarterly by the employer to the National Social Security Fund. Corporate income is taxed at a flat rate of 35%. Other taxes on business include a professional license tax on commercial profits; a tax on services, levied on gross turnover; taxes on the production, manufacture, and commercial presentation of goods; an income tax on transferable securities, levied on dividend distributions; and a municipal tax, levied on rent. Agricultural taxes on farm products, livestock, and fruit trees are also imposed. There is also a value-added tax that varies from 6–29%, with a standard rate of 17%.

37CUSTOMS AND DUTIES

In 1959, Tunisia withdrew from the French Customs Union and the Franco-Tunisian Economic and Financial Convention of 3 June 1955. A surviving trade convention provided for duty-free entry of Tunisian products into France; suspended in 1964, following the nationalization of French-owned farmlands, this agreement has since been restored. The maximum basic customs tariff has been reduced to 43%, with additional temporary customs duties of up to 30% from 1992 to 1994 to protect local goods during this transitional phase. These temporary duties will be lowered 10% per year and ultimately eliminated.

In 1969, Tunisia was granted associate membership in the EC. Under the accord, which was renewed in 1976 and 1983, the EC countries removed customs duties and quotas on nearly all of Tunisia's industrial exports. Tunisia is a full member of GATT.

38FOREIGN INVESTMENT

In 1972, a new investment law provided special benefits to companies manufacturing commodities for export, a regulation that stimulated some foreign involvement, particularly in the textile industry. Incentives consist of partial or total tax exemption for periods of 10–20 years, as well as exemption from customs and import duties on raw materials and equipment. A similar law to encourage investment in industries producing for local markets was enacted in 1974 and amended in 1981; the statute requires that such firms exhibit partial (in many cases majority) Tunisian ownership. A 1981 law offers incentives for investment in less-developed regions. Kuwait, Sa'udi Arabia, Qatar, the United Arab Emirates, and Algeria participate with Tunisia in development banks to channel Arab investment funds. New foreign direct investment was estimated at $147.5 million in 1987.

A new investment code, to replace the codes of 1972 and 1974, was passed in 1989, offering further tax and customs concessions to local as well as foreign investors, particularly in export-oriented enterprises. Tunisian law stil prohibits ownership of land by non-Tunisians, although a special 40-year land lease system permits agricultural development by foreign companies.

39ECONOMIC DEVELOPMENT

A 10-year plan adopted in 1962 proposed an average annual increase in the GNP of 6.5%, with a net investment of D896 million (about one-half devoted to infrastructure and one-fourth to agriculture). Total gross investment for the period 1962–71 was estimated at D1,176.8 million.

The plan for 1973–76 proposed increasing investments by 75% over the previous plan; investments were to reach D1,200 million, or about 22% of the GNP for the four-year period. An annual growth rate of 6.6% was targeted for the period. Fully 75% of the plan's investments were to be financed with international aid.

Total investment under the 1977–81 plan was projected at D4,200 million, of which manufacturing industries received the largest single allocation, D950 million. Once again, the burden of financing the program fell on external sources, with Arab funds accounting for 30% of the anticipated foreign capital. Actual growth came close to the target of 7.5% a year in real terms. The development plan for 1982–86 set forth three main goals: employment growth, regional development, and balance of payments equilibrium. Some 33% of the total expenditure of D8 billion was to be invested in labor-intensive industries. Performance fell far short of the goal of 6% a year in real growth.

The inauguration of the 1987–91 development plan followed the foreign exchange crisis of 1986, and the adoption of an IMF sponsored economic rehabilitation scheme. It called for expenditure of D10.4 billion in public spending, with another D5.3 billion from private sources and D6 billion from abroad. Services were to receive 39%, agriculture 19%, and manufacturing 16%.

Real annual growth of 4% was projected. While this target was easily reached in 1987, GDP growth dropped to 1.4 in 1988 and increased to 3.1% in 1989. The 1992–96 development plan envisaged average annual GDP growth of 6%, based on strong expansion in the manufacturing industry (8.7%) and tourism (22.3%). The plan calls for further cuts in consumer subsidies and the privatization of many state assets.

Between 1953 and 1986, gross public assistance from multilateral sources totaled over $2 billion. Aid from the US accounted for another $1.1 billion over the same period. France was the leading bilateral donor in the 1980s, providing 22% of total aid, 1980–85, and Fr855 million in 1986. Foreign donors were expected to meet Tunisia's call for $450 million in grants and loans in 1987 to alleviate its payments problems. The IMF extended two loans worth SDR218.39 million in 1986 and the IBRD granted $300 million in loans in 1986–87.

Disbursements of aid from OECD countries, Arab countries, and international agencies reached $427.4 million in 1988. Italy has replaced France as chief source of bilateral aid, as the dispute has continued between Tunisia and Paris over both the level and the type of assistance provided.

Tunisia's external debt rose steadily during the 1980s, from $3.5 billion (equivalent to 41.6% of GDP) at the end of 1980 to $6.7 billion (73.5%) in 1987, and to $9.2 billion in 1992 (these figures do not reflect debt increased by the high level of military purchases in the mid–1980s, mostly from the US). The debt service ratio (debt service to exports of goods and services) was approximately 22% in 1990. Outstanding foreign debt could rise to $10 billion in 1994, but debt servicing is likely to account for no more than 18% of exported goods and services.

40SOCIAL DEVELOPMENT

The Agricultural Labor Code of 20 April 1956 grants agricultural workers family allowances and old age pensions. During 1960–64, the government instituted a social security system to which both employers and workers contribute. It is administered by the National Social Security Fund, which provides benefits including maternity payments, family allowances, disability and life insurance, and old age insurance. Polygamy was prohibited in 1957, and Tunisian women enjoy full civil and political rights under the law. Educational and employment opportunities are growing steadily. In 1992, women constituted about 25% of the work force, including 21% of civil servants. In 1993, the Personal Status Code was liberalized to further increase women's legal rights in areas including transmission of citizenship, employment, and spousal abuse. Abortions during the first trimester are permitted. The fertility rate was 4.5 in the mid-1980s.

41HEALTH

Health conditions have shown significant improvement in recent years, although diet and sanitation remain deficient. Epidemics have virtually disappeared, and the incidence of contagious diseases has been considerably reduced. In 1990, there were 55 cases per 100,000 people of tuberculosis reported. Immunization rates for children up to one year old in 1992 were: tuberculosis (80%); diphtheria, pertussis, and tetanus (95%); polio (95%); and measles (87%).

In 1991, Tunisia had 4,482 physicians, 913 dentists, and 1,252 midwives. In 1990, there were 19,837 nurses. As of 1992, there were 53 doctors per 100,000 people, with a nurse to doctor ratio of 2.7. In the same year, there were 12 hospital beds per 1,000 people. Free health services are available to about 70% of the population, with about 90% of the population having access to health care services in 1992. Total expenditures in 1990 for health care were $614 million.

The government supports a family planning program. Tunisia's birth rate in 1993 was 27.1 per 1,000 people, and about 50% of

married women (ages 15 to 49) use contraception. There were 230,000 births in 1992. Infant mortality was 32 per 1,000 live births in 1992; maternal mortality was 70 per 100,000 live births in 1991; and general mortality was 6.4 per 1,000 people in 1993. Average life expectancy was 68 years in 1992.

42HOUSING

The natural increase of population, augmented by the migration of rural dwellers to urban areas, has caused serious housing problems. Squatter communities, called gourbvilles, have sprung up in urban regions. The rate of housing construction lags far behind the need.

The government has spent well over D1 billion on workers' housing. Since the mid-1960s, trade unions have provided new housing for members. Financial assistance to needy homeowners is provided by a national housing fund. Residential rents were frozen by the government in early 1983. As of 1984, 71% of housing units were traditional structures, or "dar," 14% were "villas" (detached homes), 9% were the squatter homes called "gourli," and 5% were apartments. In the same year, 79% of all dwellings were owner occupied, 13% were rented, and 9% were occupied rent free. Total investment in housing for 1993 was projected at D615 for approximately 40,100 units, up from D550 for 38,600 units in 1992.

43EDUCATION

On becoming independent in 1956, Tunisia inherited a small but efficient educational system based on French and, to a lesser extent, Islamic influence. In 1958, the government nationalized most of the existing facilities; remaining private institutions were subject to government regulation. In the same year the government began a comprehensive plan for educational development to achieve universal, free, compulsory primary education and a significant expansion of the secondary school system. In 1984, almost all school-age boys and 87% of eligible girls were enrolled in educational institutions; the proportions for secondary schools, however, were only 37% and 26%, respectively. Arabic is the language of instruction in early primary grades but is later replaced by French. In 1991 there were 1,426,215 students and 54,013 teachers in 3,971 primary schools; there were 589,674 pupils and 34,808 instructors in secondary institutions. The University of Tunis was founded on 31 March 1960; in 1986/87, it had 29,573 students and 4,105 full-time teachers. Tunisians studying at foreign universities numbered about 10,000 in 1985. All higher level institutions in 1991 had 76,097 students and 4,941 instructors. The 1990 adult literacy rate was 65.3%. Of this rate, men were estimated at 74.2% and women at 56.3%.

44LIBRARIES AND MUSEUMS

The National Library in Tunis has over 700,000 volumes, including collections of rare Arabic and Oriental manuscripts. Tunis also has a large central library and a smaller public library. The University of Tunis library has 220,000 volumes. The Arab League Documentation and Information Center, with 25,000 volumes, has been housed at Tunis since 1980.

The Bardo National Museum, founded in Tunis in 1888, has the largest collection of Roman mosaics in the world. Another fine collection is located at the museum in Sousse, which contains archaeological remains dating from the 6th century BC to the 6th century AD. Other museums are in Monastir, Sfax, Qairouan, Maktar, Sbeitla, Sousse, and Carthage. The National Institute of Archaeology is located in Tunis.

45MEDIA

Tunisia's well-developed postal, telephone, and telegraph system is government-operated and links all the important cities. A marine cable connects Tunisia with France, and a land cable links it with Algeria and Morocco. In 1991 there were 333,185 telephones. The government-owned Tunisian Radio-Television Broadcasting (ERTT) broadcasts in Arabic, French, and Italian over one national station, one international station, and five regional stations. There are four television channels, and a fifth was being set up in Sfax in 1993. Relay stations bring in programs from Italian television. In 1991 there were an estimated 1,640,000 radios and 650,000 television sets in use.

Government permits are required for distribution of publications. Criticism of high government officials or fundamental state institutions can result in seizure or suspension of the offending publication. The leading dailies, all published in Tunis, are shown in the following table, with 1991 circulations:

	LANGUAGE	CIRCULATION
As-Sabah	Arabic	70,000
L'Action	French	NA
Al 'Amal	Arabic	NA
Le Temps	French	42,000
La Presse	French	40,000

46ORGANIZATIONS

There are chambers of commerce in Tunis, Sfax, Sousse, and Bizerte; the Tunisian Union of Industry, Commerce, and Crafts, a national association of trade federations and business interests, is in Tunis. The National Union of Tunisian Women promotes greater participation by women in economic, political, and cultural affairs. Other large organizations are the Tunisian General Union of Students and the National Union of Tunisian Farmers.

47TOURISM, TRAVEL, AND RECREATION

Tourism is Tunisia's leading net earner of foreign exchange. Nationals of many countries may visit Tunisia for up to four months without a visa. Hotel beds numbered 123,188 in 1991, rooms numbered 61,594, and the occupancy rate was 37.6 percent. In 1991, 3,224,015 visitors went to Tunisia, 1,086,564 from Europe and 911,836 from Africa. Tourist expenditures reached $685 million that year. Tunisia's cosmopolitan capital city, the ruins of Carthage, the ancient Muslim and Jewish quarters of Jerba, and the modern coastal resorts in the vicinity of Monastir are among the main tourist attractions.

48FAMOUS TUNISIANS

Ancient Carthage was located near the site of modern Tunis. Its most famous leader was Hannibal (247–183 BC), the general who campaigned in Italy for several years (218–211 BC) but who was defeated by the Romans under Scipio Africanus at Zama in 202 BC. The dominant figure of modern Tunisia is Habib Bourguiba (Habib bin 'Ali ar-Rugaybah, b.1903); he led Tunisia to independence, formed its first government, and was president from 1957 to 1987. Mongi Slim (1908–69) served as president of the 16th session of the UN General Assembly (1961–62). Mohamed Mzali (b.1925) has served in numerous government posts, including prime minister in 1980–86. Gen. Zine el 'Abidine Ben 'Ali; (b.1936) assumed the presidency in 1987.

Tunisia's noteworthy literary figures include Albert Memmi (b.1915), the author of *The Statue of Salt* (1957), who writes in French; and Mahmoud Messadi (b.1911), who writes in Arabic. Prominent Tunisian painters are Ammar Farhat (b.1911) and Jallah bin 'Abdallah (b.1921).

49DEPENDENCIES

Tunisia has no territories or colonies.

50BIBLIOGRAPHY

Anderson, Lisa. *The State and Social Transformation in Tunisia and Libya, 1830–1980.* Princeton, N.J.: Princeton University Press, 1986.

Brown, Leon Carl. *The Tunisia of Ahmad Bey, 1837–1855.* Princeton, N.J.: Princeton University Press, 1974.

Ling, Dwight D. *Tunisia, from Protectorate to Republic.* Bloomington: Indiana University Press, 1967.

Moore, Clement H. *Tunisia since Independence: The Dynamics of One-Party Government.* Westport, Conn.: Greenwood, 1982.

Moudoud, E. *Modernization, the State, and Regional Disparity in Developing Countries: Tunisia in Historical Perspective, 1881–1982.* Boulder, Colo.: Westview Press, 1989.

Nabli, Mustapha K. and Jeffrey B. Nugent (eds.). *The New Institutional Economics and Development: Theory and Applications to Tunisia.* New York: Elsevier Science Publishing Co., 1989.

Nelson, Harold D (ed.). *Tunisia: A Country Study.* 3rd ed. Washington, D.C.: Dept. of the Army, 1988.

Perkins, Kenneth J. *Historical Dictionary of Tunisia.* Metuchen, N.J.: Scarecrow Press, 1989.

Salem, Norma. *Habib Bourguiba, Islam, and the Creation of Tunisia.* Wolfeboro, N.H.: Longwood, 1984.

Zartman, I. William (ed.). *Tunisia: The Political Economy of Reform.* Boulder, Colo.: L. Rienner, 1991.

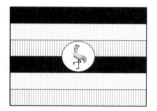

UGANDA

Republic of Uganda

CAPITAL: Kampala.

FLAG: The national flag consists of six equal horizontal stripes of black, yellow, red, black, yellow, and red (from top to bottom); at the center, within a white circle, is a crested crane, the national bird of Uganda.

ANTHEM: Begins "O Uganda! May God uphold thee."

MONETARY UNIT: The new Uganda shilling (NUSh) was introduced in May 1987 with a value equal to 100 old Uganda shillings. NUSh1 = $0.01612 (or $1 = NUSh62.03). There are coins of 1, 2, and 5 shillings, and notes of 10, 20, 50, 100, 200, 500, and 1,000 shillings.

WEIGHTS AND MEASURES: The metric system is now in use.

HOLIDAYS: New Year's Day, 1 January; Labor Day, 1 May; Martyrs' Day, 3 June; Independence Day, 9 October; Christmas Day, 25 December; Boxing Day, 26 December. Movable holidays include Good Friday, Easter Monday, 'Id al-Fitr, and 'Id al-'Adha'.

TIME: 3 PM = noon GMT.

¹LOCATION, SIZE, AND EXTENT

A landlocked country in east-central Africa, situated north and northwest of Lake Victoria, Uganda has a total area of 236,040 sq km (91,136 sq mi), of which 42,383 sq km (16,364 sq mi) is inland water or swamp. Comparatively, the area occupied by Uganda is slightly smaller than the state of Oregon. It extends 787 km (489 mi) NNE–SSW and 486 km (302 mi) ESE–WNW. Bounded on the N by Sudan, on the E by Kenya, on the S by Tanzania and Rwanda, and on the W by Zaire, Uganda has a total boundary length of 2,688 km (1,676 mi).

²TOPOGRAPHY

The greater part of Uganda consists of a plateau 800 to 2,000 m (2,600–6,600 ft) in height. Along the western border, in the Ruwenzori Mountains, Margherita Peak reaches a height of 5,109 m (16,762 ft), while on the eastern frontier Mount Elgon rises to 4,321 m (14,178 ft). By contrast, the Western Rift Valley, which runs from north to south through the western half of the country, is below 910 m (3,000 ft) on the surface of Lake Edward and Lake George and 621 m (2,036 ft) on the surface of Lake Albert (L. Mobutu Sese Seko). The White Nile has its source in Lake Victoria; as the Victoria Nile, it runs northward through Lake Kyoga and then westward to Lake Albert, from which it emerges as the Albert Nile to resume its northward course to the Sudan.

³CLIMATE

Although Uganda is on the equator, its climate is warm rather than hot, and temperatures vary little throughout the year. Most of the territory receives an annual rainfall of at least 100 cm (40 in). At Entebbe, mean annual rainfall is 162 cm (64 in); in the northeast, it is only 69 cm (27 in). Temperature generally varies by altitude; on Lake Albert, the mean annual maximum is 29°C (84°F) and the mean annual minimum 22°C (72°F). At Kabale in the southwest, 1,250 m (4,100 ft) higher, the mean annual maximum is 23°C (73°F), and the mean annual minimum 10°C (50°F). At Kampala, these extremes are 27°C (81°F) and 17°C (63°F).

⁴FLORA AND FAUNA

In the southern half of Uganda, the natural vegetation has been largely replaced by cultivated plots, in which plantain is the most prominent. There are, however, scattered patches of thick forest or of elephant grass and mvuli trees, providing excellent timber.

The cooler western highlands contain a higher proportion of long grass and forest. In the extreme southwest, however, cultivation is intensive even on the high mountain slopes. In the drier northern region, short grasses appear, and there are areas of open woodland; thorn trees and borassus palms also grow.

Elephant, hippopotamus, buffalo, cob, topi, and a number of varieties of monkeys are all plentiful, while lion, giraffe, and rhinoceros also are to be seen. At least 15 mammal species are found only in Uganda.

The birds of Uganda include the crowned crane (the national emblem), bulbul, weaver, crow, shrike, heron, egret, ibis, guinea fowl, mouse bird, lourie, hornbill, pigeon, dove, bee-eater, hoopoe, darter, lily-trotter, marabou stork, kingfisher, fish eagle, and kite.

There are relatively few varieties of fish, but the lakes and rivers contain plentiful stocks of tilapia, Nile perch, catfish, lungfish, elephant snout fish, and other species. Crocodiles, too, are found in many areas and are particularly evident along the Nile between the Kabalega (Murchison) Falls and Lake Albert. There is a wide variety of snakes, but the more dangerous varieties are rarely observed.

⁵ENVIRONMENT

Major environmental problems in Uganda include overgrazing, deforestation, and primitive agricultural methods, all of which lead to soil erosion. Attempts at controlling the propagation of tsetse flies have resulted in the use of hazardous chemicals. The nation's water supply is threatened by toxic industrial pollutants; mercury from mining activity is also found in the water supply. Uganda has 15.8 cu mi of water with 70% used for farming and 8% used for industrial activity. Roughly 40% of the nation's city dwellers and 70% of the people living in rural areas do not have pure water. Forests and woodlands were reduced by two-thirds between 1962 and 1977. By 1985, 193 square miles of forests were eliminated. Poaching of protected animals is widespread. Uganda's three national parks total over 6,300 sq km (2,400 sq mi). In 1994, 16 of the nation's mammal species and 12 of the nation's bird species were endangered, as well as 11 species of plants. Endangered species include the mountain gorilla, northern white rhinoceros, black rhinoceros, and Nile crocodile.

6 POPULATION

The most recent census in Uganda, in January 1991, registered a population of 16,671,705. In 1994, the estimated population was 20,848,480, and 23,401,000 was projected for the year 2000, assuming a crude birthrate of 48 per 1,000 population and a crude death rate of 20.6, for a net natural increase of 27.4, over 1995–2000. The annual increase is about 3%, with the growth rate about 5.3% a year in urban areas. Estimated population density in 1994 was 88 per sq km (229 per sq mi) of land. The northern, eastern, and western regions are less densely populated than the region along the north shore of Lake Victoria. At the time of the 1991 census, Kampala, the capital and largest city, had a population of 773,463. Other major cities were Jinja, 60,979; Masaka, 49,070; and Mbale, 53,634. Only 12.5% of the population lived in urban areas in 1995.

7 MIGRATION

Expulsion of Asian noncitizens was decreed by the Amin government in 1972; almost all the nation's 74,000 Asians, both citizens and noncitizens, emigrated during the Amin regime. In 1982, the government enacted the Expropriated Properties Bill, which provided for the restoration of property to Asians expelled under Amin. About 6,000 Asians had returned by 1983. At the end of 1992 there were 196,300 registered African refugees in Uganda, of which 92,100 were Sudanese, 85,800 Rwandese, and 15,600 Zairians. Perhaps another 150,000 refugees were unregistered.

After the fall of the Amin regime, as many as 240,000 people from Amin's West Nile district may have fled to Zaire and the Sudan. Many of them returned to Uganda in 1983; government campaigns against guerrillas, however, displaced thousands more, and at the end of 1986 there were an estimated 170,000 Ugandan refugees in Sudan and 23,000 in Zaire. The refugee population in Zaire remained steady, but the number in the Sudan had dropped to 3,800 by the end of 1992.

8 ETHNIC GROUPS

Uganda's ethnic groups are most broadly distinguished by language. In southern Uganda, most of the population speak Bantu languages. Sudanic speakers inhabit the northwest; Nilotic speakers, principally the Acholi and Langi, the north and the Iteso and Karamajong in the northeast. The Baganda, who populate the northern shore of Lake Victoria, constitute the largest single ethnic group in Uganda (about 17% of the total population). Other important tribal groups include the Iteso, Banyoro, Banyankole, Batoro, Basoga, Bakiga, Banyaruanda, Langi, Bagisu, and Acholi. Perhaps 6% of the population (not counting refugees) is of Rwandan descent, either Tutsi or Hutu. Most of them live in the south.

With the forced emigration of Asian noncitizens from Uganda beginning in autumn 1972, the Asian population, composed of about 74,000 persons of Indian or Pakistani origin, diminished rapidly, and it was estimated that fewer than 500 Asians remained in Uganda in 1975. Some of them returned in the 1980s, however, and in 1989 the population was estimated at about 10,000. There are also small numbers of Europeans and Arabs.

9 LANGUAGES

English is the official language. Bantu languages, particularly Luganda (the language of the Baganda), are widespread in the southern, western, and central areas. Nilotic languages are common in the north and northeast, and Central Sudanic clusters exist in the northwest. Kiswahili and Arabic are also widely spoken.

10 RELIGIONS

About 62% of the population is Christian; 41% Roman Catholic; and 22% Protestant (mostly Anglican). About 5% is Muslim. The rest practice traditional African religions, which are more common in the north and west of Uganda.

In 1969, Pope Paul VI visited Uganda and canonized 22 Roman Catholics martyred in 1884–85. More than 42 religious sects, mostly Christian, were banned by President Idi Amin Dada (a Muslim); the ban was lifted after Amin's fall in 1979. In 1993, Pope John Paul II visited Uganda as part of his 10th African tour and spoke on the problem of AIDS, which at that time afflicted almost 9% of the population.

11 TRANSPORTATION

A landlocked country, Uganda depends on links with Tanzania and Kenya for access to the sea. The main rail line runs from Tororo in the east through Jinja and Kampala to the Kilembe copper mines near Kasese. The northwest line runs from Tororo to Pakwach. Eastward from Tororo, the line crosses into Kenya and runs to the port of Mombasa. Both lines were in need of repair in 1987, and parts of the northern line were not running because of rebel activity. There is a total of 1,286 km (799 mi) of track in Uganda.

In 1991 there were 26,200 km (16,280 mi) of roads, 8% of them surfaced. There are an additional 5,849 km (3,635 mi) of gravel, crushed stone, and laterite roads; the remainder are earth roads and tracks. In 1991 there were 12,865 passenger cars and 12,933 trucks and buses in Uganda. Many were not in service due to damage, shortages of fuel and spare parts, and closing of repair and maintenance facilities.

Steamships formerly carried cargo and passengers along the country's major lakes and navigable rivers, but there is no regular service on the Nile. As of 1987, three Ugandan train ferries were plying Lake Victoria, connecting at Kisumu, Kenya, and Mwanza, Tanzania.

Uganda's international airport which serviced about 122,000 passengers in 1990, is at Entebbe.

12 HISTORY

San-like peoples were among the Uganda region's earliest inhabitants. Over the centuries, however, they were overcome by waves of migrants, beginning with the Cushitic speakers, who probably penetrated the area around 1000 BC. In the first millennium AD, Bantu-speaking peoples moved into the highland areas of East Africa, where they cultivated the banana as a food crop. After AD 100, two other migrations filtered through the area: Nilotic-speaking Sudanic people and Luo speakers.

In the region south and west of the Nile, a number of polities formed, most of them strongly centralized. North and east of the Nile, political organization tended to be decentralized. In the south, the kingdom of Bunyoro was the most powerful and extensive, but in the 18th century the neighboring kingdom of Buganda began to challenge its supremacy. The two states were engaged in a critical power struggle when the British explorers John Hanning Speke and J. A. Grant reached Buganda in 1862. They had been preceded some years earlier by Arab ivory and slave traders. Other foreigners soon followed. Sir Samuel Baker entered Uganda from the north shortly after Speke's departure. Baker described a body of water which he named Lake Albert. Baker returned to Uganda in 1872–73 as a representative of the Egyptian government, which was pursuing a policy of expansion up the Nile. The first Christian missionaries, members of the Church Missionary Society of Great Britain, came to Buganda in 1877. They were followed in 1879 by the Roman Catholic White Fathers.

The missionaries were welcomed by the kabaka (ruler) of Buganda, Mutesa I, who hoped to gain their support or the support of their countrymen against the Egyptian threat from the north. When the missionaries displayed no interest in military matters and the Egyptian danger was removed by the Mahdist rising in the Sudan in the early 1880s, Mutesa became less amenable. His son, Mwanga, who succeeded Mutesa on the latter's death in 1884, was even more hostile, fearing the influence exerted over his subjects by both the missionaries and the Arab traders. The kabaka, therefore, began to persecute the Bagandan adherents of Christianity and Islam. Both sets of converts joined forces to drive the kabaka from his country in 1888. This brief alliance soon came to an end; a few weeks later, the Christians were expelled by the Muslims. Mwanga then appealed to the Christians for help, and they finally succeeded in restoring him to power early in 1890.

In 1888, the Imperial British East African Co. was granted a charter and authorized to administer the British sphere of East Africa. The Anglo-German agreement of 1890 officially outlined imperial spheres of influence in East Africa. By that agreement, what is now Uganda and Kenya were to be considered British spheres and Tanganyika a German sphere. In 1890, Capt. F. D. Lugard was sent to Buganda to establish the company's influence there. Lugard obtained Mwanga's agreement to a treaty that placed Buganda under the company's protection. Shortly afterward, however, lack of funds compelled the company to withdraw its representatives from Buganda.

In 1894, the kingdom of Buganda became a British protectorate, which was extended in 1896 to cover Bunyoro and most of what is now Uganda. In 1897, Mwanga led a revolt against British encroachments; he was quickly defeated and deposed. His infant son, Daudi Chwa, succeeded him, and a regency was established to govern Buganda under British supervision. Under the Uganda Agreement of 1900, Buganda was ruled indirectly by the British, who in turn used the Baganda leadership as agents to extend British control indirectly throughout Uganda. The agreement confirmed the privileged position of Buganda in Uganda and of the traditional chiefs in Buganda. Subsequent treaties for indirect rule were concluded with the remaining kingdoms over a period of years.

Buganda's rebuff of British policies following World War II marked the beginning of a conflict over the place of Buganda within the future evolution of the territory. Kabaka Mutesa II was deposed in 1953 when he refused to force his chiefs to cooperate with the British. He was restored to power in 1955 under a compromise agreement.

The problem of an acceptable role for Buganda within a united Uganda remained unsettled up to the constitutional conference convened in London in October 1961. It was agreed to place Buganda in a federal relationship to the central government. It was also decided at this conference that Uganda should obtain independence on 9 October 1962. At a second constitutional conference in June 1962, Buganda agreed to scale down its demands over financial matters and ended its threats of secession from the central government. In August, a federal relationship with the kingdom of Ankole was agreed upon, with plans to use the agreement as a model for dealing with the remaining two kingdoms, Bunyoro and Toro.

On 9 October 1963, an amendment to the constitution abolished the post of governor-general and replaced it with that of president. Sir Edward Mutesa (Kabaka Mutesa II of Buganda) became Uganda's first president. In February 1966, the 1962 constitution was suspended and the prime minister, Milton Obote, assumed all powers of government. Parliament formally abrogated the 1962 constitution on 15 April 1966 and adopted a new constitution, which created the post of president and commander-in-chief; Obote was elected to fill this position on the same day.

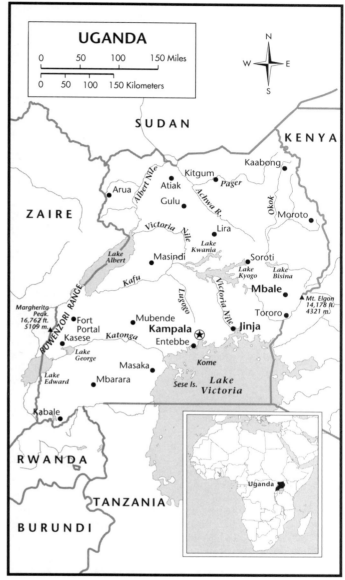

LOCATION: 4°7′N to 1°30′s; 29°33′ to 35°20′E. **BOUNDARY LENGTHS:** Sudan, 470 km (292 mi); Kenya, 850 km (528 mi); Tanzania, 418 km (260 mi); Rwanda, 169 km (105 mi); Zaire, 764 km (475 mi).

Obote declared a state of emergency in Buganda following a clash between the police and dissident Baganda protesting the new constitution. On 24 May, Ugandan troops took control of the kabaka's palace, and the kabaka fled the country.

Further constitutional changes proposed in June 1967 were adopted by Parliament sitting as a constituent assembly. The new constitution abolished the federal relationship of Buganda and the other kingdoms, making Uganda a unitary state. Uganda became a republic with an executive president, who would be concurrently head of state and of government.

In December 1969, President Obote was shot and wounded in Kampala, reportedly by supporters of the former kabaka. Parliament declared a state of emergency on 22 December 1969. Ten opposition leaders were arrested and all opposition parties were banned.

Amin Seizes Power

On 25 January 1971, while Obote was out of the country, Maj. Gen. Idi Amin led a successful military coup; Obote was received by Tanzania as a political exile. The Second Republic of Uganda was proclaimed on 17 March 1971, with Amin as president. In September 1972, Ugandans who had followed Obote into exile in Tanzania staged an abortive invasion. They were immediately overpowered, but tensions between Uganda and Tanzania remained high.

The expulsion of Asian noncitizens from Uganda in August 1972 also caused international tension, especially with the UK. Relations with the UK were further aggravated by the expulsion of numerous British nationals in 1973 and by the nationalization of UK-owned enterprises beginning in December 1972. An Israeli commando raid on Entebbe Airport on 3–4 July 1976, which freed 91 Israeli passengers and 12 crew members held captive by pro-Palestinian radicals in a hijacked aircraft, was a severe blow to the prestige of Amin, who was suspected of collusion with the hijackers (20 Ugandan troops were killed during the raid).

Under Amin, Uganda suffered a reign of terror that had claimed 50,000 to 300,000 lives by 1977, according to Amnesty International. The expulsion of the Asians took a heavy toll on the economy, especially on trade. Agricultural and industrial production also fell, and educational and health facilities suffered from the loss of skilled personnel. The collapse in 1977, essentially because of political differences, of the 10-year-old East African Community (its members were Kenya, Tanzania, and Uganda) also dealt a blow to Uganda's economy.

In late October 1978, Ugandan forces invaded Tanzanian territory, but Tanzanian forces, supported by anti-Amin rebels, struck back and by January 1979 had entered Ugandan territory. Kampala was taken on 11 April 1979, and all of Uganda was cleared of Amin's forces by the end of May; Amin fled first to Libya, which had given him military support, and later to Sa'udi Arabia. Yusuf K. Lule, an educator, formed a provisional government but was ousted on 20 June in favor of Godfrey Binaisa. On 13 May 1980, a military takeover ousted Binaisa and installed Paulo Muwanga. Parliamentary elections administered by Muwanga and other supporters of Obote, who returned from exile in Tanzania, were held on 10 December 1980. The election results, which opponents claimed were fraudulent, gave Obote's Uganda People's Congress (UPC) a clear majority, and he was sworn in as president on 15 December 1980. A period of reconstruction followed, and Tanzanian troops left in mid-1981. Security remained precarious, however. An undisciplined soldiery committed many outrages, and antigovernment guerrilla groups, especially the National Resistance Army (NRA), which was supported from abroad by Lule and Binaisa, remained active.

Obote's second term in office was marked by continued fighting between the army and guerrilla factions. As many as 100,000 or more people may have died as a result of massacres, starvation, and actions that impeded relief operations. International groups denounced the regime for human rights abuses. On 27 July 1985, Obote was overthrown in a military coup and Lt. Gen. Tito Okello, commander of the armed forces, was installed as president.

The NRA continued fighting, however, and on 26 January 1986 it occupied Kampala; three days later, NRA leader Yoweri Museveni assumed the presidency. By April the National Resistance Movement (NRM) government was in control of most of the country, but armed supporters of the Obote, Amin, and Okello regimes remained active in northern and northeastern Uganda, as well as opposition from Karamojong separatists and prophetic religious movements, most notably the Holy Spirit rebels of Alice Lakwena in 1987.

After 1990, most of the insurgency had lost strength or been militarily silenced. Except for tiny groups of bandits, rebel military action had ceased. However, Museveni resisted introducing a multiparty constitution advocating "no-party government" instead. By 1992, work on a draft constitution had progressed.

As late as August 1992, parliament formalized the ban on party politics which officials of the UPC and DP (both abolished by Museveni in 1986) rejected at a press conference. Nonetheless, parties became more active, despite the ban and police action.

In April 1993, parliament legislated the basis for nonparty elections to choose a constituent assembly which will consider the draft constitution released in December 1992 by an appointed commission. In a secret ballot election on 28 March 1994, Ugandans directly elected 214 delegates to the 288-member assembly. There are also 10 delegates appointed by the president and 56 representing interest groups. In addition, each party which contested the 1980 election will be able to send two delegates. General elections are to be held at the end of 1994. The NRM, which favors a no-party model of government, won about 150 seats in the assembly.

The government has introduced constitutional changes allowing the Baganda to restore their monarchy (purely for ceremonial purposes). Ronald Mutebi, son of the former king, was installed as Kabaka on 31 July 1993. The monarchies had been abolished in the 1967 constitution. A second king was restored and a third was rejected by government.

[13]GOVERNMENT

Following the coup of 25 January 1971, led by Maj. Gen. Amin, those provisions of the 1967 constitution dealing with the executive and legislature were suspended, and Amin ruled by decree. As commander-in-chief of the armed forces and president of the military government, he exercised virtually all power.

Following Amin's defeat, the Uganda High Court in 1980 declared a modified version of the 1967 constitution to be the law of the land. The constitution was amended in May 1985, but it was suspended with the fall of the Obote government in July, when the National Assembly was dissolved. A 270-person National Resistance Council was established in 1986 to act as the nation's legislative body pending the holding of elections. Nonpartisan elections for the NRC were held in February 1989. There are now 382 members, 216 elected and 166 appointed by the president. An appointed cabinet (including members of the banned opposition parties) advises the president. He also seeks advice from and consensus with key interest groups and institutions on important policy issues, especially from the National Resistance Army.

Throughout 1992, work progressed (after several delays) on a new draft constitution. By December, government had introduced legislation providing for the election of a nonpartisan constituent assembly that would meet in 1993. It envisioned a 180-member body with ensured representation for special interest groups (including 10 seats for the Army, 8 for women, and 4 seats for youth). Again, delays postponed that election until 28 March 1994. The current government's term expires on 25 January 1995.

[14]POLITICAL PARTIES

The Uganda People's Congress (UPC), founded in 1959, was the leading political party of the pre-Amin era. At the time of independence it formed a ruling coalition with the Kabaka Yekka (The King Only), which drew its support from the Baganda. The opposition party was the Democratic Party (DP), founded in 1953.

The marriage of convenience between the UPC and the Kabaka Yekka deteriorated, and in February 1966, Prime Minister Milton Obote, who had been the head of the UPC, suspended the constitution, deposed the president and vice-president, and began a move to power which culminated in the proclamation of the Republic of Uganda under a new constitution adopted in September 1967. The political situation under Obote continued to deteriorate, and after an attempt on his life, Obote's government banned the opposition parties and arrested 10 of their leaders. Uganda was subsequently declared a one-party state, the UPC remaining as the only legal party. After the military overthrow of the Obote government on 25 January 1971, Maj. Gen. Amin outlawed all political parties.

After the overthrow of Amin, four political parties took part in the parliamentary elections held in December 1980. The UPC was declared to have won 74 seats in the National Assembly; the DP, 51; the Uganda Patriotic Movement, 1; and the Conservative Party, 0. Some DP members later defected to the UPC. These parties, as well as Yoweri Museveni's National Resistance Movement and the Uganda Freedom Movement, were represented in the cabinet appointed in 1986. The government ordered all parties to suspend active operations, however, and mandated that elections would not be held before 1989.

By 1991, however, party activity, although banned, began to increase. Top officials of the DP and UPC were arrested in January 1992. Museveni insisted that no party activity could precede the new constitution. In August, the DP and UPC held a joint press conference to denounce parliament's formalization of the ban. The referendum scheduled for March 1994 was to remain nonpartisan. The Ugandan People's Democratic Movement (UPDM) operates from exile, even though the government signed a peace agreement with it in July 1990.

15 LOCAL GOVERNMENT

Until the adoption of the 1967 constitution, local government in Buganda was conducted on behalf of the kabaka by six ministers, advised by the lukiko (Buganda council) and by a hierarchy of chiefs. With the abolition of the federal system of government in 1967, Buganda was divided into four districts, and the kabaka's government was dissolved. The federal status of the kingdoms of Ankole, Bunyoro, and Toro was also abolished. Under that constitution, Uganda was divided into 18 districts.

In 1973, President Amin instituted a new system of provincial government establishing 10 provinces (Nile, Northern, Karamoja, Eastern, North Buganda, Busoga, South Buganda, Western, Southern, and Kampala) subdivided into 26 districts. Later Kampala became Central Province, and the number of districts increased to 33 by 1980.

Under the Museveni government established in 1986, National Resistance Movement committees were playing a leading role in local and district affairs. In early March 1992, local council elections were held nationwide. They had originally been scheduled for 1991. Political parties were not allowed to campaign, although many candidates could be identified as members of particular parties.

16 JUDICIAL SYSTEM

At the lowest level are three classes of courts presided over by magistrates. Above these are the chief magistrate's court, which hears appeals from magistrates. The High Court hears appeals and has full criminal and civil jurisdiction. It consists of a chief justice and a number of puisne justices. The three-member Court of Appeal hears appeals from the High Court. A military court system handles offenses involving military personnel. Village resistance councils (RC's) mediated disputes involving land ownership and creditor claims. These councils have at times overstepped their authority in order to hear criminal cases including murder and rape. RC decisions are appealable to magistrate's courts, but ignorance of the right to appeal and the time and cost involved make such appeals rare.

Judicial procedure is based on the British model. In practice, a large backlog of cases delays access to a speedy trial.

Although the president retains some control of appointments to the judiciary, the courts appear to engage in independent decision-making and the government normally complies with court decisions.

17 ARMED FORCES

After Amin's regime was overthrown, a Commonwealth training force was sent to reorganize the army, which proved difficult. In 1987, the National Resistance Army (NRA) was established as the national army in the wake of another civil war. Thousands of defeated guerillas were given amnesty and integrated into the NRA, swelling its ranks to as many as 70,000–100,000 men, armed with antique US, UK, and Russian weapons. The operational readiness of Ugandan tanks, APCs, artillery, AT and AD missiles, and 10 combat aircraft is doubtful. No reliable fiscal data exists for defense.

18 INTERNATIONAL COOPERATION

On 25 October 1962, Uganda became the 110th member of the UN; it is a member of ECA and all the nonregional specialized agencies except IMO. Uganda participated in the establishment of the African Development Bank and is a member of the Commonwealth of Nations, G-77, and OAU. Kampala was OAU headquarters for the 1975 summit meeting, and President Amin became OAU president for 1975/76. Uganda was a signatory to the Lomé Convention with the EC and is also a signatory of GATT and the Law of the Sea.

19 ECONOMY

Uganda's economy is agriculture based, with rural poverty a continuing problem. The mining, industrial and tourist sectors are only minor contributors to GDP. The upheavals of the 1970s and the troubles of the early 1980s left the economy in disarray. However, an economic reform process begun in 1986 has resulted in important progress. Over the past three years the government has made significant strides in liberalizing markets, although some administrative controls remain. The economic growth rate averaged about 7% in 1993. By showing its commitment to economic reform the government has gained the confidence of international lending agencies. These results point to visible improvement in the economic environment in Uganda.

20 INCOME

In 1992 Uganda's GNP was $2,949 million at current prices, or $170 per capita. For the period 1985–92 the average inflation rate was 91.1%, resulting in a real growth rate in per capita GNP of 1.8%.

In 1992 the GDP was $3,164 million in current US dollars. It is estimated that agriculture, hunting, forestry, and fishing contributed 67% to GDP; manufacturing, 4%; construction, 3%; wholesale and retail trade, 12%; transport, storage, and communication, 4%; finance, insurance, real estate, and business services, 3%; and community, social, and personal services, 7%.

21 LABOR

The vast majority of economically active Ugandans work outside the monetary economy. Agriculture engaged over 90% of the total population of 16.7 million in 1991. Manufacturing employed 62,555 persons in 1990, accounting for 2% of total employment.

Working conditions, hours of work, and paid holidays are negotiated with the unions. The Uganda Trades Union Congress was dissolved in 1973 and replaced by the National Organization of Trade Unions, which all unions are required to join. NOTU is independent of the government.

22 AGRICULTURE

Uganda's economy is predominantly agrarian; 52% of the GDP, 80% of the employed labor force, and almost all export earnings are derived from the agricultural sector. A total of 6,750,000 ha (16,679,250 acres), or one-third of the land area, was under cultivation in 1991. Subsistence production remains the pattern; 70% of the area under cultivation is used to produce locally consumed food crops. Women provide over half of agricultural labor, traditionally focusing on food rather than cash crop production. The monetary value of market crops is exceeded by the estimated value of subsistence agriculture. Plantains, cassava, sweet potatoes, and bananas are the major food crops. In 1992, food production estimates included plantains, 8 million tons; cassava, 3.7 million tons; sweet potatoes, 1.7 million tons; bananas, 570,000 tons; finger millet, 593,000 tons; corn, 595,000 tons; sorghum, 375,000 tons; beans, 402,000 tons; and potatoes, 257,000 tons.

Although coffee is still the primary export earner for Uganda, receipts in 1992 fell to $98 million, their lowest level in over a decade. From 1990 to 1992, coffee exports averaged 72% of total exports annually. Production of robusta, which was cultivated by the Baganda before the arrival of the Arabs and British, and some Arabica varieties of coffee provides the most important single source of income for more than 1 million Ugandan farmers and is the principal earner of foreign exchange. Export crop production reached a peak in 1969. Estimated production of major cash crops in 1992 included coffee, 180,000 tons; cotton (lint), 11,000 tons; tea, 9,000 tons; raw sugar, 49,000 tons; and tobacco, 6,000 tons.

23ANIMAL HUSBANDRY

Uganda had an estimated 5,100,000 head of cattle, 3,350,000 goats, 1,980,000 sheep, and 880,000 hogs in 1992, as well as about 20 million chickens. An estimated 536,000 cattle, 1,173,000 goats, and 792,000 sheep were slaughtered in 1992; meat production was an estimated 193,000 tons. The tsetse fly, which infests about 30% of Uganda, limits livestock production, and cattle rustling remains a problem. The livestock sector had been disrupted by armed rebels, but the United Nations, the European Community, Denmark, and several international development banks are contributing to its revitalization.

24FISHING

Many persons find employment in fishing and the marketing of fish, and many fishermen sell their catch to the main distribution centers. Most fish are caught from dugouts or hand-propelled canoes. Lake Victoria and Lake Kyoga are the major commercial fishing areas. In 1991, the total catch was estimated at 254,900 tons. The fishing industry has benefited from a large ice-making plant at Soroti.

25FORESTRY

Forests covered 5,510,000 ha (13,615,000 acres) in 1991. About half of the forested area is savanna woodland. In 1991, production of roundwood was estimated at 15.7 million cu m. About 87% is used for fuel.

26MINING

Uganda is not richly endowed with minerals. Extraction of copper was the only large-scale mining operation; after reaching a high of about 18,000 tons in 1964, production was halted in 1980. In 1991, a pilot study was begun by the Ugandan and French governments and Barclays Metals Ltd. of the United Kingdom to process the Kilembe Mine tailings for cobalt, using a natural strain of bacteria to separate the cobalt metal from the mine tailings. Small quantities of wolfram, tin, tungsten, and phosphates are also mined. Limestone is quarried for use in cement, and salt is obtained by evaporation of lakes and brine wells.

27ENERGY AND POWER

Hydroelectric facilities are ample, permitting export of energy to neighboring countries. In the early 1990s, hydroelectric potential was estimated at nearly 200,000 kw. The almost exclusive source of power is the Owen Falls Hydroelectric Scheme along the Victoria Nile, northwest of Jinja, which has an installed capacity of 162,000 kw. A total of 783 million kwh (almost all hydroelectric) was generated in 1991, compared with the 1971 peak of 816 million kwh; 112 million kwh were exported to Kenya. As of 1992, only 3–5% of the population was estimated to have access to electricity. Fuel wood and charcoal supply 95% of required energy.

28INDUSTRY

Production of most industrial products declined in 1973, largely because of the expulsion of skilled Asian personnel. A precipitous decline followed, with output in 1985 little more than a third of the postindependence peak levels of 1970–72. Average capacity utilization was probably under 30% in 1992. Among the industries affected were cotton, coffee, tea, sugar, tobacco, edible oils, dairy products, grain milling, brewing, vehicle assembly, textiles, steel, metal products, cement, soap, shoes, animal feed, fertilizers, paint, and matches.

Though this sector has been slow to recover, there are areas of promising activity. The textile industry suffers from a lack of skilled labor but is being encouraged by funds from the European Community and the Arab Development Bank. General Motors is assembling vehicles in Uganda, and Lonrho has returned to manage its previously owned brewery, to build an oil pipeline, and to join in agricultural marketing efforts. Coca-Cola, Pepsi, and Schweppes are producing soft drinks. A new tannery will make Uganda self-sufficient in leather products. Batteries, canned foods, pharmaceuticals, and salt are among the other products being produced in Uganda's industrial sector.

29SCIENCE AND TECHNOLOGY

Uganda has a medical association, a child malnutrition unit, and agriculture and forestry research stations in Kampala. An animal health center and the Geological Survey and Mines Department are in Entebbe. Makerere University has faculties of science, agriculture and forestry, technology, medicine, and veterinary science. Uganda Polytechnic Kyambogo has 1,000 students. Mbarara University of Science and Technology has a faculty of medicine.

30DOMESTIC TRADE

Kampala is Uganda's main commercial center, but many concerns have their head or regional offices in Nairobi, Kenya. Business hours are from 8 or 8:15 AM to 12:30 PM and from 2 to 5 PM. Shops close on Sundays. Banking hours are 8:30 AM to 12:30 PM, Monday–Friday.

31FOREIGN TRADE

Coffee has often provided Uganda with a favorable balance of trade. Since 1987, however, with the exception of 1991, the trade balance has been negative. In recent years, coffee has been by far the most important export (91.2% of total exports in 1990) and the principal earner of foreign exchange. Principal exports include coffee, cotton, and corn. Principal imports include capital and intermediate goods; food, beverages, and tobacco; and vehicles.

In 1989, Uganda's leading export partner was the Netherlands (16.2%), followed closely by the United States (15.8%), France (13.2%), and the United Kingdom. Imports came primarily from Kenya (31.4%), the United Kingdom (20.1%), and Germany (15.1%). In 1986–87, countertrade agreements worth at least $80.7 million were negotiated with Cuba, Libya, Egypt, and other countries.

32BALANCE OF PAYMENTS

Uganda had a favorable balance of payments in the 1930s and throughout the postwar years—an unusual feature in an underdeveloped country. The favorable balance with the rest of the world, however, was diminished by deficits in trade with Kenya and Tanzania following independence. Under the second five-year plan (1966–71), Uganda's payments position declined, and during the 1970s, years of deficit outnumbered those of surplus; moreover, the deficits were larger than the surpluses. Normally a trade surplus offsets substantial capital and services deficits, but poor trade performances and mounting debt service led to a loss of reserves in the 1980s. From 1986 to 1990, merchandise exports fell by 56% (due largely to plummeting coffee prices), while merchandise imports increased by 30%, so that the trade deficit widened rapidly from $69 million to $440 million in just a few years. In 1992 Uganda's merchandise imports amounted to about $500 million, more than three times the value of its exports. This trade imbalance yields a current account deficit equivalent to 5% of GDP.

In 1992 merchandise exports totaled $151.2 million and imports $421.9 million. The merchandise trade balance was $-270.7 million.

33BANKING AND SECURITIES

The Bank of Uganda was established on 16 May 1966 as the bank of issue, undertaking the function previously served by the East African Currency Board in Nairobi. In July 1965, the Uganda Commercial Bank Act replaced the Uganda Credit and Savings Bank Ordinance of 1950. The newly created government-owned Uganda Commercial Bank assumed all assets and liabilities of the Uganda Credit and Savings Bank. The Bank provided a full commercial banking service, complementary to and in competition with the existing commercial banks in the country. In 1987, it had 57 branches.

As of 1992 there were nine other commercial banks in Uganda, six of them foreign. The Uganda Development Bank is a government bank that channels long-term loans from foreign sources to Ugandan businesses. The East African Development Bank, the last remnant of the defunct East African Community, obtains funds from abroad for Kenya, Tanzania, and Uganda.

34INSURANCE

As of 1987, the government-owned National Insurance Corp. of Uganda, the Uganda American Insurance Co. Ltd., and the East Africa General Insurance Co. Ltd. were doing business in Uganda.

35PUBLIC FINANCE

The fiscal year runs from 1 July to 30 June. The main sources of government revenue are the export duties on coffee and cotton, import duties, income and profit taxes, excise taxes, and sales taxes. Deficits are chronic. The IMF, World Bank and other donors have bolstered public revenues since 1987. Decreased revenues in 1992 caused the deficit to rise sharply. As a result, the government borrowed heavily from the central bank, thus exacerbating inflation. Outstanding debt (including arrears) amounted to $2.7 billion in mid-1992.

36TAXATION

Individual income is taxed progressively at rates ranging from 10% to 50%, and corporate income is taxed at 40%. Social security taxes are paid by both employers (10% of gross wages) and employees (5%).

37CUSTOMS AND DUTIES

All foreign importers must be registered with the Ministry of Commerce, and all imports and exports require licenses. As a party to the Lomé Convention, Uganda benefits from EC tariff preferences for its goods. Import duties are levied ad valorem at 12 different rates.

38FOREIGN INVESTMENT

A 1982 law provided for restoration of expropriated property to Asians who return and for compensation to those who do not; a number of large Asian-owned enterprises have resumed operations as joint ventures in which the government holds 51% ownership. The United Kingdom group Mitchell Cotts also regained its nationalized property by participating in a similar joint venture. Further measures were taken in 1991 to recompense Asian Ugandans, and a new investment code designed to protect foreigners was issued in 1990.

39ECONOMIC DEVELOPMENT

Uganda's economic development policy for the 1990s was outlined in the Economic Recovery Program for 1988–92. State investment was lowered by 42% from the previous plan and the export sector was to be revived, particularly the nontraditional export sector. The investment budget was divided among the transport and communications sector (27%), social infrastructure (25.7%), agriculture (23.8%), and the industry and tourism sector (17.2%).

40SOCIAL DEVELOPMENT

Responsibility for social welfare rests primarily with the Ministry of Culture and Community Development, but voluntary agencies play an ancillary role. The Ministry sponsors community development self-help projects, which are intended to involve the population in development schemes and to raise the standard of living.

Women are accorded equal rights, but tradition limits their exercise of them. It is estimated that women who survive their childbearing years bear an average of seven children. Abortion is legal on broad health grounds.

There was little regard for human rights under the Amin regime. Amnesty International estimated the number of Ugandans killed between 1971 and 1977 at 50,000 to 300,000. During 1980–85, the UPC government engaged in mass arrests of suspected guerrillas, and there were reports of killings and torture by government security forces.

41HEALTH

Although medical treatment in government hospitals and dispensaries is free, facilities deteriorated greatly under Amin's rule, and following the 1978–79 war of liberation, many hospitals were left without medicine or beds. Venereal disease continues to be a problem in the adult population, and AIDS became a severe problem in the 1980s, with an estimated 800,000 Ugandans HIV-positive in 1989. Containment of other serious diseases, such as cholera, dysentery, tuberculosis, malaria, schistosomiasis, sleeping sickness, typhus, and leprosy, is made difficult by poor sanitation and unclean water. The most serious obstacle to health has arisen from nutritional deficiencies, particularly among children.

In 1990, there were 300 cases of tuberculosis per 100,000 people. Immunization rates for 1992 for children up to one year old were high: tuberculosis (98%); diphtheria, pertussis, and tetanus (72%); polio (72%); and measles (70%).

In 1992, there were 4 physicians and 8 hospital beds per 100,000 inhabitants. In 1990, the total health care expenditures were $95 million, with an estimated 61% of the population having access to health care services in 1992.

In 1993, Uganda was planning the following health care projects: rehabilitation of buildings, equipment, fittings, and services; institutional support and training; designs for 5 district hospitals and 10 rural centers; and a mental health rehabilitation study. The country also plans to focus on health care awareness and education—in particular, family planning and AIDS.

42HOUSING

Most of the inhabitants live in thatched huts with mud and wattle walls, but styles of building vary from group to group. Even in rural areas, however, corrugated iron is used extensively as a roofing material. In urban centers, sun-baked mud bricks, concrete blocks, and even fired bricks were encouraged by the government, which was responsible for a number of housing schemes prior to the Amin era. In that period, housing was neglected, and there was considerable damage to the nation's housing stock during the 1978–79 war. The National Housing and Construction Corp., a government agency founded in 1964, builds residential housing. According to the latest available information for 1980–88, the total number of housing units was 3,100,000 with 5.1 people per dwelling.

43EDUCATION

The school system generally comprises a seven-year primary course, a four-year junior secondary course, and a two-year senior secondary course for those who qualify. Those who do not choose to attend secondary schools may attend technical schools. The government hopes to ensure at least four years of education for every child who wishes to go to school, and in the more densely populated areas this has already been achieved, but in the 1980s, following the war, many primary students were attending schools without windows, chairs, books, or writing materials. Many of the senior schools are boarding establishments, and bursaries are available from local authorities and various groups for qualified candidates unable to pay the fees. Primary schools are financed from central government grants, local government funds, and fees from pupils. All senior secondary schools, technical schools, and training colleges receive direct grants-in-aid; in addition, secondary school fees are collected by the headmasters.

In 1988 there were 7,905 primary schools. At the primary level there were 2,632,764 pupils and 75,561 teachers in 1988, and at the secondary level, 260,069 pupils and 15,437 teachers. During the same year, enrollment in teacher-training schools was 13,179 and there were 6,556 students in the various technical and vocational institutions.

Makerere College, the University College of East Africa (founded 1921), became Makerere University in 1970. Situated on the outskirts of Kampala, it prepares students for degrees in the arts, sciences, and agriculture and for advanced diplomas in medicine, education, engineering, law, and veterinary science. In 1990 there were 15,578 pupils and 1,555 teachers in all higher level institutions. In 1990, the adult literacy rate was 48.3% (males: 62.2% and females: 34.9%).

44LIBRARIES AND MUSEUMS

Makerere University has the largest and most comprehensive library in East Africa. It consists of a central library with over 400,000 volumes, which functions as the National Reference Library, and the Albert Cook Library of Medicine with over 22,000 volumes, which functions as the National Library of Medicine. The university also has specialized libraries in the fields of technology, education, social sciences, and farm management. The Public Libraries Board, founded in 1964, administers the Uganda Library Service, with 20 branches and 110,000 volumes.

The Uganda Museum, founded in 1908 on the outskirts of Kampala, contains an excellent anthropological collection. The museum conducts a regular education service in collaboration with the Uganda Society. It has a fine collection of East African musical instruments and a growing collection of archaeological specimens. The Zoological Museum at Makerere University has a collection of rock fossils, birds, and mammals indigenous to Uganda, and the university's geology department has natural history collections. Entebbe has botanical gardens, a zoo, an aquarium, and a game and fisheries museum. There are also two fine arts museums in Kampala, regional folk museums at Kabale, Mbarara, and Soroti, a variety of agricultural and forestry collections, and three national park museums.

45MEDIA

Radio Uganda, founded in 1954, controls radio broadcasting in the country, while television is in the hands of the Uganda Television Service; both operate as part of the Ministry of Information and Broadcasting. Radio Uganda broadcasts daily in 22 languages, including English, French, Swahili, and local languages; television programs are in English, Swahili, and Luganda. In 1991 there were about 1,975,000 radios and about 187,000 television sets. In the same year, there were 61,046 telephones.

The government-operated *New Vision*, with a 1991 circulation of 30,000 is published in English in Kampala. Other dailies, all published in Kampala (with 1991 circulation figures), are *The Star*(13,000*)*, *Munno*(14,000*)*, *Ngabo*(15,000*)*, and *Taifa Empya*(4,000*)*. Weeklies in Kampala include the *Equator, The Economy, Mulengera, Taifa Uganda,* and *Weekly Topic.*

46ORGANIZATIONS

The Uganda Society is the oldest and most prominent cultural organization. There is also a National Chamber of Commerce and Industry and an employers' federation. The cooperative movement is extensive.

47TOURISM, TRAVEL, AND RECREATION

Tourism facilities are adequate in Kampala but limited in other areas. There were 4,567 hotel beds in 1991, with a 32% occupancy rate, and tourism receipts totaled US$15 million. In 1991, 69,000 tourists visited Uganda, down from 85,000 in 1971. Wildlife is the major tourist attraction. Tourists require a passport, visa, and yellow fever inoculation.

48FAMOUS UGANDANS

Kabaka Mutesa I (r.1856–84) contributed to Uganda's modern development. Sir Apollo Kagwa, chief minister (1890–1926) to Kabaka Mwanga and his successor, Kabaka Daudi Chwa, was one of the dominant figures in Uganda's history. Mukama Kabarega of Bunyoro (r.1896–99) led his people against British and Buganda forces until captured and exiled in 1899; he died in exile in 1923. Apollo Milton Obote (b.1924), founder of the UPC and prime minister from 1962 to 1966, overthrew the first president, Sir Edward Frederick Mutesa (Kabaka Mutesa II of Buganda, 1924–69), and was himself president of Uganda from 1966 to 1971 and from 1980 to 1985. Maj. Gen. Idi Amin Dada (b.1925) overthrew Obote in 1971 and led a military government until he was ousted in 1979 by Tanzanian forces and Ugandan rebels. Yoweri Museveni (b.1944), leader of the National Resistance Movement, became president in 1986.

49DEPENDENCIES

Uganda has no territories or colonies.

50BIBLIOGRAPHY

Byrnes, Rita M. (ed.). *Uganda: A Country Study.* 2d ed. Washington, D.C.: Library of Congress, 1992.

Hansen, Holger Bernt and Michael Twaddle (eds.). *Uganda Now: Between Decay & Development.* Athens: Ohio University Press, 1988.

Kaberuka, Will. *The Political Economy of Uganda, 1890–1979: A Case Study of Colonialism and Underdevelopment.* New York: Vantage Press, 1990.

Mutibwa, Phares Mukasa. *Uganda since Independence: A Story of Unfulfilled Hopes.* London: Hurst & Co., 1992.

Omara-Otunnu, Amii. *Politics and the Military in Uganda, 1890–1985.* New York: St. Martin's, 1987.

Smith, George I. *The Ghosts of Kampala: The Rise and Fall of Idi Amin.* New York: St. Martin's, 1980.

Twaddle, Michael. *Kakungulu & the Creation of Uganda, 1868–1928.* Athens, OH: Ohio University Press, 1993.

UNITED KINGDOM
AFRICAN DEPENDENCIES

BRITISH INDIAN OCEAN TERRITORY

In November 1965, the UK created a new colony, the British Indian Ocean Territory, from three island groups (Aldabra, Farquhar, and Des Roches) and the Chagos Archipelago (formerly a dependency of Mauritius). Aldabra, Farquhar, and Des Roches became part of independent Seychelles in 1976.

The chief island of the Chagos Archipelago is Diego Garcia, on which the US maintains a naval base under an agreement with the British. The expressed intent of the US to expand its naval base in order to strengthen the US military presence in the Indian Ocean and thereby secure the oil routes from the Persian Gulf was a sensitive international question in the late 1970s and early 1980s.

The Chagos Archipelago is located at 6°s and 72°E and covers a total area of 54,400 sq km (21,000 sq mi), although the land area is only 60 sq km (23 sq mi). Diego Garcia is both the largest island (44 sq km/17 sq mi) and the most southerly, lying nearly 1,770 km (1,100 mi) east of Mahé, the main island of the Seychelles; it is also the only populated island in the territory. The average temperature on Diego Garcia is 27°c (81°F); annual rainfall ranges from 230 to 255 cm (90–100 in).

France took possession of the Chagos Archipelago during the 18th century but ceded it to the UK in 1814. It was administered as a dependency of Mauritius until 1965. Initially the archipelago was exploited for copra by slave laborers from Mauritius; after emancipation in the 19th century, they became contract employees. Some of them, now known as Ilois, stayed on and became permanent residents. The UK bought the copra plantations from the private owners in 1967 and decided to close them down; some 1,200 Ilois were removed to Mauritius during 1967–73. In 1982, after prolonged negotiation, the UK granted £4 million to the Ilois on Mauritius, whose government agreed to provide land worth £1 million for their permanent resettlement.

In 1980, the government of Mauritius demanded that Diego Garcia revert to its control, arguing that the UK had violated an understanding allegedly given in 1967 that the island would not be used as a military base. The UK government denied giving any such assurance.

ST. HELENA

St. Helena, a British colony 122 sq km (47 sq mi) in area, is a mountainous island in the South Atlantic Ocean at approximately 16°s and 5°45′w, about 1,930 km (1,200 mi) from the west coast of Africa. The maximum elevation, at Diana's Peak, is 828 m (2,717 ft). Southeast trade winds give the island a pleasant climate, despite its tropical location. The temperature at Jamestown, the capital, on the north coast, ranges from 18° to 29°c (65–85°F); inland, as the elevation rises, temperatures are somewhat cooler. Rainfall ranges to an annual maximum of about 100 cm (40 in). The population, of mixed origin, was estimated at 6,193 in 1986. The language is English, and the majority of people are Anglicans. There are 10 Anglican churches, 4 Baptist chapels, a Roman Catholic church, and a Seventh-Day Adventist church.

Jamestown has open anchorages but no port facilities. The St. Helena Shipping Co. provides passenger and cargo service from the UK and South Africa. There is no airport. St. Helena has 105

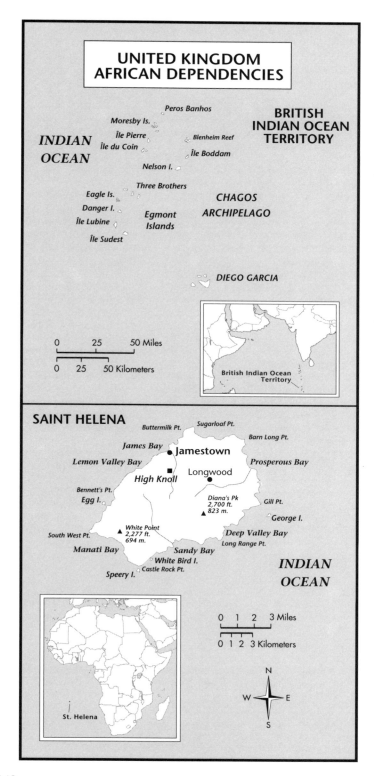

km (65 mi) of all-weather roads, 87 km (54 mi) of which have been bituminized.

Uninhabited when first sighted by the Portuguese navigator João da Nova Castella in 1502, and claimed by the Dutch in 1633, the island was garrisoned in 1659 by the British East India Company, captured by the Dutch in 1673, and retaken that same year by the English. It became famous as the place of Napoleon's exile, from 1815 until his death in 1821, and passed to the crown in 1834.

The island is administered by a governor, with the aid of a Legislative Council that includes, in addition to the governor, 2 ex-officio and 12 elected members. General elections were held in 1968, 1972, 1976, 1980, and 1984. Council committees, a majority of whose members belong to the Legislative Council, are appointed by the governor and charged with executive powers and general supervision of government departments. The Supreme Court of St. Helena, headed by a chief justice, has full criminal and civil jurisdiction. Trial is by a jury of eight. Other judicial institutions include a magistrate's court, a small claims court, and a juvenile court.

St. Helena coins of 1, 2, 5, 10, and 50 pence and 1 pound and notes of 5 and 10 pounds are legal tender; their value is on a par with their UK equivalents.

The domestic economy is based on agriculture. The main crops are potatoes, sweet potatoes, corn, and vegetables. There are no exploitable minerals, and virtually all timber is imported. St. Helena also imports all of its consumer and capital goods. The UK and South Africa are St. Helena's best customers and suppliers. Imports came to US$2.4 million in 1992; exports (fish) were US$23,900.

The colony's revenues in the early 1990s were US$3.2 million. Expenditures in the early 1990s totaled US$2.9 million. Domestic revenues include succession and death duties, an entertainment tax, a head tax, taxes on motor vehicles and on shops, and personal income and company taxes. The graduated personal income tax rate ranges from 10% to 30%. The company tax was 25% of net distributable profits.

There is an unemployment relief system, and workers' compensation is paid for death or disablement. The sole labor union, the St. Helena General Workers' Union, had about 472 members in 1992; approximately two-thirds of the labor force works for the government. Health facilities include a hospital of 54 beds as well as six clinics and a mental hospital.

The population is entirely literate. Education is free and compulsory between the ages of 5 and 15. There are 8 primary schools and one high school. A free public library is located in Jamestown, and there are branch libraries in several rural districts. Longwood House, Napoleon's home in exile, is now French property and a museum. The colony had 550 telephones in 1992. Cable and Wireless Ltd. provides telegraph communications between St. Helena, Cape Town, and Ascension Island. Radio receivers in use numbered about 1,500 in 1992. The government maintains a broadcasting station, a weekly newspaper, and monthly film shows in each district.

Dependencies of St. Helena are Tristan da Cunha and Ascension, which are inhabited, and Gough Island, the three Nightingale Islands, and Inaccessible Island, which are not. Tristan da Cunha, at 37°15′s and 12°30′w, approximately 2,400 km (1,500 mi) ssw of St. Helena, is a partly wooded volcanic island, with an area of 98 sq km (38 sq mi), reaching a maximum elevation of 2,060 m (6,760 ft). Annual rainfall averages 168 cm (66 in) on the coast. The population numbers around 300, nearly all of whom traced their ancestry to members of an English garrison sent to the island in 1816. Communications are limited to a few calls by ships each year and to a wireless station in daily contact with Cape Town. There is also a local broadcasting and radiotelephone service. A closed-circuit television system was introduced in 1983.

A South African rock lobster (crayfish) company operates a fish-freezing factory on the island. This facility replaced a cannery that was destroyed by a volcanic eruption in October 1961 which forced the inhabitants to evacuate the island. They were resettled near Southampton, England, in January 1962. Owing to their previous isolation, however, the islanders were particularly vulnerable to respiratory diseases, and many of them became ill because of the English climate. In March 1963, an advance group returned to Tristan da Cunha to repair some of the damaged property and to plant potatoes, the staple subsistence crop; the remaining islanders returned by the end of the year.

An island council consists of an administrator (who also serves as a magistrate), three appointed members, and eight elected members. Considerable revenue is derived from the sale of stamps; however, the fishing industry provides the chief source of livelihood. Development aid ended in 1980, and since then the island has financed its own projects.

Ascension, at 7°56′s and 14°25′w, about 1,131 km (703 mi) NW of St. Helena, is a bleak volcanic island with an area of 88 sq km (34 sq mi). The island's highest peak, Green Mountain, is 859 m (2,817 ft) above sea level. Ascension became a dependency of St. Helena in 1922 and is an important telecommunications station. In 1942, during World War II, the US established an air base on the island. A US National Aeronautics and Space Administration (NASA) tracking station and a British Broadcasting Corp. (BBC) relay station were established in 1966. British forces used the island in 1982 as a staging area for the recovery of the Falkland Islands from Argentine occupation, and a new Royal Air Force camp was completed in 1984. The population of Ascension, excluding British military personnel, totals around 1,000.

Sea turtles come to the island between December and May to lay their eggs. Wild goats and partridges abound. Ascension is the breeding ground of the sooty tern, the "wide-awake bird."

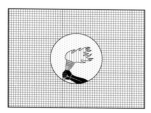

ZAIRE

Republic of Zaire
République du Zaïre

CAPITAL: Kinshasa.

FLAG: The flag adopted on 27 October 1971 is green with a yellow circle in the center; inside the circle is a forearm and hand clasping a red lighted torch.

ANTHEM: *Song of Independence.*

MONETARY UNIT: The zaire (z), a paper currency introduced in 1967, is divided into 100 makuta (singular: likuta); 1 likuta is divided into 100 sengi. There are coins of 10 sengi and 1, 5, 10, and 20 makuta, and notes of 5, 10, 50, 100, 500, 1,000, 2,000, 5,000, 10,000, 50,000, 100,000, 200,000, 500,000, 1,000,000, and 5,000,000 zaires. z1 = $0.0077 (or $1 = z129.68).

WEIGHTS AND MEASURES: The metric system is the legal standard.

HOLIDAYS: New Year's Day, 1 January; Commemoration of Martyrs of Independence, 4 January; Labor Day, 1 May; Anniversary of the Popular Movement of the Revolution, 20 May; Promulgation of the 1967 Constitution, 24 June; Independence Day, 30 June; Parents' Day, 1 August; Youth Day and Birthday of President Mobutu, 14 October; Anniversary of Zaire, 27 October; Army Day, 17 November; the Anniversary of the Regime, 24 November; and Christmas Day, 25 December.

TIME: In Kinshasa, 1 PM = noon GMT; in Lubumbashi, 2 PM = noon GMT.

¹LOCATION, SIZE, AND EXTENT

Zaire (formerly the Democratic Republic of the Congo) is situated in central Africa, and is crossed by the equator in its north-central region. It is the third-largest country on the continent, covering an area of 2,345,410 sq km (905,568 sq mi), with a length of 2,276 km (1,414 mi) SSE–NNW and a width of 2,236 km (1,389 mi) ENE–WSW. Comparatively, the area occupied by Zaire is slightly more than one-quarter the size of the US. On the N it is bounded by the Central African Republic, on the NE by Sudan, on the E by Uganda, Rwanda, Burundi, and Tanzania, on the SE and S by Zambia, on the SW by Angola, and on the W by the Cabinda enclave of Angola and the Congo, with a total boundary length of 10,308 km (6,405 mi). Its extreme western portion is a narrow wedge terminating in a strip of coastline along the Atlantic Ocean. Zaire and Zambia dispute the border to the east of Lake Mweru. Zaire's capital city, Kinshasa, is located in the western part of the country.

²TOPOGRAPHY

The principal river is the Zaire (formerly Congo), which flows 4,398 km (2,733 mi) from its headwaters to its estuary. The gigantic semicircular bend in the river, which is called the Lualaba in its upper course, delineates a central depression known as the cuvette, with an average altitude of about 400 m (1,300 ft). Around this densely forested section, which covers nearly half the area of the country, plateaus rise gradually to heights of 900–1,000 m (2,950–3,280 ft) to the north and south. The highest altitudes are found along the eastern fringe of the country, on the edge of the Great Rift Valley, where dislocation of the strata has produced important volcanic and mountain masses, the most notable of which is Margherita Peak, on the border with Uganda, rising to 5,109 m (16,762 ft), third highest in Africa.

Savanna and park forest vegetation predominate north and south of the equatorial forest belt; the southern savanna belt is far more extensive than the northern one. All major rivers are tributaries of the Zaire; these include the Lomami, the Aruwimi or Ituri, the Ubangi, the Uélé, the Kasai, the Sankuru, the Lulua, the Kwango, and the Kwilu. The largest lakes include Tanganyika, Albert (L. Mobutu Sese Seko), Edward, Kivu, and Mweru, all of which form parts of the eastern border. Other large lakes are Mai-Ndombe and Tumba.

³CLIMATE

The climate is tropically hot and humid in the lower western and central regions, with frequent heavy rains from October or November through May south of the equator and from April to November in the north, while along the equator itself there is only one season. In the cuvette, temperatures average 24°C (75°F), with high humidity and almost no seasonal variation. Annual rainfall is between 130 cm and 200 cm (51–79 in). In the northern and southern plateaus there are wet and dry seasons, with temperatures slightly cooler in the latter and annual rainfall of 100–160 cm (39–63 in). The eastern highlands have temperatures averaging 18°C (64°F) and 24°C (75°F), depending on the season. Rainfall averages 120–180 cm (47–71 in).

⁴FLORA AND FAUNA

The flora and fauna of Zaire include some 95% of all the varieties found in Africa. Among the many species of trees are the red cedar, mahogany, oak, walnut, the silk-cotton tree, and various palms. Orchids, lilies, lobelias, and gladioli are some of the flowers found, along with shrubs and plants of the euphorbia and landolphia families. Larger species of mammals include the lion, elephant, buffalo, rhinoceros, zebra, leopard, cheetah, gorilla, chimpanzee, wild boar, giraffe, okapi, and wild hog. The baboon and many kinds of monkeys are common, as are the jackal, hyena, civet, porcupine, squirrel, rabbit, and rat. Hippopotamuses and crocodiles are found in the rivers. Large snakes include the python, puff adder, and tree cobra. Lizards and chameleons are among the numerous small reptiles.

Birds are mainly of species common to much of Africa. They include the eagle, vulture, owl, goose, duck, parrot, whidah and other weaver birds, pigeon, sunbird, cuckoo, and swift, along with the crane, heron, stork, pelican, and cormorant. The rivers and lakes have many kinds of fish, among them catfish, tigerfish, and electric eels. Insects include various dragonflies, bees, wasps, beetles, mosquitoes, and the tsetse fly, as well as scorpions, spiders, centipedes, ants, and termites.

5ENVIRONMENT

In 1986 there were 9 national parks, and the total protected area covered 8,827,000 ha (21,812,000 acres). Deforestation is caused by increased farming activity and the nation's dependency on wood for fuel. By 1985, 1,429 square miles of forestland had been lost. There were four Natural World Heritage Sites and 3 biosphere reserves in 1986. The main environmental problem is poor water and sanitation systems, which result in the spread of insect- and rodent-borne diseases. The water pollution problem is caused by untreated sewage, along with industrial chemicals and mining by-products. The nation has 244.5 cu mi of water with 17% used for farming activities and 25% used for industrial purposes. Roughly one-third of the nation's city dwellers and 76% of the people living in rural areas do not have pure water. In 1994, 31 of Zaire's mammal species and 27 of its bird species are endangered as well as 3 types of plants. Endangered species in Zaire include the Marunga sunbird and the northern white and northern square-lipped rhinoceros.

6POPULATION

According to census figures, the population in 1984 was 29,916,800. A US Census Bureau estimate put the population at 41,691,200 in mid-1994. A population of 50,970,000 was projected for the year 2000, assuming a crude birthrate of 44.7 per 1,000 population, a crude death rate of 14.1, and a net natural increase of 33.6 during 1995–2000. Density, on the basis of the 1994 estimate, was 17.8 persons per sq km (46 per sq mi). The annual rate of increase in the early 1990s was 3.2%. About 48% of the population is under 15 years of age. Kinshasa, the capital, had an estimated population of 3,455,000 in 1990. Other large cities are Lubumbashi; Mbuji-Mayi; Kolwezi; Kananga; and Kisangani. The population was about 29% urban in 1995.

7MIGRATION

Political tensions and crises in neighboring African countries have resulted in large-scale migration to Zaire. Many refugees were resettled in Zaire through the aid of outside governments, private relief organizations, the UN, and UN-related agencies. At the end of 1992 there were 391,100 UNHCR-registered refugees in Zaire, including 198,000 from Angola, 21,100 from Uganda, 50,900 from Rwanda, and 9,500 from Burundi.

After a general amnesty for refugees and political exiles in 1978, some 200,000 Zairians were repatriated from Angola, Zambia, Sudan, Tanzania, and Europe. There were 60,200 officially registered Zairians living in neighboring countries at the end of 1992, including 25,800 in Burundi, 16,000 in Tanzania, 15,600 in Uganda, and 2,300 in Sudan.

8ETHNIC GROUPS

Bantu-speaking peoples form about 80% of the population. Most of the rest are Sudanic-speaking groups in the north and northeast. In the cuvette are found about 80,000–100,000 Pygmies. Among the Bantu-speaking peoples, no one group forms more than 10% of the population. The major groups are the Kongo, or Bakongo, in Lower Zaire; the Luba, or Baluba, in East Kasai and Shaba; the Mongo and related groups in the cuvette area; the Lunda and Chokwe in Bandundu and West Kasai; the Bemba and Hemba in Shaba; and the Kwango and Kasai in Bandundu. Non-

Africans include Belgians, Greeks, Lebanese, and Asian Indians; they may have numbered 200,000 in the early 1990s.

9LANGUAGES

As many as 700 languages and dialects are spoken in Zaire. Serving as regional linguae francae are four African languages: Lingala is used in the north from Kisangani to Kinshasa, as well as in the armed forces, and is being deliberately promoted by the present administration; Swahili, in the Kingwana dialect, is used in the east; Kikongo in Lower Zaire; and Tshiluba in the south-central area. In addition, Lomongo is widely spoken in the cuvette. French is the official language and is widely used in government and commerce.

10RELIGIONS

Roman Catholic and Protestant missions have long been active in the country, and in 1990, it was estimated that 50.6% of the population was Roman Catholic. About 28% was Protestant in 1989. Officially recognized denominations are the Roman Catholic Church; the Church of Christ in Zaire, which purports to encompass all Protestant denominations; and the Kimbangist Church, which claims to be the largest independent African church on the continent. There is a Muslim minority in the northeast, numbering approximately 450,000. The rest adhere mostly to traditional African beliefs.

During the 1970s, the regime of President Mobutu moved to curb the influence of the Roman Catholic Church. All church-affiliated schools and voluntary associations were either disbanded or taken over by the state. The power of the Church was further eroded in 1974 with the cancellation of religious holidays, and as of January 1975, religious instruction in primary and secondary schools was abolished. As of the mid-1980s, however, the Roman Catholic Church, along with the smaller churches, remained independent of government apparatus.

11TRANSPORTATION

Inland waterways—rivers and lakes—are the main channels of transportation. No single railroad runs the full length of the country, and paved highways are few and short. Lack of adequate transportation is a major problem affecting the development of Zaire's vast area. While the rivers, particularly the Zaire and its tributaries, are mostly navigable, they are blocked at various points from through navigation by cataracts and waterfalls, making it necessary to move goods by rail or road between the navigable sections. Principal river ports are Kinshasa, Ilebo, Mbandaka, Kisangani, Kalemie, Ubundu, and Kindu. A total of 16,037 km (9,965 mi) of river and lake waterways are in service. The chief seaport and only deepwater port is Matadi on the Zaire River, 148 km (92 mi) from the Atlantic Ocean. Boma and Banana, also on the Zaire below Matadi, are the only other seaports. The Zaire Maritime Co. is the national shipping line. Zaire had one merchant vessel at the end of 1991, totaling 13,000 GRT.

In 1985 there was about 146,500 km (91,000 mi) of roads, but most of this was mere track; of 49,000 km (30,400 mi) of true road, only 2,800 km (1,740 mi) was bitumenized. One of the major routes was from Kinshasa to Lubumbashi. The road network was in a state of deterioration in the mid-1980s. Motor vehicles in 1991 included 100,000 passenger cars and 90,000 commercial vehicles.

There were 5,254 km (3,265 mi) of railway in 1991. Among the most important internal links are Lubumbashi–Ilebo, Kingala–Kindu, Ubundu–Kisangani, and Kinshasa–Matadi. In the early 1980s, the Kinshasa–Matadi line was being extended by a Japanese company. A road and rail bridge across the Zaire River at Matadi was completed in 1983. The southeastern network connects with the Angolan and Zambian railroad systems. In

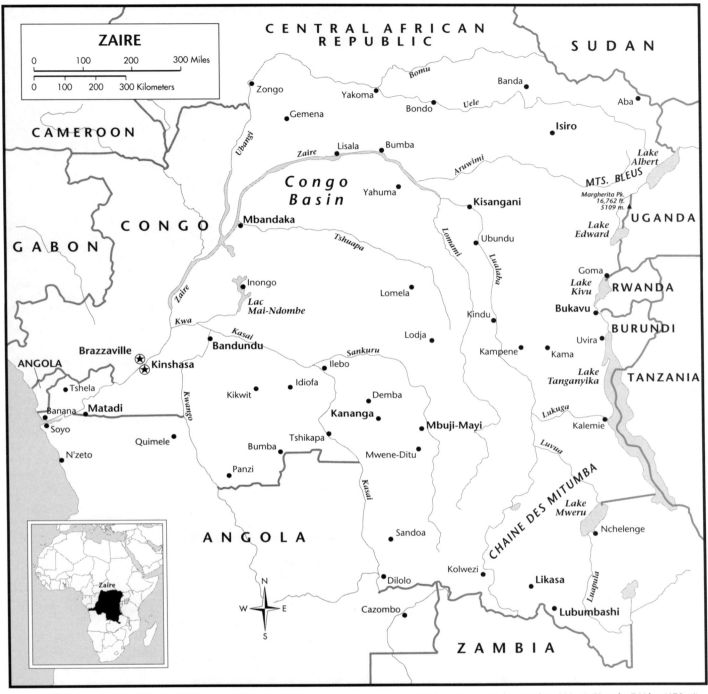

ZAIRE

| 0 | 100 | 200 | 300 Miles |
| 0 | 100 | 200 | 300 Kilometers |

LOCATION: 5°28′N to 13°27′S; 12°12′ to 31°18′E. **BOUNDARY LENGTHS:** Central African Republic, 1,577 km (980 mi); Sudan, 628 km (390 mi); Uganda, 764 km (475 mi); Rwanda, 217 km (135 mi); Burundi, 233 km (145 mi); Tanzania, 459 km (285 mi); Zambia, 2,107 km (1,309 mi); Angola, 2,285 km (1,420 mi); Atlantic coastline, 40 km (25 mi); Cabinda, 225 km (140 mi); Congo, 1,625 km (1,010 mi). **TERRITORIAL SEA LIMIT:** 12 mi.

1974, all railroads were consolidated under a single state-controlled corporation, SNCZ.

Air transport has become an important factor in the country's economy. Zaire has five international airports—N'Djili (Kinshasa), Luano (Lubumbashi), and airports at Bukavu, Goma, and Kisangani—which can accommodate long-distance jet aircraft. There are numerous other airfields and landing strips. The national airline, Air Zaïre, was organized in 1961 and has flights to European and African cities, as well as within the country. Zaïre Aéro Service and Scibe Airlift Cargo Zaire also offer domestic and international flights. Civil aviation performed 240 million passenger-km and 29 million freight ton-km of service in 1992.

¹²HISTORY

The earliest inhabitants of the area now called Zaire are believed to have been Pygmy tribes who lived by hunting and gathering food and using stone tools. Bantu-speaking peoples entered from the west by AD 150, while non-Bantu-speakers penetrated what is now northern Zaire from the north. These peoples brought with them agriculture and developed iron tools. In 1482, the Portuguese navigator Diogo Cão visited the mouth of the Zaire (Congo) River, marking the first known European contact with the region, but this did not lead to penetration of the interior. The Portuguese confined their relations to the Kongo kingdom, which ruled the area near the mouth of the Zaire River as well as what is now the coast of northern Angola. A lucrative slave trade developed.

In the 16th century, the powerful Luba state developed in what is now Shaba Province; soon afterward, a Lunda state was established in what is now south-central Zaire. In 1789, a Portuguese explorer, José Lacerdu e Almeida, explored the cuvette and penetrated as far as Shaba, where he learned of the rich copper mines. A thriving Arab trade in slaves and ivory reached the Luba country from the east in the late 1850s or early 1860s.

The Scottish explorer David Livingstone reached the upper course of the Zaire in 1871, when his whereabouts became unknown and Welsh-American explorer Henry M. Stanley, commisioned by a US newspaper, located and rescued him (in modern Tanzania). In 1876–77, after the death of Livingstone, Stanley followed the river from the point that Livingstone had reached to its mouth. King Leopold II of Belgium commissioned Stanley to undertake further explorations and to make treaties with the tribal chiefs. In 1878, the monarch formed the International Association of the Congo, a development company, with himself as the chief stockholder. The Berlin Conference of 1884–85 recognized the Independent State of the Congo, set up by Leopold under his personal rule, and its ultimate boundaries were established by treaties with other colonial powers.

International criticism and investigation of the treatment of the inhabitants, particularly on the rubber plantations, resulted in 1908 in the end of personal rule; the territory was transferred to Belgium as a colony called the Belgian Congo, and in that year a law known as the Colonial Charter set up its basic structure of government.

The rise of nationalism in the various African territories following World War II seemed to have bypassed the colony, which remained without self-government (except for a few large cities) until 1959. Then Congolese demanded independence and rioted, first in Léopoldville (now Kinshasa) and then in other parts of the colony. Following the first outbreaks, the Belgian government outlined a program for the gradual attainment of self-rule in the colony, but as the independence movement persisted and grew, Belgium agreed to grant the Congo its independence in mid-1960 and to assist in the training of Congolese administrators, as well as to continue economic and other aid after independence.

The newly independent Republic of the Congo was inaugurated on 30 June 1960, with Joseph Kasavubu as its first head of state and Patrice Lumumba its first premier. It was immediately confronted by massive economic, political, and social problems. A week after independence the armed forces mutinied, and separatist movements and intertribal conflict threatened to split the country. Following the mutiny and the ousting of its European officers, the Congolese National Army became an undisciplined and uncertain force, with groups of solidiers supporting various political and military leaders.

A major blow to the new republic was the secession of mineral-rich Katanga (now Shaba) Province, announced on 11 July 1960 by Moïse Tshombe, head of the provincial government. The central government was hamstrung by the loss of revenues from its richest province and by the departure of Belgian civil servants, doctors, teachers, and technicians. After some assaults on Belgian nationals, Belgium sent paratroopers into the Congo, which appealed to the UN for help. Faced with the threatened collapse of a new nation, the UN responded with what grew into a program of massive assistance—financial, military, administrative, and technical. It established the UN Operation for the Congo

(UNOC), sent in a UN military force (made up of contingents volunteered by nonmajor powers), and furnished considerable numbers of experts in administration, teachers, doctors, and other skilled personnel.

In September 1960, Kasavubu dismissed Lumumba as premier, and Lumumba announced that he had dismissed Kasavubu as head of state. The parliament subsequently rescinded both dismissals. Kasavubu then dismissed the parliament and with Col. Joseph-Désiré Mobutu, the army's newly appointed chief of staff, succeeded in taking Lumumba prisoner. UN troops did not interfere. As demands for Lumumba's release mounted, Lumumba was secretly handed over to the Katanga authorities, who had him put to death early in 1961. Shortly afterward, the UN Security Council for the first time authorized UN forces in the Congo to use force if necessary, as a "last resort," to prevent civil war from occurring.

In September 1961, after Katanga forces fired on UN troops seeking to secure the removal of foreign mercenaries, UN Secretary-General Dag Hammarskjöld flew to the Congo, where he boarded a plane for Northern Rhodesia (now Zambia) to meet with Tshombe. The plane crashed, killing him and all others on board. In December 1962, Katanga forces in Elisabethville (now Lubumbashi) opened sustained fire on UN troops. The UN troops then began broad-scale military operations to disarm the Katanga forces throughout the province. As they neared the completion of their task, Tshombe capitulated, and the secession of Katanga was ended on 14 January 1963.

Almost immediately, a new insurrection, in the form of a series of rebellions, broke out. The rebels at one point exercised de facto control over more than half the country. As UN troops were withdrawn on 30 June 1964, the self-exiled Tshombe was recalled and offered the position of prime minister, largely at US and Belgian instigation. Tshombe promptly recruited several hundred white mercenaries to spearhead the demoralized national army. Rebel-held Stanleyville (now Kisangani) was recaptured in November 1964, when a US-airlifted contingent of Belgian paratroopers disarmed the insurgents. Widespread government reprisals against the population followed. By then, the rebellion had been contained.

Mobutu Assumes Power

Tshombe's attempt to establish a nationwide political base was successful in parliamentary elections held in early 1965, but on 13 October 1965 he was removed from office by Kasavubu, who attempted to replace him with Evariste Kimba, also from Katanga. When Kimba was not endorsed by the parliament, Gen. Mobutu, commander-in-chief of the Congolese National Army, seized power in a coup d'état on 24 November 1965 and assumed the presidency.

A new constitution adopted in June 1967 instituted a centralized presidential form of government, coupled with the creation of a new political movement, the Popular Movement of the Revolution (Mouvement Populaire de la Révolution—MPR). Tshombe's hopes for a comeback were dashed when he was kidnapped in June 1967 and imprisoned in Algeria, where he died two years later. His supporters, led by French and Belgian mercenaries, mutinied again in July 1967 but were finally defeated in November, in part because of logistical support of Mobutu extended by the US government. Other sources of opposition were summarily dealt with in 1968 with the disbanding of independent labor and student organizations.

The country was officially transformed into a one-party state in 1970. In 1971, the name of the country was changed from Congo to Zaire. (This name, an inaccurate rendition of the Kikongo word for "river," had been given by 16th-century Portuguese navigators to the river that later came to be known as the Congo.) This turned out to be the first step in a campaign of national "authenticity," which led not only to the Africanization of all European toponyms (a process that had already been applied to major cities in 1966) but also to the banning of Christian names (Mobutu himself changed his name to Mobutu Sese Seko).

Mobutu was elected without opposition to a new seven-year term as president in 1977, but he continued to face opposition, both external and internal. Former Katangan gendarmes, who had earlier fled to Angola, invaded Shaba Province on 8 March 1977. Mobutu, charging that Cuba and the former USSR were behind the invasion, enlisted the aid of 1,500 Moroccan troops. The incursion was quelled by late May. In May 1978, however, the rebels again invaded Shaba and occupied Kolwezi, a key mining center. French paratroopers retook Kolwezi on 19 May and were later joined by Belgian troops, but several hundred foreigners and Zairians were killed during the eight-day rebel occupation. Troops from Morocco, Gabon, and Senegal replaced the French and Belgians in June; Zairian troops later reoccupied the region.

In 1981, Premier Nguza Karl-I-Bond resigned and became spokesman for an opposition group based in Belgium; however, he returned to Zaire in 1985 and was appointed ambassador to the US in 1986. In June 1982, thirteen former parliament members were jailed allegedly for trying to organize an opposition party. They were released in 1983, as part of an announced amnesty for political detainees and exiles, but 6 of the 13 were sent into internal exile in 1986.

In 1982, Mobutu resumed diplomatic ties with Israel, which had been broken in 1974; five Arab nations quickly cut ties with Zaire, and $350 million in promised Arab aid to Zaire was blocked. In 1983, Zaire sent 2,700 troops to Chad to aid the government against Libyan-backed rebels; they were withdrawn in 1984. Mobutu was reelected "unopposed" to a new seven-year presidential term in July 1984. In 1986 and 1987 there were reports that the US was using an airbase in Zaire to supply weapons to the antigovernment guerrillas in neighboring Angola; Mobutu denied these charges and affirmed his support of the Angolan government.

For their support of western positions through the Cold War, Zaire, and in particular Mobutu, were handsomely rewarded. Western aid and investment and state seizures of private property have made some individuals extraordinarily wealthy. Mobutu allegedly is now the wealthiest person in Africa, with a fortune estimated at $5 billion, most of which is safely outside Zaire. However, widely publicized human rights violations in the late 1980s have put Mobutu on the defensive. He lobbies the US Congress vigorously, conducts public relations campaigns in Europe and North America and, until the collapse of his authority in the 1990s, managed to gain support from abroad. French and Belgian troops intervened in the Kinshasa unrest of 1990.

To head off critics, Mobutu promised to create a multiparty Third Republic. But, in fact, he raised the level of repression. He originally hoped to create two new parties, both of which reflected his own political philosophy and were to join with his own MPR. Those opposed to Mobutu rejected this scheme. But the opposition was divided into a score of parties. With the army in disarray and disorder growing, Mobutu was forced to call a National Conference of some 2,800 delegates in September 1991 to draft a new constitution. Some 130 opposition parties joined together as the Sacred Union. Mobutu on several occasions suspended the Conference, but it continued to meet. It often failed to arrive at a consensus. When it did, Mobutu thwarted its decisions. As Zaire became paralyzed by this power struggle, the social and economic infrastructure disintegrated. Mobutu himself abandoned his presidential palace for the security of his yacht on the Congo River.

In November 1991, Mobutu split the Sacred Union by naming Nguza Karl-I-Bond of the Union of Federalists and Independent Republicans (UFERI) as prime minister. Nguza closed the National Conference in February 1992. Pressure from inside and from western aid donors forced Mobutu to allow the Conference to resume in April. It sought to draft a new constitution and threatened to rename Zaire "Congo." On 14 August 1992, the Sacred Union got the Conference to elect Etienne Tshisekedi of the Union for Democracy and Social Progress (UDPS) as prime minister of a transitional government. Mobutu, who countered by forming a new government under his control and dismissing Tshisekedi in December 1992, controlled the army, the central bank, and the police. Continuing the struggle for control of the state, the Conference drafted a constitution and set a referendum date for April 1993, but it was never held. In March, Mobutu called a conclave of political leaders and named Faustin Birindwa as prime minister. The High Council of the Republic, the interim legislature, continued to recognize Tshisekedi as did Zaire's principal economic partners abroad. Mobutu was able to incite ethnic violence through "ethnic cleansing policies," thereby dividing his opponents and then using his armed forces to quell the violence.

Two parallel governments attempt to rule Zaire. One controls the country's wealth and the media, the other has a popular following and professed support from western governments. In September 1993, there was a minor breakthrough. Thanks to UN mediation, the rival powers agreed on a draft constitution for the Third Republic. The two legislatures were to combine into a single, 700-person assembly. New presidential and parliamentary elections were promised. However in January 1994, Mobutu dissolved both governments and a joint sitting of the two legislatures, (the HCR-Parliament of Transition). It met on January 19 and appointed the Roman Catholic archbishop of Kisangani as its president. Tshisekedi organized a successful, one-day strike in Kinshasa.

In 1993, Mobutu's Bank of Zaire introduced new currency on three occasions, but it soon became worthless. Merchants would not accept it and riots broke out when soldiers could not spend their pay. French and Belgian troops were deployed in Kinshasa to help restore order as foreigners fled. Public employees also went on strike because of the economic conditions. Anarchy, corruption, uncontrolled violence and poverty now prevail. Government authority has dissolved, leaving the country to pillaging soldiers and roaming gangs. The situation has led one journalist to call Zaire "a stateless country." Shaba province has declared its autonomy. AIDS is rife. The struggle of two rival claimants to power continues though neither can mount much overt support, yet the stalemate continues.

13GOVERNMENT

A basic law (loi fondamentale) was adopted in early 1960, before independence, pending the adoption of a permanent constitution by a constituent assembly. It provided for a division of executive powers between the head of state (president) and the head of government (premier). The premier and a cabinet known as the Council of Ministers were both responsible to the bicameral legislature on all matters of policy. This document was replaced by a constitution adopted in 1964 and modeled closely on the 1958 constitution of the French Fifth Republic. Under its terms, the president determined and directed the policy of the state and had the power to appoint and dismiss the prime minister. The powers of the parliament were sharply reduced. After his takeover in November 1965, Gen. Mobutu initially adhered to the 1964 constitution, but in October 1966 he combined the office of prime minister with the presidency. In June 1967, a new constitution was promulgated. It provided for a highly centralized form of presidential government and virtually eliminated the autonomy that provincial authorities had previously exercised.

The constitution was further amended on 23 December 1970, when the MPR was proclaimed the sole party of the republic.

MPR primacy over all other national institutions, which resulted from the 1970 establishment of a single-party system, was affirmed in constitutions promulgated in 1974 and 1978. Instead of directly electing the president of the republic, voters confirmed the choice made by the MPR for its chairman, who automatically became the head of state and head of the government. The president's leading role in national affairs was further institutionalized by constitutional provisions that made him the formal head of the Political Bureau, of the Party Congress, and of the National Executive and National Legislative councils.

Organs of the MPR included the 80-member Central Committee, created in 1980 as the policy-making center for both party and government; the 16-member Political Bureau; the Party Congress, which was supposed to meet every five years; the National Executive Council (or cabinet); and the National Legislative Council, a unicameral body with 310 members. The Legislative Council was elected by universal suffrage from MPR-approved candidates. In practice, however, most government functions were directly controlled by President Mobutu through his personal entourage and through numerous aides and advisers. The constitution was last amended in April 1990 to permit the formation of alternative parties.

Starting in 1990, this autocratic structure began to unravel. Mobutu is now challenged by a rival government and he is unable to secure compliance with his decrees. In September 1993, the transitional Tshisekedi government elected by the National Conference in August 1992 and the Mobutu forces agreed on a draft constitution for the Third Republic and on an electoral process leading to a popular government in 1995. However, on 14 January 1994, Mobutu dismissed both governments and rival parliaments, a move that had little effect on the nation. Zaire has, as it has since 1992, two ineffectual governments, neither of which is capable of carrying out policy.

A rival legislature, the 435-member High Council of the Republic (HCR) was established by the National Conference in December, 1992, and a government set up by the HCR and headed by Prime Minister Tshisekedi claims to rule. Yet the army has evicted his officers from government facilities. Mobutu has repeatedly tried to remove Tshisekedi from office, but Tshisekedi refuses to recognize Mobutu's authority to do so. Mobutu has de facto control of the administration but it is unable to act effectively. As a result of this stalemate, the government has virtually collapsed.

[14]POLITICAL PARTIES

Political activity was sharply restricted during the colonial period, but several dozen political parties had sprung into existence by early 1960, most of them small and based on local or ethnic organizations.

Only one party of the more than 20 that entered the May 1960 elections emerged with an effective national organization. This was the National Congolese Movement (Mouvement National Congolais—MNC), whose leader, Patrice Lumumba, similarly emerged as the only personality with a national following. Although the MNC captured only 30% of the popular vote, it formed alliances with two regional parties and controlled 64 of the 137 seats in the House of Representatives. The national government subsequently organized in June 1960, however, won the backing of a much broader (although less cohesive) coalition which included, among others, Joseph Kasavubu's Bakongo Alliance (Alliance des Bakongo—ABAKO), the largest of the ethnic parties. Kasavubu became the country's head of state and in September 1960 ousted Lumumba from the premiership. After Tshombe's accession to the post of prime minister in 1964, national and provincial elections were scheduled. In a rather belated effort to organize national support for his policies, Tshombe persuaded some 40-odd local formations to go to the polls under the hastily improvised label of the National Congolese Convention (Convention Nationale Congolaise—CONACO). The elections, held in March–April 1965, gave CONACO 106 of the 166 seats in the lower house of the legislature. Kasavubu's subsequent dismissal of Tshombe in October 1965 and the failure of his handpicked successor, Evariste Kimba, to secure majority support in the CONACO-controlled lower house led to a complete stalemate, which was finally resolved only by Mobutu's seizure of power on 25 November 1965.

The new regime initially suspended all political parties, but in April 1967, Mobutu created the Popular Movement of the Revolution (Mouvement Populaire de la Révolution—MPR) in order to develop a political base for his regime. The constitution promulgated in June 1967 provided for the existence of "no more than two" political parties. However, all attempts to organize an opposition party to the MPR were summarily repressed, and the facade of bipartisanship was officially abandoned on 23 December 1970, when a constitutional amendment formally transformed the country into a single-party state. The chairman of the MPR automatically holds the office of head of state and head of the government after approval by the voters. Party and state are effectively one, and every citizen is automatically a member of the MPR.

Of the four exiled opposition groups headquartered in Brussels, the Union for Democracy and Social Progress (Union pour la Démocratie et du Progrès Social—UDPS) appeared to be the most significant.

The constitution was amended to permit party activity in April 1990. By the time the National Conference was called in September 1991, several parties had emerged. The most important among them combined to form a coalition known as the Sacred Union. These include the UDPS, the Union of Federalists and Independent Republicans (UFERI), the Unified Lumumbist Party (PALU) of Antoine Gizenga, and the Social Democratic Christian Party (PDSC). UFERI was later pried away from the Sacred Union by Mobutu's offer of the prime ministership to UFERI's Nguza Karl-I-Bond in November, 1991. Every one of Mobutu's prime ministers since 1991 has been lured from the upper echelons of opposition parties. Mobutu is still able to "buy off" his critics. Pro-Mobutu parties belong to the Forces Politique de Conclave (FPC).

[15]LOCAL GOVERNMENT

Since independence, the number of provinces has been as low as 6 and as high as 21, with an autonomous capital district at Kinshasa (formerly Léopoldville). In 1966, the number of provinces was cut back to 12, later to 8, and then to 10. At the same time, provincial autonomy, considerable in the republic's early years, was virtually eliminated following the adoption of a new constitution in 1967. The major divisions, now called regions, are Bas-Zaire, Bandundu, Equateur, Haut-Zaire, Nord-Kivu, Shaba (formerly Katanga), Kasai-Oriental, Maniema and Sud-Kivu, and Kasai-Occidental. These are now administered directly by regional commissioners. The regions are divided into 37 subregions (the former districts), of which 13 are major towns and their environs. These are further subdivided into 134 zones. Urban zones contain localities, while rural zones contain collectivities (chiefdoms), which in turn contain rural localities (groups of villages). Kinshasa, although autonomous, is organized like a region with subregions and zones.

Local administration was for years virtually coterminous with the local branch of the MPR. Regional, subregional, and zone commissioners are appointed by the central government and may not be natives of the units they head. There are rural and urban councils. Urban councils were elected in 1977 and 1982; rural councils were elected in 1982. But the current breakdown of government leaves the operation of local government in doubt.

16 JUDICIAL SYSTEM

The legal system is based on both Belgian and tribal law. The courts include courts of first instance, appellate courts, a Supreme Court and the Court of State Security. Many disputes are adjudicated at the local level by administrative officials or traditional authorities.

Although 1977 amendments to the Constitution and the new Constitution proposed in 1992 guarantee an independent judiciary, in practice the President and the Government have been able to influence court decisions.

The Constitution guarantees defendants the right to counsel and a public trial. Appellate review is afforded in all cases except those involving national security and serious crimes adjudicated by the Court of State Security.

17 ARMED FORCES

There was an army of 26,000 in 1993, composed of 2 divisions and 5 brigades. The navy of 1,300 had about 24 patrol craft. There was an air force of 1,800 personnel, with 28 combat aircraft. Paramilitary forces, composed of the gendarmerie, numbered about 25,000, and there was a civil guard of 10,000. Foreign Advisers from Europe and Asia, help train Zairian troops and paramilitary units. In 1988 Zaire spent $49 million on defense, probably less than 1% of GDP.

18 INTERNATIONAL COOPERATION

Zaire (then known as the Congo) was admitted to membership in the UN on 20 September 1960. It is a member of ECA and all the nonregional specialized agencies and is a signatory to GATT and the Law of the Sea. Zaire is also a member of the African Development Bank, G-77, and the OAU. It joined OCAM, the organization of Francophonic African states, in 1964, but withdrew in 1972. In 1964, it became an associated member of the EC. Zaire is a member of the International Council of Copper Exporting Countries. Zaire, Rwanda, and Burundi form the Economic Community of the Great Lakes Countries.

19 ECONOMY

Zaire has a wealth of natural resources that should provide the foundation for a stable economy. However, in September 1991 mutinous military troops looted all major urban centers bringing the economy to a virtual standstill. A large government deficit, primarily to pay salaries for the military and civil servants, was financed by printing currency. Hyperinflation, rapid devaluation, and abandonment of the formal economy ensued. As a result of the accompanying widespread uncertainty and civil disorder, most businesses that are unable to leave the country have adopted a defensive stance, minimizing their exposure in Zaire and waiting for an upturn in the economy.

When operational, Zaire's economy is mixed. The state dominates the mining and utility sectors, but private industry is dominant elsewhere. Except for petroleum products, utilities, and parts of the transportation sector, market-determined prices are the norm, and many parastatal enterprises compete with private ones. Although Zaire possesses large amounts of unused agricultural land, its urban population is dependent on imported food due to the lack of a transportation network. Foreign exchange for food and other imports is generated primarily through export of diamonds, crude petroleum, and coffee.

20 INCOME

In 1992 Zaire's GNP was $235 per capita. For the period 1985–92 the average inflation rate was 35.0%. In 1992 the GDP was $920 million in current US dollars; of that total it is estimated that mining contributed 21.1%, services 22.4%, and commerce 17.4%. Agriculture accounted for 9.5% and manufacturing 1.6%.

21 LABOR

Unemployment and underemployment have remained serious problems for Zaire. In 1991 there was an estimated labor force of 20,000,000; perhaps fewer than 20% were wage and salary workers. Agriculture employs 80% of the population, with the modern sector employing only about 400,000 persons.

On 23 June 1967, all unions were disbanded and superseded by a single state-controlled labor organization, the National Union of Congolese Workers, later renamed the National Union of Zairian Workers (Union Nationale des Travailleurs du Zaïre—UNTZA). In 1986, UNTZA had an estimated membership of more than 1 million. Since 24 April 1990, when political pluralism was permitted, the UNTZA has disaffiliated itself from the Popular Movement for the Revolution (MPR). The official workweek is six days (48 hours). Unionization stands at about 20%.

22 AGRICULTURE

The agricultural sector supports 71.5% of the labor force and accounts for 11.7% of the GDP (1988). The principal crops are cassava, yams, plantains, rice, and maize. The country is not drought-prone but is handicapped by a poor internal transportation system, which impedes the development of an effective national urban food-supply system.

In 1991, land under annual or perennial crops constituted only 3.4% of Zaire's land area. Agriculture is divided into two basic sectors: subsistence, which employs the vast majority of the work force, and commercial, which is export-oriented and conducted on plantations.

Subsistence farming involves 4 million families on plots averaging 1.6 ha (4 acres), usually a little larger in Savanna areas than in the rain forest. Subsistence farmers produce mainly manioc, corn, tubers, and sorghum. In 1992, food-crop production included manioc, 18,300,000 tons; sugarcane, 1,150,000 tons; corn, 920,000 tons; peanuts, 440,000 tons; and rice, 365,000 tons. In 1992, plantains totaled 1,830,000 tons; sweet potatoes, 380,000 tons; bananas, 405,000 tons; yams, 310,000 tons; and pineapples, 145,000 tons. Domestic food production has been insufficient to meet the country's needs, and many basic food products have had to be imported.

The production of cash crops was severely disrupted by the wave of civil disorder that engulfed the country between 1960 and 1967, and production fell again after many small foreign-owned plantations were nationalized in 1973–74. As of 1992, the production of Zaire's principal cash crops (coffee, rubber, palm oil, cocoa, tea) was mostly back in private hands. Commercial farmers number some 300,000, with holdings between 12 and 250 ha (30 and 618 acres). Coffee is Zaire's third most important export (after copper and crude oil) and is the leading agricultural export. An estimated 98,000 tons were produced in 1992 (down from 120,000 tons in 1990); 80% of production comes from the provinces of Haut Zaire, Equateur, and Kivu. Only 10% to 15% of production is arabica coffee, the vast majority being robusta; coffee exports are mostly sold to Italy, France, Belgium, and Switzerland. The collapse of the International Coffee Agreement in 1989 quickly led to a doubling of exports by Zaire, whereupon the surplus entering the world market drove down prices rapidly. Whereas 102,000 tons of coffee exported in 1990 had a value of $1,080 million, by 1992, 104,268 tons of coffee exports were only worth $609 million.

Rubber is the second most important export cash crop. The plantation crop has been slowly recovering from nationalization. Some plantations are now replanting for the first time in over 20 years. In 1992, production amounted to 11,000 tons. Palm oil production is concentrated in three large operations, two of them foreign-owned. Production in 1992 totaled 183,000 tons. Palm oil production remains profitable in Zaire due to a 100% tax on competing imported oil. The production of cotton engages about

250,000 farmers, who annually produce 22,000–26,000 tons. Domestic production, however, is not sufficient for the country's textile manufacturers. Other cash crops produced in 1992 were 4,000 tons of tobacco, 3,000 tons of tea, and 4,000 tons of cocoa.

23ANIMAL HUSBANDRY

In 1992, local meat production was an estimated 212,000 tons, but only half of the meat demand is met domestically. The number of head of cattle in 1992 was estimated at 1,650,000, found in the higher eastern regions, above the range of the tsetse fly. ONDE, a state agency, manages large ranches, mainly in Shaba and West Kasai. The number of goats in 1992 was estimated at 3,080,000; hogs totaled 840,000, and sheep 920,000.

24FISHING

Fish are the single most important source of animal protein in Zaire. Total production of marine, river, and lake fisheries in 1991 was estimated at 160,000 tons, all but 2,000 tons from inland waters. PEMARZA, a state agency, carries on marine fishing.

25FORESTRY

Forest and woodland covers over three-quarters of the total land area of Zaire. Zaire possesses vast timber resources, and commercial development of the country's 61 million ha (150 million acres) of exploitable wooded area is only beginning. For a long time, the Mayumbe area of Lower Zaire was the major center of timber exploitation, but this area is in the process of total depletion. In recent years, the far more extensive forest regions of the central cuvette and of the Ubangi River Valley have increasingly been tapped. Roundwood removals were estimated at 40,079,000 cu m in 1991, about 93% for fuel. Some 14 species are presently being harvested. Exports of forest products in 1992 totaled $23.8 million, or only 3% of total exports. Foreign capital is necessary in order for forestry to expand, and the government recognizes that changes in tax structure and export procedures will be needed to facilitate economic growth.

26MINING

Mining is by far the most important sector of the export-oriented economy. In 1991, the mining industry was damaged by the decrease in production of copper and cobalt, the two major mineral exports. Zaire is a leading producer of cobalt and the world's second largest producer of diamonds. Other minerals include zinc, tin, manganese, gold, silver, cadmium, tantalum, and tungsten. Uranium for the first US atomic bomb was mined in Zaire.

During the colonial period, mineral rights for the most part were vested in two charter companies, in which the state was a major shareholder, and in a number of railroad companies. Mining concessions were granted by the chartered companies or by the colonial government. The most important mining firms were subsidiaries of Belgian holding companies. Less than 20% of the conceded areas were actually being exploited, despite the fact that many undeveloped regions were known to hold significant deposits. In this fashion, mining companies such as the dominant Mining Union of Haut Katanga (UMHK) sought to husband their resources and to maintain stable levels of production in order to avoid a depreciation of their products and an early exhaustion of their reserves. Thus, copper production was held to around 300,000 tons a year. Ore-processing methods, meanwhile, were steadily improved, with electrolytic processing coming into widespread use by independence.

Mining was the one sector of the economy that did not suffer a marked decline during the 1960–67 period of disruption and conflict. Output of some important minerals, notably copper, remained steady or even rose.

In 1966, UMHK was stripped of all its mining concessions, which were turned over to a state-owned corporation renamed GECAMINES in 1971. GECAMINES mines copper, zinc, cobalt, silver, uranium, and cadmium. UMHK was eventually compensated for its nationalized assets, and management of the Katanga mines was contracted out by the government to the Belgian corporation SGM (controlled by the same financial interests as UMHK), which had been handling the refining and marketing of Katanga copper. In 1973, Zaire assumed control of the Belgium diamond-mining firm Mining Company of Bakwanga, and all other foreign mining concerns were instructed to sell 50% of their shares to the government. Some of the unexploited copper deposits taken over by the government have been contracted to foreign corporations operating in partnership with the government of Zaire.

Copper is produced exclusively in the Shaba Region (formerly Katanga; *shaba* means "copper" in Swahili). Output (recoverable copper content of ores and concentrates) in 1991 was 8,620,000 tons, down from 15,363,000 tons in 1988. The 33% drop in production from 1990 to 1991 was caused by a cave-in in September 1990 at GECAMINES' Kamato mine.

Until 1986, Zaire was the world's leading producer of industrial diamonds. The chief diamond-producing center is Mbuji-Mayi in East Kasai. Société Minière de Bakwanga (MIBA), 80% government owned, produced 19.0 million carats, down from 23.3 million carats in 1986; private artisanal diamond miners may be extracting up to 15 million carats annually in the Tshikapa region. MIBA sells its output to a subsidiary of the DeBeers Consolidated Mines group under contract. Diamonds from artisanal miners are purchased by buyers or are smuggled abroad—an estimated $400 million in diamonds and gold exit Zaire annually in this manner.

The output of cobalt from mined ore was reported at about 20,900 tons in 1991 (down from 42,700 tons in 1987). Zinc metal production from mined output fell from 172,000 tons in 1969 to 81,400 tons in 1991. Production of cassiterite (tin ore) was 1,635 tons in 1991, compared with 7,502 tons in 1974. Cassiterite is mined in the Shaba and Kivu regions.

Low-grade coal from Shaba came to 60,000 tons in 1991. Much of it is used by the cement plant at Kalemie. High-grade coal and coke are imported for metallurgy.

Other production figures estimated for 1991 were tantalum, 16 tons; columbium, 15 tons; silver, 80,000 kg; wolfram (tungsten), 15,000 kg; and gold, 8,800 kg. Small-scale diamond and gold mining was legalized in October 1982 in an effort to get the proceeds recorded and into the banks. Many peasants, teachers, and students left their previous pursuits to go prospecting.

Over half of Zaire's mineral exports must take a circuitous route by river and railway from Shaba to Matadi, because the Benguela railway to Angola has effectively been closed since 1975. Most of the rest goes south by rail to South Africa, which is an important source of imports.

27ENERGY AND POWER

Offshore oil production began in 1975. In 1992, eight Atlantic Ocean and Zaire River estuary oil fields were in operation, run by two consortia: one composed of Zaire Gulf Oil Co. (Chevron), Teikoku Co. (a Japanese company), and Union Oil Co.; the other composed of Petrofina and Shell Oil Co. Production in 1992 totaled 9.9 million barrels, down from 10.6 million in 1990. Proven reserves amount to 127.7 million barrels, with offshore reserves accounting for only 20%. Large quantities of methane gas have been located at Lake Kivu, which is shared with Rwanda. Oil product imports consist of gasoline, jet fuel, kerosene, aviation gas, fuel oil, and liquefied petroleum gas.

Zaire has vast resources for the development of hydroelectric power: its potential is thought to exceed 100 million kw. In fact, less than 3% of that potential has been harnessed. In 1991, installed capacity came to 2,831,000 kw, of which only 59,000 kw was thermal. Production was 6,168 million kwh, of which more than half was used for mining and metallurgy in Shaba, and 198 million kwh was exported.

The most important hydroelectric site is at Inga, on the lower Zaire River, which provides most of installed capacity. A high-voltage transmission line more than 1,700 km (1,100 mi) long, to carry some of the surplus power generated at Inga to the mining centers of the southeast, was completed in 1982. Only about 2% of the population has access to electricity.

28 INDUSTRY

Manufacturing came to only 2% of GDP in 1988, and it has been hard hit since then due to foreign exchange problems and a decline in local purchasing power due to the hyperinflation of the 1989-1993 period. Much of Zaire's industry is the processing of agricultural products (sugar, flour) and mineral-bearing ore (copper, zinc, petroleum, cement). The production of consumer goods (beer, soft drinks, textiles) plays a leading role in the sector as well.

A five-year investment in the copper smelter in Shaba was completed in 1990. However, the center was severely damaged by political unrest in 1992–93 and has virtually ceased operation. The Maluju steel mill was unprofitable and closed in 1986. The Muanda refinery has operated at 12% of capacity for a variety of technical and financial reasons.

29 SCIENCE AND TECHNOLOGY

Belgium is the chief source of Zaire's technical aid. The General Commission on Atomic Energy, conducting research in peaceful application of atomic energy, is in Kinshasa, as are the Geographic Institute of Zaire, the Institute of Tropical Medicine, the National Institute for the Study of Agronomical Research, the Institute of Nature Conservation, the Geological Service, and France's Bureau of Geological and Mineral Research. The University of Kinshasa has faculties of sciences, polytechnic, medicine, and pharmacy. The University of Kisangani has faculties of science and medicine. The University of Lubumbashi has faculties of sciences, polytechnic, and veterinary medicine. In addition, five university-level institutes offer training in information science, agronomy, and medicine.

30 DOMESTIC TRADE

In 1973, Asians and Europeans were barred from any commercial activity in five of the country's eight regions. Shortly thereafter, a deliberate policy of Zairization of the retail sector was introduced. Under these measures, expatriates were barred from a wide range of business activities, mostly in the retail and service sectors. During the 1970s and 1980s, a large parallel, or black, market also operated.

Kinshasa, connected by rail with Matadi, the main port of entry, is the principal general distribution center for mining equipment and the chief center for trade with Zambia and South Africa. Kisangani is a major distribution and marketing center for the northeast. Other commercial centers are Likasi, Kolwezi, Kananga, Mbandaka, and Matadi.

The domestic economy is in disarray due to political unrest. Merchants refused to accept the new currencies that were repeatedly issued by the Bank of Zaire in 1993, and riots ensued when soldiers were unable to spend their pay.

Usual business hours are from 7:30 AM to 12:30 PM and from 2:30 to 5 PM, Monday through Friday, and 7:30 AM to noon on Saturday. Most correspondence and advertising are in French.

31 FOREIGN TRADE

Zaire has traditionally had a favorable trade balance, albeit one highly sensitive to changes in the world market prices for copper

and cobalt, two of its principal exports. Principal exports in 1985 (in millions of US dollars) were as follows:

Copper	636.8
Crude oil	310.9
Cobalt	224.6
Diamonds	202.0
Coffee	96.6
Other exports	418.1
TOTAL	1,889.0

Principal imports in 1985 (in millions of dollars) were as follows:

Machinery and transport equipment	472.2
Food, drink, and tobacco	342.9
Mineral oils	281.1
Chemicals	74.6
Other imports	311.2
TOTAL	1,482.0

Belgium is Zaire's most important trade partner, accounting for about 32% of total exports and about 22% of total imports in 1985. European Community countries together accounted for about 61% of total trade.

32 BALANCE OF PAYMENTS

Zaire's favorable trade balance is more than offset by a large deficit in services. Substantial illegal exports, imports, and transfers of capital and profits abroad are unrecorded. In August 1991, the government permitted the zaire, the national currency, to float because the central bank had exhausted its foreign exchange reserves. By statute, the government no longer controls the import or export of capital or the foreign exchange markets.

33 BANKING AND SECURITIES

The Bank of Zaire serves as the country's central bank and bank of issue. In 1993, the commercial banks in Zaire included the Zairian Commercial Bank, the Union Banks of Zaire, Barclays Bank (Zaire), the Bank of Paris and the Low Countries, the Bank of Kinshasa, Citibank (Zaire), and Grindlays International Bank of Zaire. The only public savings banks were the People's Bank and the General Savings Fund of Zaire. There is also a state-owned National Fund of Savings and Real Estate Credit. In 1992, total money bank reserves stood at US$156.7 million; demand, time, and foreign currency deposits totaled z1,077 million. An indication of the deterioration of economic life was a strong disinclination by the public to keep money in banks. There are no securities exchanges in Zaire.

34 INSURANCE

In 1959 there were eight insurance firms, each representing many foreign companies. Workers' compensation was the only form of compulsory insurance in the territory. In 1967, all private insurance companies were abolished and replaced by the state-owned National Society of Insurance. In 1986, 40% of non-life premiums were written for automotive insurance, 32.9% for commercial transport coverage, and 21.4% for fire insurance.

35 PUBLIC FINANCE

Public finance in Zaire from the late 1970s to the mid-1980s was characterized by uncontrolled spending, poor tax collection, and large deficits, often covered by creating new money. Expenditures are almost entirely current. The state owned copper mining company typically has generated one-third of the government's revenue.

Since 1976, Zaire's external debt has been rescheduled frequently, but the nation continued to fall behind on payments. In

1981, for example, OECD members deferred $345 million of $715 million due them, and in 1982 only an estimated $250 million of the $946 million due was paid. The IMF extended a standby credit of $1.06 billion in 1981, but within a few months blocked it because conditions on which it was based, including cuts in public spending, had not been met. In late 1983, Zaire accepted an IMF austerity plan that included a currency devaluation of almost 80%, in exchange for $350 million in credits over 15 months. At the end of 1985, Zaire's debt was almost $6 billion. In May 1986, Zaire received a new standby IMF credit of $256 million, but it was blocked six months later when Mobutu placed a ceiling on debt payments. In May 1987, a new IMF loan was made, in return for tax hikes and an increase in prices for petroleum products. Most of about $600 million due to Zaire's creditors in 1986 was rescheduled. Even after debt rescheduling, the fiscal deficit grew from 0.3% of GDP in 1984–86 to 6.3% in 1988. The government's refusal to curb spending stalled the stabilization effort by 1989. Political unrest and transition in 1990 led to the abandonment of fiscal management and public sector reforms, which resulted in hyperinflation and discontinued investment. By 1992, the fiscal cash deficit was estimated at $1.3 billion, financed by monetary creation and the accumulation of both domestic and foreign arrears.

The following table shows actual revenues and expenditures for 1990 and 1991 in billions of zaires.

	1990	1991
REVENUE AND GRANTS		
Tax revenue	632	6,268
Non-tax revenue	46	786
Grants	145	1,586
TOTAL	824	8,640
EXPENDITURES & LENDING MINUS REPAYMENTS	1,260	28,985
Deficit/Surplus	−437	−20,345

In 1991 Zaire's total public debt stood at z170,377 million, of which z147,172 million was financed abroad.

36 TAXATION

In 1993, personal income was taxed progressively, with a 50% ceiling on total payable tax. The corporate tax rate was 50% of taxable profits. Profits of branches of foreign corporations were subject to the same rate of taxation. There was also an 18% sales tax on local services and a 3% to 20% tax on the wholesale price of local manufacturing. An employment tax of 33% is imposed on services by foreigners. Other taxes include an educational tax, property tax, and a transfer tax.

37 CUSTOMS AND DUTIES

Import tariffs consist of a turnover tax of up to 20% and general customs duties (15–50%). The latter include a fiscal duty (5–50% but 180% for luxury items); a 3% statistical tax; and a consumption tax that varies based on the item. Soft drinks and alcoholic beverages are subject to an excise tax ranging from 32% to 100%. Zaire is associated with the EC countries through the Lomé Convention, which provides for the reduction of tariff barriers between the signatories and EC members.

38 FOREIGN INVESTMENT

Beginning in 1966, when the Mobutu government began to assert control over the economy, foreign firms with assets and operations predominantly based in Zaire were ordered to incorporate under national law and to transfer their headquarters to Zaire. For a time, a liberal investment code enacted in 1969 encouraged private investments, which rose to z136.2 million in 1971. In 1973, however, Asians and Europeans were barred from any commercial activity in five of the country's eight regions. Shortly thereafter, a deliberate policy of Zairization of the retail sector was introduced. Under these measures, expatriates were barred from a wide range of business activities, mostly in the retail and service sectors. Foreigners affected by this policy were compelled to sell their interests to Zairian nationals, many of whom turned out to be officials of the national party. Many of the new owners had little or no business experience, and quite a few of them simply liquidated the stock and never repaid the low-interest loans extended by the government for acquisition of the businesses. More frequently, Zairization involved some form of mixed ownership, with the government usually the major shareholder but with management remaining in largely foreign hands.

Generally poor results brought new changes. The investment code of 1979, updated in 1986, provides for tax holidays of up to five years, guaranteed repatriation of capital and profits, and exoneration of sales tax and customs duties on new equipment that cannot be supplied by local industry. These concessions apply mainly to industrial concerns, and each company must negotiate benefits. New foreign direct investment in 1985 totaled $61.9 million.

39 ECONOMIC DEVELOPMENT

The announced priorities of the Mobutu government have been economic nationalism and the development of an infrastructure appropriate to an industrial economy. Infrastructural development would involve the extension of the country's hydroelectric potential, transportation network, harbor facilities, and oil-refining capability, as well as the development of basic industries such as iron and aluminum smelters and cement plants. However, many development plans have been poorly planned and mismanaged.

Development expenditures are usually made year by year and despite occasional, vaguely conceived three-year plans, little progress has been made over the years. The development horizon in Zaire appears limitless in each of its principal sectors. Since 1992, however, any semblance of economic planning and development management has evaporated. The currency is out of control, and change for the better seems unlikely until the political situation stabilizes.

40 SOCIAL DEVELOPMENT

Social security is handled by the National Social Security Institute, an autonomous public agency created in 1961 and controlled by the Labor and Social Security Department. In addition to pension funds, the institute administers compensation for accidents and illness; old age, disability, and death benefits; and family allowances.

The Department of Social Affairs administers a number of welfare agencies. One of its divisions, created in 1968, supervises the activities of the many social centers that endeavor to develop a sense of community spirit in urban and rural neighborhoods throughout the country. They also offer vocational training for unemployed youths, adult education programs, and a number of activities for women. However, the Roman Catholic Church still provides most of the nation's welfare and social programs.

Abortion is legal to save the mother's life. Only 1% of married couples practiced contraception in 1984. A married woman must obtain her husband's authorization before opening a bank account, accepting a job, obtaining a passport, or renting or selling real estate.

Even during the relatively calm years of Mobutu's unchallenged rule, there were frequent reports of arbitrary arrests, detention without charges, and extortion. President Mobutu occasionally issued general amnesties for political detainees and exiles. But since the open protests of 1990, unlawful detention, assassination, ethnic violence incited by Mobutu's political operatives, and random shootings and beatings have become commonplace. Prosecution for such activities is rare.

41 HEALTH

The departure of large numbers of European medical personnel in mid-1960 left the country's health services greatly weakened. Not a single African doctor had been graduated at the time of independence. In 1960, 90 doctors of 28 nationalities recruited by WHO were working in the country. WHO emphasis was on the training of Zairian health workers, to prepare them to run their own health services. In 1990, there were 1.6 beds per 1,000 people. Medical personnel in 1990 included 2,469 physicians, 59 pharmacists, 41 dentists, and 27,601 nurses. Most facilities are concentrated in the major cities. Total health care expenditures were $179 million in 1990. In 1992, only 26% of the population had access to health care services.

Diseases include malaria, trypanosomiasis, onchocerciasis, schistosomiasis, tuberculosis, measles, leprosy, dysentery, typhoid, and hookworm; acquired immune deficiency syndrome (AIDS) has also been recognized and, in 1987, tests indicated that 9% of babies were born with the virus. Malnutrition is a serious health problem, especially among children.

In 1990, there were 333 cases of tuberculosis reported per 100,000 people. In 1992, children up to one year old were immunized against tuberculosis (65%); diphtheria, pertussis, and tetanus (32%); polio (31%); and measles (31%). In 1991, an estimated 39% of the population had access to safe water, and only 23% had adequate sanitation.

In 1993 the birth rate was 47.5 per 1,000 people with only an estimated 1% of married women (ages 15 to 49) using contraception. Average life expectancy was 52 years. Infant mortality was 121 per 1,000 live births in 1992; maternal mortality was 800 per 100,000 live births in 1991; and general mortality was 14.6 per 1,000 people in 1993.

42 HOUSING

The massive urban influx that began after independence led to a fourfold increase in the population of Kinshasa, creating a massive housing problem that is still far from solved. Tens of thousands of squatters are crowded into squalid shantytowns on the outskirts of the capital. Other, more prosperous migrants have built themselves permanent dwellings. Unable to control the spread of unauthorized and generally substandard construction or to come up with adequate alternatives, the government tolerated what it could not prevent and began extending basic utilities to the new settlements.

Housing falls under the responsibility of the Department of Public Health and Social Affairs. Public housing and home-building loans sponsored by the National Housing Office still cover no more than a tiny fraction of the country's massive housing needs. As of 1984, 52% of housing units were traditional one-room adobe, straw, or mud structures, and 45% were modern houses of durable or semi-durable material containing one or more rooms.

43 EDUCATION

The colonial system of education became notable for its failure to provide university training for Africans, although the rate of elementary school attendance under the Belgians was one of the highest in Africa (56% in 1959). This figure was deceptive, however, since most elementary schooling was limited to the first two grades. Fewer than 10% of school-age children completed the six-year elementary cycle. Understandably, one of the chief efforts of the successive governments of Zaire has been to push as many schoolchildren as possible beyond the threshold of the two-year cycle. This effort has accounted for a massive increase in elementary-school population since 1960.

Education is compulsory between ages 6 and 12. Primary-school enrollment, which was 1,403,572 in 1958/59, rose to 4,356,516 in 1987. The percentage of girls enrolled in the primary-school system also increased. The development of secondary education has also been dramatic: the number of secondary-school students rose from 38,000 in 1960–61 to 1,066,350 in 1987. In 1990 adult illiteracy was 28.2% (males: 16.4% and females: 39.3%).

University education was virtually nonexistent in the Belgian Congo prior to the mid-1950s. Up to that time, only a handful of Africans had been permitted to enroll in Belgian universities. Teacher-training institutions, religious seminaries, and advanced technical training in medicine, agronomy, and public administration were available, but did not lead to recognized university degrees. The Catholic University of Lovanium at Kinshasa (affiliated with the Catholic University of Louvain in Belgium) was organized in 1953. The State University of the Belgian Congo and Ruanda-Urundi at Lubumbashi was set up in 1955. A third university was established at Kisangani under Protestant auspices in 1962. A number of specialized institutes of higher learning were also created following independence.

In August 1971, the existing institutes and the three universities were amalgamated into a single national university system, the National University of Zaire, organized into three separate campuses located in Kinshasa, Lubumbashi, and Kisangani. The three campuses were reorganized as separate universities in 1981. In 1988 all higher level institutions had 3,873 teaching staff and 61,422 pupils. Zaire also has numerous university institutes, including ones specializing in agriculture, applied technology, business, and the arts.

44 LIBRARIES AND MUSEUMS

The largest libraries are at the Universities of Lubumbashi and Kisangani, with 300,000 volumes each. The library at the University of Kinshasa has over 90,000 volumes. Smaller academic libraries are attached to various specialized university institutes. The Kinshasa Public Library has 24,000 volumes.

The Museum of Anthropology, Academy of Fine Arts, and Prehistoric Museum are in Kinshasa, and regional museums are in Lubumbashi, Kisangani, Kananga, Mbandaka, and other cities.

45 MEDIA

The postal, telephone, and telegraph services are owned and operated by the government. Telephones in 1991 numbered 32,116. An earth-satellite station was inaugurated at Matadi in 1985. Radio and television transmission is under the control of the government-owned La Voix du Zaïre, Radio Candip (for educational broadcasts), and Zaïre Télévision, with headquarters in Kinshasa. Broadcasts are in French and in African languages. In 1991 there were some 3.7 million radios and 41,000 television sets.

Major newspapers are only nominally privately owned. Journalists must be members of the state-controlled union to practice their profession. In 1972, a drastic reorganization of the secular press led to the demise of 27 of the country's remaining 33 newspapers. In March 1973, in the wake of the conflict between church and state, 31 religious publications were suspended. The press today is firmly under MPR control. The largest dailies, with 1992 circulations, are La Dépêche in Lubumbashi, 20,000; Courrier d'Afrique in Kinshasa, 15,000; and L'Essor du Zaïre in Lubumbashi, 10,000. Other dailies are Centre-Afrique (Bukavu), Le Stanleyvillois (Kisangani), Taifa (Lubumbashi), Mjumbe (Lubumbashi), and Salongo (Kinshasa).

46 ORGANIZATIONS

Since coming to power, the Mobutu regime has attempted to control and centralize all voluntary organizations. The Corps of Volunteers of the Republic (CVR), a semipolitical movement directly under the control of President Mobutu, was created in February 1966. Its objectives were to promote "national reconstruction" and to "awaken national consciousness." The relative lack of enthusiasm generated by the CVR led to its being taken over in April 1967 by the MPR, which created a youth section for the ruling party—the Young Popular Movement of the Revolution.

Mobutu's conflict with the Roman Catholic Church provided the government with an excuse to ban all independent youth associations (most of which were church-related) and to replace them with party-controlled organizations. Student associations have been similarly disbanded and superseded by an MPR-affiliated agency. In fact, virtually every public organization in Zaire is now technically linked to the single party or headed by a party representative. ANEZA, the national association of private enterprises, with nearly 1,000 members, has absorbed all chambers of commerce.

47TOURISM, TRAVEL, AND RECREATION

Virunga National Park in the Virunga Mountains is one of the best game preserves in Africa and is particularly noted for lions, elephants, and hippopotamuses. Kahuzi-Biega Park, west of Lake Kivu, is one of the last refuges of the endangered mountain gorilla. Kinshasa has two zoos and a presidential garden. In 1989 there were 51,000 tourist arrivals, and tourist receipts came to US$6 million. There were 21,824 hotel rooms and 27,262 beds. However, tourism has suffered in recent years due to political and economic crises.

Tourists and visitors are required to have a passport with a valid visa. A certificate of inoculation against yellow fever and cholera is required for entry into Zaire.

48FAMOUS ZAIRIANS

In the period of the transition to independence, two Zairian political leaders emerged as national figures: Joseph Kasavubu (1917–69), head of the ABAKO party, became the first chief of state; Patrice Emery Lumumba (1926–61) became the new nation's first premier, and his subsequent murder made him a revolutionary martyr in Communist and many third-world countries. In 1960, Moïse Kapenda Tshombe (1919–69), who headed the government of Katanga Province, became prominent when he declared Katanga an independent state with himself as its president and maintained the secession until early 1963. Gen. Mobutu Sese Seko (Joseph-Désiré Mobutu, b.1930), commander-in-chief of the Congolese National Army from 1961 to 1965, assumed the presidency after he deposed President Kasavubu on 25 November 1965. The MPR party congress promoted Mobutu to the rank of field marshal in December 1982.

49DEPENDENCIES

Zaire has no territories or colonies.

50BIBLIOGRAPHY

Abi-Saab, Georges. *The United Nations Operation in the Congo, 1960–64.* New York: Oxford University Press, 1979.

American University. *Zaire: A Country Study.* Washington, D.C.: Government Printing Office. 3rd ed., 1979.

Anstey, Roger. *King Leopold's Legacy: The Congo under Belgian Rule, 1908–1960.* London: Oxford University Press, 1966.

Bobb, F. Scott. *Historical Dictionary of Zaire.* Metuchen, N.J.: Scarecrow Press, 1988.

Bustin, Édouard. *Lunda under Belgian Rule.* Cambridge, Mass.: Harvard University Press, 1975.

Callaghy, Thomas M. *The State-Society Struggle: Zaire in Comparative Perspective.* New York: Columbia University Press, 1984.

Elliot, Jeffrey M. and Mervyn M. Dymally (eds.). *Voices of Zaire: Rhetoric or Reality.* New York: Washington Institute Press, 1990.

Gérard-Libois, Jules. *Katanga Secession.* Madison: University of Wisconsin Press, 1966.

Gann, Lewis H., and Peter J. Duignan. *The Rulers of Belgian Africa: 1884 to 1914.* Princeton, N.J.: Princeton University Press, 1979.

Gibbs, David N. *The Political Economy of Third World Intervention: Mines, Money, and US Policy in the Congo Crisis.* Chicago: University of Chicago Press, 1991.

Gran, Guy. *Zaire: The Political Economy of Underdevelopment.* New York: Praeger, 1979.

Harms, Robert W. *River of Wealth, River of Sorrow: The Central Zaire Basin in the Era of the Slave and Ivory Trade, 1500 to 1891.* New Haven, Conn.: Yale University Press, 1981.

Heinz, G., and H. Donnay. *Lumumba: The Last Fifty Days.* New York: Grove, 1969.

Hyland, Paul. *The Black Heart: A Voyage into Central Africa.* London: Gollancz, 1988.

Kanza, Thomas. *The Rise and Fall of Patrice Lumumba.* Cambridge, Mass.: Schenkman, 1979.

La Fontaine, J. S. *City Politics: A Study of Léopoldville, 1962–1963.* Cambridge: Cambridge University Press, 1970.

Lefever, Ernest W. *Uncertain Mandate: Politics of the UN Congo Operation.* Baltimore: Johns Hopkins Press, 1967.

Lemarchand, René. *Political Awakening in the Congo.* Westport, Conn.: Greenwood, 1982 (orig. 1964).

Leslie, Winsome J. *Zaire: Continuity and Political Change in an Oppressive State.* Boulder, Colo.: Westview Press, 1993.

MacGaffey, Janet. *Entrepreneurs and Parasites: The Struggle for Indigenous Capitalism in Zaire.* New York: Cambridge University Press, 1987.

Markowitz, Marvin D. *Cross and Sword: The Political Role of Christian Missions in the Belgian Congo, 1908–1960.* Stanford, Calif.: Hoover Institution Press, 1973.

McGaffey, Wyatt. *Custom and Government in the Lower Congo.* Berkeley: University of California Press, 1970.

McGaffey, Wyatt. *Modern Congo Prophets: Religion in a Plural Society.* Bloomington: Indiana University Press, 1983.

Mokoli, Mondonga M. *State against Development: The Experience of Post-1965 Zaire.* Westport, CT: Greenwood Press, 1992.

Nelson, Jack E. *Christian Missionizing and Social Transformation: A History of Conflict and Change in Eastern Zaire.* New York: Praeger, 1992.

Nkrumah, Kwame. *Challenge of the Congo: A Case Study of Foreign Pressures in an Independent State.* London: Nelson, 1967.

Reefe, Thomas O. *The Rainbow and the Kings: A History of the Luba Empire to 1891.* Berkeley: University of California Press, 1981.

Thornton, John. *The Kingdom of Kongo: Civil War and Transition, 1641–1718.* Madison: University of Wisconsin Press, 1983.

Turnbull, Colin M. *Lonely African.* New York: Touchstone Books, 1968.

Varon, Bension. *Zaire: Current Economic Situation and Constraints.* Washington, D.C.: World Bank, 1980.

Weissman, Stephen R. *American Foreign Policy in the Congo, 1960–1964.* Ithaca, N.Y.: Cornell University Press, 1974.

Zaire in Pictures. Minneapolis: Lerner, 1992.

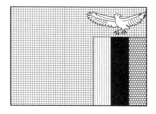

ZAMBIA

Republic of Zambia

CAPITAL: Lusaka.

FLAG: The flag is green, with a tricolor of dark red, black, and orange vertical stripes at the lower corner of the fly, topped by a golden flying eagle.

ANTHEM: *Stand and Sing for Zambia.*

MONETARY UNIT: The kwacha (K) of 100 ngwee replaced the Zambian pound (z₤) on 15 January 1968. There are coins of 1, 2, 5, 10, 20, and 50 ngwee, and notes of 1, 2, 5, 10, 20, 50, 100, and 500 kwacha. K1 = $0.1202 (or $1 = K8.3216).

WEIGHTS AND MEASURES: The metric system is used.

HOLIDAYS: New Year's Day, 1 January; Youth Day, 11 March; Labor Day, 1 May; African Freedom Day, 24 May; Heroes' Day, 1st Monday after 1st weekend in July; Unity Day, Tuesday after Heroes' Day; Farmers' Day, 5 August; Independence Day, 24 October; Christmas, 25 December. Movable religious holidays include Good Friday and Easter Monday.

TIME: 2 PM = noon GMT.

¹LOCATION, SIZE, AND EXTENT

A landlocked country in southcentral Africa, Zambia has an area of 752,610 sq km (290,584 sq mi), with a maximum length of 1,206 km (749 mi) E–W and a maximum width of 815 km (506 mi) N–S. Comparatively, the area occupied by Zambia is slightly larger than the state of Texas. Bounded on the NE by Tanzania, on the E by Malawi, on the SE by Mozambique and Zimbabwe, on the S by Zimbabwe, Botswana, and Namibia (South West Africa), on the W by Angola, and on the W by Zaire, Zambia has a total boundary length of 5,664 km (3,519 mi).

Zambia's capital city, Lusaka, is located in the southcentral part of the country.

²TOPOGRAPHY

Most of the landmass in Zambia is a high plateau lying between 910 and 1,370 m (3,000–4,500 ft) above sea level. In the northeast, the Muchinga Mountains exceed 1,800 m (5,900 ft) in height. Elevations below 610 m (2,000 ft) are encountered in the valleys of the major river systems. Plateau land in the northeastern and eastern parts of the country is broken by the low-lying Luangwa River, and in the western half by the Kafue River. Both rivers are tributaries of the upper Zambezi, the major waterway of the area. The frequent occurrence of rapids and falls prevents through navigation of the Zambezi.

There are three large natural lakes—Bangweulu, Mweru, and Tanganyika—all in the northern area. Lake Bangweulu and the swamps at its southern end cover about 9,840 sq km (3,800 sq mi) and are drained by the Luapula River. Kariba, one of the world's largest man-made lakes, is on the southern border; it was formed by the impoundment of the Zambezi by the construction of the Kariba Dam.

³CLIMATE

Although Zambia lies within the tropics, much of it has a pleasant climate because of the altitude. Temperatures are highest in the valleys of the Zambezi, Luangwa, and Kafue and by the shores of Lakes Tanganyika, Mweru, and Bangweulu.

There are wide seasonal variations in temperature and rainfall. October is the hottest month. The main rainy season starts in mid-November, with heavy tropical storms lasting well into April. The northern and northwestern provinces have an annual rainfall of about 125 cm (50 in), while areas in the far south have as little as 75 cm (30 in). May to mid-August is the cool season, after which temperatures rise rapidly. September is very dry.

Daytime temperatures may range from 23° to 31°C (73–88°F), dropping at night to as low as 5°C (41°F) in June and July. Lusaka, at 1,250 m (4,100 ft), has an average minimum of 9°C (48°F) and an average maximum of 23°C (73°F) in July, with averages of 17°C (63°F) and 26°C (79°F), respectively, in January; normal annual rainfall is 81 cm (32 in).

⁴FLORA AND FAUNA

Most of the territory is plateau, and the prevailing type of vegetation is open woodland or savanna. Acacia and baobab trees, thorn trees and bushes, and tall perennial grasses are widespread, becoming coarser and sparser in the drier areas to the south. To the north and east grows a thin forest. The southwest has forests of Zambian teak (*Baikiaea plurijuga*).

The national parks and game reserves, such as the Kafue National Park, conserve the wildlife threatened by settlement. The Cookson's wildebeest, Senga Kob, Thornicroft giraffe, and red lechwe are unique to Zambia. The many varieties of buck include kudu, impala, duiker, and sten. In Luangwa Valley can be found giraffe, zebra, rhinoceros, elephant, baboon, monkey, hyena, wolf, and lion. Among the nocturnal animals are serval and civet cat, genet, and jackal. Other mammals include the honey badger, ant bear, rock rabbit, warthog, and bush pig.

Zambia has a wealth of bird life, including the eagle, gull, tern, kingfisher, swift, redwing, lark, babbler, sunbird, weaver, red-billed quelea (in Luangwa Valley), stork, goose, plover, skimmer, bee-eater, wagtail, sparrow, swallow, thrush, shrike, nightingale, dove, nightjar, and an occasional ostrich. White pelican, flamingo, heron, ibis, and the crowned crane are found in the game reserves.

There are more than 150 recorded species of reptiles, including 78 species of snakes and 66 of lizards. Among them are the crocodile, tortoise, turtle, terrapin, gecko, agama, nonvenomous python, mamba, viper, and adder. The range of species of fish is also wide and includes bream, snoutfish, butterfish, tigerfish, bottlenose, gorgefish, mudfish, catfish, barbel, "vundu," squeaker, whitebait, perch, carp, bass, and "utaka" (of the sardine type). Insect types number in the thousands, and many are peculiar to the area. The Copperbelt region and the swamps of Lake Bangweulu are especially rich in insect life.

5ENVIRONMENT

Both traditional and modern farming methods in Zambia involve clearing large areas of forest. As of 1985, the nation had lost 270 square miles of forestland, mainly to slash-and-burn agriculture but also to firewood gathering and charcoal production. Consequent erosion results in the loss of up to 3 million tons of topsoil annually. The growth of a single crop on agricultural land and the use of fertilizers threaten the soil and contribute to acidification. Lack of adequate water-treatment facilities contributes to the prevalence of bilharziasis and other parasitic infections. Water pollution is a problem due to contamination by sewage and toxic industrial chemicals. The nation has 23.0 cu mi of water supply, of which 26% is used for farming and 11% for industry. Roughly one-fourth of Zambia's city dwellers and 57% of the people living in rural areas do not have pure water.

The Copperbelt region, Zambia's mineral-extraction and refining center, is prone to pollution, including acid rain, and buildup of toxins in the soil near many smelters poses a threat to food crops. Air pollution is created by the use of oil products for cars and coal in industrial activity. Wildlife is endangered in some areas by hunting and poaching, although the National Parks and Wildlife Act (1982) mandates automatic imprisonment for trading illicitly in elephant tusks and rhinoceros horns. In 1994, 10 of the nation's mammal species, including the black rhinoceros, and 10 bird species were threatened, as well as 1 type of plant.

6POPULATION

In 1990, the population was 7,818,447, according to a census report that the UN adjusted upward by 4%. In 1994, the population was estimated at 9,371,621. The projected population for the year 2000 was 10,672,000, assuming a crude birthrate of 44.1 per 1,000 population, a crude death rate of 18.4, and a net natural increase of 25.7 during 1995–2000. As of 1994, the population was 43% urban and 57% rural. Lusaka, the capital, had 979,000 inhabitants in 1990. Estimates for other cities in 1989 included Kitwe (495,000), Ndola (467,000), Mufulira (206,000), Chingola (201,000), and Kabwe (210,000). The main urban concentrations were in the Copperbelt mining complex. Overall, Zambia in 1994 had a population density of 12.5 per sq km (32.3 per sq mi). The annual growth rate in 1990–95 was 2.8%.

7MIGRATION

Before independence, the size of the European population waxed and waned with the fortunes of the mining industry. During the political upheavals of the mid-1960s, many Europeans in the mining industries left Zambia. A sizable number of refugees from southern Africa fled to Zambia, and many exiled African nationalist organizations established offices in Lusaka. At the end of 1992, there were an estimated 142,100 refugees in Zambia, including 101,800 Angolans and 26,300 Mozambicans.

8ETHNIC GROUPS

The African community, more than 99% of Zambia's total population, belongs to various Bantu groups. (The term "Bantu" refers roughly to all peoples in whose language the root *ntu* means "man.") The Bemba group—37% of the African population—

inhabits the Northern and Copperbelt provinces. Other African societies include the Tonga (19%), Lunda (12%), Nyanja (11%), Mambwe (8%), and Lozi or Barotse (7%). In all, there are at least 73 different African societal classifications.

The Europeans, numbering about 17,000 in 1984, are mainly of British stock, either immigrants or their descendants from the UK or South Africa. Other European groups include those of Dutch, Italian, and Greek descent. Counting Asians, mainly migrants from the Indian subcontinent, and people of mixed race, there were about 60,000 non-Africans in 1986.

9LANGUAGES

Some 80 different languages have been identified, most of them of the Bantu family. For educational and administrative purposes, seven main languages are recognized: Bemba, Lozi, Lunda, Kaonde, Luvale, Tonga, and Nyanja. Bemba, with its various dialects, is widely spoken in northern Zambia and is the lingua franca in the Copperbelt. The Ila and Tonga tongues predominate in the Southern Province. English is the official language.

10RELIGIONS

An estimated 70% of the population follows African tribal religions, while 20% professes some form of Christianity, more than one-third being Roman Catholics. Others belong to indigenous African churches, the Jehovah's Witnesses, or other Protestant denominations, including the United Church of Zambia, Christian Brethren, Reformed Church of Zambia, and Seventh-day Adventists. Many Zambian churches combine traditional animistic practices with the Christian faith. In 1965, an indigenous sect, the Lumpa Church, was banned after clashes with government troops resulted in the loss of about 700 lives. Proselytizing by members of the Jehovah's Witnesses has been banned by the government. In 1982, Roman Catholic Archbishop Emmanuel Milingo was recalled to Rome by the Vatican, which reportedly believed that his faith-healing sessions amounted to witchcraft.

11TRANSPORTATION

Almost all of Zambia's industries, commercial agriculture, and major cities are located along the rail lines, which are often paralleled by highways. The Zambia Railways system consists of 1,266 km (787 mi) of 3'6' gauge track. The rail link with the Atlantic via the Katanga and Benguela railways to Lobito Bay in Angola has been affected by instability in Angola since the mid-1970s. Construction began in October 1970 on the Tazara railway, a 1,860-km (1,156-mi) line linking Dar es Salaam in Tanzania with Kapiri Mposhi, north of Lusaka; intended to lessen Zambian dependence on the white-minority regimes of Rhodesia and South Africa, the line (890 km/553 mi of which is in Zambia) was completed and commissioned in July 1976. Equipment and operational problems have kept the railway from reaching its full potential, however, and rail cargo links with South Africa and Mozambique ports, passing through Zimbabwe, remain important for Zambian commerce.

Zambia had 36,370 km (22,600 mi) of roadway in 1991, of which 18% was paved. The principal routes were the Great North Road (809 km/503 mi), running from Kapiri Mposhi through Tanzania to Dar es Salaam, with a connecting road in Zambia from Kapiri Mposhi south to Livingstone (Maramba); the Great East Road (586 km/364 mi), from Lusaka to Chipata and thence to the Malawi border, with a connecting road (583 km/362 mi) from Mongu to Lusaka; the Zaire Border Road, from Kapiri Mposhi on the Great North Road through the Copperbelt region to Katanga, Zaire; and the Kafue-Harare (Zimbabwe) road. Road services continue to play an important role in transporting copper and general cargo to and from Dar es Salaam. Transport services on the main routes also are provided by the National Transport Corp. of Zambia, the state-owned freight and

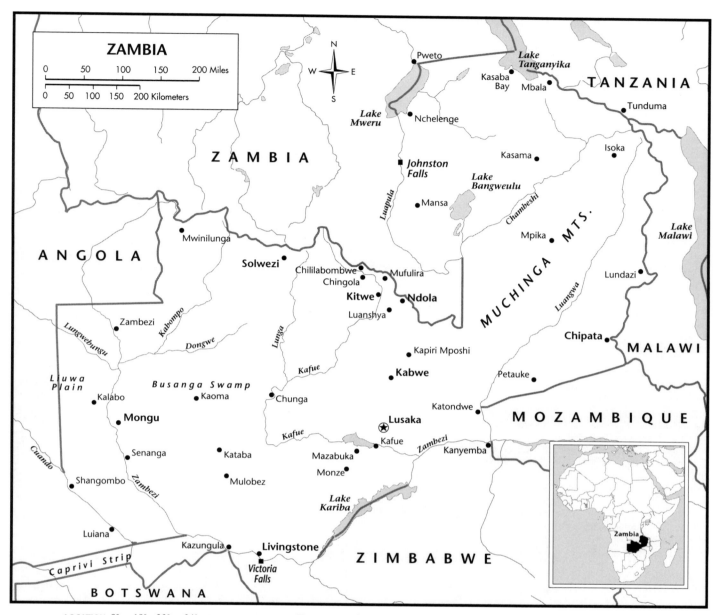

ZAMBIA

| 0 | 50 | 100 | 150 | 200 Miles |
| 0 | 50 | 100 | 150 | 200 Kilometers |

LOCATION: 9° to 18°s; 23° to 34°E. **BOUNDARY LENGTHS:** Tanzania, 322 km (200 mi); Malawi, 746 km (464 mi); Mozambique, 424 km (263 mi); Zimbabwe, 739 km (459 mi); Namibia (South West Africa), 203 km (126 mi); Angola, 1,086 km (675 mi); Zaire, 2,107 km (1,309 mi).

passenger transport service. The United Bus Co. of Zambia is the largest passenger carrier. In 1991, there were 170,000 registered motor vehicles, including 100,000 passenger cars.

Faced with rising costs and high debt obligations, state-owned Zambia Airways, the national airline, had operating revenues in 1990 of $140.8 million, but expenses of $176.5 million. The line carried 246,000 passengers in 1992. Zambia Airways provides international service from Lusaka to several African and European countries, as well as domestic service to 17 Zambian centers.

Mpulungu on Lake Tanganyika is Zambia's only port and receives goods supplied through Tanzania. There are several fishing harbors on Kariba Lake.

12HISTORY

The history of Zambia before the 19th century can be studied only through archaeology and oral traditions. Iron working and agriculture were practiced in some parts of Zambia by about AD 100. By AD 900, mining and trading were evident in southern

Zambia. Between the 15th century (or possibly earlier) and the 18th century, various groups of Bantu migrants from the southern Congo (now Zaire) settled in Zambia. By the beginning of the 19th century, three large-scale political units existed in Zambia, in three different types of geographic environment. On the northeast plateau between the valleys of the Luapula and Luangwa, the Bemba had established a system of chieftainships; the Lunda kingdom of Kazembe was in the Luapula Valley; and the kingdom of the Lozi was in the far west, in the floodplain of the upper Zambezi.

Zambia was affected by 2 "invasions" in the mid-19th century. Shaka's Zulu empire in South Africa set in motion a series of migrations, commonly referred to as the mfecane; groups of peoples, including the Ngoni, were forced to migrate north across the Zambezi in order to avoid the Zulu raids and conquests. The other invasion came in the form of traders from the north—Nyamwezi, Arabs, and Swahili—drawing Zambia into long-distance trading systems.

The first significant European contact was through Christian missionaries. David Livingstone explored the region near Lake Bangweulu extensively from 1851 to his death in 1873. In 1884, François Coillard, a French Protestant missionary, settled in Barotseland (now the Western Province).

In the 1890s, Cecil Rhodes' British South Africa Company, which had already established itself to the south, extended its charter to the lands north of the Zambezi. From 1891 to the end of 1923, the territory—known as Northern Rhodesia—was ruled by this private company. Efforts to stimulate European settlement were disappointing, since anticipated discoveries of mineral wealth failed to materialize.

In the 1920s, new methods of exploiting the extensive mineral deposits in the Copperbelt region transformed the economic life of the territory. Development of these ore bodies, although hampered by the Great Depression, reversed the roles of the two Rhodesias. Northern Rhodesia, formerly viewed as an economic liability in any projected merger with Southern Rhodesia, now was seen as a source of wealth. European settlements rose rapidly, spurred directly by the requirements of the mining industry and indirectly by the subsequent expansion of the economy.

Before federation in 1953, the political development of the territory focused on two issues: the relationship of the European settlers with the colonial authorities on the one hand, and that between the settlers and the Africans on the other. The European settler community pressed for a greater voice in the colony's affairs. The major political issue involving the relations between Europeans and Africans concerned the allocation of land. Commissions on land policy designated the areas adjacent to the railway line as crown land. Although there was no legal bar to the acquisition of crown land by Africans, the effect of the arrangement was to exclude them from the commercially most attractive acreage.

In 1953, Northern Rhodesia became a member of the Federation of Rhodesia and Nyasaland. Even though the overwhelming majority of Africans in the territory was opposed to the federal arrangement, the British government decided that Northern Rhodesia would participate in the federation. In 1960, a royal commission reported that, despite clear economic benefits, the majority of Africans in both Northern Rhodesia and Nyasaland was opposed to the continuance of federation in its present form. In early 1962, Nyasaland's desire to secede from the federation was acknowledged by the British government.

Following its initiation into the federation, the government of Northern Rhodesia underwent constitutional changes, with a growing emphasis on African representation. Africans had not been represented on the Legislative Council until 1948, when two were named to that body. An enlarged Legislative Council, convened in 1954 just after the formation of the federation, included four Africans selected by the African Representative Council. A new constitution, introduced in January 1959, aimed at replacing the council with a political system based on a greater degree of cooperation between the races.

Discussions on a revision of this constitution began in December 1960 but were brought to an early close by disagreement between the European-dominated United Federal Party and the United National Independence Party (UNIP). But agreement was finally reached, and a new constitution came into effect in September 1962. Elections later that year produced an African majority in the Legislative Council, which then called for secession from the federation, full internal self-government under a new constitution, and a new National Assembly based on a broader, more democratic franchise.

The Republic of Zambia is Born

On 31 December 1963, the Federation of Rhodesia and Nyasaland was formally dissolved. On 24 October 1964, Northern Rhodesia became an independent republic, and its name was changed to Zambia. Kenneth Kaunda, the leader of the ruling UNIP, became the nation's first president. Kaunda was reelected in 1969, 1973, 1978, and 1983, surviving a series of coup attempts during 1980–81.

During the 1970s, Zambia played a key role in the movement toward black majority rule in Rhodesia. Zambia's border with Rhodesia was closed from 1973 to 1978 by Kaunda in retaliation for Rhodesian raids into Zambia; the raids were intended to impede the infiltration of Patriotic Front guerrillas into Rhodesia from their Zambian bases. The emergence of independent, black-ruled Zimbabwe eased the political pressure, but a drastic decline of world copper prices in the early 1980s, coupled with a severe drought, left Zambia in a perilous economic position. The continuing civil war in Angola also had repercussions in Zambia, bringing disruption of Zambian trade routes and casualties among Zambians along the border.

A South African air raid near Lusaka on 19 May 1986 was aimed at curbing Zambia's support for black nationalist groups in exile there. Later in the year, Kaunda supported Commonwealth sanctions against South Africa but did not take action himself, since Zambia is heavily dependent on imports from South Africa.

Riots, the worst since independence, broke out on 9 December 1986 in protest against the removal of subsidies for cornmeal, which had caused the price to rise by 120%; 15 people were killed, hundreds were injured, and hundreds of shops were looted. Peace returned two days later when Kaunda restored the subsidy and nationalized the grain-milling industry. He also ruled thenceforth with state of emergency powers. Reduction in government spending in order to reduce the deficit had been demanded by the International Monetary Fund, along with the devaluation of the currency, as a condition for extending new loans to enable Zambia to pay for essential imports. On 1 May 1987, Kaunda rejected the IMF conditions for a new financing package of about $300 million. He limited payments on the foreign debt to well under 10% of export earnings and established a new fixed currency rate of eight kwacha to the dollar. This did little to improve the economy or the popularity of Kaunda and UNIP.

By early 1989, Zambia, in consultation with the IMF and the World Bank, developed a new economic reform plan. In early 1991, Zambia qualified for World Bank assistance for the first time since 1987, although this was later suspended. By 1990, a growing opposition to UNIP's monopoly of power had coalesced in the Movement for Multiparty Democracy (MMD). A number of UNIP defectors and major labor leaders came together to pressure Kaunda to hold multiparty elections. In December 1990, after a tumultuous year that included riots in Lusaka and a coup attempt, Kaunda signed legislation ending UNIP's legal monopoly of power.

After difficult negotiations between the government and opposition groups, Zambia enacted a new constitution in August 1991. It enlarged the National Assembly, established an electoral commission, and allowed for more than one presidential candidate. Candidates no longer are required to be UNIP members. In September, Kaunda announced the date for Zambia's first multiparty parliamentary and presidential elections in 19 years. On 31 October and 1 November 1991, the 27-year long state of emergency was terminated. Frederick J. T. Chiluba (MMD) defeated Kaunda, 81% to 15%. The MMD won over 125 of the 150 elected seats in the Assembly. UNIP won 25 seats, although UNIP swept the Eastern Province, winning 19 seats there.

Despite the change of government, the economy still sputtered. Chiluba's austerity measures may have been popular with Zambia's creditors, but not with its people. Likewise, his privatization plans alarmed the unions, his original base of support. Chiluba's

MMD in power became autocratic and corrupt. Kaunda, his family, and UNIP officials were harassed. The press began to criticize Chiluba's government and Chiluba lashed back. An Anticorruption Commission investigated three senior cabinet ministers suspected of abuse of office.

UNIP remained the principal target of Chiluba's wrath. In February 1993, a document known as "Operation Zero Option" was leaked to the press. Allegedly written by Kaunda loyalists, it called for a campaign of strikes, riots and crime to destabilize the government. On 4 March 1993, government declared a three-month state of emergency and detained 26 UNIP members, including three of Kaunda's sons. Chiluba lifted the state of emergency on May 25 and released all but eight of the detainees, whom he charged with offenses from treason to possession of seditious documents.

13 GOVERNMENT

From 1953 to 1963, Northern Rhodesia was a protectorate under the jurisdiction of the British crown, within the Federation of Rhodesia and Nyasaland. On 24 October 1964, it became an independent republic. The constitution of January 1964 was amended in 1968 and in 1972, when it was officially announced that Zambia would become a one-party "participatory democracy," with the sole party the ruling United National Independence Party. A new constitution was drafted and received presidential assent in August 1973.

Under the 1973 constitution, the president of the Republic of Zambia is head of state and commander-in-chief of the armed forces, as well as president of the UNIP. Once chosen by the ruling party, the president must be confirmed by a majority of the electorate, voting by universal adult suffrage at age 18. No limitation is placed on the length of the president's tenure in office.

The prime minister is the leader of government business and an ex officio member of the UNIP Central Committee. As provided in the constitution, the Central Committee consists of not more than 25 members, 20 to be elected at the party's general conference, held every five years, and 3 to be nominated by the president, who is also a member. Cabinet decisions are subordinate to those of the UNIP Central Committee.

The parliament consists of the president and a National Assembly of 125 elected members. Up to 10 additional members of the National Assembly may be nominated by the president. All Assembly members must be UNIP members, and their candidacy must be approved by the party's Central Committee. The normal life of the Assembly is five years. To become law, a bill requires presidential assent. The constitution also provides for a House of Chiefs of 27 members, 4 each from the Northern, Western, Southern, and Eastern provinces, 3 each from the Northwestern, Luapula, and Central provinces, and 2 from the Copperbelt Province. It submits resolutions to be debated by the Assembly and considers matters referred to it by the president.

A Bill of Rights, guaranteeing the fundamental freedom and rights of the individual, is included in the 1973 constitution. However, if at any time the president feels the security of the state is threatened, he has the power to proclaim a state of emergency.

In August 1991, a new constitution was promulgated. The president is now elected directly by universal suffrage and may serve a maximum of two five-year terms. The National Assembly has 150 directly elected members and up to eight appointed by the president, also for five-year terms. Candidates for office no longer are required to be UNIP members.

14 POLITICAL PARTIES

African nationalism began to rise in Northern Rhodesia after World War II. African welfare associations, founded before the war, developed rapidly into political organizations. In 1946, representatives from 14 welfare societies formed the Federation of Welfare Societies. In 1948, the federation was reconstituted as the Northern Rhodesia Congress. It became the North Rhodesian African National Congress (ANC) in 1951 under the leadership of Harry Nkumbula. In 1958, dissatisfaction with Nkumbula's leadership gave rise to a breakaway movement led by the party's secretary-general, Kenneth Kaunda. Kaunda formed the Zambia African National Congress, which was declared illegal the following year. In 1960, the United National Independence Party (UNIP) was formed under Kaunda's leadership. UNIP received a majority of the popular votes in the 1962 elections and formed the first government after independence. The ANC became the chief opposition party.

In 1967, the United Party (UP) was formed by Nalumino Mundia, a Lozi who had been dismissed from the cabinet in 1966. Its support came mainly from Barotseland in the southwest, where the UP promised to restore the power of the chiefs. After violence erupted in the Copperbelt, Kaunda banned the UP as a "threat to public security and peace," and Mundia and his principal officers were arrested. In August 1968, the UP was declared illegal. Mundia was released in 1969, joined the UNIP in 1974, and was named prime minister in 1981.

In the general elections of December 1969, the UNIP won 81 seats in the National Assembly, the ANC 23, and independents 1. Kaunda was reelected president. The elections were followed by violence and political unrest. At the opening of the new Assembly, the speaker refused to recognize the ANC as the official opposition. With the proclamation of a one-party state in December 1972, UNIP became the only legal party in Zambia. The ANC was assimilated into UNIP; the United Progressive Party, formed in August 1971, was summarily disbanded by the government, and its founder, Simon Kapwepwe, briefly arrested.

On 5 December 1973, the first presidential elections held under the new constitution brought the reelection of Kaunda to a third term with 85% of the vote. Voters also filled the 125 elective seats in the National Assembly. In 1975, the UNIP declared its ranks open to former followers of banned parties, but in 1978 candidacy was restricted to those with five years' continuous UNIP membership. National Assembly and presidential elections were held in December 1978, with Kaunda, again unopposed, receiving 80.5% of the vote. In the elections of October 1983, Kaunda's share of the total rose to 93%. A total of 766 candidates ran for the 125 Assembly seats.

After considerable social unrest in 1986 and again in 1990, the Kaunda government came under domestic and international pressure to end UNIP's monopoly on legitimate partisan activity. A Movement for Multiparty Democracy (MMD) was formed and led by trade unionists and defectors from UNIP. Finally, in December 1990, Kaunda signed into law a bill legalizing opposition political parties. In the new constitution adopted in August 1991, candidates are no longer required to belong to UNIP.

These changes paved the way to multiparty presidential and parliamentary elections on 31 October and 1 November 1991, the first in 19 years. The MMD's leader, Frederick Chiluba, easily won the presidency, 81% to 15% for Kaunda. The MMD got 125 seats to 15 for UNIP in the National Assembly.

Since then, the MMD government has harassed and briefly detained UNIP militants, including Kaunda and his family. Kaunda stepped down as UNIP leader in August 1992. New opposition parties have been formed: the Multi-Racial Party (MRP), the National Democratic Alliance (NADA), the United Democratic Party, the United Democratic Congress Party, the latter two headed by former top UNIP leaders. The National Party (also with prominent ex-MMD figures) was created in August 1993 and won four seats in the Assembly in 1993–94 by-elections. Even within the MMD there is a breakaway group, the Caucus for National Unity, to root out corruption in government.

The MMD continues with its free market reforms, including privatization of the parastatal corporations and encouragement of foreign investment. With the exception of UNIP, more than 30 opposition parties operate without governmental interference. However, MMD is under great pressure to remove top officers, even of cabinet rank, who are alleged to be involved in drug trafficking.

15LOCAL GOVERNMENT
Zambia is divided into nine provinces (including the special province of Lusaka), administered by officials appointed by the central government. Each province is further divided into districts, presided over by district secretaries. Around 55% of Zambians live in towns and cities, one of the highest rates in Africa. Lusaka has a city council, and the other large towns have councils or town management boards; most townships, however, are directly administered by government officers. Local elections in urban areas are organized on a ward system with universal adult suffrage. Local urban authorities can levy taxes, borrow money, and own and manage housing projects. They control roads, water, power, town planning, health facilities, and other public services within their areas.

Administrative districts lying outside municipal and township areas are governed by rural councils, consisting of members elected by universal adult suffrage and a minority of nominated members, mainly chiefs, appointed by the under minister of the interior. Councils have evolved from the former Native Authorities, which were constituted on a tribal basis. The rural councils have frequently cut across African societal boundaries in order to establish larger and more viable units. The functions and powers of rural councils are similar to those of the urban local authorities.

16JUDICIAL SYSTEM
The law is administered by a High Court, consisting of a chief justice and 16 puisne judges. Resident magistrate's courts are also established at various centers. The law administered in these courts is founded upon British common law. The local courts deal mainly with customary law, especially cases relating to marriage, property, and inheritance. Under the constitution of 1973, the Supreme Court is the highest court in Zambia and serves as the final court of appeal. The chief justice and other judges are appointed by the president. In consultation with the prime minister, the president also appoints the director of public prosecution and the attorney general, the latter being the principal legal adviser to the government. The independence of the judiciary has been respected by the Movement for Multiparty Democracy (MMD) government.

17ARMED FORCES
As of 1993, the strength of the armed forces was 24,000; paramilitary forces, consisting of two police battalions, totaled 1,400. The army numbered 20,000; the air force had 4,000 personnel and 67 combat aircraft. In 1979, Zambia signed a major arms agreement with the former USSR, who supplied its military equipment. Military service is voluntary. No reliable fiscal data is available, but defense spending is estimated at around $200 million a year.

18INTERNATIONAL COOPERATION
Zambia joined the UN on 1 December 1964 and participates in ECA and all the nonregional specialized agencies except IMO. It belongs to the African Development Bank, Commonwealth of Nations, G-77, and OAU, and is a signatory of GATT and the Law of the Sea. Located in Zambia are the headquarters of the International Red Locust Control Organization for Central and Southern Africa, as well as an office of the UN High Commissioner of Refugees and a regional office of the UN Institute for Namibia, established to provide training for future administrators of an independent Namibian state. Zambia belongs to the Southern African Development Coordinating Conference (SADCC) and the Preferential Trade Area for Eastern and Southern Africa. While supporting liberation movements, Zambia has played a pivotal role in the search for détente in southern Africa.

19ECONOMY
As of 1994, the Zambian economy is in a precarious state. High inflation, severe drought, declining export prices, and failed economic policies have all taken their toll. After steady declines in per capita GDP, Zambia in 1992 was redesignated a least developed country by the United Nations. The impact of inflation on the poor, the middle class, and business has eroded public support for the government's reform policies. However, the inflation rate recently dropped dramatically, the first sign that tight monetary and fiscal policies were beginning to have an effect. After the drought of 1992, agricultural production rebounded with record harvests of many crops, but the Government's tight cash budget policy limited its capacity to purchase the crops. The key copper industry maintained production levels, but depressed world prices kept revenues at lower levels. Consequently, the expected recovery of the early 1990s has been slow to appear.

20INCOME
In 1992, Zambia's GNP was $2,580 million at current prices, or $290 per capita. For the period 1985–92 the average inflation rate was 69.1%, resulting in a real growth rate in per capita GNP of –2.1%.

In 1992, the GDP was $470 million in current US dollars. It is estimated that agriculture, hunting, forestry, and fishing contributed 12% to GDP; mining and quarrying, 14%; manufacturing, 26%; electricity, gas, and water, 1%; construction, 5%; wholesale and retail trade, 10%; transport, storage, and communication, 7%; finance, insurance, real estate, and business services, 11%; community, social, and personal services, 8%; and other sources 6%.

21LABOR
In 1992, recorded employment in Zambia totaled 300,000 persons, of whom 15% were engaged in mining, about 31% in services, 6% in construction, 7% each in commerce, finance, and transportation/communication, 14% in manufacturing, and 13% in other sectors. The majority of Zambian laborers work not as wage earners but in subsistence agriculture. Unemployment is estimated at more than one-third of the potential labor force.

The Labor Department is responsible for employment exchange services and for enforcing protective labor legislation. About 60% of wage earners are unionized. There were at least 19 labor unions in 1992, most of them affiliated with the Zambia Congress of Trade Unions (ZCTU). In 1985, all strikes were banned in essential sectors. Strikes were common in 1992 as workers' salaries and conditions of service were undercut by harsh economic conditions and large cost of living increases.

22AGRICULTURE
The development of commercial farming followed the construction of the railroad in the early 20th century, but the main stimulus did not come until World War II, when it was necessary to ensure a maximum output of copper and to minimize the shipping space required for food imports. Food production continued to expand as the copper industry helped raise living standards. Additional European immigration in the 1950s, as well as programs to diversify the economy, gave rise to the production for export of tobacco, cotton, and peanuts. However, partly because of the rapidly rising population, agricultural output never reached the point of meeting domestic food requirements. Only 5% of the

land area is cultivated at any time, although a much larger area is potentially arable.

The majority of Zambia's population engages in subsistence farming. The principal subsistence crops are corn, sorghum, and cassava, while the main cash crops are tobacco, corn, sugarcane, peanuts, and cotton. In 1992, liberalized marketing began for most crops, but because of the 1991/92 drought, corn marketing remained under government control. A bountiful 1993 harvest was expected to make a solid recovery from the drought.

Production of tobacco, the most important export crop, was estimated at 10,000 tons in 1993, the largest on record and double the 1992 harvest. Marketed corn production in 1992 was 464,000 tons (down from 1,096,000 tons in 1991). Cotton production reached 10,000 tons of fiber. Also marketed in 1992 were 1,150,000 tons of sugarcane, 6,000 tons of sunflowers, 21,000 tons of peanuts, and 62,000 tons of wheat.

23ANIMAL HUSBANDRY

The estimated livestock population in 1992 included 3,095,000 head of cattle, 623,000 sheep and goats, and 290,000 hogs. Cattle production in certain regions is limited by sleeping sickness, carried by the tsetse fly. During 1992, cattle slaughterings totaled 254,000 head.

24FISHING

Because Zambia's inland waters are a valuable source of food and employment, the fishing industry plays an important part in the rural economy. Large quantities of fish, most of which are transported by rail to processing centers, are frozen or dried. Major quantities are obtained from Bangweulu, Tanganyika, and Mweru lakes, and from the Kafue and Luapula rivers. The catch in 1991 was 65,945 tons.

25FORESTRY

About 40% of Zambia was covered by woodland in the early 1990s; commercial exploitation is concentrated in the southwest and in the Copperbelt. Roundwood production was about 13,719,000 cu m in 1991, 94% of it for fuel needs.

26MINING

Mining is central to Zambia's economy; the nation was the world's fourth largest producer of copper and second leading producer of cobalt in 1991. In 1969, the country's two major copper mining companies, Nchanga Consolidated Copper Mines (NCCM) and Roan Consolidated Mines (RCM), were 51% nationalized, and in 1974 they were reorganized under management appointed by the government. They were merged into Zambia Consolidated Copper Mines (ZCCM) in 1982. Full responsibility for the country's entire metal sales was taken up in 1974 by a new and wholly government-owned organization, the Metal Marketing Corp. The government-established Zambia Industrial and Mining Corp. holds the government's mining and industrial portfolio, while its subsidiary, the Mining and Development Corp., administers all mines other than the ZCCM ones and handles other industrial projects. The October 1991 elections resulted in the dismissal of many government officials, including the head of ZCCM. The new government is seeking to privatize parastatal organizations.

With world copper demand declining from the effects of recession or slow growth in industrial countries, Zambian output fell during the 1980s. The mining industry was also plagued with labor unrest and transportation difficulties, including port and rail congestion, and shortages of spare parts, raw materials, and fuel. In 1991, copper content of concentrates mined amounted to 345,519 tons, down from 403,450 tons in 1987.

Coal production fell from 579,000 tons in 1980 to 345,000 tons in 1991. Zinc output fell from 30,287 tons in 1987 to 19,825 in 1991. Lead output also dropped from 12,510 tons in 1987 to 9,084 tons in 1991. The production of cobalt from mined concentrates fell from 7,365 tons in 1987 to 6,991 tons in 1991. Minor quantities of silver, gold, selenium, iron ore, feldspar, and tin are produced. Gemstones, in the form of amethysts and emeralds, are also mined.

27ENERGY AND POWER

As of 1984, the mining industry was the largest consumer of energy, accounting for more than 48% of the total commercial energy demand. The main source of electricity was hydropower (70%), followed by petroleum products (20%), and coal (10%). A total of 7,775 million kwh of electricity was produced in 1991; Zambia exported about 19% of its production to Zimbabwe. In 1992, due to drought, Zambia imported electricity from Zaire. Electricity exports to Zimbabwe resumed in 1993.

The Kafue Power Station was commissioned in 1978, guaranteeing self-sufficiency in electricity even at times of low rainfall. This power station brought the total installed capacity in Zambia to more than 1,600 Mw, compared with 600 Mw in 1971. Installed capacity had risen to 2,436 Mw (92% hydro) by 1991.

Crude oil is imported by means of a leaking pipeline from Tanzania. As of 1993, the World Bank was involved in financing the rehabilitation of the pipeline. An inefficient refinery at Ndola may need to be shut down soon, especially if Zambia elects to bring in finished products by pipeline.

28INDUSTRY

In the industrial sector, 9.8% of the labor force produces 38.2% of GDP. In 1990 the food, beverage, and tobacco industry accounted for 37% of industrial ouput, textiles and clothing for 12%, and chemicals for 11%. Apart from copper refining, the most important industries are those connected with the manufacture of sulfuric acid, fertilizer, glass, batteries, cigarettes, textiles, yarn, glycerine, vehicle and tractor assembling, sawmilling, wood and joinery manufacture, tire retreading, processing of food and drink, and the manufacture of cement and cement products. Nitrogen Chemicals of Zambia, which produces fertilizer, is the largest non-mining enterprise.

To assist in the establishment of manufacturing and processing industries, the government has formed the Industrial Development Corp. of Zambia (INDECO). Together with its subsidiaries, INDECO accounted for about 75% of all Zambian industrial activity in 1991.

Zambia is self-sufficient in energy, with the Kafue Gorge hydroelectric center the biggest contributor. Output is, however, affected by drought.

29SCIENCE AND TECHNOLOGY

The National Council for Scientific Research advises the government on scientific matters and coordinates and disseminates the results of the Zambian research effort. Scientific learned societies include the Engineering Institution of Zambia. Research institutes specialize in fisheries, veterinary science, geology, agriculture, forestry and forest products, tropical diseases, pneumoconiosis, and red locust control. The University of Zambia at Lusaka has schools of natural sciences, engineering, medicine, agriculture, and mines. Copperbelt University has schools of environmental studies and technology. In addition, three colleges offer courses in agriculture and engineering.

30DOMESTIC TRADE

Centers of trading activity are the main towns along the rail line. The requirements of most sizable retail firms are imported directly. Serving African consumers, the small retailer conducts most of the wholesale business in imported goods; indeed, a local company often acts as agent, wholesaler, retailer, and distributor. Since independence, trading activity has increased both in the hinterland and in the urban areas, especially in Lusaka. Government licenses are required for general dealers and for some municipal businesses. The government controls most agricultural wholesaling and, through parastatal agencies, large wholesale and retail chains.

Normal business hours are from 8 AM to 12:30 PM and 2 to 4:30 PM, Monday–Friday. Banks are open from 8:15 AM to 12:45 PM on most weekdays, but close at noon on Thursdays and 11 AM on Saturdays.

31 FOREIGN TRADE

Copper is by far the leading export item, accounting for к6,845,200 million of Zambia's total exports of к8,058,653 million (84.9%) in 1987. Other leading export commodities were cobalt, zinc, and lead. Of Zambia's total import bill of к1,610 million in 1985, oil accounted for 30.6%; other major imports include machinery and transport equipment and basic manufactured goods.

Zambia's leading export partner in 1985 was Japan (23.1%), followed by the United Kingdom (7.4%) and China (6.8%). Imports arrived from South Africa (18.7%), the United Kingdom (15.3%), the United States (9.3%), and Japan (5.3%).

32 BALANCE OF PAYMENTS

Zambian trade is normally in rough balance, with a slight surplus. However, a heavy debt burden gives the country a current account deficit, and hard currency is often in short supply. In 1992, imports rose to $1,268 million, with 85% of the increase due to corn imports because of drought.

In 1991 merchandise exports totaled $1,172 million and imports $752 million. The merchandise trade balance was $420 million. The following table summarizes Zambia's balance of payments for 1990 and 1991 (in millions of US dollars):

	1990	1991
CURRENT ACCOUNT		
Goods, services, and income	−974	−546
Unrequited transfers	377	239
TOTALS	−597	−307
CAPITAL ACCOUNT		
Direct investment	203	34
Other long-term capital	507	21
Other short-term capital	−222	−45
Exceptional financing	−68	249
Reserves	−144	−62
TOTALS	275	197
Errors and omissions	322	110
Total change in reserves	−30	−24

33 BANKING AND SECURITIES

In November 1970, the Zambian government announced that it would take a majority interest in all banks operating in Zambia; however, the banking proposals were later modified so that the government became majority shareholder through the State Finance and Development Corp. of the already state-owned Zambia National Commercial Bank Ltd. (ZNCB) and the Commercial Bank of Zambia. Foreign-owned banks were required to incorporate in Zambia. Any commercial bank wholly or partly owned by the government had to have capitalization of not less than к500,000; any other commercial bank had to have not less than к2 million, and at least half the directors had to be residents of Zambia. The Bank of Zambia, the central bank, sets and controls all currency and banking activities in the country. The leading commercial banks are subsidiaries of Barclays, Grindlays, and The Standard Bank.

The money supply, as measured by M2, totaled к48,357 million as of 1993. Commercial banks had total assets of us$205.5 million at the end of 1993.

34 INSURANCE

On 1 January 1972, the Zambia State Insurance Corp. (ZSIC) took over all insurance transactions in Zambia. The operations of ZSIC cover fire, marine, aviation, accident, motor vehicle, and life insurance. All imports must be insured with this agency. Life insurance in force totaled к2.84 billion in 1992.

35 PUBLIC FINANCE

With its heavy dependency on copper, Zambia is able to show comfortable surpluses in its public accounts only when the mining industry is prosperous. From 1985 to 1987, Zambia attempted to implement a structural reform program, sponsored by the IBRD and IMF. In 1987, however, the government stopped the program and reverted to deficit spending and monetary creation. By 1992, a new government was committed to curtailing public expenditures through privatization and decreasing the civil service; the primary fiscal deficit that year was estimated at к19 billion or 3% of GDP.

In 1987, Zambia's total public debt stood at к27,512.1 million of which к20,459.3 million was financed abroad. Total debt at the end of 1991 amounted to us$7.3 billion; excluding short-term debt, Zambia's debt is one of the highest per capita in the world.

36 TAXATION

As of 1993, the income tax rate ranged from 15% to 35%. The company tax was 40–45% of net income, but only 15% on agricultural activities. A sales tax on most goods ranged from 15% to 20% and a capital gains tax was scheduled to go into effect within the year.

37 CUSTOMS AND DUTIES

Tariff schedules give preferential treatment to imports from the UK and other Commonwealth countries. Rebates are allowed on certain capital goods and on most materials used in local manufacturing industries. Tariff protection also is accorded to selected new industries. Most imports require licenses. Import duties for goods not exempted ranged from 15% to 100% of value in 1993. Most goods are also subject to a 15% sales tax. In 1991, the government created customs-free zones at Lusaka, Livingstone, and Ndola.

38 FOREIGN INVESTMENT

In the past, the heaviest concentrations of foreign private capital in Zambia were in the mining enterprises of the Copperbelt, now 51% nationalized. Although tax holidays have been offered as incentives, Zambia's highly socialized economy has not been conducive to private foreign investment, and exchange controls have made the repatriation of profits and dividends difficult.

Laws concerning retention of foreign exchange have been consistent, achieving full liberalization only recently. In 1983, exporters of non-traditional items could keep 50% of earned foreign exchange to finance imported inputs. This resulted in a five-fold increase in non-metal exports. This provision was revoked in 1987. The Investment Act of 1991 provided for a 70% foreign exchange retention during the first three years of a license, 60% in the next two years, and 50% for the rest of the license's term. This act was subsequently revised to allow for full retention of foreign exchange earnings.

39 ECONOMIC DEVELOPMENT

Zambia's primary development object is the implementation of the current structural adjustment agreement. Controlling inflation (207% in 1992) is the first priority, followed by faster implementation of social sector programs, legal and civil service reform, and privatization. New investment has been slow to form as investors await anticipated lower inflation rates. The lack of administrative capacity lies at the heart of the delays.

40 SOCIAL DEVELOPMENT

Social welfare services are provided by the government in association with local authorities and voluntary agencies. Statutory and remedial welfare services include emergency relief, care for the aged, protection of children, adoption, and probation. Group work and community development services are the responsibility of the local authorities, who are assisted by government technicians and grants-in-aid. A national provident fund, begun in October 1966, requires employers and employees to make contributions toward a worker's retirement at age 55. The Zambia Youth Service operates specially constructed camps that provide vocational training for unemployed and unskilled youth.

In 1972, Zambia adopted a law allowing abortion for social or medical reasons; it has been implemented on a very limited scale, at least in part because of lack of equipment and trained staff. The fertility rate in the mid-1990s was 6.7, and the birthrate is among the highest in the world.

Human rights abuses, including beatings and even the killing of persons in police custody, have prompted protest and the creation of a Commission of Inquiry to investigate. There are also government efforts to curb the press and a tendency for the press to censor itself. The offices of the *Weekly Post* have been attacked several times. In May 1994, the editor and a reporter of the *Post* was arrested for a headline that called Chiluba a "twit."

41 HEALTH

In 1964, responsibility for public health was transferred from the federation to Zambian authorities. Since then, the government has developed a health plan centered on specialist hospitals, with general and regional hospitals dealing with less complicated cases. At a lower level, district hospitals treat common medical and surgical cases. Rural health centers and clinics with outpatient facilities have been established throughout the country. Services to Zambian nationals are free at the rural health centers and clinics and at hospitals at the large urban centers. Due to government spending restrictions, the public health care sector has suffered from a severe shortage of doctors, medicine, and medical equipment and supplies.

As of 1992, government records indicate 9 hospitals and a few small outpatient clinics. Zambia produces locally 25% of the pharmaceuticals it consumes. Medical personnel in 1990 included 713 doctors, 26 dentists, 24 pharmacists, 1,503 nurses, and 311 midwives. The population per doctor in that year was 11,290, and per nursing professional was 600.

Malaria and tuberculosis are major health problems, and hookworm and schistosomiasis afflict a large proportion of the population. There were 345 cases of tuberculosis per 100,000 people reported in 1990. In 1991, only 53% of the population had access to safe water, and a mere 37% had adequate sanitation. In 1992, children up to one year old were immunized against tuberculosis (83%); diphtheria, pertussis, and tetanus (57%); polio (59%); and measles (56%).

Average life expectancy in 1992 was estimated at only 45 years (a decline since 1984). The infant mortality rate that year was 113 per 1,000 live births (an increase since 1984); the maternal mortality rate was 150 per 100,000 live births in 1991; and the general mortality rate was 18 per 1,000 people in 1993. In mid-1986, blood surveys indicated that 15% of the population was carrying the AIDS virus. In 1992, an estimated 75% of the population had access to health care services and, in 1990, Zambia spent only $117 million on health care.

42 HOUSING

Widespread instances of overcrowding and slum growth have for many years focused government attention on urban housing problems. Local authorities have statutory responsibility for housing and housing management. The Zambia National Building Society makes loans to local agencies for the financing of approved schemes, and the National Housing Authority established a special fund to support self-help projects for low-income earners. Mining companies have constructed townships for the families of African workers in the Copperbelt. About 67% of the population had access to safe water in the mid-1980s. According to the latest available information for 1980–88, total housing units numbered 1,410,000 with 4.9 people per dwelling.

43 EDUCATION

Most of the nation's schools are operated by local authorities or by missions and are aided by the central government. A small number of schools are directly administered by the government. Primary education lasts for seven years and is compulsory. Secondary education is for five years. In 1990, 1,461,206 pupils were in 3,587 primary schools and in 1988, 170,299 students attended secondary schools. Adult literacy rates in 1990 were 80.8% for men and 65.3% for women. In 1990, 4,669 students were in teacher training and 3,313 students were in vocational. (UNESCO estimates.) The University of Zambia was established in 1965. Other institutions of higher learning include technical colleges and a two-year college of agriculture. All higher level institutions had 15,343 pupils in 1990.

44 LIBRARIES AND MUSEUMS

The Zambia Library Service maintains 900 library centers, 6 regional libraries, 6 branch libraries, and a central library with 500,000 volumes. The Lusaka Urban District Libraries has 145,000 volumes, and the Ndola Public Library has 90,000. The National Archives of Zambia maintains a library of about 20,000 volumes. The University of Zambia has holdings of more than 300,000 books.

The National Museum, located in Livingstone, has displays on natural history, archaeology, ethnography, recent history, African art, metallurgy, and memorabilia relating to David Livingstone. The Eastern Cataract Field Museum near Victoria Falls concentrates on archaeology and geology, including illustrations of the formation of the falls and the Stone Age sequence in the area. Lusaka has the Art Center and the Military and Police Museum of Zambia. The Moto Moto Museum in Mbala (founded in 1974) exhibits ethnography and history materials. The Copperbelt Museum at Ndola exhibits geological and historical items as well as ethnic art.

45 MEDIA

The central government is responsible for postal and telecommunication services. A direct radiotelegraph circuit has been established between Lusaka and London, and direct telephone links are in operation to all neighboring countries. About 95,281 telephones were in use in 1991. The Zambia Broadcasting Service, which provides radio programs in English and seven local languages, and Zambian Television are government owned and operated. In 1991 there were 680,000 radio receivers and 217,000 television receivers.

Zambia has two daily newspapers: the UNIP-owned *Times of Zambia*, founded in Ndola in 1943 and with an estimated 1991 circulation of 45,000; and the government-owned *Zambia Daily Mail*, published in Lusaka, with a circulation of 25,000.

46 ORGANIZATIONS

Professional and learned societies include the Wildlife Conservation Society of Zambia, the Zambia Library Association, and the

Zambia Medical Association, all in Lusaka. Among service organizations are the Lions, Rotary, Jaycees, Professional Women's Club, and Women's Institute. Business groups include chambers of commerce in the major towns.

⁴⁷TOURISM, TRAVEL, AND RECREATION

One of the most impressive tourist attractions in Zambia is *Mosioa-Tunya* ("the smoke that thunders")—Victoria Falls. In 1972, a new national park system created 17 parks covering 8% of the entire country. The Kafue National Park, one of the largest in Africa, with 22,500 sq km (8,700 sq mi) of bush, forest, and plain, is well-served with tourist facilities. South Luangwa National Park is another outstanding wildlife area. In 1990, Zambia received 141,004 foreign visitors, 74% from Africa and 16% from Europe. In 1991, there were 3,962 hotel rooms with 6,889 beds and a 54% occupancy rate, and tourism receipts totaled US$35 million. Nationals of Commonwealth countries do not need visas. Precautions against malaria are advisable, and travelers who have passed through areas subject to yellow fever or cholera must have vaccinations.

⁴⁸FAMOUS ZAMBIANS

Kenneth David Kaunda (b.1924) has been Zambia's president since independence. Nalumino Mundia (b.1927), long prominent in Zambian political affairs, was prime minister 1981–85, when he became ambassador to the US.

⁴⁹DEPENDENCIES

Zambia has no territories or colonies.

⁵⁰BIBLIOGRAPHY

American University. *Area Handbook for Zambia*. 3rd ed. Washington, D.C.: Government Printing Office, 1979.

Anglin, Douglas G., and Timothy Shaw. *Zambia's Foreign Policy: Studies in Diplomacy and Dependence*. Boulder, Colo.: Westview, 1979.

Burdette, Marcia M. *Zambia: Between Two Worlds*. Boulder, Colo.: Westview Press, 1988.

Chan, Stephen. *Kaunda and Southern Africa: Image and Reality in Foreign Policy*. New York: British Academic Press, 1992.

Chanock, Martin. *Law, Custom, and Social Order: The Colonial Experience in Malawi and Zambia*. New York: Cambridge University Press, 1985.

Fagan, Brian (ed.). *A Short History of Zambia*. New York: Oxford University Press, 1968.

Getzel, Cheryl, *et al.* (eds.). *The Dynamics of the One-Party State in Zambia*. Wolfeboro, N.H.: Longwood Publishing Group, 1984.

Grotpeter, John J. *Historical Dictionary of Zambia*. Metuchen, N.J.: Scarecrow, 1979.

Hamalengwa, M. *Class Struggles in Zambia, 1889–1989, & The Fall of Kenneth Kaunda, 1990–1991*. Lanham, Md.: University Press of America, 1992.

Hansen, Karen Tranberg. *Distant Companions: Servants and Employers in Zambia, 1900–1985*. Ithaca: Cornell University Press, 1989.

Kaunda, Kenneth. *Letter to My Children*. London: Longman, 1963.

———. *Zambia Shall Be Free*. New York: Praeger, 1963.

Pettman, Jan. *Zambia: Security and Conflict*. New York: St. Martin's, 1974.

Rotberg, Robert I. *The Rise of Nationalism in Central Africa: The Making of Malawi and Zambia, 1873–1964*. Cambridge, Mass.: Harvard University Press, 1965.

Tordoff, William (ed.). *Government and Politics in Zambia*. Berkeley: University of California Press, 1974.

Tordoff, William. *Administration in Zambia*. Madison: University of Wisconsin Press, 1981.

ZIMBABWE

Republic of Zimbabwe

CAPITAL: Harare.

FLAG: The flag has seven equal horizontal stripes of green, yellow, red, black, red, yellow, and green. At the hoist is a white triangle, which contains a representation in yellow of the bird of Zimbabwe, superimposed on a red star.

ANTHEM: *God Bless Africa.*

MONETARY UNIT: The Zimbabwe dollar (z$) is a paper currency of 100 cents. There are coins of 1, 5, 10, 20, and 50 cents and 1 dollar, and notes of 2, 5, 10, and 20 dollars. z$1 = US$0.0057 (or US$1 = z$175.00).

WEIGHTS AND MEASURES: The metric system is used.

HOLIDAYS: New Year's Day, 1 January; Independence Day, 18 April; Workers' Day, 1 May; Africa Day, 25 May; Heroes' Days, 11–13 August; Christmas Day, 25 December; Boxing Day, 26 December. Movable holidays are Good Friday, Holy Saturday, Easter Monday, and Whitmonday.

TIME: 2 PM = noon GMT.

¹LOCATION, SIZE, AND EXTENT

A landlocked country of southcentral Africa, Zimbabwe (formerly Rhodesia) lies between the Zambezi River on the N and the Limpopo River on the S. It has an area of 390,580 sq km (150,804 sq mi), with a length of 852 km (529 mi) WNW–ESE and a width of 710 km (441 mi) NNE–SSW. Comparatively, the area occupied by Zimbabwe is slightly larger than the state of Montana. Bounded on the N and E by Mozambique, on the S by the Republic of South Africa, on the SW by Botswana, and on the NW and N by Zambia, Zimbabwe has a total boundary length of 3,066 km (1,905 mi). Zimbabwe's capital city, Harare, is located in the northeast part of the country.

²TOPOGRAPHY

Most of Zimbabwe is rolling plateau, with over 75% of it lying between 600 and 1,500 m (2,000–5,000 ft) above sea level, and almost all of it over 300 m (1,000 ft). The area of high plateau, known as the highveld, is some 650 km (400 mi) long by 80 km (50 mi) wide, and stretches northeast to southwest at 1,200 to 1,675 m (4,000–5,500 ft). This culminates in the northeast in the Inyanga mountains, reaching the country's highest point at Mt. Inyangani, 2,592 m (8,504 ft). On either side of the highveld is the middleveld, a plateau ranging from about 600 to 1,200 m (2,000–4,000 ft) in height. Below 610 m (2,000 ft) are areas making up the lowveld, wide and grassy plains in the basins of the Zambezi and the Limpopo.

The highveld is a central ridge forming the country's watershed, with streams flowing southeast to the Limpopo and Sabi rivers and northwest into the Zambezi. Only the largest of the many rivers have an all-year-round flow of water.

³CLIMATE

Altitude and relief greatly affect both temperature and rainfall in Zimbabwe. The higher areas in the east and the highveld receive more rainfall and are cooler than the lower areas. Temperatures on the highveld vary from 12–13°C (54–55°F) in winter to 24°C (75°F) in summer. On the lowveld the temperatures are usually 6°C (11°F) higher, and summer temperatures in the Zambezi and Limpopo valleys average between 32° and 38°C (90–100°F). Rainfall decreases from east to west. The eastern mountains receive more than 100 cm (40 in) annually, while Harare has 81 cm (32 in) and Bulawayo 61 cm (24 in). The south and southwest receive little rainfall. Seasonal shortages of water are common.

The summer rainy season lasts from November to March. It is followed by a transitional season, during which both rainfall and temperatures decrease. The cool, dry season follows, lasting from mid-May to mid-August. Finally, there is the warm, dry season, which lasts until the onset of the rains.

⁴FLORA AND FAUNA

The country is mostly savanna, although the moist and mountainous east supports tropical evergreen and hardwood forests. Trees include teak and mahogany, knobthorn, msasa, and baobab. Among the numerous flowers and shrubs are hibiscus, spider lily, leonotus, cassia, tree wisteria, and dombeya.

Mammals include elephant, lion, buffalo, hippopotamus, rhinoceros, gorilla, chimpanzee, baboon, okapi, giraffe, kudu, duiker, eland, sable, gemsbok, waterbuck, zebra, warthog, lynx, aardvark, porcupine, fox, badger, otter, hare, bat, shrew, and scaly anteater.

Snakes and lizards abound. The largest lizard, the water monitor, is found in many rivers, as are several species of crocodile. About 500 species of birds include the ant-thrush, barbet, bee-eater, bishop bird, bulbul, bush-warbler, drongo, emerald cuckoo, grouse, gray lourie, and pheasant.

⁵ENVIRONMENT

Among the most serious of Zimbabwe's environmental problems is erosion of its agricultural lands and deforestation. By 1992, deforestation was progressing at the rate of 70,000–100,000 ha per year, or about 1.5% of the nation's forestland. The confinement of the African population to less productive lands before independence put severe pressure on these lands, as much as half of which may have been irreversibly damaged.

Air and water pollution result from the combined effects of transportation vehicles, mining, fertilizers, and the cement industry. Zimbabwe contributes 0.1% of the world's total gas emissions, and its cities produce 0.5 million tons of solid waste per year. Zimbabwe has been estimated to have the highest DDT concentrations in the world in its agricultural produce.

In 1994, nine of the nation's mammal species and six bird species were endangered, as well as 96 types of plants. Zimbabwe has about half of the world's population of black rhinoceroses, an endangered species. For protection, the government has adopted a policy of shooting poachers on sight.

[6] POPULATION

According to census figures based on a sample, the population as of August 1992 was 10,401,767, of which about 97.6% was African, 2% European, and 0.4% Asian or of mixed race. The population was estimated at 11,669,803 in 1994 and projected to be 13,194,000 in the year 2000, assuming a crude birthrate of 37.6 per 1,000 population, a crude death rate of 10.8, and a net natural increase of 26.8 during 1995–2000. Population density in 1994 was 29.9 per sq km (77.5 per sq mi). The largest cities, with their populations at the time of the 1992 census, were Harare (formerly Salisbury), 1,478,810, and Bulawayo, 620,936. Other cities included Chitungwiza, Gweru (formerly Gwelo), and Mutare (formerly Umtali).

[7] MIGRATION

By early 1987, about 110,000 whites were estimated to have remained in Zimbabwe, about half the number on independence in 1980. There were also about 25,000 Coloured (of mixed race) and 10,000 Asians. Some 1.5 million people who had left for neighboring states during the civil war returned after independence, putting considerable strain on the new nation. In addition, by the end of 1992, famine and civil war in Mozambique had driven an estimated 136,600 Mozambicans into Zimbabwe. In 1991 there were 24,442 Zimbabwe-born whites and 13,568 blacks living in South Africa.

[8] ETHNIC GROUPS

Africans in Zimbabwe are mainly related to the two major Bantu-speaking groups, the Shona (about 77% of the population) and the Ndebele (about 18%). Of the former group, the Korekore predominate in the north, the Zezuru are in the center around Harare, the Karanga are in the south, the Ndau and Manyika in the east, the Kalanga in the west; the Rozwi are spread throughout the country. The various clans of the Ndebele, more recent immigrants from the south, occupy the area around Bulawayo and Gwanda. Other groups include the Tonga near Kariba Lake, and the Sotho, Venda, and Hlengwe along the southern border.

Europeans are almost entirely either immigrants from the UK or South Africa or their descendants; those from South Africa include a substantial number of South African Dutch (Afrikaner) descent. There are small groups of Portuguese, Italians, and other Europeans, as well as Asians and peoples of mixed ancestry.

[9] LANGUAGES

The Shona speak dialects of the same Bantu language, Shona. There are six major dialects: Karanga, Zezuru, Korekore, Manyika, Ndau, and Kalanga. The Ndebele speak modified versions of Ndebele (or Sindebele), which belongs to the Nguni group of southeast Bantu languages.

English, the official language, is spoken by most Europeans and by an increasing number of Africans.

[10] RELIGIONS

About 55% of the total population was Christian as of 1993. Traditional religious practices are still followed by at least 40%

of the population. Of professing Christians, Protestants constitute some 17%, adherents of African indigenous churches, 14%, and Roman Catholics, 8.7%. There are several Jewish congregations in Harare and Bulawayo. A small percentage of the population is Muslim, and there are some Baha'is and Hindus.

[11] TRANSPORTATION

In 1991, the National Railways of Zimbabwe, a public corporation, operated 4,304 km (2,675 mi) of rail lines. Rail links exist with Zambia, Mozambique, Botswana, and the Republic of South Africa. Electrification of the railroads was begun following independence. There were 85,237 km (52,966 mi) of road in 1991, of which 15,0800 km (9,800 mi) were classified as paved. In 1991 there were 265,000 motor vehicles in use, including 200,000 passenger cars.

Zimbabwe operates domestic, regional, and European flights. Harare and Bulawayo are the principal airports. In 1992, total scheduled traffic included 810 million passenger-km and 139 million freight ton-km of flight. Zimbabwe's international cargo airline, Affretair, flew some 2 million km (1,242,800 mi) in 1991, performing 48.6 million freight ton-km of service.

[12] HISTORY

Evidence of Stone Age cultures dating back 100,000 years has been found, and it is thought that the San people, now living mostly in the Kalahari Desert, are the descendants of Zimbabwe's original inhabitants. The remains of ironworking cultures that date back to AD 300 have been discovered. Little is known of the early ironworkers, but it is believed that they were farmers, herdsmen, and hunters who lived in small groups. They put pressure on the San by gradually taking over the land. With the arrival of the Bantu-speaking Shona from the north between the 10th and 11th centuries AD, the San were driven out or killed, and the early ironworkers were incorporated into the invading groups. The Shona gradually developed gold and ivory trade with the coast, and by the mid-15th century had established a strong empire, with its capital at the ancient city of Zimbabwe. This empire, known as Munhumutapa, split by the end of the century, the southern part becoming the Urozwi Empire, which flourished for two centuries.

By the time the British began arriving in the mid-19th century, the Shona people had long been subjected to slave raids. The once-powerful Urozwi Empire had been destroyed in the 1830s by the Ndebele, who, under Mzilikaze, had fled from the Zulus in South Africa. David Livingstone, a Scottish missionary and explorer, was chiefly responsible for opening the whole region to European penetration. His explorations in the 1850s focused public attention on Central Africa, and his reports on the slave trade stimulated missionary activity. In 1858, after visiting Mzilikaze, Robert Moffat, Livingstone's father-in-law, established Inyati Mission, the first permanent European settlement in what is now Zimbabwe.

To forestall Portuguese and Boer expansion, both the British government and Cecil Rhodes actively sought to acquire territory. Rhodes, whose fortune had been made through diamond mining in South Africa, became especially active in gaining mineral rights and in sending settlers into Matabeleland (the area occupied by the Ndebele people) and Mashonaland (the area occupied by the Shona people). In 1888, Lobengula, king of the Ndebele, accepted a treaty with Great Britain and granted to Charles Rudd, one of Rhodes's agents, exclusive mineral rights to the lands he controlled. Gold was already known to exist in Mashonaland, so, with the grant of rights, Rhodes was able to obtain a royal charter for his British South Africa Company (BSAC) in 1889. The BSAC sent a group of settlers with a force of European police into Mashonaland, where they founded the town of Salisbury (now Harare). Rhodes gained the right to dispose of land to

LOCATION: 15°37′ to 22°25′s; 25°14′ to 33°4′E. **BOUNDARY LENGTHS:** Mozambique, 1,223 km (760 mi); South Africa, 225 km (140 mi); Botswana, 813 km (505 mi); Zambia, 727 km (452 mi).

settlers (a right he was already exercising de facto). With the defeat of the Ndebele and the Shona between 1893 and 1897, Europeans were guaranteed unimpeded settlement. The name Rhodesia was common usage by 1895.

Under BSAC administration, British settlement continued, but conflicts arose between the settlers and the company. In 1923, Southern Rhodesia was annexed to the crown; its African inhabitants thereby became British subjects, and the colony received its basic constitution. Ten years later, the BSAC ceded its mineral rights to the territory's government for £2 million.

After the onset of self-government, the major issue in Southern Rhodesia was the relationship between the European settlers and the African population. The British government, besides controlling the colony's foreign affairs, retained certain powers to safeguard the rights of Africans. In 1930, however, Southern Rhodesia adopted a land apportionment act which was accepted by the British government. Under this measure, about half the total land area, including all the mining and industrial regions and all the areas served by railroads or roads, was reserved for

Europeans. Most of the rest was designated as Tribal Trust Land, native purchase land, or unassigned land. Later acts firmly entrenched the policy of dividing land on a racial basis.

In 1953, the Central African Federation was formed, consisting of the three British territories of Northern Rhodesia (now Zambia), Nyasaland (now Malawi), and Southern Rhodesia, with each territory retaining its original constitutional status. In 1962, in spite of the opposition of the federal prime minister, Sir Roy Welensky, Nyasaland and Northern Rhodesia withdrew from the federation with British approval. The federation disbanded in 1963. Southern Rhodesia, although legally still a colony, sought an independent course under the name of Rhodesia.

Political agitation in Rhodesia increased after the UK's granting of independence to Malawi and Zambia. The white-settler government demanded formalization of independence, which it claimed had been in effect since 1923. The African nationalists also demanded independence, but under conditions of universal franchise and African majority rule. The British government refused to yield to settler demands without amendments to the colony's constitution, including a graduated extension of the franchise leading to eventual African rule. Negotiations repeatedly broke down, and on 5 November 1965, Rhodesian Prime Minister Ian Smith declared a state of emergency. On 11 November, the Smith government issued a unilateral declaration of independence (since known as UDI). The British government viewed UDI as illegal and imposed limited economic sanctions, but these measures did not bring about the desired results. In December, the UN Security Council passed a resolution calling for selective mandatory sanctions against Rhodesia. Further attempts at a negotiated settlement ended in failure. In a referendum held on 20 June 1969, the Rhodesian electorate—92% white—approved the establishment of a republic.

The British governor-general, Sir Humphrey Gibbs, resigned on 24 June 1969. The Legislative Council passed the constitution bill in November, and Rhodesia declared itself a republic on 2 March 1970. The UK called the declaration illegal, and 11 countries closed their consulates in Rhodesia. The UN Security Council called on member states not to recognize any acts by the illegal regime and condemned Portugal and South Africa for maintaining relations with Rhodesia.

Problems in Rhodesia deepened after UDI, largely as a result of regional and international political pressure, African nationalist demands, and African guerrilla activities. Members of the African National Council (ANC), an African nationalist group, were increasingly subjected to persecution and arrest. Nevertheless, guerrilla activity continued. The principal African nationalist groups, besides the ANC, were the Zimbabwe African People's Union (ZAPU), and the Zimbabwe African National Union (ZANU).

A meeting took place in Geneva in October 1976 between the British and Smith governments and four African nationalist groups. Prominent at the meeting were Joshua Nkomo, the leader of ZAPU; Robert Mugabe, leader of ZANU; Bishop Abel Muzorewa of the ANC; and the Reverend Ndabaningi Sithole, former leader of ZANU. Nkomo and Mugabe had previously formed an alliance, the Patriotic Front. The conference was unable to find the basis for a national settlement; but on 3 March 1978, the Smith regime signed an internal agreement with Muzorewa, Sithole, and other leaders, providing for qualified majority rule and universal suffrage. Although Bishop Muzorewa, whose party won a majority in the elections of April 1979, became the first black prime minister of the country (now renamed Zimbabwe-Rhodesia), the Patriotic Front continued fighting.

Meanwhile, the British government had begun new consultations on the conflict, and at the Commonwealth of Nations Conference in Lusaka, Zambia, in August 1979, committed itself to seeking a settlement. Negotiations that began at Lancaster House, in England, on 10 September resulted in an agreement, by 21 December, on a new, democratic constitution, democratic elections, and independence. On 10 December, the Zimbabwe-Rhodesian parliament had dissolved itself, and the country reverted to formal colonial status during the transition period before independence. That month, sanctions were lifted and a cease-fire declared. Following elections held in February, Robert Mugabe became the first prime minister and formed a coalition government that included Joshua Nkomo. The independent nation of Zimbabwe was proclaimed on 18 April 1980, and the new parliament opened on 14 May 1980.

Independence and Factionalism

Following independence, Zimbabwe initially made significant economic and social progress, but internal dissent became increasingly evident. The long-simmering rivalry erupted between Mugabe's dominant ZANU-Patriotic Front Party, which represented the majority Shona tribes, and Nkomo's ZAPU, which had

the support of the minority Ndebele. A major point of contention was Mugabe's intention to make Zimbabwe a one-party state. Mugabe ousted Nkomo from the cabinet in February 1982 after the discovery of arms caches that were alleged to be part of a ZAPU-led coup attempt. On 8 March 1983, Nkomo went into exile, but returned to Parliament in August.

Meanwhile, internal security worsened, especially in Matabeleland, where Nkomo supporters resorted to terrorism. The government responded by jailing suspected dissidents, using emergency powers dating from the period of white rule, and by military campaigns against the terrorists. The government's Fifth Brigade, trained by the Democratic People's Republic of Korea and loyal to Mugabe, was accused of numerous atrocities against civilians in Matabeleland during 1983. By early 1984, it was reported that many residents in Matabeleland were starving as a result of the military's interruption of food supplies to the area.

Armed dissidents continued to operate in Matabeleland until 1987, and food supplies in the area continued to be inadequate. A round of particularly brutal killings—men, women, and children—occurred late in the year. The violence abated after the two largest political parties, ZANU and ZAPU, agreed to merge in December 1987.

A growing problem, however, was the political instability of Zimbabwe's neighbors to the south and east. In 1986, South African forces raided the premises of the South African black-liberation African National Congress in Harare, and 10,000 Zimbabwean troops were deployed in Mozambique, seeking to keep antigovernment forces in that country from severing Zimbabwe's rail, road, and oil-pipeline links with the port of Beira in Mozambique. Although Beira is the closest port to land-locked Zimbabwe, because of the guerrilla war in Mozambique about 85% of Zimbabwe's foreign trade was passing through South Africa instead.

Despite its reputed commitment to socialism, the Mugabe government has been slow to dismantle the socioeconomic structures of the old Rhodesia. Until 1990, the government's hands were tied by the Lancaster House accords. Private property, most particularly large white-owned estates, could not be confiscated without fair market compensation. Nevertheless, economic progress was solid and Zimbabwe seemed to have come to terms with its settler minority. There has been only modest resettlement of the landless (52,000 out of 162,000 landless families from 1980 to 1990) and when white farmers were bought out, often black politicians were the beneficiaries. Just over 4,000 white farmers still own more than one-third of the land, often the best land.

In March 1992, a controversial Land Acquisition Act was passed calling for the government to purchase half of the mostly white-owned commercial farming land at below-market prices, without the right of appeal, in order to redistribute land to black peasants. However, the government continued to move slowly and not until April 1993 was it announced that 70 farms, totaling 470,000 acres, would be purchased. Unease among whites grew, and fear of even worse unemployment, already estimated at around 40%. Economic conditions also threatened to untrack the Economic Structural Adjustment Program (ESAP) designed by the IMF and the World Bank. ESAP pressed for a market-driven economy, reduction of the civil service, and an end to price controls and commodity subsidies. It also sought to improve incentives for foreign investors by reducing government spending, reducing tariffs, and ending artificial supports for the currency.

In this faltering economic situation, opposition to Mugabe grew. In January 1992, Sithole returned from seven years of self-imposed exile in the US. In July, Ian Smith chaired a meeting of Rhodesian-era parties seeking to form a coalition in opposition to Mugabe. Sithole and his ZANU-Ndonga Party, the United African National Congress, the largely-white Conservative Alliance, and Edgar Tekere's Zimbabwe Unity Movement (ZUM) were included. Students, church leaders, trade unionists, and the media began to speak out. In May 1992 a new pressure group, the Forum for Democratic Reform, was launched in preparation for the 1995 elections. It evolved into the Forum Party, which advocates free enterprise, clean government, respect for human rights, and a drastic reduction of state control of the economy.

In the March 1990 elections, Mugabe was reelected with 78.3% of the vote. ZUM's candidate, Tekere, received about 21.7% of the vote. For parliament, ZANU-PF got 117 seats; ZUM, two seats; and ZANU-Ndonga, one seat. There was a sharp drop in voter participation, and the election was marred by restrictions on opposition activity and open intimidation of opposition voters. At first, Mugabe insisted that the results were a mandate to establish a one-party state. In 1991, however, growing opposition abroad and domestically, even within ZANU-PF itself, forced him to postpone his plans. Within Zimbabwe, many have come to believe that the overcentralization of power would be a betrayal of the revolution. With a slumping economy, compounded by an extensive drought in 1991 and 1992, the Mugabe government is losing support. It has responded by restriction of human and political rights, weakening the Bill of Rights, placing checks on the heretofore independent judiciary, and tampering with voters' rolls and opposition party financing. It even suspended the investigation into the 1982–87 Matabeleland Crisis, a decision that prompted a November 1993 reprimand by the OAU's Human Rights Commission.

¹³GOVERNMENT

Under the constitution that took effect on 18 April 1980, independent Zimbabwe has a bicameral Parliament. The lower house, the House of Assembly, had 100 members, 20 of whom were elected by white voters, and 80 by persons on the common voters' roll, which included all voters except whites. The upper house, or Senate, had 40 members, 14 of whom were chosen by the 80 Assembly members elected from the common roll, 10 by the 20 white Assembly members, 10 by the Council of Chiefs, and 6 nominated by the president on the advice of the prime minister. The racial basis of Parliament could not be amended until 1987 unless by unanimous vote of Parliament; amendment afterward needed only a 70% vote of the Assembly. During the first 10 years of independence, the Declaration of Rights in the Constitution could be amended only by a unanimous vote of the Assembly; amendment of other clauses required a 70% majority. In August 1987, as soon as the constitution allowed, the separate representation for whites in Parliament was abolished and the 20 seats were temporarily filled by representatives selected by the other 80 members. The two houses of Parliament were merged after the 1990 elections into a chamber of 150 members, 120 elected by popular vote, 10 traditional chiefs, eight provincial governors, and 12 appointed by the president. Its term of office is five years. At the same time, another constitutional change created an executive presidency and abolished the office of prime minister. ZANU leader Robert Mugabe assumed the presidency on 1 December 1987 and was reelected in March 1990.

Parliament sits for a maximum of 5 years. The president is directly elected for a 6-year term and may be reelected. There is universal suffrage from age 18.

¹⁴POLITICAL PARTIES

The Rhodesian Front Party, which dominated politics from its formation in March 1962 until the establishment of majority rule in 1979, advocated racial separation, division of land on a racial basis, and the protection of the Rhodesian whites. The party won all 20 Assembly seats reserved for whites in both the 1979 and 1980 elections, and in 1981, it changed its name to the Republican Front Party (RFP). Ian Smith, who served (1964–79) as prime minister, remained as party leader until his suspension from Parliament in 1987. He was succeeded by Mark Partridge. The name of the party had previously been changed again to the Conservative Alliance Zimbabwe (CAZ). The CAZ won 15 of the 20 seats allotted to whites in the 1985 elections.

The principal black parties in Zimbabwean politics originated in the struggle for independence on a tribal basis. The Zimbabwe African People's Union (ZAPU) was formed in December 1961 and led by Joshua Nkomo. It was split in July 1963 by the creation of the Zimbabwe African National Union (ZANU), led by the Reverend Ndabaningi Sithole, and later by Robert Mugabe. ZAPU's constituency was eventually reduced to the Ndebele minority, while ZANU gained wide support among the Shona tribes. Both ZAPU and ZANU took up arms against the government and in 1976 allied themselves in the Patriotic Front (PF).

After Bishop Abel Muzorewa accepted the Smith government's proposal for an internal constitutional settlement in 1978, his followers, now known as the United African National Council (UANC), emerged as the major party. In elections on 17–21 April 1979, the UANC captured a majority of 51 seats in the new Assembly, and Muzorewa became the nation's first black prime minister. The elections, however, were boycotted by the PF, which continued its armed opposition to the government.

Under British auspices, a new constitutional settlement obtained PF approval in 1979, and the elections of 27–29 February 1980 were contested by nine parties, including ZANU-Patriotic Front, led by Robert Mugabe, and ZAPU (which registered under the name Popular Front). Of the 80 Assembly seats elected from the common rolls, ZANU-Patriotic Front took 57, Popular Front (or ZAPU) 20, and UNAC 3. In the July 1985 elections, ZANU-PF won 63 seats, PF-ZAPU, 15. After much enmity and bitterness during most of the 1980s, ZAPU and ZANU finally agreed to merge in late 1987 under the name of ZANU and the merger was consummated in December, 1989.

President Mugabe declared his intention to make Zimbabwe a one-party state by 1990. He regarded his party's victory in the 1990 elections as a mandate to proceed with his plans to establish ZANU-PF as the only legal party. He was soon turned away from that scheme by strong pressure from creditor governments abroad and a chorus of opposition domestically, including from within ZANU-PF. Zimbabwe got caught up in the general press throughout tropical Africa for greater decentralization of power and competitive party politics.

New parties began to emerge in the late 1980s and early 1990s in preparation for the expected elections in 1995. Tekere's Zimbabwe Unity Movement (ZUM) contested the 1990 elections with some success. The UANC, still led by Muzorewa, merged with ZUM in January 1994. In January, long-time Mugabe rival Sithole returned from exile and created his own party, also using the ZANU rubic of ZANU-Ndonga or sometimes ZANU-Sithole.

In March 1993, former Chief Justice Enoch Dumbutshena launched the Forum Party, an outgrowth of the pressure group, Forum for Democratic Reform. The CAZ is still active, as is the Democratic Party, which has emerged from a split within ZUM.

¹⁵LOCAL GOVERNMENT

Each of the eight provinces of Zimbabwe is administered by a provincial commissioner appointed by the central government. Local services are provided by city, town, and rural councils. The Ministry of Local Government, Rural and Urban Planning is charged with ensuring the establishment of local authorities where necessary and local adherence to legislation.

¹⁶JUDICIAL SYSTEM

The legal system is based on Roman-Dutch law and has been influenced by the system of South Africa. A four-member Supreme Court, headed by the chief justice, has original jurisdiction over alleged violations of fundamental rights guaranteed in the constitution and appellate jurisdiction over other matters. There is a High Court consisting of general and appellate divisions. Below the High Court are regional magistrate's courts with civil jurisdiction and magistrate's courts with both civil and criminal jurisdiction. Before independence, separate African courts had jurisdiction over cases involving traditional law and custom. Beginning in 1981, these courts were integrated into the national system.

The chief justice of the High Court is appointed by the president upon recommendation of the Judicial Service Commission. The Commission also advises the president on the appointment of the other judges.

In 1990 the Customary Law and Local Courts Act established a unitary court system made up of headmen's courts, chiefs' courts, magisterial courts, the High Court, and the Supreme Court. Under this system, customary law cases can be appealed through all levels to the Supreme Court. The judiciary has earned a reputation for independence from the executive branch.

[17]ARMED FORCES

After independence, a new army was formed by integration of the former Rhodesian Security Force and the two guerrilla armies, ZANLA (the military wing of ZANU) and ZIPRA (the military wing of ZAPU). Many former ZIPRA members, however, began deserting to the insurgents' ranks in 1982 to protest government treatment of their former leader, Joshua Nkomo.

Regular armed forces numbered 48,500 in 1993. The army had 6,000 troops organized into 26 infantry battalions, 1 artillery regiment, 1 armored regiment, 1 engineer regiment, and supporting units. The air force had 2,500 personnel and 36 combat aircraft. Paramilitary forces included the Zimbabwe Republic Police Force, with 15,000 members, and the Police Support Unit with 2,000 members. The national militia came to 4,000. Estimated defense expenditures for 1991 were $412 milliion or 6% of GDP.

Zimbabwe provides 3,000 soldiers for the defense of Mozambique.

[18]INTERNATIONAL COOPERATION

Zimbabwe became a UN member on 25 August 1980 and belongs to ECA and all the nonregional specialized agencies except IAEA and IMO. It is also a member of the African Development Bank, the Commonwealth of Nations, G-77, the OAU, the Southern African Defense Co-ordinating Commission (SADCC), and the Preferential Trade Association (PTA) for eastern and southern Africa. Zimbabwe is a signatory of GATT and the Law of the Sea.

[19]ECONOMY

Zimbabwe has developed one of the most diverse economies in Africa. It has abundant agricultural and mineral resources and a well-developed industrial sector and infrastructure. Average annual growth during the first post-independence decade was 2.9%. However, problems abound. The Government has remained committed to the Economic Structural Adjustment Program (ESAP), despite severe hardships the Program caused average Zimbabweans. Although Zimbabwe began to recover from the effects of the devastating 1991–92 drought, which caused a decline of between 8% and 9% in the GDP, the unemployment rate is almost 45% and thousands remain chronically dependent on food support. Although the need for land reform is widely accepted, the 1992 Land Acquisition Act has been implemented along racial lines. Zimbabwe's external debt rose considerably in the 1980s. The debt-service ratio in 1991 stood at 27.2%. In conjunction with the IMF, Zimbabwe drew up a 1991–1995 economic reform plan. Central to this program was the reduction of the civil service by 25% with some 32,000 jobs to be eliminated by 1994.

[20]INCOME

In 1992, Zimbabwe's GNP was $5,896 million at current prices, or $570 per capita. For the period 1985–92 the average inflation rate was 17.6%, resulting in a real growth rate in per capita GNP of –0.6%.

In 1992, the GDP was $5,690 million in current US dollars. It is estimated that agriculture, hunting, forestry, and fishing contributed 17% to GDP; mining and quarrying, 6%; manufacturing, 23%; electricity, gas, and water, 3%; construction, 2%; wholesale and retail trade, 9%; transport, storage, and communication, 6%; finance, insurance, real estate, and business services, 5%; community, social, and personal services, 15%; and other sources 15%.

[21]LABOR

In 1991, there were 1,187,300 employed civilians in Zimbabwe; 681,400 in services, 266,500 in industry, and 239,400 in agriculture. The total labor force is estimated at 2.75 million, or 27% of the total population. Average monthly nonagricultural earnings in 1992 were z$932.30. Average wages were lowest in agriculture (z$203.30 in 1991). Since independence, a priority of the government's wage policy has been reduction of the huge variation in earnings among workers, partly by increasing minimum wages and by controlling increases in higher wage brackets. Growing unemployment remains a serious problem as new jobs fail to keep pace with the number of new job seekers; the unemployment rate in 1991 was believed to be at least 17–31%.

In 1981, the Zimbabwe Congress of Trade Unions (ZCTU) was formed as an umbrella organization for all trade unions and to promote the formation of a single trade union for each industry. As of 1992, about 21% of the salaried work force were members of the 35 unions which formed the ZCTU. Spontaneous strikes and lockouts are banned. Government-mandated worker committees carry out many functions performed by unions elsewhere, and annual wage increases are mandated for all workers.

[22]AGRICULTURE

Since 1991, Zimbabwean agriculture has undergone a fundamental transition away from artificial producer and consumer prices, which were set far below world market levels. Many commercial farms changed from corn, cotton, and oilseed production to tobacco and horticultural activities because the government refused to permit producer prices to keep pace with rising input prices. Some 239,400 individuals (20%) were engaged in agriculture in 1991, including 4,000 commercial farmers, who are mostly descendants of European colonists.

In 1992, drought severely affected the output of every crop except tobacco. Corn, wheat, cotton, oilseed, coffee, and sugar outputs all declined by at least 75%. Tobacco production in 1992 exceeded 200,000 tons, and the expected 1993 production should top 220,000 tons, further contributing to oversupply of the leaf on the world market and consequent tumbling prices. Corn production in 1992 totaled only 362,000 tons, down from 1,586,000 tons in 1991 because of the drought. In normal years, Zimbabwe is one of Africa's largest corn exporters.

Quantities of cotton both for export and to supply domestic textile manufacture sharply expanded before the most recent drought. In 1992, cotton production totaled 27,000 tons, down from 72,000 tons in 1991. Marketed production figures of other crops in 1991 and 1992 (respectively) were wheat, 259 and 81 tons; sorghum, about 68 and 29 tons; soybeans, 111 and 51 tons; peanuts, 107 and 34 tons; coffee, 12 and 4 tons; and sugarcane, 3,236 and 300. Rice, potatoes, tea, and pyrethrum are also grown.

[23]ANIMAL HUSBANDRY

In 1992, some 4,700,000 head of cattle, 580,000 sheep, 290,000 hogs, and 2,570,000 goats were held. Chickens numbered about

13 million. Livestock raising is an important industry, which has been helped by increased diversification initiated after 1965. In 1992, cattle slaughterings totaled 440,000 head; sheep, 38,000 head; pigs, 203,000 head. Fresh milk production from cows totaled 415,000 tons.

24FISHING

There is some commercial fishing on Kariba Lake. Rural Zimbabweans fish the smaller lakes and rivers. The total catch in 1991 was estimated at 22,155 tons.

25FORESTRY

In 1991, 49% of Zimbabwe's land area was estimated to be forest or woodland, but this classification included scattered tree savanna and considerable areas of grassland likely to be reforested in the foreseeable future. Forestry is gaining importance in Zimbabwe. There are hardwood forests in the western part of the country and in the Victoria Falls area. About 100,000 tons of teak, mahogany, and mukwa (kiaat) are cut annually. Roundwood production totaled 7.9 million cu m in 1991; sawn wood production was 190,000 cu m (in 1984). Softwood afforestation projects have been undertaken in the eastern districts to supply local needs heretofore met by imports; however, the loss of woodlands may be as high as 1.5% per year.

26MINING

Zimbabwe is a world leader in the production of lithium, asbestos, and chromium. Zimbabwe has more than half of the world's known reserves of chromium. In order of value, the most important minerals in 1991 were gold, asbestos, nickel, coal, copper, chromite, tin, and silver. Coal deposits in the Hwange area are substantial, and nickel production has increased significantly since 1965. Palladium, zinc, lead, cobalt, barite, quartz, and talc are also among the more than three dozen minerals mined in Zimbabwe. Mineral output in 1991 included coal, 5,616,000 tons; chromium ore, 563,634 tons; asbestos, 141,697 tons; copper, 14,420 tons; nickel, 12,371 tons; and gold, 17,820 kg. More than 90% of mineral output is exported.

Gold accounted for 33% of mineral export earnings in 1991; the mining sector accounted for 7% of the GDP of $6.4 billion, and 40% of total foreign exchange in 1991. In the late 1960s and early 1970s, copper had replaced gold and asbestos as the most valuable mineral, but its production has not kept pace with that of other minerals. The Mining (Alluvial Gold, Public Streams) regulations of 1991 legalized gold panning, but all gold panners must sell their gold to the Reserve Bank of Zimbabwe; the sale of gold to private individuals is illegal. The new code also permits unlimited foreign exchange to companies that export more than 75% of their production, and mining companies are now allowed to keep 5% of their export earnings in order to buy imported raw materials.

27ENERGY AND POWER

Zimbabwe relies heavily on hydroelectricity and coal for its energy needs. Wood is also still important. Petroleum accounts for only 9% of Zimbabwe's total energy consumption, but provides most motor fuels. A pipeline from the Mozambique port of Beira to Mutare provides the majority of Zimbabwe's refined petroleum and diesel oil; the rest comes from South Africa. Mobil's recent exploration in the Zambezi Valley has showed some promise for locating natural gas reserves, but not for oil. Coal reserves in Zimbabwe are estimated at 30 billion tons. Production in 1991 totaled 5.6 million tons, with much of that amount going to the coal-fired Hwange plant for electricity production. In 1982, a plant producing ethanol from sugarcane opened and now produces some 20% of motor fuel requirements. The use of solar energy is increasing.

Power production was virtually all from coal-burning thermal plants until the construction of a 666,000 kw hydroelectric power project at Kariba Gorge on the Zambezi River, begun in 1955 as a joint undertaking with Zambia and the UK. Electrical production is shared with Zambia and, as of 1991, Zimbabwe imported about 9% of its total electricity requirements from the Zambian side. In 1991, Zimbabwe produced 9,565 million kwh. Installed capacity that year was 2,038,000 kw.

28INDUSTRY

Zimbabwe has a substantial and diverse manufacturing base, which is partly a legacy of the international sanctions imposed over the five years prior to independence. The manufacturing sector accounted for 26% of GDP in 1991, when the volume index of manufacturing reached 144. The index fell to 123 in 1992 and declined further in 1993. Wood and furniture products measured substantial gains in 1991, while other key sectors (clothing, chemicals, petroleum and metal products) registered declines.

Zimbabwe has a substantial cotton and textile industry and metal and engineering sector. The building materials industry has been expanded. Other leading industries are food processing, sugar refining, tobacco, clothing, chemicals, beverages, industrial coke, cement, pig iron and crude steel, nitrogenous and phosphate fertilizers, unwrought nickel and tin, wood pulp and furniture.

Zimbabwe's national generating capacity is 1,900 Mw (1989) from thermal and hydroelectric sources. Maximum demand is 1,400 Mw. As growth in demand is anticipated, extensions of the country's power generating capacity were agreed to in 1991. The 1992 drought lowered hydroelectric production significantly, forcing Zimbabwe to make emergency power purchases from Zaire and Zambia.

29SCIENCE AND TECHNOLOGY

Much of Zimbabwe's research effort is directed at improvements in agriculture. The government's budget for agricultural research is administered by the Agricultural Research Council. In Harare, at the Blair Research Laboratory, simple, innovative technologies are being developed to improve Zimbabwe's water supply and sewage disposal. Other research organizations, all in Harare, include the Geological Survey of Zimbabwe, the Institute of Mining Research, and the Public Health Laboratory. The National University of Science and Technology has 549 students. Degrees in agriculture and polytechnic studies are offered by 7 colleges.

30DOMESTIC TRADE

Harare and Bulawayo are the country's principal distribution centers. They are linked by rail and road to smaller towns that serve as centers for their immediate rural areas. Head offices of most of the large companies are in one or the other of the two cities.

Business hours are generally from 8 AM to 5 PM Monday through Saturday. Banks are open from 8:30 AM to 2 PM Monday–Friday, except on Wednesday, when they close at noon. Saturday banking hours are from 8:30 to 11 AM.

31FOREIGN TRADE

Total exports reached 3,659.5 million Zimbabwe dollars in 1990 while imports cost z$3,937.8 million. Deficits were recorded in 1989 and 1990, surpluses in the years 1984–88. Gold was the export leader in 1991 (13.6%), followed by tobacco (12.7%), cotton, textiles, ferro-alloys, food and live animals, crude inedible non-food materials, nickel, asbestos, copper, sugar, and iron and steel bars, ingots and billets.

During 1990, Germany took 11.6% of Zimbabwe's exports; the United Kingdom, 10.8%; and South Africa (8.9%). Imports came mainly from South Africa, 20.2%; the United Kingdom, 11.7%; and the United States, 10.6%.

32 BALANCE OF PAYMENTS

Zimbabwe's imports grew by 23% in 1991 from 1990, and are expected to rise by 10% annually through 1995, reflecting a relaxation of import controls and the inflow of capital goods needed for investment. Exports remained static in 1991, but are expected to rise by 12–14% annually through 1995. The rapid rise of the current account deficit since 1989 has been caused primarily by the surge in imports from the creation of the Open General Import License (OGIL) list of items possible for importation without first obtaining a foreign exchange allocation from the government. With huge pent-up demand and future uncertainty about the program, importers rushed to take advantage of the opportunity, often hoarding several years' supply of items, which caused the trade deficit to balloon.

In 1991, merchandise exports totaled US$1,693.8 million and imports US$1,645.7 million. The merchandise trade balance was US$48.1 million. The following table summarizes Zimbabwe's balance of payments for 1990 and 1991 (in millions of US dollars):

	1990	1991
CURRENT ACCOUNT		
Goods, services, and income	−276.7	−587.4
Unrequited transfers	105.1	98.0
TOTALS	−171.6	−489.4
CAPITAL ACCOUNT		
Direct investment	−12.2	2.8
Portfolio investment	−21.7	7.3
Other long-term capital	164.4	272.0
Other short-term capital	—	125.8
Other liabilities	14.6	—
Reserves	7.4	105.2
TOTALS	152.5	513.1
Errors and omissions	19.1	−23.6
Total change in reserves	23.4	317.4

33 BANKING AND SECURITIES

The Reserve Bank of Zimbabwe administers all monetary and exchange controls and is the sole bank of issue. As of 1993, foreign assets amounted to z$3,545.2 million. The Zimbabwe Development Bank was established in 1983 as a development finance institution.

Commercial banks include Barclays Bank International, Standard Bank, Zimbank, Bank of Credit and Commerce Zimbabwe (43% government owned), and Grindlays Bank. There are four merchant banks and three discount houses that deal with government-issued Treasury bills. The Post Office Savings Bank is an important savings institution. The money supply, as measured by M2, amounted to z$91,238 million in 1993.

The Zimbabwe Stock Exchange, with floors in Harare, deals in government securities and the securities of many privately owned companies.

34 INSURANCE

Insurance companies must be registered with and licensed by the Registrar of Insurance, make security deposits with the Treasury, file annual financial reports, and observe other government regulations.

Principal types of insurance written are life, fire, automobile, employers' liability, and accident. Automobile third-party liability is compulsory. There were some 50 insurance companies doing business in Zimbabwe in the mid-1980s. Per capita premiums totaled US$32.2, or 5.2% of GDP, in 1990.

35 PUBLIC FINANCE

Zimbabwe derives its principal revenues from income taxes, sales tax, customs and excise duties, and interest, dividends, and profits. Principal categories of expenditure are education, defense, debt service, and agriculture. Budgets for the 1970s and the 1980s were generally in deficit. Escalating fiscal deficits in the 1980s led to the implementation early in 1991 of an extensive reform program, which focuses on fiscal deficit reduction and minetary reforms. A severe drought in 1992, however, set back the program; the deficit rose to more than 10% of GDP in 1993.

The following table shows actual revenues and expenditures for 1990 and 1991 in millions of Zimbabwe dollars.

	1990	1991
REVENUE AND GRANTS		
Tax revenue	4,367.0	5,906.0
Non-tax revenue	522.3	604.4
Capital revenue	9.6	10.7
Grants	138.2	250.0
TOTAL	5,307.1	6,771.1
EXPENDITURES & LENDING MINUS REPAYMENTS		
Expenditures	5,872.3	7,418.7
Lending Minus Repayments	572.6	782.7
TOTAL	6,444.9	8,201.4
Deficit/Surplus	−1,137.8	−1,430.3

In 1990, Zimbabwe's total public debt stood at z$10,411.8 million, of which z$4,036.7 million was financed abroad.

36 TAXATION

The primary tax on individuals is an income tax, which is based on a graduated scale of rates up to a prescribed limit (z$45,000 in 1993), above which the maximum rate applies (55% in 1993). Companies are taxed at a flat percentage of taxable income—42.5% in 1992/93. In recent years, a surcharge has been added to the income tax.

A sales tax, imposed at the retail stage, is applied to most goods except for food; in 1990, it ranged from 10–20%. Other taxes include a vehicle tax, a betting tax, taxes on dividends and branch profits, capital goods, and stamp, transfer, and estate duties. There are excise duties on alcoholic beverages, cigarettes, and tobacco.

37 CUSTOMS AND DUTIES

Zimbabwe uses the GATT system of tariff codes. Duties mostly range between 15% and 20% but can go as high as 60%. Duties on certain imports from Botswana and PTA countries are reduced. Other import taxes include a surtax of 20% on c.i.f. value, a sales tax if the importer is the end-user, and anti-dumping duties as specified in the Customs and Excise Act.

38 FOREIGN INVESTMENT

According to the foreign investment code published in October 1982, at least 20% of a new venture must be Zimbabwean-owned and should have shares available to the government if requested. In most cases, the government demands a majority share of any joint venture it enters. Foreign investors must get permission from the Foreign Investment Committee and the Ministry of Finance, Economic Planning, and Development, for the development of any new enterprise in Zimbabwe. The government is particularly receptive to joint ventures in rural areas that use local raw materials and labor intensive methods, and some tax incentives are offered.

Absentee investments in agriculture are discouraged and underutilized land is subject to fair-value purchase by the government for redistribution to family farmers. This policy affects primarily 50% of the 11 million ha of agricultural estates created prior to independence and is being contested in Zimbabwe's courts. The banking sector is diverse, with foreign banks well represented.

39ECONOMIC DEVELOPMENT

Since independence, the primary goal has been to redress socio-economic imbalance and restructure the economy while maintaining growth. At the same time, the government wishes to avoid alienating its white population, whose skills remain important to the economy. The government has so far rejected nationalization but has rather purchased shares in various enterprises (e.g., the national newspaper chain and Zimbank).

A three-year transitional development plan was adopted for 1982–85. It called for investments of z$6,100 million (59% in the public sector) and assumed an average net growth rate of 8% per year. Manufacturing was to receive 23% of total investment, transport 14%, and agriculture 13%. Total investment fell 30% short of this goal. The Five-Year Development Plan for 1986–90 called for an annual growth rate of 5.1%, with z$7,126 million in investments, of which some 60% would be from public-sector investment and 40% would come from foreign sources. Education, defense, and debt service are the largest categories of government spending.

Since independence, Zimbabwe has received large amounts of foreign aid. The United Kingdom and other Western nations are the major sources of bilateral aid. The World Bank, the United States, the European Community, the former Soviet Union, China, and the former Yugoslavia have all contributed substantial amounts.

40SOCIAL DEVELOPMENT

The Ministry of Labour, Manpower Planning and Social Welfare deals with child welfare, delinquency, adoption, family problems, refugees, the aged, and public assistance. There are some government and industrial pension programs. Voluntary welfare organizations providing facilities for the aged, the handicapped, and care of children receive some government assistance. Workers' compensation is provided to those Africans whose earnings fall below a set minimum yearly wage. Problems include a low standard of living among rural Africans.

On 10 December 1982, the Legal Age of Majority Act conferred majority status on Zimbabwean black women. Previously, they had been considered under the guardianship of either fathers or husbands. It was estimated in the mid-1990s that women would bear 5.3 children if they lived through their childbearing years. Abortion is permitted on limited grounds.

There have been numerous reports of human rights violations. In 1984, the Mugabe government announced the discovery of mass graves of more than 4,000 civilians and guerrillas allegedly killed by the Smith regime during the civil war. There have also been reports of atrocities and torture under the Mugabe government. The 1965 Emergency Powers Act, which the Mugabe government has continued to renew, allows persons to be detained indefinitely if they are suspected of being a threat to national security. Human rights groups have accused the regime of abuses that include summary executions, torture, beatings, arbitrary arrests, and officially condoned mob violence. As many as 3,000 political opponents were detained without trial in 1985, including 4 members of Parliament, with probably 1,000 being held at any particular time. In addition, from 1982 to 1987, the crisis in Matabeleland, put down ruthlessly by the Army's 5th Brigade, led to mass killings of hundreds of government opponents. The report of a commission investigating this uprising remains secret.

41HEALTH

All health services are the responsibility of the Ministry of Health, which is responsible for 50% of total health care expenditures (z$416 million in 1990) provided by local authorities (with Ministry of Health grants), mission churches (also with grants), and industrial organizations and private services. About 85% of the population had access to health care services in 1992.

The government has declared its intention to provide free medical services for all. In 1982, those earning less than z$150 a month were eligible for free health care. Prior to independence, facilities for Africans were free, but these were greatly inferior to those available to Europeans. Zimbabwe has been focusing on building and/or upgrading rural health care centers and district hospitals and expanding rural health programs, such as immunization, control of diarrheal diseases, training of health care workers, and improving the supply and affordability of essential drugs. The local pharmaceutical industry is well developed. The Ministry of National Supplies operates the Government Medical Stores, which procures on behalf of the Ministry of Health. There were four tiers of health care delivery in Zimbabwe as of 1992: (1) 56 rural hospitals, and 927 health centers (public and private) providing preventive and curative services; (2) 55 district hospitals; (3) 8 provincial and 4 general hospitals; and (4) 5 central hospitals located in major cities. Medical personnel in 1990 included 1,320 doctors (1 per 7,180 people), 131 dentists, 347 pharmacists, 6,116 nurses (1 per 1,000 people), and 2,651 certified midwives.

Tuberculosis has been a major health problem (207 reported cases per 100,000 people in 1990). Local campaigns are under way to control schistosomiasis, which affects a large percentage of the African population. In 1990, 12% of children under 5 years old were considered malnourished. In 1991, 84% of the population had access to safe water, but only 40% had adequate sanitation.

There were 434,000 births in 1992. Zimbabwe's 1993 birth rate was 40.6 per 1,000 people with about 43% of married women (ages 15 to 49) using contraception. Maternal mortality rates were high as of 1990, and the disease pattern was one of mainly preventable diseases. The country has a very young population (47% under 15 years in 1990). Fertility rates are high, and the population is forecast to rise to 11.9 million by the year 2000. Infant mortality was 60 per 1,000 live births in 1992, and life expectancy was only 56 years. General mortality was 11 per 1,000 in 1993.

42HOUSING

In rural areas, Africans live in villages and on farms in housing that is mainly of brick or mud and stick construction with thatch or metal roofs. The villages are usually small (except for the massive protected villages), with fewer than 100 inhabitants. Urban housing is generally of brick. According to the latest available information for 1980–88, total housing units numbered 2,000,000 with 4.2 people per dwelling.

43EDUCATION

Adult literacy rates in 1990 were 73.7% for men and 60.3% for women. A unitary system of education under the Ministry of Education has replaced the dual system of separate educational facilities for Africans and non-Africans formerly maintained by the Rhodesian government. Education is free and compulsory for 8 years between the ages of 7 and 15. Secondary education is for 6 years.

In 1986/87, expenditures on education were estimated at z$698 million. In 1992 there were 2,301,642 students in 4,567 primary schools with 60,834 teachers. The same year, general secondary schools had 657,344 students. In 1991, students in secondary schools numbered 710,619 with 25,225 teachers.

The University of Zimbabwe provides higher education on a multiracial basis; there were 9 colleges in 1987. In 1992, there were 3,076 teaching staff and 61,553 students in all higher level institutions.

⁴⁴LIBRARIES AND MUSEUMS

The National Free Library of Zimbabwe (formerly of Rhodesia) was founded in 1943 in Bulawayo as a national lending library and center for interlibrary loans. It has over 90,000 volumes. Also in Bulawayo is the Public Library, with 98,000 volumes. Other libraries include the Harare City Library, the Turner Memorial Library in Mutare, the Library of Parliament, and libraries in more than a dozen smaller towns. The National Archives of Zimbabwe, located in Harare, receives a copy of every book published in Zimbabwe, as does the Bulawayo Public Library. There were more than 150,000 registered public library users using 76 public libraries in 1989. The library at the University of Zimbabwe is the largest in the country, with 500,000 volumes in the main library and branches.

The Zimbabwe Museum of Natural History at Bulawayo has geologic, ethnographic, historical, and zoological collections. Located in Harare are the Zimbabwe Museum of Human Sciences, with archaeological, historical, zoological, and other collections, and the National Gallery of Zimbabwe, which displays works of national, regional, and European art.

⁴⁵MEDIA

The Ministry of Information, Posts and Telecommunications provides telephone, telegraph, and postal services. In 1991 there were 286,600 telephones, about 3 per 100 population. Radio Zimbabwe broadcasts over 2 AM and 3 FM channels, and government-produced television programs are broadcast from Harare and Bulawayo. In 1991 there were 860,000 radios and 270,000 television sets.

There are 2 daily papers and more than 40 periodicals published in Zimbabwe. The dailies, with their 1991 circulations, are the *Herald* (Harare), 110,000; and the *Chronicle* (Bulawayo), 41,000.

⁴⁶ORGANIZATIONS

The government encourages the development of agricultural and other cooperatives, which are seen as a means of improving the subsistence economy. The Zimbabwe National Chamber of Commerce has many branches.

⁴⁷TOURISM, TRAVEL, AND RECREATION

Tourist attractions include Victoria Falls and the Kariba Dam on the Zambezi River, numerous wildlife sanctuaries and game reserves, including Hwange National Park, the eastern highlands, the Matobo Hills, and the Zimbabwe ruins near Masvingo. There are safari areas in the Zambezi Valley below the Kariba Dam, and at Tuli, and resort, camping, and fishing facilities.

Tourism receipts for 1990 totaled approximately US$47 million. In 1991, 513,580 tourists visited Zimbabwe, 39% from South Africa, 29% from Zambia, and 9% from Europe. There were 4,147 hotel rooms with 6,919 beds and a 50% occupancy rate. South African visitors still account for the largest share of the tourist trade and political progress in that country brightens the outlook for tourism in Zimbabwe. Tourists not from Commonwealth countries are expected to have both passports and visas. A certificate of vaccination against yellow fever is required for those visitors who are arriving from one of the infected areas.

⁴⁸FAMOUS ZIMBABWEANS

The country's former name, Rhodesia, was derived from Cecil John Rhodes (1853–1902), whose company administered the area during the late 19th and early 20th centuries.

Lobengula (1833–94), king of the Ndebele, whose grant of the minerals concession in his territory to Rhodes in 1888 led to European settlement, headed an unsuccessful rebellion of his people against the settlers in 1893. Prominent African nationalist leaders are Joshua Nkomo (b.1917), leader of ZAPU; Bishop Abel Muzorewa (b.1925) of the United Methodist Church, who became the nation's first black prime minister in 1979; and ZANU leader Robert Gabriel Mugabe (b.1924), who became prime minister after independence. Ian Smith (b.1919) was prime minister from 1964 to 1979. Many of the early works of the British novelist Doris Lessing (b.1919) are set in the Rhodesia where she grew up.

⁴⁹DEPENDENCIES

Zimbabwe has no territories or colonies.

⁵⁰BIBLIOGRAPHY

American University. *Zimbabwe: A Country Study.* Washington, D.C.: Government Printing Office, 1983.

Bowman, Larry W. *Politics in Rhodesia: White Power in an African State.* Cambridge, Mass.: Harvard University Press, 1973.

Cheney, Patricia. *The Land and People of Zimbabwe.* New York: Lippincott, 1990.

Herbst, Jeffrey Ira. *State Politics in Zimbabwe.* Berkeley: University of California Press, 1990.

Kennedy, Dane Keith. *Islands of White: Settler Society and Culture in Kenya and Southern Rhodesia, 1890–1939.* Durham, N.C.: Duke University Press, 1987.

Kriger, Norma J. *Zimbabwe's Guerrilla War: Peasant Voices.* New York: Cambridge University Press, 1992.

Mason, Philip. *The Birth of a Dilemma: The Conquest and Settlement of Rhodesia.* London: Oxford University Press, 1958.

Nkala, Jericho C. *The United Nations, International Law and the Rhodesian Independence Crisis.* London: Oxford University Press, 1985.

Nkomo, Joshua. *The Story of My Life.* London: Mowbrays, 1984.

O'Toole, Thomas. *Zimbabwe in Pictures.* Minneapolis: Lerner Pub. Co., 1988.

Phimister, I. R. *An Economic and Social History of Zimbabwe, 1890–1948: Capital Accumulation and Class Struggle.* New York: Longman, 1988.

Potts, Deborah. *Zimbabwe.* Santa Barbara, Calif.: Clio Press, 1993.

Tamarkin, M. *The Making of Zimbabwe: Decolonization in Regional and International Politics.* Savage, MD: F. Cass, 1990.

Weiss, Ruth. *Zimbabwe and the New Elite.* New York: British Academic Press, 1994.

INDEX TO COUNTRIES AND TERRITORIES

This alphabetical list includes countries and dependencies (colonies, protectorates, and other territories) described in the encyclopedia. Countries and territories described in their own articles are followed by the continental volume (printed in *italics*) in which each appears, along with the volume number and first page of the article. For example, Argentina, which begins on page 7 of *Americas* (Volume 3), is listed this way: Argentina—*Americas* 3:7. Dependencies are listed here with the title of the volume in which they are treated, followed by the name of the article in which they are dealt with. In a few cases, an alternative name for the same place is given in parentheses at the end of the entry. The name of the volume *Asia and Oceania* is abbreviated in this list to *Asia*.

ISBN 0-8103-9880-X

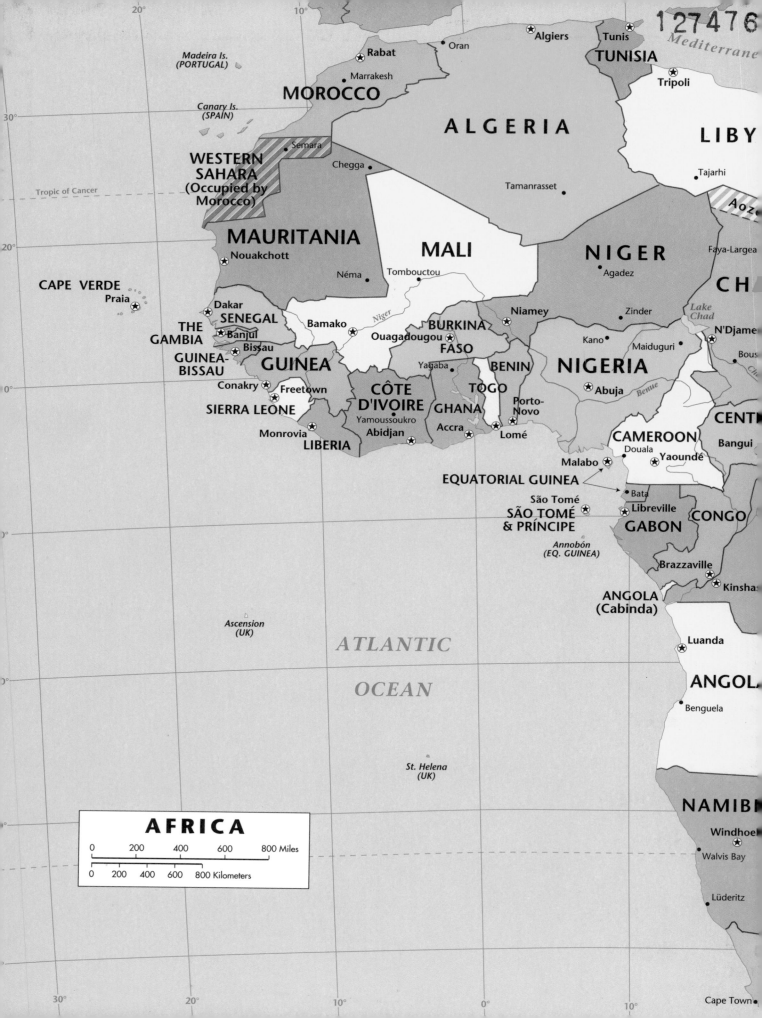